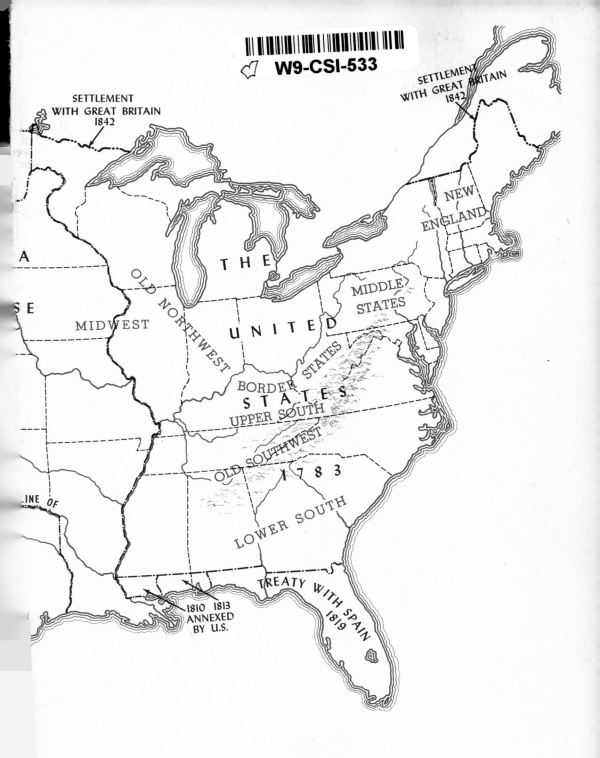

SETTLEMENT
WITH GREAT BRITAIN
1842

SETTLEMENT
WITH GREAT BRITAIN
1842

NEW
ENGLAND

THE

MIDDLE
STATES

MIDWEST

OLD NORTHWEST

UNITED

BORDER STATES

STATES
UPPER SOUTH

OLD SOUTHWEST

1 7 8 3

LINE OF

LOWER SOUTH

TREATY WITH SPAIN
1819

1810 1813
ANNEXED
BY U.S.

TERRITORIAL GROWTH OF THE
UNITED STATES

RISE OF THE AMERICAN REPUBLIC

RISE OF THE
AMERICAN
REPUBLIC

JOHN RICHARD ALDEN

Professor of History, Duke University

HARPER & ROW, PUBLISHERS
New York, Evanston, and London

RISE OF THE AMERICAN REPUBLIC

C–N

LIBRARY OF CONGRESS CATALOG CARD NUMBER: 63–11296

FOR ANNE

CONTENTS

ILLUSTRATIONS

MAPS

1 THE FIRST AMERICANS

When in the memorable summer of 1492 Christopher Columbus sailed from the Canary Islands into the "Ocean Sea," he expected to find Cathay (China) and Cipangu (Japan). However, instead of Chinese and neighboring peoples, on the shores of the Caribbean he found red men descended from Asians so changed in the American environment that they formed a new variety of mankind. Believing that he had reached outlying parts of the Orient, the bold and skillful sailor fancied that the dark-eyed, brown-skinned folk that he met on the beaches of the Bahamas were inhabitants of India. He called them Indians, and the name endures, to the continuing distress of anthropologists, historians, and others who must use the same word to designate the inhabitants of the great Asian subcontinent and the first settlers in the New World. The word "Amerind," coined to distinguish the American Indian from the Asian Indian, has not come into general use.

Certainly the red men were not then in a world new to them. They had entered the Americas at least twenty thousand years before Columbus appeared from the east. It has often been claimed that they were not the first inhabitants of the Americas, but no valid evidence of the existence of

1

a more ancient people has ever been found. It is evident enough that there was physical contact between the Americas on the one hand and Europe and Asia on the other, in the dim distant past, because the fauna and flora of the Americas are in general strikingly similar to those of the other continents. With respect to humankind, however, it must now be believed that the first men to traverse the virgin lands and waters between Alaska and Cape Horn were descendants of Asians who ventured eastward from Siberia. It is conceivable that others of Oriental origin reached the Americas by way of the central Pacific and the south Pacific, but the distances and the difficulties of such routes suggest strongly that they were not used. It has been urged that there was once in the south Pacific a continent of Mu, now largely vanished into the sea, which served as a steppingstone to the Americas from the west. According to this fanciful theory, the curious statues and writings found on Easter Island in the south Pacific are remains of that lost continent. Actually, Easter Island was peopled by Polynesians advancing from the west; so far as is known, it was the point of farthest Polynesian penetration. The continent of Mu as a link between Asia and the Americas is quite as mythical as the continent of Atlantis performing the same service between the Americas and Europe. Nor need any credence be placed in the fanciful theory that the red men are the offspring of the ten Lost Tribes of Israel. It may reasonably be assumed that Asians passed over the relatively small obstacles between Siberia and Alaska in scattered groups, and that they and their progeny moved eastward and southward, populating both the Americas and the adjacent islands. Geography and the obvious physical similarities between the later Indians and the Asian peoples point clearly to this conclusion. Remains of settlements made by the Indians in the United States, as many as eight or ten thousands of years prior to the birth of Christ, have been found and studied by devoted scholars. The veil which covers the early history of the American Indians is slowly lifting as anthropologists, employing modern scientific techniques such as Carbon 14-dating, delve more extensively into the remains of early Indian villages.

The Indians were not numerous in Columbus' day; there were probably fewer than there are at the present time. In round numbers there were perhaps 1,000,000 in what are now the United States and Canada, 4,000,000 in Mexico and Central America, and 5,000,000 in South America. Nor were they multiplying rapidly in North America when Europeans established permanent contact with them. It would appear that their birth rate in the northern part of the New World was low. Early European observers accounted for the small size of the Indian family by a supposed lack of ardor in the Indian male, who was presumably so devoted to the glories of the hunt and warfare that he chose to be domestically ascetic. At any rate, it is true that the indignities and barbarities inflicted upon captives by the red men did not include ravishing of female prisoners; and Indian families were not so large as those of European colonials. However, the explanation of the fewness and of the slow increase of the Indians is doubtless to be found principally in their economy, which did not provide them with assured and abundant food. North and east of the Rio Grande waters the Indians were still primarily hunters. Although they commonly lived in villages, they practiced agriculture only incidentally, producing garden stuffs rather than grain; and their only domestic animal was the dog. It is well known that the Indian male in the eastern part of what is now the United States spent little time in growing crops, these chores being left to the women, boys, and men who were too old to hunt or fight, and who had little to offer in council. Feast and famine were alternately the lot of the Indians. They had not learned to preserve food in great quantity; they knew well how to bear hunger. Indeed, they were uniformly accustomed to face misfortunes of all sorts with stoic unconcern, even with pleasure. The Indian warrior exulted because as a captive he could suffer unflinchingly the cruellest torments that might be inflicted upon him; equally staunch was the Indian woman, who shared his hardships with equanimity and assisted him in torturing his prisoners. The world has known no more courageous people.

During the thousands of years which elapsed between the appearance of the Indians and the coming of the white man, hundreds of Indian tribes, or nations, developed in North America. Various languages and sub-languages also evolved, as well as differing religions and complex social and political structures. In general, these Indians made less progress toward civilization than did the tribes of Central and South America. The Inca of the Andean highlands were superb organizers and magnificent builders; the Maya of southeastern Mexico and Guatemala were remarkable astronomers, making calendars of amazing accuracy; and the Aztec in the valley of Mexico developed a stable and well-ordered society. They were peoples who had learned how to maintain a constant food supply, essential for physical security and the creation of leisure, which were in turn required for cultural improvement. Those Indians had also managed to create political institutions which endured for long periods of time. It was otherwise to the north, where the Indians were frequently threatened with extinction by starvation, hardship, and warfare. To be sure, the Natchez nation in the lower Mississippi Valley had progressed so far religiously as to worship the sun, while the Iroquois had established a relatively stable confederacy in the valley of the Mohawk River and the Finger Lakes region of New York. We cannot know what the Delaware, Cherokee, Sioux, and Ottawa might have achieved had they not been interrupted by the intrusion of the Europeans. At any rate, the art of writing was unknown to them and to their neighbors, although they had learned to use wampum beads as a mnemonic aid. Twentieth-century Americans, seeking peace of mind in a difficult and troubled world, found it among Hopi tribesmen. But personal tranquillity is doubtless in some measure a proof of cultural stagnation. The Europeans learned from the North American Indians how to cultivate corn (maize), potatoes, tomatoes, and other products of the soil; otherwise the first inhabitants of the northern part of the New World had relatively little to give to their conquerors.

EARLY CONTACTS WITH THE NEW WORLD

There was little contact between the Indians and Europeans before 1492. The red men did not paddle their canoes across the sea into the mouth of the Rhine, and it is to be doubted that whites, except for the Norse voyagers, reached the western shores of the Atlantic before the dauntless Genoese. Many dubious claims of "discovery" of the New World prior to the time of Columbus have been put forth, and scraps of evidence have been presented to prove them valid. National conceit, naïveté, and chicanery are the chief supports of such claims, which have come from the Irish, Welsh, French, English, Danish, Polish, and Portuguese. An Irish St. Brendan is said to have sailed off to the west in the sixth century A.D., to have found America, and to have returned to Ireland. European maps of the Atlantic in the fifteenth century displayed a St. Brendan's Island or Islands in the middle of the ocean, but it is altogether likely that the saint's voyage across the ocean is mythical. It has been claimed that the Welsh Prince Madoc set off across the Atlantic about the year 1170, that he reached North America, and that his voyage led to the creation of Welsh colonies on that continent, even that the Mandan tribe of Indians in the upper Missouri valley was at least partly of Welsh descent—perhaps so, after visits from white traders in the nineteenth century. The Madoc story is actually a pure and amusing fabrication, which was concocted long after Columbus had reached the New World. Frenchmen are said to have fished off the shores of Newfoundland before 1492, not telling the world because they wished to avoid competition. Another tale has English sailors from Bristol finding their way to the Grand Banks before Columbus reached the Bahamas, their "discovery" being kept quiet for the same and other reasons. It has been reported that Captain Jean Cousin of the French port of Dieppe sailed off to the west in 1488, found land beyond the ocean, and returned to tell his tale. A similar story has a Danish ship preceding Cousin by twelve years. Another has it that the Danish "discovery" was really Polish because the ship's pilot was a Polish navigator. In the year 1486 there was a "secret" Portuguese voyage across the Atlantic—so secret that it very likely did not occur at all. Columbus was supposedly inspired by the findings of the Portuguese. More believable is the story contained in the extraordinary Zeno narratives published in Italy in the sixteenth century, which chronicle possible journeys of Faroe Island explorers to and in the New World, to "Dromio," and other regions conceivably located in America. In the main, it would appear that evidence for contact between Europe and the Americas in the Christian era before the 1492 voyage of Columbus is not much more convincing than that for contact between Africa and the Americas, or between Asia and the Americas. All are extremely doubtful, save for contacts presumably made by the Norse.

NORSE EXPLORATIONS

About the year 1073 Adam of Bremen, a monk who wrote a history of the archbishopric of Hamburg, inserted in his chronicle a reference to Vinland, a country recently entered by the Norsemen. Presumably this was the Vinland discovered by Leif Ericson, in all likelihood a part of the New World. That North America was reached by Ericson and other Norsemen is, of course, supported by the geography of the north Atlantic world, with the Faroe and Shetland Islands, Iceland, and Greenland acting as stepping-stones between North America and Scandinavia. It is well known that the Norsemen occupied all of these, reaching the southwest coast of Greenland by 985. Remains of at least one of their settlements upon that coast still exist. It may be that the climate of that region was then milder than it now is, and that the westward advance and colonization by the Norse were less difficult than they would appear to be. For the intrepid Scandinavian adventurers who made their way in open ships to Greenland, a further advance to Labrador or Newfoundland would have been nothing remarkable; and their sagas tell us that they did reach territories quite clearly in the western hemisphere. The sagas, in this case historical rather than fictional, were originally oral narratives handed down from generation to generation, eventually being reduced to writing. Two of the sagas still preserved describe Leif Ericson's voyage to Vinland as well as other later voyages to the same place. These histories are supported by incidental references to Vinland and persons who went there in several other sagas which tell of the progress of Norse settlements in Iceland and Greenland.

The evidence of the sagas, taken together, is impressive. The two principal narratives say that Bjarni Herjulfson, a Norse voyager proceeding westward to Greenland in 986, was blown off his course to the southward, turned to the north, and saw land upon his left as he proceeded to his destination. He and his men may well have been the first Europeans to see an American shore. These sagas also report that Leif Ericson in 1000 or 1002, either purposefully seeking the coast reported by Herjulfson or being driven upon it in the same fashion as his predecessor, found Vinland, an area where wild grapes abounded. According to this story, Leif returned to Greenland and other venturers sought the new country he had explored.

Data are given not only of Vinland, but of Helluland and Markland, regions traversed between Vinland and Greenland. None of these has been certainly identified, although too-confident investigators have located them in this area or that. The narratives are too brief to permit us to know more than that Vinland lay somewhere between Labrador and Chesapeake Bay. However, surprisingly explicit information is offered about the natives with whom the Norse traded and fought, the "Skraelings" (barbarians); concerning the plants and animals of Vinland; and about the length of the day in that region. These and other descriptive statements suggest quite positively that Leif Ericson and those who followed him entered the north-eastern part of North America.

Records in the Scandinavian world, unfortunately scanty, suggest that contact between Greenland and Vinland may have been long maintained; and American scholars of Scandinavian descent, with others, have been tempted to write, not merely about Norse discoveries, but also about a Norse empire in North America. Hence arises some degree of credence in the famous Kensington (Minnesota) Stone, the Newport (Rhode Island) Tower, and other objects as remains of the Norsemen. It is altogether likely that the Kensington Stone, which received much public attention after its discovery in 1898, and chronicles in runic writing the sad fate of Norse adventurers in Minnesota in the year 1362, carried no message until late in the nineteenth century. Experts familiar with runes find those upon the stone to be peculiar, and it is most unlikely that they were carved in the fourteenth century. The stone tower at Newport, thought by enthusiasts to be the central part of a Norse church, is rather certainly what is left of an unusual stone windmill erected by Governor Benedict Arnold of Rhode Island in the seventeenth century. One should avoid tilting against it; and a stone reported to have been found in nearby Narragansett Bay in the 1920s bearing the name of Leif Ericson and "MI"—the year 1001—must be considered with skepticism. These United States have had their full share of myth-makers, cranks, and practical jokers who enjoy playing upon the credulity of more sober folk. All are obstacles in the pursuit of historical truth. Heady wine continues to come from Vinland, and it is possible to imbibe too freely of it. The Northmen in all likelihood did not settle in any large number in Vinland; it is not known that they remained there very long, and no blue-eyed Indians were afterward found by explorers such as Columbus, Captain John Smith, and Samuel de Champlain, who were inclined to look for wonders to report. The Indians did not even remember the Norsemen, unless one chooses to believe that Quetzalcoatl, the "Fair God" of the Aztecs, was a lingering memory of some Norse chieftain; nor was the Algonquin Indian tongue enriched with Scandinavian terms. However long the Norse continued to pass between Vinland and Greenland, permanent and fruitful settlement was not achieved. The link vanished, leaving no surely authentic trace, save in the sagas. In fact, the Norse colonies on Greenland themselves disappeared in the fifteenth century and were temporarily forgotten, together with Vinland.

To the Norsemen, Vinland was not a New World, but merely another country beyond Greenland. They did not claim to have found a New World; and in a sense they did not discover it, since their activities were fundamentally without result. A letter written by Columbus—it has been attacked as a forgery—says that in 1477 he made a voyage to the waters off Iceland. In consequence, it has been inferred that he went ashore on the great island, that he learned of Vinland, and, therefore, that he knew he would find America when he set out from Spain. However, it is not known that he set foot on Iceland; its inhabitants could hardly have told him about unimportant and forgotten Vinland, much less a New World. Sailing almost due west from Spain, Columbus obviously was not searching for Vinland, and the familiar story that he was attempting to chart a new path to the Orient is not only sensible, but assuredly true.

Commonly it is assumed that even relatively solid information about America gained from the Norse voyages could hardly have led to colonization of the Americas, because Europe was not yet prepared to make the necessary efforts. Lack of stable and powerful governments, of capital, of reliable and maneuverable ocean-going ships, of geographical knowledge, of scientific instruments necessary for skillful sailing—all of these have been cited as major obstacles in the path of peopling the New World from Europe in the eleventh century and in those immediately following. Nevertheless, one may envisage a slow but ultimately successful advance into the Americas during the medieval period. Possibly progress toward the removal of each of these hindrances might have tended to weaken the others. In any case, rapid exploitation of the Norse "discovery" that was not really a discovery was impossible. However, toward the close of the fifteenth century conditions in Europe were far more favorable than they had been earlier, both for crossing the Atlantic and for peopling the Americas. Indeed, with the advantage of hindsight, we may say that these events had then become inevitable, that they could not be long delayed. All of which takes no credit from Columbus, who must ever remain a mighty figure in the annals of mankind.

FIFTEENTH-CENTURY EXPLORATIONS

Before the end of the fifteenth century most of the modern European states bordering upon the Atlantic had made their appearance and had acquired in large measure political stability under the leadership of their royal families. The power of the feudal nobility was waning, and local allegiances were giving way to national ones. In England the Wars of the

Roses not only decimated the ranks of the lords but brought to the throne in 1485 the first of the dominating Tudors, Henry VII. With the support of a rising middle class he and his strong-headed descendants governed firmly as "bosses" for more than a century. Less surely in control of France were the Valois kings, but the same political phenomena existed in that country in a lesser degree. There the nobility longer retained more of their ancient independence and the middle class attained influence more slowly and less effectively. The shifting tides of events were nevertheless with the French kings. Among the Valois were the potent rulers, Francis I (1515–1547) and Henry II (1547–1559). After the coming to the throne of the Bourbons in 1589 the French state received impressive leadership from Henry IV (1589–1610), the astute Cardinals Richelieu and Mazarin, and Louis XIV (1643–1715).

In Spain the growth of royal power was greater than it was in England. The foundation of the Spanish monarchy was laid by the marriage of Ferdinand of Aragon and Isabella of Castile in 1469, this union bringing together two able rulers and the two major Spanish principalities. Together Ferdinand and Isabella brought under their dominion almost all of modern Spain, their triumphs including the destruction of the last Moorish kingdom, Granada, in 1492. Their descendants inherited both Spain and claim to the bulk of the New World. Their grandson, Charles I (1516–1556), who inherited suzerainty over the Low Countries and was Holy Roman Emperor as Charles V, and Philip II (1556–1598) held sway over extensive European territories and rapidly increasing colonial possessions, chiefly in the Americas. During the reign of Charles I the authority of the Spanish crown passed beyond challenge at home. Royal power was firmly established even earlier in Portugal, where Prince Henry the Navigator and Emanuel the Great supplied leadership in the discovery of new lands and the building of a far-spread Portuguese Empire.

Monarchs so entrenched at home that they were accepted as rulers almost in the nature of things and even by divine right, were able, of course, to supply stable government in regions beyond the seas. Efforts toward exploration and settlement could accordingly be better organized and longer maintained, all the more because these princes were able to contribute from their treasuries, at least on some occasions. Moreover, they were able to offer rewards in the form of titles and revenues to persons who were willing to risk their lives and their fortunes in ventures beyond the sea.

Another factor which made passage across the Atlantic possible was increased knowledge. The west Europeans had learned how to build ships that were larger, safer, and more maneuverable, although they were clumsy and not easily handled according to later standards. The compass had been, and was in common use among navigators; moreover, by means of the astrolabe, they were able roughly to measure latitude. Sailors had become accustomed to relatively long voyages along the shores of Europe and Africa, and had acquired some confidence that seas not yet traversed were like those which were familiar to them. Educated men and navigators were well aware of the spherical shape of the earth. China and Japan had become known to the west Europeans, especially through the publication of the *Travels of Marco Polo;* India likewise was within their ken; the Canaries and the Azores had been discovered and occupied by Spain and Portugal respectively; and the Portuguese had brought the west coast of Africa within the view of the Europeans. It was not merely that specific knowledge and skills had been accumulated; interest in things intellectual was greater and more widespread than it had been for several centuries, and the spirit of inquiry was at a high level. The so-called Renaissance had long been in progress, and it was spreading northward. Its effects were discernible not only among scholars and artists, but in the courts of princes, in the counting-houses of merchants, in the castles of the nobility, and among sea captains and pilots.

There were also economic means and motivation which had not existed earlier. Trade had burgeoned in Europe, and capital had accumulated among merchants and bankers who sought opportunities for profitable investment. Even the expansion of the Turkish Empire in western Asia stimulated the west Europeans to look southward and westward for new economic opportunities. Long established in Asia Minor and Syria, the Turks had occupied the lower Balkans, and had captured Constantinople in 1453. Toward the end of the fifteenth century they were pushing both northward and southward, and Egypt, which finally fell to them in 1517, was threatened by their aggressive forces. The Turks had closed the routes hitherto used by Europeans to reach eastern and southern Asia, except for the Red Sea passageway, and even that was in peril. Commerce with the Orient, especially because it brought much-desired spices into Europe, had been strikingly profitable, and had been partly responsible for the rise to wealth of the port cities of Venice and Genoa. The spreading Turkish barrier not only injured the trade of European merchants, but inspired Europeans to think of finding a new and open route to the Orient.

THE PORTUGUESE

The Portuguese found a new path to Asia before the century had closed. By the year 1350 the west coast of Africa had been explored as far as Cape Bojador. Under the leadership of Prince Henry the Navigator, a member of the Portuguese royal family, they steadily pushed on southward from 1419 to 1460. Prince Henry not only maintained an astronomical laboratory at the southern tip of Portugal, but developed a school for the study of geography and the training of navigators. After his death, the Portuguese explored below the equator, and in 1486 Bartholomew Diaz rounded the

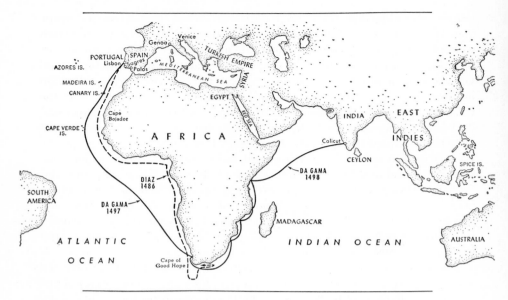

PORTUGUESE EXPLORATION (ASIA AND AFRICA)

southern tip of Africa, to which he gave the name of the Cape of Storms. King John II of Portugal, realizing that a way to Asia had probably been opened, gave to the promontory a more suitable title, the Cape of Good Hope. Twelve years later his optimistic prediction was realized when Vasco da Gama rounded the Cape and made his way to Calicut in India. The Portuguese promptly followed up da Gama's discovery, and sent ships and soldiers for trade and conquest to the shores of the Indian Ocean. Before long they had established posts in India and had built an empire in the Spice Islands in the East Indies. Had not Columbus anticipated them, the Portuguese must also have found the New World as a result of their voyages to the Orient, for their ships could hardly have failed to find the shores of the "hump" of Brazil.

John II, prescient regarding the Portuguese advance around Africa, was less farseeing with regard to exploration to the westward, and so had no part in the discovery of the Americas. Christopher Columbus urged him to support an expedition to find a western passage to the Orient, but the king refused, failing to take advantage of the opportunity which was eventually seized by Queen Isabella of Castile. Columbus, born in Genoa in 1451, was a weaver in his youth, but soon turned to the sea. After much voyaging, studying, and discussion with other navigators, he had come to believe in a simple but remarkable theory, that a ship sailing directly westward from Spain or Portugal must strike the shores of eastern Asia. He was well aware of the shape of the earth, and his conclusion was, of course, quite right. Courageous, bold, and avid for wealth, position, and fame, he was eager to lead an expedition out into the Atlantic. He realized that a voyage to the westward would be risky; its dangers were greater than he thought. While he knew the shape of the earth, he underestimated its size, and believed that the outlying shores of eastern Asia were about twenty-four hundred miles from those of Portugal and Spain. He also hoped to find in the Atlantic an island or islands where he might stop for rest and refreshment. Even so, the voyage which he projected was extremely hazardous, and profit from it most uncertain. In part, Columbus was doubtless refused sponsorship by King John because the Italian sailor demanded handsome rewards, should he be successful.

COLUMBUS

Failing to secure the support of the Portuguese monarch, unsuccessful perhaps in efforts to win the help of the rulers of France and England, Columbus energetically sought the approval of Queen Isabella. Her advisers long argued against the scheme of the impetuous Italian, but his self-assurance, the logic of his proposal, and the possibility of immense gains at last had their effect. After the kingdom of Granada had been conquered, the queen felt able to embark upon the venture, and she entered into a contract with Columbus. By this agreement Columbus was to become Admiral of the "Ocean Sea" through which he passed and Viceroy of all new regions which he might discover, unless they already belonged to a Christian prince. He was also to have a share in any profits of the expedition, other shares to go to the queen and to private persons who joined with her and Columbus in financing the voyage. Officially commissioned by Isabella, Columbus had little difficulty in securing the necessary ships, sailors, and supplies. The Pinzon brothers of Palos, a port in southwestern Spain, lent their talents and invested money in the enterprise and at last, on August 3, 1492, Columbus slipped out of Palos. His three small ships, the *Santa Maria,* the *Pinta,* and the *Niña,* carried ninety sailors, these being chiefly Spanish, although the crews had an international flavor. Most were convicts and debtors who had been pressed into service.

After an uneventful trip to the Canary Islands, Columbus took on fresh water and then sailed off to the westward into the unknown ocean. The trade winds steadily blew the ships onward in very fine weather, and the little squadron made its way without incident into the Sargasso Sea. Its weedy waters made the sailors think that they were near land, only to disappoint them when the ships passed beyond it. As the wind continued to blow constantly from the east, the sailors became more and more restless as the ships plowed farther into the unknown. They were not afraid they would fall over the edge of the earth, but they were concerned that they might not find winds which would enable them to return home. They began to murmur among themselves; to quiet them, Columbus falsified his ship's log. When he entered the distance he had covered during a day, he reduced the figure—but it was actually reasonably correct, because he was making more rapid progress than he calculated. Of course, no St. Brendan's Island appeared on the water, nor did Columbus and his men see a mythical island of Antillia, which cartographers had placed on maps of the time. When Columbus reached the area where he expected to find Japan or China, there was nothing to be seen but ocean. He pressed on amid the mounting complaints of his sailors, but found it necessary to hint that he would soon turn about if land were not found. At last signs appeared that the ships were approaching land, parts of trees in the water and birds overhead. Crowding on all sail and turning toward the northwest, Columbus drove forward rapidly, risking running aground in the uncharted waters. Early in the morning of October 12 a lookout saw land in the distance, and the news spread rapidly through the ships. As they approached the shore, Columbus and his officers put on their finest clothing, so that they would be suitably clad when they met the native ruler or one of his representatives. Going ashore in small boats, they gave thanks to God that they had reached their destination. There they met naked brownskinned people, who gazed upon them with awe, for they fancied that the strange, bearded, well-clothed strangers had come down from the skies. Columbus had reached one of the Bahama Islands, which he called San Salvador, probably the one which is now known as Watling Island.

The gentle folk Columbus met on San Salvador were nothing like the Asians he had expected to find, and their huts were not the palaces described by Marco Polo. Clearly, he had not reached his goal. He believed, however, that he had found an outlying part of Asia, and that a little further search would bring him to the cities of the rich and gorgeous East. The natives were friendly, and there was an exchange of information by sign language, but he learned little from them. To them and their neighbors he casually gave the name Indians, and he called the region they inhabited "the Indies." So began the European invasion of the Americas.

For the Indians, the coming of the white man meant catastrophe, for they could neither effectively defend their way of life, nor could they readily adapt themselves to the white man's ways. They were numerous enough to have made a desperate struggle for their freedom, but they lacked the weapons and especially the discipline of the Europeans. What was even more serious, because of feuds among themselves, they were seldom able to unite in defense of their homeland. In fact, the Indians not only wasted their strength in fighting each other, but also often served in the field as allies of the Europeans against their own people. Resistance was all the more difficult because the diseases of the whites, especially smallpox and tuberculosis, decimated the red men. Moreover, with the passage of time, the Indians came to copy the Europeans with respect to weapons, clothing, and the use of alcohol. When they learned to rely upon the gun, to wear the white man's coat, and to drink the white man's rum or brandy, they became ultimately dependent upon the Europeans. In the end it made little difference to the Indian whether he dealt with Spaniard, Frenchman, or Englishman, for the result was always the same: he was forced to accept tribal extinction or inferior status in the white man's society. Much has been written about the differences between Spanish, Dutch, French, and English relations with the red men, and there were interesting dissimilarities. The Spanish and Portuguese intermarried most freely with the natives, in the case of the Spanish partly because the immigration of women from Spain was long officially discouraged. The French, also intermarrying freely with the Indians, were more adept than other Europeans in Indian diplomacy. The English excelled in trading with the Indians, for they were better able than other Europeans to supply the red men with guns, ammunition, clothing, and liquor, at a profit to themselves, if not to the Indians. Nevertheless, all Europeans, when they were strong enough to do so, insisted that the Indians make way for the white man. In those parts of the Americas lying south of the Rio Grande, because the Spanish and Portuguese did not migrate to the New World in large numbers in colonial times, Indian culture survived to some degree under European rule; north of the Rio Grande, Indian culture remains only in vestige, for the red men came to form only a small part of a vast population.

2 FRANCE AND ENGLAND
CHALLENGE SPAIN

After visiting San Salvador, other islands in the Bahamas, and Cuba, which he thought to be China—he also saw mermaids off its coast—Columbus explored the island of Haiti. Losing one of his ships, he built a fort there and garrisoned it with 37 men for whom there was no room in the remaining vessels. They were to stay until Columbus could return from Spain, but they were slain by the Indians, for the long conflict between the red men and the Europeans had already begun. Columbus and the two remaining ships made their way northward into the Atlantic and after many adventures reached Spain. En route, Columbus was forced into Lisbon harbor by a storm. He announced there, and again when he reached Spain, that he had found a new route to Asia. King John II of Portugal did not believe him. He was of the opinion that Columbus had landed on islands south and west of the Azores in an area conceded by the rulers of Spain, in 1455 and again by the Treaty of Alcaçovas in 1479, to be within a Portuguese sphere of influence. The Portuguese king considered im-

14

prisoning Columbus but permitted him to proceed to Palos when he was assured that Isabella and Ferdinand planned no encroachment on his domains.

It had long been the custom of Europeans to secure grants from the papacy for lands conquered from the heathen, and it was the pope who had officially announced the line between Portuguese and Spanish spheres in Africa and its offshore islands in 1455. Now Pope Alexander VI, of the Spanish family of Borgia, was asked to sanctify Isabella's claims to the lands found by Columbus. Accordingly, he issued three decrees which declared that all territories west of a line drawn north and south at a distance of 100 leagues west of the Azores were to be exclusively exploited by the Spanish, except when such lands should be ruled by Christian princes. Lands reserved for the Portuguese Crown since 1455 were thus limited on the west— too narrowly limited, in the opinion of John II, who protested energetically. The result was a concession by the monarchs of Spain which proved to be expensive. In the Treaty of Tordesillas of 1494 the line was pushed westward to a point 370 leagues beyond the Cape Verde Islands. By this new arrangement, which was given papal sanction twelve years later, the eastern part of Brazil fell to Portugal. In the year 1500 Pedro Alvares Cabral with a Portuguese fleet en route to India sailed farther to the west than usual, either by design or by accident, and struck the Brazilian coast. With this discovery began Portugal's American empire.

Columbus brought back to Spain gold dust, parrots, some Indians, and assurances that great wealth was easy to find in the Indies. His sailors apparently brought syphilis to Spain; it seems to have been a mild disease among the red men, but it soon raged through all of western Europe. He was sent back to the Caribbean as soon as preparations could be made, this time with a squadron of ships and hundreds of men. The city of Santo Domingo, the first permanent European colony in the Americas, was established in 1496. However, he found no great wealth. On a third voyage he reached the mainland of South America at the mouth of the Orinoco River, but again he found neither Japan nor riches. Moreover, he was unable even to maintain order among his followers, and a royal official arrested him and sent him back to Spain as a prisoner. Freed, he made a fourth and final voyage, exploring the coast of Central America in 1502. Deprived of most of the honors and emoluments which had been promised him, he died in modest circumstances in 1506. His descendants, however, were elevated to the nobility and pensioned by the Spanish Crown. It would seem that he never knew he had found a new world, and by a quirk of unkind fate neither of the continents he discovered bears his name. The year after his death the German geographer Martin Waldseemüller, in the belief that the Florentine Amerigo Vespucci had been first to land on the

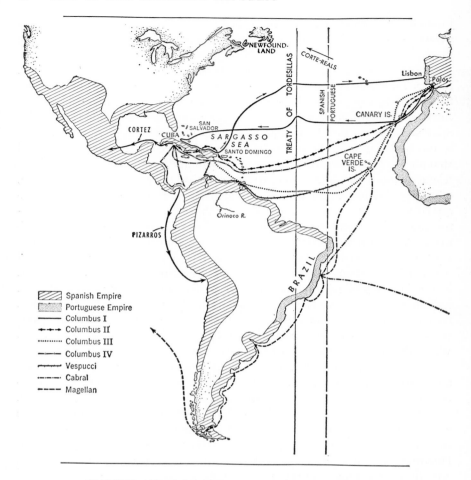

SPANISH AND PORTUGUESE IN THE NEW WORLD

mainland south of the Caribbean, suggested that that region be named for him. Waldseemüller had his way, and the name America gradually spread to cover both continents of the New World.

THE SPANISH EMPIRE

Within a century after Columbus' first voyage, Spain won a magnificent empire in the New World. From her ports explorer after explorer crossed the Atlantic in search of a short route to the Orient, which of course was never found. When it became apparent that there was no passageway through Central America, the search broadened and Spanish navigators probed along the shores of both North and South America. One of them, Ferdinand Magellan, a Portuguese pilot in Spanish pay, led an expedition through the straits which bear his name and thence on to the Philippines. There he was killed in battle with the natives, but one of his ships returned to Spain in 1521 after a three-year voyage, thus completing the first circumnavigation of the globe. The Spanish also quickly conquered and occupied the islands of the Caribbean. Their inhabitants, except for the cannibalistic and warlike Caribs, were not remarkable for their proficiency in battle, while superior armor, weapons, and military discipline gave the Spanish an immense advantage. In the harsh fate of the Arawaks, the peace-loving people of the Caribbean, the "Black Legend" of Spanish cruelty had its origins. However, it should be said that the Arawaks suffered more from sickness and labor, to which they were unaccustomed, than from the guns and swords of their conquerors. Negro slaves were soon imported from Africa to replace them.

With variations and exceptions the tale of the Spanish Conquistadores in the islands was repeated again and again on the American mainlands. Bold soldiers, crusaders for Christ, and treasure-seekers, the Spaniards gained control of Mexico, Central America, and all of South America except Brazil, by 1580. Their empire endured on the mainlands for three centuries, and indeed came to an end only when Spain was forced to give up Cuba and Puerto Rico in 1898. With amazing rapidity they also made their way northward into territory which later became part of the United States while their sailors explored the coasts of California and Oregon before 1550. In 1541 Francisco Vasques de Coronado with an army of nearly 300 men set out from Mexico to find the fabulously rich "seven cities of Cíbola." Not finding them in Arizona, he pushed east into New Mexico, where he sought another glittering objective, Quivira, a city with gold-paved streets. On he journeyed through Texas and Oklahoma into central Kansas. Returning unhappily to Mexico, he left no settlement behind him. Other explorers followed in his wake, however, and a colony was founded in New Mexico in 1598. Santa Fé became its capital eleven years afterward.

The Spanish entered the southeastern part of the United States a generation before Coronado began his remarkable journey, but did not form a permanent settlement there until 1565. Juan Ponce de Léon landed in Florida in 1513, and returned eight years later, seeking a land of lucre called Bimini, and a fountain of eternal youth which might revive his old and worn body. He and his men were attacked by Indians and driven to sea, Ponce de Léon being mortally wounded. Pánfilo de Narváez, who led a large group of men and women to Tampa Bay in 1528, encountered no happier fate. Three years afterward Hernando de Soto, seeking treasure with 600 men, began an amazing journey which took him through Florida, Georgia, and South Carolina, thence westward across the Mississippi in

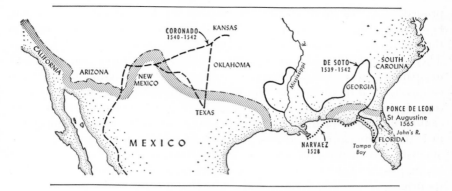

SPANISH MAINLAND EXPLORERS

search of a will-o'-the-wisp. Disgusted at the failure of attempts to found a colony in Florida, the Spanish ruler, Philip II, announced in 1561 that no further efforts should be made. However, the Spanish did establish a permanent colony four years later, largely as a defensive measure. French Huguenots, locating on the St. John's River in Northern Florida, had begun to attack Spanish treasure ships passing between the tip of the peninsula and Cuba on their way northward. From that island Pedro Menéndez de Avilés, with a small army, founded St. Augustine and drove off the French. The town survived and became the capital of the Spanish province of Florida.

The Spanish also tried to establish themselves on the coasts of the Carolinas and Virginia, but in vain. Efforts to found colonies in the Carolinas in 1526 and 1566 failed, and another undertaken by Spanish Jesuits in Virginia after 1570 met a similar fate. The absence of metallic treasures in the area, bitter opposition from the Indians, waning aggressiveness of the Spanish, and doubtless the defeat of the Great Armada in 1588, all contributed to the abandonment of efforts to occupy lands to the north of Florida. Only a few missions in Georgia were successful, and they were given up in the next century. A vast and rich region along the north Atlantic was thus left vacant of Europeans. Opportunity was extended to the French, Dutch, and English, and they did not fail to take advantage of it.

The Spanish empire in the Americas was largely the creation of individuals, rather than of the Spanish Crown. Occasionally the Conquistadores received financial help from the government, but in the main they had to develop their own sinews of war in order to win glory, wealth, and power. Nor were the missionaries who did so much to Christianize the Indians generally supported by the Crown. The characteristic title of the Conquistadores was Adelantado, which indicates that its bearer was entitled to conquer in a certain area. The Adelantado was often guaranteed certain privileges of great value in the event that his enterprise should be successful. Hernán Cortés, who conquered the valley of Mexico, the Pizarros, who overthrew the Incas in Peru, and others of their amazing breed were not permitted to govern for long. Some Conquistadores, like the Pizarros, bitterly resented the establishment of a royal regime and actually fought against royal officials, but always unsuccessfully. The Spanish empire was gradually organized into viceroyalties and smaller units.

For many decades the "Indies" brought great wealth to the Spanish Crown. The king received a fifth of the products of the mines, including precious stones as well as the remarkably rich silver deposits of Mexico and the Andean highlands. His income from sales and other taxes imposed upon his subjects in the New World was also large, and sales monopolies added to the royal treasury. Charles I, the grandson of Ferdinand and Isabella, and for a time his son Philip II, seemed to possess sources of almost inexhaustible wealth and to hold the west in fee as Venice once held the east. Treasure ships from the Indies began to deposit quantities of precious metals in Spanish ports in 1523 and became the wonders of the sixteenth century. However, in the long run the precious metals may have been injurious rather than beneficial to Spain, in part because they encouraged the Crown to neglect commerce and to limit its development in the American colonies. This is not to suggest that Spain merely exploited her colonies or that she failed as a colonizing nation. Her record in the New World, though uneven, is more impressive than it is commonly considered by North Americans. There is the fact that her empire endured for 300 years. Moreover, Spanish institutions, language, and culture were effectively transplanted. In further defense of the Spanish it may be said that they were not peculiarly vicious in their relations with the Indians and Negroes. There was greater intellectual freedom and progress in colonial Spanish America than has been generally recognized. Its commerce was severely restricted by orders from Madrid, but it must be recalled that England, France, and Holland did not offer freedom of trade to their New World subjects.

Did Spain in the last analysis gain from the riches from across the Atlantic? Since foreigners were barred from trade with the Indies, Spanish merchants easily made money by purchasing non-Spanish goods and sending them off to the colonies at greatly increased prices. This system left little incentive for Spanish manufacturers. Moreover, the flow of seemingly easy wealth into the royal coffers doubtless helped to persuade the Spanish rulers that the economy could be neglected, that they were opulent, and that they could engage in long, expensive, and finally unsuccessful wars in Europe. Spain did not flourish, except temporarily, because of her magnificent American domains. During the reign of Philip II Spain entered upon a long period of decline which was punctuated in 1588 by the humiliating failure of the Great Armada. Soon after the middle of the seventeenth century France secured military ascendancy on the European continent. There was to be a revival of national power under the Bourbons after 1700, but it only served to arrest the decline, and Spain continued to lag behind other European powers.

PORTUGUESE SETTLEMENTS

Even in the days of greatest Spanish energy and power, the active Portuguese insisted upon the execution of the Treaty of Tordesillas and occupied a large part of South America. For many years after the landfall of Cabral, the Crown of Portugal displayed little interest in Brazil, since Portuguese ventures in India and the East Indies were very profitable at the time. Nevertheless, the voyage of Cabral was followed by various others, organized principally to secure the red dyewood from which the name Brazil is derived. Portuguese merchants gradually established little trading posts along the Brazilian coast, and various males, going ashore of their own volition or marooned because of misbehavior aboard ship, "went native." These intermarried with the Indians and are often referred to as the "grandfathers" of Brazil, since their daughters became wives for later comers. At length Portuguese interest in Brazil increased, partly because profits from the eastern empire were less than anticipated, and partly because Portuguese jealousy was aroused by the appearance of Spaniards and French on its coasts. In 1530 King John III sent out Martim Affonso de Sousa as governor with wide powers and a band of 400 settlers. Sousa established the first permanent settlement, at São Vicente, and has been called the father of Brazil. Gradually the Portuguese occupied the shores of their vast colony, warding off attempts by the French and Dutch to seize segments or all of it. Brazil became Portuguese in language and in culture, although that culture was of course influenced by the Indians and by Negroes who were imported as slaves. The colony prospered moderately, and eventually expanded far beyond the line of Tordesillas, for the Portuguese did not hesitate to encroach upon lands which that treaty had awarded to Spain.

The Portuguese confined most of their efforts to Brazil, but the line of demarcation enabled them to claim Newfoundland and Labrador as well. Learning that John Cabot, sailing for Henry VII of England, had found land in northeastern North America, the Portuguese Captain Gaspar Corte-Real sailed to the northwest, finding "a land which was very cool and with great woods." He disappeared on a second journey thither in 1501. In the following year his brother Miguel went in search of him, and he also vanished. In 1503 the Portuguese king sent out an expedition to try to find the lost brothers. It did not meet with success, and Portugal lost interest in Labrador and Newfoundland. Only the Portuguese origin of the former name reminds us that her hardy sailors crossed the northern Atlantic only eight years after the first voyage of Columbus.

Spain's exclusive claim to the lands and seas beyond the line of Tordesillas was never recognized by the European states north of the Pyrenees—not even when Spanish strength was at its zenith in the sixteenth century. No crowned heads in central Europe were able to challenge the division of the New World into Spanish and Portuguese spheres of influence; indeed, Germany and Italy did not exist as national states. However, the leaders of England, France, and the Dutch republic, later those of Sweden and Denmark, displayed little respect for priority in discovery and none at all for papal sanction. Francis I of France cynically suggested that he would accept the settlement of Tordesillas when its makers produced a will of Adam barring his French descendants from the Americas. Discovery might enable a nation to claim new lands, but only permanent occupation permitted them to be held. The rulers north of the Pyrenees did not allow the Portuguese to retain Brazil nor the Spanish to dominate a large part of the New World without long struggles. Eventually, they occupied most of North America, many islands in the Caribbean, and minor areas in Central and South America. Roman Catholic princes displayed no more concern for papal authority than did the Protestants; they did display an equal lust for treasure and territory.

FRENCH EXPLORERS

France made an early and vain effort to settle on that part of the North American coast that had not been occupied by Spain. In 1524, commissioned by Francis I, Giovanni Verrazano set sail across the Atlantic on a voyage of exploration. He entered Delaware Bay, then moved northward into New York Bay (he was probably the first European to enter it), followed the coast as far to the northeast as Cape Breton Island, and returned safely to France, where he reported favorably upon his findings. In 1534 Francis I sent out Jacques Cartier, a hardy mariner of Saint-Malo, toward the area last visited by Verrazano, where gold and other wealth presumably were to be had. He was also to search for a northwest passage to Asia. Cartier visited the west coast of Newfoundland and touched upon Prince Edward Island, but returned home without finding the mouth of the St. Lawrence River. He returned in the following year, however, discovered the river, and pushed inland as far as the Indian village of Hochelaga, at the site of modern Montreal. There Indians who were apparently members of the powerful Iroquois Indian confederacy, told him of a kingdom named Saguenay, which was off to the west and which possessed great wealth. The kingdom was as enticing as the seven cities of Cíbola had been to Coronado, and Cartier yearned to go in search of it. However, winter was approaching, so he returned to France to tell the great news, taking with him an Indian chief from Hochelaga to support his story.

The treasures of Saguenay also charmed Francis. Learning that Francis proposed to send settlers to the St. Lawrence, Charles I protested against an intrusion into territory which he insisted was Spanish. Francis was not to be deterred, and appointed the Sieur de Roberval viceroy of a colony of Canada-to-be, with Cartier as commander of ships under him. In 1541 Cartier again sailed into the St. Lawrence, established a post on the river below Montreal, and pushed up the river to find Saguenay. He failed, and set off for France once more. Meeting an expedition under Roberval en route, he refused to accompany it, and went on to Europe. Roberval and his followers reoccupied Cartier's base, where they endured a harsh winter in 1542–1543. They too searched vainly for Saguenay, abandoned the enterprise, and finally made their way back to France. The Crown of France ignored Canada for almost the next half-century. In addition to the discouraging reports from Cartier and Roberval, civil wars at home made royal efforts toward American colonization difficult, if not impossible.

However, religious strife, the major cause of conflict within France after 1560, did lead to French attempts to settle in other parts of the Americas. Protestant followers of John Calvin were numerous in France, especially among the merchants, the artisans, and the lower nobility. Intermittent persecution failed to prevent a rapid spread of Calvinist doctrines and for a time one-tenth or more of Frenchmen were Huguenots, as Calvinists were known in France. At mid-century, however, the future in France seemed dark for them, and some turned to emigration to America in order to secure religious freedom. They were the first persons to depart for the New World to escape religious persecution. They were permitted by the Crown to try to found colonies in both South and North America, but they were given little assistance. They tried to build an "Antarctic France" after 1556 in the area of Rio de Janeiro, but were finally driven off by the Portuguese. In 1562 they attempted to found a settlement at Port Royal, South Carolina, and again failed. Two years later two groups of Huguenot settlers went to the St. John's River in northern Florida to found a "New France." These were decimated and scattered by the Spanish. The Huguenots then temporarily abandoned their efforts to settle in North America. A more enduring New France was to develop in the St. Lawrence Valley after the end of the century. More than a century later French Protestants again appeared in South Carolina; this time they came with the blessing of the English government and contributed to the growth of the English rather than the French empire.

ENGLISH EXPLORERS

The part played by England in the New World in the sixteenth century was very much like that of France. The English sent out exploring expeditions earlier than did the French, but their efforts to colonize began later. Like the French, they failed to create a permanent colony until after the end of that century.

It was Henry VII, the first of the Tudors, who took the first step toward building an English empire. In 1497 he sponsored a westward voyage from Bristol in search of a route to Asia. John Cabot, a Venetian navigator, along with certain persons of Bristol planned and financed the project. The Venetian made his way across the north Atlantic in the *Matthew* with a crew of only 18 men. He struck the American coast somewhere near Newfoundland and ran along it to the southwest for several hundred miles. He claimed the region for his royal master, returned safely to his home port, and gave out reports of the magnificent fishing grounds off Newfoundland and New England. Henry was pleased, and rewarded Cabot with a present of £10 and a pension of £20 per annum, substantial gifts for a king who was not noted for financial extravagance. He also gave permission for a second voyage, which Cabot and his supporters undertook, again at their own expense. Accordingly, in 1498 Cabot set sail with five ships and several hundred men. Whether he completed the journey is not known, but some of his men came back to England after exploring the coast from Nova Scotia as far south as Delaware Bay, and possibly as far as the Carolinas. Neither Henry nor Cabot nor the seafaring people of Bristol followed up these journeys of exploration. The only immediate result was the beginning of English cod fishing off the coast of Newfoundland, a business which afterward gave impetus to colonization. Nevertheless the Cabot voyages were important, for they gave England a claim to the east coast of North America on the basis of first discovery.

Henry VIII displayed no more interest in the New World than had his father. He was chiefly occupied with warfare and diplomacy at home, and during the early years of his reign he was generally on good terms with the rulers of Spain, who were relatives of his first wife, Catherine of Aragon. When he wished to free himself from Catherine and the papacy refused him an annulment, he made himself head of the English Church. In this way he unintentionally brought the Protestant revolt to England, which was shaken by bitter religious conflicts until after the accession of Elizabeth I in 1558. This struggle was perhaps enough in itself to occupy the energies of the English. Moreover, Elizabeth's elder half-sister and predecessor, Mary Tudor, was a Roman Catholic and wife of Philip II; she would not dream

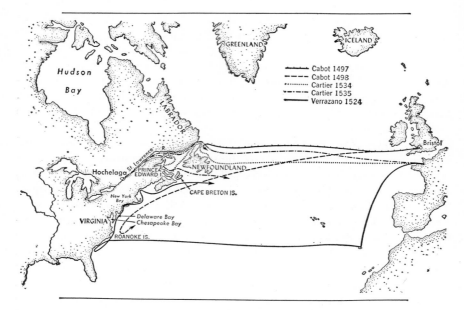

FIRST FRENCH AND ENGLISH EXPLORERS

of challenging her beloved husband's claim to hegemony in the New World. There is some doubt that even a united England would have been strong enough to colonize successfully before the era of Elizabeth. Nevertheless, events were pointing toward England's entrance into the contest for wealth and empire in the Americas. Henry VIII had established the English navy, as well as a record in English royal marriages, and the years between 1558 and 1562 brought a decided shift in English conditions and policy. Immediately before her death in 1558, Mary abandoned Calais to France and so put an end to England's European possessions and ambitions, an event which permitted her successor to devote herself to other matters.

The early years of the reign of Elizabeth brought the permanent establishment of the Anglican Church, one which occupied a position halfway between those of Rome and Calvin, and which soon won the allegiance of most Englishmen. By 1562 the Anglican Church was formally and firmly embedded in English law—if Elizabeth could hold her throne against the Catholic Mary Stuart, Queen of Scots and against the Catholic Philip II, who had been Mary Tudor's husband. It is a striking fact that in the same year, 1562, John Hawkins took a long step toward creating an English empire in America by voyaging to the Caribbean to sell Negro slaves, an enterprise which found no favor at the court of Spain. Thereafter, though assuring Philip of her friendship and even suggesting her affection, Elizabeth haltingly moved toward an assault against Spain in the New World, and then into open warfare against Philip in Europe.

John Hawkins' first journey to America was dictated by a desire for peaceful and profitable commerce. English merchants had long thought of the Spanish colonies as areas in which they might trade to great advantage. They had held back, partly because Spanish decrees forbade traffic between Spanish colonials and foreigners, and partly because they feared that such traffic would lead Philip to close the ports of old Spain and the Low Countries, where they did a profitable business. Hawkins and certain London merchants chose to take the chance of reprisal, hoping that Philip would see some advantage for Spain in their enterprises, and that he would withdraw or fail to carry out his own decrees. With English merchandise and 400 Negro slaves from the coast of Africa, Hawkins appeared off Haiti in 1563. The Spanish planters wanted his Negroes and goods, and dealt with him in spite of the royal prohibition. He did a splendid business and carried off a fine return cargo and orders for future deliveries. Philip was deeply angered by Hawkins' intrusion, renewed the prohibition, and ordered his officials in the Caribbean to see to it that Hawkins and others like him were prevented from violating it again. However, Hawkins was pleased by the results of his first voyage and returned to the Spanish colonies the next year, going to the mainland of northern South America—the Spanish Main. The inhabitants feared to trade with him, although some doubtless desired to do so; moreover, Crown officials undertook to prevent traffic, though with no great eagerness. Hawkins insisted upon doing business, even if he had to employ arms, and again he was successful. A third voyage brought an open break between England and Spain in the New World. In 1568 the English adventurer went back to the Caribbean with eight ships, two of which actually belonged to Queen Elizabeth, who thus became a partner in an enterprise certain to arouse the hostility of the Spanish king. Again Hawkins trafficked on the Spanish Main, but he was driven by storm to a Mexican port, where he sought and was given permission to refit. There he was assailed and routed by a fleet arriving from Spain. Only four of his ships, including one captained by his kinsman, Francis Drake, returned safely to England. Believing that they had been victims of treachery, Hawkins and Drake determined upon revenge. "El Draco" was all the more vengeful because he, like Hawkins, was an ardent Protestant.

After 1568 Drake and other English freebooters coursed the Caribbean in search of plunder rather than trade. In 1572 Drake attacked Nombre de Dios and Cartagena, captured several Spanish ships, and made his way across the isthmus of Panama, where he seized a mule train loaded with precious metals. Five years later he began his famous voyage round the world. He ravaged the west coast of Spanish America, accumulated an amazing booty, and returned to England by way of the Cape of Good Hope. He shared his spoils with Queen Elizabeth, who knighted him upon the deck of his ship, *Golden Hind*. In 1585 he returned to the Caribbean with a large fleet and a commission from the queen, capturing Cartagena a second time and destroying St. Augustine. After Philip II became king of Portugal as well as of Spain in 1580, English captains ravaged Portuguese settlements in Brazil as well. They injured Spain and at the same time enriched themselves when their ventures were successful, as they commonly were. Meanwhile, like the French before them, the English sought a northwest passage to Asia. In the 1570s Martin Frobisher made three voyages to the north of Newfoundland and actually found a passage, though it was hardly usable, in the Arctic Ocean; and John Davis soon afterward penetrated into the strait that bears his name. However, the practical result of their labors was to direct English attention to the southward.

The first English effort to colonize in America came in 1578. It was Sir Humphrey Gilbert, half-brother of the renowned Walter Raleigh, who was responsible for that first attempt. Chiefly interested first in finding a northwest passage, then in schemes to attack Spanish shipping and ports, Gilbert ultimately came to lay most emphasis upon colonization. On June 11, 1578, Queen Elizabeth gave him a patent for North America, authorizing him and his heirs "to discover, search, finde out and viewe such remote heathen and barbarous landes, countries and territories not actually possessed of any Christian prince or people. . . . And the same to have hould occupie and enjoye to him his heires and assignes forever with all comodities jurisdiccions and royalties both by sea and land." They were given full governmental authority in those lands, with two important exceptions, that those who should settle in America were "to have and enjoye all the priviledges of free denizens and parsons natyve of England," and that their "statutes, lawes and ordenances" were to be as consistent as might be with "the forme of the lawes and pollicies of England." The rights of Gilbert were to expire unless he established a colony within six years. In return for the powers granted to him, Gilbert agreed to give the Crown one-fifth of the products of all mines that might be found. It was further stipulated that the Crown was not responsible for any actions of the patentees hostile to any Christian ruler, a proviso which was suggested by Gilbert himself. In other words, if the venture were successful, Elizabeth could officially accept responsibility; if it failed, she could wash her hands of it.

Enlisting the aid of several associates, including Raleigh, and with crews of adventurers and pirates, Gilbert set sail before the end of 1578 with a heavily armed squadron of seven ships. Evidently his intentions upon this first voyage were to explore, to establish a base, and to use it to attack the Spanish. However, the expedition was a failure, for storms and internal dissension prevented a journey across the ocean. Two years later Gilbert sent Simon Fernandez, a Portuguese pilot, across the Atlantic to secure information in the *Squirrel,* a tiny ship of 8 tons with a crew of only eleven men. Fernandez actually accomplished his mission, returning to report that he had found Indians living in round houses. He had probably landed on the coast of New England. However, Gilbert had to accomplish more than this, for the end of the six-year period of his patent was approaching. In June, 1583, he could once more set sail for North America, with five ships and 260 men. Lacking sufficient supplies to proceed farther, he had to put in at Newfoundland. There, where fishermen had long sojourned between fishing trips, he established a post which he hoped would enable him to retain his patent right. Sailing to the southwest with two ships, he found nothing. Changing his course for England, he and his two ships were stricken by storm. One ship returned safely to England, but the one that carried Gilbert was never again seen. Gilbert's ventures were completely unsuccessful, and he lost both fortune and life in them.

Walter Raleigh, courtier, warrior, sailor, explorer, adventurer, colonial entrepreneur extraordinary, famous for his interest in tobacco (which was actually introduced into England in quantity by Drake), stepped into the shoes of his half-brother. A favorite of Queen Elizabeth and a man of wealth, he asked for and was given a royal charter in March, 1584. It substantially endowed him with the same rights as had been possessed by Gilbert, and it placed him under the same restrictions. He too was required to establish a colony within six years in order to maintain his privileges. Raleigh moved promptly, sending Captains Philip Amadas and Arthur Barlow on a voyage of exploration. They reached the coast of North Carolina in July. There they traded with the Indians and made a survey of Roanoke Island. They returned to England with two Indian captives and a small rope of pearls. One of their leaders reported that the lands were "the most plentifull, sweete, fruitfull, and wholsome of all the worlde," and that the Indians were "most gentle, loving, and faithfull, voide of all guile and treason, and such as live after the maner of the golden age. . . ." They reported that the climate was mild, and that Roanoke and neighboring islands were located in an enclosed and protected sea. The only lack for a colony was a fine harbor. Their handsome descriptions were joyfully received, and Raleigh promptly attached the name Virginia to the coast of North America to honor the queen, who indicated her pleasure by knighting her shrewd courtier.

Raleigh drove on. He secured the help of Richard Hakluyt the younger, an extraordinary propagandist, for an all-important attempt to persuade Elizabeth to support a colony in Virginia with royal funds. Hakluyt presented to her his famous *Discourse on the Western Planting,* in which he asserted that England would profit mightily, not only from a successful venture at Roanoke, but from other colonies along the east coast of North America. He contended that Spain's power was based upon the wealth of her American possessions, and that English colonies in America would be ideal bases from which to attack Spanish shipping and to find a northwest passage. They would also serve to advance the cause of Protestantism. Above all, they would lay the foundations for a vast commerce between England and America at a time when English traders were meeting serious competition elsewhere. His arguments, though not new, were cogent and well presented. However, Elizabeth, never one to lavish money, believed she could not afford to adopt Hakluyt's proposal. The European situation was tense, and open warfare with Philip II was approaching. She gave her blessing to Raleigh, but no more. Her successors were to follow the same policy with few exceptions during several generations.

Accordingly, Raleigh had to proceed as best he might, with such help as he could get from private persons. Richard Hakluyt the elder prepared a lengthy paper on the best way to form a string of settlements along the shores of Virginia. He urged a careful survey of natural resources, and stressed the possibilities of agriculture and commerce rather than mineral wealth, although he did indicate faith in quick returns. Guided by his suggestions, Raleigh sent Sir Richard Grenville with seven ships and many men back to Roanoke Island. Grenville reached his destination in June, 1585, and departed for England in August, leaving more than 100 men on the island. They included Ralph Lane as commander, John White, an artist who made splendid water colors of the neighboring Indians, and Thomas Hariot, who later published the first book concerning English America. Lane and his men did much exploring, as far to the north as Chesapeake Bay, traded with the Indians, and tried to grow sugar cane. In September, 1585, Lane was optimistic. The mainland of North Carolina, he said, had "the goodliest soyle under the cope of heaven . . . it is the goodliest and most pleasing territorie of the world . . . and the climate so wholsome, that wee had not one sicke since we touched the land here." In the spring, however, the English adventurers became involved in open warfare with the Indians and discouraged about their prospects because Grenville's return with supplies and reinforcements was delayed. Lane came to believe that "the discovery of a good Mine . . . or a passage to the South-sea, or some way to it, and nothing els can bring this Countrey in request to be inhabited by our nation." In June, 1586, Drake stopped off at Roanoke, generously offering either to carry Raleigh's people back to England or to give them a ship loaded with supplies. The ship in question being damaged by a storm, they decided to accompany him homeward. For "feare they should be left behinde they left all things confusedly, as if they had beene chased from thence by a mighty army; and no doubt so they were; for the hand of God came upon them for the cruelty and outrages committed by some of them against the native inhabitants of that countrey." By ill fortune, Grenville arrived only two weeks after their departure. He left a holding force of only 15 men at Roanoke, a reckless step in view of the Indian fighting which had occurred earlier, and also departed.

In 1587 Raleigh, apparently with the support of other private persons, made another effort to put down roots in America. He sent three ships with ample supplies and 68 men, 17 women, and 9 children. They were to go ashore on Chesapeake Bay, Roanoke now being considered an unsuitable spot. The artist, John White, was to serve as governor, and was to control the colony with the aid of twelve assistants, who were to serve as a council. The ships went by way of the West Indies to Roanoke to pick up the 15 men left there the previous year. Only the bones of one were found, a direful portent. Moreover, they could not proceed to Chesapeake Bay, because Simon Fernandez refused to pilot them thither, saying that the season was too late. It was decided, instead, to locate on the mainland 50 miles from Roanoke. In August the ships set off for England. Before they departed, Governor White's daughter, Eleanor Dare, gave birth to a child appropriately named Virginia, the first of English stock to be born on American soil. She left no descendants to claim exalted social position as a consequence, for the settlers were never again seen by Europeans. They were probably slain by the Indians; some may have been permitted to live, being adopted according to Indian custom. The approach of full-scale war between England and Spain distracted Raleigh's attention and also made it difficult for him to send reinforcements. One expedition was ruined when Queen Elizabeth took his ships for national uses; another was forced back into port by a Spanish attack. At last John White managed to return to Roanoke in 1590 as a passenger in a small English squadron going to the Caribbean. He and his associates found only a message left behind by the lost colonists, the word *Croatoan*. Croatoan was the name of a nearby Indian chief and tribe; and it had been agreed in 1587 that the colonists should leave such a message to indicate their location if they left Roanoke. White was able to make only a brief search. A longer one would probably have been of little avail, except to secure news of the deaths of the settlers. The squadron moved on to sea, and Raleigh's ill-fated Virginia project came to an end. He could afford to do no more, at least for a time. He insisted, however, that he would live long enough "to see the English nation planted there," and so he did.

BERMUDAS or SUMMER'S Is

3 VIRGINIA AND PLYMOUTH

The first decade of the seventeenth century was a period of extraordinary activity for empire building in North America. Permanent colonies were planted at Jamestown by the English, at Quebec by the French, and the Dutch explored New Netherland, all between 1607 and 1609. Conditions had become more favorable for English colonization than they had been before, as old motives for colonization became stronger and new ones appeared. Moreover, a new device helpful in organizing for colonial settlement had been developed in the form of the company. Hostility toward

Spain and the desire for bases for attacks on her shipping and settlements continued as before. Thoughtful men believed, as in the past, that colonization should be encouraged so that English people could flourish and multiply in America. The hope that a passageway to the Orient could be found through North America had not died. Profits from fishing off the coasts of New England and Newfoundland were large, and some men believed that stations or settlements on those coasts would make fishing even more profitable. Moreover, it was still thought that gold and silver might be found in North America as they had been in Mexico and South America. Dreams of easy mineral wealth encouraged adventurers to gamble heavily. Some foresaw great riches from commerce between the colonies and mother country. Others saw in colonization a cure for overpopulation at home. While the population in England was not large, perhaps about 4,000,000, it is true that these included large numbers who were unemployed, vagrants, and convicts. Were such people to find new places beyond the seas, they would increase the wealth and security of the mother country and at the same time do something for themselves. Still further, they would not be a burden upon the public purse at home.

No doubt the English practice of enclosure, which drove people from the land at a time when they could not find employment in the cities, contributed to the desire of many persons to emigrate. A little later, the desire for land became an impelling motive, for in England the chances of the average man to acquire it were not good. They were even less on the continent of Europe. As it became apparent that land ownership could be achieved in America, peasants, small farmers, and for that matter village, town, and city folk, began to dream of getting lands for themselves and for their descendants. Eventually, indeed, land was the great magnet which was to draw tens of millions of people to North America.

Religion also became a powerful factor in building the English empire in America. The Anglican Church was, of course, a middle way. However, it persecuted not only Roman Catholics, but also Protestants who for one reason or another found it unsatisfactory. Accordingly the Puritans, those who wished to purify the Church of England, and the Separatists, Protestants who had no hope of changing it to suit their wishes, found in America religious freedom for themselves and a chance to deny it to others. On the other hand, when the Puritans were in power in England, as they were from 1642 to 1660, Anglicans often fled to areas where they might worship freely, especially Virginia and Maryland.

The company was of value in successful colonization because it permitted larger efforts, over longer periods of time. As we have already seen, Sir Walter Raleigh failed because he lacked funds to continue his expensive projects. The company had slowly developed in the sixteenth century, and had become a familiar device in England for pooling capital and risks by

1600. In such a combination the stockholders or freemen met quarterly to choose assistants—or as we would say, directors—and a treasurer or governor, who corresponded to today's president and directed operations. The East India Company, established at the beginning of the seventeenth century, had governmental authority as well as commercial privileges, and enjoyed extraordinary success, which impressed venturers of all sorts in London and in England generally. Indeed, Sir Thomas Smythe, a principal founder of the colony of Virginia, was also the first governor of the East India Company.

In 1606 Smythe and various other men who had been interested in Raleigh's ventures, together with others who dreamed of gaining wealth from the New World, founded the London Company of Virginia. Among its leaders were Robert Rich, the Earl of Warwick, and Sir Edwin Sandys. That same year Sir John Popham, a Somerset lawyer and Chief Justice of England, joined with Sir Ferdinando Gorges, Governor of the Port of Plymouth to organize a Plymouth Company. Its members came chiefly from southwestern England, especially from Plymouth and Bristol. Several persons belonged to both companies. The stockholders of the London combination hoped to find quick prosperity in mines in the region of Chesapeake Bay, and in attacks on Spanish commerce. The people of the Plymouth Company, on the other hand, were more interested in the fisheries off New England and Newfoundland, and in the proceeds of lumbering and fur trading. The two groups sought royal favor together, and obtained it in 1606 when James I granted a royal charter to both. The long war with Spain had ended only a few months earlier, and James was reluctant to enter upon a policy certain to offend the Spanish Crown. Nevertheless, although the Spanish were unwilling to admit the right of Englishmen to settle anywhere in the New World, the king ventured to grant a large part of North America to the two English groups.

By the charter of 1606 the London Company was given all that part of North America between latitude 34° and 38°, stretching from sea to sea. The Plymouth Company was given the region between 41° and 45° of north latitude, also sea to sea. Both companies were authorized to settle their respective areas as they saw fit. Both could establish colonies in the region between their exclusive jurisdictions, so long as the settlements of one were no nearer than fifty miles to those of the other. Each was to organize a governing council within its domains in America. These councils were to operate under the direction of the companies in both economic and political matters. However, they also were to act under the direction of a royal council, which was to sit in London; actually, the royal council consisted chiefly of members of the two companies.

The Plymouth Company never succeeded in founding a permanent colony within its territory. In 1607 it sent an expedition led by George Popham and Raleigh Gilbert which established a post on the coast of Maine. However, this settlement endured only a few months, the hardships of a New England winter promptly putting an end to it. Thereafter, Sir Ferdinando Gorges, the leading spirit in the Company, continued to do what he could to exploit its rights. He authorized fishing and trading vessels to visit the coast of New England and to explore it. He advertised the region, with valuable assistance from Captain John Smith, who visited it in 1614 and two years later published *The Description of New England,* a volume phrased in the language of a real estate prospectus. It is worth noting that Smith, so famous in the annals of Virginia, was the person who gave New England its name. After 1620 the Plymouth Company, reorganized as the Council of New England, became an extremely important body by making grants to other organizations and individuals that did successfully occupy various points in New England. It therefore turned out that the Plymouth Company, although it did no settling itself, was by no means unimportant in the settlement of North America.

THE SETTLEMENT OF VIRGINIA

The London Company of Virginia was far more active, and established a permanent settlement in its territory within a few months. It prepared three ships which set out from London toward the close of 1606, and reached Chesapeake Bay the following April. Less than a month later 120 colonists from the ships began to throw up huts at Jamestown on the James River. All were men, and most were dead within three years from hardship, Indian attacks, and disease. Many others who followed them to Chesapeake Bay in 1608 and 1609 met the same fate. By 1610 the survivors despaired of success and actually set off down the river for England. As they came out into Chesapeake Bay, however, they met ships bringing more settlers and supplies, and they turned back to try again.

Meanwhile, the Company had secured a new charter from the Crown. By this document of 1609 the boundaries of its dominions were altered. Henceforth it was to have all the territory between lines beginning at points 200 miles north and south of Point Comfort and running west and northwest sea to sea. Another important change in the new charter relieved the Company of reporting to the royal council, which was abolished. The Anglican Church was legally established in the new colony. Still further amendments were made in 1612.

The Company sent out reinforcements in 1610 and in the following years, and indeed the stockholders sank large sums into the colony. However, they were losers in the end. The mines did not materialize. When a

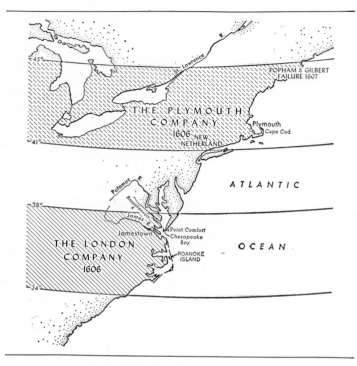

VIRGINIA AND PLYMOUTH COLONIES

shipload of gold was sent from Virginia to England, the contents turned out to be only iron pyrites. Profits were inevitably delayed and ephemeral, because the wealth of Virginia was agricultural rather than mineral.

Those who came to Virginia on the first three ships in the spring of 1607 endured almost intolerable hardships. They chose Jamestown as the site for their first settlement because the James River was deep along the shore at that spot, and it was therefore easy to anchor ships there. However, Jamestown actually was located on a low island, where malaria inevitably flourished. Weak from a long voyage and suffering from scurvy, the settlers were in no condition for the hardships which they were forced to undergo. Their supplies of food soon ran low. Fresh food was plentiful in the woods and waters around them, but the supply could not consistently be maintained. Neighboring Indians soon taught them how to grow corn and other vegetables, but the labor of growing crops, of building huts, of hunting, and of exploring were grievous burdens to the settlers, who were in general unaccustomed to manual toil. Many of the first settlers were called "gentlemen," which term indicates that they came from substantial families. Their relatives were doubtless glad to know that they were beyond the seas, for many were younger sons and ne'er-do-wells for whom there was no future at home. They were commonly imbued with the get-rich-quick spirit and better prepared to fight than to work. It would have been better for the colony had they been carpenters, masons, and experienced farmers. Captain John Smith, a tower of strength during the few months he spent in the colony, even had to persuade some of these gentlemen that cutting down trees was a sport, to get them to swing axes. Added trouble came from the fact that the first settlers were all male; women were necessary for the colony, but none appeared on the banks of the James for some time. Of course the Indians were a menace as well as a help. Happily, they and their "Emperor" Powhatan did not immediately resolve to drive the colonists into the sea. Had they attempted to do so, they must have succeeded. However, except for occasional minor outbreaks, the Indians were quiet, and not until 1622 was there a general attack upon the colony. Then it was nearly destroyed, but after fifteen years of planting and growth it was able to withstand a vigorous attack, although a part of Jamestown itself was ruined.

With the passing years and the appearance of women and more settlers, with experience in growing crops, with added know-how for survival in its strange new environment, the colony slowly achieved stability. By 1614 its future was virtually assured. In that year John Rolfe sent a shipment of mild Virginia tobacco to England, where it was welcomed and sold at a good profit. The settlers had found the Indians using tobacco chiefly for ceremonial purposes, but the sort grown by Powhatan and his friends was strong and unpalatable to Europeans. However, Rolfe imported leaf from the West Indies which was much milder and much more pleasing to Europeans, and it grew very well in Virginia. Tobacco had already been introduced into England by Sir Francis Drake, and the demand for it had increased. Indeed, men everywhere were to find the soothing weed infinitely attractive. The cash and credit obtained by Virginians who followed Rolfe's example enabled them to clear more land, grow more tobacco, and to build themselves better homes. Although the Virginians raised wheat, other crops, and cattle, tobacco continued to be the basic crop along the shores of Chesapeake Bay for many generations. The banks of the James, the York, the Rappahannock, and the Potomac rivers were occupied by planters who steadily pushed inland as more and more land was put into production.

The social structure of Virginia also changed with the passing years. More and more men who were prepared to work appeared in the colony. The Company sent out artisans who were, of course, far more useful than the upper-middle-class folk who had formed the first contingent of settlers. The colony likewise gained from the establishment of family life.

In 1619 a new source of labor appeared when a Dutch ship captain brought the first load of Negroes into Chesapeake Bay. Technically they were for some years servants rather than slaves. However, with the passage of time they became legally slaves, their status being utterly different from that of the Europeans who were brought in as servants. Both races might have been happier had the Negroes not been imported, but the introduction of slavery was hardly to be avoided. Even in the attempt at colonizing Roanoke Island the use of Negro slaves from the West Indies was considered by Sir Francis Drake. Had the Roanoke experiment been successful, the Negro would have appeared at the very beginning of English colonization. As it was, only twelve years intervened between the settlement of the whites and the coming of the Negro. In any case by 1619 the basic elements of Virginia society had appeared, the gentleman, the yeoman, and the Negro.

Meanwhile the colony achieved political stability. In the early years the council was riven by dissension and its members quarreled furiously among themselves. However, after 1610 a governor ruled sternly; order was what was needed, and it was given by Sir Thomas Dale and other firm-handed officials. In 1618 a great change came when the Company, under the leadership of Sir Edwin Sandys, instructed a new governor to have the settlers participate in governing the colony. Sir George Yeardley was ordered to invite each of the small settlements in the colony to send two men to Jamestown to assist him in making political, executive, and judicial decisions. The result was the calling of the House of Burgesses in 1619. The meeting of the elected legislative body in English America was, of course, a momentous event; it became an example for all other English colonies. The Company instructed its governors to call the burgesses into session so long as the Company endured. When the colony became the property of the Crown in 1625, the first royal governor was also instructed to call representatives to Jamestown to assist him in government. The burgesses met irregularly until 1639; then the governor was instructed to call the representatives into session at regular intervals. Eventually the House of Burgesses ceased to exercise executive and judicial authority and became a purely legislative body.

The year 1619 was thus a turning point in the history of Virginia. The appearance of the House of Burgesses and of the Negro were important enough. Moreover, it was at this same time that the tobacco industry became stabilized, for the government undertook to prevent the raising of tobacco in England and also levied high tariffs upon foreign tobaccos, thus reserving the English market for the Virginia product. It may even be said that Virginia's political, social, and economic future was settled for generations by events at the close of the second decade of the century.

Just as the future of the colony seemed more or less assured, the London Company of Virginia was deprived of its charter. Because the Company never did make spectacular profits, it had become increasingly difficult to secure new funds to invest in the colony. Financial losses led to dissatisfaction among the shareholders, which was increased by struggles for control of the Company. Intrigue followed wrangling, and wrangling followed intrigue. The king decided to intervene and proposed various reforms and changes, which, however, were rejected by the Company. At last the government intervened decisively, annulling its charter rights in 1624. This drastic action was once thought to result from enmity between the king and Sir Edwin Sandys, who was the leader of the Company at the time. It was believed that the Crown used this way to punish Sandys, who was an opponent of royal power. However, the Crown had been given ample excuse for interference in the affairs of the Company, which, it must be confessed, was badly operated. In any case, after 1625 Virginia was governed principally by a governor chosen by the Crown, a council assisting him in executive affairs, a second council assisting him in legislative affairs, and the House of Burgesses.

Too much may be made of the hardships and the vicissitudes of early Virginia. Great as they were, they were not so great to those who endured them as they would seem to persons of the twentieth century. For most Englishmen of the seventeenth century life was both hard and uncertain. While it is true that four-fifths of those who came to Virginia during the decade after 1607 lost their lives, it is also true that many of them would not have survived that same decade in old England. Moreover, the first Virginians were building not only for themselves but for their children, better than they could have done in old England.

THE PILGRIMS AND PLYMOUTH

In the twentieth century Americans who do not live in the South sometimes find it difficult to believe that the first permanent English settlement was established in Virginia. So much is known, and there is so much misinformation about the Pilgrims of Plymouth that it is frequently assumed that they formed the first English settlement in North America. Actually, of course, the Pilgrims did not reach Cape Cod until after the House of Burgesses had begun to function on the banks of the James.

The Pilgrim colony had its roots in religious strife in England. After the re-establishment of the Anglican Church in the early years of the reign of Elizabeth that Church persecuted Protestants as well as Roman Catholics. Many Englishmen toward the end of the sixteenth century believed that the Anglican Church, though an improvement over the Roman Church, was not the true one. They fancied that its forms of worship were too dignified, too ornate, and too papist. They also found its system of government unsatisfactory, and felt that archbishops, bishops, deans, and other officials of the Anglican Church were no great improvement over similar Roman Catholic dignitaries. Moreover, although the Anglican Church in its Thirty-Nine Articles allowed ample room for doctrinal differences, there were many who insisted that it should adopt the doctrines of John Calvin. The word *Puritan* has frequently been used to designate all Protestants who for any reason wished to change or remodel the established Church. It has also been used to indicate a Calvinistic approach to religion and to life. In this broader sense the Pilgrims were Puritans, and indeed historians commonly described them as Puritans until the middle of the nineteenth century. However, if the word Puritan is used in its narrower sense—and it will be so employed herein—then the Pilgrims were *Separatists* rather than Puritans.

The Separatists were folk of the Calvinist persuasion who believed that the Anglican Church was far from being the true Church; that it was beyond reform. Accordingly they thought that the true Church must be built again from new foundations. For them the unit of Church government was generally the congregation, which was to govern itself under the leadership of its own clergy and elders. They would have no hierarchy above the individual congregations.

The first leader of the Separatists was Robert Browne. He later returned to the orthodox Church of England, but many of those whom he had converted to the Separatist way persisted in it. Moreover, Separatism was taken up in Cambridge University in the early years of the seventeenth century, producing many eminent men, both clergy and laymen. Among them was the Reverend John Smyth, who established a Separatist congregation at Gainsborough in Lincolnshire about the year 1605. A year or two later the Reverend Richard Clyfton, also a Cambridge man, founded another one not far away, at Scrooby in Nottinghamshire. Although the fact is not established, it is likely that both of these congregations were inspired by Smyth. In any case, both were persecuted, and as a result Smyth and his Gainsborough flock emigrated to Amsterdam in Holland. The flight of Smyth and his people served as an example for the Scrooby congregation, and its members also began to move to Holland in 1607.

The Scrooby Church was a remarkable one. Clyfton was perhaps no great man, but his Cambridge-educated fellow pastor, the Reverend John Robinson, was a superior person. Gentle and lovable, he was admired and respected by the flock. William Brewster, a man of gentle birth who was the leading elder of the congregation, was also a man of character and talents; he also had attended Cambridge, although he had not graduated. Others among the few scores of persons at Scrooby were plain folk, farmers, workmen, and artisans. Even among these there were people of stature, if not of polish. Conspicuous among them was William Bradford, a self-educated man who later wrote a classic if prejudiced history of the Scrooby congregation and of its adventures in the Old and New Worlds.

In 1607 Holland was the only country in Europe which offered substantial religious freedom. The Dutch were in the main ardent Calvinists, but they were opposed to persecution on the ground of religion, perhaps because the teachings of their great leader, William of Orange, called for religious freedom. They offered asylum to Jews as well as to Separatists and French Protestants. They had not yet won their independence from the kings of Spain, but were well on the road to political freedom. Since Holland was close at hand and her people were more like the English than were other Europeans, it is readily understood why the Scrooby Pilgrims sought refuge there. They intended to embark at the port of Boston, but officials were warned of their plan. At that time under a law passed in 1598 no one could leave England without a royal license. They had no such license; law officers stopped them, arrested some of them, and forced them to return to their homes.

In the spring of 1608 the Scrooby congregation set out again, this time to embark in a Dutch vessel near Grimsby on the Humber River. After some members of it had gone on board, police captured and dispersed the others. The Dutch captain promptly put to sea and finally reached Amsterdam. Those who were captured near Grimsby were soon released by the Privy Council of James I, evidently in the belief that it was just as well that the troublesome Separatists leave England. Doubtless to officials they were a nuisance and not worth serious persecution. By 1608 then, the Scrooby congregation was gathered in Amsterdam. However, they did not remain in that city, partly because the Separatists who had preceded them were engaged in furious religious controversy. The following year they moved on to the attractive city of Leyden in north central Holland. Leyden lay inland, and possessed no major economic opportunities, although it did contain a famous university. The Pilgrims were without means and had to find any employment they could. William Brewster taught English at the university and later became a publisher of books banned in England. The others had to adopt less exalted occupations; they became brewers, printers, hatters, and cloth and silk makers.

The Pilgrims made a decent living, but only as a result of long and arduous labor which included toil even by young children. Forced to compete with the Dutch under a language handicap, they could not hope to prosper soon. Their hardships were so great that some could not endure them, preferring to return to England and possibly to prison. Bradford says that men and women became prematurely aged because of incessant labor. As the years passed, the Pilgrims accordingly became more and more worried about their economic future. They were also concerned because they must in time become absorbed in the Dutch population. They were failing to win converts among the Dutch; indeed, some of their own children threatened to switch to the Dutch religion, which was much like their own, but nevertheless foreign to them. Certainly they were not building the church of God of which they had dreamed. Still another reason for unhappiness in Holland was that the truce of 1609 between the king of Spain and the Dutch was to expire in 1621. As the end of the truce approached, the resumption of warfare was to be expected, with Leyden a possible scene of hostilities.

With the "great hope and inward zeall they had of laying some good foundation, or at least to make some way therunto, for the propagating and advancing the gospell of the Kingdom of Christ" the Pilgrims began to think of migrating to America, "yea, tho they should be as stepping stones unto others for the performing of so great a work." There would be economic opportunity for them in America, and they could live again as Englishmen if they could get permission to settle in English territory. Many were reluctant to go and would have preferred to remain in Holland or even to return to England. However, the majority eventually decided to go somewhere in the Americas. They considered settling in English Guiana, but correctly concluded that its climate was too unfavorable and that it was too vulnerable to Spanish attack. After much discussion they decided tentatively to settle in the territory of the London Company of Virginia if suitable arrangements could be made, including an assurance of religious toleration from James I. Through friends in England they began negotiations with various officials in London in 1617. The Dutch, learning of their plans, suggested that they migrate to New Netherland, which had been explored by Henry Hudson in 1609. The Dutch proposal was tentatively turned down, as was a suggestion that they migrate to the lands of the Plymouth Company in New England.

At length, through the influence of Sir Edwin Sandys, the Pilgrims secured permission to form a settlement in Virginia, receiving a patent in 1619 by the London Company. Although James I would not officially promise them religious freedom, he sent confidential assurances through intermediaries that he would not bother them if they should choose to settle in Virginia. Lacking funds, they entered into an agreement with a group of London merchants headed by Thomas Weston who agreed to finance them, the investors to be repaid with interest and to have a monopoly in whatever trade the Pilgrims should establish with England. Finally, in 1620 all was ready. At the last moment many of the Pilgrims decided not to go, or at least to wait for a more favorable opportunity. Indeed, there was not enough room for all to go on the ship which picked up the voyagers at Delftshaven in July, 1620. Fewer than 40 out of more than 200 of the congregation embarked. John Robinson, who had become its religious leader, did not go, perhaps because of his health, or perhaps because the flock at Leyden needed him. The voyagers set out without a clergyman and were without a fixed pastor in America for several years. When they did obtain one, he was a man of heretical views and had to be removed. Actually, Brewster was the real religious head of the colony for many years.

At Southampton, England, the voyagers were joined by other Separatists, by employees of the London merchants, and by individuals desiring to emigrate for economic reasons. Two ships were provided, the *Speedwell* and the *Mayflower,* and both set sail on August 5. However, the *Speedwell* leaked badly, and in the end turned out to be unsafe and unusable. At last the *Mayflower,* a ship of 180 tons, set out alone with only 101 passengers, less than half of them from Leyden. The crossing was stormy, and the vessel reached Cape Cod in poor condition, with its passengers exhausted. They decided not to go on to Virginia because of their weakness and because of the weather. Instead they determined to go to New Netherland. They actually set out for the Dutch colony, but were driven back by a storm. Thereupon they dropped anchor inside Cape Cod in November and sent out parties to find a suitable place to put down. At length they chose a site on the low, sandy shores of Plymouth, where there was a good water supply. During December they built huts and worked to make themselves as safe and comfortable as possible before the height of winter.

It is well known that the original group of Pilgrims suffered terribly during the winter of 1620 and 1621. Scurvy, malnutrition, and exposure carried off more than half of them. In the summer and fall of 1621 things went better. Samoset and Squanto, Indians who had accompanied earlier voyagers to England and who had been taught English, showed them how to plant corn, how to fish, and were of help in many other ways. They managed to get through the winter of 1621 fairly well and afterward had no periods of short rations. Later they were joined by more Separatists from Leyden and from England, and the colony grew steadily, though not very quickly, in numbers. Thomas Weston and his associates continued to send some supplies. Fortunately, the Indians in the neighborhood had been almost wiped out by plague in 1617, and Captain Myles Standish and his Pilgrim army could deal effectively with those few survivors who were hostile.

At first the Plymouth colony operated on a company basis. However, it soon moved toward complete individual enterprise. Then the settlers began to prosper moderately through farming, fishing, and trading with the Indians, eventually accumulating enough to pay off their debts to the Weston merchants. In 1691, when the colony became a part of Massachusetts, it contained no more than 7000 people. Indeed, its importance has often been exaggerated.

Since they landed in New England rather than Virginia, the Pilgrims were without legal status. However, in 1621 they were authorized by the Council of New England to stay there and to manage their own affairs by majority rule. Nine years later, after divorcing themselves from the London merchants, they received a direct grant of land and definite boundaries in the so-called "Old Charter," which is still preserved at Plymouth. In effect Plymouth became a "corporate" colony, although it never had a charter authorizing it to form a government. Before landing, the Pilgrims had realized that they had no authority to establish one, and undertook to create some sort of political order through the Mayflower Compact. This document was all the more necessary because some of the non-Separatists who accompanied them threatened to do as they pleased, once the voyage was over. Almost all were persuaded to sign the compact, in which they agreed to obey a government to be formed. Pilgrims and strangers, as the non-Separatists were called, quickly undertook to establish a church and to elect a governor, John Carver. Carver died in the spring of 1621, and was replaced by William Bradford, who was thereafter the principal leader of the colony and served as governor most of the time until his death in 1657. A company system of government was established, the governor and the assistants being chosen by the freemen, who had to be church members. When new villages were formed, the system was continued. However, after 1643 the freemen no longer participated directly in law-making. Instead, the several towns elected representatives who met with the governor and the assistants to legislate for the colony. The Separatists remained the dominant group in the colony, with some of the strangers joining the church to become full partners in the holy experiment and in public affairs. Other non-Separatists, although they did not become members of the church, were satisfied to let the "saints" manage the business of the colony. Plymouth was not a complete democracy; leadership actually came from the governor and the assistants. After 1636 the colony had a code of laws prepared and promulgated so that the settlers knew their obligations in the courts of the colony. Thus the Pilgrims solved their economic and political problems, although they were unable to establish a true and dominant church in America. They were too few to impose their religious ways upon others, but they did secure religious freedom for themselves.

4 THE PURITANS AND THE CALVERTS

The successful settlement of Plymouth should not be looked upon as an isolated event. In the decade of the 1620s English colonies were founded all along the coast of northeastern North America. The year in which the Pilgrims sailed for America was the same in which Sir William Alexander obtained a grant of Nova Scotia from James I. Colonists sent out by Alexander captured Quebec from the French. Unfortunately for the British empire, Quebec, taken from France at a time when England and France were at war, was returned in a peace treaty of 1632. However, Alexander never quite lost his grip upon Nova Scotia, and it remained a debatable land between England and France. Newfoundland was a scene of English activities in that decade. Moreover the Council of New England through various grants to groups and individuals made possible the establishment of several small settlements on the coast of Massachusetts. Weymouth was founded in 1622 by Thomas Weston, and was fostered by Robert Gorges, who brought a company of settlers to that place the following year. Weymouth grew very slowly, but some settlers did stay on there permanently.

The best known of these small settlements is one made at Braintree in 1625. Thomas Morton, a lawyer of the Anglican persuasion, soon became the principal figure in the tiny colony which came to bear the name Merriemount. Morton and his associates were tremendously unpopular among the Pilgrims, partly because they lived a gay and dissolute life. They built a maypole and frolicked around it with Indian girls, consuming large amounts of liquor. The Pilgrims were not prohibitionists, so were hardly unhappy because Morton and his friends imbibed alcohol. They were aggrieved because the Morton group was dissolute. More important, they were injured by Morton's economic activities, for he sold both liquor and firearms to the neighboring Indians. It was not at all unlikely that those firearms would sooner or later be leveled at the Pilgrims themselves, and they resolved to put a stop to this traffic. In 1628 Myles Standish arrested Morton and broke up his settlement. Morton promptly returned. A few years later the Puritans of Massachusetts Bay again dispersed the settlers. Morton went off to England and eventually returned to settle on the coast of Maine, where he died in poverty. However, his Merriemount colony was never entirely deserted.

THE MASSACHUSETTS BAY COLONY

Less colorful but with far more important results was a settlement of the Dorchester Company of southwestern England in 1623 on the northern coast of Massachusetts at Cape Ann. It was the fruit of the efforts of the Reverend John White, a conservative Puritan who was interested in establishing a colony both for fishing and for spreading the true gospel. It soon collapsed, but some of the settlers led by Roger Conant moved southward and in 1626 founded Salem, which became a permanent settlement. Meanwhile, the Dorchester Company raised needed capital among London merchants and Puritan country gentlemen in the east of England. It was successful in attracting new recruits, and was reorganized as the New England Company, then as the Massachusetts Bay Company. Although the Puritans were a minority in the new combination, they became the dominant element.

In the late 1620s the Puritans were more persecuted than they had been in the past by the Anglican Church. They were also unhappy about the political situation in England, for they belonged to a Parliamentary party which opposed King Charles I and was not very successful at that time.

Moreover, some of their principal leaders, being country gentlemen, were in economic distress. Thus there were religious, political, and economic reasons why they were dissatisfied in England. Accordingly some of them, clergymen and gentlemen, conceived that they had much to gain by settling in New England. The Massachusetts Bay Company was their vehicle. The Dorchester people and the London merchants who had joined the Company for profit did not ardently oppose this scheme. In 1628 the Company secured a grant of lands about Massachusetts Bay from the Council for New England. Then in the following year it somehow or other obtained a charter directly from the Crown. This charter gave to the Massachusetts Bay Company all the lands between boundaries beginning at points three miles north of the Merrimac River and three miles south of the Charles River and running from sea to sea. It was also authorized to organize itself in the customary way. Presumably the Company was to hold its meetings and carry out its functions in London; however, there was no express stipulation in the charter compelling it to meet in that city. This omission was doubtless not a matter of chance, and it may be believed that the Puritans were preparing to take the charter and Company with them across the ocean. Why that significant omission was not rectified by Crown officials is a mystery. Bribery may be the explanation, or the Crown's officers may not have been sufficiently watchful for its interests.

In 1629 the Company sent John Endicott to Massachusetts Bay to assume control of the small settlements already established there by the Dorchester Company. In the following year over seventeen ships carrying more than 1000 persons and ample supplies of food and tools sailed for Massachusetts Bay. The Reverend John Cotton, who was himself soon to follow, delivered a farewell sermon saying: "Moreover I will appoint a place for my people Israel, and will plant them, and move no more; neither shall the children of wickedness afflict them anymore, as before time." In the ships were John Winthrop, the governor of the Company, its vice-governor, several other stockholders, and various other gentlemen, clergymen, scholars, and many plain folk. A great transplanting had begun, for these ships were followed by many more which brought thousands of Puritans and others who emigrated for economic reasons to the shores of Massachusetts Bay by 1640. The charter of the Company was carried across the ocean in the first ships.

The emigration of the Puritans and their allies was carefully organized and was rather quickly successful. Inevitably there were hardships, but they were not on the scale of those endured by the Pilgrims. Town after town, each containing a congregation and built about a church, appeared on the shores of Massachusetts Bay. Within a few years Boston became the center of the new colony. Something like two hundred of the Puritans who crossed in 1630 died before the end of that year, but the remainder soon

EARLY SETTLERS IN NEW ENGLAND

prospered, as did those who came later. The soil about Massachusetts Bay is thin and studded with rocks, but the Puritans made it produce enough for their own needs. Unable to depend upon agriculture as the sole means of subsistence, they soon turned to lumbering, fishing, and trading with the Indians. There were ample supplies of timber near the coast suitable for the building of ships, and the Puritans had launched their first one by 1631. They found fishing particularly lucrative, for the waters off New England and Newfoundland furnished a plentiful supply of codfish which was in great demand, particularly in the Mediterranean countries. Before long the colony's ships were making regular appearances in the West Indies and England, as well as in the Mediterranean, and fishing had become one of the foundations of its sound and diversified economy.

Technically, the Puritans were members of the Church of England when they emigrated. However, they had to build a church of their own, starting from scratch. There were no recognized Anglican officials, at least no high officials, among them. Following the example of Plymouth, they established a church congregation by covenant, and then formed others from the first one. While they followed the Pilgrims' lead, they claimed for some time that the Massachusetts Bay churches were not Separatist. Authority was vested in the congregations, especially in their elders and in the customary two clergymen. Thus the Puritans in America were called Congregationalists.

Although the Massachusetts Bay Company was described in its charter as a body "corporate and politique," it was not intended that the charter should serve as a constitution for an American colony. However, the leaders of the Puritans, under the guidance of John Winthrop, undertook to use it for that purpose. It gave the Company authority to make and execute laws, to appoint officers, to administer justice, and to grant lands. The charter also provided that the stockholders, or freemen, meeting four times each year in a General Court were to choose assistants, or councillors, and a governor. Major decisions were to be made by the freemen meeting together with the assistants and the governor. The consent of at least seven assistants out of eighteen was necessary for action by the Company. It might seem that these provisions gave enough authority to Winthrop and the other leaders who controlled the few Company members in the colony. They would, of course, occupy the assistantships and supply the governor. However, the leaders feared that the arrangements made by the charter would vest too much power in the common folk whom they distrusted. Winthrop desired a system in which the godly and most responsible among the common folk would help elect persons of piety, education, and social standing. Once elected, these people should continue to exercise power indefinitely. Common folk should be pleased to recognize them as wise and superior. So that those folk would not make evil use of the charter, Winthrop and his supporters kept its provisions secret.

As a General Court attended by the few freemen in the colony in October, 1630, it was decided that the assistants were to have the power to elect the governor and with his consent to make and execute laws and to appoint magistrates. These arrangements definitely violated the provisions of the charter. Dissatisfaction immediately appeared among the settlers: 109 demanded that they be made freemen in 1631, threatening to leave the colony unless their requests were granted. Their demand was reluctantly allowed. Aware that other and similar demands would be made, Governor Winthrop and the assistants enacted a law in 1631 which required church membership for all those who would be freemen. This restriction assured a relatively small electorate, and one that would be reliable from Winthrop's viewpoint. A person did not easily become a member of a church, since he had to be approved by the congregation, the elders, and the clergymen, who put applicants through exacting tests. The suffrage was more generously given for local affairs. After 1647 persons who had been baptized and who were of good repute were even could even serve as selectmen. After 1661 by the Halfway Covenant persons who had been baptized and who were of good repute were even allowed to vote for members of the General Court, by that time organized as a colonial assembly.

Of course, the right to vote did not mean everything in Massachusetts Bay. If the voters could only elect the assistants and the governors, they could hardly force their wishes upon the government. As early as 1632 objections came from Watertown against paying taxes levied by the governor and the assistants. The complainers were forced to apologize for their "insolence." Two years later, however, a general protest arose in the colony against arbitrary rule and taxation. Two representatives sent by each town came to Boston and demanded to see the charter. Winthrop and his friends had to comply. It was apparent that its provisions had been violated. Winthrop unhappily explained that this was so because there were too many freemen to function as a governing body. He was compelled, nevertheless, to agree that government henceforth should be in accordance with the charter. To meet his argument of unwieldiness, the General Court authorized the freemen to act through representatives holding proxies, two or three from each town. It was also stipulated that election of the governor was in the future to be by "papers" rather than by voice. The change was hardly revolutionary. Under the charter seven assistants had the power to prevent the representatives of the voters from taking action displeasing to the Puritan oligarchy. There followed a struggle between the governor and the assistants on one side and the representatives of the voters on the other. In 1644 a contest developed over the ownership of a pig between Mrs. Sherman, a widow, and Robert Keaynes, a wealthy merchant. The representatives sided with the widow, and the assistants with the merchant. This conflict was ultimately resolved in favor of the oligarchy. In 1645 it was agreed that there should be two houses in Massachusetts Bay, the assistants forming a council, or upper house, and retaining their veto power. However an important restriction was placed upon the oligarchy three years later. Before 1648 magistrates in the colony had decided cases on their own judgment, using at will common law, Massachusetts statutes, or Biblical precepts. After that year they were forced to follow laws made by the General Court, containing the "laws and liberties of Massachusetts."

There were other causes for political dissatisfaction. Relations between church and state were so close that Massachusetts Bay was a semitheocracy. It has been mentioned that church members were the only voters after

1631. A law of 1635 required all persons to attend church; one of 1636 provided for the taxation of all persons to support the churches, and another of the same year forbade the establishment of new churches without the approval of the clergy and of the General Court. The ordinary courts, with clergymen sitting alongside magistrates on the bench, punished heresy. The General Court did likewise. The Puritan oligarchy was decidedly intolerant. It is notorious that four Quakers who refused to leave and stay away from Massachusetts Bay were executed in 1658 and 1659. Winthrop was not fond of punishing heretics, but John Endicott and others were fanatics who sometimes had their way. Many folk in Massachusetts Bay had come for economic betterment, not to establish the kingdom of God on earth according to the Puritan prescription. Besides, even among orthodox Puritans, some believed that too close a union between church and state was undesirable. However, the Puritan oligarchy in general saw in their semitheocracy political safety as well as the salvation of souls. In 1651, the General Court gave its approval to the Cambridge Platform, which called for an association of the churches of the colony, toward preventing heresy.

The close union between church and state in Massachusetts Bay is more readily understood when it is realized that the colony was endangered both within and without. There were many settlers who would have gone their own religious way had they been permitted to do so. Such persons were also likely to be critics of the existing governmental system. The orthodox in Massachusetts Bay, being threatened by action from England, insisted upon unity within the colony and strove with considerable success to attain it. From its very beginning the colony was assailed by Thomas Morton, Sir Ferdinando Gorges, Captain John Mason, and others whose interests were threatened or injured by it. In 1633 a Commission for Foreign Plantations was organized in England as a subcommittee of the Privy Council to look after colonial affairs. This body, headed by William Laud, Anglican archenemy of the Puritans, demanded that the Massachusetts Bay charter be brought back to England. When the Massachusetts Bay leaders refused to comply, the Commission declared the charter invalid. Thereupon suit was brought in an English court against the charter, a writ of *quo warranto* being issued in 1637. Massachusetts Bay did not even bother to defend itself against the suit, and a decision declaring the charter void was handed down. At the same time Gorges was appointed Governor General of New England, and it was expected that he would go there to enforce the decision of the English court. He failed to make the voyage, and the colony ignored the decision. It must be conceded that Massachusetts Bay behaved truculently toward England. It was also high-handed in its dealings with hostile persons and other groups claiming lands and powers in New England. Vigorous action would doubtless have been taken against the Bay Colony except that Charles I, Laud, and other supporters of the Crown had their hands full with religious and political troubles at home. The beginning of the English Civil War in 1642 relieved the colony of serious pressure from England for nearly twenty years, for the Parliamentary party and dictator Oliver Cromwell were generally friendly. Not until after the return of the Stuarts to the throne in 1660 in the person of Charles II was the colony again menaced from London. Accordingly, it proceeded in its own independent way for a full generation, so far as English pressure was concerned.

Meanwhile, Massachusetts Bay fathered, or stepfathered, with some assistance from Plymouth Colony and England, the settlement of Rhode Island, Connecticut, New Hampshire, and Maine.

RHODE ISLAND

Rhode Island was founded by persons who were unhappy religiously and politically in Massachusetts Bay and in Plymouth. Chief among them was Roger Williams, a brilliant young clergyman who had come out to Plymouth in 1631. Of Welsh stock, Williams was a graduate of Cambridge University. Like so many other young men at Cambridge, he became a Puritan. Lovable, quickwitted, fond of intellectual controversy, courageous, Williams became a marked man when still a student at the university. He was soon singled out for Anglican persecution and was warned by friends that he would do well to leave England. Hence his appearance at Plymouth and his employment a few months later as a clergyman at Salem. Williams was welcomed as a valuable recruit in Massachusetts Bay. However, he soon became a thorn in the flesh of the orthodox there. He was not satisfied that the Congregational system in Massachusetts Bay perfectly represented God's will. He was also disturbed by the very close relationship between it and the state. He believed that church government in the colony was too autocratic.

Challenging the church, he inevitably also attacked the state with which it was so intimately associated. This attack was direct as well as indirect. The colony claimed to own all land within its boundaries by virtue of its charter. While the Indians were usually compensated when their lands were taken by the settlers, they were paid as a matter of expediency rather than justice. Williams asserted that the charter did not confer ownership upon the colony, that lands were the property of the Indians, and that they must be purchased in order to secure title. Thus Williams assailed the powers that were in the colony on religious, political, and economic grounds. He was highly persuasive; he acquired followers; and he was dangerous. He was forced to appear before the General Court in 1635 to face charges of heresy and treason. He was found guilty and ordered banished to England. However, he was informed by his friend John Winthrop that he would not be molested if he moved beyond the southern boundary of Massachusetts Bay, so he proceeded to the shores of Narragansett Bay in 1636. Later the same year he and some friends founded the town of Providence on land that he had already purchased from the Indians. It grew slowly but steadily, and from it other towns soon developed nearby.

In Providence Williams' political and religious ideas underwent further change. By 1638 he had become a Seeker, that is a person who believed that the true church had not yet appeared anywhere. For a time he was attracted to Baptist ideas, and helped to found the first Baptist Church in America. In general, however, his theology remained orthodoxly Calvinist until the end of his life. In Massachusetts Bay Williams had not preached complete religious freedom, but in Rhode Island he thundered against tithes, laws requiring attendance at public worship, and persecution for heresy. There he insisted upon separation of church and state, or rather that the state should give equal protection to all forms of religious faith. He practiced what he preached. Williams found the teachings of the Society of Friends to be abominable but when Quakers appeared in Rhode Island, he insisted that they should not be molested.

In politics too, Williams was a generous-minded man. In 1636 he entered into a compact which called for the establishment of government in Providence on the basis of majority rule. The compact demanded protection for the rights of individuals, barred religious legislation, and gave the right to vote to all heads of families. To a degree the remarkable Williams was in seventeenth-century America what Thomas Jefferson was in the next century.

Another founder of Rhode Island was Mrs. Anne Hutchinson, also an exile from Massachusetts Bay. As a member of the church at Boston Mrs. Hutchinson slipped into difficulties because she was a good woman. The mother of many children, she knew that other mothers were frequently unable to attend services on Sunday. She therefore began to hold meetings at her home on Thursday to tell the ladies and some of the men what the clergyman had preached on the preceding Sunday. Before long she was not merely repeating what she had heard on Sunday but adding her own comments. She urged her listeners to embrace the "covenant of grace" instead of the orthodox "covenant of works." It was inevitable that Mrs. Hutchinson, lacking a thorough theological education, should eventually utter heresy. No great trouble would have ensued had she not acquired followers, but the Reverend John Wheelwright, her brother-in-law, became one of her adherents, as did a number of plain folk. The orthodox clergy began to show concern about this ignorant woman who dared to assert her opinions as against her betters. She responded by plunging deeper into heresy, finally claiming even the power of prophecy. In this she went far too far, and in 1637 she was called before the General Court and told that she must leave the colony. Wheelwright was also ordered to leave. Mrs. Hutchinson and a few followers accordingly moved southward to Rhode Island and established the town of Portsmouth in 1638. A little later she moved to Connecticut, where she was slain by Indians in 1642. Her settlement at Portsmouth, however, was permanent.

A third builder of Rhode Island was William Coddington, one of Mrs. Hutchinson's followers who quarreled bitterly with another settler, Samuel Gorton. In disgust he left Portsmouth and established Newport in the year 1639. Eventually Coddington became a Quaker; Newport flourished and became the principal town of Rhode Island in the colonial period.

Samuel Gorton, originally a grocer in London, was a fourth architect of Rhode Island. He was a religious crank who converted his clergyman's wife to unorthodox views. In 1638 he fled from Plymouth to Portsmouth, where this "proud and pestilent seducer" quarreled with Coddington. Moving to Pawtuxet, then under the leadership of Williams, he caused so much commotion that thirteen of Williams' followers asked Massachusetts Bay to deal with him. He fled to Shawomet on the west shore of Narragansett Bay, where he founded Warwick in 1643. There too he was a trouble-maker, stirring up warfare among the neighboring Indians. That same year officers of the New England Confederation arrested him and carried him to Boston for trial on charges of heresy and treason. Convicted, he was banished to England. In England, however, a Parliamentary board established to look after colonial affairs granted him the lands he had settled at Shawomet, and at the same time ordered that he and his friends were not to be molested. He was thus enabled to return to Warwick, and his settlement survived.

From the four towns mentioned grew Rhode Island and Providence Plantations. Its settlements were constantly threatened by interference from Massachusetts Bay. One of the reasons for the establishment of the Confederation of New England in 1643 was to destroy such independent settlements. In 1644 Williams obtained a charter from the Parliamentary commissioners for the colonies which recognized the right of the Rhode Islanders to the lands which they occupied and authorized them to set up political institutions by majority vote. In consequence in a convention in 1647 representatives from the four original towns adopted a constitution. The democratic town governments already established were to function as before. In addition there was to be a representative assembly with members elected annually. The delegates were to choose four assistants and a president. Since all laws were to be initiated by the towns and had to be approved by each town, Rhode Island acquired a federal system of government. This constitution also provided for freedom of conscience in religion. The return of the Stuarts in 1660 nullified the charter from the Parliamentary commission. Fortunately for the Rhode Islanders, they obtained a royal charter in 1663 which contained substantially the same provisions as that of 1644. Although they were long looked upon as heretics and adherents of anarchy, Williams saw their situation through different eyes. He said in 1654: "We have long drunk of the cup of as great liberties as any people we can hear of under the whole heaven."

CONNECTICUT AND NORTHERN NEW ENGLAND

The settlement of Connecticut was actually undertaken shortly before that of Rhode Island. Again dissatisfaction in Massachusetts Bay and Plymouth were causes for the migration. However the migrants were impelled by economic considerations rather than by decrees of exile. The relatively small amounts of good land about Boston and Plymouth were soon occupied. News brought back by traders and explorers that the Connecticut River valley contained rich lands was especially attractive to persons who were mildly dissatisfied with the position of church and state in Massachusetts Bay. One of these was the Reverend Thomas Hooker of Newtown (Cambridge), who did not like to see clergymen sitting on the bench with magistrates and participating in the making of legal decisions. Moreover Hooker seems to have entertained some doubt that the suffrage should be restricted to orthodox church members. In any case, he asked permission from the General Court to emigrate to the Connecticut valley in 1634. In the following year permission was granted, with the stipulation that the emigrants continue to accept the authority of Massachusetts Bay. A small group of settlers promptly made their way to the valley and in 1636 Hooker led an exodus westward. Hartford, Windsor, and Wethersfield were soon founded in what is now northern Connecticut, as was Springfield, just across the boundary in Massachusetts.

The Bay Colony organized a commission to govern these new towns, but since all but Springfield turned out to be outside the boundaries of Massachusetts, their settlers ignored it. Deputies from the three Connecticut towns formed a general assembly in the year 1637. In the following year it adopted the "Fundamental Orders of Connecticut," a constitution which was approved by the towns in 1639. It provided for a corporate system of government in the Connecticut River colony. It did not require that the voter be a church member, the suffrage being granted by the General Court. The General Court was to consist of deputies chosen in the towns, with a governor and assistants elected annually. The veto power was withheld from the governor, and the General Court could convene itself and could be dissolved only by its members. A veto power was conceded to the assistants after 1645, and they retained it when they formed a separate house in 1698. In practice, the system of government in the Connecticut River colony differed but little from that in Massachusetts Bay. Nor was the position of the Congregational Church fundamentally different from that of the church in the older colony.

The Connecticut River colony expanded materially within twenty-five years and became the basis for Connecticut. New towns appeared about the original three. Saybrook, founded in 1635 at the mouth of the Connecticut River by English Puritans under the leadership of Lord Saye and Sele, Lord Brooke, and the Earl of Warwick, was added as a result of purchase in the year 1644, and five years later the town of Southampton on Long Island, settled in 1640 by Puritans from Connecticut, was also added.

In 1662 the New Haven colony, together with its outlying settlements, was likewise absorbed into Connecticut. The town of New Haven was founded in 1638 by the Reverend John Davenport and Theophilus Eaton, devout Puritans who had crossed from England to Boston the year before. Disliking the dissension they found in Massachusetts Bay, and pleased by reports of the natural wealth of Connecticut, they pushed on westward, seeking to establish a true Bible Commonwealth. New Haven prospered almost from the beginning and other towns soon developed about it, spreading westward as far as Greenwich. In 1643 a constitution was established; only church members were allowed to vote, and once again a General Court appeared. Puritanism was even more devout in New Haven than it was in Massachusetts Bay, the Bible being commonly used to decide cases in the courts. The New Haven colony was not confined to what is now Connecticut: it included the town of Southold on eastern Long Island, established in 1640.

None of the settlements in what is now Connecticut possessed any legal governing authority until 1662. Then John Winthrop, Jr., secured from Charles II a charter establishing a colony of Connecticut, which included both the Connecticut River towns and those of New Haven north of Long Island Sound. In effect, the Connecticut River towns maintained the institutions they had already established and absorbed the neighboring settlements to the southward. The colony founded by Davenport and Eaton objected, but to no avail. Thus appeared the virtually autonomous colony of Connecticut. Why the Crown permitted such a large degree of self-government remains a mystery. Less difficult to understand is the growth of Connecticut. Rich lands, trading with the Indians, shipbuilding and commerce, together with industry and thrift, assured an early prosperity.

Northern New England was settled less rapidly than southern. In 1622 the Council of New England granted what is now New Hampshire and Maine to Captain John Mason and Sir Ferdinando Gorges. Seven years later the two men agreed that Mason should have New Hampshire and

Gorges Maine. This arrangement was later approved in London. As the proprietor of New Hampshire Mason was not active. However, two towns —Dover and Portsmouth—did gradually develop on its seacoast after 1623. In 1637 the Reverend John Wheelwright with other exiles from Massachusetts Bay founded Exeter. Hampton was settled three years later by orthodox Puritans from Massachusetts Bay. Thereafter New Hampshire gradually grew, a newer and less prosperous Massachusetts Bay. The early history of Maine was somewhat similar. Before the death of Gorges in 1647 several towns appeared in southern Maine, York, Kittery, Wells, and Saco. Farming and fishing were the bases of a modest development.

Massachusetts Bay laid claim to both New Hampshire and Maine, partly by charter right and partly on the basis of purchase from the proprietors. By 1643 the claim to New Hampshire had been effectively asserted, although the Mason family long protested in vain. However, in 1677 an English court declared that Massachusetts Bay held no legal title, and New Hampshire was made a royal colony two years later. Massachusetts Bay similarly asserted control of Maine during the years of 1656–1658. After Charles II's ascension to the throne, a grandson of Gorges effectively challenged the pretensions of the Bay colony, and in 1677 the Privy Council recognized his right to Maine. But before the region could be royalized, Massachusetts Bay hastily and secretly bought out the Gorges family rights, with the result that Maine became a part of Massachusetts and remained so until 1820.

A striking event in the early history of New England was the establishment of the Confederation of New England in 1643, its members being the Connecticut River towns, New Haven, Plymouth, and Massachusetts Bay. It was to provide for defense against the Indians, especially the Narragansett nation. They were a serious menace, which was not finally removed until King Philip's War in 1675 and 1676. The danger of French advance from the north was another reason, as was a persistent and nagging quarrel with the Dutch, whose occupation of the Hudson River valley was never recognized by the English and whose claims to territory as far east as the Connecticut River were deeply resented. The framers of the Confederation also saw it as a means of dealing with the heretics of Rhode Island and with the proprietors of Maine and New Hampshire. Obviously in union there would be strength. Delegates from the four colonies meeting at Boston agreed to form a perpetual league of friendship and defense. It was agreed that there should be a directorate of eight men, two from each of the members—all being churchmen. The eight were authorized to manage Indian affairs and defense, and specifically to make treaties of war and peace, with six votes being necessary to carry any measure. It was agreed that military costs should be based upon population and apportioned accordingly. It was also stipulated that the colonies should undertake to return escaped prisoners and slaves, and that a will probated in one colony should be recognized in the others. This league operated actively for some years and then gradually sank into desuetude. Perhaps it was not of fundamental importance, but it did prove the value of centralization in meeting common colonial problems.

THE CALVERTS AND MARYLAND

The founding of Maryland was almost simultaneous with that of Connecticut, although the former was not intended as a haven for Puritans. While the Mason and Gorges families derived no substantial profits from their activities in New England, the Calvert family did very well indeed as proprietors of Maryland. Maryland was founded by George Calvert, Lord Baltimore, and his son Cecilius. The elder Calvert was a liberal-minded man, a high official under James I, an Oxford graduate, and a speculator in American projects. When he announced that he was a Roman Catholic, in 1624, he was barred from a public career in England, so devoted himself to colony building. Between 1620 and 1627 he vainly tried to develop one which he called Avalon in Newfoundland. Turning his attention southward, he appeared in Virginia in 1629 to look over the lands immediately north of the Potomac River. When the charter of the London Company had been annulled in 1624 the king had indicated that the boundaries of the Virginia colony would not be altered to its injury. Nevertheless, the Virginians became alarmed. They treated Baltimore well, but drove him from Virginia by demanding that he take an oath of supremacy, which no self-respecting Roman Catholic could utter. Before he left, however, he saw enough of the land about Chesapeake Bay to persuade him that he must have some of it.

Returning to England, Baltimore petitioned the Crown for a proprietary grant for a colony to be called Maryland in honor of Charles I's wife, Henrietta Maria. The king was decidedly sympathetic, and a charter was issued in 1632. It conveyed to Baltimore and his descendants about 10 million acres of land bordered on the south by the Potomac, on the west by a line running through the source of the Potomac, and on the north by the 40th parallel (which gave the Baltimores a claim to Philadelphia which they could not make good). They were also given extensive political and social powers, which were approximately the same as had been exercised by the Bishop of Durham when he was made a semi-independent ruler to fight more effectively against the wild Scots in the Middle Ages. In general, they were authorized to set up a feudal principality and to rule it like overlords of the Middle Ages. However, there were some restrictions, including a requirement that Maryland laws were to be made only with the advice and assent of the colony's freeholders. In addition it was stipulated that there might be appeals from Maryland to English courts. In return for these handsome privileges the Baltimores were to give the king each year two Indian arrows and one-fifth of all the products of the mines discovered in the colony.

While the charter was being prepared, George Calvert died, and his son, Cecilius, succeeded him. The second Lord Baltimore, like his father, saw in the Maryland project not only possibilities of profit, but also an American refuge for Roman Catholics. Under his direction two ships, the *Ark* and the *Dove,* set out for Chesapeake Bay with over 200 settlers, about half of whom were Roman Catholic. They arrived safely and founded the town of St. Marys in 1634. Other emigrants followed, and many settlers moved northward from Virginia into the new colony, especially after 1640. The majority of the settlers from Virginia were Protestants; in fact Protestants were in the majority from the beginning.

The early emigrants to Maryland suffered no great hardships, for Virginia served as a source for supplies, and tobacco could be grown as easily north of the Potomac as south of it. However, social, religious, and political troubles soon developed. While Leonard Calvert, illegitimate half-brother of Cecilius, governed ably for many years, the colony became restless under his rule. The Baltimores undertook to set up a true feudal system, making large grants and sales of lands to the few persons who could pay quit rents and maintain estates tilled by tenants. The system was disliked by persons who could not secure grants, and there was tension between the grantees and their tenants, especially since the former were usually Roman Catholic, while the latter were commonly Protestant.

Religious difficulties must have arisen in any case, not only because of the peculiar landlord-tenant relationship, but also from attempts by the Jesuits to make Maryland into a definitely Roman Catholic colony. On the one hand, the Baltimores had to soothe the Protestants; on the other, they had to restrain the zealous Jesuits. Whatever shortcomings the early Baltimore family may have had, its religious policy was liberal and enlightened. In 1649 the proprietor urged the assembly to pass a law requiring religious toleration; all persons professing belief in Christianity were to be permitted to worship freely. Penalties were laid down against those who might interfere with this freedom, and also against persons who should use exasperating epithets such as "heretic," "idolater," and "popish priest." To these generous provisions the Protestant lower house added another that was decidedly illiberal. It demanded the death penalty for all those who should refuse to subscribe to the doctrine of the Trinity. There could not be many such persons, and in practice the Maryland statute of religious toleration was a landmark on the road to religious liberty.

Political troubles were also almost inevitable. As early as 1635 representatives elected by the settlers participated in the business of government. By 1650 these formed a lower house of assembly; an upper house or council and the governor were chosen by the proprietor. Since the interests of the settlers unavoidably clashed with those of the proprietor, and since the majority members of the lower house were Protestant, while the governor and most of the council were Roman Catholic, there was chronic controversy. This was inflamed by the Baltimores' attempt to deny the lower house the right to initiate legislation, a right it eventually secured.

The Baltimores lost control of their American principality for a few years during the Commonwealth period. After the execution of Charles I, the governor proclaimed the accession of his son, Charles II, thereby giving the Protestants an excuse for revolt. They secured help from Virginia, and from a fleet under control of the English Parliament that appeared in Chesapeake Bay in 1652. Its presence compelled recognition of the authority of Parliament over both Virginia and Maryland. It also enabled the Protestant majority to assume control of Maryland. The new regime promptly repealed the Toleration Act of 1649, but in 1658 the English government restored the Baltimore regime, and the law was as promptly restored.

Partly because of the policy of the Baltimores, holders of large land grants in Maryland tended to become a landed aristocracy. That tendency was increased by the introduction of tobacco growing and of Negro slavery. The earliest settlements gradually became strikingly similar economically and socially to those of Tidewater Virginia. True, the influence and the fame of the Maryland aristocrats were less than those of their fellows in Virginia, because central and western Maryland were eventually settled by small landholding farmers.

ENGLISH COLONIES IN THE CARIBBEAN

It should not be assumed that English colonizing before the Restoration of 1660 was confined to the mainland of North America. Bermuda was explored and was developed by a Bermuda Company not long after the founding of Jamestown. The Caribbean area was attractive to English adventurers, speculators, and Puritans. The Puritans made a determined, though unsuccessful, effort to occupy Providence Island in the Caribbean. In the middle of the 1620s part of the island of St. Christopher became English territory; and the occupation of Barbados, Grenada, Barbuda, Montserrat, and other West Indian islands rapidly followed. An expedition sent out against the Spaniards by Oliver Cromwell captured Jamaica in 1655. These islands were more attractive to many Englishmen than was the mainland. Settlement was attempted even in Guiana, unsuccessfully. These tropical colonies did not prosper at first. However, the settlers soon turned to the production of sugar cane. There was a large and growing market on the mainland and in Europe for sugar, molasses, and the rum which was made from molasses. The sugar plantation with gangs of Negro slaves replaced the small farms which had been characteristic of the islands in their early years. Accordingly the islands acquired an aristocracy of wealthy landowners, many of whom were also absentees residing in England and managing their American estates through agents. Except for Jamaica, the islands were under proprietary rule until 1672, when they were royalized, acquiring a system of government like that in Virginia. Trade between these tropical outposts of empire and the mainland colonies increased as the seventeenth century wore on, and seemed to be almost vital to the mainland colonists in the following century. Moreover, settlers moved from the islands to the mainland, especially to Carolina.

t' Fort nieuw Amsterdam op de Manhatans

5 THE ENGLISH COLONIES 1660–1689

Six of the original thirteen colonies were established between 1607 and 1660; between 1660 and the English "Glorious Revolution" of 1688 six others appeared. One of them was New York, taken from the Dutch in 1664; the others were settled by the English themselves. The older English colonies on the Atlantic flourished, although they had their troubles.

THE OLDER COLONIES

VIRGINIA

During the generation between the accession of Charles II in 1660 and the dethronement of James II in 1688 Virginia was plagued with economic difficulties because of her reliance upon tobacco as a cash crop. Overproduction of the "yellow weed" caused an economic crisis. An attempt to limit production failed, and an improvement in the situation came only when the demand caught up with the size of the crop. Also very disturbing in Virginia was a political quarrel which ended in Bacon's Rebellion in 1676. Tension developed between the coastal or Tidewater people and those of the more recently settled Piedmont area inland. There were various reasons for conflict. A planter aristocracy holding Negro slaves was beginning to appear in the Tidewater, while the Piedmont was as yet largely inhabited by small farmers. The people of the Piedmont were poor, less educated, less cultivated, and less English than those who lived near the shores of the Chesapeake. They were also doubtless somewhat more democratic in their social and political views. Suffering from harassing Indian attacks, they sought assistance from the legislature and the governor, Sir William Berkeley. Aid was refused to them, and they had to deal with the Indians as best they could. Exasperated by the refusal of Berkeley and the Tidewater to help, they rose in revolt and marched upon Jamestown in 1676. Led by Nathaniel Bacon, a recent immigrant from England, they swept aside feeble opposition and occupied the colonial capital, Berkeley fleeing across Chesapeake Bay to the eastern shore. At the moment of triumph Bacon suddenly died and, lacking leadership, his followers began to desert the cause. Berkeley was soon able to regain control of Jamestown and to exact vengeance from the insurgents, several of whose leaders he had hanged. "Bacon's Rebellion" was not a struggle between Englishmen and Americans, but was rather one between two American factions, one of which was supported by English officials. Its collapse led to a strengthening of royal power in Virginia. After 1680 the governor was no longer dependent upon the good will of the House of Burgesses for his salary. It was thenceforth paid from an export duty on tobacco, a tax which could not be repealed without the consent of the governor. Thereafter the House of Burgesses no longer performed judicial functions. The suffrage was also restricted, to freeholders. The Piedmont and popular government had suffered a setback, though hardly a decisive defeat.

MARYLAND

During the same period Maryland encountered similar troubles, together with others that were peculiarly her own. She too suffered from bad conditions in the tobacco business and had to wait until a larger demand for tobacco brought a return of prosperity. After the return of the Baltimore regime in 1658 the wrangling between landlords and tenants, between Protestants and Roman Catholics, and between the proprietors and their people continued. The lower house sought to limit the authority of the Baltimores and to compel them to bear a larger part of public expenses. The proprietors, supported by the governor and the council, strenuously resisted. Much legislation approved by the lower house was vetoed by the proprietor, who also struck at the "popular" party by raising the requirement for voting to the possession of property worth £40. There was a feeble revolt in 1676, doubtless suggested by the uprising across the Potomac. Thirteen years later the Protestant enemies of the Baltimores again rose in rebellion, this time successfully. Receiving the news of the Glorious Revolution of 1688 and of the accession of William and Mary to the throne, the Council of Maryland refused to proclaim the new king and queen. This decision was made in the midst of wild rumors of a conspiracy organized by the exiled James II and Louis XIV of France which would bring French troops and hordes of Indians across the frontiers of the English colonies. It was rumored that many officials in the English colonies were parties to the plot, the Baltimores and their followers being among those suspected of complicity. The Protestants under John Coode easily seized control of Maryland. Governmental powers were placed in the hands of a Convention and an executive committee of loyal adherents of William and Mary. Their conduct was not displeasing to William, who organized a royal government which endured until the Baltimore family saw the wisdom of the Anglican way twenty-five years later.

NEW ENGLAND

Although shaken by King Philip's War, New England also prospered during the Restoration. There was a steady growth in numbers, and in the riches of this world; and with it doubtless some decrease in concern about the world beyond death. Conspicuous was the burgeoning of maritime trade. Ships from Boston and Newport unfurled their sails in the harbors of Lisbon and Liverpool, and on the shores of Maryland and Madagascar. Men of wealth were seen in Boston streets and the comforts, if not the luxuries, of seventeenth-century life became fairly common east of the Hudson.

Prosperity did not bring political peace to New England. Because the Crown gave charters to Connecticut and Rhode Island in the early years of the Restoration it might be concluded that the English government was satisfied with them. The fact was otherwise. The king and his ministers were increasingly unhappy because their authority was flouted, especially in Massachusetts Bay. That colony provoked London dignitaries in various ways. Its harsh treatment of Quakers, and its persecution of members of the Anglican Church aroused resentment in the imperial capital, as did its attempt to swallow up Maine and New Hampshire. When the New Englanders gave asylum to Edward Whalley and William Goffe, instrumental in the execution of Charles I, leaders in London were not pleased. More important, the merchants of Massachusetts Bay were competing effectively in maritime trade with those of England; and they refused to obey the English Navigation Acts, laws designed to restrict their activities. The General Court of Massachusetts Bay even asserted that Parliament had no authority to pass such acts. At one time Massachusetts Bay actually refused to fly the English flag, except in the outer reaches of Boston harbor where it could not be seen from the shore. In sum, the colony truculently questioned English authority both before and after 1660. English officials sent to the colonies to investigate were rudely treated. When Edward Randolph, appointed collector of customs, appeared in New England in 1681, Massachusetts Bay refused to concede that he had the right to collect duties, and fined and imprisoned his deputies. At long last English officials moved decisively. Suit was brought against Massachusetts Bay in an English Court and its charter was declared void in 1684.

In February, 1685, Charles II died and the throne passed to his younger brother, James II, formerly the Duke of York. James may not have been a wise man, but he was a vigorous one. He undertook not only to deal sternly with the Massachusetts Bay Puritans, but to place all of New England, New York, and New Jersey under the control of a royal governor and council. Between 1686 and 1688 he created the Dominion of New England, placing over it as a presumably permanent governor the Anglican Sir Edmund Andros, who was given English troops to compel obedience. The charters of Connecticut and Rhode Island were set aside, along with that of Massachusetts Bay. For a time New England seemed to accept the inevitable. Formed in part for unity against the French and to deal with the Indians, the Dominion proved useful for those purposes. From the first, however, the Andros regime was bitterly resented throughout New England, and especially in Massachusetts Bay. Andros could hardly have pleased the Bay people, and he made no serious effort to do so. Restrained only by the advice of his council, he ruled arbitrarily. He needlessly questioned the legality of land titles in the colony, and he forced a Congregational church in Boston to let its facilities be used for Anglican services. By the fall of 1688 leaders in Massachusetts Bay were plotting revolt. By the following spring it was known in Boston that William and Mary had ascended the English throne. In April, claiming to be adherents of William and Mary and falsely accusing Andros of being a Roman Catholic, prominent clergymen and laymen in Massachusetts Bay called upon their brethren to take up arms. They responded; and Andros' soldiers, believing that the governor was involved in the rumored conspiracy which had so affected public opinion in Maryland, declined to fight. He became a prisoner and after vain efforts to escape was finally shipped off to England. The governments which had existed before his arrival were promptly restored in Connecticut and Rhode Island.

William III was well aware that the people of Massachusetts Bay had risen not only against James II, but against English authority in general. Accordingly, he insisted that the Massachusetts Bay charter was dead; in 1691 he issued a new charter, creating a colony of Massachusetts, which included the Bay, Plymouth, and Maine. It was to have a royal governor, a lower house of assembly elected by voters meeting only a property requirement, and an upper chamber chosen jointly by the lower house and the governor. The Congregational Church remained official in Massachusetts, but freedom of worship was extended to all Protestants. Royal authority was asserted much more effectively in New England after 1691 than it had been before 1684.

NEW COLONIES

The English empire in North America thrived and expanded in the period of the Restoration. The gap between the old colonies on the Chesapeake and in Massachusetts was closed by the new provinces of New York, New Jersey, Pennsylvania, and Delaware; and the foundations of the Carolinas were solidly laid on the shores of Albemarle Sound and Charleston Bay. By 1688 the Atlantic coastline between the Kennebec and Savannah rivers was tightly in the English grasp.

THE DUTCH AND NEW YORK

New York was not a new colony, but a Dutch one under new ownership. It will be recalled that New York harbor was entered as early as 1525, by Verrazano, sailing in the service of France. However, it was not until 1609 that New York Bay and the Hudson River were visited again by Europeans, this time by Henry Hudson, an English sea captain in Dutch pay. Seeking a passage eastward to Asia by way of the Arctic Ocean, Hudson was forced to turn back by a mutiny in his crew. His men agreed to accompany him on a voyage across the Atlantic in an attempt to find a westward passage to Asia. Hence the appearance of Hudson and his ship, the *Halfmoon*, beside Manhattan. After spending a month trading with the Indians, he sailed for Holland. Stopping off in England, he was arrested as a not very patriotic Englishman. Permitted to report to his Dutch employers, he urged that they exploit his findings, that great profit might be made from growing tobacco in the valley of the Hudson. Five years later Dutch traders built Fort Nassau just south of modern Albany, this post being replaced by Fort Orange, where Albany now stands, in 1618. In 1614 the Dutch also explored Long Island Sound and the Delaware River, and they laid claim to all lands between the Connecticut and Delaware rivers. To this area they gave the name New Netherland. Little was done to develop New Netherland until it became the property of the Dutch West India Company in 1621. Formed under the leadership of William Usselinx, a Protestant refugee from Flanders, it had for its purposes more effective attacks upon Spanish and Portuguese colonies in the New World, the establishment of Dutch colonies therein, and amassing of wealth for its members through plunder and trade. Partly public, partly private, it was given a monopoly of trade between the west coast of Africa and the eastern shores of the

Americas, and full governmental powers. Tendered some public money and ships, the Company embarked upon a remarkable career. Its attacks upon Spanish treasure secured lucre, and it made a strenuous but vain effort to wrest Brazil from the Portuguese. It also established Dutch colonies in the Caribbean and on the northern coast of South America. New Netherland was actually not a major interest of the Company, which was interested in profits rather than in peopling. Nevertheless in 1624 it sent out the ship *New Netherland* which carried settlers to the Delaware River, to Fort Orange, the lower Connecticut River, and Governor's Island in New York harbor. A fort was built on Manhattan the following year, and the island was purchased from the Indians in 1626 by Peter Minuit. There grew the town of New Amsterdam, which became the capital of the colony. New Netherland grew slowly, because the Company failed to foster immigration and discouraged farming. However, the Dutch eagerly sought trade; Fort Orange became the center of a rich traffic with the Iroquois, and New Amsterdam became a base for business with the adjacent English colonies. Settlers continued to come from Holland, although in general the Dutch were satisfied to remain in their own country. Moreover, the Company welcomed English, Germans, Flemings, French Protestants, and Jews as well. New Netherland therefore became cosmopolitan, although the bulk of the inhabitants were Dutch. When it became New York it contained perhaps seven thousand persons.

New Netherland was arbitrarily and ill-governed. The inhabitants had little to say about their political destinies. Power was vested in a governor appointed by the Company, which chose even the clergymen and teachers. The governors appear as quaint and colorful characters in the writings of Washington Irving, but to the people they ruled they were inefficient, capricious, and dictatorial. Perhaps the best of them was the last, Peter Stuyvesant, who was courageous though ill-tempered. Once and again the settlers petitioned for a representative assembly, but the Company ignored their wishes.

Of special importance was the land policy of the Company, which encouraged the establishment of manors in much the same way that the Baltimores did in Maryland. In 1629 the Company offered the famous patroonships to persons who would undertake to people the Hudson Valley with tenants. A patroon might thus obtain a domain twelve miles long on one bank of the Hudson or six miles in length on both sides of the river. Only one of the patroons, Kiliaen Van Rensselaer, an Amsterdam diamond merchant, secured a permanent estate. However, the Company continued to make large grants of lands to favored persons, thus encouraging the growth of a landed aristocracy and discouraging the development of a small farmer class.

Although New Netherland was not seriously molested by the English for decades, from the English point of view it did not legally exist. English attack upon it was therefore likely. The colony was also menaced on the north by the French, who pushed southward from the St. Lawrence. However, the Iroquois nation traded with the Dutch, became their allies, and were supplied with Dutch firearms. They held back the French and also dealt harshly with Indian enemies of the Dutch. While the colony remained insecure, it did expand, absorbing New Sweden in 1655. Denmark and Sweden were not very active in the race for empire in America, although the former did acquire the Virgin Islands, and a Swedish company organized by William Usselinx and Peter Minuit planted a few scores of Swedes on the Delaware River after 1638. Their presence was offensive to the Dutch, who considered the Delaware's banks their own property. In 1655 Stuyvesant, parading military force on the Delaware, secured the peaceful surrender of New Sweden.

Nine years later Stuyvesant himself saw an English squadron and English troops in New York Bay, and was told that he must surrender New Netherland. The presence of the Dutch between the Connecticut River and Chesapeake Bay increasingly irritated English officials, all the more so because the Dutch ignored the English Navigation Acts. In 1663 Charles II, although England and Holland were at peace, made his brother James, Duke of York, proprietor of New Netherland, eastern Long Island, islands off the coast of New England, and what is now northern Maine. He also supplied the forces necessary to back up his brother's claim. The doughty Stuyvesant wished to fight, but there was no lust for combat among his people, and he yielded to necessity. Only on the Delaware were a few shots fired in the defense of New Netherland. As a result of the Anglo-Dutch War which followed, New Netherland became New York. Nine years later, in another Anglo-Dutch War, a Dutch expedition seized New York. Again there was no resistance, but New York was returned to England in the peace treaty which ended that conflict in 1674, New Netherland again becoming New York, and New Amsterdam, New York town.

To later generations the Swedes bequeathed the log cabin. The legacy left by the Dutch was more imposing. To the American language New Netherland gave such words as cookie, stoop, boss, and placenames such as Nassau and Brooklyn. New Netherland families, Schuylers, Bayards, and Roosevelts, were to give leaders to the American republic. From the colonial Dutch also came the custom of exchanging gifts at Christmas, and the celebration of New Year's Day with the Tom-and-Jerry. Of greater immediate importance, the Dutch kept the Hudson Valley out of French hands until English ones were free to seize it; and they passed on to the English the alliance they had formed with the Iroquois.

As Duke of York, and after 1685 as King of England, James gave New

York efficient but arbitrary government and religious toleration. Before long he was confronted with a demand for a legislature in which representatives of the inhabitants should form one house. He tried to dodge the issue by setting up a Court of Assizes, composed of appointed justices of the peace, which he hoped would be accepted by the colonists. They were not deceived and insisted upon having a true assembly. In 1683, one was finally called together. It promptly prepared a "Charter of Libertyes and Privileges," in effect a constitution for the colony, and asked James to approve it. After some hesitation, he denied the request after he ascended the throne. Instead he made New York a part of the Dominion of New England.

There was much unrest in New York even before the news came of the Glorious Revolution. James's refusal to permit New Yorkers to participate in government was, of course, disturbing to the settlers. The Dutch were unhappy because they were not permitted to trade freely with Holland, a privilege they believed they had secured by treaty when New Netherland became New York. The Puritans on eastern Long Island, torn away from Connecticut in 1664, had not yet reconciled themselves to the change. Dutch and English colonists alike were aggrieved because several of the officers sent to New York by James were Roman Catholics. In New York as elsewhere in the English colonies the rumor of a Catholic-French-Indian conspiracy flew about. Popular feeling ran high against James, whose lieutenant governor, Francis Nicholson, fled to England. Thereupon the governor's council claimed authority to rule. However, Jacob Leisler, a prominent citizen of German descent who had married a wealthy Dutch widow, seized control with the support of the Long Island English and the poorer Dutch. He claimed he was supporting William and Mary, indeed that he had been invested with authority by William. He locked up wealthy merchants and landowners who opposed him. When soldiers under a Major Ingoldesby sent out by William arrived in New York, Leisler refused to disband his militia and actually resisted Ingoldesby at the cost of a few casualties. Similarly, when Henry Sloughter, appointed governor by William, appeared, Leisler recognized his authority only under duress. Accused of treason by Nicholas Bayard, Peter Schuyler, and other local enemies, he was tried, found guilty, and executed before the English government could consider an application for pardon. His son-in-law, Jacob Milborne, met the same cruel fate. Whatever Leisler's motives, he can hardly qualify as a defender of American liberties against English tyranny. At any rate, New York, a royal province after James ascended the throne, remained one. However, William agreed to the establishment of a popular branch of the legislature, and New York acquired the standard form of government for a royal colony.

THE QUAKER COLONIES

Throughout the seventeenth century there was much carelessness in London about American real estate. In 1665 James gave New Jersey, then inhabited only by Indians, a few Dutch across from Manhattan, and a few English along the Delaware, to his friends Lord John Berkeley and Sir George Carteret. They divided the present between them, Berkeley taking West Jersey, Carteret, East Jersey. Both men tried to enlist settlers, neither with remarkable success. Nor did either profit greatly. In 1673 Berkeley sold his rights to a Quaker, Edward Byllinge, from whom they passed eventually to a group of Quakers. In 1680 the Carteret family conveyed East Jersey to a second company, in which Quakers were prominent. The two Jerseys grew steadily under the management of the two groups of owners, and continued to flourish when the two companies merged. Representative bodies were early set up in both territories. Whether or not the later proprietors had power to govern was doubtful; at any rate the two colonies were finally united as the royal province of New Jersey in 1702. Land not yet disposed of, however, remained in the hands of the proprietors, and does to the present day.

Pennsylvania and Delaware had a stronger Quaker complexion than New Jersey, being the properties of William Penn. The Quakers, or more properly the Society of Friends, first became conspicuous in England in the 1650s, the principal founder of the sect being George Fox. They stressed the "inner light" as the guide to salvation, and considered both clergy and sacraments unnecessary. They also emphasized simplicity in garb and speech, and in literal obedience to the scriptures, refused to swear oaths. They were opposed to the use of arms because the Bible said, "Thou shalt not kill." Those beliefs and behavior seemed extraordinary and fantastic to most other folk in the seventeenth century, and the Quakers were widely persecuted. Partly because of that persecution the sect grew rapidly for a generation or so.

Among early Quaker converts was William Penn, the son of a wealthy admiral of Welsh descent. He became the most famous of all the Friends. Born in 1644, Penn might well have been merely another English aristocrat, but one of some distinction, because he possessed physical vigor, intellectual ability, courage, and a kindly spirit. Among his tutors was the Quaker Thomas Loe, who instructed him in the tenets of the Friends, as well as in more mundane lore. Sent on to Oxford University, Penn was again exposed to Quaker influence. The academic authorities suggested to his father that the university would be improved by the absence of his son, and William departed without his degree. The admiral sent Penn to Paris, where he pursued his studies, including the religious ones. Returning home, he soon committed himself permanently to the Society of Friends.

No quiet convert, Penn zealously preached the word; breaking religious laws, he was sent to jail several times. The admiral threatened to disinherit him; instead he left him in 1670 a large estate, and a debt of £16,000 owed to him by the Crown. Like his father, William was a good friend of Charles II and James, Duke of York. A quarrel between Quakers claiming ownership of West Jersey drew his attention sharply to America, for he served as an arbitrator between the opposing parties. Indeed, he became a leading figure in the affairs of West Jersey, and probably had something to do with the making of the surprisingly liberal constitution given that colony in 1677. His attention settled on the region west of the Delaware, still largely vacant of Europeans. There he planned to start a proprietary colony as a means of enriching himself and his family, and as a refuge for oppressed Quakers. In 1681, Charles II, in exchange for cancelling the debt owed to Penn by the Crown, gave him Pennsylvania, which was to extend 100 leagues westward from the Delaware, between the 40th and 43rd parallels. Emulating his brother, the Duke of York gave him Delaware, which James claimed by right of conquest.

The rights of Penn and his descendants as proprietors of Pennsylvania were less handsomely defined than were those of the Baltimores in Maryland, since London officials had been irked by the independent attitude of the Calverts. Nevertheless, the Penns were free to dispose of the lands within their domain, and were authorized to make laws and levy taxes with the "advice, assent and approbation" of the freemen or their representatives. The laws of Pennsylvania were to be as nearly as possible "agreeable to the Laws and Statutes, and Rights of this Our Kingdome of England." They were to be sent to England within five years for inspection, and might be disallowed by the Privy Council. The right to tax was reserved to the Crown and Parliament, and the charter specifically provided for the maintenance of the royal customs service in the colony. Observance of the Navigation Acts was demanded, and the proprietor was required to keep an agent in London. Appeals to London from Pennsylvania courts were to be permitted in all cases. It was further stipulated that any twenty Anglicans desiring to establish a church and to employ a clergyman be permitted to do so. Unaware of Pennsylvania's bituminous and anthracite wealth, officers of the Crown inserted the customary requirement that one-fifth of the gold and silver found in the colony must go to the Crown.

Penn exploited his grant promptly, sending to America Quakers who founded Chester in 1681 and Philadelphia the following year. English, Welsh, and German Quakers were conspicuous among the first settlers, the Germans being largely responsible for the founding of Germantown in 1683. Penn had traveled in Europe as a Quaker missionary, and had made many friends. Extolling the opportunities to be had in Pennsylvania, he

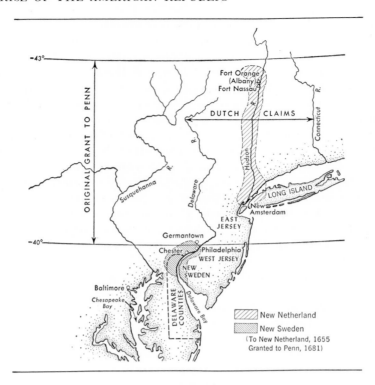

THE QUAKER COLONIES

advertised his colony extensively through his European acquaintances. Mennonites were among those who put down roots at Germantown, and members of other German Protestant sects soon committed themselves to the "holy experiment." French Huguenots also made their way up the Delaware. The first settlers in Pennsylvania were sober and industrious folk; and the colony flourished from the beginning. Well tilled, the lands of southeastern Pennsylvania assured an early prosperity; the Delaware was a broad and easy route to the outside world. For many years relations with the neighboring Indians were peaceful; at the same time, the warlike Iroquois protected Pennsylvania against French attacks from the north.

To govern his domains Penn soon prepared a constitution, the "Frame of Government." This famous document is obviously the product of a liberal mind. In it Penn astutely argued that government should mean a rule of law, not one of men. There was to be toleration for all who believed in God, and no one was to suffer the death penalty except for murder or treason. The machinery of Penn's government deserves less praise, because it was cumbersome. At the head of the state was to be the proprietor, or a governor acting for him with the advice of an executive council; there were to be two legislative bodies, a council to propose laws, and an assembly to accept or reject them. Both houses were to be elected by the freemen, these to include any man who had a small cultivated freehold, as well as anyone who rented 100 acres and tilled as many as ten. The "Frame of Government" could be amended by a six-sevenths vote of both houses.

There were troubles between Penn and his people, these being increased by Penn's natural desire to secure a profit from his investment, and by his paternalistic attitude toward them. He altered the constitution several times; and after 1701 Pennsylvania had a one-house legislature. At that time Delaware, which as "the three lower counties" had been considered as a unit with Pennsylvania, acquired its own assembly. Thereafter it led its own political life, although the two colonies continued to have the same governor until the coming of independence.

Whether or not Penn would be able to cling to his proprietary rights was long doubtful. As a friend of James II, he was deprived of his governmental authority in 1692. In fact, at that time he made himself obscure in London so as to escape the attention of royal officers. However, his charter was fully restored two years later. Afterward he almost lost Pennsylvania to his own steward, an unscrupulous man who managed to make it appear that Penn was indebted to him. That menace was also removed. Another threat existed in the Penns' Quakerism, which hardly made them popular in London. It was not until Penn's heirs became Anglican that the family's American rights and privileges became securely established.

THE CAROLINAS

The English Empire on the North American mainland was consolidated and also expanded to the southward during the period of the Restoration. When Charles II ascended the throne, the region between Virginia and Spanish Florida was almost unoccupied, save for the Indians. The Spanish, it will be recalled, made no attempt to occupy Virginia after 1572, although they long refused to admit English rights there. The Dons did send soldiers and missionaries into what later became the Carolinas and Georgia, but their bases were not put to effective use; under the pressure of Indian attacks, they withdrew into northern Florida a few months after the accession of Charles. By that time Virginians pushing south in search of fresh lands had, probably unknowingly, crossed the Old Dominion's boundaries and were planting themselves in some numbers on the shores of Albemarle Sound, in what is now North Carolina. The coastline southward for hundreds of miles was vacant of Europeans, although those shores were not unknown. As early as 1629 Charles I had given Sir Robert Heath the territory between latitude 35 degrees and 31 degrees, but Heath and his successors were never active. Heath had intended to found a colony, but in 1663, his rights were set aside, and Charles II gave permission to a group of eight proprietors to establish a colony of Carolina.

The moving spirit in the Carolina project was, originally, a planter from Barbados, John Colleton. Colleton believed that the region would readily produce silk, wine, olives, and other semitropical fruits which could profitably be sold in England. He expected successful occupation of the region to bring both personal and national profit. He was not sufficiently wealthy and influential to get a proprietary grant by himself; accordingly, he enlisted seven partners, Sir William Berkeley, Lord John Berkeley, Sir George Carteret, Sir Anthony Ashley Cooper, the Earl of Craven, the Earl of Clarendon, and the Earl of Albemarle. The King could not deny the wishes of these wealthy and loyal gentlemen; in a charter of 1663 he gave them the territory between 31 degrees and 36 degrees of north latitude, from sea to sea, with rights and privileges similar to those granted to the Baltimores thirty years earlier. Special provisions exempted semitropical products from Carolina from duties in England for seven years; the Anglican Church was to be official, but the proprietors were permitted to offer religious toleration; and they could create titles of nobility which differed from those currently used in England. Two years later the charter was revised, the northern limit of Carolina being moved to 36 degrees 30 minutes, so as to include existing settlements on Albemarle Sound; and religious toleration was required.

The Carolina proprietors were always more interested in profits and power than they were in making investments toward those ends. They gave their permission, but no financial help, to New Englanders who tried to settle at the mouth of the Cape Fear River in 1663, and to a group of Barbadians under Sir John Yeamans, who wanted to settle in the same locale two years later. Both efforts failed, partly because of the poverty of the lands in the area.

In 1669 the proprietors stirred themselves, and sent out three ships carrying settlers and supplies; these included beer which was too hastily consumed, before the ships were ten days out of port. The crews and immigrants had to drink water thereafter, until they reached Barbados, where the ships picked up more passengers. The expedition proceeded to the mainland and a colony was established in 1670 on the south side of the Ashley River some distance above its mouth, being named Charlestown (Charleston). Ten years later the settlement was moved bodily to the peninsula between the Ashley and Cooper rivers on the shores of Charleston Bay, which offered the finest harbor between Virginia and Florida. Charlestown became the nucleus of settlements which soon came to be

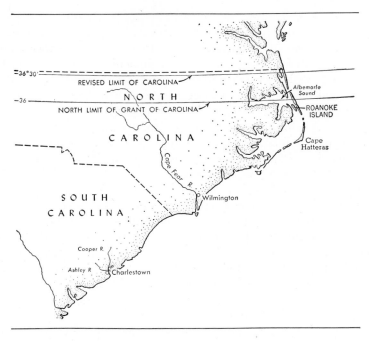

THE CAROLINAS

known as South Carolina. The first immigrants were followed by others from England and from the English West Indies; French Huguenots, driven from their native country, appeared in numbers after 1680. There were also Scottish Highlanders, who founded Stuart Town to the southward in 1684, but who were driven back toward Charlestown by the Spanish; even New England supplied some folk.

The olives did not prosper, and silks seen in Charlestown were those brought with them by the settlers. Nevertheless, farming and cattle raising provided sustenance in the early years, while trade with the Indians brought in money. Vast herds of deer coursed through the southern woodlands and savannahs; the Indians were pleased to exchange deer skins for guns, ammunition, clothing, rum, and trinkets. The skins were readily sold in England and on the Continent, where they were used to make leather goods and clothing. The famed South Carolina aristocracy soon began to appear, the proprietors trying to establish three orders of nobility—the seigneurs, landgraves, and caciques. These sobriquets were not much valued, although they were used well into the eighteenth century. The proprietors also made large grants of land to favored persons such as themselves, in an effort to create feudal manors. Negro slavery in the West Indian style was introduced, but the plantation was not of importance in

South Carolina until after the introduction of rice-growing, about 1691.

Meanwhile, to the northeast the settlements about Albemarle Sound became the nucleus of North Carolina. From them there was a slow expansion to the west and southwest, growth being retarded by lack of a fine port and easily developed natural resources. Again the inhabitants were of varied background. Relatively isolated, they prospered only moderately, through farming, cattle raising, lumbering, and producing tar, pitch, and turpentine. While North Carolina had her incipient aristocrats, throughout the colonial period small farmers were her dominant element. Their number was larger in proportion and in power than was to be found in Virginia or South Carolina.

The original plans for government in the Carolinas were drawn up by Anthony Ashley Cooper, the Earl of Shaftesbury, probably with the help of John Locke, later a famous philosopher, but then a young man. They were extraordinarily complicated, indeed unworkable. Executive authority was placed in a council, for which each proprietor chose a member. At its head was a governor, who was to be chosen by the Palatine, or leading proprietor. However, the senior proprietor present in Carolina was himself entitled to serve as governor. The council was to submit legislation to an assembly elected by the voters, the assembly being denied the right to initiate laws. In practice, the Fundamental Constitutions was both unwieldy and too favorable to the interests of the proprietors. It was modified again and again.

From the beginning the Carolinas had separate councils and assemblies, because their settlements were distant from each other. By 1711, each had its own governor and council, chosen by the proprietors, and an elected lower house, which forcefully claimed the right to initiate legislation. North and South Carolina had definitely entered upon different paths.

At the time of the Glorious Revolution the English Empire in North America was firmly planted between the Kennebec and Savannah rivers. As yet, the English had made little progress into the interior. The Indians remained formidable; the Spanish remained a threat of sorts on the south; and the French constituted a serious menace. Nevertheless, the English colonies had grown almost beyond the power of their enemies to destroy.

6 BRITAIN'S AMERICAN EMPIRE 1689–1763

Precisely a century after the planting at Jamestown, the English Empire became the British Empire. England and Scotland, hitherto united only in allegiance to the same royal family, by the Act of Union of 1707 joined to form the United Kingdom of Great Britain. Instead of being treated as foreigners in the empire, the Scots became full partners in it; in fact, it was facetiously said afterward that they had taken over England and her possessions. Certainly the Act of Union did not interrupt the growth of the empire; nor was there any basic change in colonial policy. From the beginning the English overseas possessions were expected to contribute to the wealth and power of the mother country. The colonies, together with the home islands, were looked upon as parts of an economic community, each part serving the others, but with the prosperity of the central part receiving priority. It was assumed in London that colonists retained the personal rights of Englishmen, and they were allowed to participate in the management of their own domestic affairs through representatives in elected assemblies. It was also assumed in London, however, that such assemblies existed only by virtue of gracious permission, and that Crown and Parliament possessed the same authority in the colonies that they did in England.

75

The empire expanded and thrived between the Glorious Revolution of 1688 and the beginning of the American one in 1763. The colonies on the American mainland, sharing in the prosperity and pride of empire, matured, and their people secured for themselves larger political powers at the expense of the mother country. By 1763, indeed, they were so numerous and so used to participating in the direction of their own political destinies that they could hardly have been long held within the empire, save by their own consent.

In a sense the empire, like Topsy, "just growed." Its British leaders did not devote their chief efforts to it, but national interests were seldom out of their minds, and they steadily strove to secure treasure, trade, and territory at the expense of other European nations, especially Spain, the Netherlands, and France. These rivalries, coupled with political and religious conflicts, provoked intermittent warfare, from which Britain emerged as the great victor in 1763, and as the possessor of the greatest empire in modern European times.

During the century following the first voyage of John Hawkins to the Caribbean, Spain was the most feared and most detested enemy. Although Spanish power waned in Europe after the defeat of the Great Armada and the Spanish empire gradually ceased to expand, it was some time before the English realized that the Spanish were no longer vigorous nor venturesome. Despite growing weakness, the Spanish continued to play an important part in European affairs, and insisted until 1670 that the Englishmen who had settled in the Caribbean and along the Chesapeake were interlopers on territory that was rightfully Spanish. Then Spain was forced to admit, in the Treaty of Madrid, that the English settlements in America were legal. Thereafter, England's great colonial rival was France, although the English continued to seize Spanish possessions. After 1700, when the French Bourbons ascended the Spanish throne, the Spanish Bourbons were forced to become involved in the wars between their French relatives and England.

In the middle of the seventeenth century the English became embroiled with other aspirants for trade and empire, the Dutch, who were formidable antagonists. In Europe the Dutch had made a country from the sea; they sought with equal energy to build an empire, and they wrestled with the English for territory in the East and West Indies and on the mainland of North America. They likewise competed with the English for maritime commerce. The two peoples fell to blows, even though they had common interests in European affairs, and although both were Protestant. A series of naval wars brought no decisive victory, but the Dutch were too few to maintain the contest. In addition, they were threatened at home by French aggression after 1661, when Louis XIV, the "Sun King," took up the reins of government. That monarch sought as "natural boundaries" the

Rhine, the Alps, and the Pyrenees, and the Dutch had to defend themselves against invading French armies. They needed the assistance of the English, who became convinced that they must give it, since they were alarmed lest France dominate the Low Countries and ultimately the Continent. Abandoning New Netherland and colonial competition with the English, the Dutch entered into a defensive alliance with them in 1674. Thereafter they tried to maintain and exploit rather than to expand their possessions overseas.

In the end the English found the French far more formidable opponents than either the Spanish or the Dutch. France was united, prosperous, and powerful, and the absolute monarchy of the Bourbons was firmly established when Louis XIV assumed the management of French policy. Vain, able, and aggressive, he strove throughout his long reign, which endured until 1715, to establish French hegemony in Europe and to develop the empire which he had inherited. His policies were pushed, though with less vigor, in the time of his successor, Louis XV. They aroused bitter opposition in London, and led to a series of great wars, collectively known as the Second Hundred Years' War, which ended in ultimate disaster for France.

THE SECOND HUNDRED YEARS' WAR

Under Louis XIV the growth of French Canada was fostered; Guadeloupe, Martinique, the eastern portion of Haiti, and other Caribbean sugar islands were occupied; and efforts were made to push into Nova Scotia, Newfoundland, and the Hudson Bay country. Extensive explorations were undertaken in the North American interior by Father Marquette, Joliet, LaSalle, and others. The French established the course of the Mississippi River. Detroit was founded by them in 1702. A French expedition under the Sieur d'Iberville founded Biloxi in 1699 and Mobile a year later, laying the groundwork for the colony of Louisiana. The French laid claim to all territory between the Rockies and the Appalachian divide, and to Texas as well. In 1718 under Louis XV they built New Orleans, which became the capital of Louisiana. By 1750 they were trying to prevent English expansion by building a chain of forts running from Niagara to the forks of the Ohio and thence southward. By that time they were also seriously competing with the English for trading stations on the west coast of Africa. They were already established in India, at Pondicherry and Chandernagore, from which bases they were trying to secure both trade and territory. There, too, they encountered the English, who were pursuing similar objectives from centers at Bombay and Madras.

In the Second Hundred Years' War France had several obvious advantages, including larger population, large and well-led armies, and greater wealth. She also derived strength from allies. On the other hand,

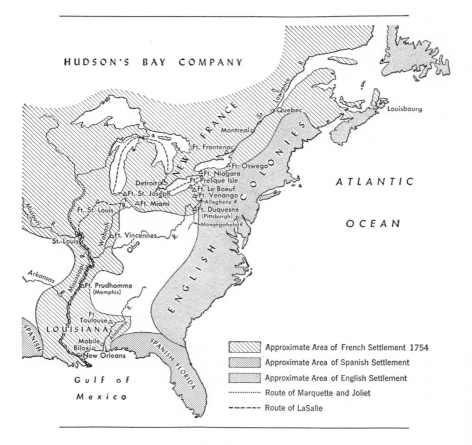

THE FRENCH IN NORTH AMERICA

France was pursuing two goals at the same time, ascendancy in Europe and expansion overseas; the two proving to be beyond her powers. European princes allied themselves with the British to protect themselves from French aggression. The British had a major advantage in sea power which could be employed both to defend the home islands and overseas possessions, as well as to assail the French empire. Happily for the British, their leaders recognized the value of sea power and laid increasing emphasis upon the maritime conflict.

In North America the British were in a peculiarly favorable position. As late as 1754 British colonists, and politicians in London as well, feared encirclement by the French, who might be able to drive the colonists into the sea. They were unduly alarmed. Canada, the core of French strength, actually contained fewer than 60,000 persons, most of them concentrated between Quebec and Montreal. Arbitrary government, religious intolerance, a land policy which discriminated against the small farmer, and a relatively harsh climate had slowed its growth. Louisiana, so impressive on the map, was far weaker than Canada, containing no more than 7000 French inhabitants. There, too, French policy had interfered with rather than encouraged development, and the riches of the Mississippi Valley had not been effectively exploited. French troops, together with the brave Canadian militia, were indeed formidable antagonists. Moreover, they were supported by many Indian tribes, because the French did not seize the lands of the red men and were generally more adept in dealing with the Indians than were the British. Yet the English colonists outnumbered their French neighbors by 20 to 1, and far surpassed them in wealth. The British had their own friends among the Indians, notably the Iroquois in the north, and the Cherokee, Chickasaw, and the Creek in the south. The British influenced chiefs and won friends among the Indians because they could offer superior trade goods at cheaper prices. In fact, many of the Indian nations were so dependent upon the British for trade goods that they were subject to economic coercion. That the French could continue the contest in North America so long must be explained in part by the lack of centralized control in the British colonies, which found it difficult to act in concert save in great emergencies.

The long Anglo-French struggle included four major wars, all with issues that were both European and colonial. At the time of the Glorious Revolution Louis XIV was at war with several German princes. He gave asylum to James II, and assisted him in his efforts to regain the throne. They proved to be in vain; an army led by James in Ireland being utterly crushed by William at the Battle of the Boyne in 1690. England, Holland, and German princes opposing Louis' advance toward the Rhine combined effectively against him, and after several years of hard fighting compelled him to make peace at Ryswick in 1697. This conflict, known in Europe as the War of the League of Augsburg and in America as King William's War, brought no decisive results in Europe or in America, where it consisted largely of border affrays.

QUEEN ANNE'S WAR

A second and greater convulsion began in 1702, the Spanish Crown and Spanish possessions in the Old and New Worlds being the major stakes. Charles II of Spain died in 1700, leaving no male heir. In anticipation of his death, William III and Louis XVI had made earnest efforts to arrange for a peaceful partition of the Spanish lands to which members of the ruling houses of France and Bavaria, and of the Holy Roman Empire, the Austrian Habsburgs, had claims by virtue of descent from princesses of the Spanish royal family. It was evident that Spain and her possessions could not go either to a Bourbon or a Habsburg without destroying the balance of power in Europe, and that either of those solutions must lead to war. The negotiations between William and Louis were fruitless. When it became known that Charles had indicated in his will that he was to be succeeded by the Bourbon Prince Philip, Louis' great-grandson, Louis announced that Philip had become ruler of Spain and all her territories, saying that the Pyrenees no longer existed. The Habsburg family promptly began hostilities in behalf of its own claimant, being joined by other German rulers and by Holland and England, neither of which could feel safe with Europe dominated by the Bourbons. Nor could the English contemplate without grave concern a possible union of the French and Spanish empires. An arduous and exhausting conflict, labeled the War of the Spanish Succession in Europe and Queen Anne's War in America ensued. John Churchill, Duke of Marlborough, led the British and Dutch troops and humbled Louis' generals in the Low Countries, while British armies and fleets won important victories elsewhere. Britain made peace with Spain and France at Utrecht in 1713. Philip was allowed to become King of Spain, but with the proviso that France and Spain were never to be united under one ruler. Britain received for her efforts Gibraltar and Minorca, one of the Balearic Islands, which gave her control of the western Mediterranean. In addition, France recognized British ownership of the Hudson Bay country, Newfoundland, and Nova Scotia. Spain also gave Britain a monopoly on the slave trade between Africa and the Spanish possessions in the New World, together with the right to send to them each year one merchant ship. The commercial concessions, like the territorial gains, were important, since the Spanish colonies had hitherto been legally closed to British merchants.

During the three decades after the peace of Utrecht, Britain and France were at peace, although that period brought indecisive contests between Britain and Spain. However, Anglo-French rivalry continued, markedly in North America and in India.

SETTLING GEORGIA

Listening to warnings from South Carolina of French and Spanish "aggressions," the British government arranged to build and garrison with British regulars Fort Frederica on the Altamaha River in Georgia in 1721. This post was to serve as an outwork against the French in Louisiana and the Spanish in Florida. Largely for the same purpose, the Crown granted a charter for a new colony of Georgia in 1732. Many men, philanthropists, politicians, and military people, and especially the benevolent-minded General James Oglethorpe, had pushed for its creation. They wanted British occupation of the land between the Savannah River and the out-

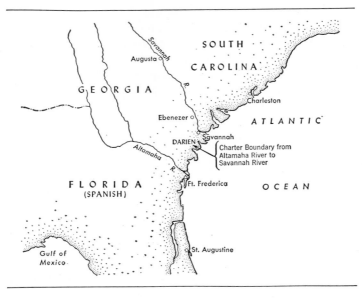

SETTLEMENT OF GEORGIA

posts of Spanish Florida. It contained no European settlements; a bulwark would thus be erected for the defense of the southern colonies. Georgia would also serve as a base from which the British could compete more effectively with the Spanish and French for the trade with the southern Indian tribes. It was also expected to supply semitropical fruits, silk, and wines, which were much desired in Britain. The proponents of this plan urged, ardently, that the colony be used as a haven for debtors and other unfortunates. Debtors in England and her colonies were commonly punished by being tossed into prison where they could do neither themselves, their families, nor the public any good; where, indeed, they were a burden upon the public. In Georgia they could be of service to the state and to their families as farmers and soldiers. The arguments offered by Oglethorpe and his associates were very appealing. Hence the charter was granted, setting the limits of Georgia at the Savannah on the north, the Altamaha on the south, and the Pacific on the west. The colony was to be governed by trustees who were not to profit personally; the trustees were to appoint officials to serve in the colony, no provision being made for immediate participation in government by the settlers. After twenty-one years the colony was to be taken over by the Crown. Unlike earlier colonies, Georgia was given assistance from the British Treasury, which for some years helped the colony by annual grants which ranged from £8000 to

£26,000. Indeed the grants, eventually reduced to something less than £5000, were continued until Georgia became an independent state. A regiment of troops was also supplied, and benevolent persons privately gave about £20,000 for the project.

Under the leadership of Oglethorpe, 135 settlers including some debtors proceeded to Georgia, where they founded Savannah in 1733. A contingent of German Lutherans founded Ebenezer in 1734; three years later, another of Scottish Highlanders settled at Darien. Many Carolinians ventured across the Savannah; Indian traders from South Carolina were principally responsible for the establishment of Augusta in 1735. The great hopes of Georgia's sponsors were not realized either entirely or immediately. The colony grew slowly, becoming, in effect, a younger South Carolina. Nevertheless, the colony became a permanent one, and served as a barrier against Spanish attack, and also as a staging ground for an unsuccessful British expedition against St. Augustine.

THE WAR OF JENKINS' EAR

The third great conflict of the Second Hundred Years' War began for the British in 1739, when they slipped into military contest with Spain. The causes were largely commercial, although the ostensible reason for war was the supposed cruelty of the Spanish to one Captain Jenkins, who claimed that they had cut off his ear. This War of Jenkins' Ear later merged into the War of the Austrian Succession, which began in the following year.

In 1740 the possessions of the Austrian Habsburgs were inherited by a woman, Maria Theresa; and Frederick the Great of Prussia, with support from Louis XV because of the traditional hostility between the Bourbons and the Austrian Habsburgs, undertook to wrest the fertile province of Silesia from Maria Theresa. Britain supported the queen, and took up arms against France in 1744. Thereafter, the British fought against both the Spanish and the French until the making of a general peace at Aix-la-Chapelle in 1748. English attacks upon the Spanish empire were largely unsuccessful. The French conquered a large part of Belgium, then part of the dominions of Maria Theresa. The British did gain one striking success in America, Massachusetts militia under William Pepperrell and a British naval squadron under Commodore Peter Warren capturing the great French fort of Louisbourg in 1745. It was located on Cape Breton Island, and had been erected to serve as protection for the mouth of the St. Lawrence and for Canada. Had Louisbourg been retained by the British, the position of the French in Canada must have been greatly weakened. Instead, it was returned to France in exchange for the return of Bourbon conquests in Belgium to Maria Theresa, for Britain was eager to prevent French expansion into the Low Countries.

THE FRENCH AND INDIAN WAR

The war firmly established the Hanoverian family on the throne of Britain. Its right to rule had been denied by both the son and grandson of James II, exiles in France. George I, a Protestant descendant of James I, was placed on the throne in 1714, when the Protestant Queen Anne died without direct heirs. The son of James II, the Old Pretender, had stirred up an uprising in Scotland in 1715; in 1745 Charles Edward, the Young Pretender undertook to unseat George II, failing utterly.

The peace of Aix-la-Chapelle turned out to be only an armistice during which the major European states, in a "diplomatic revolution," rearranged their alliances. Maria Theresa refused to admit that Silesia was finally lost, and prepared for another struggle. She secured the support of France, Russia, Sweden, and of several minor German rulers against Frederick; meanwhile, Britain and Hanover moved toward friendship with Prussia, which was consummated by an Anglo-Prussian alliance in 1756.

The fighting between Britain and France was already in progress, having begun where the Allegheny and Monongahela Rivers join to form the Ohio, in the summer of 1754. French troops moving southward to build a fort at that strategic spot encountered militiamen under George Washington who had been sent westward by Lieutenant-Governor Robert Dinwiddie of Virginia for the same purpose. After an initial success, Washington, faced by superior force, was compelled to capitulate and to retreat. The French built Fort Duquesne, later Pittsburgh, on the spot. The British Cabinet responded by sending Major General Edward Braddock to America with two regiments of redcoats and instructions to drive the French from Fort Duquesne. The French were also to be driven from Fort Niagara. The war began dismally for the British. In the campaign of 1755, colonial militia and Iroquois warriors under William Johnson defeated an army of French and Indians near Crown Point in upper New York but the British expedition against Niagara bogged down, and Braddock met overwhelming disaster and death. On July 9, as he approached Fort Duquesne with his regulars and militia who had joined him, they were assailed and routed by a much smaller body of French and Indians. Mortally wounded, Braddock died shortly after the Battle of the Monongahela. Meanwhile hostilities began on the Atlantic Ocean, and became general in the spring of 1756, when Britain and France exchanged declarations of war. Because the conflict continued until 1763, it is commonly described as the Seven Years' War in Europe; in America it was designated the French and Indian War.

The Seven Years' War also began badly in Europe for the British and their Prussian allies. In 1757, however, the indomitable Frederick, virtually surrounded by enemies of overwhelming strength, inflicted heavy losses upon his Austrian and French foes at Rossbach and Leuthen. That year Britain acquired a great war leader in the person of William Pitt the Elder, who was the principal man in the Cabinet until 1761. Imperious, untiring, magnificent in oratory, and a shrewd judge of men, Pitt infused great energy into the British war effort, enlarged the army and the navy, and gave them younger and abler commanding officers. Pitt put into the field forces under the Duke of Brunswick which protected Hanover and Prussia against the French; he also supplied Frederick generously with funds. Relieved from pressure on the west, Frederick displayed an extraordinary genius and desperate determination, and staved off assaults by the Austrians and Russians until 1761. Then Tsarina Elizabeth of Russia died and was replaced by Peter II. Peter fervently admired the Prussian king, and withdrew from the war. When Peter was assassinated, his widow, Catherine the Great, continued his policy of neutrality. His resources almost exhausted, Frederick was able to hang on until Maria Theresa abandoned the fray. Thus Frederick emerged victorious, even though he lost his British subsidy when Pitt fell from power. Pitt resigned because George III, who became king in 1760, together with influential British politicians, refused to support him in a design to attack Spain and to crush the Bourbons. Spain, long neutral, came to the assistance of France in 1762, invading Portugal, Britain's ally. The result was disastrous for the Spanish Bourbons. British and Portuguese soldiers successfully defended Portugal; having struck heavy blows at the French empire, British soldiers and tars turned their attention to the Spanish one.

When Pitt came into authority, the tide of warfare changed on the seas and in the colonial world. The British navy inflicted defeat upon the French, making a French invasion of Britain impossible and preventing the French from sending reinforcements and supplies to their colonies. On the other hand, Britain was able to pour men and ships into colonial warfare. This turn of events was symbolized by Robert Clive's overwhelming victory over allies of France at Plassey in India in 1757. Four years later, the French possessions in India were in British hands.

The tide did not turn quite so quickly in North America. The British colonies there were unable to make a united effort. To achieve unity, delegates from seven of them had met at Albany in 1754 and had drawn up a Plan of Union. This called for an American council headed by a British official, to be responsible for the common defense and to have the power to tax for that purpose. But the Plan of Union pleased neither the imperial government nor the American assemblies. However, in accordance with a recommendation by the Albany Congress, management of relations with the Iroquois, so important to military success, was entrusted to William Johnson, a veteran Indian trader and agent, and a skillful diplomat. After 1756, as superintendent for the Iroquois and their allies,

Johnson won friends for the British and secured important military assistance from the Six Nations. Edmund Atkin strove to do the same kind of job among the red men south of the Ohio, but with less success. Unity in military command was also largely achieved under a succession of British commanders in chief who followed Braddock. The Indian superintendents operated under his direction, as did thousands of American militiamen. Reinforcements of redcoats streamed across the ocean, and the Anglo-American forces, supported by the Iroquois, brought increasing pressure upon French Canada. Between 1756 and 1758, the Marquis de Montcalm, the bold and able leader of the French forces in Canada, dealt heavy blows at the redcoats and colonials, capturing Oswego and Fort William Henry, and bloodily repulsing a British army at Ticonderoga. Then Anglo-American power began to tell. In 1758 the wings of the French in Canada were clipped; General John Forbes captured Fort Duquesne, and a British fleet and army retook the great fortress of Louisbourg. The following year General Jeffery Amherst drove the French out of New York, advancing toward Montreal. Meanwhile, General James Wolfe and Admiral Charles Saunders moved up the St. Lawrence to assail the French stronghold at Quebec. In a memorable British victory on the Plains of Abraham, both Montcalm and Wolfe were mortally wounded. The French defenders fled into the city, but were soon forced to surrender, in September, 1759. A French counterattack was unsuccessful. In September, 1760, British forces converged upon Montreal and the last French stronghold was forced to surrender.

After the fall of Montreal British attention turned toward the capture of New Orleans and Louisiana. Hitherto, Louisiana had suffered only from the efforts of the British navy, which cut off supplies as well as reinforcements. Taking advantage of bungling Indian diplomacy on the part of the British, French agents from Louisiana had been able to stir up the Cherokee to attack the frontiers of the southern British colonies. In the ensuing Anglo-Cherokee War of 1760 and 1761, colonials and British regulars had to invade and to ravage the country of the Cherokee before the Indians would admit defeat. Nor were the British able to move against New Orleans in 1762, for they were busy taking Havana from the Spanish. An expedition against New Orleans was planned for the following year, but before it could get under way, France and Spain decided to abandon the struggle, and peace was made at Paris in February, 1763. Britain nevertheless obtained eastern Louisiana.

Beaten, disorganized, and exhausted, the French and Spanish Bourbons were forced to make vast concessions to Britain. To regain Havana, Spain ceded to Britain her ancient colony of Florida. France abandoned her ambitions in India, thus opening the way for British exploitation of that subcontinent. Louis XV also ceded some sugar islands in the Caribbean.

Most important of all, France withdrew from the North American continent, Britain receiving Canada and all French territory east of the Mississippi, save for the town of New Orleans. During the peace negotiations, Louis made a present of New Orleans and Louisiana west of the Mississippi to his cousin Charles III of Spain, partly to liquidate the French empire on the continent, and partly to compensate Spain for the loss of Florida. The gift was not a remarkably generous one, in view of the fact that Louisiana had brought France expense rather than profit. It was therefore of doubtful value to Spain, although it acted as a barrier against the British for the Spanish possessions to the south. The triumph of the British in the long struggle with France was, of course, of extraordinary importance, conceivably even greater than that of the Americans in the War of Independence. Among other decisions, it was determined that North America was to be British rather than French, or British-American rather than French-American, a conclusion with far-reaching consequences.

In the year 1763, the British empire was wealthy, impressive, and powerful, and its potentialities were immense. Modern Europe had known nothing like it, and Britain was envied and feared in the courts of European rulers. Twenty years later, that empire lay almost in ruins, for Britain had lost her most valuable possessions, the Thirteen Colonies; indeed, all the lands between the Atlantic and the Mississippi. Such a great overturn must be explained largely in terms of shortsighted colonial policy. The British were efficient enough in dealing with European rivals, but they were unable to understand their own people beyond the Atlantic.

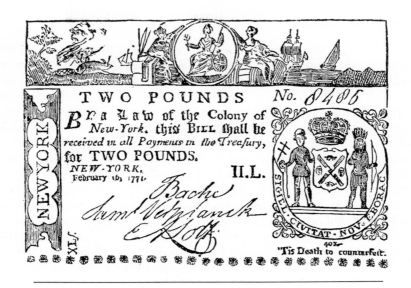

7 THE MATURE COLONIES

Before 1763 there was almost no doubt in London regarding the power of Crown and Parliament to rule over the empire. From its beginning it was conceded that the American colonists possessed the "rights of Englishmen," in the same fashion as did Englishmen at home. When the Parliament of 1650 passed an act asserting that its authority extended over the colonies, colonial claims and charter rights to the contrary notwithstanding, it merely stated what seemed to be an obvious fact in London. Charters could be revoked in theory, and often were in practice. Colonial assemblies established under their provisions, or in any other fashion, did not exist as a matter of absolute right; rather, they were permitted to function. In accordance with this view, the assemblies in the royal colonies met and acted only because the governor, following his instructions, permitted them to do so. They could deal only with domestic affairs, and even in that area they were subject to direction from London.

ENGLISH MERCANTILISTIC POLICY

Parliament began to regulate the maritime commerce of the colonists as early as 1650, and later undertook to impose controls upon colonial manufacturing and currency. The act of 1650 forbade foreign ships to go to the colonies, except with the permission of the Council of State. In the following year Parliament enacted the first of its famous Navigation Acts. This statute was intended to encourage the growth of the English (in-

87

cluding colonial) merchant marine at the expense of foreign competitors, particularly the Dutch. It declared that goods carried to England or to the English colonies from foreign ports in Asia, Africa, or America must be carried in English ships. They must have English captains and the majority of crew members must be English. Merchandise from Europe must be transported in similar fashion, except that it might be shipped in vessels of the country producing the goods. Thus the Dutch would be severely cramped, since they could carry only the products of the Netherlands. Further, trade between parts of the empire was restricted to English merchantmen. Nine years later, after the collapse of the Puritan Commonwealth, this act was replaced by another containing the same restrictions and several additional ones. The provision requiring an English majority in a ship's crew was raised, so that three quarters of the crew had to be English. Foreign vessels were entirely barred from trade with the colonies. Perhaps even more important were new clauses which declared that certain "enumerated articles" such as sugar, cotton, indigo, tobacco, ginger, and dyewoods, produced in an English colony could be shipped only to another English colony or to England. The major purpose of these restrictions was to insure insofar as possible a reliable supply of these basic commodities for England; secondly, English merchants would profit from selling them on the European continent. Later rice, molasses, tar, furs, and deerskins were added to the list of enumerated articles. Another Navigation Act, often called the Staple Act, in 1663 required that with minor exceptions all European goods destined for the colonies had to be landed in England. This arrangement permitted English merchants to handle and sell the goods at a profit, at the same time increasing the proceeds of English import and export duties. Navigation Acts of 1673 and 1696 contained additional stipulations to make it as certain as possible that the laws of 1660 and 1663 would be obeyed. American overseas trade was further confined by the Molasses Act of 1733, which placed a duty of sixpence per gallon on molasses brought to the American mainland from the foreign islands in the West Indies. This tax was to force the colonials to buy their molasses, important because it was the basic ingredient in rum, from British planters who could not produce it as cheaply as could the French, Spanish, and Dutch.

Parliament also placed limits upon American manufacturing. By a law of 1699 the colonials were forbidden to export wool and woolen goods from one colony to another, or to England. They were to make woolen stuffs only for local consumption. Similarly, in the Hat Act of 1732 the size of establishments making hats in America was severely limited, and the exportation of hats from one colony to another or to Britain was forbidden. By the Iron Act of 1750 the colonials were told that they must not increase their steel output, although they might cast iron and freely make bar iron to send to the factories of Birmingham and Sheffield for processing and finishing. The intent of this measure was obviously to remove colonial competition in steel and finished iron products.

In 1740, Parliament undertook to impose mild restrictions upon colonial banking. Eleven years later it passed a law regulating paper currency in New England. Such currency was often put out by colonies without the proper amount of gold or silver behind it, and tended to depreciate in value. Moreover, the colonials frequently made it legal tender, that is, currency which could be used to pay debts, and which creditors had to accept as payment. The act forbade legal tender provisions, and stipulated that paper currencies in New England were to be soundly supported in the future.

On casual inspection, the economic legislation of Parliament may seem to be grossly discriminatory against the colonists and selfishly directed toward enhancing the prosperity of the mother country at the expense of her American progeny. To be sure, English politicians believed in the doctrines of mercantilism. True, they wanted to accumulate bullion, cash, and credit in the mother country, and they tried to compel the colonists to produce raw materials rather than finished goods. They strove to assist the English merchant, and as time went on, they sought increasingly to develop manufacturing at home while discouraging it in the colonies, which they tried to maintain as markets for finished goods and producers of raw materials. In general, when there was a serious conflict between the interests of the two, those of the Englishmen at home would be served, the decision being justified on the score that the mother country contributed disproportionately to the expenses of imperial defense. Decisions in favor of the homeland as against the colonies were also psychologically justified on the assumption that colonials were inferior simply because they were colonials.

However, it should be observed that English politicians thought of the empire as an economic community, with each of its parts serving the others, and that they offered favors to Englishmen at a distance as well as to those at home. The Navigation Acts encouraged the development of the shipping of Boston as well as that of Bristol. In the eighteenth century a full third of the British merchant marine was colonial, and more than one third of its vessels were built in the American colonies. The Americans were injured to some degree by being forced to buy goods from English merchants. The tobacco growers about Chesapeake Bay, nine-tenths of whose exported products was smoked on the European continent, lost heavily because they had to sell to English merchants. On the other hand, much of their trade must have been so channeled even in the absence of coercive laws. Nor were the restrictions on manufacturing so vital as they may appear, at least not as reasons for seeking American independence. The Americans were very largely an agricultural people and few of them were interested in manufacturing before the achievement of independence. The Iron Act was looked upon by some colonials as an unjust law, but it was less onerous than might be supposed, simply because its provisions were often evaded. Indeed, the Americans generally found ways and means to circumvent the Acts of Trade and Navigation with impunity. American commerce and manufacturing were far less burdened in practice than they were on paper. It is significant that the Americans did not look upon the Acts of Trade and Navigation as a grievance that required prompt remedy, even in 1774 and 1775 when they were disposed to define their rights in very broad terms.

It should not be forgotten that Parliament gave important assistance to American producers of raw materials. Especially important were bounties offered to encourage the processing of naval stores, tar, pitch, and turpentine, and to the growers of indigo. There is no doubt that the bounty on indigo contributed materially to the remarkable prosperity of South Carolina planters after 1750.

Whatever may have been the effects of British mercantile policy in America or elsewhere, there can be no doubt that the American colonies prospered. In fact, Professor Arthur M. Schlesinger has expressed the opinion that the fifty-year period between 1713 and 1763 was the "golden age of the American merchant."

COLONIAL GOVERNMENTS

Seeking to make the empire a well-rounded economic community, persons responsible for policy in England gradually became convinced of the need for royalizing the colonial governments. During the seventeenth century they slowly learned that proprietary and corporate colonies were difficult to control. The existence of three types of colonies, proprietary, corporate, and royal, created awkward problems in colonial management. They did not fail to observe that the Acts of Trade and Navigation were violated more frequently in the colonies which were not royally organized. Hence the royal system became an accepted ideal in London before the Glorious Revolution of 1688, and remained so. The ideal was never reached because of English respect for legal rights, resistance by the proprietors and the corporate colonies, and lack of energy in London. Accordingly, Connecticut and Rhode Island regained their charters after the Glorious Revolution; the Penn family was permitted to rule Pennsylvania and Delaware until the coming of independence; and the Calverts, losing their governmental powers after the Glorious Revolution, not only recovered them when the family became Anglican in 1715, but also clung to them until the day of independence. However, at the request of her inhabitants, South Carolina was royalized in 1719, partly because her proprietors were bad managers, and partly because they failed to provide for an effective defense against hostile Indians. For much the same reasons, North Carolina was given a royal system ten years later. After the rule of the trustees was terminated in 1751, Georgia also acquired a royal governor and council. Thus eight of the original thirteen colonies became royal in form, as did almost all other British possessions in the New World.

Centralization of power became an ideal along with royalization, but no real progress was made toward achieving it. It became obvious that cheaper and better management, more fruitful Indian diplomacy, and more effective defense could be had by lessening the number of colonies or by creating a colonial federation. The Dominion of New England was, of course, directed toward those ends. Its collapse did not mean that the ideal of centralization was abandoned. On the contrary, many schemes for realizing it made their appearance in the eighteenth century, including the Albany Plan of Union. Again, colonial resistance, legal difficulties, and lack of a driving force in London prevented the transformation of wish into reality. Eventually the colonists created their own union.

Had all thirteen colonies been royal in form, British authority would not have been much greater at the beginning of the American Revolution than it actually was. In domestic affairs Connecticut and Rhode Island were largely self-governed, and with respect to local questions in the proprietary provinces Britain exercised influence rather than power. Actually, by 1763 British control was far from firm, even in the royal colonies. To be sure, their governors, appointed by the Crown, had impressive authority. These dignitaries possessed a veto power, commanded the provincial army and navy, appointed various minor officials, and could call elections for, prorogue, and dissolve the assembly. The granting of lands was also largely under their direction. The members of the council, whose consent was necessary for all legislation, were also chosen by the Crown (except in Massachusetts), usually upon the recommendation of the governor. Various other officers, such as judges of the higher courts, treasurers, and secretaries, were also selected in London. Moreover, these provincial office holders inevitably received the support of some colonials, if only because of the patronage and favors which they could dispense. In every royal colony there was a "court party" which tended to support the governor on most issues. The customs officers were political allies of the governor, as were the Indian superintendents and commanders in chief of the British army in the later colonial period. British authority was still further protected by the requirement that appeals be permitted from the highest colonial courts to London, and that all laws made in the royal colonies were subject to disallowance—similar to veto—by the Privy Council. Nevertheless, the popular element in government in the royal colonies, the lower house, had become dominant, at least in situations where British and American interests clashed.

GROWTH OF THE COLONIES

In 1763 the American colonists were neither few, nor poor, nor unsophisticated. By that time both Tidewater and Piedmont from southern Maine to Georgia were well settled; indeed Americans were already crossing over the Appalachians into the valley of the Mississippi. On an average, population doubled every twenty-three years during the colonial period, and there were between 1.5 and 2 million persons in the Thirteen Colonies in 1763. This extraordinary increase was based in part upon a remarkably high birth rate. In the colonial period children were an asset rather than an economic burden, and there was opportunity for them in a rapidly expanding economy. Besides, birth control was unknown, and the social diseases were far less common west of the Atlantic than they were in the Old World. Spinsters and bachelors, widows and widowers could not be comfortable or happy in the colonial environment. Adults were almost invariably married folk; the Americans married early and often, and their progeny was numerous. Benjamin Franklin was one of a family of 18 children. In consequence, despite a heavy mortality rate among children and adults, one may with some plausibility refer to an "unnatural" increase among the colonists.

Immigration continued to add substantially to the population. The British government welcomed to the colonies Protestants from the European continent as well as from the British Isles, and it discouraged Roman Catholics only by restricting British citizenship to persons who would take an oath of allegiance unacceptable to Catholics. Indeed, the British government not only opened wide the door for immigrants, but forced thousands to pass through it. These were persons convicted of crime in Britain and given a choice between execution and transportation. Their services were sold and they were bound to work for American masters during a period of seven years, after which they were free to embark upon a new life. The colonial governments also welcomed Protestant immigrants, extending aid and even gifts of land. Had they been able to do so, the American assemblies might have put a stop to the traffic in convicts, but preventive laws would have been unacceptable to the Privy Council. Late in the colonial period, many Americans, especially in Pennsylvania, Delaware, and the Upper South, came to believe that the oceanic slave trade should be limited or abolished. However, American laws to limit that traffic were usually disallowed by the Privy Council, which sought to

protect the interests of British slave traders. In general, then, those who
wished to go to America were encouraged rather than prevented. Offering
economic opportunity, religious toleration, and a large measure of political
freedom, the colonies became a land of Canaan for tens of thousands of
people in the Old World. Above all, they were drawn to America because
of the relative ease with which they could own land.

By 1763, except in Georgia, the lower house in the eight royal colonies
had become dominant in domestic matters. In these affairs the colonists
assumed that their assemblies had the same powers and privileges as did
the House of Commons in England. They existed and functioned, not
because they were permitted to do so, but because they were based upon
the right of Englishmen to be governed by their own representatives. The
Americans did not see their assemblies as the English did. Everywhere the
lower house sought to follow the example of the House of Commons in
form and in function, even using its name. It successfully asserted its
control over finances. Once the purse strings were in its hands, the lower
house was able to impose its will upon the governor and the council in
most local questions, although the governor struggled to maintain the royal
prerogative. Contests between him and the popular branch were frequent,
and the king's man was sometimes the loser. Power lost by one governor
was seldom regained by his successors, and every victory won by the lower
house tended to lead toward another. Governors, able or mediocre, came
and went, but the lower house seemed to go on forever in its drive for
additional power. Ultimately, the representatives of the voters even seized
part of the executive authority, indicating not only the purposes for which
money should be spent, but naming the persons who should handle it.
The Commons House of South Carolina in 1774 actually managed to put
paper currency in circulation, despite disapproval by both the governor
and the upper house. Some royal governors who heeded instructions
from home rather than the wishes of the colonists suffered, because the
lower house forgot to vote funds for their salaries. The intelligent ones
were acutely conscious of the waning influence of Britain in the royal
colonies, especially in situations where British and American interests
clashed. After 1763 the royal governor could no longer be considered a
pillar of strength for the British Empire.

8 LIFE IN THE COLONIES

By the year 1763 the word "American" was in common use to designate inhabitants of the British colonies in America. That it was frequently used is to be explained in part by its convenience, but in a larger degree because the term was a name for a new people. In earlier times the Americans were merely Englishmen in America. However, the word acquired a new meaning, and those who used it had come to recognize that the Americans were not just British people who happened to live on the western side of the Atlantic. A few years later, Hector St. Jean de Crévecoeur was to ask the pregnant question, "What then is this American, this new man?" While others did not perceive so sharply the differences which had arisen between the British and the Americans, divergences between the two were sensed both in Britain and America. It was felt with good reason that the inhabitants of the Thirteen Colonies were much alike, hence that they could all be properly called Americans. It was evident enough that the Maine mariner and the Maryland planter were not cast in precisely the same mold, and that there were dissimilarities between the Savannah merchant and the trader of Salem. Nevertheless, the Americans were fundamentally like each other, and variant from others, even the British.

At the end of the Seven Years' War the Americans were in the main of British stock, about half of their forebears being English and smaller fractions Scottish and Scotch-Irish. Their British ancestors probably numbered somewhat less than two-thirds of the whole. The second largest element was African, for something like 20 percent of all Americans were Negro. German strains were also in evidence, forming perhaps seven or eight percent of the total. Conspicuous on the American family tree were the Dutch, French, Welsh, Swiss, Swedes, Finns, and Jews. The "melting pot" was already boiling, for intermarriage between the British and other European elements was a striking phenomenon. An American of that time might have English, French, Dutch, and German grandparents. Nor were there lacking unions between whites and Negroes, although intermarriage between the two was uncommon. Negroes were increasingly mulattos and quadroons rather than pure African in descent.

Naturally, the English language and English culture were dominant. Here and there in enclaves where the Germans and the Dutch were numerous, their languages long persisted. Dutch was spoken in the vicinity of Albany as late as 1800, and German was used even longer in parts of Pennsylvania. With these minor exceptions, English—and much the same sort of English—was used throughout the colonies. Similarly, the non-English element among the whites adapted themselves to English ways and adjusted to English institutions. Even the Negroes were strongly affected by the dominant influence of the English. How pervasive that influence was is shown in a statement of Governor William Livingston of New Jersey, who had three Dutch grandparents and only one Scottish, that he was "Anglo-Saxon."

But if the non-English elements intermarried with and tended to become like the English ones, all Americans became less and less like the English in the mother country. With every passing year from the founding of Jamestown the gap widened, the homeland becoming increasingly remote and alien. After the passage of six generations, the magnitude of the change was not fully understood by most Americans, who steadily retained an attachment to the "old country." On the other hand, the internal differences among the colonists, their clashing economic systems, their divergent societies, and their political, religious, and cultural dissimilarities were better known. Contemporary observers noted that commercial and cultural exchange between the colonies was not great, but that there were broad channels of trade and culture between some of the colonies, particularly the Southern ones, and England. Some of these observers saw American political union of any sort as impossible. Actually, the colonists underwent a host of common experiences not encountered in Britain or Europe; the great bulk of them were people of the land; economic, social, and intellectual ties between them gradually became stronger; and they had common enemies in the Indians, the Spanish, and the French. Perhaps no factor contributes more to that community of sentiment which is the foundation of the national state than the existence of common and dangerous foes. The long-continued struggles for power between the colonials and British officials also tended to unify the Americans. When hostility toward Britain increased after 1763, American nationalism bloomed like a flower in the spring sun.

At the beginning of the era of independence (1763–1789) the colonies may be divided into three, or even four, sections: the South; New England; the middle colonies; and the frontier. It is profitable to examine each in some detail.

THE CULTURE OF THE SOUTH

The South, although that word was not used for a geographical area until after the achievement of independence, was a region distinct from the middle colonies and New England. It included Georgia, the Carolinas, Virginia, and Maryland, the last being more closely tied to her Southern neighbors than she was in later years. The Southern colonists were less English than those of New England, more so than those of the middle colonies. The Virginians were largely English and Negro, the latter forming about forty percent of the population. In Virginia's western counties there were important elements of Scotch-Irish and Germans who had come southward from Pennsylvania after 1725. Maryland was similarly peopled, except that her Negroes were proportionately somewhat fewer. The inhabitants of North Carolina, South Carolina, and Georgia were heterogeneous, the English being numerous in all three, and especially on the coastal plain or Tidewater. In the interior, above the Fall Line on the Piedmont, the Scotch-Irish settled in large numbers toward the middle of the eighteenth century, being joined by smaller contingents of Germans. Scottish settlers, including Highlanders who fled across the ocean after the collapse of their rebellions in 1715 and 1745, also formed an important minority. Less numerous, but not without influence, were the French Huguenots who concentrated in South Carolina. The proportion of Negroes was the same in North Carolina and Georgia as in Maryland; in South Carolina they formed half or more of the total population. In that part of the Low Country (the coastal plain of South Carolina, southern

North Carolina and northern Georgia) centering on Charleston, Negroes outnumbered whites by as many as six to one. In general, there were far greater numbers of Negroes along the Tidewater than on the Piedmont.

In 1763 no city in the South, save for Charleston, had as many as 10,000 people. There were a number of flourishing towns and villages, such as Norfolk, Winchester, and Savannah, but the Southerners as a whole lived on the land. In Maryland and Virginia their principal crop was tobacco, 100 million pounds of which was exported annually from the Chesapeake area. In South Carolina the principal products were rice and indigo, the dye-plant being very profitable because of a British bounty given to enable its planters to compete with growers in the foreign islands of the West Indies. The economy of North Carolina, like her population, was diversified, the small farm being characteristic in much of the colony. Small farms were also to be found in numbers in the interior parts of Maryland, Virginia, and South Carolina. Georgia was as yet a frontier colony, being in essence a younger South Carolina. Iron was mined in Maryland, and both iron and lead in Virginia. However, manufacturing in the South was largely confined to the processing of raw materials and to the making of clothing, weapons, tools, and liquors for local consumption.

SOUTHERN SOCIAL CLASSES

Dominant in Southern society were the plantation owners, such as the Carrolls of Maryland, the Carters, Randolphs, and Lees of Virginia, and the Middletons, Draytons, and Pinckneys of South Carolina. Some hundreds of families formed a true aristocracy, at least according to American standards. They were concentrated about the shores of Chesapeake Bay and in the Low Country of South Carolina. There were few titles of nobility among them, and their position was based upon wealth, chiefly in land and slaves, rather than upon hereditary superiority. These families commonly owned several plantations, each being worked by some dozens of slaves. Although this aristocracy did not despise wealth secured by other means, it depended largely upon tobacco in the region of the Chesapeake and upon rice and indigo in the Carolina Low Country. Its members lived well, in comfortable and even elegant mansions; in Virginia and Maryland they lived in the country, but in South Carolina they divided their time between their estates and their town houses in Charleston. Many were well educated, although only a few possessed college degrees. Some were graduates of William and Mary and a few had graduated from colleges in the northern colonies. Perhaps as many attended universities in Britain and Europe. Athletic, devoted to horsemanship and hunting, fond of cards and dancing, these men also devoted themselves to public service. These aristocrats formed a ruling class, directing the course of local government and playing important roles in colonial affairs. Their neighbors looked to them for leadership in public questions, and were given it.

Below the aristocracy in the Southern social structure was a substantial middle class, composed of lesser planters, small farmers, merchants and traders, professional folk, and mechanics. Persons in this middle class who acquired wealth readily advanced into the ranks of the aristocracy; George Washington was one who did. At the bottom of white society were those people, far fewer in number, who were later described as "poor white trash." These were poor, ignorant, and often ill-behaved. The bond servants formed a special group among the whites, since their social status was determined after their period of service by their industry, ability, thrift, and good fortune, or lack of it.

At the very bottom of the social structure were the Negroes, who were, with minor exceptions, slaves. Some were employed as servants and artisans, but most were fieldhands, who worked under the direction of their owner or of his overseer. Their original homes were on the west coast of Africa, where they formed various nations and tribes; these differed from each other in physique, language, and culture. Some of the slaves were born in Africa and more were steadily imported in the notorious slave ships, which carried them through the horrors of the "Middle Passage." Others came from the West Indies, and of course many were born in the mainland colonies. Although the status of the Negro in the first years of Virginia is uncertain, it was, within a generation, that of a slave, unless he had been legally freed. Plainly clad and rudely fed, the fieldhand performed most of the physical labor on the Southern Tidewater. Were he a servant or a mechanic, he fared better. He withstood the heat of the southern summers well, and usually remained cheerful despite his status. Occasionally the Negroes rose in revolt, but always in vain. Their presence in large numbers alarmed many thoughtful whites who believed that the South suffered because her immigrants were Negro rather than white, and who foresaw racial troubles extending into the distant future.

It has been said that in the colonial South all ladies and gentlemen were Anglicans, but that not all Anglicans were ladies and gentlemen. The ruling class was indeed Anglican, with but few exceptions, and the Church of England was officially established in all of the Southern colonies. Nowhere did it command the affection of a majority, except possibly in Virginia. It was nevertheless given a privileged position, especially in the Old Dominion, where it was supported by levies upon the public, and where a marriage not performed by an Anglican clergyman was of doubtful legality. Presbyterians and Baptists of one sort or another were also numerous in the South, especially on the Piedmont. Less conspicuous were Lutherans, Moravians, and French Calvinists. Anglican services were dignified, and Anglican sermons were suffused with learning, although it was not always the learning of the rector. Presbyterian clergymen were also often men of stature and scholars, as were the Lutheran clergy. However, there was "enthusiasm" among the Presbyterians and Baptists, for many of whom Christianity was chiefly emotional. Religious fervor and revivalism were more characteristic of the Piedmont than of the Tidewater. In both regions there was much indifference, notoriously among those who were Anglicans by inheritance. Deism was winning converts among the more sophisticated planters and merchants. Nevertheless, it should be stressed that there was devoted adherence to Puritan ideals and the Puritan moral code in the South, especially in the middle class.

Culturally, the South lagged somewhat behind the other regions. No doubt this fact is explained in part by the fewness of Southern cities and towns, and in the far South the climate was doubtless an adverse factor. Another was the Negroes, who when they came to America were on a cultural level comparable to that achieved by the ancestors of their white masters about two thousand years earlier. Illiteracy was common among the whites, and nearly universal among the Negroes, who were not permitted, much less encouraged, to learn to read and write. There were a few elementary schools maintained at public expense, and there were many private schools whose masters and mistresses tried to teach the mysteries of reading, writing, and arithmetic. Education at the secondary level was largely through private tutoring, so was usually confined to the children of families of means. Even for them it was reserved to the males. It was thought sufficient for a girl, even one of a wealthy family, to go beyond the three R's only so far as to play a musical instrument, to sketch, and to dance. Only men went to college, and but few of them. Intellectuals like Thomas Jefferson and James Madison were freaks, even among the aristocracy. Even the Southern magnates, like Washington, were not usually exposed to much formal learning; they often read extensively, imbibed knowledge through social intercourse, in the courts, and in the legislature. Nor did the South nurture literary and scientific genius, although there was widespread interest in literature, the theatre, painting, music, and science. To be sure, cultivated talent and genius, save in the area of politics, were rare everywhere in colonial America.

LIFE IN NEW ENGLAND

New England at the beginning of the Revolutionary era was peopled almost entirely by persons of English descent. Travelers observed that the villages and cities of the Yankees were more like those of Old England than were any others in the colonies. The New Englanders extracted as much wealth as possible from their relatively thin lands. They also sought riches from the sea and were remarkably successful as traders, both on land and sea. Industrious, thrifty, aggressive, and shrewd, they could make much from relatively little, and they prospered exceedingly. In 1763 most were still farmers, but many of them were merchants, mechanics, sailors, fishermen, and traders. For the Yankees—that name was already in use— the village was still the principal center, although Boston and Newport had developed into cities, the former being second only to Philadelphia in the colonies. From many places along their seaboard the New Englanders carried on an extensive maritime commerce; they carried lumber and fish to the West Indies, sailed ships to England, took cod to the Mediterranean, transported slaves from Africa to America, and brought home molasses and sugar from the West Indies. From a mercantilist point of view, the New England colonies were less valuable to the empire than were the Southern ones. Except for timber and ships, they produced little that was desired in Great Britain. Their merchants competed with the British, because the New Englander chose to prosper rather than to obey to the letter and the spirit the Acts of Navigation.

The social structure in Yankee-land, though superficially like that in the South, was actually quite different. There was an aristocracy, but its members were not necessarily large landowners. Merchants were conspicuous in it, together with a few lawyers, clergymen, and office holders. While wealth and standing through land ownership were preferred in the South, in New England money and status were more often derived from trade, perhaps coupled with land. So pervasive was the influence of money that the clergy, save for its leaders, was no longer recognized as belonging to the highest social stratum. Toward the middle of the eighteenth century the men of the cloth had been forced to take second place to those of the business offices. The aristocracy of New England was relatively small, and the gap between it and the middle class was slight and easily crossed. Most of the Yankees, however, must be described as belonging to a middle class, which included a large number of landowning farmers, artisans, traders, and fishermen. Few whites in New England were desperately poor, and New England was hardly conscious of any "poor white trash." Neither bond servants nor slaves were numerous above Long Island Sound, except that the slave traders of Rhode Island had brought home part of their human cargoes.

RELIGION

New England was far more homogeneous religiously than was the South. The great majority of the Yankees were Congregationalists, either in terms of church membership or tradition. Baptists, Anglicans, and Quakers were minority groups of some importance. Except in Rhode Island, the Congregational Church was firmly established by law and was supported by the state. Nevertheless, the religious complexion of New England had altered during the eighteenth century. The old Puritanism, with its emphasis on learning and logic as well as faith, was much weaker than it once had been. Emotional and revivalist Christianity had appeared in New England as well as in the colonies to the south. In the 1740s and 1750s that outburst of emotional religion called the Great Awakening manifested itself in Worcester and Springfield as well as in Philadelphia and Savannah. Indeed, for a time the most gifted of the Congregationalist divines, the Reverend Jonathan Edwards, a philosopher as well as a theologian, was closely associated with the Great Awakening. The established church also suffered attack from a different quarter, from the world of science. Accepting the universe as described by Sir Isaac Newton and his followers, New England intellectuals, like their fellows abroad, were turning to deism, striving to find their creator through study of the universe rather than the revelation of the Scriptures. Unitarians, who denied the Trinity and whose religious views often differed little from those of the deist, were increasingly in evidence. Doubtless the greater prosperity and security gained since the seventeenth century helped undermine the old Church, which, it will be recalled, never did enjoy the allegiance of all the inhabitants. Life was longer and more comfortable than it had once been, and death was at a greater distance. Moreover, the Yankees' contacts with the outside world were far greater than those of their ancestors. Even the clergy wandered from the old way; Yale was founded in 1701 because Harvard had become heretical. Not that Puritanism had vanished, or that the Congregational clergy had become impotent. Ministers remained greatly respected and continued to exert influence second only to that of men of wealth. Certainly the Puritan outlook and moral code, adhered to by many south as well as east of the Hudson, continued to play large roles in American civilization until the twentieth century.

EDUCATION AND THE ARTS

In the field of education New England early took and held the lead in terms both of quantity and quality. The Rhode Islanders, fearing state control over education—thought control—lagged behind their neighbors, relying on private action. With Massachusetts leading the way, the rest of New England looked upon teaching the young as a public responsibility. In Puritan New England schools were used not only to improve the individual but to plant in him Puritan religious concepts and allegiance to the Puritan way of life. The concentration of population in villages made it easier to take collective action. Social divisions were not so sharp in New England that families of means insisted upon special instruction for their children. As early as 1642 the Massachusetts General Court required all to see to it that their children were taught to read; and five years later that body ordered every town containing as many as fifty families to employ a schoolmaster to teach the children to read and write, or to pay a fine of five pounds. Some towns preferred to pay the fine rather than hire a teacher, but many elementary schools did appear in the Bay colony. The example of Massachusetts was copied substantially throughout New England, except, of course, in Rhode Island. Proficiency in reading and writing became common in the Yankee country. Moreover, government encouraged education at a more advanced level, Massachusetts providing for a Latin Grammar School as early as 1647, and for the establishment of several academies in the eighteenth century. These academies, which were privately operated and which flourished after 1750, offered instruction not only in Latin and Greek, but also in English composition and literature, mathematics, modern languages, and science. Such a program was both liberal and practical. Only for a few sons of well-to-do families was a collegiate education possible. Harvard and Yale were founded primarily to insure a supply of competent clergymen. Before 1700 Harvard began to lay stress upon literature and philosophy in addition to the classics, and Yale was founded by persons dissatisfied with the change. But the same influences which broadened the curriculum at Cambridge eventually made themselves felt at New Haven. These two Congregationalist colleges were the only ones in being in New England at the end of the Seven Years' War, but the College of Rhode Island, later Brown University, was established in 1765, and Dartmouth appeared four years later as a school for the instruction of both white and Indian boys.

It is hardly surprising that New England took and maintained the lead culturally in the colonies. Her people enjoyed superiority in their general level of information, and in literacy New England could bear comparison to Old England. This is not to say that the Yankees produced many outstanding men in literature, science, and the arts by the end of the colonial period, at least not according to British and European standards. New England had produced no John Locke, no Samuel Johnson, no Henry Fielding, no Sir Joshua Reynolds. The inferiority of America as compared with Britain was to arouse American envy and anger after their separation. Lamented the American poet, Philip Freneau:

> Can we never be thought
>   to have learning or grace
> Unless it be brought
>   from that damnable place?

Nevertheless, it will hardly do to describe as a great poet Anne Bradstreet of Massachusetts, whose volume *The Tenth Muse Lately Sprung Up in America, or Several Poems* was published in London in 1650. She wrote with unconscious humor;

> The windy cholick oft my bowels rend,
>   to break the darksome prison where it's penned.
> The Cramp and Gout doth sadly torture me,
>   and the restraining, lame Ciatiaca.

On occasion she could write delightfully, as when she objected to the masculine opinion that woman's place is in the home:

> I am obnoxious to each carping tongue
>   who says my hand a needle better fits . . .

The poetry of Edward Taylor, which did not come to light until 1937, is of a much higher order. Taylor, a minister of Westfield, Massachusetts, occupied himself with things metaphysical, and has received much praise from the followers of T. S. Eliot, also preoccupied by such matters. It has been claimed that Taylor belongs in the company of John Donne, although his reputation may sink with passing time. Certainly, too much praise may be heaped upon Cotton Mather, even though that scholar presciently asserted that disease was caused by small, invisible animals. Likewise, the talents and achievements of Jonathan Edwards have sometimes been exaggerated; as a philosopher he cannot stand comparison with his British contemporaries, George Berkeley and David Hume. Save in the world of politics, the time was yet distant when American men of intellect could reasonably be described as the equals of their British and European counterparts.

LOCAL GOVERNMENT

New England is noted for the manner in which local government was carried on. The basic unit was the town, that is, the village and its immediate vicinity. In this respect New England contrasted with the Southern colonies, where the county and parish dealt with local problems. Not that the county was unknown in New England, but that government by the town became important in Yankee-land as nowhere else. Doubtless the New Englanders first established such communities in part because they were familiar with similar ones in old England; also, the members of a church congregation tended to settle in close proximity one to another. Conceivably, more effective defense against the Indians may have had something to do with the planning of such communities. Towns founded later were frequently laid out by land speculators. Whatever the reasons for their formation, the village green with its church, school house, and rows of neat homes, became a characteristic of the landscape. Much has been written about the political democracy in these towns, and with some justice. From an early time the suffrage was broader in purely local affairs than it was in connection with the election of members of the general court in Massachusetts. In fact, persons who were not church members were not only permitted to vote, but were compelled to take part in town meetings and to participate in the solution of local questions. The town meeting, which gathered at least once each year, chose the selectmen and other officers, passed local ordinances, and offered a forum in which the inhabitants could express their wishes and opinions. Too much may be made of such meetings, for it is obvious that all citizens did not carry equal weight and that the wealthier must often have exerted greater influence than their less prosperous fellows. Even so, more men could more effectively express their opinions in town meetings than in any other legislative body in America.

THE MIDDLE COLONIES

In terms of national background, the middle colonies—New York, New Jersey, Pennsylvania, and Delaware—contained a population more diverse even than that of the South by 1763. Prominent among the non-British elements were the Germans, who began to settle in the Mohawk Valley in numbers in 1709, and moved in thousands a little later in the century into Pennsylvania, where they became known as the "Pennsylvania Dutch." They eventually numbered about one-third of Pennsylvania's population. Almost simultaneously the Scotch-Irish began their great migration from Ulster; after trying New England and New York, they too entered Pennsylvania, in numbers almost as large as the Germans. They settled immediately to the west of the Germans, on the frontier, in what is now the central part of the state. About 1725 both the Germans and the Scotch-Irish began to push southward into Maryland, eventually moving as far as Georgia. The Dutch were another important minority, and there were some Welsh, Swedes, Protestant French, and Jews in the middle colonies. Negroes were hardly to be found, except in the city of New York and Delaware.

In social structure the middle colonies were more like New England than the South. They too had their aristocrats with wealth based both upon the land and on trade. The middle colonies had rich lands and fine harbors, and many men prospered from the combination. Lands were frequently held in large estates, especially in New York, and their possessors, such as the Livingstons, the Van Rensselaers, and the De Lanceys attained great prestige and power. Intermingled with them at the peak of the social structure were the families of the merchants who sold the colonies' wheat and meat abroad. The merchant of Philadelphia was no less proud and hardly less respected than the great landowner of the Hudson Valley. Like New England, the middle colonies had a very large middle class of prosperous farmers, traders, professional folk, and artisans. However, bond servants and tenants on great estates were more frequently found there than in New England. In general, social lines were somewhat more sharply drawn in the middle colonies than they were to the eastward, but not so clearly as they were to the south.

The middle colonies' great variety in national background, economic activity, and social organization was reflected in their religion. In three counties of New York there was an established church, that being Anglican, but no sect had the allegiance of a majority of the population in any one colony. Churches and meeting-houses of Lutherans, Congregationalists, Presbyterians, Mennonites, Dunkards, Moravians, Anglicans, Baptists, and of Dutch and German Calvinists studded the land; a Jewish synagogue was established in New York as early as 1655. Freedom to worship was assured to everyone, and the state did not inflict any serious penalty upon the nonconformist. Nevertheless, religious belief was in part the cause of a long and bitter political controversy in Pennsylvania during the Anglo-French wars. In that colony, before it was very old, the Quakers became a minority, although they continued to dominate the region around Philadelphia. Thanks to unfair apportionment of seats, whereby the older parts of Pennsylvania were overrepresented in the Assembly, the Quakers controlled the Assembly until the Seven Years' War was well under way. Also, they enjoyed the support of the Germans, some of whom were opposed to warfare and most of whom looked to the Friends as "good people" for leadership. Averse to waging war and sheltered from attacks by the Indians and the French by the presence of the Scotch-Irish and the Germans on the frontier, the Quakers failed to provide adequately for the defense of the colony. Given insufficient military assistance by the Assembly, suffering severely from Indian attacks at the beginning of the Seven Years' War, the frontier folk furiously assailed the Quakers. The conflict between them was resolved to a degree in 1757, when the Friends in the Assembly, faced by a threat that Parliament would require an oath of allegiance from all Assembly members, chose not to present themselves before the voters. Quakers later returned to the legislature, but they did not again effectively control it until after the war. The pacifism of the Friends could not be given a fair trial.

EDUCATION AND THE ARTS

The middle American country made steady progress in letters, the sciences, and the arts. The value of education was as clearly recognized as it was in New England. New Netherland had its public schools, and the Scotch-Irish, like the Dutch, were devoted to learning. The Quakers, in their early days inclined to look upon education as corruptive, came to be fosterers of it, at least of those subjects which did not appear to them to be frivolous. Provision for instruction in the middle colonies was largely private, but schools for teaching the elementary subjects were available in some numbers. Nor was education at the secondary level entirely neglected, although it was reserved, as in New England, largely for sons of prosperous families. The Academy at Philadelphia, which was inspired by Benjamin Franklin and opened its doors in 1751, offered excellent instruction. It emphasized the classics, although Franklin urged a broader program toward a more liberal education. Afterward the Academy became the University of Pennsylvania. Even before the founding of the Academy, in 1746, Princeton University was established as the College of New Jersey, being devoted to the instruction of young men, and especially to the production of Presbyterian clergymen. In 1754 Columbia College was founded; it was called King's College, New York being an Anglican stronghold. Twelve years later Queen's College, afterward Rutgers University, appeared at New Brunswick in New Jersey; it became an intellectual and religious fortress of the Dutch Reformed Church.

Assuredly the middle colonies had their fair share of distinguished men, including Cadwallader Colden, born in Scotland, but during most of his long life a royal official in New York; John Bartram of Pennsylvania, a gifted botanist; and Franklin, the greatest American of his generation. While Colden attempted in vain to improve upon the physics of Sir Isaac Newton, Franklin made major contributions in the study of electricity. Born in Boston in 1706, Franklin emigrated as a youth to Philadelphia, where he achieved signal success as a printer and as publisher of the *Pennsylvania Gazette.* Achieving a substantial estate, he was able to retire from private business at the age of 42. As a young man he had labored to improve himself, and he was to continue to do so throughout life. His early career was not one of unalloyed success. He afterward confessed to some shortcomings in behavior, "errata" as he called them; the result of one of his "errata" was an illegitimate son, William, whose mother remains unknown. William Franklin brought lifelong embarrassment to his father, although he was a person of respectable abilities, and became royal governor of New Jersey. He eventually turned Tory and died in exile in England.

In his early middle age Benjamin Franklin had fewer frailties, and his intellectual powers were well developed. Soon after the middle of the century, Franklin suddenly became famous in the Western world because of his demonstration that lightning was an electrical discharge, and because of his invention of the lightning rod. His studies and reports on the nature and behavior of electricity were far more important and were valued by scientists who could appreciate and use his insights. He was a worthy follower of Newton. Even as he attained an international reputation as a scientist, he was becoming a politician of more than local repute. The Albany Plan of Union was essentially his creation; he went to London as an agent for Pennsylvania in 1757, remaining in Britain, except for a brief period from 1762 to 1764, almost until the outbreak of the War of Independence. He was a stout defender and potent propagandist for American rights in London; later, he appeared as an astute and skillful diplomat in Paris.

THE OLD WEST

While we have divided the colonies into regions from north to south, it may also be observed that there were eastern and western divisions; these were roughly separated by the Fall Line. The Old West, the region between the Fall Line and the Appalachian divide, was inhabited chiefly by small landowning farmers until after the Revolution; in the wealthier and more sophisticated society along the coast large merchants and planters were more conspicuous and influential. The people of the Old West were poorer than their fellows on the coast and were frequently indebted to them. Schools and educational opportunities were fewer and the cultural level lower in the interior than they were on the coastal plain. The Tidewater had more contacts with Britain, while the people of the Old West were more affected by the American frontier environment. They tended to develop and to adhere to beliefs in social equality and political democracy, concepts which lacked appeal for prosperous merchants and proud planters. Political differences between the two regions were inevitable, the first being Bacon's Rebellion. The apportionment of seats in the lower house of assembly was a source of bitter controversy in the colonies from Pennsylvania to Georgia; the Tidewater leaders were often reluctant to concede to newer settlements the representation they deserved on the basis of population. They did not wish to lose power and dignity, and they feared that if the Piedmont people gained control in the assembly, they would use it to place a larger part of the tax burden upon the Tidewater. At the same time they might secure for themselves benefits from the expenditure of public money.

The struggle between East and West was apparently not sharp in New England in the eighteenth century. Indeed, it seems that the seacoast was actually underrepresented in terms of population in the General Court of Massachusetts. In Pennsylvania, however, the contest was acrimonious, and was heightened by the Quakers' pacifism and disinterest in defense of the frontier. There was less tension in Virginia, where Bacon's Rebellion may have reminded both Tidewater and Piedmont of the value of sweet reason. Doubtless the "Old Guard" of planters who dominated the House of Burgesses was more solicitous of Piedmont interests than were Quaker merchants for the welfare of the Scotch-Irish in the valleys of central Pennsylvania. Tension became acute in the Carolinas and led to physical violence after 1760. In South Carolina the aristocratic planters

THE FALL LINE OF RIVERS

of the Low Country long refused representation based on population to the Up Country, declining for many years even to create new assembly districts above the Fall Line. They did not even permit courts or jails on the Piedmont until 1773; by that time the population of the interior, excluding Negroes, was probably larger than that on the coast. Serious fighting was averted only by the influence of Lieutenant Governor William Bull II, who did his best to soothe the outraged feelings of the Up Country people, and successfully insisted that they have courts and a few voices in the legislature. In North Carolina hostility between the two regions brought open warfare. In the Tarheel colony the Piedmont was seriously underrepresented, and had a special grievance in that its county offices were filled by Tidewater men who exacted heavy fees for their services. After 1765 a movement to secure redress of real and fancied injuries gained remarkable impetus. Those who participated were called "Regulators," a term first used in South Carolina, since their purpose was to regulate matters, especially fees. Riots raged for several years, public officials being rudely treated and forced, in a degree, to mend their ways. Eventually, after threats of force, some concessions were made by the assembly, but quiet did not come until the Regulators had been crushed in the battle of the Alamance in 1771. Six Regulators were hanged as traitors, their fate being a warning to their fellows. Thereafter, the Piedmont became calm, although hostility toward the Tidewater did not vanish.

9 ORIGINS OF THE REVOLUTION

THE EMPIRE IN 1763

When the Seven Years' War officially came to an end in February, 1763, British power and pride were at a peak. The British Empire, more impressive than any other since the days of the Romans, included not only the eastern third of North America, but also valuable sugar islands in the Caribbean, Gibraltar, and Minorca, trading stations on the west coast of Africa, and secure footholds in India. The British merchant marine was flourishing and had surpassed all others. The Industrial Revolution was already well under way in the home islands, British manufacturers far outstripping their continental rivals. Even France was hard put to it to match Britain in commercial wealth. Moreover, the economic and political outlook seemed far more favorable for Britain than for her European rivals. From the military point of view, the prospect seemed particularly bright, for the British navy equalled the French and Spanish combined, and the British army, though small in size, was highly respected for its fighting qualities. The armed forces of France and Spain were shattered and disorganized, and Prussia was exhausted from her travails in the Seven Years' War. British prestige was at a summit, and Britain was feared and respected as she never had been before, even in the day of Cromwell. Twenty years later she had lost the most valuable of all her colonies and had signed the humiliating treaties at Paris which have been said to mark the end of the first British Empire and the beginning of a second one. So astonishing an overturn in the affairs of men is to be explained in part by the incompetence of George III and the British politicians, who quarreled among themselves and failed to secure allies against the day when France and Spain would try to reverse the verdict of the Seven Years' War. Their incompetence drove the Thirteen Colonies, the most valuable of all British possessions, into revolt.

In the very midst of the overwhelming military triumphs of 1759 and 1760, some realistic-minded English pamphleteers insisted that Britain's hold upon the Thirteen Colonies was none too secure. They contended that Canada, then falling before British arms, should be returned to France. They also believed that Britain should take from France tropical sugar islands rather than what they called the snowy wastes of Canada. Above all, they argued that the people of the Thirteen Colonies would appreciate the benefits of membership in the British Empire so long as they were threatened by French Canada. Once that menace were removed, they said, the Americans would no longer need British military assistance, and would turn toward thoughts of independence; they would be more concerned about their rights within the British Empire than about their duties toward the empire. However, William Pitt was certain that the Americans were firmly loyal, and he wished to avoid having to conquer Canada a third time. Like his brilliant commander at Quebec, James Wolfe, he dreamed of a North America entirely British. While it can hardly be said that the acquisition of Canada made the loss of the Thirteen Colonies inevitable, it is no doubt true that the departure of the French from the St. Lawrence left the Americans less dependent on the empire and less concerned with their obligations to it.

THE ARMY IN AMERICA

The Seven Years' War had hardly ended when British politicians embarked upon new measures which provoked discontent in the Thirteen Colonies and finally drove them into revolt. When hostilities ceased, a Cabinet headed by John Stuart, Earl of Bute, once the king's tutor and his loyal follower, undertook to reduce the size of the British army. It had grown immensely during the war and contained more than one hundred regiments at the close of hostilities. The national debt had risen rapidly during the war, to £130 million, a staggering figure for that time. Since even the interest upon such a debt seemed a heavy obligation, it might have been expected that the Cabinet would call for a return to the prewar establishment. Instead, the Bute ministry asked Parliament to promise support for seventy-five regiments, to which Parliament readily agreed. A large part of the increase in the peacetime army resulted from a decision to maintain substantial garrison forces in North America. Britain had never kept more than 3100 redcoats in North America in time of peace, but it was now determined that sixteen regiments of perhaps 6000 men should be on permanent duty for the protection of the colonies and a few adjacent islands. These troops were to serve under a commander in chief stationed at New York. This command was held by Sir Jeffery Amherst until November, 1763, and from that time until after the outbreak of the War of Independence by General Thomas Gage. The reasons for doubling the garrison forces in North America are unknown. It may be that British politicians casually thought that so large an empire deserved a larger peacetime army than in the past, and that they stationed the troops approximately where they were when the war ended. They later said that the valley of the St. Lawrence, occupied by 60,000 French Canadians, must be garrisoned; that troops would be necessary for defense against the Indians; that many strategic posts in the interior ought to be maintained for protection and to encourage and regulate Indian trade; that troops would be useful for defense of the Floridas against possible Spanish attack from Cuba and Louisiana, or to attack New Orleans in the event of another conflict with Spain; and lastly, that all of the garrison force would be valuable in the event of a future war in which the Bourbons could expect aid from Indian allies. It was not intended that this army be used against the British colonists, although one anonymous writer suggested that its presence would remind the Americans of their firm allegiance to Britain.

Since it had not been thought necessary to keep a considerable force of redcoats in North America before 1754, when the French, Spaniards, and Indians had been far more formidable enemies, this new military policy was a remarkable departure. It planted seeds of future trouble between America and Great Britain. It was doubtful that so large an army was needed, and the Americans were not asked whether they wanted it. Furthermore, it was assumed in London that the Americans should eventually pay for its upkeep on the dubious ground that it was maintained for their protection. The British felt that American taxes were low and that the Americans were prosperous and unburdened by heavy debts, while the British themselves suffered from both heavy debts and taxes; a British land tax had risen from two to four shillings per acre as a result of the Seven Years' War. More than £200,000 per annum was needed to support this army, and somehow or other it had to be extracted from American pockets. That the Americans would willingly undertake such a burden was highly doubtful. Moreover, the very presence of the army was likely to create ill will between the colonists and the mother country, while British politicians might be tempted to use the army against the Americans in the event of serious dispute. It would seem that the decision to keep sixteen regiments of redcoats in America was hastily and thoughtlessly made, that it led toward the destruction rather than the preservation of the British Empire in America. Had the Bute ministry permitted the Americans to take more responsibility for their own defense, they must have been more appreciative of the value of their connection with Britain.

THE GRENVILLE MEASURES

In April, 1763, the Bute ministry fell and was followed by a Cabinet formed by George Grenville and the Duke of Bedford in which Grenville was the king's first minister. Grenville was an honest, courageous, stubborn, and opinionated man with a reputation for competence in affairs of money. He let it be known that his government would be both efficient and economical. He turned out to be a vigorous administrator, but not genuinely thrifty. Had he been truly devoted to economy, he would at least have considered reversing the decision to maintain a large garrison force in America. There is no evidence that he did so. Instead, he began to search for ways to make the Americans pay for its support. They were not quickly found, and he and his colleagues proceeded first to the solution of other colonial problems. Between 1763 and 1765 a series of laws and decrees affecting America poured forth from London; taken together, they formed a new colonial program, and constituted a striking departure from past policies. Grenville displayed more energy than wisdom.

THE PROCLAMATION LINE OF 1763

One of the most important of the new measures was the royal Proclamation of October 7, 1763, which established three new royal colonies, Quebec in the valley of the St. Lawrence River; East Florida, which included the peninsula of Florida and a narrow strip of territory stretching westward along the Gulf of Mexico; and West Florida, a thin band of territory along the Gulf between the Chattahoochee and Mississippi rivers. Far more important to the colonists, it set aside the entire interior of British North America as a reservation for the Indians. White settlement west of the Appalachian divide was forbidden, and Indian tribes were recognized as communal owners of the lands they occupied, which in several cases lay east of the mountains. Private purchases of Indian lands were declared to be illegal, and sales of such lands were to be made only at public meetings presided over by royal officials. The major reason for this famous proclamation was undoubtedly a desire to prevent Indian wars, which were often caused by encroachments upon Indian lands. Pontiac's War had broken out the preceding spring and was then in bloody progress; it undoubtedly acted as a stimulus to action. Another reason for the proclamation was the belief held by some members of the ministry that British economic interests would be served by it. They thought that the Americans, being kept east of the Appalachians, would remain an agricultural people purchasing British manufactured goods. By this line of reasoning, if the area west of the divide were occupied, the older settlements would turn to manufacturing in competition with British manufacturers. The proclamation immediately aroused discontent among thousands of land-hungry Americans who were eager to settle to the westward, and who had little liking or respect for the Indians. The measure was promptly denounced as unjust, and a violation of colonial rights. Land speculators joined in the chorus of protests. Influential Americans had long profited by taking title to soil in the unsettled interior, using it or selling it profitably as pioneers moved in. Especially addicted to such speculations were the Virginia planters, some of whom had obtained large grants beyond the Appalachians even before the Seven Years' War. The speculators included Washington, Lees, and other Virginia clans; their ventures were endangered, or at least temporarily hindered, by the proclamation. The speculators proceeded with their schemes, despite the order from London, and settlers swarmed over the mountains into the upper Ohio Valley. In 1765 British troops were used to drive squatters out of southwestern Pennsylvania, but resentment was so fierce that General Gage did not dare to use the troops a second time when the frontiersmen again advanced into the forbidden territory.

Toward preserving peace with the red men, the Grenville-Bedford ministry also undertook to keep the royal Indian superintendents permanently in office, to bring order and efficiency into diplomatic relations with the Indians. A plan to put the regulation of the Indian trade largely under the control of these officials was drawn up in 1764. Although this scheme was never formally approved, the superintendents took it upon themselves, with the support of General Gage, to bring as much order as possible into the trade. Their activities won no friends for Britain, except among the Indians, for the superintendents generally defended the interests of the red men. Their behavior was assailed as discriminatory, and it was claimed that they exercised powers which properly belonged to the

NORTH AMERICA EAST OF THE MISSISSIPPI, 1763

colonial governors and assemblies. After 1768 they gave up their efforts to regulate trade, but remained unpopular because they tried to offer some degree of protection to the lands of the Indians.

THE QUARTERING ACT

Creating discontent among the pioneers and land speculators, the Grenville-Bedford ministry carried through several measures which were especially exasperating to people on the seacoast. Among them was the Quartering Act, passed in 1765 at the request of General Gage. After 1763 some colonists urged redcoats to desert, telling them that the Mutiny Act, which annually provided for the maintenance of the British Army, did not apply in America, hence that the soldiers were not legally subject to military discipline. By the law of 1765 the Mutiny Act was specifically extended to America. In addition, the colonists were called upon to furnish quarters and supplies to the troops in somewhat the same fashion as in England. There innkeepers were compelled to furnish quarters, food, and drink to the troops on certain occasions. Now it was required that the colonies supply quarters, firewood, candles, cider or beer, and other small items that the Grenville-Bedford measure listed, to soldiers stationed in the settled parts of America. The colonial assemblies were in effect ordered to vote any necessary funds. The sums demanded were not immediately large, since most of the troops were on duty at forts in the interior, but the law took it for granted that American assemblies must obey Parliament and that money could be abstracted from the pockets of the Americans without their consent.

THE SUGAR ACT

A greater cause for discontent among the Americans was the Sugar Act of 1764. Owners of sugar plantations in the British West Indies, who had influence in London, urged that decisive action be taken to prevent them from buying molasses in the French, Spanish, and other foreign islands in the Caribbean. Together with changes in duties on wines and sugar, the Sugar Act imposed an import tax of threepence per gallon upon molasses brought to the mainland from the foreign islands. This duty had a double purpose, which was indicated in the act itself. It was believed that the duty was sufficient to limit the trade with the foreigners; however, some of the colonials would continue to trade with the foreign islands and would pay the duty, thus providing a revenue. The second purpose was a novelty because the mainland colonists had never before been taxed by Parliament, except for the purpose of regulating trade. The receipts from the duty were to be used for the support of the British army in America. Protests came promptly from the northern and middle colonies, and also from North Carolina. The molasses tax was sharply condemned, not only because it would severely injure the trade with the West Indies, but also because it would diminish the flow of Spanish and French currency to the mainland. The Thirteen Colonies were chronically short of currency, and French and Spanish coins had served a very real need. Here and there, the tax was assailed as being unconstitutional, and as a violation of the rights of Englishmen on the ground that it was "taxation without representation." It was so condemned by a Boston town meeting and by the assembly of New York.

Had the Sugar Act been looked upon as another Molasses Act, to be evaded almost at will, its passage might have aroused no great feeling.

However, the Grenville-Bedford ministry made it clear that the government intended to collect the duty and also to enforce the Acts of Navigation, so long ignored by the colonists. The Sugar Act authorized the use of admiralty courts for those accused of violations. Hitherto, offenders had frequently escaped when tried in colonial courts, because sympathetic juries could commonly find grounds for acquittal. However, juries were not used in the admiralty courts, and their judges would hardly be lenient with offenders. Further, the ministry "shook up" the customs service in America, striving to make it more efficient. In 1763 that service collected no more than £2000 at an expense of at least £7000. It was riddled with "honest graft" and with plain thievery. Several of its officers were men who had never been in America, men who drew their pay in England and performed their duties through deputies hired at modest salaries. Grenville insisted that the absentee office holders, upon pain of dismissal, proceed to America to do their work, and a British naval squadron stationed at Halifax was ordered to help them. He also let it be known that he wanted all customs men to exhibit both zeal and honesty, although he did not undertake a similar cleanup at home, where there was a veritable Augean stable of graft and corruption.

THE CURRENCY ACT

Another Grenville measure which created serious colonial discontent was the Currency Act of 1764. The colonists suffered from a chronic lack of a circulating medium, in part because of an unfavorable balance of trade with Britain. They early hit upon the issuance of paper money to be used as currency. The paper put forth by various colonies, together with the coins brought in from Spanish and French islands in the Caribbean, had provided a satisfactory supply. But as we have seen, several of the colonies had issued paper money without adequate support, and these monies had tended to diminish in value. Moreover, some of the colonies had declared their paper currency legal tender. Thus, colonial paper currency was likely to fluctuate in value, and to offer opportunities to debtors to take advantage of their creditors. In 1751 Parliament had forbidden the New England colonies to issue or reissue unsupported paper currency or to use paper money as legal tender. The law of 1764 extended these prohibitions to all the colonies, being especially aimed at Virginia, which was then preparing to embark upon a paper money program. It is obvious that the Sugar Act and the new Currency Act deprived the colonists of needed currency, just when they were called upon to shoulder a substantial part of the cost of the defense of the British Empire. When Grenville introduced the Sugar Act, he let it be known that he was also considering a stamp tax for America, thus informing the colonists that their cup of woes would be filled to the brim.

THE STAMP ACT

In the spring of 1764 Grenville announced that he would call for an American stamp tax the next year, unless the Americans suggested some other means by which they would provide perhaps £50,000 or £60,000 annually for the support of the army in America. He did not mean what he said, for he never indicated to the several colonies what sums each would be expected to supply. It was therefore impossible for any colony to find out what was expected of it. Grenville was really determined from the first to have the stamp tax in any case. At that time all of the colonies had agents in London to represent them. When Grenville asked some of these agents for alternative proposals, they suggested that the ministry ask each of the American assemblies for a proper contribution as it had in the past.

This scheme Grenville rejected, for it was most unlikely that all of the assemblies would make satisfactory annual contributions. Indeed, it seemed probable that some would vote little or no money, thus encouraging the others to diminish or to abandon their contributions. Such a system would certainly not provide a reliable revenue; after 1781 a similar system in the Articles of Confederation was to fail rather miserably. Benjamin Franklin, then agent for Pennsylvania, offered another alternative, a statesmanlike proposal. This was that the British government set up a bank in the colonies; this bank was to have the authority to issue a paper currency. Lent at interest, it would bring a large profit to government; it would at the same time provide the colonists with useful and widely circulating paper currency. Grenville rejected Franklin's astute plan; he must have the stamp tax.

To make the stamp tax more palatable, Grenville considered adding American members to the House of Commons. Had this step been taken, the colonists could not have complained about taxation without representation. But such a change would have required much time, and it was extremely doubtful that Parliament would ever give its approval. It was not to be expected that members of Parliament, who, like all Europeans, looked upon their brethren in the New World as inferiors, would accept them as political equals. Besides, the presence of any number of Americans in the House of Commons would give the colonials great influence in British affairs generally. Instead, Grenville proceeded with his original plan, disregarding protests which poured into London from the colonies. Assembly after American assembly denounced the proposed stamp tax as unjust, the majority likewise insisting that it was unconstitutional, on the ground that it was the right of an Englishman to be taxed only through his own representatives. They continued to hit at the Sugar Act as unfair and injurious to commerce, and some of them to hint that it too was unconstitutional. Nevertheless, in the spring of 1765 Grenville introduced his measure, which was modeled on an English levy.

The Stamp Act required that the colonists purchase stamps to be placed upon legal documents, ship clearance papers, playing cards, insurance policies, newspapers, and other items. The cost of the stamps varied, the rates being generally lower than those in England. They were substantial for college diplomas, commissions to office, and legal documents, while much less expensive stamps were required for articles of apprenticeship, playing cards, dice, and newspapers. Heavy fines and forfeitures were provided for infractions of the law. The concept of a colonial stamp tax was not new; indeed, such a tax had been suggested more than forty years earlier. Nor was the House of Commons shocked by the proposal. Members were pleased to think that the colonists would be compelled to shoulder part of the burdens of the Empire. There was vigorous opposition from a rather small minority, in which Colonel Isaac Barré was conspicuous. Barré was an officer who had served in America during the Seven Years' War and had become acquainted with Americans and their views. Moreover, he had a personal grudge against Grenville, who had deprived him of a lucrative office. Barré inveighed against the tax as an enormous injustice to the Americans, whom he described as "sons of liberty," and predicted that they would resist rather than pay the tax. But neither Grenville nor the majority in the House paid much heed to Barré and other members who opposed the tax. It was taken for granted that Parliament had the power to levy the tax, and likewise that the tax was just. Except for Barré, hardly anyone believed that the colonists would actually resist. Only about fifty members of the House voted against the law, both British officials and Americans then in England assuming there would be no difficulty in collecting the tax. To make it somewhat more acceptable, Grenville undertook to appoint Americans as stamp distributors, and he asked American agents in London to recommend persons for these profitable posts. Benjamin Franklin did not expect trouble and urged the selection of his friend John Hughes as stamp distributor for Pennsylvania, and of another friend, Jared Ingersoll, for a similar office in Connecticut. His advice to the colonists was that they pay the tax and make up their losses by the practice of thrift. In London it seemed that Grenville had found a simple, inexpensive, and effective method of prying money from the Americans.

It is evident enough that the Grenville measures formed a program, that they made a pattern, and that British colonial policy had entered upon a new course. Despite protests against each of the parts of the program, it was not certain what action the Americans would take. They reacted violently, the great majority finding in the Grenville measures not only a new policy, but a pattern of tyranny. Americans detested the stamp tax above all, and determined to resist it. It was the fiery orator Patrick Henry, who led the colonists into open defiance of British authority. When news of the passage of the Stamp Act reached Virginia late in May, 1765, the House of Burgesses was in session. Most of the members had gone home, some perhaps departing so as to avoid having to take a stand with respect to the tax. It was, after all, one thing to assail the tax before it was passed, quite another thing to struggle against it after it had been enacted into law by Parliament. Among the members still at Williamsburg, there were some who were not eager to challenge British authority decisively. Patrick Henry, a new member, insisted that the House stand forth vigorously to defend the rights of Englishmen in Virginia. He introduced seven resolutions which flatly denounced the tax as unconstitutional and declared that the law should be disobeyed. In defense of his resolutions he delivered a stirring oration in which he called for resistance to the will of Parliament. He was not quite so vigorous in his language as he was once supposed to have been, but he was emphatic enough. The Burgesses did not pass all of his resolutions, but they did endorse those which labelled the Stamp Act contrary to the rights of Englishmen and Virginians. Spurred on by Henry and speaking for Britain's oldest American colony, the House hinted that Virginia was prepared to take steps to prevent the execution of the Act. The Massachusetts General Court swiftly followed the example of the Burgesses, and issued a call for a congress of all the colonies to meet at New York in the fall and to speak for all the Americans. Thereafter, the stamp tax and other Grenville measures were enthusiastically attacked in legislature after American legislature, in the three dozen colonial newspapers, in the pulpit, in public gatherings, before grand juries, and in pamphlets. The Americans made it abundantly clear that they believed that such a tax could be imposed upon them only by their own assemblies. They insisted that it was the right of an American as well as an Englishman to be taxed only when the legislative body laying the tax contained a member from his neighborhood. They did not unequivocally say that the Sugar Act violated their rights precisely as the Stamp Act did, although they might logically have done so. The Stamp Act Congress, containing delegates from seven colonies, met in New York in the early fall of 1765. It specifically declared the Stamp Act to be unconstitutional, described the Sugar Act as economically injurious, and denounced the latter because it extended the use of admiralty courts. It failed to designate the Sugar Act in unmistakable language as violating colonial rights. However, the Congress did ask the Crown and Parliament to repeal both laws.

AMERICA DEFIES BRITAIN

The colonists did not content themselves with respectful requests for repeal of the hated Stamp Act. The tax was not to go into effect until

November 1, and there was time to organize resistance. The colonists hit upon two effective methods to prevent execution of the Act. The law could hardly be carried into effect without stamp distributors. The men appointed to these posts were almost invariably colonists, and as such were subject to social, economic, and physical pressures. In colony after colony during the summer and fall they were urged either to refuse appointment or to resign their commissions. Frequently these requests were supported by threats of mob violence, and no distributor in the Thirteen Colonies dared to ignore the threats of his neighbors, for fear that he and his family might suffer. To make sure that the stamps would not be sold, the colonists also undertook to make them unavailable. The little papers were shipped from England; mobs prevented their unloading, destroyed them, or compelled their recipients to store them away and promise that they would not be sold. A few were sold in Georgia, and the Stamp Act was enforced in Nova Scotia, Quebec, and the Floridas. However, none was used in twelve of the Thirteen Colonies.

Successful resistance to the Stamp Act was impossible in the Floridas and Nova Scotia, where the civilian population was small, and where British troops and sailors were available in strength. Nor did the French Canadians resist, for the cry "no taxation without representation" meant little to them. Stamps were also sold in Georgia for a brief period, because of special circumstances in that colony. Georgia received annually from the British treasury £4000 or £5000 toward her governmental expenses, and her people could hardly claim that they were being treated unjustly. Georgia had about seventy "rangers" in royal pay, and there were two small British warships at Savannah when the crisis came. The population was still small, and the governor, James Wright, was an able and determined man. Sentiment was more divided in Georgia than it was elsewhere in the Thirteen Colonies; Governor Wright insisted that the stamps be sold, and employed the rangers and sailors from His Majesty's ships to maintain order. He was momentarily successful, forcing ships that sailed from Savannah to carry stamped clearance papers. However, Wright soon abandoned his efforts in the face of mounting public anger.

In the other old British colonies on the mainland the governors found it impossible to coerce their rebellious charges. It was obviously useless for them to call upon the town watches, the sheriffs, or the militia, since they were all American. Nor could they prevent the destruction of property belonging to stamp distributors, or to the few persons who publicly asserted that the tax should be paid. In New York a mob even destroyed a coach and sleigh belonging to the royal lieutenant governor before his very eyes. Repression was possible only with British warships and soldiers, and there were too few on the American coast to accomplish much. In distress three British governors urged General Gage to use the army against the colonists, on the assumption that a rebellion was in progress. Gage refused, on the ground that the Americans were rioting rather than rebelling. He said he would furnish troops to serve under civilian direction if formally requested to do so. The governors could not make such a request without the consent of their councils; these were composed of Americans and refused to give their approval. Accordingly, the army could not be used. Actually, at the time Gage had very few soldiers available for duty in the settled parts of the Thirteen Colonies. Helpless and resentful, he did order about four hundred men from the frontier into the middle colonies, so that they would be available in grave emergency. Thus began a movement of the troops into the towns of the Thirteen Colonies, a movement which was soon to supply additional reasons for colonial discontent.

The colonists not only prevented the execution of the Stamp Act but found an effective way to secure its repeal. In October, 1765, the towns-folk of New York in a public meeting pledged themselves to buy no more British goods until the detested tax should be removed. The New Yorkers' example was followed extensively throughout the colonies, and orders for British goods fell off sharply during the following winter. At the same time Americans indebted to British merchants displayed even greater reluctance than usual in making payment. As a result, British manufacturers and merchants, who had not yet recovered from their postwar difficulties, were made even more unhappy. As the colonists had expected, they petitioned for the repeal of the tax.

The American situation posed a difficult problem for the British government. Had George Grenville had his way, the response of Britain would have been certain and prompt. Grenville believed that American constitutional arguments against the stamp tax were without foundation; that America was in rebellion; and that the Americans should be made to obey. But Grenville was no longer Prime Minister, having been forced out of office by George III in July, 1765, because of a dispute between them over English domestic issues. Grenville exercised sway only over a small segment of the Whig Party, which was split into several factions at the time. One of these, headed by the Duke of Bedford, had helped to carry through the Grenville measures. Another, led by the Marquis of Rockingham, saw the American constitutional position as untenable, but contended that the tax should be removed to help British manufacturers and merchants in their distress and to please and soothe the colonists. Rockingham had succeeded Grenville as Prime Minister, and he and his Cabinet urged repeal. They received ardent support from a fourth group of Whigs led by William Pitt, who found the American argument against the Stamp Act quite convincing and who also pushed for repeal. Still another faction, later called "the King's Friends" because they looked to George III for leadership, did not take a positive stand.

The king was inclined to favor coercion, but permitted his personal followers to vote as they wished. Rockingham and Pitt, whose opinion had a profound effect upon public opinion, finally had their way, the stamp tax being set aside in March of 1766. Parliament yielded with the greatest reluctance, however, and simultaneously passed the Declaratory Act, which received the support of all except the Pittites, and asserted the right of Parliament to legislate for America "in all cases whatsoever." It was evident that the prevailing British view of the rights of Englishmen in America differed sharply from that held by Americans. That the British government did not accept the American constitutional argument was shown in the spring of 1766 in laws as well as words. The American assemblies were "required" to compensate those persons who had lost property as the result of mob action. The duty on molasses was reduced from threepence to one penny per gallon, but was applied to all molasses imported into America, whether from the British or foreign islands. The duty on molasses thus became purely a revenue measure. More trouble was to come.

10 THE COMING OF THE REVOLUTION

The Americans paid little heed to the Declaratory Act; displayed only irritation because they had to compensate those who had lost property in the Stamp Act riots; and had little to say about the molasses duty of 1766. Rejoicing over repeal of the Stamp Act, they celebrated the happy occasion with feasts, parades, and bonfires. Nevertheless, within eighteen months Britain and her colonies were again seriously at odds. The tensions caused by British western policy continued; the Quartering Act led to sharp quarrels in several colonies, especially in New York, which complied with the law only when threatened with the loss of its "privilege" of holding legislative meetings; and squabbles arose because British customs officers performed their duties with unaccustomed zeal. The standing army was increasingly a source of discord because it was more and more concentrated in the seacoast, three regiments being constantly on duty in the middle colonies after 1768. Other large contingents were stationed in Halifax and St. Augustine, where they were readily available for service in the Thirteen Colonies. The army was doubtless moved eastward in part to save trouble and expense, but the move made it readily available for service against the colonists. The temptation to use it for that purpose was enhanced, and a part of it was sent to Boston to maintain order as early as the fall of 1768. However, the Townshend Acts were the principal causes of the second Anglo-American crisis, which began in 1767 and lasted until 1770.

THE TOWNSHEND ACTS

It is not likely that the Rockingham ministry would have done anything seriously to upset the Americans, but it was driven from power in the summer of 1766 by George III and William Pitt. The king and the "Great Commoner" joined forces to create a Cabinet of "All the Talents," a government presumably including the ablest men regardless of party or factional affiliation. The new ministry was composed principally of Pittites and King's Friends. Pitt expected to dominate it as the newly made Earl of Chatham, but he found it impossible to attend to business because he suffered intensely from the gout and was compelled to retire to Bath for medical treatment. His young disciple, the Earl of Grafton, was Prime Minister, but devoted himself to a mistress rather than to politics. Charles Townshend, Chancellor of the Exchequer, came forward to fill the vacuum. He was plagued early in 1767 by demands in the House of Commons that the financial burden of maintaining the British army in America be lightened or lifted from the shoulders of the British taxpayer. Townshend was a brilliant mimic, and had a reputation for cleverness; unfortunately, he lacked wisdom. The colonists had not made it clear that they regarded an import duty to get revenue as unconstitutional, or that they saw no difference between such an "external" duty and an "internal" levy such as the Stamp Act. Blandly announcing that the colonists had drawn such a distinction, although he himself was unable to do so, Townshend answered his critics by proposing new duties upon red and white lead, painters' colors, certain kinds of paper, and tea brought into American ports. The proceeds were to be used to defray part of the expense of the army, and he expected something like £40,000 per annum to be raised in this way. Parliament, continuing to harbor resentment against the colonists, heartily gave its consent to the new taxes. Next, Townshend let it be known that the proceeds of the taxes would be used first to pay the salaries of some royal officials in America, so that they would no longer be dependent upon colonial assemblies for their salaries; only the remainder would be devoted to military costs. According to his revised plan, the duties would produce very little toward the needs of the army; it would, of course, tend to buttress British authority in America. In the spring of 1767 Townshend also persuaded Parliament to establish a Board of Customs Commissioners in Boston. This Board was to have control over all the customs officers in America, and it was believed that this step would bring greater efficiency into that service, hitherto directed from London.

The colonists agreed with Charles Townshend that there was no constitutional difference between internal and external levies to raise revenue. Forced to take a stand, they declared both to be beyond the powers of Parliament. This view was expressed in a series of essays called "Letters from a Farmer in Pennsylvania" which appeared in the colonial newspapers. They were written by John Dickinson, a wealthy lawyer and gentleman farmer who posed as a simple, poor, but honest man of the land. Dickinson declared that taxes for revenue could not be imposed upon the Americans by Parliament, whether they were internal or external. Any such tax would violate the rights of Englishmen. However, Dickinson admitted the constitutionality of taxes used as weapons to regulate trade. He described the new customs commissioners as officials who would become petty tyrants, and he assailed Townshend's plan to pay royal officials in America with British rather than colonial funds. This last he saw as subversive of established custom and as a scheme to enlarge British influence in America. The colonists, subscribing widely to the principles put forth by Dickinson, again sought to force the repeal of the detested British legislation by economic coercion. A boycott of British goods was undertaken for the second time, committees in port after port undertaking its enforcement. Many colonials were averse to the step; these were chiefly merchants who disliked interruption of trade and who had been alarmed by the rioting of mechanics and workmen during the Stamp Act troubles. Despite these objections, the boycott began in New England in the fall of 1767. Its spread southward was very gradual, and it was not well established in the far South until 1769. Many merchants were forced into the program only by economic, social, and political pressure; nevertheless, the boycott was quite effective and orders for British goods were cut in half. It had the desired effect, as British manufacturers and merchants soon began to urge repeal of the Townshend duties. But the British economy was in better shape than it had been three years earlier, and the petitions for repeal were neither so numerous nor so fervent as those of the Stamp Act crisis.

REDCOATS IN BOSTON

There was no "Townshend Act Congress," although many colonists desired one, because the governors, under instructions from London, prevented the assemblies from meeting to choose delegates. However, there was rioting, especially in Boston, where the Commissioners of Customs provided targets for American attack. Those officials would have been unpopular in any case, but they became more so because they zealously did their duty after November, 1767. Feeling against them was running high by the following March, when some of their underlings were violently threatened by a mob. That the commissioners were in any real danger is very doubtful, but they claimed that they were, and appealed for military protection. As a result, warships were sent to Boston, and the British Cabinet ordered General Gage to put one or more regiments into the city. Whether or not their alarm was real, the commissioners in June seized the sloop *Liberty,* owned by John Hancock, charging that it had been operated so as to violate the Navigation Acts. Technically, Hancock may have been a "smuggler," but it is not unlikely that he was the intended victim of a frameup. Subordinate customs officials were promptly assailed, and the commissioners fled to Castle William in Boston Harbor, where they were safe under the guns of British warships. Once more they clamored for troops, and the Cabinet ordered two regiments stationed in Ireland to proceed to Boston. Accordingly, in the fall of 1768, redcoats began to move into the city, and four regiments had arrived by spring.

Stationing a British garrison in Boston, was, of course, a hazardous step. The employment of redcoats was certain to arouse resentment, both in the city and throughout the colonies. Moreover, at least minor clashes between the soldiers and civilians could hardly be avoided. British commanders strove to preserve strict discipline and to prevent their men from quarreling with the townspeople, but were unable to prevent incidents. Samuel Adams, who was making a reputation as a defender of American rights in Massachusetts, did not pour oil on troubled waters. With some associates he put out "A Journal of the Times," a serial account of events in Boston which appeared in colonial newspapers for more than a year. "A Journal of the Times" pictured the British troops as rude, profane, and arrogant assailants of Boston men and women. As time went on, fracases between soldiers and townsfolk increased in numbers and in violence, each affair leading to another. In February, 1770, occurred the first death of the American Revolution. A mob gathered around the house of a customs informer, one Ebenezer Richardson, who fired his musket from a window, mortally wounding a boy who was among his tormenters. By March 5, excitement was running high, and it was apparent that a serious clash could not be prevented unless the troops left the city. The royal governor, Thomas Hutchinson, insisted that the troops remain. That evening, rioting men and boys assaulted a British sentinel and a party of troops who came to his rescue in front of the Customs House. The troops fired into the crowd, slaying five and wounding six others. Only the withdrawal of the soldiers to Castle William at Hutchinson's request prevented further and more serious fighting. Long afterward, the Americans who lost their lives in the "Boston Massacre" were looked upon as martyrs in the United States; however, the British troops could logically plead self-defense. A Massachusetts court in the fall of 1770 acquitted their commander, Captain Robert Preston, on a charge of murder, since he had not commanded his men to fire. His men were also tried. All were freed on the ground of self-defense, except for two, who were found guilty of manslaughter and who received light punishment. Wherever lay the responsibility for this bloody affair, it served to widen the gap between Britain and America.

The first response of Cabinet and Parliament to resistance against the Townshend laws was vigorous, but their attitude softened with the passing months. There was talk in London of altering the constitution of Massachusetts so as to make that colony more respectful to British authority. The House of Commons even suggested that the persons most responsible for the tumults in Boston be brought to England for trial as traitors. However, the decision to send redcoats to Boston was the only drastic measure adopted. The pleas of the British businessmen were heard with some sympathy. More important, the Cabinet itself was badly divided over the proper course to pursue regarding America. The ministry became increasingly one of the King's Friends between 1767 and 1770, Lord North succeeding Townshend as Chancellor of the Exchequer and the Earl of Hillsborough being appointed as a new Secretary of State for the Colonies. But not all of the King's Friends favored coercion, and the stand taken by Lord North proved to be decisive. North was a likeable, intelligent, well-educated, and witty man who did not enjoy trouble. He was not a man of firm will, and was later to come under the personal domination of George III. In the spring of 1769 North declared that the Townshend duties ought to be rescinded, not because they were unconstitutional, but because they injured British commerce. He received support from the Duke of Grafton and other members of the ministry. In consequence, it was announced that the obnoxious duties would be repealed, except for the tax on tea. That was retained, not to secure revenue, but to assert by example Parliament's right to levy import duties in America. Francis Bernard, who had been extremely unpopular as royal governor of Massachusetts, was recalled and made a baronet to compensate him for his sufferings in Boston; he was replaced by Thomas Hutchinson, Massachusetts-born, but equally loyal to Britain. Instructions were sent to General Gage authorizing him to remove the troops from Boston. Some were kept in the town, however, until the Boston Massacre. As we have seen, Hutchinson believed they were necessary to maintain order in the city. Early in 1770, the ministry was again reconstructed, all the important posts being filled by the King's Friends, with Lord North as Prime Minister. On March 5, the very day of the Boston massacre, North urged the Commons to repeal the Townshend duties save for that on tea, and the House promptly did so.

LULL BEFORE THE STORM, 1770–1773

The second Anglo-American crisis thereupon drew quickly to an end. Some of the colonists, including Samuel Adams, demanded that the boycott on British goods be continued until the tax on tea should be removed. They wanted total victory over Parliament. A second group desired to end the boycott immediately, on the ground that American demands had been substantially met. A third body of colonists contended that the boycott should henceforth be confined only to Townshend-taxed tea. In the summer and fall of 1770, their view prevailed, and normal economic relations were reestablished between the colonies and the mother country. There were sighs of relief on both sides of the Atlantic.

The years from 1770 to 1773 were ones of political quiet and prosperity in America. In Massachusetts Samuel Adams strove desperately to fan the embers of discontent into flame. He convinced himself that America must seek independence to escape British tyranny, and provoked Governor Hutchinson into irritating debates over the rights of the colonists as opposed to those of Britain. He also made much of an announcement from London in 1772 that salaries of royal officials in Massachusetts would henceforth be paid by the British treasury. To stir up popular feeling, he organized committees of correspondence in several Massachusetts towns. These were supplemented the following year by similar committees set up by the assemblies in several colonies, the House of Burgesses being the first to set up such a group. In the summer of 1772 the burning of the British revenue cutter *Gaspee* off Providence created a flurry of excitement. This was done by aggressive citizens who disliked the zeal with which the commander of the vessel enforced the Navigation Acts. The British government sent a commission to discover the perpetrators of the crime, but it could find no one in Providence who knew anything about the affair. In general, the colonists refused to make much out of little. In fact, neither John Adams nor George Washington objected to drinking tea made from Townshend-taxed leaves. John Hancock snubbed his old friend, Samuel Adams, because Adams insisted on quarreling with Britain.

The British government could not let well enough alone. Early in 1774, Alexander Wedderburn, the British Solicitor General, savagely denounced Benjamin Franklin before the Privy Council, describing him as a thief, a Bostonian, and a plotter for American independence. Franklin's offense was that he had returned to Massachusetts certain letters from Governor Hutchinson to a British official, in which Hutchinson had suggested that means ought to be found to curb the activities of Samuel Adams and his like. At the same time Franklin was deprived of an office which he had long held, that of Deputy Postmaster General in America.

THE BOSTON TEA PARTY

If the attack upon Franklin was foolish, Parliament, under the leadership of Lord North, had passed an equally foolish measure several months earlier. In 1773 the British East India Company was in financial straits: it had 17 million pounds of tea in its warehouses, and its officials devised a scheme to sell the aromatic stuff to the Americans. For the most part the colonists had been using Dutch tea smuggled into their ports, because it was far cheaper than the English variety. Under British law the East India Company had been forced to carry its tea to England, to pay a duty of 12 pence per pound there, and to sell it in England. The Company asked North to arrange for the removal of the duty, and to let it sell tea directly to the Americans. It also asked for the removal of the Townshend duty. North gave his blessing to the scheme, but insisted that the Townshend duty be retained. He calculated that the Company, paying only the Townshend duty, could sell its tea in America cheaper than the Dutch could. Thus the Company would receive much needed help, and the Americans would buy the lower-priced British tea. If they did so, they would seriously violate their own principle of "no taxation without representation," because of the Townshend duty. Parliament readily passed the necessary legislation, and in the fall of 1773 ships carrying the tea of "John Company" approached the American shores.

The trap which Lord North too casually prepared for the colonists was readily recognized by them. If the Company's tea were landed, it would almost certainly be purchased at one place or another, and if some of the colonists bought it, others would follow their example. Successful resistance required that the tea be treated as the stamps had been eight years earlier— that drastic action be taken. Merchants and other cautious folk might have served as a restraining force, but many merchants were offended because "John Company" had designated only a few favored men to distribute its tea in each colony. The Bostonians led the way. The captains of three vessels bringing tea to Boston were told that they must carry it away; Governor Hutchinson insisted that it be landed or seized for nonpayment of customs duties. When it became likely that the customs men would seize the tea and dispose of it at sale, a band of townsfolk dressed like Mohawk Indians boarded the three vessels and threw £15,000 worth of tea into the harbor, on December 16, 1773. The Boston "Tea Party" was followed by similar festivities throughout the colonies, although it was not usually necessary to destroy the tea. Some of the ships carrying it were turned back;

one shipload was stored in a warehouse in Charleston and afterward sold to finance the Patriot war effort.

ACTS OF COERCION

The news of the American "tea parties" aroused sharp resentment in London, not only because the colonists denied the authority of Parliament, but also because they had destroyed private British property. Some British politicians who had hitherto looked upon the Americans with friendly eyes decided that this time they had gone too far. Again there was talk in the Cabinet of arresting American "traitors." Eventually, in the spring of 1774, a policy of "moderate" repression was adopted. It was directed against Boston and Massachusetts, which were thought to be the centers of American resistance. They were to be punished and to serve as examples for the Americans in general. Since it was impossible to discover and seize the men who had dumped the tea into Boston Harbor, Parliament undertook to make the entire city suffer. It passed a "Port Bill" which closed Boston Harbor to commerce until such time as Boston should indicate that it had due respect for British authority. Payment for the destroyed tea would have been good evidence for such a change of heart. In a Massachusetts Government Act, Parliament declared that the Council of Massachusetts should henceforth be chosen by the Crown, that town meetings were to be held only once a year, unless the governor permitted others, and that jury panels were to be selected by the sheriffs rather than by town meetings. The Quartering Act was revised to make it as certain as possible that British troops in Massachusetts would be housed and partly supplied by the colony. A fourth "coercive" act provided that British officials, charged with crime resulting from efforts to enforce the first three laws could, with the permission of the governor, be tried in a colony other than Massachusetts, or in Britain. At the same time Parliament approved the Quebec Act, which was not intended as a punitive measure, but which was considered one by the Americans, who looked upon it as one of the "Intolerable Acts." The Quebec Act announced that the colony on the St. Lawrence was to be ruled for the time being by a governor and royal council. It recognized the right of the Roman Catholic Church to collect tithes in Canada, and extended the boundaries of Quebec to the Ohio River on the south and the Mississippi on the west, provided that no existing legal colonial boundary was to be altered. Many Americans were angry because Roman Catholicism was favored in Canada, and many objected that the people of Quebec had been denied the right to participate in the making of their own laws. Moreover, the extension of Quebec to the southwest was looked upon as contrary to the charter claims in the Old Northwest of Virginia and other colonies. Doubtless Americans had little valid reason to complain of the Quebec Act, but it was otherwise with the steps taken against Boston and Massachusetts. The Cabinet made it clear that the Coercive Acts were to be enforced. General Gage was appointed Governor of Massachusetts, and was ordered to keep in Boston four or more regiments—enough to control the city and colony.

There were many persons in Boston and Massachusetts who urged that the city or the colony pay for the pleasure of the Boston Tea Party. Reports of the Intolerable Acts and the appearance of Governor Gage and some redcoats in Boston in May, 1774, caused a shift in sentiment. A Boston town meeting declined by a small majority to pay for the tea. Instead, it undertook to alleviate the sufferings of the poor who would be put out of work by the Port Bill. The harbor was closed in June, and distress became common. When Gage tried to persuade the General Court to pay for the tea, that body defied him, issuing a call for the First Continental Congress. In August, when the names of the new members of the Council became known, mob violence flamed everywhere outside of Boston; the new officials were compelled to refuse or resign their appointments, or to flee into the city for refuge. Royal authority collapsed beyond the British lines, and Gage thought it imprudent to try to restore it. He built entrenchments across the neck which then connected Boston with the mainland, brought in reinforcements as rapidly as possible, tried to preserve quiet in the city, and wrote home for instructions. He described the situation in gloomy words, saying that New England would fight rather than bow to Britain. He also pointed out that a large army would be needed, if it were decided to employ land forces against the Yankees. It was to be feared, he said, that the New Englanders would be supported by the other colonists. He waited until April, 1775, for orders. Meanwhile, the lower house of the Massachusetts legislature met, in October, 1774, and assumed control of the colony outside of Boston. It provided for the collection of taxes, appointed a committee of safety, and began to collect supplies and to train militia for the trouble to come. It was, in effect, a revolutionary regime.

RESISTANCE: THE FIRST CONTINENTAL CONGRESS

The colonies rallied to the support of Massachusetts, and all except Georgia sent delegates to the First Continental Congress, which met at Philadelphia in the fall of 1774. Among the delegates were George Washington, Patrick Henry, and Richard Henry Lee of Virginia, John and Samuel Adams of Massachusetts, John Jay and Philip Livingston of New York, John and Edward Rutledge, and Christopher Gadsden of South Carolina, and Joseph Galloway, John Dickinson, and Thomas Mifflin of Pennsylvania. The situation was alarming, and armed hostilities not unlikely. In consequence, many colonists, both in and out of the Congress, were disposed to seek some kind of accommodation. Toward that end,

Galloway offered a plan by which the colonial assemblies would elect representatives to serve on a grand American council, presided over by a British official. The council would have power to act in all but local matters. The British presiding officer would have a veto power; on the other hand, Parliament would be forbidden to tax Americans without the consent of the council. This scheme, which did not provide for redress of past grievances, was defeated by a small majority. Instead the Congress forthrightly demanded the repeal of a long list of laws passed by Parliament after 1763, all being described as arbitrary and unconstitutional. The delegates declared that they would be pleased to return to the "good old days" of 1763 and that they would accept imperial regulation of American maritime commerce. They appealed alike to the rights of Englishmen and to the rights of mankind, and in addresses to the king and to the people of Great Britain urged that their wishes be met. To punctuate their demands, they adopted an "Association" which called for nonimportation and nonconsumption of British goods after December 1, 1774, and for nonexportation of goods except rice to Britain and to the British West Indies after September, 1775. These restrictions were to continue in force until Britain mended her ways. The Association was to be enforced by local committees throughout the colonies. Provision was also made for the meeting of a second Congress in Philadelphia in May, 1775, which would act as need then indicated.

In the winter of 1774 and 1775 the colonists divided ever more sharply into two groups, the Patriots and the Tories, the latter being those who were disposed to support Britain in the event of an armed clash. The Tories were definitely in the minority, and were unable to prevent rigid enforcement of the Association. The Loyalists, as the Tories called themselves, were subjected to all sorts of pressures, some of the more obnoxious ones being coated with tar and feathers. In colony after colony, the lower house, emulating that of Massachusetts, began to reach out for complete legislative and executive powers. State governments were rapidly emerging.

RESORT TO MILITARY FORCE

In the winter of 1774 and 1775 the British government, receiving the ominous news from America, made a fateful decision. British opinion was divided and there was disagreement as to the proper course to pursue in both Cabinet and Parliament. A minority, led by the Earl of Chatham and Edmund Burke, declared that the use of force would lead to the gravest consequences, and urged that Britain again undertake to conciliate rather than coerce the colonists. It was pointed out that a trial by force was to be avoided in any case, and that the outcome of such a clash was by no means certain. The Americans would fight and fight well; moreover, it was only too likely that France and Spain would attack Britain if she became deeply involved in a contest with the colonists. Lord North was not eager to try to overrun the colonies with troops, for at the moment Britain had too few for the task. But George III and the majority of the Cabinet insisted that British sovereignty had been challenged and that it must be defended. They believed that many Americans, when faced with a choice, would support Britain, and that the colonial malcontents could not successfully resist the British army. They refused to concede that Britain's difficulties were great enough to tempt France and Spain into another war. Lord North undertook to execute the will of his master and of his colleagues, and Parliament gave large majorities to measures for military and economic coercion. Arrangements were made to send additional troops to America, and Massachusetts was declared to be in a state of rebellion. The New Englanders were forbidden to fish on the Grand Banks of Newfoundland or to carry on overseas trade except with Britain and the British West Indies. At the insistence of Lord North, Parliament reluctantly gave its approval to his famous Conciliatory Resolution as a gesture toward accommodation with the colonists. By this resolution, any American colony in which the legislature contributed its fair share toward the expenses of imperial defense would be exempted from Parliamentary taxation for revenue; also, any sums collected for the purpose of regulating trade in such a colony would be credited to it. This proposal was not pleasing to Parliament and could hardly satisfy the Americans. It was addressed, not to the First Continental Congress, but to the individual colonies. If it were accepted by one or more, and rejected by the others, it would create dissension among the Americans. More seriously, it denied to the colonial legislatures the right to decide whether to tax or not to tax for imperial defense. It did not impress the Americans as a sincere effort toward composing Anglo-American disputes.

Perhaps the most important of all the British decisions, certainly the one which brought the most rapid response, was an order to General Gage to "do something" with the 5000 troops he had collected in Boston. In mid-April he received a letter from the Cabinet telling him that he had been too cautious, and that if he thought it wise, he should proclaim martial law. He was ordered to suppress "riots," enlist Tory troops, and arrest the leaders of the Massachusetts Patriots, even if he thought such a step would lead to hostilities. He was told that an early trial by arms was preferable to a contest at a later time when the Americans would be better prepared for a struggle.

What was Gage to do? Some of the Massachusetts Patriot leaders were out of reach, and he apparently made no effort to seize those who were in Boston and the vicinity. He knew—the Cabinet did not when it sent out its decisive orders—that the Patriots were gathering military stores at Concord, about twenty miles from Boston. He decided to send out a column of troops to destroy the supplies. If they succeeded without serious incident, well and good; if they were attacked, the burden of beginning hostilities would be upon the colonists. Accordingly, about 700 British soldiers quietly slipped out of Boston on the night of April 18 and moved into Lexington at dawn on the following morning. Their progress was marked by observers, and word of their approach was carried before them by messengers, particularly Paul Revere. As the British advance guard trudged through Lexington, it discovered a small band of American militia under Captain Jonas Parker on the village green. Major John Pitcairn, commander of the British advance guard, ordered the Americans to lay down their weapons and disperse. The militiamen began to move away, but retained their weapons; shooting began, whether by the British or by an American, is not known. Certainly the British did most of the shooting, firing at the Americans until they were beyond range. Several militiamen were slain and more were wounded, the British suffering only minor casualties. The redcoats marched on to Concord, destroyed part of the stores gathered there, skirmished again with Patriot militia, and turned back toward Boston. Meanwhile, the alarm was spreading rapidly through the countryside, and several thousand Patriots in scattered groups undertook to intercept the British column. Hiding behind houses, trees, and stone walls, they inflicted heavy losses on the column before it reached Lexington. The British were unable to retaliate effectively, but at Lexington they were rescued by a relief force sent out from Boston by General Gage. As the combined British contingents moved back toward the city, the unequal fight continued, the Americans continuing their unorthodox tactics. Finally the regulars escaped their pursuers and found their way to Bunker Hill, where they were safe from immediate attack. Within a few days thousands of Yankees were camped about Boston, and the city was invested. After Lexington and Concord there was talk of reconciliation, and many plans were proposed for the purpose. But the war had already begun, and it did not end until American independence had been achieved.

11 THE WAR OF INDEPENDENCE

The War of Independence, which began in the chilly dawn at Lexington, lasted eight years. Until July 2, 1776, the Americans struggled, at least officially, for their rights within the British Empire. They were not at first subjected to severe military trials, because Britain was unable to put large land forces in motion for more than a year. Then on the very day when the Americans declared their independence, the British began major offensive operations which continued until the winter of 1777 and gravely threatened the existence of the new American Republic. A third phase of the war began when France became the ally of the United States on February 6, 1778, the conflict widening and becoming truly international. France came to blows with Britain in June, 1778, as did Spain in 1779, and Holland in 1780. The entrance of France plunged Britain into many difficulties, forcing the British army in America to limit its aggressive activities to the Southern states. Those came to a sudden halt in Yorktown in October, 1781, and there was little fighting thereafter, except with Indian allies of the British and at the peace tables.

The Second Continental Congress gave direction to the American war effort. It convened at Philadelphia on May 10, 1775, its membership much the same as that of its predecessor, except that it now included Benjamin Franklin. Not long afterward it received another valuable recruit in

Thomas Jefferson. It had been expected that the Congress would speak for all America; it did far more than that. It promptly "adopted" the New England army around Boston, and later established a Continental army, appointing Washington as its commander in chief; a few months later the Congress established an American navy and a marine corps. It set up a "constitutional" postal service, opened negotiations with the Indians, began to print paper money, and declared American independence. Later, it borrowed money, and executed the alliance with France. In effect, the Congress, together with its committees and its civil servants, served as the first national government of the United States.

The states made their appearance at the same time. Between 1774 and 1776 the colonial assemblies disappeared one by one, and were replaced by conventions and congresses, revolutionary bodies which took governmental authority upon themselves. The officials of the royal and proprietary colonies also vanished, departing sometimes with dignity but on occasion amid threats and recriminations. The British governors were replaced by executive committees and councils manned by Patriots. The new state regimes worked closely with the Congress toward winning the war against Britain. Each of them raised militia who helped the Continental army. All were replaced before the end of the war, each of the states acquiring a constitution and organized government thereunder.

FIRST PHASE: PATRIOT VICTORIES

For more than a year after Lexington and Concord, the British were unable to move vigorously against the American rebels. Although the British fleet in American waters could not be effectively challenged by the Americans, it was small; at the beginning of hostilities the army could do little more than hold Boston. Much time was needed for Britain to collect and to send reinforcements across the Atlantic. Seeking help wherever it could be found, British officials in America strove to enlist Tories and Indian allies, and promised freedom to Negro slaves who would serve under His Majesty's colors. Lord Dunmore, the last royal governor of Virginia, was able to carry on warfare against the coasts of the Old Dominion until the summer of 1776, with a few regulars, some Tories, and "Royal Ethiopians." Arousing fears of a slave insurrection, he won little beyond the hatred of the Patriots. Governor Josiah Martin of North Carolina, believing that a British expedition was en route to his aid, called upon the Tories of North Carolina to rally around him in January, 1776. More than a thousand, chiefly recent immigrants from the Scottish Highlands, responded, but the British forces did not appear, and in February the Tories were completely defeated in the Battle of Moore's Creek Bridge. Loyalists were also active in South Carolina, but a display of Patriot power soon persuaded them to

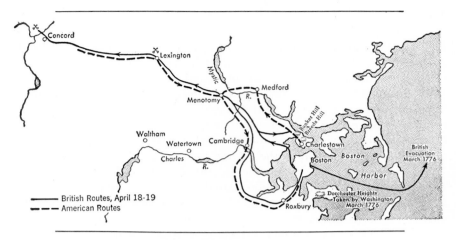

THE BOSTON AREA, 1775–1776

lie low. Later the Tories and the Indians performed useful military services against the Patriots. British use of the red men posed harassing problems for the Americans, although it was of very doubtful wisdom, since the employment of the Indians, like the use of the slaves, infuriated the Patriots against Britain.

Taking advantage of British weakness, the Americans strove to drive them from Boston and also from Canada. On June 17, 1775, General Gage was alarmed by news that New England militiamen had occupied Breed's Hill north of Boston. From that eminence the Patriots, if they should secure artillery, would be able to throw cannon shot into the city and force the evacuation of the British army, as well as withdrawal of British warships from the harbor. Gage sent General William Howe to drive the Patriots from the hill. Howe accomplished his mission, but only after a savage struggle called the Battle of Bunker Hill, in which the British suffered 1054 casualties; 45 percent of their troops engaged. Thereafter Gage and Howe, who succeeded him in Boston, refrained from even local adventures. Washington, who assumed command of the Americans in the first days of July, once and again considered an attack upon the British. Despite his superiority in numbers, he could not move effectively against them until he had acquired cannon. Securing artillery captured at Fort Ticonderoga, he seized Dorchester Heights south of Boston early in March, 1776. From those hills he could bombard the city into submission. Rather than attempt to drive the Americans off the heights, since little could be achieved at Boston in any case, the British sailed away to Halifax on March 17. The anniversary of "Evacuation Day," which is also St. Patrick's Day, was afterward celebrated with zeal by the Irish of Boston.

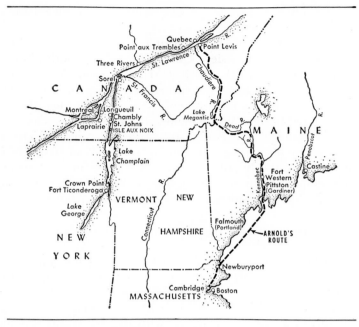

AMERICAN INVASION OF CANADA, 1775–1776

CAMPAIGN IN CANADA

Even before the war began, some New Englanders were planning to make Quebec into a fourteenth colony. The capture of the weakly defended Fort Ticonderoga by "Green Mountain Boys" under Ethan Allen, accompanied by Benedict Arnold, opened the way for an American advance northward along Lake Champlain. Patriot leaders were eager to secure the support of the French Canadians and to close the St. Lawrence to the British. In the late summer of 1775, Arnold led more than a thousand men northward from Washington's camp into the woods of Maine, toward the city of Quebec. Meanwhile, General Richard Montgomery with a larger force pushed forward from Lake Champlain against Montreal. Despite extraordinary difficulties, Arnold reached the St. Lawrence with most of his men. Overcoming vigorous British resistance and capturing Montreal, Montgomery also made his appearance with his surviving troops outside of the fortress-city of Quebec. But Guy Carleton, governor and military commander in Canada, had managed to collect within its walls a motley garrison of British regulars, marines, sailors, Tories, and French Canadians. With hardly more than one thousand men available for duty, Montgomery and Arnold undertook to storm the city from two directions on the last day of 1775. Leading one of the attacks, Montgomery was killed early in the day, and his men failed to push on; Arnold was wounded leading the second assault, and his followers, after making their way into the city, were either captured or driven back. Thereafter Arnold continued, with other American commanders, to besiege Quebec for many months, but it could not be taken, and the arrival of British reinforcements forced the Americans to withdraw in the following spring. In consequence, Canada, so recently added to the British empire, remained within it when the Thirteen Colonies separated from it. While most of the French Canadians remained neutral in the struggle, the Patriots nevertheless reaped a rich dividend from their Canadian campaign. Sending a large body of troops to Canada to rescue Carleton, the British later had to transfer most of them to the Thirteen Colonies. Their march southward in 1777 gave the Patriots a chance to strike a decisive blow, a chance they did not fail to seize.

SECOND PHASE: BRITAIN ON THE OFFENSIVE

It had not been expected generally in Britain that the Americans could effectively resist the British army. The bad news of Lexington, Concord, and Bunker Hill caused considerable alarm. Some men feared that George III was trying to make himself a more or less benevolent despot in Britain, and sympathized, at least to a degree, with the Americans. Among them were Chatham and Edmund Burke, who urged that reconciliation be attempted. The king and his friends, doubtless with the consent of the majority of the British people, determined to continue the struggle and to exert greater force. General Gage was replaced, the troops in Canada being put under the command of Guy Carleton and those in the Thirteen Colonies under General Howe, an arrangement which turned out to be a happy one for the Americans. Lord George Germain was made Colonial Secretary, and vigorously pushed the war effort. Several thousand troops were collected for service in America, but enlistments were slow because the war was not popular in Britain. Therefore the Cabinet sought troops on the European continent. Through a series of treaties with several princelings of western Germany, Britain purchased the services of about 30,000 German soldiers. These mercenaries were known as the Hessians in America, because a large proportion of them came from the state of Hesse-Cassel. The fleet in America was also strengthened and placed under the command of Richard, Lord Howe, elder brother of the general and Britain's most distinguished admiral. The colonies were declared in a state of rebellion as early as August, 1775. In November, Parliament passed the Prohibitory Act which placed the Thirteen Colonies under naval blockade, authorizing Admiral Howe to seize American sailors and ships attempting to put to sea. The Howe brothers were given a general pardoning power, as well as authority to lift the naval blockade when the rebellion should be crushed. At the restoration of the peace Rhode Island and Connecticut were to be royalized, and Lord North's Conciliatory Resolution was to be used as the basis for settling the question of imperial taxation.

CAMPAIGNS OF 1776

Under Lord Germain, Britain put what were, for her, large forces in motion for the campaign of 1776. Ten thousand troops were sent to the St. Lawrence to drive the Americans out of Canada and to pursue them down the Lake Champlain–Hudson River passageway. If possible, these troops, under the command of Guy Carleton, were to attack New England from the northwest, while the main British army was to land in New York and push into Yankee-land from the southwest. Arrangements were also made to send a small naval squadron and an army of 3000 to the Southern colonies. There they were to establish contact with the Loyalists and strike an effective blow before the beginning of the great British effort at New York. They were to remain only briefly in the South, and were then to join General Howe. That commander and his brother were to gather the bulk of the British land and sea forces at New York, which was the strategic center of the colonies, insofar as they had one. As we have seen, their first task after taking that city was to drive the New Englanders out of the war.

The Patriots were easily driven out of Canada, and were forced to retreat to Ticonderoga. However, Benedict Arnold delayed Carleton's advance by building a fleet on Lake Champlain, making it necessary for Carleton also to construct ships. The British general was able to build a more powerful squadron and to destroy Arnold's vessels in the Battle of Valcour Island. However, these operations required time, and October was well advanced before he was free to move his troops against Ticonderoga, held by a dispirited American garrison. Fortunately for that garrison, Carleton decided to postpone further advance until 1777 because of his long supply line and the approach of winter. Meanwhile, the British Southern expedition moved against Charleston. It arrived too late and in too small force to achieve any results. No Loyalists came forth to meet the British, and their warships were so badly damaged (June 28, 1776) in an attempt to reduce a fort on Sullivan's Island in Charleston's harbor that they had to abandon the project.

In the summer of 1776 the Howe brothers collected their forces in New York harbor, troops coming in from Halifax, from England, from Charleston, and from Chesapeake Bay. Ultimately they totaled about 35,000, an immense army for the Britain of that day. Washington, anticipating that New York would be General Howe's first objective, had dug in there and attempted to hold off the British, in an awkward position and with inferior forces. On August 27 General Howe routed the American

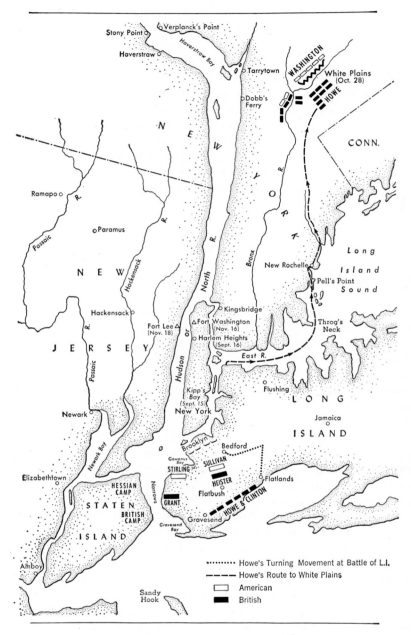

Stony Point ○
Verplanck's Point ○
Haverstraw Bay
Haverstraw ○
Tarrytown ○
WASHINGTON
White Plains (Oct. 28)
HOWE
Dobb's Ferry ○
CONN.
N E W
Ramapo ○   R.
Paramus ○
Passaic
Hackensack R.
NEW
North   R.
Bronx
New Rochelle ○
Pell's Point
Y O R K
Long   Island   Sound
Hackensack ○
Kingsbridge ○
Fort Lee △ (Nov. 18)
△ Fort Washington (Nov. 16)
Harlem Heights (Sept. 16) ○
Throg's Neck
J E R S E Y
Passaic R.
Hudson   or   North   R.
East R.
Kipp's Bay (Sept. 15)
Flushing ○
Newark
New York
L O N G
Jamaica ○
Newark Bay
Brooklyn
Bedford ○
I S L A N D
Elizabethtown ○
Gowanus Bay
SULLIVAN
STIRLING
HEISTER
Flatlands ○
HESSIAN CAMP
Narrows
Flatbush ○
STATEN
GRANT
HOWE & CLINTON
BRITISH CAMP
Gravesend Bay
Gravesend ○
I S L A N D
Amboy ○
Sandy Hook

•••••••••• Howe's Turning Movement at Battle of L.I.
– – – – – Howe's Route to White Plains
☐ American
■ British

NEW YORK CAMPAIGN, 1776

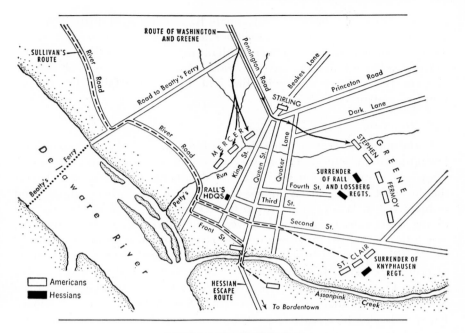

BATTLE OF TRENTON

left wing in the Battle of Long Island; in September he occupied New York City; in October he pursued Washington through Westchester County. Washington's army was melting away, his militia disappearing by thousands. Nevertheless, he was able to inflict a check upon Howe in the Battle of White Plains, persuading Howe to postpone his invasion of New England. Turning westward suddenly, Howe swiftly captured Fort Washington on the northern end of Manhattan Island on November 16, together with its garrison of 3000 men and large quantities of supplies. The loss of Fort Washington was a crushing blow to the Patriots, and the British were able to advance across New Jersey. Washington did what he could to hold them back, but was compelled to flee beyond the Delaware River. He feared that the British would drive on against Philadelphia. Instead, as winter had already begun, Howe chose to go into winter quarters, posting garrisons of Hessians along the east bank of the Delaware and keeping the bulk of his troops in New York and eastern New Jersey. The Patriot cause was in great peril and American morale at a low level after a long series of defeats. Receiving a small number of reinforcements, Washington boldly took the offensive, surprising the garrison of Hessians at Trenton on December 26 and capturing more than 1000 of them. A week later he was gravely threatened by Lord Cornwallis, who had come up with British reinforcements. Washington eluded his British antagonist, marched around Cornwallis, brushed aside small British forces at Princeton, and made his way north to Morristown. There early in January he settled down for the winter. He had been brilliant on occasion, and almost always fortunate. Patriot morale was restored, for the Americans had learned that the British were not invincible. The British had failed to take advantage of their best opportunities.

CAMPAIGNS OF 1777

In the spring of 1777 the British again took the offensive, but under less favorable circumstances. Before they were able to move, the Continental army was reorganized on the basis of enlistments for three years or for the duration of the war. Weapons, clothing, blankets, other supplies, and cash arrived in Washington's camp from France. These were secretly sent to the Americans by a French government eager to aggravate Britain's difficulties, but as yet unwilling to take part openly in the war. Meanwhile, the British gained little in strength and abandoned their well-conceived plan of 1776. Germain permitted General Howe to substitute Philadelphia for New England as his first objective, and the Howe brothers set sail from New York for Philadelphia late in July. New York City and Newport, Rhode Island, which had been taken at the end of the campaign of 1776, were left protected by garrisons under General Sir Henry Clinton. The bulk of the Canadian army was entrusted to General John Burgoyne, who was ordered to proceed to Albany, where he was to establish contact with General Howe at the end of their respectively successful campaigns.

The new British plan, if such it may be called, was ill-conceived in over-confidence. Division in command and difficulty in communication also played their parts in causing the British bungling, which dispersed rather than concentrated the British war effort. Should Burgoyne get into trouble in his advance through the wilderness to Albany, he could expect no important help from the main British army en route to Philadelphia, unless Washington tried to ruin the British scheme by gathering all his available forces on the Hudson and forcing Howe to follow him. Washington chose to devote himself to the defense of Pennsylvania, leaving that of New England and New York to a second American army which gathered south of Lake Champlain. "Gentleman Johnny" Burgoyne reached Albany, but as a prisoner.

In August, a great British armada moved up Chesapeake Bay and landed 15,000 troops under General Howe at its northern extremity. Washington strove to delay Howe's advance toward Philadelphia with a smaller army, but was outflanked and defeated at the Battle of Brandywine. The British general occupied the Quaker city on September 26, concentrating his men to the westward. He was forced to use part of his army, in conjunction with the British fleet, to capture American forts along the Delaware River in

BRITISH STRATEGY, 1777

order to establish a sure line of communications and supplies. Perhaps with his success at Trenton in mind, Washington took advantage of Howe's temporary weakness, and suddenly attacked the British at Germantown on October 4. The British were not firmly entrenched and were surprised, but managed to drive him off. Howe was unable to take the field again until late in the year, and winter put an end to his activities. Defeated but by no means destroyed, Washington's army could go into winter quarters at Valley Forge content with a very respectable showing.

CAMPAIGNS IN NEW YORK

Before Washington's weary Continentals trudged off into winter quarters, Burgoyne met a crushing disaster. He ordered Colonel Barry St. Leger with a mixed force of 2000 redcoats, Tories, and Indians, to move against Albany from the west by way of Lake Ontario and the Mohawk Valley. Burgoyne himself led about 8000 men, chiefly redcoats and Hessians, southward from Lake Champlain. He captured Ticonderoga with ease

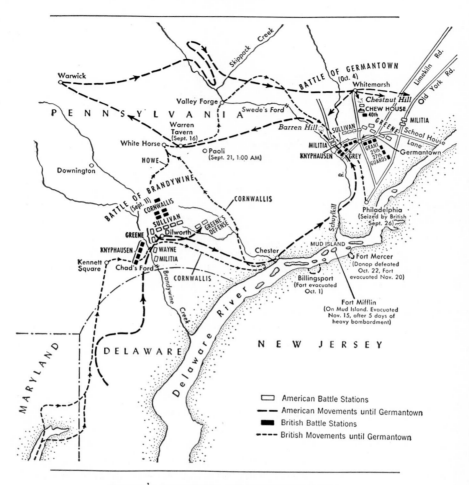

HOWE'S INVASION OF PENNSYLVANIA

early in July and moved on into the valley of the Hudson, creating panic among the Patriots. At first General Philip Schuyler, commanding the American army in the north, could only slow Burgoyne's advance by felling trees and turning creeks across Burgoyne's route. Then the tide began to turn. An American garrison at Fort Stanwix blocked St. Leger's progress along the Mohawk. At the bloody battle of Oriskany St. Leger defeated a relieving force of American militia which came up under the leadership of General Nicholas Herkimer. However, he suffered heavy losses, and news of a second relief army advancing up the Mohawk under Benedict Arnold made his Indian allies retreat. St. Leger was then forced to fall back to Lake Ontario. Meanwhile, Burgoyne's own army became enmeshed in ever greater difficulties. A detachment sent out to secure supplies was routed at Bennington, Vermont, by New Hampshire militia under General John Stark. A second body of troops sent to the assistance of the first was also beaten and driven back, with heavy losses. In mid-September Burgoyne pushed down the west bank of the Hudson toward Albany, but storm clouds were gathering about him. The northern American army, under a new commander, General Horatio Gates, was entrenched at Bemis Heights, and barred his path. Thousands of New England militiamen, alarmed for the safety of their homes and their families, were swarming to Gates's assistance and were threatening the British line of communication. In their desperation, the Patriots had become formidable, and Burgoyne was now in real trouble. Rather than retreat, he tried to turn Gates's left flank on September 19, but was driven back in the first Battle of Freeman's Farm. He tried again on October 7, and this time he suffered a stunning defeat, again at Freeman's Farm. It was then too late for him to fall back to Canada, and his only hope lay in an advance up the Hudson from New York City by General Clinton. Clinton did not have enough men to effect a rescue, but he was able to make a sufficient show of force on the lower Hudson to secure easier terms for Burgoyne. Surrounded by overwhelmingly superior Patriot forces, Burgoyne laid down his arms on October 17, signing a convention in which he promised that his men would never again

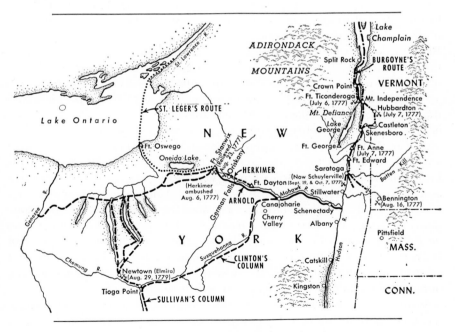

CAMPAIGNS IN NEW YORK STATE

bear arms against the Patriots. Actually, for one reason or another, his redcoats and Hessians became full prisoners. The convention of Saratoga was a tremendous blow to British arms and pride, and, like Trenton, marked a turning point in the war.

THIRD PHASE: ALLIES AND VICTORY

When news reached the eastern side of the Atlantic that Washington's army had safely survived the campaign of 1777 and that Burgoyne had laid down his arms at Saratoga, the war entered upon a new phase, rapidly spreading over a large part of the globe. Much as they desired to take advantage of Britain's distress, France and Spain had long refrained from open involvement in the war, for various reasons. From the very beginning of the Anglo-American troubles, France watched closely for an opportunity to avenge the humiliations visited upon her in the Seven Years' War and to make up for the losses she had suffered in that struggle. The French navy had been rebuilt, and new vigor had been infused into the French army. Hostilities had hardly begun when the Count de Vergennes, the French foreign minister, undertook to persuade his fellow ministers and the youthful Louis XVI to put the forces of France in motion. Louis opposed the step, partly because he thought it immoral to attack a brother monarch who was in difficulties. The Baron de Turgot, the minister of finance, also objected; mindful of the low state of the French treasury, he insisted that France could not afford a major war. He claimed that the British colonies were in any case like leaves on a tree, that it was not worth the effort to tear them from the tree because they would eventually fall of their own accord. The fact that the Americans were republicans was another stumbling block, for the example of a successful republic across the Atlantic might weaken the French absolute monarchy. Besides, Spain held back, and the French ministers wanted Spanish assistance. There was also fear that the Patriots might not be in dead earnest, that they might abandon their rebellion just as France entered it. Accordingly, while France hesitated to take the plunge, Vergennes persuaded his colleagues and his royal master to send secret aid to the Americans, even before they asked for it. The foreign minister arranged to establish a fictitious company, Rodrigue Hortalez et Cie, headed by the famous playwright, Caron de Beaumarchais, who was also a bold adventurer and the trusted agent of Vergennes. Through Beaumarchais large quantities of supplies, and even of cash were hurried off to America by the French Crown; the king of Spain also made minor contributions through Beaumarchais.

While American defeats in 1776 and 1777 persuaded the French government to maintain its neutrality, the American cause became increasingly popular in France, thanks in large part to the efforts of Benjamin Franklin.

Appointed by Congress, along with Silas Deane and Dr. Arthur Lee, to solicit a French alliance, Franklin reached France in November, 1776. The Philadelphian did everything possible to create good will for the United States. As a scientist, he was welcomed by French scientists, and as a philosopher he hobnobbed with followers of Voltaire, whom he did not scruple to kiss on both cheeks. Disciples of Jean Jacques Rousseau, influential at the French Court, chose to look upon him as the embodiment of Rousseau's ideal man of nature, so he dressed simply and did not correct their error. Discovering that the ladies carried a good deal of weight, he played the part of an elderly but charming gallant. When at last word of victory at Saratoga and the good news of Germantown reached Paris, the French Crown took the decisive step without even waiting for Spain to act. On February 6, 1778, the American commissioners signed two treaties with Vergennes. By the first, France recognized the independence of the United States and entered into commercial agreements with the new republic. In the second treaty, on the correct assumption that the first one would precipitate an Anglo-French war, France and the United States formed a military alliance, promising to continue hostilities until the independence of the United States had been assured. France forever renounced all claim to territory between the Atlantic Ocean and the Mississippi, including Canada, and guaranteed the integrity of American territory as it should be at the close of the war. In return, the United States promised to assist France in defending her West Indian possessions against British attack at any future time. The parties were not to make peace separately. The new allies were in complete accord as to their objectives, as the French desired American trade rather than territory, for they believed that American independence would bring them great economic gains and would cripple British power. Britain responded to French recognition of American independence as expected, and hostilities between Britain and France began in June, 1778.

In April, 1779, Spain also entered the war. Under the able monarch Charles III, Spanish power had revived after 1763, but the same factors which had prevented France from taking open action had their influence at Madrid. And Charles's ministers had additional reasons for avoiding embroilment. They feared that the appearance of the United States among the family of nations would stimulate revolt in the Spanish colonies. They foresaw, too, that the United States would be more aggressive in attacking Spain's New World empire than the British had ever been. They were therefore firmly against recognizing American independence. However, Vergennes finally persuaded the Spanish to take up arms by promising to continue the war until Spain had regained Gibraltar from Britain. Offering to mediate on terms which the British promptly rejected, Charles III then put his troops and ships in motion.

The entry of the Bourbon monarchs into the war forced Britain to fight in the English Channel, on the Atlantic, in the West Indies, in the Mediterranean, in Africa, and also in India, where a native rebellion was assisted by a French fleet. The extension of the war brought Britain only one ally, feeble Portugal. The princes of central Europe were coolly neutral, and the Baltic states formed a League of Armed Neutrality to protect their merchant shipping against British interference. Because Holland was a member of the League and because she could do more damage to Britain as a neutral than as a belligerent, George III declared war upon the Netherlands in 1780. Britain was thus diplomatically isolated, thanks to the work of Vergennes. So it was that she faced a ring of enemies in the later years of the War of Independence.

The news which caused joy in Paris in December, 1777, brought consternation to London. Again and again Lord North tried to resign, while the public clamored for the Earl of Chatham to take the helm. George III bent only slightly before this pressure; he persuaded North to remain in office, insisted that Britain deal with her ancient enemies as best she might, and permitted North to make a new offer of conciliation to the Patriots. In the spring of 1778 a commission, headed by the Earl of Carlisle was sent to America to offer terms to Congress, including forgiveness for past offenses and substantial autonomy within the British Empire. The British emissaries reached the Delaware River after the Congress had unanimously ratified the French alliance, and at a time when the British army and navy were preparing to evacuate Philadelphia. What they had to offer was too little and too late. They returned to England in disgust and disappointment.

The approach of hostilities with France also persuaded George III and the British Cabinet that their forces on the American mainland must go on the defensive, at least temporarily. This decision seemed necessary because of the danger that a French fleet, superior to that under Admiral Howe, might soon appear on the American coast. General Henry Clinton, succeeding William Howe, was ordered to evacuate Philadelphia, to assume a defensive position at New York or another suitable spot to the eastward, and to send part of his army to the West Indies. On June 18 Clinton and the bulk of his army began a march across New Jersey toward New York City. Word of his departure brought great joy at Valley Forge. Washington's army had undergone terrible hardships during the winter but had revived, as usual, with the coming of spring. Washington himself had had special personal difficulties, for he had been assailed in Congress and out as incompetent because he had failed to win victories in 1777. It has been charged that there was a plot to force his removal, the so-called "Conway Cabal"; evidence of such a plot is lacking. In any case, the Virginian had easily survived the attacks upon his record. With an army

equal in strength to that of Clinton, he pursued the British commander.
A battle at Monmouth Courthouse in New Jersey resulted in a draw, and
Clinton was able to reach New York without further incident, although
Washington's army had demonstrated its quality.

After 1778 Clinton conducted no major operations in the northern states,
contenting himself for more than two years with raids, blockade, and
attempts to seduce Patriot leaders. He was able to win over Benedict
Arnold, who undertook to turn the American base at West Point over
to the British. However, Arnold's treachery was discovered, and he was
forced to flee to New York for refuge. Nor was Clinton's war of endurance
effective, for the British raids exasperated rather than weakened the
Patriots, who proved as able as Britain to endure a protracted conflict.
Moreover, the British army was itself exposed to attack. The small fleet
which Britain maintained at New York was not strong enough to deal
with a powerful French fleet. Should the French blockade the British army
or a part of it from the sea, it might well be trapped. Only the skill and
courage of Admiral Howe, together with good fortune, had warded off
thrusts by a powerful French fleet under the Comte d'Estaing in the
summer of 1778. Two years later, after the British had evacuated Newport,
Clinton could not prevent the establishment at that place of a small French
squadron and army of 5000 men.

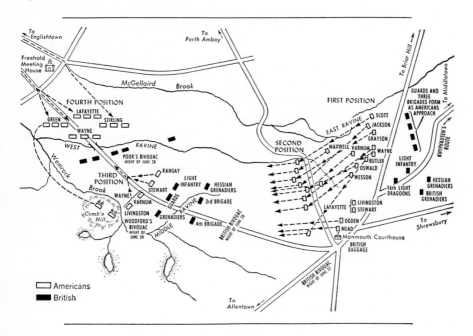

BATTLE OF MONMOUTH

VICTORY IN THE SOUTH

Clinton was nevertheless strong enough to risk a limited offensive in the far South, where he hoped the British would receive effective assistance from the many Loyalists. Savannah was taken before the end of 1778, and Charleston, with more than 5000 prisoners, fell to an army led by Clinton himself, in May, 1780. Forced to return to New York, Clinton gave the British command in the Southern states to Lord Cornwallis. While Clinton thought in terms of occupying the sea-coast and hurting the Southern Patriots as much as possible at a small cost, Cornwallis was a bold and energetic officer, who believed that a general ought to fight. After the fall of Charleston, Patriot resistance in the South almost collapsed. On August 16 at Camden, South Carolina, Cornwallis easily routed a mixed force of Continentals and militia which General Horatio Gates had led southward in a vain attempt to drive the British back toward the sea. Controlling the interior of South Carolina and Georgia by means of a chain of garrisoned forts, and greatly encouraged by the victory at Camden, Cornwallis undertook to invade North Carolina. However, he was forced to retreat from the "North State" when an auxiliary force of more than 1000 Tories covering his left flank under Major Patrick Ferguson was surrounded and destroyed by backwoods riflemen at King's Mountain.

King's Mountain was a Southern equivalent of the Battle of Bennington, and Cornwallis had reason to fear that he might encounter the fate of Burgoyne. Recovering from the shocks of disasters at Charleston and Camden, the Southern Patriots turned ever more effectively to guerrilla warfare under redoubtable leaders such as Francis Marion, Thomas Sumter, and Andrew Pickens. These American partisans picked off small detachments of British troops, interrupted supply lines, and dealt harshly with Loyalists who dared to take up arms. At the same time the Congress and Washington sent such supplies and small bodies of troops as they could spare to the rescue of the Southerners. With them came General Nathanael Greene, who assumed command of the Continentals and cooperating forces of militia in the South. Greene was bold, resourceful, and staunch. However, Cornwallis was not satisfied to hold the British conquests in the Carolinas and Georgia. When he received reinforcements he again pushed northward in the winter of 1780–1781. Again he received a rude shock. Greene's small army having been divided into two parts, Cornwallis sent out his venturesome subordinate, Colonel Banastre Tarleton, to attack one of them under General Daniel Morgan. In January, 1781, Tarleton caught up with Morgan at Cowpens, but was driven back and smashed by hard-fighting Continentals and sharp-shooting militia riflemen. The response of Cornwallis was to try to catch and destroy Greene's forces. Fleeing before him, Greene led Cornwallis on a wild chase to the Virginia

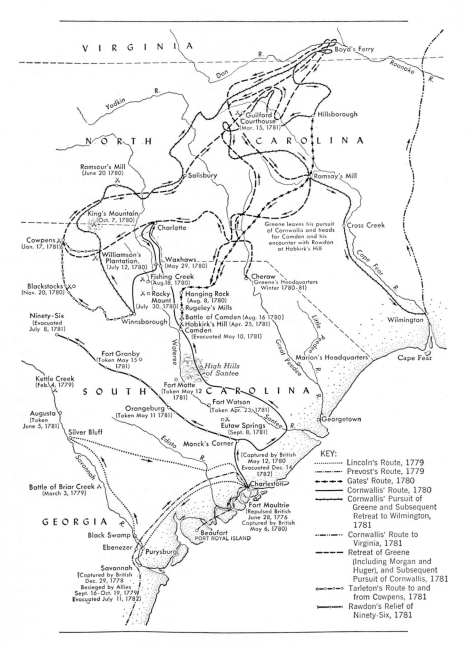

V I R G I N I A

Don R.

Boyd's Ferry

Roanoke R.

Yadkin R.

N O R T H   C A R O L I N A

Guilford Courthouse (Mar. 15, 1781)

Hillsborough

Ramsour's Mill (June 20 1780)

Salisbury

Ramsay's Mill

Cross Creek

King's Mountain (Oct. 7, 1780)

Charlotte

Greene leaves his pursuit of Cornwallis and heads for Camden and his encounter with Rawdon at Hobkirk's Hill

Cape Fear R.

Cowpens (Jan. 17, 1781)

Williamson's Plantation (July 12, 1780)

Waxhaws (May 29, 1780)

Cheraw (Greene's Headquarters Winter 1780-81)

Blackstocks (Nov. 20, 1780)

Fishing Creek (Aug.18, 1780)

Rocky Mount (July 30, 1780)

Hanging Rock (Aug. 8, 1780)
Rugeley's Mills
Battle of Camden (Aug. 16 1780)
Hobkirk's Hill (Apr. 25, 1781)
Camden (Evacuated May 10, 1781)

Little Peedee R.

Wilmington

Ninety-Six (Evacuated July 8, 1781)

Winnsborough

Wateree R.

High Hills of Santee

Great Peedee R.

Marion's Headquarters

Cape Fear

Fort Granby (Taken May 15 1781)

Kettle Creek (Feb. 4, 1779)

S O U T H   C A R O L I N A

Fort Motte (Taken May 12 1781)

Fort Watson (Taken Apr. 23, 1781)

Santee R.

Georgetown

Augusta (Taken June 5, 1781)

Silver Bluff

Orangeburg (Taken May 11 1781)

Eutaw Springs (Sept. 8, 1781)

Edisto R.

Monck's Corner

Battle of Briar Creek (March 3, 1779)

Savannah R.

G E O R G I A

Black Swamp

Ebenezer

Purysburg

Beaufort
PORT ROYAL ISLAND

(Captured by British May 12, 1780 Evacuated Dec. 14 1782)

Charleston

Fort Moultrie (Repulsed British June 28, 1776 Captured by British May 6, 1780)

Savannah (Captured by British Dec. 29, 1778 Besieged by Allies Sept. 16-Oct. 19, 1779 Evacuated July 11, 1782)

KEY:

.... Lincoln's Route, 1779
–·–·–·– Prevost's Route, 1779
◄–◄–◄ Gates' Route, 1780
——— Cornwallis' Route, 1780
–•–•–• Cornwallis' Pursuit of Greene and Subsequent Retreat to Wilmington, 1781
–··–··– Cornwallis' Route to Virginia, 1781
– – – – Retreat of Greene (Including Morgan and Huger), and Subsequent Pursuit of Cornwallis, 1781
o–o–o–o Tarleton's Route to and from Cowpens, 1781
├–■–■–┤ Rawdon's Relief of Ninety-Six, 1781

THE CAROLINAS AND GEORGIA

border, where Cornwallis finally realized that pursuit was useless and dangerous. His army was wasting away from disease, hardships, and casualties at the hands of the Patriots. When he fell back, Greene, reinforced, advanced and offered battle at Guilford Courthouse in March, 1781. A drawn battle followed, the British suffering losses which they could ill afford.

Unable to maintain himself in the interior of North Carolina, instead of retreating to protect the earlier British conquests in the far South, Cornwallis marched off to Wilmington and thence into Virginia with the remains of his army, about 1500 men. After his departure, Greene undertook to reduce the British strongholds in South Carolina and Georgia, with the assistance of the Southern partisans. The British garrisons, supported by numerous bands of Tory irregulars, fought desperately and Greene was unable to win a victory in the open field. He was defeated at Hobkirk's Hill and secured no more than a draw in the bloody battle of Eutaw Springs. However, the British were compelled to surrender or evacuate all their posts in the interior, and held only Charleston and Savannah by the end of 1781.

Meanwhile, Cornwallis met an unhappy fate on the shores of Chesapeake Bay. Adding British raiding forces which he found in Virginia to his troops from the Carolinas, he had about 7000 men and dreamed of doing great things in the Old Dominion. He wanted to make Virginia the main theatre of war, while Clinton wanted him to move the bulk of his men to the northward. In the summer of 1781 the two discussed strategy by correspondence, and Cornwallis vainly tried to destroy small Patriot forces under the Marquis de Lafayette. While Cornwallis was digging in at Yorktown, the event which Clinton had feared for so long came to pass. A mighty French fleet of 28 warships under Admiral de Grasse had made its way across the Atlantic to the West Indies. Then, following a plan made by Washington and the French command, De Grasse proceeded to the mouth of the Chesapeake, which he reached at the end of August. Moving in concert, Washington and the bulk of the Continentals which had long been stationed about New York, together with the French army at Newport under Count Rochambeau, marched quietly and swiftly for Virginia. The French squadron at Newport sailed for the same destination. The British admirals in the West Indies had not sent enough reinforcements to enable the fleet based at New York to deal with De Grasse. British Admirals Hood and Graves led a fleet to the Chesapeake, but were worsted in an engagement with De Grasse, and sailed off to New York for repairs and reinforcements. So Cornwallis was cut off by sea, the two French fleets combining to prevent his escape by water. Escape by land had also become impossible, as 8000 French regulars from Newport and the West Indies, together with about 9000 Continentals and militia-

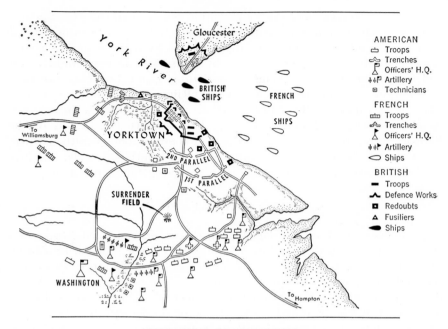

AMERICAN
🛏 Troops
🏕 Trenches
⚑ Officers' H.Q.
⚒ Artillery
▣ Technicians

FRENCH
🏠 Troops
🏕 Trenches
⚑ Officers' H.Q.
⚒ Artillery
⬭ Ships

BRITISH
▬ Troops
⚓ Defence Works
◼ Redoubts
▲ Fusiliers
◗ Ships

THE SIEGE OF YORKTOWN

men, had closed in on him. At last the British fleet, with Clinton and several thousand troops, set sail from New York. En route, Clinton learned that he was too late. Cornwallis had asked for terms on October 17, and had surrendered all his forces two days later. The end of the first British Empire had come.

After Yorktown the British army undertook no further offensives, for it was obvious that Britain had lost the war in America. Her Indian allies did not abandon the struggle so quickly. Most of the tribes east of the Mississippi had taken the warpath against the Patriots. They had long been aware that their homes, their hunting grounds, and their independence were threatened by the onrushing tide of American pioneers. One after another, the Six Nations, the Shawnee, the Cherokee, the Creek, and other tribes took up the hatchet, eagerly aligning themselves with King George in spite of American efforts to keep them neutral. Supplied with guns, ammunition, tomahawks, and rum by British agents, the Indians vengefully assailed the American frontiers after 1776, slaughtering and torturing hundreds of Americans. With the help of bands of Tories and redcoat detachments they threatened to drive the Americans back over the Appalachian Ridge. But the American frontiersmen fought back desperately, and received help from state governments and from Congress. The Cherokee country was thrice raided, and Cherokee power was permanently reduced by Southern Patriots. The Six Nations suffered similarly in 1779, when an American army under General John Sullivan devastated their towns and fields and broke their morale. Even the distant Shawnee saw their villages and lands ravaged by Kentucky riflemen. Amid blood and horror the frontier settlements of Kentucky and Tennessee not only held on, but grew in numbers and power. Riflemen under George Rogers Clark even captured "Hair-Buyer" Henry Hamilton and a British garrison at Vincennes, Indiana in 1779. The punitive expeditions of the Patriots drove the Indians into despair; they responded with a flurry of attacks which caused further agonies on the frontiers in 1782, but they could not shake the firm American grip on wide lands south of the Ohio.

THE PARIS TREATIES

The news of Yorktown brought down the Cabinet of Lord North, who at last escaped from the clutches of George III. A new ministry headed by the Marquis of Rockingham carried on the war against France, Spain, and Holland, and opened peace negotiations with the Americans. When Rockingham died, he was succeeded by the Earl of Shelburne, a disciple of the Earl of Chatham and a veteran foe of the American policy of the King's Friends. Emissaries sent to Paris by the Rockingham and Shelburne Cabinets had the doubtful pleasure of negotiating with Benjamin Franklin, John Jay, John Adams, and Henry Laurens, who had been appointed, with Thomas Jefferson, by Congress to deal with the British. Jefferson had been held up in America by the illness and death of his wife. His services were not essential, since Franklin, who had become the American minister to France in 1778, was capable of handling the task by himself despite his advanced age. He received solid support from Jay and Adams, although these last occasionally gave the impression that they were two bulls in a china shop. Honest and able, they lacked the polish and the finesse as well as the charm and wit of the old Philadelphian.

The British emissaries in Paris were eager to drive a wedge between the Americans and the Bourbons, hoping thereby to secure some advantage for Britain. During most of 1782 they continued to hope that the Americans would finally accept something less than complete independence, or at least enter into some sort of loose alliance with Britain. So grateful was Congress for French aid that the American delegates had been ordered to consult with Vergennes and to follow his advice upon all critical points. However, the Patriots knew that Spain was trying to keep the Americans away from the Mississippi or even to confine them to the region east of the Alleghenies, and they sensed that Vergennes looked with some favor upon the wishes of Spain. Franco-Spanish forces had failed to take Gibraltar, France had grown weary of the war, and Vergennes was trying to placate the Spanish and persuade them to make peace. America's amateur diplomats, with Franklin taking the lead, therefore agreed to bargain separately with the British. They entered into a preliminary treaty in November, 1782, which became final in the general peace settlement in 1783.

The Americans obtained very advantageous terms. The independence of the United States was recognized, and its boundaries were generously drawn. The American limit on the west was set at the Mississippi River; the northern boundaries of New England and New York were liberally defined; and the United States was to include the Old Northwest, its northern line much the same as it is today. On the south the frontier ran up the St. Marys River, still the boundary between Florida and Georgia, thence westward to the Apalachicola River west of Tallahassee. If Britain retained West Florida, the boundary between that colony and the United States was to follow a line running eastward from the mouth of the Yazoo River, which enters the Mississippi at Vicksburg; on the other hand, should West Florida become Spanish, the line was to be farther south along the thirty-first parallel. The Americans also secured the right to fish on the Grand Banks of Newfoundland. They were compelled to make some promises on the part of the United States, agreeing that British merchants "meet with no lawful impediment" in trying to collect debts owed to them by American citizens, and that Congress would "earnestly recommend" to the states that they cease to persecute Loyalists and return property taken from them during the war. Reporting the terms of the treaty to Congress, the Patriot emissaries asserted that they were very favorable to the United States, a judgment which has never been challenged.

That Britain gave so much and asked so little in the preliminary treaty is to be explained largely by her desire to end an exhausting and fruitless war. As negotiations continued, Britain's military situation improved somewhat. France and Spain also suffered severely from the effects of the conflict, and agreed to put an end to hostilities, even though they had not achieved all of their objectives. Since the Spanish had captured Mobile and Pensacola, Britain ceded the Floridas to Spain, and also the island of Minorca in the Mediterranean. France obtained no important concessions for herself, and the expense of the war severely injured her national finances and helped to bring on the French Revolution in 1789. The French did not secure the anticipated extensive trade with the United States after the war. Nevertheless, Vergennes could console himself with the thought that the final peace treaties which were signed at Paris in September, 1783, humiliated and weakened France's traditional enemy across the Channel. Other Frenchmen were later to rejoice because, in the War of Independence, France had struck a mighty blow for the rights of mankind.

At the close of the Revolutionary War the independence of the United States was recognized by all the European powers. The triumph of the Patriots marked a turning point in modern history, not merely because of what it meant for the Americans, but also because of its influence upon the fate of peoples around the world. The American Revolution brought the first break in the European colonial system. It inspired and continues to inspire colonials of all colors to seek freedom from European domination. From it sprang the first modern republican system of government in a large nation. Continuing to thrive in the vastness of the United States generation after generation, republicanism was a threat to monarchism, dictatorship, and aristocracy everywhere. The Declaration of Independence remains a battlecry for those who seek political and social justice.

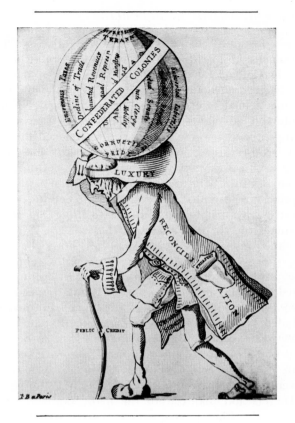

12 THE NEW ORDER

During and immediately after the War of Independence civil reconstruction went on at such a pace that scholars have been tempted to think in terms of two American revolutions, one external and the other internal. The word *revolution* is doubtless too handsome a term to describe the internal changes of the 1770s and 1780s. One may think, however, of a continuing revolution that acquired impetus during those decades and has not ceased today. Certainly the political, social, and economic changes accompanying independence portended the arrival of a new order.

The process of civil reconstruction may be said to have begun even before the shooting at Lexington. From the beginning of the war the Patriots had known that they were not in complete agreement regarding their objectives. Among them was a group of conservatives, these being the men who envisioned few changes beyond those made necessary by the separation from Britain. A handful of the conservatives would have been prepared to replace the British monarchy by an American one, and an army officer, one Colonel Lewis Nicola, actually suggested to Washington in 1782 that the general should make himself master of the United States. Washington was a moderate conservative and rejected Nicola's proposal as unthinkable and ridiculous, for with the bulk of the conservatives and the American people as a whole, he was firmly attached to the republican principle. The conservatives, while not opposed to some types of social reform, feared political changes which would give political power to the masses of men of little education or property. They wished insofar as possible to preserve the political status quo antebellum, with the power formerly exercised by Britain passing over to those Americans who had been dominant in the colonial assemblies before 1775.

Opposed to the conservatives were the radicals, who believed that victory should bring universal manhood suffrage, generally representative government, the protection of personal rights, social leveling, abolition of state-supported churches, and other reforms. While the leaders of the conservatives were to be found among the wealthy merchants and planters, the radicals included few men of note, being generally small farmers and tradesmen. Between conservatives and radicals was a third group, who may be called liberals, who sought reform and improvement but opposed the immediate establishment of popular democracy. Conspicuous among the liberals were Thomas Jefferson, James Madison, and other intellectuals among the lawyers and planters. In the many political contests of the 1770s and 1780s the liberals frequently secured a dominant influence, leading the way toward the more democratic America which was to come. Which is not to say that Americans of the Revolutionary generation were cast in three tight molds of thought; there was infinite variation among the three groups, and there were men whose views almost defy classification. That there was diversity of opinion, boldly expressed, testifies to the health of the American body politic in that era.

THE ARTICLES OF CONFEDERATION

On one point the Patriots were generally well agreed; that all governments should rest upon written constitutions. The war had hardly begun when the Second Continental Congress undertook to make a constitution for the United States, while the Revolutionary bodies in the thirteen colony-states began to prepare constitutions for them. The first of these basic documents, including the Articles of Confederation, were made by legislative bodies occupied by many duties, which included waging the war. Their members were often chosen in elections in which constitution-making was not an issue, and state constitutions were often adopted without prior approval by the voters. Before long it was contended, by Jefferson among others, that constitutions should be drawn only by conventions specially elected for the purpose, and that they should go into effect only when sanctioned by the voters. With Massachusetts and New Hampshire leading the way, the constitutional convention and referendum became fundamental parts of the American political machinery before 1789.

It will be recalled that the Second Continental Congress, recognizing the need for an American union to win and maintain independence, had appointed a committee to draw up a constitution for a central American government as early as June, 1776. The committee was made up of one delegate from each of the colony-states, the most influential member being John Dickinson. It quite promptly brought in a draft of the Articles of Confederation, but this Dickinson Draft did not please the Congress. It was disliked chiefly because its sponsors apparently anticipated the creation of a powerful central government. Except that the Dickinson Draft's national congress did not have the power to tax, it was to be largely the arbiter of its own authority with respect to the states. The Congress proceeded to revise the draft drastically, and sent the Articles of Confederation to the several state legislatures for ratification in 1777. The revised document provided for the continuance of the Second Continental Congress upon a constitutional basis. There was to be a one-house congress containing two to seven delegates from each of the states, these being chosen by the state legislatures. Each state delegation was to have one vote. The Congress was to have power to maintain an army and navy, to conduct foreign relations, to make treaties with foreign powers, to issue currency, to declare war and peace, and to handle Indian affairs, except that it must not intrude upon the rights of the states in dealing with the red men. The major grants of power were to be exercised only with nine state delegations concurring, a simple majority being necessary for minor matters. The Congress was not given the power to tax; it was to requisition money from the states, which were to supply funds in proportion to the value of the improved lands within their boundaries. Independence and sovereignty were guaranteed to the states, except to the degree that authority was vested in the central government. No provision was made for an executive, and national courts were to be established only to deal with specific disputes between the states. It was declared that the union embodied in these articles was to be "perpetual," and that the constitution could be amended only by the consent of the legislatures of all thirteen states. Special provisions asserted that the "free inhabitants" of one state were "entitled to all privileges and immunities in the several states," that they should have free ingress and egress to and from the respective states, and that they should enjoy similar privileges of trade and commerce. Extradition of persons accused of crime was provided for, and each state was to extend full faith and credit to the records, acts, and judicial decisions of every other state. Another special clause, which was long to delay ratification, declared that "no state shall be deprived of territory for the benefit of the United States."

LAND CLAIMS

The state legislatures found various faults in the Articles of Confederation and proposed amendments to remedy them. New Englanders did not like the system of requisitioning solely on the basis of the value of improved lands, and wished that property in the form of slaves also be taken into account. The South Carolina assembly, led by William Henry Drayton, felt that the powers of the central government would be too great, and urged that no important measure enacted by the Congress should become law without the consent of eleven of the state delegations. Thus the interests of the South would be protected, the delegations from any three Southern states being sufficient to prevent action hostile to that section. The Congress refused to consider these or other amendments, insisting upon ratification without change. Most of the states acceded before many months had passed, although several were reluctant because of the clause which guaranteed the lands of each individual state against claims by the United States. Maryland, in fact, positively refused to accept the Articles unless that clause were removed. The difficulty was that the clause safeguarded states' claims to ownership of lands between the Appalachians and the Mississippi. There were seven such "landed states"—Massachusetts, Connecticut, New York, Virginia, the Carolinas, and Georgia—basing their pretensions on colonial charters, laws, and Indian treaties. New York claimed control over the territories of the Six Nations and their allies, on the ground that the Six Nations were tributary to New York. Georgia's claim was founded on her charter and British law. The remainder of the landed states relied upon charter rights. Most impressive of the claims was Virginia's, for it included not only Kentucky but all of the Old Northwest. The landless states, led by Maryland, contended that Trans-Appalachia should be the property of the American people rather than of individual states, since it would have to be won by common sacrifice. Of course this argument was sound. It was obvious enough that if western lands were distributed by the state of Virginia, Marylanders would be at a disadvantage in competing with Virginians for those lands.

There were two other reasons for the opposition from the landless states. These were small—especially Maryland, Delaware, and New Jersey—and they jealously wished to prevent the disparity in size between themselves and their neighbors from increasing. Besides, influential speculators in the landless states who had purchased lands from the Indians knew that these transactions would be considered illegal by the governments of the landed

THE UNITED STATES AFTER 1783

states. Nevertheless the need for union was so great that all of the landless states except for Maryland ratified the Articles; Maryland absolutely refused to give consent unless her wishes were met. There was merit in her contention, and union without her was undesirable. At last, on October 10, 1780, the Virginians, supported by the New Yorkers, gave their consent to a momentous resolution in order to satisfy the landless states. This declared that all unappropriated lands beyond the mountains should be sold for the common benefit of the United States, and that they should be "settled and formed into distinct republican states, which shall become members of the federal union, and have the same rights of sovereignty, freedom, and independence, as the other states." With Virginia again in the van the landed states gave life to this resolution by making substantial concessions of their claims, one after another, beginning in 1781. As a result, Maryland approved the Articles of Confederation on March 1 of that year, and the constitution was put into effect. A union was thus created with a central government which, at least after 1783, controlled a western empire. The union under the Articles of Confederation proved to be weak, but the common possession of the west strengthened the bonds of sentiment between Americans. The making of new states in the west later strengthened the Union and enlarged the area of popular government in the United States.

PROBLEMS OF FINANCE

Progress was made during the war toward the creation of a more satisfactory central government and also toward the solution of the western problem. However, the Congress was plagued both before and after adoption of the Articles of Confederation with vexing difficulties which often could not be resolved. Lacking constitutional authority before 1781, the Congress was nevertheless compelled to supply leadership for the Patriot cause. Given the circumstances, its war record was creditable, and American triumphs in arms and diplomacy belong in no small part to that body, although its achievements lack the glamor of Washington's military victories or Franklin's diplomatic ones. One problem seemed almost insoluble, that of finance. Loans and gifts from France and Spain helped to supply the sinews of war, and individual states also made important contributions toward that end. Yet the Congress had somehow or other to find large additional sums, and it hit upon the familiar colonial expedient of issuing inadequately supported paper money. Perhaps there was no alternative. In any case, more and more Continental currency was put into circulation after 1775, and by 1780 it totaled more than $200,000,000. Inevitably, it depreciated in value as the war went on; declining rapidly after 1777, it became virtually worthless by 1780, when it was substantially repudiated. The Continental currency served as an indirect means of taxation, but it hardly strengthened the credit of the United States. Because Congress could find no effective way of transmuting American wealth into readily usable form, the Continental army—and American officials—were often ill-paid or unpaid, while the army was frequently without sufficient food, clothing, shelter, and weapons. The sufferings of the troops in winter encampments at Valley Forge and Morristown were heart-rending. Perhaps it might have functioned more efficiently had not Washington, Franklin,

Jefferson, and John Adams left it for other duties. At any rate, it is likely that the delegates achieved as much as was possible under the circumstances.

STATE GOVERNMENT

Most governmental authority rested in the states from 1776 to 1789, and it was the states that were largely responsible for the so-called "Internal Revolution." In general, the new state governments looked very much like the colonial regimes they succeeded, with a president or governor taking the place of a royal or proprietary executive. Most of the states established two-house legislatures, and the bicameral system eventually became almost universal. Judges were appointed, or elected by the legislature or by the voters. In some states the governor functioned in important matters only with the consent of a council. Theoretically, in accordance with the teachings of John Locke and other contemporary political philosophers, legislative, executive, and judicial powers were divided; in practice, the governor had little authority, the judiciary even less, and the assembly was dominant. The fear of executive tyranny, derived in part from past experience with royal governors, was so great that the veto power was almost uniformly withheld from the new governors, American though they were.

The Revolution did not bring with it immediately political democracy. In no state was universal manhood suffrage established, but in almost every one the right to vote was more generously granted than it had been in colonial times. Property and tax-paying qualifications remained, but in several states they were such that enterprising free white males could meet them with little difficulty. Legislative districts were redrawn so that representation was determined by population more than it had hitherto been, although interior areas in the South continued to have less than they deserved. State capitals tended to move westward toward the center of population. Property qualifications for office-holding were established in some of the states as a result of conservative influence. In some cases these were surprisingly high, but the prevailing tendency was to open the road to office to anyone who had the right to vote. In several of the new commonwealths, the upper house, or senate, was made a bulwark for the protection of property. In sum, the state governments were more responsive to the people as a whole than had been the colonial regimes they followed. Indeed, universal manhood suffrage was not far distant, being embodied in a constitution drawn up for Vermont in 1777 and in the basic documents of Kentucky and Tennessee, which became part of the Union in 1792 and 1796.

A striking feature of the new order was the adoption of a Bill of Rights in every one of the thirteen commonwealths. Jealous of their personal rights, the Patriots insisted that they must be put beyond peril. They were listed—the right to trial by jury, the right to petition, the right to the writ of habeas corpus, and many more—either in the state constitution or in special legislation considered as sacred as a constitutional provision. It is probably true that freedom of speech, of press, and of person was safer, except in the case of Tories, from 1776 to 1789 than in any other period of American history, since neither the national nor the state governments possessed coercive authority. It should go without saying that the press on occasion behaved irresponsibly.

CHURCH AND STATE

One of the great changes accompanying separation from Britain was the substantial achievement of religious freedom. Every one of the colonies had had religious discrimination. It had been mild in Rhode Island, Pennsylvania, New Jersey, and Delaware, and more onerous in Massachusetts, Connecticut, and Virginia. Except in Rhode Island, the Congregational Church was supported by government throughout New England, and the Anglican Church was official in three New York counties and in all of the colonies from Maryland southward. Freedom of worship was denied nowhere, but Protestants in general, or Protestants of a particular sect, were favored everywhere. Many of the Revolutionary leaders, including Jefferson, Franklin, John Adams, Tom Paine, and Ethan Allen, whether conservatives or liberals, were Unitarians or deists. Many more, of more orthodox belief, could not believe that any one sect exclusively possessed the Truth and the Way. These people wanted, insofar as possible, to make religion a private affair, to divorce church and state. For them liberty meant not only the right to worship or not to worship as one chose, but also the right to deny support to any church or theology. The major ties between church and government were cut soon after the War of Independence, although the last links did not disappear in Massachusetts and Connecticut until the nineteenth century was well under way. In some states, as in Delaware, it continued to be required that public officials believe in the Trinity. However, such intolerances vanished before long. They were no more important than the barring of clergymen from office in other states. The Anglican Church (Episcopalian after 1783) was temporarily deprived of support from public funds in Virginia as early as 1776, but struggled strenuously for some years to regain the favored position. When it became apparent to the Anglican clergy that the prewar situation could not be restored, they joined with Presbyterian and other clergymen in a drive for public support for all Christian churches. This "general assessment" scheme secured the ardent backing of Patrick Henry and was approved by Washington and the young lawyer John Marshall.

The plan was sanctioned by a large majority in the Virginia legislature in 1784, but James Madison and other liberals managed to stave off any action. The Baptists and thousands of Presbyterian laymen and clergymen rallied behind Madison. In 1786 the scheme was definitely set aside, and the assembly enacted the Statute of Religious Liberty written by Jefferson, which declared:

That truth is great and will prevail if left to herself, that she is the proper and sufficient antagonist to errors, and has nothing to fear from the conflict, unless by human interposition disarmed of her natural weapons, free argument and debate, errors ceasing to be dangerous when it is permitted freely to contradict them.

Be it enacted by the General Assembly, that no man shall be compelled to frequent or support any religious worship, place, or ministry whatsoever, nor shall be enforced, restrained, molested, or burthened in his body or goods, nor shall otherwise suffer on account of his religious opinions or belief; but that all men shall be free to profess, and by argument to maintain, their opinion in matters of religion, and that the same shall in no wise diminish, enlarge, or affect their civil capacities.

The Statute of Religious Liberty also proclaimed:

That the rights hereby asserted are of the natural rights of mankind, and that if any act shall hereafter be passed to repeal the present, or to narrow its operation, such act will be an infringement of natural right.

SOCIAL AND ECONOMIC PROBLEMS

Jefferson, who had faith in the future as well as a knack for politics, was also conspicuous in a successful movement against primogeniture and entail, institutions which were the twin props of European aristocracy, and which were almost universally supported by law in the colonies in 1775. In Virginia an owner could place both his lands and his slaves under entail; that is, he could restrict inheritance to a specified line of heirs, and thus compel his descendants to preserve the bulk of his estate intact. Under primogeniture, in effect throughout the colonies, if a person died intestate, his eldest son was assured either a double share in the inheritance or the whole of it. While it is true that there were legal devices by which an entail could be set aside, American society had given its consent to the concentration and perpetuation of wealth in certain families, and even in individual branches of families. The guarantee of wealth within a family, generation after generation, would assure to at least some of its members social prestige, education, and political influence as well. With Jefferson leading the way toward equality, Revolutionary reformers put an end to primogeniture and entail in all the states within thirty years after Lexington. Thereafter family property could be kept relatively intact by will only; in the twentieth century federal and state inheritance taxes were to make it somewhat difficult to maintain family wealth even by that means. The abolition of primogeniture and entail opened the way to a broader distribution of property, dealt a blow to the principle of aristocracy, and helped prevent inequality in political influence.

Hereditary titles and honors also aroused the displeasure of the Revolutionary reformers. Only a few Americans had acquired titles under the British regime, and it did not seem likely that additional ones would be created in numbers, either by American or European governments. Nevertheless, to make sure that such evils should not become serious, they were expressly forbidden in some of the state constitutions. Georgia refused the right to vote to any person claiming a title. The Articles of Confederation denied both to the United States and to the several states the power to grant any "title of nobility," and decreed that federal or state office-holders were not to accept such dignities from any foreign country. The Constitution of 1787 also barred American titles, and American dukes, viscounts, and barons were effectively outlawed. When the Society of the Cincinnati, composed of Revolutionary officers, was organized in 1783, its constitution confined membership to officers and eldest sons among their descendants; this last arrangement aroused a storm of protest, and Washington persuaded the national assembly of the Society to abandon it. Like other peoples, Americans have desired honors and distinctions. These needs have been met by the creation of countless fraternities, clubs, societies, and associations, none of which has produced serious hereditary distinctions. They have offered a measure of stability to individuals in a fluid society, and have often done good and great works. It has been said that the Americans, unable to establish firmly any superiority based on birth, have become "a nation of joiners."

EQUALITY: EDUCATION AND LAND

The Revolutionary ferment also led to demands for kinder treatment of debtors, improvement in prisons, revision and softening of criminal codes, and increased public expenditures for education. Many Patriot leaders realized that the new order required that the benefits of education should be extended to those less affluent, so that they might better participate in public affairs. Said John Adams in 1776: "Laws for the liberal education of youth, especially of the lower class of people, are so extremely wise and useful, that, to a humane and generous mind, no expense for this purpose would be thought extravagant." In a "Bill for the Diffusion of Knowledge" Jefferson proposed in 1779 that Virginia spend generously to establish public schools for elementary instruction and for a university to be formed from the College of William and Mary. His desire was that Virginia provide elementary education for the masses, secondary instruction for the more gifted, and a liberal education at the university level for the most gifted, who would be very few. In constitutions, laws, and resolutions, the states endorsed the principle of increased support for public instruction; Congress did likewise, declaring in the Northwest Ordinance of 1787 that "Religion, morality, and knowledge, being necessary to good government and the happiness of mankind, schools and the means of education shall forever be encouraged." Schools and colleges to be supported in whole or in part by the public were widely planned, and some actually opened their doors to students. However, practice did not match theory until a later time. The war interfered with education, and money to finance it was not easily found until postwar economic difficulties had been solved. One educational project of the Revolutionary generation, that of a national university, remains unexecuted today.

Had the war started a vast redistribution of property, and especially of land, the use of the term "Internal Revolution" would be positively justified. There was no such immense overturn. Some persons, especially Tories, lost their property in the upheaval, but these did not form a large fraction of the population. Some Patriots built fortunes during the war; these were usually merchants who started with some means and profited from dealing in scarce goods that had to be imported from abroad. Many thousands of acres of land were confiscated from Loyalists and sold to Patriots, at least some of whom were tenants who thus managed to become landowners. While the war brought economic fluidity, shifts in wealth were moderate rather than extraordinary. Possibly the most important economic change was the method by which unoccupied western lands were disposed of by the government. It will be recalled that in colonial times persons who had influence with the governor and his council, or with officials in London, had frequently obtained thousands of western acres at little or no expense. As a result of the Revolution, these lands were distributed by the states, and particularly by the American central government. After 1776, speculators often found favor at both the state and national capitals, but the poorer man had a better chance to secure a farm at a moderate price. The small farmer received increasingly generous treatment from the federal government after 1820; and tens of thousands were given homesteads after 1862.

SLAVERY

Inevitably talk about "the natural rights of mankind" led many leaders and common folk to believe that Negro slavery must be abolished. British and Tory propagandists, including Doctor Samuel Johnson, pointed out that while the Patriots struggled for their own freedom, they held the Negroes in bondage. Well aware of the inconsistency, Washington, Jefferson, Monroe, Gates, Hamilton, Laurens, and other Patriots from all parts of the Union felt that eventually slavery must go. This was not entirely because of the difficulty of reconciling their political philosophy with the existence of slavery—such a reconciliation was achieved to a degree by the Virginia Convention in 1776 on the ground that the Negroes had never been partners in a compact—but because they were convinced that slavery was a vicious institution, both for the Negroes and for their white masters. It was evident enough that slavery made inevitable widespread and sometimes cruel abuse of the blacks by the whites. It was also recognized that the masters suffered morally and economically; that power corrupted the owner; and that in the long run slave labor was unprofitable. In the Northern states, where there were few Negroes whose presence as freemen would create a serious problem, at least in the immediate future, there were few defenders of slavery. In 1780 Pennsylvania provided for its gradual abolition by a constitutional provision; four years later it was outlawed in Massachusetts on the ground that the state constitution asserted that "all men are free and equal," and within thirty years slavery was either dead or on the road to extinction in all of the Northern states. Moreover, it was forbidden in the Old Northwest by the Ordinance of 1787, and never flourished in that region.

Below the Mason-Dixon line, however, slavery continued and eventually struck even deeper roots. The many great Southerners of the Revolutionary generation were indeed sharply opposed to human bondage, but their sentiments were not shared by the majority among the Southern whites. In the far South slavery seemed at the time profitable for the whites, and even in the Upper South it was feared that the first effects of emancipation would be injurious to the interests of the slaveowners. James Monroe declared that he had leisure to pursue his public career only because he was supported by slave labor. Southern whites generally realized that relations between themselves and masses of free Negroes would present many problems, and that the solutions might not always lie in the hands of the whites. Rather than face the problems of a free society, many Southerners preferred to defend slavery; others believed that action must be taken, but chose to postpone it until such time as emancipation might be effected with less difficulty for the whites. Only in Virginia and Maryland, where there was stronger evidence that slavery was unprofitable, could any step be taken promptly. In the Chesapeake states manumission, the freeing of a slave by his master, was made legally possible, by Virginia in 1782 and somewhat later by Maryland. Under these laws thousands of Negroes were emancipated, but Virginia soon placed serious limits upon the right of the master to free his slaves, and the institution remained firmly entrenched below the Mason-Dixon line. Although slavery was not ardently or effectively opposed in the states where it was important, the slave trade from Africa and the West Indies was brought to a halt. The horrors of the oceanic slave trade, in which Rhode Islanders had vied with Charlestonians and Liverpool merchants, had long aroused indignation among generous-minded people, and several colonial assemblies had tried to stop the importation of slaves from across the ocean. However, these laws had been almost uniformly disallowed by the British Privy Council. The boycotts established by the colonists, especially the Association of 1774, had interfered seriously with progress of the slave trade, and the war limited it severely. At any rate, several of the emerging states outlawed the importation of slaves by sea as soon as they could. Both Virginia and Maryland enacted preventive laws, which were sanctioned by some men who usually approved of slavery, on the grounds that the supply of labor was adequate and the value of slaves would be reduced by further importations. Within a generation the Carolinas and Georgia also passed restrictive legislation which virtually stopped the traffic. Action was slower in the far South because many slaves had been carried away by the British during the war, and because it was claimed that more slaves were needed to clear and develop lands in the interior. Federal prohibition of the trade was permitted by the Constitution of 1787 and put into law twenty years later. It definitely cut off the supply of Negroes from Africa and the West Indies, although there were minor illegal efforts to revive the traffic shortly before the Civil War. The problem of racial relations was eased, but of course it continued to be an extraordinarily difficult one, since the Negroes already present, like their white neighbors, and in similar quantity, had progeny. The Negroes were in the United States to stay. Many whites, including Jefferson, and later Abraham Lincoln, thought of exporting them to Africa as the best solution. Wishing to believe that the endowments of the two races were equal, Jefferson never could quite convince himself that such was the case. Further, he feared that the Negroes, once freed in the United States, would remember their many wrongs and would seek vengeance to the third and fourth generation. The rancor which Jefferson expected from the Negroes has seldom appeared, while their abilities are more highly esteemed by modern observers than they were in his day. It is now commonly accepted that differences are cultural rather than hereditary; such was the view taken by Jefferson's great rival, Alexander Hamilton.

TREATMENT OF THE TORIES

If the Negroes did not immediately receive their full share of the benefits of the Revolution, the Tories were given their full share of its sufferings. They were detested by the Patriots, even by such moderate-minded men as Washington and Franklin; they were the more disliked because they had once been neighbors and friends. Forming perhaps one quarter of the population, they were at once dangerous to the Patriots and extremely useful to the British. They obstructed the Patriot war effort, supplied the redcoats with foodstuffs and information, served as spies and as guides for British troops, and took the field in large numbers, perhaps as many as thirty thousand. Whether as partisans or as "provincials" in British pay, the Loyalists fought well. The American states dealt harshly with them, and they were forbidden to vote, hold office, practice the professions, or refuse to accept worthless Patriot currency. In 1777 the Congress recommended to the states that they seize and sell Tory property to help finance the war. The states needed no urging, and every one of them declared forfeit Tory lands and other valuables. Sometimes the Tories were merely fined according to the value of their property; often they lost possession entirely. Even the end of hostilities did not put an end to the punishment visited upon them by the Patriots, for several of the states ignored the peace treaty's recommendation that they cease to persecute the Loyalists. Their tale of woe also included banishment, for the states exiled their leaders and many others who declined to take a patriot oath of allegiance.

Perhaps fifty thousand Tories were forced into or chose exile. Many of them settled in Ontario and the Maritime Provinces of Canada, others in Britain, and a few in the West Indies. They were assisted by Britain to secure new homes, and several million pounds were granted to them by the British treasury in part compensation for their property losses. They and their descendants became ardent defenders of the British Empire. Happily for the United States, they were not a peculiarly valuable or select group; they came from all sections of American society and were indistinguishable from the Patriots in wealth, education, social status, or in talent. Nor did the majority, who remained in the United States, have an easy time of it after the war, for many Patriots found it difficult to accept even the mildest and least offensive of Loyalists as peaceful neighbors. However, many Loyalists who lived quietly and behaved prudently during the war escaped punishment. Many preferred the British connection, but were not disposed to make any great sacrifice for it, and almost all accepted the military verdict of the War of Independence as final. There were no Tory revolts after 1783, and within a decade the Tories remaining in the United States had been quite effectively merged with the Patriots. Becoming reconciled to the Patriot triumph, in the end most participated fully in the benefits of the Revolution.

ECONOMIC STRESSES

The Americans of the postwar years, even those who had been ardent Patriots, did not immediately enter upon an era of private prosperity and public well-being. The years from 1783 to 1789 brought economic and political troubles as well as beneficent reforms. However, these troubles had largely vanished or been removed by 1789, when an effective American national government began to function.

The postwar years were ones of economic stress and strain, for the war had created large public debts, brought forth issues of depreciating currency by both the federal and state governments, and had generally dislocated the economy. With the return of peace merchants and farmers expected a rapid return to the general prosperity of the years immediately before 1775. Southern planters borrowed to put new lands into cultivation, and merchants ordered large quantities of goods on credit. Both were encouraged by the British, who had goods and cash and who were eager to resume business with America. The French and Spanish could not offer credit, so could not compete with the British; hence the French reaped no major economic benefits from their efforts in the war. It soon developed that the Americans had been overly optimistic and that good markets for their products and wares were lacking. Although the state treasuries were partly filled by the sales of Tory and western lands, the legislatures were forced to tax heavily to meet current expenses, and some of them had to raise their levies to a peak to pay off debts accumulated during the war. In some states the burden of taxation became almost crushing, and seizures of homes and lands for nonpayment of taxes became common. The situation was not improved by efforts of the radicals to ease the load of debt by putting out large quantities of new unsupported currency. As legal tender in Rhode Island, such money persuaded creditors to flee from debtors; issued in moderate quantity and with public support in South Carolina, it proved beneficial; everywhere it provoked heated debate and political dissatisfaction. In 1785 and 1786 the United States were in the throes of a depression which gradually lifted as most of the states put their financial houses in order and the natural wealth of the nation asserted itself. By 1789 the Americans were again relatively prosperous.

EXTERNAL AFFAIRS

INDIANS AND SPAIN

The troubles of the 1780s were not merely economic, for relations with the Indians and with foreign nations presented awkward and vexing problems for the Congress. The red men of Trans-Appalachia were unhappy after 1783, some of the tribes refusing to put down the hatchet when their ally George III ordered his sailors and soldiers to cease fire. The Shawnee and other northwestern tribesmen continued their raids across the Ohio throughout the decade, being encouraged by British merchants who supplied them with the tools of war from Canada and by the presence of British troops in several posts on American soil along the Great Lakes. Congress vainly tried to placate these Indians and as vainly tried to frighten them into peaceful behavior by a display of military force. In the Old Southwest the situation was roughly similar. There a part of the Cherokee Nation was unwilling to accept defeat, and struggled desperately under the leadership of Dragging Canoe to preserve their ancient independence and power. The "Chickamauga," as Dragging Canoe's followers were called, were on occasion supported by other Cherokee and were able to carry on bitter warfare against the settlers of east and middle Tennessee. The Creek were also restive, some joining the Chickamauga while others indulged themselves in raids along the frontiers of Georgia. Both the Creek and the Cherokee obtained ammunition and weapons from British merchants in the Spanish Floridas, and Spanish officials along the Gulf Coast neither urged the Indians to make peace nor refused them entertainment and asylum in Spanish territory. After much savage fighting, in which the pioneers of Tennessee were ably led by men such as John (Nolichucky Jack) Sevier, the Cherokee were effectively reduced, although the Creek remained a major menace.

The pioneers of Kentucky and Tennessee had other grievances against Spain. In an attempt to stem the advancing tide of American settlement, Spain not only sought hegemony over the Southwestern Indians, but also used her control of the mouth of the Mississippi as an economic weapon. Most products that the American settlers had to sell could not be sent eastward to market because of the difficulties of terrain, and had to be shipped by way of the great river. In the 1780s they had little to send out, but they were given cause for future concern when, in the middle of the decade, Spain forbade them the use of the lower stretches of the Mississippi, and then, in 1787, permitted passage only upon payment of a heavy tariff. At the same time the governor at New Orleans and other Spanish officials let it be known that the Kentuckians and Tennesseeans would be better treated if they allied themselves with the Spanish Crown. Disgusted by the failure of Virginia and the Congress to support them adequately in their struggles against the Indians, the British, and the Spanish, a few Kentuckians considered some sort of connection with Spain, for their own benefit rather than that of Spain. The great majority really desired to create a new state in the Union, so that they could practice self-government and deal more effectively with their own problems. They also wanted the United States to pursue a more vigorous policy with respect to Spain, to compel the Spanish to open up the river. The response of the Tennesseeans was similar. Indeed in 1784 the inhabitants of eastern Tennessee, without the consent of North Carolina, organized a "State of Franklin" which endured dubiously for about four years.

Unable to placate the Southwestern Indians because Georgia and other Southern states refused their support, Congress could not force the Spanish to open the Mississippi. The United States had no legal right to the use of that part of the river which flowed through Spanish territory. Threats to Spain would be to no avail, since there was no military power to support them. Moreover, some Northern members of Congress did not care whether or not the river was open to American shipping, and in some cases they were actually opposed to it because they were jealous of the growth of the South. When Don Diego de Gardoqui came to the United States as a Spanish envoy in 1785, John Jay, Secretary in charge of foreign affairs, proposed that the United States agree not to press for the opening of the river during a twenty-five year period in return for trade concessions on the part of Spain. This bargain was so bitterly condemned by Southerners in Congress that it was not carried out. Nor could Congress persuade Spain to accept the American interpretation of the boundary between the United States and West Florida. The Spanish court insisted that the northern limit of West Florida be the same as it was when the British held the province, and would not accept the thirty-first parallel. Nor could Congress effectively prevent Spanish intrigues among the Creek. The Muskogee warriors, under the leadership of their half-breed chief, "King" Alexander McGillivray, continued their close relations with British merchants and Spanish officials. McGillivray would not enter into a treaty of friendship with the United States until 1790, when he finally consented to sign such an agreement with President Washington at New York City.

RELATIONS WITH BRITAIN

The central government under the Articles of Confederation had no greater success in dealing with Britain than it had with Spain. Anti-American feeling ran high in Britain after the war because it was felt that Britain had been humiliated and sorely injured by her ungrateful colonists. It was also widely believed that Britain had been too generous in making the peace. When American merchants sought to continue to trade with the British West Indies, they were sharply reminded that they had become foreigners and that the Acts of Navigation applied to them just as they did to the French and Dutch. Their traffic with Britain's Caribbean islands was limited to suit British interests, and American trade with the islands did not flourish as it had in the past. But the British government was not content to treat Americans as the foreigners they had certainly become; they were treated as unimportant foreigners. Britain did not even bother to send a minister to the United States for some years. More seriously, while the peace negotiations were still in progress, orders were sent to British officials in Canada not to give up the chain of forts including Michilimackinac, Detroit, and Niagara, which stretched along the Great Lakes–St. Lawrence waterway, even though they were on American soil. The purpose was to assist Canadian fur traders against American competitors so long as might be possible and convenient. As it turned out, British troops remained in the posts for thirteen years after the war. Excuses were easily found for keeping them on American territory. These usually took the form of arguments that the Americans had failed to execute provisions of the peace treaties concerning treatment of the Loyalists and debts owed by Americans to British merchants. The states did place obstacles in the path of British creditors seeking to collect from their American debtors, and in several cases they ignored the congressional recommendation that they cease to punish the Loyalists. Britain was thus given pretext, if not a good reason, for holding the forts. The posts became not only centers for the Indian trade, but bases from which anti-American propaganda was spread among the red men of the Old Northwest. Protests by the United States were fruitless, and as Minister to the Court of St. James, John Adams received very cool treatment, which he returned in kind.

The British claimed—with some justice—that it was idle to negotiate with an American government which lacked authority to carry out its pledges. The Congress did not have effective control over commerce with foreign nations, nor did it have power to regulate commerce between states. It was unable to prevent a tariff war between New York and Connecticut, and it had no right to intervene in a dispute between Maryland and Virginia over the use of the Potomac River. In fact, the central government lacked not only constitutional power, but also money with which it could act. It will be recalled that its operations were to be financed by requisitions upon the states, these to be paid in proportion to the value of improved lands. Even when willing, the states of the 1780s were sometimes unable to meet this obligation, and they were not always willing. When one fulfilled its pledge and another did not, the first was likely to stop or diminish its payment. The result was that the central government was chronically so short of funds that it was threatened by bankruptcy. Pleas to the state legislatures did not have the desired effect, and there was no way to force them to contribute.

WESTWARD EXPANSION

If by 1787 the central government seemed almost ready to expire from anemia, nevertheless in that year the Congress did achieve a remarkable triumph in domestic affairs. It did not need money to establish government and sell lands in the vast territory which gradually came under its control beyond the Appalachians after 1781. In 1785 the Congress laid the foundation of the land system of the United States, providing for the division of national lands into townships six miles square, which were in turn divided into thirty-six sections one mile square. The ordinance also stipulated that in every township section number 16 should be set aside for the support of public schools. Congress had already begun to consider blueprints for governments in the nation's western empire. Between 1781 and 1786 Virginia and all of the states to the northward, except

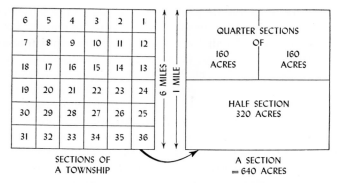

THE PUBLIC LAND SURVEY SYSTEM

Connecticut, ceded their rights in the Old Northwest to the central government. In April, 1784, expecting that all of the states would soon abandon their western claims, Congress passed an ordinance prepared by Jefferson which called for the rapid organization of self-government and the formation of new states beyond the mountains. Provision was made for their admission to the Union as soon as their populations justified that step. The Ordinance of 1784 was not executed, but its principles were inserted in the great Ordinance of 1787 which laid the groundwork for the settlement and development of the Old Northwest. The Ohio Company, formed in Boston in 1786 to buy western lands and to promote their settlement, pushed Congress into action. Among the leaders of the company was Dr. Manasseh Cutler, who in the early summer of 1787 made an offer to Congress for a vast tract of land north of the Ohio River. The company proposed to pay for the land, not in cash, but in certificates of indebtedness, which were documents acknowledging debts owed by the United States for goods and services. Congress listened attentively to Cutler, who was both a Doctor of Divinity and a shrewd man at business. On July 13 it passed the great Ordinance which laid down the colonial policy the United States was to follow until the end of the nineteenth century.

The Old Northwest was temporarily governed by a governor and three judges, appointed by Congress, who were to carry out those laws of the thirteen states they thought most appropriate. When the territory should contain five thousand free male adults, a territorial legislature was to be elected by the inhabitants and empowered to govern the territory along with the governor and a council. Neither territorial officials nor territorial legislature was to interfere with the personal freedoms of the settlers, who were protected by a bill of rights. It was also declared there should be "neither slavery nor involuntary servitude" in the region, this provision having the support of both Northerners and Southerners in Congress. It is not likely that slavery would have spread north of the Ohio in any event, but the ordinance made doubly sure that it would stop at the river, since prevention in the territorial state was equivalent to permanent prevention. The ordinance also stipulated that not less than three and no more than five states were eventually to be created within the territory. When any one of the areas intended for statehood contained as many as sixty thousand free persons, it was to be recognized as a state, admitted into the Union, and be a full equal of the original thirteen. Congress thus proclaimed that the Old Northwest was not to remain a colonial region, and that persons moving into it took with them their right of self-government, their personal liberties, and equality with the inhabitants of the original states. The same arrangements being made for the Old Southwest and the region between the Mississippi and the Pacific Ocean, the United States was to hold no colonies until the American flag flew over islands in the Caribbean and the Pacific.

FAILURE OF THE ARTICLES

The weakness of the central government under the Articles of Confederation was recognized and deplored by men such as Washington and Hamilton even before the Articles went into effect, and the great Virginian called for creation of a stronger union in his farewell message to his army. Within a few months after adoption of the Articles, Congress proposed an amendment which would give itself the power to levy an import tax. Along with existing sources of revenue, such a levy would have provided sufficient funds for the central government to function decently for some years. The amendment was ratified by twelve states, but the smallest state, Rhode Island, refused its consent. While pressure was being brought upon Rhode Island to reconsider, Virginia's approval was withdrawn. The amendment thus failed, and another which would have given Congress the power to impose import duties and which would have altered the basis for state contributions to the central treasury was not endorsed by the states. Once and again the Congress considered other amendments, but none was ever ratified. The requirement of unanimous consent by the states was an almost insuperable obstacle; it was perhaps the greatest defect in the Articles. It is conceivable that, had it not been for this provision, the Articles might have been revised so as to serve as a workable federal constitution. Since that road to change was effectively barred, those who desired to strengthen the central regime were forced to seek other means.

Sentiment favoring a stronger central government increased with the passing years, and the means to create one were found. The conservatives had been inclined to favor a powerful central regime from 1776 onward, and they became increasingly devoted to that concept. Planters and merchants who had lent money to the United States and held certificates of indebtedness obviously had a far better chance of being paid by such a government than by the existing one. In states dominated by radicals and liberals the conservatives quite logically desired the transfer of power from the state capitals to the national one, where they might have greater success in their political battles. Also, a strong central government could be given power to prevent the issuance of cheap paper money and making it legal tender. The conservatives were shocked into action by Shays' Rebellion in Massachusetts in 1786. So frequently was property seized and sold for nonpayment of taxes that the farmers of the western part of the state, under the leadership of a Revolutionary veteran named Daniel Shays, in desperation used threats and violence to stop such sales. Order was not restored until Governor James Bowdoin called out the militia, whose march into the disturbed region finally persuaded the rebels that they must cease to resist the law. The conservatives were not entirely or even principally motivated by personal and factional considerations. It seemed obvious to them that a stronger central government could better protect American commerce with foreign countries, remove bars against the free flow of trade within the nation, more emphatically assert the dignity of the United States and of the American people, and more effectively provide for defense and expansion. Since the troubles of the 1780s were laid with some justice on "the government," many common people began to offer the conservatives increasing support. In many cases, liberals likewise reached the conclusion that the central government must be strengthened, although they would hardly go so far in making changes as the conservatives.

It is certainly not surprising that the demand for governmental change gained momentum during and immediately after the depression of 1785 and 1786. The means for reform developed in rather curious fashion. In 1785 commissioners appointed by Maryland and Virginia met at Mt. Vernon to settle the quarrel between the two states over the navigation of the Potomac. Thereupon it was suggested that all the states send representatives to a convention to be held at Annapolis to find means to remove barriers against interstate trade. Under Madison's leadership the Virginia commissioners issued the invitation, but only five states sent representatives. However, among them were Madison and Alexander Hamilton from New York; these two men, undaunted because the meeting could not achieve the purpose for which it was called, persuaded their fellow delegates to move boldly toward a larger objective. The Annapolis gathering urged the several states to send delegates to a convention to meet at Philadelphia in May, 1787, which should "take into consideration the situation of the United States, to devise such further provisions as shall appear to them necessary to render the constitution of the federal government adequate to exigencies of the Union; and to report such an act for that purpose to the United States in Congress assembled, as, when agreed to by them, and afterwards confirmed by the legislatures of every state, will effectually provide for the same." The response to the call was favorable, and Congress endorsed the proposal, issuing invitations in February, 1787. The convention, asserted Congress, was to meet for the sole and express purpose of revising the Articles of Confederation. Except for Rhode Island, the state legislatures responded by electing delegates, fifty-five of whom later appeared in Philadelphia. The delegates had a great opportunity, and they made the most of it.

13 A MORE PERFECT UNION

The constitutional convention met at Philadelphia on May 25, 1787, and labored until September 17. It was a remarkably distinguished body of men, for with a few exceptions the states had sent their ablest leaders. The convention lacked the services of Jefferson and John Adams, then abroad as ministers to France and Great Britain, but it contained some genius and a great deal of solid talent. In the Virginia delegation were Washington, Madison, Edmund Randolph, and George Mason. From Pennsylvania came James Wilson, a Scottish-born lawyer versed in history and political philosophy, Gouverneur Morris, a brilliant debater and lucid stylist, and Robert Morris, who had long served as the chief financial agent for Congress. John Dickinson represented Delaware. Connecticut furnished three able, moderate, and responsible men: Roger Sherman, a self-made man, Oliver Ellsworth, a distinguished lawyer, and William Samuel Johnson, a liberally educated scholar. From South Carolina came John Rutledge, an astute lawyer, trusted as was no other man in his state, and the indomitable leader of South Carolina in the War of Independence, Charles Cotesworth Pinckney, Revolutionary officer, man of honor, conciliatory and reliable politician, and his cousin, the gifted young Charles Pinckney. Among the Massachusetts delegates was Rufus King, an ardent advocate of a strong central government. Of the three delegates from New York, only Hamilton was an outstanding figure, and he could offer little help in the convention, partly because his colleagues, John Lansing and Robert Yates, outvoted him, and partly because his political philosophy—he praised constitutional monarchy and aristocracy as theoretically ideal—was quite unacceptable to the rest of the delegates. There were in the convention some men who contributed little, such as Lansing and Yates, Elbridge Gerry of Massachusetts, who did not seem to know what he wanted, Luther Martin of Maryland, who talked windily and obstructively, and others who are little remembered except for their participation in the convention. Nevertheless, as a whole the delegates were remarkable for ability, character, education, and experience, and they wrought extremely well.

WRITING THE CONSTITUTION

The first step taken by the convention was to choose as its president Washington, who was not adept at political maneuvering or masterly in debate, but who lent dignity to the convention and to its work, the prestige of the most trusted and most respected American. A second important decision was to proceed in secret, so that the delegates could quietly express their opinions and compose their differences, not "playing to the gallery" and not disturbed or swayed by public clamor. Much of the work was done in committee and in informal Committee of the Whole. Voting, when necessary, was by states, as it was in the Congress. Moving with surprising speed, the convention on May 30 made its greatest decision of all. It unanimously passed a resolution asserting that no "merely federal" union was capable of providing for the "common defence, security of liberty, and general welfare." Another resolution, which declared "that a National Government ought to be established consisting of a supreme Legislative, Executive, and Judiciary," was adopted by a substantial majority, with New York divided and Connecticut opposed. As Madison nicely explained, the meaning of this language was that the United States should have a new government, partly federal and partly national. This decision turned out to be final, and to carry it out the delegates chose to prepare a new Constitution rather than try to revise the Articles of Confederation.

THE VIRGINIA PLAN

Although the decision to create a strong central government stood, it was seriously questioned in succeeding weeks. There also followed bitter arguments regarding methods of choosing legislative members and the executive, and also about what their powers should be. The Virginia delegation arrived early at Philadelphia, drafted a plan for a new system, this being largely the work of Madison, and presented it to the convention. The Virginia Plan served as the basis of the Constitution that was presently prepared, but several of its provisions aroused strenuous opposition and had to be altered or dropped. It called for the creation of a bicameral Congress, the lower house (which became the House of Representatives) based on population or wealth, and an upper chamber (which became the Senate) selected by the first body, from persons nominated by the state assemblies. There was to be an executive, not described in detail, and national courts; the executive and the judges were to be chosen by Congress. That body was to have all the powers possessed by Congress under the Articles of Confederation, and was also authorized "to legislate in all cases to which the separate States are incompetent, or in which the harmony of the United States may be interrupted by the exercise" of state authority. The executive, together with a convenient number of the judges, was to form a council to revise bills passed by Congress, and was given a veto.

SMALL STATES VERSUS LARGE

The Virginia Plan was vehemently attacked on two grounds, that it placed the small states under the domination of the large ones, and that it gave too great authority to the central government. It is evident that the second objection was well founded, since the central government would have been substantially able to do whatever it pleased; the plan opened the way for the reduction of the states to minor political units. However, it was the first objection which was most serious at the moment. Delegates from the small states were alarmed lest the large states exercise control over the lower house and thus over the whole central government. Massachusetts, Pennsylvania, and Virginia, with perhaps some support from other states, could secure a majority in the lower house and use it for their own benefit and to the injury of the other states. The men from the small states rallied in support of an alternate plan presented by the New Jersey delegation, led by William Paterson. The New Jersey Plan would have given to Congress the same powers it had under the Articles of Confederation, plus authority to levy import and stamp duties and to regulate interstate and foreign commerce. It also contained arrangements for the federal executive and judiciary, and a significant assertion that congressional laws and national treaties should be "supreme law," with state judges to be bound thereby. The small state program also authorized the central government to use force against the states, if necessary, to assert its constitutional authority. Above all, the New Jersey Plan called for equal representation of the states in a one-house Congress. Thus it appealed both to those who feared large state domination and to opponents of excessive concentration of power in the central government. One of its supporters, Gunning Bedford of Delaware, went so far as to say that the small states, if their wishes were ignored, knew of a foreign power that would be glad to take them by the hand.

Madison, speaking on behalf of proportional representation, pointed out that the fears of the small-state men were based on a mistaken notion that the interests of the large states were identical, and that their numbers would form a solid bloc. He asserted what is now accepted as obvious, that members would vote in accordance with sectional, economic, and social interests. Hence members of Congress from Massachusetts and Connecticut were much more likely to see eye to eye than were those of Massachusetts and Virginia. New Jersey representatives would probably vote with those from Pennsylvania more often than with New Hampshireites. Madison's sensible arguments did not prevail, and compromise was necessary. While there was a majority for proportional representation, the wishes of the small states could not be ignored if a constitution was to be completed and ratified. The solution was the "Great Compromise," often called the Connecticut Compromise because it was vigorously endorsed by the representatives of the Nutmeg State. According to this settlement the House of Representatives was to have representation in proportion to population, while the states were to be equal in the Senate, each having two senators who would vote individually. Eventually, as a result, densely populated New York and thinly peopled New Mexico were to have the same voices in the upper house. While the disparity is obviously "undemocratic," the evil is by no means an unmitigated one. The immediate consequence of the "Great Compromise" was to end the struggle into which the men of the small states had plunged the convention. Thereafter Paterson and his associates were as willing to give large powers to the central government as were their fellow delegates, since they did not fear that those powers would be used against them. Some delegates continued to fear too great a concentration of authority in the national capital, but these were in a decided minority.

FEDERAL POWERS

In July the convention was able to move on to the far more fundamental questions of the scope of federal authority and of the manner in which it should be exercised. The second question was brilliantly solved by placing the states and the federal government side by side, both resting upon the people, and giving the former direct authority over the people. Thus the citizen became responsible for and to both the states and the nation. The first problem, that of federal authority, was also solved in splendid fashion. The too vague and too wide grants of power to the central government in the Virginia Plan—certainly too extensive to win public approval—were set aside. Instead, the convention gave the national government ample authority for the needs of the day and indicated the scope of this authority as precisely as possible by listing the powers of Congress and defining with considerable precision the powers of the executive and of the judiciary. Prohibitions placed upon the central government and the states further clarified the distribution of authority. In addition to the powers granted by the Articles of Confederation, Congress was permitted to regulate commerce with foreign countries and between the states, to levy import and excise taxes, to impose direct taxes and indirect taxes, to manage Indian affairs, to issue and control currency, to establish a uniform rule of naturalization and uniform bankruptcy laws, to fix weights and measures, to regulate the militia and to make use of it "to execute the laws of the Union, suppress insurrections and repel invasions," and with its taxing power to provide for "the common defence and general welfare of the United States."

SECTIONAL COMPROMISE

Sectional differences between North and South appeared even before the Declaration of Independence, and have not yet ceased. As soon as the two were joined in a Union, their economic and social divergences, based fundamentally upon climate, created political clashes. So serious were the differences that a shrewd Tory observer, James Anderson, was able in 1776 to predict the Civil War, the nature of its issues, and its result. Between 1775 and 1787, the North and South fought over the use of Negro troops, slaves in the apportionment of contributions to the central treasury, the opening of the Mississippi, and slavery in the national lands south of the Ohio. In 1787 Southern leaders were inclined to believe that their section would surpass the North in size and population—Kentucky and Tennessee were already largely settled while the occupation of the Old Northwest had not yet begun—but they nevertheless desired constitutional safeguards against possible Northern domination of the central government. In the convention the delegates from South Carolina and Georgia were especially eager for such protective clauses, although they also desired a powerful central government. They feared that Congress would foster Northern commercial interests at the expense of Southern agriculture, and that the burden of national taxation would be distributed to the disadvantage of the South. This concern was shared to a degree by delegates from the Upper South. Sectional feeling flared in the convention when Gouverneur Morris and other Northerners tried to secure clauses which would deny to the west—at that time the Old Southwest—representation in congress on the basis of numbers. Southern delegates, led by Madison and George Mason, were well aware that Morris' proposal was directed against the South as well as the West, and vigorously opposed and defeated it.

The counting of slaves was also warmly debated and created two issues that perplexed the convention. Southerners wanted them to be counted for purposes of representation, but not for direct taxation, including poll taxes; Northerners contended that slaves should be included with whites for purposes of direct taxation, but not for congressional representation. However, neither side was adamant. The convention used a formula developed by Madison four years earlier, and decided that three-fifths of the slaves should be counted for purposes of apportionment, and that the same fraction be used for direct taxes.

Further troubles were to come. Southerners were opposed to export taxes because they would rest more heavily upon the South than upon the North, and they urged that the power to levy such taxes be denied to Congress. They also feared navigation acts which would give Northerners a virtual monopoly of Southern maritime trade and increase freight rates for the Southerners. They wanted a constitutional clause which would require the vote of two-thirds of both houses of Congress to pass such legislation, thus making passage impossible without Southern consent. Northerners were opposed to these special provisions, both because they wished to protect their own interests, and because they wanted to strengthen rather than weaken central authority. Another serious clash came because Northerners, vigorously backed by Virginians and Marylanders, insisted that the central government should definitely put an end to the oceanic slave trade. Men from the far South, especially Charles Cotesworth Pinckney, urged that the trade be continued until a supposed need for slave labor in South Carolina and Georgia was met. Pinckney further argued that the problem should be dealt with by the states, and expressed belief that South Carolina and Georgia, if left free to act, would eventually cut off the traffic of their own volition. The convention was deadlocked on these issues until the Connecticut delegation again led the way to compromise by indicating its willingness to accept something less than immediate abolition of the slave trade. The men from the Deep South were also disposed to make some sacrifice in order to achieve agreement. A special committee brought before the convention a series of proposals which were substantially approved. Thus was arranged a bargain whereby Congress was forbidden to levy export taxes, while navigation acts could be passed by a simple majority vote. Federal action against the slave trade was barred until the Constitution had been in effect for twenty years, and Congress was permitted to collect a tax of not more than $10 upon each slave imported before that time.

SEPARATION OF POWERS

Many questions of less dangerous nature faced the convention as it strove to provide for the executive. After some hesitation the delegates agreed that executive authority should be placed in the hands of a single man, the President. With the consent of a majority of the Senate, he was given power to appoint the heads of the departments, emissaries to foreign countries, officers in the armed services, and various other civil officers; he was made commander in chief of the army and the navy; he was to have authority to veto bills passed by Congress, except that his veto could be overridden when a two-thirds majority in both houses so desired; and he was generally entrusted with the execution of the will of the national government. The convention had difficulty in settling on the means of choosing the President, the length of his term, and his eligibility for more than one term. At one stage in the deliberations it was decided that he should serve for seven years without the privilege of a second term. Finally, his term was established at four years, and nothing was said to prevent him from serving two or more terms. The convention was not satisfied with letting Congress choose the President, and election by popular vote was thought to be inexpedient, especially since that would give the states no part in the choice. It would also place a heavy responsibility upon the voter, whose judgment was not always to be trusted. In the end an extremely complicated system of election was devised, which endures substantially unchanged today. Presidential electors were to be chosen in each state as its legislature should direct, their number to equal the number of Representatives plus the number of Senators from that state. The electors were to meet at the state capitals, and each was to vote for two persons for the Presidency. The votes of the electors were to be counted before both houses of Congress. The person having the largest electoral vote, and a majority of the electors was to be elected. In the event that no one had a majority, or two men were tied, the House of Representatives was to make the choice, voting by states. Should there be a tie, the House would select one of the two men; if no person had a majority the House was to make its choice from among the five highest men. The man having the second largest vote of the electors was to be the Vice-President; were there a tie for the Vice-Presidency it was to be resolved by the Senate. It was expected that the electors would exercise their independent judgment, that they would usually fail to give a majority for the Presidency to any one person, and that the President would therefore normally be chosen by the House of Representatives from men nominated by the electors. The system was to create many difficulties, some of which were removed later by constitutional amendment. Not the least defect in it is that the American people as a whole do not and never did quite understand it.

Vesting the judicial power of the United States in a Supreme Court and such other inferior courts as Congress might establish, the Constitution provided for an independent judiciary. Federal judges were to be chosen by the President with the consent of the Senate and were to serve during good behavior, which normally means for life. The jurisdiction of the federal courts was generously defined, that of the Supreme Court including cases in which two or more states were parties. State judges were instructed to obey the federal Constitution. The Constitution "and the laws of the United States, which shall be made in pursuance thereof; and all treaties made, or which shall be made, under the authority of the United States" were declared to be "the Supreme Law of the land." The Constitution was not only law, but supreme law, to be enforced in the courts. The way was thus opened for judicial interpretation of the Constitution, with the federal Supreme Court as the body which would play the leading part in such interpretation.

Dividing federal authority neatly among the legislative, executive, and judicial branches, the convention devised a system of checks and balances to prevent any one of the three, particularly the executive, from becoming too powerful at the expense of the others. Carrying out the principle of separation of powers, the convention felt it necessary to make sure so far as possible that each branch was subject to some degree of control by the others. Accordingly, the President was given a veto power, while Congress was authorized to impeach both the President and federal judges. The House of Representatives was to bring the charges, the Senate to try the accused, and a two-thirds majority was to be necessary for conviction. The judiciary, when deciding cases, was tendered the power to set aside as illegal both acts of Congress and decisions of the President when, in the opinion of the judges, they violated the Constitution, "the Supreme Law of the Land." While it has been contended in the twentieth century that the separation of powers, together with checks and balances, prevents the federal government from taking necessarily swift and decisive action, that thesis is debatable; certainly for several generations after 1787 the evil against which most Americans wished to be protected was the concentration of power in the hands of one man or a few men.

It has often been contended that the Constitution was the work of the conservatives, that its provisions were undemocratic, and that its adoption marked a conservative reaction. Certainly the Constitution was made in general by men of property, and the conservatives were in a majority in the convention. It is also true that the Constitution contains provisions much desired by the conservatives, such as those which forbade the states to coin money, put forth currency, or to make anything but gold and silver coin legal tender. A clause which prevented the states from passing laws "impairing the obligation of contracts" was also obviously a conservative device. These clauses, however, were not offensive to the liberal way of thought. Nor were the arrangements for the election of the Congress or the President markedly less democratic than were current methods for choosing state lawmakers and governors. Those who could vote for members of the lower house in the state legislature could also vote for members of the House of Representatives. True, United States senators were to be elected by members of the state legislatures rather than by the voters, but the Senates of some of the states were also chosen indirectly. There were no property qualifications for holding federal office, although these were common in the states. While the President was to be indirectly elected, the voters could have some part in the choice of the chief executive, and they could increase their role by bringing pressure upon their state legislature, since the latter decided how the electors were to be selected. On the whole, the federal Constitution was less democratic than those of North Carolina and Virginia, but more democratic than those of Maryland and New York.

ADOPTING THE CONSTITUTION

The Constitution could not be adopted without popular endorsement. Put into excellent form by a committee in which Gouverneur Morris was the leader, it was forwarded to the old Congress and to the states for approval. The convention declared that the Constitution should be considered by state conventions rather than by state legislatures, as required by the Articles of Confederation, and also that it should go into effect as soon as nine state conventions had ratified it. It may be contended that these arrangements violated the Articles of Confederation and that the Constitution of 1787 is unconstitutional. On the other hand, it cannot be denied that state conventions chosen solely to consider the Constitution were more democratic than consideration by the state legislatures. The qualifications for voting for members of the conventions were not less generous than those for electing members of the lower houses of the state legislatures. The use of conventions, as Madison pointed out, would assure a solid basis of popular consent for the Constitution, since the people of the United States would express their wishes through delegates especially chosen for the purpose. If the federal convention of 1787 displayed lack of reverence for the Articles of Confederation, its behavior may be condoned. The method of ratification was not only democratic, but it was accepted by the state legislatures, approved by a very large part of public opinion, and successfully put into effect.

The Constitution of 1787 was later described by the British statesman, William E. Gladstone, as the greatest piece of political craftsmanship ever struck off at one time by the hand of man, and the document has been superlatively praised by hosts of critics, American and foreign. With some important changes, it has withstood the trials of more than one and a half centuries, an extraordinary record. Yet the men who made it did not think of it as perfect, or even close to perfection; it had many faults, but it was the best constitution they could make under the circumstances. Some delegates opposed its adoption and left Philadelphia before the document was finished, and of the forty-two men who were present at the last sessions, three refused to sign it. The thirty-nine delegates who put their signatures to it were aware of defects in it, and even found flaws which did not exist. Nevertheless, they were quite convinced that they had performed their task competently, and that their handiwork deserved public approval. The first public reaction was to the same effect, but strenuous opposition to the Constitution soon developed.

THE PROS AND CONS

It was not at all difficult to find faults in the Constitution, and nearly every part of it was eventually denounced in the newspapers, in pamphlets, in mass meetings, in the state legislatures, and in the state conventions. The powers given to the President were too great, his term of office was too long, and the way was open for him to become a dictator; senators should be chosen by popular vote rather than by the state legislatures; federal judges should hold office for short fixed periods rather than for life; and so on and on. The three most serious criticisms were that the Constitution contained no Bill of Rights to protect the individual against federal tyranny; that power was excessively concentrated in the central government at the expense of the states; and that the South did not receive enough safeguards against Northern ascendancy. The radicals tended to oppose ratification while the liberals were divided. As was to be expected, the conservatives stoutly championed the document. Small farmers were often against it, as were state officers, who feared that adoption might mean a lessening of their own influence and importance. Merchants, wealthy planters, lawyers, and the prosperous were generally in favor of it. Thus people on the seacoast tended to favor adoption, while those in the interior tended to be opposed. Since the Tidewater was commonly overrepresented in the conventions as it was in the state legislatures, the friends of the Constitution could often send more delegates to the conventions than their own numbers warranted. Happily, those who were dissatisfied with the Constitution were divided into two camps, some being firmly convinced that the central government already had enough powers under the Articles of Confederation, while others believed that the new Constitution might be acceptable with more or less extensive changes. The champions of the Constitution eventually secured sufficient support from this second group to achieve ratification. To some extent, members of this group were won over by the arguments of the Constitution's defenders, for whom the famous *Federalist Papers,* written by Hamilton, Madison, and John Jay supplied an arsenal of arguments. These 77 essays appeared in the newspapers, cogently analyzed the Constitution, and effectively defended all its major provisions. Less persuasive were the "Letters of a Federal

Farmer," written by Richard Henry Lee, which put the case against the document.

ACCEPTANCE, STATE BY STATE

The Federalists, as the friends of the Constitution are called, won easy victories in several of the state conventions. Delaware approved by a unanimous vote on December 7, 1787, New Jersey followed without dissent on December 18, as did Georgia on January 2. Pennsylvania also gave an early endorsement. There the Anti-Federalists, knowing that they could not prevail in a convention, struggled in the state legislature to prevent election of a convention. They did not have a majority in the legislature, but could prevent the establishment of a quorum. The Federalists solved that difficulty by seizing two Anti-Federalist members and holding them in their seats until a quorum was made, then voted through the call for the election. As had been expected, the Federalists, being especially strong in Philadelphia, won an easy victory, and Pennsylvania gave its sanction on December 12 by a vote of 46 to 23. Connecticut also ratified quickly by 128 to 40.

The Constitution faced its first great test in Massachusetts. Endorsement by that state was vital because of her wealth and population. When the Massachusetts convention met, on January 9, 1788, the Anti-Federalists seemed to have a solid majority, estimated at 192 to 144. John Hancock and Samuel Adams were not enthusiastic for the Constitution and the chances for a favorable verdict did not seem good. A suggestion to Hancock that he would be a suitable candidate for the Vice-Presidency under the new regime is said to have had some effect upon him. Adams and many of the Anti-Federalists were especially concerned because the Constitution lacked a Bill of Rights. They were not satisfied by assertions that the powers of the federal government, being enumerated in the Constitution, could not be expanded or even used to the injury of personal rights. It seems that the omission occurred largely because the makers of the document thought the protections listed in a Bill of Rights unnecessary. The Massachusetts Federalists insisted upon ratification without amendments, since additional provisions would cloud the issue and doubtless force the calling of another national convention. They won over Adams and some of the Anti-Federalists by promising to give their support, as soon as the Constitution should be put into effect, to a list of amendments protecting personal rights and reserving to the states or to the people all powers "not expressly delegated" by the Constitution to the central government. In this way the Federalists managed to obtain a majority. The final vote in Massachusetts was nevertheless close, 187 to 168.

The next trial of strength, in New Hampshire, in February, was inde-

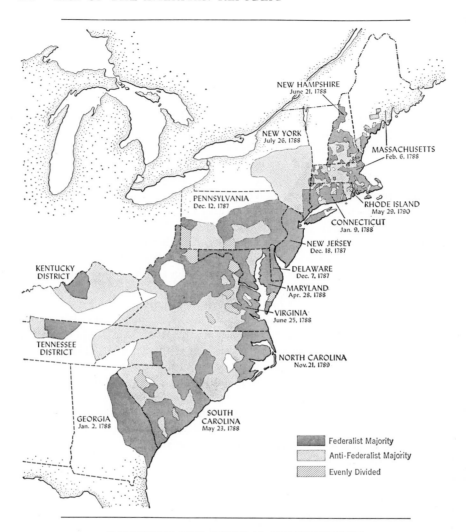

RATIFYING THE FEDERAL CONSTITUTION

cisive. So powerful was the opposition, employing the same arguments that had been used in Massachusetts, that the Federalists were forced to accept postponement of voting until June rather than risk immediate defeat. However, the Federalists were easily victorious at the polls in Maryland, and her convention voted aye by the heavy majority of 63 to 11 on April 28. South Carolina likewise offered an emphatic endorsement a month later. However, men from South Carolina's Piedmont, led by a wealthy planter named Rawlins Lowndes, denounced the Constitution because they felt that, among other faults, it did not offer protection enough to Southern interests. Both in the state legislature and in the state convention the men who had represented South Carolina at Philadelphia defended the Constitution on the ground that it had been necessary to make some concessions in order to secure some agreement; they also contended that no important Southern interest had been bargained away and that there was no disposition in the North to do injustice to the South. The planters and the merchants of Charleston, heavily overrepresented in terms of population in both the legislature and the convention, rallied behind the Federalist champions John Rutledge, Charles Cotesworth Pinckney, John Barnwell, and others; the vote was carried by a majority of 149 to 73. The Federalists obtained approval of a ninth state when the New Hampshire convention reconvened on June 18. They followed the tactic employed by the Massachusetts Federalists, offering to recommend twelve amendments, to be acted upon after the Constitution was put into effect. On June 21 the Constitution was sanctioned by a vote of 57 to 47, the twelve amendments also being proposed for consideration.

VIRGINIA'S DECISION

Although New Hampshire's vote brought the number of states which had ratified to nine, the figure set as the minimum for putting the Constitution into operation, it was obvious enough that there could be no new union without Virginia, the largest and most populous of the states. Virginia's action would in all probability be decisive, and it was not at all certain which way the Old Dominion would go. Opinion in Virginia was sharply divided; there the Anti-Federalists mustered all the arguments which were brought against the Constitution elsewhere, and especially the contention that Southern interests were in grave danger. And the Anti-Federalists found a leader in Patrick Henry, who had lost none of his magical oratory, none of his remarkable ability to appeal to the passions of his listeners. Henry was seconded by George Mason, a devout liberal who sincerely believed that the Constitution was a menace to personal liberty, and who feared that the South would suffer under it. Indeed, to protect the South, Mason had suggested in the constitutional convention that there be three presidents, one from New England, one from the Middle States, and one from the South, and that each of them possess a veto power. Refusing to sign the Constitution, Mason had returned to Virginia to do what he could to prevent its adoption. Allied to Henry and Mason were John Tyler and two of Virginia's war heroes, William Grayson and James Monroe. Henry himself was so vigorous in championing Southern interests that the Virginia Federalists suspected him of trying to form a separate Southern union. That such was the case is doubtful, but he did insist that the Constitution should not be approved unless a Bill of Rights and twenty other amendments, most of them designed to protect the South, were made part of it. His amendments would have given the South power to prevent hostile laws, and to ward off treaties injurious to Southern interests. He would not accept a promise of later amendment, insisted that the Constitution must be changed before it was approved by the Virginia convention. When that body met on June 2, the Federalists and the Anti-Federalists were almost evenly divided. That part of Virginia north of the James River, and the region of the Shenandoah Valley had voted for men supporting the Constitution; southern Virginia and Kentucky had done the opposite. However, the Federalists were ably led by Madison, Edmund Randolph, Edmund Pendleton, and "Light-Horse" Harry Lee. Randolph was of particular importance to the Federalists, not only because of the prestige of the great Randolph clan, but because he was a recent convert. In the federal convention he had refused to sign the Constitution, and had returned to Virginia convinced that it must be altered before it could be adopted. Reconsidering, he had come to the conclusion that ratification, with all of its supposed faults, was preferable to any attempt to perfect it before it was adopted, since such an effort might make the formation of a satisfactory union impossible.

Luckily for the Federalists, Henry made an error in tactics in the convention, urging that the members examine the Constitution clause by clause. Henry excelled in argument when he could employ seductive generalities, not when he had to debate about detail. His florid and emotional speeches were rebutted by Madison, who quietly and dryly demolished many of his arguments. When Henry posed as the great champion of liberty, as he had so often in the past, "Light-Horse" Harry Lee rudely denied that the defense of liberty was Henry's special province. He was not too modest to point out that he had fought throughout the war for liberty, and that he would match his military record against that of Henry. The Federalists not only held their own in debate but were fortified by solid support from Washington. There could be no real doubt that Washington would be chosen as the first President under the Constitution, and delicacy forbade him to seek election to the convention. Nevertheless, it was well known that this most respected of all Americans desired ratification; the fact that he would in all likelihood be the first President reduced alarm for Southern interests. At last, on June 25, the Virginia convention ratified by the narrow margin of 89 to 79. However, the Federalists were forced, as in Massachusetts and New Hampshire, to promise support for amendments, particularly for a Bill of Rights. The convention, in fact, urged passage not only of a Bill of Rights, but also of Henry's amendments for protection of the South.

The action of Virginia was decisive. The New York convention, meeting at Poughkeepsie on June 17, was easily dominated by the Anti-Federalists, who had the support of the farmers and rural magnates of the Hudson River Valley, and who were led by George Clinton, New York's principal war hero and a trusted and competent politician. The Federalists were outnumbered two to one, but were ably directed by Hamilton, who eloquently extolled the merits of the Constitution, which he considered far from perfect but far superior to the Articles of Confederation. Hamilton strove to postpone a decision until news could be received of the action taken by New Hampshire and Virginia. He was successful to a degree, because some of the Anti-Federalists were themselves eager to know which way the wind was blowing. When word came that New Hampshire, and more important, Virginia, had voted aye, the Anti-Federalists' majority collapsed. Again, ratification depending on prior amendment was defeated, and the Constitution was approved by 30 votes to 27 on July 26. Again a series of changes was offered for consideration.

On September 13, 1787, although North Carolina and Rhode Island were still outside the fold, the old Congress, in one of its last acts, undertook to set the new federal government in motion. It seemed that North Carolina and Rhode Island must be affected by the "band wagon" impulse, that they could hardly remain outside the new Union. The old Congress chose New York City as a temporary capital for the new national government to be, set dates for the appointment of presidential electors and for their balloting, and announced that the first Congress under the Constitution would convene on March 4, 1789, thus establishing that date for the beginning of the presidential term. A North Carolina convention, which met on July 21, 1788, had refused its sanction to the Constitution. The wealthy planters and merchants were unable to convince the numerous small farmers that their fears for personal liberty and Southern interests were unfounded. By a vote of two to one the convention demanded prior amendments containing a Bill of Rights and protection for the South. After the new government had begun to function, various factors wrought a great shift in sentiment in the state. For some months North Carolina was presumably an independent republic, but it could not remain so. Fear of tariff discrimination and information that the chances for a federal Bill of Rights were good, helped to change the minds of many Anti-Federalists, and a second convention gave its approval to the Constitution by a large majority on November 21, 1789.

Nowhere was opposition to the Constitution stronger than it was in Rhode Island, where the radicals were a potent force. In February, 1788, the state legislature refused even to call a convention, and instead ordered a popular referendum upon the Constitution. The Federalists refused to take part in the referendum, and the vote was overwhelmingly against the Constitution. Rhode Island could no more pursue an independent course than could North Carolina, but she was slow to reverse her stand. The forces which impelled North Carolina to alter her verdict finally made themselves felt in Rhode Island, and in January, 1790, her legislature called a convention. On May 29 that body, by a vote of 34 to 32, carried the state into the new Union.

Historians have often speculated on what the result might have been, had the Constitution been submitted to popular vote. Probably it would have been defeated in several states. It is nevertheless true that the merits of the Constitution were the deciding factors. Nationalistic sentiment, belief that the troubles of the 1780s were caused in part by the weakness of the central government, realization that prosperity, defense, and national interests would be advanced by the creation of a stronger central government, all of these convinced men from all walks of life that the Constitution ought to be put in force. The proponents of the Constitution had the better arguments, as debates in the conventions clearly demonstrated. The Constitution was ratified because the case for it was strong, not because it subserved the interests of particular persons and groups—although it did that too. It is a striking fact that the Anti-Federalists, after briefly striving to secure a second and revisory federal convention, accepted their defeat with little rancor. Perhaps even more remarkable than the splendid work done by the framers in the federal convention, was the manner in which the American people made their decision. The Constitution was not imposed upon them; they freely debated its merits and its shortcomings; they refrained from violence, except in minor and isolated cases, and the transition from the Confederation to the permanent Union was achieved without resort to arms, in almost ideal republican fashion.

14 A STRONGER CENTRAL GOVERNMENT

In the first elections under the Constitution its friends elected the chief executive and won control of both houses of Congress. When the votes of the presidential electors were counted, it was discovered, to no one's surprise, that Washington had been unanimously elected to the Presidency. John Adams, having the second largest number of electoral votes, became Vice-President. In the spring of 1789 Washington traveled north from Mount Vernon to New York City. His progress was marked by public celebrations and he was joyfully received in the new temporary national capital. The House of Representatives and the Senate had been organized before his arrival on April 23, and John Adams had already taken office as Vice-President. On the balcony of Federal Hall the great man soberly took his oath of office, and shortly afterward he soberly delivered the first inaugural address in the Senate chamber of that building. The new government then promptly proceeded to business.

THE FIRST PRESIDENT

Immediately after Washington's death, "Light-Horse" Harry Lee in an oration before Congress described him as "first in war, first in peace, and first in the hearts of his countrymen." When public men pass from the human scene, they are commonly fulsomely praised, their serious defects

197

being ignored or passed over lightly. Lee's eloquent appraisal has stood the test of time and investigation by scholars of later generations, although Americans were to find in Abraham Lincoln a more sympathetic and more appealing person. Little is known of the inward life of Washington. He did not wear his heart upon his sleeve, and he was shy, reserved, and even cold in the presence of strangers. He was not brilliant in intellect, graceful of phrase, or witty; he had no charm, and to some he seemed dull and conventional, both in thought and behavior. Washington was born on February 22, 1732 into a middle-class Virginia family, and was 57 years of age when he entered the presidential office. Little is known of his early years—there is no reliable information concerning his boyhood conduct in connection with cherry-trees or telling lies. He had little formal schooling, but learned to express himself decently in speech and in writing. As a surveyor and militia officer, and as the intimate of the aristocratic Fairfax family, he acquired knowledge of the ways of men along with the manners of the gentleman. In the Braddock campaign and later as a colonel of Virginia militia, he demonstrated courage, good judgment, and reliability. Acquiring Mount Vernon from the estate of his elder brother Lawrence, he also moved into the Virginia aristocracy, in which his position was firmly established by his marriage to Martha Dandridge Custis in 1759. The marriage was hardly a romantic one, for Martha Custis was a widow with two children, and they were married only seven months after the death of her first husband. Doubtless their marriage was one of both affection and convenience; at any rate, it has never been suggested that he broke his vow of fidelity. After the Seven Years' War, Washington engaged extensively in western land speculation and acquired tens of thousands of acres in what is now southwestern Pennsylvania and West Virginia. A generation later he reaped substantial profits from these invest-ments. Earning the trust of his fellow Virginians in civil as well as military matters, he emerged as a steadfast defender of American rights during the decade from 1765 to 1775. Called to the high command in the Continental army, he again displayed steady courage, unswerving devotion to the cause, and remarkable perseverance in the face of disaster. He was not a superbly gifted military commander, but he learned the art of warfare as the Anglo-American struggle progressed. Above all, he was a general who believed in fighting, and he and his men learned to fight very well. It is unlikely that any other American could have done better as commander in chief.

Those who knew Washington well were aware that he was not without minor faults. He had a bad temper, which he was usually able to control, and he did not suffer without complaining. Like other human beings, he occasionally sought to evade responsibility for his own errors, as he did in connection with the loss of Fort Washington in 1776. After the War of Independence he was the idol of veterans and public alike, as both sensed that he was utterly trustworthy. In no other American leader could be found Washington's great qualities of solid understanding, good judgment, physical and moral courage, modesty, and unswerving allegiance to honor and public service. No longer young when he became President, he had lost his teeth and was not so vigorous as he had been in his youth. It has been said that Washington rendered greater service as President than he did in the War of Independence. Such is probably not the case, for the trials which the United States underwent during his stay in the Presidency, serious as they were, were not of the first order. The principal task of the American people immediately after 1789 was to reap the full benefit from the labors and sacrifices of the preceding decades. Washington played a great part in securing these benefits, and also in planning for the American future.

WASHINGTON'S ADMINISTRATION

It was soon evident that the new central government was to be strikingly different from the one which it succeeded. The Congress quickly provided for customs duties which assured a steady and reliable revenue, large enough so that current expenses were covered and a surplus made available for other needs. The means for operation were thus provided, and the new regime, unlike the old one, contained men who could and would make use of them. As promptly as possible Washington gathered around him four principal advisers, and before many months had passed, they began to meet as the Cabinet, an institution not provided for by the Constitution, but one which proved extremely useful and which has become a permanent part of the government. As his Secretary of State, Washington chose Thomas Jefferson, easily the best man available for that post, both in talents and in experience. He secured the services of the young and brilliant Alexander Hamilton as Secretary of the Treasury; his Secretary of War was the reliable Henry Knox, who had displayed constancy on many battlefields; as his Attorney General, Washington selected Edmund Randolph, important more because of his wealth and his influence than because of his abilities. As other minor offices in the executive department were created, Washington filled them with able and responsible men, trusted Revolutionary veterans, and experienced public servants. Similarly, when it became necessary to nominate men for judicial offices, his choices were almost uniformly respectable, although he could not always get the most gifted men, because the federal bench had not yet acquired prestige and power. The new central government soon acquired stability and authority, and it moved vigorously to deal with both domestic and international problems. The Constitution provided a framework for a better American order; during Washington's two terms, flesh and muscle grew upon the skeleton, and the central government emerged as a lusty, assertive, efficient, and honest machine. The outlook was all the brighter because the Anti-Federalists had more or less gracefully accepted the verdict against them, and because the hard times of the middle 1780s had vanished.

THE BILL OF RIGHTS

One of the first tasks taken up by Congress was to draft a federal Bill of Rights. In line with the promises made to the Anti-Federalists in the struggle over ratification, Congress soon submitted twelve constitutional amendments, these being sponsored by James Madison in the House of Representatives. By 1791 ten of the proposed amendments had secured the required approval of three quarters of the state legislatures, and were incorporated into the constitution. The federal Bill of Rights contained in them is similar in form to those which protect the individual against the tyranny of the states. Among other provisions, Congress is forbidden to establish a church, to prohibit the free exercise of religion, to abridge freedom of speech, the press, the right of assembly, and the right of petition. The citizen's right to keep and bear arms is assured, and individuals are protected against "unreasonable searches and seizures." General warrants are forbidden; double jeopardy is outlawed; the right to trial by jury is guaranteed, together with other protections in criminal cases; excessive bails, fines, and cruel and unusual punishments are forbidden; private property is not to be taken for public use without just compensation; and no person is to "be deprived of life, liberty, or property, without due process of law." The ninth and tenth amendments were attempts to defend generally the rights of the people and the authority of the states. In the first of these it was asserted that "The Enumeration in the Constitution of certain rights, shall not be construed to deny or disparage others retained by the people." In the tenth amendment it was declared that "The powers not delegated to the United States by the Constitution, nor prohibited by it to the States, are reserved to the States respectively, or to the people." Thus, on paper at least, the personal freedoms of the individual were protected against tyranny on the part of the central government as well as by the states. After the Civil War the Fourteenth Amendment was to supply further powerful protection against arbitrary action by the states.

While the rights of the individual have frequently been violated by both the federal government and the states since 1791, the constitutional protections have commonly shielded the innocent, the weak, and the unorthodox from political and judicial oppression; on occasion, as the founding fathers expected, they have also proved to be a bulwark covering criminals against just punishment. It was assumed by the constitution-builders of the eighteenth century that it was more important to protect one innocent person than to punish many guilty ones.

THE FEDERAL JUDICIARY

Another of the basic constructive works of the first Congress was the Judiciary Act of September, 1789. The Constitution provided for a Supreme Court and defined its original jurisdiction, but left it to the Congress to establish other federal courts and to define their jurisdictions. The Judiciary Act established at least one district court in every state to serve as trial courts. Above them were circuit courts, which could hear appeals. The Supreme Court was given five judges, and was tendered appellate jurisdiction. Arrangements were made for writs, so that appeals could be appropriately made from one court to another. Since it was believed that the federal courts would not have a vast amount of business, the circuit courts were not staffed by separate judges; each was to be presided over by two judges of the Supreme Court and one federal district judge. John Jay, the first Chief Justice of the United States, took office on September 26, 1789, and the federal courts soon began to function. As had been expected, they were not very busy for some years, and they did not at first command dignity and prestige.

HAMILTON AND HIS PROGRAM

Washington's domestic policies were largely supplied by Alexander Hamilton, who was fertile in planning and who enjoyed the confidence of the chief executive. Hamilton's influence was not confined to the treasury; indeed Washington sought and often followed his advice on a wide variety of questions, both domestic and foreign. Born illegitimately on the West Indian island of Nevis in 1755, Hamilton was under 35 years of age when he took office at the treasury. Of Scottish and French ancestry, he had migrated to the mainland as a youth; he had made an enviable reputation as an officer in the Continental army, serving for several years as Washington's aide-de-camp. In 1780 he had married Elizabeth Schuyler, daughter of General Philip Schuyler, and had thus become attached to one of the great families of New York. After the War of Independence, he became a prominent lawyer, and also engaged successfully in politics. His role in the making and adoption of the Constitution has already been mentioned. Of middle height, slender, graceful, he was gay, charming, and intellectually gifted. Although he was a debater of marked ability, he had no feeling for the beauty of language, and he wrote rather tediously. He was, however, remarkably skillful in planning, and astute in finding the means to execute his projects. He thought logically, he possessed great moral courage, he was honest about money, and he was apt to be impatient with men whose talents were inferior to his own. In youth he had been an adventurer, lustful for success and military glory; he continued to seek them in his maturity. Despite the circumstances of his birth, as an army officer and the husband of Elizabeth Schuyler he had acquired lofty social status; he was possibly all the more determined to assert his own superiority because he had been forced to begin life under a cloud, through no fault of his own.

Hamilton was far more conscious of the defects of mankind than he was of human ideals, and he believed profoundly in the principle of aristocracy. In an imperfect world unlikely to improve, he insisted that authority should rest in the qualified few, of whom, of course, he was one. He was "realistic" even about the qualified few. They would be governed by their own interests, hence government must care for those interests to secure their solid support. He proposed to use the power of the central government to foster American industry and commerce, and from that development to gain the support of manufacturers, merchants, lawyers, wealthy planters, and men of means in general.

THE NATIONAL DEBT

In a series of reports to Congress in 1790 and 1791, Hamilton presented his program and secured adoption of important parts of it, but only after bitter contests which led to the creation of the first American political parties. In January, 1790, he urged that the United States pay all of the national debts piled up before 1789 at par, and also the debts of the states incurred in wagering the War of Independence. He desired that the holders of national and state securities be compensated with new United States bonds. Thus the credit of the central government would be established beyond cavil, and the possessors of the new bonds, men of wealth and influence, would find it to their interest to support the new government. There could be no sound objection to the payment of the nation's debts owed to foreigners, chiefly the French and Dutch, and these Congress readily agreed to pay, to a total of about $11,700,000. It was otherwise with that portion of the national debt owed to Americans, which totaled more than $44 million and was largely in the form of "certificates of indebtedness." These certificates, issued in return for goods and services, had sunk in value during the 1780s. The original holders in many cases had been forced to sell them at prices far below par, even as low as 15 percent of their face value. Shrewd speculators had bought up the paper and would profit handsomely, while the original holders, who had helped the United States in times of greatest need, would not. James Madison, indignant because Hamilton's scheme would enrich the speculators, urged that it be revised so that the original holders of the certificates would be re-warded according to their deserts. Hamilton contended that it would be almost impossible to devise and execute a plan which would achieve Madison's purpose—in this matter, at least, he had doubts concerning his own powers. Congress supported Hamilton by a large majority, some members hastily sending out agents to buy up certificates at low prices before it became known that they were to be refunded at par. Madison and others even more strenuously opposed assumption of the state debts, of which Hamilton proposed to pay $21,500,000. Some of the states, especially in the South, had paid off large parts of their war debts, while others, including the New England states, had not. There was objection not only on the ground of favoritism, but also on the ground that transfer of the debts to the federal government would increase its authority. Although the measure was defeated in the House of Representatives by a close vote, Hamilton persevered. The Virginians wished to have the national capital located on the Potomac River, but lacked the votes to achieve their purpose. Hamilton and Madison entered into a bargain, arranged by Jefferson, whereby Madison supplied enough votes to assure federal assumption of the state debts, while Hamilton's support for moving the capital southward helped carry the day for the Virginians. Accordingly, arrangements were made to establish the District of Columbia, to use Philadelphia as a temporary capital for ten years, and to remove the central government to Washington in 1800. At the time the selection of a site on the Potomac seemed sensible enough, but with the subsequent increase in federal activity, the warmth and high humidity of the long Washington summers became serious obstacles to government efficiency. Assumption of the state debts was also a doubtful measure. It was hardly necessary to establish the credit of the United States, and the favoritism which inevitably accompanied it caused serious dissension.

THE BANK OF THE UNITED STATES

Shortly before Christmas in 1790 Hamilton presented to the House of Representatives a report in which he urged the creation of a Bank of the United States. He asked that Congress charter the bank for a period of twenty years. It was to be both a private bank and a public institution, the United States to hold twenty percent of the $10 million of capital stock, with private investors having the remainder. It was to have the right to carry on the usual banking operations, and to issue a paper currency. It would also serve as a depository for federal funds, and would be able to lend money to the federal government in case of need. It was modeled upon the Bank of England, although Hamilton declared that it was essentially more like the Bank of Amsterdam. Hamilton correctly predicted that such a bank, supported by the prestige of the national government, would supply a stable and widely circulating paper currency, which was sorely needed.

However, the measure was bitterly attacked by Jefferson, Madison, and other men in public life. Again Hamilton had devised a scheme which would achieve important public purposes. However, it might also enrich a few private persons, for it was obvious that those who could afford to buy stock in the bank were likely to profit from its connection with the government, since the national bank was certain to have greater prestige and greater opportunities for profitable investment than other banks. Again the cry of favoritism was raised; and it is quite true that the genius of Hamilton was equal to producing a plan which would have achieved his public purposes without enriching a few privileged investors. Jefferson and Madison also opposed the measure because it gave advantage to businessmen over those who lived on the land, and to Northerners over Southerners. Moreover, they looked upon the bank as another device for excessive concentration of power in the central government. Still further, Jefferson denounced the measure as unconstitutional, pointing out in an opinion requested by Washington that the Constitution contained no reference to such a bank, that Congress had not been specifically given the power to incorporate, and that the Tenth Amendment, then in process of adoption, declared that "the powers not delegated to the United States by the Constitution, nor prohibited by it to the States, are reserved to the States respectively, or to the people." Opposed to the expansion of federal authority, at least when it was to be exercised by Hamilton, Jefferson called for "strict construction" of the Constitution. In defense of the constitutionality of the bank, Hamilton contended in a paper prepared for Washington that the creation of the bank could be justified on the basis of "implied powers." The enumerated powers gave Congress the right to regulate currency, and to provide for the borrowing of money. The bank would be a useful instrument for safeguarding public funds, for borrowing money, and for regulating currency. He neatly stated the doctrine of implied powers: "If the *end* be clearly comprehended within any of the specified powers, and if the measure have an obvious relation to that *end*, if it is not forbidden by any particular provision of the constitution, it may safely be deemed to come within the compass of the national authority." In support of this line of thought, he cited Article I, Section 8, of the Constitution, which declared that the Congress was to have power to "make all Laws which shall be necessary and proper for carrying into Execution" the delegated powers. In rebuttal Jefferson argued that the bank was not "necessary and proper," that "convenient" and "necessary" were not synonyms. Jefferson's position was doubtless superior in logic, but Washington, uncertain of the constitutional merits of the dispute, decided to support his Secretary of the Treasury, since his department was the one directly affected. Congress also followed Hamilton's leadership and the bank was established, with speculators jostling each other to secure stock in it. Investors did not profit so handsomely as they had expected, but after some initial difficulties, the bank operated successfully until the expiration of its charter.

THE WHISKEY TAX

Another of Hamilton's measures which stimulated controversy was the excise tax on the manufacture of distilled liquors, which Congress imposed at his urging. He sponsored the tax in part to increase federal revenue, and in part to exert national authority. The tax was certain to be unpopular, there being in those days no prohibitionists to support it. Hamilton expected that backwoods farmers would offer some resistance, and so they did. Among them whiskey was not only consumed in quantity, but was also used as a medium of exchange in lieu of money. As early as 1792 farmers in the South and in western Pennsylvania held meetings in which they denounced the tax. By 1794 backwoodsmen in western Pennsylvania were threatening armed resistance, thus creating the opportunity which Hamilton had sought for the federal government to flex its muscles. When the farmers gathered in arms, despite proclamations from Washington ordering them to disperse and return to their homes, the President called out the militia in Pennsylvania and neighboring states, placed it under the command of "Light-Horse" Harry Lee, and ordered him to suppress the rebellion. The appearance of the army persuaded the farmers that the law must be obeyed, and the disorders promptly came to an end. Two of the leaders of the "Whiskey Rebellion" were tried and convicted on charges of treason, but were pardoned by Washington.

Not all of the Hamilton program was carried out. Toward achieving prosperity and a well-rounded economy, Hamilton submitted a report on manufactures to the House of Representatives in December, 1791. In this document he called for a protective tariff that would enable American manufacturers to compete successfully with European, especially the British. He also proposed a system of bounties to encourage agriculture, and the building of roads and canals under federal sponsorship. He was unable to muster powerful support for these measures, which Jefferson, Madison, and their followers considered to be unwise, unnecessary, conducive to federal tyranny, and unconstitutional.

THE FIRST POLITICAL PARTIES

By 1792, indeed, the Hamilton program had brought about the creation of two political factions, which soon became the first political parties. Supporting the program were merchants, lawyers, manufacturers, speculators, wealthy planters, men who leaned toward aristocracy and conservatism, and many others, including New England farmers who wanted public order and stability. The Federalists, as they came to be called, were most numerous in New England and the coastal areas to the southward. While they generally supported Hamilton's ventures, the rank and file admired rather than trusted him; John Adams, who had less sympathy for aristocracy and privilege than did Hamilton, became the most popular Federalist in public life.

JEFFERSON AND THE DEMOCRATIC-REPUBLICANS

The faction which opposed the Federalists was organized by Jefferson and Madison, who were close personal and political friends, and who made an alliance with the potent George Clinton of New York before Washington's first term had ended. The party which grew from this alliance was given the name "Republican" by its supporters, while it was called the "Democratic Party" by its opponents, the words "democratic" and "democracy" signifying mob rule at that time. The Democratic-Republican Party attracted as followers, mechanics, reformers, and men who had received few or no favors from the federal government. It was the strongest in the South and in the interior, weakest on the coast and in New England. Although dislike for favoritism and corruption, both of which appeared at the national capital within a few months after Washington's inauguration, was a powerful cementing force among them, the Democratic-Republicans were not merely dissatisfied "outs." The principles to which Jefferson gave allegiance were the dominant philosophy of the party. He believed that humankind was basically good and capable of improvement, and that it was safe to entrust political power to the average man because in the long run he would come to the right decisions. Jefferson was particularly disposed to place faith in the freeholding farmer, who was presumably sturdy, honest, and independent-minded. He hoped that the United States would remain fundamentally agrarian, and he favored doing nothing to encourage industry or the expansion of commerce; these, he thought, debased the men who engaged in them. In Jefferson there was also a distrust of government, which he saw as a necessary evil. The concentration of power in the central government which Hamilton so greatly desired alarmed the Virginian, all the more because Hamilton's program offered special favors to "insiders" and was accompanied by public corruption. A devoted republican, but not a believer in "democracy" as it afterward developed in the United States, he was enlightened, progressive, and civilized—in sum, a liberal. The doctrine of "strict construction" of the Constitution did not form the core of his political philosophy; rather it was the means by which he strove to prevent the remodeling of the United

States on the Hamilton formula, and to promote his own ideal America.

By 1792 the Democratic-Republicans and the Federalists were engaged in heated political warfare. Jefferson and Hamilton, each assisted by other writers, were belaboring each other in the newspapers and in pamphlets. Political charges and countercharges not only filled the public prints, but echoed in the halls of Congress. Federalists denounced Jefferson as an enemy of the Constitution and as one who intrigued against the administration of which he was a part. Jefferson's followers not only assailed the Hamilton program, but attacked its author's character, claiming that he profited personally from his position as Secretary of the Treasury. An investigation disclosed only that Hamilton had carried on an illicit affair with one Mrs. James Reynolds; he had scrupulously avoided using his knowledge of public business to fill his own purse. Although he was a very successful lawyer in the last years of his life, he died a poor man.

Deeply disturbed by the quarrel between his confidential advisers, Washington tried to compose their differences, but in vain. In fact, because Washington had sided with Hamilton rather than with him, Jefferson informed the President that he would resign his office after the election of 1792. Although Washington's sympathies lay with the Federalists, and control of Congress was bitterly contested in that election, Jefferson and his followers did not seek to prevent a second term for Washington. On the contrary, Jefferson urged the President to seek reelection, because Washington was a great unifying force in the nation. In any case, Washington could not have been defeated. No elector voted against him, but John Adams, the Federalist candidate for the Vice-Presidency, was opposed by the Democratic-Republican George Clinton, Adams winning by 77 votes to 50. Soon afterward Jefferson temporarily retired to private life, in July, 1793, and Hamilton withdrew from the Cabinet in January, 1795. The departure of the two men from the circle of Washington's advisers did not lessen the violence of political warfare, indeed it may have added to its heat.

PROSPERITY AND EXPANSION

The clouds of partisan strife cannot hide the fact that the new national government, nourished by the proceeds from its customs duties and the excise tax, relieved by the redistribution of its debts, and capably administered by Washington and his associates, was remarkably successful. The economic health of the nation became once more apparent, and even the western problems which had been so trying in the period of the Confederation became less onerous. With settlers continuing to move westward, Vermont (1791), Kentucky (1792), and Tennessee (1796) became states, and eastern Ohio was rapidly occupied. In 1790 Washington received Alexander McGillivray, king of the Creek Indians, in New York, and entered into a treaty of friendship which tended to soothe irritations in the Old Southwest. The President was forced to resort to the sword in order to secure a measure of quiet north of the Ohio. In 1791, an expedition led by the veteran General Arthur St. Clair marched against the tribes of the Old Northwest, but was checked and forced to fall back. The humiliating defeat of St. Clair at the hands of the red men drove the new government to increased effort, and General "Mad Anthony" Wayne was entrusted with the task of retrieving the situation. Chosen for the assignment because of his boldness and his lust for fighting, Wayne, nevertheless refused to march until he was well prepared. Gathering a new army, he patiently trained it until it had acquired firm discipline, then moved forward in 1794. The northwestern Indians under Chief Little Turtle withdrew before him, but finally turned to face him in the Maumee Valley, near the present Toledo, Ohio. In the Battle of Fallen Timbers which followed, the Indians were routed. A fort which the British had built on the Maumee refused to give them refuge; the disheartened red men were compelled to make peace and an extensive cession of territory at Greenville in the following year. The American advance into the Old Northwest continued, and within twenty years the power of the tribes in that region was to be utterly broken. During that same period the Creek were also to go down in final defeat. Neither red men nor European palefaces could stem the onrush of American expansion.

15 FOREIGN ENTANGLEMENTS AND
DOMESTIC POLITICS

REVOLUTION AND WAR IN EUROPE

The year 1789 marked the achievement of stability in the American union, and also the beginning of the French Revolution, which convulsed France and then all of Europe. The fall of the Bastille on July 14, 1789 signaled the collapse of absolute monarchy in France, and Louis XVI became a constitutional monarch two years later. This political change was accompanied by sweeping social reforms, both being resisted by the Crown, most of the nobles, and a large part of the clergy, for they bitterly resented the loss of their ancient powers and privileges. Disorder and bloodshed disturbed not only the French people, but the peoples and rulers of Europe generally. The Hohenzollern king of Prussia and the Habsburg Holy Roman Emperor in Vienna, conscious that the old regime in France could not go down without the most serious repercussions in their own territories, undertook to restore the royal authority of Louis XVI, and their armies began to advance toward Paris in 1792. They never reached the French capital, and their invasions on behalf of their brother monarch led to the creation of the first French Republic. A Convention which had been called to prepare a constitution for France ordered the imprisonment and then the execution of the king, waged ferocious war against internal enemies, and struggled desperately against foreign foes. Britain, appalled by the overthrow of the old regime in France and fearing that the French republicans would not only export their political ideals but seek the expansion of France, entered the war as an ally of the Habsburgs and the Hohenzollerns. There followed the Reign of Terror, in which the Convention and its committees executed thousands of supposed opponents of the republic. The French Revolutionists proved able not only to defend their country, but to carry the war to the lands of their enemies. The theatre of warfare constantly widened, and Europe suffered constant military, political, and social upheaval until 1815. France remained technically a republic under the Directory (1795–1799) and the Consulate (1800–1804), but Napoleon Bonaparte became the master of the nation in 1799 and officially its emperor in 1804. Under his brilliant leadership France threatened dominance of all of Europe. Against France and Napoleon Britain struggled bitterly, making full use of her sea power, raising up alliances against the French, and pouring money into the war effort. The United States could not but be affected by the mighty contest, especially since the exercise of British sea power injured both American purses and persons.

THE WAR AND AMERICAN SHIPPING

The struggle between revolutionary France and her enemies endured for twenty-three years and involved the United States because of economic, sentimental, and ideological interests. Moreover, American security was directly affected, favorably if both France and Britain should be weakened by the contest, unfavorably if one or the other were overwhelmingly triumphant. Since the Americans traded extensively with both antagonists and their empires, the American economy could not but be influenced. Both the producers of raw materials in the United States and the owners of the ships that carried them on the Atlantic expected to continue these activities, despite the war, and indeed hoped to secure more profitable markets as a result of the conflict. Presumably both the British and French would want American products even more than in time of peace. During the War of Independence the United States had espoused the doctrine of "free ships, free goods," which meant that neutral vessels would not be molested by belligerents in war time. But the British had not accepted this principle, for it would have deprived the royal navy of the right to prevent war materials from reaching France and her allies. In 1793 the British

Privy Council authorized the seizure and search of American vessels suspected of taking goods to French colonies or of carrying French colonial products to France. These orders were effectively and high-handedly enforced, and the American merchant marine suffered as a consequence. Before long the French began to consider ways and means whereby American trade with "perfidious Albion" might be interrupted.

The British Orders in Council created another American grievance, for they authorized the impressment of British sailors employed on American merchant vessels. Britain badly needed sailors for her navy, and they were difficult to secure, for British tars were poorly paid and harshly treated. Pressgangs had long "enlisted" men in British ports, and their operations in the British Isles had become accepted by need and by custom. However, impressment in American ports had been bitterly resented since before the era of independence, and the forceable seizure of British nationals from American ships aroused indignation in the United States. The British government took the view that such kidnappings ought to be welcomed by the United States, since the men carried off would strengthen Britain in her fight against French anarchy and despotism. Americans protested that grabbing a British seaman from an American ship, whether a merchant sailor or a deserter from the royal navy, was the same as an invasion of American territory. Such seizures were all the more exasperating because it was not always possible to tell the difference between American and British sailors, and British naval parties often carried off bona fide American citizens. Impressment was both insulting and injurious to the new nation, and the practice could not fail to arouse hatred against Britain. Damage which the French inflicted upon the American merchant marine, grievous though it might be, did not include the "shanghaiing" of American sailors.

Sentimentally, at the beginning of the long struggle, the Americans were inclined to favor France, because of France's aid in the War of Independence, as well as the legacy of hostility toward Britain which derived from the same war. Accordingly, some Americans were disposed to look upon the European conflict as a continuation of the contest which had temporarily ended at Yorktown. On the other hand, the ancient distrust of France, which had been so pervasive among the Americans as colonials, persisted, especially in New England. American ideological sympathies were badly divided, for many Americans believed that the British were fighting for order and decency, while as many fancied the cause of France to be that of liberty and humanity. Those who favored the British stressed the executions of Louis XVI, Queen Marie Antoinette, and countless others in France; the French assault against organized religion; and the French destruction of property rights. The champions of France conceded excesses and untoward events in the Revolution, but insisted that France was struggling in behalf of republicanism, social equality, and personal freedom. As the war proceeded, more and more of the American people took sides, and John Adams afterward estimated that one-third of the Americans were pro-British, one-third were pro-French, and one-third were neutral. Whatever their bias, Americans generally did not wish to enter the war on one side or the other.

NEUTRALITY

The pro-British element in the United States was largely in the Federalist camp, while those who favored the French were principally followers of Jefferson and Madison. Thus the parties already taking shape on domestic issues found themselves at odds on foreign policy as well. In the spring of 1793 Washington asked the advice of his Cabinet as to the course which the United States should pursue. He was especially concerned lest the nation be dragged into the war by its pledge in the Franco-American alliance of 1778 to help defend France's West Indian islands against British attack. Hamilton advised that the United States maintain neutrality, although his sympathies lay with the British. He contended that the treaty of 1778 had lapsed, since it had been made with a French government that no longer existed; therefore the United States was no longer obliged to assist in the defense of the French islands. Jefferson, whose sentiments were pro-French, also counseled neutrality. Unlike Hamilton, he correctly argued that the treaty was still in force, on the principle that governments inherit the obligations of their predecessors. He pointed out, however, that the United States need not feel compelled to help the French resist British aggression in the Caribbean, because it could be claimed with some justice that France had failed to execute certain other sections of the alliance. As it turned out, France did not, then or later, demand American help in the protection of her possessions, so the question of the meaning and validity of the alliance was never settled. There could be no doubt as to the desire of the American people as a whole for neutrality, and on April 22 Washington issued the Neutrality Proclamation, in which he warned American citizens to avoid hostile acts against any of the warring nations.

THE GENÊT AFFAIR

It was far easier to proclaim neutrality than it was to maintain it. The ignorance and impudence of Edmond Charles Genêt, first minister of the French Republic to the United States, promptly brought on a crisis in Franco-American relations. Landing in South Carolina two weeks before the issuance of the proclamation, Genêt had come to the United States to win American friendship and to negotiate a new commercial treaty, or at least so his instructions said. Genêt, who should have known better, assumed that the Americans would do whatever France desired; that they and their government must be eager to help mankind through the French cause. He was perhaps misled by warm receptions which he had received as he traveled northward to Philadelphia. En route he commissioned four American vessels as French privateers and laid plans to raise armies to attack the Floridas and Louisiana in behalf of France, Spain being at the time one of France's enemies. In Philadelphia Washington received Genêt coolly, and Secretary of State Jefferson told the French minister that he could not commission American troops and ships for French service. After pledging himself to behave, Genêt nevertheless proceeded to send out another privateer, despite a protest from Jefferson. Pro-French elements were voicing their sentiments through a host of newly formed Democratic societies, and in the belief that the course of the President was unpopular, Genêt even threatened to appeal over his head to the people. These antics sadly embarrassed Jefferson, Madison, and even the Democratic societies. Washington and his Cabinet decided to demand the recall of the reckless diplomat. However, by this time Genêt's friends had fallen from power in Paris, and his enemies, the Jacobins, had replaced them. The Jacobins sent a new minister to Philadelphia, with instructions to ship Genêt home under arrest. In France Genêt might have faced the guillotine, and he was not at all eager to leave the United States. Putting aside the vexations which the clumsy Frenchman had heaped upon him, Washington generously offered him asylum as a political refugee. Possibly sobered by his experiences, Genêt married a daughter of Governor George Clinton, settled down as a gentleman farmer, and later achieved some fame as a useful inventor.

ANGLO-AMERICAN RELATIONS

The Genêt affair had hardly ended when relations with Britain entered upon a period of acute strain. The British should have been pleased by the passage of the Neutrality Act of June, 1794, which forbade the enlistment of American citizens in the armies of foreign countries and the preparation of armed vessels in American harbors for foreign service. The Act indicated the eagerness of the United States to avoid involvement in the war. Two months earlier it had been learned that the British Orders in Council which interfered so seriously with American maritime trade had been revoked, and an embargo which Congress had placed upon American shipping in protest against the orders had been lifted. At the same time Washington, with the approval of the Senate, had appointed Chief Justice John Jay as a special envoy to London in the hope that he would be able to achieve a settlement of the major troubles between the two nations. However Jay did not find a yielding spirit in the British capital. Hamilton had indiscreetly informed George Hammond, newly arrived in Philadelphia as the first British minister to the United States, that there was no danger of the United States going to war to secure the redress of remaining grievances. This information was relayed to his superiors by Hammond, and convinced them that it was not necessary to make any important concessions in their dealings with Jay. Instead, they flattered Jay, whom they found susceptible to sweet words, and secured his approval of a treaty which was on the surface highly favorable to Britain. The treaty, signed in November, 1794, said nothing about impressment and nothing about the encouragement which British officials had offered to the Indians of the Old Northwest. It contained a number of complex commercial provisions which were generally favorable to Britain. British exports to the United States were to receive a most-favored-nation treatment. American vessels were to be permitted to trade in the British East Indies, and American ships carrying less than seventy tons were to be allowed to visit the British West Indies, provided that they did not load cotton, sugar, or molasses in the Caribbean. The pre-Revolutionary debts owed by Americans to British merchants, a dispute concerning the northeastern boundary between the United States and Canada, and payment for illegal seizures of American ships were to be settled later by joint commissions. (Actually, a large part of the debts owed by American citizens to British citizens was eventually paid by the American government.) Britain promised to evacuate her troops from the forts which she still held on American soil in the Great Lakes region as speedily as possible.

There was no doubt that Jay, handicapped by Hamilton's assurance to Hammond and by his own vanity, had made a bad bargain. Indeed, Lord Grenville, the British Secretary of State who had dealt with Jay, had done in the American at almost every turn. The commercial provisions of the treaty were highly favorable to Britain; the silence concerning impressment and the rights of neutrals was also a British triumph; and the very fact of its signing, although it did not technically conflict with the terms of the Franco-American alliance of 1778, aroused anti-American feeling in Paris. As it turned out, the commercial provisions were not quite so injurious to the United States as they first appeared to be, because the British chose not to enforce the seventy-ton limit for American ships going to His Majesty's islands in the Caribbean. But at the time the only major concession secured by Jay was Britain's agreement to remove her men from the American side of the Great Lakes.

When the terms of the agreement became known in the United States, there was a tumultuous uproar against it, the Democratic-Republicans denouncing it in most violent language. Even John Rutledge, a Federalist recently appointed as Chief Justice of the United States, joined in the chorus of disapproval. When the President consulted his Cabinet, Edmund Randolph, who had succeeded Jefferson as Secretary of State, advised

Washington not to sign the treaty. Most of the Federalists favored ratification, although they reluctantly admitted that the agreement was not what it should be. Washington coolly assessed the situation and saw that it was better to accept a bad bargain and maintain the peace than to refuse it and very likely become involved in a war with Britain. He foresaw that time and growing American power would eventually compel the British to be more liberal in their treatment of American goods and American persons on the seas. He also realized that the withdrawal of the British from the northwestern posts was of the first importance to the United States, since it would open up the rich territories of the Old Northwest as far as the shores of Lake Superior. American rights on the seas and markets for American goods beyond them could wait; continued British occupation of the Old Northwest might permanently limit the growth of the United States. Accordingly the President firmly requested the Senate to ratify the treaty, and despite resistance by the Democratic-Republicans, the necessary two-thirds majority was secured. The followers of Jefferson and Madison then tried to prevent the treaty from going into effect by denying funds necessary to carry out its provisions. They claimed that the House of Representatives could cancel the bargain since the appropriations needed the approval of that body. Washington insisted that the lower house should accept the agreement made by the President and the Senate in good faith, and the requisite funds were finally voted. Thus in the summer of 1795 the danger of war with Britain was temporarily reduced; in the following year the redcoats withdrew from American soil to Canada.

PINCKNEY'S TREATY

If the wars of the French Revolution and Napoleon brought embarrassments to the United States, they also brought opportunities and solid gains. It may even be contended that Britain would have clung to the northwestern forts indefinitely had she not been involved in war with France. Certainly, the conflict in Europe impelled Spain to make important concessions to the American republic. In 1795 Spain withdrew her support from France's enemies and sought instead French friendship. At the urging of James Monroe, who was then minister to France, the French government recommended to the Spanish that they undertake to appease the Americans. Kentuckians and Tennesseeans were threatening to open up the Mississippi River by force if necessary, and the ministers of the Spanish monarch concluded that it would be well to avoid serious trouble with the United States. As a result, Thomas Pinckney, sent as an envoy extraordinary to Madrid, was able to secure extensive concessions from Spain in the Treaty of San Lorenzo, often known as Pinckney's Treaty, which was signed in October, 1795. With the United States offering nothing in return, Spain gave up the right to interfere with American navigation on

THE OLD NORTHWEST AND THE OLD SOUTHWEST

the Mississippi, and permitted Americans to use New Orleans as a place of deposit for goods passing down the river en route to sea. At the end of three years, the right of deposit was to be renewed, either at New Orleans or some other port. Spain also recognized the American claim that the thirty-first parallel was the boundary between West Florida and the United States. Still further, the Spanish monarchy promised to restrain Indians residing in Spanish possessions from raiding American territory. Pinckney's Treaty was a triumph for American diplomacy and was, of course, joyfully approved by the President and the Senate. Whatever may be said about the inability of the American government to secure rights and privileges for Americans on the high seas and abroad at the beginning of the European struggle, it is a striking fact that the British retreated from the Old Northwest and the Spaniards from the Old Southwest by 1796, only seven years after the United States had secured a strong central government. The contention of friends of the Constitution in 1787 and 1788 that its adoption would promote the security and growth of the nation was soon proven to be correct.

THE ELECTION OF 1796: THE FAREWELL ADDRESS

As the election of 1796 approached, the Federalists would have been delighted to support Washington for a third term in the Presidency. But Washington was 64 years of age, disgusted with the vexations of public office, exasperated by attacks from the Democratic-Republicans, and eager finally to return to Mount Vernon. Although his espousal of the Federalist cause had won him many political enemies, so that he might not have been able to win reelection by a unanimous electoral vote, he could not have failed to win a third term had he wished it. Actually, it is not at all certain that the Democratic-Republicans could have secured the choice of even one anti-Washington elector. Removing himself from the presidential contest, Washington published in a newspaper his "Farewell Address," which had long been in process of preparation and which was written in part by Madison and Hamilton for him. The counsel which the great Virginian gave to the American people with respect to foreign affairs is well known, or rather, should be well known. With his usual good judgment, he advised his compatriots to steer clear of "permanent alliances" and involvement in European affairs. A moderate-sized army and navy would provide for the ordinary needs of defense. Said he, "we may safely trust to temporary alliances for extraordinary emergencies." It is apparent that Washington understood the impossibility of complete isolation, and that he wished the United States to profit by rather than to lose because of the troubles and agonies of Europe.

It is not commonly observed that the "Farewell Address" also most soberly and very emphatically denounced sectionalism. Washington said:

It is of infinite moment that you should properly estimate the immense value of your national Union to your collective and individual happiness; that you should cherish cordial, habitual and immoveable attachment to it; accustoming yourselves to think and speak of it as of the palladium of your political safety and prosperity; watching for its preservation in jealous anxiety; discountenancing whatever may suggest even a suspicion that it can in any event be abandoned, and indignantly frowning upon the first dawning of every attempt to alienate any portion of our country from the rest, or to enfeeble the sacred ties which now link together the various parts.

Washington continued,

The name *American,* which belongs to you, in your national capacity, must always exalt the just pride of patriotism, more than appellations derived from local discriminations. With slight shades of difference, you have the same religion, manners, habits, and political principles. You have in a common cause fought and triumphed together. The independence and liberty you possess are the work of joint councils, and joint efforts; of common dangers, sufferings and successes.

But, added the President, however powerful were such sentiments, they were far less important than the interests which bound together the nation, for "every portion of our country finds the most commanding motives for carefully guarding and preserving the union of the whole." He saw the North profiting from manufacturing and carrying the raw and precious materials of the South; on the other hand, the South gained as the North supplied new markets for her raw materials at home and abroad. Similarly, the West provided, and would increasingly provide, markets for the goods made in the East; in turn, the East would not only offer to the West "supplies requisite to its growth and comfort," but military protection and political influence which would secure for the West "the secure enjoyment of indispensable outlets for its own productions." Washington was utterly against political parties organized on geographical bases, and he warned against sectional "jealousies and heartburnings." Unlike his contemporary, Patrick Henry, Washington was utterly unable to glory on one occasion in the name American, and on another to try to pit one section against another. He was not, as Daniel Webster later became, first a sectionalist and then a nationalist; nor was he like John C. Calhoun, who was a nationalist and later a sectionalist. The towering Virginian was steadily devoted to the nation from its birth to his death. When he died in retirement three years later, his detractors, who were not few while he occupied the Presidential office, joined in the universal lament.

THE ADAMS ADMINISTRATION

Had the Federalists, girding for the Presidential campaign of 1796, given their support to their next outstanding leader after Washington, they must have chosen Alexander Hamilton. Although Hamilton had continued to exercise great influence upon governmental policy even after his resignation from the treasury in January, 1795, he was not popular in the nation as a whole, and was not well liked even in his own party. Rank and file Federalists in New England were firmly behind John Adams, and the party chose the safe and sound moderate conservative from rural Quincy rather than the gifted financier and manipulator from New York. For the Vice-Presidency, as a counterbalance to Adams, the Federalists put forward Thomas Pinckney, freshly home from his diplomatic victory at San Lorenzo and admired as a worthy and spirited member of the Southern seaboard aristocracy. Against these men, with their impressive records, the Democratic-Republicans offered Jefferson, whose talents, political and other, were so impressive that he was unrivalled in his party, even by Madison. For the Vice-Presidency they wanted Aaron Burr, a Revolutionary veteran and astute lawyer who was molding a machine for the party in New York

City. Both parties had the "balanced" tickets which American politicians later came to believe necessary for success at the polls. The unpopularity of the Jay treaty was a handicap to the Federalists, and they were hampered by scheming on the part of Hamilton. Jealous of Adams, Hamilton undertook to arrange for some Federalist presidential electors to vote for Pinckney, but not for Adams. Thus Pinckney might have secured a majority and more votes than Adams in the electoral college, and might have won the Presidency, since at that time there was no legal distinction between an electoral ballot cast for the Presidency and another cast for the Vice-Presidency. When Hamilton's scheme became known, all of the Federalist electors felt compelled to vote for Adams and some of them refused to vote for Pinckney. The election was bitterly fought, and the result very close, Adams receiving 71 electoral votes, Jefferson 68, Pinckney 59, and Burr 30. In consequence the Democratic-Republican Jefferson became Vice-President and the presiding officer of the Senate, while his old friend and enemy Adams became the chief executive.

After they had retired from public office Jefferson and John Adams, urged on by their mutual friend Dr. Benjamin Rush, engaged in correspondence in which the New Englander frequently asserted that he had been misunderstood and vilified by the Democratic-Republicans. He continued to be irritated because they had said that in his mature years he had abandoned the principles of the Revolution; Adams protested that his thought and behavior from 1789 to 1801 were completely consistent with the philosophy he had expressed in 1776. It cannot be denied that he had reason to complain, for like all great public figures, he had been unjustly assailed. A plump little man and a conceited one, with a penchant for feeling himself abused, Adams was never a monarchist, as his political enemies claimed. Nor was he a believer in special privilege for those of family and money, as were so many Federalists. He had no affection for the sort of aristocracy which attracted Hamilton, whom he disliked personally, and he believed in an aristocracy of virtue rather than one of heredity and wealth. He believed that men of character and ability should be accepted as superior and as leaders by their fellows; in his aristocracy of virtue he would himself be a shining light. Honest and moderate in his conservatism, Adams turned out to be a worthy and respectable chief executive, despite his famous foibles. He restrained the extremists among the Federalists and prevented them from leading the nation into an unnecessary and dangerous war with France—which would have permitted them to raise a large army and to proceed with military adventures which might conceivably be undertaken, even against fellow Americans of the Democratic-Republican persuasion. Adams was neither a fortunate nor a happy President, but in the last analysis he was a successful one.

UNDECLARED WAR WITH FRANCE

In March, 1797, "Honest John" inherited not only Washington's Cabinet, which he chose to continue in office, but the hostility of the Democratic-Republicans, and an awkward situation which rapidly developed into a crisis with respect to France. He found himself involved in a struggle for control within his own party, in which two Cabinet members, Timothy Pickering and James McHenry, proved to be friends of Hamilton rather than of the President; he was also in bitter conflict with Jefferson and his followers, who assailed him as they had never dared to attack Washington; and the nation was involved in an undeclared war with France which endured for two years.

Angry because the United States had concluded the Jay treaty with Britain, a new French government, the Directory, was interfering with American shipping and even refused to receive Charles Cotesworth Pinckney, who had been appointed minister to France by Washington and who had arrived in Paris toward the end of 1796. Trying to reach some sort of settlement, Adams appointed a commission of three, Pinckney, John Marshall, and Elbridge Gerry, to negotiate with the French. Gerry was a prominent Democratic-Republican from New England, and was named in order to secure support for the commission from his party. When the three sought to discuss Franco-American problems with the French foreign minister, Talleyrand, in October, 1797, they were put off by that wily diplomat. Later in the same month they were called upon by three emissaries who indicated that Talleyrand would have nothing to say to them until they agreed that the United States would pay a bribe of $240,000 and lend France a substantial sum of money. The American envoys contemptuously refused the demands of the three Frenchmen, to whom they referred as X, Y, and Z. Pinckney and Marshall left Paris in disgust, Gerry remaining in the hope of salvaging something from the wreck, especially since Talleyrand threatened a declaration of war against the United States. Gerry achieved nothing beyond the suspicions of Federalists at home, and the news of the insulting treatment given him and his fellow commissioners provoked angry American resentment. In the spring of 1798 many Federalists demanded a declaration of war against the French. The embarrassed Democratic-Republicans lacked the strength to restrain them, but in this case Adams refused to go along with his own party. If France wanted war, he would let France begin it. However, he favored preparation for conflict, and the Federalists arranged for the establishment of the Navy Department, the building of a number of frigates, and the raising of an army. Washington came out of retirement to accept command of the new army. At his insistence Hamilton was given second rank, although Adams distrusted him and would have preferred Henry Knox, the efficient

head of the Continental artillery in the War of Independence. Had the
army taken the field, in view of Washington's age and declining physical
strength, Hamilton would have had a long-sought opportunity to display
military talents which he fancied he possessed. Congress also declared the
treaties of 1778 with France to be null and void. Had the French been
eager to engage in formal warfare, a French declaration would have followed. Instead, the French continued to harass American shipping, which
led to American retaliation by force. After the capture of the American
merchantman *Retaliation* by the French in November, 1798, the new
American frigates sought revenge. In the following February one of them,
the *Constellation,* under Captain Thomas Truxtun, fought and captured
the French warship *L'Insurgent.* A year later the same frigate struggled to
a draw with the French ship *La Vengeance.* The undeclared war on the
ocean demonstrated the quality of the new American navy, but brought
no benefit to France.

Meanwhile, Hamilton continued to demand all-out war against the
French, while his friends Pickering and McHenry clamored for it in the
Cabinet. To their consternation, Adams refused to let the war become
official and more deadly without making one last effort to secure agree-
ment. Receiving a confidential assurance from Talleyrand that a new
American minister would be received with respect, the President named to
the post a moderate Federalist, William Vans Murray of Maryland in
February, 1799. Despite the entreaties and the anguish of belligerent Federalists, he went further, and sent a new commission to deal with the
French. Its members, Murray, William R. Davie, and Chief Justice Oliver
Ellsworth, were politely greeted in the French capital. Napoleon had seized
control of France as First Consul by his famous coup d'état at the end of
1799, and was eager to put an end to the Franco-American crisis. Toward
easing the situation, he agreed to the so-called Convention of 1800, which
among other things definitely put an end to American responsibility in the
defense of the French West Indian Islands. In fact, as finally ratified by
the Senate, the Convention of 1800 voided both of the treaties of 1778.
Thereafter relations between the two former allies improved, until Napoleon, as emperor after 1804, undertook to wage all-out warfare against
Britain.

THE ALIEN AND SEDITION ACTS

While he prevented war with France by his cautious conduct, Adams
failed to stop another project of the extreme Federalists. In the late spring
and early summer of 1798, when excitement over the X, Y, Z, affair was at
a high pitch, the most partisan of the Federalists undertook to crush
Democratic-Republican resistance. Because immigrants tended to join the
Democratic-Republicans, the Federalist-dominated Congress lengthened

the period of residence required before citizenship could be obtained from five years to fourteen years. An Alien Act gave the President the power to deport any alien he considered a menace to the United States, or any foreigner who, in his opinion, harbored "treasonable or secret" hostility against the United States. Of far greater importance was the extraordinary Sedition Act of July, 1798, which not only forbade seditious combinations against the United States, but also threatened to interfere with the constitutional right of assembly. Above all, the law was remarkable because it provided for the punishment of persons who should publish "any false, scandalous and malicious writing" which might cause the American people to hold the government, Congress, or the President in disrepute. Publishing such writings was made a misdemeanor punishable by a fine up to $2000 and imprisonment not to exceed two years. It was obviously the intention of the more fanatical Federalists to silence Democratic-Republican editors, and so to injure their party. The President gave his approval to all of these measures, including the Sedition Act, for he had been grievously abused by the newspapers of the Jefferson camp. Nevertheless, despite the fact that it permitted a defendant to justify his words on the score that he was telling the truth, the Sedition Act clearly violated the freedom of the press guaranteed by the Constitution. Moreover, the law was executed in courts presided over by Federalist judges who were only too often bitterly partisan and who gave glad encouragement to equally partisan federal district attorneys. No fewer than twenty-five Democratic-Republican publishers were prosecuted under the law, and ten of them were convicted. Particularly obnoxious was the behavior of Judge Samuel Chase, who made it clear to jury and public alike that any Democratic-Republican who was critical in print of the Adams administration or of any of its parts was by that very fact a criminal. Several Jeffersonian editors went to prison, and more were fined. Thus the federal courts were used as instruments of tyranny, and the independence of the press was gravely threatened.

But the vigorous execution of the Sedition Act did not seriously injure the Democratic-Republicans, who resorted to extreme measures to defend themselves and to continue as an effective opposition party. They assailed the Federalist laws as unnecessary for the defense of the United States, as wicked, arbitrary, and contrary to the Constitution. In desperation they appealed to the states to stand forth in defense of the rights of the citizen. The Virginia assembly, under the control of Democratic-Republicans, resolved that a state had the right and the duty "to interpose" in defense of an individual suffering from the unconstitutional exercise of national power. Democratic-Republicans in the Kentucky legislature employed more vigorous language from the pen of Jefferson. They said that every state had "an equal right to judge for itself, as well of infractions as of the mode and measure of redress," whenever the national government should try to exert authority not specifically delegated to it by the Constitution. When the assemblies of other states protested against the Kentucky doctrine, they came forth with an even more vigorous resolution, in 1799, which asserted that "a nullification . . . of all unauthorized acts done under color of" the Constitution was "the rightful remedy." In seeking to erect a defense against the arbitrary Sedition Act, Jefferson and the Kentuckians went far toward the doctrines of nullification and secession afterward so vigorously championed by John C. Calhoun.

THE ELECTION OF 1800

It is conceivable that the repressive Federalist legislation of 1798, and especially the Sedition Act and harsh treatment meted out to Democratic-Republican publishers by the Federalist judges, injured rather than aided the party of Adams and Hamilton. Moreover, the Federalists were engaged in an intra-party feud as the election of 1800 approached. In the spring of that year Adams drove both Timothy Pickering and James McHenry from office on the ground that they had been disloyal to him and agents of Hamilton. The animosity between the two Federalist leaders hardly benefited their party, already under fire on various scores, including the Sedition Act, high taxes to finance the undeclared war against France, and the contempt which ultra-Federalists only too often expressed for the poor and the lowborn. Grievances accumulated during eleven years of Federalist rule weighed heavily upon the followers of Adams and Hamilton, and the prospect for party success became darker as the election drew near. Even then, Hamilton indulged his dislike for Adams by engaging in an intrigue similar to the one which he had carried on in 1796. The Federalists had no choice but to support Adams for a second term, and they put up for the Vice-Presidency the popular Charles Cotesworth Pinckney, brother of Thomas Pinckney. Hamilton hoped that the Federalists would secure a majority in the electoral college, but that some of their electors would fail to vote for Adams, while all would vote for Pinckney, who would become the chief executive. News of the scheme leaked out, as in 1796, and it had to be abandoned. All of the Federalist electors cast their votes for Adams, and one of them refused to vote for Pinckney. In the end, it mattered not how the Federalist electors voted, because the Democratic-Republicans won majorities in both houses of Congress, the Presidency, and the Vice-Presidency. They rallied again behind Jefferson and Aaron Burr, both of whom received 73 electoral votes to 65 for Adams and 64 for Pinckney.

But had the Democratic-Republicans really secured the Presidency? Although they had intended that Burr become Vice-President, he was legally tied with Jefferson for the Presidency, and the House of Representatives had to choose between the two. The House which had to decide was not the newly elected Democratic-Republican one, which would not meet for many months, but the existing "lame duck" House, which contained a Federalist majority. The decision might have been made easy if Burr had announced that he would not accept the Presidency, in view of the fact that his party had intended him for the second office. However, Burr kept silence, thereby indicating that he might be willing to accept the Presidency. Even so, the House should have had no real difficulty in making its choice, since it was obvious that the great majority of the Democratic-Republicans supported Burr for the second office rather than for the first. The Federalists in the House should have set aside partisanship and joined with their Democratic-Republican colleagues in a prompt choice of the Virginian. However, they could not bring themselves to do so, for feeling against Jefferson ran high among them. Some evidently hoped to strike a bargain with Burr, receiving promises of concessions from him in return for their votes, but Burr refused to deal with them. Other Federalists hoped to prevent a decision between the two Democratic-Republicans, thus paving the way for the continuance of Adams in the Presidency. Voting by states as prescribed by the Constitution, the House cast thirty-five ballots without reaching any decision; the Federalists stood by Burr, while the Democratic-Republicans backed the acknowledged leader of their party.

At last it became apparent to some of the more thoughtful Federalists that they might lose rather than gain if Burr were elected over Jefferson. It had become obvious enough that the Democratic-Republicans would not permit Adams to remain in office after the close of his term. James Monroe, then governor of Virginia, was saying that any attempt to keep Adams in the White House would bring Virginia troops to Washington. Hamilton profoundly disliked Burr, and found the New Yorker even more objectionable than Jefferson; and he finally threw his influence in favor of the Virginian. There was an unsuccessful attempt on the part of some Federalists to obtain concessions from Jefferson in return for switching their votes. On the thirty-sixth ballot enough Federalists either voted for Jefferson or abstained from voting so that he secured a majority of the state delegations. Accordingly, he assumed the high office on March 4, Adams glumly retiring to Massachusetts and permanently to private life. By a strange coincidence he and Jefferson died within a few hours of each other on the fiftieth anniversary of the Declaration of Independence in 1826.

Alexander Hamilton, younger than his two rivals, was dead more than twenty years before them. Continuing his law practice in New York after 1801, he maintained his interest in politics. New York Federalists considered making overtures to Burr in order to make way against the Democratic-Republicans, but Hamilton vigorously opposed such an alliance. His dislike of Burr was intense, and he indulged himself in remarks unflattering to Burr, both as a public figure and as a private person. Burr demanded either an apology or satisfaction on the dueling ground. Hamilton had served as a second in a duel during the War of Independence, and as late as 1795 he had himself sent a similar demand to an acquaintance by whom he thought himself injured. However, Hamilton had lost a son in a duel resulting from a political quarrel, and he had come to look upon personal combats on the "field of honor" as senseless. Yet he would not retract the opinions he had expressed about Burr's character, and Burr insisted that he fight. Equipped with pistols, the two men faced each other on a dueling ground at Weehawken, New Jersey, on July 10, 1804. Burr fired first, his bullet striking Hamilton in the liver and mortally wounding him. Perhaps Hamilton did not intend to shoot; at any rate, his pistol fired into the air. He died the next day, leaving behind him a large family in distress. Immediately before the fatal duel he had bemoaned the American trend toward democracy; had he lived longer, Hamilton must have felt continuous disappointment over the course of public affairs. So ended an adventurous and spectacular career.

16 JEFFERSON IN DOMESTIC POWER

Afterward, assessing the results of the election of 1800, Jefferson said that the Democratic-Republican triumph brought "as real a revolution in the principles of our government as that of 1776 was in its form." If the word "revolution" be rather narrowly defined, Jefferson's judgment was quite correct. The Federalists had used the power of the federal government to achieve order and stability; under Jefferson the national authority was dedicated to liberty and to a more democratic republicanism. Concern for the freedom of the many replaced devotion to the interests of the few. Simplicity in manners replaced Federalist snobbishness. The farmer and the Southerner came to the political forefront. Great as the change was, it was not accompanied by violence, and the useful foundations erected by the Federalists were not destroyed. Commerce and industry were not persecuted; the newly won authority of the central government was not dissipated; and the federal treasury was strengthened rather than looted. Nor did the Democratic-Republicans fail to use the strength of the new nation to defend the rights and interests of Americans on the seas and abroad.

THE JEFFERSON REGIME

Nearly 58 years of age when he assumed the duties of the Presidency, Jefferson had already proven his devotion to liberty, his genius with the pen, and his unusual gifts as a diplomat and politician. On his inaugural day he made it clear that he was a statesman who could rise above party politics, even though his opinions of his political enemies were not noted for remarkable charity. Leaving his boarding house, he walked in republican simplicity through the dust of the streets of the new city of Washington to the Capitol to take the oath of office and to announce the course which he proposed to follow. He expressed profound faith in the strength and future of the United States. There was, he said, no cause for alarm because party conflicts had recently been heated and bitter. He reminded his countrymen that "We are all Republicans—we are all Federalists." He felt it quite unnecessary to take drastic measures to safeguard the Union or its republican form of government against internal enemies. "If there be any among us who would wish to dissolve this Union or to change its republican form, let them stand undisturbed as monuments of the safety with which error of opinion may be tolerated where reason is left free to combat it." The rights of the minority must be respected, but the will of the majority must prevail. Elections were the republican method of correcting abuses, and it was necessary that there be "absolute acquiescence in the decisions of the majority." Jefferson urged the support of the states "in all their rights," for they were "the most competent" for "domestic concerns and the surest bulwarks against anti-republican tendencies." Nevertheless, he desired "the preservation of the general government in its whole constitutional vigor, as the sheet anchor of our peace at home and safety abroad." For the rest, he would have honesty and frugality in public life, and would avoid "entangling alliances" with foreign powers. Jefferson followed the course which he had described, veering only slightly from it when on occasion he was misled by prejudice. It would be difficult to demonstrate that he would have done better had he led his followers on any other path.

THE CABINET

To assist him, Jefferson called into service an able Cabinet, in which James Madison and Albert Gallatin were the most conspicuous members. With the help of Nathaniel Macon and John Randolph of Roanoke—and of other men when Macon and Randolph broke with the President over the doctrine of strict interpretation of the Constitution—he steadily maintained leadership of the Congress. Madison served as Secretary of State, and the two were on remarkably friendly terms and worked harmoniously together, both on foreign and domestic problems. Indeed, since Jefferson was a widower, Madison's wife Dolley served as the President's official hostess when one was needed. Gallatin, Swiss-born, wealthy, well-educated, and devoted to the public service, performed superbly in the treasury. Heartily sharing Jefferson's desire to reduce public expenses and the national debt, he worked efficiently toward both goals. In consequence, the debt (which had actually increased from 1789 to 1801) was lowered from $83 million to $57 million in the next eight years, this despite the fact that the Jeffersonians annulled all of the internal levies, including the hated tax on whiskey, which the Federalists had imposed. This record was all the more startling because it was necessary to pay for the Louisiana Purchase and the Tripolitan War during that period. However, the policy of thrift was dangerous, in that it was applied to the army, which was half-starved; fortunately the Tripolitan War compelled Jefferson and Gallatin to give decent support to the navy. Gallatin also carried through a fundamental reform in financial management, insisting that Congress cease to appropriate money in lump sums, and that funds be allocated for specific purposes. This reform, which proved permanent, deprived the executive branch of the opportunity to spend public funds in ways that were not approved by the legislature. Mr. Gallatin was a remarkably businesslike man in a regime which otherwise was characterized by the simplicity and homely elegance of government as it was practiced in Virginia.

FEDERALIST CONTROL OF COURTS

Actually, Jefferson and his allies did not have absolute mastery over the machinery in Washington, although Jefferson overwhelmingly defeated Charles Cotesworth Pinckney in the election of 1804 and the Democratic-Republicans continuously controlled both houses of Congress for many years. They removed ardent and conspicuous Federalists from office in the executive departments, not without some embarrassment, and replaced them with loyal and presumably deserving Democratic-Republicans. Jefferson felt it necessary to push out his enemies, since, as he said, few of them died and none resigned. However, he would not sanction dismissal of all Federalists from the executive branch, despite clamorous office-seeking by the presumably faithful of his own party.

But the Democratic-Republicans did not secure control of the federal judiciary in 1801, and the Supreme Court long remained a Federalist stronghold. The federal judges, holding their places on the bench during good behavior, were all Federalists, and could not easily be restored to private life. Moreover, President Adams and the Federalist party had done everything possible to turn the judiciary into a Federalist stronghold during the closing weeks of his Presidency. They hoped to use the federal courts to fight a delaying action against Jefferson and his cohorts until the happy day came when the Federalists should again be victorious at the polls. On January 20, 1801, Adams had appointed as Chief Justice of the United States, John Marshall, then serving as Secretary of State. The redoubtable Marshall was a brilliant and utterly devoted Federalist, a cousin but a personal enemy of Jefferson, and was to dominate the Supreme Court during most of the 34 years of life which remained to him. Toward tightening their grip upon the judiciary and providing safe posts for deserving party members, the Federalists had also pushed through the Judiciary Act of February, 1801. This measure called for a reduction of the number of justices of the Supreme Court from six to five when a vacancy should occur. Thus, it was hoped, Jefferson would be unable to appoint even one of his friends to the high court for some years. The law also created sixteen new circuit courts of appeal, each to be presided over by a judge especially appointed for the purpose. In addition, the new courts were provided with various marshals, bailiffs, and clerks. To provide still further for loyal party members, the Federalists in another law established 42 offices of justice of the peace in the District of Columbia. Appointments to these were to be for five-year terms. In the closing days of his Presidency, "Honest John" Adams and Secretary of State Marshall, with the help of the Senate, were frantically busy filling the new posts which had thus been created. On the day before Jefferson was inaugurated Marshall was engaged in making out commissions as late as nine o'clock of the evening; rumor had it that he actually worked until midnight. Accordingly, some of the appointees not inappropriately received the sobriquet "Midnight Judges." Oddly enough, Marshall, who was not remarkable for his industry, failed to complete all of the commissions, this omission leading to an extraordinary and significant lawsuit.

Thus Jefferson was faced by an enlarged and hostile judiciary, and he could not forget that the Federalist judges had vigorously and venomously enforced the Sedition Act against Democratic-Republican editors. He permitted that hated law to expire, arranging for the federal government to pay back the fines which had been imposed upon the editors. Thoroughly exasperated, he embarked upon a campaign to cleanse the judiciary of his most determined foes.

THE EXECUTIVE VERSUS THE COURTS

It was not easy to compel Federalists to doff their judicial robes, because of the protection given the judiciary by the Constitution. A beginning was made in April, 1802, when the Jeffersonians passed a new Judiciary Act, which stipulated that the number of Supreme Court justices was to be increased again to six, and wiped out the circuit court which had so recently been established. The circuit court system provided for in the

Judiciary Act of 1789 was again put into operation. It could have been argued that the law of 1802 was unconstitutional in that it deprived the new Federalist circuit judges of posts which they were entitled to hold subject to "good behavior." To such a contention, the Jeffersonians would have answered that Congress had the power to destroy as well as to create courts—that the loss of their offices by the judges was only an unfortunate consequence, that a judge had no right to sit upon a bench which did not exist. The Federalists did not raise the issue, partly because the act of 1802 also prevented a meeting of the Supreme Court for many months. When it did convene, its members prudently decided that it was not politically wise to challenge the law, and they went forth on circuit as they had before 1801.

IMPEACHMENT

In March, 1804, the Democratic-Republicans wielded another weapon against the Federalist judges, impeachment. The Constitution, to be sure, provided that the judges could be "removed from Office on Impeachment for, and Conviction of, Treason, Bribery, or other high Crimes and Misdemeanors." Against some of the judges it could readily be shown that they had behaved as passionate partisans on the bench and that, regardless of the evidence, they had made sure that certain Democratic-Republican editors were found guilty of violating the Sedition Act. Also, they had browbeaten both counsel for the defense and juries, arbitrarily and indecently. However, they had not been guilty of either major or minor crimes according to any legal definition. Jefferson and his advisers claimed that the framers of the Constitution could not have intended that the grounds for impeachment be restricted only to those specifically mentioned, since such an interpretation would put the judges quite definitely beyond the reach of the legislative and executive branches. Consequently, they insisted that there must be good reasons for impeachment not mentioned in the Constitution. Accordingly, they arranged to bring charges in the House of Representatives against John Pickering, a judge in the New Hampshire district court. Pickering had behaved very badly indeed, and they hoped both to secure his conviction and to pave the way for proceedings against other men who had, in their opinion, conducted themselves in an even more vicious manner. The House of Representatives did impeach Pickering; he was found guilty by the Senate and removed from office. However, testimony indicated that he was not responsible for his rather astonishing misbehavior (which included drunkenness on the bench), and that he was actually insane. Jefferson and his associates then proceeded against Samuel Chase, Associate Justice of the Supreme Court, whom they utterly detested. The House voted to impeach him, but some Democratic-Republicans in the Senate refused to vote against him on the grounds that his behavior, however reprehensible, was not criminal. When they joined with the Federalist senators to vote for acquittal, it was not possible to secure the two-thirds majority required for conviction. This made it apparent that it was useless for the Democratic-Republican leadership to move against any other Federalist judge, despite the Pickering verdict.

The result of Jefferson's campaign was a victory for the Federalists, and the position of the federal judiciary was buttressed rather than weakened. As the years passed, Jefferson and his successors could gradually replace Federalist justices of the Supreme Court by Democratic-Republicans, but in some instances the new appointees adopted the philosophy of John Marshall and became his loyal supporters. Among them was the scholarly Joseph Story, who outdid Marshall as a defender of nationalist principles, of property rights, and of the authority of the Supreme Court as against the state courts. With the passage of time the clash between the executive and legislative branches on the one side, and the judicial branch on the other lessened as the Democratic-Republicans realized that there was no grave danger in the expansion of federal power when they exercised it. They trusted themselves not to establish a wicked tyranny on the banks of the Potomac.

MARBURY V. MADISON

Only the sagest and most dispassionate of observers in the year 1803 could have predicted the outcome when William Marbury asked the Supreme Court to issue a writ of mandamus against James Madison. Marbury was one of those inconspicuous persons who have on occasion become as famous as the mighty in American history. A loyal Federalist, he was appointed one of the justices of the peace for the District of Columbia by the Federalists in the "lame duck" session of 1801. More accurately, he was nominated by President Adams and approved by the Senate for the minor judgeship in the Federal District. However, in the last hours of the Adams regime John Marshall as Secretary of State was unable or failed to deliver Marbury's commission. When Madison succeeded Marshall, he found the commission, along with others, ready for delivery. Jefferson and Madison agreed that the document should be withheld, although they made no effort to prevent the execution of other last-minute appointments made by the Federalists. They took the view that Marbury had no right to claim the post unless he received the commission, and that the President had the power to cancel the appointment up to the moment when Marbury should receive the document. Feeling abused because he had been deprived of the honors and emoluments of the post, Marbury believed that he could force the delivery of the commission by judicial process. Despite advice to the contrary by leading Federalists, he formally requested the Supreme Court to order Madison to give it to him. He thus placed the Court, and especially Chief Justice Marshall, in an awkward situation; with Jefferson's backing Madison had made it known that he would refuse to obey such a writ. There was no way in which Madison and Jefferson could be forced to recognize the authority of the Court, and issuance of an ignored writ would subject the Court to ridicule. Jefferson would show no mercy to Marshall, even though both were descended from the house of Randolph, and the Chief Justice had served as Jefferson's lawyer when he first began to practice law. For whatever reason, the two men had broken their friendship, and had become personal as well as political enemies. The lanky, lean Virginian with the keen little black eyes who presided over the Court cleverly found a way to thwart his cousin and at the same time to assert the authority of the Court as it had not been done before. He produced an extraordinary opinion which his judicial brethren unanimously endorsed.

Had Marshall and his colleagues behaved in truly judicial fashion, the decision which they rendered would first have answered the question, did the Court have jurisdiction? Instead, Marshall began by asking whether Marbury was entitled to his post, and answered in the affirmative, thus condemning the behavior of Jefferson and Madison. Then Marshall put a second query: was there any legal remedy available to Marbury? The reply was that there was one, that there must be one. Finally, Marshall proceeded to the legal part of his opinion, and propounded a third question: did the Supreme Court have the authority to issue a writ of mandamus in behalf of Marbury? He replied in the negative. Marbury based his case on Section 13 of the Judiciary Act of 1789, which authorized the Supreme Court "to issue . . . writs of *mandamus* . . . to . . . persons holding office under the authority of the United States." Clearly the intent of Section 13 was to supply the Court with a judicial weapon for cases where it already had jurisdiction under the Constitution. Accordingly, it was necessary only for Marshall to say that the Court could not rule upon the Marbury-Madison controversy, since its original jurisdiction was confined to cases in which one or more of the parties was a state or a representative of a foreign country. Thus, as had been hinted earlier in the opinion, Marbury should have begun his suit in a lower federal court. However, while denying the writ to Marbury, Marshall took the view that it was the intent of Congress in Section 13 to add to the original jurisdiction of the Court. Thus, he said, there was a conflict between the Constitution and Section 13. The answer seemed clear to him and to his colleagues; Congress had exceeded its authority in passing Section 13. Since there was conflict between the Constitution, "the supreme law of the land," and one part of a law passed by Congress, the latter must be set aside as null and void.

Judges in lower federal courts had hitherto asserted the power of the federal judiciary to set aside acts of Congress on the ground that they violated the Constitution. For the first time the Supreme Court now officially sanctioned that doctrine. Marshall had found it possible to assert most emphatically the power of the Supreme Court, at the same time depriving Jefferson and Madison of an opportunity to strike at it. It has been contended that the decision in *Marbury* v. *Madison* was not fundamentally important, because the Court had declared unconstitutional only a part of an act of Congress which applied exclusively to the judiciary. However, the logic applied by Marshall could clearly be extended to laws affecting the other two branches of the federal government, and likewise to state laws and to the actions of state officials. A precedent had been set, and lawyers and judges are fond of precedent. It was to be more than fifty years before the Supreme Court again declared a federal law to be null and void because it conflicted with the Constitution. Later, however, the Court more and more frequently declared congressional legislation void because of conflict with "the supreme law of the land." Jefferson, and Andrew Jackson and Franklin D. Roosevelt after him, could logically argue that all three branches of the federal government should have the right to interpret the Constitution, but the Supreme Court, because it is the highest court of appeal, has frequently had the last word. Toward the end of the nineteenth century the Court became very nearly a "third chamber."

THE LOUISIANA PURCHASE

Napoleon's wars against coalitions devised by Britain brought distress to the Democratic-Republicans, just as the wars between Britain and her allies and the French Republic had created troubles for the Federalists; but the agonies of Europe also gave opportunities to the United States. The year 1803 was memorable not only for the exasperating business of *Marbury* v. *Madison,* but also for the purchase of Louisiana, one of Jefferson's greatest achievements. Strangely enough, the United States secured Louisiana, not from weak Spain, but from powerful France.

During the wars of the 1790s, Spanish politicians had become increasingly weary of the problems which the possession of New Orleans and Louisiana imposed upon them. Spain spent more money on Louisiana than she received from it, and the colony caused almost continuous friction with the United States. It was obvious that Louisiana could not be defended against a determined attack by the United States, France, or Britain. Moreover, it was useful to Spain largely as a barrier against assaults upon Spanish territories in Mexico and the Caribbean Sea. After 1795, Spanish politicians were willing to consider returning the colony to France in the thought that France might then interpose her strength between the remainder of the Spanish empire and the aggressive British and Americans. Besides, Spain could expect lands elsewhere by way of compensation. Meanwhile, a dream of rebuilding the French empire attracted the imagination of the French leaders, who regretted that Louisiana had been given to Spain in 1762. Napoleon, whose ambitions knew no limits, was fascinated by the vision and strove to make it a reality. In his behalf Talleyrand astutely appealed to the Spanish Crown: "Let the Court of Madrid cede these districts [Louisiana] to France, and from that moment the power of America is bounded by the limit which it may suit the interests and the tranquillity of France and Spain to assign her. The French Republic . . . will be a wall of brass forever impenetrable to the combined efforts of England and America." In exchange for Louisiana Napoleon proposed to give the Italian kingdom of Tuscany to the son-in-law of the Spanish monarch, Charles IV. Charles's advisers considered this a good bargain and accepted it for their master in the secret treaty of San Ildefonso, signed on October 1, 1800. The transaction was not completed, however, until 1802, because the French dictator failed to deliver Tuscany, and Charles was reluctant to give up Louisiana without receiving his price. At last Napoleon, promising that the territory would never be abandoned to a third power, insisted that the cession be made. Accordingly, the Spanish king signed an order on October 15, 1802, directing his officials in Louisiana to turn the colony over to the French. So after forty years all of the territory between the Rockies and the Mississippi, and from New Orleans along the Gulf Coast eastward to Mobile, again became French soil.

The Franco-Spanish bargain could not be kept entirely secret, and reports concerning it reached the United States as early as 1801. Alarmed, Jefferson unofficially and quietly urged the French to abandon the deal, pointing out that a France holding New Orleans and the west bank of the Mississippi could hardly fail to become an enemy of the United States. Jefferson's advice, of course, was not taken in Paris. Concern in America became general when it was learned that the Spanish had suspended the right of deposit at New Orleans in October, 1802. Having begun to make extensive use of the Mississippi to export raw materials, the Americans of Trans-Appalachia were furious. Some of the more violent spirits among them talked of marching upon New Orleans, as if it were not a deadly serious matter to assault Spain or France. Cooler heads urged prompt action on the part of the federal government. While the more fanatical Federalists rejoiced over his predicament, Jefferson had been thinking about the matter and had found a possible remedy, which he hardly dared hope would be successful. Of one thing he was sure; the French must not be allowed to hold New Orleans. Said he: "There is on the globe one single spot, the possessor of which is our natural and habitual enemy. It is New

Orleans. . . . The day that France takes possession of New Orleans, fixes the sentence which is to restrain her [the United States] forever within her low-water mark. . . . From that moment, we must marry ourselves to the British fleet and nation." Late in 1802 Jefferson made it clear to French and Spanish diplomats in Washington that the United States was deeply offended by the Treaty of San Ildefonso. He played upon the fears of the Spanish by emphasizing the westerners' threats of a march upon New Orleans, and he was gracious to British representatives, thus hinting that French occupation of New Orleans might lead to an Anglo-American alliance. Congress took an even more vigorous step, authorizing the President to ask the state governors to raise 80,000 militia. In January, 1803, Jefferson played his trump card, although it hardly seemed likely to win. With the consent of the Senate, he sent James Monroe as a special envoy to France with instructions to try to buy New Orleans and West Florida, and with permission to pay as much as $10 million for them. Robert R. Livingston, the American minister in Paris, was to work with Monroe toward making the purchase. Jefferson wrote to the two men to tell them that "the future destinies of this Republic" rested upon the success or failure of their mission. Should it fail, they were to open discussions with the British toward the making of an alliance.

It was not to be expected that Livingston and Monroe would achieve their goal, but fortune suddenly changed in favor of the United States. Napoleon was learning that restoration of the French empire in the New World was likely to be both expensive and risky. He had hoped to regain control of Haiti as well as Louisiana; in fact Haiti, or Santo Domingo, was looked upon in Paris as an almost indispensable steppingstone to New Orleans. But it had proved to be extraordinarily difficult to put down a Negro revolt which began on the island in 1795 and which consumed French money and men in staggering numbers. An army which Napoleon sent to Haiti under the direction of his brother-in-law suffered 50,000 dead, chiefly as the result of yellow fever. Without Haiti, Louisiana lost much of its value to France. Moreover, a peace treaty recently made with Britain at Amiens obviously would not endure. As soon as the war resumed, it was to be expected that the British would undertake the conquest of New Orleans. Angry and disgusted because of the failure of his colonial enterprise, the French emperor had decided to liquidate it, to devote his full attention to his enemies in Europe. He much preferred that Louisiana go to the United States rather than to Britain, and the United States was obviously eager to purchase it. Contemptuously ignoring his promise to Spain not to let it pass to a third power, he ordered Talleyrand to ask Livingston how much the American government would pay for all of Louisiana. Livingston consulted Monroe, newly arrived in Paris, and the two saw a heaven-sent opportunity for the United States. They exceeded their instructions, and offered to pay $11,250,000 for the colony. In addition, they pledged the United States to pay about $3,750,000 to American citizens who held claims against the French government because of its depredations upon American shipping. Napoleon agreed to the bargain, and a treaty containing these terms was signed on May 2, 1803. There can be no doubt that Livingston and Monroe, purchasing Louisiana at a total cost of $15 million, had indeed secured a bargain.

REACTION AT HOME

The good news of the treaty and the happy tidings that Napoleon was abandoning his American empire were neither good nor happy for the more extreme New England Federalists. They were already disturbed because political power seemed to be passing to the South and the West, and feared that the addition of Louisiana and new states made from it would permanently reduce New England's influence in the Union; it would also enable the agrarian Democratic-Republicans to cling indefinitely to authority in Washington. Led by Timothy Pickering, the "Essex Junto" of Massachusetts consequently began to consider withdrawing New England, New York, and New Jersey from the Union and founding a separate Federalist nation. The great majority of the northern Federalists would have no part in the scheme, and indeed knew nothing of it. Alexander Hamilton delivered a heavy blow against it by refusing to support Aaron Burr for the governorship of New York—the Junto had hoped to find a useful ally in Burr.

If but few Federalists harbored thoughts of leaving the Union, more of them were opposed to ratifying the treaty, and some reached the conclusion that it violated the Constitution. They pointed out that the Constitution did not specifically authorize the acquisition of new territory, and denounced the purchase with the strict constructionist arguments which the Democratic-Republicans had so warmly advanced a decade earlier. In fact, deprived of control of the central government and so weakened that they were unlikely to regain it, the Federalists were generally turning away from the doctrine of implied powers. American parties out of power were to display the same tendency to assail the growth of national authority until the twentieth century. Jefferson and the Democratic-Republicans, of course, wished to consummate the purchase, but they too were plagued by the problem of constitutional interpretation. They could constitutionally justify acceptance of the treaty on the basis of implied powers, since the federal government was authorized both to make treaties and to wage war. Since territory is commonly lost or gained through warfare and treaties, it was reasonable to assume that the framers of the Constitution did not intend to bar American expansion by such means. Many Democratic-Republicans, setting aside their fondly defended strict constructionism, now appealed to the Hamiltonian liberal interpretation of national powers. Even members of the Cabinet tended to change their constitutional theory to fit the situation. But Jefferson could not persuade himself to be so obviously inconsistent; for the President, the logical thing to do was to seek a constitutional amendment which would specifically give to the central government the right to acquire and to govern territory. But that would require much time, and Jefferson felt that he could not wait. Napoleon's offer to sell might be withdrawn at any time. Concluding that the treaty was of doubtful constitutionality, Jefferson nevertheless urged the Senate to endorse it. He hoped that the good sense of the American people would prevent untoward results from the violation of the Constitution. In effect, he placed the defense of the nation's paramount interest above the Constitution. The Senate sanctioned the treaty in October, 1803, and the House of Representatives was not slow in offering its assistance toward procuring the necessary funds. Before the end of the following year William Claiborne arrived in New Orleans to be formally inducted into office as the first governor of the Territory of Louisiana.

LOUISIANA'S BOUNDARIES

Jefferson and his friends knew that they had secured an empire for the United States and that they had doubled American territory at the cost of only $15 million. They would have been hard pressed to describe its terrain, its resources, or its people. They could not even describe its boundaries, beyond saying that in general they were the Rocky Mountains on the west and the Mississippi River on the east. It turned out that most of Louisiana was rich and pleasing, its resources were vast, and its French and Indian inhabitants were worthy additions to the American population. As for the uncertain limits of the new possession, it was to the advantage of the United States that they were not clearly laid down, as Napoleon had hinted to Livingston and Monroe when they sought a more precise description than they had been given. In effect, the French dictator had suggested to the Americans that they might well be able to impose upon Spain their own definitions of the boundaries between Louisiana and the Spanish holdings in Mexico and the Floridas.

What the United States had bought was the Louisiana that was given by France to Spain in 1762 and which had been returned to France in 1800. Livingston satisfied himself that it included West Florida, together with Mobile and Pensacola. It was reasonable for the United States to contend that Mobile had been a part of Louisiana until 1763, although Spain claimed it and land west of it. However, Jefferson preferred not to conduct a scholarly investigation to discover whether or not West Florida was included in the purchase, but simply to assert ownership of it. When Spain should be in difficulties, her government would see the wisdom of

THE LOUISIANA PURCHASE

accepting compensation in return for recognizing American pretensions. As it happened, that part of West Florida lying west of the Perdido River soon became American territory, and without any concession to Spain. In 1810, American frontiersmen who had settled between the Pearl River and the Mississippi revolted, drove out the local Spanish officials, and asserted their independence from Spain. Jefferson had vainly tried to create a situation in which Spain would be forced to sell. Madison, his successor, asked to act by the revolutionists, simply announced that West Florida as far east as the Perdido River was American soil. Spain protested bitterly, and to some avail, for Madison did not quite dare to move immediately against Spanish-held Mobile. However, three years later, when Spain was in dire distress, the American General James Wilkinson occupied Mobile without encountering resistance. Successful in insisting on their own interpretation of Louisiana's boundary on the east, Americans also tried to push the western bounds of Louisiana far toward the setting sun. The French had long claimed, but not very effectively, that Texas was a part of

Louisiana. The claim was revived by the United States and turned out to be useful in bargaining with Spain for the remainder of the Floridas. The passage of another generation and a revolution in Texas ultimately led to the annexation of that region also to the United States.

WESTWARD EXPLORATION

While Jefferson the politician and diplomat strove to enlarge the limits of Louisiana, Jefferson the politician and amateur scientist sent out exploring parties to discover as much as possible about its geography and resources. As early as January, 1803, he asked Congress to supply funds for an expedition to the westward for the purpose of winning friends and increasing trade among the Indians. The money was voted, and the President chose as joint commanders of the enterprise Meriwether Lewis, his private secretary, and William Clark, brother of George Rogers Clark. In the spring of 1804 Lewis and Clark led a party of 27 men, chiefly soldiers, up the Missouri River. Wintering in the Mandan Indian villages in what is now North Dakota, the explorers were joined by an Indian woman named Sacagawea, who was to be of great assistance as an interpreter. The following year they pushed on to the sources of the Missouri, and thence to the Columbia River, arriving on the shores of the Pacific in November. Thirteen years earlier the American Captain Robert Gray had discovered and explored the great river, which was named after his ship. The Lewis and Clark party gave the United States a second argument in support of a claim to the Columbia valley. Lewis and Clark safely made the return journey in 1806, bringing with them maps, drawings, journals, and reports bearing a vast quantity of information. They had served Jefferson very well.

Somewhat less fortunate as an explorer was Zebulon M. Pike, who was sent out by General James Wilkinson to find the source of the Mississippi River, while Lewis and Clark were threading their way from the Rockies to the Pacific. Pike failed in his mission. He also failed in a second expedition which he undertook in 1806 and 1807. He pushed on into Colorado, where he discovered the famous peak named after him, and thence into New Mexico, invading Spanish soil. He was seized by the Spanish at Santa Fé and was imprisoned for a short time, but was able to publish an extensive report on his findings after his release. A storehouse of valuable information came from the efforts of Lewis and Clark and of Pike, but much remained to be learned about Louisiana and the Oregon region. Jefferson hoped that Louisiana would supply so much rich land that the American people would remain a nation of farmers indefinitely. Precise knowledge of Louisiana accumulated only slowly, but hunters and settlers did not wait for accurate descriptions or for the development of transportation facilities. Within less than a century the Louisiana territory was fully occupied, and with it the valley of the Columbia and the Great Southwest.

"THE BURR CONSPIRACY"

It was perhaps easier for Lewis and Clark to find their way across the Rockies than it is for historians to discover the truth about the so-called "Burr Conspiracy." The shot which killed Alexander Hamilton also ruined Burr's political career, because he was looked upon as a murderer by many people, particularly in the Northern states. Although dueling had not been uncommon among Revolutionary officers—resort to the field of honor continued to be fashionable in the South for several decades— Hamilton's death was so shocking that Northern opinion refused to excuse Burr for doing what many others had done before. Ostracized and under indictment for murder in New York and New Jersey, the Vice-President of the United States unhappily turned from politics to a new adventure. Exactly what it involved remains unknown, but soon after the duel Burr approached the British minister in Washington, asking him for money, presumably to finance a movement to separate western territory from the United States. The British envoy, Anthony Merry, prudently refused to advance the funds, but for reasons that are not clear his Spanish counterpart did give Burr a little money. In the summer of 1805 Burr made a tour of the Mississippi Valley and conferred with General Wilkinson, commander of the American troops in the region. A year later he appeared at Blennerhasset's Island in the upper Ohio River, where he conversed at length with its owner and his friend, Harman Blennerhasset. After Burr left for Tennessee, some 60 men gathered on the island, and moved down the Ohio in a small flotilla of flatboats. Joining this poorly armed group, Burr led them down the Mississippi.

What Burr intended to do with this trifling force remains even now a mystery. He himself claimed that he proposed to found a colony of congenial spirits in the Arkansas region. There is evidence that he intended to enter Texas and establish an independent empire on Spanish soil; some scholars believe that he planned to cut off some territory from the American union. The first information about the expedition led Jefferson to issue a proclamation warning its members not to violate Spanish soil. However, when informed by Wilkinson that Burr intended to seize American territory, the President issued orders for his arrest. As the expedition approached Natchez, Burr learned that Wilkinson, who had participated in the formation of the scheme, had turned against him and had denounced him as a traitor. To proceed further would have been foolhardy; Burr could expect only arrest at New Orleans. Leaving his men to scatter, he fled toward Spanish Florida, but was caught before he could reach the border and probable safety.

An epidemic of indictments broke out against Burr and his chief lieutenants, and various legal proceedings were taken against them. By far the most important was Burr's trial on the charge of treason in the United States Circuit Court in Richmond, Virginia, in August, 1807. It was held amid political excitement; the Democratic-Republicans ardently desired Burr's conviction, while the Federalists, who were strong in Richmond, ardently wished for his acquittal. One of Jefferson's followers, John Randolph of Roanoke, was the foreman of the grand jury which returned the indictment; and Jefferson urged the federal district attorney to do everything possible to secure Burr's conviction. After the struggle for the Presidency in the House of Representatives in 1801, Jefferson was by no means fond of his running mate. But if the Democratic-Republicans were able to bring pressure against the disappointed adventurer, the Federalists held the trump card, for Chief Justice Marshall himself presided over the trial. Marshall had an opportunity to strike against Jefferson, and it cannot be doubted that he took advantage of it. The Constitution declares that treason against the United States consists "only in levying War against them, or in adhering to their Enemies, giving them Aid and Comfort." It also asserts that "No Person shall be convicted of Treason unless on the Testimony of two Witnesses to the same overt Act, or on Confession in open Court." Marshall, who had vainly attempted to subpoena the President as a witness, insisted upon a rigid interpretation of the constitutional requirement that there be two witnesses to the same overt act. The prosecution could not produce two persons who could testify that they had seen Burr perform such an act. As a result, on September 1, the jury brought in the interesting verdict, "not guilty by any evidence submitted to us." Thus acquitted, Burr hastened off to Europe to escape further prosecutions, returning after some years to die quietly and almost obscurely as a New York City lawyer. Since his intention remains doubtful, it is well that he was found innocent. It was also well that, whatever the reasons for his interpretation, Marshall insisted upon direct evidence for conviction on a charge of treason. Too often men had suffered for treason in Europe on the basis of indirect and inadequate evidence. Happily, treason trials did not become conspicuous in the American scene until the middle of the twentieth century.

17 ECONOMIC AND SOCIAL PROGRESS

Important though the "Revolution of 1800" and the purchase of Louisiana were, it may well be that the most important fact about the United States from 1789 to 1815 was that the Americans, continuing their colonial habit of remarkable increase, doubled in numbers. When Washington took office, the Union contained fewer than 4 million souls; in 1815 there were about 8 million within its borders. This burgeoning population was, of course, accompanied by an increase in the number and size of its settled areas and by its economic growth. It should go without saying that the American people in 1815 were far more powerful in a military way than they had been a quarter of a century earlier, and that they were far safer from external attacks than they had been in 1789. Such is the fact, although historians have habitually assumed that the American republic was weak when it was created and that it continued to be so. It is fairly obvious that

242

the Americans possessed great defensive military strength at the time of the War of Independence, and that there were far more and equally vigorous Americans with every passing decade.

POPULATION AND THE LAND

It may even be said that the central fact of the period was a high American birth rate, for the rapid increase in numbers is not to be explained by immigration. Europeans continued to cross the Atlantic to find new homes, but they did not swarm across as had the Germans and the Scotch-Irish in the eighteenth century. Political changes drove persons of one group or another out of France, and the Negro rebellion in Haiti forced other Frenchmen to seek refuge on the American mainland. Troubles at home impelled a few Irish Roman Catholics to emigrate, and the British Isles and Germany continued to send forth new settlers. Nevertheless, restrained by the exigencies of war, Europeans tended to remain at home, and it is likely that there were fewer than 200,000 immigrants during the whole generation. In some years there were fewer than 5000 of them, not so many as were to enter the United States in a single day a century later. In sum, the American of 1815 was clearly not "a new man," but the American of 1789, altering with his environment.

Doubling within 25 years, the American population shifted its weight, and the North moved past the South in numbers. The western parts of Virginia, Kentucky, and Tennessee continued to draw settlers, but those of New York and Pennsylvania, and eastern Ohio as well, were peopled far more rapidly. The hope which Southerners entertained in 1789 that the Southern states would not only continue to hold a slight advantage in population, but that it would actually increase, proved to be an illusion. The first census in 1790 indicated that just over 50 percent of the American people lived below the Mason-Dixon line; thereafter census after census told a story of ever-increasing inferiority for the South. True, New England long failed even to keep pace with the South, for the number of Yankees remained almost stationary for many years. This fact did not mean that New Englanders had ceased to breed. It meant, instead, that immigrants were avoiding Yankee-land, which was already thickly settled, so far as agriculture was concerned by 1790, and that New England was exporting population. The Yankees had begun their invasion of New York City, but went in far larger numbers into upstate New York, northern Pennsylvania, and northern Ohio.

It was the Middle States that grew phenomenally in the last decade of the eighteenth century and the early years of the nineteenth. Tens of thousands of settlers, moving in from New England, from the older parts of New York, and from Europe, occupied the pleasant and fertile Finger

Lakes region and pushed on toward Lakes Ontario and Erie. The population of New York quadrupled between 1790 and 1820, and the state became the largest in the Union in terms of numbers, a distinction which it was to continue to enjoy into the second half of the twentieth century. New York City kept pace with the state and surpassed Philadelphia in numbers in 1820.

In 1815 Southerners were not alarmed by the rapid growth of the North. In the decade of the 1790s, to be sure, Southerners had resented federal favors to the Northern merchant marine, which had received preferential treatment as against foreign shipping in tonnage duties. Moreover, and more seriously, the assumption of state debts and the creation of the first Bank of the United States had aroused feeling below the Mason-Dixon line. But the "Revolution of 1800" not only put a President sympathetic to Southern interests in the White House, but also brought into national power the Democratic-Republican party, in which the South had the preponderant influence. It was New England that manifested a most vigorous sectionalism during the war of 1812.

Federalists' fears that the West would fill up rapidly and that New England and Federalism would steadily become less important were well founded, for the American population shifted materially toward the Mississippi before 1815, and failed to carry with it the Federalist faith. Five new states, Vermont (1791), Kentucky (1792), Tennessee (1796), Ohio (1803), and Louisiana (1812) joined the original thirteen, sending to the national capital men who were disciples of Jefferson, and some who were even more friendly toward political democracy than was Jefferson. The course of empire was not moving as rapidly westward as it did later in the century, but it was moving.

Had the federal government made it easy for the settler to acquire a homestead, the westward movement must have been more rapid. But neither the states possessing unoccupied lands nor the national government sought to plant people on land they owned—this despite Jefferson's allegiance to the independent farmer as the basis of the best society. The states sold land to speculators in order to get money, and revenue from the sale of land was also sought by Congress. The Land Ordinance of 1785 stipulated that federal land should be sold in quantities of 640 acres or more, at a price of $1 per acre, requirements which made purchases difficult for the great majority of farmers. A federal land law of 1796 contained similar requirements, and only 50 thousand acres were sold in a four-year period under that act. As governor of the Northwest Territory, William Henry Harrison urged that purchase of federal lands be made easier. He was supported by Albert Gallatin, and in 1800 Congress authorized the sale of plots of 320 acres at $2 per acre, the purchaser putting down $160 in cash and paying the balance over a period of years. But even this more liberal arrangement was not generous enough for the average man seeking a homestead. He often wanted only 160 acres, or sometimes as little as 80 or 100. Frequently he did not have the cash even to pay for 160 acres; and a law of 1804 which reduced the minimum plot to that size did not make homestead purchasing easy. Accordingly, settlers continued to purchase chiefly from land companies which had acquired much of the available public domain. Some took possession at least temporarily by squatting on unoccupied land. It was not until 1820 that the federal government began to sell land under terms which were easily met. After that year it was necessary to buy only 80 acres, and the price was set as low as $1.25 per acre. The act of 1820 required payment in cash, but an 80-acre homestead could now be acquired for as little as $100. Under this arrangement the speculator lost most of his advantage over the settler. There should be no great sorrow over the unhappy fate of the man who could not purchase public lands before 1820, for he did have an opportunity to buy from private owners. Certainly, his chance of earning a decent livelihood on the soil were infinitely better than they would have been in England or on the European continent, where, after a lifetime of toil and thrift, a tenant was almost invariably still a tenant.

COMMERCE—FOREIGN AND DOMESTIC

If the ambition of most Americans remained the acquisition of a good farm, it was nevertheless true that more and more of their fellows were turning to commerce and industry. Despite interference by the Europeans, American maritime traffic flourished, the profits from successful voyages across the Atlantic more than making up for frequent seizures of ships and cargoes by Britain and France. American wheat, flour, tobacco, rice, lumber, and fish usually found ready markets in the European world, especially in Britain, which continued to be the best customer of the United States. Finished goods were brought into American ports in large quantities, mainly from Britain, but also from Holland and Germany. Wines were imported from the Mediterranean, coffee and indigo from Spanish America, and spices and tea from the East Indies and China. As early as 1784 the American ship *Empress of China* made her way to the Far East, thus starting a lucrative trade with the Orient. Merchantmen from New England and New York, making voyages that lasted for as long as two years, appeared in the harbors of China, Sumatra, and Arabia. The profits were frequently as high as 100 percent, and some American merchants made fortunes from them. Maritime commerce expanded so rapidly that there was one million tons of American shipping by 1805. About half was owned in New England, where Boston port continued to flourish, but New York City profited greatly from the expansion of sea traffic and replaced Philadelphia as the center of American maritime trade. Together with New York, however, many a smaller port prospered, including Philadelphia, Baltimore, Providence, Albany, and Sag Harbor. After 1803 they were joined by New Orleans, through which increasing commerce funneled between the Mississippi Valley and the outside world. New Orleans and Baltimore became centers of a growing exchange between the United States and the Latin American countries after 1807. By 1815 there was not much oceanic water untraversed by American vessels: Tahiti and Tripoli, Liverpool and Lisbon, Shanghai and St. Petersburg—all knew the American sailor. In widely scattered places the Americans had displayed an affinity for the sea and for traffic upon it—in the War of 1812 they also proved beyond any doubt that they could fight on deep water.

Internal trade flourished with the external, and communities far removed from salt water increased in numbers and in size. Cargo-carrying on the Ohio gave impetus to the growth of Pittsburgh. Lexington flourished in Kentucky's bluegrass country. Lancaster, Pennsylvania profited from traffic on the roads. Richmond as the capital of Virginia grew into a comfortable small city. Towns and cities grew in the North rather than in the South, which clung stoutly to agriculture as a way of life.

Of special importance to the inland urban centers—they also contributed to the development of the coastal ports—were the turnpikes, which became popular soon after the close of the War of Independence. While New York and Pennsylvania were already beginning to assume some responsibility for building and improving roads, these were almost universally neglected by government. In 1785 Maryland and Virginia discovered a method of developing roads without spending tax money. By collecting tolls at stations placed at suitable intervals, it was possible to make the users pay for roads. Such toll roads, or turnpikes, had already been successful in England, and quickly caught the public fancy in the United States. The usual procedure was to charter a company and to authorize it to charge certain fees over a period of years, or indefinitely, in return for building and maintaining a road. Such a company built a highway of stone covered with gravel between Philadelphia and Lancaster in the years 1792–1794. It has been widened and resurfaced, but is still called the Lancaster Pike. A little later other companies were building good roads in New England and in the Middle States. Massachusetts chartered no fewer than one hundred companies before 1813—not all of them, of course, being as active with gravel as they were with paper. The new highways were accompanied by new bridges, which replaced awkward and expensive ferries at various river crossings. Self-educated engineers built astonishingly good and large wooden bridges over the Charles River at Boston and over the Schuylkill at Philadelphia. One bridge over the Schuylkill had an arch 340 feet in length. To protect such structures from the elements, they were often built with wooden roofs, and the covered bridge became an everyday sight for the traveler. Like the turnpikes, the bridges were usually erected by companies which were organized as profit-making ventures.

The states were slow to invest public funds in road building, and early in the nineteenth century it seemed likely that the federal government would have to assume major responsibility for construction not undertaken by private companies. When Ohio was admitted to the Union in 1803, the federal government agreed to use 5 percent of the funds derived from the sale of public lands in that state toward constructing roads from the Atlantic watershed over the Appalachians and across the Ohio River. The plan, rather surprisingly, was partly executed, and the Cumberland Road was built between Cumberland, Maryland, and Wheeling, Virginia, after 1810. As a result, since Baltimore and Cumberland were connected by a turnpike, it became possible to travel in some comfort from Chesapeake Bay to the banks of the Ohio. But the Cumberland Road, or as it was often called, the National Road, was the only one to receive federal help for decades. Gallatin, whose devotion to Democratic-Republican principles and fondness for thrift did not prevent him from making long-range plans, proposed to Congress in 1808 a program calling for the expenditure of $16 million of federal funds to improve American communications. However, the constitutional scruples of many of his fellow party members, together with difficulty in finding the money, eventually defeated Gallatin's scheme and others like it. More than a century passed before the federal government heartily engaged in road improvement.

Meanwhile, communication by water was entering upon a new era, that of the steamboat, although that vessel was not in common use before 1815. John Fitch launched a successful steamboat on the Delaware River as early as 1787, and James Rumsey another on the Potomac in the same year. Fifteen years later John Stevens designed a screw propeller, which was used successfully on the *Phoenix* six years afterward. However, the first truly successful steamboat was Robert Fulton's *Clermont,* which churned its way from New York to Albany in thirty-two hours in August, 1807. Soon afterward, with support from several wealthy capitalists, Fulton was able to schedule regular trips between the two cities. Improved and enlarged, the steamboat with its thrashing propellers soon became a familiar sight on the American rivers, although sailing ships continued to carry the bulk of maritime traffic during the next several decades.

THE COTTON GIN

Inventions contributed to the development of agriculture and industry as well as of commerce. Well known are the results of Eli Whitney's invention of the cotton gin; they can hardly be exaggerated. Toward the end of the eighteenth century Great Britain had machines to manufacture large quantities of cotton, and there was a splendid market for gotton goods, growing along with the population. Cotton itself, however, was not available in suitably large quantity. After the War of Independence the demand for it in England was satisfied in part by imports of long-staple cotton from the Carolinas and Georgia. This type of cotton could be grown only on the coasts and islands of those states, and it was not possible to produce enough to keep the English machines busy. Large quantities of the short-staple cotton could easily be grown in the interior, but the seeds of that kind of plant were so tightly wrapped in the cotton that their removal was costly in time and money. Accordingly, the production of the short-staple variety was not profitable. Immediately after the War of Independence several inventors had sought to develop a machine which would easily and cheaply separate the seed from the lint. In 1793, as the world knows, young Eli Whitney invented the successful cotton gin, thus defeating his competitors, who promptly appropriated the basic features of his machine and prevented him from making a fortune. He and they manufactured large numbers of gins, which in turn made possible the accumulation of fortunes by many planters in the nineteenth century. Between 1794 and 1804 the cotton crop was multiplied eight times, and cotton-growing became basic in the South Atlantic states. Long before 1815 production of the "white weed" had spread westward as far as the Natchez region of Mississippi. At the close of the War of 1812 cotton was not yet king in the Southern states, but it was preparing to ascend the throne.

THE ARTS

Although it grew steadily in terms of numbers, wealth, power, and stability, the United States, as one might expect, lagged culturally during the quarter-century which followed Washington's inauguration. While it is possible to mention various American cultural "firsts" which occurred during that period, literary and artistic genius did not, perhaps could not, flourish. In 1789 William Hill Brown published *The Power of Sympathy,* usually considered the first American novel. Three years later Hugh Henry Brackenridge put forth his *Modern Chivalry,* a volume of some quality which satirized life on the frontier. As the eighteenth century came to a close Charles Brockden Brown published a series of Gothic romances which achieved popularity and insured him a place in histories of American literature. In 1809 came forth Washington Irving's satirical, able, and appealing *History of New York . . . by Diedrich Knickerbocker.* However, Irving's literary career was just beginning at that time, and his more impressive works lay in the future. The charm which is to be found in the *Knickerbocker* history is also present in Joel Barlow's *Hasty Pudding,* an attractive poem by an author who is better known for his longer and not very interesting production *The Columbiad*. Barlow was a romantic and a revolutionary; less exotic was John Howard Payne, whose plays began to appear on American stages early in the nineteenth century, and whose "Home, Sweet Home" written in Paris, later made him an American immortal.

The period from 1789 to 1815 was more noteworthy for artistic achievement than it was for literary genius. Gilbert Stuart, after extensive study in England, returned to America in 1792, and became the great American portrait painter of his time. Possessing both technical knowledge and a mastery of color, Stuart painted many of the great men of the era, as well as some who were not so impressive. One of his many portraits of Washington has been seen by almost all Americans, either in the original or in copies. Charles Willson Peale, along with his brother and his three sons, were all painters, with Charles the best of the clan. He combined operating a Natural History Museum in Philadelphia with limning many Revolutionary worthies. Scenes and personalities of the War of Independence were the forte of John Trumbull, who, like Stuart, worked in London in the studio of Benjamin West. Trumbull's "The Battle of Bunker's Hill" and his "The Declaration of Independence" are his most famous productions. Not so well known as Stuart or Trumbull, but bolder (or less prudent), John Vanderlyn painted not only historical scenes but in 1810 his "Ariadne," one of the earliest nudes done in America. In an America that feared any kind of immorality, it ruined his reputation and his career.

America long continued to excel in the spread of information rather than in individual cultural achievement. Newspapers multiplied in great numbers in the closing years of the eighteenth century and the first ones of the nineteenth, while magazines that lasted for more than an issue or two appeared for the first time. Tax money was not available for the support of libraries, but colleges and other private bodies continued to collect and preserve books. It was said in 1818 that "all the libraries in America would not furnish materials for a work like Gibbon's *Decline and Fall of the Roman Empire*." Certainly the Americans were collecting and preserving materials concerning the decline and fall of the first British Empire, for they were fascinated by the history of the Revolution. Few people will now contend that the origins and development of the American Republic are less important objects of study than the withering and collapse of the western and eastern Roman Empires in the fifth and fifteenth centuries. To be sure, America had no equivalent to Gibbon, nor would she have one for generations. To one acute observer, whose comment was often repeated during many decades, America was to Europe as Rome was to Greece. The comparison was to irk Americans, but was it not flattering to them that they should be compared to a people who for so long maintained order in an otherwise chaotic world?

Eating well and drinking plentifully, decently clad and suitably housed, able to read but not to write in the grand manner, the early American is hardly to be described culturally in superlatives. But if one uses sober language about him, it should not be forgotten that he lived in comfort and freedom elsewhere enjoyed only by fortunate minorities. To say that life was good for the Long Island farmer, the Philadelphia merchant, the Carolina planter, the New England artisan, the Tennessee frontiersman, is not to confess to being swayed by sentimental nostalgia.

18 THE WAR OF 1812

Thanks to the good sense of John Adams, the Federalists did not make the mistake of going to war with France, despite the hostility so many of them felt toward that country. Would the Democratic-Republicans, in power after 1801, become involved in conflict with Britain, which was so heartily disliked by many of them? The Jeffersonians displayed more restraint in their dealings with England than the Federalists had in theirs with France, but they finally had to ask the nation to take up arms when Britannia not only insisted upon ruling the waves but haughtily refused to let Americans traverse her watery domains in peace. In the twentieth century it may be thought that the maintenance of self-respect is insufficient cause for a nation to go to war. It was otherwise in the early part of the nineteenth century, and it is not too much to say that the United States was compelled by British arrogance to seek redress by cannon and bayonet.

Certainly the Democratic-Republicans manifested no lust for major military adventures during their first decade in office. They had no love for armies or navies—even for American ones—for they believed that great military establishments were by their very nature enemies of liberty. They had feared that the large army which Hamilton had tried to raise during

251

the undeclared war with France would be used against them, in threat if not in deed. They therefore neglected the land forces of the United States, although they did found the Military Academy at West Point in 1802. Nor were they builders of fleets, contenting themselves with the navy which had been bequeathed to them by the Federalists. They wished to avoid war, the maintenance of large standing armies and fleets, and the spending of money.

TO THE SHORES OF TRIPOLI

It must not be thought, however, that in the field of foreign affairs the Jeffersonians were fuzzy-minded idealists who shrank from realities. On the contrary, they persistently sought advantage for the United States in the troubles of Europe; nor would they bend the knee before the pirates who ruled the Barbary states of North Africa. Britain and France were accustomed to securing safe passage for their merchant vessels in the Mediterranean by paying bribes to the pirate "princes" of Morocco, Algiers, Tunis, and Tripoli. Under Federalist rule the United States, following the example of Britain and France, also paid tribute to these robber-rulers, who managed both to fill their treasuries with European money and their stock of slaves with European captives. The Washington and Adams administrations bowed before their demands according to unhallowed custom.

Jefferson was opposed to lavishing abroad the money he found so difficult to save at home, and he was particularly reluctant to pay the $200,000 extorted from the United States every year. When, in 1801, the ruler of Tripoli demanded even more money than he had been receiving, Jefferson indignantly refused, and when Tripoli declared war, the peace-loving President accepted the challenge and ordered the American navy to blockade "the shores of Tripoli." United States marines were afterward to sing about the exploits of the Corps on the northern coast of Africa, and not without reason. The skimpy American naval forces were not able to crush resistance in Tripoli, but they performed brilliantly. After four years of intermittent hostilities Tripoli was glad to release three hundred captive American sailors in return for $60,000 in cash and a payment of not more than $6000 whenever a new American consul should appear in Tripoli Harbor. Ten years later, after the appearance in the Mediterranean of a squadron under Commodore Stephen Decatur, all the "princes" of North Africa were forced to abandon their levies upon American shipping. So the American navy dealt fittingly with blackmailers whom the great powers of Europe could not or would not attack. During the fighting before 1805 American sailors and marines gained in experience and confidence, and were therefore better prepared for the time when they would be compelled to fight their British counterparts.

NEUTRALITY AND ECONOMIC WARFARE

Before that time came, American civil officers sought for several years to avoid war with England and to protect the rights of American citizens on the seas. At last the arrogance of a Britain that behaved as if America were not truly independent, persuaded the Jeffersonians that America must take up arms. The great European war resumed in 1803, with Napoleon and various allies wrestling with Britain and her allies for supremacy. The conflict raged for another dozen years, with England as mistress of the seas and Napoleon master of the European mainland. England's greatest admiral, Lord Nelson, established her naval supremacy in the Battle of Trafalgar in 1805, decisively defeating the combined fleets of France and Spain. To make their naval dominance more certain the British destroyed the Danish fleet by a surprise attack in 1807, lest it be used against them. Thereafter almost the only warships off the coasts of Europe were British ones. Seeking to force Napoleon into submission, the British resumed their efforts to cut off France's maritime trade, to deprive her of foodstuffs and raw materials, and to prevent her from sending goods to overseas markets. Resorting again to the weapon of blockade, Britain in 1806 issued Orders in Council which declared a part of the French coast closed to neutral shipping; next, all of the French shores were included, and finally, all the coasts of Europe under French control. There was one exception to the rule, one which could hardly please neutrals desiring to trade with France: a neutral vessel which paid duties at a British port could proceed to a French one. In decrees announced from Berlin and Milan, Napoleon retaliated by forbidding all trade with the British Isles and ordering the seizure of any ship that traded with the islands or paid duties at one of their ports.

There followed full-scale economic warfare, even though on occasion both antagonists found it expedient to wink at violations of their own rules; Napoleon had to ignore his own decrees to get himself some new overcoats from London. Of course, if the neutrals behaved in accordance with British orders and French decrees, they could not engage in maritime commerce with the British Isles or western Europe. Chief among the neutrals was the United States, and American merchants and farmers were the principal sufferers. The resumption of the war had enlarged markets for American foodstuffs and raw materials, and many Americans had profited from the war until the issuance of the British orders and the French decrees. Thereafter both the British and French seized dozens of American vessels trying to carry on trade despite the interdicts. The United States protested bitterly, contending that the antagonists were depriving the American merchant marine of its rights under international law, and urged that the offensive rules be withdrawn or modified. That Britain and France ignored international law was not surprising, for neither seemed disposed to forgo any useful weapon. The greatest injuries to American shipping were inflicted by the British, since their war vessels were numerous enough to permit effective patrolling of the water approaches to Europe.

IMPRESSMENT AND EMBARGO

Britain again resorted to the impressment of American seamen, for her navy needed sailors even more desperately than it had in the 1790s. Even before the British blockade of the European continent, America prepared to strike back with the weapon which had proved so effective against Britain before 1775, a boycott of British goods. In April, 1806, Congress passed an act which forbade the importation from England of various goods and products. However, the law was suspended until December, 1807, for it was hoped in Washington that the threat of using it would bring Britain to terms. But Britain refused to make any concession of importance, and in June, 1807, the commander of her frigate *Leopard* flagrantly violated international law in an impressment quarrel. Off Norfolk, Virginia, he demanded that Commodore James Barron of the United States frigate *Chesapeake* surrender four men whom he claimed were deserters from the Royal Navy. Barron quite properly refused to give up the men or to permit his vessel to be searched. Thereupon, the *Leopard* opened fire, killing three men and wounding eighteen more; Barron, whose ship was not ready for action, was forced to give up the supposed deserters. This impudent and wanton attack upon an American war vessel was cause enough for war, and an outraged Congress clamored for it.

Jefferson was not ready for a trial by arms, nor was the country, and he sought redress by economic means. The United States demanded and finally received compensation for the attack upon the *Chesapeake*, in 1811. The Non-Importation Act was invoked, and was then quickly replaced by the Embargo Act, which in effect forbade all commerce with European nations. This famous law was in effect between December, 1807, and March, 1809. While it prostrated American maritime trade and severely injured American agriculture, it did not force either Britain or France to repent. The British could get along without American raw materials and without American markets for British goods. Napoleon actually used the law for his own purposes. When American merchantmen appeared in ports under his control, he ordered their seizure, on the ground that they must be ships belonging to no nation. He was able to take many such vessels, since American merchants frequently preferred to break the law and to take the risk of British or French seizure to letting their ships lie idle in port. The loss of one ship was often compensated for by the profits from two or three uninterrupted voyages.

The Embargo Act was imposed by congressmen from the South and

West; it was intensely detested in the more commercial parts of the country. In New England it was denounced as arbitrary and unconstitutional, and Governor Jonathan Trumbull of Connecticut declared that the states should "interpose" to protect their citizens against the tyranny of Washington. In a minority position, New England threatened to behave as had Virginia and Kenucky in 1798. The New England Federalists, moving toward the defense of states' rights and limiting federal authority over foreign commerce, received no support from the courts. A Federalist district court judge in Massachusetts declared that, regardless of its merits, the Embargo Act was constitutional.

Jefferson soon recognized that the law was not accomplishing its purpose and that it was needlessly injurious. In consequence, it was repealed and replaced by a Non-Intercourse Act in March, 1809. By this law the interdict was confined to Britain and France, and the President was authorized to resume trade with either of those nations if it should cease to infringe upon American rights. Again, the law failed to have the desired effect, so in May, 1810, Congress adopted a slightly different approach. Macon's Bill No. 2 authorized the opening of trade with either Britain or France if either withdrew offensive restrictions on commerce; in such a situation it authorized continued barring of trade with the other power. But this weapon was just as ineffective as the others. Indeed, Napoleon accepted the bargain offered, but seized American shipping at the very time that the United States was carrying out its promise to prevent trade with Britain. Moreover, Britain was exasperated by the transaction, and showed her displeasure by a renewal of impressments. Eventually, British politicians did realize that they must make some concessions to the United States, for British industry and commerce were suffering from the loss of American markets and raw materials. Besides, it was evident after the American elections of 1810 that a war spirit was rising in the United States. On June 16, 1812, it was announced in London that the detested Orders in Council were to be suspended, and they were set aside a week later. It was too late. Unaware that the British were about to take action, Congress had declared war, the resolution being passed by the House of Representatives on June 4 and by the Senate on June 18. Once begun, the war could not quickly be stopped.

THE WAR

Wars are seldom accurately named, and the second conflict between America and Britain is no exception to the rule. It is often called the Second War for Independence, although, because of the very advantageous defensive position of the United States, independence was not at stake. Nor is another title for it, the War of 1812, entirely precise, since it continued until 1815. Moreover, hostilities began in 1811. On May 1 of that year the British frigate *Guerrière* impressed an American citizen from an American ship just outside New York harbor. Thereupon Captain John Rodgers with the American frigate *President* was ordered to the area to protect American merchant sailors. As Rodgers proceeded to his station, he saw a British warship, which he thought to be the *Guerrière*. It fled before him, and being overtaken, refused to identify itself. Rodgers then opened fire. The ship which he attacked was not the *Guerrière,* but the *Little Belt,* a much smaller vessel. The *Little Belt* was far outmatched, and was soon disabled; 9 members of her crew were killed, and 23 were wounded.

WAR HAWKS AND THE WEST

Also in the spring of 1811, army muskets and frontier rifles were being readied for action against Britain's red-skinned allies in the Old Northwest. There the great Shawnee Chief Tecumseh and his brother the Prophet, with the immoral support of the British from Canada, were preparing for a last-ditch defense of their territory. Toward that end they were trying to create a great Indian confederacy, and also to secure British military help. Alarmed by their activities, the Governor of the Indiana Territory, William Henry Harrison, moved against their capital on Tippecanoe Creek with about one thousand men in the fall. Tecumseh happened to be on a mission in the Old Southwest in search of allies, but his people responded in typical Indian fashion. On November 7 they made a surprise attack on Harrison, who was encamped within a mile of their principal village. The battle continued through the day, with both sides suffering heavily. The Americans were almost ready to concede defeat when the Indians fell back, and on the following day Harrison was able to put Tecumseh's capital to the torch.

Returning home, Tecumseh prepared to renew the struggle, but avoided a major clash until his British friends should be ready to take the field. Since Harrison was temporarily unable to muster forces strong enough to take the offensive, the frontier remained relatively quiet for some months after the battle. However, the settlers in the Ohio Valley and on the south shores of Lake Erie continued to demand that Tecumseh's forest empire be destroyed and his British friends driven from Ontario. They wanted the Indian menace removed; land-hungry, they also wanted possession of Ontario, the "Garden of Canada." Their demands did not abate when the British formally withdrew their support from Tecumseh, and when hostilities were resumed the following year, they cried "On to Canada."

Meanwhile, a somewhat similar situation was moving the Old Southwest in the direction of warfare. There the Creek and other Indians, at odds with American frontiersmen, were strengthened by trading with Panton, Leslie and Company, a British firm operating in the Spanish Floridas.

There also American expansionists saw in foreign hands rich lands they desired for themselves. Spain, overrun by the troops of Napoleon, was quite unable to defend her territories east of the Mississippi. In 1810 Southern frontiersmen captured Baton Rouge and established a Republic of West Florida. This aggressive act received the hearty approval of President Madison and of Congress, which took the next step in May, 1812, declaring West Florida to be an American property. Its capital, Mobile, still remained in Spanish hands, but Southern expansionists proposed not only to take that town but also to seize East Florida. In addition, they wanted a final settlement with the Creek which would reduce those warriors to impotence.

The War of 1812 was not waged for the sole purpose of defending the rights of American sailors and ships on the ocean. The men who pushed the declaration of war through Congress in June, 1812, were not merchants from New England and New York. They were Southerners and Westerners, young men who had been elected in 1810, commonly newcomers on the national political scene. These "War Hawks," as they were called, included Henry Clay of Kentucky, John C. Calhoun of South Carolina, Felix Grundy of Tennessee, and Peter B. Porter of western New York. Congressmen from the North, and especially those from New England, strenuously opposed the declaration. Chiefly Federalists, they contended that it was as logical to wage war against Napoleon as it was against Britain. The majority for the declaration in the House of Representatives was only 79 to 49, and that in the Senate was only 19 to 13. However, the War Hawks were not merely expansionists using British abuses against American sailors and shipping as excuses for a war to grab rich lands owned by a foreign power. There can be no doubt that these new young men hoped to wrest Ontario from Britain and both Floridas from weakened Spain, which was then a British ally. But it should be recalled that both Ontario and the Floridas had served as refuges and military storehouses for hostile Indians. Also, the British had injured American agriculture as well as American commerce, a fact of which the War Hawks were not unaware. Less influenced by considerations of dollars and cents than their older colleagues from the seaboard, and less concerned for the havoc of warfare, these ardent young patriots bitterly resented the indignities heaped upon the United States by Britain. They won the support of Madison, but were unable to gain that of the New England Federalists, who would bitterly describe the conflict as "Mr. Madison's War."

LACK OF PREPARATION

Although a general war had long threatened, the United States was quite unprepared for it in 1812. The nation was especially unready financially, for it could not support its military efforts by taxation and was unable to borrow as freely as necessary. The dismantling of the First Bank of the United States in 1811 had deprived the country of an institution which might have been useful in solving the problem of money and credit. The financial problem was aggravated by the diminishing customs receipts caused by the interruption of trade. Also embarrassing was the refusal of New England, then the nation's financial center, to purchase national securities. So awkward was the question of finances that the federal government could be described as nearly bankrupt in 1814—its difficulties resembling those which perplexed Congress in the later years of the War of Independence.

Enmeshed in many troubles, the nation also suffered from the unreadiness of the army and navy. The army, such as it was, was led by officers who had never possessed ability or who had lost it through too many years of inactivity. The naval officers were of a superior order, but the navy did not have enough ships, there being only 16 fighting vessels in service at the beginning of the conflict. Besides, the largest were frigates of 44 guns, for the United States had not built ships-of-the-line to match those with 64 guns and more possessed by Britain.

The nation also was weakened by internal strife, the Federalists of New York and especially those of New England declining to share fully in the war effort. In language that must have astonished his predecessor, Samuel Adams, Governor Strong of Massachusetts in June, 1812, called for a public fast to deplore the war "against the nation from which we are descended." The war was officially denounced by the legislatures of Massachusetts and Connecticut, both of which discouraged enlistments in the federal service and tried to prevent the use of their militia against the enemy. Indeed, New England merchants gave aid and comfort to the British by selling supplies to their forces in Canada and to their warships off the coast. But all of these handicaps did not bring ultimate disaster, partly because Britain had to devote her chief efforts to the struggle against Napoleon until the spring of 1814, and partly because of America's excellent defensive position. The war began with a series of stunning American victories at sea and spectacular defeats on land; it ended with the navy bottled up in Atlantic harbors and the army triumphant in battle at New Orleans.

NAVAL VICTORIES

In 1812 and 1813, before Britain could bring her superior maritime power to bear, the tiny American navy astonished the world. The American frigates, sturdily built and somewhat more heavily armed than their British counterparts, emerged triumphant in single-ship encounters. The *Constitution* under Captain Isaac Hull brought laurels and joy to the navy by wrecking the *Guerrière* in a half-hour duel off Nova Scotia in August, 1812. The *United States* under Captain Stephen Decatur captured the

British frigate *Macedonian* in October of the same year, and in December the *Constitution,* now commanded by Captain William Bainbridge, sank the frigate *Java.* Smaller American war vessels were also usually victorious in duels with British ships of the same size. There was glory, even in defeat. When the ill-fated *Chesapeake* was captured by the *Shannon,* her dying Captain Lawrence gave as his last order, "Don't give up the ship!" The British navy had not suffered so many defeats when fighting on equal terms since the time, 150 years earlier, when the Dutch had challenged them in the Strait of Dover. One by one, "Old Ironsides" and her sister frigates were penned in harbor by Britain's growing American fleet, but not until they had given a rude shock to the assumption of British superiority on the sea. Nor did the bottling up of American frigates bring an end to British troubles on the water, for American cruisers and privateers continued to assail British merchant shipping throughout the war. No fewer than 825 British merchantmen had been taken by the summer of 1814. Infesting even the English Channel, the privateers forced the British to use the convoy system and drove British insurance rates to very high levels. Nor were the exploits of American sailors confined to salt water, for they also won decisive triumphs on Lakes Erie and Champlain.

THE OLD NORTHWEST

To a degree the successes of American sailors in 1812 compensated for dismal failures in the warfare on land. The major theatres of conflict for the army lay on the frontiers between the United States and Canada until the war was near its close. American military leaders hoped for an early conquest of Canada, and American armies advanced from Detroit into western Ontario, across the Niagara River, and along the shores of Lake Champlain toward Montreal. But the success of these movements required trained troops and vigorous commanders; as might have been expected, the Canadians resisted bravely. The armies on Niagara and beside Lake Champlain made no progress, one reason being that in both of them some of the militia refused to serve beyond the Canadian boundary. Unimpressive as were their records, the commanders of these forces were not compelled to report disaster. Less fortunate was General William Hull, an uncle of Captain Isaac Hull, who had to tell his superiors in Washington that he and his army at Detroit had become prisoners of war. After crossing the Detroit River with more than 2000 men in July, Hull found himself confronted by General Isaac Brock with a Canadian force nearly as large as his own, while his rear was threatened by Tecumseh's Indian warriors. Retreating to Detroit, Hull was surrounded there by the Canadians and Indians. Alarmed lest a successful attack lead to an Indian massacre, Hull surrendered to Brock on August 16 without firing a shot. That Hull was afterward found guilty of cowardice and neglect of duty and was sentenced to death by a court-martial—the penalty was not exacted because of his age and his service in the War of Independence—did not improve the situation of the American forces in the Old Northwest. American forts on Mackinac Island and on the site of Chicago (Fort Dearborn) had fallen to the British even before Detroit, and they and their Indian allies were free to invade Indiana and Ohio.

Nor did 1813 bring much better fortune to the American forces operating in New York State. No progress was made toward Montreal, and the fighting on the Niagara frontier remained indecisive. There new officers were coming forward, including General Jacob Brown, a stout militiaman, and General Winfield Scott, a regular army man. Brown and Scott held their own in hard fought battles, but were unable to penetrate far into Canada.

Meanwhile, the tide of war changed decisively in favor of the Americans in the Old Northwest. William Henry Harrison assumed command of all American troops in that area in the fall of 1812. Part of his army was badly defeated in the Battle of the Raisin River the following January; in the struggle and in an Indian massacre that followed about 400 Americans were slain and another 500 taken prisoner. But Harrison persisted, and he successfully defended Fort Meigs at the mouth of the Maumee River in the following May. In August Major George Croghan held Fort Stephenson on the Sandusky River against British assaults.

Next, Captain Oliver Hazard Perry gave evidence that not all New Englanders were opposed to the war. Sent to win command of Lake Erie, which was indispensable if Harrison was to achieve any success, Perry managed to put ten vessels mounting 55 guns in commission at Presque Isle. On September 10 a British squadron under Captain Robert Barkley which had hitherto controlled the lake challenged Perry to battle at Put In Bay. Barkley's six vessels carried 65 guns—his vessels and his guns being somewhat smaller than Perry's. There followed a three-hour struggle, one of the hardest-fought naval engagements of the war. When Perry's flagship was so riddled by shot that it was forced out of action, he removed to another ship and resumed the struggle. He won an overwhelming victory, smashing or capturing all of the British vessels, and he joyfully reported to Harrison, "We have met the enemy and they are ours." Harrison was then able to march swiftly forward to Detroit, which was evacuated by the British General Henry Proctor without a fight. Proctor and Tecumseh retreated to the Thames River in Ontario, where they turned to offer battle on October 5. They were overwhelmed swiftly, their forces were captured or scattered, and Tecumseh himself was killed. Thereafter the Shawnee and their warrior allies abandoned the fight. The British continued to hold Mackinac Island until the end of the war, but they were unable to make another attack upon Detroit. By 1814 they had other more important objects in view.

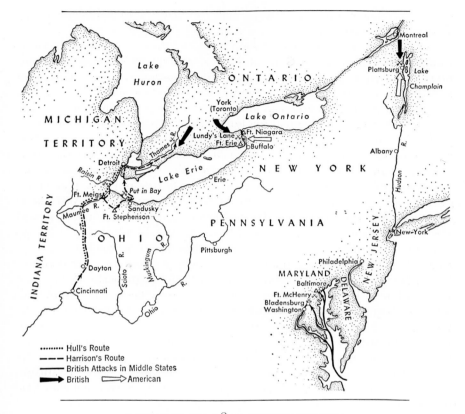

THE WAR OF 1812 IN THE NORTH

THE NORTHEAST, 1814

During 1812 and 1813 Britain was so heavily engaged with Napoleonic France that she was unable to muster large forces for the war in America. Only when Napoleon's empire was reduced to the Island of Elba in April, 1814, was it possible for her to take the offensive in the New World. Up to that time the British navy had blockaded only the Middle and Southern states, partly because of a shortage of ships and partly because London hoped the New Englanders would become more and more separated from their fellow Americans if they were treated well. Now the blockade was extended to cover all of the American coast. Fourteen thousand troops, veterans of the European wars, were sent across the ocean, so that the king's soldiers could move to the attack on the Canadian boundary, the shores of Chesapeake Bay, and the banks of the lower Mississippi. They were checked by General Jacob Brown in the hard-fought battle of Lundy's Lane on the Niagara frontier on July 25, and also before Fort Erie, which they vainly tried to take in August.

But Niagara was only a side show for the British. Their great effort came in September, when General Sir George Prevost led 11,000 veterans down the west coast of Lake Champlain, supported from the lake by a squadron of four ships and twelve gunboats. This little fleet under Captain George Downie carried 800 men and 90 guns; it had to win control of the lake if Prevost was to penetrate far into American territory. To stop Prevost's army there were only 3300 American troops under General Alexander Macomb at Plattsburg. On the lake, however, Captain Thomas Macdonough had a flotilla which matched Downie's in strength, except that Macdonough's guns were of shorter range. Anchoring opposite Plattsburg, Macdonough awaited an attack by Downie. Meanwhile, Prevost drove Macomb southward and secured a position from which he could bombard the American squadron from its rear. He failed to take advantage of his opportunity, leaving the British fleet unsupported. On September 11 it engaged that of Macdonough in a naval battle which lasted for more than two hours. In the Battle of Lake Champlain Macdonough performed as had Perry at Put In Bay. All the larger British ships were destroyed or captured, and the British gunboats had to seek safety in flight. The lake came decisively under American control, and Prevost had no choice but to fall back toward Montreal. Thus the war along the Canadian boundary ended in a stalemate: both the earlier American offensives and the later British ones had failed. Peculiarly enough, the Americans had been more successful on water than on land; Britannia was unable to rule the waves of Lakes Erie or Champlain.

THE MIDDLE STATES, 1814

While Prevost was moving southward, a British force entered Chesapeake Bay to divert American attention and if possible to raid Washington and Baltimore. The former was very weakly defended, and on August 24, 4000 British troops quickly routed a motley army of 7000 Americans under General William H. Winder at Bladensburg, just north of the capital. They also overcame sturdy resistance by Commodore Joshua Barney with 400 sailors and some artillery on the outskirts of Washington on the 24th and 25th. President Madison, members of his Cabinet, and the American militia routed at Bladensburg fled into Virginia. The British, remembering that an American raiding force had burned the government buildings at York (afterward Toronto), put the Capitol, the White House, and most of the federal offices to the torch. After doing as much damage as possible, they turned against Baltimore, where they were stopped by large forces collected under General Samuel Smith. Their fleet then undertook to open up the harbor by bombarding Fort McHenry, which protected it, into submission. During the night of September 13–14 shot and shell fell steadily on the fort, but in the morning "Old Glory" still flew above its ramparts. Francis Scott Key, an American civilian who watched the scene, hastened to pen and paper and wrote "The Star Spangled Banner" to celebrate the occasion. Put to music not quite singable for most Americans, it thrilled the nation and finally became the national anthem by act of Congress in 1931. Key's exultation was not premature, for the British had been effectively checked. They lingered on in Chesapeake Bay for another month, at last turning away to sea.

NEW ORLEANS

Injurious to American pride though the burning of Washington was, British depredations on the Potomac were not militarily important. Far more serious was their attempt to take New Orleans, which was defended by General Andrew Jackson.

Andrew Jackson had already won a great reputation as a leader of militia in the Old Southwest. Like Jacob Brown, he had no more than local repute

JACKSON IN THE SOUTHWEST

when the war began, although he had held various civil offices in Tennessee. Upon him fell the principal burden of dealing with the Creek Indians. The most warlike of all the red men in the Old Southwest, the Creek had carried on desultory hostilities against American frontiersmen ever since the War of Independence. As advancing white settlements threatened their shrinking hunting grounds, they became increasingly desperate. Urged on by the "Red Sticks," a faction desiring an all-out struggle against the whites, the Creek took up arms in July, 1813. At the end of August they captured Fort Mims on the Alabama River, massacring 250 of its defenders. Jackson collected militia from Tennessee, Georgia, and Mississippi, and marched against them in the fall. In a series of bloody engagements which followed, the Tennessee volunteers, who formed the bulk of Jackson's forces, were not always victorious. However, in March Jackson and General John Coffee led 3000 men against the Creek stronghold at Horseshoe Bend on the Tallapoosa River, sweeping over the defenses of the Indians and killing perhaps 900 warriors. Although the Creek did not immediately sue for peace, their power was permanently broken, and the war virtually came to a close for them in August.

Meanwhile, Jackson had become commander of all American forces in the Old Southwest, responsible for the defense of Mobile, after its seizure from the Spanish by General Wilkinson, and also for that of New Orleans. President Madison had put the right man in the right spot. In December, 1814, a British fleet put 7500 regulars ashore above the mouth of the Mississippi: many of them had served in the Chesapeake. Under Sir Edward Pakenham, a brother-in-law of the Duke of Wellington, they moved up the east bank toward New Orleans, Jackson hastily collected all available forces, including even Jean Lafitte and his pirates, who knew something about the use of artillery. A born leader of men and stern disciplinarian, Jackson was determined to win, and his motley army shared his resolution. With about 4500 men, including veterans of frontier fighting from Tennessee and Kentucky, he built a line of breastworks across a narrow spot between the east bank of the Mississippi and a cypress swamp. The west side of the river he covered with smaller forces. On January 8 Pakenham attacked. He sent a detachment against Jackson's right flank, but it was checked. He personally led 5300 redcoats in a direct assault upon the breastworks, only to be driven back by Jackson's artillery and infantry fire. A second charge by Pakenham was bloodily repulsed. Within a half-hour the British sustained more than 2000 casualties; Pakenham himself was among the dead. Jackson had only 21 killed and wounded. It was obvious to Pakenham's successor, General John Lambert, that the British had failed, and he and the remains of the British army sailed away three weeks later. Jackson's stunning victory made him, even above Harrison and Brown, the great American hero of the war.

THE RETURN TO PEACE

Although Jackson was not aware of it, peace had already been made with Britain, and his great triumph was won after the war's end. The news of New Orleans reached Washington almost at the same time as a report that American commissioners had signed a treaty with British representatives at Ghent in Belgium. The rejoicing in Washington was witnessed, if not entirely shared, by three messengers who had come from New England to demand that the Constitution be altered so that in the future no other war or major obligation be taken on without the consent of that region. As the war had continued, discontent had mounted east of the Hudson, and had led to threats of nullification and separation. While Jackson's army was gathering at New Orleans, twenty-five delegates representing most of New England gathered at Hartford to consider ways to compel the national government to behave in acceptable fashion. The Hartford Convention at length drew up a list of constitutional amendments which the messengers carried to Washington. Had these been enacted, the authority of the central government must have been crippled. They provided for a two-thirds majority in Congress for the admission of new states, for an embargo (limited at any case to sixty days), and for a declaration of war, except in the event of invasion. Representatives and direct taxes were to be on the basis of free population—slaves were not to be counted. The Presidency was to be held by one person for no more than one term, and two persons from the same state were not to occupy it for successive terms—there had been too many Virginians in the White House. This was not treason, but a most vigorous expression of sectionalism. Had the demands been made a year earlier, when the war was going badly, and Congress was considering a military draft, President Madison and his regime must have been sadly embarrassed. As it was, New England and the Federalists who presumed to speak for her spoke just as their cause's foundation had disappeared.

THE TREATY OF GHENT

The war had hardly been formally declared when efforts began to restore peace. In the fall of 1812 Tsar Alexander, allied with Britain against Napoleon, offered his services as mediator. Lord Castlereagh, the English Foreign Secretary, wanted no meddling from the Tsar, so refused the offer. In the following November, however, he proposed direct negotiations. President Madison agreed and sent to Ghent as peace commissioners John Quincy Adams, James A. Bayard, Albert Gallatin, Henry Clay, and Jonathan Russell. In August, 1814 they began discussions with a British delegation. It was impossible to secure an agreement for several months because the British were not prepared to make any concessions regarding American maritime grievances. Indeed, they demanded the cession of a vast territory along the Canadian frontier and formation of a neutral Indian country as a buffer in the Old Northwest. Such large claims, based on reports of British military victories, were utterly unacceptable to the Americans, who wanted the boundary between the United States and Canada restored as it was before the war. The news of Macdonough's success on Lake Champlain softened the British attitude. Britain's greatest general, the Duke of Wellington, told the Cabinet that the military situation was not sufficiently favorable for Britain to insist upon a cession of territory. Nor did he think any decisive victory could be won unless very large forces were sent to America. His sobering advice made it possible to reach an understanding. The Americans abandoned their demands for redress of grievances, the British theirs for American territory. On December 24 a treaty was signed calling for the release of prisoners and the return of all conquered lands. Approved by Madison and unanimously ratified by the Senate in February, this treaty was more favorable for the United States than appears at first sight. The Anglo-French wars were drawing to an end. The issues of blockade and impressment would fade as growing American power provided protection for American interests in the future. Moreover, although Canada remained British, Mobile and most of West Florida remained American. In fact, so great was Spain's weakness, that all of the Floridas would soon come under the American flag.

The Treaty of Ghent was only the first of a series of agreements which insured more friendly Anglo-American relations for the immediate future. A commercial convention of 1815 opened the British East Indies to American shipping and removed discriminatory duties against American maritime trade. In 1818, President Monroe and Lord Castlereagh ended a threatened armaments race on the Great Lakes by the so-called Rush-Bagot Agreement, which restricted naval forces on the Great Lakes and Lake Champlain to police purposes. The names of Richard Rush, acting Secretary of State, and Charles Bagot, British minister to the United States, acquired a measure of immortality; the agreement not only put an end to an arms race at that time, but led to permanent removal of large armed forces from the Canadian-American frontier. Action was also taken in the so-called Convention of 1818, signed on October 20, to settle the course of much of that boundary. By its terms the line was set at the forty-ninth parallel between the Lake of the Woods and the Rocky Mountains. It also provided that the Oregon region—the vast territory between the Rockies and the Pacific bordered on the south by the forty-second parallel and on the north by Alaska—which both countries claimed, should be jointly ruled for a period of ten years. This agreement could be extended

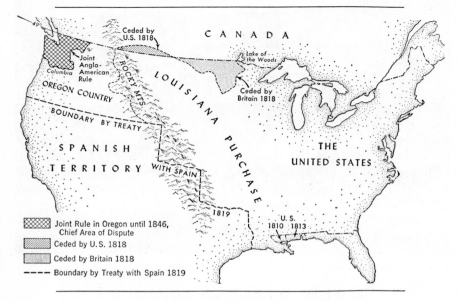

TREATIES AFTER THE WAR OF 1812

if necessary, and it was continued until 1846. In addition, the Convention of 1818 settled questions regarding the rights of American fishermen off the coasts of Newfoundland and Labrador. In sum, the Treaty of Ghent and agreements which followed it solved some awkward questions and helped toward future Anglo-American friendship.

19 A NEW WESTERN DEMOCRACY

While "Mr. Madison's War" was not a second war for political independence, its conclusion ended a twenty-five year period during which too many Federalists looked with fondness upon Britain and too many Democratic-Republicans saw American destiny as tightly linked with that of France. While America continued to accept British cultural leadership after 1815 (despite the wishes of many of her people), her national policy was no longer affected seriously by passionate attachments to British or French ideologies. Despite some humiliations and embarrassments, the war gave proof of the nation's increasing strength, and its outcome made possible continued rapid growth. Americans could now devote themselves to peace during a long generation, and they took advantage of their opportunity. The years from 1815 to 1829 saw relative political quiet, prosperity (save for a banking panic in 1819), and remarkable increases in population, economic power, and in settlements beyond the Appalachians. During that era the Floridas finally came under the American flag, and the United States declared itself the protector of the New World against the Old. During most of the period a new nationalism pervaded the country. Sectionalism waned in New England but was to revive as Southerners found their local interests threatened by the federal government.

POPULATION AND ECONOMIC GROWTH

For fifteen years after the War of 1812 the phenomenal population growth which had characterized the colonial and early national periods continued unabated. Immigrants continued to be relatively few, coming from the European areas which had supplied settlers in colonial times. But natural increase was almost amazing; the 4 million Americans of 1790 became more than 7 million by 1810, and almost 13 million by 1830. In forty years the Americans multiplied more than threefold. As the numbers of Americans mounted, so did the number of acres under cultivation. Immediately after the war there was a great westward surge of pioneers to the Mississippi and beyond. When Tecumseh's confederacy collapsed, the way was opened for the occupation of most of the Old Northwest. Treaties deprived the Indians of their claims to Ohio, the southeastern half of Michigan, and most of Indiana and Illinois. Tens of thousands of Southerners moved into the wooded and hilly lands in the southern parts of Ohio, Indiana, and Illinois. The lure of open lands, dislike of slavery, and the advance of the great cotton plantations led these Southerners across the Ohio, in such large numbers that Indiana acquired something of a Southern complexion. Meanwhile, pioneers from the Middle and New England states poured across the prairies of northern Ohio, Indiana, and Illinois. Somewhat later they swept into southern Michigan, occupying its "oak openings" and rich lake bottoms. The National Road from Cumberland to Wheeling (later extended to Vandalia, Illinois) was crowded with Conestoga wagons, as were other less famous roads. Boats and flatboats carried pioneers down the Ohio. A large part of America was in motion, and the result was the rapid appearance of new states beyond the Alleghenies. There were only four in 1815, Kentucky, Tennessee, Ohio, and Louisiana. These were joined by Indiana (1816), and Illinois (1818), and within another generation by Michigan and Wisconsin.

Nor was this great westward movement confined to the Old Northwest. Missouri, half Southern and half Northern, achieved statehood in 1820. The Old Southwest also experienced a rapid advance of settlements, for the power of the Indians had been broken, and their lands had become available to the whites. Pioneers from the seaboard South found rich new cotton lands in the "Black Belt" of Mississippi, which became a state in 1817, and Alabama, which followed two years later. There was, of course, a people who suffered from these migrations—the Indians who were displaced. They were forced to sell their hunting grounds and villages to the federal government, which in turn sold them cheaply to the pioneers. By 1825 it had become federal policy that the red men must move beyond the Mississippi. Here and there they were permitted to remain on reserva-

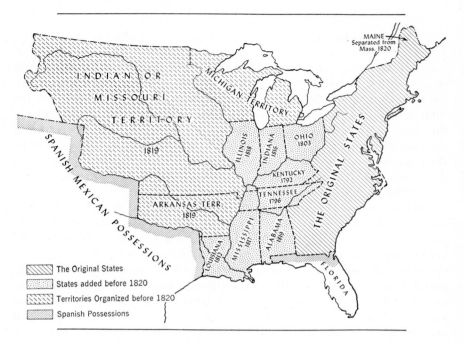

ADDITIONS TO THE STATES BEFORE 1820

tions set aside for them east of the river, and the Seminole preserved their independence for some years in the swamps of the Everglades. In 1832 Chief Black Hawk and his people tried to return to their ancestral homes in Illinois, but they were attacked and routed in the so-called Black Hawk War; this time they were driven beyond the great river for good. They and other Indians who wanted to stay in their old haunts faced forced migration, a "trail of tears" extending to the edges of the Great Plains.

Occupation of the regions between the Ohio River and the Great Lakes, and from the Tennessee River to the Gulf of Mexico inevitably brought a great expansion in agriculture. In the Old Northwest "general farming" was the rule, with wheat, corn, and cattle the principal products. The Midwest became the "bread basket" of America, with Cincinnati in the role later made famous by Chicago, that of the principal butcher of the nation. The centers of wheat and corn began to move westward from New York and Pennsylvania. Meanwhile, cotton virtually conquered the Old Southwest. It will be recalled that before the War of Independence tobacco, rice, and indigo had been, with corn, basic in the South. British law destroyed the market for indigo in England before 1800, and its production swiftly came to an end. Rice continued to be important in South Carolina and Georgia, while tobacco cultivation spread to Kentucky and Tennessee, and flourished. But the era of cotton and of the "Old South" had begun. Whitney's invention of the cotton gin made large-scale production possible, while the rapid growth in the British population as a result of the Industrial Revolution, plus the swift expansion of the United States, created ever larger demands for clothing. Accordingly, the "white weed" spread through the South Carolina Piedmont before 1800, and on into Tennessee and the Gulf States. At the beginning of the nineteenth century the nation produced 100,000 bales of cotton each year; thirty years later the annual production had reached beyond 700,000 bales. Cotton had not yet become king, but it was surely an heir-apparent.

URBANIZATION AND INDUSTRY

As the farmer and planter moved to the west, his friends and relatives remained on the family homestead or moved into town to engage in commerce or manufacturing. The movement toward urbanization, afterward so striking a feature of the American scene, had already begun in New England and the Middle States. Small at the end of the revolution, both Philadelphia and New York contained more than 100,000 people by 1820, and New York already gave signs of becoming the metropolis of the New World. The swift burgeoning of the cities was accompanied by a rapid growth in commerce and stimulated by the rise of manufacturing and the factory. As early as 1790, using machinery devised by Richard Arkwright, Samuel Slater had used power to spin cotton at Pawtucket, Rhode Island, and the production of cotton goods was to flourish in New England until

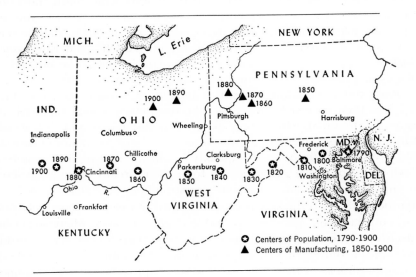

WESTWARD MOVEMENT OF POPULATION AND MANUFACTURING

the twentieth century. The factory had appeared in Massachusetts before 1815, becoming a more and more conspicuous part of the landscape in the Middle and Northern states as time went on. In Pennsylvania the iron industry, beginning to make extensive use of coal and to refine its process of production, grew remarkably. Making machinery, especially for cotton manufacture, became an important new enterprise. Machine-made paper was turned out as early as 1817 in Delaware. A new principle which was to have the most far-reaching effects, the use of interchangeable parts in manufacturing, was worked out by the ingenious Eli Whitney as early as 1798. Manufacturing was encouraged by the restrictions placed upon shipping between 1807 and 1814, and also by protective tariffs, the first of which was enacted before the end of the War of 1812. America's 87 cotton mills and 14 woolen mills of 1810 multiplied before 1830.

COMMERCE

Stimulated by the remarkable growth of manufacturing, both foreign and domestic commerce flourished. The annual value of imported goods averaged nearly $100 million immediately after the War of 1812, and more than $70 million per annum during the decade of the 1820s. In that decade the value of exported goods was almost precisely equal to that of those that entered the country. The merchant marine expanded steadily, reaching a total of more than one million tons of shipping by 1830. New York and New Orleans assumed ever greater importance as centers of oceanic trade, with New York tending to become *the* entrance to America. Internal commerce kept pace with external, and Pittsburgh, Cincinnati, and Louisville became great inland emporia. Goods moved over a widening and improving network of roads, on rivers, on the Great Lakes, and through such canals as Governor DeWitt Clinton's "big ditch" (the Erie Canal), which was opened between Albany and Buffalo in 1825. The building of turnpikes, profitable for a time, was continued on an impressive scale for about thirty years, and more than 4000 miles of such well-paved highways had been opened by 1821. But the turnpike was soon replaced to a degree by the canal, which could be used by the new steamboats. Robert Fulton's *Clermont,* pushing its way from New York to Albany, fascinated bold investors. Fulton's success quickly led to the Age of the Steamboat, which ended only when competition from the railroads became too severe for inland water traffic. Although the steamboat *Savannah* crossed the Atlantic in 1819, sailing vessels long continued to carry most oceanic trade. It was otherwise on America's navigable rivers and lakes, where steam had a decisive advantage over sail. The steamboat *Washington* made the first trip from Pittsburgh to New Orleans in 1815, beginning a remarkable era of transportation on the Ohio and the Mississippi; the story of steamboat

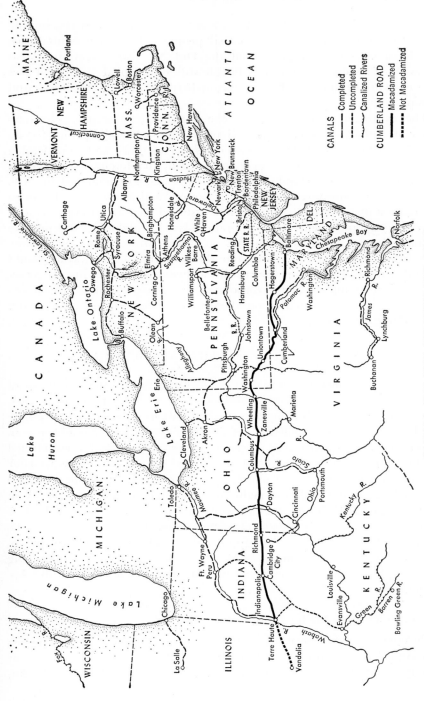

CANALS AND THE CUMBERLAND ROAD

CANALS
— — — Completed
— · — · — Uncompleted
·········· Canalized Rivers

CUMBERLAND ROAD
━━━━━ Macadamized
▪▪▪▪▪ Not Macadamized

traffic on the Great Lakes, while less romantic, was almost equally impressive. After the opening of the Erie Canal, people and products poured back and forth between New York and the Old Northwest, and the Great Lakes—St. Lawrence Waterway (though still interrupted between Lakes Erie and Ontario) became a water avenue between the Old Northwest and Europe.

The exuberant growth of American agriculture, industry, and commerce after the War of 1812 was only partly checked by the panic of 1819, and the recently founded stock exchanges of New York and Philadelphia hummed with activity. Banks were chartered by the dozens by the various states, and the Second Bank of the United States was organized in 1816. The clearing house was established in Boston, and a few banks began to pay interest upon deposits. Corporations assumed great importance, as state after state adopted general incorporation laws, abandoning the practice of chartering by special action of the legislature. Most of the new corporations were engaged in commerce, but the corporate device was afterward extended to the field of manufacturing with remarkable results. Together with the increasing use of the corporation came life insurance, which was made available in the cities on the eastern seaboard, and much later throughout the nation.

SOCIAL AND INTELLECTUAL AMERICA

Nor was American progress during the fifteen years after the Peace of Ghent confined to things physical and financial. Newspapers and magazines, especially the former, became relatively numerous, offering to the public words in quantity and sometimes of quality. There were also advances in education, with Massachusetts especially active. In 1821 Boston established the first high school with a liberal program of courses; and six years later a Massachusetts state law demanded that every town of more than five hundred people establish and maintain a high school. Another novelty in 1821 was Emma Willard's establishment at Troy, New York, of a Female Seminary, the first high school for women in the United States. With the founding of the University of Virginia in 1819 under Jefferson's leadership, the state university movement acquired new impetus, Virginia supplying an example which was soon to be copied by the states west of the Appalachians.

LITERATURE—"THE KNICKERBOCKER SCHOOL"

Devoted to the spread of information and interested in learning and the arts, Americans also contributed some originality, for their culture was not merely derivative. The "Flowering of New England" had not yet begun, and was not to begin until the 1830s, although intellectual activity was not totally absent. The Unitarians under the leadership of William Ellery Channing were assailing the stronghold of Congregationalist orthodoxy with success. It was New York, however, with its "Knickerbocker School" that supplied the leaders in American literature, notably Washington Irving and James Fenimore Cooper. Irving had made a reputation as early as 1809 it will be recalled, with his *History of New York . . . by Diedrich Knickerbocker*. He achieved added fame a decade later with the appearance of *The Sketch Book,* which included the American classic tales of "Rip Van Winkle" and "The Legend of Sleepy Hollow." While living in Europe, Irving wrote a fine life of Columbus, and continued to produce tales and sketches based upon English and European themes. Returning to America in 1832, he wrote appealingly about western exploration and produced a respectable biography of Washington. While his historical writings have largely been superseded, his fiction has a lasting humor and enduring charm.

Cooper was the first genuinely important American novelist. Irving had appeal; Cooper, power. From upstate New York, Cooper chose as the theme of his first novel, *Precaution,* life in English society, with which he was not sufficiently familiar to display his talents. Turning quickly to the American scene, in 1821 he published *The Spy,* a tale of the American Revolution. Two years later, with the appearance of *The Pioneers,* he began his great series of *Leatherstocking Tales,* which he continued with *The Last of the Mohicans, The Pathfinder, The Deerslayer,* and *The Prairie.* In these novels of the American frontier the hero was Natty Bumppo, a brave and noble man of nature. Writing about familiar things, Cooper effectively mingled romance and realistic description of life on the frontier among the Indians. While he became unpopular among his fellow Americans because he campaigned vigorously for recognition of the principle of aristocracy, his "Western" stories became part of the stouter stock of American literature. They have continued to be widely read, especially in Europe, where they have been considered basically important descriptions of American life, not only as it was in 1800, but as it was in 1900. Less significant, but also interesting, were Cooper's novels of the sea, including *The Pilot,* and his "social" novels, such as *Satanstoe.*

Also in the Knickerbocker School, although he did his best work in Massachusetts before removing to New York City, was William Cullen Bryant, whose fine talents as a lyric poet were finally submerged in newspaper work. However, the young Bryant published his "Thanatopsis" in 1817, and in the following year his splendid poem "To a Waterfowl," a classic and doubtless his masterpiece. With the appearance of Irving, Cooper, Bryant, and many lesser figures it could no longer be said that

American writers were merely pale copyists of the Europeans, especially of the English. It is pleasant to relate that the writings of these gifted Americans, unlike those of so many men of genius, were popular in their own time, and that these men did not starve in garrets.

THE UNCOUTH AMERICAN

Although the productions of the Knickerbocker School—along with John Howard Payne's "Home Sweet Home"—were well received in their own time, it should not be assumed that the Americans had become a highly cultivated people. As a whole they preferred Parson Mason Weems's homely and slapdash biography of Washington, with its famous fictional cherry tree story, to Irving's life of Columbus. The novels of Sir Walter Scott and the poetry of Lord Byron, even if widely read in America, were not to be found in every log house on the frontier, nor always in the homes of Southern aristocrats or New England merchants. The American masses were not sophisticated or remarkably well informed, albeit as well acquainted with public affairs, literature, and the arts and sciences as the majority of the British or Europeans. If one were to accept the opinions expressed by English travelers who visited the United States after 1815, one would have to conclude that Americans in general were a rough, ignorant, and boastful people. Occasionally such travelers, who could sometimes produce two volumes on the basis of two months of journey, stressed the fine manners of the Southern aristocracy or the zeal for learning displayed in Boston; stress was more likely to be upon the ungrammatical speech of the westerner, the sanitary shortcomings of American taverns, the roughness of roads, profanity on the steamboat, and lack of gentlemanly polish almost everywhere. In her *Domestic Manners of The Americans* Frances Trollope described them, chiefly on the basis of a residence in Cincinnati, as a people who were basically vulgar, and not entirely without reason. To be sure, travelers suffering from the many inconveniences that were characteristic of American travel often transferred their spleen to paper. Doubtless it was asking too much to expect Americans to behave like idealized English ladies and gentlemen. Even so, there were real crudities in American life, which increased in proportion as one moved westward. American table manners left something to be desired, although little on the table. As a whole, the Americans were not genteel; and the less informed they were, the more likely they were to brag about the superiority of God's country and its inhabitants over the effete peoples of Europe. The travelers did not always observe that the Americans enjoyed a fundamental well-being, that their crudities (exaggerated) were almost inevitable, or that those crudities were largely superficial and would pass with time.

POLITICAL DEMOCRACY

Especially disconcerting to some English travelers was the American insistence that men (except for Negro slaves) were equal. The manner in which the Americans boasted of equality with kings and aristocrats might be discourteous and vulgar, but the fact that he was free to boast was proof that political democracy had arrived in the United States. And so it had, at least by the year 1830. By that time the nation had moved from the relatively conservative republicanism of Revolutionary times through the liberal republicanism of Jefferson to Jacksonian democracy.

While long strides were taken toward true representative government during the epoch of the Revolution, political authority tended to remain in the hands of the men of property and education. The voter's usual role was to make a choice between such men. In office they frequently acted according to their own information and their own consciences rather than in accordance with the sentiments of their constituents. They usually looked on themselves as trustees of the public good rather than as agents for the mass of private citizens. The triumph of the Jeffersonians in 1800 brought into national power a new group of propertied and educated men who were more responsive to the wishes of the common people. Jefferson and his allies offered government for the people rather than government by the people. Gradually, however, the liberal-spirited republicanism of the Jeffersonians altered, as the rank and file in his party acquired power at the expense of its elite. Because the same change did not occur in the same degree among the Federalists, their party became more "snobbish" and finally died.

THE SUFFRAGE AND ELECTIONS

Most remarkable in the advance toward political democracy after the Revolution was the broadening of the suffrage. Most of the original state constitutions restricted the right to vote to property owners, while the others denied the suffrage to those who did not pay taxes. But such barriers were either lowered or removed in the constitutions of states formed after 1789. In the settlements beyond the Appalachians there was economic and social leveling which opened the way for equality of all white men at the polls; after the War of 1812 all new state constitutions provided for white manhood suffrage. Moreover, the abolition of property and tax-paying requirements proceeded in the seaboard states. White manhood suffrage was established in New Jersey in 1807, and in Maryland in 1810. Between 1818 and 1821 property qualifications were destroyed in Connecticut, Massachusetts, and New York. Only in Rhode Island did the property requirement linger. There the franchise was refused to all but freeholders and their eldest sons until 1843, the suffrage being broadened only after those who had been refused the right to vote had risen in rebellion under the leadership of Thomas W. Dorr.

The movement toward political democracy was not confined to the expansion of the suffrage, for it was accompanied by changes in public machinery which enlarged the influence of the voter. Although "gerrymandering" acquired its name early in the nineteenth century (offering a doubtful tribute to the memory of Elbridge Gerry), there was at that time a marked trend toward districting on the basis of numbers. The western areas of the original states secured representation more in proportion to their population, and beyond the mountains one part of a new state was not normally favored at the expense of another.

Changes were also made in the method of choosing the President and the Vice-President. In 1788 Washington was both nominated and elected by the electors, who had been chosen by the state legislatures. However, party caucuses in Congress soon took over the right to nominate for these offices—a practice which continued until 1824, when various state legislatures placed the names of candidates before the public. By 1840 the national party conventions had come into existence, nominating candidates and drawing up platforms upon which they might stand or fall. By that time candidates were likely to be men with strong support among the party's rank and file. Meanwhile, the presidential electors had also been made more responsible to the voters. More and more often they were chosen directly by the voters rather than by the legislatures, South Carolina and Delaware being the only states to follow the original practice after 1828. Thus the electors became party nominees, pledged to cast their ballots for their party's candidates. In other words, they largely lost their discretionary power and became instruments to register the wishes of the voters—although now and then a willful elector might try to cast his ballots against the will of his party.

ELECTION OF JUDGES

Many people came to believe that judges as well as legislators and public executives should be elected rather than appointed; state after state made the change, compelling the judges to leave their benches occasionally for some campaigning. Whether state judges should be elected or selected has been disputed ever since; election has generally received the stronger support, although lawyers usually prefer appointment, especially for the highest state courts.

While there are two sides to the question, it can be asserted with great force that the increasing use of the elective method often brought into office persons unqualified by training, educaton, and character. The belief that any man could perform the duties of any office became too prevalent. Too often the man in office chose to follow capricious opinions of his constituents rather than his own good judgment, since he had rather be elected than right. With political democracy came the "spoils system," the practice of changing public officials wholesale after the defeat of one party by another at the polls. In 1831 Senator William L. Marcy of New York coined the famous slogan "to the victor belongs the spoils," which remained a guiding principle for American politicians until it was finally limited by the establishment of civil service systems.

That political democracy brought an improvement in the quality of men in public office, including the highest offices in the land, is a doubtful proposition. It may well be that the voter of the nineteenth century—and he did vote—was less qualified in terms of education and information to exercise the suffrage than had been his predecessor of the eighteenth century. The politicians he supported were likely to be pleasing rather than potent; it is likely that American political leadership was at a higher level in the eighteenth and twentieth centuries than it was in the intervening time.

POLITICS: JEFFERSON TO JACKSON

The new democracy had definitely arrived in 1828 with the election to the Presidency of Andrew Jackson. Before Jackson was swept into the White House on a tumultuous wave of popular support, the Democratic-Republican Party had won its final triumph over the Federalists, becoming the only major party, and had then split into factions which eventually developed into two new parties. Long before the War of 1812 Federalists had begun to desert to the Democratic-Republican camp, among them the vigorous and able John Quincy Adams, son of Jefferson's friend and bitter political rival. They took with them some Federalist notions which many Jeffersonians adopted as they gradually became less hostile to the exercise of national power. As the party of Jefferson moved away from strict construction of the Constitution, states' rights, and agrarianism, some of its Southern supporters became alarmed. Finding intellectual inspiration in the writings of John Taylor of Caroline and a congressional leader in the person of John Randolph of Roanoke, these so-called "Old Republicans" struggled to return the party to its original course. In consequence, the party split roughly into three groups, the "Old Republicans," opposite to them a body of nationalists and activists, and in the middle, moderates led by Jefferson and Madison, and later by Monroe. The moderates easily nominated and elected Madison in 1808. Four years later, Madison encountered stiff opposition because of the strong anti-war feeling among the northern Democratic-Republicans. These put forth as a Presidential candidate DeWitt Clinton, a nephew of George Clinton, who had inherited some of his uncle's prestige and who had abilities of his own. The Federalists also rallied behind Clinton, and the contest in the electoral college was quite close, Clinton carrying all of the states north of the Potomac except Pennsylvania and Vermont. Madison had 128 votes, and Clinton, 89. Again in 1816 dissension appeared in the Democratic-Republican Party when many of its newer men backed William H. Crawford against Monroe. Monroe won the nomination by a rather small margin in a congressional caucus, 65 to 54. However, at the polls, Monroe won an easy victory over Rufus King, the last Presidential candidate to be named by the Federalist Party. King carried only Massachusetts and Connecticut. In 1820 Monroe was almost unopposed, receiving all of the electoral votes save one, which was cast for John Quincy Adams by William Plumer of New Hampshire. With the collapse of the Federalist Party, political passions diminished, and as early as 1817 a Boston newspaper announced that the nation had entered upon an "era of good feelings"—a phrase which was to fasten itself to the period when Monroe was in the Presidency. But factional warfare and personal rivalries within the Democratic-Republican Party continued, and were to cause bitter contests for the Presidency in 1824 and again in 1828.

20 "THE ERA OF GOOD FEELINGS"

The collapse of the Federalist party, the "Era of Good Feelings," the advance toward political democracy, all were associated with a new nationalism which pervaded the nation during the decade after 1815. The sectionalism so vigorously manifested in New England during the war came to a sudden end with the news of Jackson's victory at New Orleans and the signing of the Treaty of Ghent. New England repented her behavior, especially since the federal government soon began to push measures, including a protective tariff, which promoted her interests. Moreover, the War Hawks did not cease to be nationalists with the coming of peace; Henry Clay and John C. Calhoun were as eager to use federal powers to assist the nation's growth after 1815 as they had been to employ them against the British. Indeed, the younger men in politics, whether they had long been nursed in the Democratic-Republican tradition or were only recently divorced from the Federalist party, were very generally enthusiastic champions of federal action to promote the nation's prosperity. They also favored territorial expansion, and they were disposed to assert America's wishes vigorously in the arena of international affairs.

They were also keen to push President Madison, who seemed to them too cautious and too conservative, into action. They did not fully share the opinions of Madison entertained by the writer James K. Paulding, who described him as "a confoundedly sensible fellow, and talks about every thing like a professor."

THE NEW NATIONALISM

Not every rising young man in American politics was a devout nationalist. Daniel Webster, beginning a colorful career, was at first opposed to tariffs for protection; but the "Godlike Daniel," whose conduct did not quite live up to his majestic appearance, learned before many years had passed that what was good for the New England manufacturer was good for New England and the nation. Most typical of the "new nationalists" were Henry Clay and John Quincy Adams, Clay being the principal architect of their program for internal affairs, while Adams championed American interests in international relations. Clay developed what was afterward known as "the American system," which called for protective tariffs and federal action to build roads and canals; he also favored the Bank of the United States. For a time Calhoun was as nationalist-minded as Clay, although he later became a supporter of states' rights, when he realized that the economic welfare of South Carolina was not promoted equally with that of Massachusetts by protective tariffs. Supporting the "new nationalists" was a large body of public opinion, for promotion of American prosperity, expansion, and well-being, together with an aggressive foreign policy, had great popular appeal. However, the older political leaders were not always eager to embrace the program of the younger men, partly because they believed that the Constitution could not be decently interpreted to permit the younger men's program for domestic growth. A little later, the nationalist movement met heavy opposition in the South, where it came to be widely believed that the "American system" was actually a Northern one.

Not all nationalists supported precisely the same program, and many of their measures were defeated in Congress. Some of them wanted an enlarged regular army; but when President Madison proposed in 1815 that the army should contain 20,000 men, the Congress reduced his figure by half. In 1825 President John Quincy Adams called for government encouragement of agriculture, commerce, and manufacturing, and for legislation in behalf of the arts, sciences, and literature. He recommended the establishment of a national university and an astronomical observatory. But the most important measures supported by the new nationalists were the creation of a Second Bank of the United States, a protective tariff, and federal action toward the building of roads and canals. They were not able to push this last through on a large scale, but they did succeed in making the Second Bank of the United States, and they obtained protective tariffs, which encouraged the infant American industry.

THE SECOND BANK OF THE UNITED STATES

The War of 1812 made it only too clear that the nation needed a sound, standard paper currency, and that it was essential that there be some means whereby the federal government could borrow large sums of money in times of emergency. Even before the end of the fighting a plan for a Second Bank of the United States was proposed by Secretary of the Treasury Alexander Dallas and sanctioned by Congress in January, 1815. Because of obvious defects in Dallas' arrangements, Madison vetoed the bill. However, he recommended that Congress prepare a more suitable law, and Calhoun and Clay proceeded to action early in 1816. As a result, in March Congress voted to establish the Second Bank of the United States. It was Calhoun who introduced the necessary bill and Clay gave it powerful support, although he had voted against rechartering the First Bank of the United States in 1811—Clay had some little difficulty explaining why he thought such a bank was unconstitutional in 1811, but constitutional in 1816.

The Second Bank of the United States was modeled upon the first one, but had a much larger capital, $35 million, of which the federal government held one-fifth. The President named five of its twenty-five directors. The new bank was to serve as a depository for federal funds, was authorized to issue paper currency, and was permitted to engage in private banking operations. Since it seemed likely that the bank would earn large profits for its stockholders, it was required to pay the federal government a bonus of $1,500,000. It did not flourish immediately, but prospered after 1819 under the management of Langdon Cheves and his successor, Nicholas Biddle. It eventually had no fewer than twenty-five branches, and, as intended, it did supply a sound paper currency. But it had many enemies, some opposing it from the first because they thought it unconstitutional and as much devoted to the private interests of its stockholders as the welfare of the public. It acquired more foes because it competed all too effectively with private banks and especially because in the course of its operations it frequently exposed the paper currencies put out by its rivals as untrustworthy or even worthless. It was unjustly blamed for the panic of 1819, and it became known in many quarters as "The Monster," a name coined by Thomas Hart Benton of Missouri. Eventually, Andrew Jackson was to come forth like St. George with his sword to stab the dragon to death.

PROTECTIVE TARIFFS

As we have seen, Daniel Webster as a young politician was opposed to protective tariffs, fearing that they would injure the merchants of Massachusetts, but later changed his mind with respect to protection. On the other hand, Calhoun would become bitterly hostile to protection, although he fought for it in 1816. At that time, Calhoun believed that his native South Carolina, possessing many streams where water power could be developed, could grow into a Southern manufacturing center with the whole Southern interior as a market. American manufacturing was still in its infancy, and could hardly compete on equal terms with British competition. Accordingly, support for protection appeared in most parts of the nation, the only major opposition coming from the merchants of New England. Accordingly, the so-called Tariff of 1816 was enacted in April of that year, placing duties on twenty-five percent of imported woolens, cotton goods, and iron products. The duties on some other goods were as high as thirty percent, and no commodity was taxed at less than fifteen percent. These taxes were not high enough to prevent the importation of British goods, but they assured to American industry a substantial share of the domestic market. Before long industry passed from infancy to adolescence in New England and the Middle States, but it failed to grow rapidly in the South. Below the Mason-Dixon Line protection became unpopular within a decade, and it acquired enemies among Western farmers and consumers.

INTERNAL IMPROVEMENTS

Temperatures were so low in the year 1816 that snow fell in New England in midsummer, but there was no lack of ardor in Congress. Nationalists in it not only plumped for protection, and pushed through the charter for the Second Bank of the United States, but also strove to provide for "internal improvements" at federal expense. Roads and canals were badly needed, especially beyond the Appalachians. Private enterprise did not have enough capital to undertake many major projects, and profit from them was in any case doubtful. Nor could the states undertake vast ventures, for their funds were limited and their authority ceased at their boundaries. Accordingly, when men from Trans-Appalachia and from the Middle Atlantic states clamored for federal action, it seemed likely that they would achieve their goal. Ultimately they failed because New England and the seaboard Southern states were generally opposed to spending federal funds for roads and canals, since those regions would bear much of the cost and receive few of the immediate benefits.

Besides, there were constitutional difficulties, for it was doubtful that the makers of the Constitution intended to permit the use of federal moneys for such purposes. As early as 1806, Jefferson had proposed that

Congress spend surplus federal funds for education, roads, rivers, and canals, but he had also thought a constitutional amendment necessary before action could be taken, since he believed that under the Constitution federal money could be expended only for the purposes specifically enumerated in that document. At that time Congress was less worried about the Constitution than was the President, and it authorized the building of the Cumberland Road as far west as the Mississippi River. After the War of 1812, President Madison renewed the recommendations of Jefferson and again Congress displayed less concern for constitutional scruples than did the President. In December, 1816, Calhoun introduced a "Bonus Bill" which provided for the use of $1,500,000 paid to the Treasury by the Second Bank of the United States as a bonus for its charter and also for the use of any dividends paid to the Treasury by the Bank for "internal improvements." Stiffly opposed by New England and the seaboard South, the measure received small majorities in both houses, but was vetoed by Madison, who continued to insist that Congress could not appropriate money except in the execution of enumerated powers. Supporters of the Bonus Bill contended that the spending power was limited only by the general welfare clause of the Constitution, and some of them asserted that Congress had the right not only to spend for building roads and canals, but even to authorize federal construction. However, Madison's veto was not overridden.

Nor were the champions of federal spending for transportation able to secure adoption of their program after Monroe entered the White House. Taking a broader view of the Constitution than had Madison, Monroe conceded that Congress could appropriate funds to encourage road and canal building, but he believed that the federal government could not manage or control such facilities. Moreover, opposition to "internal improvements" continued in the halls of Congress, and the movement for federal spending for transportation gradually lost headway, although some funds were supplied to help the states carry out smaller local programs. The time was not yet ripe for the large-scale spending of federal money toward the promotion of the general welfare.

THE SUPREME COURT

The nationalist spirit which dominated Congress also pervaded the Supreme Court. Indeed, that tribunal had been nationalist in sentiment from the beginning, the views of most of the justices being little affected by the triumph of Jeffersonian Republicanism. Justice Joseph Story, appointed by Madison and an able lawyer and scholar, was no more friendly to states' rights than was Marshall. Except for William Johnson, the justices named by Jefferson and his immediate successors tended to follow the leadership of Chief Justice Marshall, whose devotion to nationalism did not lessen when it diminished among his fellow Federalists. Under Marshall's leadership the Court not only looked with favor upon the expansion of federal authority, but also defended the rights and privileges of individuals against the states. In *Fletcher* v. *Peck* (1810) the Marshall Court insisted that a huge grant of land made by the legislature of Georgia in the Yazoo region was irrevocable, although greedy speculators had engaged in wholesale bribery of Georgia lawmakers in order to obtain it. The Court asserted that the grant by the legislature constituted a contract and declared that the contract clause of the Constitution was applicable. However, it would seem that the clause was actually intended to apply only to contracts between private persons. Moreover, the Court might have ruled that the circumstances under which the contract was secured made it void.

In 1819 in the celebrated case of *Dartmouth College* v. *Woodward* the Court again used the contract clause to limit state authority. It ruled that the charter of the college, granted by King George III in 1769, was a contract, binding upon the legislature of the state of New Hampshire. Accordingly, an attempt by that legislature to take over the management of the college was declared illegal. Thus, powerful protection was extended to private institutions of learning in general. The educational consequences of the decision were in the long run beneficial, since it is doubtless desirable to maintain both public and private institutions of learning. However, the sanctity which the Marshall Court extended to the charter of Dartmouth College was also given to the charters of corporations, and it is doubtful that they should have received it. Historians have urged that the Court was too solicitous for vested interests. To be sure, it remained possible for the states to reserve authority to themselves in corporation charters granted in the future, so that they would not be cramped by the contract clause. On the other hand, since a corporation chartered in one state could carry on its activities in others, it continued to be possible for a corporation to evade strict supervision by securing a charter from a state in which the laws of incorporation were lenient.

The Marshall Court also circumscribed the authority of the states by insisting that a case involving interpretation of the Constitution could be appealed from the highest court of any state to the Supreme Court. That right of appeal had been denied by the highest court of Virginia, but it was vigorously asserted by the Supreme Court in *Cohens* v. *Virginia* (1816). An even more striking assertion of federal authority came in the memorable case of *McCulloch* v. *Maryland* (1819). Enemies of the Second Bank of the United States and champions of Maryland's state banks undertook to tax a Baltimore branch of the national bank. McCulloch, cashier of the branch, refused to pay the tax; the courts of Maryland declared that he must. He appealed to the United States Supreme Court, contending that the tax violated the Constitution. His lawyers received a sympathetic hearing, and in an opinion written by Marshall the tax was condemned as being beyond Maryland's authority. The Court ruled that the Bank of the United States was a federal instrument, that the power to tax involved the power to destroy, and that if a state could tax a federal instrument, it could also destroy the whole American federal system. Therefore, the tax violated the Constitution, even though it did not conflict with any specific provision of that document. To prove that the National Bank was a federal agency, the Court adhered to the doctrine of implied powers, put forward by Alexander Hamilton in defense of chartering the First Bank of the United States. Said Marshall, "Let the end be legitimate, let it be within the scope of the Constitution, and all means which are appropriate, which are plainly adapted to that end, which are not prohibited, but consistent with the letter and spirit of the Constitution, are constitutional." Thus this doctrine, which by implication made possible a vast expansion of federal power without resorting to the amendment process, was given solemn sanction by the Court.

An important application of the doctrine of implied powers was made as early as 1828 when in the case of *American Insurance Company* v. *Cantor,* the Court held that the right to acquire territory could be inferred from the powers to make war and treaties. The Marshall Court also reached a generous interpretation of the authority of the federal government over interstate commerce in the case of *Gibbons* v. *Ogden* (1824), when the State of New York was denied the right to establish a monopoly of steamboat traffic on the Hudson River between New York and New Jersey. Before Marshall died in 1835, nationalist sentiment in the Court was weakening, but the precedents laid down under his guiding influence were to have enduring consequence.

FOREIGN AFFAIRS

As we should expect, the nationalistic spirit so evident in domestic affairs immediately after 1815 was even more manifest in foreign relations. Hence the acquisition of all parts of the Floridas which remained under Spanish rule after 1813, and the announcement to a rather astonished world of the Monroe Doctrine. Continuing to cast covetous eyes upon Pensacola, St. Augustine, and the Florida peninsula, American politicians finally gained them peacefully by taking advantage of Spanish weakness.

SPAIN'S NEW WORLD PROBLEMS

Spain was thrown into convulsions when Napoleon invaded it and placed his brother Joseph upon its throne, in 1808. With the help of an English army, the Spanish people finally drove Joseph's French troops back over the Pyrenees, and the collapse of the Napoleonic empire returned the Bourbons to Madrid in the person of Ferdinand VII. But Spain remained troubled, since Ferdinand was an unenlightened despot, refusing to accept liberal reforms sought by many of his people. More important for the United States, the end of the Napoleonic wars did not bring peace in the Spanish possessions in the New World. As early as the American Revolution, those who lived under Spanish rule in the Americas displayed discontent. When Joseph became King of Spain, some of them set up governments which proclaimed allegiance to Ferdinand. Their real goal, however, was independence, and when Ferdinand became firmly established on the Spanish throne, they refused to recognize his authority. Spanish officials had been unable to check the revolutionary movements before 1815, and although Ferdinand could send veteran troops across the ocean after that year, even with the help of elements loyal to Spain, they could not crush the revolutionists. Warfare continued in Spain's American dominions for a decade, ending only when Ferdinand was forced to abandon the struggle. Because of the turmoil at home and in her New World empire, Spain lacked the strength even to keep order in those parts of the Floridas remaining to her. The Creek and Seminole long used Spanish territory as a refuge between attacks upon American frontier settlements, while they secured supplies by trading with resident British merchants.

Unable to prevent the raids upon American soil, Spain gave an excellent excuse for American invasion. In 1817 General Andrew Jackson, who had the task of dealing with the Indians, was authorized to pursue them, if necessary, into Spanish territory. His formal orders warned him not to take any of the Spanish posts in the Floridas. In the spring of 1818 he drove across the frontier, captured and executed two British subjects, Alexander Arbuthnot and Robert Ambrister, on the ground that they had encouraged and supplied the red men with weapons. Next he occupied Pensacola, claiming that he had received the tacit approval of his superiors in Washington to the seizure of the town.

Jackson's aggressive behavior was assailed in London, Madrid, and Washington, but it was defended by Secretary of State John Quincy Adams. Jackson was ordered to withdraw to American soil, but Adams informed the Spanish government that Jackson's conduct was justified by Spain's failure to keep order in her Floridas. Should a similar situation arise in the future, he could not guarantee that Jackson would withdraw a second time. He suggested a solution, the cession of those territories to the United States. Spain prudently chose to get what she could for them rather than lose them without compensation. Accordingly, Spain and the United States signed a treaty in 1819 which provided for a general boundary settlement. By its terms Pensacola and the peninsula of Florida became American soil, and Spain abandoned her claim to the Oregon region. In return, the United States renounced a dubious claim to Texas, and the boundary between the United States and Spanish Mexico was made to follow a line beginning at the mouth of the Sabine River and running north and west to the forty-second parallel. Another provision stipulated that the United States would assume the burden of compensating Americans who had claims for damages against Spain, to the sum of five million dollars. The treaty was ratified in 1821.

THE MONROE DOCTRINE

The difficulties into which Spain was plunged by the revolutionary movements in her American possessions opened the way for the acquisition of Florida, but those same difficulties also made possible armed intervention in the New World by the European great powers. That possibility in turn led to the Monroe Doctrine, the cornerstone of American foreign policy until the twentieth century. After 1815 the tide of war ebbed and flowed in the Spanish colonies, the revolutionists very gradually gaining superiority over the forces of Spain and the loyal colonials. As it became likely that the Spanish Americans, except in Cuba and Puerto Rico, would achieve their independence, concern arose at several royal courts. Kings and their counselors were alarmed lest the establishment of independent republics in Spanish America supply an example for the peoples of Europe.

After Napoleon was sent off to St. Helena, the rulers of the nations which had defeated him undertook to prevent his return and to make certain that there would be no second French Republic. Toward these ends Russia, Prussia, Austria, and Britain signed on November 20, 1815, the Quadruple Alliance. These great powers proclaimed their allegiance to the principle of "legitimacy," and pledged themselves to use force to prevent the revival of a dictatorial or republican regime in France. They had put Louis XVIII, a Bourbon and younger brother of Louis XVI, on the French throne. In 1818, satisfied that the new Bourbon government was reasonably stable, they permitted France to enter the alliance. Thereafter, this combination on several occasions used diplomacy and even force to suppress liberal revolutionary movements in Italy and Spain in the name of "legitimacy." The use of Austrian troops in Italy and French regulars in Spain in defense of the status quo aroused concern in London. Nevertheless, fearful that the contagion of revolution might spread from Spanish America to Europe, the great powers on the European continent began to consider the possibility of armed intervention in behalf to Spain. It is doubtful that they would have acted, but the possibility aroused alarm both in Britain and the United States. The British politicians then in power were conservative enough, but they were not in accord with the rulers of Russia, Austria, and Prussia, who were downright reactionary. Besides, they feared that French troops sent to bolster the Spanish forces in the New World might be used to run up the French flag. The revolutionists had thrown open the ports under their control to British trade, they had borrowed money from British bankers, and British volunteers were helping them, both on land and sea. Should Spain regain control of her colonies, or should they fall to France, British trade with them would probably be cut off and British investments lost. Seeking to prevent intervention, George Canning, the British Foreign Secretary, proposed in August, 1823, that Britain and the United States jointly declare their opposition.

From the beginning the sympathies of the United States lay with the revolutionists. Hostility toward Spain, a liking for fellow republicans, a desire for trade with Latin America, and a wish to reduce European influence in the New World, all aroused friendship for the revolutionists. In the spring of 1822 America took steps toward recognizing the independence of some of the new republics proclaimed by them. The specter of European fleets in Spanish American harbors that threatened in London seemed to be almost a reality on the Potomac in 1823. Secretary of War Calhoun was especially alarmed, and even Secretary of State John Quincy Adams, who was not feverish in temperament, believed that the Alliance's threat posed a "fearful question." Concern in Washington was somewhat increased by the fact that Tsar Alexander I had recently asserted claim to the northwestern part of North America, declaring that Russian Alaska extended south as far as the fifty-first parallel, thus putting in a bid for part of the Oregon country.

Considering the British invitation to join in common action, President Monroe sought the advice of Jefferson and Madison. While not distinguished for fondness for Britain, those former Presidents said they believed the situation was so serious that the invitation should be accepted. However, John Quincy Adams, astutely estimating that the Alliance would not move and that Britain would act if the continental powers did choose to move, whether or not the United States agreed to a common front, urged that the United States act independently of Britain. In December, 1823, in a message to Congress, Monroe spelled out the American policy that was to be called the Monroe Doctrine. Acting separately, the United States was able to declare against British as well as European aggression in America; by announcing his policy to Congress rather than in diplomatic notes, Monroe also deprived the European rulers of an opportunity to denounce that policy. In the message, credit for which must go to both Monroe and Adams, four principles were laid down: that intervention by any European power in behalf of Spain would be looked upon as a "manifestation of an unfriendly disposition toward the United States";

that the United States would consider any attempt on the part of the Quadruple Alliance to extend its monarchical system "to any portion of this hemisphere as dangerous to our peace and safety"; that the American continents were "henceforth not to be considered as subjects for future colonization by any European powers"; and that America would not interfere in "the internal concerns" of the European nations. Thus the United States stood forth as the protector of the New World, denouncing aggression by the Alliance, and Russian or even British expansion. It did so without running any great risk of having to take up arms, for Adams' calculation that the United States would not have to back its words with deeds was quite correct.

Whatever danger there might have been that the Alliance would put soldiers and ships in motion had been dissipated before Monroe's statement. Not waiting for an answer to his invitation, Canning had obtained a promise from France in October that she would not take part in a European crusade against the Spanish Americans. The behavior of the United States was looked upon as impudent in the courts at Vienna and St. Petersburg, and Canning could not but feel that he had been used as a cat's-paw by the unreliable Americans. He made the best of the situation by boasting that he had brought forth a new world to balance the old. The princes of the Alliance had to content themselves with the suppression of liberalism at home. By 1826 the Spanish Americans had destroyed the last army of Ferdinand VII and republics had been formed between the Oregon region and Cape Horn. Meanwhile, the royal family of Portugal, realizing that Brazil must be granted her independence, smoothly made the best of the situation by recognizing one of themselves as the first Emperor of Brazil.

Securing their independence, the Latin American peoples quite rightly gave credit to Britain rather than to the United States for assistance. They were not much impressed by Monroe's doctrine; when it eventually became a cornerstone of American foreign policy, they protested against it as being one-sided. They would not accept the United States as overlord of the New World, and feared lest it become a cover for Yankee aggression ultimately to spread throughout Latin America. Not until the twentieth century was well advanced did the United States and the nations below the Rio Grande become partners in maintaining peace in the New World.

SECTIONALISM

The Monroe Doctrine was a striking expression of American nationalism in the arena of foreign affairs. In domestic matters the nationalist tide had already encountered opposing currents of sectionalism, and its progress had been checked. The conflict between East and West, perhaps more properly between New England and the West, evident in the fight over the Bonus Bill of 1816, continued and sharpened. The admission of new states beyond the Appalachians had never been favored by New England because each such admission comparatively reduced New England's influence in national affairs. Nor had New Englanders ever become quite reconciled to the three-fifths clause with respect to representation, since they looked upon it as a special and unjust favor to the South and the Southwest. That the new states flocked to the standard of the Democratic-Republicans was an added grievance in the old Federalist stronghold. On the other hand, there was strong feeling in the West, especially below the Ohio River, against the Northeast, and especially New England, on both political and economic grounds. Western debtors had no love for Eastern creditors, and in 1819 when the Second Bank of the United States exposed the weakness of many badly run Western banks and took action which caused the collapse of some of them, it was assumed beyond the Alleghenies that New England had used its money power to injure the West. So the ancient struggle between East and West that had so early appeared in American history continued; in one form or another, it would persist into the twentieth century.

THE MISSOURI COMPROMISE

Of far greater importance was the North–South conflict, which flared into a near-crisis over the question of the admission of Missouri as a state. In March, 1818, a petition from the Missouri Territory asking for statehood was received in Washington. It quickly brought on a bitter clash between North and South which endured until 1820. James Talmadge, Jr. of New York precipitated a controversy by offering two amendments to a House of Representatives bill for Missouri statehood. These would have required that the state of Missouri prevent the further importation of Negro slaves and that she provide for the gradual emancipation of slaves then living within her bounds. These amendments would have compelled Missouri to become a free state, regardless of the wishes of her people. In any case the amendments must have been opposed in Congress by men from the South, since the free states already had a majority in the House of Representatives and since the Senate was equally divided between free and slave States. Besides, if Missouri became a free state, an extended Mason-Dixon line was likely to run toward the south in the rest of the Louisiana Territory, which was not yet organized. But they had other reasons for fighting against the Talmadge proposals. They believed that Missouri as a state should have full equality with the other states, and that the nature of the Union so required. Above all, they were exasperated because the champions of the amendments vigorously assailed the institution of slavery on moral grounds. Although slavery had virtually disappeared in the North, the institution had not hitherto been attacked by Northerners in the halls of Congress. Southern sentiment had probably not shifted very much from what it was before the era of independence, although the production of cotton by slave labor was increasingly profitable. Many Southerners deplored slavery's existence and favored its destruction; many others looked upon it as a necessary evil. At any rate, the assault by the Northerner politicos immediately led to the creation of a solid Southern bloc. After bitter debate the Talmadge amendments passed the House of Representatives by a strictly sectional vote, but they failed in the Senate, where a few Northern senators joined with their Southern colleagues to defeat them.

The dispute did not die, but spread throughout the nation. It continued for many months in Washington, until the people of the district of Maine opened a path to compromise by petitioning for the separation of Maine from Massachusetts and admission of Maine as a state. It then became possible to set aside the Talmadge amendments, and to provide for the admission of both Maine and Missouri without restrictions with respect to slavery. The so-called Missouri Compromise thus provided for the entrance into the Union of a new free state and a new slave state in accordance with the sentiments of the people of Maine and Missouri. To secure Northern consent, the compromise contained a third very important provision, that slavery be forbidden in all that part of the Louisiana Territory (save for Missouri) which lay north of the line thirty-six degrees, thirty minutes. Thus slavery was to be barred from the greater part of the vast region purchased from France. Quarreling over Missouri was resumed in 1821, because the constitution presented for approval by Missouri declared that free Negroes were not to enter the state, but that problem was solved by Congress when it declared that Missouri was not to deny such rights to United States citizens. No one could say with assurance that free Negroes were or were not citizens of the United States. The struggles over Missouri then came to an end, and debates over the morality of slavery ceased for some years.

The quarrel over Missouri was remarkably intense while it lasted, and aroused the deepest concern among thoughtful men. Said Jefferson: "This momentous question, like the fire bell in the night, awakened and filled me with terror. I considered it at once as the knell of the Union. It is hushed, indeed, for the moment. But this is a reprieve only, not a final sentence." Declared Thomas W. Cobb of Georgia: "We have kindled a fire which all the waters of the ocean cannot put out, which seas of blood can only extinguish." Both Clay and Calhoun feared that the controversy might lead to the destruction of the Union; they were alarmed because North and South, hitherto at odds principally on economic issues, had opened a quarrel upon a moral question. Jefferson clearly explained why he feared impending tragedy. "A geographical line coinciding with a marked principle, moral and political, once conceived and held up to the angry passions of men, will never be obliterated; and every new irritation will mark it deeper and deeper." John Quincy Adams agreed with Jefferson and Calhoun that sectional strife would become more bitter in the future, but believed nevertheless that he would prefer civil war to the continuance of slavery. Southern politicians had a special cause for alarm in that congressmen from the Old Northwest had sided with those of the Northeast, and it was apparent that on the question of the morality of slavery the South could not rely upon support from the region between the Ohio and the Great Lakes. The Jeffersonians had ruled by allying the South and the West. It was now apparent that the South's majority position in Washington would be gravely endangered by the reappearance of slavery as a major question in American politics.

21 ANDREW JACKSON, DEMOCRATIC KING

The "Era of Good Feelings" which never quite existed came to an end when President John Quincy Adams chose as his Secretary of State Henry Clay. He thereby mortally offended Andrew Jackson, who made Adams's four years in the Presidency most unpleasant for him and then deprived him of the office in the election of 1828. Succeeding Adams, Jackson "reigned" in Washington for eight years.

THE ELECTION OF 1824

As the election of 1824 approached, no fewer than five leaders of the Democratic-Republican party indicated their willingness to occupy the White House when Monroe vacated it. In remembrance of things past, William Henry Crawford of Georgia seemed to be the most suitable candidate. Not of Virginia as were Jefferson, Madison, and Monroe, he had nevertheless been born there; his political principles, while not unfriendly to protection, were in general like those of the inhabitants of the executive mansion for the last quarter century; he had served well enough in several executive offices, including that of Secretary of the Treasury; and he had been nominated by a congressional caucus. Nevertheless, Crawford was vigorously challenged by John Quincy Adams, Henry Clay, John C. Calhoun, and Andrew Jackson. Crawford's popularity lay with the older politicians in the party rather than with the voters, and the caucus which nominated him was a minority group. Clay, also a Virginian by birth, had many friends in the West, especially in Kentucky, while Adams was the favorite of New England. Calhoun's views were much like those of Adams and Clay at that time, all three favoring protection, internal improvements, and the Second Bank of the United States; he was especially respected and liked in the South. Intellectually gifted, courageous, and trustworthy, he sought the support of the voters rather than the party leaders. This appeal might have been successful, but it was also employed by Jackson, and Calhoun could not compete with the hero of New Orleans in a popularity contest. Realizing that such was the situation, Calhoun lowered his sights, sought the Vice-Presidency, and secured it without serious contest.

Jackson proved to be a formidable antagonist at the polls. He had no program to offer, since he had no fixed opinions on the great political questions of the day. He had served in civil offices, had been a United States Senator and member of the highest court of Tennessee, but his record in non-military posts had been undistinguished. Not yet a champion of the "common man," he was by the standards of 1788, 1800, or 1808, quite unfitted for the Presidency. He was poorly educated and had not been born a gentleman. He obviously did have the most important qualification of all, courage. Admired for his war record, he was an idol in the South and West. Nominated by the legislatures of Tennessee and Pennsylvania, he led his competitors in both popular and electoral votes, but he failed to secure a majority in the electoral college.

Since no candidate had a majority, the burden and the joy of choosing the President fell to the House of Representatives, which under the Twelfth Amendment had to make its choice from among the three leaders. Clay, who had run fourth, was therefore out of the running. He had much influence in the House, and chose to exercise it. Since Crawford had suffered a paralytic stroke, the decision actually lay between Jackson and Adams. The political views of Clay and Adams were much alike, and Clay had hardly enjoyed being beaten by Jackson in the election in the West. He came out in support of the Massachusetts man; many in Congress who looked upon Jackson as an upstart also rallied behind Adams, who was chosen on the first ballot, receiving the votes of thirteen states, while Jackson carried seven and Crawford four. Uproar followed, for Jackson's friends, insisting that as the popular favorite he should have been elected, promptly accused Clay and Adams of making a "corrupt bargain." They refused to believe that Clay, the whiskey-drinking, poker-playing, long and lean gentleman from Kentucky, could prefer the rotund, stiff, and sober Adams to their Tennessee idol. They claimed that Adams had undertaken to make Clay Secretary of State in return for his support, but were unable to bring forth any evidence in support of their charge, and none has ever been found. When Adams did actually appoint Clay to the first post in the Cabinet, which he doubtless did in good conscience, they regarded the charge as proven. Eventually, Jackson himself came to believe that a wicked deal had been made, and he declared political war upon Adams and Clay. There followed a permanent division of the Democratic-Republican party, the friends of Jackson and Calhoun gradually organizing the Democratic party, while the supporters of Adams and Clay similarly organized as National Republicans.

ADAMS IN OFFICE

Subjected to bitter partisan attack, John Quincy Adams was not happy in the White House. The cry of "corrupt bargain" continued to echo in Congress, John Randolph of Roanoke asserting in poignant phrase that the Adams–Clay alliance was a union "of the Puritan with the black-leg." Furiously resentful, Clay demandad that the brilliant but erratic Randolph either retract his insult or exchange bullets on the dueling ground. Randolph refused to withdraw his offensive remarks, and the two gentlemen traded shots, without physical damage to either. Clay had proven his courage, but he had not convinced his enemies of his integrity. He fought back as best he could, but Adams refused to use all the weapons at his command against their detractors. He might reasonably have replaced many of Jackson's and Calhoun's friends in federal office with his own. Instead, in perverse high-mindedness, Adams let remain all who did their duty, including ardent admirers of his enemies. Nor would he stoop to maneuvers which might have turned the followers of Jackson and those of Calhoun against each other, thus failing to take advantage of rivalry and jealousy which existed between them.

Adams unfolded a program for national action to encourage industry, commerce, education, science, and the arts, but Congress refused to accept his leadership. In the spring of 1828 he was able to sign a new protective tariff bill into law, but it was not his own measure. Indeed, as John Randolph wittily declared, "the bill referred to manufactures of no sort or kind, but the manufacture of a President of the United States." It was concocted by Jackson's followers for the purpose of injuring Adams and smoothing Jackson's way to the White House. In 1827 there was a clamor in the Middle States for higher barriers against the importation of foreign goods. Jackson, bitterly hostile to Adams and Clay, had begun the campaign of 1828 almost as soon as Adams entered the Presidency. The

Jacksonites, assuming that New England would rally behind Adams and that the South would favor Jackson, believed that the contest would be decided in the Middle States. To win them, they devised a bill which set very high duties on iron, hemp, flax, and raw materials, one which offered much to the Middle States and little to New England. They calculated that the bill would be defeated, with New England and the South joining to oppose it, for the agrarian South had turned against protection, chiefly on the ground that it favored the manufacturer against the consumer, the manufacturer usually being Northern, the consumer often Southern. They hoped that the Middle States protectionists would blame Adams for the defeat, and that they would turn toward Jackson. This devious scheme was ultimately successful, but not in the way that the schemers had planned. By 1828 New England had accepted the principle of protection, and her men in Congress voted for the bill, even though it was not to the immediate advantage of their region. In consequence, the bill became a law. As it turned out, the Jacksonians received credit for it in the Middle States, even though the true champions of protection were to be found in the following of Adams and Clay.

1829: A WESTERNER IN WASHINGTON

The passage of the tariff contributed toward a victory for General Jackson over Mr. Adams at the polls some months later. Whether or not the unprincipled maneuvering of the Jacksonians in Congress was essential to that triumph is doubtful. Jackson had been nominated by the legislature of Tennessee as early as 1825, and a very able group of politicians and editors, including Amos Kendall, Duff Green, John H. Eaton, and James Buchanan, had been campaigning for him for many long months. They made much of Jackson as a hero and as a common man risen to greatness; neither they nor he took any firm stand on any immediate issue so as to lose votes. They abused Adams unmercifully. He behaved with dignity; his followers, not so well organized as Jackson's, assailed Jackson's public record and also his private life. The recent broadening of the suffrage was doubtless to Jackson's advantage, for he had greater appeal to the new voters. He secured nearly 650,000 popular votes, Adams somewhat more than 500,000; he had 178 electoral votes, Adams only 83. The victor of New Orleans carried Pennsylvania, and received more than half of New York's electoral votes. It is interesting to note that he did not need this Northern support to win, and that it came in large part from workmen and farmers. He swept the South and West; their votes were sufficient to secure the Presidency for him.

Inauguration Day in 1829 was a remarkable one. John Quincy Adams behaved coolly and correctly, and the new President conducted himself like a Southern gentleman. After the ceremony had been finished, however, there was a wild celebration. Common folk who cared little for appearances invaded a reception at the White House, uproarious and triumphant. They spilled wine and food about, ruined furniture and draperies, and broke windows. To guests accustomed to the decorum of the past, they looked like the mob invading the Tuileries in the early days of the French Revolution. More thoughtful persons wondered whether Andrew Jackson was equal to the tasks before him, whether he would be a barracks President.

"KING ANDREW" OR "OLD HICKORY"

When Andrew Jackson left the White House after an eight-year residence, Henry Clay declared that he had swept through Washington like "a tropical tornado." As the old hero returned to Nashville and his beloved home, the Hermitage, the federal government still stood and it was stronger than it had been when he entered the Presidency. A mighty force, Jackson destroyed, but he also built, and that extraordinary man was surely one of the better Presidents of the United States. He was in his own time bitterly hated and greatly loved. He was not well fitted to the Presidency, yet performed brilliantly in it at times; he was not well informed upon public questions, but he was a clever politician; he became more and more democratic in his outlook without ceasing to be dictatorial in his own behavior. "King Andrew" to his enemies, he was "Old Hickory" among the tens of thousands of plain folk who thought of him as one of themselves. Divergence of opinion concerning Jackson has continued, among historians, most of whom have looked upon him with kindly eyes and have not dwelled upon his remarkable deficiencies.

Almost sixty-two years old when he became President, Jackson was a Carolinian by birth. Whether he was born in North or South Carolina is a matter of dispute; some South Carolinians are not eager to claim him as their own. Lanky and lean, he was of the same general physique as John Marshall, Henry Clay, and Abraham Lincoln. Of Scotch-Irish ancestry, he was reared in the backwoods of the Carolinas in much the same fashion that Lincoln later grew up in rural Indiana and Illinois. Unlike Lincoln, however, he had no great love for books, and he made little effort toward self-education, contenting himself with little formal schooling and scanty reading to prepare for a career as a lawyer. As a lawyer he was not outstanding, but he made his way upward in private and public life with surprising speed, prospering both as a planter and as a politician. It has been mentioned earlier that he did not distinguish himself as a Congressman and Senator from Tennessee, or as a justice of the State Supreme Court. He was not yet remarkable as a champion of the common man. He was well known as a man of inflexible will, of imperious habit, and of fighting blood. He classified his Tennessee acquaintances as friends or enemies, was loyal and generous to those whom he liked, unrelentingly harsh to those who did not please him. Not making fine distinctions between men in Tennessee, he also failed to make them in Washington.

Jackson had been noted for fighting long before he led troops against the Indians and British. He served as a boy in the War of Independence and as a militia officer for long years before he achieved fame as a general. He had won notoriety for engaging in physical contests with his personal foes before the Battle of Horseshoe Bend. He was nearly killed in a tavern brawl, and he slew one Charles Dickenson in a duel. Always sensitive on points of honor, he was chivalrous toward ladies and especially to his own wife, Rachel Donelson. She had been married to one Jason Robards, whom she divorced. She married Jackson before she had actually secured a divorce, being misinformed about the status of her suit. Thereafter, malicious gossips, including her husband's enemies, said that she had lived in sin with him for many months before she actually became his wife. Dickenson presumed upon his proficiency as a superb pistol shot when he joined in questioning her virtue. Jackson demanded satisfaction, faced Dickenson on the dueling ground, and made up for his lack of skill with a pistol by wearing a large cloak during the encounter. Dickenson fired first and damaged the cloak rather than Jackson; Jackson then took lengthy aim, shot, and mortally wounded his antagonist.

The courage and iron will which Jackson displayed in private contests was put to better use on the battlefield. In the Presidency he was still the same Jackson, although he had added some gentlemanly polish to his presence. He still had difficulties with spelling and pronunciation, and he had no knowledge of banking or public finance. When Harvard College gave him an honorary degree, John Quincy Adams was disgusted by the behavior of his alma mater, and described his rival as a "barbarian." Let us rather say that Jackson's education, formal and informal, was incomplete, that his defects were more than counterbalanced by his great qualities, and that he was a mighty figure in an age when the level of American political leadership was not very high. Men far inferior to him would later occupy the White House.

THE CABINET

Those who feel that a President is not equal to his burdens frequently find consolation in the wishful thought that he will recognize superior wisdom in his Cabinet members and will execute their policies. During the first two years of Jackon's administration neither Adams nor any other person aware of Jackson's deficiencies could find comfort in the hope that his Cabinet would compensate for them. That body was of limited ability, and Jackson soon ceased even to call it into session. Instead he sought the informal advice of political cronies such as William B. Lewis, Amos Kendall, Andrew J. Donelson, and others who as a group formed the famous "Kitchen Cabinet." This little clique was not distinguished for dignity but it was not without political abilities, and most of its members were sturdily loyal to the head cook. After 1831 policy was made in the parlor as well as in the kitchen, the Cabinet regaining much of its earlier prestige. This change did not come about because Jackson concluded that the "Kitchen Cabinet" was unseemly, or because he learned that his official counselors had fine talents. It came as the result of a squabble over the character of Mrs. John H. Eaton, which led to the creation of an almost entirely new Cabinet containing able men in whom Jackson could place his trust.

Daughter of a Washington innkeeper, Peggy O'Neale married Secretary of War Eaton only four months after the death of her first husband. Tongues wagged in the nation's capital. It was said that the attractive Peggy had been too friendly with Eaton before her first husband's decease, and the wives of Jackson's first Cabinet refused to entertain the Eatons. "King Andrew" remembered the abuse heaped upon his own wife, who had died before he entered the Presidency, and chivalrously came forward to the defense of Peggy, whom he liked. He insisted that she receive the same social treatment as the wives of other Cabinet members; when those ladies still refused to accept her, Jackson arranged for the resignations of their husbands. Only one member survived the slaughter. One other, Secretary of State Martin Van Buren, profited from the affair. A widower, he was quite willing to entertain Mrs. Eaton, and did so. He offered his resignation to help Jackson get rid of his colleagues, and thus he won Jackson's enduring gratitude. The Peggy Eaton controversy brought into the Cabinet the gifted Edward Livingston of Louisiana as Secretary of State and the able Roger B. Taney as Attorney General; and it also explains in large part why Jackson named Van Buren as his successor.

THE SPOILS SYSTEM

If Jackson was not a thoroughgoing democrat politically when he entered the Presidency, he soon became one. Before long he came forth as the champion of all the people, against special privilege for the few. He saw no need to act in behalf of industrial and commercial labor, although the lot of such labor was often a hard one, posing serious questions for a politician of penetrating mind. In other respects, however, he behaved in accordance with the principles and prejudices of the new democracy. He sincerely believed that one man was as good as another in most public offices, and that lengthy tenure of office was unhealthy. Besides, being eager to reward his friends and punish his enemies, he introduced the spoils system into Washington. He did not actually make a clean sweep of Adams' and Clay's supporters, removing less than one-fifth of those who held federal appointments in 1829, but during his eight years in the Presidency he did discharge many of the more conspicuous supporters of his foes; his example, copied and later expanded, served to fasten the spoils system upon the federal government. This contribution to political science does not stamp him as a statesman.

THE WEST AND THE INDIANS

Far less susceptible to criticism was Jackson's handling of Western problems. Although governmental expenses climbed during his Presidency, the nation's income mounted even more rapidly, thus burdening the Treasury with surplus funds, the disposition of which posed a problem. They could not even be applied to reducing the national debt, which was very low and actually disappeared in 1835, for the first and the last time in the history of the nation. The availability of money encouraged the advocates of internal improvements at federal expense to push their projects. With moderation unusual for him, Jackson vetoed a bill calling for the expenditure of $150,000 to build a turnpike in Kentucky. But this so-called Maysville Road veto, which was in part a slap at Henry Clay, meant mainly that Jackson was opposed to spending federal money for a road within the boundaries of one state. He freely consented to federal expenditures for the development of rivers and harbors. Even more popular in the West was his land policy, since he tried successfully to make it easy for the average citizen to purchase national lands. It is not surprising that Jackson retained the affection of the Western people, especially since he pleased them with his vigorous action toward pushing the Indians beyond the Mississippi, thus opening up large regions to exploitation.

Jackson hoped to persuade the red men remaining in the Old Northwest and Old Southwest peacefully to abandon their historic hunting grounds in exchange for Western regions not yet coveted by white men. This policy was carried out even though it brought great suffering upon the Indians. Threatened by force and seduced by cash as well as a promise of unmolested possession of rich lands beyond the Mississippi, the Creek, Choctaw, Chickasaw, and Cherokee signed treaties by which they agreed to emigrate. The Indian Territory, part of which afterward became Oklahoma, was set aside for them, and most of them peacefully made the long trek to their new homes. However, some of the Indians agreed to go into exile only with great reluctance, the Cherokee holding out as long as possible against heavy pressure. They had taken long strides toward the white man's civilization since the War of Independence, and their language had been reduced to writing. Struggling to remain in Georgia, they refused to recognize the state's authority over them, and they were supported by the United States Supreme Court, which ruled in 1832 in the

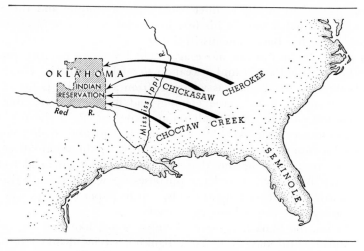

MIGRATION OF SOUTHERN INDIANS

case of *Worcester* v. *Georgia* that Georgia did not in fact have jurisdiction over them. But Georgia defied the Court successfully, for Jackson refused to do anything toward executing its verdict. He is said to have declared: "John Marshall has made his decision, now let him enforce it."

The only Southern tribe which resisted removal with some success was the Seminole nation, which preferred to fight for its liberty under its Chief Osceola. He was captured by trickery and put in prison at Charleston, where he died; his people fought on for eight years (1835–1843) from their fastnesses in the swamps of the Everglades. In the end they were permitted to remain in their watery wilderness, for it was not yet desired by the white men. The Sac and Fox of the Old Northwest also resisted. As we have seen, their return eastward in an attempt to live peacefully on part of their ancient territory was in vain. Under Black Hawk they were able to offer only feeble resistance when assailed in force. The pathetic tale arouses the sympathy of those who believe that there is but one mankind and that the red men should have been permitted to maintain their own culture in friendship with the whites. It must be admitted that it was hardly necessary to push them far beyond the Mississippi after their military power had been broken. Andrew Jackson was not entirely out of sympathy with those whites who believed that a good Indian was a dead one.

THE BANK OF THE UNITED STATES

Champion for Peggy O'Neale and the Western farmer, ardent exponent of the spoils system, Jackson was hardly a champion of the "common man" until he engaged in deadly conflict with Nicholas Biddle and the Second Bank of the United States. In his first inaugural address he declared that he considered the Bank unconstitutional and not very useful to the public. However, he did not move against it for many months, probably because he could not easily find a weapon to wield against it. There could be no doubt that the Bank was well run from a financial point of view; indeed, it would have had fewer enemies had Biddle, its very able President, been less efficient. A Philadelphian experienced in the diplomatic service, Biddle was both likeable and able. He had also made something of a name for himself in the world of literature. As the dominating figure in the Bank after 1823, he put that institution on its financial feet, and thereafter the Bank well served the purposes for which it was created. It provided a safe deposit for federal funds, and its paper currency was sound and fully acceptable throughout the nation.

Nevertheless, the Bank had many enemies. Some, like Jackson, believed it to be unconstitutional; New York banking circles disliked it because its heart was in Philadelphia; idealists detested it because the persons who held its stock profited from its connection with government. Especially vehement among its foes were those who operated banks chartered by the states and who were unable to compete with Biddle's bank, which had branches in the major cities and towns. Besides, many state banks had carelessly or dishonestly put forth paper money beyond their power to redeem; by discounting it or refusing to accept it, Biddle's bank exposed the weakness and even the worthlessness of much of this paper currency. That Biddle's institution performed a service to the public by checking the money manufacturers among its competitors was well understood by thoughtful persons; its good service in this respect was not fully appreciated by Jackson. Historians offer another charge against the Bank, that its dealings with men in public life were tinged by corruption. It has been pointed out that it lent money to members of Congress against their salaries, that it helped finance a newspaper established by the friends of Calhoun to attack Jackson, and that Daniel Webster, who as a Senator vigorously defended the Bank, quietly accepted retainer fees as one of its lawyers. While such transactions were not above reproach, they did not in themselves make the Bank a "Monster."

THE BANK AND THE ELECTION OF 1832

In February, 1831, Biddle was goaded and persuaded into doing battle with Jackson. An attack upon the Bank in the Senate by Thomas Hart Benton of Missouri, an earlier foe of Jackson who had become "Old Hickory's" political ally, vexed Biddle. He listened to Henry Clay, that perennial seeker of the Presidency, who believed that he could be elected to it in 1832 if Jackson could be made to appear as an enemy of the Bank and of sound banking practices. He persuaded Biddle to ask for a new charter, although the existing one would not expire for five years. Clay calculated that friends of the Bank were in a majority in both houses of Congress, that the bill for rechartering would pass, and that Jackson would then veto the bill. He could then be assailed in the campaign of 1832 as a foe of good banking and sound currency. The Kentuckian was sure that former supporters of John Quincy Adams and the more conservative elements in American society generally would rally behind him. All these things happened. The bill was approved by the Senate, 28–20, and by the House, 107–86, in the early summer of 1831. Jackson responded to the challenge with a veto and an accompanying message which declared that Congress could not constitutionally charter or recharter the Bank, that the Bank was a fortress of monopolism, and that it was largely unnecessary. He thus accepted the gauntlet which Clay and Biddle had thrown down, and recharter of the Bank became a great issue in the election.

Before the contest began, Clay's chances were enhanced by defections from Jackson's following. South Carolina, exasperated because Jackson had not come out as an enemy of protective tariffs, threw its electoral votes to John Floyd of Virginia. Moreover, the appearance of the remarkable Anti-Masonic party was to Clay's benefit. The Masonic Order had incurred the jealousy and suspicion of many who were barred from membership. When one William Morgan, who had announced that he would expose the secrets and the "depravity" of the Order, vanished in New York State in 1826, it was generally assumed that he had been murdered by the Masons. By 1830 the Anti-Masons were politically powerful in New York, and by 1831 they had organized a national party. First to believe that secret societies were a grave menace in the United States, the Anti-Masons also held the first national nominating convention and offered the first party platform. They put forward for the Presidency the distinguished lawyer William Wirt of Maryland. The appearance of this third party— it was the first third party—injured Jackson's chances, since the President was a member of the Masonic Order. Copying the example of the Anti-Masons, both the National Republicans and Democrats met in national conventions, the former, of course, endorsing Henry Clay. The Democrats enthusiastically nominated Jackson, with Martin Van Buren for the Vice-Presidency. The campaign which followed was bitter and nasty, the characters of all the contestants being savagely assailed. The outcome was an unpleasant surprise for Clay, although, as had been expected, the wealthy and conservative elements in the nation rallied behind him. There were more farmers and workers than there were bankers, lawyers, and merchants, and they gave Jackson an easy victory. He had 680,000 popular votes to 530,000 for Clay, who received only 49 electoral votes to his 219. William Wirt led only in Vermont, and the Anti-Masonic party vanished four years later. Of much greater significance was the fact that South Carolina cast her ballots for Floyd; that state had not only turned away from Jackson, but was preparing an ominous challenge to the authority of the federal government.

POLITICAL VICTORY AND BANKING PROBLEMS

Although Jackson had won a great personal triumph, Biddle's Bank still had many friends in the House of Representatives, and the President's enemies were still in the majority in the Senate. Nevertheless, inflexibly determined to fight the Bank to a finish, Jackson considered ways and means to strike a decisive blow at it. It was not easy to hit, since the Bank's charter was beyond attack and seemed to offer protection against any assault by the President. Some members of Jackson's Cabinet felt that nothing should or could be done before the expiration of the charter in 1836. Even so, Jackson found a bludgeon to use. The Bank would be sorely injured if the federal monies were removed from its vaults, for such action would indicate that the Bank lacked the confidence of those responsible for safeguarding federal funds. There was some doubt that such a step was consistent with the spirit, if not the letter, of the charter. Another difficulty was that the funds, if removed from Biddle's care, must be placed in state banks, many of which lacked reputations for sound banking practices. Nevertheless, Jackson insisted upon withdrawing the deposits. When Secretary of the Treasury Louis McLane indicated that he was unwilling to give the necessary orders, the President moved him to the State Department and appointed William J. Duane Secretary of the Treasury. When Duane refused to act, Jackson replaced him with Roger B. Taney of Maryland, who heartily supported the President's decision. In September, 1833, Taney announced that no further funds would be entrusted to the Bank of the United States, and began the process of withdrawal, placing federal monies in no fewer than 23 state banks before the end of the year.

The removal of the deposits was in fact a heavy blow to the Bank of the United States. Biddle fought back as best he could, tightening credit to the serious embarrassment of various state banks and to the injury of the nation's economy. When Jackson saw to it that the charter was not renewed in 1836, Biddle secured a new one from the state of Pennsylvania and continued operations until 1841. While he was no expert in politics, he was proficient in banking, and neither stockholders nor depositors who trusted him lost money as a result.

Jackson's foes in Congress used the removal of the deposits as the basis of an extended attack upon him. He had often been described as a would-be dictator, and Clay had even contended that the President had exceeded his authority by vetoing the bill for recharter of the Bank. The Kentuckian had claimed that the President did not have the authority to veto the bill on the ground of unconstitutionality since its legality had already been established by the Supreme Court in *McCulloch* v. *Maryland;* he also had argued that a President could not exercise his veto merely because he thought a measure unwise. Now Clay and other Senate friends of the Bank demanded that Jackson produce a paper which he had read to his Cabinet giving his reasons for the removal of the deposits. Jackson had quite rightly insisted that there were no constitutional limitations upon the veto power. He had also quite logically insisted that, since he was responsible for the management of the executive branch of government, members of the Cabinet were merely his advisers and he had the power to remove them. To the Senate's demand he gave a peremptory refusal, asserting that he had yet to learn "under what Constitutional authority" the Senate "had a right to require of me an account of a communication, either verbally or in writing, made to the heads of Departments acting as a Cabinet council." In March, 1834, the Senate passed a resolution offered by Clay which solemnly censured Jackson, declaring that "the President, in the late Executive proceedings in relation to the public revenue, has assumed upon himself authority and power not conferred by the Constitution and Laws, but in derogation of both." Jackson responded that if the charge made in the resolution of censure were true it offered grounds for impeachment; he challenged his opponents to bring him to trial, but the Senate refused even to consider his reply. However, time and the elections of 1834 and 1836 strengthened the cause of the President. In June, 1836, Congress passed the Deposit Act, which in effect was a compromise. It provided by law for the placing of federal funds in state banks. Thus, Congress asserted its right to put the funds where it wanted to, but located them according to Jackson's wishes. In January, 1837, the Senate ceased to feud with him, expunging from its records the resolution in which it had censured him.

Although "King Andrew" triumphed over the Second Bank of the United States, he did not display a command of the problems of currency and banking. As the Bank gradually lost its power, the restraining influence which it had helpfully exercised upon currency-making by the state banks diminished. Nor did the placing of the federal funds in some of the state banks discourage them from their efforts to turn paper into money. Both the "pet banks" which received federal funds and many others indulged freely in issuing paper money weakly supported by commercial notes. The officers of some not only knowingly put forth bad currency, but also postponed the day of reckoning by choosing a difficult spot to reach as the place where the paper money could be redeemed. The circulation of doubtful and even worthless bills vastly increased. Such bills were accepted at federal offices in payment for public lands in quantities so large that they came to be called "land-office money." Sales of public lands brought into the Treasury somewhat more than $2,600,000 in 1832, but almost $24,900,000 by 1836; the government was obviously exchanging good land for bad money. While Jackson believed that the public domain should be distributed at low rates, he fancied that it ought not to be given away, nor disposed of for trifling sums. In July, 1836, he accordingly ordered the Treasury to issue the famous "Specie Circular" which declared that, with only one special exception, the public lands were to be sold henceforth only for gold or silver. In force for nearly two years, this order made it sure that the federal government would receive honest money at its land offices. It had other far-reaching effects, for it exposed the weakness of much of the paper money then circulating, including that of the "pet banks"; it caused the hoarding of hard money; and it stimulated runs upon the state banks that brought scores of them down in collapse. Panic in banking was followed by a general depression, which was bequeathed with the Presidency to Van Buren. Jackson had slain the "Monster," but neither he nor his confidential advisers knew how to supply a stable paper money equal to the needs of the nation.

22 JACKSON: NULLIFICATION AND NATIONALISM

Asked in what state he was born, Andrew Jackson wavered between North and South Carolina; nor do we know which side of the boundary was his home. Beyond a doubt as President he gave his ultimate allegiance neither to South Carolina nor to any other state. In his later thirties he had listened to the siren call of Aaron Burr, although he did not actively participate in the "Burr Conspiracy." It may reasonably be guessed that when he became a national military hero he also became completely dedicated to the nation, his personal glory mingled with that of the Union. In the arena of politics, in the campaigns of 1824 and 1828, he was looked upon by many strict interpreters of the Constitution and states' rights men as a friend and even as a champion. He was at no time a nationalist of the stripe of Hamilton or Marshall. In the Presidency he gave comfort to states' rights men when he attacked the constitutionality of the Second Bank of the United States; on the other hand, he declared that import duties for protection against foreign goods were constitutional. If his views on the relationship between the federal government and the states were moderate, they may also be described as rather confusing. Time and trial were to prove that he

309

was utterly devoted to the Union, even if he was not quite sure about its nature. The same man who would not lift a finger to support the Supreme Court's effort to protect the Cherokee against Georgia prepared to wield the sword when South Carolina sought to nullify laws of the United States.

THE NULLIFICATION CONTROVERSY

For a full generation after the Constitution was adopted the South Carolinians were generally happy in the Union. There was some wavering between nationalism and states' rights, but the Palmetto State neither indulged in passing resolutions such as those put forth by Virginia and Kentucky in 1798, nor participated in any convention like that held at Hartford in 1814. Nevertheless, South Carolina became the ardent champion of nullification in 1828 and challenged the authority of the federal government while Jackson was in the White House. The fundamental reason why the state threw down the gauntlet was economic jealousy arising from some hard facts. In 1816 and for some years after, Calhoun and other South Carolinians had supported protective tariffs in the belief that their state would become an industrial center supplying finished goods to the Southern interior. However, various circumstances delayed the rise of industry in South Carolina, where the factory remained an unusual sight until the twentieth century. The state did not profit from protection after 1816, and her people came to believe that they were positively injured by tariffs which benefited Northern manufacturing enterprises. Certainly protection tended to increase the prices of finished goods, whether those goods were made in Britain or in New England. Nor could it reasonably be said that any benefits derived by Northern industry flowed very rapidly across the Mason-Dixon Line. From the viewpoint of South Carolina protection had still another disadvantage; that Britain, suffering from American trade barriers, might eventually purchase less of their raw materials, especially cotton, from Southerners. Concern became all the greater because the state did not recover quickly from the panic of 1819 and because her lands were less productive than those of the newer states to the westward.

With the passing years even those South Carolinians who, like Calhoun, had once pushed aggressively for tariff barriers, changed their minds. By 1827 a small but vociferous minority was vigorously demanding that the protective principle be abandoned. In July of that year, one of its leaders, Thomas Cooper, publicly declared that if the federal government continued to favor Northern industry at Southern expense the South must consider whether it was worthwhile to remain in the Union. Thus the Tariff of 1828 received the closest scrutiny in South Carolina. When it became clear that the "Tariff of Abominations" contained no concessions to South Carolina, her legislature swiftly adopted resolutions which denounced it as unjust, oppressive, and unconstitutional. In addition the lawmakers at Columbia arranged for printing the "South Carolina Exposition and Protest," a long anonymous essay by Calhoun which contained a very carefully reasoned doctrine of nullification. The legislature thus made clear its adherence to that doctrine.

CALHOUN'S "EXPOSITION AND PROTEST"

Calhoun's "Protest" was one against the tariff of 1828 in particular and the principle of protection in general. No longer a devoted nationalist, he agreed with Thomas Cooper that protective tariffs were both unjust and unconstitutional. While it is obvious enough that his interpretation of the Constitution had altered remarkably, we should not dwell upon the inconsistency, since the same sort of thing is to be found in the careers of many American leaders, including Justices of the United States Supreme Court. Possibly, consistency in principle can be based upon an inability to learn. Which is not to say that Calhoun's later interpretation of the Constitution was necessarily the correct one. In any event, concluding that the tariff of 1828 was unconstitutional, but that it would be difficult to get Congress to alter it substantially, Calhoun offered in his "Exposition" an analysis of the nature of the American Union which offered a remedy: the nullification of a federal law by a state. He claimed that a state constitutional convention could lawfully prevent a federal law which it considered unconstitutional from being enforced within the boundaries of the state. By preventing the execution of the law the state could force the federal government to reconsider its policy. It could repeal or modify the law; or the constitutionality of the law could be established beyond doubt by constitutional amendment.

To prove that a state had the power to nullify, Calhoun offered a closely reasoned line of argument. Seeing the original thirteen as independent and sovereign when they ratified the Constitution, he pointed out that each had entered the Union as the result of action by its ratifying convention. Accordingly, each of those conventions was a sovereign body which altered the constitution of a state so as to give power to the federal government. Through their separate constitutional conventions, the states entered into a contract from which the federal government derived certain powers, which were enumerated in the Constitution. Each state by constitutional convention retained its sovereignty, and if the federal government exceeded its delegated powers and broke the contract, each state had the right to "interpose" and to nullify in a state constitutional convention, and so compel the federal government to honor the contract.

Calhoun thus furnished a weapon for the South Carolinians who were disposed to take the most vigorous action against protective tariffs. He himself was not yet ready to threaten to take South Carolina out of the Union, although other men in his state were making such threats. Even so, he was soon to carry his doctrine still further and to supply arguments for the right of secession. Developing the thesis of "concurrent majorities," he would claim that a national majority must respect and act in accord with the wishes of a state majority. This contention led to the conclusion that in the event of persistent violation of the contract by a national majority, a state constitutional convention could lawfully take a state out of the Union.

WEBSTER, JACKSON, AND THE UNION

The doctrine which Calhoun put forth at Columbia was soon challenged in the District of Columbia. In January, 1830, during a Senate discussion of a resolution offered by Samuel A. Foote of Connecticut, which would temporarily have restricted sale of public lands in the West, Robert Y. Hayne of South Carolina and Daniel Webster of Massachusetts became involved in a sectional dispute. Hayne, together with Thomas Hart Benton of Missouri, claimed that New England had steadily opposed measures for the settlement and prosperity of the West. Denying the charge, Webster counterattacked, saying that Southerners too frequently spoke of the Union as if they were indifferent to it. There followed a memorable debate in which Hayne eloquently expounded the Calhoun doctrine and Webster even more eloquently assailed it. Once a strict constructionist, now Webster as a nationalist had all the zeal of a convert. Toward destroying the Calhoun thesis, he claimed that the American nation had existed before 1787 and that the state conventions which ratified the Constitution expressed the will of the American people as a whole rather than the wishes of the peoples of the separate states. He asserted that the resulting compact divided sovereignty between the federal government and the states, all of them deriving their power ultimately from the sovereign American people. In the event of disagreement over federal authority under the Constitution, the question should be settled by federal courts or resolved through the amending process. Such a question could not be settled by a state constitutional convention. Nowhere specifically mentioned in the Constitution, the doctrine of nullification was a threat to the very existence of the Union. In a stirring climax he called for allegiance to "Liberty *and* Union, now and forever, one and inseparable!" Half concealed in Webster's stretches of high-flown rhetoric was effective criticism of the Calhounian argument.

Andrew Jackson was not a brilliant lawyer, a fine orator, or a profound political philosopher, but he recognized clearly that the doctrine of nullification posed a threat to the nation and he acted accordingly. While he was not a believer in a powerful central government, he was utterly opposed to anything which endangered the existence of the Union. When Southerners had a Jefferson Day dinner in Washington in April, 1830, and offered toasts to states' rights, he flatly challenged them, offering as his own toast: "Our Union: It must be preserved." Calhoun answered the President: "The Union, next to our liberty, most dear. May we always remember that it can only be preserved by distributing equally the benefits and burdens of the Union." Having taken his stand, Jackson, as might be expected, did not waver. Soon afterward he learned that Calhoun, whom he had credited for defending his behavior in Florida before the Cabinet in 1818, had actually favored punishing him. Moreover, the Calhouns were among those who refused to receive Mrs. Eaton, so Jackson came to look upon Calhoun as both a political and a personal enemy. In his annual message of 1830, Jackson decisively affirmed the constitutionality of protective tariffs, but recommended that the rates established two years earlier be lowered. Congress failed to follow his advice and a new Tariff Law, passed in 1832, differed little from the Tariff of Abominations of 1828.

COERCION

Some Jacksonians, and perhaps the President himself, believed that the Tariff of 1832 would allay discontent in South Carolina because its rates were somewhat lower than those of 1828. They badly misjudged sentiment in that state, for the advocates of nullification had secured control of its government and were determined to do battle. In the election of 1832, the "Nullies" won an overwhelming victory over a Unionist party led by Joel Poinsett, securing more than a two-thirds majority in the state legislature. Called into special session, that body quickly arranged for a convention which met in November and was completely in the hands of the nullifiers, who had a majority of more than five to one. Led by Chancellor William Harper, Robert Y. Hayne, George McDuffie, and others, the convention displayed both passion and determination by undertaking to put nullification into practice, challenging the federal government to do its worst. It passed an ordinance declaring that the Tariffs of 1828 and 1832 were null and void within the state, and that they could not be enforced within it after February 1, 1833. The convention also declared that the ordinance could not be challenged in the Supreme Court of the United States. Finally, it unequivocally denied the right of the federal government to use force or economic reprisal to compel obedience to the tariff laws. Should it undertake military or economic coercion, "The people of this State will thenceforth hold themselves absolved from all further obligations to maintain or preserve their political connexion with the people of the other States, and will forthwith proceed to organize a separate Government, and do all other acts and things which sovereign and independent States may of right do." The convention's action was ardently supported by the legislature, which voted money to buy arms and arrange for the enlistment of volunteers.

By setting February 1 as the time when nullification would take effect, South Carolina gave the federal government time to reconsider, repent, and repeal its protective tariffs. For Jackson there was nothing to reconsider or repent. In a message to Congress on December 4, he again recommended that the protective barriers be lowered, pointing out that this step would be particularly appropriate in view of the fact that the national debt had almost disappeared and the federal government was somewhat embarrassed because it had funds beyond its needs. His friends in Congress promptly began to prepare a bill toward reduction of the rates, and consideration of it began in the House of Representatives early in 1833. Action was delayed because Henry Clay, partly to spite Jackson and partly to please Calhoun, who had resigned the Vice-Presidency to take a seat in the Senate, insisted upon taking the business into his own hands. He introduced his own bill, which called for rate reductions at two-year intervals until 1842, when there would be a maximum duty of 20 percent. This measure aroused bitterness in Daniel Webster and other advocates of protection, but it pleased the South and especially South Carolina. It also received support from moderates who wished to conciliate the Palmetto State. Passed by Congress, it was signed by Jackson on March 2, 1833.

While extending a conciliatory hand with respect to tariffs, Jackson also brandished a club over South Carolina, with the blessing of Congress. The language which he used in urging the tariff reductions was soft and friendly; the terms which he privately applied to nullification and nullifiers were plain and harsh. He referred to the leaders as madmen on the verge of committing treason, and he made it clear that he was prepared to use force to compel obedience to federal laws. Even as he moved toward tariff reform he issued a "Proclamation to the People of South Carolina" prepared by his trusted friend, Secretary of State Edward Livingston. It solemnly declared that nullification and secession were legally indefensible. Webster's arguments were used to support this view. Jackson warned the South Carolinians that they would not be happy if they achieved independence and that they could not secure it except by force of arms. Said he:

The laws of the United States must be executed. I have no discretionary power on the subject; my duty is emphatically pronounced in the Constitution. Those who told you that you might peaceably prevent their execution deceived you; they could not have been deceived themselves. They know that a forceable opposition could alone prevent the execution of the laws, and they know that such opposition must be repelled. Their object is disunion. But be not deceived by names. Disunion by armed force is *treason*. Are you really ready to incur its guilt?

Jackson had already put the scanty federal forces in South Carolina on the alert and had placed them under the command of the reliable Winfield Scott. It was evident that he was willing to resort to arms; moreover, at his request Congress passed the Force Bill, which pledged it to support military coercion.

Gunfire was postponed in Charleston Harbor for nearly thirty years. It was not necessary for federal troops to take the field, since the "Nullies" softened their stand as soon as tariff reduction became likely. Receiving no support from the other Southern states, they answered Jackson's "Proclamation" with counterblasts, but they suspended the Ordinance of Nullification late in January, 1833. When the news came in March that the new tariff law and the Force Bill had been passed, the South Carolina state convention quickly responded by repealing the ordinance and passing a new one which declared the Force Bill null and void. The "Nullies," for the time being at least, had the last word, for there was no need for the federal government to make use of the Force Bill. On the other hand, it is evident enough that the doctrines of nullification and secession had been directly and vigorously challenged.

JACKSON'S FOREIGN POLICIES

RELATIONS WITH FRANCE

Conciliatory but firm in dealing with the South Carolinians who quarreled with the federal government, Jackson quite consistently was merely firm in difficulties which arose between the United States and a foreign country, France. After the Napoleonic Wars the United States insisted that France recompense Americans who had suffered property losses from illegal seizures of ships and cargoes during the conflict. At length, in 1831, France responded to the pressure, and agreed to a treaty in which the two nations promised to provide funds to pay proper claims of American citizens against France and of French citizens against the United States. France was to pay 25,000,000 francs in six annual installments, and the United States 1,500,000 francs in the same fashion. Making financial arrangements on the assumption that France would scrupulously make payment, Jackson was embarrassed and angry when the French National Assembly failed to vote funds for the first installment. In December, 1834, he recommended to Congress that French property be seized if the payments were not forthcoming. Thereupon the French legislature voted funds on condition that the President withdraw certain statements in his message which it considered insulting to France. If the government of King Louis Philippe expected the President to be impressed, it was sorely mistaken. In his message to Congress of 1835 Jackson flatly refused to withdraw the offensive statements, and again urged that reprisals be made on French property if France still failed to meet her obligations. However, he indicated that the United States was willing to accept mediation by a third party. Great Britain offered to serve as a friend and neutral, and an agreement was reached by which France promptly made four payments. Jackson had successfully asserted the dignity of the United States.

THE TEXAS QUESTION

In view of Jackson's determined stand against France, it is mildly surprising that he moved cautiously when Americans who moved into Texas after 1820 rose in revolt against Mexico, defeated President Santa Anna, and established the Republic of Texas in 1836. Although the Texans were led by Sam Houston, Jackson's comrade and old friend, the President neither inspired nor resisted them. He wanted Texas for the United States, and he had earlier tried to buy it from Mexico. However, any attempt to bring the Republic of Texas under the American flag would not only exasperate Mexico, but permit Jackson's political enemies in the Northern states to charge that he had taken advantage of a weak neighbor to expand the empire of slavery to the westward. Although the Texans desired annexation to the United States, he would not even officially recognize the Republic of Texas until March 3, 1837, the day before he left the Presidency. He left the problems of delicate relations with Texas and Mexico to his successors.

VAN BUREN AND THE PANIC OF 1837

There can be no doubt that Jackson's behavior with respect to Texas and Mexico was softer because 1836 was a major election year. As the end of his second term and seventh decade of life approached, he looked forward with pleasure toward retirement to his beloved Hermitage, outside Nashville. But he could not leave Washington without doing everything in his power to assure the continuance of his policies and of Democratic ascendancy on the Potomac. He insisted that his party name his trusted lieutenant Martin Van Buren for the Presidency; as usual Jackson had his way. To Van Buren, a respectable New York politician without remarkable talents except for vote-getting, he bequeathed a devoted party. He could not make Van Buren into a military hero, but he could give him a great following of farmers, workmen, and intellectuals who were devoted to political democracy and republican equality, for the Democratic party was more than the shadow of one great man; indeed, it had given to Jackson more than it had received from him. Van Buren needed its strength to win, for he had no compelling personal appeal. Inheriting his mighty and good friend's following, Van Buren also inherited many and diverse political enemies who had collected in a new political party, the Whigs, in 1834.

Like the Democratic party, the Whigs contained various and jarring elements, including champions of protection, advocates of internal improvements by federal action, friends of a national bank, Southern defenders of states' rights, and foes of political democracy. It acquired strength as a gentleman's party, and as one devoted to the economic growth of the nation. Established in every state, the Whig party became truly national and played a major role in American politics for more than twenty years. However, its discordant parts were not sufficiently fused to permit a campaign in behalf of a single presidential candidate in 1836. Instead, the Whigs sought to defeat Van Buren by putting up regionally popular candidates, especially chosen to take advantage of regional discontents. They supported Hugh L. White of Tennessee, General William Henry Harrison of Ohio, and Daniel Webster. Since South Carolina nominated and gave her electoral votes to Willie P. Mangum, no fewer than five men received votes in the electoral college. Van Buren carried 15 of the 26 states and had an easy majority in the electoral count, 170 votes in a total of 294. However, the total popular vote cast for the several Whig leaders almost matched that for Van Buren. Especially attractive at the polls was General Harrison, who with both Whig and Anti-Masonic support, received almost 550,000 votes to Van Buren's 761,000. Thoughtful Whig politicians drew the inevitable conclusion that the military hero had a very special appeal throughout the nation.

Short, plump, quite bald, Martin Van Buren used the razor sparingly, and was described by people who did not love him as "Sweet Sandy Whiskers." He was assuredly not a great President, but he was a respectable one. Unfortunately, he took office at an unhappy time. Economic storm warnings were already flying when he was inaugurated, and a severe depression was under way as early as April, 1837. Feverish speculation in land, excessive optimism on the stock market, bad banking practices, a fall in the price of cotton, and other circumstances, including Jackson's "Specie Circular," brought on panic, bank failures, the destruction of credit and faith, closing of factories, unemployment in the cities, and distress upon farm and plantation. Had he been a Whig, Van Buren might have urged a resurrection of a Bank of the United States and increased protection as measures to restore prosperity. As a loyal Jacksonian, he pursued a policy of hard money and called for a law which would remove the federal funds from the "pet" state banks, some of which were in default. The so-called Independent Treasury system, which placed government funds in several federal repositories, was established in 1840. These measures were not calculated to restore prosperity; Van Buren merely waited for time and economic forces to cure the nation's pocketbook illness. These remedies eventually did their work, but the depression continued until 1841, and lingered even longer in the South and West. Since he could point to no great achievement in foreign affairs, which he had managed cautiously and correctly, Van Buren could not be confident of reelection. Rather, since the public tended to place the blame for its troubles on him, he would almost certainly be defeated if the Whigs did not defeat themselves.

"TIPPECANOE AND TYLER TOO"

The embarrassments which mounted about Van Buren brought political joy to the Whigs. For the third time Henry Clay sought to secure the Presidency. As early as December, 1837, he declared in the language of the politician, that he would be "again forced into the Presidential arena." But the prize continued to elude him, because influential northern Whigs wished to make sure of Van Buren's downfall. They insisted that a military idol must be nominated; some clamored for William Henry Harrison and others for Winfield Scott, both leaders being Virginians and martial figures of the War of 1812. Clay could also claim Virginia birth, but he had helped to begin and end the war rather than to fight it. Scott's friends turned to Harrison, and "Old Tippecanoe" won the nomination. Toward getting a balanced ticket and all possible votes, the Whigs then named for the Vice-Presidency a Virginian who had climbed the political ladder in the state where he was born, John Tyler, a defender of states' rights. A better combination for attracting votes could hardly have been conceived. Moreover, the Whigs waged an astute campaign for "Tippecanoe and Tyler too." A Democratic newspaper nastily called Harrison the sort of man who would be happiest living in a log cabin and imbibing hard cider; he actually lived in a commodious farmhouse in Ohio, but his partisans saw an opportunity to identify him as a man of the people. They made the log cabin and the hard cider jug his emblems, while falsely assailing Van Buren as a soft-fingered aristocrat who lived luxuriously and drank expensive wines in the White House. Thus they stole the Jacksonians' thunder and almost made white seem black and black seem white. Actually, Van Buren came of plain folk and was a self-made man, while Harrison was one of *the* Virginia Harrisons. The Whigs won a decisive victory, carrying 19 of the 26 states and securing an easy plurality of the popular vote; they also captured both Houses of Congress. It could hardly be said that they had halted the march of Jacksonian democracy; that march had lost impetus even before the election. The Whigs were to reap only bitter fruit from their victory, and another Jackson protegé would secure the Presidency after four years of frustration for the party in power.

23 THE OLD SOUTH AND A NEW NORTH

About the year 1820 what we call the Old South, that is, the South that undertook to break away from the Union and to make a new nation, made its appearance. This Old South stretched from the Mason-Dixon Line to the Gulf of Mexico, and as far west as the plains of Texas by 1845. Fundamentally it was merely an enlarged South, its economy and social order remaining basically the same as they had been in Revolutionary times. Cotton rather than tobacco was its chief crop, but it retained its peculiar agricultural economy and its special social order. However, the gap between the North and the South of John C. Calhoun and Jefferson Davis was greater than that between the North and the South of Washington and John Rutledge, as the North became increasingly commercial and industrial. Ill feeling between the two sections mounted, leading finally to civil war. That conflict arose primarily because North and South could not agree on what to do about Negro slavery.

THE COTTON KINGDOM

In the Old South cotton was easily king. The demand for clothing rose rapidly in the first half of the century as the population of the world increased; cotton mills, especially in England, strove to meet the demand. Their machines were fed principally by cotton from the South, which produced 731,000 bales in 1830, 2,133,000 in 1850, and 5,387,000 in 1859. The heart of the Cotton Kingdom was the tier of states stretching from Georgia to Louisiana; especially productive was the "Black Belt" of rich soil extending across Alabama. South Carolina, which had produced half of the crop at the opening of the century, was only sixth among the states in the production of cotton in 1860; Texas was growing more cotton than South Carolina by the beginning of the Civil War. Immense quantities of the white stuff went from the wharves of Mobile and New Orleans to Liverpool and Manchester. Second to cotton was tobacco, the cultivation of which spread westward and southward after the War of Independence. The production of tobacco did not keep pace with that of cotton, although it became important in Kentucky and Tennessee. In 1859 Virginia still led in tobacco, raising 124,000,000 pounds while Kentucky was second with 108,000,000 pounds. Much less important in the economy of the Old South were rice, which continued to come from the Low Country of the Carolinas and Georgia, and sugar, of which Louisiana grew nearly a quarter of a million pounds annually as the Civil War approached. As ever, corn was a basic crop in the South, but not for export. More than 40 percent of the total value of American exports was in cotton by 1840, and in the years immediately before the Civil War the proportion was more than half. In 1860, New Orleans and New York sent forth exports of equal worth, although New York easily excelled in imports.

The economy of the Old South was both stable and prosperous, but it did not keep pace with that of the Northern states. The Old Northwest flourished, producing more than 400,000,000 bushels of corn, or about half of the nation's crop by 1860; it also produced 95 million bushels of wheat. The older Northern states, while falling behind in corn and wheat, continued to lead the nation, however, with respect to other grains, potatoes, butter, cheese, and milk. While growing far less for export than his Southern counterpart, the Northern farmer did very well. The agriculture of the North was better balanced, more diversified than that of the South; and if the Northern farmer commonly "mined" the soil, like his Southern counterpart, wheat and corn did not exhaust it as did cotton and tobacco. Moreover, the Old South lagged far behind in manufacturing, which became ever more important and by 1859 was worth more in dollars than American agriculture as a whole. In that year, hardly more than one-tenth of American industrial machines clanked and clattered below the Mason-Dixon Line. Cotton manufacturing, flour milling, and iron-making were the principal industries, bringing wealth to New England, Pennsylvania, and the Old Northwest rather than to the South. Factories were by no means unknown in the South, but Southerners preferred to seek wealth through the accumulation of land and slaves. The Southern states also made far less progress in railroad building than did the North. The South was likewise falling behind steadily in population, containing only about half as many people as the North at the beginning of the Civil War.

THE SOUTHERN CLASSES

In many Southern memories and not a few Northern ones, the Old South was a vista of broad plantations owned by wealthy aristocrats, tilled by cheerful and faithful slaves, adorned by splendid mansions, but not defiled by the cabins of the Negroes. This view also includes magnolia blossoms, Southern belles, Stephen Collins Foster, and nostalgia. Romantic and tender, that Old South necessarily had some slight traces of woe, which were furnished by occasional cruelties to the slaves and by the presence of poor white trash. Another traditional memory, surviving chiefly in the North, would have it that the Old South was an unprogressive and poverty-stricken land where brutal overseers abused the Negro slaves while their masters and mistresses idled away the hours with fox-hunting, dancing, and mint juleps. The Southern scene was not simple, although charming, nor uniformly cheerful. Actually, the great plantation with its numerous slaves was real enough, and so was the mansion which sheltered its owner, but few Southern whites lived in this lordly fashion. The storied plantation could be found, especially in Alabama and in the Natchez district of Mississippi. However, smaller holdings were the rule and a majority of Southern families owned no slaves whatever in 1860. There were fewer than 400,000 slaveholders in all, and most of them owned few Negroes. The most common agricultural units consisted of white family farms and larger farms (or small plantations) worked by the proprietors with a few slaves. It is apparent that the Southern agricultural population contained many plain farmers and many prosperous ones (who may be thought of as subplanters), as well as planter aristocrats, poor whites, and Negroes. There was on the Southern countryside a sturdy middle-class, a fact which helps to explain the military strength of the Confederacy.

The Southern aristocracy was much as it had been in the eighteenth century, being composed of wealthy planters, together with small contingents of merchants and industrialists. It contained relatively few persons, as an aristocracy should. Its most conspicuous members were the great planters, who were much less numerous than is sometimes supposed, since fewer than 2300 owned more than 100 slaves. There were, of course, more than 2300 families among the gentry, for it included many who owned scores rather than hundreds of slaves. However, it is evident that not many of them were truly lords of the land. Like the aristocracy of the Revolutionary period, that of the Old South was not uniformly composed of families that had possessed wealth for generations; included were the newly rich, particularly in the states lying west and south of the Appalachians. Not always accustomed to great wealth, the aristocrats of the Old South were more notable for their courtesy than for their culture, although there were some liberally educated men who remind us of Jefferson and Madison. Its women were charming and skilled in the arts of attracting men and managing a household rather than in public affairs or criticism of the Romantic poets. Their husbands were better educated, so far as formal instruction was concerned, but did not form an intellectual elite. The rich planter was necessarily a man of affairs rather than one of the study, a man who learned from the world about him rather than from that of the past. His outlook was narrower than that of the Tidewater aristocrat of the preceding century—were not American men of wealth generally more cramped in their views in the nineteenth century than they had been in the eighteenth? The male aristocrat was able enough, even though he might be less concerned with money-making than the Northern merchants or industrialists. He hunted and fought rather than studied and thought; he was not so fond of dueling as legend declares, but he took pride in physical courage. He and his wife were better liked by English travelers than were other sorts of Americans, in some part because they were quite like the English squire and his lady.

Far removed from the aristocracy in all except distance were the "poor whites," who then, as earlier and later, were more visible in Southern society than their numbers warranted. Their cabins and shanties were as much a part of the Southern landscape as were the mansions of the great planters, and there were more of them. Living on lands that never had been rich, or had been ruined by bad use, they were not only poor, but shiftless, diseased, and addicted to violence. Suffering from inferior diet, pellagra, and hookworm, most were sorry specimens of humanity. Indolent, ill-dressed, and usually illiterate, they existed monotonously and miserably, having energy for little more than ferocious quarrels and the procreation of their kind. Their like in the twentieth century have come to be thought of as dwellers upon Erskine Caldwell's *Tobacco Road;* one may think of the "clay eaters," as they were sometimes called in the nineteenth century, as residents upon a Cotton Highway.

There was in the Old South a most important middle class, which has often received less attention than it deserves. It contained the plain farmers, prosperous planters without enough land or slaves to be placed in the aristocracy, merchants, traders, clergymen, lawyers, physicians, teachers, and mechanics. To this class belonged a majority of the Southern whites. Possibly it has attracted little interest because its constituents were relatively prosaic, having neither the romantic qualities of the aristocracy nor the dramatic ones of the poor whites. Nevertheless, that middle class was the spine of the South, and a sturdy one. As has been suggested, it contained great variations, and its limits cannot be defined with great precision. The lesser planters at the top could be and sometimes have been placed in the aristocracy. The plain farmers at the bottom are sometimes confused with the poor whites, although the difference between the two was generally easily observable; the farmer did not display the apathy, the laziness, or the coarseness of the poor white. Rather, the Southern farmer bore a strong resemblance to his Northern counterpart. From this middle class the aristocracy received recruits and from it were recruited many of the Confederate soldiers and sailors who fought so bravely in the Civil War. Many of its members owned no slaves whatever, and many more owned only a few. The middle class as a whole had little or nothing at economic stake in slavery, which is not to say that it was willing to see the institution destroyed.

SLAVERY

No one will be surprised by the statement that the Negroes were a large element in the Old South. Although there were free Negroes, a few of whom actually owned slaves, the great mass was in servitude. Actually, the slave population of the United States did not keep pace with the white in the nineteenth century, thanks in part to the enforcement of the federal act of 1807 forbidding importations from abroad. Although that law was occasionally violated, especially during the years immediately before the Civil War, the number of American Negroes was not materially increased by forced immigration after federal intervention. The slaves multiplied nearly sixfold between 1790 and 1860, increasing from around 700,000 at the time of Washington's inauguration to 2,000,000 in 1830, and almost 4,000,000 in 1860. During the same period of 70 years, however, the white population multiplied about eight times. Nevertheless, it is obvious enough that the institution of slavery was flourishing. It would neither die nor be easily destroyed because the Negroes were failing to reproduce. Nor was there any hope after 1830 that slavery and the larger puzzle of relations between white and colored could be brought to an end by sending Negroes abroad, since sending 2,000,000 persons across the Atlantic would have been an immense task.

The Negro slaves of the Old South were not what they had once been, for time and circumstance had altered them. Many had white blood, for white men had contributed importantly to the growth of the slave population. Among the slaves were many mulattoes (half Negro and half white), quadroons (one-quarter Negro and three-quarters white), octaroons (one-eighth Negro and seven-eighths white), and other mixed stocks in varying fractions. Slaves with red hair and blue eyes were not unknown, and masters and mistresses were sometimes waited upon by slaves who were their half-brothers and half-sisters. One slave recalled that there were servants in Thomas Jefferson's household who much resembled Jefferson's father-in-law. Moving biologically closer to the white race, the slaves had also been increasingly affected by the American environment, becoming less and less African culturally. A minority had learned to read and write, and they were no longer restricted to toil in the fields or domestic work. Although most were still employed in simple and monotonous labor in tobacco rows, cotton fields, or rice marshes, some were carpenters, masons, clerks, factory hands, stage drivers, and railroad men. It is clear that the Negro's position was improving in the South, even though he and his fellows formed the "mudsills" of society.

There was at the time, and has been since, much discussion about the lot of the slaves. Northern and Negro historians are likely to dwell upon the darker side of slavery, while those of Southern white background see more clearly the cloud's silver lining. No simple description will suffice; it is obvious that the slave lived neither in idyllic content under the loving care of gentle masters and mistresses, nor was he merely treated as a brute. His condition varied from place to place, and from time to time, depending upon innumerable circumstances. A household servant or a hired-out mechanic usually fared better than a field hand, and a slave was commonly better off in Virginia than he was in Alabama. In general, it may be said that slavery inevitably was a vicious institution, and that its evils were mitigated by the humane qualities of many owners and by the need to preserve the property value in the slave. The masters were usually decent people, and some were generously indulgent, treating their Negroes as family dependents. In the nature of things, another minority grossly abused their slaves. The fact that slaves were valuable especially improved the treatment that they received, since owners valued their own property. A sturdy young Negro male suitable for work in the fields was worth $300 at the opening of the nineteenth century, and his price gradually mounted, ranging between $1200 and $1800 in 1860. At the beginning of the Civil War an owner could get as much as $500 or $600 per annum for the services of a skilled artisan. So useful were such workers that they were often paid small additional sums, and every now and then one of them was able to purchase his freedom. It should be stressed, however, that palliating forces were not sufficient to justify the ownership of one man by another.

A case has often been presented in defense of slavery. Here it can be put only briefly. Its basic arguments are that the slave was commonly gently treated, that he had security, being cared for from the cradle to the grave; that, with exceptions, he was not yet ready for freedom; and that he was usually content with his lot. It is pointed out that he was largely relieved of cares, that he was on the whole cheerful, and that he loved rather than hated his proprietor. Instances enough of his loyalty and devotion to his master and mistress have been adduced.

If much more could be said in behalf of the institution, in justice one must admit that its evils easily surpassed its merits. The relationship between master and slave was inherently vicious; and it was not well that the slave should be almost absolutely subject to the will of his owner, however intelligent and indulgent that owner might be. Moreover, masters and mistresses were not usually saintly, and a few of them, inevitably, were downright wicked. Power commonly corrupts, and the authority of the proprietors was sometimes abused. Public opinion and his own economic value were the only protections of the slave against a cruel master, for he could not appeal to the courts. Beating and flogging of slaves were by no means unknown, and an owner who killed one of his slaves was likely to escape punishment. If the slave possessed a measure of security with respect to food, lodging, and clothing, he was not sumptuously fed, comfortably housed, or very well clothed. He was seldom permitted to learn to read and write, the teaching of slaves being commonly forbidden by law after 1830. Owners often discouraged marriage among their slaves, so depriving them of a stable family life.

One of the worst features of the institution was the trading in slaves. Men, women, and children were sold at public auction; and members of a family were sometimes bought by different persons, the father being separated from the mother and the children. An especially pitiful and not uncommon sight was a file of slaves, chained together, walking unwillingly from the Upper to the Lower South. Such scenes became familiar because there was a surplus supply of slave labor in the northern reaches of the South and a need for more hands in the Gulf states. They were the more tragic because the slaves were treated with much less indulgence in the Lower South, where they were more likely to be assigned to large workgangs on large plantations. Nor were the slaves the only persons who suffered from slavery, for the owners, both male and female, were tempted to become idle, imperious, capricious, and even brutal.

Although slavery may be defended as supplying a bridge by which the Negroes moved from African barbarism to Western civilization, it was not for the Negro an ideal means. He was probably more resigned to than contented with his lot. He often ran away from his master, and occasionally he joined in desperate and ferocious revolts, despite the impossibility of success. Most famous of such uprisings was the Nat Turner Insurrection in Southampton County, Virginia, in August, 1831. During a ten-day period Negroes led by Turner, one of their preachers, killed 57 whites, including men, women, and children. Hastening to arms, the whites tracked down the insurgents, slew perhaps 100 and captured, tried, and executed Turner and 19 of his followers. No thoughtful Southerner could comfortably ponder a future in which slavery endured; nor could he accept the passage of the Negro from slavery to freedom as the solution of every difficulty arising from the presence of two races in close proximity, with the Negroes being nearly as numerous as the whites in several Southern states.

THE NORTH: INDUSTRY AND IMMIGRATION

If the social structure of the Old South was unhealthy, that of the contemporary North was hardly ideal. On the whole, however, society in the Northern states was less stratified, more fluid, and more wholesome. There was greater wealth than in the Southern states, and its distribution was more equal. Northern society had fewer elements of glamor and drama, and historians have not lavished the attention upon it which they have given to the Old South. To the casual observer, the Northern society might seem to be humdrum and banal. The Northern states most decidedly were not unattractive to immigrants from Europe, who much preferred to settle in them rather than south of the Mason-Dixon Line. They were seeking new and better homes, not color or romance. Northern society was based upon an economy that was diversified as well as prosperous.

In the North, commerce and industry grew apace, and with them the Northern towns and cities. River and canal traffic, given impetus by the development of the steamboat, continued to expand until the middle of the century. The traffic which passed up and down the Hudson and through the Erie Canal after 1826 carried large numbers of people and great quantities of goods. River commerce thrived on the Ohio River after the appearance of the first steamboat there in 1815, and the Mississippi became a thriving artery in 1837. Canal-building practically ceased in the depression which began in 1837; it was not resumed, not for lack of business, but because of competition from the railroads. Although the first railroad using George Stephenson's steam locomotive appeared in England in 1825, the Americans quickly became the railroad builders of the world. A Baltimore and Ohio locomotive made a thirteen mile trip in 1830. Ten years later there were 3328 miles of railroad in the United States and in all of Europe only 1818 miles. After another decade there were 9000 miles of track in the nation, the bulk of them in the Northern states.

Inventions also stimulated agriculture and industry. Reapers invented by Cyrus McCormick and Obed Hussey in the 1830s made the harvesting of grain far easier and quicker. The steel plough was put forth by John Deere in 1837; the hot blast iron furnace using anthracite coal appeared three years later; and in 1844 Samuel F. B. Morse successfully demonstrated his telegraph system, which carried a message from Baltimore to Washington. Many other new or improved devices appeared before the mid-century, including that useful gadget, the safety pin. The use of interchangeable parts in manufacturing, practiced by Eli Whitney and Simeon North in the production of weapons at the beginning of the century, spread increasingly; machines propelled by steam power were more and more used to make them; and the factory became no uncommon sight, especially in New England. The furnaces of Pennsylvania poured forth iron, and factories produced cotton goods, locomotives, farm implements, and other machinery in imposing quantities. With the rise of commerce and industry came the big city, the population of New York multiplying eight times between 1820 and 1860, and moving past the one million mark as the Civil War approached. Philadelphia then contained more than 500,000 persons, and Baltimore more than 200,000.

Unless it be argued—and it has been—that an agrarian society is the ideal one, the New North made much more rapid progress during the 1830s and 1840s than did the Old South, for the mighty advances were in commerce and industry, which were far more Northern than they were Southern. Also, the North far outdistanced the South in attracting immigrants, if for no other reason than that they did not want to compete with slave labor. The number of persons entering the United States from Europe strikingly increased during the 1830s and 1840s, rising from 20,322 in 1830 to 369,980 in 1850. Principal in this so-called "Old Immigration" were the Irish and the Germans, much smaller contingents coming from Scandinavia, the Netherlands, and Britain. The Irish tended to settle in eastern cities, more of them finding employment on the railroads than on police forces; although many of them were driven from Ireland by the "potato famine," they did not in general turn to farming to be sure of a supply of food in America. The Germans settled in such large numbers in some Midwestern cities, such as Cincinnati, St. Louis, and Milwaukee, that they gave to those cities a distinct German flavor; still more of the Germans, however, settled on Midwestern farms. The "Old Immigrants" gave new vigor and added variety to American society, and it has been suggested jocosely (and even seriously) that the brave Irish and Germans formed the backbone of the Union armies in the Civil War. Certainly the South suffered because so few of the "Old Immigrants" came to that region.

Despite the rise to wealth of merchants and industrialists in the New North, the social structure there was not immediately and materially altered. Society remained more fluid than it was in the Old South, and the Northern country men of wealth were replaced to a degree by the owners of railroads, shops, and factories. But the new men of money, such as John Jacob Astor, did not claim to be aristocrats and were not considered such at the time; they were rich middle-class people, and they were not disdainful of the counter and the factory bench. Nor did the nonowning workers in commerce and industry quickly sink into a city proleteriat, since many of them were not completely dependent upon their jobs for a livelihood. To be sure, the so-called American working class had made its appearance and was increasing in numbers. Much more numerous were the land-owning farmers, who continued to form the backbone of Northern society, especially in the regions beyond the Alleghenies. The fat lands of lower Michigan, Indiana, Illinois, Wisconsin, and Iowa were a richer equivalent of the Southern "Black Belt." If one son of a New England family went to the city in search of opportunity, another remained on the farm, and a third passed westward to secure his own homestead. Northern society re-mained substantially an open one, most of its people being of the middling sort, with people at the extremes of wealth and poverty relatively few. There was a great sturdiness in it, which would be displayed in the grind-ing trial of the Civil War.

24 NEW ENGLAND RENAISSANCE AND ABOLITIONIST REFORMATION

The two decades preceding the mid-century were remarkable not only for American physical and economic growth, but also for a cultural flowering and a great reform movement. By 1835 the "New England Renaissance" was well under way; the assaults of the abolitionists upon slavery had started, although they seemed to be making little progress; and reformers were working for all sorts of improvements upon the American scene. The age of Jacksonian triumph was the age in which Edgar Allan Poe displayed his fertile genius; it also saw the start of Ralph Waldo Emerson's solid and enduring influence, while Nathaniel Hawthorne and Herman Melville flourished, artistically if not financially. This was also the era of great historians like William Hickling Prescott, of Henry Thoreau and William Gilmore Simms, as well as of great scientists, including John James Audubon, the student of birds, and Matthew Fontaine Maury, the distinguished oceanographer. The advance of science in general was marked by the founding of the Smithsonian Institution in 1846. Among the principal reformers were Horace Mann, Dorothea Dix, Theodore Parker, Arthur and Lewis Tappan, William Lloyd Garrison, and Theodore

Dwight Weld. The achievements of the reformers were not immediately so impressive as those of the writers, the artists, and the scientists, but with the passage of time they would exert a profound influence—among other things, helping to bring on the Civil War and destroy slavery.

INTELLECTUAL LIFE

In the 1830s and 1840s Boston was the hub of the American intellectual universe, spokes from the hub extending into the New England hinterland. That Boston was the intellectual capital during these years, and remained so until after the Civil War, is to be explained in significant part by the rise of Unitarianism, followed by that of Transcendentalism. Immediately after the War of 1812 Unitarianism thrived there under the guiding genius of William Ellery Channing, a dignified and noble figure who was the moving spirit in the founding of the Unitarian Association (or Church). Unitarianism assailed the orthodox Congregationalist doctrines of the depravity of man, predestination, and the vengeance of God, preaching instead the dignity and worth of man, the freedom of his will, his moral responsibility, his perfectibility, and the love and mercy of God. Although not new, these doctrines were immensely stimulating, and when Unitarianism began to lose some of its early vigor, Transcendentalism supplied another guiding force. Its high priest and seer was Ralph Waldo Emerson, who found the orthodoxy of Unitarianism superior to that of Congregationalism, but unsatisfactory nevertheless. A graduate of Harvard, teacher, philosopher, poet, essayist, and lecturer, he was also briefly a clergyman. Abandoning the pulpit because he could not conscientiously administer the Lord's Supper, Emerson became the great champion of Transcendentalism when he published his essay *Nature* in 1836. Not a highly systematic philosophy, and not precisely the same thing to all of its adherents, Transcendentalism laid heavy stress upon the divine in man and upon his ability to reach universal truth by the study of a mystic Nature. Its insistence that the individual should rely upon himself and make up his own mind appealed to intellectuals, who were both liberated and stimulated by its doctrines. Emerson spread them far and wide through his writings and his lectures. Boldly attacking tenets imposed by authority and by group opinion, he urged the American scholar to stop bowing down before European learning and to strike out for himself. He supplied a potent and healthy ferment.

Even more assertive than Emerson about individualism in practice was Thoreau, who challenged the tyranny of an order based on material values and who would not pay taxes to support the Mexican War, which he thought to be unjust, preferring to spend some hours in jail. He proved that it was possible to achieve personal freedom by restricting personal wants to the absolute necessities, living quietly, inexpensively, and fruitfully for two years in a cabin near Walden Pond. His answer to the problem of overweening materialism was that of a strong soul; it is not for weaker folk, beguiled by comforts and gadgets, and it is especially difficult for a family. In any event, Thoreau's retirement from the world gave him material for that fine book *Walden* which he published in 1854.

LITERARY FIGURES

Much less affected by Transcendentalism were the novelists Hawthorne and Melville, the latter being as much New York Dutch as he was New England Yankee. Neither subscribed to Emersonian optimism, and both were much concerned with the problems of evil. In his best books, dealing with old New England, Hawthorne offered themes of sin and remorse. A fine craftsman, though one of rather narrow interests, he came into his full powers just at the mid-century, publishing his most distinguished book, *The Scarlet Letter,* in 1850, while other volumes followed rapidly. Melville, who as a sailor had visited the South Pacific, used his experiences as the raw materials for a series of great novels, beginning with *Typee* in 1846. Most famous of his works is *Moby Dick,* which describes a whaling voyage and has for its theme a tragic struggle between man and Nature-God. Long dependent upon public jobs for his livelihood, Hawthorne finally won fame during his own lifetime; Melville's genius was too involved and too esoteric to secure prompt appreciation; his reputation had to wait until the twentieth century. Contemporary with Hawthorne and Melville was William Gilmore Simms of South Carolina, a prolific writer of historical romances and other works with Southern settings. The public cared little more for Simms than it did for Melville; it purchased *The Scarlet Letter* in quantity, but it also gave preference to Maria Monk's *Awful Disclosures,* a dreadful tale of frightening events in a Montreal nunnery, published in 1837, and Susan B. Warner's *The Wide, Wide World,* an undistinguished novel of 1850.

The New England of the 1830s and 1840s produced talented essayists and historians as well as novelists. Oliver Wendell Holmes, with too many interests to be profound in any one, wrote witty and charming essays, amusing verse, and the stirring *Old Ironsides,* which saved the frigate *Constitution* from destruction and made possible its preservation for posterity. James Russell Lowell, like Holmes a writer of both prose and poetry, used Yankee dialect in the *Bigelow Papers* to satirize the Mexican War and slavery. *The Vision of Sir Launfal* was and remains his most appealing poem. Emerson was a writer of pithy essays and austere poetry, as well as an intellectual leader. In *Two Years Before the Mast* Richard Henry Dana, Jr., wrote about life at sea.

Especially to be remembered among the historians were Prescott, George

Bancroft, and Richard Hildreth. Prescott was of the so-called romantic school of history, striving to achieve color and drama, not without success; his histories of Spain in the time of Ferdinand and Isabella and of the Spanish conquests of Mexico and Peru continue to attract readers, although they have been factually superseded. Bancroft, a devoted Democrat who helped Andrew Jackson prepare state papers and who had a career in diplomacy, was a "scientific historian," having been a student in Germany in his youth. Like his German mentors, he was a prodigious searcher for facts. He began to publish his imposing *History of the United States* in 1834, a massive work which eventually reached eleven volumes and the ratification of the Constitution. His industry exceeded his objectivity, for he conceived that God specially favored America and the Americans; and his writing is marred by ancestor-worship and rhetoric. His magisterial work was very popular in his own time, and it is still a storehouse of information. Using the same title as Bancroft, Hildreth covered the same ground, but carried on to the year 1821, in six volumes. Dry and sober, he was remarkably accurate, a forerunner of those many historians of the nineteenth and twentieth centuries who wrote for themselves (a worthy enterprise) rather than for the "general reader." Immediately before the mid-century there began to appear the writings of the almost ideal historian, Francis Parkman, who combined meticulous scholarship with fine prose. Of him more later.

Something has been said about the poetry of the New England Renaissance. We may not leave the subject without mentioning John Greenleaf Whittier, whose ballads and narrative poetry concerning New England and whose assaults upon slavery, in verse, eventually attained a remarkable popularity. His *Ichabod,* inspired by what Whittier thought to be Daniel Webster's defection from the cause of freedom in 1850, retains its power and passion. Even more attractive to the public than the verses of Whittier were those of Henry Wadsworth Longfellow, the most popular of American poets, but one who lacked depth and genius. He was splendidly educated and had genuine intellectual gifts, although somehow he failed to feel the tragedy of life. He was a happy man, a loveable one, who wrote tunefully and sometimes touchingly. Few American school children have not been pleasantly exposed to *Evangeline, The Song of Hiawatha,* and *The Village Blacksmith,* while high school students for generations were thrilled by his *Excelsior.* During his long life—he published his first volume of poetry in 1839 and died in 1882—American critics hoped that he would become a great poet. In the twentieth century his very real talents were often overlooked because he was not a towering genius. At least he did not starve in a garret.

Two years younger than Longfellow and twenty-four days older than Abraham Lincoln, Edgar Allan Poe had many of the attributes of genius, and his life was filled with the poverty, neglect, ill-health, and suffering which, according to folklore, must be the lot of the first-rate writer and artist. Though born in Boston, he was of Southern rather than Yankee background, and he was by far the most distinguished Southern man of letters of his time—and one of the greatest in the nation. An orphan at the age of three, he was brought up by well-to-do foster parents in Richmond. He was briefly a student at the University of Virginia, leaving because he had accumulated embarrassing gambling debts, and for a few months he was a cadet at West Point, being dismissed for gross neglect of duty. He could not make a decent living as an editor, critic, or writer; turning to alcohol to smother his sorrows, he could not properly care for his wife and son, and at the age of 40 he was carried home half-conscious from a Baltimore barroom to die. He was utterly devoted to literature, was a critic of high order, wrote splendid short stories, was one of the principal parents of the detective branch of fiction, and above all, was a lyric poet of the first rank. *The Murders in the Rue Morgue, The Gold Bug,* "The Raven," and "Annabelle Lee," along with other Poe writings, are classics not always fully appreciated because they are so familiar. There is tinkling in his poetry; it is also hauntingly hypnotic. Poe was endowed with analytical power, fond of creating scenes of horror, and dominated by the beauty of melancholy. He was not at home in New York City or Philadelphia, where he spent most of his adult years, nor has his work been as highly appreciated in America as it has been abroad, especially in France. Almost ignored in his own time, that creator of almost too seductive melody is still somewhat foreign in his own country.

RELIGION AND REVIVALS

Intellectual ferment, increased by the rise of Transcendentalism, stimulated demands for many kinds of social reform, its effect reaching far beyond the worlds of religion, philosophy, and literature. Also productive of impulses toward renovating American society were European influences and American Protestant revivalism. In England and on the Continent individuals and groups were working for specific reforms in education, family life, conditions of labor, and in many other areas. One of their great goals was the abolition of slavery. Other persons and associations, doubting that it was worthwhile to strike only at particular evils, urged a complete change in the way of life in the western world, and advocated the establishment of socialist and utopian communities toward that end. The propaganda from east of the Atlantic by those who would remold human institutions, such as Charles Fourier, who wished to bring happiness to humanity by organizing it in ideal communities called phalansteries, infected Americans conscious of the shortcomings of their own society, including Horace Greeley and the prominent Unitarian clergyman of Boston, George Ripley. Fervor for reform in America, if not ideas for achieving it, came from evangelical ferment, which was never lacking after the Great Awakening, and boiled among the Protestants in the 1820s and 1830s. Intense revivalist activity stimulated the growth of the Methodist and Baptist Churches, and led to the sending of missionaries among the Indians at home and to the Polynesians and other exotic peoples abroad. Immense throngs gathered at camp meetings to listen to such fiery preachers as Peter Cartwright, Charles G. Finney, or James B. Finley. From this religious effervescence came quarrels and divisions in the old sects, the founding of new ones, and a social gospel generations before the term was coined. Out of it came the preaching of William Miller (who inaccurately prophesied the second coming of Christ in 1843 and 1844), the founding of the Adventist Church, and the rise of the Seventh-Day Adventists, who combined an aversion to warfare with seemly piety. From it also came the Church of Latter-Day Saints, that of the Mormons, based upon revelations accorded to Joseph Smith.

This robust Protestantism objected violently to proselyting in the United States on the part of the Roman Catholic Church; its activities were disliked the more because it was gaining strength with the arrival of tens of thousands of Irish immigrants. It was belabored from the pulpit and by the pens of the Reverend Lyman Beecher and Samuel F. B. Morse. So intense was feeling between the camps of Christians that Protestants and Roman Catholics fought in the streets of Philadelphia in 1844, their battle leaving about twenty dead and some one hundred injured, and ending only when state militia imposed upon them a Christian peace. More seemly and more profitable to society were the struggles which men and women of good faith waged for good causes, such as the preservation of peace, women's rights, public education, the improvement of the lot of orphans and the insane, and the enhancement of public morality. Most important of all was a massive and long continued abolitionist campaign against Negro slavery.

REFORMERS AND UTOPIAS

Reformers passionately promoting change, if not genuine improvement, are sometimes humorless folk, and more than other men and women they are addicted to absurd notions. To their contemporaries they often seem impractical idealists, more or less lunatic. To the worldly-wise they may be at once exasperating, amusing, and admirable. So it was with those of the 1830s and 1840s. Organizing a myriad of societies, clubs, and associations devoted to this, that, and the other purpose, they poured forth streams of propaganda, some of it as ill-contrived as some of their schemes for bettering mankind. Nevertheless, in the seamed web of their organizations—for the same persons were to be found in many of them—were men and women willing, even eager, to go to jail, to be mobbed, and to be martyred in order to translate their ideals into reality. They were certainly given to oddities. Many were interested in the "science" of phrenology, and Horace Greeley soberly suggested that railroad workers ought to be employed in accordance with the bumps on their heads. Dr. Sylvester Graham, seeking to foster more sturdy bodies as well as sharper intellects, urged all to exert themselves to achieve physical symmetry, to rid themselves of fat, and to eat wholewheat bread, a foodstuff which continued to be known by this name for generations. One of his followers tried to attain perfection by living on a diet of that bread with water for an entire year—obesity if not vitality was doubtless purged from him. Some of the reformers, aware that the tight corsets worn by females of that time enabled them to blush prettily, but cramped their supply of oxygen, begged their wearers to choose suitable clothing. A society was formed to protect the morals of sailors when their ships were in port. If a fraction of the improvers was orthodoxly Calvinist and committed to belief in the depravity of man and woman, they nevertheless endeavored to perfect both.

Some American reformers tried to rebuild society from its foundations rather than repair parts of the structure. These believed that freedom and happiness could be attained only through social living under systems advocated by Robert Owen, Charles Fourier, and other pre-Marxian collectivist philosophers. Toward finding the ideal society based on love and work in common, they established dozens of more-or-less socialist communities, including the well-known one at New Harmony, Indiana, formed under Owen's leadership in 1825; the Brook Farm Colony initiated by George Ripley outside of Boston; and many of the "phalansteries" advocated by Fourier. In these communities attempts were made to share equally the physical labor, the fruits thereof, and cultural opportunities; occasionally and temporarily the inhabitants lived contentedly in Arcadia.

Ripley's Brook Farm experiment was fairly successful at first, its colonists being homogeneous, well educated, and well behaved. Among them were Nathaniel Hawthorne and Richard Henry Dana. A splendid school maintained there attracted students from far and wide, and its profits reduced the problem of finances, a major difficulty in every such colony. Nevertheless, Brook Farm endured only five years. When physical tasks were dealt out, Ripley allowed each member to make his or her choice, he himself assuming those that remained; the burden of dealing with manure fell upon him. Hawthorne, who had hoped that life in the community would enable him to make the most of his genius, discovered that hard physical toil and intellectual endeavor were not well suited to each other, so he departed. The colony began to collapse when cranks were permitted to join it, and the experiment was abandoned when its newest and largest building burned in 1846. Even so, that colony lasted longer than most. Dana was bitterly disillusioned by his experiences at Brook Farm. Even with the best of intentions, communal life had its drawbacks. Lack of money, human selfishness, and physical hardships made success unlikely; besides, the participants were frequently unbalanced folk. Some, looking upon marriage as a fetter upon freedom, thought it not unreasonable to share wives and husbands as well as goods. Within a generation the idealistic communities virtually disappeared. Residence in them did have value for at least a few of the colonists, who returned, stimulated and matured, to the normal American way of life.

SOCIAL REFORM

The reformers were more successful, though by no means uniformly so, when they aimed at specific abuses, for in assailing them it was possible to secure more support from the public. A campaign in behalf of women's rights, including the suffrage, made little progress because women did not bitterly resent social, legal, and political discriminations against them; looked upon as intellectually inferior by the males, they were generally satisfied to accept men as their superiors in theory and even in practice. It should not be assumed that they were not without great influence, nor that they were usually desperately melancholy in domestic bondage. Among the achievements of those who fought for women's rights was the acceptance of females as students at Oberlin College in 1833, and the founding three years later of the first permanent college for women, Mount Holyoke, then called the Mount Holyoke Female Seminary. There were marked advances in public education, notably at the elementary level, thanks in large part to the efforts of Horace Mann, who as Secretary of the Board of Education in Massachusetts founded the first state normal school in the United States. He also worked diligently to make teaching a profession, secured the passage of Massachusetts laws requiring greater financial support for public schools and a minimum school year of six months, and helped to found some dozens of high schools. The example of Massachusetts was gradually copied elsewhere. Less impressive headway was made at the college level, for the state universities which began to appear in numbers west of the Appalachians remained ill-nourished and weak. Nor were the private and denominational colleges as many or as splendid as they might have been, loved as they might be by their alumni. Informal education was furthered by the rise of the lyceum of which there were 3000 by 1834. Through the lyceum lectures were offered by many of the scholars of the day, including Emerson. Learning was also spread through cheap newspapers and increasing numbers of magazines. The cynical and the aristocratic-minded may doubt that the increase in newspaper reading was a social advance.

While there have always been Americans resentful of restrictions upon alcoholic liquors, there has long been the problem of excessive use of them. It was not generally recognized to be a serious one early in the nineteenth century, when even clergymen had their tot of rum. By the 1830s the evils of addiction were widely recognized; the American Temperance Union, with powerful support from Protestant churches, moved vigorously after 1836; and Neal Dow was instrumental in procuring the passage of state-wide prohibition in Maine ten years later. By 1855 no fewer than thirteen states were struggling to regulate the traffic in liquor.

There were still other reform drives that enjoyed great success. Dorothea Dix rendered an immense service to troubled humanity, being personally responsible for the founding or enlargement of hospitals for the insane in no fewer than fifteen states. She was also one of many benevolent-minded persons whose efforts turned some prisons into penitentiaries. Incarceration for debt was forbidden by one state after another, a change heartily welcomed by the working man and the improvident. But if the working man had reason to rejoice over this or that piece of social correction, his lot tended to worsen rather than to improve. As factories burgeoned, more men, women, and children became more dependent upon wages earned in them for their subsistence. Less secure economically, they commonly suffered from the notorious evils of early industrialism, long hours of work, low pay, dangerous machines, and unhealthy working conditions. Trade unions had appeared before the end of the eighteenth century, and with them the organized strike, both becoming more common in the 1830s and 1840s. However, the bulk of American labor remained unorganized and it was not easy even to secure legal recognition of the union and the strike. President Jackson ordered the army to break a strike among Irish laborers building a canal in Maryland in 1834. A working man's party came into existence as early as 1828, but it and others like it were able to win only local and temporary victories at the polls. The ten-hour day was gradually established in public service, and several states established it as a maximum before the Civil War. However, the work-week of 60 hours and more continued to be standard, and female and child labor were not given sufficient protection. The state of the workmen might have been even less satisfactory, had it not been for the existence of open lands in the West which attracted tens of thousands of persons and reduced the number of hands available for factories and mines. When reformers assailed Negro slavery, its defenders retorted that many workers in the Northern states were "white slaves"; in that clever phrase, there was a bit of exaggeration.

Seeking to repair the fabric of society by such devices as the Bloomer costume to release females from thralldom, by lectures, and by securing pledges of temperance, the reformers were too serious-minded to offer the most pleasant companionship. Nevertheless, the forces they mobilized for betterment were not trifling. In the most important of all their endless activities, a crusade against Negro slavery, they shook the nation and compelled it to consider whether or not the Southern institution should endure. Their efforts eventually led to the strengthening of opinion against it in the Northern states, sharpened the conflict between the North and South, and ultimately contributed to the outbreak of civil warfare in 1861. It is difficult to believe that if the North and South had been untroubled by difference over slavery, they would have resorted to arms in the spring of that year; that slavery became such a burning question must be explained in considerable part by the long campaign against it waged by reformer-abolitionists.

SLAVERY: "NECESSARY EVIL"

When the reformers embarked upon the cause to which they brought so much passion and devotion, slavery was as solidly established in the South as it had ever been. Many Northerners were unconcerned by the continued existence of the institution. Some of them defended it, some looked upon it as a "necessary evil," many hoped for a painless and gradual extinction, and a very few, especially Quakers, were calling for political action to put an end to it. Opinion in the South was also mixed. Sentiment there was more favorable to the institution because its destruction might bring immediate financial loss, and it certainly would not remove the difficulties created by the presence in close relationship of the two races. Were one to judge by the number of abolitionist societies in being in the year 1830, the belief that slavery must be destroyed had more adherents in the South than in the North, but such groups were not generally active in either section. Unquestionably, many Southerners considered slavery an evil, but they were not sufficiently numerous or vigorous to do anything to eradicate it. In 1831 and 1832 the Virginia Assembly considered several measures for emancipation of the slaves in the Old Dominion, defeating all of them by small majorities. Thereafter, however, no proposal pointing toward emancipation was seriously weighed in any Southern state before the Civil War. The view that slavery was a "necessary evil" acquired new believers in the South; moreover, defenders of slavery became more numerous and more articulate, their ranks being swelled by Southern reaction against abolitionist propaganda from the North. By 1830, as indicated above, it was evident that the solution of the problem by emancipation coupled with colonization was an unlikely one. To free the Negro and send him back to Africa had once seemed to be a suitable program to many whites, including Jefferson, Madison, Monroe, and John Marshall. Abraham Lincoln was to subscribe to it for a time: to execute the plan, the American Colonization Society was founded in 1817. That body sent free Negroes to Sierra Leone and then to Monrovia, settled in 1822, which became the nucleus of the independent Republic of Liberia. The Society was able to send no more than 12,000 persons to Africa before the Civil War, mostly because it lacked funds to act on a larger scale. A Mississippi Colonization Society was established in 1831, but was far less active. A total of about 15,000 Negroes went back to Africa before 1860. It should be observed that those who favored colonization were not necessarily friends of the Negro.

THE ABOLITIONISTS

Principal among the reformers who became active abolitionists were William Lloyd Garrison, Theodore Dwight Weld, and the wealthy merchants of New York, Arthur and Lewis Tappan, whose money helped to carry out many abolitionist projects. Other important figures were Wendell Phillips, William Jay, Gerrit Smith, and James G. Birney, these being only a few of many leaders. We may say that the abolitionist movement was definitely under way on January 1, 1831, when Garrison published the first number of *The Liberator,* which promptly became the chief propaganda organ of a militant group that gathered around him. He and his allies demanded the immediate abolition of slavery. Theodore Weld, who was the outstanding abolitionist west of the Alleghenies, was somewhat more moderate, calling for "immediate emancipation, gradually accomplished." Both men were humorless, able, and devoted; at the time Garrison was much better known, partly because Weld preferred obscurity, and partly because his labors were done chiefly in small colleges and towns of the Old Northwest. Weld, of old New England stock, added to the forces of the abolitionists by converting and enlisting preachers and others in the cause. As a mature student at Lane Theological Seminary in Cincinnati, at Oberlin College, and afterward as a professional organizer, he was responsible for sending out many abolitionist "missionaries." Garrison attracted national attention through his paper, denouncing slavery in harsh language. Threatened by mobbing, as were many of the abolitionists, he refused to be silenced. He announced, "I will not retreat a single inch— AND I WILL BE HEARD."

Challenged on the ground that the Constitution prevented national action against slavery, Garrison irreverently described that document as a "covenant with Hell." If other abolitionists usually employed somewhat less violent language, they were all forthright in their denunciations of the institution. They declared slavery to be contrary to the will of God, who had created men both free and equal; that the ownership of one person by another was a sin; and that slavery debased both master and man. They would not admit that the Constitution was an absolute bar preventing federal action against slavery, proclaiming that there was a "higher law" than the Constitution, to be found in the Declaration of Independence. They asserted that slavery hindered the economic progress of the South. They dwelt upon the beatings and floggings of slaves by their owners and overseers; in a book called *Slavery As It Is* Weld presented gruesome and real scenes of brutality, without troubling himself to point out that they were exceptional cases. As time went on the abolitionists added new charges; that the Southerners were enemies of freedom of speech and the press; that they plotted to extend slavery by acquiring new territory; and that they sought to dominate the nation. Not content with words, they helped to purchase the freedom of some slaves, and they worked for the Underground Railroad, which was a secret network of routes and hiding places to help slaves escape to the North.

Garrison and some of his friends refrained from entering the political arena. Other abolitionists created the Liberty Party in 1840, putting up as its candidate for the Presidency, Birney, an Alabama slaveholder who had turned against Negro bondage and had established a new home in Michigan. The emergence of the new party was greeted with derision and laughter, and Birney offered no competition to William Henry Harrison or Martin Van Buren. Four years later the Liberty Party ticket, with Birney again at its head, received 65,000 votes. Enough of its votes in New York were withheld from Henry Clay to give victory in the state and national contest to James K. Polk. Thereafter the abolitionists preferred to work through parties not made up only of themselves.

By many people in the Northern states the abolitionists were looked upon as incendiaries, mad men and women. Mobs assailed them, injuring a number of them and killing Elijah P. Lovejoy, who lost his life while trying to defend his press at Alton, Illinois, in 1837. Martyrdom won a few converts for abolition, but the cause was supported by only a small minority in the Northern states before the Civil War. However, the abolitionists compelled thought and discussion about slavery, and their agitations undoubtedly helped to persuade many Northerners both that slavery should not be permitted to spread and that it must not endure indefinitely. Antislavery feeling mounted slowly but steadily north of the Mason-Dixon Line between 1830 and 1860.

THE SOUTHERN REACTION

The abolitionist crusade coincided with and contributed to a shift in Southern attitudes toward Negro servitude. The vehemence of the assaults upon both slavery and slaveholders in newspapers, pamphlets, and books which flooded Washington and the Southern states exasperated many Southerners and impelled them to defend both themselves and the institution. Unfortunately the crusaders who condemned the slaveowners were outsiders who took a "holier-than-thou" pose; it was also true that they had nothing to lose, at least immediately, as a result of emancipation. Nor did they admit that the entire nation had been responsible for the introduction of slaves from abroad and that the entire nation ought to make whatever sacrifices were necessary for restoring the slaves to freedom. In particular they did not suggest that the Northerners, as brethren of the Southerners, ought to open their purses through taxation to help compensate the slaveowners, as proprietors had been reimbursed when slavery was abolished in the British Empire in 1833. So violent was the Southern reaction that abolitionists, whether Southern or Northern, were forced to flee beyond the Mason-Dixon Line. Indignant Southerners demanded that abolitionist propaganda be barred from the mails, and their postmasters refused to deliver it; in Georgia a law was passed calling for the execution of persons found guilty of publishing "literature" tending to incite a slave revolt. Southerners in Congress demanded that it refuse to receive a rising flood of abolitionist petitions calling for the destruction of the slave trade and slavery in the District of Columbia. The Senate prudently decided to go through the form of accepting the papers, although until after the Mexican War sentiment was strongly against taking either step. The House of Representatives took a different course, passing the "Gag Resolution" in 1836, renewing it each year until 1844. This resolution required that all papers submitted regarding slavery be "laid upon the table" and ignored. The House thereby in effect denied to the crusaders the right of petition guaranteed by the Constitution, a fact which the abolitionists made much of. John Quincy Adams, serving in the House for many years after his retirement from the Presidency, denounced the resolution as unconstitutional in session after session, and at last persuaded a majority of his colleagues to abandon it. He despised the abolitionists, but he was determined to insist upon their rights as citizens. Fearing Negro insurrections, the Southern states, one after another, tightened the provisions of their slave codes, which were laws forbidding the slaves to hold meetings, to travel without a permit, or to receive more than a minimum of schooling. In most of the Southern states changes in the codes also limited the movement of free Negroes and the right of a master to release his slave.

It was even more serious that Southerners, provoked by the abolitionist attacks, increasingly tried to claim that slavery was a "positive good." Men such as Professor Thomas R. Dew of the College of William and Mary and Chancellor William Harper of the Supreme Court of South Carolina came out as champions of slavery, praising rather than deprecating it, and promptly acquired a following. They contended that the Negro was fundamentally inferior to the white man, that slavery was sanctioned by the Holy Scriptures, that it was tacitly approved by the Constitution, that the slaves, having social security, were better off than the "white slaves" in the factories and mines of the North, and that the economy of the South was sounder and more productive than that of the North. After 1831 the gap in opinion between the North and South regarding slavery widened. Henceforth Southern leaders could not publicly urge that an end be put to the institution, although quiet opinion against it continued below the Mason-Dixon Line. Those who considered it a "positive good" and those who considered it a "necessary evil" expressed the dominant opinions in the Southern states. The growing division of opinion between North and South caused the division of the Methodist Church into two parts in 1845, and led to a virtual separation of Southern and Northern Baptists in the same year. The ties between North and South were beginning to loosen.

25 MANIFEST DESTINY

No other great nation ever expanded so quickly and so easily as did the American Republic in the first half of the nineteenth century. Within a period of fifty years its western boundary moved from the Mississippi to the Pacific Ocean and the Union became three times as large as it had been in 1800. The empires of Texas, of the Pacific Northwest, of California, of the Rocky Mountain region, and of the Southwest all came under the American flag in the fifth decade of the century, the limits of the United States in the central part of North America being more or less permanently established with the Gadsden Purchase of 1853. Those vast territories were acquired and settled with comparatively small cost in blood. Serious as were the wars with Mexico and the Indians which accompanied conquest and occupation, they did not match the struggles undergone by other expanding nations. However, the new acquisitions did supply North and South with new issues with respect to slavery, and moral questions about them were largely responsible for a national crisis in 1850 and contributed toward the clash of arms in 1861.

WESTWARD MOVEMENT

Sometimes we think of American continental expansion as if waves of pioneers gradually rolled on westward until they reached the Pacific. This picture has its merits, but it is not exactly applicable. On occasion a westward advance leaped rather than flooded, the area between the older and the new settlements being occupied later. So it was in most of the western half of the nation. During the 1830s and 1840s Arkansas, Michigan, Wisconsin, and Iowa became so well peopled that they were formed into states. Pioneers in large numbers moved into Minnesota and Texas, but did not immediately begin the task of farming or ranching on the Great Plains. Except for the Mormons, the immigrants considered the Plains and the region of the Rocky Mountains to be vexing and dangerous obstacles to be conquered in order to reach new lands of Canaan in Oregon and California. Settlers sank deep roots in the Willamette River Valley of Oregon and in the San Joaquin Valley of California before there were substantial settlements on the banks of Nebraska's Platte River or in the valleys of the Rockies.

To some degree occupation of the Great Plains was delayed because their southern reaches were set aside as an Indian reservation in 1825. More formidable as a bar to occupation was a widespread belief that the Plains were not suited to tillage; uninformed folk in the East believed they were "deserts" as late as 1830. On the other hand, Oregon and California were thought to be paradises which would produce lush crops, together with enough people who would gladly purchase whatever the farmers and ranchers might have to sell. Strangely enough, despite sentiment against settling on the Plains, which, to be sure, were almost treeless, both they and the mountains to their west were quite thoroughly explored before it was concluded that they were unattractive places to live. Explorers under both public and private sponsorship traversed both regions after the Lewis and Clark expedition, and they became well known to hunters and trappers who wandered through them in search of beaver after the War of 1812. Hunters in the employ of the British Hudson's Bay Company tramped through the northern Rockies, where they encountered eager-beaver seekers whose headquarters were at St. Louis. From St. Louis and from Taos, in New Mexico, American trappers made their way across the vast Plains and through the passes of the Rockies, across the deserts of Nevada, and into the mountain valleys of California. Among them was Jedediah Smith who found a way through the Rockies at the South Pass; "Cannibal Phil" Gardner, who on one occasion was forced to eat an Indian companion in order to survive, and who in another similar emergency devoured his In-

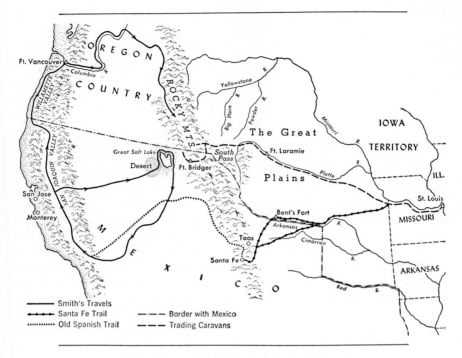

LAND OF THE MOUNTAIN MEN

dian wife; and Captain Benjamin L. E. Bonneville, whose adventures became the basis for a book by Washington Irving.

Trapping proved so profitable that the Rocky Mountain Fur Company was organized to exploit it, while John Jacob Astor's American Fur Company moved its major scene of activity from the upper Great Lakes region to the Rockies. Reaching its peak in the 1830s, the traffic in beaver skins diminished rapidly thereafter because the pond-builders were nearly wiped out. But before that happened the trappers had acquired an immense fund of information about the terrain between the fringes of settlement west of the Mississippi and the Mexican villages of Los Angeles, Monterey, and San Francisco, in California. Knowledge of the southern Great Plains and Rockies was also gained through the extensive trade which sprang up between Missouri and New Mexico, which began in 1821, flourished for a decade, and dwindled away before the Mexican War. From villages in western Missouri, traders with manufactured goods in Murphy wagons opened up the Santa Fé Trail to the capital of New Mexico, where they exchanged their goods for furs, mules, gold, and silver. At length the Mexican government forbade such caravans to go to Santa Fé, but not before the traders had acquired information about New Mexico and thoughts of peopling it with Americans. Although the trappers' and traders' familiarity with the Great Plains and Rockies did not immediately lead to the occupation of those regions, it was of great service in helping immigrants reach the Pacific coast.

AMERICANS IN TEXAS

Before the westward-moving Americans were firmly established in the Oregon country and California, they had not only planted themselves in Texas, but had founded the independent Republic of Texas. A few had seeped into Texas from Louisiana and Arkansas as early as 1815, when the United States still claimed that region as part of the Louisiana Purchase. But colonization of importance began with the Austins, Moses and Stephen, father and son. Moses Austin was a Connecticut man who had drifted westward to Missouri while it was a part of the Spanish Empire and had become a Spanish citizen there. It was he who conceived the idea of building a colony of Americans on the fertile Texas coastal plain. A few months before Mexico gained its independence from Spain, he secured the approval of the last Spanish Governor of Texas, but he died before he could make use of it. His son took up the scheme and carried it out with remarkable success, being responsible for the eventual establishment of several American communities in the valleys of the Brazos and Colorado Rivers. Stephen Austin brought in 150 settlers before the end of the year 1821. Forced to deal thereafter with the government of Mexico, which had inherited from Spain all the territory between the United States on the northeast, the Oregon country on the north, and the Pacific on the west, Austin exhibited genius as a negotiator. In 1823 he was formally granted authority to bring 300 American families into Texas provided they were virtuous, and willing to accept the Roman Catholic faith. Before the end of the year he had these families, the "Old Three Hundred," planted. He soon secured authority to import more hundreds of families; other promoters also secured permission to bring in settlers, for Mexican officials were eager to people Texas, which had been thinly settled so long as it was a part of the Spanish Empire. Austin selected his colonists carefully, managed his own affairs skillfully, and formed small communities that flourished. Newspaper advertisements by him and other entrepreneurs helped to create a "Texas Fever," so that Texas had more than 8000 Anglo-Saxons, almost entirely from the Southern states, by 1830. A string of settlements from the Sabine River to the San Antonio River Valley prospered, since eastern Texas proved ideal for growing cotton.

However, by the 1830s tension was rising between the immigrants and the Mexican Republic. Troubles could not be avoided, even though the majority of the immigrants was willing to give loyalty to Mexico, for the ways of the Mexican and the American were too alien to one another. The Americans did not become Roman Catholics, and they rather despised the Mexicans among whom they lived. Increasingly alarmed less the Americans become too numerous and too powerful, the Mexican government began to discourage new settlements and also passed a law against slavery, these measures being heartily disliked by the Americans, who had brought Negro slaves with them. Another source of unhappiness for the Americans was a change in the Mexican system of government. Of a federal style which allowed them local freedom when they entered Texas, the Mexican Republic shifted to a unitarian form, with authority concentrated in Mexico City. In consequence the Americans came to fear they would suffer under a Mexican tyranny. When Austin went to Mexico City to protest, he was tossed into prison for eight months. In 1834 General Antonio Lopez de Santa Anna, President and dictator of Mexico, undertook to reduce the foreigners to obedience by sending troops into Texas. Fighting ensued, followed by the founding of the Republic of Texas.

THE REVOLUTION IN TEXAS

The Texan Revolution began on the last day of June, 1835, when hot-headed settlers under William B. Travis bloodlessly captured one of Santa Anna's detachments at Anahuac. The majority of the Americans in Texas disapproved of Travis' aggressiveness, but they took up arms when it became evident that the Mexican dictator had no desire for conciliation and intended to use force to establish his authority. By October they had compelled the surrender of all Mexican forces in Texas, and in November they established a provisional government, appointing Sam Houston to command its fighting men. They were not yet committed to independence, for the prevailing sentiment favored local freedom within Mexico. However, they had shed Mexican blood, and it became obvious during the following winter that Santa Anna was planning to lead an army against them and they could expect little mercy from him. Able, quixotic, treacherous, and cruel, he considered himself to be a Mexican Napoleon.

In a drafty shed in the tiny village of Washington on March 2, 1836, delegates from the twelve American communities in Texas issued a Declaration of Independence. They also prepared a constitution for a Republic of Texas, and made Sam Houston commander in chief of its nonexistent army. These actions were taken in a mood of desperation, for a small garrison of Texans was then besieged at San Antonio by a Mexican army of 4000 men personally led by Santa Anna. These 187 Texans were under Travis' command and included the famous frontiersman Davy Crockett, and Jim Bowie, who is remembered in some part for his Bowie knife. Besieged in the Alamo, an abandoned Spanish mission, Travis and his rifle-

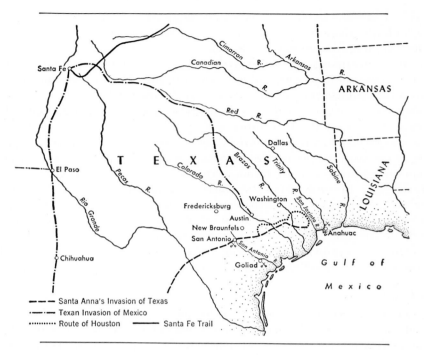

TEXAN REVOLUTION

men again and again drove the Mexican soldiers back from the walls. When it became evident that they could expect no help from the outside, they resolved to sell their lives as dearly as possible, since the angered Santa Anna, infuriated by his heavy losses, announced that no quarter would be given. At last, on March 6, after being twice repulsed, the Mexican troops swarmed over the walls of the mission. They had to take its interior bit by bit, the Texans fighting to the last man.

Santa Anna's triumph cost him heavily, for the Texan garrison had killed more than 1500 of his men before its resistance ended. The refusal of the Mexican President to permit quarter and the heroic stand made by Travis and his comrades steeled the Texans for desperate efforts. "Remember the Alamo" became their battle cry, one which afterwards unfailingly thrilled Texans and all Americans.

The Texans were unable to avenge the Alamo immediately; in fact, they suffered another heavy blow on March 19, when 350 of them were surrounded and surrendered to a greatly superior Mexican force at Goliad. A week after their surrender, presumably on orders from Santa Anna, they were massacred in cold blood. The agonized Texans demanded that Houston quickly attack Santa Anna, but the veteran fighter from Ten-

nessee prudently retreated eastward, followed by the Mexicans. Families
fled as the Mexican general advanced, but his forces dwindled while little
groups of determined men joined Houston. At last, when he was ready,
Houston turned and attacked. He had 783 men, some of whom were
Americans who had hurried across the frontier to help their brethren. On
the day of decision Santa Anna had about 1200 soldiers. On April 21
Houston assailed the Mexican army on the banks of the San Jacinto River.
Moving forward while a band played "Will You Come to the Bower I
Have Shaded For You," Houston and his army furiously charged and
routed the Mexicans. Within fifteen minutes all resistance had ceased, with
nearly half of Santa Anna's troops dead and most of the remainder prisoners. The Texans had only nine killed and thirty-four wounded. After
the battle the Texans discovered Santa Anna hiding in the underbrush.

THE REPUBLIC OF TEXAS

Although there was intermittent fighting between Texas and Mexico for
some years thereafter, the battle of San Jacinto turned out to be decisive.
In order to secure his freedom Santa Anna signed a treaty acknowledging
the independence of Texas. The Mexican Congress refused to approve it,
but its efforts to reconquer Texas were feeble.

The inhabitants of the infant republic held the first election under their
constitution a few months after San Jacinto, naming as their President
Houston, who announced himself to be in favor of governmental thrift and
annexation to the United States. The voters made it clear that they also
desired the union of the American and Texan republics. As has been mentioned above, Andrew Jackson also desired union, but took no steps toward
it, partly to avoid trouble with Mexico, and partly to avert a bitter political
contest at home. He would go only so far as to recognize the new nation,
although like John Quincy Adams before him, he had earlier tried to buy
Texas from Mexico. American recognition insured Texas freedom from
Mexico, but its entrance into the American Union was delayed and finally
arranged by President John Tyler.

The Lone Star republic endured and prospered for almost a decade.
Houston nursed its scanty funds, strove to keep peace with the wily
Comanche and with Mexico, and to eschew risky adventures. His successor,
Mirabeau B. Lamar, who became President in 1840, was more aggressive,
seeking to expand the territory of the new country, to force recognition by
Mexico, and to secure both official recognition and support from European
nations. He conceived that Texas would be more or less permanently independent. During his regime Texas fell into serious debt; an attempt to
conquer New Mexico by means of a "trading" expedition failed miserably;
troops sent southward toward Old Mexico were defeated, many of them
being captured and badly abused as prisoners. Nevertheless the infant

commonwealth grew rapidly in numbers and wealth. After 1836 it offered a square mile of land to every bachelor immigrant, and twice as much to the head of a family. Later it offered attractive concessions to promoters who would bring in groups of pioneers, causing rush by road and by water from Louisiana and Arkansas. More than 2000 Frenchmen were sent by the promoter, Henri Castro, and about 5000 Germans had made their appearance before 1846, building New Braunfels and Fredericksburg. Within ten years the population increased from 30,000 to 142,000, created an orderly, if lusty, society, acquiring schools, newspapers, jails, and the other trappings of civilization. The Texans also began to export cotton in quantity. To most of them only one thing was necessary to assure their welfare—annexation to the United States.

TO THE PACIFIC

Losing Texas, Mexico was also given reason to fear for the safety of New Mexico and California, even before Texas became a part of the United States. New Mexico had a much larger population of Mexicans and Indians than did Texas; it did not have such large areas of fertile and well-watered land; its people were poverty-stricken; and it was of little interest to the Americans as an area of colonization. But Mirabeau Lamar's designs upon New Mexico, and mild American interest in the region as a result of commerce on the Santa Fé Trail suggested to officials in Mexico City that they ought to be concerned for the safety of Sante Fé; they also had good cause to fear that California would be wrested from them.

California (often designated as Upper California to distinguish it from Lower California, the peninsula which remained in Mexican hands after 1848), almost beckoned for invasion after 1835. Earlier its settlements had not been much more than a string of missions stretching north as far as San Francisco, but these had been largely disbanded, vast ranches taking their places. Their Mexican owners had become rich by raising cattle, with the local Indians supplying the necessary labor. Life was easy and happy enough for both owner and worker, and the soft climates of central and southern California were enjoyed by a somnolent society. There was no briskness in California, except in the field of politics. The population was scanty and after 1835 local officials paid little attention to those in Mexico City, who were preoccupied with other things, and to whom California was far away. Between 1835 and 1845 there was a "Decade of Revolution," during which native Californians and Mexicans followed each other in office in bewildering succession. The political situation and the charms of California beguiled both American pioneers and politicians. By the 1840s California was ripe for American plucking, for that paradise on the Pacific was guarded by little more than distance, mountains, and deserts. These were

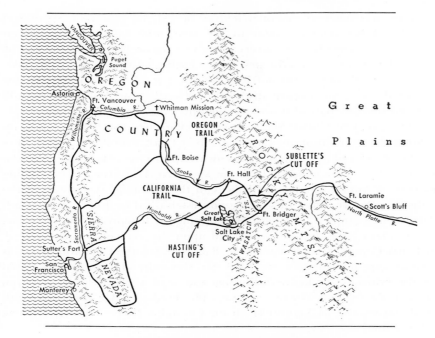

THE OREGON AND CALIFORNIA TRAILS

formidable barriers indeed, but not insuperable. Before 1843 the Americans entered singly and in small groups, by land and by sea; thereafter they came in larger bands, especially by way of the Overland Trails. The American government was moving toward annexation as early as 1842.

In the early 1840s immigrants going to California mingled with others moving toward the Oregon country on the Overland Trails. Oregon was then even more seductive than California, and pioneer parties risking the hardships and dangers of the Great Plains and Rockies headed for the Columbia River Valley more frequently than for that of the Sacramento. The Oregon Trail, traces of which were still to be seen a century later, has kept its romantic fame; it was only a wagon-track, but it was also a highway of empire. Use of it enabled so many Americans to put themselves down on the south side of the Columbia River that the American claim to the Oregon country was immensely strengthened and American title to a large part of it was assured.

THE OREGON CONTROVERSY

It will be recalled that Britain and the United States in their Convention of 1818 established a condominium over the Oregon country for a period of ten years, renewable at the will of both parties. In 1829 this joint occupation was renewed for an indefinite period. By that time Spain had abandoned her tenuous claim to the area, and Russia her somewhat stronger one. The Oregon country was a vast region limited on the east by the Rocky Mountains, on the west by the Pacific, on the south by the forty-second parallel, and on the north by the line 54°40'. Both nations claimed the whole of it on bases of discovery and settlement, but neither could contend that any part of it was occupied by more than a few dozen people before 1840. The United States based its claim upon several grounds, including the explorations of Captain Robert Gray, who discovered the Columbia River and named it after his own ship in 1792. The explorations of Lewis and Clark were used to back the American claim, as was the founding in 1811 of Astoria, the first settlement in the region, at the mouth of the Columbia. Astoria was a fur-trading post established by John Jacob Astor's Pacific Fur Company. Among other arguments, Britain adduced the fact that Captain James Cook had touched upon the coast of Oregon in 1778, and that Captain George Vancouver had ascended the Columbia River as early as 1792, immediately after Gray. Sir Alexander MacKenzie had moved up the Fraser River in the following year, and a British post had been built in the interior as early as 1805. The Hudson's Bay Company, with headquarters at Fort Vancouver on the Columbia River, was active in the river valley.

Actually, neither nation hoped to secure all of the Oregon region, but both wanted the northern part of the lower Columbia Valley. This situation was greatly affected by the appearance of Americans in numbers. Immigration was stimulated by the activities of missionaries sent out by American Methodists and Presbyterians to Christianize the Indians in the southern part of the Oregon country. Methodist missionary Jason Lee reached Vancouver in 1824, and Methodists Samuel Parker and Marcus Whitman began their labors soon afterward by the great bend of the Columbia to the eastward. In the early 1830s farmers following fur traders had begun moving into the Willamette River Valley by the hundreds. By 1843 they were numerous enough to form a local and provisional government; two years later they numbered 5000 persons. The presence of so many Americans immediately south of the Columbia River helped to put an end to the fur trade in the surrounding territory, and the Hudson's Bay Company abandoned Fort Vancouver for a post on Puget Sound. Their presence also persuaded officers of the Company and high British officials that it would be extremely difficult to prevent Americans from moving across the Columbia. The Oregon question contributed to serious tension between the United States and Britain during the first half of the 1840s. However, American expansion toward the northwest, unlike American pushing toward the southwest, did not lead to warfare.

THE OREGON CONTROVERSY

THE MORMON COLONY OF DESERET

Nor did the occupation of Utah by the Mormon colonists of Deseret in 1848 cause serious trouble. This remarkable enterprise had its origin in the teachings of Joseph Smith, who, on the basis of a personal revelation, published the *Book of Mormon* and founded the Church of the Latter-Day Saints in upstate New York in the year 1830. As a new apostle, Smith promptly acquired a large following, for he preached an earnest and worthy Christianity which appealed to plain folk. But he also advocated polygamy, and he and his followers were soon forced to flee westward, first to Ohio and then to Missouri. Driven from Missouri, they established themselves in Nauvoo, Illinois. There they were again persecuted and Smith was lynched in the jail at Carthage in 1838.

Smith's responsibilities fell upon Brigham Young, who was then the senior member of the Quorum of the Twelve Apostles, the executive body of the Mormon Church. Intellectually gifted and dauntless, Young not only sent out missionaries who won many converts both in the United States and abroad, but he also organized a series of mass migrations of his people to the shores of the Great Salt Lake in Utah. The first of these took place in 1848. In Utah Young hoped not only to create a peaceful asylum for his following, but also to create an ideal society. Many humorous references have been made to his domestic life, including some by Mark Twain, who reported that Young had a bed six feet long and ninety-six feet wide, for Young had about twenty wives and fifty-six children. A minor merit of the Mormon colony was that it contained no females unhappy because they were spinsters. It had other splendid qualities, for the Latter-Day Saints irrigated the desert and made it bloom, building a prosperous social order in which want and crime were almost unknown. When it became evident that the federal government would undertake to extend its authority over Utah, Young dreamed of bringing more thousands of Mormons to Deseret and of strengthening it so that it might secure recognition as an independent nation, but he was unable to achieve so much. He accepted the inevitable and an appointment as governor of the federal Territory of Utah in 1850. Later the Latter-Day Saints abandoned the theory and practice of polygamy. They continued to prosper, and a century after the settling of Deseret Mormon men and women included intellectually distinguished as well as sober and pious people.

POLITICS: JOHN TYLER VERSUS HENRY CLAY

Many difficulties arose with expansion toward the Pacific, and Presidents John Tyler and James K. Polk, unlike Jackson and Van Buren, had to deal with them. Both men favored the acquisitions of new territory; arrangements to add Texas to the Union were made in Tyler's time; and the remainder of the Southwest together with the Pacific Northwest came under the American flag during Polk's Presidency. They helped to make the American "Manifest Destiny" a reality.

Tyler was the first of seven Vice-Presidents who inherited the authority of the chief executive in the century from 1841 to 1945. Although Charles Dickens did not find many American gentlemen on his first visit to the United States, he discovered one in Tyler. The Virginian never achieved great popularity, for his views on domestic questions led him into a bitter feud with Henry Clay, and he was condemned by his own Whig Party. Before he left the Presidency, he had become associated with the Democrats rather than with the party that had happily nominated him for the Vice-Presidency in 1840. William Henry Harrison, feeble at the age of 68, was overwhelmed by the responsibilities and burdens of the Presidency, and died of pneumonia on April 4, 1841, precisely a month after taking office. He had made it clear, especially in his inaugural address, that he would follow rather than lead the principal Whigs in Congress. Clay expected to be the power beside the throne, with Harrison executing his wishes. He insisted that Tyler play the role which Harrison had accepted, but Tyler was his own man, and stubbornly clung to his own principles, which were at variance with those of the Kentuckian. The Whigs had nominated Tyler merely to get Southern votes, ignoring the fact that he was a states' rights man, that he was not a supporter of Clay's American System. The Whigs now paid a heavy price for their "balanced" ticket. In the summer of 1841 Van Buren's sub-treasury system was abolished, but an attempt by Clay and his friends to charter a Fiscal Bank of the United States (in effect a third Bank of the United States), failed because of the President's opposition. He vetoed two chartering bills, chiefly because neither required a state's permission for the establishment of a branch of the bank within its boundaries, a restriction which Tyler had demanded. Since the vetoes were supported by the Democrats, Clay and his allies could not secure the necessary two-thirds majority in both Houses of Congress to override the President. Most of the members of his Cabinet promptly resigned in protest, and Tyler was virtually read out of his party. In 1842 he gave his consent to a new tariff law which raised rates substantially, to the levels established in 1832, this despite Southern discontent with the measure. However, he turned increasingly toward the Democrats, especially those who came from the South, and Calhoun became his Secretary of State in the spring of 1844. Another curious result of the clash among the Whigs was that federal funds, for lack of any other arrangement, had to be placed in private banks for safekeeping until 1846, when the Democrats reestablished the sub-treasuries.

WEBSTER AS SECRETARY OF STATE

Tyler's record in foreign affairs was better than in domestic ones. When the Henry Clay Whigs deserted the Cabinet, Secretary of State Daniel Webster could not immediately give up his post. He was busily engaged in negotiations with Britain which he felt he must bring to successful close before leaving office. Not that Webster was able to reach an agreement with the British over Oregon. Like his predecessors, he offered to divide the region at the forty-ninth parallel, but the British continued to refuse such a compromise, largely because they wanted a good harbor on Puget Sound. However, Webster was successful in securing more friendly Anglo-American relations and managed to reach a decent solution to a troublesome problem which had arisen between the two nations over the boundary between Maine and Canada.

In the late 1830s England and America were at odds over several issues, and there was ill feeling in both countries, continuing into the following decade. Dozens of books written about America by British travelers, often in the vein of Mrs. Trollope, had aroused deep resentment, especially since the Americans quite naturally disliked adverse criticism, just or unjust.

American denunciations of aristocratic and effete England did not do much to improve that country's opinion of America. The fact that both American states and individuals failed to meet their obligations to British creditors after the panic of 1837 irritated London.

New Yorkers who were eager to extend American-style freedom to Canada did not soothe wounded English feelings. They gave assistance to the Canadians under William Lyon Mackenzie, who took part in an unsuccessful rebellion in 1837. American violations of neutrality provoked reprisals by Canadian forces, and uproar continued for many months until President Van Buren used federal power to restrain the aggressive New Yorkers. In 1841 their emotions were again aroused, as were those of the Canadians and British officials, when Canadian Alexander McLeod was tried in a New York court for killing an American sympathizer of the rebels on the southern side of the boundary. Fortunately for the cause of good will between the two nations, McLeod was acquitted.

Perhaps even more dangerous was a quarrel over the boundary between Maine and the Canadian province of New Brunswick which flowered into the "Aroostook War" in 1839. The frontier there was so badly described in the Paris peace treaty of 1783 that its true course could not be ascertained, and possession of several thousand square miles of territory was disputed. Britain wanted it so as to keep open military communication with Canada in the winter. In 1839 Maine farmers and Canadian lumbermen challenged each other in the doubtful area, and both Maine and New Brunswick called out militia. An American agent was arrested by the Canadians, and feeling ran so high in Congress that it voted $10,000,000 and authorized the raising of 50,000 men to deal with the emergency. Fortunately, no blood was shed in the "war," but the exasperating boundary question remained. Webster, with Tyler's support, attacked the thorny problem. In 1842 he worked out a treaty with Lord Ashburton, special British Minister to the United States, which divided the disputed region between the parties and dealt with other minor boundary problems. The Webster-Ashburton Treaty was not popular in either England or America, but in both countries good sense permitted its ratification. Rather oddly, the British and American governments were the more willing to compromise because each had evidence in the form of maps which favored the claim of the other. Later research demonstrated that the United States lost several thousand square miles of woodlands to which it was entitled, but it has not been claimed that they were worth a war.

Tyler and his advisers prudently bargained with Britain, but they were not so cautious in dealing with Mexico. California and Texas lured them on to more and more decisive action. In 1842 Webster twice tried to buy San Francisco from Mexico, but in vain. In the same year Commodore Thomas ap Catesby Jones, commander of the American naval squadron in

Extreme American Claim
Extreme British Claim
Final Boundary

WEBSTER AND ASHBURTON SPLIT THE DIFFERENCE

the Pacific, being informed that the United States was at war with Mexico, sailed into the harbor of Monterey, seized control of the village, and raised the American flag over it. Unfortunately for Jones, the rumor upon which he acted was false. He was forced to withdraw, and his action was disowned by his superiors, who conveyed their regrets to the Mexican government. It was not quite time to pluck the California plum. Nor was it possible to secure Texas immediately, although the Tyler regime moved more and more decisively toward that goal with eventual success. To some degree the United States was forced to act, for there was increased danger that the Texans would become accustomed to their independent republic and lose interest in annexation to the Union. A Texan minority which favored continued independence was receiving warm encouragement from Britain and France, both of which considered a separate Texas to be to their advantage. Neither took any particular delight in American expansion, and both wanted trade with Texas, which was likely to grow so long as Texas was independent and certain to be somewhat interrupted if Texas became a part of the American Union and moved behind American tariff barriers. The British were especially eager to preserve the independence of Texas, which they hoped could be used to establish a balance of power in North America. Even British abolitionists came out against the annexation of Texas to the United States; they hoped that the Texans could be persuaded to emancipate their slaves in exchange for British loans, and that Texas could then be used as a base for attacking slavery in the United States.

TYLER AND ANNEXATION

In 1843 Tyler determined that Texas must be brought into the Union. Abel Upshur, who had succeeded Webster as Secretary of State, prepared a treaty toward that end. To try to annex Texas was certain to create a storm at home, for Whigs, abolitionists, and anti-slavery men were certain to oppose it. Annexation would inevitably be denounced as imperialistic, the more immoral because Texas would be a slave state. Besides, the entrance of the republic into the American Union would in all probability lead to war with Mexico, since that country had never recognized its independence and had officially declared that annexation must bring war. Nevertheless, Tyler proceeded, entrusting the business of the treaty to Calhoun, whom he brought into the State Department after the death of Upshur. Presenting the proposed treaty to the Senate in the spring of 1844, Tyler's Democratic Secretary of State gave convincing proof that his best talents did not run toward diplomacy. He urged that the Senate approve it to thwart British schemes to abolish slavery in Texas, so that slavery would be defended both in Texas and in the Southern states. His arguments were so unhappily presented and so much disliked in and out of the Senate that the treaty was condemned by a vote of 35 to 16. Every Whig except one opposed it, together with seven Democrats. Even some Southerners voted against it. But the treaty was not dead, for it became apparent within a few months that there was powerful sentiment in the nation for acquiring Texas, and with it all of Oregon, California, and all the vast territories in between. In the summer and fall of 1844 "Manifest Destiny" captured the American imagination.

At the very moment when American opinion seemed to be strongly against the annexation of Texas, it was actually shifting toward a democratic imperialism which called for expansion to the Pacific. The phrase "Manifest Destiny," coined by John L. O'Sullivan, a New York editor, did not achieve popularity until 1846. O'Sullivan declared that it was "our manifest destiny to overspread and possess the whole of the continent which Providence has given us for the development of the great experiment of liberty and confederated self-government entrusted to us." But the belief that the Americans were a chosen people who had the right and duty to plant themselves on the shores of the Pacific had become popular by 1844.

The "area of liberty" must be enlarged. It was apparent that the thinly peopled northern provinces of Mexico had been meant for the Americans; and surely it was not intended on high that monarchical Britain should own Oregon. The American Republic ought to extend to its natural boundary on the west.

A DARK HORSE AND MANIFEST DESTINY

As yet not formed into a doctrine, the ideas and feelings which were later condensed into O'Sullivan's stirring phrase profoundly influenced the political campaign of 1844. Rather oddly, the leading candidates for the Presidency failed to feel the force of the ground swell of expansionism, were opposed to aggressive measures which might lead to war with Mexico or Britain, or both, and lost out to a "dark horse." Henry Clay was nominated by the Whigs, but his cautious stand on the Texas question cost him valuable votes and probably the election. He announced himself to be for annexing Texas, at the same time saying that it ought to be done so as to avoid a war with Mexico. So he lost the support of some who were determined that Texas be added to the Union and of some who insisted that that slave republic should not be. Going on record as being against annexation, Martin Van Buren did not even obtain the nomination of his party. Among others, Andrew Jackson insisted that the Democrats name for the Presidency a man pledged to get Texas. The result was the nomination by the Democrats of James K. Polk of Tennessee, the first "dark horse" candidate for the Presidency—actually Polk was by no means an unknown, for he had already been Speaker of the House of Representatives. In their platform the Democrats came out positively for expansion, asserting that all of Oregon rightly belonged to the United States and calling for "the reoccupation of Oregon, and the reannexation of Texas at the earliest practicable period," so appealing to Northern as well as Southern expansionist sentiment. The election was closely contested, Polk winning by a narrow margin in both the popular and electoral counts. The struggle was decided in New York State where Birney's Liberty Party ticket received almost 16,000 votes, drawing most of them away from Clay, who lost the state to Polk by a bare 5000. Had he carried New York, he would have had a majority of seven in the electoral college. As it was, Polk and his party came into power committed to aggressive action. They assumed they had a mandate for it, although the result of the election could be interpreted otherwise.

President Tyler and Secretary of State Calhoun, who continued in office until March, 1845, not only concluded that the election had given a mandate, but that the annexation of Texas need not be delayed until Polk entered the White House. They took advantage of the shift in American opinion and of public excitement caused by news that Britain and France were doing everything they could short of military intervention to assure the continuance of the Republic of Texas. Once more they brought forth their treaty for uniting the American and Texan Republics, although there was no hope that they could secure the two-thirds majority of the Senate necessary for approval of it. They found a way around the constitutional requirement, which afterward became a favored device of the makers of foreign policy. There was a simple majority in favor of annexation in both Houses of Congress. Accordingly, Polk and Calhoun obtained the passage of a joint resolution which authorized the negotiation of the treaty with Texas. By its terms, Texas was to become a state immediately upon ratification, was to keep her public lands, and to pay her own debts. Texas was given authority to form four new states from her territory at any future time, a provision which later interested the Democrats when they did not have a majority in the Senate. The majorities in favor of the joint resolution were not impressive, but the business was now substantially done. In October, 1845, the agreement was endorsed by a constitutional convention in Texas and the Republic was accepted as a state by Congress two months later.

In his inaugural address President Polk bluntly announced that all of the Oregon region belonged to the United States, and his statement was received with enthusiasm by many who were willing to fight England for a boundary as far north as 54°40'. But Polk was a cool and shrewd politician, as well as a man of ability and determination. The annexation of Texas would very likely bring on a war with Mexico, and he had set his heart upon acquiring California, which could hardly be done without offending Mexico. He did not want war also with England. Polk arranged for American withdrawal from the treaty authorizing joint British and American rule in Oregon, but he did not rashly send troops across the Columbia River. The British Cabinet had time to reconsider its Oregon policy. There was no desire in London for an American war, and before the end of 1845 the British Cabinet indicated that it was prepared to consider partition of Oregon at the forty-ninth parallel. Since the American government had repeatedly announced its willingness to accept such a division before 1844, Polk finally decided that the compromise could be accepted, despite the fact that he had pledged himself to get all of Oregon. An Anglo-American treaty providing for partition with a boundary following the forty-ninth parallel from the Rocky Mountains to salt water, and thence around the southern end of Vancouver Island, was signed in 1846. This despite furious protests from Lewis Cass and Stephen A. Douglas, Democratic Senators from Michigan and Illinois who pointed out that Polk had not kept his word. That he should have done so is doubtful, especially since the settlement was not disadvantageous to the United States and since it was worth-while to avoid war with Britain.

WAR WITH MEXICO

Certainly Polk did not try very hard to avert war with Mexico. He was resolved not only to have Texas, but to establish its southern boundary on the Rio Grande itself, even though Mexico still refused to recognize the loss of Texas and placed its southern limit at the Nueces River. He was also determined to get California and all the territory in between. In October, 1845, he appointed as his special agent Thomas O. Larkin, an American residing in California, instructing him confidentially to persuade the Californians either to form an independent republic under American protection, or to ask for permission to enter the American Union. In the summer of 1846, John Charles Frémont and a party of sixty men surveying for the American government, joined and supported American settlers who had proclaimed the "Republic of California" in June.

Meanwhile, Polk sent John Slidell as a special envoy to Mexico City to try to buy from Mexico all of her territory and claims to the territory above the Rio Grande and the thirty-second parallel. Appointed in November, 1845, Slidell was told that he could offer in exchange for title to the great area (approximately the same as would be acquired from Mexico in 1848), $30,000,000 and payment by the United States of several million dollars more in claims of American citizens against Mexico. In January, 1846, while Slidell was seeking to open negotiations in Mexico City, Polk also ordered General Zachary Taylor, who commanded an "Army of Observation" in Texas, to lead it across the Nueces River to the banks of the Rio Grande. In March Taylor accordingly moved into the strip of territory claimed by both Mexico and the United States between the two rivers. Before he did so, Slidell learned that his own mission was in vain. The men then in control of Mexico would not listen to his proposals; they ordered American immigrants barred from California; and they gave the Mexican general in command on the Rio Grande authority to use force to assert Mexico's right to all territory south of the Nueces River. They expected war to follow. Believing that distance and American disunity would operate powerfully in favor of Mexico, they also hoped to win it. They also erred when they guessed that they would be helped by outbreak of an Anglo-American war.

On April 25, 1846, Mexican troops attacked one of Taylor's detachments north of the Rio Grande, killing eleven men. By May 9 President Polk had decided that war with Mexico was inevitable. During the evening he so informed his Cabinet, saying that he believed he ought to ask Congress to issue a declaration immediately. Ample causes for declaring war, he said, were to be found in Mexico's refusal even to consider the claims of American citizens against it, the very cold treatment given Slidell by Mexican officials, and other minor grievances. Only George Bancroft disagreed with the President's view; he advised Polk to wait until Mexico had supplied a better reason by taking a hostile step. After the meeting had ended Polk received news of the Mexican attack upon Taylor. He promptly prepared a message to Congress calling upon it to declare war. Listing many charges against Mexico, he offered as the principal one that "Mexico . . . has invaded our territory and shed American blood upon the American soil." On May 12 Congress complied, all of the Democrats and most of the Whigs voting for the declaration. Congress also authorized the raising of 50,000 men and supplied $10,000,000 toward military expenses.

There was widespread enthusiasm for the war, warmest in the South. Far more men volunteered for service than could be used, although the war was not terribly popular in New England, where it was commonly believed that the United States was the aggressor and that in large part the conflict was the result of a desire on the part of Polk and other Southerners to spread slavery. Many Northern Whigs condemned Polk's behavior, and Abraham Lincoln as a recently elected member of the House of Representatives again and again introduced a resolution asking the President to name the "spot" on American soil where Mexican troops had shed American blood. It is true that the Mexican government was not adverse to hostility; on the other hand, Polk was clearly determined to carry the American flag to the Pacific, and he made no serious effort to prevent the clash of arms. In any case it is doubtful that war could long have been averted.

START OF THE WAR: CALIFORNIA AND NEW MEXICO

Had the Mexican army been as generously equipped in other ways as it was with generals, it would have been difficult indeed to overcome Mexican resistance. Mexico's deserts and mountains were formidable obstacles, all the more massive because of the lack of good roads in the country. Moreover, heat, cold, and disease were allies of Mexico. Neither side possessed more than a few thousand well-trained regular troops, although of course the United States had great superiority in numbers and wealth. Its armies were much better equipped, and their power compelled Mexico to seek peace after two years of war. A striking feature of the war was the high quality of the American officers, both senior and junior, among the latter being many of the men who afterward won fame in both Union and Confederate forces during the Civil War. Among them were Robert E. Lee, Ulysses S. Grant, Thomas J. Jackson, William T. Sherman, George B. McClelland, and Joseph E. Johnston. Another well-known officer who fought in the war was Santa Anna, who was in exile in Havana when the struggle began. He was eager to return to Mexico and to power, and American emissaries helped him to go home with the understanding that he would do all he could to bring the war to a close on terms satisfactory to the United States. Before the end of 1846 the General was firmly in control of the Mexican forces; he cheated on his bargain, doing all he could to check the American armies advancing into Mexico.

American military plans called for blockade of the Mexican coasts by naval squadrons, which was easily achieved, and an advance southward from the Rio Grande by an army under Zachary Taylor. New Mexico was to be taken by a smaller force under General Stephen Kearny. The seizure of California would be accomplished by a combination of forces, including a detachment to be led from New Mexico by Kearny, sailors from the American squadron in the Pacific, scouts under John C. Frémont, and volunteers from among the American settlers. If it proved necessary to put an end to Mexican resistance, Mexico City was to be captured by an army advancing westward from Vera Cruz.

Moving forward from Fort Leavenworth, Kansas, with an "Army of the West" of 1700 men, Kearny occupied Santa Fé on August 18, without a

ROUTES OF

- − − Kearny
- +−+ Doniphan
- −ı−ı Stockton
- ·········· Fremont-Gillespie
- - - - Taylor
- —— Scott
- —ı— Sloat

CAMPAIGNS OF THE MEXICAN WAR

struggle. The Mexican population afterward took up arms, but was reduced to obedience by General Sterling Price. Meanwhile, Kearny moved on to California with only 100 men, having been informed that no more were needed. Arriving in Southern California, Kearny's men were enough to settle the issue there. In California, too, there was at first no resistance against the American forces. The American flag was raised over Monterey on July 7 by Commodore John D. Sloat, and heterogeneous American forces captured all of the principal places within a few weeks. However, the Mexicans rallied and recaptured Los Angeles, Santa Barbara, and San Diego. Collecting a mixed force of cavalry, sailors, marines, and civilian volunteers, 559 in all, Kearny retook the three villages, and on January 13, 1847, the last of the Mexicans laid down their arms in accord with the Treaty of Cahuenga, which was arranged by Frémont.

CAMPAIGNS IN MEXICO

New Mexico and California were secured without great convulsions, but Zachary Taylor had no easy time of it. With about 2300 men he drove back a Mexican army of approximately 6000 at Palo Alto on May 8, 1846, and routed it on the following day in the Battle of Resaca de la Palma. Reinforced, he then advanced south of the Rio Grande, capturing Monterrey in September. He remained there for several months. Meanwhile, Colonel Alexander W. Doniphan with a small force of Missouri volunteer cavalrymen moved southward from Santa Fé, captured El Paso, and fought his way to Chihuahua. A week before Doniphan finished his remarkable exploit, Taylor, having sent the bulk of his army to Vera Cruz to take part in an advance against Mexico City, was assailed at Buena Vista by Santa Anna with an army greatly superior in numbers. After hard fighting on February 22 and 23, Taylor's 4800 men drove off Santa Anna's army of 15,000. There was no further important fighting immediately south of the Rio Grande, since Taylor had been ordered to act on the defensive only.

Much to Taylor's disappointment, his superiors decided that Mexican resistance would not cease until Mexico City had been captured, and that it must be approached from the east rather than from the north. "Rough and Ready" Taylor was not happy that General Winfield Scott, the ranking officer in the army, was entrusted with the task of taking the Mexican capital; he wanted the glory that might come to "Fuss and Feathers" Scott. And that veteran, who had performed so superbly in the War of 1812, again displayed his quality and did have the glory of entering Mexico City and of bringing the war to a close.

Scott landed near Vera Cruz with 10,000 men in March, 1847, and with help of a naval squadron captured it before the end of the month. Moving westward into the interior, he was confronted at Cerro Gordo by Santa Anna with about 13,000 men. There on April 18 Scott's army enveloped that of Santa Anna, driving it off after hard hand-to-hand fighting. Scott captured more than 3000 Mexicans; his own losses were 63 killed, 337 wounded. Moving on through the mountains to Puebla, he was forced to wait several months for reinforcements, but in August he entered the Valley of Mexico. Santa Anna had collected about 20,000 men to defend the Mexican capital. Mexican positions at Contreras and Churubusco were stormed on August 19 and 20. In these battles the American army had relatively heavy losses, 133 killed, 865 wounded, and 40 missing. However, the Mexicans suffered more than 7000 casualties, and Santa Anna asked for an armistice, which was granted on August 24. But the peace terms offered to the Mexican government by Nicholas P. Trist, who accompanied Scott and who had been entrusted with the task of making the peace treaty, were rejected by Mexican commissioners. Resuming hostilities, Scott fought his way to the City, overcoming stout resistance, especially on the heights of Chapultepec, where 100 cadets of the Mexican military college fought with great bravery, some throwing themselves down from the heights rather than surrender. With an army reduced to only 6000 men, Scott occupied the capital on September 13, marines under his command establishing themselves in "The Halls of Montezuma." Santa Anna, resigning the Presidency, tried to continue the struggle. His successors in power faced the hard fact that Mexico had lost the war, and the Mexican commissioners discussed peace terms with Trist. Although his authority to bargain had been cancelled by orders from Washington, Trist sensibly acted without authority. On February 2, 1848, in a little village just outside Mexico City, the Treaty of Guadalupe Hidalgo was signed.

By the agreement of Guadalupe Hidalgo, Mexico ceded Texas and her northwestern provinces, almost 2,000,000 square miles of territory. The boundary between the two nations was set as it is at present, except that the Panhandle of New Mexico and southern Arizona were retained by Mexico and became American territory as a result of the Gadsden Purchase five years later. In return for the cession by Mexico, the United States agreed to pay to that country $15,000,000 and also to meet the claims of American citizens against Mexico, these being found to amount to about $3,250,000. Although the treaty gave the United States virtually all the territory Polk had sought to obtain at the beginning of the war, Secretary of State James Buchanan and some Senators expressed themselves against ratification; "Manifest Destiny" for them in the early months of 1848 required that all of Mexico be annexed. Polk sensibly urged that the magnificent empire which would become American under the treaty was sufficient. It was ratified by the Senate by a vote of 38 to 14 in March, and two months later by the Mexican Congress.

The war had cost the United States about 13,000 dead, chiefly from disease, more than 4000 wounded, and nearly $100,000,000 for immediate military expenses. To the costs must be added pensions to the soldiers and their dependents continuing into the twentieth century, and much more important, a legacy of ill will toward the United States in Mexico in particular, and in Latin America in general. Afterward, those in Latin America who wished an example of "Yankee Imperialism" could cite the seizure of Mexico's northern provinces by the aggressive North Americans. In the main, however, the Treaty of Guadalupe Hidalgo was accepted in Mexico as final, except for minor boundary changes. In 1853 the Mexican government accepted $10,000,000 in payment for the Gadsden Purchase, sought by the United States to permit the building of a railroad from the Mississippi to southern California on American soil south of the Rockies. So the continuous territory of the continental United States acquired its present boundaries.

26 THE MID-CENTURY CRISIS

Expansion to the Pacific, and particularly the Mexican War, diverted American attention to a degree from domestic troubles, but it also raised new issues with respect to slavery. Those issues, added to existing ones, quickly precipitated a national crisis. Among the new questions which stirred sectional feelings were: Should California be admitted to the Union as a free state? Ought slavery be barred from the territory of Oregon? Should it be permitted, barred, or encouraged in the region between Texas and California? Ought the claim of the state of Texas to all lands east of the upper Rio Grande be recognized, thus assuring the westward spread of slavery into half of New Mexico? These questions were the more difficult because they appeared at a time when older issues concerning slavery had become acute. As the mid-century approached, anti-slavery people were insistently urging that Congress put an end to the slave trade in the District of Columbia, destroy slavery itself in Washington, and forbid domestic traffic in Negroes entirely. On the other hand, Southerners were demanding congressional action to help slaveowners catch and bring back fugitive slaves seeking refuge in the Northern states and Canada. Ill feeling over each issue was transferred to all the others, and compromise was made difficult by the demand of abolitionists that slavery be completely erased

367

and by the appeals of ardent Southern defenders of the institution who insisted that the federal government not only protect it but even try to spread its benefits. North and South came near to blows in the year 1850.

FUGITIVE SLAVES

After the Mexican War national policy regarding fugitive slaves became of the first importance. What to do about the Negroes who escaped from the South was a question almost as fraught with serious consequences between 1848 and 1860 as the question of the status of slavery in the territories of the United States, both being hotly contested. Not that slaves were fleeing in masses from all parts of the South, for the fugitives were relatively few and came chiefly from the Upper South. Although fewer than 25,000 actually escaped before the Civil War, the flight of slaves toward freedom nevertheless became of the first concern. If many attained freedom, owners would sustain heavy economic losses and the institution itself would be endangered. Accordingly, the dominant Southern opinion insisted that everything possible be done to prevent them from crossing the Mason-Dixon Line and to assure their return if they did escape. It was the duty of the federal government and of the Northern states to assist Southerners whose property had taken to its heels. On the other hand, ever since the founding of the Republic, there had been many in the Northern states who were not eager to return runaways to servitude, and their number increased with each passing decade. This despite the fact that the Constitution declared that the fugitives should be "delivered up" to their owners. Nor were Northerners admirers of the federal Fugitive Slave Law of 1793. The law called upon both federal and state officers to assist slave owners in regaining possession of their property. However, after 1820 several Northern states passed "personal liberty" acts which not only withdrew the assistance of their officers, but also required a slaveowner to establish his claim to a runaway by legal processes.

From the beginning of the Republic, as early as 1786, some Northerners not only refused to aid slaveowners in catching their property, but helped to move the property beyond the owner's reach. These friends of the fugitives gradually increased in number after the War of 1812, and more rapidly after the beginning of the abolitionist crusade. By 1830 they had organized the "Underground Railroad," a number of paths to freedom, together with way stations and conductors. By obscure roads and often under cover of night they escorted the runaways to spots in the North where they were unlikely to be found, and especially to Canada, where slavery was illegal. Free Negroes and runaways even ventured below the Mason-Dixon Line to procure traffic for the Underground Railroad. Those who ran it were looked upon as troublemakers and thieves by many Southerners.

These were disturbed by the decision of the United States Supreme Court in the case of *Prigg* v. *Pennsylvania* in 1842, which declared that a state could not prevent a slaveowner from regaining his property, but that a state was not obliged to help him secure it. Thereafter, the Northern states enacted more "personal liberty" laws. Southerners like Calhoun insisted in vain, though with some logic, that the Supreme Court had erred and that it was the states' duty to help apprehend runaway slaves, just as they were bound to assist in apprehending persons accused of crimes. After the Mexican War defenders of "Southern rights" therefore pressed hard in Congress for a stringent federal fugitive slave law, but encountered strong resistance, although the slave owners could cite the Prigg case as proof that Congress was constitutionally bound to act.

SLAVERY IN THE TERRITORIES

Whether or not there should be slavery in the territories of the United States, a burning question in 1820, was one of small importance for the next quarter of a century. Nor was there during that period any serious quarrel over the admission of states with or without slavery; free and slave states were accepted in equal numbers, until controversy flared over the annexation of the State of Texas. The settlement of the Oregon dispute with Britain and the Mexican cession led to furious struggles over the status of slavery in the region west of the Rockies. In 1847 Oregon was made into a territory, but only after a warm debate in Congress concerning slavery's legal position within it. The same issue was raised in connection with the establishment of territorial governments in the Mexican cession— indeed it was brought up long before the Mexican flag came down. By 1849 California was seeking admission as a free state, providing another troublesome question. It may be somewhat surprising that there should have been any serious contest over the legal standing of slavery in the Oregon Territory, since it was most unlikely that Negro bondage would be introduced into it. The region was obviously unsuitable for a plantation economy; Southerners had no desire to take slaves into it; and the settlers wanted it forbidden. The reason for the conflict was that by 1847 many Southerners as a matter of principle were demanding recognition of the constitutional right of a slaveowner to take into and keep his property in any region except the free states. Others, preferring political peace to a struggle over a theoretical point, were willing to let Oregon become a free territory, and it was made one.

THE WILMOT PROVISO

It was far more difficult, and for a time seemingly impossible, to reach a settlement between North and South with respect to the regions acquired from Mexico. The war with Mexico had hardly begun when an obscure Congressman from Pennsylvania, Democrat David Wilmot, made sure that his name would not be forgotten by introducing an amendment to a bill giving President Polk $2,000,000 to use toward persuading Mexico to lay down arms and to cede her northwestern provinces with Texas. His amendment, known as the Wilmot Proviso, declared that neither slavery nor involuntary servitude should ever be permitted in any territory acquired from Mexico through use of the money. The Northerners had a majority in the House of Representatives, and Whigs among them pushed the Proviso, not only because they believed in its principle, but because it would embarrass Polk and the Democrats. It passed the House by a vote of 87 to 64, but the Senate, where Northerners and Southerners were equal in number, refused to consider it in the summer of 1846. But the northern Whigs would not let the Proviso die and called for it in more stringent form in 1847, demanding that slavery be positively forbidden in any territory, except for Texas, secured from Mexico. The prohibition was approved by the House, defeated in the Senate by a vote of 31 to 21. However, agitation for it continued, some of its supporters charging that a Southern "slaveocracy" was seeking to extend its dominion into all the territories of the United States, Old Mexico, and Central America. The accusation was bitterly resented by Southerners, especially by the Southern Democrats at whom it was aimed. Some, led by Calhoun, responded by taking an extreme stand in behalf of slavery. These denied that there was any conspiracy to spread the institution, although they proclaimed it to be beneficial. They subscribed to a set of doctrines advanced by Calhoun in February, 1847, which mingled states' rights with the defense of slavery. Calhoun declared that all territories were the common property of the states; that Congress, being merely an agent of the states, could not deprive a state of its equal right in a territory by forbidding slavery within it; and that such a law was therefore unconstitutional. He claimed that he and his friends were merely "repelling attacks . . . all we ask is to be let alone; but if trampled upon, it will be idle to expect that we will not resist it." Moderates from both sides of the Mason-Dixon Line tried hard to find an acceptable middle ground, but failed. They suggested in vain that the Missouri compromise line of 36°30' be extended westward to the Pacific. In December, 1847, General Lewis Cass, who was to be nominated for the Presidency by the Democrats the following year, offered another solution which afterward achieved great popularity among moderate-minded men. In his "Nicholson Letter" Cass urged that the principle of "popular sovereignty," often vulgarly known as "squatter sovereignty," be applied. He advocated that, in accordance with the spirit of democracy, the settlers in a territory be allowed to decide for themselves whether or not they wanted slavery. This proposal was no more acceptable to extremists than was a dividing line.

THE ELECTION OF 1848

The presidential election of 1848 did not soothe sectional dissension, but it did offer evidence that the voters on both sides of the Mason-Dixon Line were not yet ready to settle the quarrel over slavery in the territories to please either David Wilmot or John C. Calhoun. Most of the leaders in both parties, wishing to win at the polls, fought against candidates and platform planks that would alienate large numbers of voters in order to satisfy extremists. Since Polk had announced that he would serve for only one term, the Democrats turned to Lewis Cass, a respectable and conservative man, popular in the Old Northwest. Their platform said nothing about slavery in the territories. In their national convention the Whigs also ignored the issue and nominated a man who had said nothing about it. Remembering the attraction William Henry Harrison had had for the voters, they wanted a military hero. They had two to chose from, Zachary Taylor and Winfield Scott. "Rough and Ready" seemed a more appealing figure than "Old Fuss and Feathers." Therefore they nominated Taylor, offering a platform that consisted largely of a recital of his military record and achievements. The Virginia-born general, who owned more than 100 slaves in Louisiana and who was utterly devoted to the Union, was the victor, and not entirely because he had defeated Santa Anna at Buena Vista.

There were Northerners in both parties who found both Cass and Taylor to be utterly unacceptable. "Barnburners," anti-slavery men among the Democrats, and "Conscience" Whigs formed a third party, which the abolitionists also joined. This Free Soil Party denounced the aggressions of the "slaveocracy," declared allegiance to the Wilmot Proviso, and called for "Free Soil, Free Speech, Free Labor, and Free Men." It also favored free homesteads for actual settlers. It named for the Presidency Van Buren, who had appeal for the "Barnburners," most numerous in New York. Although the Free Soil Party was unable to win electoral votes, Van Buren received almost 300,000 popular votes, and more than Cass in New York. Taylor had a small plurality nationally, carried New York, and obtained a majority in the electoral college, 163 to 127. Had Cass carried New York, he would have been the winner. Chosen with Taylor was the Whig vice-presidential candidate, Millard Fillmore of New York. As we shall see, the Free Soil Party soon lost headway, but the 300,000 votes which it had secured demonstrated the force of Northern sentiment against the spread of slavery. Many Northerners were unwilling to cast their ballots for Cass, "a Northern man with Southern principles," or for Taylor, "a Southern man with Southern principles." The appearance of the Free Soil Party foreshadowed that of the Republican Party.

Although practically all Southerners and most Northerners cast their ballots in 1848 for Cass or Taylor, despite the silence of the Democratic and Whig platforms with respect to slavery, sectional antagonism mounted during the campaign and afterward. It rose high in the winter of 1849–1850, with California supplying a new and most important issue by applying for admission as a free state. Controversy over slavery was so acute in the House of Representatives in December that it required three weeks and 63 ballots to elect a Speaker. By that time passionate Southerners were talking about secession and the creation of an independent Southern republic; Northern extremists were saying either that the South must yield or that the North should separate from the South. Taylor, who was actually a Southerner with Northern principles, added fuel to the flames by urging the admission of California as a free state. He also made it clear in his message to Congress, of December 1849, that disunionists would receive no comfort from him. However the Union might be menaced, he declared, "I shall stand by it and maintain it in its integrity to the full extent of the obligations imposed and the powers conferred upon me by the Constitution."

THE CALIFORNIA GOLD RUSH

It was, of course, the discovery of gold and the subsequent "Gold Rush" to California that swiftly brought a request for statehood from the shores of the Pacific. In January, 1848, nine days before the signing of the Treaty of Guadalupe Hidalgo, gold was found by one James W. Marshall while he was building a sawmill for Johann Augustus Sutter on one of the tributaries of the Sacramento River. The news spread rapidly, and it soon became evident that the precious stuff lay on the bottom of many of the streams pouring into the Sacramento. There followed rapidly a rush from all parts of California. Discoveries were made again and again, the precious metal being found in large quantities when miners dug into the banks of the streams or explored the hills and mountains from which they sprang. In the summer of 1848 men stirred by dreams of great wealth began to make their way toward California from the Mississippi Valley and from the Atlantic seaboard. When President Polk announced in a message to Congress of December, 1848, that gold had indeed been found, the "Gold Rush" began in earnest. Thousands of men scrambled westward on the Santa Fé and Overland Trails toward the diggings, singing Stephen Foster's "O, Susannah!"

> I'll scrape the mountains clean, old girl,
> I'll drain the rivers dry.

I'm off for Californi-ay.
Susannah, don't you cry.

Other fortune seekers traveled from New Orleans by sea to Vera Cruz, made their way across Mexico, and took ship (when they could find one) from Acapulco to San Francisco. From the Atlantic seaboard thousands went by ship to Panama, across the isthmus on foot, in small boats, and on burros, also finishing their journey by sea. Many others from the east coast sailed around Cape Horn. One ship, the *Eureka,* took 59 passengers from Cleveland, Ohio, by way of the St. Lawrence River to the Atlantic, reaching San Francisco by way of Cape Horn after a voyage of 264 days.

By the end of 1849 perhaps 100,000 persons had reached the gold fields. For most of them there could be no quick fortune in yellow treasure, although tens of millions of dollars worth of it were found in 1849 and again in 1850. The "rushers" became farmers, merchants, and politicians as well as miners. They established order in part by organizing "Vigilante" groups that dealt summarily with criminals. They held a convention at Monterey in the fall of 1849, which prepared a state constitution forbidding slavery. It was approved by the voters in November, and a petition for statehood was promptly sent off to Washington. The "Forty-niners" had not brought slaves with them and did not want them. Accustomed to swift action, they wanted statehood without delay.

The California petition, favored by Taylor and Northern enemies of slavery, alarmed those Southerners who were already deeply aroused by anti-slavery attacks. Hitherto they had been sure that they could prevent passage of laws against slavery, since the slave and free states had been equally represented in the Senate. So long as that situation prevailed, they could check legislative assaults upon slavery, especially since they had been able to rely upon the support of some Northern Senators. If California came in as a free state, the formal balance would be upset, and its restoration would be unlikely, at least in the near future. The House of Representatives had already approved a bill forbidding the slave trade in the District of Columbia, but that measure, like the Wilmot Proviso, had been set aside by the Senate. The admission of California as a free state threatened the Southern bulwark in that body, and Taylor's behavior made it only too clear that the South could not rely upon the President for support. In the spring of 1850 Southerners who were unwilling to risk Northern dominance in Washington turned increasingly to thoughts of secession. Robert Barnwell Rhett of South Carolina, William L. Yancey of Alabama, and other ardent champions for the South openly campaigned for separation from the Union. They hoped to advance their cause by means of the Nashville Convention, which had been called by the legislature of Mississippi, and to which all the slave states had been invited to send delegates. The Convention was to meet in June.

THE COMPROMISE OF 1850

Must there be disunion and perhaps civil war as well? Older and cooler politicians from both sides of the Mason-Dixon Line earnestly urged compromise, and they found leaders in Clay, Webster, and the Democratic Senator from Illinois, Stephen A. Douglas. Ever devoted to the nation, aged and weary, having finally abandoned his hope of securing the Presidency, Clay came forward once more as the great pacifier. Toward the close of January, 1850, he introduced in the Senate a series of resolutions toward a sectional bargain. These called for the admission of California as a free state, payment of the public debt of Texas, with Texas abandoning her claim to the eastern half of New Mexico, and territorial organization of the region between Texas and California without any stipulation regarding slavery. They also called for prohibition of the slave trade but no interference with existing slavery in the District of Columbia, a declaration that Congress lacked authority to regulate the interstate traffic in slaves, and an effective law for the return of fugitive slaves. In support of this bargain Clay called upon all to make concessions for the common good. He urged that Northern anti-slavery men be satisfied because of the provisions regarding California and the vast region to its eastward, for which it was quite unnecessary to ask a Wilmot Proviso, since soil and climate dictated that slavery could not exist there. He warned ardent champions of the South that secession was illegal and declared that they should consider decisive federal action for the return of fugitive slaves a major concession to the South.

Clay's plan and his arguments did not satisfy Calhoun, who was even nearer to the grave than was the Kentuckian. Unable to stand, he offered his opinion in a speech read for him by Senator James M. Mason of Virginia. Calhoun was well aware that Clay's compromise would weaken the position of the South, and that the admission of a free California would be a decisive defeat for his section. He saw clearly that the South was slipping more and more into a minority position, and he felt certain that the North would use its power. There could be, he said, only one remedy. If the South were to remain satisfied in the Union, there would have to be a constitutional amendment which would assure to it the ability to prevent Northern aggressions. Although he did not say so, he believed that a suitable arrangement for the protection of "Southern rights" would be the election of two Presidents, one Northern and the other Southern, each possessing a veto.

Clay received no help from Calhoun, but Daniel Webster came forward to join him, calling for compromise in his great speech of March 7. It must be conceded that Webster offered both eloquence and personal sacrifice in this, his last great oration, for he knew he would be savagely assailed in Massachusetts and by his fellow Northern Whigs if he did not insist upon the Wilmot Proviso. He nevertheless bravely supported Clay. "I wish to speak today," he said, "not as a Massachusetts man, nor as a Northern man, but as an American." While he was opposed to the spread of slavery into the region between California and Texas, he would not demand the passage of a law to forbid it, nor should his Northern brethren. Like Clay, he asserted that God himself had ordained that slavery could not flourish there, having so made the area that it was utterly unsuitable for plantation slavery. Nothing could be gained by trying to enact a law sanctioning the Divine Ordinance, and efforts to achieve it only exasperated Southerners; to preserve the Union, both sides ought to restrain their emotions. Webster was immediately subjected to brutal abuse from the Northern states, including his own Massachusetts; in *Ichabod* Whittier described him as a fallen angel; Emerson denounced him; and abolitionist Theodore Parker declared that he knew of "no deed in American history done by a son of New England to which I can compare this but the act of Benedict Arnold." However, more sober second thought could lead only to the conclusion that Webster had spoken honestly and sensibly. He helped to mold Northern opinion toward acceptance of Clay's compromise, although his fellow Northern Whigs in Congress refused to vote for provisions favorable or satisfactory to the South.

Despite the prestige of Clay and Webster, it seemed unlikely for many weeks that the Compromise would be approved. There were bitter debates, especially over the question of regulating slavery in the mountains and deserts of New Mexico, Arizona, Utah, and Nevada. Whig Senator William H. Seward of New York asserted that the Wilmot Proviso must be enacted and that acceptance of anything less was "radically wrong and essentially vicious." He went on to say that even the Constitution must not be allowed to protect slavery, since there was a "higher law" against that institution. On the other hand, Senator Jefferson Davis of Mississippi insisted that the South must have its equal rights in the territories and contended that the Constitution, by its Fifth Amendment, declaring that "No person shall be . . . deprived of liberty, life or property without due process of law," gave an owner the right to take his slave lawfully into any territory.

When Clay put his bargain into the form of three bills, one calling for the admission of a free California, a second to prohibit the slave trade in the District of Columbia, and a third, the so-called "Omnibus Bill," to deal with the territorial question, the defeat of all three seemed certain. However, Northern Democrats led by Stephen Douglas and Lewis Cass rallied to the cause of compromise, and Douglas devised a method by which the bargain could be made into law. In the form of large units, Clay's arrangements would fail, being defeated by a combination of Northerners and Southerners in opposition for different reasons. Douglas divided them into five bills, making it possible to secure a majority for each of them. Thus some of the measures could be passed by the conciliators with the support of vigorous Southern sectionalists, and others by the moderates with the help of aggressive anti-slavery men. Even this clever maneuvering did not assure victory to the compromisers, but Douglas urgently campaigned for votes in the capitol cloakrooms and finally secured the necessary majorities. Meanwhile death removed another obstacle to compromise. President Taylor was averse to making any concession to the South with respect to slavery in the territories. He died of cholera on July 9, and was succeeded by Millard Fillmore, who was an advocate of conciliation. Early in September the five bills were approved by both Houses of Congress and were signed into law by Fillmore. Taken together they afterward came to be known as the Compromise of 1850.

The terms of the Compromise differed somewhat from the proposals made by Clay. California, of course, became a free state, with the result that the balance between North and South in the Senate was permanently destroyed. Texas received $10,000,000 in return for accepting her present boundary on the west. Territories of Utah and New Mexico were established, nothing being said about slavery in either, except that appeals from decisions in their territorial courts about the status of slaves might be made to the federal Supreme Court. (No such appeals were made. In fact, as Clay and Webster had predicted, very few slaves were taken into Utah and New Mexico.) The slave trade in the District of Columbia was barred, a measure warmly endorsed by all moderate-minded men, since the sight of sales in the national capital could not fail to arouse emotion. The Fugitive Slave Law adopted was remarkably stringent, for it did everything possible to assure an owner of the return of his property. Indeed, it became easily possible through this new federal machinery to secure Negroes who were either free or the property of another owner. Special United States Commissioners were authorized to arrange for the arrest of fugitives and for their return to their owners, after a brief hearing. A white man who claimed to own a Negro had to do little more than declare under oath that the Negro was his property in order to secure him. Fugitives were not allowed to testify to prove that they were actually free men. The commissioners were authorized to enlist posses to assist them, and citizens who tried to help slaves escape were declared subject to a fine of $1000 and imprisonment for six months. So far as federal law could do it, this measure assured the return of runaways to their Southern masters. While it was presumably as important to the South as the addition of a free state was to the North, the law was to prove to be of very doubtful value.

With the adoption of the Compromise of 1850 sectional controversy over slavery temporarily waned. Even its approach soothed tempers in the

TERRITORIAL SLAVERY, 1850 AND 1854

South. The Nashville Convention in June, 1850, was attended chiefly by men from Tennessee with scattered delegates from the Lower South. Most of the states of the Upper South were not represented at all. Even so, the delegates declared that they would be satisfied by an extension of the Missouri Compromise line of 36°30′ across the territory acquired from Mexico. A second convention held in Nashville in November denounced the Compromise and proclaimed the right of secession, but it was attended by only a handful of persons. More typical of the Southern attitude was a platform prepared by a Georgia convention in December, 1850. This "Georgia Platform" declared that Georgia, not entirely pleased with the Compromise, nevertheless accepted it as "a permanent adjustment." Its signers asserted that they would resist further attacks upon slavery in Congress, taking Georgia out of the Union if such attacks were made.

In the North, too, opinion moderated temporarily with the realization that the Union had been gravely threatened by disruption. Leaders in both parties sought to have the Compromise accepted as a final settlement of sectional controversy, and both Whigs and Democrats gave allegiance to it in their platforms in the campaign of 1852. Both parties nominated men who could not be accused of holding violent opinions concerning slavery. The Democrats named Franklin Pierce of New Hampshire, an inoffensive politician. Trying once more to make political capital out of military glory, the Whigs put forward General Winfield Scott. This time their strategy failed, for their party was beginning to collapse, chiefly because of sectional tension. Some cautious Northern Whigs preferred to vote for Pierce rather than Scott, while many Southern Whigs, unhappy because slavery had been heavily assailed by Whigs such as William H. Seward, also drifted into the Democratic camp. The Free Soil Party, deserted by Martin Van Buren, obtained hardly more than 150,000 votes; Scott had nearly 1,400,000, and Pierce 1,600,000. In the electoral college Pierce won easily, 254 to 42. When he entered the White House, there was on the docket no great political question concerning slavery. However, *Uncle Tom's Cabin* had already appeared, and within a few months Stephen Douglas would unwittingly reopen the passion-arousing question of slavery in the territories of the United States.

27 A DECADE OF MATERIAL ADVANCE

Had it not been for the early resurrection of the slavery troubles buried by the Compromise of 1850, the decade of the 1850s would have been a happy one in American history. The nation prospered remarkably, recovering swiftly from a banking panic in 1857 which could not seriously disturb an economy that was both stable and expansive. American industry continued to develop rapidly; cotton grew abundantly and brought high prices; railroad building was undertaken on a larger scale; the settlement of the Rocky Mountain region and of the Great Plains began; and maritime commerce burgeoned. The 1850s also witnessed the emergence of a major poet of democracy, Walt Whitman. However, the work of that peculiarly American genius was hardly noticed; along with other feeble sentimental narratives the nation was reading that tearful and bad novel, Uncle Tom's Cabin and was quarreling furiously, not about its literary quality, but about the authenticity of its descriptions of slavery, slaves, and masters. The thoughtful doubted that the American people and their leaders would find satisfactory solutions to the problems of slavery. Whitman exulted in the onward march of a vast and free republic. A few years later he was sadly to nurse sick and wounded soldiers in Washington while the fate of the Union hung in the balance.

COMMERCE AND SETTLEMENT

RAILROADS

Especially important in the economic scene of the 1850s was railroad building, made possible by the easy availability of capital supplied largely by British investors, and by the gold mines of California. Thousands of miles of track were laid east of the Mississippi. The Chicago and Rock Island Railroad crossed the great river in 1856; even earlier the railroad that was later known as the Missouri Pacific had begun to move westward from St. Louis toward Kansas City. The Louisville and Nashville Railroad, chartered in 1850, was completed between its terminals nine years later, and the Illinois Central linked Chicago and Cairo as early as 1856. Several plans were made for the building of railroads from the Mississippi to the Pacific, although none was actually undertaken until the following decade. Notable was federal assistance in the form of land grants to the states of Illinois, Mississippi, and Alabama for the construction of railroads between Chicago and Mobile in 1850. Within seven years about 21,000,000 acres of land were so given. Another development was railroad consolidation in the longer-settled parts of the nation. The New York Central, created in 1853, combined three railroads that reached from New York City to Buffalo. It soon became possible to travel all the way from New York to Chicago by rail; the Pennsylvania established a link between Pittsburgh and Philadelphia in 1858, thus connecting Philadelphia with the Ohio Valley; and the Baltimore and Ohio opened up a through line from Baltimore to St. Louis.

Southern railroad builders were much less active than those of the Northern states. However, through service was established between Washington and Richmond on the east and Memphis and New Orleans on the west by way of Chattanooga. There was no through line across the Lower South at the beginning of the Civil War, although there was a network of railroads which converged on Atlanta. It has been contended that the establishment of railroad connections between the Middle Atlantic states and the Old Northwest so tightened economic links between the two regions that it assured the adherence of the latter to the Union in the Civil War. Actually, most Americans north of the Ohio would have supported it without such economic ties. They also carried on business, by water and rail, with New Orleans in particular and the lower Mississippi Valley in general. Surely railroad building did give the Union a great advantage in its struggle with Confederacy, for the web of railroads in the Northern states permitted rapid transportation of men and supplies. Of special value to the Union was the continuous line of the Baltimore and Ohio

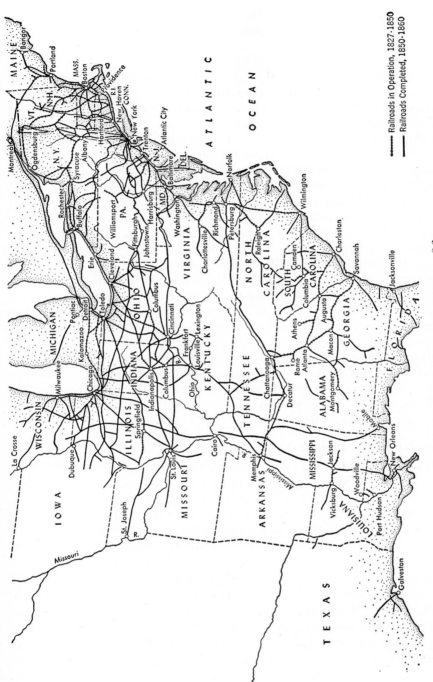

RAILROAD LINES IN OPERATION, 1860

•••••• Railroads in Operation, 1827-1850
——— Railroads Completed, 1850-1860

from Chesapeake Bay to the Mississippi, which made relatively easy the transfer of troops and guns from one theater of warfare to another.

AGE OF THE CLIPPERS

Infinitely more beautiful than the "Iron Horse" and its clattering cars of the 1850s was the swift and graceful clipper ship which brought glory and profit to the American merchant marine. That long, slim, greyhound of the sea for a time promised to give the Americans supremacy in oceanic trade, for the clipper had generous cargo space behind her sharp prow while her towering sails carried her on with amazing speed. The first clipper launched at New York in 1845 astonished the sailing world by making the voyage around Cape Horn to China in 92 days and returning in only 88. The *Sea Witch* later sailed from Hong Kong to New York in only 73 days and made a round trip between New York and San Francisco in only 97 days. The *Flying Cloud,* the fastest sailing merchantman ever launched, reduced the time between New York and San Francisco to 88 days. Carrying manufactured goods to California and to China, bringing back tea, silk, and gold, the clippers also brought magnificent returns to their owners. Alas, their heyday was short-lived, for the more prosaic steamship would usurp their place. Moreover, traffic passed from American vessels to British, for the British were less reluctant to turn from sail to steam. Besides, the British merchant marine was encouraged by public subsidies, while that of the United States was forced to rely upon private resources. The British were moving toward an easy supremacy in oceanic trade as the Civil War approached, and the heavy losses inflicted upon the American merchant marine by Confederate cruisers during the war reduced it to a decided inferiority.

THE WEST AND IMMIGRATION

Immediately before the Civil War, the horse, pulling a wagon or a stagecoach, was the Western equivalent of the clipper on the oceans. Men dreamed of laying rails and running trains from New Orleans across Texas to San Diego, from Memphis to Los Angeles, from St. Louis and Chicago to San Francisco, and from Minnesota to Puget Sound, but for some years travel and trade in the West were carried on by the original kind of horse power. California and Oregon grew steadily in numbers and wealth through the 1850s—especially the former. Late in the decade a new gold rush into Colorado and a silver rush into Nevada brought rapid settlement in both areas. The Comstock Lode in Nevada, which yielded $300,000,000 worth of silver and gold within twenty years, was one of the most astonishing mining discoveries of all times. Men rode to the new "diggings" on horseback or by stagecoach, and families continued to move westward by covered wagon. Freighting companies had begun to carry large quantities of goods across the plains even before 1850 and flourished during the following ten years. In the fall of 1858 stage coach and mail service was opened between Tipton, Missouri and San Francisco, the trip between the two being made in less than 25 days. Two years later the famous "Pony Express" carried mail from the lower Missouri River to San Francisco in less than ten days. While the gap between the settlements in the first tier of states west of the Mississippi and those beyond the Great Plains was bridged, travel and communications between them remained expensive, uncertain, and dangerous. By 1854 pioneers were moving into eastern Kansas and Nebraska, but the Great Plains Indians had not yet been conquered. However, within another generation both the Plains and their Indian inhabitants were overrun by new waves of settlers carried westward and supplied by railroads.

Important—and romantic—as the development of the West was before the Civil War, it was the work of relatively few people, and the advance toward the setting sun created no ghost cities east of the Mississippi. On the contrary, cities grew amazingly, the population of the Republic soaring from 22,000,000 to 31,500,000 between 1850 and 1860. Many more persons entered the Eastern states from Europe than departed from them to Colorado, Nevada, and the Pacific Coast. The "Old Immigration," so impressive in the 1840s, continued through the 1850s. In fact, it actually increased, more than 2,500,000 persons coming to the United States during the decade of the 1850s. That Ireland offered little opportunity and was overpopulated was an almost inescapable conclusion after 1846, when the potato crop failed and famine threatened the Emerald Isle. From Cork and Dublin the Roman Catholic Irish swarmed across the ocean, as many as 221,000 in the single year 1851. The collapse of the liberal revolution in Germany in 1848 had the same effect as the potato famine in Ireland, driving the Germans by tens of thousands across the sea in search of opportunity and freedom. 350,000 came to America during the two years 1853 and 1854. These "Forty-eighters" were immediately even more valuable acquisitions than the Irish, for they brought with them as great a devotion to liberty, together with proficiencies in philosophy and music, all of which enriched American civilization. A striking figure among them was Carl Schurz, who was to become a conspicuous liberal in national politics.

THE "YOUNG AMERICA" MOVEMENT

KNOW-NOTHINGS AND NATIVISM

The continuance of the "Old Immigration" on an even larger scale brought with it a striking increase in the nativism which had manifested itself in the 1840s. Some of the German newcomers and nearly all of the Irish were Roman Catholics, and were accordingly more difficult to assimilate than other immigrants. The ancient prejudice against the Roman Catholic Church harbored by those of older American stocks, coupled with distaste for the peculiar ways of the "foreigners" and concern over the economic competition which they offered—wages failed to keep up with prices in the 1850s—led to a steadily rising tide of feeling against the new-comers, especially against the Irish. Immediately after 1850 nativism swept through the nation. Its adherents formed a secret society, "The Supreme Order of the Star-Spangled Banner," chapters of which appeared in many cities. The Order had the usual hocus-pocus of clandestine fraternities, including secret passwords and a confidential grip. For its members patriotism demanded limits upon immigration, higher standards for naturalization, and exclusion from public office of both Roman Catholics and the foreign-born. When asked about the rituals, leadership, and purpose of the Order, the initiated replied to outsiders, "I know nothing." So strong was the appeal of Know-Nothingism that its followers were able to form an American Party which dominated elections in several Northern states in 1854 and 1855. For a time, until reason began to reassert its sway, the Know-Nothing political phalanx threatened to become one of the two major parties in the nation.

One might assume that the national indigestion which proceeded from expansion to the Pacific, together with other ills in the American body politic, would swiftly have brought a revulsion against the democratic imperialism which swept the country immediately before the Mexican War. Such was not the case, for aggressive democracy only gradually lost its appeal. Indeed, after the Treaty of Guadalupe Hidalgo there was for a few years a clamor for even more territory and also for action to spread the benefits of freedom in both the Old World and the New. Some enthusiasts for "Manifest Destiny" began a "Young America" movement, the purpose of which was to carry the American flag and the blessings of liberty into all of Mexico, Central America, and the islands of the Caribbean Sea.

Although the Gadsden Purchase was not accompanied by other acquisitions in the 1850s, the United States continued to display vigor in foreign affairs until troubles at home absorbed all of its energy. Sympathy for the liberal revolutionists of 1848 in Europe pervaded America. The efforts of the Hungarians to throw off the rule of the Austrian Habsburgs were warmly applauded and arrangements were hastily made to recognize the independence of Hungary. When the Habsburg government protested against interference in its domestic affairs, it was informed by Secretary of State Webster that the American Republic had a right to be and was deeply interested in the attempts of Europeans to overthrow monarchical, oppressive, and foreign regimes. The European revolutions, said Webster, "appeared to have their origin in those great ideas of responsible and popular governments on which the American Constitutions themselves are founded." Webster continued contemptuously and rudely, "The power of this Republic, at the present moment, is spread over a region, one of the richest and most fertile on the globe and of an extent in comparison with which the possessions of the House of Habsburg are but as a patch on the earth's surface." When the Hungarian revolution was put down by the Habsburgs with the help of Russian armies, its famous leader, Louis Kossuth, fled to Turkey for refuge. However, he was not safe, as demands were made upon the Sultan that he give up Kossuth for execution. An American warship was sent to Turkey and brought him westward to safety. Afterward he was greeted as a hero—which he was—in a struggle for the rights of mankind. Bumptious as Webster was, the screaming of the eagle at the Emperor Franz Josef did no harm, although it did not prevent savage punishment of the defeated Hungarians by their conquerors.

EXPANSION IN THE PACIFIC AND CARIBBEAN

The vigor of "Young America" was also displayed, with the most far-reaching consequences, on the shores of Asia. Trade with China, begun immediately after the War of Independence and continuing to be very profitable, could not but make American merchants desire to traffic with the Japanese, too. However, the Japanese Empire had closed its doors to foreigners in the seventeenth century and strangers were still barred when Millard Fillmore became President. The Japanese were not even hospitable to American merchant sailors who sought refuge on the islands of the Rising Sun because of shipwreck or other maritime disaster; they wished to be left completely alone. However, Japan could not maintain her isolation for very long. It was brought swiftly and decisively to an end when Fillmore sent Commodore Matthew C. Perry across the Pacific to try to secure better treatment for American nationals and to find some basis for trade. Perry reached Tokyo Bay in the summer of 1853, informed emissaries of the Japanese Emperor of his mission and sailed away, giving the Emperor and his advisers some months to consider the situation of their country. Returning to Japan with a fleet of seven ships the following March, he again conferred with Japanese officials and gave them presents of a telegraph set and a miniature railroad for their imperial master. These gifts were looked upon as impressive evidence of the achievements of Western civilization, and the Emperor gave his consent to the Treaty of Kanagawa, which was signed on March 31. In it the Japanese Empire promised asylum to shipwrecked American sailors and opened two ports to American shipping. Perry's work was continued by the aggressive Townsend Harris, sent as Consul General to Japan, who secured the opening of a third harbor in 1857 and of more in the following year, together with the establishment of formal diplomatic relations between the two countries. The statesmen of the Empire, realizing that they could not prevent the coming of the Westerners, soon sagely resolved to make full use of the inventions, machines, and military methods of the Occident to protect Japan against attack and to secure a future as prosperous as possible. Within half a century Japan became an important world power.

Both America and "Young America" desired economic empire in the Pacific; moreover, expansionists sought the annexation of the Hawaiian Islands. By the mid-century American missionaries had Christianized the Polynesians of those idyllic islands in the central Pacific; they were also frequented by Yankee whalers, sailors, and failures, some of whom had happily intermarried with the friendly native women. American merchants were well established in Honolulu, which resembled to a degree a New England town. As early as 1842 the United States declared that the archipelago would not be allowed to become the property of a foreign power. Britain and France, interested in the islands, especially because of their strategic location, were warned off, then and later. In 1854 Secretary of State William Marcy conceived that the time had come to run up the American flag. He negotiated a treaty of annexation with the native king. However, it contained a provision requiring that Hawaii become a state immediately, doubtless inserted by advisers of the ruler to prevent ratification in Washington. The treaty was set aside by Marcy. The islands would become American, but not until a long generation had passed.

There was keen opposition in the United States to the acquisition of Pacific outposts, and the nation also ultimately refused to support the program of southward expansion advocated by "Young America." At the mid-century America was more interested than ever in the lands on the shores of the Caribbean Sea, partly because of a desire to establish swifter communications between the Atlantic and Pacific, and partly because aggressive Southerners wished to increase the domains of slavery. Seeking to bring together the east and west coasts, President Polk tried to open up three routes across Mexico and Central America. He obtained the right to protect transit across Panama from the Republic of Colombia, which then owned the Isthmus. In return for a guarantee of Colombian sovereignty, Americans were allowed to build a railroad across Panama, which was completed in 1855. There was also some American interest in building a railroad across the Mexican isthmus of Tehuantepec, permission for which was eventually obtained in the Gadsden Purchase Treaty, but never used. Much more attractive to Polk was a scheme to build a canal across Nicaragua. Agents whom he sent to that country actually secured the signing of two treaties authorizing the United States to dig a canal, but the scheme was vigorously opposed by Britain. The British had long claimed the territory on the eastern coast of Nicaragua through which a canal would have to pass, and they too were eager to build one. Rather than precipitate a struggle with Britain, Polk refrained from sending either of the treaties negotiated for him to the Senate.

President Taylor was even more eager to avoid conflict, and he gave his consent to the Clayton-Bulwer Treaty of 1850, which abated Anglo-American antagonism in Central America. In this remarkable agreement, each nation promised that it would never seek exclusive control over an isthmian canal, or fortify one. If either country built one, the citizens of the other were to be allowed to use it on the same terms as those of the building nation. Both powers also pledged themselves to refrain from occupying, colonizing, or asserting dominion over any part of Central America.

The Clayton-Bulwer Treaty served to soften rivalry between Britain and the United States in the area for fifty years. It did not, however, put an end to American activity in Nicaragua. In 1855, at a time when that country was convulsed by civil war, an adventurer named William Walker led a filibustering expedition into it, declared himself dictator, made Negro slavery legal, and asked for American recognition. When he came out in favor of slavery, he made it impossible for President Pierce to accord him official recognition. Driven out of Nicaragua in 1857, he quickly organized another expedition to that troubled country, but was driven off by the American navy, since his adventures had become too embarrassing to the United States. When that restless man landed a third time with an "army," this time in Honduras, he was captured and executed.

Nor were American—chiefly Southern—designs upon Cuba carried out. That fertile island was only feebly held by a Spain that could not defend it, and lustful eyes looked at it from across the Straits of Florida. It was all the more enticing because slaves could be employed upon its sugar plantations. Southern imperialists were especially eager to acquire Cuba because they believed as many as five states could be carved out of the island, so making it possible for the South to regain and maintain equality in the Senate for a generation or more. The Southern expansionists received some support from Northerners avid for national growth. Accordingly, General Narciso López, a Nicaraguan adventurer, undertook to raise a rebellion on the island, badly governed by the Spanish. He proposed to drive them from it and to arrange for a union of Cuba with the United States. Using New Orleans as a base, he thrice planned military expeditions, enlisting among others restless American veterans of the Mexican War. His first thrust, in 1849, was stopped by officials at New Orleans; the following year he reached Cuba, but was driven away; in 1851 he went again to the island with 500 men. That was the last of his attempts, for he was captured and executed with 50 of his followers. There was a cry for war against Spain, especially from the South, and also excitement in

Madrid, which diminished when Secretary of State Webster offered official regret for insults offered to the Spanish flag and damage done to the Spanish consulate in New Orleans.

Three years later, with troubled conditions continuing in Cuba, Pierre Soulé, John Y. Mason, and James Buchanan, the American ministers to Spain, France, and England, met at Ostend in Belgium under instructions from Washington to consider policy with respect to Cuba. The result was the extraordinary Ostend Manifesto of October, 1854, in which the three envoys declared that acquisition of the island was necessary to protect the institution of slavery, that the United States ought to try to buy Cuba, and that if Spain refused, "Then by every law human and divine, we shall be justified in wresting it from Spain if we possess the power." This pronunciamento, obviously the work of Senator Soulé, so nakedly combined expansion with slavery that Secretary of State Marcy disowned it, forcing Soulé to resign his post. Publication of the Manifesto aroused a furor in the Northern states, and attempts to get Cuba had to be abandoned. If he gained by securing the Presidency, Buchanan profited from the incident, for he was thereafter persona grata to Southern champions of slavery, who helped elect him in 1856. In any event, Cuba, torn and wracked by economic troubles and insurrections, remained under the Spanish flag for another generation. Soulé's attempt to force the Spanish to sell it convinced many Northerners that the Southerners generally were actively trying to spread slavery.

AMERICAN LITERATURE

The exuberant spirit that characterized "Young America's" efforts to spread the benefits of American liberty (including slavery), abroad was not confined to schemes of expansion. It was remarkably displayed when the great poet of democracy, Walt Whitman, published his *Leaves of Grass* in 1855. Then only 36 years of age, the Anglo-Dutch "good, gray poet" was not gray-haired, and many doubted for a long time that he was either good or a poet. Born on Long Island, he had been a printer, a teacher, the writer of a novel preaching temperance, and something of a wanderer. Now he came forth with a kind of free verse which had many of the merits and faults of the Republic from which he sprang. His poetry was boastful, often crude, sometimes merely prose in the guise of verse; it could be described, as Whitman himself conceded, as "a barbaric yawp." But Whitman's poetry was far more than a raucous noise; it also had majesty, tenderness, and beauty. Whitman was an authentic genius, no pale reflector of English poetry, but a robust American who struck out on his own. Despising the sentimentality and conventionalism then so characteristic of American writing, he urged his readers to live fully, freely, and bravely.

He extolled comradeship in freedom, described the American landscape in magnificent phrases, lauded democracy, and urged peace among mankind. One may be offended by his egotism and discouraged by his crudities; one may feel that his education and his experience confined him too closely to things American. On the other hand, one must kindly despise those who secured his dismissal from a clerkship in the Department of the Interior because he had written an "obscene" book, and must pay highest tribute to his peculiar genius. In the first edition of *Leaves of Grass* and in the many poems Whitman afterward added to it there is exalting as well as exulting. Ever memorable will be many of his lines, including his "Song of Myself," "Democratic Vistas," and "When Lilacs Last in the Dooryard Bloom'd."

The appearance of Whitman in a decade when Hawthorne, Melville, Emerson, Thoreau, and many other distinguished literary figures were active made the 1850s a great era in American literature. To that galaxy must be added the name of Francis Parkman, America's greatest historian, whose superb histories of the Anglo-French struggle for North America began to appear in 1851. Two years earlier Parkman had published *The California and Oregon Trail,* which he had traversed after his graduation from the Harvard Law School in 1846. The Bostonian Parkman was of a frail constitution, and his journey to the West sapped his strength. After his return to Boston, he suffered a nervous breakdown from which he never completely recovered. He was also plagued by bad eyesight that verged at times upon blindness. However, he would not let his weaknesses reduce him to invalidism. Rich enough to employ a secretary and to pay for copies of thousands of records from British, French, and American archives, he proceeded unsteadily with his great work, which began with the *History of the Conspiracy of Pontiac* and ended after four decades of study and writing with *A Half-Century of Conflict* in 1892. There have been sounder scholars and perhaps men more gifted with the pen, but no American historian has surpassed him in both content and style. Faults may readily be found in Parkman's substance; the mighty contest between France and England was for him largely limited to the northern English colonies and Canada, for as a Bostonian he knew little and cared less about South Carolina and Louisiana; he preferred action to analysis, and he could never quite appreciate things French and Roman Catholic, although he caught their drama and romance. It is also true that his prose was sometimes purple; but if the writing of history is not a literary activity of the highest order—the earthy, brilliant, and often mistaken Dr. Samuel Johnson declared that an author could not do much with the stuff of history—it is nevertheless most difficult, as any of those who attempt it seriously will testify. All considered, Parkman's shortcomings are minor, and his *Pioneers of France in the New World, Montcalm and Wolfe,* and other volumes remain American classics. They were read in the author's own time, and they have continued to fascinate both the scholar and the general reader.

POPULAR READING

Let it not be thought that the American reader devoured Parkman's chronicle of Pontiac's War as he did Charles Dickens' *Oliver Twist* or Sir Walter Scott's *Ivanhoe.* Along with the writings of those gifted novelists, the American reader liked and bought feeble prose and worse verse. In some part such was the case because the readers were women who had never been given the opportunity to learn the difference between the literary good and bad; if masculine discrimination was sharper (which is doubtful), there was not much of it. The bestsellers of the 1850s were not the works of Whitman, Parkman, or even Hawthorne, but books of decorum (etiquette); magazines for females, such as *Godey's Lady's Book,* which had a larger circulation than any other magazine on the globe; and syrupy, sentimental, and quite undistinguished novels. As Hawthorne, who envied their royalties, said, these novels were written "by a d—d mob of scribbling women." Among them was *The Lamplighter* by Maria Cummins, which was far below the level of fiction in the popular women's magazines of the twentieth century. The most popular novels appearing in 1859 were *Beulah* by Augusta Jane Evans, and *The Hidden Hand* by Mrs. E. D. E. N. Southworth. Most popular of the American poets, along with Longfellow, was Lydia Huntley Sigourney, "The Sweet Singer of Hartford," whose verse carried tears and high moral principles. Almost amazingly attractive to the public were the productions of Timothy Shay Arthur, who published dozens of tracts and stories depicting the evils of addiction to alcohol. More than a million copies of his writings were sold during the decade, the most famous being *Ten Nights in a Bar-Room and What I Saw There,* which long continued to warn its agitated readers of the abysses into which alcoholics only too often sank.

THE LITERATURE OF SLAVERY

During the Civil War, some ten years after the publication of *Uncle Tom's Cabin, or Life Among the Lowly,* Abraham Lincoln is said to have remarked upon meeting the author that she was the little woman who had begun a big war. That Mrs. Harriet Elizabeth Beecher Stowe was personally responsible for the great American tragedy one must doubt. It is likely that Lincoln, who had become only too familiar with the complexities of human affairs, was merely offering a bit of kind flattery to the college professor's wife who had done so much to stir up sectional feeling over slavery. Daughter of the Reverend Lyman Beecher, sister of the Reverend Henry Ward Beecher, wife of Calvin E. Stowe, a Biblical professor at Bowdoin College, the little lady caused commotion when she published the first of a string of immature novels at the age of 40. One of those "scribbling women" whose productions so exasperated Hawthorne, Mrs. Stowe had heard much talk about slavery for twenty years. Technically not quite an abolitionist, she was profoundly disturbed by the passage of the Fugitive Slave Law of 1850, and began to put out *Uncle Tom's Cabin* by installments in June, 1851, in the *National Era,* an anti-slavery newspaper published in Washington, D.C. In the following year it appeared in book form, and then began its extraordinary career as a popular work. More than 300,000 copies were sold within twelve months; its sales eventually ran into the millions; and stage plays based upon it enjoyed a vast and enduring vogue. Its immediate effect was to dramatize the sufferings of the slaves. The wicked overseer Simon Legree, the gentle and lovable Uncle Tom, Little Eva, and Eliza crossing the ice, became the subjects of intense discussion as the ills of slavery were brought home to Northern readers as never before. On the other hand the lachrymose novel exasperated many Southern readers who pointed out that it portrayed Negro bondage in darker colors than were warranted.

Uncle Tom's Cabin revived controversy over slavery at the very time when conservative politicians seemed to have successfully set it aside. One must believe that their efforts would have been in vain in any case, and that Mrs. Stowe's novel merely happened to be one of several potent instruments that gave new life to sectional antagonism. Feeling was not diminished by Southern attacks upon *Uncle Tom's Cabin,* nor by the appearance of a systematic defense of slavery by George Fitzhugh in *Sociology for the South; or The Failure of Free Society* (1854), and *Cannibals All! or Slaves Without Masters* (1857). Fitzhugh, like Chancellor Harper and Professor Dew before him, insisted that Southern economy and society were superior to Northern. He was supported in verse by William J. Grayson, who published, in 1854, *The Hireling and The Slave:*

> How small the choice, from cradle to the grave,
> Between the lot of Hireling and of Slave!
> To each alike applies the stern decree,
> That man shall labour; whether bond or free,
> For all that toil, the recompense we claim—
> Food, fire, a home and clothing—is the same.
>
> And yet the life, so unassailed,
> So blest with moderate work, with ample fare,
> With all the goods the proper Hireling needs,
> The happier slave on each plantation leads. . . .

It is unlikely that these productions, or others like them, seriously altered Southern opinion. They described it rather than formed it. Nor was that opinion changed much by the appearance of Hinton Rowan Helper's *Impending Crisis of the South, and How to Meet It* in 1857. North Carolinian Helper denounced slavery on the ground that it grievously injured the Southern economy. One may suspect that Northern and Southern attitudes had become relatively fixed by 1850, that those attitudes were not materially affected by words, and that it was settled as early as 1850 that North and South would come to blows in the absence of statesmanship of the highest order.

THE FUGITIVE SLAVE LAW

One feels that the execution of the Fugitive Slave Law of 1850 was basically more important in the revival of sectional antagonism than writings for and against Negro bondage. The pen may indeed be stronger than the sword in the long run, but is it immediately more potent? Federal commissioners entrusted with the task of executing the Fugitive Slave Law tried to do their duty, but were opposed in the Northern states. Wisconsin not only tried to execute a "personal liberty" law but sought to interpose its authority as a sovereign state in defense of the runaways. Abolitionists supplied lawyers to defend them and organized mobs to rescue them from their owners and from the federal officers. They received widespread support from persons who were not necessarily dedicated to the destruction of slavery, but whose sympathies were deeply aroused by the fugitives' efforts to obtain freedom. Tens of thousands of Northerners agreed with Emerson that the law was one "which no man can obey, or abet in obeying, without loss of self-respect and forfeiture of the name of gentleman." Peculiarly exasperating to them were the efforts of a few Southerners to capture free Negroes and to take them into slavery. The Underground Railroad laid more track, employed more conductors, and ran more trains. Each year after passage of the law between 500 and 1000 fleeing Negroes were moved along its routes to safety in Northern hiding places and Canada. Feeling in the North became so strong that the managers of the railroad were able to carry on their operations almost openly, and the federal law was often successfully defied. Feeling also rose in the South, which was thus deprived of the benefits of the one major concession it had received in the Compromise of 1850. It was felt there that the North had broken a solemn bargain. Ardent defenders of slavery contended that the institution itself was threatened—both they and the abolitionists exaggerated the number of the runaways. In sum, efforts to carry out the law led to commotion and to increasing distrust between North and South.

By 1853 it was evident that tension over slavery was again rising. Then, strangely, one of those who had labored diligently and successfully for the

Compromise, unwisely and doubtless unwittingly revived the question of slavery in the territories. Stephen Douglas pushed through Congress his Kansas-Nebraska bill, a measure which led to "Bleeding Kansas," the formation of the Republican Party, further loosening of the ties between North and South, and at length to secession and Civil War.

28 THE NATION DIVIDED

There have been respected historians who have argued that the Civil War resulted from a clash for supremacy between the Southern planter aristocracy on the one side, and Northern industrial and commercial magnates on the other. While it is true that the power exerted by the Southern aristocracy in Washington was almost destroyed by the war and that the Northern magnates were exalted, it is certain that the two groups did not consciously provoke the war in order to settle the question of supremacy. One must also doubt very seriously that they engaged in such a deadly contest to settle the question of supremacy even unconsciously. That there was rivalry between the two is clear enough. They had long disagreed regarding the need for protective tariffs, but this was an issue about which feelings were not sufficiently bitter to cause a conflagration, important as it was to both parties. Nor was there any other economic dispute so serious that it could be settled only by the force of arms. Indeed, there was no combination of economic difference sufficient to persuade the Northern magnates, consciously or unconsciously, that resort must be made to force. In fact, in the 1840s and 1850s the Northern businessman was commonly opposed to sectional contests, fearing their consequences. He did not become positively allied with Northern anti-slavery people until 1860, by which time secession and Civil War had become quite certain. Nor need we assume that the planter aristocracy was determined to dominate. It was assertive, but allied with other Southern elements for "Southern rights" rather than for class mastery.

While the divergent economic systems of the North and the South caused certain problems, it was ultimately slavery that drove the sections apart and led them into a military struggle. The institution had to be shattered, for it was accompanied by massive social injustice. If North and South were to continue in peace and harmony, it was necessary that they should agree on some means to bring it to an end. Accordingly, Northerners had to come forward with a plan conceived and offered in such a way that it could have sufficient acceptance in the South to make it workable. Instead, the campaign to limit slavery without much concern for Southern feeling gained strength in the North, and Southern determination to defend slavery hardened.

TERRITORIAL SLAVERY AGAIN

The question of territorial slavery had contributed so importantly to the section crisis at mid-century that one would not expect a compromiser of 1850 to do anything toward reviving it. Nevertheless, it was resuscitated early in 1854, and the man above all responsible for its reappearance was none other than Stephen Douglas, who had labored so diligently to soothe the South and the North four years before. Of small but powerful figure, the "Little Giant" had many of the qualities of greatness. Only 40 years old at the beginning of 1854, he was a Vermont-born teacher and lawyer who had risen rapidly to his position as a Senator from Illinois. He had almost boundless energy; he was a skillful politician; and he was a brilliant debater. He had already achieved prominence among the Northern Democrats, and was looked upon as a possible Presidential candidate in the not distant future. He was ambitious, and it may be guessed that he hoped eventually to live in the White House. He was not a great man—was there one among those prominent in American political life during the decade before the inauguration of Abraham Lincoln? In view of the fact that Douglas was adept in political management, he had one extraordinary defect; he had no strong feelings about slavery, and he was not truly aware that other men did. He would not learn until too late that those feelings were fundamental in most people and that his every action should take them into account.

THE KANSAS-NEBRASKA ACT

In January, 1854, Douglas began to push through Congress the bill which eventually became the Kansas-Nebraska Act. It called for the establishment of the Territory of Kansas and also for one of Nebraska, the latter to include all of the Louisiana Purchase north of Kansas not hitherto organized. The Missouri Compromise line of 36°30' was specifically repealed, and the people of the two territories were to decide for themselves whether slavery should exist in them, except that cases concerning slaves in the territorial courts might be appealed for decision to the federal Supreme Court. In effect, popular sovereignty was substituted for division along the 36°30' line. The measure was carried by the votes of the Southern Democrats, with the support of a few Northern Democrats and Southern Whigs, and it was signed into law by President Pierce. It was, however, bitterly assailed both in and out of Congress, and soon led to the birth of the Republican Party. Douglas later declared that after that session of Congress he could have made his way home from Washington to Chicago by the light from effigies of him burning along his route.

Why such intense Northern feeling against the Kansas-Nebraska Act? The reason was that it had been made possible for slavery to exist legally in both territories, although it had been barred by the Missouri Compromise. Moreover, it was hoped by Southerners and feared by many Northerners that as a consequence of the legal change, slavery would actually be carried into Kansas, lying directly west of the slave state Missouri. The law and its principal author were savagely denounced, the first described as a conspiracy to spread slavery and the second as one of the chief plotters. Senators Charles Sumner of Massachusetts and Salmon P. Chase of Ohio claimed that Douglas had sold himself to the Southerners in the hope of securing their support for his presidential ambitions. They asserted that the Missouri Compromise was a sacred agreement which had been wantonly violated. Northern Whigs, Northern Democrats, Free-Soilers, and abolitionists joined in the chorus of denunciation.

While Douglas did wish to have Southern friends in his party, and while he was surely interested in the Presidency, personal ambition does not explain his behavior. He wanted to open up that part of the Louisiana Purchase that was unsettled and still remained an Indian reservation, in order to smooth the way for the building of a transcontinental railroad from Chicago to San Francisco. It was then becoming apparent that the federal government would eventually subsidize a railroad from the Mississippi Valley to the Pacific coast, and he was eager for the selection of Chicago as its eastern terminus. He had many friends and supporters in

Chicago, and he himself owned property that would become more valuable if Chicago were chosen as the terminus. Douglas had another reason for wishing to see the rest of the Louisiana Purchase organized; he was chairman of the Senate Committee on Territories, and he prided himself upon the number of territories and states he was helping to establish. It is likely that he wanted organized government on the Great Plains chiefly to make it easier to build a railroad across them. Originally he would have been satisfied with the creation of one territorial government of Nebraska, together with recognition of the principle of popular sovereignty within it. In order to secure the necessary votes for his project, he had taken steps to please the Southerners who would have preferred that the eastern terminus of the proposed railroad be at New Orleans or at Memphis. To gain their support he had consented to a change in his plan that specifically provided for repeal of the Missouri Compromise line, and also the creation of two territories instead of one. Since both were obviously unsuited for plantations, he did not expect slavery to spread into either territory, but he was willing that they be theoretically opened up to slavery in order to satisfy the Southerners. He contended that popular sovereignty was a democratic solution to a vexing theoretical problem, and that it had the great advantage of taking the problem away from Washington. He was puzzled when the act was so vehemently attacked, for it had not occurred to him that it would arouse Northern passions. His wife owned slaves; he himself was neither a friend nor an enemy of slavery; later he was to say that he did not care whether slavery was voted up or down.

THE REPUBLICAN PARTY

Douglas was correct enough in predicting that slavery would not actually spread into either Kansas or Nebraska. No more than a few dozen slaves were brought into the valley of the Kaw, and none into that of the Platte. He was also able to defend popular sovereignty in the two territories on the ground that his arrangement was somewhat like that made for the territories of Utah and New Mexico in 1850, whereby the settlers were not told whether or not they could have slaves. Nevertheless, the "Little Giant's" law was open to assault from the North on the ground of principle. Many opponents felt outraged, and indignation meetings were held everywhere above the Mason-Dixon Line. Northern Whigs and Democrats in large numbers resolved to leave their parties because they believed they were too friendly to slavery. Many joined the Know-Nothings in the American Party temporarily, but soon left it, since it also contained moderates and defenders of slavery. Most of the unhappy Northern Democrats and Whigs, joining with Free-Soilers and abolitionists, chose to found a new party, and they were swiftly and almost amazingly successful. In the summer of 1854, in mass meetings throughout the Northern states, they pledged themselves to support candidates for state and federal offices who would oppose the spread of slavery in the territories; they denounced the Fugitive Slave Law of 1850, and inveighed against Douglas' supposed conspiracy to bring slavery to the Great Plains. At first their candidates were announced as representing the "People's Party," the "Independent Party," and the "Republican Party." The first two titles were soon dropped, since the name of Thomas Jefferson's party inevitably had great appeal.

It has been claimed that the Republican Party was founded at a mass meeting in February, 1854, at Ripon, Wisconsin. It is also asserted that Jackson, Michigan, was its birthplace, because there under the oaks in the following July the Republicans organized on a statewide basis. Other towns and cities give themselves the honor of supplying the birthplace for the party. Actually it was born in the hearts of tens of thousands of men living in all the Northern states. Since both the Whigs and the Know-Nothings were dividing because they could not agree with respect to slavery, the Republican Party could not fail to acquire a great following in the North, although no one could have predicted that it would become and remain the great rival of the Democratic Party. In its early years its appeal was almost entirely to enemies of slavery, but what an appeal it had! Northern extremists could not fail to rally to it, since they had nowhere else to go. At the same time, Northern men who wished to think of themselves as both firm and moderate enemies of the institution could join it, for it demanded only that the spread of slavery be prevented. Whig Abraham Lincoln hesitated before joining it, but other cautious Whigs such as Edward Bates and Orville H. Browning quickly entered it, along with bitter enemies of slavery such as Charles Sumner, Salmon P. Chase, and George Julian. By 1856 the party was in power in several Northern states and was able to make a great fight for the Presidency and control of Congress.

THE FAILURE OF POPULAR SOVEREIGNTY IN KANSAS

The rapid growth of the Republican Party is also explained to a degree by the dismal failure of popular sovereignty in Kansas. Douglas had hoped that settlement of that territory would take place in the usual way. Had that occurred, and had the settlers been permitted freely to decide whether or not they wanted slavery, Kansas would have become a free territory without much squabble. But the enemies of slavery in the North and its friends in the South would not let the settlers proceed in a normal course. Instead, both insisted upon having their way in Kansas, which before many months had passed became "Bleeding Kansas." To make sure that it would become a free territory and eventually a free state, Eli Thayer organized the Massachusetts Emigrant Aid Society, soon renamed the New England Emigrant Aid Company, to send Yankees across the Missouri. By 1857 the Society had helped more than 2000 people to establish themselves in the territory. Their principal settlement was at Lawrence, which long retained a New England flavor. Other thousands of Northerners moved into Kansas, attracted by its fertile lands as well as by the opportunity to strike a blow at Negro servitude. Meanwhile, the supporters of slavery sought to colonize Kansas with slave owners and slaves, but were unsuccessful because Kansas was quite unsuitable for growing cotton or tobacco. Colonel Jefferson Buford of Alabama, by spending his own fortune, was finally able to lead 300 Southerners into the territory in 1856, but they found little to interest them, and did not even found a Southern community. Indeed, but few Southerners made new homes for themselves in Kansas, those who did being chiefly from Missouri.

Unfortunately, armed bands of Missourians who did not care to live in Kansas frequently entered the territory to try to make it officially a slave region, and their appeal to violence provoked the settlers from the Northern states to arm themselves. Buford's men had come carrying Bibles; the Missourians bore rifles; Thayer's Emigrant Aid Company supplied the Northerners with "Beecher's Bibles," which were similar to the weapons of the Missourians rather than those of Buford's men. Minor clashes between the partisans occurred in the early months of 1855. In March about 5000 "Missouri Border Ruffians" entered Kansas, voted in an election, and saw to it that the territory acquired a pro-slavery legislature. Declaring the election illegal, the pioneers from the North held a convention in the following autumn at Topeka, which prepared a constitution prohibiting slavery, and also the entrance of free Negroes into the territory. (Like many Northerners, they wanted the Negroes to be free and far away.) The Northerners then held an election, ratified their constitution, and chose a governor and a legislature of their own.

Thereafter, for five years, there was governmental confusion in Kansas. President Pierce, following the lead of his Secretary of War, Jefferson Davis, and Stephen Douglas, gave his blessing to the Southern faction, but it could not secure effective control of the territory. In November and December of 1855 came the "Wakarusa War," a series of armed brawls between the Missouri Borderers and the Northern settlers in Lawrence and its vicinity. The following May fighting was resumed. "Border Ruffians," Kickapoo Rangers, and Buford men (now armed with guns rather than Bibles) captured and sacked Lawrence. Only two lives were lost, but wild excitement followed. The fanatical and mentally unbalanced abolitionist John Brown made his entrance into history when he and his four sons and two other men sought revenge. Three days after the capture of Lawrence they seized and executed five pro-slavery settlers at Pottawatomie Creek.

Thereafter the two parties attacked one another's strongholds and engaged in bitter guerilla warfare. Quiet did not come until the territorial governor called in federal troops. More than 200 persons were killed in the strife in Kansas before the end of 1856. Neither party was able to secure supremacy; the men from the North were more numerous, but their opponents received the stronger support from Washington.

Kansas was a cockpit, and the bloodshed there helped to drive North and South farther apart, for violence, as usual, begot violence. Resort to force was made even in the halls of Congress while the pro-slavery men were burning and pillaging Lawrence. While they were putting the torch to that village, Senator Charles Sumner of Massachusetts delivered a philippic in Washington against the "slave oligarchy," denouncing its "rape" of Kansas. In his "The Crime Against Kansas" speech in the Senate Sumner also descended to insult, referring unfavorably to the character of his absent colleague from South Carolina, Andrew P. Butler, and comparing Butler's state to a woman of the streets. His unworthy performance provoked one even worse. Representative Preston S. Brooks, a nephew of Butler, resented the aspersions cast upon his relative and his state. On May 22, he entered the Senate Chamber, surprised Sumner at his desk, and beat him on the head with a cane until Sumner fell unconscious to the floor. He did not stop until Stephen Douglas and others restrained him. This unhappy incident created much ill feeling. In the North many looked upon Sumner as a hero who had sacrificed himself in a great cause. He was so badly injured that he was unable to return to his duties for three years. On the other hand, many Southerners felt that Brooks had behaved quite properly. When he resigned his seat in order to give the voters in his district an opportunity to express their opinion, they reelected him by a handsome majority. Moreover, since he had broken his cane, many Southern admirers made him presents of new ones.

THE CAMPAIGN OF 1856

The public scene had an ugly look at the beginning of the campaign of 1856, and the campaign's outcome did not promise permanent improvement. The Democrats, meeting at Cincinnati in June, managed to shelve their sectional difference temporarily and to agree upon a platform and a candidate. They praised the Kansas-Nebraska Act as a fair compromise, but they refused to nominate its author, Douglas, or Pierce, who had stoutly supported it. Instead, they named the veteran politician James Buchanan, who as minister to England had escaped involvement in the sectional turmoil. "Old Buck," a bachelor and a Pennsylvanian, was not unacceptable to the Northern Democrats who had clung to their party, and he was eminently pleasing to the Southerners in it, although he believed slavery to be morally wrong. It will be recalled that he had participated in issuing the Ostend Manifesto. He had never said a word offensive to the adherents of slavery. He had the support of many cautious Northern businessmen and bankers, especially in Pennsylvania. Joined with him on the Democratic ticket was John C. Breckenridge of Kentucky. So the Democrats were able to offer a "national" program and candidates.

The Republicans also held their convention in June, at Philadelphia. They, too, declared that they spoke for the nation, but they had among them only a few delegates from the South, those being from Kentucky and Maryland. In their platform they denied the "authority of Congress, of a Territorial Legislature, of any individual or association of individuals to give legal assistance to slavery in any territory of the United States." They asserted that Congress had complete power over the territories, and that it had the "right and the duty" to prohibit within them those twin relics of barbarism, polygamy and slavery. They denounced the repeal of the Missouri Compromise line, popular sovereignty, and the Democrats generally. They called for the building of a transcontinental railroad and federal spending for internal improvements. They passed over their outstanding leaders, who had acquired enemies, as must all vigorous men long in public life. They nominated for the Presidency the army officer, explorer, and adventurer, John C. Frémont. Illegitimate, but a glamorous figure, Frémont was also attractive because he had married the beautiful daughter of the potent Democratic Senator from Missouri, Thomas Hart Benton. For the Vice-Presidency the Convention considered Abraham Lincoln of Illinois, who had lately joined the party, but finally chose William L. Dayton of New Jersey.

There was a third important party in the campaign, for the Whigs, although they had lost heavily both to the Democrats and the Republicans, were still numerous. Their more cautious and more conservative members would not go to the Democrats in the South nor to the Republicans in the North. Joined by many Know-Nothings, they rallied behind Millard Fillmore and called for sectional harmony. They secured 874,534 popular votes for Fillmore; Frémont had 1,335,264; and Buchanan 1,838,169. In the electoral college Buchanan had 174, Frémont 114, and Fillmore 8. The result alarmed thoughtful men who sought peace, for it was evident that the Whig Party, which had had a national following, was dying, and that the Republican Party, without appeal in the South, had become swiftly and truly powerful in the North. Frémont carried 11 free states, and Buchanan only 4, Pennsylvania, New Jersey, Indiana, and Illinois. Despite their numerical inferiority the Republicans had come very close to winning the Presidency, and it was evident that they had a good chance to gain it in 1860. If they did, how would the South respond? The answer had already been given by some enthusiasts for "Southern rights." Governor Henry

Wise of Virginia had declared that if the "Black Republican" Frémont were elected the South must leave the Union to form an independent "Confederacy." It would depart from the Union, if possible, peacefully and quietly, but if necessary "in war and blood." The peacemakers in politics were obviously losing power and influence.

THE SUPREME COURT AND SLAVERY

In his inaugural address Buchanan congratulated the nation upon the remarkable prosperity which it enjoyed, and hinted that a decision had been reached by the Supreme Court regarding the status of slavery in the territories which ought to be accepted as final. Two days later, on March 6, 1857, the Court handed down its decision, together with a series of opinions, in the case of *Scott* v. *Sandford.* "Scott" was Dred Scott, a Negro; "Sandford" was John Sanford (his name was misspelled in the official report), his supposed owner. Two Supreme Court judges had informed Buchanan that it had settled Scott's status and had also defined the authority of Congress over the territories. They were guilty of impropriety and Buchanan of wishful thinking. The pleasure which he felt because of the nation's flourishing economy vanished in a panic that began in August when the Ohio Life and Trust Company closed its doors with enormous liabilities amounting to $7,000,000. Thereafter, runs were made upon many principal banks in the Northern states; for a time payments were legally suspended in several of them. Confidence was not restored until the year had closed. There were more than 5000 failures in commerce and industry, and widespread unemployment and suffering among the workers. As it happened, the South, with its special economy, suffered much less than the North, which was proof of the virtues of slavery to its ardent defenders. Then prosperity returned. Buchanan's hope that the decision of the Supreme Court would solve the question of slavery in the territories proved to have no foundation whatever.

The Dred Scott case was treated in a remarkable way by the Supreme Court. Originally a slave in Missouri, Scott had been taken by a former master, Dr. John Emerson, into Illinois in 1834 and then into Minnesota, living for about four years in regions declared to be free by the Northwest Ordinance and in territory proclaimed free by the Missouri Compromise. In 1846, after returning to Missouri, he sued for his freedom in the state courts on the grounds that he had resided in a free state and in a free territory. A Missouri lower court upheld his claim, but the Supreme Court of that state disallowed it. In 1852, with the help of Sanford, who did not value his services as a slave and intended to free him in any event, he appealed to a federal district court and then to the nation's highest tribunal. His plea could easily have been rejected on the score of precedent without causing a commotion. In the case of *Strader* v. *Graham* seven years earlier the Supreme Court had accepted the decision of a state Supreme Court as final regarding the status of a Negro resident in that state. The majority of the justices, being of Southern background, were disposed to turn down Scott's appeal on the basis of that precedent. However, two of them, Benjamin R. Curtis and John McLean, Northerners, not only dissented, but insisted upon writing opinions asserting both that Scott was entitled to freedom and that Congress was constitutionally empowered to regulate slavery in the territories. Chief Justice Roger B. Taney and other members then determined to present equally elaborate analyses of the Constitution to prove that Scott was a slave and that Congress lacked authority to prevent a slave owner from taking his property into any territory. The result was that every one of the nine justices wrote an opinion.

Dred Scott lost his appeal by seven votes to two, being freed soon afterward by Mr. Sanford. However, Curtis and McLean contended that Scott became a free Negro when he resided in Illinois; if not, he became one in the Louisiana territory in the 1830s under the Missouri Compromise law; that as such he was a citizen and entitled to sue in the federal courts; and that the Supreme Court must recognize him to be a free man. They argued that the Missouri Compromise line was constitutional, because Congress had been given power in the Constitution "to dispose of and make all needful Rules and Regulations respecting the Territory or other Property belonging to the United States," also because it obtained authority over territories through implied powers when it acquired them.

Taney, supported in the main by five other justices, offered an elaborate historical and constitutional disquisition in which he reached very different conclusions. He ruled against Scott's appeal on three different grounds: that the Negro's status had been settled by the Supreme Court of Missouri, that a free Negro was not a citizen of the United States and could not sue in the federal Courts, and that Scott was a slave despite his residence in Illinois and the Louisiana Territory, and as such certainly did not have legal access to those courts. His contention that a free Negro was not a citizen of the United States, even though he might be a citizen of a state, was to be savagely criticized. His third argument was to create fury, for if accepted it established an extreme version of "Southern rights" with respect to slavery in the territories. Curtis and McLean had made a good case for complete Congressional authority over the territories in theory, and they had been able to list fourteen instances in which the federal lawmakers had forbidden slavery in one territory or another. However, Taney declared that practice did not determine, and that Congress could not prevent an owner from taking his slave into and keeping him in a federal territory. Adopting a line of argument earlier presented by Jefferson Davis, he said that a slave was property; that the Fifth Amendment to the Constitution forbade the federal government to deprive any person of property "without due process of law"; and that a law which prevented a slave owner from making use of his property in a territory was therefore unconstitutional. The Missouri Compromise line had been, from his point of view, null and void from the beginning.

It is not surprising that Taney immediately became the object of a storm of abuse from the North. He was biased; his history was bad; his logic was worse; and his law was outrageous. Actually Taney's history, logic, law, and behavior were about as good as those of McLean and Curtis. However, if it were generally accepted, that part of his opinion regarding the power of Congress over slavery in the territories would have been a crushing blow to the Republicans, for they would not have been able to proceed against it without a constitutional amendment giving Congress authority to do so. Many of their leaders proclaimed it to be *obiter dictum,* a statement irrelevant to the case and therefore of no constitutional significance. Much less respectful of the Supreme Court than they usually were afterward, the Republicans made it clear that they would proceed with their program.

The embarrassed and angry Republicans defied the Supreme Court and kept their ranks, and the Dred Scott decision ultimately gave them a political advantage, for it led to an unresolvable clash in the Democratic Party between the champions of "Southern rights" and those of popular sovereignty. Before that decision many defenders of "Southern rights" did not realize that Stephen Douglas was not a friend of slavery or that popular sovereignty was not intended to encourage its spread. They secured a clear presentation of Douglas' views in 1857 and 1858 when he insisted that popular sovereignty be honestly put into practice in Kansas, even though his doctrine was inconsistent with the Taney opinion, and though the results would be a free territory and State of Kansas. In 1857 the pro-slavery party in Kansas, despite the wishes of the majority of the settlers, prepared the Lecompton Constitution, which gave approval to slavery, and secured its adoption by trickery. Had it been approved by Congress, Kansas would have become a slave state, at least in form. President Buchanan urged that the Lecompton document be endorsed, but Douglas insisted that it was utterly contrary to the wishes of the majority of the people of Kansas and that it be rejected. Buchanan and his Southern Democratic friends then pushed through Congress the English Bill, supposedly a compromise. It provided that the Kansans should vote on the Lecompton Constitution in an honest election, but offered economic favors if it were approved. The bait was not taken in Kansas, and the document was voted down by a majority of more than 5 to 1, statehood for Kansas being postponed until 1861. The breach between Douglas and his followers on the one hand, and Buchanan and the Democratic defenders of "Southern rights" on the other, became a yawning gap when Douglas boldly challenged the Taney opinion in a contest with Abraham Lincoln for the Senate in 1858.

LINCOLN: MAN AND POLITICIAN

Seeking reelection to the Senate, Douglas was confronted on the hustings in Illinois during the late summer and fall of 1858 by a formidable antagonist. Lincoln was not yet well known nationally—he became so as a result of the contest—but he was no obscure or unsuccessful man in his own state. Of humble background, born in Kentucky and reared among plain folk in that state, Indiana, and Illinois, he was a self-made and amazingly well made man. The legends which have grown up about his childhood, youth, and young manhood are shabby when compared to the known facts. Even the sad tale, for which there is no good evidence, of his tragic love for Anne Rutledge is sickly stuff in the light of the history of his love for his wife, Mary Todd. In view of the time and place, the hardships which Lincoln underwent as a boy and a young man were not unique. What is remarkable is the splendor of his maturing personality. Farm worker, railsplitter, storekeeper, surveyor, captain of volunteers in the Black Hawk War, he was only 27 when he was admitted to the Bar. As a lawyer he was successful from the beginning, and he was early recognized in Springfield and on the circuit as a rising young man. He had made the most of his cultural opportunities, and he was not merely a story-telling, homespun, backwoods lawyer when the well-educated and personable Mary Todd became his bride. The Lincolns had children and troubles, but he moved steadily upward in the Illinois world. The lanky, gaunt husband, despite susceptibility to fits of melancholia, acquired poise and dignity, while retaining the modesty, good humor, and zest for jokes which he had displayed when young. He had held only one important public office, serving one term as a Congressman. When he confronted Douglas he was no frontier democrat; he had been a loyal Whig, and he was a quite conservative Republican. In a speech at Peoria in 1854, he had come out against the extension of slavery in the territories, but had acquitted the South of charges that it had conspired to expand the domain of Negro bondage. He did not call for repeal of the Fugitive Slave Law of 1850, but for revision of it toward giving the Negro legal justice. He said that he favored gradual emancipation of the slaves. He asserted emphatically that he had no prejudice against the Southern people, saying that he did not know all the answers to all the problems raised by slavery, and that he could not blame the Southerners for failure to solve them.

Relatively conservative in his approach toward slavery, Lincoln was nevertheless vigorous—and eloquent—in his campaign against Douglas. In the heat of politicking he used noble but provocative language. Accepting the Republican nomination, he declared:

A house divided against itself cannot stand. I believe this Government cannot endure permanently half-slave and half-free. I do not expect the Union to be dissolved—I do not expect the house to fall, but I do expect that it will cease to be divided. It will become all one thing or all the other. Either the opponents of slavery will arrest a further spread of it and place it where the public mind shall rest in the belief that it is in the course of ultimate extinction; or its advocates will push it forward till it shall become alike lawful in all the States, old as well as new —North as well as South.

THE LINCOLN-DOUGLAS DEBATES

Lincoln did not coin the phrase "irrepressible conflict"—that honor belonged to William H. Seward—but he subscribed to Seward's thesis. When Douglas accepted his challenge to a series of seven debates in the small towns of Illinois, Lincoln continued to express himself in strong language. Although he rejected the proposition that the Negro was the equal of the white man, he denounced slavery as "a moral, a social, and a political wrong." When Douglas attacked him as an "incendiary" because he had declared that slavery would either expand or die, Lincoln clung to his position. Lincoln also displayed a splendid talent for politicking, in which, indeed, he was a master. He forced Douglas to declare himself with respect to the Taney opinion, which embarrassed the advocates of popular sovereignty as well as the Republicans. If Congress could not prevent slavery in the territories, how could it be done by a territorial legislature, created by Congress and certainly possessing no greater authority than its creator? In the second of the Lincoln-Douglas debates at Freeport, Lincoln put a formal question to Douglas: "Can the people of a United States Territory, in any lawful way, against the wish of any citizen of the United States, exclude slavery from its limits prior to the formation of a State Constitution?" The "Little Giant," refusing to abandon his doctrine, insisted that it could be and that it ought to be executed regardless of the Supreme Court decision. His answer was clever and practical:

I answer emphatically as Mr. Lincoln has heard me answer a hundred times from every stump in Illinois, that in my opinion the people of a Territory can, by lawful means, exclude slavery from their limits prior to the formation of a State Constitution. Mr. Lincoln knew that I had answered that question over and over again. . . . It matters not which way the Supreme Court may hereafter decide . . . the people have the lawful means to introduce it or exclude it as they please for the reason that slavery cannot exist a day or an hour anywhere, unless it is supported by local police regulations. Those police regulations can only be established by the local legislature; and if people are opposed to slavery, they will elect representatives to that body who will by unfriendly legislation actually prevent the introduction of it into their midst.

It was true enough that a territorial legislature could provide for slavery by law, and that it could also substantially prevent it by not enacting a slave code, without which Negro bondage could hardly exist. It was also true, as Douglas said, that Nature herself had proclaimed that slavery could not flourish in Kansas or Nebraska. However, Douglas' "Freeport Doctrine," repeated again and again, injured the political prospects of its author and led to a schism in his party, although it satisfied most of the Illinois Democrats. The Southern Democrats learned that, if he was not an enemy of slavery, he was not its friend, and that he favored evasion of a Supreme Court decision in order to maintain his doctrine of popular sovereignty. Two years more and they would demand that he and the Northern Democrats who supported him specifically declare their acceptance of the Taney doctrine.

Of course, Douglas was able to embarrass Lincoln by asking him how he could reconcile his position on slavery in the territories with that of the Supreme Court. Lincoln, like other Republicans, had to say that he did not accept Taney's opinion as final, and that the Dred Scott decision might be overruled in another future case, even by constitutional amendment. But here Douglas won only debating points, for nearly all Republicans were determined to defy the Supreme Court. It may be said that Douglas held his own intellectually in the debates, but that he met a major political defeat. He was reelected to the Senate by the Illinois legislature, in which the Democrats had a majority, despite the fact that the Republicans secured a larger popular vote than the Democrats. However, Douglas lost the Presidency in 1860, and his astute antagonist won it.

The unchallengeable estimate of thoughtful mankind is that President Lincoln was a statesman of the very first order, as well as a singularly appealing human being. He was a magnificent person in 1858, but was he then, or in 1860, the man of transcendent vision that he was during the Civil War? One can hardly accept Douglas' description of Lincoln in 1858 as an "incendiary." Can it be argued that Lincoln should have been aware that the nation was moving steadily toward Civil War, that the North should have taken a more conciliatory attitude to avert it? While Lincoln and Douglas were engaging in forensics in Illinois, a society was formed in Cleveland, Ohio, to campaign for emancipation of all the slaves, with their owners to be compensated by the federal government. Looking back, we may be quite sure that positive action on the part of the North, on the basis that slavery was a common responsibility, would have been necessary to prevent a military contest, for Southern wills and hearts were hardening. Neither Lincoln nor his party adopted a program of compensated emancipation until the Civil War was under way. If the owners had been paid an average of $500 for each slave the cost to the federal government would have been immense, about $1,375,000,000, a staggering sum for a nation with an annual budget of $75,000,000. Of course, the Civil War cost far more, and hundreds of thousands of lives as well. It is perhaps too much to ask of Lincoln and his party that they should have proposed freedom for the slaves and payment to their owners. We see the future dimly, even the wisest of us. It is certainly difficult to believe that Robert E. Lee and many other Southerners would have turned away from a North offering to share in a common economic sacrifice in order to put an end to slavery.

THE ROAD TO WAR

The rift between North and South continued to widen. Although Douglas survived the Republican onslaught in the autumn of 1858, the Republicans were very successful in the Northern elections that year, securing control even of President Buchanan's Pennsylvania. Their chances of winning the Presidency in 1860 were much improved, a fact which stiffened the attitude of the North toward the South. On the other hand, hostility toward the North increased below the Mason-Dixon Line, especially among the Democrats, who were becoming more insistent that their party unequivocally stand forth for "Southern rights." Abolitionist John Brown helped to widen the gap. Collecting funds from New England and New York abolitionists, including Theodore Parker and wealthy Gerrit Smith, he concocted a harebrained scheme to foment a slave revolt in the South. In the fall of 1858 he gathered 21 men, including five Negroes, at the Kennedy farm across the Potomac River from Harper's Ferry. On October 16 he and his followers seized the arsenal at Harper's Ferry, and called upon the slaves in its neighborhood to join them and to fight for their freedom. Not a single slave responded, and Brown and his men were soon surrounded and besieged in the Arsenal. After two days of fighting, the survivors were compelled to surrender to United States marines led by Colonel Robert E. Lee. Tried for treason against the State of Virginia, Brown was found guilty and was hanged on December 2. Several of his followers later encountered the same fate. Although moderate-minded Northerners saw Brown as a reckless fanatic, many others looked upon him as a hero ready to sacrifice himself in a great cause. His soul would go marching on. His desperate enterprise caused consternation and horror in the South, and Southerners erroneously but naturally concluded that there were many John Browns in the Northern states. Southern extremists began to urge insistently, as Jefferson Davis and William L. Yancey had earlier, that the African slave trade be revived.

More ominous were resolutions passed by the legislatures of Alabama and Florida early in 1860 which declared that the election of a "Black Republican" President the following autumn would be reason enough for secession from the Union. Arrangements for raising militia were made in

South Carolina, Mississippi, and other states in the Lower South. It was evident to the thoughtful observer that the election of a Republican to the Presidency was indeed likely to bring an effort to secede in the tier of states stretching from South Carolina to Florida and westward to Texas. In those states there were still many who believed that such drastic action should not be taken merely because of the occupation of the White House by a Republican. Moreover, in the Upper South, sentiment for disunion was much weaker.

THE CAMPAIGN OF 1860

The campaign of 1860 began under very troubled skies; the storm burst before Republican President Lincoln entered the executive mansion.

In the spring of 1860 the Democrats, convulsed by sectional strife, were unable to agree upon a platform and a Presidential candidate, and no fewer than four important parties sought the favor of the voters in the campaign of that year. When the Democrats met in national convention at Charleston, South Carolina, in April, their Southern wing demanded that the party pledge itself to the protection of slavery in the territories. Most of the Northern Democrats, giving their allegiance to Douglas and popular sovereignty, refused to make the promise, and delegates from eight Southern states thereupon left the convention. Those who remained, because of the party rule which required a two-thirds majority for nominations (in effect from 1836 to 1932), were unable to name anyone for the Presidency after 67 ballots. Adjourning until June, they met again in Baltimore, and finally settled upon Douglas and Herschel V. Johnson of Georgia for the Presidency and Vice-Presidency. Another group of dissatisfied Southerners left that meeting. Then Democrats representing the bulk of their party in the South held a separate convention at Baltimore, called for federal action to establish "Southern rights" and to secure Cuba, and nominated John C. Breckenridge for the Presidency, with Joseph Lane of Oregon for the Vice-Presidency. In the meantime, a group of conservatives, including former Whigs and Know-Nothings, had also held a convention at Baltimore—which must have had a surfeit of politicians that spring—and had created the Constitutional Union Party. For the two highest national offices they supported John Bell of Tennessee and Edward Everett of Massachusetts; they condemned sectional parties, and urged loyalty to the Constitution and the Union.

The Republicans met at Chicago and adopted a platform which assured them of victory in the Northern states, and with it, control of the White House. To their original plank that slavery must be kept from spreading, they added others which could not fail to attract additional votes. They called for a free homestead law, certain to gain ballots for them in the Old Northwest and on the Pacific coast, and they came out for a protective tariff, which pleased Eastern industrialists and proved to wealthy Northerners that they were responsible folk. They spoke out against nativism, urging that recent immigrants be given treatment equal to that accorded to the descendants of earlier ones, thus appealing strongly to the "Old Immigration." There were four principal aspirants for their Presidential nomination, William H. Seward, Salmon P. Chase, Edward Bates, and Abraham Lincoln. While Seward was the most widely known, he had been in public life long enough to accumulate many enemies. Both Seward and Chase seemed to the more cautious Republicans unnecessarily aggressive with respect to slavery. They liked Lincoln and Bates, Lincoln more than Bates. Lincoln's "managers" at the convention, chief of whom was David Davis, maneuvered realistically for him. They promised a Cabinet position to Simon Cameron, who controlled the Pennsylvania delegation, in return for his support; they half-promised another Cabinet post to Caleb Smith in exchange for the votes of Indiana, and they similarly procured support in the Ohio delegation by pledging federal appointments. Seward led at first, but Lincoln was nominated on the third ballot. To balance the ticket the Republicans named Hannibal Hamlin of Maine for the Vice-Presidency.

In the campaign that followed, the principal contestants in the Northern states were Lincoln and Douglas; in the South the contest was chiefly between Breckenridge and Bell. Lincoln received a trifle less than 40 percent of the popular vote. The ballots cast numbered, for Lincoln, 1,866,352; for Douglas 1,375,157; for Breckenridge, 849,781; and for Bell, 589,581. Because the popular vote for Lincoln was cast almost entirely in the Northern states he ran steadily ahead of Douglas, and secured an easy majority in the electoral college. There he had 180 votes from 18 free states; Douglas had only 12 votes, three from New Jersey, and nine from Missouri. Bell carried three states in the Upper South, securing 39 electoral votes, and Breckenridge was victorious in 11 slave states which gave him 72. The results of the elections to the House of Representatives and the Senate reflected public opinion, and the Republicans failed to secure a majority in either branch of Congress. It should be remarked that Lincoln would have triumphed even if all the popular votes for his rivals had been cast for only one of them.

It was observed by Douglas during the campaign that he could not win and that the South was moving rapidly toward secession. Touring the South, he found most of the followers of Breckenridge threatening secession if Lincoln were chosen. Moreover, although many Bell men in the Upper South were opposing disunion, those in the Lower South were saying that they would not oppose secession if President Lincoln and his party acted against Southern interests. Declaring his own devotion to the Union and assuring his listeners that he would not countenance secession, he urged that the South be patient and refrain from trying to destroy the nation. He spoke in vain, for at last the secession movement had begun.

SECESSION AND CONFEDERACY

The South Carolina legislature was in session when it became apparent that Lincoln had been elected, and unanimously voted to call a state convention, which met on December 20. That body, asserting both the right of revolution and the Calhoun doctrine of constitutional secession, unanimously declared that the ratification of the Constitution by the South Carolina Convention of 1788 was rescinded, and that the "union now subsisting between South Carolina and the other states, under the name of the 'United States of America' is hereby dissolved." South Carolina would not wait to find out whether Lincoln and the Republicans would actually take steps against slavery. Her people made their decision amidst wild enthusiasm, and six other states in the Deep South followed her example within six weeks. By February 1, 1861, Mississippi, Florida, Alabama, Georgia, Louisiana, and Texas had also passed ordinances of secession. The opposition of cautious men was swept aside and enthusiasm for "Southern rights" became devotion to the Southern Confederacy. Orators spoke in rhapsodies about a Southern empire which would become great in the world. When cooler men expressed their opinion that separation from the Union would not be achieved without an armed struggle, the advocates of secession declared that it would hardly be necessary to fight; if it were, they would sacrifice everything in a noble cause.

Secession and some sort of Southern union, were, of course, inextricably linked, for a string of independent republics could not endure. The seven seceding states sent delegates to a convention which met at Montgomery, Alabama, in February, 1861. This body acted as a provisional Congress for the Confederate States of America, chose Jefferson Davis as their temporary President and Alexander H. Stephens as their temporary Vice-President, and drafted a constitution for a new federation. Modeled upon the Constitution of the United States, it stressed "the sovereign and independent character of its states." It sanctioned slavery and established safeguards to preserve it. However, it forbade any external trading in slaves, except with the United States. It contained one basic improvement upon the Constitution of 1787; the President was empowered to veto individual items in appropriation bills. The document did not mention anything about the right of a state to secede, but that right was assumed. Before the end of 1861, elections were held in the Confederacy in which Davis and Stephens were given six-year terms in their offices and the members of the "permanent" Confederate Congress were chosen. Before that body met the capital of the Confederacy was moved to Richmond. By that time, eleven states had joined the Confederacy, for Virginia, North Carolina, Tennessee, and Arkansas had cast their lots with the Lower South in the spring of 1861.

The secession of the Lower Southern states was accompanied by the seizure of a number of federal forts along the coast, and a "lame duck" President and Congress were confronted by an extraordinary crisis. On the advice of his Attorney General, Buchanan declared that secession was legally impossible, but that he had no constitutional authority to use force against the seceders. There were last minute efforts to secure a compromise, by Northern Democrats and men from the Upper South. In December, 1860, Senator John J. Crittenden of Kentucky proposed that slavery be permitted in the territories south of the line 36° 30', forbidden north of it. The Republicans, following the leadership of Lincoln, opposed the measure, and the bill died in a Senate committee. Thereupon, those who sought to pacify called a Peace Convention, which met at Washington in February. Men attended from most of the Northern states and from the Upper South. They drafted a more detailed compromise, but it was in vain, for the Republicans would not recede from their position with regard to slavery in the territories. Congress did not act upon the plan submitted to it by the Conference. It had become too late to talk; on the other hand, action against the seceders was postponed until Lincoln took office. Fort after fort was seized by troops of the seceded states, but without much bloodshed. When South Carolina demanded that the forts in Charleston harbor be surrendered, Major Robert Anderson, commanding the Federal troops there, established himself and a garrison in Fort Sumter and prepared to resist as best he might. Buchanan sent reinforcements and provisions southward for him in the unarmed ship *Star of the West*. It was driven off by shore batteries manned by South Carolina troops. What to do about Fort Sumter was one of the questions which faced Lincoln in the week after his inauguration.

LINCOLN'S FIRST MONTHS

In the early months of 1861 militias were arming and training everywhere, and Lincoln was unable to proceed to Washington in dignity. Informed that he would be attacked in Baltimore, he secretly took a special train which brought him safely into the capital on February 23. On March 4 he delivered his First Inaugural Address, one of his greatest speeches. Many Northerners, including even some abolitionists, were willing to let the seceders go in peace. They could not, said Lincoln. He declared that he would not interfere with the institution of slavery in the states where it existed. He denounced the doctrine of secession as unconstitutional and productive of anarchy. He admitted that the Southerners could appeal to the right of revolution, but he reminded them that the federal government also had the right to assert its authority. He said that a separation of the Union was impossible, physically as well as constitutionally, and he made it clear that if necessary, he would use force against the secessionists. He called upon the Southerners to pause, consider, and work with their brethren "to adjust, in the best way, all our present difficulties." He ended with an eloquent appeal:

In *your* hands, my dissatisfied fellow-countrymen, and not in *mine* is the momentous issue of civil war. The government will not assail *you*. You can have no conflict without your being yourselves the aggressors. *You* have no oath registered in Heaven to destroy the government, while *I* shall have the most solemn one to 'preserve, protect, and defend' it.

I am loath to close. We are not enemies but friends. We must not be enemies. Though passion may have strained, it must not break our bonds of affection. The mystic chords of memory, stretching from every battlefield and patriot grave to every living heart and hearthstone, all over this broad land, will yet swell the chorus of the Union, when again touched, as surely they will be, by the better angels of our nature.

Lincoln's eloquence could have no effect upon enthusiastic Confederates, and the nation drifted rapidly toward internecine war. Lincoln's Secretary of State, Seward, urged the President to provoke a contest with England in the desperate hope that the South might rally behind the Stars and Stripes against a European foe. Lincoln rejected Seward's dangerous advice and determined to face squarely the ultimate danger at home. The garrison at Fort Sumter was running short of supplies, and would soon be forced to surrender if it was not helped. On April 6, he sent notice to South Carolina that a supply ship would soon sail. Unwilling that the fort should remain under Union control and fearing that Lincoln intended to introduce more troops into the fort, South Carolina officials, on April 11 demanded its surrender. Major Anderson refused, although he admitted that he must do so soon for lack of provisions—he was not aware that they were being sent to him. The following day South Carolina troops under the command of General Pierre G. T. Beauregard opened artillery fire upon the fort, and the Civil War had begun. After 34 hours of bombardment, to which Anderson was quite unable to reply, he was forced to surrender. Miraculously, no one in the garrison was slain, although one of Anderson's men was killed while helping to fire a last salute. Two days later Lincoln declared that an "insurrection" existed in the South, and called for 75,000 volunteers to help suppress it. It has been contended that Lincoln, desiring war, tricked the South Carolinians into firing the first shots. Proof for this charge is lacking, and we may acquit him of intentional deceit in view of the essential honesty which he so often manifested. There can be no doubt that he expected war.

SECESSION OF THE UPPER SOUTH

The firing upon Fort Sumter forced the people of the Upper South to choose between the Union and the Confederacy. Sentiment there had been sharply and bitterly divided during the fateful winter of 1860–1861. Tens of thousands were for the Union, first and last; many favored swift secession; and many sympathized with the Confederates but would not take their stand with them until the federal government moved aggressively. Between April 17 and May 20 Virginia, Arkansas, Tennessee, and North Carolina successively passed ordinances of secession and joined the Confederacy. The Confederacy was thereby immensely strengthened, but a minority in each of the four states clung to and fought for the Union. Its adherents were numerous in western North Carolina and in eastern Tennessee, where slaves were few.

THE BORDER STATES

In western Virginia the friends of the Union were in the majority, and with the help of Federal troops they eventually formed the new state of West Virginia, admitted in 1863. All the other states in which there were slaves, Delaware, Maryland, Kentucky, and Missouri, never left it. In Maryland and Missouri the Federals were in the majority, and they were given political and military support by Lincoln, with the result that both were saved to the Union. So was Kentucky, in which the Federals were the stronger. Many Kentuckians would have preferred to be neutral, but troops entered the state from both the South and the North. The Union forces were the more powerful, and they established Federal control of the state, although it supplied tens of thousands of men to the Confederate army. In one slave state of 1861 there was no hesitation; Delaware would supply a few soldiers to the Confederacy, but her people very generally continued their allegiance to the old flag.

There were men in the North as well as in the South who were not sorry that the clash would be settled by arms, but their joy was not felt by the majority on either side. In fact, it was desperately difficult for many thousands to choose between the Union and the Confederacy, and some never made a choice. Robert E. Lee, no champion of slavery, and a veteran army officer, was offered the post of commander in chief of the Union armies, but finally and reluctantly cast his lot with his Virginia friends and neighbors. Another Virginia army officer of splendid character and abilities, George H. Thomas, turned away from his state and offered his services to the nation. So difficult it was to decide in the border commonwealths that brothers fought in opposing armies. For them, indeed, the war was a civil one, a struggle between brethren. Several names have been given to the sanguinary conflict which raged in America between 1861 and 1865.

There are those who passionately insist that it ought to be called the "War between the States"; and some, following the lead of Edward Channing, use the term, "The War for Southern Independence." Because "Civil War" has the advantage of brevity, and because the conflict was between parties that formed one people both earlier and later, it is herein used. An added argument in favor of it is that it does not stigmatize the beliefs and conduct of honorable men on either side. However the mighty struggle which began at Fort Sumter may be designated, it cost the American people 600,000 lives, more than any other of the wars in which they have participated.

29 THE WAR FOR THE UNION: FIRST PHASE

If the outcome of a war could be predicted by totting up the men and the resources of the antagonists, the destruction of the Confederacy was inevitable. However, superiority in men, machines, and money does not assure a military victory, and it is obvious enough that the Confederacy, enduring for four years, was not doomed to failure from its beginning. There are those who believe that the chance of survival for a Southern nation was never very good, and that the military conflict was prolonged only because of the superb leadership of the Confederate generals and the gallantry of the Southern soldiers. Actually, the entire war considered, the South cannot be shown to have possessed an advantage either in military genius or in the quality of its manhood. Both sides had both strengths and weaknesses, and it is not at all impossible that, given better management, the Confederacy might have become a more or less permanent member of the family of nations.

THE ANTAGONISTS COMPARED

The North had major advantages in numbers, in industrial power, railroads, capital, and foodstuffs. It had five men for every two in the Confederacy; counting whites only, the North had four men to one. The population

of the Confederacy was roughly 9,000,000, opposed to 23,000,000 in the
states which clung to the Union. Northern industry was vastly more
productive than Southern, at least ten times larger in terms of output. The
North also enjoyed superiority with respect to transportation by water, and
more especially by land. It was rich in merchant shipping, and the United
States Navy, never successfully challenged by the Confederacy, made it possible to carry large numbers of men and quantities of supplies on both salt
and fresh water. Of special value to the Union cause was the network of
railroads which covered the Northern states. There were three through
lines between the east coast and the Old Northwest, making possible a relatively rapid transfer of troops and military materials from one theater of
warfare to another. The North also controlled various lines running into
the Confederacy that proved useful as avenues of penetration. There was
ample wealth in the North to sustain a great and continuous war effort,
and the region also contained all the metals necessary for warfare, together
with farms which could offer abundant food. In sum, the North had a
well-balanced and prosperous economy. Moreover, along with an ample
supply of mechanics and engineers, the Northern states, despite the number
of large cities in them, contained hundreds of thousands of hardy men on
the land who were vigorous and accustomed to the use of guns. From the
logging camps of Michigan, the farms of Ohio, the mines of Pennsylvania,

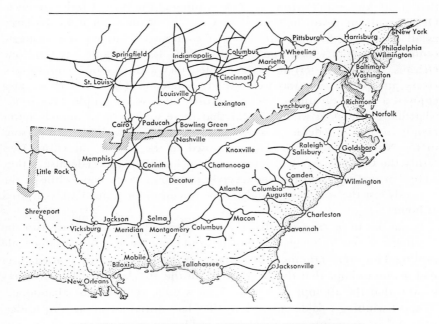

MAIN RAIL LINES OF MILITARY IMPORTANCE

and the rocky hills of New England the North would draw sturdy soldiers, as good as any in the world.

The fundamental military weaknesses of the Confederacy are evident. and its sources of strength not so apparent. Serious as industrial inferiority was for the South, the Confederate armies lacked neither guns nor ammunition until the closing months of the war. A supply of sorts was on hand at the beginning of the conflict. It was added to by Southern factories, especially the Tredegar Iron Works of Richmond; it was improved by captures from the Federal forces; and it was increased by importations from Europe. The Southern railroads were inadequate, Texas and Florida not even being connected with the rest of the Confederacy by rail. There was only one through line connecting Richmond with the Mississippi by way of Chattanooga, and Charleston was not connected with the eastern bank of the lower Mississippi River until the beginning of hostilities. Traveling by rail from Meridian, Mississippi, to Montgomery for his inauguration, Jefferson Davis had to go by way of Chattanooga and Atlanta. Let it be observed, however, that Union armies, as they moved forward into the Confederacy, also encountered a difficult transportation problem. Southern agriculture was not of the sort which could easily supply the vast quantities of foodstuffs needed by the Confederate armies; yet it proved to be good enough so that they were not starved into submission.

All in all, the military situation of the Confederacy was something like that of the American Patriots at the beginning of the War of Independence. Of great advantage to the Confederacy was its vastness, for it was as large as all of western Europe. Moreover, it contained relatively few strategic centers, the loss of which would be disastrous. Its only large city was New Orleans. Besides, the terrain of the Confederacy with its mountains, forests, rivers, and poor roads, was well suited to defense. The Confederacy also enjoyed a slight advantage over the North because its people were somewhat more united—it would appear that there were proportionately fewer people in the Confederacy who did not support it than there were persons in the Northern states who were opposed to the Union war effort. Certainly the Confederates had much more to lose than the Federals; if they were defeated they must suffer severely in almost every way, while if the Federals lost the war they would not be obviously or immediately injured at home.

It was not to be expected that the Confederate forces would overrun the Northern states, although the North would not be free from large-scale raiding. However, standing substantially on the defensive, the Confederates had reason to hope that they could contain the attacks of the Union forces so well that the attempt to subdue them would eventually be abandoned. Toward winning this defensive war, they had initial advantages in leadership and in acquaintance with firearms. They had about 1000 officers, 300 of whom had been educated at West Point and 700 in Southern military academies; among them were several brilliant and many able commanders, including Robert E. Lee, Joseph E. Johnston, Albert Sidney Johnston, Thomas (Stonewall) Jackson, and others less famous. As it happened, the Union was unfortunate in its first choices of commanders in the field, and its ablest men, Ulysses S. Grant, William Tecumseh Sherman, and George H. Thomas, were only gradually advanced to the highest commands. Somewhat more accustomed to the use of guns than was his Northern counterpart, the Confederate soldier at first had a slight superiority, which, however, soon vanished.

A special source of hope for the Confederacy was that England and France would soon recognize its independence. Such recognition, even by England alone, would bring with it ample military supplies from abroad, foreign financial support, the breaking of the Union blockade of the Southern seacoasts, in all likelihood a war between England and the Union, and quite surely Southern independence. England and France might have done for the Confederacy what France did for the Patriots in the War of Independence, but the Confederacy never received foreign recognition and was granted sympathy rather than important help by England and France. Fundamentally the Southerners had to rely upon themselves, and they were ultimately unable to hold off the increasingly powerful armies which the Union put into the field.

THE WAR AT SEA

The tides of warfare on land swept back and forth until 1864, when they began to run steadily against the Confederacy. On the water, however, the Union enjoyed superiority at the outset, and was never effectively challenged. The Union Navy in 1861 had only 23 steamships and 7500 officers and men; none of its vessels was armored, and many of its officers were old and old-fashioned in their thinking about naval warfare. Nevertheless, the Union had the beginnings of a powerful navy and rapidly produced ships, engines, and trained seamen. The Confederacy had very few experienced officers at the beginning of the war, for Southerners in the Navy, like David Farragut, generally clung to their allegiance to the old flag; they had carried it to distant places, and they were more devoted to the nation than were the Southerners who had served it on land. There was not even one factory in the South which could produce a marine engine, and facilities in the Confederacy for making ships and armor were totally inadequate. The North promptly began to turn out gunboats and carrying craft which were very useful on the Mississippi River and its tributaries, where they powerfully strengthened Union armies. From Northern shipyards also came dozens of larger vessels which made possible the severing of the Confederacy at the Mississippi; the capture or closing of Southern ports; and the maintenance of a naval blockade from Chesapeake Bay to the mouth of the Mississippi. Before the end of the war the Union Navy commissioned more than 670 ships, of which about one in ten was armored.

The Confederacy's only real hope for success against the Federal Navy lay in the swift development of new weapons and of new and more formidable warcraft. The Southerners made good use of torpedoes and of mines, but they could not be employed in great enough numbers to inflict truly serious losses upon the Union Navy. Momentarily, in 1862, Stephen Mallory, the Confederate Secretary of the Navy, believed that he had found the means to cripple Federal power on the seas. Most of the Federal vessels were wooden. Mallory had the *U.S.S. Merrimac,* which had been sunk near Norfolk, Virginia, raised from the water, fitted with cannon, and covered with iron sheathing thick enough to repel any shot which might be fired against it. Mallory hoped that the *Merrimac,* renamed *Virginia,* would be able to destroy the wooden shipping of the Union Navy without serious damage to herself. His thinking was sound enough. Attacking unarmored Union war vessels in Chesapeake Bay, the *Virginia* quickly sank two of them at the cost of only two men. Her commander was preparing to continue the easy work of destruction when he was suddenly confronted by a Federal ironclad, the *Monitor,* for the Union Navy had also been experimenting. The inventor John Ericson had developed this "cheesebox on a raft," a small vessel which rose only thirty inches above the water, was covered with iron, and carried heavy guns in a revolving metal turret. In the ensuing engagement the *Virginia* and the *Monitor* cannonaded one another for four hours. The heavy shot of the Confederate vessel bounced off the *Monitor,* and her return fire did no serious damage to the *Virginia.* So effective was the armor of the two ships that only three Yankees and eleven Confederates were wounded, not a man being killed. Before the *Virginia* could resume her career, Federal troops seized her anchorage, forcing the Confederates to dismantle the vessel. The Confederates later built about fifteen other ironclads, but none of them was ever able to put to sea. On the other hand, the Union Navy soon had several ships like the *Monitor* in operation, and Union dominance of the waters adjacent to the Confederacy continued. Ships like the *Monitor* could not stand heavy seas, and it was said of them that they had "negative flotation." However, they were very effective against Confederate forts defending harbors and rivers, and they opened the way for successful attacks upon Southern ports.

BLOCKADE

So great was the superiority of the Union Navy that, with the help of troops supplied by the Army, it was able to close off seven of the major Confederate harbors by 1862. Thereafter, the only major ports controlled by the Confederates were Charleston, Mobile, and Wilmington. Charleston was cut off from the sea by the Union capture of Fort Wagoner in 1863; Admiral Farragut deprived the Confederates of the use of Mobile Bay the following year; and Fort Fisher, which covered the traffic of Wilmington, fell to the Federals early in 1865. The Federal Navy not only helped to capture and close the portals of the Confederacy; it also maintained an off-shore blockade which was proclaimed by President Lincoln in 1861. That blockade was for some time only a paper one, for the Navy did not have enough ships to guard the long Southern coastline. It gradually became more effective, although Confederate "blockade runners" continued to pass through it until the very end of the war. These were swift ships which slipped out to Nassau in the Bahama Islands and to other neutral ports, carrying cotton and other goods and returning with military supplies. As late as 1864, about four-fifths of these voyages were safely completed, and it has been estimated that the Confederacy was able to export $200,000,000 worth of goods despite the blockade. There can be no doubt, however, that it grievously injured the Confederacy. Southern commerce with the outside world dwindled away steadily during the war. Oddly enough, cargoes which were brought in through the blockade often contained luxury goods of no military value whatsoever. It would be too much to say that the Confederacy was strangled into submission because it was cut off from the outside world, but it was seriously weakened.

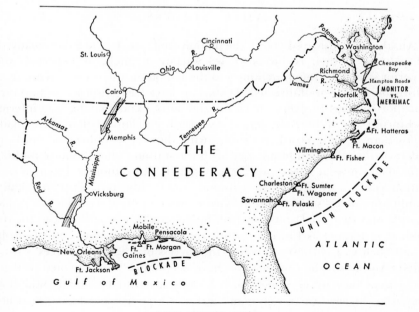

THE NAVAL WAR

Like the Patriots in the War of Independence, the Confederates, unable to build a fighting fleet, resorted to raids on Northern maritime commerce. Building swift cruisers at home and buying others in England, the Confederates hoped to strike at the Northern merchant marine so vigorously that the Union would have to lift the blockade to protect it. The cruisers, especially five which were built in England, were remarkably successful, capturing 261 Union sailing vessels. The American merchant marine was so badly damaged by these attacks that more than half of it sought foreign registration. Particularly efficient was Captain Raphael Semmes of the *Sumter* and the *Alabama,* who was a scourge to the Federals on the seas. The *Alabama* was finally destroyed off the French coast by the Union iron-clad *Kearsarge.* The *Shenandoah,* built in Glasgow, under the command of Captain James I. Waddell, perhaps did even more damage to the Union. It circumnavigated the globe, captured 40 vessels, and continued to hunt down Northern whalers in the Pacific long after Robert E. Lee had surrendered. Grievous as was the damage inflicted by the Confederate raiders, they did not achieve their great purpose. The Union did not rely on its merchant marine to win the war, and Lincoln and his advisers wisely refused to abandon the blockade in order to protect it. The Confederate cruisers dealt blows from which the merchant marine recovered only after the passage of decades, but they could not force open the water approaches to the Confederacy.

CIVILIAN LEADERS

All things considered, both the Union and the Confederacy made as efficient use of their resources for sea warfare as might be expected, and superior strength brought triumph to the Union on the oceans. Were their efforts on land as well directed? Historians have been disposed to find serious shortcomings in Jefferson Davis, and to contend that he was inferior to Lincoln as a military leader. It has also been claimed that Davis made a less than perfect record in dealing with the civil problems of the Confederacy, these being intermingled with the military ones. Because nothing fails like failure, it is easy to reach too harsh an opinion of Davis. Had a nation come into permanent existence under his leadership, his faults would appear less serious and his virtues more impressive. It has been said against him that, cold and dignified, he did not arouse enthusiasm for the Confederate cause as Lincoln did for that of the Union. But did Lincoln arouse such vast enthusiasm before the success of the Union forces was assured? And could the Confederates have been much more devoted to their cause than they were? Some North Carolinians and Georgians said that they were engaged in "a rich man's war and a poor man's fight." Was not the same assertion made in Ohio and New York?

It has been pointed out that Davis' Cabinet was not distinguished for ability, and that only Judah P. Benjamin, who held several offices in it at one time or another, was extremely able. It was indeed a Cabinet chosen more for political reasons than for the possession of genius by its members. Were Lincoln's confidential advisers far more gifted? They also were chosen in large part for political reasons, three of its original members having been rivals of Lincoln for the Republican nomination in 1860 and two having swung support to Lincoln at the right time in the Chicago convention. As Secretary of State the intelligent but erratic Seward was something less than great; Simon Cameron as Secretary of War left much to be desired; and Salmon P. Chase in the Treasury, while not incapable, was something less than utterly loyal to the President. Edwin M. Stanton, who replaced Cameron at the War Office, was intelligent and vigorous, but he was not a great military minister. Gideon Welles, in charge of the Navy, was both reliable and competent. Again, however the Confederate Cabinet would have looked as good as or better than the Federal one, had the Confederacy endured. The men in the Union Cabinet had the means with which to do their work, and they did not have to be brilliant to turn in a satisfactory performance. It has been charged that Davis played favorites in appointing officers to the high command in the Confederate Army, and that he promoted one or two incompetent commanders, while failing to make full use of the talents of some abler men. He made some poor choices, as did Lincoln; both also appointed men of military genius to the highest posts. It cannot be shown that the Confederate and Federal "brass" were of very different alloys. Both Presidents displayed courage and utter determination. They were also curiously alike in their feeling for the man in the ranks; like Lincoln, Davis freely pardoned soldiers who had been sentenced to death because they had fallen asleep on sentry duty out of sheer weariness. Perhaps the most valid charges against Davis are that he tried to finance the Confederate war effort by printing money and by borrowing rather than taxing, and that he permitted the Southern railroads to fall into disrepair at a time when their services were essential to a successful defense. Not a towering figure, Davis was a respectable one; he is overshadowed among the Confederates by the noble Lee; he did not have the stature that makes easy forgiveness of occasional failures by men of the caliber of Lincoln and Lee.

THE FIRST FIGHTING, 1861

It has been suggested that the war on land posed great difficulties for the Union. It had to hold the Border States, Missouri, Kentucky, and Maryland, together with the city of Washington, prevent damaging raids by Confederate armies on the offensive, and overrun the Confederacy. Its difficulties were aggravated by the Confederate decision to establish the Southern capital at Richmond, hardly 100 miles from Washington. It has been argued that the Southerners were unwise to commit themselves to the defense of a capital so far to the north. It would seem that they were wise to place it on the James River and to defend it with determination, because in any case they could not afford to let half of Virginia pass under Federal control without a major struggle. Besides, the concentration of Confederate forces enabled them to threaten Washington with a frontal attack from the south, and also with flanking movements from the Shenandoah Valley. Several Northern commanders had to face the awkward problem of driving the Confederates from Richmond, at the same time protecting Washington. This problem proved to be insoluble until the Northern Army of the Potomac became so much stronger than the Confederate Army of Northern Virginia that it could perform both tasks at the same time. Compelled to engage in large-scale fighting in northern Virginia, the Union forces had greater freedom of movement elsewhere. Their offensive efforts were largely directed by geography and the location of railroad lines. With Union strength on the water, it was clear enough that an attempt should be made to control the entire Mississippi River, thus splitting the Confederacy into two parts. It was also clear that the capture of Chattanooga and Atlanta would virtually again split the Confederacy by destroying railroad communications between the South Atlantic seaboard and the states of the Old Southwest. Accordingly, the Union forces had three major objectives on land. It was a long time before all were achieved.

The greatest agony the American people had known, or would know for at least another century, endured for four years. However, there was relatively little fighting in 1861, since both sides rather expected easy victory and failed to make great efforts until the spring of the following year. It was difficult to believe in the spring of 1861 that the nation was actually slipping into the grimmest and bloodiest of its conflicts. It was hoped against hope in the South that the Union would permit the peaceful departure of the Confederate States, and that if the Union armies moved, they could be held off without extreme sacrifice. It was thoughtlessly asserted below the Mason-Dixon Line that one Southerner could whip five Yankees. To the north of the Line there was a wishful expectation that Federal troops would swiftly seize Richmond and arrest Jefferson Davis, fomenter of a feeble insurrection. The optimists on the Union side were soon shocked into some sense of reality; not long afterward it also became apparent to supporters of the Confederacy that they were engaged in a major struggle.

Enlarging the regular army and calling for 75,000 volunteers after the capture of Fort Sumter, Lincoln soon put the Federal forces in motion on land. They first engaged Confederate troops on June 10, 1861, and part of them suffered defeat in the first great battle of the war at Bull Run on July 21. Driven by Northern clamor for a swift advance into Richmond, General Irvin McDowell with more than 20,000 Federal soldiers moved southward into Virginia. Confronted by a nearly equal Confederate army under General Pierre Beauregard at Bull Run, McDowell skillfully opened an attack upon the Confederate left flank. He was on the verge of victory when Confederate reinforcements from the Shenandoah Valley suddenly appeared on the field. Part of them under General Thomas J. Jackson checked the charging Union troops; "Stonewall" Jackson made his bow in history. Others followed, joining in a counterattack which drove the Federals northward in utter confusion. There was no pursuit, for the victors were weary and unprepared to follow up their success. In the end, the Union possibly obtained greater benefits from its defeat at Bull Run than the Confederacy did from its victory, for the Union was stimulated to immediate and great effort. Hundreds of thousands of men were called to the colors, and the Union undertook to wage the war in grim earnest. There could be no further attempt to move against Richmond in 1861, but a powerful Federal army gathered in northern Virginia for a major advance the following spring.

Elsewhere, the Union forces were much more successful in 1861, keeping the states of Maryland, Kentucky, and Missouri in the Union, although in all three there were tens of thousands of sympathizers with the Confederacy. An attempt to keep Kentucky neutral failed, and in the three commonwealths Union supporters gained control with the aid of the Federal troops. Moreover, friends of the Union in western Virginia rallied to the advancing Federal armies and helped drive the Confederates eastward and southward. So strong was Union sentiment in that part of the country that it was possible to establish a rump "loyal" legislature of Virginia, which gave its consent to the formation of the new state of West Virginia in 1863. There was warm Union feeling not only in West Virginia, but in all the southern Appalachian highlands. Winston County, Alabama, even tried to secede from that state, but was informed that secession could be overdone.

CAMPAIGNS OF 1862: THE WEST

The war was bloody enough in 1862 to satisfy the most sanguinary; both sides poured more and more men into the conflict. Union soldiers and sailors steadily pushed forward on and near the Mississippi River; the tide of battle surged back and forth in the central arena of Kentucky and Tennessee; and the Union Army of the Potomac continued to meet frustration in the rolling hills, woods, and swamps of Virginia. At the end of the year, although it had suffered heavy blows, the Confederacy was strong in heart and high in hope. Encouraging for the Union were the capture of New

Orleans and the checking in Maryland of an attempted invasion of the North by General Robert E. Lee and the Army of Northern Virginia. War-weariness was only beginning, whether in the Confederacy or in the North.

On the Mississippi the Union scored major victories in 1862, and its forces also secured a tight grip upon central Tennessee. Early in the year Federal land and water forces under General Ulysses S. Grant and Commodore Andrew H. Foote began to advance southward from the Ohio River through western Kentucky. On February 6 gunboats under Foote captured almost without a struggle Fort Henry, which had been built to prevent the Federals from using the Tennessee River. Grant and Foote then promptly moved against Fort Donelson, which was only twelve miles away and had been erected to close off the Cumberland River to Union shipping. Fort Donelson was sturdily constructed and garrisoned by 18,000 Confederates under General John B. Floyd. Foote's gunboats were unable to force the surrender of the garrison, but Grant surrounded the fort with his troops on February 13. Disheartened, most of the Confederate commanders agreed to surrender two days later. That night part of the garrison slipped through the lines to safety, but General Simon B. Buckner surrendered the fort and 14,000 men to Grant. The Confederacy had suffered a heavy blow; the way was open for a Federal advance against Nashville, and Foote's gunboats were freed for further attacks along the Mississippi. They moved down the great river, assaulting and capturing Island No. 10, which the Confederates had fortified to defend its upper reaches.

Meanwhile, another Union naval squadron under David Farragut moved up the Mississippi from its mouth. Farragut ran past Confederate forts intended to bar his progress and captured New Orleans in April. A Union army under General Benjamin F. Butler then occupied the city, while Farragut pushed on up the river. By the end of the year, although the Confederates still held a strong position at Vicksburg, Mississippi, the river was substantially in Federal hands and the South was quite effectively split in two. Thereafter the Confederates west of the Mississippi were of little help to those east of it. Indeed, enough pressure was kept against them so that they had all they could do to defend themselves. In 1862 they were driven back from Missouri by a strong Union army commanded by General John C. Frémont and later by General Samuel Curtis.

Although the capture of Forts Henry and Donelson opened the way for an easy capture of Nashville, the further progress of the Union armies southward from that city was slow and bloody. Discovering that Grant had advanced with only part of the Union army, leaving the remainder under General Carlos Buell well to the rear, the brilliant Confederate commander Albert Sidney Johnston suddenly assailed Grant near Pittsburg Landing early on the morning of April 6. That Union hero, completely surprised,

THE WAR IN THE WEST, 1862

was actually several miles away from his men when the action began.
Johnston's 40,000 troops, in bitter fighting, drove back the Federal men
and tried to pin them against the Tennessee River. But fortune did not
favor Johnston in the Battle of Shiloh, as the action came to be called.
Rallying the soldiers in blue, Grant fought back desperately and hung on
until reinforcements could reach him from Buell. Johnston was killed, and
was succeeded by Beauregard, who failed to receive hoped-for help en route
from Arkansas. Beauregard resumed hostilities on the next morning, but
was forced back as Union strength grew ever greater. Thereafter, the
Federals advanced as far to the south as Corinth, Mississippi, where they
cut one of the main Confederate railroad lines; they also seized Memphis.
In August, General Braxton Bragg led the men in gray northward from
Chattanooga in a massive counterthrust. Joined by a detachment from
Knoxville, under General Kirby Smith, he swept on into Kentucky, toward
Louisville. Caught unprepared, Buell hastily gathered troops to defend
Kentucky, and attacked Bragg at Perryville on October 8. Buell was re-
pulsed, but he received reinforcements, and the Confederate general was

compelled to fall back toward Chattanooga, followed by General W. S. Rosecrans, who had replaced the unsuccessful Buell. On December 31, Rosecrans and Bragg clashed furiously at Stone's River near Murfreesboro. A Confederate attack drove back Rosecrans, but he did not retreat. When Bragg again took the offensive, on January 2, he was repelled with heavy losses and had no choice but to fall back toward Alabama, having failed to break the Union grip upon central and western Tennessee. Losses at both Shiloh and Stone's River were very heavy; the Federal casualties at Stone's River were nearly 13,000, those of the Confederates almost 12,000, while at Shiloh the antagonists had actually lost even more heavily. The South could not afford to fight such battles as well as the Union could.

CAMPAIGNS OF 1862: THE EAST

On the eastern side of the Appalachians in 1862, Confederate generals performed brilliantly, and the Federal forces gained no decisive advantage. However, the Union poured more men into the struggle there, and the South had to strain to defend its capital. After the first battle of Bull Run, General George B. McClellan began to prepare the Union troops on the Potomac for a powerful offensive. A professional and veteran officer, he instilled discipline and developed the morale of the Union troops. After January, 1862, he and other Federal commanders received energetic support from the War Department, taken over from Cameron by Edwin M. Stanton, who sent forward men and supplies in large numbers. Many on the Union side hoped that McClellan would drive hard against Richmond. Lincoln even ordered the "Little Napoleon," as McClellan was known, to begin an offensive on February 22. But McClellan was not yet ready—it has been said by some military critics that he was never ready to act and that he was, indeed, better fitted to be an Inspector General than a field commander.

When McClellan did move, in March, he followed a plan which President Lincoln heartily disliked. Lincoln urged the General to push directly southward from the Potomac toward Richmond, which would make Washington safe and, at the same time, threaten the Confederate capital. Well aware of the several rivers which run from west to east across that part of Virginia between the two cities, aware too of the woods, swamps, and rough country within it, McClellan preferred the easier approach to Richmond from the east, by way of the peninsula between the James and York Rivers. McClellan was in the right, provided the Union had strength enough to defend Washington and at the same time to give him sufficient men to overcome Confederate resistance east of Richmond. His plan was afterwards successfully executed by Grant. However, in 1862 it was doubtful that the Federal armies could be divided into two parts, each strong

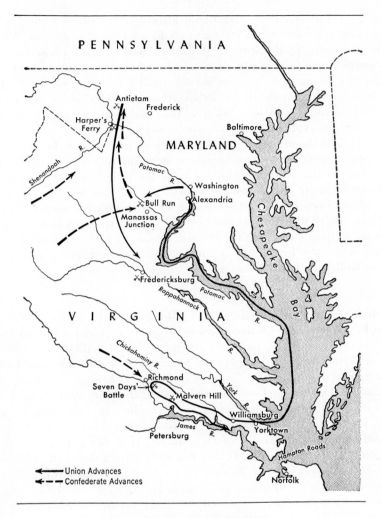

CAMPAIGNS IN THE EAST

enough for its task; if the Confederates advanced upon Washington while McClellan lay east of Richmond, it was doubtful that he could be of assistance. On the other hand, there can be no assurance that Lincoln's plan was better conceived. Perhaps Union success was impossible until such time as its armies enjoyed a clear superiority over their opponents in Virginia. As it was, Lincoln permitted McClellan to undertake his offensive from the Chesapeake, but insisted that a smaller army under General McDowell be stationed between Washington and the main Confederate army. The results were not very fortunate for the Union.

McClellan did not seize Richmond, although his advance guards took posts within five miles of the city, and could see it in the distance. Moving up the peninsula in the spring, McClellan was at first opposed by only small forces which he might have brushed aside. Exaggerating the strength of the Confederates who confronted him under General Joseph E. Johnston, he advanced slowly in the expectation that McDowell would move south to join him. He divided his army into two parts, one on the northern bank of the Chickahominy River, which was to establish a junction with McDowell, and the other on the south bank of that stream. McDowell did not appear; moreover, Johnston saw a splendid opportunity to strike a heavy blow at the Union troops south of the river, since reinforcements could not be easily sent across the Chickahominy. On May 31 he opened his attack at Seven Pines, and for a time seemed to have a major victory in his hands; but reinforcements reached the Union troops in time to relieve the pressure upon them, and the Confederate army had to fall back. Losses on both sides were heavy, and Johnston was wounded, being replaced by General Robert E. Lee.

SOUTHERN GENERALS: LEE AND JACKSON

With the coming into command of "Marse Robert," as Lee came to be known by his men, the Confederates in Virginia acquired a superb leader. In addition, "Stonewall" Jackson had emerged as a brilliant officer as the result of extraordinary exploits in the Shenandoah Valley. Lee and Jackson were a formidable pair. A professor at the Virginia Military Institute at the outbreak of the war, Jackson was iron-willed, intrepid, swift-moving, and fertile in stratagems. He has never been excelled in leadership of small armies; had he had the opportunity, he would also doubtless have made a splendid record as a director of large forces. It is beyond cavil that Lee managed the Army of Northern Virginia with remarkable skill. The son of "Light-Horse Harry" Lee of Revolutionary War fame, he was both a great professional soldier and a fine gentleman. His strategy and tactics on this or that occasion have been censured; William Tecumseh Sherman, a good judge of military men, believed that Lee sacrificed too much in order to defend Richmond, and many writers have found fault with Lee's management of his men at Gettysburg. He was not quite a Caesar or Napoleon, but his career as a commander in Virginia was studded with victories, and it is unlikely that any other man in his place could have done more. The trust which his officers and men had in him, and the devotion which they gave to him made the Army of Northern Virginia far more powerful than its numbers warranted. He became the great hero, and eventually the very personification of the Confederacy.

Lee was quickly able to take the offensive, thanks to Jackson, who had brought consternation to the Union forces with a startling display of generalship in the Shenandoah. While McClellan was slowly moving westward toward Richmond, Jackson, with only 18,000 men, dealt with more than double that number of Federal troops in the beautiful valley. He not only held back one army under Frémont in West Virginia, but won victory after victory over another led by General Nathaniel P. Banks, and finally drove it across the Potomac. Stanton was so alarmed for the safety of Washington that he sent out a hasty call for militia to defend it, and 20,000 troops were detached from McDowell's army to help stop Jackson. Jackson countered by taking some of his troops and rapidly joining Lee to help against McClellan. Enjoying a temporary numerical superiority, Lee strove to inflict a heavy blow upon McClellan. Confederate cavalry under the gallant James E. B. "Jeb" Stuart rode completely around the Union army. On June 26 Lee began a series of attacks which continued until July 1; in those Seven Days' Battles the Federal army was gradually forced back to a base at Malvern Hill on the James River. McClellan's men successfully withstood the last of the attacks. Unable to accomplish anything more, Lee withdrew toward Richmond. He had saved the Confederate capital, and his offensive persuaded the powers in Washington to move McClellan's army back to the Potomac. The cost, which the Confederacy could hardly afford, was heavy, about 22,000 casualties; McClellan's losses were about 16,000.

NORTHERN OFFICERS

Returning to the strategy of a southward advance from the Potomac, Lincoln and his advisers removed McClellan from command, replacing him with General John Pope. McClellan had not done too badly, but not nearly so well as the President had expected. Besides, he had treated Lincoln with disdain. Alas for Lincoln and the Union cause, Pope had far less ability than McClellan, and he soon encountered defeat. Before the Union army could be regrouped in northern Virginia, Lee and Jackson moved northward by way of the Shenandoah Valley. Jackson struck at Pope's flank and rear near Manassas Junction. Hitting back at that elusive commander, Pope was suddenly confronted by the entire Confederate Army and was driven away in the second Battle of Bull Run. Camped outside Washington, Pope was removed by Lincoln, who in desperation put McClellan back in command. To Lincoln the situation seemed almost desperate.

After the second Battle of Bull Run, Lee might cautiously have remained on the defensive, conserving his strength for future trials. Instead, he felt strong enough to undertake a major offensive, and moved northward. On September 15, Jackson captured Harper's Ferry and a Union garrison of 11,000 men. However, as Lee crossed the Potomac into Maryland, intending to isolate Washington from the west and perhaps also to take Harrisburg in Pennsylvania, McClellan gradually collected large forces to oppose him. Checked in some minor engagements, Lee with only 40,000 men was attacked by McClellan with 70,000 at Antietam on September 17. Lee managed to withstand the Federal assaults, each side losing almost 12,000 men. Had McClellan continued his attacks, Lee must have been in serious trouble, especially since the Potomac made retreat difficult for him. Mc-Clellan permitted Lee to retreat unmolested across the river and back to Virginia. Deeply disappointed by Lee's escape, Lincoln again changed generals, giving McClellan's command to General Ambrose E. Burnside. Burnside won greater fame by his sideburns than by his skill as a leader. Given a vast force of 113,000 men, he found nothing better to do with them than to make a frontal attack upon Lee's 75,000, in strong entrenchments at Fredericksburg. There on December 13 Lee's Confederates, posted on high hills, rather easily checked desperate charges by Burnside. The Army of the Potomac lost about 11,000 men and Lee only half so many. Sadly, Lincoln once more changed generals, raising to the high command in Virginia, General Joseph Hooker, who had a reputation for aggressiveness and who was known as "Fighting Joe." By that time winter had come, and Hooker did no fighting until the spring of 1863.

With the close of the campaign of 1862, the war entered upon a new phase. Hitherto, in order to conciliate supporters of the Union who were not hostile to slavery, Lincoln had carefully proclaimed the preservation of the Union to be his sole aim. On January 1, 1863, he issued his Emancipation Proclamation, declaring all slaves within the Confederate lines free. Thenceforward, the Union forces fought for two goals, the saving of a nation and the freedom of the black race in America.

30 THE WAR AT HOME AND ABROAD

For the majority of people on both sides, hardly any sacrifice was too great to win the Civil War, and both North and South freely spent money as well as blood in the vast contest. To a degree civil liberties were sacrificed, together with states' rights, for on neither side would the leaders suffer defeat because of individual and constitutional scruples. On neither side of the Mason-Dixon Line was opposition to the war entirely suppressed, because it was too powerful in both the South and the North. However, despite disunity at home, both the Union and the Confederacy were able to make prodigious war efforts. It has been suggested that the South ultimately lost because its people were unwilling to abandon all for their cause; yet the Southern people did indeed offer "the last full measure of devotion." And if there were hundreds of thousands of Northerners who were lukewarm or opposed to the Union cause, it should not be forgotten that the people as a whole gave extraordinarily in behalf of ideals many of

433

them considered to be almost holy. Many soldiers on both sides came to wonder why they were shooting at each other, but there was fervency, too, in the ranks of the Blue and the Gray, as well as passionate loyalty to the men at the front in Northern and Southern homes. Hence it was that veterans of the conflict were afterward venerated, and who will say that they deserved less?

MEN AND SUPPLIES

If there was on both sides a genuine willingness to fight, it is nevertheless true that both the South and the North had to resort to conscription to fill the ranks of their armies. The drafting of men on such a vast scale was unprecedented in America, forced military service in the past having been confined to colonies and states. In the first months men volunteered in such numbers that sometimes they could not be used immediately and other tens of thousands put on uniform of their own free will in the later years of the struggle. But the needs for men were immense, and the fallen, the wounded, and the captured had to be replaced. Also, it was recognized both in Richmond and in Washington that an attempt should be made to secure equality of sacrifice; further, the draft made it possible to estimate the number of men available in the future and enabled military planners to do their work more intelligently. Desertions—one man in ten in both the Union and Confederate armies departed from duty without permission— also stimulated conscription.

THE SOUTH AND THE DRAFT

First to draft men was the Confederacy. By an act of its Congress in April, 1862, it declared every white man between the ages of 18 and 35 subject to military service for three years. It required each of the Southern states to supply men in proportion to its population. The law was bitterly condemned in North Carolina, South Carolina, and Georgia on the ground that it infringed upon states' rights. Governor Joseph E. Brown of Georgia denounced it as a blow to liberty, and Governor Zebulon B. Vance of North Carolina reluctantly enforced it in his state. The law was also censured because it gave exemption to clergymen, teachers, newspaper editors, druggists, and owners and overseers controlling twenty or more slaves. That men rich enough to own twenty slaves were excused rankled among the poorer whites. It was officially claimed that the presence of such owners or their overseers was necessary to keep order among the slaves; the plain farmer, well aware that the war was being fought to defend slavery, was often inclined to find injustice in an act which exempted the slaveholders. The fact that the wealthy planters generally volunteered did not entirely remove his sense of injustice. Nor was the exemption of newspaper editors universally applauded below the Mason-Dixon Line. Moreover, the law permitted a conscript to send a substitute, an arrangement which was also condemned as favoritism for the rich, since the substitute normally had to be purchased.

A second conscription act passed by the Confederate Congress early in 1864 was not much more satisfactory; it also contained disliked exemptions for physicians, newspaper editors, clergymen, overseers of plantations worked by fifteen or more slaves, and state employees certified by a governor to be necessary for the management of public affairs. The law was widely defied, as governors and courts refused to enforce it. The Confederate Congress declared the writ of habeas corpus suspended to prevent legal action in behalf of unwilling conscripts, but in vain. By the fall of 1864 the law was a dead letter, the supply of men available for service was falling low indeed, and a clamor arose for calling Negroes to the colors. In March, 1865, President Davis was authorized to call upon the Southern states for 300,000 men, without respect to color. Only a few slaves became Confederate soldiers, for the war was then drawing mercilessly and mercifully to an end.

THE NORTH AND THE DRAFT

The draft was equally unpopular in the North, perhaps even more so. The first Union Conscription Act, passed in March, 1863, declared all men between the ages of 20 and 45 to be subject to military service. Again, however, there were complaints of discrimination, because a drafted man could be excused upon payment of $300 or procurement of a substitute. There were other inequitable exemptions on the basis of family obligations. Procurement of a substitute, which was permitted until the act was revised in February, 1864, was a particular cause of discontent. Under the law of 1863 the states were divided into districts, each of which was to supply a quota of men. It could be filled by volunteers as well as draftees, and in many districts the requirement was met by volunteers. Indeed, the great majority of the men who fought for the Union were volunteers. However, freedom from military service for a money payment, which men of wealth took advantage of with some frequency, was a scandal. Moreover, permitting substitutes had disturbing effects. Since anyone could be offered as a substitute, some men made a business of supplying them where needed, even procuring them in England and Ireland. Such substitutes received a bounty when accepted for service; many of them deserted, sold their services a second time, again deserted, and even repeated the process a dozen times. The "bounty-jumper" did not materially add to the strength of the armies, and it was well for the Union cause that it was not entirely dependent upon drafted men. During the years 1863 and 1864 about 835,000 men offered themselves to their country. The draft was peculiarly unpopular in New

York City, where the war was also unpopular. In July, 1863, anti-draft riots broke out in the city and continued for four days. Negroes were attacked and killed, and much property was destroyed, men, women, and boys participating in the orgy. The police were helpless, and thousands of Federal troops had to be sent into it to restore order. There were disturbances in other Northern cities. Drafting continued, and toward the end of the war the quality of the Union soldier tended to deteriorate, as did that of the men under Lee and Johnston. Even so, the Union derived an enormous advantage from conscription because it had more men. Its superiority in that respect actually increased during the war, since immigration from Europe to the Northern states was not stopped by the hostilities. Many newly arrived Irish and Germans gave their lives for the Union; so many fought for it that Confederates with some reason could refer to the "mercenary" and "foreign" Federal armies.

SUPPLYING THE ARMIES

How were the great numbers of men in the armies and navies fed, clothed, and supplied with weapons? Rather surprisingly, by turning from cotton-growing to the production of food, the Confederates, with the loyal help of their slaves, managed to produce enough grain and meat for their armed forces. Securing some military materials abroad, they were able to furnish enough clothing and weapons so that, as far as supplies were concerned, the Confederate forces could have gone on fighting indefinitely. The Southern armies also made good use of captured Federal supplies and equipment. After the spring of 1864, the soldiers in gray began to suffer seriously for lack of food and clothing, but the chief reason was the collapse of the Southern railroads, worn out by heavy use and cut to pieces by advancing Federal armies. It was much easier for the Union to care for its fighting men. The rich farm lands above the Mason-Dixon Line were tilled by men, women, and boys, who made greater use of labor-saving devices and who produced crops throughout the struggle. In fact, they grew so much wheat and corn that the Union was able to export large quantities to the British Isles and western Europe, which were troubled by poor harvests. Production was encouraged by the passage of the Homestead Act in May, 1862, in accordance with the Republican campaign promise two years earlier. This generous law offered to every adult male who was the head of a family, whether a citizen or an alien who had announced his intention to become one, 160 acres of land upon payment of a registration fee, and residence upon the land for five years. Such a homestead could also be secured on the basis of residence for six months and payment of $1.25 an acre. Thousands took early advantage of the Act, and Northern farms spread westward across the Missouri River. Northern factories poured forth clothing, weapons, blankets, tents, and ammunition. There were very few strikes in Northern industry, the owners of which often prospered by executing government contracts.

THE COST OF WAR

How to finance the war effort was a problem to both sides, but a far more difficult one for the Confederacy than it was for the Union. Perhaps the government at Richmond did not attack the problem with sufficient energy. The Confederate Congress did not levy taxes until 1863, at that time imposing a 10 percent levy upon Southern property to be paid "in kind." Instead of taxing, which would have been disagreeable and possibly unproductive of either large sums of money or vast quantities of goods, Jefferson Davis and the Confederate Congress relied principally upon loans and the printing of paper currency. The Southern people gladly lent more than $100,000,000; even greater loans could have been secured had the South possessed a strong banking system. About $15,000,000 in loans was obtained from Confederate sympathizers in England and France at the height of the war. The printing of paper money, which began as early as March, 1861, added largely to the Confederate treasury, although its depreciation, which soon set in, also created confusion. Not made legal tender, the Confederate notes were issued in ever greater quantity, until they reached a paper value of more than $1,000,000,000. Despite the eagerness of the Southern government and its zealous supporters to maintain this money at par, its value soon began to wane and continued to decrease as the chances of Confederate success diminished. By 1863 the Confederate dollar was worth only one-third of the Federal one; before Lee's surrender at Appomattox one Union dollar could be exchanged for fifty Confederate dollars. Prudent people in the Confederacy hoarded "Yankee" money during the war, for it was not likely to lose value entirely.

The federal government, with far greater wealth to tap, found the means to carry on the conflict without excessive suffering. The Lincoln government secured large sums by taxation, although it also resorted to borrowing and the issuance of paper money. Beginning with the Morrill Tariff of March, 1861, the federal government steadily raised rates on imported goods, thus securing money, carrying out a Republican campaign pledge of 1860, and offering protection to Northern industry. The Union Congress, for the first time, in August, 1861, imposed an income tax which required the payment of 3 percent upon incomes above $800 per annum. Later the tax was increased, and with other internal levies it supplied nearly one-quarter of the Federal expenses during the war. However, the bulk of them was borne by receipts from loans and the emission of paper money, the famous "greenbacks." Creating the National Banking System in 1863, the Union government sold vast quantities of bonds to its member banks, permitting them to issue national banking notes up to 90 percent of the value of the bonds which they held. Thus a double purpose was served, the sale of the bonds, and the issue of a much-needed stable paper money. Reforming the national currency under the pressure of war in 1865, Congress also destroyed state bank notes by imposing a tax of 10 percent upon them. On the other hand, beginning in 1862, it put forth an ever increasing stream of greenbacks, which were legal tender but not supported by precious metal or bonds. About $450,000,000 in greenback money was issued; its value fluctuated during and after the war, but it served its purpose and had a happier fate than the Confederate currency. The national debt rose during the war to nearly $3,000,000,000, but the Union was not threatened with bankruptcy. There was no Confederate debt at the end of the war; had there been one, it could have been paid off only with extreme difficulty.

The suffering caused by the struggle was immense, and it was not confined to the front lines. The tragic toll of casualties brought mourning everywhere. The hundreds of thousands of graves of the dead, about 350,000 of Union men, and perhaps 250,000 of Confederate, studded the American landscape. Hastily set up hospitals were crowded with the wounded and the sick, and tens of thousands of soldiers who survived the war lived on crippled and maimed. The wounded often died from lack of sanitation and medical knowledge, and with them the sick. Volunteer nurses such as Clara Barton and the poet Walt Whitman toiled endlessly to lessen the suffering, and military officers strove to secure better care, although their efforts were partly in vain. The day of penicillin, and even of surgical cleanliness, was still far in the future. Far worse than the hospitals were the prison camps, both in the North and in the South, in which thousands of men pined and died. Under the best of circumstances, the captured soldier suffered in confinement, and those who guarded him were not always gentle. Prisoners who tried to escape were likely to be very closely confined. After the war Confederate soldiers would tell of indignities and horrors they underwent in Federal prisons; even more dreadful histories were related by Union men who were freed at the close of the conflict. Inevitably, the captive in Confederate hands fared somewhat worse than the Southerner captured by the Union, because the South often did not have generous supplies of food and clothing, even for its own troops. The sufferings of Federal prisoners in the camp at Andersonville, Georgia, were so great that supporters of the Union became convinced that they were inflicted deliberately. Nearly 13,000 men died there. The actual explanation of the tragedy was ignorance, incompetence, and poverty, but convinced that the prisoners had been intentionally starved and otherwise cruelly treated, Union officials demanded vengeance after the war. In consequence, the commandant of the camp, Captain Henry Wirz, was accused of conspiring to murder the prisoners in his care, was found guilty by a military court, and was hanged. Trials of the vanquished by the victors are not coolly conducted.

THE HOME FRONT

Civilians also felt the hardships of war, for only too many families had lost a father or a son. In addition, those who lived in the arenas of battle could lose crops, cattle, and home. Only a small part of the Confederacy east of the Mississippi escaped the ravages of warfare, and much destruction was done in Arkansas and Louisiana. Heavy damage was also inflicted upon civilians in the Border States that remained in the Union. The southern parts of Indiana and Ohio felt the raids of General John Morgan and the Confederate cavalry; while "Jeb" Stuart's horsemen swept through that part of Pennsylvania around Gettysburg. To most of the South the war brought poverty, even in areas not traversed by soldiers. Nor did the Northerners who were removed from the scenes of fighting prosper uniformly, for inflation took its toll everywhere. During the war prices in the Northern states more than doubled, but wages increased less than half as much. Many Northerners were as poor at the end of the conflict as they were at its beginning; in the Confederacy few amassed any wealth.

DISSENSION BEHIND THE LINES

Neither Lincoln nor Jefferson Davis could do much toward alleviating the misery of a war that could not be ended by compromise; nor were Federal and Confederate lawmakers able to do more than try to secure some measure of equality in sacrifice, even that being often beyond reach. As the fighting went on and on, unhappiness and dissension increased in both the North and the South. The anti-Confederate sentiment so widespread in the hills of the southern Appalachians at the beginning of the war did not diminish with the passage of time, and may have increased. In the hill country and on both sides of it secret societies gradually appeared which called for peace and sometimes rendered assistance to the Union armies. In the hills, indeed, men openly fought for the Union cause. If the people of the southern lowlands generally remained loyal to the Confederacy until the very end, they too felt war weariness. Davis was condemned and reviled, branded as incompetent, and in the same breath denounced as a dictator. Lincoln was similarly abused, being described as a combination of buffoon and baboon. Davis was made to appear to be a cold-hearted aristocrat, Lincoln as a coarse and ignorant backwoodsman. Davis was more fortunate than Lincoln in that he was not compelled to deal with any opposing political party; he was attacked only by individuals and factions. In the North, too, there were secret societies, such as the Knights of the Golden Circle, which sought to bring the war to a swift end, and which offered aid and comfort to the enemy. Made up of people who had opposed the war from its inception and of others who lost the will to fight as it continued, these societies secured tens of thousands of members and threatened internal revolt by 1863, especially in Ohio, Indiana, and Illinois. Moreover, even among the stoutest supporters of the Union, Lincoln was blamed for defeat and denied credit for victory, since such great sacrifices over so long a time brought such seemingly small results. He was blamed by the zealous for war profiteers, of whom there were many, and for the men of means (sometimes the same as the profiteers) who managed to evade military service.

Distressing to the gentle and merciful Lincoln was the charge that he dictatorially violated the Constitution. Trying to do all that might decently be done to crush Confederate resistance, he made ample use of the armed forces as their commander in chief, freely employing executive authority in civil matters. Both he and the federal Congress, which also displayed determination to win the war, stretched their powers under the Constitution in unprecedented fashion. Both were accused of gross violations of that basic document, especially by Northern Confederate sympathizers and others who opposed the continuance of the war, and by men devoted to the preservation of civil rights. Lincoln was more bitterly attacked than the Congress, being assailed as a would-be dictator. In the spring of 1861 he enlarged the regular army without approval by Congress; later he suspended the writ of habeas corpus, which he hardly had the authority to do, in order to deal more effectively with men who endangered the war effort; he permitted the Army to arrest persons suspected of disloyalty and to try them in military courts when civil ones were open, and to punish them; and he insisted that Northern newspapers refrain from what he considered treasonable and seditious publication. He was accordingly denounced for interference with freedom of speech and press, for arbitrary imprisonment, and for the establishment of military rule. Both he and the Congress were vehemently attacked on the ground that conscription was not authorized by the Constitution, although their authority to wage war quite clearly sanctioned forced service. Admitted that Lincoln occasionally exceeded his constitutional powers, but it must be remembered that he often had provocation, and that he might have dealt far more harshly than he did with friends of the Confederacy behind the Union lines. Thus there was an uproar when Clement L. Vallandingham, a prominent Democratic politician in Ohio, was arrested, tried by a military court in Cincinnati, and sentenced to imprisonment for the duration of the war for uttering disloyal sentiments. Vallandingham had publicly and very forcefully urged that the Union make peace with the Confederacy. Somewhat amused as well as irritated by the great concern for

Vallandigham's rights, Lincoln arranged to export him to the Confederacy, where the President fancied he would be at home. When Vallandigham later returned to Ohio by way of Canada, he was not further molested. Lincoln considered his treatment of the "Copperheads" —Northerners who gave direct or indirect support to the Confederacy— to be lenient, pointing out that a Union soldier who gave heed to their propaganda and deserted was subject to execution. In any event, Lincoln acted upon the principle that the preservation of the Union was more important than relatively minor and temporary breaches of the Constitution. Jefferson had once announced the same doctrine. There must be great concern for the protection of personal rights and the maintenance of law in national emergencies; on the other hand, it will be conceded that a Constitution without a country is of limited value.

NORTHERN POLITICS, 1864

Lincoln was also plagued by bitter party warfare until the election of 1864. As the war went on, political allegiances changed, but Lincoln was still an object of savage partisan attack, and his reelection in 1864 was doubtful almost to the last days of the campaign. Once the war had begun, the Republicans quite readily committed themselves to its vigorous prosecution, but the Northern Democrats and other opposition groups could not so easily agree upon a stand with respect to the conflict. Some who were devoted to the Union moved into the Republican party, especially in the Border States. However, most Northern Democrats remained in their party, and offered a vigorous if not always loyal opposition. Unfortunately for the Union, Stephen Douglas, who had never wavered in his allegiance and who showed his loyalty by appearing on the platform at Lincoln's first inauguration, died not long afterward. There was no one among his followers who could immediately replace him, and his party divided into two wings, united only by a common political history and antipathy toward the Republicans. The majority of the Northern Democrats supported the war effort, and were known indeed as "War Democrats." However, others in the party were eager for peace at almost any price, and some found no great fault in the Confederacy. Standing both for the war effort and against it, the Democrats did very well in the off-year elections of 1862, winning 75 seats in the House of Representatives and the governorships of some important states, including New York. Retaining control of the Congress by no great margin, Lincoln and his followers were again seriously challenged two years later. The Republicans and their allies then formed a National Union Party, nominating Republican Lincoln for the Presidency, and Democrat Andrew Johnson of Tennessee for the Vice-Presidency. The Democrats named General George McClellan and George

H. Pendleton of Ohio. They called for both peace and the preservation of the Union, goals which were hardly reconcilable but had a powerful appeal. McClellan had no love for Lincoln; he personally was for continuing the war until the Confederacy should be crushed; and he wanted the Presidency. He accepted the leadership of the Democratic party, but repudiated its platform. His chances for attaining his ambition seemed good in the late summer and autumn, when the North was war-weary, and when there existed a dearth of military victories for the Union arms. But before the ballots were cast a Federal army under General William Tecumseh Sherman captured Atlanta and General Philip H. Sheridan finally drove the Confederate forces from the valley of the Shenandoah. Lincoln won an easy victory in the electoral college, 221 votes to 12, although his majority in the popular vote was only 400,000 in a total of 4,000,000. With him was elected a Republican Congress, and thereafter there was no chance of negotiating peace with the Confederacy.

The Democrats were not responsible for all of Lincoln's political troubles in wartime. More moderate than many of his fellow Republicans in 1860, Lincoln was cautious and conservative in the Presidency, sometimes almost overwhelmed by his cares. Trying to mobilize discordant elements, he sought to avoid extreme measures which would deprive the Union of any of its much needed adherents. In particular, he refused for many months to take any decisive step against slavery, to avoid offending the many friends of the Union in the Border States who owned slaves and felt no hostility to the institution. He thereby brought upon himself the condemnation of the abolitionists. Nor would Lincoln consent to waging a ruthless war, as passionate men in his party demanded. He himself was perhaps as much Southern as he was Northern, having been born only a few miles from the birthplace of Jefferson Davis; close relatives of Mrs. Lincoln served in the Confederate Army, and the President felt no hate for Southerners.

A Radical Republican faction which demanded swift and decisive movement, both against slavery and the Confederacy, developed early in the war and helped to make Lincoln's days and nights miserable. The Radicals were potent in Congress; forming a joint committee on the conduct of the war before the end of 1861, they used it as a vehicle to harass the President. Through it they hoped to manage the war; they failed to achieve that purpose, but Lincoln was not assuredly the master of his party until the Confederacy began to totter. The Radicals even tried to force the President to dismiss William Seward from the State Department, despite Lincoln's obvious faith in him. They also clamored for the demotion and discharge of Army officers who were not hostile to slavery. Conversely, they pushed for the promotion of officers whose chief merits were political rather than martial. They carried on intrigues with Salmon P. Chase, the Secretary of the Treasury, who believed that one term was enough for Lincoln and that his successor ought to be a certain well qualified Cabinet member. After Lincoln's second nomination in 1864 some of the Radicals even planned to organize a third party; they did not do so only because they realized they could not get enough popular support to secure control of the Presidency. As the war drew to its end, they made it clear that they were disposed to deal harshly with the defeated Confederates. Again Lincoln felt otherwise.

THE EMANCIPATION PROCLAMATION

Though Lincoln is commonly known as the "Great Emancipator," his views on slavery and the Negro differed from those of the Radicals, many of whom believed that slavery must be eradicated as soon as possible and that the Negroes should promptly be given all the rights of citizens, with the suffrage. Nevertheless, he sanctioned measure after measure against slavery, and when he considered the time to be ripe he issued his extraordinary Emancipation Proclamation. Early in the war he had to restrain generals of the Radical persuasion who exceeded their authority and struck against the institution. In May, 1861, General Benjamin F. Butler at Fortress Monroe, Virginia, declared that slaves who fled into his lines were "contraband of war" and that they would not be sent back to their owners. In August of that year General John C. Frémont proclaimed that the slaves of Missourians in arms against the Union were free; and in May, 1862, General David Hunter announced the end of Negro servitude in his department, which included the coasts of South Carolina, Georgia, and Florida. Lincoln felt compelled to modify the orders of Frémont and Hunter on the ground that they had moved precipitously, even illegally. However, the President and Congress did not fail to act against the institution. In August, 1861, a confiscation law was passed which declared that slaves fighting for the Confederacy or laboring in support of its military effort were free. In the summer of 1862 a second confiscation law proclaimed the liberation of all slaves belonging to persons who committed treason or actively supported the Confederacy. Even earlier, in June, 1862, ignoring the Dred Scott decision, Congress had abolished Negro servitude in the territories of the United States. Moreover, Lincoln moved against slavery in the District of Columbia and the Border States as soon as action could be taken without sapping the strength of the Union. For the Federal District and for the Border States, he favored emancipation with payment to the owners for their property. In April, 1862, Congress provided for emancipation with compensation in the District of Columbia, and thereafter the President urged the governors and legislators of the Border States to take similar action, promising Federal assistance. In December, 1862, he asked Congress to propose a Constitutional amendment which would provide for freeing the slaves in the Border country with payment of the owners, but that body failed to respond. Nor did the executives or legislators of the area move decisively, and its slaves remained in servitude until the close of the war.

Tenderness for the feelings of men who supported the Union but who opposed drastic measures against slavery long kept Lincoln from hitting hard at the institution. However, as the Union grip upon the Border States became firmer, it became safer for Lincoln to strike at it. In fact, it became increasingly apparent to the President as 1862 wore on, that a major attack upon slavery would strengthen rather than injure the cause of the Union. There was then a well-founded fear in Washington that England and France would intervene on behalf of the Confederacy. But if the Union made it clear that it was devoted not only to the preservation of the United States but to the destruction of slavery, humanitarian sentiment in England would make it difficult for the English government to give open support to the Confederacy. Since France would not move without England, a major attack upon slavery might prevent hostile behavior on the part of both.

By July, 1862, Lincoln had decided to issue the Emancipation Proclamation, but it seemed wise to him to defer it, for the Confederacy was then militarily prosperous and he wished to avoid the charge that the Proclamation was a measure of desperation. After the Battle of Antietam, and after Lee had been checked, though hardly defeated, the President announced that the Proclamation would be issued on January 1, 1863. It declared that all slaves in Southern regions still held by the Confederate armies were "thenceforward, and forever free." It has often been pointed out that the document set free no slaves immediately, since those behind the Union armies were specifically exempted. Also, it is readily apparent that the measure differed in no important way from the second confiscation act. The Proclamation was even of doubtful constitutionality, since it could be defended only on the basis that it was a proper exercise of the power of the President as commander in chief. But the importance of the Proclamation did not lie in the number of slaves it freed or did not free. It served as a notice to America and the rest of the world that the Union was embarked upon a crusade against slavery. The Federal cause acquired a new moral dignity, for it thereafter embraced not only suppression of the Confederacy, but also struggle in behalf of the rights of mankind. Nor should it be forgotten that the slaves behind the Confederate entrenchments acquired freedom, in fact if not in law, as the Union armies penetrated ever more deeply into the South. Their status and that of slaves everywhere was placed beyond serious question by the enactment of the Thirteenth Amendment to the Constitution in 1865, which forbade both slavery and involuntary servitude.

THE WAR AND EUROPE

The leaders of the Confederacy hoped for intervention by England and France until the war was well advanced, and Lincoln and his advisers were long menaced by it. The Emperor Napoleon III favored the Confederacy from the beginning of the conflict, and was disposed to act energetically in its behalf if Britain would do likewise. He did not dare to move alone. Important in determining his attitude was his spectacular attempt to establish a French-dominated empire in Mexico with the unfortunate Archduke Maximilian of Austria upon its throne. That astonishing adventure unquestionably defied the Monroe Doctrine, and it was denounced again and again by Lincoln and Secretary of State Seward. It was obvious that, if the Confederacy disappeared, the United States would insist upon the departure of the French troops who maintained Maximilian's regime. His empire could not be defended against attack by a united America. Accordingly, although many Frenchmen favored the Union, Napoleon was quite willing to intervene, at least until he became gravely concerned because of European troubles, including the rise of Prussian power in central Europe and the spectre of a united Germany on France's northeastern boundary.

Intervention by England was by no means an impossibility, for the men in power in London both disliked the American Republic and liked the Confederacy. They were Whigs, led by Lord Palmerston, Earl Russell, and other aristocrats who had never felt affection for American democracy. They wished to see it fail, all the more because they were faced at home by an insistent demand for extension of the suffrage, at least to the English lower middle class. It would be easier to refuse that demand if it could be shown that government of the people had dismally failed in America. On the other hand, the Southern aristocrats were congenial to Palmerston and Russell. Besides, even in 1861, it seemed likely that a united America would eventually become more important than England; were the United States divided into two parts, there would be no nation in the New World to challenge English superiority. There were also economic reasons why the Confederacy quickly acquired friends in London. Independent, the South would certainly for many years refrain from imposing heavy duties upon English manufactured goods, and would indeed welcome their importation. It could reasonably be hoped that the Southerners would prefer to buy finished products from the English rather than the Yankees, for they could pay for those products by selling their cotton in England.

These various considerations convinced many Southerners that English aid was likely, even that England would surely act in their behalf. It was even believed that England could be forced to intervene, that her need for cotton would compel it. "Cotton is king," they proclaimed. The manufacture of cotton textiles was of the first economic importance in England, perhaps one Englishman in every five depending on it, directly or indirectly, for his living. Assuming that England must have cotton in order to avoid economic disaster, that the fluffy stuff could be supplied with regularity and in sufficient quantity only by the Confederacy, the worshipers of "King Cotton" were positive of English aid. As it turned out, although England's entrance into the war remained a possibility for more than two years, Southern cotton was not a decisive force. In the first place, the English, a perverse people, were not quite so influenced by economic interests as had been expected; even the workers in the cotton factories would not demand that British policy be based upon the preservation of their jobs. And the English machines did not long stand idle because of a lack of the "white weed." In 1861 there was actually in England a glut of textile goods, the market for them having been well filled; the Southern bumper crop of 1860 was available when the machines were again set in motion, and when more was needed it was obtained in some quantity from Egypt and India. The cotton raised in the South after the beginning of the war was not essential to England.

There were other forces and considerations which worked against a pro-Confederate British policy. Among the poorer Englishmen, including the factory hands, there was much good will for the American Republic, indeed hope that England would be remolded politically and socially in accordance with American principles of equality. English radicals such as Richard Cobden and John Bright were vigorous champions of the North. A conflict with the Union would have been by no means universally popular; and, aware that any decisive action in favor of the Confederacy must bring war with the Union, the English leaders had to consider the grave consequences that might follow. Had the British government recognized the independence of the South, the Union would surely have declared war upon England. The entrance of England into the conflict in its early stages would doubtless have assured the success of the Confederate nation. It would also have brought the destruction by Federal cruisers of the British merchant marine that was flourishing while Confederate cruisers were sweeping Union shipping from the seas. It was also likely that war would lead to a successful Union invasion of Canada. The fundamental decision which the English government had to make was by no means an easy one.

THE TRENT AFFAIR

The chance that England might interfere lasted until 1863. Although reason dictated to authorities in Washington and in London that they should move cautiously, it long remained possible that a hasty act in one city or the other would precipitate hostilities. Even the recognition by England of the Confederacy as a belligerent, which it undoubtedly was, aroused bitterness in the North. A crisis arose before the end of 1861 because of the imprudence of Charles Wilkes, captain of the Union sloop *San Jacinto.* Wilkes learned that James M. Mason and John Slidell, who had been appointed as commissioners by the Confederate government to seek help and recognition in Europe, had reached Havana and were sailing from Havana for England on board the *Trent,* a British steamer. Slidell's talents as a diplomat were highly respected, and Wilkes was eager to prevent him from reaching London. Without sufficient thought for the consequences, he stopped the *Trent* with gunfire, boarded her, and carried off the Confederate emissaries in definite violation of international law. He had exceeded even the aggressiveness of the British in dealing with American ships and crews during the wars of the French Revolution and against Napoleon. But, bringing Mason and Slidell home, he was received as a hero, was promoted, and was given an official vote of thanks by the House of Representatives. In London his behavior was bitterly condemned, and the British Foreign Secretary, Earl Russell, sent a message which demanded the release of the two men and an apology to Britain. He told the British minister in Washington to wait seven days for a satisfactory reply; if one was not forthcoming, he was to return home immediately. Only the intervention of Prince Albert, husband of Queen Victoria, prevented even more drastic action in London. Confronted by Russell's demand, Lincoln and Seward chose to comply, despite clamor about them to dare the British to do their worst. Prudence dictated that the British should not be unnecessarily offended, and both the President and the Secretary of State were well aware that Wilkes' action was not readily defensible. Announcing that Mason and Slidell would be released, Seward slyly declared his pleasure that Britain had finally agreed with the United States that there were legal limits to seizures upon the high seas.

MEDIATION AND AID TO THE CONFEDERACY

In the fall of 1862 Lords Palmerston and Russell for a time considered a step which must have brought on a second crisis. On the assumption that Union arms were failing, they considered mediation and an attempt to persuade the federal government that it could not conquer the Confederacy and that it ought to recognize the independence of the South. William Ewart Gladstone, after Palmerston and Russell the most important man in the British Cabinet, agreed with them. An attempt at mediation would quite certainly have led to a declaration of war from Washington; it is questionable whether Palmerston and Russell were aware of the danger. Learning of the setback which Lee had sustained at Antietam, they decided not to offer their services, at least for the time being. When Napoleon III did formally offer to mediate early in 1864, he was peremptorily informed that such intervention on his part would be looked upon by the United States as a hostile act, that is, that it would be followed by a declaration of war.

The news of the Emancipation Proclamation had an impressive effect upon British opinion, and made Palmerston and Russell more careful. It still remained possible, however, that Britain would blunder into war without desiring it because of the activities of her shipbuilders. Clever Confederate agents had made arrangements by which the cruisers *Florida*, *Shenandoah*, and *Alabama* were built in British shipyards. Ostensibly constructed to carry merchandise, these were actually intended to be war vessels. After leaving the yards, they were taken over by Confederate crews and fitted with cannon; such cruisers destroyed more than 250 American merchant craft during the war. Charles Francis Adams, Lincoln's minister in London, protested again and again against the activities of the shipbuilders, insisting that the British government, by permitting them to continue, was committing an unneutral act. The British Cabinet was slow to move, partly because it had no desire to help the Union, and partly because it was difficult to prove legally that the ships were intended to be war vessels. Despite convincing evidence offered by Adams that the *Alabama* was built for military use, British officials negligently permitted her to go to sea. As American merchant vessels sank beneath the waves, Adams began to present bills for damage to Her Majesty's Government, and anti-British feeling rose so high in the North that the Federal Congress authorized the building of privateers, which could be used only to attack British maritime commerce. Alarmed, at last the British Cabinet did act. In April, 1863, it seized the *Alexandra*, which was being built to serve as another *Alabama*. The British government was unable to prove that the *Alexandra* was legally a Confederate ship, and its owners sued and obtained damages for illegal seizure of private property.

Rendered cautious by this discomfiting setback, the British Cabinet was reluctant to move when the Laird firm at Birkenhead began to build two "rams" for the Confederacy. These were ironclad steamers armed with a sharp metal bow to cut through enemy craft, and were to be armed with nine-inch guns. It was believed by many, including Adams, that these ships were a formidable menace. It has even been suggested that they might have broken the blockade of the Confederacy and so perhaps have insured independence for the South. Had they reached the sea, had they been supplied with crews and guns, and had they reached the American coast, they might indeed have achieved something, though it was hardly likely that they could have disposed of the entire Union Navy. Since they could hardly have crossed the Atlantic before the end of 1863, it is most unlikely that they could have saved the Confederacy, already staggering under Union attack. Believing that the rams posed a great danger, Adams insisted that the British government prevent them from taking to sea. Although everyone knew the purpose for which the rams were being built, the Confederate agents created difficulties for British officials by preparing papers showing that the ships were being constructed not for the South, but for France. Next they let it be known that the ruler of Egypt would receive them. Still later they sold them to a French company with the understanding that they would be turned over to Confederates at the appropriate time. Again Lord Russell was confronted with a legal problem, and again he moved slowly. At last, losing patience, Adams sent him a most solemn letter of warning on September 5, 1863. Assuming that the British government had decided not to do anything about the ships, and that they would be permitted to depart, he wrote to Russell: "It would be superfluous in me to point out to your Lordship that this is war." As it turned out, the minister's warning was quite unnecessary; two days earlier Russell had given orders to keep the ships in port. So the crisis of the Laird rams passed. In the following year, Napoleon III let the Confederates build a ram at a French port, but it arrived in America as the war was drawing to its close, and it accomplished nothing.

No European government except that of Tsarist Russia displayed friendship toward the Union during the Civil War, and Russia evinced sympathy for the Union only because she was on bad terms with Britain and France in 1863 and 1864. Russian naval craft were sent to America so that they might attack British shipping in the event that the Tsarist Empire and Britain fell to blows, but their presence gave the Unionists encouragement. They bitterly resented the hostility manifested toward them by Britain and France. The time soon came when Napoleon III could be called to a reckoning, and he was humiliatingly forced to withdraw his troops from Mexico. Nothing of that sort occurred with respect to England. The tide of English sentiment turned steadily toward the Union because of the appeal to the English conscience of the crusade against slavery. When the news of the assassination of Lincoln reached London there was an outpouring of sorrow. Thereafter relations between England and America would more than once be tense, but mutual respect and good sense triumphed over the memory of old wrongs and new jealousies.

31 THE FALL OF THE CONFEDERACY

In the spring of 1863, the Union armies, becoming ever more powerful, drove deep into the Confederacy west of the Appalachians and could not be forced back; on the eastern front the Army of the Potomac underwent another humiliating defeat at Chancellorsville, but held off the attack of Lee at Gettysburg in July. The same year which saw the end of the Confederacy's hopes for foreign intervention also brought the turning of the military tide against it. The troops in gray struggled desperately to fend off the assaults of the advancing Federals through 1864, but without ultimate success. It was apparent by the beginning of 1865 that the weeks of the Confederacy were numbered, and that it would not long endure after weather permitted the Federals to move forward once more. Its death agonies began at Appomattox on April 9 and ended before the close of May. As it crumbled, Lincoln was murdered, and the task of restoring and rebuilding fell to feebler and less subtle hands. The tragedy of the

American people ended with its principal actor newly dead and buried at Springfield, where he had spent his happiest years.

WAR IN THE WEST, 1863

The name of Ulysses S. Grant is writ large upon the history of Union triumphs during the last two years of the Civil War. A failure as a civilian, the convivial general had done well but not brilliantly in the first campaigns of the conflict. There would never be anything Napoleonic about him, except briefly at Vicksburg, where he shone as a master of the art of warfare. His performance there was not repeated, but the steady com-

THE UNION TAKES THE MISSISSIPPI

petence he brought into the Union high command would finally suffice to bring decisive victory to the Army of the Potomac. He was confronted by a difficult problem on the Mississippi in the early weeks of 1863. On the heights of Vicksburg was an army under General John C. Pemberton under orders from Jefferson Davis to defend the city, which with Port Hudson down the river prevented free Union use of the Mississippi. Strongly fortified and protected on both the north and the east by swamps, Vicksburg seemed able to withstand major attacks, and there were Confederate forces gathering at Jackson which could be expected to attempt to come to Pemberton's aid. After initial failures, Grant found a remarkable way to reduce the city. Toward the end of March he left his supply base at Memphis, crossed over to the west bank of the Mississippi and moved below Vicksburg. Meanwhile, a Union river squadron ran past the city's batteries overlooking the river and joined him. Then Grant recrossed the river to its eastern bank, marching eastward and northward. In May he won a series of battles, driving Pemberton with 30,000 men back behind the lines into Vicksburg, while at the same time pushing General Joseph E. Johnston back to Jackson and beyond. Then, having Johnston out of the way, he tried to storm Vicksburg; failing twice, he brought up more and more troops and besieged the city, bombarding it for six weeks. Pemberton's supplies became ever more scanty, and knowing that no help would come, the Confederate general surrendered his army on July 4. Four days later Port Hudson also fell before Union arms. The Confederacy had suffered a stunning blow. Thereafter, the Mississippi was completely controlled by the Union. What was perhaps even more serious to the Confederacy was that it had lost 40,000 men, while Grant's casualties were only one-quarter as large.

WAR IN THE EAST, 1863

Without a Grant to lead it, the Army of the Potomac in 1863 encountered disastrous defeat and won a great victory. Toward the end of April "Fighting Joe" Hooker moved southward across the Rappahannock River with 130,000 men, a formidable and veteran army. He was given all the fighting that he could take by Lee with forces only half so large. Choosing not to wait for a Federal attack, Lee sent Stonewall Jackson marching to the westward to attack Hooker's right wing and rear. As usual, Jackson carried out his assignment with efficiency and celerity. On May 2 at Chancellorsville he opened an attack which caught Hooker unprepared, while Lee began to push forward against the Union front. The Federal right wing fell back in confusion, and only a determined stand by General Alfred Pleasanton deprived Lee of a major triumph. As it was, Hooker felt it to be necessary to withdraw toward Washington. The Federal and Confederate losses were about equal, each side sustaining about 11,000 casualties. However, the figures are deceptive, for Stonewall Jackson was one of the Confederates listed among the dead, wounded, and captured. While reconnoitering he had been accidentally shot by his own men; he was mortally wounded and died a few days after the battle. Lee had lost his good left arm, and it may well be that the military balance sheet of Chancellorsville was ultimately in favor of the Union. There was only one Stonewall Jackson in the Confederate forces; he could not be replaced.

Had Jackson lived on, it cannot be said that the outcome of the war would have been different, for despite its defeats, the Army of the Potomac became stronger rather than weaker with the passage of time. Its power was soon demonstrated, when Lee determined to take the offensive. The Confederate general a second time moved northward by way of the Shenan-

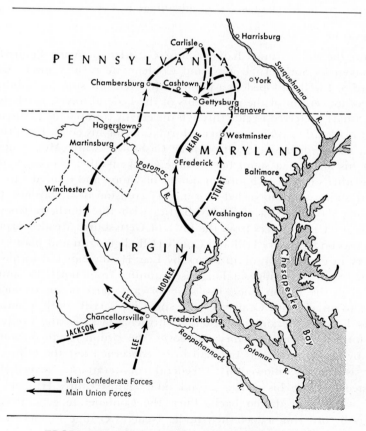

FROM CHANCELLORSVILLE TO GETTYSBURG

doah, Maryland, and then into southern Pennsylvania to bring the war home to the North. Had fortune favored him, he might have captured Harrisburg or approached Washington from the west. But the chances for a truly effective thrust were actually not good. Hooker proposed to take advantage of the fact that Lee had left Richmond exposed and to send an army against it. However, Lincoln and his advisers did not think that Washington was a suitable exchange for Richmond, and Hooker was ordered to deal with Lee. He moved northward rapidly, keeping his army between Lee and Washington. Now the strength of the Union began to appear. Lincoln called for 100,000 volunteers for six months service, and the call was heeded. It turned out that their help was not needed, for Hooker had enough men to hold off the Southern general, or even to crush him. But "Fighting Joe" did not fight; after a quarrel with General Henry Halleck, commander in chief of all the Union armies, he resigned his commission and was replaced by General George Gordon Meade. It does not appear that the change was of advantage to Lee.

GETTYSBURG

Before the end of June Chambersburg, Carlisle, and York, Pennsylvania, were taken by Southern troops, and Confederate cavalry under General Richard S. Ewell galloped to a point within ten miles of Harrisburg. But Lee was not certain of the movements of the Federal forces, partly because "Jeb" Stuart preferred to ride through the enemy countryside to disrupt the Union rear, rather than to gather information for his chief. Lee prudently took a strong defensive position near Cashtown, while Meade began to gather his men for a stand before Pipe Creek; neither was eager to fight on the other's terms. A chance encounter of Union and Confederate troops at Gettysburg on June 30 led to a mighty collision of the armies. On the following day began a three-day battle, with the Southern troops first driving the Union forces from the town of Gettysburg. Meade's army then took posts on Cemetery Hill and Culp's Hill, digging in and planting their artillery in expectation of an attack by Lee. He did not fail to move. Occupying Seminary Ridge, a long rise running from north to south and parallel to the Union lines, Lee sent forward parts of his command on July 2 to attack both Cemetery Hill and Culp's Hill. Both assaults were repulsed, and it became evident that further attacks by the Confederates were unlikely to bring victory; moreover, the Union troops outnumbered Lee's by 15,000 men, and Lee had to be concerned lest the failure of another assault be followed by a Federal counterattack. Nevertheless, he persisted, sending his men a second time against Culp's Hill on July 3. They were again driven back. Then the Confederate general gambled heavily by ordering 15,000 men under General George E. Pickett against the Union center in the afternoon of the same day. As the brave South-

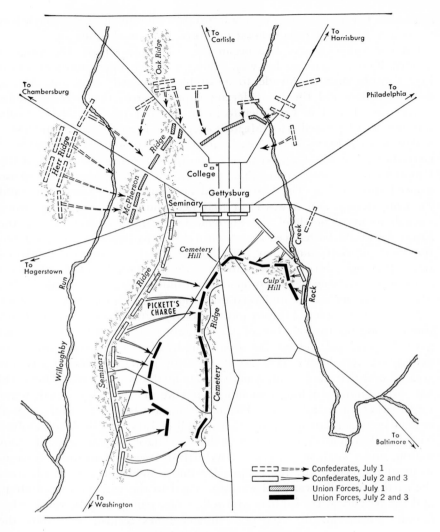

To Carlisle

To Harrisburg

To Chambersburg

Oak Ridge

To Philadelphia

Herr Ridge

Ridge

McPherson

College

Gettysburg

Seminary

Creek

To Hagerstown

Cemetery Hill

Culp's Hill

Run

Ridge

PICKETT'S CHARGE

Rock

Willoughby

Seminary

Ridge

Cemetery

To Baltimore

To Washington

<table>
<tr><td>Confederates, July 1</td></tr>
<tr><td>Confederates, July 2 and 3</td></tr>
<tr><td>Union Forces, July 1</td></tr>
<tr><td>Union Forces, July 2 and 3</td></tr>
</table>

THE BATTLE OF GETTYSBURG

erners moved across the valley between the two armies, then pushed forward in three lines up the slope toward Cemetery Ridge, they were battered by artillery and rifle fire. Pushing on and on despite their thinning ranks, the Confederates climbed toward the height where the Union troops awaited them. No more than 100 of them reached it, and they were driven back by rifle fire and the bayonet. Pickett's charge, almost doomed to failure from the beginning, did not come near success. Pickett's men fell back to Seminary Ridge, rejoining their disappointed comrades. Lee now unhappily made preparations to meet counterthrusts by Meade, but the Union general cautiously remained quiet.

On the following day Lee began the inevitable retreat. He found a flooded Potomac barring his way. Seeing a golden opportunity to crush Lee, Lincoln ordered Meade to assail his weakened army, but Meade delayed action and the Confederates slipped across the river when its waters subsided. The Confederate army was not crushed, and Lincoln was not at all pleased with Meade's behavior. Even so, the Confederacy had suffered a heavy blow. Nearly 4000 Southern soldiers were slain at Gettysburg, and about 24,000 were wounded or missing. The losses of the Union were also heavy, more than 3000 killed, and approximately 20,000 injured and missing. The Union could far better afford men than could the Confederacy, and it was clear that Lee would never again be strong enough to move north of the Potomac in great force, and that in the future he would be reduced almost entirely to the defensive. So great was the shock of Gettysburg that both Meade and Lee chose to recuperate rather than fight during the remainder of 1863. In fact, Meade would never again lead the Army of the Potomac as an independent commander. After March, 1864, he served under Grant, who became commander in chief.

In November, 1863, Lincoln went to Gettysburg to join in a ceremony commemorating the sacrifice of the Union dead. Since Edward Everett gave the principal address, the usual lengthy one of that time, the President spoke very briefly. His speech, carefully prepared, may well be the greatest ever delivered by an American. He modestly declared, "The world will little know, nor long remember what we say here, but it can never forget what they did here." His touching words are at least as well remembered as their deeds. Many, if not all of Lincoln's listeners resolved with the President that "these dead shall not have died in vain—that this nation, under God, shall have a new birth of freedom; and that Government of the people, by the people, for the people shall not perish from the earth." Yet afterward aid was begrudged to the widows, the children, and the parents of the soldiers who fell at Gettysburg and on many a less famous battlefield. In later years it sometimes seemed that only the politicians who wanted the votes of the living veterans gave worthwhile homage to the men who did not survive the war. Nevertheless, Lincoln's voice and words would be remembered by the generous of heart for generations.

THE WAR IN TENNESSEE

Gettysburg and Vicksburg did not represent the total progress of the Union armies in 1863, for the Federal troops pushing toward Atlanta also battered forward. They too engaged in fierce fighting, and the blows which they inflicted upon the Confederacy injured it seriously. In June General Rosecrans moved from the Federal base at Nashville against Chattanooga, approaching it from the southwest and menacing the communication line between Chattanooga and Atlanta. General Braxton Bragg, commanding the defending Confederates, had no choice but to retreat or to fight. He was quite willing to do battle, for Lee had sent a corps under General James Longstreet to his assistance, and his troops outnumbered Rosecrans' 66,000 to 58,000. Deserting Chattanooga, which was promptly occupied by the Federals, Bragg assailed the Union army at Chickamauga on September 18 and 19. The Confederates took advantage of mistakes on the part of the Federal command which weakened the Union center; they

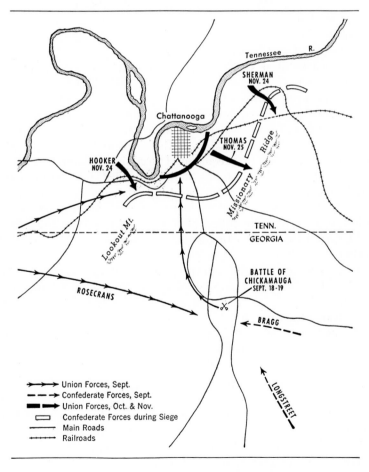

BATTLES IN TENNESSEE, 1863

attacked it, broke through, and finally drove both the Federal center and right wing back in confusion. But as they fell back into Chattanooga on the 19th, the Union left wing under General George H. Thomas held its ground. In six hours of fighting, despite assault from almost every quarter, Thomas' men withstood all attacks, inflicting heavy losses upon the Confederates. Not until nightfall, after his ammunition had been exhausted, did Thomas fall back unmolested and in good order to Chattanooga. Bragg had won a victory—or had he? Heavy Union losses included more than 1600 men killed, but Bragg's were even greater, more than 2300 slain. Since each side had about 15,000 wounded or missing, Chickamauga was one of the bloodiest battles of the war. The Confederacy could not afford such Pyrrhic victories, and Bragg's men, decimated in the struggle, unhappily realized that their immense effort had failed to crush a Federal army smaller than their own. On the other hand, the Federals had acquired another great general, or rather came to recognize the worth of Thomas, the "Rock of Chickamauga."

For some weeks after Chickamauga it did indeed appear that Bragg would reap a rich reward, for Rosecrans sat idle in Chattanooga while Bragg occupied nearby hills which permitted him to cut off Chattanooga's communications by railroad and by way of the Tennessee River. In consequence, the Federal army was for a time threatened by starvation. Rosecrans knew that he must break out of the town and prepared a plan for that purpose, but failed to execute it. Placed in command of all Union armies west of the Appalachians, Grant hurried to Chattanooga, put Thomas in the place of Rosecrans, and quickly opened up a supply line to Nashville. Bringing in reinforcements, Grant took the offensive with the Union army and drove Bragg off Lookout Mountain and other hills south of Chattanooga. When Bragg gathered his men on Missionary Ridge for another stand, Thomas began an attack to clear the base of the ridge, preparatory to further assault. However, Thomas' men not only did their task quickly, but continued on, climbing the ridge and driving the Confederates from it en route. Chattanooga was now firmly in Union hands, and an advance against Atlanta in 1864 became feasible. Meanwhile, Knoxville and its surrounding area had passed into Federal hands, so that Tennessee was completely under Union control.

CAMPAIGNS OF 1864

In the spring of 1864 massive and well led Federal armies moved against Confederate ones that were weaker but well officered. Assuming command of all Union armies in March, Grant personally took charge of the Army of the Potomac, and undertook to deal with Lee; under him were the workmanlike Meade and the dashing General Philip Sheridan, who would prove to be most useful in the Shenandoah Valley. The Union army at Chattanooga was placed under General William Tecumseh Sherman, an alert, astute, and imaginative man who had not yet won major laurels, but who was soon to exhibit military qualities of the highest order. Opposing him was General Joseph E. Johnston, doubtless an equally able man, who had replaced Bragg. Under Sherman was the redoubtable Thomas. Since that part of the Confederacy immediately east of the Mississippi had been fairly well cleared of Confederate troops, it was possible to send powerful reinforcements to Sherman. Grant was also supplied with new troops so that both he and Sherman enjoyed a superiority of approximately two to one over their opponents. The two Union generals made good use of this strength, and Sheridan and Thomas performed brilliantly. With all their genius and all the forces they could gather, Lee and Johnston were not able to make way against Grant and Sherman. There would be no more Federal retreats. At the end of the year Lee still held Richmond, but the Confederacy was collapsing behind him.

GRANT AND LEE IN VIRGINIA

Only too well aware that he could hardly hope to excel Lee in maneuver, Grant proposed to hammer away at him until his Army of Northern Virginia could stand no more. Based upon the fact that he had far more men than Lee, his plan must bring heavy losses to both sides, losses which the Union could grudgingly afford, but the Confederacy could not. He obstinately executed the plan. Sending an army under General Benjamin F. Butler up the James River to threaten Richmond from the east, and another under General Franz Sigel to conquer the Shenandoah Valley, Grant put in motion the bulk of his forces, more than 100,000 men, directly against the Confederate capital. Lee countered by placing Pierre Beauregard east of Richmond with an army of 30,000 men to oppose Butler, sent General Jubal A. Early against Sigel, and personally undertook with 60,000 men to hold off the main Federal army. Early in May Grant crossed the Rapidan, entering the Wilderness, a region well described by its name; in that rough and wooded country Lee boldly assailed Grant's right flank, bedeviled Grant's men by his skillful thrusts, and inflicted more than 18,000 casualties in a three-day battle. However, Lee's own losses were about 10,000 and Grant did not retreat. He held his ground, then moved forward again, trying to outflank the Confederate general at Spotsylvania Courthouse. He failed to deceive Lee, and was repulsed after five days of heavy fighting. Again Grant's army suffered severely, but he kept pushing forward to his left. At the Chickahominy River the Union general attacked again, and there in the battle of Cold Harbor during the first three days of June, he was again held off by a well-entrenched Lee.

Cold Harbor seemed to be almost a butchering of Grant's army. His

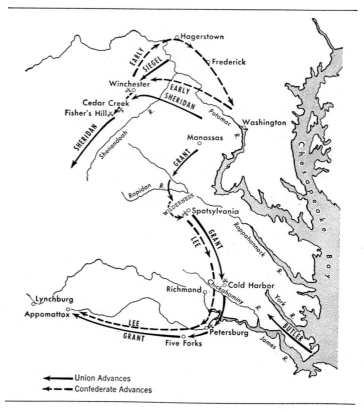

EASTERN CAMPAIGNS, 1864–1865

losses there, with those he had already suffered, added up to about 60,000 men, or as many as Lee had when the campaign began. But Grant was dogged, and he was doubtless right; the gaps in his ranks could be filled. Lee's casualties amounted to nearly half of the total forces with which he had begun the year, and he could not fully replace the brave Confederates who had sacrificed themselves against the battering of the Union army. Lee's forces were beginning to bleed away. Still moving forward to his left, Grant at last placed some men south of the James River in June, in an attempt to do what McClellan had attempted two years earlier, to move against Richmond from the east and south. On the 14th of that month Grant began a four-day attack upon Petersburg, but failed to take it. Fortifying Petersburg heavily, Lee entrenched his army so thoroughly that Grant was forced to besiege rather than to attack him. There the two armies faced each other for eight months, carrying on trench warfare and bombarding each other, while Lee's strength slowly ebbed away.

Two years earlier, when McClellan threatened Richmond, Stonewall Jackson had forced his retirement by threatening Washington from the Shenandoah. In 1864 Jubal Early undertook to repeat the exploits of the great Stonewall. For a time he seemed capable of duplicating the performance; he defeated Sigel in the valley on May 15th, and when General David Hunter succeeded Sigel, he pushed Hunter back into West Virginia. Then, early in July, he crossed the Potomac, swept through Hagerstown and Frederick, and advanced southeastward into the District of Columbia. By July 11 he was within five miles of Washington. The Federal capital fell into a momentary panic, for the troops available to defend it were hardly strong enough to stop Early. But this crisis did not shake Grant's determination to take Richmond, and he merely sent back two divisions which, with the troops available in Washington, forced Early to retreat into the Shenandoah. That was only the beginning of Early's misfortunes. In August the vigorous General Philip Sheridan was placed in charge of the Union troops in the valley. On September 19 he defeated Early at Winchester, and three days later he again worsted the Confederate general at Fisher's Hill. On October 19, while Sheridan was 20 miles away, Early surprised his army at Cedar Creek, and drove it from the field. However, Sheridan hastened forward, reorganized his troops about him, counterattacked, and inflicted another decisive defeat upon Early. The Confederate general was thereafter unable to offer much resistance, and Sheridan pushed on southward through the valley. To make sure that it would not again be used for a Confederate approach to Washington, he swept the valley clean of foodstuffs and livestock, so that, as the saying went, even a crow would have found it necessary to carry his rations with him in order to travel through the Shenandoah. There was no further threat to Washington.

SHERMAN IN GEORGIA

Although the year 1864 ended with Lee still holding on grimly at Richmond and Petersburg, the sun of the Confederacy was setting. By that time Sherman was loose in Georgia and the Confederacy had no army worthy of the name west of the Appalachians. Given 100,000 men, Sherman set out from Chattanooga in May, for Atlanta. Johnston, with about 60,000 men, skillfully fought defensive actions, but Sherman made good use of his superior strength, outflanking Johnston and steadily forcing him back. Meanwhile, Sherman carefully developed his communication lines, rebuilding railroads and bridges and protecting them with forts, to assure the safety of the rear of his army. Soon after the middle of July the Union army approached Atlanta. As it trudged forward, Johnston was superseded by General John B. Hood, because Jefferson Davis had lost faith in his delaying tactics. Certainly Hood was aggressive; he attacked Sherman twice, on July 20 and again on July 22, but was driven back with heavy losses on both occasions. He then dug in at Atlanta and managed to hold it for almost six weeks. Threatened with encirclement, he was forced to evacuate the city, which Sherman occupied on September 2, amid fires and confusion splendidly described in Margaret Mitchell's extraordinarily popular novel, *Gone With the Wind*. Atlanta then had fewer than 10,000 inhabitants, being by no means the great city it afterward became. However, because of its strategic location and its importance as a railroad junction, it was in a sense the heart of the Confederacy, just as Richmond was its head. Its capture by Sherman was therefore a staggering blow to the South, and the news of its fall brought rejoicing throughout the Union.

Rendered desperate by the loss of Atlanta, General Hood sought to retrieve all that had been lost by a daring advance into Tennessee. Moving to the west and then northward toward Nashville, he hoped to destroy Sherman's communications and to force the Union general to follow him, just as Bragg had compelled Buell to pursue him into Kentucky in 1862. Sherman refused to panic; he believed that the Union had enough men in Tennessee to deal with Hood, and he had faith in George Thomas. Accordingly, he felt free to move on from Atlanta, sending Thomas back to deal with Hood. There was no important obstacle between Atlanta and Savannah. Setting out for the sea with 62,000 men, Sherman marched steadily eastward. His men moved on a front as wide as 60 miles, living on the country, destroying factories, warehouses, bridges, railroads, and public buildings as they went. They also looted happily. After devastating the countryside, Sherman appeared before Savannah on September 10th. When a Union naval squadron came to his help, feeble Confederate forces trying to defend the city evacuated it and it fell to Sherman on December 22. Its capture was, of course, a handsome Christmas present for Lincoln, as it has been so often described. There was little to prevent Sherman from moving into South Carolina early in 1865.

While Sherman's army jubilantly tramped from the hills of Atlanta to the Georgia seacoast, Thomas had to face the aggressive Hood. With 40,000 men the Confederate general pushed on through southern Tennessee. On November 30 he was confronted at Franklin by a part of Thomas' forces under General John M. Schofield. Hood attacked and was roughly repulsed, losing more than 5000 men in killed and wounded. The able and prudent Schofield then withdrew to Nashville, where Thomas was mustering all possible strength. Hood followed, and found Thomas firmly entrenched. When Hood failed to attack promptly, Thomas patiently made his preparations for battle; he would not hurry into fighting despite frantic urging from Grant and Secretary of War Stanton. At last he was ready, and he assailed Hood on December 15th. Hood's army was

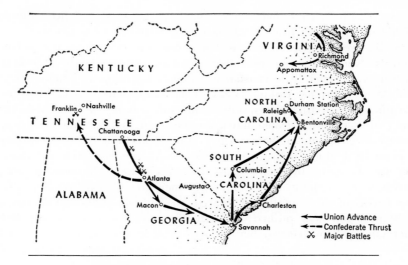

THE END OF THE CONFEDERACY

driven back and routed, so badly defeated that it was not thereafter active in the war. The "Rock of Chickamauga" was not soft at Nashville. One may well ask whether the Virginian Thomas might not have shone as one of the very greatest generals of the Civil War, had he had more opportunity to display his talents.

THE COMING OF THE END

In the early weeks of 1865 Confederate morale sank lower and lower. To inspire the men in gray, Jefferson Davis and the Confederate Congress arranged to appoint Lee as commander in chief of all the Southern forces; the change might have been useful had it occurred at an earlier time, but it came too late to have any effect. In desperation Davis sent an emissary to Europe to tell the English and French governments that the Confederacy was prepared to put an end to slavery in return for their assistance, but in vain, for they who would not recognize the Confederacy when its star was in the ascendant refused to interfere when the star was falling. In order to strengthen the Southerners' will to resist, Davis also permitted a delegation headed by Vice-President Alexander Stephens to go to Hampton Roads to confer with Lincoln and Seward regarding peace negotiations. Davis knew what Stephens did not, that Lincoln would accept nothing less than complete submission to the federal government; he hoped that Lincoln's refusal to discuss terms would drive the Confederates to greater efforts. Lincoln did say that the war could not end until Federal victory was fully conceded, but the news of his stand had little influence within the Southern lines. Nothing now availed the Confederacy.

While Lee clung stubbornly to Richmond and Petersburg in the face of Grant's ever increasing pressure, Sherman advanced northward from Savannah. He met little resistance in South Carolina and soon after the middle of February Columbia and Charleston fell. Feeling that South Carolina was peculiarly responsible for the making of the Confederacy, the Union troops wreaked havoc as they marched, setting fire to more than a dozen towns in their path; Columbia also felt the torch, probably applied by Union hands, although Sherman afterward claimed that the city was set ablaze by fleeing Confederates. On went Sherman into North Carolina, where Johnston gathered old men and boys to bar his path. In the battle of Bentonville on March 19 and 20 Johnston offered stiff resistance, but was pushed back by Sherman's superior army. Before Sherman could proceed farther, the end came in Virginia.

SURRENDER

At last Lee could defend Richmond no longer. On March 25 he tried to break through Grant's lines by attacking Fort Steadman to the east of Petersburg, but was repulsed. On April 1, he attacked a second time, striking at Grant's left wing at Five Forks, but again in vain. With his army dwindling away, Lee abandoned both Richmond and Petersburg on the following day and retreated southwestward in the hope of reaching Lynchburg. If he managed to reach that town, he planned to go southward to North Carolina to join Johnston in making a last stand. But the Confederate general could not escape with his army. Sheridan's cavalry swept around Lee's weary infantry and barred their path to the west, while Grant pushed on from Richmond. Lee now had fewer than 30,000 men. He might conceivably have forced his way with a small part of them through Sheridan's horsemen, and might have fled on to the Appalachians to carry on guerrilla warfare, but to what avail? The Confederate commander had never done less than his duty, however painful that might be; he knew that further resistance was useless, and he accepted the inevitable. Grant requested him to surrender on April 7. Lee asked what terms Grant had to offer. The two generals met at Appomattox Courthouse on April 9. Grant was as generous as he could be to his great antagonist, and Lee promptly accepted his terms. All of Lee's army surrendered, but his troops were all placed on parole and permitted to go home. Moreover, Lee's officers were permitted to keep their pistols and swords, and the Confederates who owned horses or mules were allowed to take them away. They would be needed, Grant and Lee agreed, for the spring plowing. Lee rode sadly away to private life. Later he accepted the presidency of the college which afterward was renamed in his honor

Washington and Lee University. Dignified in defeat, he died full of honors five years later; his leadership had given nobility to the Confederacy.

When Lee laid down his arms, continued resistance by other Confederate commanders became clearly useless and they too surrendered, one by one. Johnston gave up the struggle on April 18, signing terms for himself and his 37,000 men with Sherman at the Bennett House near Durham Station in North Carolina. He received from Sherman the same liberal treatment. On May 4 and May 26 the remaining Confederate forces in the lower South were formally surrendered in Alabama and at New Orleans respectively.

Some of the Confederate troops preferred to go into exile rather than to accept the military verdict against them, fleeing to Mexico, Brazil, the West Indies and England; a few Confederate officials who felt they could not again live under the Union flag or who feared punishment also hurried away to foreign lands. One of them was the remarkable Judah P. Benjamin, who not only succeeded in reaching England, but as a man in his sixties began a new and brilliantly successful career as a lawyer. One who was captured trying to escape was Jefferson Davis, who was trapped by Union troops as he fled through Georgia. Soon accused of treason, he was imprisoned in Fortress Monroe, but the leader of the "Johnny Rebs" was never brought to trial, and was finally permitted to return to civil life. Like Lee, he behaved with dignity under crushing misfortune.

DEATH OF THE CONFEDERACY AND LINCOLN

There remained the mighty task of reconstructing the American nation, and of restoring order in the Southern states. Never as prosperous as the Northern states, they were now poverty-stricken, and their finances in confusion. The Southern people were also in bad straits, most of those who had possessed wealth before the war having become poor. The Southern railroads were badly disorganized; cattle and pigs had almost vanished in several parts of the South; factories and homes had been destroyed; and financial credit for a time was almost unobtainable. Worst of all, a quarter of a million of the best of Southern manhood was gone, a tragic loss which would be felt for generations. In addition, the vast problem of establishing a society in which the whites and the freed Negroes must live side by side imposed a heavy burden. Only the Negroes had an immediately darker economic future than the Southern whites, but they had the consolation of escaping from servitude. It was a long time before the Southern whites regained their feet politically, even longer before they attained any measure of prosperity. The lot of the Negro continued to be an unhappy one, although it slowly improved, far into the twentieth century.

It has often been said, and it bears repeating, that had Lincoln lived, he would have performed most valuable service in reconstruction. There was no hate for the South or for Southerners in that magnanimous man. In his second inaugural address, given as the war was drawing to its close, he had begged the Union to forgive its enemies. "With malice toward none; with charity for all" he would "bind up the nation's wounds" and "do all which may achieve and cherish a just and lasting peace." He had even earlier displayed his generous feelings toward the South in deeds as well as words. In December, 1863 he had announced a plan for reorganizing the South after the defeat of the Confederates. With few exceptions, he would pardon all those Southerners who took a new oath of loyalty, and he would recognize as legal any state government in the South established by persons taking that oath, provided that they formed one-tenth of those who voted in 1860, and provided that they forbade slavery. In July, 1864, he vetoed the Wade-Davis bill, which demanded that nothing be done toward political restoration in any Southern state until a majority of its voters swore that they had been loyal in the past and that they would be faithful in the future. Lincoln's veto of that measure was of the pocket variety—that is, he held the bill unsigned until Congress adjourned—and the Republican Radicals who pushed it through Congress were unable to enact it against his will. They could and did bitterly denounce him for softness toward rebels and for offering a helping hand to the Democratic Party, which would presumably control most of the state governments set up under the President's arrangements. Had Lincoln lived, he might not have had his own way with respect to the South, but it is likely that he could have prevented the adoption of the harshest measures proposed by the Radicals. During the war he had grown from a likeable and competent politician to one of great stature, and his prestige was immense by the end of the conflict.

Suddenly the President was dead. He visited Richmond on April 5, after its evacuation by Lee, and was greeted with respect by the whites and with joy by the Negroes. Receiving the news of Appomattox in Washington, he again called for conciliation with the South. While Lincoln was considering means to restore the South, the actor John Wilkes Booth, Lewis Powell, and other conspirators were madly planning to revive the Confederacy by murdering him, Seward, and other Union leaders. On April 14 Lincoln went to see the play *Our American Cousin* at Ford's Theater. While Powell quietly slipped into Seward's home and severely wounded the Secretary of State, Booth made his way to Ford's Theater, fired a bullet into the President's head, and fled. Unconscious and mortally injured, the President died in a house across the street from the theater the following morning. Pursued, Booth was surrounded in a barn near Bowling Green, Virginia, and died there, probably a suicide. Four of his fellow conspirators—if they were all guilty—were afterward hanged. Andrew Johnson became President of the United States.

When Lincoln was gone there was an outpouring of grief such as the American people had never before felt over the loss of one man. Winner on no great battlefield, humble in origin, unfamiliar with fine schools and royal courts, he became one of the few truly great of the world. Afterward, whatever censure might be heaped upon America, it could be said that it had produced Abraham Lincoln.

32 THE RADICALS AND THE SOUTH

ANDREW JOHNSON

At Lincoln's second inauguration Andrew Johnson became Vice-President and was drunk. He was not a toper, but he was not equal to the immense burden which fell upon him when Lincoln was murdered six weeks later. Like the "Rail-splitter," he was assuredly a man of the people; were humble origins the key to greatness, he might have attained stature with Lincoln, or at least with Jackson. His rise in the world was an American dream. Born in North Carolina, reared in Tennessee, he was in his youth a tailor. Marrying a good woman who taught him to read and write, he entered politics as a Democrat and champion of the rights of the common man against the wealthy planters of Tennessee. Moving steadily up the political ladder, he became Governor of Tennessee, and then one of its Senators in Washington. In the crisis of 1861 he stubbornly clung to the Union, and he served under Lincoln as military governor of Tennessee. In the American way he was nominated along with Lincoln in 1864 so that the Unionist party could attract the votes of Democrats. It is

468

to be suspected that his merits as a possible successor to Lincoln were not scrupulously weighed. Johnson had fine qualities, a good understanding, honesty, and courage. He also had weaknesses, for he lacked the sense of balance and humor so conspicuous in Lincoln, and he was accustomed to deal harshly with his political enemies—he had several of the virtues and faults of Andrew Jackson. Johnson was not well fitted for the tasks that fell to him, and he labored under a heavy handicap, for he was a Democrat surrounded by Republicans. The Unionist party began to fade as soon as the war ended, and the Republicans in it, considering Johnson both a Democrat and an accidental President, were not disposed to accept his leadership. Adopting Lincoln's generous stand toward the defeated South, Johnson soon offended the Radical element among the Republicans. There followed a bitter struggle between Johnson and the Radicals; he received support from some moderate Republicans and from the Democrats, but he was defeated. What was far worse, the problem of dealing with the conquered South, difficult enough in any case, was attacked by Washington for some years in a vengeful rather than a charitable spirit. The South continued to pay heavily for its attempt to secure independence.

JOHNSON AND RECONSTRUCTION

During Johnson's first days in office, the Radicals hoped that he would be their man, for he had been not only a firm adherent to the Union, but a stubborn enemy of the Southern planter aristocracy. They were soon disappointed, since the President had no desire to punish all the Southern whites because of the sins of some of them, and because he was not eager to exalt the Negroes at the expense of their former masters. Johnson neglected to call Congress into special session—it would not regularly meet until December, 1865; he amended Lincoln's plan for Southern reconstruction so as to humiliate wealthy Southerners; and he put this altered scheme into effect, hoping to present it as an accomplished fact when Congress met. He officially recognized state governments set up in Tennessee, Arkansas, Louisiana, and Virginia in accordance with Lincoln's wishes. Appointing temporary governors for the other seven members of the Confederacy, he authorized them to arrange for the resurrection of loyal governments. They were to call constitutional conventions composed of men chosen by voters who had taken an oath of loyalty to the United States. Each convention was required to alter the constitution of the state in which it sat by abolishing slavery and by repudiating any debt the state had accumulated in support of the Southern cause. These things done, the usual elections could be held, including those of members of the national House of Representatives and Senate. Johnson hoped that the men thus selected would be accepted by Congress when it convened. He proposed to punish only a few thousands of prominent Southerners, including those who possessed more than $20,000 in property, for their devotion to the Confederacy. They would be deprived of the right to hold office and to vote, but they could ask him for pardon. Accordingly, the Southern states were "reconstructed" in the summer and fall of 1865, except for Texas, which executed the Johnson plan in the spring of 1866. Meanwhile, Johnson had the pleasure of receiving petition after petition for pardon from formerly conspicuous Confederates; satisfied that they had been sufficiently humiliated, he granted the pardons.

When Congress convened, it quickly challenged the work of Johnson and substantially undid it. Its members had long been restive because Lincoln had accumulated and exercised great power during the war, and they were disposed to prevent Johnson from "usurping" authority from the legislative branch. Many were determined to punish the South and the Southerners. Some of the Radicals, feeling that freedom was not enough for the Negroes, insisted that they should be recognized as the equals of whites, and that their citizenship should be placed beyond question. The Republicans generally feared that the Democrats would profit politically in the South if the work of Johnson were accepted; they were alarmed lest the Democrats should soon gain control of the nation and steal the fruits of victory from those who had sacrificed in behalf of the Union. Since the three-fifths clause in the Constitution would no longer be effective, the South would have a larger representation in the House than it had had in 1860. The Radicals were the more unhappy because the new Johnson regimes in the South had sent to Congress men who had been forthright in behalf of the Confederacy, even its Vice-President, Alexander Stephens, who had been elected Senator from Georgia. The Radicals soon had another reason for discontent. In the fall and winter of 1865 the new Southern legislatures began to enact "Black Codes" which repressed vagrancy among the freed Negroes and which compelled them to work—for the whites. While there was a need to deal with Negroes who wandered about and who fancied that liberty meant only relief from toil, provisions of some of the "Black Codes" were remarkably harsh, and Northern friends of the Negroes concluded that the makers of the codes were merely trying to revive Negro servitude in altered form.

STATUS OF THE SOUTH

The Radicals not only disliked the fruit of Johnson's plan, but condemned the plan itself as an infringement upon the authority of Congress. Both Lincoln and Johnson had acted on the assumption that the Southern states were constitutionally indestructible, that they had never left the Union, and that, having been temporarily out of their proper relationship to it, they could be placed back in good standing by relatively gentle executive fiat. Senator Charles Sumner, who had no cause to love the South, took a different view in 1865; by seceding, he said, they had committed "suicide." Thaddeus Stevens, then just making his bid for fame at the age of 73, was an even more fanatical enemy of the South than was Sumner. A Representative from Pennsylvania, Stevens had been a vigorous anti-slavery man before 1860, and he nourished a dislike for the Southern planter aristocracy which did not vanish with the Confederacy. In temperament he had some things in common with Andrew Johnson. Stevens proclaimed the Southern states to be "conquered provinces," an interpretation of their status which was in effect much like that of Sumner. According to either view, the Southern states had vanished and must be created anew; since only Congress had the power to admit new states, both Sumner and Stevens asserted that only the legislature had the power to undertake political reconstruction.

While Lincoln and Johnson may have been more accurate in their interpretation of the nature of the Union—the United States Supreme Court in 1869 spoke of "an indestructible Union of indestructible states"—Stevens, Sumner, and the body of Radicals who gathered behind them had their way. They formed a joint committee of fifteen members which was dominated by Stevens and which undertook to fashion policy for the South and the Negro. Under its leadership Congress refused to seat the men who had been elected to national office by the Johnson regimes in the South. In the first six months of 1866 that body quarreled ever more acrimoniously with Johnson. In February it passed a law to enlarge the powers of the Freedman's Bureau, which had been established a year earlier to provide temporary care for newly freed Negroes and to assist them to find means to support themselves. Congress wished to give the Bureau authority to bring before military courts Southerners violating the civil rights of the Negroes. The President vetoed the measure, declaring that the arrangement for military trial violated the Fifth Amendment to the Constitution, and that Congress could not properly legislate when eleven states were not represented in it through no fault of their own. In July the Congress passed the bill over the President's veto. In April the legislators sought better means to protect the Negro, passing a Civil Rights bill which ostensibly granted citizenship to all Negroes and guaranteed them the civil rights of all other persons born in the United States. That Congress could constitutionally enact such a law was very doubtful, and its sponsors were aware of the fact. Nevertheless, when Johnson vetoed it on the ground that it violated the supreme law of the land—a view with which the United States Supreme Court concurred in 1883—its sponsors again managed to override the President's veto.

THE FOURTEENTH AMENDMENT

To make sure that the Constitution would not be used against them, the Radical leaders then pushed through Congress the famous Fourteenth Amendment. It defined American citizenship and definitely gave it to all Negroes, for it declared that "All persons born or naturalized in the United States, and subject to the jurisdiction thereof, are citizens of the United States and of the State wherein they reside." It also offered protection of "the privileges or immunities of citizens of the United States" against state law. It further declared that no state could "deprive any person of life, liberty, or property, without due process of law; nor deny to any person within its jurisdiction the equal protection of the laws." Almost inevitably, the defenses erected by the Amendment were phrased in general terms and therefore subject to later interpretation. It is noteworthy too, that, being offered to "citizens," they protected whites as well as Negroes, and corporations as well, since they fall for many purposes within the legal definition of "citizens." Congress intended only to defend the Negroes, but it opened the way for a multitude of lawsuits against the states by Negroes, by whites, and by corporations.

Congress also sought to compel the Southern states to let the Negroes vote by stipulating that any state which barred part of its males over 21 from voting, "except for rebellion or crime," would be deprived of representation in Congress in proportion to the number who were refused the suffrage. This provision was not workable and was never enforced. In addition, the Amendment struck at men who had taken an oath of allegiance before the Civil War and who had actively supported the Confederacy. They were barred from all federal and state offices, but could regain the right to hold such offices by action of Congress, a two-thirds majority being required. Still further, all debts contracted in behalf of the Confederacy were declared illegal. Johnson could do no more than denounce the Amendment, and it was promptly presented to the states for ratification.

By the summer of 1866 the battle line between Johnson and the Radicals was sharply drawn. Keenly adverse to the Fourteenth Amendment and hoping that the President would win the contest, the members of the Southern legislatures chosen under the Lincoln-Johnson plan, except for those of Tennessee, refused to ratify the Amendment. The Radicals rewarded Tennessee by accepting her Senators and Representatives in the halls of Congress, and more vehemently assailed Johnson. The President did not gain the allegiance of many Republicans. With some allies he tried to build a permanent National Union party of moderate men, but a convention held at Philadelphia for that purpose achieved nothing. Most of the support which the President received came from the Democrats. The Radicals actually profited from a speaking tour which Johnson made in August and September, for he denounced them in intemperate language. In the elections which followed in November, the Republicans won an impressive victory, securing majorities greater than two-thirds in both houses of Congress. Since the Radicals controlled the more moderate Republicans, they became masters of Congress. Radical with respect to the South and the Negroes, they had convinced Northern bankers, merchants, and industrialists that they could be trusted not to indulge in radical practices with respect to taxation, currency, and finance. Where Northern interests were directly affected, the Radicals were cautious, and they had a great following not only in the business community, but also among farmers and veterans of the Union army.

CONGRESS AND RECONSTRUCTION

Flushed with their triumph, Stevens, Sumner, and their cohorts proceeded to begin over again in the South, except for Tennessee, already remolded to their satisfaction and governed by Radicals. In March, 1867, they drove through Congress and over Johnson's veto the First Reconstruction Act. It was a drastic measure which divided the South into five military districts, each of them temporarily under military law. All of the Southern states, with the usual exception of Tennessee, had to establish new governments according to a prescribed formula. Each had to hold a constitutional convention elected by universal manhood suffrage, only former Confederates who had taken an oath of loyalty to the Union before 1861 being barred from the polls. Under this arrangement Negroes could vote. In addition it was required that the conventions alter the state constitutions so as to give Negroes the suffrage, also that the conventions ratify the Fourteenth Amendment. Only after all these things had been done would Congress accept Senators and Representatives sent to Washington by the Southern states. Appalled by the terms of this act, Southern leaders commonly refused to execute it. Thereupon the Radicals pushed through a series of additional laws which gave added authority to the generals commanding in the five military districts, and which made it as sure as possible that the Radicals would have their own way. Although Johnson doubted the constitutionality of all these congressional measures, he prudently put them into effect.

The result was remarkable. Under the rules laid down by Congress the army carried out a new registration of the voters in the ten recalcitrant states, and found that Negroes formed a majority in five of them. With the help and under the leadership of "scalawags," Southern whites disposed to bow to the will of Congress, and "carpetbaggers," Northerners who came

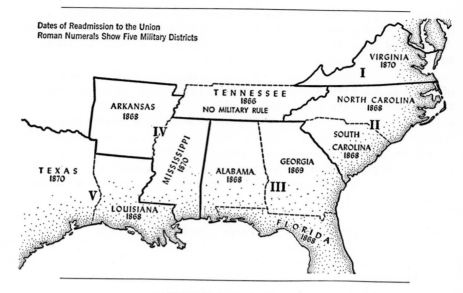

Dates of Readmission to the Union
Roman Numerals Show Five Military Districts

VIRGINIA
1870
I

TENNESSEE
1866
NO MILITARY RULE

ARKANSAS
1868

NORTH CAROLINA
1868

IV

MISSISSIPPI
1870

SOUTH
CAROLINA
1868

II

TEXAS
1870

ALABAMA
1868

GEORGIA
1869

V

III

LOUISIANA
1868

FLORIDA
1868

REJOINING THE UNION

south to work with the Negroes, they had majorities in the other five. By the end of 1868 seven of the Southern states had been reformed in compliance with the demands of Congress, which recognized them and let them return to the fold early in 1869. The other three, Mississippi, Texas, and Virginia, were denied readmission because they did not refuse the vote to "disloyal" whites. After yielding to congressional pressure, Georgia defied Congress by expelling Negroes from her legislature, and was compelled to go through the process of political reconstruction a third time.

The states of Georgia (1869), Texas, Mississippi, and Virginia (1870) were finally accepted into the federal family only after they had submitted and had ratified the Fifteenth Amendment. Aware that nothing which had been done thus far assured equality to the Negroes at polling places in the South, Congress tried to give them the right to vote by a specific constitutional provision. The Amendment, approved by Congress in February, 1869, and ratified by the states during the following year, forbade any state to deprive a citizen of the right to the suffrage because of race, color, or previous condition of servitude. In time Southern whites would find means to prevent Negroes from voting, but for the moment they voted in large numbers.

CARPETBAGGER REGIMES

An immediate result of the congressional policy was the establishment of the notorious "carpetbagger" regimes in the South, dominated by Radicals, and dependent upon military force and the ballots of illiterate and ignorant Negroes. They could hardly have become respectable, and they did not. They were not totally vicious, for strains of idealism ran alike through carpetbaggers, scalawags, and Negroes. The carpetbaggers were almost invariably the leaders; in fact, the scalawags soon deserted the Radicals, because they were bitterly attacked by their white neighbors as traitors to their own. Under the guidance of carpetbagger governors the Radicals provided not only for protection of the Negro, but for free public schools, something largely new in the South, and for orphanages and asylums. They also supplied funds to encourage the building of railroads. In the main, however, the carpetbagger regimes failed distressingly and dismally. Some of the Northerners who flocked into the South to help the Negro were likewise eager to help themselves, and others were almost entirely swayed by a desire for personal gain. Nor was there any lack of looters among the scalawags and Negroes, the latter receiving only scraps and being in some part excusable because in their innocence they followed the example of rapacious whites.

Impoverished by the war, the Southern states became ridden by extravagance and graft, and were driven deeply into debt. Taxes were multiplied. The graft had its humorous aspects; in South Carolina the legislature gave the Speaker of the House $1000 because he had lost that sum on a horse race. The manager of a railroad owned by the State of Georgia managed to save $30,000 a year out of his salary of $3,000, by the exercise of rigid economy. But robbery and waste were far too real and too serious to be merely amusing; they were particularly evident in the building and operation of state-owned railroads which ran few and poor trains at the expense to the public of many millions of dollars. The Carolinas, Georgia, and Louisiana suffered peculiarly from the rapacity of the carpetbaggers. Nor was the popularity of the Radical governments in the South increased because of their support from Federal troops and Negro militia, which were used to stifle discontented whites. When the carpetbagger regimes finally vanished, the state debt of North Carolina had been increased from $16,000,000 to $40,000,000, that of South Carolina from $6,000,000 to $25,000,000, and that of Louisiana from $6,000,000 to nearly $50,000,000.

IMPEACHMENT

Not content with their triumph over President Johnson with respect to policy toward the conquered South, the Radicals boldly impeached him. In February, 1868, the House of Representatives brought a series of eleven charges against him, the most important being that he had broken a law of 1867 which required the President to issue all military orders through the General of the Army; and that he had violated the Tenure of Office act of the same year, which declared that the President could not remove officials appointed with the consent of the Senate without securing its approval. Since Congress had made violation of those statutes by the President a crime, Johnson had exposed himself to the process of impeachment by disobeying them. The law requiring the President to transmit his orders only through the General of the Army, who was then U. S. Grant, was clearly unconstitutional, for it contravened the President's authority as commander in chief of the armed services. The Tenure of Office act was also of doubtful constitutionality, for it had become generally recognized that the President had the right to remove executive officers without consulting the Senate (later the Supreme Court of the United States ruled that the President had that power). Aware that the Radicals were trying to trap him, Johnson had moved cautiously for some months. At length, however, convinced that the two laws were unconstitutional, he challenged them. On February 21 he dismissed Secretary of War Stanton, and with good reason, for Stanton was an ally of the Radicals in the President's very Cabinet.

The charges against Johnson were specious, for it was quite clear that he had committed no crime of the sort which the Constitution prescribed as a suitable basis for impeachment. Nevertheless, it long remained doubtful whether he would be convicted or acquitted. The Radicals quite readily obtained the necessary majority to impeach him in the House of Representatives, and it seemed likely for some weeks that they would secure the necessary two-thirds vote in the Senate for conviction. However, Chief Justice Salmon P. Chase, who had been appointed by Lincoln to succeed Taney and who presided over the trial in the Senate, conducted it with fairness and dignity. Moreover, the lawyers for Johnson's defense riddled the case against him. The President's fate rested with the moderate Republicans, who were under heavy pressure from the Radicals.

In the end, the President narrowly won an acquittal. The decisive vote came on the eleventh of the charges, which brought together all of the President's supposed "crimes." Twelve Democratic Senators who could have only sympathy for Johnson voted nay, and with them seven Republicans; thirty-five Republicans announced themselves for conviction. Johnson was thus found innocent by one vote. There is evidence that two of those Republicans who voted against Johnson would have voted in his behalf had it been necessary; at any rate, the outcome was close. Those Republican Senators who had behaved in accordance with their consciences had prevented a tragic injustice; although they were punished politically by their party, they had earned the gratitude of the nation.

Neither the President nor the Supreme Court of the United States was able to challenge the Radicals effectively. When the Court was asked to consider whether or not the military tribunals in the South were constitutional, it tended to avoid the issue. When it did agree to consider a case involving the validity of basic parts of the Reconstruction laws, Congress in March, 1868, deprived it of jurisdiction. The following year the Court in *Texas* v. *White* took the view that the states were indissoluble, but nevertheless refused to condemn any of the acts.

GRANT THE PRESIDENT

Nor were the Radicals checked at the polls, despite the loss of Thaddeus Stevens by death, in 1868. By that time the Republican Party was losing popularity because of the excesses of the Radicals in their dealings with the South and with President Johnson. It was also under fire because it stood for a sound and restricted currency. Farmers and other debtors were clamoring for the issuance of more paper money to ease their burdens; the United States Treasury was reducing the number of greenback dollars in circulation. Facing defeat, the Republicans resorted to the already traditional vote-getter, the military hero, and nominated U. S. Grant for the Presidency. He had once been a Democrat of sorts, had never been active in politics, and had never given much study to public affairs. The platform upon which he ran endorsed Radical reconstruction and sound money, but carefully avoided commitment on other important issues. "Vote as you fought" was the Republican campaign cry, and it was effective. The Democrats might logically have chosen Johnson to oppose Grant, but he had been too long associated with the Republicans to please them; besides he could not win. Instead, they nominated Horatio Seymour, a respectable man who had been governor of New York, but one who had won no military laurels. They denounced Radical reconstruction and displayed some sympathy for currency inflation, to Seymour's discomfort. With only eight Southern states taking part in the election, six of them and the nation voted for Grant, who won an easy victory in the electoral college, 214 to 80. That the Republicans badly needed Grant's personal popularity, however, was indicated by the narrowness of his margin in the popular ballots, where his majority was only slightly more than 300,000 out of a total of 5,715,000. Had it not been for the votes of the Negroes, he would probably have had fewer popular votes than Seymour. The Republican and Democratic parties were nearly equal in strength, and they were to remain so for a generation, although the Democrats won the Presidency only twice between the Civil War and the election of 1912.

Ulysses S. Grant was the first of the Ohio dynasty of Presidents; when the merits of Presidents have been weighed, he has commonly been given a place at or near the bottom. Since the United States has survived many chief executives of mediocre abilities, it might be inferred that Grant must have been very incapable. Such was not the case, for he displayed intelligence as a military man and—quite diversely—as a writer. Nor did he lack either physical or moral courage, the former proven on battlefields enough, the latter superbly demonstrated when, suffering from a fatal cancer, the General doggedly wrote his memoirs in order to pay his debts and to care for his family. But the General was a decent and kindly man who did not apply himself very vigorously to his Presidential duties, which he disliked. He was unduly respectful toward men of money, and accepted their advice too easily. He was too trusting when he permitted his affection for relatives and friends to affect his judgment; and while he was personally honest, he was a little callous about corruption in public life. Because of his generosity toward Lee at Appomattox, because he had announced that he desired peace in the South, and because he had been moderate or indifferent to politics, the Southern whites hoped the Radical regimes would be destroyed, or at least improved, with Grant in the White House. They were terribly disappointed, for after a conciliatory gesture or two, the new President aligned himself with the Radicals. The low estimate which historians have of Grant is based in part upon his policy with respect to the South.

FROM RADICALISM TO THE SOLID SOUTH

It must be admitted that the Southern situation which confronted Grant in the spring of 1869 was a difficult one, aggravated by the recent passage of the Fifteenth Amendment. It was quite clear that the Republicans pushed it through largely because the Negro vote was so helpful to them in the election of 1868, and because it was likely to be valuable in the future. The party leaders wished to keep their grip on the Southern states, and Grant would not stand in their way. He saw nothing dubious in the procedure by which four of the Southern states were required to ratify the Amendment before they were "readmitted" to the Union, nor did he object to the use of troops to maintain the Radical regimes in power. Republican policy toward the South did soften before Grant left office, but not because the President insisted on it; the change came because the policy was obviously failing to attain its objectives, and because it was costing the party friends in the North. A demand that peace and quiet be restored in the South was gaining strength north of the Mason-Dixon Line.

Despite the efforts of the Republicans in Washington the carpetbagger governments began to collapse in 1870. The Negroes and many of the poor Southern whites who had supported them became lukewarm and even hostile as they became increasingly aware that the carpetbaggers were using them to make great personal profits. Many whites who had voted for carpetbaggers and scalawags to prevent the return to authority of the planter aristocracy came to believe that the order which existed before

1860 was preferable to domination by the carpetbaggers and their Negro adherents. The Ku Klux Klan, the Knights of the White Camellia, the Order of the White Rose, and other secret societies that brought terror to the Negroes, especially the more credulous ones, also weakened the support of the Radical governments. The Klan, founded in Pulaski, Tennessee, in 1866, was the largest, most effective, and most famous of these. Carefully organized throughout the South under a "Grand Wizard," "Grand Dragon," "Grand Giants," and similarly designated officers, the Klansmen dressed themselves in ghostly and ghastly costumes, rode through the countryside at night, and threatened Negroes with dire punishment if they continued to help the carpetbaggers. When threats failed, they resorted to violence, beating and murdering the Negroes who refused to be intimidated. Congressional legislation against the secret societies had little effect, even though the Army was used to enforce it, for it was difficult to catch the nightraiders and to identify them. The Klan gradually disappeared, more because its excesses made it unpopular among the Southern whites than for any other reason. However, it did undoubtedly serve to keep Negroes away from the polls and so helped the enemies of the Radicals to win elections.

Far more important toward reducing the Negro vote was economic coercion. Most of the Negroes worked for or rented lands from whites, and often they were in debt to whites. When they were told, as they increasingly were, that they would suffer economically unless they stayed away from the polls, many felt that they had to comply. Organized in Conservative parties, the white enemies of the Radicals overthrew all of the carpetbagger regimes except those in South Carolina, Florida, and Louisiana between 1870 and 1874. After another three years the entire South would be under the control of the whites.

The establishment, or restoration, of "white supremacy" in the South brought with it domination of the South by the Democratic party. Before the Civil War the Democrats had been sturdily challenged there by the Whigs. Since the Radicals in the South were, or became, Republicans, the Conservatives inevitably associated themselves with the Democrats. The Democratic Solid South made its first appearance in 1876, although the electoral votes of South Carolina, Florida, and Louisiana were counted for the Republican Presidential candidate.

33 THE GROWTH OF THE NATION

Confirming the verdict of the Civil War that the nation was more important than the states, the Republicans used—and sometimes abused—national power in the restoration of the South. During the twelve years after Appomattox they also used national resources to encourage the building of a transcontinental railroad, although in other respects they did not seek to extend the authority of the federal government. They dealt efficiently with the problem of the national debt, which had been vastly increased by the war; they did not do badly in meeting currency difficulties; and they functioned effectively in the field of foreign affairs. While corruption, caused in part by postwar disillusionment, flourished in Washington during Grant's Presidency, the collapse of public morality in the national capital did not prevent economic progress.

ECONOMIC GROWTH

An oversimplified interpretation of the course of American history has it that the Civil War was basically a contest for control of the republic between the Southern aristocracy and Northern "Big Business," and that the Yankees triumphed. Actually, "Big Business" did not exist during or immediately following the war; certainly Republican politicians did not know that they were dominated by it. While their policies were generally pleasing to Northern manufacturers, it does not follow that the Republicans deliberately favored banking, commerce, and industry at the expense of the farmer, laborer, and the general welfare. In the long, troubled decade after the Civil War, it is doubtful that the Democrats would have done any better. The Republicans may be criticized because they believed in tariffs for protection, and because they maintained the high wartime duties justified by the need for revenue, and even increased them. In 1869 the average rate upon imports was 47 percent. Although rates were lowered in 1870 and again in 1872, they were restored in 1875 substantially to the levels of 1869. In any event, the duties gave handsome sums to government, which, despite the lowering of excise taxes and the abolition of levies upon inheritances and incomes, balanced federal budgets and even created surpluses.

Something may also be said in behalf of the way in which the Republicans managed the national debt and currency problems. The debt amounted to nearly $2,846,000,000 in 1865. Some of the Democrats endorsed the "Ohio Idea" of George H. Pendleton, which called for the issuance of greenback currency to pay off the debt; all that can be said for the idea is that the nation did need a larger supply of currency. Denouncing Pendleton's plan, the Republicans took care of the national debt by floating issues of long-term government bonds which national banks could use as security for issuing more notes. The need for currency in the growing nation was not fully taken care of; reliance upon national bank notes for currency was also open to objection on the ground that their circulation was dependent upon the national debt rather than economic requirements. The Republicans would not substantially increase the quantity of greenbacks, and finally reduced the amount in circulation to $300,000,000 in 1875. Besides, in 1873 they placed the United States on a gold standard, preventing for the time being the coinage of silver dollars. They gave the nation sound money, but not enough of it. Nevertheless, the country, except for the South, prospered immediately after the Civil War. There was no depression until 1873 brought a "Panic" caused in part by overspeculation in railroads. It began with the collapse of the powerful house of Jay Cooke and Company, which was followed by many business failures, a rapid fall in prices, and widespread unemployment that lasted for about five years.

It has often been said that American industry was remarkably stimulated by the Civil War, as it was afterward by World War I and World War II. Actually, there was no giant growth in American manufacturing between

1861 and 1865, although the economy of the North and the West prospered both during and after the conflict. Economic progress was spurred not only by military needs, but also by the inventions of ingenious minds. In 1864 George M. Pullman built his "Pioneer," the first railroad car especially made to permit passengers to sleep; three years later he organized his Pullman Palace Car Company. Meanwhile, Thaddeus Lowe had invented the first machine to make artificial ice, a device which eventually led to a better American diet. Between 1868 and 1872 George Westinghouse developed an air-brake which made railroad travel far safer, the first of his many major contributions to American industry. A vacuum cleaner was patented as early as 1869, and the manufacturing of shoes was greatly improved by new machines developed during and immediately after the war. Soon afterward Stephen Dudley Field invented an electrically powered street car which was put into use in New York City in 1874. By 1876 Alexander Graham Bell invented the telephone, which was soon put to general use and abuse. Meanwhile, other inventions of the pre-Civil War period were perfected and eagerly exploited, while the factory became ever more important in American life.

Other contributions to the wealth of the nation came from the discovery of oil, first secured through a well dug by Edwin L. Drake at Titusville, Pennsylvania, in 1859. Petroleum soon replaced whale-oil in lamps in American homes; before long, in fact, oil and petroleum became interchangeable words. New discoveries of gold in the Rocky Mountain region added to the national treasure. Less glamorous, but ultimately of great value, was the sowing of wheat and corn on the plains of Nebraska and Kansas. Riches also came from the cattle industry which began to flourish on the Great Plains immediately after the Civil War.

RAILROADING

A most spectacular factor in American growth in the postwar years was railroad building, especially to the west of the Mississippi. Before President Grant left office, one transcontinental line had been finished and three others were under construction. Three of these were subsidized by the federal government—the states had earlier offered substantial assistance to railroad builders. The first transcontinental route to be completed ran between Nebraska and California. The Union Pacific Railroad was authorized by Congress in 1862 to lay rails from Nebraska westward, and the Central Pacific was permitted to put them down from California eastward, the trackage to be joined in Utah. In the law by which Congress granted the right of way to the two railroads, to encourage them to proceed quickly, each was given ten alternate sections of public domain per mile, on both sides of their tracks. Two years later these grants of land were doubled. Thus spurred on, the iron horses moved rapidly toward one another after

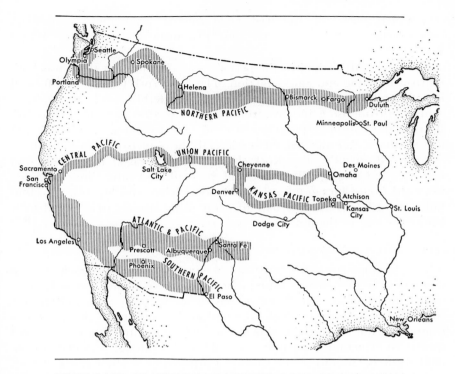

FIRST LAND GRANTS TO TRANSCONTINENTAL RAILWAYS

the war. Chinese laborers worked diligently on the western line and Irish ones on the eastern, and in May, 1869, the two railroads formed a junction at Promontory Point in Utah.

The Northern Pacific Railroad, chartered in 1864 to build a line between Duluth, Minnesota, and Portland, Oregon, made less rapid progress, not being finished until 1883. It was given twenty sections per mile in the states through which it ran, forty sections per mile in the territories. The Atcheson, Topeka, and Santa Fé Railroad made about equal progress. Nourished by 3 million acres of land in alternate sections in Kansas, it finally reached Los Angeles in 1883. A year earlier New Orleans and Los Angeles had been joined by rails, the Southern Pacific controlling an important part of the trackage; it also received a large quantity of land, about 24 million acres. The federal government further assisted the western railroads by lending them many millions of dollars. In justice to the railroads, it should be recalled that these loans were all repaid with interest and that the roads which received land grants in turn agreed to carry soldiers and United States property without cost to the nation. Although they were later allowed to charge half of the usual rates, the federal government eventually received great benefit from the arrangement, because the special rates were not discontinued until after World War II.

East of the Mississippi in the period from 1865 to 1877 there was both railroad building and amalgamation. The New York Central was formed in 1867 under the leadership of Cornelius Vanderbilt, while the Pennsylvania Railroad also gained control of several smaller lines and expanded. By 1873 the Baltimore and Ohio stretched as far west as Cincinnati, and the Southern Railway offered service all the way from Washington to Atlanta. Meanwhile, the Rock Island, the Chicago, Burlington and Quincy, the Chicago, Milwaukee and St. Paul, and other lines extended westward from Chicago toward the Missouri River and beyond. A web of railroad tracks covered the nation; many other strands were added to it before the end of the nineteenth century.

SPECULATION AND CORRUPTION

The development of the railroads was accompanied by much reckless speculation in their stocks. Entrepreneurs waged economic battles for control of this line or that. More serious so far as the public welfare was concerned, was the graft which appeared in the building of the first transcontinental line. Both the Union Pacific and the Central Pacific employed special construction companies to build their trackage. Scandal accompanied the operations of the Crocker Corporation of the Central Pacific, and the Credit Mobilier of the Union Pacific became notorious. The Credit Mobilier was carefully organized so that the profits of construction would go to the promoters of the Union Pacific rather than to its stockholders. Moreover, in 1872 several important Republican politicians, including Schuyler Colfax, Henry Wilson, and James A. Garfield, were accused of accepting stock in the Credit Mobilier in return for their political influence. Colfax was Vice-President at the time and was soon succeeded by Wilson; nine years later Garfield became President. Their guilt was never established, but that of other lesser Republicans was.

Corruption in public life was, of course, confined neither to the affairs of the new bigger business nor to Washington. It was widespread, to be found in the Northern state capitals as well as in the carpetbagger governments. In New York City the notorious "Tweed Ring," led by Tammany boss William Marcy Tweed, looted the city treasury. Before their plundering was stopped as the result of a campaign led by *The New York Times*, the ring stole something like $100,000,000. When it was exposed, most of its members fled to Europe to spend their gains, although Tweed himself was convicted of embezzlement in 1872 and died in prison six years later.

During the eight years of Grant's Presidency corruption was brought to light again and again. In 1869 the daring speculators Jay Gould and

"Jubilee Jim" Fisk sought to secure a corner on the nation's gold, hoping eventually to dispose of their holdings in the precious metal with vast profit to themselves. They could not control the market if the federal government chose to sell its gold. They therefore persuaded Abel R. Corbin, Grant's brother-in-law, a lobbyist by occupation, to do what he could toward preventing such selling. Corbin was unable to get Grant's promise to prevent it, but Gould and Fisk passed the word about that the President would not interfere with their operations. The price of gold soared on the market; then Grant ordered the treasury to sell, and the Gould-Fisk corner collapsed. The Credit Mobilier scandal of 1872 was quickly followed by the "Salary Grab" act, which raised the salary of the President from $25,000 to $50,000, and that of members of Congress from $5000 to $7500. It also enlarged the salaries of the Justices of the Supreme Court. The increases were not unreasonable—the President's salary had not been altered since 1789—but they were made in a time of economic stress, when Congress was in low repute among thoughtful men. In 1874, under the lash of adverse public opinion, its members were constrained to reduce their pay to its former level. In the same year the Secretary of the Treasury had to resign to escape a vote of censure in the House of Representatives.

The exposure of the "Whiskey Ring" came in 1875. Formed originally in St. Louis but soon at work in other cities, the "Whiskey Ring" was composed of internal revenue officers and distillers who conspired to defraud the government of excise taxes. As a result, no fewer than 238 persons were eventually indicted, including General Orville E. Babcock, Grant's own private secretary. The President used his influence to ward off Babcock's conviction. And still the revelations of misconduct continued. In 1876 it became known that Secretary of War William W. Belknap had accepted bribes in connection with the sale of trading posts in the Indian Territory. Impeached by the House of Representatives, Belknap resigned his post in an attempt to avoid trial. Nevertheless, the Senate considered the case against him; he was acquitted, but on the technical ground that the Senate lacked jurisdiction because he was no longer in the federal service.

POSTWAR DIPLOMACY

Happily, the post-bellum record of the Republicans in foreign affairs, though a spotty one, was definitely superior to their performance in things domestic. Secretary of State Seward, who continued in office throughout Johnson's Presidency, committed no irretrievable errors, and Hamilton Fish, who followed him in the Grant regime, did very well, despite many difficulties, including his President. In Johnson's time the United States acquired the Island of Midway and Alaska; Fish won a great diplomatic triumph by persuading England to pay the *Alabama* claims, labored diligently and successfully toward improving relations between America and England, and behaved circumspectly with regard to troubles in the Caribbean region. The two New York Republicans were most respectable men.

NAPOLEON III AND MEXICO

Recovering from the wounds he had received at the time of Lincoln's assassination, Seward was little altered; he continued to vacillate between prudence and harebrained schemes, between modesty and truculence. He completed one piece of unfinished business by bringing steadily increasing pressure upon the Emperor Napoleon III to withdraw his troops from Mexico. In 1867, Napoleon was weary of his Mexican adventure; resistance against his puppet Emperor Maximilian by Mexican republicans under Benito Juarez was becoming stronger rather than weaker; affairs in Europe wore a troubled aspect; and the French ruler did not wish to become entangled in a contest with the United States. Even though the Union troops had been largely disbanded and the American treasury was not full, Napoleon had no desire for a major war which he could hardly hope to win west of the Atlantic. Seward's language in dealing with him was extremely careful; the Secretary did not even refer specifically to the Monroe Doctrine. At last Napoleon reluctantly called home his French soldiers, advising Maximilian to withdraw with them. That young prince refused to desert the Mexicans who had rallied about him and carried on a hopeless struggle against Juarez. He was finally captured and shot. Juarez became something of a Mexican Lincoln; Seward wished that he had spared Maximilian.

SEWARD'S ICEBOX

The achievement which assured Seward a place in history was the purchase of Alaska. Midway Island, which was taken for the United States by an American naval officer in 1867, the year in which Alaska was purchased, was not secured through any action on Seward's part. That the Secretary of State was responsible only for obtaining Alaska is a trifle surprising, in view of the fact that he was a feverish annexationist. No American Secretary of State was more lustful for territory than Seward, who dreamed of the day when the Stars and Stripes would fly over both Americas and the islands between. But the times and circumstances were against him, for the nation was almost glutted with land and was suffering from postwar disillusion; besides, as a loyal supporter of President Johnson, Seward had difficulty in getting help from Congress for his schemes of expansion. Seeking a naval base in the Caribbean, he tried to secure the Bay of Samaná from the Dominican Republic, which not only offered to turn over Samaná, but the whole country. Seward was stopped by Congress, the

House of Representatives indicating that it believed the Dominican Republic would bring more trouble than it was worth. He encountered a similar misfortune in an attempt to buy the Virgin Islands, then the property of Denmark. The Danish government was willing to sell them, provided the inhabitants of the islands gave consent, for $7,500,000. It signed the necessary treaty and the people of the islands gladly voted for annexation to the United States. Again, Congress refused to support Seward; the Senate would not ratify the treaty, and the House of Representatives refused to supply the requisite funds.

The Secretary fared much better in his "Arctic" enterprise than in his Caribbean ones. It is a matter of perennial surprise that the only difficulties in the way of securing Alaska were internal. However, there were the same objections to the acquisition of Alaska as there were to obtaining the tropical islands. Besides, Congress was learning to distrust Mr. Seward's sanguine schemes for annexing lands here, there, and everywhere in the New World. In the end, nevertheless, Congress did support Seward in the purchase of the vast Russian colony. There was no problem of getting Russian consent, for the government of Tsar Alexander II was eager to dispose of it. The Russian-American Company, which had managed the huge peninsula for Russia, was facing bankruptcy, and Alexander's ministers were averse to assuming direct control of it, for they knew it would be a liability, at least temporarily. They were aware that Alaska possessed precious metals, but believed they could not be exploited until the distant future. They knew that Britain could seize it easily, in the event of an Anglo-Russian war, and they also foresaw an American advance into Alaska. Accordingly, the Russian minister in Washington let it be known that his master might be coaxed into selling it. Seward leaped at the chance, so eager to buy that he did not quibble about the price. It was set at $7,200,000; although Seward was ignorant of the fact, Russia would have accepted as little as $5,000,000. A treaty of purchase was hastily prepared and presented to the Senate in April of 1867. At first the treaty was vehemently attacked in the press, largely because of ignorance of Alaska and its possibilities. How could anyone think of buying "Walrussia," an iceberg, an icehouse, an icebox? However, Seward began an "educational" campaign, dwelling upon the vast resources of Alaska, the wisdom of taking it before Britain should act, and the advantage at one and the same time of procuring Russia's withdrawal from the New World and of cementing friendship with her. He won over Charles Sumner, whose influence helped to persuade the Senate to endorse the treaty, which was done by an overwhelming majority of 37 to 2.

The consent of the House of Representatives was also necessary because of the money involved. That body long hesitated, finding almost every conceivable objection to the purchase. Gradually the weight of argument swung in favor of purchase. It was said in behalf of the bargain that it was a means to recompense Russia for the friendship she had displayed toward the Union during the Civil War. According to Russian documents, some members of the House were convinced through gifts of Russian money. In the end, the House gave its approval by a handsome majority, 113 to 43. The weary Russian minister asked to be transferred so that he could breathe a "purer atmosphere" than that of Washington.

HAMILTON FISH: CUBA AND THE PACIFIC

Hamilton Fish was no empire builder; he spent much time and energy preventing American expansion into the Caribbean. Nevertheless, further steps toward getting possessions in the Pacific were taken while he was Grant's Secretary of State. A rebellion against Spain in Cuba, which began in 1868, offered the same temptation to intervene to which the United States succumbed thirty years later. American sympathy went out to the Cuban rebels, who were permitted to organize military expeditions on the American mainland. When American citizens, chiefly naturalized Cubans, were captured and shot by the Spanish army, demands arose for energetic action on behalf of the oppressed Cubans struggling for liberty against a vicious Old World monarchy. It was urged that the United States declare war upon Spain, or at least recognize the Cuban rebels as belligerents, an action which would doubtless have led to war, since Spain was not in a mood to accept American interference. Although the Cubans were very weak militarily, President Grant and many members of Congress were eager to intervene. In August, 1869, Grant actually signed a proclamation recognizing the rebels as belligerents, and ordered Fish to issue it. Instead, Fish withheld the announcement, then successfully undertook to convince the President of the wisdom of maintaining neutrality. A year later, threatening to resign unless Grant supported him, Fish persuaded the President to send a message to Congress strongly recommending neutrality. A resolution in the House of Representatives calling for recognition of the rebels as belligerents was then narrowly defeated.

In the fall of 1873 danger of a war with Spain again mounted as a result of the *Virginius* incident. The ship *Virginius,* operated by Cuban insurgents and carrying revolutionists and munitions, was captured at sea by a Spanish war vessel and taken into the harbor of Santiago in Cuba. There the Spanish shot 53 passengers and crew members, including Americans and Englishmen, as pirates. Unaware of the true character of the *Virginius,* Fish demanded an apology and swift redress for the lives of the Americans executed. Then, learning that the *Virginius* was not rightfully sailing under the American flag, he prudently moderated his demands and accepted $80,000 as compensation to the families of the slain American citizens. War with Spain was averted.

Fish also helped Senator Charles Sumner to prevent the acquisition of a naval base in the Bay of Samaná. Grant had opposed Seward's scheme to buy the Virgin Islands because he disliked Seward, but he eagerly sought to get the naval base in the Dominican Republic. Fish could not restrain him; however, as chairman of the Senate Committee on Foreign Relations, Sumner fought against the President's project, and in 1870 he secured Senate rejection of a treaty calling for the annexation of the little and troubled republic. Again the United States escaped involvement in the Caribbean.

In the Pacific, however, the tale was different. American interest in the Samoan Islands in the South Pacific was rising, and the Navy believed that the splendid harbor of Pago Pago on the island of Tutuila was a fine location for a naval base. In 1872 an American naval officer signed a treaty with a Samoan chief which gave the United States the right to establish the base at Pago Pago in return for American protection. The Senate refused to endorse the treaty, but the State Department, offering its support to the Navy, continued to seek friends for the United States in the islands. The eventual result was a treaty made in 1878, by which the United States secured the right to build the base, in return pledging its good offices for composing any troubles which might arise between the Samoans and other powers. The nation was at least half-committed to an imperial outpost in the South Pacific. Relations between America and Hawaii also became much closer during Grant's second term, so that the eventual annexation of the island kingdom became almost inevitable. A trade reciprocity treaty with the native ruler was turned down by the Senate in 1867, but eight years later the Senate gave its sanction to another and far-reaching document. It permitted duty-free exportation of sugar from the islands to the United States; in return, the crown of Hawaii promised to make no territorial concession to any other power. The result was the sale of large quantities of Hawaiian sugar in the United States and a strong economic link between America and Hawaii.

ANGLO-AMERICAN RELATIONS

The dignified, responsible, and cool Fish shone brightly in dealing with Britain, achieving results beyond the reach of the more brilliant but erratic Seward. After Appomattox relations between America and England continued to be strained. On the westward side of the Atlantic it was not forgotten that England had shown favor toward the Confederacy, and resentment continued at a high level in the North because Britain had permitted the building of Confederate cruisers in her ports. On the other hand, the designs of some Americans upon Canada aroused feeling both in Canada and in Britain. Important in the founding of the Dominion of Canada in 1867 was a desire to ward off annexation by the Americans. One quarrel over a boundary and another over the Grand Banks fisheries caused a feeling of concern in London, Ottawa, and Washington. Especially offensive to Canada and to Britain were attempted invasions of Canada by the Fenians in 1866 and 1870. The Fenians were members of a brotherhood of Irish revolutionists who sought to achieve Irish independence by attacking Canada. Without much respect for realities, they hoped that they could conquer Canada and exchange it for the freedom of Ireland, or that they might entangle the United States and England in a war which would lead to the independence of Ireland. Fenianism attracted much support from Irish-Americans, who brought their hatred of Britain with them across the ocean, although only a few hundred volunteered for military service. The first Fenian invasion was easily checked by the Canadians, and a second was ruined when a United States marshal arrested its leader. Although the Fenian movements were hardly a serious menace to Canada, they were important because British and Canadian officials felt that the United States should have prevented them.

The already awkward situation between England and America was made worse in 1869 when Sumner delivered a sensational indictment against Britain in the Senate, demanding that she pay for the losses inflicted upon the American merchant marine by Confederate cruisers built in England. He also claimed that she should pay for indirect damages done by those cruisers, and for the total cost of the war to the Union after Gettysburg, this on the assumption that the Confederacy endured two years longer because of the help it received from the British. The bill presented by Sumner amounted to several billions of dollars. Its presentation aroused anger and ridicule in England. Nevertheless, the affair of the cruisers was regretted there, partly because it was widely believed that the British government had behaved improperly, and partly because it was feared, with good reason, that America would permit the building of similar cruisers in her ports when Britain again became involved in a war with one of her European enemies. A disposition toward reaching a settlement developed in England, and Fish made conciliatory gestures.

The result, in 1871, was the extraordinary Treaty of Washington, by which the two countries agreed to submit four of their disputes, including the one about Confederate cruisers, to arbitration. The British so keenly desired an accommodation that in the treaty they expressed regret for the escape of the *Alabama,* a fact which made it easier for the Senate to give its consent. A commission which considered the American claims with respect to the cruisers made no progress for a time, because the United States presented a bill along the lines laid down in Sumner's speech, asking for direct, indirect, and resulting damages. This was doubtless done to satisfy public opinion at home. When America agreed to accept compensation for direct injuries only, it became possible to proceed, and the commission finally awarded the United States $15,000,000. The other arbitrating bodies assessed the value of British claims against the United States at nearly $7,500,000. Accordingly, the awards cost England a little more than $7,500,000. The result was not entirely satisfactory either in London or Washington, but it was accepted by both parties, and feeling between them changed for the better. It was the first time that two great nations had successfully submitted important disputes to arbitration.

DOMESTIC POLITICS

If, because of the efforts of Fish, the record of Grant was respectable in foreign affairs, it was hardly so in several other respects. Nevertheless, the General was easily reelected in 1872, despite a serious split in the Republican party. Disgusted by the Grant regime's corruption and by its policy toward the South, Horace Greeley, Carl Schurz, Edwin L. Godkin, Charles Francis Adams, and other prominent men turned against Grant and founded a Liberal Republican party in 1872. They nominated Greeley for the Presidency and called earnestly for honest government, stressing the need for civil service reform—the Grant administration had established a Civil Service Commission a year earlier, but had deprived it of any possible usefulness by giving it no money. The Democrats also named Greeley. On casual view Greeley had an excellent chance of winning. Actually, he was too stout a Republican to arouse enthusiasm among rank and file Democrats; he was too much of a professional reformer to please the conservative elements; and he had been both inconsistent and irresponsible with respect to important public questions. While the Democrats favored a low protective tariff, he was for a high one. The full story of corruption in Grant's government was not yet known. The nation voted more decisively for the General than it had four years earlier, giving him a majority of 763,000 popular votes and an easy victory in the electoral college, 286 to 66. Greeley actually received no electoral votes, since he died before they were cast and his electors voted for various Liberal Republicans.

Liberal Republicanism was a dismal failure, but the Democratic party, resuming its independence, revived and did very well in the election of 1874, winning a majority in the House of Representatives. Two years later it secured a majority of the popular vote for the Presidency, but lost it nevertheless to the Republicans.

THE HAYES-TILDEN ELECTION

The leading candidate for the Republican Presidential nomination in 1876 was James G. Blaine of Maine, a man gifted with intellectual and oratorical abilities. However, the Republican convention refused to name him, for he had not satisfactorily answered a charge of corruption brought against him. Instead, the party prudently named Rutherford B. Hayes, a moderate and respectable Ohio politician. The Democrats supported Samuel J. Tilden of New York, who had made a reputation as a reformer in the governorship of that state. There was little to choose between the two men. Tilden had a margin of about 250,000 popular votes; carrying New York, New Jersey, Connecticut, and Indiana, with most of the Southern states, he had 184 electoral votes, or one short of a majority. The returns from South Carolina, Florida, and Louisiana were disputed; carpetbagger officials who were losing control of those states reported their electoral votes for Hayes, while incoming Democrats declared that Tilden had won in all three. Two sets of electors were also named in Oregon, where the Republicans unquestionably had a majority in the popular vote, but had named as an elector a postmaster who, under the Constitution, was ineligible to serve. To replace him the Democratic governor of Oregon named a Democrat while the Republicans put forth the name of another Republican. If any one of the disputed electoral ballots was cast for Tilden, he would be the victor. The Republicans asserted that all of them belonged to Hayes, and that he had been chosen.

There followed a strange contest, for the Constitution did not provide any means to settle the dispute. It merely declared that the electoral ballots were to be opened by the President of the Senate in the presence of the Senate and the House of Representatives, and that they "shall then be counted." Who was to do the counting? It will be recalled that the upper house was controlled by the Republicans, the lower one by the Democrats. In each of the chambers the majority was determined to have its way. Finally, late in January, 1877, Congress found a way out of the deadlock. It set up an Electoral Commission to award the disputed votes. It consisted of fifteen men, five from the Senate, five from the House, and five from the Supreme Court. It was agreed that all of the judgments of the Commission needed the consent of only one of the chambers to be decisive. It was expected that the Commission would consist of seven Democrats, seven Republicans and Supreme Court Justice David Davis, who was then known as an independent in politics. However, at this point Davis was elected to the Senate by the legislature of Illinois and hastily left the bench. He had to be replaced by another justice and only Republican justices were available. Accordingly, Judge Joseph P. Bradley was named. He was at first disposed to favor the claims of Tilden, but was subjected to heavy Republican pressure. By a straight party vote of eight to seven the Commission decided all the questions before it in favor of Hayes. The Republicans on it conveniently discovered that, whatever the facts in the several disputes, it could be said that the returns sent to Washington by the officials who customarily reported them favored Hayes. Under the provisions of the law setting up the Commission, Hayes was now sure of 185 votes, for the Republican Senate in every case endorsed the findings of the Commission. But would the Democrats let him take the Presidency? Embittered Northern Democratic adherents of Tilden declared that the election was being stolen and something ought to be done. Something was done, by Hayes. During the campaign he had indicated that he favored a softening of Republican policy toward the South. Now he let it be known to Southern Democrats that as President he would appoint a Southerner to his Cabinet. He also showed friendliness toward Southern railway interests. Far more important, he would order the withdrawal of all federal troops still remaining in the South. In any case, the Southerners were in no mood to fight for Tilden, who to do him justice, did not challenge the findings of the Commission. Pleased by Hayes' pledges, the Southerners indicated that Hayes must be permitted to take office.

Hayes was as good as his word. In April he did order the departure of all federal troops from the South. By that time all of the carpetbagger governments had been driven out of power and the continuing task of reconstruction was placed largely in Southern white hands.

34 THE GREAT WEST

In the popular mind throughout the world there is no history more romantic than that of the Great American West, from the close of the Civil War to the passing of the frontier. There the Indian, brave, vengeful, and pitiful, made his last stand, General George A. Custer and the Seventh Cavalry rode to undying fame, the cowboy with his six-shooter played the role of a modern knight, while cattlemen and sheepherders fought it out. The schoolmarm from the East fell in love with and married the valiant but gentlemanly frontier hero, a Southerner by birth; there virtue was always rewarded except in the unfortunate Indian. Such is the story of *the* West so often told in "Westerns," in novels, in movies, on radio, and on television. There are important elements of truth in it: the cowtown did exist, as did the gunman, the Texas Ranger, and the rest. True, the cowboy was commonly a farmhand who spent most of his time caring for cattle rather than in glamorous adventures. Nevertheless, in a sense the history of the Great West is even more fascinating than the popular semi-legends about it. The West was conquered by railroaders, miners, hunters, sheepherders, and farmers, as well as cowboys and cavalrymen.

The last West, the vast region roughly bounded on the east by the ninety-eighth meridian of longitude, on the west by the Rocky Mountains, and by the Canadian and Mexican borders was, except to a few hunters, not much more than a formidable and forbidding obstacle on the way to the Pacific coast at the time of the Civil War. The treeless plains with their hot summer suns in cloudless skies and their sudden winter snowstorms were not yet attractive to most whites. As we have seen, most uninformed Easterners fancied that something like a desert lay between the lower Missouri River and the Rockies. Even so, that West substantially disappeared within one long generation. The provincial Easterner who believes that Nebraska is somewhere near Idaho and who is unaware of the attractions of the Plains country may be tempted to think that it was finally occupied only because the rest of the United States was rather well filled with people. To those who spend their lives in New England villages or upon the sidewalks of New York the rolling expanses of the Great Plains may still look forbidding. After the search for precious metals on the Pacific Coast and in the Rockies had lost some of its appeal as a swift road to wealth, the genuine merits of the region of the Plains were recognized and their settlement followed rapidly. The coming of the railroads, artesian wells, barbed wire, dry farming, and later, irrigation, turned the semiarid country into one of cattle and grain. The Plains could not, to be sure, offer the attractions of the prairies of Illinois, because they lack sufficient rainfall. Given water, they would form an immense Canaan; who will say that the exigencies and ingenuity of mankind will not some day supply the water?

Unlike earlier American western frontiers, that which centered upon the Great Plains was conquered by invasions of settlers from both the east and the west. The spread of mining into it was from the direction of the setting sun. By the time of the Civil War seekers for mineral wealth had followed prospectors and the news of "rich strikes" from California back into Nevada and Colorado. There followed "rushes" into Idaho, Montana, Wyoming, and the Black Hills of the Dakotas. Arizona and New Mexico were not ignored. Wherever gold or silver, or both, was found, a town quickly sprang up. At first such settlements were not much in the way of civilization. They attracted gamblers, ne'er-do-wells, keepers of saloons, and prostitutes. Robbery and murder were in their early days only too frequent. Wildest of all of them doubtless was Deadwood, which seems to have attracted a peculiarly gay, irresponsible, and vicious collection of cardsharps, adventurers, and desperados. If, however, a mining town acquired permanence—many of them did not, becoming "ghost" towns—its people established order, employing "Vigilante" justice until marshals, sheriffs, and courts were ready to assume the task of maintaining the peace. A newspaper appeared, or perhaps more than one; then came a hotel, decent women, children, shops, and schools. Towns near rich strikes even acquired mansions and "oper'y houses," although the fortunate men who became genuinely rich tended to establish themselves in San Francisco and other inviting cities. Many of the towns died because there was not enough precious metal nearby to sustain them; some lived on because of gold, silver, copper, and lead far beneath the surface, which brought in mining companies that carried on more or less permanently. Other mining centers eventually prospered because of the growth of agriculture, and some because of railroad traffic and business.

The railroads also served to help destroy the Great West, some entering it from the Pacific coast, but more from the east. To the four transcontinental lines finished or begun before the end of Grant's Presidency was soon added a fifth, eventually known as the Great Northern Railway, which stretched from the Mississippi to Tacoma, Washington, by 1893. The "iron horses" needed fuel and water, hence the building of stations at intervals on the Plains—these were actually preceded by smaller ones built for stagecoach lines or the Pony Express, which carried mail from St. Joseph, Missouri, to San Francisco as early as 1860. The building of the railroads was also accompanied by the spread of information about the economic possibilities of the West; it became known that there was something other than deserts and semideserts in the valleys of the Platte and Cimarron Rivers. Seeking to sell the lands which they had obtained from the federal government, the railroads urged people to seize opportunity in an unexploited country, giving suitably favorable pictures of the possibilities of the lands which they owned. James J. Hill, controlling the Great Northern Railway, which received no land grants, was especially active in promoting settlement along the right of way of his line. Some of the railroads even employed agents to encourage people in Europe to seek new homes on the Plains. Further, the availability of transport made possible the rise of the cattle industry and more or less profitable raising of corn and wheat for Eastern markets. In addition, they enabled hunters to ship hundreds of thousands of buffalo skins eastward and virtually to destroy the vast buffalo herds, so depriving thousands of Indians of their traditional livelihood and helping to reduce them to dependence upon the white man. With the railroads advancing from the East came the farmers in tens of thousands, flooding into Kansas, Texas, and Nebraska, and later into the Dakotas, Wyoming, and Oklahoma. Nebraska became a state in 1867; its population was hardly sufficient for the purpose, but the majority of it was Republican, and the Republicans needed votes in Washington. Meanwhile, the Cattle Kingdom, beginning in Texas, spread northward and westward, occupying most of the semiarid region between the farmers and the mountains and valleys in the Rockies. By 1890 there was no major frontier left in the United States.

THE INDIANS

Had bravery been enough to hold back the miners, the farmers, and the cattlemen, together with United States army, the occupation would have been long deferred, for the Plains Indians fought desperately for their freedom and their way of life. The Apache and Navaho of the New Southwest fought with equal courage.

It was fortunate for the whites that the principal Indian tribes of California and the Rocky Mountain region, the Diggers and the Utes, were not warlike. The Apache, the Navaho, the Comanche, the Cheyenne, the Arapaho, and the Sioux, gave the army, the cowboys, the Texas Rangers, and all other whites all the fighting they wanted. Except for the Navaho, those tribes were horsemen, adept in the use of lances and of three-foot bows. These weapons were effective enough, perhaps better than the swords and inferior rifles with which the army in the West was equipped during and immediately after the Civil War. Later, the Indians acquired guns by gift and trade, and used them with equal efficiency. Unhappily for the Indians, the whites gradually armed themselves with superior weapons, Winchester repeating rifles and Colt six-guns. The Indians long retained an advantage in mobility, for most of them lived in tepees which could be moved in a few hours, and fed and clothed themselves from the herds of buffalo. It was no coincidence that the resistance of the red men ended with the virtual extinction of the buffalo.

In popular legend the Apache have a reputation for courage, treachery, and cruelty. Cruel they were by the white man's standards, not by their own. Treachery was something they shared with the whites with whom they struggled. For raiding settlements in Texas and New Mexico, they and the Navaho were attacked and subjugated after bitter fighting during the Civil War by Union troops. The Apache were forced to go to reservations set aside for them, but many refused to accept the dullness and poverty of reservation life, fled to the open, and resumed the hopeless struggle. The massacre of 100 of them at Camp Grant in Arizona in 1871 helped to persuade the Apache that it was better to be free briefly than to die either swiftly or slowly on the reservation. The Apache did not finally bow to their fate until their savage chief Geronimo submitted in 1886.

The story was much the same for the tribes of the southern part of the Great Plains. The Cheyenne and the Arapaho began their fight for freedom in 1864, after they had been assigned to a reservation in eastern Colorado. Five hundred were suddenly attacked by Colorado militia under Colonel J. M. Chivington. In the "Chivington Massacre" which followed, all but fifty of the Indians, men, women, and children alike, were slain.

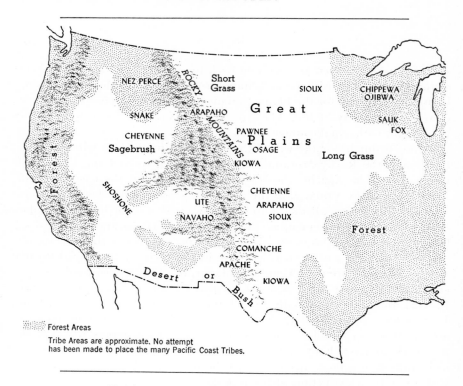

GREAT PLAINS AND MAIN INDIAN TRIBES

However, their chief, Black Kettle, escaped, and for a time carried on desultory raids against whites wherever he could find them. In 1865 the Cheyenne and Arapaho, along with the Comanche and other tribes of the southern Great Plains, made peace and accepted reservations in the Indian Territory of Oklahoma. This bargain was confirmed by federal commissioners sent out from Washington in 1867 to put an end to Indian troubles and to smooth the way for white occupation of Kansas and Nebraska. But these tribes were inevitably unhappy in Oklahoma and in 1868, armed with guns, they took to the warpath. Both Kansas and Texas felt their fury. In November, 1868, Colonel George A. Custer, leading troops and frontiersmen, surrounded several hundred Cheyenne and Arapaho warriors under Black Kettle on the banks of the Washita River. After several hours of fierce conflict, Black Kettle and more than 100 of his men were dead, the remainder fleeing to temporary safety. The southern Plains Indians fought on six years longer, carrying on bloody raids of vengeance, but had at last to yield to the army and to accept reservation life in Oklahoma.

On the Great Plains and on the eastern approaches to the Rockies lived

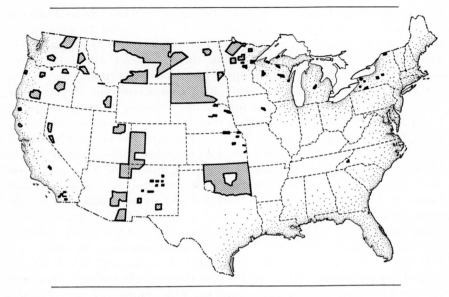

INDIAN RESERVATIONS IN 1875

the Sioux. Numerous and warlike, they were not easily brought into subjection. The poet, Eugene Field said:

> Now what in the world shall we doux
> With the bloody and murderous Sioux
> Who some time ago
> Took his arrow and bow
> And raised such a hellabelioux?

Some of the Sioux took up arms against the whites in Minnesota as early
as 1862, but were beaten and driven westward. By 1865 miners were pushing into the Sioux country from the west, and farmers were entering it
from the east. When the federal government began to build a road between
Minnesota and Montana, the Sioux took up arms under Chief Red Cloud.
There followed a three-year war in which the red men won a substantial
victory near Fort Philip Kearny in Wyoming, killing Captain W. J.
Fetterman and a detachment of 81 troops. The "First Sioux War" ended
when the federal commissioners offered the Sioux a permanent reservation
in the Dakota Territory west of the Missouri River. The Sioux accepted
the offer and signed a peace treaty at Fort Laramie, Wyoming, in the
following year.

The Sioux found life hard and unpalatable on their reservation.
Through the federal Indian Service they received spoiled meat and other
bad food, while miners and other adventurers refused to keep off the lands

reserved for them. Unable to restrain the aggressive whites, federal officials tried to restrict the movements of the Sioux. The restless Indians, under the leadership of Sitting Bull and Crazy Horse, fled into Montana, where the army had no choice but to follow them. General Alfred H. Terry organized three columns of troops which converged upon the Sioux, gathered in the valley of the Little Big Horn River. Discovering their camp, Colonel Custer, who led one of the columns, moved forward to attack before the arrival of the other two. Dividing his command into two parts, he sent one down the west bank of the river and personally led the other 265 men along its eastern bank. Thinking that the Sioux immediately before him were not numerous, he moved against their encampment on June 25. There were more than 2500 in it; they poured out to fight and Custer and his men were soon surrounded. Occupying a hill, they fought desperately to hold off repeated attacks, but all were killed. "Custer's Last Stand" was a memorable victory for the Sioux; the reckless Custer, whether devoted to duty or a gloryseeker, became a tragic and romantic hero.

However, the Sioux had triumphed over only one detachment of the federal troops. General Terry arrived on the scene in time to rescue the soldiers sent down the west bank of the Little Big Horn by Custer. Gathering the federal soldiers, he pursued the Sioux warriors, who retreated eastward. Before the end of October he trapped about 3000 of them in the Tongue River valley, and secured the surrender of most. A few, including Sitting Bull, refused to go back to the reservation, and sought freedom in Canada. Thereafter, the Sioux were generally quiet for some years. In 1890 one of their "magicians" caused a commotion among them by proclaiming that they could win back their lands and their liberty under his leadership. When troops tried to stop the "Ghost Dances" through which he was stirring up his people, the Sioux resisted. Among them was Sitting Bull, who had returned from Canada. He was killed. In the "Battle" of Wounded Knee the troops, sent out to disarm a large band of Sioux, attacked it, slaying 200 men, women, and children. The affair at Wounded Knee, a massacre rather than a fight, marked the end of serious Indian resistance in the United States.

Subdued at last by superior power, most of the American Indians had to learn to live like their conquerors. Happily, once they had lost their independence, they suffered little from social discrimination. Nevertheless, the transition from their own ways to those of the whites was difficult. They received help from eastern humanitarians who were stirred to action by Helen Hunt Jackson's *A Century of Dishonor,* a book published in 1881 which described the treatment received by the Indians from the whites in the darkest colors. Seeking to turn the Indians into homestead farmers as rapidly as possible, so that they might become economically independent, the humanitarians secured the passage of the Dawes Severalty

Act in 1887. This gave authority to the President to divide the lands of any tribe among its members, each married man to receive 160 acres, with lesser amounts going to single men, women, and children. Such lands were to be held in trust by the federal government for 25 years, to prevent unwise sales to unscrupulous whites. In addition, it was stipulated that Indians who received such individual land allotments were thenceforth citizens of the United States. The measure might not have been adopted had it not been pleasing to white speculators who hoped to obtain surpluses of tribal land not needed to provide for its members. However, the Indians profited from the surplus lands also, for proceeds from the sale of them were used to educate the Indians. The Great White Father had bestirred himself to found the Carlisle (Pennsylvania) Indian School as early as 1879 to provide training in things agricultural and mechanical for selected Indian boys. Later he offered much more substantial help by establishing elementary schools on Indian reservations.

The problems of the Indian were not solved when he came to own a piece of land, for often it was not fertile. Poverty was long the lot of many of the red men, whether they lived individually or tribally. There were striking exceptions to the rule in the Indian Territory of Oklahoma, where the discovery of oil made some individuals and the Osage tribe wealthy. A long forward step came in 1924 when all Indians were declared to be American citizens. Thereafter, seeking to help the red men toward happiness, the federal government encouraged the continuance of tribal life where it still existed, as it did in New Mexico and Arizona. Afflicted by bad conscience, it also opened the way immediately after World War II for lawsuits against itself by Indian tribes that claimed they had been insufficiently paid for lands they had ceded to the United States. Since the prices paid were often low, and since the law suits were "friendly," tribe after tribe received additional pay, the total reaching many millions of dollars. By that time there were doubtless more persons who called themselves Indians than there were at the time of the founding of Jamestown, but many of those who proudly called themselves Indians were partly white or Negro. The amalgamation of red and white was proceeding rapidly.

THE CATTLE KINGDOM

The freedom of the cowboy hardly endured beyond that of the Indian, for he was fenced in by the time the last of the great Indian tribes were confined to the reservations. The great days of the Cattle Kingdom were only from the close of the Civil War to the middle of the 1880s; then the open range disappeared, except in romance. But what a time it was while it lasted! It began immediately after the war when owners of herds of cattle in southern Texas, unable to find sufficient markets in the shattered and disorganized South, decided to try to sell beef in the North, where the war had brought a shortage. Thus began the "long drive" from southern Texas northward to railroads extending beyond the Mississippi. The first drive, which ended at Sedalia, Missouri, was not very profitable, for Indians, angry settlers, and wooded country exacted a heavy toll. Then Joseph M. McCoy, an Illinois dealer in meat, had an inspiration; he built stock-pens and other facilities at Abilene, Kansas, on the Kansas Pacific Railway, and invited the Texas cattlemen to bring their longhorns there. The route from Texas to Abilene, afterward known as the Chisholm Trail, ran through open and largely unsettled country. The result was magical. The Texans brought 35,000 steers to Abilene in 1867, 75,000 the following year, and then hundreds of thousands. As settlements and railroads advanced westward, Abilene lost business to Newton, Ellsworth, and Dodge City, but something like four million cattle reached the Kansas cowtowns before the "long drive" ended in the mid-1880s. While it lasted, the cowtowns, with their saloons, dance halls, brothels, brawls, murders, and United States marshals, became notorious and famous, for the cowboy, paid off at the end of the drive, had to have his fling. The shabby and garish cowtowns absorbed his wages in his brief sprees; while they lasted, he enjoyed himself, but not always to the liking of respectable folk who wanted peace and quiet.

With the development of refrigerated railroad cars the market for cattle widened enormously, western beef moving to the East and to Europe to feed an ever-increasing population. Raising cattle became for a time a quick road to wealth, for steers were readily and cheaply raised on the free grass of the open range, and they brought as much as nine cents per pound at Chicago, Omaha, and Kansas City. The cattlemen, abandoning the "long drive," soon moved northward to take advantage of the grassy plains and occasional valleys of Kansas, Nebraska, and eastern Colorado, as railroad service became easily available there. The Cattle Kingdom extended on to the Dakotas, Wyoming, and Montana. Breeding eastern cattle with the longhorns, their owners sent ever larger quantities of better and better beef eastward. Their profits were sometimes immense, and many an energetic and thrifty cowpoke developed a vast herd from a few head of cattle. Investment in cattle became a rage in the East and in England, and company after company was formed for the purpose. Then came collapse from overproduction, falling prices, lack of sufficient free grass, and storms that decimated the roving herds. Then came fencing, and the squeezing out of the poor and less efficient owners. The ranch appeared as a vast cattle farm, and the cowboy had to learn to pitch hay. The cattle business even shifted eastward, for it became easier and cheaper to fatten the animals on farms in the valley of the lower Missouri River and in the prairie country of the Old Northwest. A colorful chapter in the American

THE LONG DRIVE

story had ended. It would be told again and again, with omissions and additions; the Polynesian of the Island of Bora Bora would learn the techniques of a gun fight with six-shooters.

Modern man wants clothing and lamb chops as well as steak, whether whole or ground. The sheepherder, finding his occupation not very comfortable in the Ohio Valley, followed the miners to the Pacific coast, then worked his way back toward the Great Plains. He and his flock were detested by the cattlemen, for he took valuable water holes, and his woolly animals shared the wild grasses with the cows. The presence of the sheepmen and their charges was all the more resented because cattlemen believed that sheep, cropping the grass very closely, killed it. "Wars" followed, and the cowboy's revolver did not prove to be consistently more deadly than the sheepherder's rifle and shotgun. The cattleman had to learn to live with the sheepman. When he eventually found out that raising lambs could be more profitable than steers, he often learned to prefer baaing to lowing. The production of wool became important in the West.

FARMING ON THE PLAINS

The cattle country shrank far more from invasion by farmers than it did because of the inroads of the sheepherders. Firmly entrenched at the end of the Civil War in Iowa, Minnesota, and the eastern parts of Nebraska and Kansas, the farmers moved rapidly westward during the generation between 1865 and 1890. They poured into Texas, the Dakotas, and eastern Colorado, as well as into central Kansas and Nebraska. When part of the Indian Territory was opened to settlement in 1890, they rushed into it; when a second part, the Cherokee Strip, was thrown open three years later, they rapidly established themselves upon it; and they were as quick to settle when the remainder of the Territory was later made available to them. The Great West was a land of promise to the farmers of the Midwest and also to those of the Southwest, though to a lesser degree. America and Europe needed wheat, and corn as well, and both could be grown on the Plains. Wheat was so much in demand during the first fifteen years after the Civil War that its price seldom fell below $1 per bushel. It was sold in large quantities in England, more than 150,000,000 bushels in 1880. Wheat growing on the Plains posed new problems with respect both to production and processing, but they were rapidly solved. The soft winter wheat grown in the East and Midwest would not survive the cold winters on the Northern plains; it was replaced by hard spring wheat and by hard kerneled "Turkey Red" wheat imported from Russia. The newer varieties of grain required new machinery for grinding. This was developed by 1871 in Minneapolis, and ten years later mills in that city and in St. Louis and Kansas City were putting out vast quantities of "New Process Flour." Plows were improved to permit the easy cutting of the rich soil; "dry" farming—cultivation carried on so as to make the most and best use of less generous rainfall—was employed, and harvesting machines made large-scale farming possible. The grain elevator appeared beside railroad tracks, and barbed wire was invented to protect both crops and animals in a country where wood was exceedingly scarce. Windmills were improved and brought in to pull much needed water from deep in the ground. So difficulty after difficulty was conquered, and with them millions of acres of soil. During the two decades beginning in 1870, 225 million acres of land were put into cultivation in the United States, most of it in the Great West.

It should not be assumed that the Homestead Act of 1862 enabled the onrushing farmers to secure rich land easily, or that it was the sole vehicle through which the farmers became established in the West. It is likely that no more than one-ninth of the West came directly into their hands under the provisions of that law. Actually, the 160 acres which could be secured under it were not enough to support a family in central Nebraska, although they were ample in central Illinois. The Western family-sized farm therefore could not be obtained under the law. Besides, much of the best land was distributed in other ways. The railroads, it will be recalled, were granted vast acreages; large quantities were given to the states; and great areas were permitted to pass into private hands by preemption under a law of 1841 which offered the privilege of purchase to those who "squatted" on land before it was surveyed. The states frequently sold their lands to speculators, who often secured more by going through the forms of preemption. They also employed men as their agents to secure soil under the Homestead Act. The would-be settler therefore commonly had to purchase from the railroads or from speculators. Even so, he generally did well, if he survived early hardships on the Plains. Many of the pioneers did not, returning in defeat to the wooded and well-watered regions from which they came.

Those who established themselves as farmers on the Plains underwent trials which city folk, who seldom ventured to try such a life, could not have withstood. Since there were few trees, the settler had to start off in any sort of a hut, then in a sodhouse, its walls and roof chiefly of turf, and its floor the bare earth. Time and prosperity were required before wood could be brought in to build houses. Water was often carried from a creek, perhaps a muddy one, until a well could be sunk, no easy matter when underground water lay dozens or even hundreds of feet underneath the surface. Beans, bread, and salt were the food staples of the early years. Hotter suns than the pioneers had ever known beat down upon them in the summer; July winds moving from the south across wheat fields seemed to become warmer as they moved northward. The winters were colder than they were in Indiana or Kentucky, occasionally bringing violent storms that left the ground covered with heavy snows. Then the farmer had to bring his domestic animals into his sodhouse, until he became prosperous enough to build a shelter for them. Tornadoes moving from the southwest in spring and early summer sometimes destroyed the unfortunates in their paths. Especially disheartening was drought, which the pioneers had not anticipated, since rainfall was more generous than usual on the Plains immediately after the Civil War. With drought came grasshopper plagues that were both destructive and terrifying, for the hopping insects ate almost everything as they swept through the countryside. Nevertheless, most of the pioneers made good, although their lives did not become as easy as those of the farmers to the east. Too dependent upon wheat and corn, they would suffer seriously from overproduction as well as drought. With the miners, cattlemen, and sheepherders, they filled territory after territory, created state after state until the admission of Arizona and New Mexico as states in 1912 brought the total to forty-eight. A mere list of those admitted after 1865 is impressive: Nebraska, Colorado, Montana, South Dakota, North Dakota, Washington, Idaho, Wyoming, Utah, Oklahoma, New Mexico, and Arizona. To be sure, not all of them were located on the Great Plains. In a larger sense they were all part of the West.

35 THE RISE OF MODERN AMERICA

Amazing as agricultural expansion was after the Civil War, the growth of American industry and commerce was even more astonishing. By the end of the nineteenth century American industrial production was greater than that of any other nation in the world. Despite the spread of agriculture across the nation, the value of manufactured goods produced exceeded the worth of the fruits of the soil for the first time; thereafter, the gap between them widened constantly. With this extraordinary bursting of industry came a continuing increase in population which was not so great in terms of percentage as in the past, but which was massive nevertheless. In 1870 there were about 38,500,000 Americans; thirty years later there were almost 76,000,000. Contributing heavily to this increase were waves of immigration, especially from southern and eastern Europe. Toward the end of the century Europeans who sought new homes in the United States steadily numbered more than 500,000 persons annually. Commerce flourished along with industry and agriculture, and the city became ever more important in American life. At the beginning of the Civil War hardly more than 16 Americans out of 100 lived in centers having populations of 8000 or more; forty years afterward almost a third of Americans resided in such urban places. A new America, industrial, commercial, and urban emerged; with it came the beginnings of a "New Immigration" that

507

would add novel ingredients in large quantities to the Melting Pot. The course of rapid growth, like that of true love, never does run smooth, and there were jarrings enough as the face and body of the nation altered.

INDUSTRIAL GROWTH

The rise of industry in America was not in itself unique, for the same phenomenon was to be seen in western and central Europe and later in other parts of the world. What was different about it was its magnitude. Later on, America would again lead the way by moving toward a more general diffusion of the benefits of industry. Precisely why it made such rapid advances in the latter part of the nineteenth century cannot be determined. The natural resources conducive to its growth had long been available in profusion—rich lands, abundant stores of iron and almost every other valuable metal, timber in vast quantities, and oil trapped beneath the surface in almost incredible amounts. It has been remarked that the Civil War was apparently not an extraordinary stimulant. The steady progress of invention doubtless offered a major contribution. Government offered encouragement and imposed few restrictions upon industry before the twentieth century. It also helped by lending money and giving lands to the railroads. Tariffs consistently offered protection against European manufacturers until the present century was well under way, and gave assistance to an industry that was no longer "infant." Capital was available, accumulated at home and invested from abroad, for English money helped to nourish many American enterprises. There was a generous supply of labor, for immigrants constantly added to the stock of hands and skills.

Central in the expansion of American manufacturing was a host of new inventions, processes, and techniques, among them improved machinery for making shoes, flour, clothing, and cigarettes. Other developments were the harvesting "combine," the rotary drill, power shovels, railroad refrigeration cars, and the improvement and increased use of metal alloys, chemical processes, and electric power. More and more oil was found in Pennsylvania and West Virginia, later in Oklahoma, and it was refined with greater precision for more numerous uses. Most important of all was ever more effective exploitation of coal and iron. While the mining of coal had formerly been conducted chiefly on the anthracite fields of eastern Pennsylvania, now the bituminous deposits of western Pennsylvania, West Virginia, and Illinois were made to yield immense quantities of fuel. It was used to make steam power, which came to be employed far more than the familiar water power. It also served to supply hearths of the steel industry, which grew by leaps and bounds. In the 1870s and 1880s the production of steel by means of the Bessemer Process became standard, tripling during the latter decade. Even more important was the production of the open-hearth process, which readily removed sulphur and phosphorus from iron ore, thus making it possible to use ore which had formerly been almost worthless. The manufacture of steel and iron flourished in Pittsburgh and its vicinity, and to a lesser degree in the Birmingham area of Alabama, where both coal and iron ore were close at hand. With increasing exploitation of the rich iron mines in the Mesabi Range in Minnesota and other hills in Michigan's Upper Peninsula, Gary and Cleveland received the black metal by lake boats and became great steel centers. The availability of generous supplies of steel made possible innumerable improvements in manufacturing and transport.

THE CITY

Commerce, transport, and the city kept pace with manufacturing. Between the beginning of Grant's Presidency and the end of the century railroad trackage tripled; in 1900 there were 200,000 miles of tracks in the United States, more than in all of Europe. Passengers and goods moved quickly and inexpensively by train in almost every part of the nation, while the dining car and the Pullman sleeper made travel over great distances comfortable, at least for the prosperous. The department store developed to help distribute cloth and clothing, dishes and kitchen utensils, and the ten thousands of things pouring out of American factories and imported from abroad. In the larger cities it became possible to ride from one's home to shops or offices on electric trolley cars. The bicycle came into common use, especially for pleasure riding on quiet streets and country lanes. The "horseless carriage" appeared in the 1890s, but was not to come into general use until the following decade. However, quiet streets and roads became more difficult to find, especially for the city dweller. In 1860 New York City was the home of a little more than 1,000,000 persons; forty years later nearly 3,500,000 lived in it. By 1900 Chicago, rail center and butcher for a vast area, had almost 1,700,000 people, and Philadelphia, while growing much less rapidly, nevertheless housed almost 1,300,000. In the 1880s cities throughout the nation grew with astonishing rapidity, Minneapolis from 47,000 to 164,000, Omaha from 30,500 to 140,000, St. Louis from 60,000 to more than 152,000, and Birmingham, Alabama, from 3000 to more than 26,000. In a sense, the city had replaced the frontier by 1890, for the mecca of the dissatisfied from rural America had by that time become the city rather than the beguiling lands in the West.

BIG BUSINESS AND THE ROBBER BARONS

Such far-reaching changes in the very staff and stuff of American life brought with them all sorts of consequences. One was the appearance of genuine "Big Business," the formation of giant corporations, trusts, and, at the very end of the century, the holding company. The order of that generation was combination, sometimes extraordinarily vicious, to prevent competition, to secure efficiency, and to reap greater profits. The trust was a neat device by which trustees held and voted the stock of several companies for their own benefit, though not necessarily for that of the public; the holding company afterward served much the same purposes, but had larger possibilities for controlling many companies with a relatively small investment. Most famous of all the combinations were the Standard Oil of John D. Rockefeller, and the United States Steel Corporation organized by Elbert H. Gary and J. P. Morgan in 1902. Standard Oil was chartered as a company in Ohio in 1870; re-formed as a trust which was dissolved by court order in 1892, it appeared as the Standard Oil Company of New Jersey, both a holding and operating company, in 1899. It was able to monopolize oil refining for many years. The United States Steel Corporation, an immense company, controlled iron ore, shipping facilities, and steel works; capitalized at $1,400,000,000; it long dominated the iron industry. But these were only two of many economic concentrations of wealth and power. There was a "Whiskey Trust," a "Sugar Trust," and a "Lead Trust." Cornelius Vanderbilt, James J. Hill, and Edward Harriman, among others, built railroad empires, Daniel Guggenheim founded a dynasty in mining, Andrew D. Carnegie was the master of a kingdom in steel until he chose to sell out to the United States Steel Corporation, and James B. Duke acquired massive tobacco interests.

These economic giants and the men who made them have been bitterly condemned by some historians and defended, at least to a degree, by others. The case against the trusts is formidable enough. They stifled competition, driving their rivals out of existence or absorbing them; monopolizing a product or a service, they fleeced the public by charging excessively high prices; they treated labor as a commodity, grinding down men, women and children alike; they flouted the laws; they corrupted lawmakers, judges, and public officials of all sorts and ranks; and they discriminated against the farmer. Three practices of the railroads have brought especial condemnation on them: inequitable rates, "pooling," and rebates. Competing savagely, especially in the 1870s, the railroads carried on rate wars where two or more ran parallel lines. Losing money from this kind of operation, they charged higher rates in areas where they had a monopoly of the carrying business. In consequence, it was often more expensive to ship goods on a short haul than on a long one on the same railroad. The farmer in particular suffered from the discriminatory procedure. In part to reduce ruinous competition, the railroads also developed the pool, by which they divided the business in a given area, set the rates within it, and shared the profits in accordance with a predetermined formula. For the public the pool could mean poor service as well as heavier charges. The rebate was a "kickback" from a railroad to a user of its services who was powerful enough to demand special treatment. A fixed percentage of freight charges was returned to those who could command it, often secretly. A general indictment against "Big Business" has been delivered on the ground that it was simply too big for the good of the nation.

The men who led in the creation of "Big Business" have been condemned with it, for greed, ruthlessness, disregard for the interests of others, and evil conduct. The name "Robber Barons" has been attached to them. A favorite example of their conduct is John D. Rockefeller's thoroughgoing use of rebates to injure competitors; he obtained rebates from the railroads, not only upon his own oil, but also upon that of his competitors. Other charges against the business leaders include stock-watering, unscrupulous manipulation of stocks on the exchanges, and taking advantage generally of the small and innocent investor.

The "Robber Barons" and "Big Business" have been defended on the ground that they developed the powerful machines in industry and transport which enabled the nation successfully to meet the dangerous challenge of Germany and her allies in World War I. If so, they cannot receive much credit, since it was not the intention of the barons to prepare for that struggle. Other defenses of the "entrepreneurs," as they are now commonly called in America, are more cogent. It must be recalled that the "entrepreneurs" hardly differed from their like in other countries; that no ethical rules for the conduct of their activities had been established when they embarked upon them; that many of them were not unscrupulous, at least by their own standards; that they were driven to combination in some part because of ruinous competition; and also that "Big Business" was not only inevitable but that it was not unhealthy in the long run. Its bad practices could be curbed; its benefits could be spread throughout society.

What sort of people were the entrepreneurs, and to what uses were put the immense fortunes that they accumulated? They were generally not crude, self-made men, but men who began in the world with some advantages. They came from families that were not poor, and they were fairly well educated by the standards of the time. They were commonly members of the more conservative Protestant churches, Episcopalians, Presbyterians, and Congregationalists. John D. Rockefeller taught a Sunday School class. They were not addicted to keeping mistresses and most of them saw themselves as benefactors to society. They created a new American aristocracy, for much of their money has remained with their descendants. On the other hand, the benefactions received from foundations established with Rockefeller, Carnegie, Duke, Guggenheim, Henry E. Huntington, and Leland Stanford money have been enormous. In this century the Rockefeller Foundation, the Carnegie Foundation, and the Duke Endowment have had hundreds of millions of dollars to spend for the public good.

If the entrepreneurs exerted more influence, good and bad, than other men, the cities which they helped to build were also to affect the American future profoundly, both for weal and woe. They sucked in sturdy farmer stock, depriving it of relative economic independence and of touch with the soil. They tended to discourage marriage and large families; the larger they became the more they encouraged crime, for they supplied better hiding places for the criminal. They fostered misconduct in public office, for what was the public business of the mass was likely to become no one's business; and they had an adverse effect upon private morality. They also offered freedom and stimulation to writers, artists, and musicians, as cities have done in all ages. They were conducive to change in thought as well as in behavior. In politics, with their great voting power, they more readily offered support to new men and to new ideas. If they had some undesirable social qualities, they were fruitful centers for an advancing American civilization. They would have had an even more powerful impact in the political world, had not rural America refused to give city folks representation in proportion to their numbers. The farmer and the villager, attracted by the city, exaggerated its corruptive influence and tried to keep control of the state and federal governments in their own true hands.

RURAL AMERICA AND BIG BUSINESS

Rural America, fighting a long and losing struggle against the urban one, engaged the railroads in a bitter fight that started in the 1870s and dragged on for decades. At first the farmers of the Midwest carried the burden of it. Their basic difficulty was overproduction, brought on by the geographical extension of farming and by increased yields. It was aggravated by the treatment which they received from the railroads and from the owners of warehouses. At that time the railroads did not even publish their rates, and their practice of charging all the traffic would bear, regardless of the service rendered, injured the farmers peculiarly, for there was less competition between the railroads in the farm country. The farmer deeply resented paying more for a short haul than the businessman would have to pay for a longer one. Also, he was enraged when he was confronted by grain warehouses that charged identical and exorbitant rates, as nine of them in Chicago did. The remedy of the farmers was political action. Their first vehicle was the Patrons of Husbandry, better known as the Grangers, originated by Oliver H. Kelley, a government clerk, for social purposes immediately after the Civil War. With the support of businessmen in the Midwest, some of whom also suffered from railroad discrimination and were morally outraged, the Grangers held conventions denouncing monopolists and "middle men." They demanded from their state legislatures laws setting reasonable and maximum rates for both railroads and warehouses. When Republicans and Democrats in the state capitals did not move swiftly enough to please them, they formed Farmers Parties. They secured the laws they wanted between 1871 and 1874 in Illinois, Wisconsin, and Iowa, and later in other states. The charges of the railroads and the warehouses were regulated either directly by the legislature or by a commission established for the purpose.

While the farmers and their allies won a series of victories, they were not decisive. The railroads struck back, seeking power to protect their interests in the state legislatures, and also appealing to the courts. They secured the election of railroad lawyers and other friends to the legislatures; they resorted to bribery and threats against their enemies in office; and they made good, but not very successful fights at Springfield, Madison, and Lincoln. They did somewhat better in the courts, where their ingenious lawyers eventually persuaded judges that the Granger laws and others like them violated the due process clause of the Fourteenth Amendment. Under constant pressure from them, the Supreme Court of the United States did some lawmaking of its own.

How the due process clause finally came to be a bulwark against efforts of the states to regulate the railroads and economic activity in general is a curious tale. When the Supreme Court first interpreted the Fourteenth Amendment in the Slaughter House Cases of 1873, it narrowly construed the meaning of the Amendment. It held that its intention was the protection of the rights of the Negro only, doubtless a correct view historically. Further, the Court carefully pointed out that there were two kinds of citizenship, state and federal, and then ruled, probably erroneously, that the framers of the Amendment intended to protect only the rights of federal citizens. Still further, the Court indicated that these, covered by the "privileges and immunities" clause, were relatively few and that the majority of civil rights still lay within the domain of the states. The Court in recognition of historical fact, despite Chief Justice Taney's opinion to the contrary in the Dred Scott case, asserted that "due process of law" meant only that proper procedure must be followed. It refused to accept the proposition that the Fourteenth Amendment gave judges the power to rule a state law unconstitutional on the ground that it deprived a white person of "life, liberty, or property."

When the railroad lawyers failed to get state tribunals to set aside the Granger laws on constitutional grounds, they appealed to the federal judiciary. At first they were turned away. In the Granger cases, particularly *Munn* v. *Illinois,* in 1877, the Supreme Court upheld the constitutionality of the Granger laws. The police power of a state permitted it to regulate business with "a public interest." The railroads were advised to appeal "to the polls not to the courts." Nor would the Court declare itself against state regulation of intrastate commerce because the federal government had the power to regulate interstate commerce. However, with corporation lawyers flourishing and being placed upon the bench in greater numbers, the Supreme Court gradually altered its view. A majority of the justices came to insist that due process meant that justice be done in substance as well as in form, that it applied to whites and corporations as well as to Negroes, and that the courts had to prevent economic injustice done by a state through fixing rates, either by a state commission or legislature. Besides, the high court ruled that state authority could not be exercised to regulate interstate commerce. Thus the police power of the states proved to be insufficient for the regulation of the railroads. The farmers and others who wanted action against them had to go to the federal government for relief, as they did in the 1880s; and they had also to try to change again the philosophy of the Supreme Court.

LABOR

The rise of "Big Business," disconcerting to the farmer, profoundly affected American labor, skilled and unskilled. The economic lot of the working man did not worsen during the last part of the century, for, although wages remained low, prices tended to be lower still. Nevertheless, along with the farmer, the city laborer received only a small share of the new wealth. He had other reasons to be unhappy. When he had worked with his employer there was no social gulf between them, and his "boss" had taken a personal interest in him. As one of an ever-increasing body of employees of companies that became always larger, he lost personal touch with his employers. Dealing with him through intermediaries, they were tempted to look upon his toil as a commodity, and to think of him in the same fashion. There was less concern for his welfare on the part of employers who were unfamiliar with his working conditions and his life in general. As early as 1868, Congress established an eight-hour day for laborers and mechanics on the payrolls of the federal government, but the ten-hour day long remained the rule in industry. Labor became restless, especially in periods of depression such as those which began in 1873 and in 1893. Strikes and industrial violence became fairly common, and the labor union movement gained headway, although it made slow progress.

In Europe the coming of capitalistic industrialism was accompanied by the appearance of socialism, Marxian communism, and anarchism, and all of those creeds spread to America. The Socialists, whether of Marxian or other origin, were the most active. They participated in the formation of labor unions, and they also entered politics, in the belief that economic action alone would not achieve their goals. Friedrich A. Sorge, a disciple of Marx, established the American headquarters for the First International in New York City. The Socialist-Labor party was founded in 1877. However, socialism proved to have little attraction for American workers and anarchism had even less. They were not deeply stirred by the affair of the Haymarket Riot in Chicago in 1886. When police tried to break up an anarchist-communist meeting in Haymarket Square, someone threw a bomb which fatally wounded seven of the police, who responded by firing into the crowd. Of eight of the agitators found responsible for throwing the bomb, four were executed. That they and the others, who were later released from prison, were guilty remains doubtful. In any event, there was little sympathy in the ranks of American labor for those who sought, not to reform the capitalistic system, but to destroy it. American workmen were not fond of Henry Clay Frick, general manager of the Carnegie Steel Company, who did not hesitate to use force to break a strike. On the other hand, they did not applaud an attempt by a Russian-born anarchist, Alexander Berkman, to murder Frick.

There was no lack of violence between capital and labor, for working men resorted to the strike, from which developed a number of bloody incidents. The "Molly Maguires," a secret society of Irish miners that grew out of the Ancient Order of Hibernians, was responsible for various assaults and murders in eastern Pennsylvania before it was crushed in 1875. Ten of its members were hanged for murder. In 1877 came a widespread railroad strike in protest against wage cuts, which led to rioting in several cities. Federal troops were used to restore order at Martinsburg, West Virginia, where nine men were killed in a fight between strikers and state militia. They were also used in Pittsburgh, where strikers and sympathizers engaged in a battle with militia that cost twenty-six lives and much destruction of railroad property, including the Union Depot. The Haymarket "Massacre" followed an attempted general strike in Chicago. Berkman's attempt to assassinate Frick was preceded by an armed clash at Homestead, Pennsylvania, which cost seven lives, between strikers and Pinkerton men hired by Frick. Frick broke the strike by securing "scab" workers, with state militia restoring order. Two years later, during the depression which began in 1893, came another major railroad strike in the Midwest. Again, there was violence, and federal marshals and troops were sent to Chicago to restore order.

THE GROWING UNIONS

That there were great strikes does not indicate that the labor unions quickly became numerous and powerful. Weak at the time of the Civil War, they gained vigor but slowly, in some part because the convulsions that grew from strikes were blamed upon labor rather than capital. The crimes of the anarchists were also associated with unions in the public mind. Far more important, the workingman had imbibed from the cup of American individualism, and he often preferred to do his own bargaining, especially if he were skilled. Another basic reason why many workers were not fond of unionism was that they were very well satisfied with conditions as they were, and each hoped that he himself might prosper, or even become rich. It was generally believed, and not without reason, that the capable and the industrious could rise rapidly in the new economic order. The progress of the poor boy to wealth and security so often chronicled by Horatio Alger was not mere myth; and if the workingman could not always ascend the ladder of success, he could hope to put his children upon rungs of it well above the ground. Another deterrent to the growth of the unions was the impractical idealism of some of their leaders. Needless to say, unionism was not liked by the employers, who were likely to resist any combination on the part of labor.

Despite the unpopularity of the unions and the strong opposition to them, the railway brotherhoods appeared in the 1860s and 1870s and survived the depression of 1873, while various other trade unions were organized. As early as 1866, the National Labor Union was formed to secure the eight-hour day throughout the nation. It failed to achieve its goal, resolved itself into a splinter political party, and collapsed in 1872. Much larger and more potent was the Knights of Labor, founded in 1871, and a national industrial union by 1878. Or was it a union? All who worked for a living, including women and Negroes, but excluding bankers, lawyers, physicians and liquor dealers, were eligible for membership, although three-fourths of those belonging to any local unit had to be wage earners. While the Knights in the East were principally workingmen, the society, for such it may also be called, was dominated in the Midwest by farmers. Under the leadership of Terence V. Powderly the Knights sought the eight-hour day, preferring boycotts and arbitration to strikes. They favored establishment of cooperatives, with respect to both production and consumption, and actually formed more than one hundred of them. Seeking political reforms, they advocated the graduated income tax. The Knights of Labor was both a union and a fraternity with high ideals for a better America achieved through good will and social unity. By 1886 there were more than 700,000 enrolled in it. However, it had by that time begun to use the weapon of the strike, and a series of defeats persuaded most of the Knights to take off their armor. By 1893 the Knights of Labor remained only as an agrarian society. It had already been replaced as the most powerful combination in labor by the American Federation of Labor, which was founded in 1886 under the leadership of Samuel Gompers, a practical-minded immigrant who had been a cigar maker. The Federation originally contained 25 unions with approximately 150,000 members. Each union retained its autonomy within the national body. Composed of skilled workers, the Federation confined itself strictly to trade unionism. It avoided ideology, exerted itself successfully for the "aristocracy" of American workingmen. The unskilled, and the bulk of labor, remained unorganized until the twentieth century was well advanced.

THE NEW IMMIGRATION

Still another facet of a new America began to emerge in the 1880s. The vanishing of the frontier, the triumph of "Big Business," and the beginnings of successful trade unionism were accompanied by the first waves of the "New Immigration." Italians, Greeks, Slavs of many varieties, and Jews began to enter the United States in large numbers about 1885. The so-called "Old Immigration" from northwestern Europe continued, but that from southern and eastern Europe surpassed it as early as 1896. Thereafter, the influx from Italy, the Balkans, Austria-Hungary, Poland, and Russia, reached almost unbelievable proportions, with the number of new arrivals going beyond 1,000,000 in 1905. The presence of these latecomers in the cities strengthened the antagonism of rural against urban America. And their participation in the development of the unions—many became factory workers, miners, and railroad laborers—strengthened feeling against the unions. Indeed, the New Immigration gradually aroused alarm among the earlier immigrants and their descendants, and dykes would eventually be built against the swelling tide of newcomers. There was a demand for protective walls before the end of the century. It did not lead to effective action, and the composition of the American people was basically altered.

Restrictions on immigration actually began as early as 1882 with the passage of a law to exclude the Chinese. Another of the same year was designed to improve the quality of persons entering the United States from Europe. The insane and known criminals were excluded, together with persons likely to become public charges, which was not a remarkable departure from the "easy come" policy that had been followed in America from colonial times. The barring of Chinese was much more important, for it indicated a determination that the United States would not become a home for all the peoples of the world, and that it should remain Occidental. By the Burlingame Treaty of 1868 Chinese immigration had been permitted, in accordance with historic Anglo-American policy. However, when Chinese laborers began to appear on the Pacific coast in numbers, an outcry rose against them. Peculiarly alien, they were willing to work for low wages, and they aroused keen resentment among workers of European background. The usual prejudice against newcomers was far stronger with respect to the Asians than it had been or ever would be against the Europeans. It was contended that the Chinese could not be

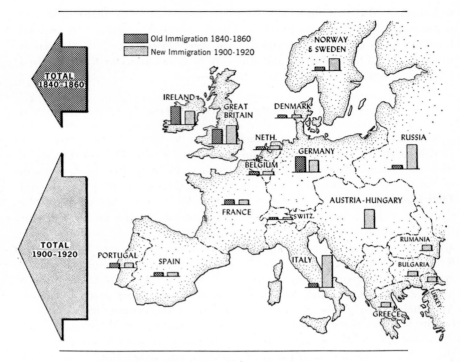

IMMIGRATION BEFORE AND AFTER THE CIVIL WAR

assimilated—they wore pigtails and they were too thrifty. As their number mounted and they began to take root, sentiment against them in California reached a high pitch. In San Francisco Denis Kearney, an Irish immigrant, organized workingmen and hoodlums for attacks upon the "heathen Chinee," who were subjected to all sorts of abuse. In 1877 rioting Kearneyites murdered several of the Chinese. A demand from the West Coast that further immigration from China be prevented brought about the abrogation of the Burlingame Treaty in 1880, and led to a substitute permitting America to "limit or suspend" entrance of the Chinese. It was followed two years later by the law already mentioned, which barred Chinese immigration for ten years. In 1882 nearly one-tenth of the population of California was Chinese. That proportion afterward diminished, for exclusion became an American principle. The government of China protested against total and permanent exclusion, but a second period of temporary suspension of Chinese immigration was followed in 1902 by an absolute bar that endured until 1943. After that, America undertook to accept as many as 150 Chinese per annum under the quota system.

In 1886, when the New Immigration began, the Statue of Liberty was dedicated on Bedloe's Island in New York harbor. In a poem by Emma Lazarus engraved upon a tablet below the "Goddess," she is represented as saying:

> Give me your tired, your poor,
> Your huddled masses yearning to breathe free,
> The wretched refuse of your teeming shore.
> Send these, the homeless, tempest-tost to me,
> I lift my lamp beside the golden door!

This noble sentiment was to wane, even with respect to Europeans, for feeling turned against the Poles, the Italians, the Jews, and other strange folk who passed the Statue of Liberty in ever growing numbers. Again nativism swelled in America. Labor disliked the competition offered by the new workers. Much more serious, Protestant America disliked the heavy increase in the Catholics in the nation and an American Protective Association appeared in the 1890s to fight against Roman Catholicism. The Jews, who came from Poland and Russia as victims of persecution, aroused antipathy. It was claimed that the new immigrants were racially inferior, although they belonged to the white race. With somewhat more logic it was contended that America would suffer by the introduction of hordes of people debased by poverty and tyranny in the Old World; there was a temptation to forget that earlier settlers also came largely from the poor and the oppressed. Nativists pointed out that anarchists and communists were being imported. They wanted, in effect, an America dominated by people descended from northwestern Europeans, and one that was Protestant, at least in tradition. They believed that American liberty and order were threatened. Toward stemming the New Immigration, and to a degree the Old, in 1891 Congress passed an act which barred paupers, those afflicted by dangerous, contagious, or loathsome disease, polygamists, and all persons whose passage was paid by others, unless those others were friends or relatives. Toward preserving the Old America, Henry Cabot Lodge in 1897 pushed through Congress a bill which would have imposed a literacy test upon all immigrants. It was clearly intended as a bar against the newer variety, who came from countries where schooling was difficult to obtain. Describing the measure as unjust, President Grover Cleveland vetoed it two days before he left office. Interest in it diminished as economic conditions improved, for the nation was not yet ready to erect high walls against newcomers.

36 THE TROUBLED SOUTH

When all of the Southern states came under the control of the Conservatives in 1877 and the last of the troops departed, the South entered upon a new course. It had been "redeemed," and its Redeemers became heroes like the Confederates of Bull Run and Chickamauga. Afterwards South Carolinians recounted with pride their exploits as unarmed "Red Shirts" under General Wade Hampton in the struggle for redemption from the carpetbaggers in their state. What followed was much less glorious, for the triumph of the Conservatives brought with it neither social peace nor prosperity. Political order was achieved, but the South increasingly became and long remained an economic colony of the North, and the racial problem continued with new complexities arising from the emancipation of the Negroes. The Democratic Solid South had made its appearance, although its votes were not sufficient to give the South a decisive voice in the affairs of the nation. However, the Democrats below the Mason-Dixon Line became so powerful that they were able to establish a one-party system and to create and sustain white supremacy, that being the desire above all of the Southern whites. The Negroes were gradually driven from the arena of politics. Had the Republicans persevered in their efforts to help the Negroes, they might have been able to participate more fully in government, but Lincoln's party lost interest in them, and remained indifferent until their votes in Northern cities became important to it. The Negroes might also have profited politically from divisions among the Southern whites. In the end, however, the Southern whites chose to accept defeat at each other's hands rather than to accept the Negroes as allies and so to give them the opportunity to gain political strength. The decision of the whites, definitely reached in the 1890s, was to let the Negro become a nonvoting and helpless Republican.

WHITE SUPREMACY

Determined to prevent the return of carpetbagger rule, the Redeemers, who before long generally changed their party name from Conservative to Democrat, did not immediately attempt wholesale denial of the vote to the Negroes. Some of them, including General Wade Hampton and Alexander Stephens, generally men of means, or at least of high social standing, urged that they be permitted to continue to cast votes. Besides, no method by which the Negroes could be disfranchised without violating the Fifteenth Amendment and without bringing down the wrath of Republican Washington could readily be found. Accordingly, tens of thousands of Negroes went to the polls until the 1890s, and here and there one could be found in public office. Nevertheless, various measures to hold down the Negro vote and its importance were taken in the late 1870s. Physical and economic coercion did not vanish; in the state legislatures gerrymandering diminished the influence of areas where numerous Negroes voted; political authority was concentrated at the state capital, local officials becoming appointive rather than elective, to prevent Negro domination of any area; registration of voters was required well in advance of elections; and residence requirements were raised, barring many Negroes who moved about to seek work. Other devices lessened the importance of the Negro voter. The ballot was made more complicated so that he could not understand it, ballot boxes in districts where Negroes were numerous often "disappeared" before their contents were counted, and white canvassers commonly brought in false returns. Moreover, bribery of Negro voters, freely practiced in the era of Radical Reconstruction, did not cease.

THE NEGRO AND THE VOTE

These measures and devices were sufficient to maintain the supremacy of the whites, so long as they were united. In the 1880s and 1890s, however, they were seriously at odds among themselves, when the Populist movement endangered the Democrats' grip upon the South. The more conservative Democrats mobilized Negro voters against Democrats who joined or supported the Populists; on the other hand, the Populists and their allies in the Democratic party displayed a disposition to call for destruction of all bars against Negro voting. Alarm spread in both the contending groups, and they put aside their differences to deal with the common enemy. They carried through legal and constitutional changes that prevented Negro voting in the South for many years. Forty years after Appomattox, feeling was greater against Negro suffrage than it was in 1875. The new contrivances by which the Negroes were effectively stripped of the vote were requirements that the voter must have paid a poll tax and that he pass a literacy test. In some states the possession of property was made a substitute for the latter. The poll tax requirement was all the more effective because the person had to go to a tax office many months before election time, pay one or two dollars, secure a receipt, and display it upon demand at the polls. Five Southern states also stipulated that the tax had to be paid for prior years. The result was that the poor and the careless, whites as well as Negroes, lost the chance to vote. Such was the intention of the conservative element in the South, which was especially responsible for the tax payment restriction. The common test for literacy was the ability to read and to explain a section of the state constitution or other political instrument. Since the examining was done by whites, the Negro, even a well-educated one, was likely to fail. A loophole was sometimes left for unlettered whites, examiners being permitted to enroll persons who could understand a section of the state constitution when it was read to them; only whites displayed such ability.

Even so, the several new barriers placed in the path of the voter, coupled with those that had been established in the past, aroused protest among the more liberal-minded whites. If the new arrangements were to last, something more had to be done to permit poor and ignorant whites to vote. The result was the famous "Grandfather Clause." It usually ordained that a man could vote, even though he could meet neither an educational nor a property prerequisite, if he, his father, or his grandfather had had the suffrage before January 1, 1867. Since Negroes did not have the ballot before that date, the obvious purpose of the Grandfather Clause was to let down the bars for poor and uneducated whites, while at the same time maintaining them for the Negroes. In some states the Grandfather Clause was somewhat less generous to the whites, for it demanded that the individuals excused be, or be descended from, a Confederate veteran. Such clauses clearly violated the Fifteenth Amendment, and they were declared unconstitutional by the United States Supreme Court in 1915. By that time, however, they had served their purpose, for whites who could take advantage of the proviso had done so and had had their names inscribed on voting lists—if they thought it worthwhile. The poll tax payment and literacy requirements, of course, were consistent with the federal Constitution. Despite the Grandfather Clause, so many hurdles had been set up for the voter that large numbers of whites, in addition to the Negroes, were discouraged from getting or keeping the franchise. The electorate in the South was commonly cut in half, even reduced to a third of what it had been in some states. After 1900, not surprisingly, Southern politicians were often conservative—and property-minded.

SOCIAL SEPARATION

Logically enough, extreme political discrimination against the Negroes was accompanied by social separation of the white and Negro races. Jim Crow grew to maturity in the 1880s and 1890s. When the carpetbagger regimes collapsed, whites and blacks still mingled rather freely in parts of the South—in the lowlands—as they had in the time of slavery. Negroes mixed with whites on trains in South Carolina, except in first class, where ladies traveled; they were not kept out of saloons patronized by whites in Mississippi; and they were sometimes fed in the same restaurants as whites, although at different tables. Northerners were then shocked by the intimacy which they observed between the two peoples in the low country of the South. Since the superiority of the whites of means, education, and greater social prestige was unchallengeable, they felt no need to put the Negroes in "their place"; so far as they were concerned, the Negroes were already in a satisfactory situation. It was not so with the homestead farmers, the workers, or any whites who increasingly had to compete with Negroes for their livelihood. As the Negroes began to move inland toward the hills to take jobs in factories on the Piedmont, and to secure whatever other employment they could, they offered competition to the less prosperous whites, who had never been on such terms with them. The former slave owner could continue to be paternal; he did not wish to be fraternal. The poorer the white man, the more hostile he was likely to be to the black; the "poor white trash," so famed for its poverty, illiteracy, and shift-lessness, especially resented the rivalry imposed by the emancipation of the Negroes. Arguments for the superiority of the white man, against mis-cegenation, and for racial separation strongly appealed to the whites who possessed relatively small property or none at all. The white man might be the father of a mulatto; if so, he nevertheless desired to keep his white and brown progeny apart. Fighting for his own rights against the more prosperous upper class, he may have been tempted to form an alliance with the Negro, but in the end he preferred to help establish a caste system in which the Negroes formed the lowest stratum.

Social segregation, becoming more common in practice in the 1880s, was sanctified by laws and more laws in the South during the generation that preceded the outbreak of World War I. Separation on trains was com-monly required by 1891; it was imposed a little later by law in schools, libraries, theaters, hotels, hospitals, insane asylums, penitentiaries, and cemeteries. The Negro was also confined to certain residential areas. He was put in his place, an inferior one, even when he was offered theoretically equal treatment. Unable to prevent the passage of the segregation laws, Negroes sought rulings from the Supreme Court that they violated the Fourteenth Amendment. They received no help from the high court. In 1883 it had ruled that the amendment offered no protection against the invasion of civil rights by private persons. In 1896, after some hesitation, it declared that segregation on railroads did not violate the amendment if equal accommodations were offered. This doctrine, spelled out in *Plessy* v. *Ferguson,* was assumed for many years to apply to all the Jim Crow laws. The Supreme Court would no more offer protection to the Negroes than would the President or the Congress. Separation of the races was also the rule outside the South, although laws requiring it were far less common.

The era in which the Southern Negro was driven from politics and forced to accept social segregation was also that in which lynching flourished. In freedom, the Negroes were often rootless. Wandering into the Southern cities, and before long into Northern ones, they were dislocated, poor, ignorant, and often unwanted. Idleness and crime became only too prevalent among them, and they committed violence against whites as well as against one another. They were assailed by mobs in cities where they congregated, and the race riot became an ugly facet of American life. So did lynching, practiced in the North but more often in the South. Some whites suffered from it, but more Negroes. Between 1889 and 1899 there was an average of 187.5 lynchings per annum. The figure fell to 92.5 during the following decade, but the practice was increasingly confined to Negro victims. It was contended in defense of lynching that its terrors would limit the brutalities committed by the Negroes and that legal processes were not swift enough to deal with those guilty of murder or rape. Torturing, slaying, and burning of the bodies of the guilty were unusual testimonies to the benefits of civilization; that some of the victims were quite innocent of wrongdoing added to the horrors of lynching. The behavior of the mobs was all the more barbarous because Southern courts were accustomed to mete out swift and stern punishment to Negroes found guilty of crimes against whites, taking lightly wrongs inflicted upon Negroes by each other and by whites.

THE SOUTHERN ECONOMY

Adding weight to every difficulty, the weakness of the Southern economy posed massive problems. Not so rich in substance as the Northern states, the Southern ones were comparatively even poorer after the Civil War than they had been in 1860. The physical damage done in the conflict, heavy expenditures from slender capital, the disruption of communications, the loss of a quarter-million of productive men, the transit of the Negroes from slave labor to free, all these contributed to Southern economic distress. In the twentieth century the United States would surprise the cynical throughout the world by assisting its fallen enemies to their feet with generous gifts of money. In 1865 the problem of reconstruction was looked upon as almost purely political; the only important financial help extended toward the South was that given through the Freedmen's Bureau, to the Negroes. Southern recovery was slow through the carpet-bagger years, and the state debts piled up by the Radical regimes retarded progress.

Coming into power immediately before the depression that began in 1873, the Redeemers had to face conditions that may properly be described as dismal. Basic was the fact that per capita wealth in the South was barely more than one-third that in the rest of the nation. The outlook was gloomy, and it improved only gradually. The long run remedies were obvious enough; diversified farming and the development of industry, as in the Northern states. Indispensable for their achievement was the creation of a system of public education. It was much easier to discern the ills of the South and their ultimate correctives than it was to do anything about them. In fact the first steps taken by the Redeemers may have served to a degree to postpone progress. They had to put the finances of the Southern states in order, which they did, in part by means of harsh retrenchment in expenditures. They "readjusted" downward the public debt in several states by refusing to pay, or paying only part of the obligations that had been fraudulently contracted during the carpetbagger regimes, this despite the complaints of bondholders and men who believed that public faith should be as much respected as private honor. To care for the debts that remained, public expenses were cut to almost irreducible levels. Public education for a time received less support than it had in the days of the carpetbaggers. Moreover, burdensome property and poll taxes were used, as of yore, to secure revenue.

THE FARMERS

For the man on the land in the South, whether white or Negro, the problem was long one of survival rather than progress. With the disappearance of the slave plantation the Southern countryside did not become one of prosperous homesteads owned by sturdy and industrious farmers. If people on the land in the upper Mississippi Valley had trouble in the latter part of the nineteenth century, they were prosperous in comparison with the agriculturists of the South. A third of all Southern horses and mules vanished as a result of the Civil War, and perhaps half of Southern farm machinery. Capital remained scarce below the Mason-Dixon Line for decades. Besides, the Southern farmer continued to suffer from the protective tariff, selling his products in a free market and purchasing in one entirely or partly closed. After the Civil War the Negroes usually became tenants of their former owners or of new men who somehow or other managed to buy plantations. Many whites also became tenants upon small farms cut out of the plantations. Without funds, they had to secure credit wherever they could, often through a country merchant. Those who owned their land often needed credit almost as badly, and secured it in the same fashion. The result was the crop-lien system, by which merchants and others who had managed to accumulate some cash or who had access to credit, made loans and accepted crops as security. So a tiller might secure seed, food, and clothing for his family, and perhaps money to pay taxes, until his cotton or tobacco was ripe. Unfortunately, this arrangement turned out to be more than a temporary one in many cases. The lender had to charge interest, and the farmer's crops might bring him just enough to pay off his debt, or even less, compelling him to borrow year after year. Escape from the system was peculiarly difficult for the tenant, for he was often also a sharecropper, who paid the landowner rent in the form of a part of his cotton, tobacco, or rice. Thus the agricultural South was restored, but prosperity did not quickly follow. It may be doubted that even those who supplied the credit actually made much money, although they have been accused of extorting heavy interest and of paying as low prices as possible for the products brought in by their debtors. In any event, the tenant, the landowner, and the lender all suffered from the arrangement, for it bolstered the one-crop agriculture characteristic of the South before the Civil War. Cotton and tobacco brought cash, and cash had to be gotten. Diversification was put off into the future. A strange result was the importation of dairy foods from the Northern states, a circumstance which provoked censure of the Southern farmer as unenlightened and shiftless; it was not recognized that he might also be helpless.

Bearing up as best they might under their many troubles, the Southern whites on the land sought comfort in religion, especially in the Baptist and Methodist churches. Many of them also looked about for political friends and found them in the farmers of the Midwest and West. Why not create an alliance like that which had existed between South and West before 1860 and which had been able to dominate in Washington? At least, something might be done toward increasing the supply of money; all farmers would profit from easier money, those in debt and the solvent ones as well. However, the farmers above the Mason-Dixon Line were not eager for the lowering of tariffs, which was much desired below it. The Yankees were attached to the Republican party and more likely to go into a third party than into the Democratic one; the Southerners were often held within the Democratic party because it stood for white supremacy. The farmers were not able to work together effectively in politics until the 1890s, and even then they were not able to secure control of the federal government. The Negroes in the South, meanwhile, lost hope of achieving anything for themselves through elections; there even developed in the Republican party in the South a "lily-white" faction which gave its allegiance to white supremacy. The Negroes needed the solace of religion even more than the rural whites.

THE NEW SOUTH

Also devoted to orthodox Protestant Christianity, the Southern middle class, whose most famous spokesman was Henry Grady of the Atlanta *Constitution,* searched for economic and social salvation in copying the northeastern part of the nation. The factory, the railroad, and commerce should be transplanted to the South, a "New South," a Yankeeized one. The South had iron ore, coal, lumber, cotton, tobacco, and water power as well. Why not turn to manufacturing? The future was with the middle class, but the immediate future was not all that the middle class could desire. Southern entrepreneurs, scraping up capital, built cotton mills and tobacco factories in the Carolinas, and also engaged in railroad building. Some prospered, and there were some Southern millionaires by the close of the century. Soon after 1900 more cotton was consumed by Southern mills than by those of New England. For a time the steel industry centered about Birmingham threatened a serious rivalry with the steel complex of Pittsburgh. But the new Southern factories were often confined to the first processing of raw materials, the final product issuing from Northern ones as in the past. Higher freight rates charged by Southern railroads—these originally justified on the ground that traffic was sparse and mileage great —made it more difficult for the manufacturers in the South to secure markets. Moreover, much of the manufacturing that developed was carried on by Northerners attracted south of the Mason-Dixon Line by cheap water power, liberal supplies of labor, low wages, and tax concessions. Southern railways were often financed in New York. The New South continued to be afflicted by a colonial economy; only the foundations for a true prosperity had been laid. So ugly were some features of the New South, its drab mill towns, its destruction of forests, and its abuse of human beings, that critics of it occasionally urged a return to the Old South, poor as it had been in worldly goods. Of course, there could be no turning back; whether it will or no, the South will become more and more like the North.

It should go without saying that the Old South did not utterly vanish with the passing of the nineteenth century. Legacies from it were traditions of good manners, honor, and gallantry, which were nourished not only by the remnants of the plantation aristocracy but also by the middle class risen to relative wealth and power. Such qualities seemed slightly archaic in the bustle of an industrial society, but they also contributed to a pervasive charm which the sensitive outsider invariably felt in the South. Toward the end of the century was added another and potent tradition, that of the "Lost Cause." After the passage of 25 years, the Confederate veterans acquired lofty stature, their shortcomings forgotten, their valor and constancy enhanced in memory. Nevertheless, the future beckoned insistently.

EDUCATION

If the economic advance of the South was slow and halting after the restoration of home rule, its educational progress was even more limited. While the public schools flourished outside the South, they did not do so within it. They were retarded by low regional income, a widely scattered population, and a disproportion between children and adults, the former being remarkably numerous. There was also the necessity of maintaining separate systems for whites and Negroes, dictated by the Jim Crow philosophy. The money that would have been necessary for the South to catch up with and to keep pace with the rest of the nation was not to be had. The South spent as generously as other regions in terms of income—even more generously. Nevertheless, at the beginning of the twentieth century one-fifth of all the white men below the Mason-Dixon Line were illiterate, as were half of the Negroes. The elementary schools were wretchedly supported, with relatively few students taught by poorly paid and inadequately prepared teachers; those for the Negroes were worse than those for the white children. High schools for whites were uncommon and were to be found chiefly in the larger cities; for Negroes they hardly existed. Nor were the Southern colleges and universities comparable to those in other regions. At that time not a single state that had been part of the Confederacy compelled children to attend school. The gap between the South and the rest of the nation would narrow only slowly in the twentieth century, thanks largely to the generosity of the Southern taxpayer, for a larger part of tax money continued to be spent for public education in the South than elsewhere.

SLOW PROGRESS OF THE NEGRO

If the immediate outlook for the Southern whites at the close of the nineteenth century was not bright, it was far less promising for the Negro. On the land he had made some progress toward ownership, but three out of four Negroes who lived in the country were still tenants or sharecroppers. In the cities and towns he was in some respects worse off than he had been a generation earlier. Then he had often been a skilled worker, but he had been increasingly barred from the crafts. In the new factories the better jobs—inferior as they were—were taken by whites. Largely confined to menial toil, the urban Negroes were relegated to slums and near-slums in which poverty, ignorance, and idleness bred crime. Improvement in the lot of the Negro would come gradually under the leadership of Booker T. Washington. Under his guidance after 1895 the Negroes refrained from protesting against racial separation and deprivation of the vote, and concentrated instead upon educational and economic advance. By accepting, temporarily, political and social discrimination, the Negroes gained support from Southern whites for their other objectives. They also received assistance from philanthropists, both Northern and Southern. The result was the gradual appearance of a separate Negro economy and social structure in the South—and in the North. A renewed and insistent demand for an end to discrimination and segregation did not come until after World War I. Leadership was then supplied by the National Association for the Advancement of Colored People, which had little power until after the death of Booker Washington in 1915.

37 THE BEGINNINGS OF NATIONAL REFORM

During the twenty years between 1876 and 1896 the Republicans and the Democrats were virtually equal in strength. Their leaders, not men of extraordinary wisdom, eagerly sought office and power, but not in order to make fundamental changes. When the Democrats did bring forward a far-reaching program of reform as a result of the depression of 1893, they were defeated at the polls. The party leaders only slowly recognized that the new America brought with it problems that they had to face. The Republicans lost interest in the Negroes, the Democrats were reluctant to urge action against agricultural distress beyond the historic remedy of tariff reduction, and neither party was eager to tackle the abuses that accompanied the rise of Big Business. Subscribing to the doctrine of laissez-faire, politicians had become accustomed to the belief that government should do as little as possible to interfere with economic processes, although it might offer assistance to economic enterprise. When they did discern evils that required correction, it was difficult for them to think in terms of political remedies. Nor were they quickly seized by a desire to act against corruption in public life, so prevalent in the new America; nearly all of them believed in the "spoils system." The parties differed with regard to the tariff, the Republicans standing for protection and the

Democrats for less protection, or for tariffs for revenue only; otherwise, it was difficult to distinguish between the two in terms of political philosophy. The Democrats urged that the Republican rascals be turned out of office, and sought to win national elections by appealing to party allegiance, recent immigrants, Roman Catholics, and dissatisfied Republicans. Toward winning the Presidency their strategy was to try for a majority by getting the electoral votes of New York and one or two other Northern states, and to carry all the states below the Mason-Dixon Line. They had no difficulty in carrying the South, but despite the support of Tammany Hall, they did not find it easy to beat the Republicans in New York. It was also hard for them to carry Indiana, upon which they concentrated because it was one of the few Northern states where traditional Democrats were almost as numerous as traditional Republicans. The leaders of the Republicans urged that the Democratic rascals be returned to private life, appealed to party loyalty, claimed credit for saving the Union, displayed solicitude for federal veterans, and attracted powerful support from the more conservative Northern elements, including farmers, merchants, and industrialists. If the issues were not all major and sharply drawn, the campaigns possessed fervor enough, and the voters very generally voted.

THE MODERATE HAYES

Rutherford B. Hayes, the second President of the Ohio Republican dynasty, compares favorably with his predecessor, and was not inferior to his immediate successors. In terms of formal education he was much better prepared for a public career than were many nineteenth-century American Presidents, for he was a graduate both of Kenyon College and of the Harvard Law School. Nor was he inexperienced in politics, for he had been governor of his native state. Nevertheless, he is not remembered as a great chief executive, but as a sensible conservative of no remarkable talents who found the duties of the Presidency rather oppressive. The Democrats did what they could to make life miserable for him, and with some success, for they controlled the House of Representatives during his term of office, and the Senate as well after 1879. He was assailed by a faction in his own party, because of a hot dispute over patronage. Restless elements among the farmers and labor turned against him because he opposed their demands for currency inflation and political reforms. Even his removal of federal troops from the South failed to win many friends for him among the Democrats, for he insisted upon retaining the right to send them back in case of need, vetoing Democratic bills that would have deprived him of the necessary authority.

Coming out against the spoils system, Hayes grievously offended Senator Roscoe Conkling of New York and other bosses of his party. Hayes sought to cleanse the New York City Customs House of corrupt practices, to place in it men qualified for their duties rather than Conkling's henchmen. When the President sought to remove two of them, Chester A. Arthur and Alonzo B. Cornell, New York's Republican senators demanded as a matter of senatorial courtesy that their colleagues refuse to approve replacements chosen by him. With help from the Democrats, Hayes won the fight in the Senate, but Conkling and other so-called Stalwarts continued their feud with him.

Hayes was also faced by disconcerting demands for currency inflation, these stimulated by the depression of 1873. A believer in sound money, he fought vigorously to prevent the cheapening of the dollar, a measure he believed both unfair to creditors and generally dangerous. He was satisfied to let the greenbacks already in circulation when he entered the Presidency, about $350,000,000 of them, remain in circulation. In fact, he gave his consent to an act of Congress of 1878 making them a permanent part of the currency. He was the more willing to accept the change because the greenbacks were approaching par with the national bank notes, and also because the federal Treasury had accumulated an ample supply of gold in support of its paper money. However, the President would go no further, although he was under heavy pressure to put out more dollars. By 1876 farmers and labor seeking an increase in the money supply had found a new vehicle for it, and powerful allies as well. They called for the free and unlimited coinage of silver at a ratio to gold of 16 to 1. This measure was vigorously pushed by mine owners exploiting handsome new discoveries of silver in Colorado, Utah, and Nevada in the middle 1870s. With the market price of silver declining as a result, the mine owners eagerly sought to compel the Treasury to buy their bullion at a fixed and good price. They, and the farm and labor elements that quickly rallied behind this program in zealous partisanship, even referred to the omission of the silver dollar from the coinage in 1873 as the "Crime of '73," as if it had been planned to injure their interests. A bill embodying the inflationist program was actually passed by the House of Representatives in 1876 and again in the following year. The second bill was passed by the Senate, but was so greatly amended by the defenders of the status quo that it did not achieve its purpose. Even as amended, this Bland-Allison Bill displeased Hayes, who vetoed it; it was passed over his veto. The act required that the Secretary of the Treasury buy not less than $2,000,000 and not more than $4,000,000 worth of silver every month at the market price, and that the silver be converted into dollars. Hayes and John Sherman, Secretary of the Treasury, saw to it that the minimum amount specified by the Bland-Allison Act was purchased, so reducing the effect of the law to a minimum.

So keen was dissatisfaction with Hayes and conservatives in both the major parties that the discontented flocked by tens of thousands into the National Greenback Party, which had been formed in 1875. Renamed the Greenback Labor Party, it drew support particularly from farmers in the Midwest and West, especially from those who had been active in the Granger movement. It received accretions from labor, in part because Hayes had used the army to suppress the rioting which accompanied the railroad strikes of 1877. The Greenbackers polled more than 1,000,000 votes in the congressional election of 1878. Thereafter, although they nominated candidates for the Presidency in 1880 and again in 1884, their strength declined rapidly, because of a return to prosperity in 1879. Before the party died, however, it adopted a program for change and reform which was eventually largely executed by the traditional parties. By 1880 the Greenbackers were calling not only for the free and unlimited coinage of silver, but for regulation of the hours of labor, female suffrage, a federal graduated income tax, and congressional regulation of interstate commerce.

GARFIELD AND ARTHUR

Long before the end of his term of office, Hayes announced that he would not be a candidate for a second one. In any case, it was doubtful that he could secure the Republican nomination, and even more that he could be reelected. Senator Conkling and the Stalwarts, desiring both victory at the polls and patronage, put forward tried and true vote-getter Ulysses S. Grant. A "Half-Breed" faction in which James G. Blaine was prominent offered opposition to the Stalwarts, and prevented Grant's nomination. Eventually, after 36 ballots the Republican convention named a "dark horse," James A. Garfield of Ohio. Since Garfield was allied to the Half-Breed wing of the party, Chester A. Arthur was named for the Vice-Presidency in order to please the Stalwarts. Heeding a growing demand from the public, the Republicans inserted in their platform a promise to undertake civil service reform, in order to prevent the Democrats from posing as champions of clean government. They needed all the strength they could muster, for the Democrats nominated Civil War hero General Winfield Scott Hancock, thus depriving the Republicans of a chance to attract votes by dwelling upon the fine war record of Garfield, who had also rendered distinguished service in the field. The chief issue in the campaign was tariffs for protection versus tariffs for revenue only. In the discussion General Hancock did not shine, for he spoke of it as a "local" question, failing to make his point, that tariff laws were dictated by the strength of many scattered interests. Garfield, college president, lawyer, and orator, as well as a veteran, made a somewhat better impression. His indiscreet transaction with the Credit Mobilier was apparently not held against him. He was the victor in an astonishingly close election, receiving 4,449,000 popular votes to 4,442,000 for Hancock. While his plurality was only 7000 votes, his margin in the electoral college was 214 to 155. The return of prosperity had made the Republican triumph possible.

It was, in the end, a tragic victory, for the Half-Breeds and Stalwarts promptly engaged in a struggle over the spoils. The new President appointed Blaine as his Secretary of State, and thereby aroused the hostility of the Stalwarts. Besides, Garfield refused to let Roscoe Conkling control patronage in New York. Ignoring protests from Conkling and Thomas Platt, the two senators from New York, he named William H. Robertson for the post of Collector of the Port of New York City. Conkling and Platt then demanded that the Senate refuse to approve Robertson's appointment, in accordance with the principle of senatorial courtesy. Failing to get the support of a majority of their colleagues, they resigned in protest, hoping that the legislature of New York would vindicate their behavior by reelecting them. Again they lost, for they were not returned to Washington; Conkling was retired to private life; Platt would regain influence and become a political boss. Then came the assassination of Garfield by Charles J. Guiteau, a crazed Stalwart who failed to secure an office and blamed the President for his ill fortune. Mortally wounded on July 2, 1881 Garfield died the following September.

The death of President Garfield proved again that the practice of selecting Vice-Presidential candidates on the basis of their vote-getting contribution was a vicious one, although both parties continued to ignore the fact that the Vice-President has a good chance to become the chief executive. Chester A. Arthur could hardly have been chosen for the Presidency on his own merits. Fortunately, sobered by the responsibility which fell upon him, he performed better than might have been expected. Giving favor neither to the Stalwarts nor the Half-Breeds, he brought into office a number of Republicans belonging to neither faction, and he served as a decent caretaker. Nor would he stand against the civil service reform made inevitable by the murder of Garfield. Early in 1883 the permanent foundation for a merit system was made by the passage of the Pendleton Act. It established the Civil Service Commission, a bipartisan board of three men, with authority to determine the virtues of office-seekers by means of competitive examinations. The law also declared that about one-tenth of the federal offices had to be filled on the basis of superior performance in the examinations, and authorized the President to extend the merit system to other posts. In addition, it forbade the collection of campaign contributions from federal employees. Although the law applied the principle of merit only to a small fraction of federal appointments, it was possible for successive Presidents to require that it be followed with respect to additional offices. Gradually a larger and larger part of the federal bureaucracy was placed under the merit system. Unfortunately, time would demonstrate that filling a job in accordance with performance on examinations did not solve every problem arising from the need for a bureaucracy.

THE ELECTION OF 1884

By 1884 the party that "saved the nation" had pretty well spent its credit, and its leaders finally pushed the voters too far. Despite the pleas of thoughtful party members who urged the nomination for the Presidency of a man committed to civil service reform and identified with good government, the Republican national convention gave its blessing to the "Plumed Knight" of Maine, James G. Blaine. Talented, magnetic, and adept on the speaker's platform, Blaine had never satisfactorily explained away charges of corrupt dealings made against him in 1876. He had been accused of using his influence as Speaker of the House of Representatives to secure a land grant for the Little Rock and Fort Smith Railroad in return for cash. It was widely believed that he had not told all the truth when he denied the accusation, and he was referred to as the "Continental Liar from the State of Maine" in the campaign of 1884. Many "Independent Republicans" thereupon indicated that they would bolt to the Democrats, if they put the name of a respectable candidate at the head of their ticket.

Sensing victory, the Democrats nominated Grover Cleveland, who had made an excellent record as mayor of Buffalo and governor of New York. He seemed to be an almost ideal candidate, not only to most of the Democrats, but to the independent Republicans, since he had administered his posts honestly and efficiently. Making good their threat to desert their party, Carl Schurz, Charles Francis Adams, Jr., George W. Curtis, and many other Republicans came out for Cleveland. Scornfully called "Mugwumps" (Indian chiefs whose egos were so big that they would not be bound by the decisions of a tribal council) by the followers of Blaine, they gave powerful support to Cleveland. They and the Democrats were much embarrassed when the champions of Blaine accused Cleveland of being the father of a child, although he was then a bachelor. The charge was doubtless true. Cleveland made no attempt to deny it, admitting that he was supporting an illegitimate child. The Mugwumps and the Democrats concluded that Blaine's unsatisfactory behavior in public life fitted him for a private one, and that Cleveland's faulty conduct in private life would not prevent him from giving good service in a public capacity. Even so, the Democratic cause suffered.

Cleveland won the election, but by a very narrow margin; carrying New York and Indiana in addition to the Solid South, he had a plurality of 62,000 popular votes. He won in the electoral college by 219 to 182. Had

Cleveland lost New York, which he carried by 1149 votes, he would have been defeated in the electoral count. He carried it despite the opposition of John Kelly, the head of Tammany Hall. It is very likely that his victory in New York resulted from a blunder committed by Blaine, one of those mistakes that give politicians nightmares. Immediately before the election the Reverend Samuel D. Burchard, at the head of a delegation of clergymen, called on the Republican candidate at his hotel in New York City. Burchard intemperately described the Democratic party as a compound of "Rum, Romanism, and Rebellion," and Blaine somehow neglected to declare that he did not agree with the sentiment so vigorously expressed. Undoubtedly, as Blaine afterward lamented, many Irish voters in New York City, learning of the incident, refused to follow the lead of Tammany Hall, and voted for Cleveland. The Democrats rejoiced over the triumph for which they had had to wait so long. During the campaign the Republicans had gleefully attacked Cleveland in verse:

> "Ma, Ma, where's my Pa?"
> "Gone to the White House,
>   Ha! Ha! Ha!"

After Cleveland had won, Democrats marching jubilantly in torchlight parades paid tribute alike to their leader, the illegitimate child, and the mother:

> Hurrah for Maria, hurrah for the kid,
> We voted for Grover,
> And we're damned glad we did.

A DEMOCRATIC PRESIDENT

Grover Cleveland was neither an intellectual nor a revolutionary reformer, but a sturdy, fat man of moderate views who was both honest and courageous. Not a great man, he performed capably. Confronted by demands from his party for a wholesale evacuation of Republicans from federal offices—the Democrats had long been deprived of the sweets of Canaan, and were determined to have them—he found it politically necessary to yield; however, he placed about 12,000 positions under civil service. Toward healing the wounds of the Civil War, he brought a Confederate into his Cabinet and gave other posts to Southerners. He also arranged for the return of captured Confederate battle flags, but rescinded his order because of the violent opposition it aroused in the North. When he removed a federal district attorney from office for just cause and the Senate objected that he had violated the Tenure of Office Act, he insisted the law was unconstitutional and secured its repeal. He dealt courageously with the related problems of an annual surplus in revenue, demands for Civil War pensions, and the tariff. In the 1880s the national government had to face an unusual problem. Its revenues ran steadily $100,000,000 per annum above its expenditures, and the excess could not even be used to reduce the national debt, which was then easily carried. To care for the perplexing surplus, Cleveland urged reduction of tariffs, a step which he also justified on the ground that Big Business profited excessively because of the high rates on imports that had been imposed by the Republicans. They were strong enough in Congress to prevent lowering of the rates. The Grand Army of the Republic, the association of Civil War veterans, had a different answer to the surplus question—spending it for pensions. The demands of the organized veterans were especially embarrassing to the President, because he had not served in the war. He did not oppose pensions for disabilities incurred in service, for which provision had been made. However, he vetoed many bills passed by Congress that awarded grants to men who had failed to establish their claims in the Bureau of Pensions. With typical moderation, he also studied and approved many such special bills. In 1887 Congress placed before him a measure which would have authorized grants to veterans who had made their living by manual labor and who had become physically unable to perform it. Cleveland again employed his veto, despite heavy pressure from the Old Soldiers. Even so, the nation was paying out about $80,000,000 per annum for pensions when he left the Presidency in 1889.

BEGINNINGS OF FEDERAL BUSINESS REGULATION

No radical, Cleveland in his first term did participate in a revolutionary decision, a major departure by the national government from the principle of laissez-faire. He signed the Interstate Commerce Act of 1887, in which an attempt was made to curb railroad abuses. Demands for such action had been welling up for more than a decade, but many politicians had continued to believe, or at least to hope, that the railroad magnates would respond to criticism and abandon the practices that had led to the Granger movement. Moreover, the railroads had influence in Congress, especially in the Senate, and they had exerted it to prevent interference. By 1885, however, it was evident both that the railroads had not abandoned their vicious ways and that the states were quite unable to force them into good behavior. A Senate investigating committee headed by Shelby M. Cullom, after a sweeping inquiry, reported that federal action had to be taken to correct the immoral conduct of the railroads, and that public opinion emphatically favored it. The Congress responded, and passed the regulatory law by heavy majorities. It declared that railroads doing business in more than one state must post their rates, make them just and reasonable, and refrain from changing them without notice. It declared pools, rate discrimination, and rebates illegal. The railroads were further forbidden to demand more money for a short haul than for a long one on the same line. The law also established the Interstate Commerce Commission, the first of many "independent" regulatory bodies to be set up by Congress. Its members were given power to investigate the behavior of the interstate railroads, to force them to give information concerning their transactions, and to compel them to make annual reports about their finances in accordance with a uniform system of accounting. The commission was, in addition, authorized to institute proceedings in equity against violators of the law in the federal courts. The law was far less stringent than it seemed, for it did not firmly empower the commission to fix rates. Railroad management was fertile in finding devices to circumvent its requirements, and more or less openly flaunted them. When the commission undertook to secure just and reasonable rates by setting maximum ones, the Supreme Court ruled that it had exceeded its authority. Ten years after the passage of the act, the commission had been reduced to little more than a fact-finding body. Nevertheless, laissez-faire had been dealt a heavy blow; precedent for national regulation had been firmly founded.

THE SECOND PRESIDENT HARRISON

No crusader, Grover Cleveland refused even to campaign for reelection in 1888; he believed that a President ought not whisk about the country shaking hands, kissing babies, and making carefully worded speeches that would please many and offend few. He would not even come out flatly for lowering tariffs in accordance with the traditional stand of his party. The Republicans, on the other hand, waged a vigorous campaign. They forthrightly championed high protective tariffs and promised handsome pensions to the Union veterans. They denounced Cleveland as niggardly in dealing with Northern veterans, and at the same time generous to the former Confederates. They collected a huge campaign fund from manufacturers who appreciated their fervent advocacy of high protection, and they effectively spread their propaganda. They also offered a respectable candidate for the Presidency in the person of Benjamin Harrison, grandson of William Henry Harrison, a colonel in the Civil War, and an Ohioborn lawyer who had climbed the political ladder in Indiana as far as the United States Senate. Their hearts were with Blaine, but they wanted to win. Harrison was a dignified and excellent speaker, although he had no love for politicking or politicians.

Toward the end of the campaign Harrison's cause was helped by a mean trick played by George A. Osgoodby, a California Republican. Posing as an Englishman who had become a naturalized citizen and calling himself "Charles F. Murchison," Osgoodby wrote a letter to the British minister in Washington, Sir Lionel Sackville-West, asking him whether Cleveland was or was not a friend to England. Sackville-West, forgetting that diplomats ought to mind their own business, replied that Cleveland was quite satisfactory to England. Osgoodby then gave the British minister's letter to Republican leaders, who published it a few days before the balloting. Cleveland promptly sent home Sackville-West, who was jaunty about his error. Osgoodby had achieved his purpose, which was to injure Cleveland among the Irish voters, who were still hostile to England. It is possible that Osgoodby's trick won the election for Harrison. He lost to Cleveland in the popular vote, the President having 5,540,050 to his 5,444,337. However, Harrison's popular votes were better distributed for gaining electoral votes, and he carried the key states of New York and Indiana, and was the victor in the electoral college, 233 to 168. Such an outcome would have been profoundly disturbing at a later time; in 1888 it was gracefully accepted by both Cleveland and the Democrats. There might have been an outcry had the differences in the parties and the candidates been sharper.

Genial and gracious among his good friends, Benjamin Harrison was not aggressive, and he was cold to politicians. He felt constrained to make Blaine his Secretary of State, and Blaine moved vigorously. In domestic affairs leadership was assumed by veteran Republican politicians, including Speaker Thomas B. Reed of the House of Representatives, who governed that body with an iron hand. They easily disposed of the surplus, put two major laws upon the books, and permitted passage of a third one. The surplus was destroyed by liberal expenditures for the improvement of rivers and harbors, new public buildings, and government services, but especially by generous outlays for pensions to the Union veterans. "God help the surplus," declared James Tanner, who served for a short time as Commissioner of Pensions under Harrison. He freely approved grants.

More important was the passage in 1890 of the Dependent Pension Act, which authorized awards to all of the surviving Old Soldiers unable to earn a living by manual labor, and also to the dependents of veterans. During Harrison's Presidency money spent for pensions rose from $81,000,000 to $157,000,000, and the number of pensioners doubled, reaching 966,000. Before he left office, the surplus had been turned into a neat deficit. The Republicans also provided most efficiently for protection against foreign industrial competition in the McKinley Tariff Act of 1890. Rates were raised to an average level of almost 50 percent, and further increases were authorized as weapons against nations discriminating against American goods. To please the farmers, who actually received little benefit from them, duties were placed upon various agricultural products. It was evident that this measure gave more protection to the powerful, and little to the weak. Accordingly, because they needed votes from the West to pass it, the Republican leaders arranged for the enacting of the Sherman Silver Purchase Act. It did not provide for the free coinage of silver, which was being demanded more and more insistently by agrarian inflationists and mining interests, but it required the Treasury to buy every month 4,500,000 ounces of silver and to pay for it with legal tender currency redeemable at the Treasury in gold or silver. The law did expand the supply of money; it also opened the way for an attack upon the national gold reserve, since in practice the new currency had to be redeemed upon demand in gold.

SHERMAN ANTI-TRUST ACT

In view of the attitude toward industry displayed by the Republicans, it may seem mildly surprising that they joined with Democrats in putting through the Sherman Anti-Trust Act, which on its face severely restricted the activities of Big Business. However, by 1890 public feeling, so potent in forcing the enactment of the Interstate Commerce law, was demanding further action, not merely against the railroads, but against "monopolies" of all sorts. Passed almost unanimously, the Sherman law forthrightly declared illegal "Every contract, combination in the form of trust or otherwise, or conspiracy, in restraint of trade or commerce among the several States, or with foreign nations." Persons convicted of violation of it could be fined up to $5000 and imprisoned for as long as a year. The federal circuit courts were empowered to take action to prevent violations. Moreover, third parties injured by those who broke the law were permitted to sue for triple damages. On the surface, the law was a drastic remedial measure, and it seems to have been the intent of Congress that it be such. Since the states were also trying to regulate the trusts, they were apparently rather effectively restricted. It was otherwise in practice, partly because the Attorney General made little effort to enforce the law for more than a decade, partly because lawyers and judges interpreted it and the Constitution so as to deprive it of much of its force. It was applied to the railroads, and later to railroad unions, although it clearly had not been intended to extend to such a "combination." More important, the United States Supreme Court declared that the law could not apply to the production of goods, on the ground that federal authority over commerce could not be exerted until goods had entered the channels of interstate trade. The Court also gradually moved toward the view that Congress meant to prevent only "unreasonable" restraint, since almost any business agreement would affect other parties to some degree. The federal government was for some years unwilling and unable to do anything very much against the trusts. The same statement may be made with respect to the states, some of which, notoriously New Jersey and Delaware, gave wide freedom to corporations formed under their laws.

AGRARIAN REVOLT

As the election of 1892 approached, the prospect was grim for the Republicans, who had managed to please only the industrialists and the Civil War pensioners. Even the owners of silver mines were not made happy by the Sherman Purchase Act, because, while government purchased more silver, its price went down nevertheless. Nor did bankers like that law. Liberal-minded men were offended because the Republicans had carried out a wholesale removal of Democrats from office, giving little more than lip service to the principle of merit. It was held against the Republicans that they had spent money too freely; the annual budget had passed $1,000,000,000. The Democrats had been supplied with heavy ammunition for the campaign. What was far worse for Harrison and his followers was that they had won the enmity of labor and the farmers. By 1890, in fact, an agrarian revolt was well under way. In the late 1880s distress returned to the land; prices of farm products fell; drought punished the settlers who had recently occupied the Great Plains; falling into debt, farmers were weighed down by mortgages and heavy interest charges; and neither of the major parties seemed to care very much. As a result, working through various farm organizations such as the Southern Alliance and the Colored Farmers' Alliance, the farmers furiously sought redress by political means. In the South the Alliance men, led by the picturesque Benjamin F. Tillman of South Carolina and Thomas Watson of Georgia, seized control of several states by taking over the Democratic party in the election of 1890. West of the Mississippi the Alliance people began to form a third party. Altogether, they sent no fewer than 44 men to Congress in 1890. In Kansas, a hotbed of discontent, the People's Party sprang into existence before the election. There Mary Ellen Lease urged the farmers to "raise less corn and more Hell!"—she might also appropriately have counseled the raising of fewer farmers. By 1892 a national People's Party had been organized and was prepared for battle. A convention of the Populists demanded free and unlimited coinage of silver at the ratio of 16 to 1; an increase in the currency of at least $50 per person; public ownership of all transportation and communication lines; a graduated income tax; direct election of United States senators; the secret ballot; the initiative; the referendum; the regulation of hours of work for industrial labor; restriction of immigration; and more. Almost every demand made by the Populists was eventually translated into law, although their program seemed to be irresponsible and even revolutionary to the majority of Republicans and Democrats in 1892.

With the Populist party cutting into the strength of the Republicans in the Midwest and West, but aligning with the Democrats in the South, the Democrats entered the campaign with justified confidence. They put forward Grover Cleveland for the third time. He effectively assailed the Republicans as caterers to inflationists while the Populists attacked them as servants of the "money power." The result was a resounding defeat for the Republicans. Cleveland received 5,554,414 popular votes, Harrison 5,190,802, and Populist Weaver 1,027,329. In the electoral college Cleveland had 277, Harrison 155, and Weaver 22. Weaver carried five states, Kansas, North Dakota, Colorado, Nevada, and Idaho. Cleveland won, besides the Solid South, Connecticut, New York, New Jersey, Delaware, Indiana, and to the surprise of all concerned, Illinois, Wisconsin, and California. The Democrats also secured control of both houses of Congress. In March, 1893, Cleveland returned to the White House for a second sojourn. Before he reentered it, the greatest depression the United States had ever known was under way.

38 THE GRAY NINETIES

The change in 1893 from Harrison and the Republicans to Cleveland and the Democrats was one from tweedledum to tweedledee, so far as the seriously dissatisfied elements in American society were concerned. The Cleveland who took the oath of office on March 4 was the same Cleveland who had left office four years earlier. He had acquired no new ideas and he had not lost his bravery; if he had changed at all, it was that he had become even less flexible than he had been in his first term. He had not found, and he never did find any fundamental fault in America. He saw only defects in government that could be removed or reduced by the application of honesty, economy, and courage. He had come to look upon himself as a statesman almost above party; he was a strong man rather than a great one. Gathering about him a Cabinet of men of his own views, he set out to reduce expenses, balance the budget, and to put the currency back on a sound footing. He also strove, but not too insistently, to lower tariffs and to expand the merit system. His second term was much less comfortable than his first one, for it coincided with the depression of

543

1893, and he retired to private life with few expressions of regret from his fellow Democrats. His party eventually deserted him for Populism and William Jennings Bryan. He left the White House in dignity and with an easy conscience, for he believed he had fought the good fight.

THE DEPRESSION OF 1893

The depression of 1893 began with a financial panic just ten days before Cleveland reentered the Presidency. Only a few months earlier, Harrison, ignoring the plight of the farmers, had informed Congress that all was well with the American economy, and that work was abundant and wages high, whether measured in terms of dollars or in buying power. Then suddenly the Philadelphia and Reading Railroad, without warning, went bankrupt. Anxiety mounted among financiers, railroad leaders, and speculators. On May 5 the National Cordage Company collapsed and created alarm that quickly led to a crash in the stock market. Banks began to call in their loans, and businesses to fail in large numbers. Railroad companies toppled incredibly, the Erie Railroad in July, the Northern Pacific in August, the Union Pacific in October, and the Atcheson, Topeka and Santa Fé in December. By the end of 1893, 500 banks and nearly 16,000 businesses had failed. The panic swelled into a depression that continued until Cleveland had left office. Between 1894 and 1897, 300 more banks fell, and with them more industrial companies. Steel companies followed the railroads into bankruptcy; by the summer of 1894 nearly 41,000 miles of railroad trackage was in the hands of receivers, who bought very little steel. There was a short upturn in 1895, then a further slackening in economic activity. By 1896 stock prices had fallen one-third, not an impressive fraction in terms of the market collapse that began in 1929, but indicative nevertheless of a long and grinding slump. The depression was peculiarly hard upon the farmers of the South and the Great Plains region, which had been distressed even before 1893, and on industrial labor, which suffered as never before from unemployment. It has been estimated that the unemployed in commerce and industry numbered at least 2,450,000 at the bottom of the depression in the winter of 1893–1894, and that they numbered about 2,000,000 in the winter of 1896–1897. It was reported that at the lowest point of the slump more than 100,000 in Chicago were without jobs. America had never known such a severe depression, and there would not be another one comparable to it until the Great Depression that began in 1929.

CAUSES OF THE DEPRESSION

What was it that staggered the American economy? Some conservative-minded people contended that it was caused by the rantings of such wild men as communists, socialists, and Populists, who destroyed public confidence. Others would have it that withdrawals of capital by foreign investors, especially English ones, between 1890 and 1896 brought on the panic and the depression. Certainly the departure of the foreign capital did contribute to the panic, although it was hardly responsible for the severity of the slump that followed. The Populists and other believers in "soft" money were sure that the principal source of trouble was the tight money policy that had been followed by both the Republicans and the Democrats. Overexpansion of the railroads and of industry was cited as a prime factor, and protective tariffs as contributing ones. The real explanation is not simple, but it is apparent that the various segments of the economy had become so intertwined that all suffered when one was in distress, and that the depression began in and spread from agriculture. The railroads, unwisely extended into areas where business was slender, and at least sometimes handicapped by "watered stock," were hit by declining farm business. Then followed the crumbling of the stock market, the failure of metropolitan banks, the breaking in consequence of smaller ones, and a general slackening in industry and commerce. In brief, there was a chain reaction, its impulse proceeding from the pinched farmers.

Cleveland entertained a narrow and shallow view of the causes of the depression, one that he shared with friends among the financiers. For him, the slump had its origin in one law; moreover, its cure lay in repealing that law. He believed that the Sherman Silver Purchase Act, requiring both the purchase and coinage of silver, had sapped faith in the desire and ability of the government to maintain the gold standard. It followed, then, that the repeal of that measure would restore confidence and permit recovery. In June, 1893, he called a special session of the Congress to meet in August. The day after issuing the summons he underwent a successful operation for cancer of the mouth, secretly, in order not to add to the public confusion; by the time Congress met, he was equipped with an artificial jaw of vulcanized rubber, but he could still clench his teeth. He demanded the repeal of the law.

It was long doubtful that Congress would comply with Cleveland's insistent request. Democrats from the South and West bitterly refused to concede that the Sherman Silver Purchase Act had been injurious; they asserted that it was defective only because it did not provide for a sufficient expansion of the currency. They were joined by Republicans from the Midwest and West, who felt as they did. With them stood the Populists. The men from the South, the Midwest, and the West cried that the troubles of the nation proceeded from an international conspiracy of bankers determined to grind down the poor. They insisted that the farmers had prospered before 1873 and that they had begun to suffer only when the bankers quietly stopped the coinage of silver in the "Crime of 1873,"

They also claimed that as debtors the farmers had to repay in scarce and more valuable money after 1873, and that the entire nation suffered from a shortage of currency. Their remedy was to put out more money. In the House of Representatives a new member from Nebraska, William Jennings Bryan, did not hesitate to challenge Cleveland. He declared:

Today, the Democratic party stands between two great forces, each inviting its support. On the one side stand the corporate interests of the nation, its moneyed institutions, passionless. They demand special legislation, favors, privileges, and immunities. . . . On the other hand stands that unnumbered throng which gave a name to the Democratic party and for which it has assumed to speak. Work-worn and dust-begrimed, they make their sad appeal. . . . Although the ones who most deserve the fostering care of Government, their cries for help too often beat in vain against the outer wall, while others less deserving find ready access to legislative halls.

The fervid and vivid oratory of the inflationists was all in vain, at least so far as immediate consequences were concerned. Men from the North and East, both Democrats and Republicans, rallied behind the President, who used the whip of patronage to secure the votes of waverers. In October the Sherman Silver Purchase Act was formally set aside.

It turned out that Cleveland did not have a prompt cure for the depression, but rather that he had merely won the first of a series of battles in a campaign to preserve a gold standard. Several hundred million dollars of greenback and silver certificates remained in circulation. The Republicans had felt constrained to make them all redeemable in gold, and Cleveland believed it necessary to continue that policy. However, he found it extremely difficult, for the public preferred gold to paper, and forced the Treasury to pay out the precious metal in exchange for the paper. To meet such demands, the Treasury had steadily maintained a gold reserve of more than $100,000,000 and it was commonly believed that the reserve ought not to fall below that value. Nevertheless, it was barely above that figure when Cleveland reentered the Presidency, and it soon began to dwindle. The demands for gold became almost frantic, and the reserve diminished to $62,000,000 by January, 1894. The reserve was restored to $100,000,000 by purchasing gold through a sale of bonds. That did little good to the Treasury, for even those who had purchased the bonds forced it to give out gold for paper. The bond issue gave only temporary relief; a second one brought the same result. At the beginning of February, 1895, the reserve was cut to less than $42,000,000, and Cleveland and his advisers were almost desperate. They met the crisis with the help of banker J. P. Morgan, and of August Belmont who represented the Rothschild banking family. They privately supplied the Treasury with 3,500,000 ounces of gold, at least half of it from Europe, taking bonds in return. They quickly sold the bonds at a profit, a fact that was disturbing. It was even more disquieting that the United States had to seek their help in order to preserve its credit. Cleveland justified the bargain on the ground that the services of the bankers were sorely needed and that their profit probably was not large. In any case, the gold reserve was again restored. Less than a year later still another sale of bonds, a public one, was necessary to replenish the reserve, but it was not seriously attacked thereafter. Cleveland had won an impressive victory for "sound" money, but the depression had not vanished.

UNEMPLOYMENT

Assuming that economic recovery would come if public confidence in American money was sustained, Cleveland refused to take any action to help the unemployed. The masses of workmen discharged did not, so he thought, present a new problem. Like most Americans, he believed that the industrious and the thrifty, if able-bodied, could care for themselves, and that everyone ought to be industrious and thrifty. With whatever private assistance was needed, the poor should get along as best they could until conditions improved. He believed that the federal government should be supported by the citizen, not the citizen by the federal government. He did not realize that in an industrial world the unemployed could not so readily endure hardships as in the past. Only too often the city factory employee neither owned a home nor had any substantial savings. He was likely to be in serious distress within a few weeks after being laid off or discharged.

Cleveland did not consider the undertaking of new public works to provide jobs for the unemployed. When a few members of Congress proposed an emission of $500,000,000 in legal tender currency, the money to be used to build roads, he displayed no enthusiasm for the proposal. When Jacob S. Coxey of Massillon, Ohio, and others organized marches of the unemployed to Washington to bring direct pressure upon government to secure both a program of road building and currency inflation, Cleveland and most other Americans became concerned. Coxey, a wealthy businessman, but a Populist, set out with his "army" of 100 unarmed men in the spring of 1894. Acquiring recruits, including 100 students from Lehigh University, and also losing some men as it moved on toward the capital, the army numbered 500 when it reached Washington. It behaved very well en route; convinced that they were struggling in behalf of a "commonwealth of Christ," Coxey's followers were idealists and cranks, not hoodlums. Sixteen other "armies" that set out for Washington that spring—only 1200 men in all reached it—were similarly composed, except for two organized on the Pacific Coast that undertook to secure railroad transportation by force. Attempting to penetrate into the Capitol to present their demands, Coxey and two other leaders of the Commonwealers were arrested for carrying banners on its grounds; and Coxey and his aide Christopher Columbus Jones were also charged with violating the law by walking on the grass. Numerous policemen who had been gathered to preserve order became excited and used their clubs upon both Coxey's men and innocent bystanders, and about 50 persons were injured as they fled. Coxey and Jones were fined $5.00 and sentenced to 20 days in jail. So ended a march which had its humorous aspects. It gave the thoughtful food for thought, for Coxey's "soldiers" were obviously decent and inoffensive men. Was it possible that something was seriously wrong in America?

Although he was against work relief, Cleveland continued to be a moderate reformer. Before he left office in 1897 he doubled the number of federal employees under the merit system; there were about 40,000 under civil service in 1893 and about 80,000 four years later. He also tried to redeem a campaign promise to lower tariffs, but with little success. Protectionist interests in the Senate were so powerful that most rates were only moderately reduced in the Wilson-Gorman Act of 1894. The President, only too well aware that it differed little from the existing McKinley Tariff Act, indicated his displeasure by letting the bill become law without his signature.

THE INCOME TAX CONTROVERSY

The Wilson-Gorman Act did contain a great reform in principle, an income tax. Cleveland endorsed it only as a means of replacing revenue lost by reductions in the import duties. The income tax was the work of men more conscious of the new America than he. It had long been evident that those who had accumulated or were amassing large and even immense fortunes were escaping taxation in proportion to their wealth. The income tax was one obvious remedy, and it had won the support of more than Populists. The tax was very moderate, 2 percent upon all income over $4000 per annum. It was vainly opposed as a revolutionary measure, which indeed it was.

The income tax of 1894 did not long remain alive on the statute books. The new levy was promptly attacked as unconstitutional by lawyers who brought it before the Supreme Court for a ruling. They contended that the tax was socialistic, communistic, and anarchistic. Despite the fact that it had upheld the constitutionality of the Civil War income tax in 1881, the Court had great difficulty in handling the case of *Pollock* v. *Farmers' Loan and Trust Company* in 1895. It declared by a vote of 6 to 2 that the tax could not be collected upon income from municipal bonds, which were constitutionally classified with state bonds. To tax the income from state and municipal bonds was in effect to tax the states and cities. A levy on income from state bonds might endanger the federal system, enabling the national government to ruin the states financially. To support this conclusion the majority of the justices cited with approval *McCulloch* v. *Maryland* and John Marshall's declaration that the power to tax involved the power to destroy. Also by a vote of 6 to 2, the Court asserted that income from real property could not constitutionally be taxed, since it would be equivalent to a tax upon the real property itself. Thus it was a direct tax, and the Constitution required that direct taxes be apportioned among the states. Accordingly, the levy on income from land was also unconstitutional. However, the Court was unable to agree whether, with these two exceptions, the new tax was consistent with the Constitution. Four justices believed that the tax was, four that it was not. Hearing the arguments a second time, it again listened to appeals from corporation lawyers to strike down a tax that was both un-American and unconstitutional. It was declared, obviously with some justification in view of later experience, that the tax would encourage cheating, that it would turn the Americans into a nation of liars; it certainly persuaded them to study bookkeeping. In one of its most bitterly condemned decisions the Court, by a vote of 5 to 4, now ruled that the income tax was completely unconstitutional. Its decision was peculiarly open to attack in that one of the judges in the majority had changed his mind at the last moment. The Supreme Court was even more conservative than Cleveland.

LABOR AND THE STRIKE

Cleveland and the Supreme Court differed not at all in their attitude toward the Chicago railroad strike of 1894. The depression brought on many strikes as well as unemployment; more than 500,000 men lost their jobs that year in attempts to improve their lot. Disorder followed, and cautious people became alarmed. In April, 125,000 United Mine Workers struck in protest against a cut in pay, but were forced to return to their picks and shovels at the new lower wages. Almost simultaneously the American Railway Union struck against James J. Hill's Great Northern Railroad, for the same reason. Arbitration that followed gave the workers most of their demands. The American Railway Union, founded by Eugene V. Debs, was unusual in that it embraced all railroad workers, skilled and unskilled. It undertook to accept as members employees of the Pullman Palace Car Company and to support them in a strike against it, against the better judgment of Debs. The leaders of the new union, hardly more than a year old, believed it to be stronger than it was, again except for Debs. Although it did have more than 150,000 members, it suffered a crushing defeat, and Debs went to prison.

The Pullman strike had a curious background. George M. Pullman looked upon his workmen as his children, and had built for them what he considered a "model town," named after himself, a few miles outside of Chicago. It was actually a model company town, in which Pullman was a feudal lord. During the depression his company encountered difficulties, but continued to make profits. Nevertheless, he reduced the pay of his workers five times within a year, but he refused to lower the high rents that he charged his employees. Desperate, they formed a grievance committee to speak for them; Pullman responded by discharging all of its members. He felt that his men were ungrateful, and he refused either to talk to their representatives or to consider arbitration, although it was urged upon him by the mayors of 50 cities. Going on strike, the Pullman workers begged for the help of the American Railway Union, which first responded by declaring that its railroadmen would not handle Pullman cars. However, the railroads then began to discharge employees who refused to handle the cars. The union then struck against the railroads. Its efforts were concentrated on Chicago and its vicinity.

The railroads centering upon Chicago broke the strike with the help of Richard Olney, Cleveland's Attorney General, and the President himself. Their officers would not move trains, even with "scab" labor, without Pullman cars, and claimed that the American Railway Union was obstructing the mails. This strategy pleased Olney, himself a member of the boards of directors of three railroads. Olney's subordinates in Chicago then secured an injunction forbidding the union and its members to interfere with the mails. Immediately after the injunction was served, a mob containing more townspeople than strikers ditched a mail train in Blue Island, Illinois. Up to that time there had been no violence in Chicago, but Cleveland, urged on by Olney, declared that there was a "reign of terror" in the city and sent 2000 soldiers to restore order. Then wild rioting broke out in Chicago; 12 people were killed, and much railroad property was destroyed. The strike was broken by the troops. Singularly enough, neither Mayor John Hopkins of Chicago nor Governor John Peter Altgeld of Illinois had asked Cleveland for help in maintaining order. In fact, Altgeld informed the President that the state militia of Illinois could keep the peace, and declared that the President had acted illegally. He received no satisfaction from Cleveland, who asserted that he was within his powers when he sent the soldiers to prevent obstruction of the mails and to counter "conspiracies . . . against commerce between the States." The Supreme Court saw the situation as Olney and Cleveland did. Eugene V. Debs and eight other officers of the American Railway Union, having disobeyed the injunction, were found guilty of contempt of court and sentenced to imprisonment. They appealed to the Supreme Court, denying that they had interfered with the mails, denying also the constitutional power of the judge who had sentenced them to issue an injunction. Their appeal was turned down. Thereafter, the injunction became a favorite weapon to use against strikers. Released from prison, Debs emerged a convert to socialism. With others he founded the Socialist party in 1900.

Their experiences in the depression of 1893 did not persuade many Americans to follow the example of Debs and become Socialists. Instead, in the elections of 1894, the voters behaved as usual, casting their ballots in accordance with party affiliation or against the Democrats because one of their number happened to be in the White House during the hard times. The Populists gained, but not remarkably; the Republicans scored an impressive victory with a majority of 140 in the House of Representatives. Somewhat discouraged, the Populists, believing that expansion of the currency was their only attractive issue, decided to place almost their whole emphasis upon it in 1896. They were encouraged by the tremendous popularity of William H. Harvey's *Coin's Financial School,* a most persuasive pamphlet published in 1894 which ascribed all of America's ills to one cause, an inadequate currency, and offered a single sovereign remedy, the free coinage of silver at the ratio to gold of 16 to 1. As the campaign of 1896 approached, it was obvious that a party calling for more money based upon silver would get many votes—so obvious that both major ones were attracted toward bimetalism. In the end the Republicans resisted its allure; the Democrats, turning against Cleveland, stole the thunder of the Populists.

CONVENTIONS AND CANDIDATES OF 1896

Meeting at St. Louis in June, 1896, the Republican national convention contained an aggressive minority, chiefly from the Rocky Mountain region and the South, that demanded the free coinage of silver. It seemed to some observers that the convention would offer at least a gesture in the direction of bimetalism, partly to win votes and partly because the leading aspirant for the Presidential nomination was William McKinley, who had not committed himself to the gold standard. However, Mark Hanna, the astute Ohio industrialist and political boss who was McKinley's most ardent supporter, made a bargain with the "sound money" men by which it was agreed that they would align themselves behind McKinley and that he would avoid heresy with respect to the currency question. Accordingly, the Republican platform called for dollars "as good as gold," declaring against free coinage of silver unless other nations formally agreed to do likewise (a most unlikely event). Silverites from the Rocky Mountain states then walked out of the convention, and McKinley was named for the Presidency without any real contest. The Republicans had committed themselves to Cleveland conservatism, with two exceptions: they declared their customary solicitude for the Northern veterans, and for effective tariff protection.

The Democrats are traditionally less inhibited than their rivals in their national conventions, and they outdid themselves in 1896 at Chicago. The party had powerful silver sentiment in it; in fact, the silverites had an easy majority. Under the leadership of Governor Altgeld the Democrats adopted a forward-looking program, calling for the free coinage of silver; abolition of national bank notes; a tariff for revenue only; a graduated income tax; enforcement of the Sherman Act; and an increase in the authority of the Interstate Commerce Commission. Their platform also denounced Cleveland's use of the army to break the railroad strike as "a crime against free institutions," and inveighed against government "by injunction as a new and highly dangerous form of oppression." Disowning Cleveland, they had an opportunity to stand forth as liberals and responsible reformers. They did not seize the opportunity, since free coinage of silver was hardly a sure and complete answer to the nation's currency problem. Had they come forth for a sound and expanded currency, committing themselves to no panacea, they must have had a powerful appeal to thoughtful, independent voters. As it was, the delegates were passionate on the silver question and less interested in others. They differed in no material way from the Populists. Moreover, the convention failed to choose a candidate who could see the necessity for calling for reform on a broad front. The delegates were enthralled by the oratory of the youthful William Jennings Bryan. Speaking in behalf of the platform and against the efforts of Cleveland Democrats to amend it, the 36-year-old Nebraskan delivered an extraordinary extemporaneous speech which he had been gradually preparing during two years. With a golden voice, graceful gestures, and passion, Bryan declared that he spoke for "the struggling masses," for the laborer, the country merchant, the village lawyer, the miner, and the farmer. Above all, he cried out for free silver coinage and the farmer. In an eloquent peroration which brought his listeners to their feet, he challenged "the idle holders of idle capital":

> You come to us and tell us that the great cities are in favor of the gold standard; we reply that the great cities rest upon our broad and fertile prairies. Burn down your cities and leave our farms, and your cities will spring up again as if by magic; but destroy our farms and the grass will grow in the streets of every city in the country. . . .
>
> If they dare to come out in the open field and defend the gold standard as a good thing, we will fight them to the uttermost. Having behind us the producing masses of this nation and the world, supported by the commercial interests, the laboring interests, and the toilers everywhere, we will answer their demand for a gold standard by saying to them: You shall not press down upon the brow of labor this crown of thorns, you shall not crucify mankind upon a cross of gold.

The delegates were swept away by Bryan's magnificent performance. Setting aside "Silver Dick" Bland of Missouri, a veteran champion of currency expansion, they named Bryan for the Presidency on the fourth ballot. This despite forebodings on the part of Altgeld. Ineligible for the Presidency because he was not a natural-born citizen of the United States, the harelipped Governor of Illinois, who knew much about mankind, if relatively little about currency, feared that Bryan had not much more than a splendid speaking ability to offer to the voters. His judgment of the Democratic candidate would eventually be shared by many others. While Bryan was not without understanding, he was unequal to the task of molding his party into one that stood for enlightened liberalism. He, too, felt that the free coinage of silver was more important than all else.

So strong was feeling on the money question that many Cleveland Democrats deserted their party, founded the National Democratic Party, and named John M. Palmer for the Presidency on a platform of allegiance to the gold standard. Even earlier, the silver Republicans under the leadership of Senator Henry M. Teller of Colorado organized themselves as the National Silver Republicans. However, they urged the election of Bryan. And what of the Populists? The issue upon which they had concentrated their affections had been stolen by the Democrats, and they were badly divided among themselves regarding the course they should take. Finally, refusing to accept the Democratic Vice-Presidential candidate, Arthur Sewall, a Maine businessman, they endorsed Bryan for the Presidency and Populist "Tom" Watson of Georgia for the Vice-Presidency. Other minor parties entered the contest, and the voters had, on the surface, a wide choice. Actually, the decision lay between Bryan and McKinley.

THE CAMPAIGN OF 1896

Bryan was far and away the most conspicuous figure in the campaign. The silver mining interests donated sufficient money to the Democrats so that he could wage a strenuous battle. Displaying astonishing stamina, he made 600 speeches in 29 states, and traveled 13,000 miles in 14 weeks. Everywhere he went large crowds came forth to listen to the "Boy Orator of the Platte," who insistently cried that the free coinage of silver would give economic justice to the masses. His vehement denunciations of the "Gold Bugs," and of the selfishness of the rich men of the East aroused enthusiasm among farmers. To sophisticated defenders of sound money he seemed at one and the same time visionary, fatuous, revolutionary, and dangerous. They freely described him as a communist and an anarchist, although the more thoughtful among them had to admire his energy. Actually, there was little of the revolutionist in him. Of Southern background, he was basically orthodox and conventional, a devout Christian.

As a boy and as a student at Illinois College he had developed natural gifts as an orator, and he was making energetic use of a superb platform style. He was not clever, nor insidious, nor a Samson trying to pull down the pillars of society.

The most sagacious figure in the campaign was not Bryan, nor William McKinley, but Mark Hanna. McKinley, the last of the Civil War heroes from Ohio to be sponsored for the Presidency by the Republicans, had abilities much like those of his rival, except in declamation. A kindly, tactful, and pious man, he had long served in the House of Representatives and fancied himself as an expert upon the tariff, with which he had had much experience. He wished to stand forth as a champion of protection, and to make the tariff the chief issue. As Republican campaign manager, Hanna took his good friend Major McKinley in hand. He persuaded his candidate not to go on speaking tours, and not to discuss public questions at length. He arranged numerous "front porch" gatherings at McKinley's home. Delegation after delegation of friendly visitors was brought to call upon McKinley and to ask suitable questions, to which he, having been informed about the questions in advance, made suitable replies. The impression created was that he was a safe, responsible, and likeable person. Hanna also collected large sums of money from industrialists and bankers to spread the Republican propaganda. Employers suggested to workers that the election of Bryan might well mean that they would lose their jobs, if they had such. Hanna was sure that he had the formula for victory,

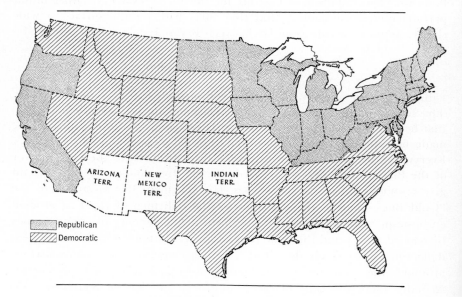

REPUBLICAN VICTORY, 1896

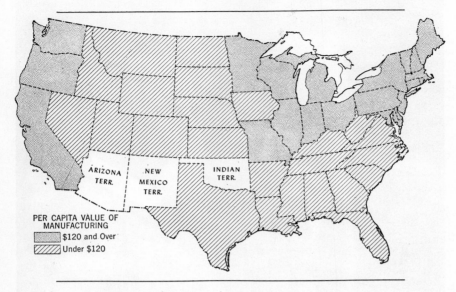

PER CAPITA VALUE OF
MANUFACTURING

[▨] $120 and Over

[▨] Under $120

CHIEF MANUFACTURING STATES, 1900

and he was right. Bryan carried the South and most of the West, and his popular vote was impressive, over 6,500,000. However, McKinley ran well ahead in the Midwest and the East, obtaining more than 7,100,000 popular votes and a substantial margin in the electoral college, 271 to 176. The Republicans also won control of both houses of Congress.

Ironically enough, the farmers who had so passionately given their loyalty to the Populists and then to Bryan secured the more generous currency they so earnestly desired soon after McKinley became President. It did not come through the coinage of silver, although he said a few words in favor of international bimetalism in his inaugural address. New mines in Australia and Alaska enhanced the supply of gold. Besides, the Republicans, officially putting the nation upon the gold standard in 1900, arranged to expand the currency somewhat by authorizing the smaller national banks, not hitherto given that privilege, to issue notes. In fact, despite the passage of the Dingley Tariff Act of 1897, which raised rates upon imported goods to a remarkably high average of 57 percent and were only moderately reduced in 1909, the farmers were entering upon a period of prosperity that would endure for two decades.

39 THE GILDED AGE AND AFTER

Were one to judge the American people by what they read and sang between the close of the Civil War and the depression of 1893, they were satisfied, simple, and sentimental; with qualifications, all three adjectives are suitable, despite the distresses of the farmers of the South and the West and those of the workmen. On the whole, the American people were well off, and they knew it. Hence their rejection of schemes of thoroughgoing reform, their gentle shifts in politics from Republican to Democrat, and from Democrat to Republican. It must not be forgotten that the lot of the American, as it had long been and as it would long continue to be, was happier than that of his fellow men. When the distinguished English observer James Bryce published *The American Commonwealth* in 1888, he correctly pointed out that life in America was basically good, and that the nation was not badly governed, except for its cities. By European standards most American farmers and workmen lived well. Social discontent rose only slowly as both the very rich and the very poor grew more numerous; even in the election of 1896, coming in the midst of hard times, William Jennings Bryan's voice was heard as that of a siren of the classical kind. There was intellectual and social ferment in the 1870s and 1880s, but the great

556

mass in the middle of American society was little affected by it until the dying years of the century. Not until the first decade of the twentieth century was there a very general conviction in America that the nation suffered from ills that required potent medicines.

LITERATURE AND THE ARTS

The best-selling books of an era are often the poor and unimportant ones, but they do supply some measure of the interests, intellectual competence, and tastes of the public. The most popular new books that appeared in America during the generation before the depression of 1893 included the sentimental *St. Elmo* of Augusta J. Evans Wilson; Louisa May Alcott's *Little Women* and *Little Men;* General Lew Wallace's *Ben Hur; The Old Swimmin'-Hole* of James Whitcomb Riley; and Frances Hodgson Burnett's *Little Lord Fauntleroy*. Widely circulated also were the rags-to-riches books of Horatio Alger, turned out with the industry that their author praised as the principal ingredient in his formula for the achievement of success and happiness. There were, to be sure, other and better books that secured many readers: the *Innocents Abroad, Tom Sawyer,* and *Huckleberry Finn* of Mark Twain; Henry George's *Progress and Poverty;* and Edward Bellamy's *Looking Backward*. It is apparent enough that the American "general reader" had not become sophisticated. He, or more likely she, preferred Will Carleton's *Over the Hills to the Poor House* to the *Democratic Vistas* of Walt Whitman. It is comforting to recall that the Holy Scriptures were read more than any other writings.

But it would be wrong to assume that all, or nearly all, was sugar and sentiment. Talent and genius will flower, perhaps not in the desert, but in the oases to be found in the driest of waste places. Paul Hamilton Hayne, living in a shack furnished with wooden crates and decorated with pictures cut from magazines, found no oasis near Augusta in Georgia, and did not become the great poet he might have been. Sidney Lanier, poor and stricken by tuberculosis, lacked the benefit of a nourishing cultural environment until his life was nearly ended. Would that he could have written more of the melodies and rhythms of "The Song of the Chattahoochee" and "The Marshes of Glynn." Happily, New England—despite at least a temporary wane in literary vitality there—and New York City continued to offer encouragement to the poet, the novelist, and the writer generally. Elsewhere, gifted literary men and women made money chiefly by writing for the newspapers. Slender help came to them from the magazines, which had small circulation, and narrow and genteel horizons. Spiritual encouragement came from Whitman, James Russell Lowell, John Greenleaf Whittier, and Oliver Wendell Holmes, all of whom lived on into the 1890s. However, literature had only one great tower of strength for the aspiring writer, William Dean Howells, who stretched out an uplifting arm from Boston and New York.

THE NEW WRITERS

The three most gifted literary people of the Gilded Age were doubtless the female poet Emily Dickinson, the humorist Mark Twain, and the novelist Henry James, if those who had already achieved greatness be excluded. Miss Dickinson was an eccentric and exotic New England spinster who was unknown in her own time. She published only two brief poems before her death in 1886, not because her verses were unappreciated, but because she shrank from offering them to the public. Only gradually did they appear in print, bringing delight to the sensitive. An old maid recluse in Amherst, Massachusetts, she felt intensely and expressed herself in splendid imagery. Her short verses about fundamentals, God, love, defeat, and death, have a peculiar power and poignancy. She wrote:

> The lightning is a yellow fork
> From tables in the sky
> By inadvertent fingers dropped,
> The awful cutlery
> Of mansions never quite disclosed
> And never quite concealed,
> The apparatus of the dark
> To ignorance revealed.

And touchingly she wrote about her own fate:

> A wife at daybreak I shall be;
> Sunrise, hast thou a flag for me?
> At midnight I am yet a maid—
> How short it takes to make it bride!
> Then, midnight I have passed from thee
> Unto the East and Victory.
>
> Midnight, "Good night!"
> I hear them call.
> The angels bustle in the hall,
> And softly my Future climbs the stair,
> I fumble at my childhood's prayer—
> So soon to be a child no more!
> Eternity, I'm coming, Sir—
> Master, I've seen that face before.

Of utterly different stuff was Samuel Langhorne Clemens, better known by his pen name of Mark Twain. For him life held no agonies until much of it had passed. Born in the small town of Hannibal, Missouri, that he immortalized with his books about Tom Sawyer and Huckleberry Finn, he

was one of those born storytellers who bring joy to their fellows, a delightful and charming humorist when at his best, which was most of the time.
Like Benjamin Franklin, he began as a printer; in his youth he was also
a pilot of river boats on the Mississippi and a miner. Printing quite logically led to reporting, and he began his rise to fame by writing newspaper
pieces. His amusing story, *The Celebrated Jumping Frog of Calaveras
County,* caught the attention of the public at the close of the Civil War.
He was sent as a travel correspondent to the Holy Land in 1867; and his
account of that journey in *Innocents Abroad* brought him a national reputation at the age of 34. This and other travel books won him immense
popularity, not only because of their humor, but because he patriotically
made fun of European art, customs, and manners. *Life on the Mississippi*
and *The Adventures of Huckleberry Finn,* in which there are well-drawn
people as well as charm and amusement, are doubtless his best books.
Twain also became an exceedingly attractive lecturer, and despite some
bad investments became a wealthy man. He was less successful as a novelist.
In his later years, he became bitter, for what reason is not clear, although
he had become deeply concerned about the injustices in American society.
He was to protest savagely against American repression of the Filipinos
after 1899. It may be that he had come to see himself as fundamentally a
failure. Although even Clemens's attempts to be funny were not always
successful, his renown as a humorist is not likely to die. His account of the
predicament in which Brigham Young found himself when he made a
present to one of his many children will ever delight parents who must
show no favoritism among their progeny. In essence, Twain, like Whitman,
was wholesomely American.

Also truly American, but of a very different stamp, was Henry James, an
East Coast sophisticate who spent most of his life in England, finally becoming a British citizen. He came from a family of means, was well-educated, and was at home in high social circles both in America and England.
A novelist, James chose to describe the lives of the wealthy on both sides of
the Atlantic. His work was not that of a lusty and exuberant genius, but
that of a careful and critical craftsman. There was little action in his books;
they were characterized by subtle analysis of personal relationships. A
favorite theme was the clash between the sturdy American and the more
sophisticated European, in which the sterling virtues of the Yankee appeared to advantage. He wrote complexly, and his books were not very
popular until psychological dissection came into vogue with the writings
of Marcel Proust and James Joyce.

REALISM

More prolific even than Twain and James was William Dean Howells,
who was for many years the most influential person in the American liter-

ary world. Born in Ohio, as a good Republican he wrote a campaign life of Lincoln in 1860 and was rewarded by an appointment as American consul at Venice. Returning home, he settled in Boston. He was the editor of the *Atlantic Monthly* for ten years, and his opinion of men and of things literary acquired great weight. The earlier of his many novels emphasized the smiling aspect of American life, the manners of the comfortable middle class from which he sprang and which he knew well. However, the gentle and decent Howells continued to mature intellectually in Boston, became convinced that all was not well in America, turned toward socialism, and decided that humanity was more important than art. He moved to New York because it had a freer atmosphere, in 1886. The new temper of his mind is shown by his denunciation of the execution of the Haymarket Riot anarchists as "the thing forever damnable before God and abominable to civilized man." Between 1887 and 1897, although he continued to use rather conventional and proper language in his novels, he described the evils of the new industrial age and its sinister impact upon rich and poor alike. In *A Hazard of New Fortunes* he described the "robber baron."

All American novelists did not move toward the newer realism with Howells. However, Hamlin Garland, who in his early career wrote about comfortable farm life in the Midwest and was afterward to stress the nobility and courage of the pioneers in that region, depicted straightforwardly the hardships endured by men and women on the same soil in *Main-Travelled Roads,* published in 1891. Romantic in his earlier and later writings, Garland was grimly realistic for a time, and even campaigned for the Populists. In 1893, Stephen Crane published at his own expense *Maggie: A Girl of the Streets,* because publishers found it too shocking—it bluntly related the story of a factory girl who was paid $5.00 per week, sought happiness in an illicit affair with a bartender, became a prostitute, and killed herself. Two years later Crane put forth the very popular story of a soldier in the Civil War, *The Red Badge of Courage,* in which the realities of war and the feelings of the soldier were realistically and imaginatively described. Nevertheless, at the turn of the century the most popular novels were commonly historical and romantic, such as Charles Major's *When Knighthood Was in Flower,* Paul Leicester Ford's *Janice Meredith,* and Mary Johnston's *To Have and To Hold.*

ARTISTS AND ARCHITECTS

Realism also slowly made its way among the artists and the architects in the Gilded Age. A new power and a new maturity came into American painting with Winslow Homer, a splendid watercolorist, who did *The Gulf Stream,* and Thomas Eakins, who did fine studies of the human body, as in *The Swimming Hole* and *Max Schmidt in a Single Scull.* Albert Pinkham Ryder was intense and imaginative, as in his *Death on a Pale Horse.* The superb etcher James A. McNeill Whistler was an American, although he spent all of his adult life abroad. Augustus Saint-Gaudens achieved fame as a sculptor in the Gilded Age. In architecture Victorian Gothic and French Renaissance styles dominated, with a Romanesque revival. However, architecture had more to offer than gingerbread and mansard roofs, for that peculiarly American building, the skyscraper, made its appearance in Chicago in the 1880s and soon afterward in New York. Louis Henri Sullivan not only helped to develop the skyscraper, but was the principal originator of modern organic architecture based on the fundamental concept that form ought to follow function.

INTELLECTUAL LIFE

Reluctant to acknowledge that anything genuinely serious was wrong with their world, the Americans generally tended to shy away from intellectuals, writers, and artists who urged that they broaden and deepen their outlook. They were encouraged to continue in their familiar patterns of thought and belief by men who had made vast fortunes. They were assured that the accumulation of these fortunes was the result of hard work, thrift, and intelligence, and that they too could move rapidly on the road to wealth. Becoming somewhat concerned because of the plight of the farmers and the appearance of fetid slums in the great cities, they were told that poverty and personal distress arose from indolence and self-indulgence, and only infrequently from misfortune, such as the early death of a family breadwinner. Such occasional tragedies could be mended by the industry of a widow, by the help of relatives, or by the efforts of energetic sons. And, were not peddling newspapers, blacking shoes, and service as a messenger boy not only useful for sustaining a poor family but sure steps toward prosperity for the boy himself? The acquisition of riches was justified by an appeal to orthodox Calvinism, which had long given its blessing both to hard work and to the accumulation of money. Opulence received powerful theological sanction from the doctrine of stewardship. The rich were stewards of God, who had seen fit to reward their efforts; imbued with His spirit, they would use their money for the public good. To do them justice, the fabulously affluent John D. Rockefeller, Sr., and Andrew Carnegie both believed in and practiced stewardship on a vast scale. To be sure, neither of them left behind progeny who had to make their way as Rockefeller and Carnegie had.

As the teachings of Charles Darwin acquired vogue in the United States after the Civil War, they too were used to support economic and social inequality. Darwin's law of the "survival of the fittest" in Nature was transplanted into the world of man; beneficial in Nature, it was so also in the affairs of men, for it was well that the strong should flourish and that the inferior should not. Getting money, much money, in competition with one's fellows was, then, blessed by both God and science.

SCIENCE AND RELIGION

In the end, nevertheless, the intellectuals and reformers of better will scored some victories in the Gilded Age and laid the foundations for others to come. The benefits of science, though not so evident as they afterward were, gave scientists some measure of immunity from attack. The opinions of the men who had developed anesthesia could not lightly be set aside as those of visionaries. They were listened to by thoughtful men and women, who were told that the earth had not been swiftly created in the year 4004 B.C., and that mankind had a much longer history than the brief one given him by Genesis. The geologists told them that the earth is very old; among them was Louis Agassiz, whose authority then seemed almost unchallengeable. Moreover, acquaintance with Darwin's *Origin of Species* confirmed what the observant had long since noticed, that man was closely related to the mammals among the animals. Darwin pointed out that man was the product of a long evolutionary process. Just how the process worked might be debated, but the law of evolution increasingly gained recognition. In consequence, literal interpretation of the Bible, of whatever version, long since rejected by the learned, was dealt a staggering blow. That man's history was that of an animal who had very slowly developed a peculiar genius was disconcerting to many. Was there then, no God of their fathers? However, many cheerfully accepted the teachings of Darwin, including the Reverend Henry Ward Beecher, pastor of a large church in Brooklyn, brother of Harriet Beecher Stowe, and the most popular preacher of his generation. Protestant clergymen in numbers began to welcome the concept of evolution as a proof of progress under the direction of God; they predicted with some confidence further advance toward perfection under the divine guidance.

Increased knowledge about evolution ultimately had profound effects that were social as well as intellectual and theological. As early as 1867, Octavius Brooks Frothingham and others of proud names and repute in Boston formed a Free Religious Association which called for a "Religion of Humanity." The society demanded that orthodox Christians cease to oppose evolution and historical criticism of the Scriptures; that there be freedom of thought; and that Christians join with all mankind to make a universal religion. Later, as the pastor of a church in New York Frothingham preached to large audiences of influential people who spread his teachings. Far more potent in spreading the Religion of Humanity was Robert G. Ingersoll, simultaneously one of the most hated and most loved men of his time. Son of a Calvinist preacher against whom he rebelled, a Civil War veteran, a lawyer, and a superb orator, Ingersoll forsook a brilliant career in politics, wealth, and respectability to work for a better world. His Religion of Humanity was also one of Democracy. He is especially remembered as a lecturer and a religious skeptic who aroused fury among orthodox Christians by his witty and penetrating analyses of the Scriptures. But Ingersoll was much more than a severe, entrancing, and convincing doubter. Speaking everywhere to crowds that paid to listen to him, he insisted that mankind must place its faith in man himself. It was idle to appeal to an unknowable God; and it was of no purpose to seek guidance in Nature, for "Nature produces man without purpose and obliterates him without regret." Ingersoll's Religion of Humanity was practical as well as philosophical. If the proper goal of mankind was its own improvement, there was much work to do. Calling for freedom of thought and faith in science, he looked forward to the day when machines would free man from want and brutal toil. But he also urged immediate action toward lessening the hours of labor and increasing the pay of workmen. There should be a more equal distribution of wealth. He hoped that one day society would cease to produce "millionaires and mendicants—gorged indolence and famished industry." Here and there all over America Ingersoll converted men to religious skepticism; he also persuaded many that there were serious ills in American life that required remedy. Blameless in personal conduct, he was condemned as Jefferson and Lincoln had been. Whatever may be said about his heresies and his orthodoxies, he was a good and lovable man.

UTOPIAN REFORMERS

Ingersoll offered no specific program to cure the economic and social ills of industrial America. Henry George and Edward Bellamy did. The remedies that they urged had serious defects, and they have not been adopted, but both men provoked thought and discussion and exercised a seminal influence. George was undoubtedly the more important of the two. Born a Philadelphian and Episcopalian, he became a sailor, then a Californian and a Jeffersonian. Unhappily observing the newly rich, he believed that economic disparity, if not corrected, would be fatal to freedom. It was not enough that men should have the right to vote and be, at least theoretically, equal before the law; they must have equal access to the riches of the earth, as the author of Nature had intended. It came to George that unearned increment of land was the great source of economic inequality, for the owners of land received the profits of progress. He had a simple prescription that must put everything right—the single tax on land, which would remove the direful economic inequity. George's social philosophy, put forth in his book *Progress and Poverty* in 1879, and in other later writings, attracted a great following. *Progress and Poverty* was purchased by hundreds of thousands of people, and single tax clubs sprang up, in England as well as in

America. Although his diagnosis of the sickness of industrial America and his prescription for it were faulty, his teachings that the sickness was serious and that government must supply the remedy dealt heavy blows to laissez-faire philosophy. When he died in New York in 1897, 100,000 people filed past his bier.

For Edward Bellamy, who published the Utopian novel *Looking Backward* in 1888, the corrective of all social ills was the "Brotherhood of Humanity," achieved through a totalitarian state. In his book he described a supposedly ideal society that existed in the year A.D. 2000, in which all persons received an equal income from government. All worked for the state until the age of 45, then retired to lives of leisure. In his Utopia individuals were distinguished from each other only by titles given in acknowledgment of special service rendered to the whole group. It was quickly pointed out by critics that Bellamy's Utopia was hostile to liberty, and enthusiasm for his new order soon waned. But Bellamy, too, helped to persuade that there were problems in America that must be attacked. State socialism did not flourish, although it had a certain romantic attraction in the Bellamy formula.

LEARNING AND THE SPREAD OF INFORMATION

Intellectual ferment and change also appeared in American colleges and universities, which were not stagnant in the Gilded Age. At Harvard, under the leadership of President Charles W. Eliot, the elective system for undergraduates was adopted, the example of Harvard being followed later everywhere in the nation. So it became possible for the undergraduate to sample learning more widely, and to a degree, to avoid intellectual toil. Graduate work was installed at The Johns Hopkins University, Harvard, Yale, the University of Michigan, and at Columbia University, among others. Doctors of philosophy educated in Germany began to train doctors of philosophy in American schools, bringing the German seminar across the Atlantic. Increasingly heavy emphasis was laid upon the "scientific" approach to learning. Sociology was introduced as a "science," thanks largely to the efforts of government clerk Lester Ward. Historians brought back from Germany a "scientific method" that promoted accuracy with respect to detail and presumably with respect to general conclusions. Among those who studied abroad was Henry Adams, scion of *the* Adams family, who wrote a classic *History of the United States During the Administrations of Jefferson and Madison*. In the end he discovered no scientific principle underlying mankind's course. Ultimately, his studies led him into profound pessimism, for he failed to find reasons to believe that America was having a healthy progress. He soon left the halls of Academe because he believed he could accomplish nothing in them; later he withdrew from the world of events to travel. *The Education of Henry Adams,* published after his death, records both his perception of his world and his despair. More optimistic was Frederick Jackson Turner, who urged that American history was not merely an extension of European, but that it contained a novel and hopeful element. In a paper read before the American Historical Association in 1893 entitled *The Significance of the Frontier in American History*, Turner contended that the outer belt of settlement immediately behind the many successive American frontiers had had a profound influence. In those areas democracy, individualism, social equality, and a spirit of cooperation flourished and gained new strength as region after region was put under cultivation. Turner also believed that the opening up of new areas provided a "safety-valve," offering opportunity to people living to the eastward and so relieving economic and social tension. Turner's arguments have been subjected to severe criticisms, the most important being that the importance of America's European background was underestimated and that the influence of the frontier regions was not clearly distinguished from the influence of the American environment as a whole. In any event, by noting that physical frontiers had substantially vanished, Turner compelled thought about a new and different America. The scientific approach to history had a discernible and direct impact upon the nation in that Woodrow Wilson as a graduate student at The Johns Hopkins University wrote a doctoral dissertation on *Congressional Government* which contained concepts he later put into practice as President. The emphasis upon the scientific method in history had another result which was less happy. Its practitioners often fancied that it was unnecessary to express themselves in pleasing language. In consequence, their writings were frequently for each other rather than for the public. What they had to say nevertheless achieved circulation through their students and through "popularizers."

There should be no question but that information and ideas spread more rapidly in the Gilded Age than hitherto, because of the growth of educational institutions. The older private colleges and universities grew larger, and new ones appeared, including Cornell University in 1867, Leland Stanford in 1885, and the University of Chicago in 1891. The land grant colleges matured and expanded in the Midwest and Far West. The state universities made rapid progress, moving into rivalry with the older private ones, with the University of Michigan leading the way. The public high school became fairly common, and elementary instruction at public expense was carried on everywhere, even in the impoverished South. As a result illiteracy was cut nearly in half between 1870 and 1900, from 20 percent to 10.7 percent.

As the Gilded Age drew to a close in the 1890s, information and ideas were circulated as never before in America, not only through lectures, books, and schools, but by means of newly founded magazines and newspapers. During this decade, *The New York Times* offered to its readers an accuracy, objectivity, and coverage of news such as no American news-paper had hitherto offered. Newspaper circulation increased immensely, and that of magazines even more remarkably. *The Review of Reviews, The Outlook, Collier's,* and the *Literary Digest* appeared beside the *Atlantic, Harper's,* and *The Nation.* While amusement, for building circulation and securing advertising, was often placed above instruction in the newspapers—comics, advice to the lovelorn, features, and large sport sections made their debut—the newspapers nevertheless became a powerful educational force. The new magazines also catered often to sensation, to the sentimental, to amusement, to escapism, although some of them were informative—some were even lively as well.

Gradually, through many means, both political and social reform acquired adherents. It was of special importance that they became more and more numerous among educated and middle-class Americans. It was also of moment that men of families long and well established came forward to supply leadership. Such men, with their thousands of dollars, felt crowded by the new rich with their millions. They could feel sympathy for the poor, the weak, and the unfortunate. They were often impelled by the spirit of *noblesse oblige.* Henry Adams felt himself helpless in industrial America, but Theodore Roosevelt went out to do battle.

40 APPROACH TO EMPIRE

In the last quarter of the nineteenth century a new wave of imperialism engulfed the great powers of Europe, Britain, France, Germany, Italy, and Russia—and Japan and America. Lust for colonies, commercial concessions, and naval bases drove those nations to empire building, and created or magnified keen rivalries among them. Other forces pushed them on: missionary activity; the desire to "civilize" the Asians, Africans, and Polynesians; and jealousy of each other. The British expanded their already farflung possessions; the French were especially active in Africa and Indo-China; and the recently united Germany sought territory in Africa and the Pacific. Except for Italy, all those powers became very interested in China; the recently formed kingdom of Italy, too weak to embark upon many expensive adventures, centered its major efforts on Africa. The rivalries that sprang from contests for empire not only increased animosities among nations, but in several cases also soothed away ancient hostilities between countries that were confronted by a common and potent competitor. By the spring of 1898 the United States had acquired Midway Island, a base in the Hawaiian Islands, and a solid claim to part of the Samoan archipelago. During the same period Anglo-American antipathies diminished remarkably. Thereafter, America was deeply involved, willy-nilly, in the affairs of the world.

AMERICA AND IMPERIALISM

Expansion beyond the North American continent was the work of no one party, although as it turned out the Republicans favored it more than did the Democrats. America became infected by imperialism for the same reasons as other countries. The virtual disappearance of good free land before the end of the century, the development of a mature industrial economy, the need and desire for markets abroad, the spirit of nationalism, and a sense of mission—these and other forces drove the United States into adventures beyond the sea. The insulation long provided by the oceans was rapidly thinning because of advances in communications, and the comfortable isolation so long enjoyed by the Americans could not in any case have endured much longer. It weakened faster because the nation pushed out over the waters that protected it.

That no party and no politician was fundamentally responsible for the formation of the American Empire is indicated by the fact that the chief instrument for building it, the navy, was strengthened and modernized with the common consent of politicians of all stripes. Neglected, along with the army, for nearly two decades after the Civil War, in the 1880s and 1890s it was supplied with iron ships to match its iron men. The Navy Department was modernized, facilities for making both ships and armament were vastly improved, and efficiency at sea was restored. At the end of the century America did not have a fleet equal to that of Britain or even to that of Germany, but it was superior to those of the other European nations. If one party was more responsible for its fashioning than the other, it was the Democrats, for it was William C. Whitney, Secretary of the Navy under Cleveland, who was the chief architect of this program in the second half of the 1880s.

A new spirit of aggressiveness entered American foreign policy when James G. Blaine was briefly Secretary of State in 1881. During the few months he was in office, he busied himself with Latin America, trying to expand the market for American finished goods there and to establish the United States as a "big sister" to the nations south of the Rio Grande. He had little immediate success, but he laid the foundations for the Pan-American Union, which was permanently established soon after he returned to the State Department in 1889. Blaine also tried to persuade Britain to nullify the Clayton-Bulwer Treaty, without success. However, he bluntly asserted, as President Hayes had before him, that an isthmian canal was of the first interest to the United States, and both he and his successors would have moved vigorously to protect that interest had it seemed likely that a canal could soon be completed. They guessed correctly that the French Company under Ferdinand de Lesseps which began to try to cut a waterway across Panama in 1879 would fail.

THE SAMOAN CRISIS

Further steps on the path to empire were taken during Cleveland's first term, although the Democratic President was not a champion of expansion. In 1887, renewing the reciprocity treaty of 1875 with the kingdom of Hawaii, the United States secured the exclusive right to build a naval base at Pearl Harbor, so strengthening American ties with the sunlit islands at the crossroads of the Pacific. The United States also became more deeply involved in the affairs of the Samoan Islands, where American interests clashed with those of Britain and Germany. The United States wanted a naval station at Pago Pago, but otherwise wished to leave the natives to themselves. However, German traders in the islands sought to bring them under the control of their fatherland, and the German government undertook to obtain a mandate over them. The British, who had also been lured to the Samoan archipelago, were willing to let the Germans dominate it if they were compensated elsewhere. When Germany refused to accept a triple protectorate proposed by the United States and staged a revolution among the natives that brought them under a pro-German faction, tension swiftly grew in the islands. The German-dominated regime discriminated against American and British traders. The three countries then sent warships to the islands, and war threatened in the faraway South Pacific. War vessels anchored near each other in Apia harbor, but did not shoot. The evident American and British determination persuaded the German chancellor, Prince von Bismarck, to negotiate, in the spring of 1889. No unfortunate incident at Apia prevented the diplomats from reaching a settlement at a conference held in Berlin. Instead, Nature intervened with a tropical hurricane that wrecked the German and American ships and drove the only British vessel on the spot out to sea. Germany gave in to the American demand, and a triple protectorate was established over the islands in June, 1889. Britain and Germany would have preferred a division of the archipelago between the three powers, but America was averse to acquiring Samoan territory. Another decade, and there would be less squeamishness in the United States.

BLAINE AS SECRETARY OF STATE

Blaine, returning to office as Secretary of State in time to see the Samoan crisis to its conclusion, prudently avoided the use of strong language in dealing with Germany and England. Like the other men involved, he was doubtless sobered by the danger of war, and he could not but feel the losses of the lives of American sailors in the hurricane. Nevertheless, "Jingo

Jim," as he came to be called, was as aggressive when serving under Harrison as he had been under Garfield and Arthur; and Harrison was of much the same mind. Blaine dealt roughly with Italy in 1891 in an affair arising from a lynching in New Orleans. The Chief of Police of that city had been murdered while investigating the activities of the Mafia Society, and eleven persons of Italian descent were accused, but acquitted. A mob slew all eleven, three of whom were citizens of Italy. That country thereupon demanded indemnity for the lynching and punishment of the lynchers. Blaine pointed out in his reply that the federal government did not have jurisdiction in the matter. When the Italian minister in Washington insisted that something be done, Blaine informed him that the Secretary of State did "not recognize the right of any government to tell the United States what it should do. We have never received orders from any foreign power and we will not begin now." Ministers were recalled home by both countries before Harrison and Blaine decided it was worthwhile to soothe Italy by paying $25,000 as an indemnity.

In a controversy with Chile, Blaine and Harrison were even more truculent. At a time when relations between America and Chile were strained because Chilean would-be revolutionists had secured arms in the United States, Captain Winfield Scott Schley of the American navy unwisely gave shore leave to some of his sailors at Valparaiso. A riot in a saloon between the sailors and Chileans ended with two sailors killed, seventeen injured, and others beaten and imprisoned. The government of Chile was slow in offering an apology for the untoward brawl. In January, 1892 Blaine demanded that it apologize for unflattering statements made by the Chilean Foreign Minister about President Harrison; otherwise, America would sever diplomatic relations. Had he not desired to make friends in Latin America, Blaine doubtless would have been even more vigorous. A few days later, while an apology from Chile was being decoded, the President suggested in a message to Congress that he would not be adverse to a declaration of war. The affair was settled by the Chilean apology and the payment by the Chilean government of cash to the injured and to the heirs of the two men who had been killed.

Also in 1892 Blaine engaged in one of those controversies with Britain that seemed almost inevitable in the nineteenth century. The issue was a rather exotic one. Canadian sealers were killing seals in the Bering Sea, a practice which threatened to exterminate those furbearing creatures. Trying to preserve and to exploit the seals—they could profitably be killed ashore without destroying the seal population—the United States seized Canadian sealing vessels and declared the Bering Sea to be under American jurisdiction. Its case was good on moral grounds, but poor in international law, upon which the British Foreign Secretary, Lord Salisbury, very carefully instructed Blaine. The upshot was an arbitrated agreement by which

America paid damages for the ship seizures and both countries agreed to limit the depredations of the sealers.

HAWAII

Blaine believed that both Cuba and the Hawaiian Islands were within an American sphere of influence. Unable to bring Cuba into a closer relationship with the United States, he was the principal figure in an almost successful attempt to annex Hawaii. The affair began with the sugar planters of the islands, mostly Americans and several of them the descendants of missionaries. They were not very happy under the easygoing, inefficient, and capricious rule of the native royal family. They succeeded in 1887 in imposing a constitution upon the Hawaiian Crown, but it was revoked in 1893 by Queen Lilioukalani, two years after she ascended the throne. The planters had another reason for unhappiness, a two cents per pound bounty upon sugar given to domestic producers in the United States by the McKinley Tariff Act of 1890. With the help of the bounty American producers could compete with those of Cuba and Hawaii. The planters on Oahu Island and others could solve both of their problems by bringing Hawaii under the American flag. Under the leadership of Sanford B. Dole, they rose in revolt against the native queen. Using a conventional imperialistic technique, John L. Stevens, the American minister to the kingdom, promptly arranged to land marines from the cruiser *Boston* to protect American lives and property. It may be guessed that Dole and the planters had made a prior agreement with Stevens. With the help of the marines the revolutionaries captured the public buildings on Oahu, and Stevens, without bothering to consult his superiors in Washington, officially recognized a government formed by the planters on the following day. Two weeks later, on February 1, Stevens proclaimed Hawaii to be an American protectorate, and ran up the Stars and Stripes in Honolulu. As President of the Republic of Hawaii Dole swiftly signed a treaty of annexation, which was promptly presented by President Harrison to the Senate. Unfortunately for Stevens and Dole, they had not been quite fast enough. The treaty was held up by Democrats in the Senate until the departure of Harrison from the Presidency. Grover Cleveland, who disliked imperialistic adventures, withdrew the document from the Senate a few days after he took office the second time.

For a time things looked black for the planters, but all was not lost. A special commissioner sent by Cleveland to Honolulu to investigate lowered the American flag and sent the marines aboard ship. He submitted a report to the President which made it clear that Stevens had been too helpful to the planters. He also asserted that most of the people of the islands were opposed to union with the United States. Cleveland's conscience was touched, and he tried to put "Queen Lil" back upon her throne, this despite a widespread clamor for annexation in American newspapers. He sent a new minister, Albert S. Willis, with instructions to try to persuade the queen and the planters to forgive and forget, with the queen resuming authority as a constitutional monarch. At length she agreed, abandoning a deeply cherished desire to cut off the heads of her enemies. However, the planters refused. Cleveland would not go so far as to use force against them and in 1894 he felt obliged to recognize officially the new Republic of Hawaii. The planters had made progress toward their objective. Time and a more complaisant President would help them to achieve it.

THE VENEZUELA DISPUTE

Curiously enough, the Cleveland who was condemned by American empire builders also played the part of the jingo in the Venezuela boundary dispute, which severely strained relations between Britain and America. Cleveland was badly advised by Richard Olney, whom he had made his Secretary of State. Moreover, he was overly swayed by his anti-imperialist sentiments and by anti-British feeling in the United States. His quarrel with Britain grew out of one between Britain and Venezuela over the boundary between Venezuela and English Guiana. The line between the two had long been a cause of controversy. The area claimed by both nations was extensive, for the contestants had enlarged their claims in order to do as well as possible in a final settlement. The British were willing to "split the difference," but were in no hurry, especially after gold was found in the disputed region. After 1887 Venezuela began insistently to press for a division through arbitration, posing as a small and helpless American nation harassed by the demands of a powerful, imperialistic, and European one. Venezuelan leaders calculated that their stand would gain approval in the United States and that they would profit from arbitration in which America played a role. Without paying too much attention to Venezuela, the British, involved in many seemingly more important questions, refused to arbitrate, since they knew that Venezuela would profit from that procedure. Nor did they welcome American "good offices" to settle the quarrel. In consequence, anti-British feeling in the United States, stimulated by clever Venezuelan propaganda, began to rise in 1894. When Congress in a joint resolution urged arbitration, Cleveland and Olney decided that the time had come to intervene. In July, 1895, Olney, with Cleveland's approval, sent off to London an astonishing note. He asserted that Britain, by interfering in the affairs of Venezuela, was violating the Monroe Doctrine —he would have been on firmer ground had he claimed that the British, by trying to expand their territory at the expense of the South American republic, were violating the noncolonization dictum of that Doctrine. The American people, continued Olney, were determined that the Doctrine be enforced. Would or would not Britain accept arbitration? The question was put with self-righteous and boastful language that could not fail to offend:

Today the United States is practically sovereign on this continent and its fiat is law upon the subjects to which it confines its interposition. Why? It is not . . . because wisdom and justice and equity are the invariable characteristics of the dealings of the United States. It is because, in addition to all other grounds, its infinite resources combined with its isolated position render it master of the situation and practically invulnerable against any or all other powers.

What sort of reply did Cleveland and Olney expect from the bombardment of historical blunder and bombast that the Secretary of State aimed at Britain? Lord Salisbury, the British Foreign Secretary, let them wait for it for four months. When he finally answered, he coolly refused arbitration. The boundary dispute had nothing to do with the Monroe Doctrine; it was only a problem of determining the "frontier of a British possession which belonged to the Throne of England long before the Republic of Venezuela came into existence." Correcting historical errors made by Olney, Salisbury wrote like a dignified and rather indifferent professor putting straight an ignorant and bumptious student. The tone of his reply was irritating, and he made no counterproposal. He goaded Cleveland and Olney to action, for they were not the sort to allow themselves to be brushed off so casually. On December 17, the President sent a message to Congress in which he declared that the United States must protect the rights of Venezuela. He asked that body to pay the expenses of an investigating commission that he would appoint to ascertain the true course of the boundary, and he announced his determination that Britain accept the findings of the commission. The money was voted amidst thunderous applause. A war fever developed in the United States, and Cleveland's challenge stirred anti-American feeling in England. However, sober second thought on both sides of the water suggested the foolishness of fighting about a region that was largely tropical jungle. Salisbury learned that he had gone too far; he supplied information to Cleveland's boundary commission, and then agreed to negotiate directly with Venezuela. Early in 1896 the excitement died down. Three years later a final settlement was reached, with a line little different from what Britain had always been willing to accept. The crisis proved to be, not one of a continuing chain, but the end of major troubles between America and England. It was becoming increasingly difficult to keep alive historical hostility toward Britain, and Irish immigration had diminished. The English had reached the conclusion that the United States had come to stay, and as England herself became more democratic, English opinion was turning toward friendship with America. Moreover, Britain's position was weakening as her European rivals became more and more powerful; she needed friends. Good feeling toward England was further fostered in America as Americans learned from experience about the perplexities of empire.

THE CUBAN REBELLION

Cleveland the anti-imperialist succumbed to the temptation to bait the British in the Venezuela frontier quarrel, but he was firmly opposed to any step that might directly involve the United States in a rebellion that broke out in Cuba in 1895. Again the United States served as a base for Cuban rebels, against Cleveland's will; again there was a desire to help the oppressed Cubans; and again Americans who lusted for that island became active. In the early months of 1896 Congress passed a resolution favoring recognition as a belligerent of a government set up by the rebels, but Cleveland ignored it. He was so determined not to be drawn into the conflict that he said there would be no war with Spain, even if Congress declared it, for he would not raise troops for it. However, the Cuban situation did not become critical for the United States until after he had left office. Had he continued in it for another year or two, it is quite possible that there would have been no Spanish-American War.

William McKinley, once a soldier, had no love for warfare. In his first inaugural address he denounced both wars and imperialism: "We want no wars of conquest; we must avoid the temptation of territorial aggression. War should never be entered upon until every agency of peace has failed; peace is preferable to war in almost every contingency." Privately, the new President was even more forthright, asserting that he wanted no part in "jingo nonsense." He unquestionably meant what he said, but there were mighty forces driving America on which even the stubborn Cleveland might not have been able to withstand, and McKinley was an amiable rather than a sturdy man. The nation had become industrial, powerful, and rich, with a population of about 75,000,000. It possessed an efficient navy. It had been at peace with the world during a long generation. Younger men in public life, such as Theodore Roosevelt and his friend Henry Cabot Lodge, conceived that America had a mission, that the nation ought to exert its strength toward improving the world. Toward that end, the acquisition of colonies and protectorates, and warfare—preferably not on a vast scale—were suitable means. Nor was the desire to spread American power and civilization confined to such younger men. The memory of the sufferings of the Civil War had faded. Hence McKinley did not object to acquiring the Hawaiian Islands. Hence the Cuban rebellion from its very beginning threatened to involve the United States more seriously than in the past. Hostility toward monarchical Spain, sympathy for the oppressed Cubans, the feeling that America had a special interest in the Caribbean, and a desire to protect American investments in sugar plantations and mills

in Cuba, all impelled the nation toward intervention. Humanitarian sentiment helped drive the United States to action, for Spain employed drastic
methods toward putting down the Cuban uprising, and atrocities committed by the Spanish were magnified by a newly developed and very influential American "yellow" press. Bungling and mischance also had their
parts in bringing on the Spanish-American War.

The Cuban rebellion was an ugly business from its beginning. Inefficient
and arbitrary, the Spanish had earned the hostility of their subjects in the
"Pearl of the Antilles." Nevertheless, Spain had tens of thousands of troops
on the island, and the revolutionaries found it impossible to stand against
them in open battle. Collecting arms and money from Cubans in the
United States as well as at home, the rebels early resorted to guerrilla warfare and to economic weapons. They ordered the owners and workers on
sugar plantations to cease work, and they undertook to punish as traitors all
persons who carried foodstuffs into the towns held by the Spanish soldiers.
They hoped to harass and to starve out the Spanish forces. The revolutionaries very energetically carried out this strategy, burning property and
plundering savagely. Bands of them roved the interior of the island doing
widespread destruction, while the Spanish held on to the seaports and most
of the larger towns. Faced by the unorthodox and all too effective rebel
strategy, Spain commissioned as Governor General a vigorous army officer,
General Valeriano Weyler. To fight them he adopted the policy of "reconcentration," ordering all faithful subjects of Spain to come to the towns
and cities. If they did not, they were to be treated as traitors. Whatever
might be said for the policy as a countermeasure, its results were most unhappy. Thousands of Cubans, especially old men, women, and children, entered the towns and cities, where no arrangements to feed and house them
had been made. They were thrust into concentration camps where they
suffered terribly from hardship, lack of food, and disease. Weyler received
the sobriquet of "the butcher" for his efforts, but they were effective militarily, and the rebels were almost crushed by the fall of 1897. In October
of that year a new and liberal-minded Spanish ministry recalled Weyler, released many persons from the concentration camps, and gave a large measure of home rule to the Cubans. The rebellion then seemed to be on the
verge of collapse.

"YELLOW JOURNALISM"

Meanwhile, whipped up by irresponsible newspaper men, sentiment for
intervention increased in the United States. Joseph Pulitzer and William
Randolph Hearst, engaged in building newspaper empires, had learned
that sensational stories, true or not, increased circulation and profits. Pulitzer's New York *World* and Hearst's New York *Journal* sent reporters to
Cuba to get shocking reports. Other New York newspapers copied their ex-

ample and Cuba became lurid front page news all over the country, for the dispatches sent back to New York from the troubled island were circulated everywhere by wire service. The "yellow" papers made it clear to the reporters that they wanted sensational reports rather than the truth, and they got what they wanted. Atrocity stories were sought with special eagerness, although the papers published anything that would arouse the emotions of their readers. They portrayed Cuba as a land suffering horrors and terrors at the hands of a brutal Spanish soldiery, magnifying many times the very real suffering resulting from Weyler's reconcentration policy. Bloodshed, rape, robbery, destruction of property, and abuse of American citizens were their constant themes. Pulitzer's *Journal* under a headline "Does Our Flag Protect Women?" described the searching of three Cuban ladies by Spanish officials on a ship carrying the American flag. To illustrate the story, the *World* also published a drawing by the artist Frederic Remington which showed the brutal Spanish males forcing one of the Cuban women to take off her clothing. It was not emphasized that the Spanish had quite reasonably boarded the ship because they had reason to believe that it might be carrying aid to the rebels; it was later disclosed that the searching, to find letters among the rebels, was done by an elderly matron in a cabin. The flood of stories, true, half-true, and false, was accompanied by editorials insisting that America intervene for the sake of civilization. Unaccustomed to such a barrage of propaganda, the American public was deeply stirred, so much so that clamor for intervention rose at the very time when the rebellion was dying down. It was not diminished by the publication in February, 1898, of a letter written by Depuy de Lôme, the Spanish minister at Washington, in which President McKinley was described as a weak seeker of popularity, a politician who waited to see which way the wind blew. The letter was a private one and had been seized in the Havana post office by a rebel agent. Nevertheless, even though de Lôme hastily resigned in order not to embarrass his country, the letter added to anti-Spanish feeling.

SINKING OF THE MAINE

Whatever else he was, McKinley was imprudent in January, 1898, when he ordered the battleship *Maine* sent to Havana. A riot had broken out there on January 12, and the American consul, Fitzhugh Lee, had reported that it might be necessary to send ships to protect American citizens and property. But the riot was not directed against Americans, and Lee had made it clear that protection was not immediately necessary. Why then was the *Maine* sent? McKinley informed de Lôme, before that gentleman left for home, that the battleship was merely paying a courtesy visit. It was not the time for such a gesture, for the Spanish ministry feared that an unlucky incident would lead to war with the United States, and did not want the warship in Havana harbor. The concern in Madrid was only too well-founded.

After riding quietly at anchor in Havana harbor for three weeks, on February 15 the *Maine* suddenly sank as the result of a tremendous explosion. More than 250 of her crew were killed. Furor followed in the United States, where the "yellow" newspapers stridently blamed Spain for the disaster, denounced that country for "treachery," and urged a declaration of war. Their opinion was shared by Assistant Secretary of the Navy Theodore Roosevelt, who was sure that the ship was sunk by "an act of dirty treachery on the part of the Spaniards." Captain Charles B. Sigsbee of the *Maine,* who survived the explosion, urged that the Spanish be not blamed until investigation had shown what was responsible. The Spanish government, its leaders aghast, hastily offered a burial ground in Cuba for the dead. But hysteria seized upon a large part of the American people, and Congress voted $50,000,000 to prepare for war before a naval court of inquiry investigating the explosion could give its report. Neither Captain Sigsbee nor Fitzhugh Lee believed that the Spanish had intentionally struck against the *Maine;* it was obvious that Spanish officials in Havana were grief-stricken. Indeed, it was most unlikely that Spanish officers had moved aggressively against the ship, since American intervention would obviously be against Spain. The court of inquiry, composed entirely of Americans, reported on March 28 after an incomplete investigation that it believed the explosion had been caused outside the *Maine,* at the same time indicating that it might have been an internal one. If it was not internal, it is more likely that the Cuban insurgents were responsible for it than that reckless Spaniards acted without orders; presumably the rebels stood to gain from American action against Spain. It is possible that the *Maine* struck a mine placed in the harbor by the Spanish, but forgotten by them. A claim advanced more than a half-century later by Cubans hostile to the United States that America had plotted the sinking of her own ship is ludicrous. Later probing into the explosion brought no clear answer. At the time, the report of the court of inquiry was generally interpreted in the United States to mean that Spain had been guilty of either gross negligence or an aggressive act. The cry, "Remember the *Maine,*" was taken up everywhere. Vengeance for the slain and justice for the Cubans were demanded as the war fever mounted higher and higher.

In the meantime, McKinley was negotiating with Spain through the American minister at Madrid, Stewart Woodford, a Civil War veteran who was eager to prevent armed conflict between the two nations. On March 27 Woodford was instructed to demand from Spain the establishment of an armistice with Cuba until October 1; abandoning of the reconcentration policy; and consideration of an arrangement whereby McKinley would settle the struggle if it had not been ended by October 1. The Spanish ministry moved slowly, because feeling against making concessions was strong in Spain. Nevertheless, to the joy of Woodford, the ministry put an end to reconcentration on April 5, and four days later directed the Spanish commander in chief in Cuba to grant an immediate suspension of fighting. The armistice was to endure as long as he thought it prudent. Spain wanted peace, since she could not hope to win a war with the United States. She made very substantial concessions, and quite obviously could be pushed to make more. McKinley might therefore have taken a firm stand for peace, informing the Congress and the American public that the Cubans must eventually have what they wanted—this despite the fact that the rebels had refused to stop fighting. The President had hitherto, with the business interests of the country, been opposed to a war with Spain. However, McKinley was appalled by the suffering in Cuba. He desired to end it, and he could not stand against the war hysteria as John Adams had a century earlier. On April 11 in a message to Congress he asked for authority to use the armed forces to put an end to the conflict in Cuba. This document, prepared before the President learned that Spain had in effect capitulated to his demands, contained a sentence toward its close, mentioning almost as an afterthought, that Spain had made the concessions. Congress accepted McKinley's peculiar invitation to act. On April 19 it passed a joint resolution, approved by the President on the following day, which declared Cuba to be free, demanded the withdrawal of the Spanish forces from the island, directed the President to use the army and navy to achieve those purposes, and proclaimed (in the Teller Amendment) that America wished neither to annex Cuba nor to control it in any way. On April 25, Congress resolved that war with Spain had existed since April 21. The Spanish government, very much against its will, and despite the concessions it had made, found itself engaged in a conflict with the powerful republic across the ocean.

If, with the advantage of hindsight, one concludes that neither McKinley nor the American people quite knew what they were doing in April, 1898, it is to their credit that their motives, so far as they knew, were not sordid. They did not seek to protect American economic interests in Cuba, nor did they want Cuba or any other territory beyond the sea. Deeply touched by the atrocities in Cuba, which had been immensely magnified by their newspapers, they sincerely believed that taking up arms against Spain was generous and humanitarian. William Jennings Bryan spoke forth for Cuban independence well before McKinley did, and for similar reasons. McKinley and Bryan were not astute men; if they were swayed by considerations of personal or party advantage, they were not fully aware of the fact. In a little time they and the American people would discover that they had taken a long step away from the American continent, that the one great step led to others, and that it was impossible to turn back.

41 A WORLD POWER

Had anyone predicted on April 1, 1898, that within two years the United States would possess an empire containing the Philippines, Guam, Wake Island, Midway, Hawaii, the Samoan island of Tutuila, Puerto Rico, and a protectorate over Cuba, he would have been considered a humorist or a wild visionary. Very few Americans could have located all of those places on a map. But the affairs of nations may take swift and unexpected turns, and the war begun by the United States to free Cuba led to the raising of the American flag over the distant, low-lying sandy shores of Wake Island. By 1900 America was playing an important role in the Far East; in fact, as the twentieth century opened, the United States emerged as a world power.

America had never been able completely to ignore Europe. As a world power the nation became more and more involved in the affairs of both Europe and Asia. The great change cannot be simply explained as a European seduction of innocent America from Eden.

WAR WITH SPAIN

The war to relieve the oppressed people of Cuba began on the other side of the world, in Manila Bay, and the Stars and Stripes floated over the capital of the Philippines by the middle of August, 1898. The clash of arms began in the Far East because Spain still owned the Philippines and had a fleet in Manila Bay. It was a weak, rusty, and antiquated fleet, but one that might have been used against American merchant shipping in the Pacific and, just conceivably, to throw a few shells at San Francisco. There was some concern in Washington lest it appear in the Atlantic to strengthen another Spanish fleet there, although there is no evidence that Spain hoped to use her Asian squadron offensively. In any case, it was decided in Washington almost a month before the beginning of the war that an American fleet under Commodore George Dewey stationed at Hong Kong should in the event of armed conflict attack the Spanish warships off Manila. On February 5, with characteristic aggressiveness, Assistant Secretary of the Navy Theodore Roosevelt, while Secretary of the Navy John D. Long was temporarily absent from the capital, cabled Dewey:

Order the squadron, except the *Monocacy* to Hong Kong. Keep full of coal. In the event of Declaration of War Spain your duty will be to see that the Spanish squadron does not leave the Asiatic coast, and then offensive operations in the Philippine Islands. Keep *Olympia* until further orders.

Mr. Long mildly rebuked Roosevelt for his impudence, but he did not withdraw the orders. Accordingly Dewey made his way into Manila Bay on April 30 with four modern cruisers and two gunboats. The following morning he attacked the Spanish squadron of ten old ships under Admiral Montojo. There was no real contest. For hours American warships sailed back and forth in front of the Spanish ones, firing into them almost at will. The Spanish fleet was destroyed, and 381 Spaniards were killed or wounded. Dewey's losses were eight men hurt by flying splinters. Before the end of the day Dewey had also silenced Spanish shore batteries. There was no longer any danger that Admiral Montojo would take the offensive anywhere. Dewey might have sailed away with the satisfaction of a job efficiently done. However, McKinley and his advisers then made a far-reaching decision, to send troops to seize Manila. More than 10,000 men were sent across the Pacific under General Wesley Merritt. The Filipinos had long been restive under Spanish rule. Taking up arms under Emilio Aguinaldo, they joined the American troops in attacking the weak Spanish land forces about Manila, and the city surrendered to Merritt on August 13. With the fall of the city Spanish resistance virtually ceased in the Philippines.

THE CUBAN CAMPAIGN

Fighting on the island of Cuba for the freedom of the Cuban people was not much more necessary than fighting on the island of Luzon had been to win freedom for the Filipinos. The American fleet in the Atlantic was far superior to the only remaining Spanish naval forces, a squadron maintained in European waters. At the beginning of the war Rear Admiral William T. Sampson commanded four battleships and two cruisers in the Atlantic, together with smaller vessels. He was soon reinforced by the battleship *Oregon,* which sped from the Pacific around South America to join him. The Spanish home fleet under Admiral Pasqual Cervera y Topete contained only four cruisers and three destroyers, and they were quite unfit for action. Spain's single battleship was laid up for repairs. All that was necessary to force Spain out of Cuba was to deal with Admiral Cervera and to blockade the island. Without hope of reinforcement, the Spanish troops must sooner or later surrender. But McKinley, Congress, and the American people were determined to fight under the palm-trees of Cuba as well as under those of Luzon, and to hit at the Spaniards wherever they were. The regular army contained only 30,000 men, but Congress authorized an increase to about 60,000, and called for 200,000 volunteers. Since the Spanish were supposed to have 155,000 men in service in Cuba, that number did not seem excessively large. It was easily raised, for the war was very popular in America. Included among the new soldiers were William Jennings Bryan, who like most of the volunteers never left the United States, and Theodore Roosevelt, who managed to win glory for himself in Cuba. Troops to move against the island were gradually gathered during the spring at Tampa, amidst wild confusion, for the army was out of practice. Perhaps it was just as well that they could not prudently be sent to the island until the spring rains had ended. When they finally began to embark in June, the first 17,000 to go scrambled aboard, helter-skelter, in complete disorder from a one-track railroad. Ill-trained and haphazardly equipped, they set out for Cuba in blue winter uniforms—not ideal for service in the tropics; in the chill of fall at Montauk on the eastern end of Long Island many of them would later be supplied with khaki summer clothing. Under the leadership of General William Shafter they sailed for Santiago on the southeast coast of Cuba, to help the navy there.

While the army was milling about in Tampa, the American Atlantic fleet under Admiral Sampson steamed about trying to find Admiral Cervera, who if he crossed the Atlantic, would be forced to stop in a harbor in Puerto Rico or Cuba to fill his coal bins. While citizens of New York, Boston, and other cities along the Atlantic seaboard begged for protection against the guns of Admiral Cervera, Sampson watched the northern shore of Cuba and Commodore Winfield Scott Schley prowled along the southern one. Cervera did come, but only on a mission of honor. He knew and the Spanish government knew that he had little chance to accomplish anything, and that his fleet would in all probability be destroyed. Determined to show bravery in a hopeless cause, the ministry ordered him not to surrender, and if necessary to go down fighting. He slipped across the ocean and sought coal and at least temporary safety in Santiago harbor, where his fleet was protected by land batteries. Finding the Spanish admiral there, Commodore Schley promptly blockaded the mouth of the harbor, and called Admiral Sampson to his aid. By June 1, Cervera was tightly bottled up in the harbor. On the other hand, Sampson was unable to break into it because a narrow channel which led in from the sea was easily defended by the Spanish. It was the task of General Shafter and the American expeditionary army, to move against Santiago from the land, and to force Cervera either to surrender or to go out to face the American fleet.

Landing unopposed on the beach at Siboney, near Santiago, Shafter and his army gradually sorted themselves out and moved forward. On July 1 he ordered General Henry W. Lawton, with 6600 men, to attack El Caney, a fortified village, and General Jacob F. Kent, with 8000 troops, to move against San Juan Hill. Possession of those two strong places would enable Shafter to prevent Spanish reinforcements from entering Santiago from the westward and would also open the way for a further assault upon the town. El Caney was defended by only 500 Spaniards, but they fought all day, killing 81 Americans and wounding 160 before they finally retreated. Meanwhile, Kent discovered that the Spanish had garrisoned not only San Juan Hill but the adjacent Kettle Hill. He divided his force into two parts and sent them forward against the Spanish garrisons. It was Lieutenant Colonel Theodore Roosevelt with his Rough Riders, college men, businessmen, and cowboys, together with dismounted Negro cavalrymen, who captured Kettle Hill, the Spanish fleeing before the Americans reached its summit. So Roosevelt became a war hero. Meanwhile, San Juan Hill had also fallen, and with little further fighting the Spanish withdrew into Santiago. However, Shafter's losses had been heavy, 225 dead and 1384 wounded, and he was discouraged rather than elated. Weighing 300 pounds, he was so fat that he could mount his horse only from a platform, and he suffered both from heat and the gout. Fearing that he could not take Santiago, where the Spanish had more troops than he did, he considered making a retreat. Roosevelt shared the general's alarm, expressing the opinion that "we are within measurable distance of a terrible military disaster; we *must* have help." Other officers suggested to Shafter that the Spanish, surrounded on land and blockaded from the sea, were in far worse straits than the Americans. His spirits lifting, the general demanded the surrender of the town on July 3.

The Spanish were indeed much worse off, for they were even running low on food and water. Concluding that the town could not hold out much longer, Cervera had already reported to the Spanish Governor-General at Havana that he must either scuttle his fleet or try uselessly to escape. Governor-General Blanco ordered him to try to escape, no matter what the consequences might be. As the Spanish ships in single file moved out of the harbor and turned westward on that same July 3, the American fleet immediately set out in pursuit. Under the command of Schley, because Admiral Sampson had gone ashore to visit Shafter, its much more powerful ships relentlessly hunted down Cervera's vessels. Three of the four Spanish cruisers were wrecked by American gunfire, and the fourth, unable to keep her engines going because of poor coal, hauled down her flag. One of Cervera's destroyers blew up, and the other surrendered. Only one American had been killed and only one wounded; 300 of the Spanish had been killed, 151 injured, and the remainder captured.

THE TREATY OF PARIS

The destruction of the Spanish fleet off Santiago maintained Spanish honor and virtually brought the war to an end. On July 17 the garrison of Santiago, about 24,000 men, surrendered, and on July 25, an American army under General Nelson A. Miles captured Puerto Rico almost without resistance. On the following day the Spanish ministry asked the United States for peace terms, and on August 12 an agreement was signed which put an end to the fighting. By its terms Spain gave up Cuba, agreed to cede Puerto Rico and one of the Ladrone Islands to the United States, and consented to the occupation of Manila by the Americans until a peace treaty should be made at Paris.

The terms of the preliminary peace indicate that the United States, having made war upon Spain largely because of humanitarian sentiment, was turning rapidly toward empire building. Such was the fact. The war brought many converts to imperialism, including President McKinley. While the fighting was still in progress, he managed the annexation of Hawaii. Those who wanted to make Hawaii a part of the United States were able to point out that the islands were of the first importance in prosecuting the war in the Philippines. A protest from Japan against American acquisition of the islands also fortified American demands for it. Many members of the Senate continued to oppose annexation, although their opposition was softening. Some of them were impressed by the argument that Hawaii had long been within an American sphere of influence, and that joining it outright to the United States would be no great change. Even so, McKinley, dusting off the treaty rejected by the Senate in 1897, prudently refrained from asking the Senate to approve it. Instead he asked that the Congress by a joint resolution authorize American signature of

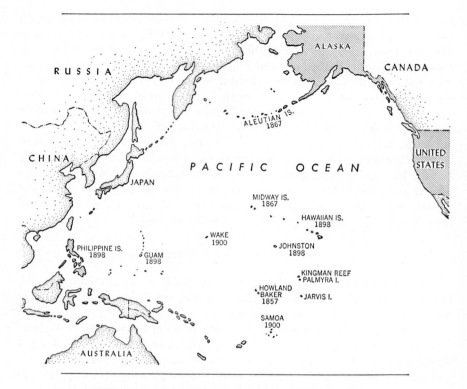

THE AMERICAN ADVANCE INTO THE PACIFIC

the treaty. His strategy was successful; the resolution, requiring simple majorities, passed both houses on July 7. Thus the war with Spain hastened the addition of Hawaii and the web of empire in the Pacific was already taking form. Three days before the passage of the resolution, American forces landed on uninhabited Wake Island, and ran up the flag over it. Even earlier, Guam, the principal island in the Ladrones, had been captured. The Spanish officials there, unaware that war had been declared, had at first believed that American gunfire against Guam was intended as a salute. Informed otherwise, they had sensibly surrendered. Hence the cession by Spain of one of the Ladrone Islands in the preliminary peace.

WHAT TO DO WITH THE PHILIPPINES

It is evident that during the summer of 1898 America was moving not only to acquire the Philippines but to establish between them and the United States a string of bases consisting of Hawaii, Midway, Wake, and Guam. Nevertheless, even after the signature of the preliminary agreement, McKinley was not certain what to do about the Philippines, although he did not doubt the wisdom of acquiring the steppingstones to them. Anti-imperialists urged that the Philippines be returned to Spain, or at least that they should not become American territory. They stressed the sordidness and the dangers of imperialism, condemning annexation of the Philippines as immoral. Imperialists answered that their acquisition would permit the spread of Christianity and of civilization to a backward area, and that America ought to assume a part of "the white man's burden." Businessmen wanted the Philippines not only for their commerce, but because the Chinese market could be approached through them. Imperialists also pointed out that the Philippines were likely to become the property of Germany, or Britain, or Japan, if America did not take them. This argument was effective with the President, who had reason to believe that Germany hoped to secure the Philippines if the United States did not take them. Germany had sent a strong naval squadron to Manila Bay to protect her citizens before American troops landed on Luzon; and its commander had unpleasantly made minor difficulties for Commodore Dewey.

At any rate, McKinley finally decided that the Philippines ought to become American. Afterward he declared that he had prayed for divine guidance, and with the help of God had reached the conclusion that the islands could not go back to Spain, since Spain had misgoverned them; that they could not be allowed to go to Germany or any other great power; that the Filipinos were unfit to govern themselves; and that America must take the islands. It was the duty of the Americans to "educate the Filipinos, and uplift and civilize and Christianize them, and by God's grace do the best we could for them as our fellow men for whom Christ died." It should be observed that the establishment of an American protectorate would have thwarted any and all designs upon the Philippines of Germany, or any other imperial power. Outright annexation, for McKinley, had to be justified on the ground that America had a duty to serve the Filipinos. He did not ask them what they wanted; it turned out that many of them did not wish to exchange Spanish masters for American ones.

Appointing peace commissioners to negotiate with the Spanish at Paris, McKinley saw to it that a majority of them favored acquisition of the Philippines. Before the negotiations began he told them that America could not "accept less than the full right and sovereignty of the Island of Luzon." Then he decided that it would be a bit awkward if the United States took Luzon, but not the many other islands of the Philippines. Accordingly, he further instructed the American commissioners: "The cession must be the whole archipelago or none. The latter is wholly inadmissible, and the former must therefore be required." The Spanish delegates at Paris were most reluctant to abandon the Philippines, but finally agreed to yield them in return for a payment of $20,000,000. In addition,

Spain formally ceded Puerto Rico and Guam to the United States as indemnity for American war losses. Spain also abandoned her title to Cuba, the status of that island being otherwise left uncertain, American annexation of it being blocked by the Teller Amendment. These several arrangements were placed in a treaty which was signed at Paris on December 10.

It was not at all certain that the Treaty of Paris would be ratified by the Senate. And it had to be approved by a two-thirds majority, for McKinley and the imperialists could not resort again to the device of the joint resolution. For a time it seemed that the champions of the treaty would not be able to get the necessary two-thirds majority. Conscious that an American empire would be established by the treaty, anti-imperialists attacked it bitterly. It was apparent that the Filipinos and other peoples who would be brought under the American flag as the result of it would not, at least immediately, be given all the rights of American citizens. Hence America was turning her back on the Declaration of Independence. Must America be merely another imperialistic nation? If she behaved tyrannously abroad, liberty must be menaced at home. The Americans ought not to follow the example of the Romans, who had abandoned their republic and their liberty for empire and their own subjugation. An anti-imperialist league, with a most distinguished list of members, including Grover Cleveland, John Sherman, Samuel Gompers, Andrew Carnegie, William James, William Dean Howells, and Mark Twain, emphatically denounced the treaty. Both Republicans and Democrats assailed it. Not the least of their arguments was their contention that ownership of the Philippines would seriously involve the United States in Far Eastern troubles.

But the anti-imperialists were too late, and as a result, too few. Many of them had carelessly failed to take a positive stand against the acquisition of Hawaii, and they could not make a logical distinction between Hawaii on the one hand and the Philippines, Guam, and Puerto Rico on the other. Moreover, the expansionists appealed speciously to the course of destiny, to duty, and to commercial advantage. Besides, they received help from William Jennings Bryan, who fervently disliked overseas empire, but urged that the treaty be accepted. With strange logic he asserted that the nation ought to accept it, and then turn away from building an empire. It seems not to have occurred to him that it would not be easy to shuffle off territories that had been so solemnly acquired. Certainly the imperialists would hardly lose strength if the document were approved. It was, on February 6, 1899, by a vote of 57 to 27, a very narrow margin. How bad Bryan's tactics were was shown eight days later, when Senator August O. Bacon proposed an amendment to the treaty by which the United States would have promised Philippine independence as soon as the Filipinos demonstrated their ability to form a stable government. The Senate was evenly divided with respect to the amendment, and it was defeated by the casting of a deciding vote by Vice-President Garret Hobart. In any case it would have had no more than a moral effect, since the treaty already had been ratified. Nevertheless, the vote upon it was significant, for it indicated that something like half the Senate desired annexation, not for the sake of the Filipinos, but for the supposed advantages that annexation gave to the United States. Many men who lent their voices and their ballots to the cause of empire would later regret their behavior. At almost the same moment that the Senate endorsed the treaty, American soldiers on Luzon began to exchange shots with Filipinos led by Aguinaldo.

The impulse toward empire did not subside with the signing of the Treaty of Paris, although it lost some of its vigor as it became apparent that expansion enmeshed the United States in novel and perplexing difficulties. Nevertheless, Wake Island was formally annexed in 1900, and the United States also definitely acquired territory in Samoa as the new century opened. In 1899 Germany had revised and renewed her proposal of ten years earlier, to divide the islands between the United States and Germany, with Britain receiving territorial compensation from Germany elsewhere in lieu of her claims in Samoa. The British agreed, and America now decided that it would be advantageous to put an end to the Samoan protectorate of the three powers. In accordance with a treaty signed by the three nations and approved by the Senate in January, 1900, the United States became the owner of several of the islands, including Tutuila and its fine harbor of Pago Pago, with Germany obtaining two other islands of less importance. Placed under the direction of the navy, American Samoa provided an important naval base in the Pacific.

THE PERMANENT COURT OF INTERNATIONAL ARBITRATION

By 1900 lust for overseas territory was waning in the United States, but the nation continued to assert itself vigorously in other affairs of the world. In the summer of 1899 America sent delegates to the First Hague Peace Conference, called by Tsar Nicholas II of Russia, toward the prevention of war and limiting the use of weapons. With twenty-five other nations the United States agreed to establish the Permanent Court of International Arbitration. However, the Conference largely failed to achieve the purposes for which it was called, because arbitration of international disputes was not made compulsory, and the jurisdiction of the Permanent Court was not extended to questions in which national honor or integrity were involved. America also insisted that quarrels arising from application of the Monroe Doctrine were not subject to settlement by the international tribunal.

THE "OPEN DOOR" IN CHINA

Much more important was American entrance into the troubled affairs of the Chinese empire. In the 1890s the Great Powers, including Japan, following Britain's example, busied themselves with securing bases and spheres of influence in China, which was weak and disorganized. It seemed that the vast nation might be carved up and divided among Russia, Britain, Germany, France, Italy, and Japan. John Hay, who had once been Lincoln's private secretary, was placed in charge of the State Department in September, 1898. He soon determined that the United States must play a role in China, although that country seemed far away and of little importance to most Americans. American trade with the Celestial Kingdom was small, and Hay might well have chosen to avoid involvement in its affairs. But like his friends Theodore Roosevelt and Senator Henry Cabot Lodge, he was convinced that America must assert herself everywhere as befitted a great and moral nation. Brilliant and aggressive, Hay won acclaim for his "Open Door" policy with respect to China. Fearing that the Great Powers possessing spheres of influence in China would establish discriminatory tariffs and impose other commercial barriers within them, Hay asked all of them formally to promise that they would permit the Chinese government to collect tariffs in their spheres of influence and that they would not favor their own subjects with respect to harbor dues and railroad rates. The replies received by Hay were polite but qualified assurances. Brushing aside the qualifications, Hay declared on March 20, 1900, that all had accepted the Open Door as "final and definitive." It was believed at home that he had won a splendid diplomatic victory, and that he had also won for the United States an equal opportunity to trade with the Chinese, even that he had done something to help preserve the political integrity of China. Actually, the Open Door was a small portal, and it had first been championed by the British. It should be observed that Hay had not assailed, but had instead recognized the vested interests of the Great Powers in China.

After the Boxer Rebellion in the spring of 1900 John Hay tried not only to open wide the door into China, but to slip in through a window. When the Chinese "Boxers" attacked the "foreign devils" and besieged many of them in the foreign legations in Peking, the United States supplied 2500 troops to the international expedition of about 20,000 men that forced its way into Peking and rescued the surrounded foreigners from the maddened Chinese. Since the Boxers had plundered and murdered, Hay feared that the Great Powers would insist upon further commercial and territorial concessions as compensation. He therefore officially announced that America opposed such indemnities. He also now asserted that trade should be free with all parts of the Chinese Empire. In some part because of his stand only a money penalty of $353,000,000 was imposed upon China, with the American share as $24,500,000. (The United States in the end accepted only about $6,500,000, the remainder being used to pay for the education of Chinese students in America.) Nevertheless, Hay came to believe that America, at least at that time, could do little or nothing to protect China. In November, 1900, urged on by the navy, he actually joined in the scramble for concessions in that country, quietly trying to get a naval base and surrounding sphere of influence at Samsah Bay in southern China. He did not succeed; Japan stopped him, bringing to his attention the fact that she had a prior claim to the area. The Japanese could not refrain from pointing out it was a little odd that he who had spoken so vigorously for the preservation of Chinese rights should seek to become one of her despoilers.

HAY AND THE CANAL

While Hay achieved no real glory as the result of his Far Eastern policy, he succeeded in 1900 and 1901 in removing one of the obstacles preventing the United States from building a canal across Central America. The military value of such a canal was dramatically emphasized in the Spanish-American War when the battleship *Oregon,* to join the Atlantic fleet, had to steam completely around South America. He therefore resumed the American effort to persuade Britain to cancel the Clayton-Bulwer Treaty. In February, 1900, he managed to get her to sign the first Hay-Pauncefote Treaty, by which the British abandoned part of their rights under the earlier agreement. However, the new arrangement displeased the Senate, largely because it did not permit America to fortify a canal. Hay then sought and obtained further concessions from the British; they cost Britain little and the English desired American friendship. A second Hay-Pauncefote Treaty, approved by the Senate the following November authorized American building and control of a canal; its neutrality was to be maintained by the United States; and it was to be used on equal terms by the ships of all nations. The first step had been taken toward opening a Yankee water link across Central America.

A CUBAN SETTLEMENT

In the meantime, America had to do something about Cuba and to provide for the government of her newly acquired possessions in the Caribbean and the Pacific. Because of the Teller Amendment of 1898, Cuba could not be decently annexed. Moreover, the Cubans obviously desired to form an independent republic. The American army kept order in Cuba until 1902, governing efficiently. Under its direction Dr. Walter Reed carried on experiments which proved that yellow fever was spread by mosquitoes, and a sanitation campaign virtually put an end to the disease in Cuba, where it had exacted an awful toll. In 1900 the Cubans were permitted to hold a constitutional convention, and they prepared for themselves a basic document, in which there was no reference to the United States. By that time American policy toward the island had been formed. It called for a protectorate over Cuba. Accordingly, the Cuban constitutional convention was informed that it must insert in its constitution a number of provisions, collectively known as the Platt Amendment, that had been voted by the American Congress. American military rule would continue until the Cubans agreed; having little choice, they did so. After the withdrawal of troops, in 1903, the Republic of Cuba went still further, signing a treaty containing the Platt Amendment. Thus it became impossible for Cuba to set aside these provisions without American consent. They required that Cuba never make a treaty with any third power that would impair Cuban independence; that the Cuban government refrain from contracting any public debt it could not pay by means of its ordinary taxes; that the United States could intervene to preserve Cuban independence and also to maintain law and order; and that Cuba would sell or lease to the United States land for naval or coaling stations. Thus possible aggression by a European power against Cuba was rather effectively prevented—it was feared in Washington that Germany hoped to gain possession of it. Thus also the United States secured permission to build a naval base at Guantanamo Bay. The suspicious-minded believed that the clauses permitting American intervention to maintain order would lead eventually to outright annexation. Instead, American sentiment turned more and more in favor of Cuban independence. America already had troubles enough within her empire. Troops went to Cuba in 1906 and again three years later to restore order, but they were withdrawn as soon as they had accomplished their mission. After a generation as a protectorate of the United States Cuba became completely independent.

GOVERNING THE PHILIPPINES AND PUERTO RICO

The news that America was acquiring title to the Philippines from Spain led to warfare between the Filipinos and the American troops stationed among them, for it was obvious to the civilized inhabitants of the islands that the United States intended to rule over them for many years to come. While many of the Filipinos, scattered on hundreds of islands, were backward and even savage, there was among them an important element that was Spanish or partly Spanish in blood. Christian, and eager for independence, the more advanced Filipinos were also ready to fight for their freedom from the United States. They rallied behind Aguinaldo, who claimed that independence had been promised to him when he took the field against the Spanish, and who was convinced that he had been used as a tool and then betrayed by the United States. About 70,000

Filipinos took up arms, and an American army of the same size needed a year to beat down their resistance. Even then guerrilla warfare continued, with the brutalities invariably resulting from it. Aguinaldo was captured in March, 1901, but the Filipinos did not lay down their muskets and machetes finally until the summer of the following year. To many Americans it was hateful to bring the benefits of civilization to the islands by means of the rifle and the bayonet. However, civil government was established, rather ironically, on July 4, 1901. A Philippine Commission headed by William Howard Taft then assumed the tasks of policing, sanitation, and public education. Eventually Taft even brought Filipinos into the Commission. It did its work well, and the Filipinos gradually became relatively content under the American flag.

Although there was nothing like the American-Filipino War in the other newly acquired possessions, liberal-minded men found reason to be unhappy because of the treatment accorded to their peoples. Hawaii, dominated by American whites, was made a territory in 1900, and its people became American citizens, although statehood was withheld for more than a half-century. Puerto Rico, under the Foraker Act of 1900, was made an "unorganized territory" under an American governor with a two-house legislature, the upper body named in Washington, the lower elected by the Puerto Ricans. They were not granted American citizenship until 1917, when Puerto Rico achieved the same status as Hawaii. The fact that the Puerto Ricans and other peoples in the American empire were looked upon and treated as subjects rather than Americans aroused concern among those in the United States, chiefly intellectuals, who believed that everyone living under the American flag ought to possess equal rights under the Constitution. However, in the Insular Cases, the United States Supreme Court declared that Congress was required to respect only certain fundamental rights in the new off-shore possessions under the Constitution. Even those were confined to substance rather than to form. Moreover, the lawmakers had the authority to withhold American citizenship and even to differentiate between parts of the empire with respect to tariffs. Not surprisingly, a nationalist movement developed in Puerto Rico, but it was deprived of any major grievance when the Puerto Ricans secured recognition as American citizens.

THE ELECTION OF 1900

Whatever the intellectuals might think, it is evident that the Americans as a whole were not disposed to vote against McKinley and the Republicans in the election of 1900 on the grounds that they had led the nation into the war with Spain and into empire building. In their platform of that year the Democrats declared that imperialism was the "paramount issue," and "that no nation can long endure half republic and half empire." Also, "that imperialism abroad will lead quickly and inevitably to despotism at home." The Democrats also called for reforms at home; action against "indefensible and intolerable" monopoly; strengthening of the Interstate Commerce Commission; an end to government by injunction; and the direct election of United States senators. The party continued to stand for the free coinage of silver, and for the second time named Bryan for the Presidency. Because he discovered that the voters had little interest in imperialism, he concentrated instead on currency and domestic reform. The Republicans forthrightly defended their record in the making of the empire, declared themselves for high protective tariffs, and gave their allegiance to the gold standard. Like the Democrats, they urged that the United States dig a canal across Central America. Conscious that they were vulnerable because they had taken no steps to improve the civil service or to regulate Big Business, they promised to do both. The Populists named their own candidate and made their own platform, but played little part in the campaign. Their issues were being taken over by the major parties, especially by the Democrats, and they were no longer important as a political group, although their party survived until 1908. For the Presidency, of course, the Republicans named McKinley. For the Vice-Presidency they chose Theodore Roosevelt, a war hero. Elected Governor of New York in 1898, Roosevelt would have preferred not to run for national office until 1904, when he might very well secure the nomination for the Presidency. However, Boss "Tom" Platt of New York wanted the troublesome Roosevelt out of the state and pushed him for the Vice-Presidency with the thought that Roosevelt's career would be buried in it. "Teddy" rather reluctantly agreed to run with McKinley. In the campaign the Republicans laid heavy stress upon the prosperity of the nation, asserting that they stood for "the full dinner pail." The economic well-being of the nation doubtless assured their victory. McKinley won again, by a somewhat larger margin than in 1896, obtaining 7,219,525 popular votes to 6,358,737 for Bryan, and 292 electoral votes against Bryan's 155. Bryan led only in the Solid South, Kentucky, Missouri, and four Rocky Mountain states. The Republicans also retained control of both houses of Congress.

Less than a year later Theodore Roosevelt was President. While attending a public reception in Buffalo, McKinley was shot and mortally wounded by an anarchist, Leon Czolgosz. McKinley died on September 14, 1901, and the ebullient Roosevelt entered the White House. He was not quite 43 years of age.

42 THE SQUARE DEAL

When the sculptor Gutzon Borglum began to carve the figures of the four greatest Americans in the Black Hills a few years after the death of Theodore Roosevelt, he placed Roosevelt side by side with Washington, Jefferson, and Lincoln. Had the four men been chosen a generation later it is unlikely that "Teddy" would have been included, for time, perspective, and scholarship had reduced his image. Nor is it likely that the first President Roosevelt will be restored to the first rank of American statesmen; yet he loomed large and was a popular idol in his own time. He will doubtless be remembered as one of the abler Presidents and even more surely as an extraordinary personality. A champion of domestic reform, a leader in the progressive movement, a preacher of morality, a maker of aggressive foreign policy, a coiner of phrases, a historian, a politician of parts—Roosevelt was all of these, and more. He was courageous, gifted, versatile, gregarious, and magnetic, yet not quite a great man. He exercised a powerful and beneficent influence at home, if not abroad; perhaps he came to the Presidential power too early in life to employ it in the best possible fashion. He had not learned to be sensitive to his own shortcomings, a fault of which much has been made, although it is not uncommon. It may be that scholars find it difficult to do justice to that forthright extrovert.

ROOSEVELT THE CONSERVATIVE

If there was an American aristocracy in the second half of the nineteenth century, Roosevelt was born into it. The Roosevelts had been settled in New York since the seventeenth century, and they had had money, though not great wealth, for several generations. Theodore was sent to Groton School and then to Harvard, and he also traveled abroad. He did not excel as a student; he was well below the middle of his class at Harvard, although as he said, only "one gentleman" performed better. It is hardly surprising that as a young man he considered himself a superior person; he never could quite accept recent immigrants, workmen, or Latin Americans as his equals. Brought up to act according to a strict code, he was also self-righteous, and never really learned to question his own motives. He might easily have become a snobbish dilettante, for he was weak and asthmatic as a child. But Roosevelt had a stubborn courage; through exercises and games he overcame his physical handicaps, and in maturity he was powerful in body and aggressive in personality. As a youth he turned toward the writing of history, publishing *The Naval War of 1812* only two years after he left Harvard. In his early 30s he put forth *The Winning of the West,* in which he displayed a characteristic contempt for the Indian. He was better qualified to make history than to write it. At the age of 24 he was elected to the New York legislature; at 28, after spending two years as a rancher in the Badlands of North Dakota, he ran unsuccessfully for mayor of New York City. He performed very well as a member of the federal Civil Service Commission and as a Police Commissioner in New York City. He was efficient as well as incorruptible in the various offices that he held before he entered the Presidency. He early won a reputation as a reformer, chiefly because he stood for integrity in public life; he did not believe that America suffered from vital ills when he inherited the White House. He had been an utterly loyal Republican, campaigning energetically for Blaine in 1884, when his friend Henry Cabot Lodge voted for Cleveland. He had been an ardent and shortsighted imperialist. Conservative leaders in the Republican party did not know what to think about him when he became President. He was obviously a practical politician, but was he malleable, and did he not have a tendency to go off on tangents? Mark Hanna feared that the "cowboy" would prove to be unreliable and unmanageable, and Hanna was a shrewd judge of men.

From the viewpoint of Hanna and conservatives like him, there was almost nothing wrong in America when Roosevelt became President. They had withstood the assaults of the Populists and the Bryan Democrats, and they were determined not to lose the fruits of their victories. Hanna as an industrialist paid good wages, and despised employers who did otherwise, but he did not think it wise to try to compel them to behave better. Although not long before his death McKinley finally reached the conclusion that tariffs had become too high and that they ought to be lowered, he did nothing to change them. In the main, the Big Business community and its supporters, including Hanna, believed that all was well and that no one ought to try to rock the boat. National wealth was increasing rapidly; it was to double within a decade. American industry had taken such strides that more manufactured goods were exported than imported. The American steel industry undersold the British in world markets as early as the mid-1890s and was moving steadily toward world leadership, which it reached by World War I. There was good reason to believe even in 1901 that New York would before long replace London as the world's financial center, and that Washington would possess greater political influence than the British capital. The American population had already swelled far beyond that of any other industrial country; it was nearly 76,000,000 in 1900, and it was increasing rapidly, reaching almost 92,000,000 in 1910. Immigration supplied cheap labor and was moving toward new peaks; it would surpass 1,000,000 during each of six years before the outbreak of World War I. Even the lot of the farmer had improved, and would continue to do so, with farm prices advancing nearly 50 percent between 1900 and 1910. During the five years immediately before World War I the farmer was to enjoy his fair share of the proceeds of the national economy; at least economic experts afterward so calculated. The workers in the towns and the cities were not faring so well, and average wages purchased somewhat less in the first decade of the twentieth century than they had in the last one of the nineteenth. On the other hand, there was little unemployment. It is not surprising that the conservatives felt the health of the United States to be excellent, and that they wished Roosevelt would emulate McKinley.

Well entrenched in Congress, in the state legislatures, and in city councils as well, the defenders of the political *status quo* nevertheless had some cause for concern, since the demands of the Populists and the Bryan Democrats were being voiced by prosperous middle class Americans, Republicans as well as Democrats. Men who had angrily condemned the Populists as cranks and wild-eyed radicals were becoming convinced that action must be taken to cleanse a generally sound nation of various evils. The progressive movement was getting under way, and was soon to gain strength. Its adherents would try both to curb bad economic practices and to extend political democracy.

THE TRUSTS

The trusts were especially exposed to attack. In 1894 Henry Demarest Lloyd had bitterly assailed the Standard Oil Company in *Wealth against*

Commonwealth, exposing both John D. Rockefeller's relentless and sometimes unscrupulous crowding out of competitors and Standard Oil's disregard for the public. Lloyd might be dismissed as a rabble-rouser; indeed,
Rockefeller's behavior was somewhat less sinful than that of other industrial giants. But even the McKinley Congress of 1898 had felt forced to
look into the trusts, and had appointed a commission for the purpose.
While the commission justified the new industrial combinations because
they put an end to harmful and wasteful competition, it had pointed out
some disconcerting facts about them. They were often capitalized at two
or three times the value of their constituent parts, their stock containing
much "water." Those who created the trusts, usually in the form of holding companies and giant corporations after 1900, accepted huge fees for
their services; and their officers were paid immense salaries. Opinion was
growing that the trusts were becoming deeply injurious by concentrating
vast power in the hands of a few, establishing monopolies, digging a deep
gulf between the rich and the poor, and flouting government as well. In
common thought, not entirely fair to the trusts, they were formed to run
competitors out of business, to raise prices to the consumer, to lower wages,
and to reap all the profits possible. Moreover, combinations in industry
and transportation were increasing, and they were coming more and more
under the control of investment banking houses, such as J. P. Morgan and
Company of New York. Bankers remote from the workers were creating
a "money trust" that controlled networks in industry and transportation
and manipulated credit throughout the nation. In 1901 the railroads were
largely under the control of a few individuals, and the United States Steel
Corporation and other huge industrial trusts had just made their appearance. The public was becoming alarmed and there was a growing insistent
demand that the Sherman Anti-Trust Act be enforced, and that the Interstate Commerce Commission be given authority. McKinley, like Cleveland,
had done nothing to curb the trusts.

Immediately after taking office, Roosevelt asserted that he would continue McKinley's policies, and so pleased the Big Business community that
had been so delighted with his predecessor. Nor did his first message to
Congress, in December, 1901, reveal a thoroughgoing reformer. In it he
described the growth of powerful corporations as "natural"; promised support toward opening foreign markets; and asked that the merchant marine
be subsidized. On the other hand, the new President cautiously suggested
that some changes should be made. He urged that immigration be checked
by educational and economic tests. He laid greater stress upon the "real
and grave evils" arising from big industry, condemning particularly the
"watering" of stock in giant corporations. He recommended that "practical efforts" be made to remedy such evils through national supervision of
corporations, and he also recommended enlargement of the powers of the

Interstate Commerce Commission, so that railroad rate discriminations might be removed. He likewise came forth for a federal program of conservation and reclamation of natural resources. While the message was not a McKinley document, neither was it one of a man dedicated to radical measures. It is evident that Roosevelt did not yet feel sure of himself in the Presidency; that he was seeking a middle way in domestic policy; and that he was eager to avoid making enemies in his party. He was a practical politician who wanted to stay in the White House; and he knew full well that, at least for the time being, he must work with the conservatives of his party if he hoped to accomplish anything.

PRESIDENT AND CONGRESS

In general, throughout the term which he inherited from McKinley, Roosevelt did maintain good relations with the conservative Republicans who dominated Congress. The Senate then was guided by Nelson W. Aldrich of Rhode Island, Orville H. Platt of Connecticut, John C. Spooner of Wisconsin, William B. Allison of Iowa, and Mark Hanna. In that body Aldrich was as influential as Hanna. His daughter had married John D. Rockefeller, Jr., and he himself was a self-made millionaire who firmly believed in government by a moneyed aristocracy. On public questions Roosevelt consulted these men, and also Joseph G. Cannon, who became Speaker of the House of Representatives in 1903 and who ruled it with an iron hand. Striving to injure the feelings of those politicians as little as possible—he never openly attacked high protective tariffs, although he had been a low-tariff man in his youth—Roosevelt secured the passage of several reform measures. In 1902 Congress followed his leadership by passing the Newlands Act, which definitely committed the federal government to the principles of conservation and reclamation of natural resources. It provided that money received from the sale of public lands in sixteen states in the West and Southwest be used for irrigation of arid regions. In the following year Congress established a Department of Commerce and Labor which contained a Bureau of Corporations, authorized to investigate and report upon the behavior of corporations making use of the channels of interstate commerce. Roosevelt forced through that measure by declaring that opposition to it was led by John D. Rockefeller. Further, he secured money to enlarge the staff of the Attorney General so that suits might be more vigorously prosecuted under the Sherman Act. It was also possible to move against rebates, for some railroad owners had become willing to give up the practice. They were presumably effectively barred by the Elkins Act, which provided punishment for all concerned in the giving or the taking of rebates.

In March, 1903, Roosevelt declared that he had great respect for Senator Aldrich, Speaker Cannon, and other conservative Republicans in Congress; he said that he had to work with them, and that he preferred to work with them instead of with "radical reformers." Nevertheless, "His Accidency," acquiring assurance on public questions, and more confident that he would receive the Republican nomination for the Presidency in 1904, was moving away from Aldrich and his associates. In affairs he could handle without the help of Congress he had already allied himself with the "radical reformers." Soon after he took office he had a conversation with J. P. Morgan, in which the powerful banker blandly indicated that he was not profoundly impressed by political men, even the President of the United States. Roosevelt was infuriated. He was also deeply angered by the behavior of George F. Baer, president of the Reading Railroad, in the anthracite coal strike of 1902. Roosevelt struck at Morgan, and he dealt vigorously with Baer and other coal mine operators.

THE NORTHERN SECURITIES CASE

Believing that bigness in industry and transport was inevitable and that it was not of much use to try to prevent it, Roosevelt would have preferred to let business combinations grow and to force good behavior on them by use and expansion of the powers of the national government. His view had much to be said for it. However, since he had difficulty even in securing permission from Congress to form the Bureau of Corporations, he could entertain no hope that the lawmakers would do anything against the trusts in the near future. Convinced that some alternative must be found to check them, he undertook to enforce the Sherman Act, even though he had no real faith in it. On February 19, 1902, Attorney General Philander Knox announced that the Department of Justice, under instructions from Roosevelt, would file a suit to force the dissolution of the Northern Securities Company. The announcement caused turmoil in Wall Street and staggered the stock market, although the news was received by the general public with pleasure, because Roosevelt was asserting the authority of the United States against the money giants. Northern Securities was the first giant holding company, formed the preceding year by J. P. Morgan, James J. Hill, and Edward H. Harriman, with the support of the Rockefeller interests, to monopolize railroad traffic in the northwestern part of the nation. It controlled the three great railroads of that region, the Northern Pacific, the Great Northern, and the Chicago, Burlington, and Quincy. Northern Securities had a capital stock of $400,000,000, of which 30 percent, according to Knox, was "water." The public would presumably pay higher rates to the monopoly so that dividends might be paid upon the "water." In 1903 a Federal Circuit Court of Appeals declared that Northern Securities violated the Sherman Law and that it must be dissolved, to the joy of the man in the street. The lawyers for Northern Securities swiftly appealed to the Supreme Court, hoping to persuade it that the combination was merely one of stock and that congressional power over commerce did not extend to such cases. They declared that it was like the "sugar trust," that it had only an "indirect" effect upon interstate trade, and reminded the Court that the "sugar trust" had been ruled beyond the scope of federal control over commerce. Their pleas almost succeeded, but the high court, by a 5-to-4 decision, asserted that any combination restraining interstate or foreign commerce, whether directly or indirectly, was subject to federal authority, and that Northern Securities must be dissolved. The Sherman Act was thus given new life, and the way was opened for further prosecutions of the trusts. But Roosevelt had won a battle rather than a war. His heart was not yet in the fight against the trusts, and he did not push other prosecutions under the Sherman law until after he had been elected to the Presidency in 1904.

THE COAL STRIKE

Taking place at a time when anthracite was of the first importance to the national economy—it was widely used both to heat homes and to secure power—the coal strike in northeastern Pennsylvania in 1902 brought on a labor crisis. In May of that year more than 50,000 of the United Mine Workers went out on strike under the leadership of John F. Mitchell. They demanded an eight-hour day, a 10–20 percent increase in pay, recognition of their union, and other minor concessions. The anthracite deposits were largely owned by the railroads of the region, and their presidents refused for months to bargain in any fashion whatever. They were determined to crush the union, and they expected to succeed with the help of the public when the coalbins of the cities on the Eastern seaboard became empty. Through the summer and into the fall the mines were quiet, the miners holding out with the help of their fellows in the soft coal fields. However, public opinion turned against the owners, whose refusal to deal with the miners was contrasted with repeated offers from them to arbitrate. The spokesmen for the owners, especially George F. Baer of the Reading Railroad, further exasperated the public by arrogant statements. Baer went so far as to proclaim that God had seen fit to give vast property to Christian men like himself, and made it clear that mere mortals ought not interfere with His arrangements. Newspapers and magazines began to demand that there be compulsory compromise, and even that the anthracite mines be nationalized.

Roosevelt was no ardent champion of labor unions, and he was utterly opposed to the closed shop. At heart he favored men of wealth rather than those who used their hands to secure a livelihood, preferring the middle class and the educated to both. It was the easier for him to use force against unions than it was to coerce owners. On the other hand, he believed that unions were the necessary counterpart of giant corporations, and that labor must be decently paid and treated, both to serve the cause of justice and to prevent social upheaval. Told by his advisers, most of whom he had inherited from McKinley, that he lacked power to intervene in the dispute, Roosevelt became more and more restive as autumn approached. At length, rejecting the contention that the President was helpless in such an emergency, he invited Mitchell and the leaders of the mine operators to a conference at the White House on October 3. At the meeting Baer and his associates refused even to discuss the strike with the union leaders who attended. They positively refused arbitration of any sort, although the unions freely agreed either to bargain directly or to accept the verdict of investigating outsiders. The railroad executives asserted that the union had been responsible for many murders; that thousands of non-union miners wanted to work; but that they were prevented from doing so by the strikers. They also claimed that it was the duty of the government to intervene in order to restore order. An injunction against the union was a proper remedy, and with it the sending of troops to keep the peace. They wanted Roosevelt to act as Cleveland had in the railroad strike of 1894, but their behavior deeply angered the President, who refused to break the strike. He let it be known that he was preparing to send 10,000 troops to seize the mines so that coal would not be lacking in the coming winter, and he arranged to have Governor William A. Stone of Pennsylvania ask for the help of the army. To have sent soldiers, even on the plea of emergency, would have stretched Presidential powers, as they were interpreted at that time, and it may be doubted that Roosevelt intended to do it; he was doubtless bluffing. In any case, it was not necessary for him to take that drastic step. After much negotiation, J. P. Morgan undertook to act for an alarmed financial and industrial community. On October 13 through agents he arranged with the President an agreement by which the miners were to resume work, and a commission appointed by Roosevelt was to settle the issues at stake. When Roosevelt chose the members of the arbitrating body, it did not meet the wishes of the union, which protested. Thereupon, compelled by the agreement to appoint an "eminent sociologist," Roosevelt chose the president of the Brotherhood of Railroad Conductors. The commission reduced the hours of the miners from ten to nine, in some cases to eight, and gave them a 10 percent increase in pay. However, the union was not given recognition, and the mine owners were pleased by a recommendation that they be permitted to raise the price of coal by 10 percent, which they did promptly. So the strike was settled. Roosevelt had set a precedent by intervening, and also by befriending labor. The immediate cost of the concessions secured by the miners was paid by the consumer, an arrangement which was also to be copied in the future.

PRESIDENT IN HIS OWN RIGHT

Roosevelt and the Republicans easily won the election of 1904. There was only one man who might have wrested the Republican nomination from Roosevelt, Mark Hanna, who was favored by Big Business. Hanna died early in the year, and Roosevelt thereafter had no rival in his party. Even had Hanna lived, it is doubtful that he could have pushed Roosevelt aside, for he was intensely popular and had carefully used his patronage to secure the choice of delegates to the Republican convention friendly to himself. As the campaign approached, Roosevelt saw to it that every Union veteran of the Civil War who had reached the age of 62 received a pension of $5.00 per month, and made friendly gestures toward J. P. Morgan, Edward H. Harriman, and other economic powers. He might be something of a reformer, but he was basically safe and sane. He was nominated unanimously on a platform that committed him to little, if anything.

Nor was Roosevelt vigorously challenged by the Democratic candidate for the Presidency, Judge Alton B. Parker of New York. William Jennings Bryan was quite willing to run against Roosevelt, but the Democrats could not bring themselves to name one who had twice been defeated. The choice for them lay between Parker, a respected jurist supported by eastern Democrats under the leadership of Grover Cleveland, and William Randolph Hearst, who attracted some reform elements among the Bryanites. Hearst was not well liked, and Parker was nominated almost by default. He was supplied with a platform almost as ambiguous as that of the Republicans, and with octogenarian Senator Henry Gassaway Davis of West Virginia as his running mate. The Democrats did forthrightly condemn the trusts and called for an increase in the authority of the Interstate Commerce Commission, but Judge Parker let it be known that he believed the regulation of Big Business should be left to the states. Parker also successfully insisted that his party abandon an equivocal plank on currency and forthrightly accept the gold standard. In the contest with Roosevelt he was clearly the more conservative of the two. Toward the close of the campaign he made an impression by charging that George B. Cortelyou, Roosevelt's friend and campaign manager, had collected a huge slush fund from the great corporations to insure victory for Roosevelt and the Republicans. That accusation was well founded, but Roosevelt deprived it of force by flatly denying it. Roosevelt came forth as the champion of "the square deal" for all, a phrase that appealed to all reformers and could cost him few votes. With respect to foreign affairs, he was able to point with pride to the fact that he had opened the way for the building of the Panama Canal. The cynical and the observant might dislike him because he so often preached morality and practiced politics. Some disliked him because he referred to himself so frequently—it was said that the Government Printing Office ran out of capital I's, used so extensively in his speeches and papers. Roosevelt, and with him the Republicans, triumphed; he received 7,628,834 popular votes to 5,840,401 for Parker. The judge received only 140 electoral ballots, Roosevelt 336. "His Accidency" had won the Presidency in his own right.

THE PROGRESSIVE ERA

On the night of victory, Roosevelt announced that he would not seek a second election. Under no circumstances, he declared, would he accept another nomination. Thereafter the elected Roosevelt moved steadily to the left. He accurately described himself as a man of the center before the election of 1904, and as a "radical" before he left the White House a little more than four years later. What happened to him? Doubtless he felt less need to seek the approval, or at least the neutrality, of the leaders of industry, commerce, and banking, since he had forsworn a third period of service in the Presidency. Another reason for his swing to the left was that his dislike for the practices of Big Business increased as he became more familiar with them. It may also be inferred that Roosevelt's instinct to fight, hitherto usually repressed, asserted itself, and that he could no longer bear compromising with J. P. Morgan and his like. Certainly one reason for Roosevelt's shifting was a tide of opinion that was carrying both Republicans and Democrats into progressivism. Roosevelt must have been impressed by the fact that 400,000 voters cast their ballots for Socialist Eugene V. Debs for the Presidency in 1904. Before he left office he was completely identified with the progressive Republicans, and he had emerged as a thoroughgoing reformer.

Roosevelt, although he became the most conspicuous of the progressives, was only one of many men and women who moved into their camp in the early years of the twentieth century. By 1905 they had won control of several cities and states, and were busy remolding them. Some, including Mayors Hazen S. Pingree of Detroit and Samuel M. Jones of Toledo, had made their appearance in city politics in the 1890s. Among those who became progressives after the turn of the century were Thomas L. Johnson, Mayor of Cleveland for eight years; Brand Whitlock, who carried on the work of Jones in Toledo; Robert M. LaFollette, who was elected Governor of Wisconsin in 1900, Albert B. Cummins, Governor of Iowa, and William S. U'Ren of Oregon, who was responsible for the adoption in his state of important changes in political machinery that were afterward widely copied. The progressive leaders were generally well-educated people of some means, even of wealth; they were essentially middle class, and they were not at all revolutionary. They campaigned to rid the cities and states of graft, corruption, and domination by bosses, by railroads, and by other economic interests; they were enemies of the trusts, and they sought extension of political democracy to secure the power to carry out their other reforms. They were responsible for municipal ownership of water, gas, and streetcar services in many cities, resorting to a limited degree of municipal socialism only because they could find no other means to remove abuses. Like Roosevelt, they wanted "the square deal" within the capitalistic framework. Again like Roosevelt, they were idealists and moralists, disliking plutocracy, but not fond of organized labor and rather unhappy because of the "New Immigration." They were, nevertheless, ardent believers in democracy, believing that a former, better America could be largely restored by making sure that the will of the voters was not thwarted. Hence, their championship of the direct primary instead of the convention to nominate for office, also their advocacy of the initiative, the referendum, and the recall in state and local government. They urged too the direct election of United States senators, because those chosen by the state legislatures were often "plutocrats" or their servants. Gradually the progressives began to seek still further reforms, such as regulation of child and female labor, limiting the hours of work for men, minimum wages, and even female suffrage. Their achievements were impressive, especially in the South and the West. The city manager type of government made its appearance; much social legislation was enacted; the secret ballot became standard; and other devices for assuring the execution of the popular will were quite widely adopted, though not in a majority of the cities or the states. They secured popular choice of United States senators in many states by enjoining the legislature to elect the victor in a primary. Through state railroad and industrial commissions they regulated business activity so effectively that those who were curbed sometimes turned toward federal regulation as the lesser of two evils, preferring to deal with one master instead of more than forty. The progressives were zealous, particularly because they had commonly been earlier supporters of the *status quo.* So LaFollette, like Roosevelt, had given his support to McKinley in 1896; other progressives had been admirers of Grover Cleveland.

The rise of the progressives was accompanied by that of the "muckrakers," as Roosevelt called them, publicists who made careers of exposing machine politics, the machinations of Big Business, graft, and social evils. They wrote exposé after exposé in popular magazines such as *Collier's, McClure's,* and the *American.* Ida M. Tarbell published a sensational *History of the Standard Oil Company* in *McClure's* after 1903. Lincoln Steffens—who in his youth had been eager to make a great fortune—published *The Shame of the Cities,* the title of which indicates the content. Two years later David Graham Phillips almost savagely assailed the upper house of Congress as a nest of privilege and corruption in *The Treason of the Sen-*

ate. The writings of the muckrakers tended to become sensational, for their authors were not objective scholars, but authors writing to make a livelihood. They were not invariably just to the individuals they attacked, but there can be no doubt that they strengthened demands for change, especially among middle class Americans.

THE PRESIDENT SWINGS TO THE LEFT

The elected President Roosevelt made ever larger proposals for reform and used steadily stronger and more unfavorable language about those who opposed his measures. He resumed his campaign against the trusts, beginning a long series of prosecutions against them under the Sherman law. In his first message to Congress after his election he urged that limits be put upon the hours of work for railroad labor; that the Interstate Commerce Commission be given power to consider complaints made against railroad rates and to establish reasonable ones after consideration of the evidence; that the Bureau of Corporations be authorized to license all interstate businesses; that it be given authority to investigate insurance; and that the District of Columbia be used as a laboratory in which to investigate the probable effects of reforms in areas beyond federal authority. Roosevelt wanted to try out in the District laws curbing child labor, establishing juvenile courts, and requiring compulsory school attendance, factory inspection, and slum clearance. When Congress failed to respond with enthusiasm, he moved farther to the left. In the congressional campaign of 1906 he shocked conservatives and constitutional lawyers as well by asserting that the federal government ought to impose "a constantly increasing supervision over and control of the great fortunes used in business," and that under the Constitution it possessed an "inherent power" to do so. He claimed that the nation could act "in all cases where the object involved was beyond the power of the several states," an extraordinary interpretation of the Constitution supporting a remarkable demand for the exercise of federal authority.

By 1907 the President was describing all great fortunes as "useless." In August of that year he condemned "certain malefactors of great wealth" whom he accused of deliberately fostering a banking panic that had shaken the country. The following December he laid down the far-reaching program afterward described by the phrase "New Nationalism." He urged upon Congress, in addition to federal incorporation laws, inheritance and income taxes, federal regulation of railroad securities, fixing of railroad rates in accordance with the physical value of railroad property, limiting the use of injunctions in labor disputes, federal investigation of major labor troubles, adherence to the eight-hour day, and compensation for killed and injured workmen. He also called for federal action against stock market gambling. In addition, he bitterly condemned "predatory wealth," and forthrightly condemned the federal courts because they had found workmen's compensation laws unconstitutional. Roosevelt was then in the very van of American reformers, except for the Socialists; his advocacy of a thoroughly regulated capitalistic society went beyond Woodrow Wilson's "New Freedom" and anticipated in a large degree the "New Deal" of his cousin, Franklin D. Roosevelt.

SOME RADICAL REFORMS

One of the reasons why Roosevelt more and more vehemently called for radical reforms was that he was able to obtain so few of them. Progressivism was gaining strength on Capitol Hill, but dominated neither house until after he had left the Presidency. Even so, three important laws were passed in the early summer of 1906, because of the pressure of public opinion. A number of the railroads had quite openly violated the Elkins Law, continuing to give rebates. A resulting outcry led to the Hepburn Act, which greatly increased the authority of the Interstate Commerce Commission, giving it power to set maximum railroad rates that were just and reasonable, these to be based upon a uniform system of accounting. Its authority was also extended to express companies, the Pullman Company, oil pipelines, and other facilities. Roosevelt and the progressives vainly sought to insert in the law a provision restricting the railroads to a fair return upon the physical value of their property. However, it did stipulate that the orders of the commission were to go into effect and were to be enforced, at least until they were set aside by the federal judiciary, thus compelling the railroads to prove unfair discrimination against them or to accept the rulings of the commission. The law also severely limited the granting of free passes, by which the railroads had secured friends in politics. Although the Hepburn Act was not so stringent as the progressives desired, it was very effective.

Almost simultaneously Congress passed the Pure Food and Drug and the Meat Inspection Acts. The first of these resulted from a campaign by the muckrakers against the menace of adulterated and mislabeled foods. Great publicity had been given to the researches of a government chemist, Harvey Wiley, who had shown that dangerous preservatives and dishonest labeling were commonly used. The act forbade the transport through the channels of interstate commerce of adulterated and misbranded foods and drugs. The Meat Inspection Law had a similar history. The muckrakers, particularly Upton Sinclair in a novel called The Jungle, had revealed that the great meat-packing companies in Chicago were indifferent to filth and that they did not scruple to sell the flesh of diseased animals. Sinclair's exposé doubtless contributed to the number of vegetarians. An investigation ordered by Roosevelt confirmed Sinclair's findings. The Meat Inspection Law followed upon a wave of public indignation. It provided for the appointment of federal inspectors who could bar diseased animals and infected and rotten meat from the facilities of interstate commerce.

Another important improvement began with the passage of the Aldrich-Vreeland Act in 1908. It followed upon the panic of the preceding year, which had threatened to blossom into a depression and which had been checked only by great efforts on the part of J. P. Morgan. The financier had managed to restore confidence in one threatened major bank after another, by coming to their aid. However, the panic, including a severe drop in the stock market, had made evident weaknesses in both the credit structure of the nation and its currency system. The law empowered the national banks to issue notes based upon state and local bonds and commercial paper for a period of six years. Although a tax was imposed upon the national bank notes so supported—it was not levied upon their notes based upon federal bonds—the supply of paper money was increased, and it was made in some degree adjustable. Of much greater significance was the forming of a Monetary Commission, of which Senator Aldrich became the head, to investigate banking and currency systems at home and abroad to secure information. Its report, submitted in 1912, was to be the basis for the Federal Reserve Act of 1913.

The Aldrich-Vreeland law was the work of Aldrich rather than of Roosevelt, who was on increasingly bad terms with the Republican majority in Congress during his last years in office. After the election of 1906 such progressive Republicans as Senators Albert J. Beveridge of Indiana, Robert M. LaFollette of Wisconsin, and Jonathan P. Dolliver of Iowa, both in the Senate and the House, rallied behind the President, but they were in a minority. More potent were Aldrich and Senator Joseph B. Foraker, the latter being in the pay of the Standard Oil Company as long as he was in the Senate. But the conservatives in Congress were unable to balk Roosevelt's program of conservation of natural resources, which he pushed with increasing vigor during his second term. Such conservation was one of Roosevelt's greatest achievements. A driving force toward preserving and making good use of the nation's natural wealth was Gifford Pinchot, head of the Forestry Service of the Department of Agriculture, who was ardently backed by the President. When Roosevelt took office, about 45,000,000 acres of national land had been set aside to preserve forests and to provide parks. While he was President, almost 150,000,000 acres were reserved, the government undertaking to save coal, oil, and other mineral deposits, together with water power sites, woods, and scenic beauties. The building of dams to supply water for irrigation and for drinking, and to furnish power, was also begun. There was widespread protest against conservation from those who wished to exploit natural resources for their personal gain. Lumbermen, oilmen, ranchers, and officers of power companies desired the freedom they had enjoyed in the past, and they were supported by laissez-faire conservatives of the East. The enemies of conservation were strong enough to push through Congress in 1907 a bill which declared that additions to the forest reserves in six Western states were not to be made without congressional approval. Before Roosevelt signed the measure, he used his executive authority to make reserves of all lands in those states that were then considered advisable by the Department of the Interior. Forbidden by Congress to set aside power sites without its specific permission, Pinchot and Roosevelt sought to thwart its will by reserving 2500 of them as "Ranger Stations." Conservation made progress despite the hostility of Congress. Roosevelt not only made liberal use of his executive authority to foster it, but arranged for National Conservation Congresses, at which governors and others devoted to the cause met annually. Thanks in large part to his efforts, no fewer than forty-one states created commissions to save and prudently develop natural resources by 1910. Few of Roosevelt's actions are less susceptible to criticism than his championship of conservation.

Leaving the White House on March 4, 1909, Roosevelt expressed the hope that his successor, William Howard Taft would follow "my policies." Taft did not act as Roosevelt had, and progressivism did not make rapid progress while he was in the Presidency. Roosevelt was to reenter the political arena as its great champion.

43 THEODORE ROOSEVELT'S
WORLD POLICY

Theodore Roosevelt was happier in foreign affairs than domestic ones. He was freer to move and could embark upon major enterprises without the consent of Congress. Moreover, he enjoyed playing a principal role on the world stage, which, in the end, he thought more important than the domestic scene. He was moved by a sense of mission, was convinced that America must take her place as one of the great powers under his leadership, and he believed that she could exert a beneficent influence almost everywhere on the globe. In the Presidency he was an unashamed imperialist, though a less ardent one than he had earlier been. In his view, all nations were engaged in a struggle to live and to expand. He fancied, however, that wars would become less frequent and that the outcome would be progress. He divided the peoples of the world into two groups, the civilized and the barbarous. The civilized were piloted by the Great Powers, and it was well that they should expand and carry civilization to their inferiors. As one of the great nations, America ought both to participate in their contests and to expand, especially since America had a generous civilization to spread. During his years in office Roosevelt saw to it that the strength of the navy was doubled; he arranged for the building of the Panama Canal; pursued a vigorous policy with respect to Latin America; and intervened in both Asiatic and European questions in unprecedented fashion. He had able Secretaries of State, John Hay until 1905, and then Elihu Root. Their advice he found helpful, but he used rather than followed it. He brought the "strenuous life," in which he gloried, into foreign affairs; he won a Nobel Peace Prize; and his behavior was such that it has been subjected to the most severe criticism. If Roosevelt's preachings were not always quite consistent with his practices in internal matters, the two were somewhat farther apart with respect to things international. He was a complex man.

THE PANAMA CANAL

For no other part of his conduct has Roosevelt been so much condemned as for the manner in which he dealt with the South American Republic of Colombia in order to secure the right to dig and control the Panama Canal. He never admitted that he had done anything unethical, and he claimed great credit because he had not permitted stupid and selfish people to prevent the building of the "Big Ditch," so useful to mankind in general and so valuable both commercially and militarily to the United States. Critics have urged that his end could have been accomplished as quickly, or almost as quickly, by more satisfactory means. The story is a complicated one.

It will be recalled that, before Roosevelt became President, John Hay had succeeded in removing the British obstacle to the building of an American canal across Central America by obtaining the cancellation of the Clayton-Bulwer Treaty. Hay was trying not only to open the way for digging the water passage, but also to get protecting bases for it and control of the Caribbean as well. Roosevelt heartily approved of what Hay had done. Attempts initiated by the Secretary of State to buy Margarita Island, the Cocos Islands in the Pacific, and a naval station from Ecuador in the Galapagos failed, for one reason and another. An effort to purchase the Virgin Islands from Denmark came closer to success; the necessary treaty was worked out in January, 1902, but in the end Denmark declined to ratify it, possibly because of pressure from Germany. Roosevelt had to accept those minor disappointments, but he could and did insist that Cuba permit the establishment of a powerful American naval base and that nothing should be allowed to prevent or postpone the building of the waterway.

CHOOSING A ROUTE

The first decision that Roosevelt and the Congress had to make after the signing of the Hay-Pauncefote Treaty on November 18, 1901, was to choose a route for the canal. The route across Panama was shorter, and the cost of construction would be lower. A canal across Nicaragua would be longer and more expensive to build, but would require fewer locks; moreover, Nicaragua was willing to sell the right to build and maintain one. While it was hoped that Colombia, which then owned the Isthmus of Panama, would make a similar bargain, there was a special difficulty to be removed if the Panama route were used. The New Panama Canal Company, which had inherited the property of de Lesseps' French company, also had acquired its right to cut a passageway across the narrow isthmus. It was asking a huge sum, more than $100,000,000, for its property and the franchise. Immediately before the signing of the Hay-Pauncefote Treaty, the Walker Commission, a body of engineers that had been appointed by McKinley to recommend one route or the other, gave its opinion in favor of the Nicaraguan one. However, the French company then quickly reduced its price to $40,000,000, thereby converting Roosevelt to Panama; the President in turn persuaded the commission to change its opinion and to come out for Panama, in January, 1902. There remained strong feeling in favor of Nicaragua in Congress, and it seemed for many months that Congress would insist on having its way. But Congress, too, changed its mind, thanks in large part to two lobbyists for the French company, William N. Cromwell, a New York lawyer, and Philippe Bunau-Varilla, a Frenchman, once the chief engineer under de Lesseps and a principal stockholder in the company. Cromwell had given $60,000 to the Republican campaign chest in 1900 in order to win friends for the Panama route. He and Bunau-Varilla went to see Roosevelt, Hay, Hanna, and other influential men in Washington. Bunau-Varilla sought to weaken the case for Nicaragua by instilling fear of volcanic activity in one of the Nicaraguan mountains. This strategy was unsuccessful until Mont Pelée on the French island of Martinique in the Caribbean suddenly erupted in May, 1902, and killed about 40,000 people. Soon afterward the Nicaraguan volcano became uneasy. The Frenchman hastily secured 90 Nicaraguan postage stamps upon which the volcano was shown belching forth smoke, and sent them to influential politicians. This clever maneuver may have had some influence. Certainly, Mark Hanna, chairman of the Republican National Committee in 1900, could not but be grateful for Cromwell's campaign contribution. At any rate, in June Congress declared in favor of securing a right of way across Panama, if the President could secure it "within a reasonable time and upon reasonable terms." Should that not be possible, he was to approach the Republic of Nicaragua.

THE U.S. IN THE CARIBBEAN

Needing only the consent of Colombia to use the Panama route, Roosevelt and John Hay ran into difficulties. That country was controlled by an aged dictator, José Marroquin, who moved slowly. His government was willing to grant permission to cut the canal, but at a higher price than the United States wished to pay, and with reservations protecting the police power of Colombia over adjacent areas. In January, 1903, Hay and Tomás Herran, representing Colombia, signed a treaty by which America was to be given a canal zone six miles wide in return for $10,000,000 in cash and an annual fee of $250,000. Colombia was theoretically to retain sovereignty over the zone, but American courts were to function within it. The American Senate gave its consent to the agreement, but the Colombian one refused, unanimously, for public feeling in the South American nation was against it. However, its government was willing to make a bargain, and proposed new terms. It wanted more money, $25,000,000; alternatively, it would accept $20,000,000 from the United States and $10,-000,000 from the French company. Colombia also continued to require that policing in the zone remain in her hands. It was clear that she was in no hurry to sell. Her bargaining position was strong, and it would actually become stronger, for the franchise of the French company would expire in 1904 or 1910, the terminal date being one or the other as Colombia might decide.

THE BUNAU-VARILLA PLOT AND REPUBLIC OF PANAMA

It would doubtless have been wise for Roosevelt to be patient and to haggle with Colombia, at the same time threatening to turn to Nicaragua. He might also have abandoned the Panama route, and might have devoted all his efforts toward securing the Nicaraguan one, which had its advantages, including its nearness. Instead, determined to build the canal across Panama, the President refused to offer Colombia anything beyond the Hay-Herran Treaty terms, and privately denounced the Colombians as "homicidal corruptionists" and "contemptible little creatures." He declared that the "blackmailers of Bogotá" must not be permitted to bar permanently a pathway of civilization. In a draft of a message to Congress prepared in October, 1903 he recommended that the United States take possession of the Panamanian isthmus and build a canal "without any further parley with Colombia," but on second thought he deleted the passage. There was another way by which America could obtain a canal zone across the isthmus, and it was being pursued, with a fair prospect of success. In the summer of 1903 Roosevelt had quietly let it be known that it would be most convenient if the Panamanians should rebel and secure their independence. A republic of Panama would doubtless be more willing to deal with the United States than was Colombia. By mid-September American newspaper and magazine writers were indicating that they favored a rebellion in Panama. The New York *Evening Post* declared, "Many public men of prominence" were "in favor of intimating to the Panama revolutionists that if they will maintain resistance long enough . . . this government will see to it that they are not run over by the superior forces of Colombia." It was broadly hinted to the Panamanians, who had earlier and vainly revolted, that they should rise again and that they might expect help from the United States. The hint did not escape Bunau-Varilla, who saw an opportunity for the French company to sell its rights before they expired.

In the fall of 1903 in the Hotel Waldorf-Astoria in New York City Bunau-Varilla plotted a Panamanian rebellion; by a liberal use of money he enlisted the services of Panama patriots, of some hundreds of firemen and Colombian soldiers stationed on the isthmus. Meanwhile, he conferred with Roosevelt, Hay, and other officials in Washington to find out for certain whether the United States would come to the help of "his army," which obviously could not withstand the forces of Colombia. Under a treaty of 1846 with Colombia the United States had undertaken to maintain the "perfect neutrality" of the isthmus in order that "free transit" be assured. The purpose was to prevent Britain, or some other third power, from taking Panama. On several earlier occasions, when Panama was in revolt American troops had been landed on the isthmus to assure the "free transit." The American soldiers had not interfered with the movements of the Colombian army. But might not the United States, under a strained interpretation of the treaty, undertake to protect "free transit" by keeping Colombian forces from the isthmus? Bunau-Varilla obtained no commitment in Washington, but he observed that strong language was employed there against Colombia. When he learned that the American cruiser *Nashville* had been ordered to the isthmus and would arrive on November 2, he concluded that it was safe to proceed with his plans. He cabled his agent in Panama, and on the following day, revolution was proclaimed. Three hours before it began the American consul at Panama City received a cable from Washington asking whether it had begun. It was quickly successful, for the American navy, under orders, kept away Colombian reinforcements in order to maintain the "free transit." On November 4, the revolutionists announced that the independent Republic of Panama had been formed; an hour after receiving the news, Roosevelt decided that the new nation should be recognized; and recognition was officially extended on November 6. Helpless, Colombia could only complain.

There was no difficulty about securing a canal zone from the Republic of Panama, for on November 13 the Frenchman Bunau-Varilla made his appearance in Washington as the official envoy of the new nation. Five days later he signed the necessary treaty, which he had persuaded the government of that republic to endorse, sight unseen. By the Hay-Bunau-Varilla Treaty, approved by the American Senate two months later, the United States obtained the right to dig a canal and was given control, "as if sovereign," in perpetuity over a zone ten miles wide across the isthmus. Included, of course, was the power to protect the canal by military force. In return, America guaranteed the independence of Panama, paid it $10,000,000, and further agreed to pay the isthmian republic an annual fee of $250,000, beginning nine years after the signing of the treaty. Digging could be begun; and the French company had secured $40,000,000, minus expenses. Cromwell set his fee at $600,000.

Immediately after the Panama *coup*, Roosevelt was bitterly condemned at home and abroad for his part in it. In the main, however, American sentiment approved his behavior, although it was widely agreed that it was open to attack on moral grounds. He was excused on the basis that Colombia's conduct had been most provoking. He himself asserted that his "every" action had been "in accordance with the highest, finest, and nicest standards of public and governmental ethics." He also declared: "If ever a Government could be said to have received a mandate from civilization . . . the United States holds that position with regard to the interoceanic canal." Adverse criticism continuing, he not only strenuously denied that he had done anything censurable, but claimed a large part of the credit for the *coup.* In 1909 he told Henry Cabot Lodge that "the vital work of getting Panama as an independent Republic . . . was done by me without the aid or advice of anyone . . . and without the knowledge of anyone." Two years later he declared before a university audience at Berkeley, California,

I am interested in the Panama Canal because I started it. If I had followed traditional, conservative methods I would have submitted a dignified State paper of probably 200 pages to Congress and the debates on it would be going on yet; but I took the Canal Zone and let Congress debate, and while the debate goes on the Canal does also.

Colombia was certain that the United States owed an apology, at least a cash indemnity. Its government several times urged that its claims be submitted to arbitration, which America steadily refused. President William Howard Taft tried, without success, to placate the Colombians without acknowledging any fault on the part of the United States. President Woodrow Wilson, as a Democrat, found it easier to believe that Roosevelt's behavior was not quite what it might have been, and concluded a treaty with the South American country in 1914 in which the United States expressed "sincere regret," and agreed to pay Colombia $25,000,000. The Senate, with Henry Cabot Lodge defending the former President, declined to endorse the agreement. Roosevelt himself protested vehemently against it. In 1921, after Roosevelt's death, the treaty was revived, with the omission of the expression of "sincere regret." The Republicans were then in power, but Lodge favored it, although as Roosevelt had pointed out, the money payment to Colombia could hardly be construed in any other way than as an admission of wrongdoing on the part of the United States. The Senate then ratified the treaty, apparently because it was desirable to please Colombia in order to secure a share in exploiting oil recently found in that country. So the unhappy affair was ended, but in Latin America enemies of the United States who thundered against "Yankee imperialism" continued to offer the Panama business as proof.

The story of the construction of the waterway is more pleasing. Progress was delayed because a contest developed between advocates of a sea level canal and men who insisted that there must be locks, and also because malaria and yellow fever took a heavy toll among workers in the Zone. Colonel William C. Gorgas cleaned up and substantially rid the region of the Canal of these diseases. In 1906 Roosevelt and Congress determined that there must be locks, and Lieutenant Colonel George W. Goethals was placed in charge of construction. The work then moved forward steadily, and the Big Ditch, forty miles long, was finished in 1914. The cost of construction was much higher than had been expected, $365,000,000. On the other hand, the Canal proved to be even more valuable militarily than had been anticipated. It greatly increased the mobility and striking power of the American navy, permitting swift transfer of warships between the Atlantic and Pacific. Toward the end of the 1950s more than 9000 merchant vessels were passing through the locks each year. Panama did not remain satisfied with the terms of the treaty of 1904, and later obtained additional concessions. In 1936 the annual fee received by Panama was raised to $430,000, and it was increased to $1,930,000 in 1955. In the latter year the United States also guaranteed equality of pay and opportunity to all workers in the Zone and undertook to build a bridge over the Pacific entrance to the Canal. Dissatisfaction arose and continued in Panama because of the perpetual lease.

THE ROOSEVELT COROLLARY

The Canal was not Roosevelt's only problem in Latin America. Tumult in Cuba also posed difficulties, offering an excuse for seizing possession of it. However, having some familiarity with Cuba and conscious of the headaches annexation would entail, he sent troops to restore order, but withdrew them as quickly as conditions permitted. More awkward for him was the trouble raised by the refusal of Cipriano Castro, dictator of Venezuela, to pay the debts his country owed to Europeans. Borrowing heavily from British, German, and Italian investors, Castro decided that it was quite unnecessary to repay them. In 1901 Germany, acting in behalf of her creditor citizens, proposed that the International Court at The Hague consider the situation and arrange for its settlement, but Castro declined to take part in such a negotiation. Roosevelt was disgusted by the behavior of the Venezuelan dictator, whom he described as an "unspeakable villainous little monkey," and let it be known that the United States would not intervene if European nations undertook to "spank" such Latin Americans who made no effort to pay their debts to foreign citizens. Accordingly, since Venezuela owed her citizens five times as much as they owed German ones, England suggested to Germany that they use force to reduce the dictator to reason. The two nations, later joined by Italy, blockaded Venezuela by means of warships; Venezuelan gunboats were captured, and the Germans sank two of them. In December, 1902, Castro hastily decided that arbitration by The Hague court was acceptable.

The financial question was thus solved, but while the negotiations were in process, the Germans bombarded a Venezuelan fort and an adjacent village. American opinion then turned rapidly against Germany. Long afterward Roosevelt recalled that he had compelled Germany to be satisfied by the money payment to her citizens and that he had threatened to send Admiral Dewey with a fleet to Venezuela if Kaiser Wilhelm II did not behave properly. Proof that Germany desired anything more than the collection of the debts and that the President delivered such a threat is lacking. In any event, suspicion increased in America that Germany sought to acquire colonies on the shores of the Caribbean, and Roosevelt moved toward intervention in Latin America to prevent European intervention. Luis M. Drago, the Foreign Minister of Argentina, considering the Venezuelan question, declared that the use of force to collect public debts ought to be declared a violation of international law. In 1907, at the Second Peace Conference at The Hague, America subscribed basically to the "Drago Doctrine." However, Roosevelt remained convinced that the best way to prevent European military action and whatever consequences might come of it, was for the United States to see to it that European nations were deprived of any cause or pretext for using force.

The question of Latin American public debts was revived in 1904, when the Dominican Republic was threatened by European action. The poor and badly governed Santo Domingo had little income beyond the receipts at its customs houses. Borrowing money from Americans and Europeans, it had pledged those receipts toward repayment and had agreed to permit foreign collection of the duties in the event of default. In 1903 Belgium, foreseeing default, had suggested that it be prevented by the establishment of an international regime that would both govern the republic and restore order in its finances. Roosevelt had rejected the proposal, not caring for an arrangement by which Europeans would take part in the government of a New World nation. The following year the Dominican Republic announced that it would give preferential treatment to its American creditors, and warm protests came from Europe. Employment of force by European countries became a distinct possibility. To prevent it, Roosevelt announced and put into effect the Roosevelt Corollary to the Monroe Doctrine. In a message to Congress in December of that year he announced that the United States had a "moral mandate" to see to it that the nations of Latin America paid their debts and met all their obligations, in order to ward off European measures that might lead to the most serious consequences. Rumor then had it that Germany might resort to arms. Roosevelt asserted that:

Chronic wrongdoing . . . may in America as elsewhere, ultimately require intervention by some civilized nation, and in the Western Hemisphere the adherence of the United States to the Monroe Doctrine may force the United States, however reluctantly, in flagrant cases of such wrongdoing or impotence, to the exercise of an international police power.

He then brought pressure upon the Dominican Republic which led to an invitation to America to take over the customs houses and to use 55 percent of their revenue to meet the demands of the creditors, the remainder to be used for ordinary governmental expenses. The Senate, with some Republicans joining the Democrats, refused to ratify a protocol embodying the arrangement. The President would not be balked and signed an executive agreement to the same effect with Santo Domingo early in 1905. Under it, Americans collected the customs duties and put the finances in order, the Senate being persuaded to give formal approval of the arrangement two years later. Roosevelt had solved an awkward difficulty. His solution was applauded by the British, and had even been suggested by them. There was little objection from the Latin American nations at the time. Afterward, when American intervention led to rather frequent landings by the marines, sentiment against the Corollary became widespread in those countries.

ANGLO-AMERICAN RELATIONS AND
THE ALASKAN BOUNDARY

Roosevelt gave little heed to the feelings of the Spanish Americans, and blustered a bit against the British, or more correctly, against the Canadians. However, he played a major part in bringing America and England into a close friendship. He was not hereditarily anti-English; though a devoted patriot and an empire builder, he saw England, not so much as a competitor to be struggled against, but as a partner in advancing civilization. On bad terms with France and Russia, Britain became disturbed when Germany began to build a powerful fleet in 1898. "Splendid isolation" no longer seemed to be a safe policy in London, and overtures were made by the British to Japan and the United States. These resulted in an alliance between England and Japan, signed in 1902. Because of American opinion against that kind of foreign entanglement, an Anglo-American alliance was out of the question, but a good understanding was possible, and the British strove to secure it. Of all the major European powers England alone made it clear that her sympathies lay with the United States in the Spanish-American War; moreover, Britain carefully avoided doing anything that might embarrass America in the Venezuelan and Dominican controversies. She again demonstrated her desire for friendship when the Alaska boundary dispute became a serious one in 1903. After the discovery of gold in the Klondike, it was learned that the best approach to the Canadian ores there was through the Alaska Panhandle. The boundary between it and Canada had never been precisely ascertained, although an Anglo-Russian treaty of 1825 clearly indicated that the line should run in such a fashion that the Panhandle would form a continuous stretch of territory. Canadians, wishing to secure possession of the Lynn Canal, which would have given them a port within the Panhandle, now claimed that the line ought to be run in a more westerly course. Canada was willing to arbitrate, but hoped to secure the salt-water port. Roosevelt was sure that

THE "IMPARTIAL JURISTS" DECIDE FOR THE U.S.

the Canadians had no case, and that they came "dangerously near black-mail." Britain and America agreed to arbitrate, each choosing three "impartial jurists of repute," the six men to make their decision by majority vote. Roosevelt appointed Elihu Root, then Secretary of War and two politicians, one of whom was Henry Cabot Lodge, well known as a hater of everything British. Nevertheless, England did not protest, but selected two Canadians and Lord Alverstone, Chief Justice of England. Through private channels Roosevelt let it be known in London that the arbitrators must not merely "split the difference," but that their decision must favor the United States. If it did not, he would send troops and run the boundary as he thought right. Such a threat in times past might well have provoked the most vigorous response; carried out, it might have led to war. However, both British and Canadian officials knew that their case was far from strong. In London it may have been suggested to Lord Alverstone that it would be as well if he did not favor the Canadian claim. He voted with the Americans, Canada receiving some minor concessions, but America retained control of the Lynn Canal and continuous territory the entire length of the Panhandle. Although Roosevelt had behaved aggressively, he was sure that his cause was just. He did not want conflict with England. While he was quite aware that America was militarily secure—he was building an ever more powerful fleet to warn off would-be enemies—it was clear enough to him that friendship with Britain and the British navy would supply additional protection to the United States. After 1903 America and England became steadily more sympathetic toward each other, so much so that it was mistakenly suspected that they had signed a secret alliance well before the outbreak of World War I.

THE FAR EAST

Believing that America must play a major role in the affairs of the world, Roosevelt intervened far more actively in Far Eastern and European questions than had any other American President. He helped to bring to an end a great war in Asia, and he strove to prevent one in Europe. Although he was awarded the Nobel Peace Prize for his efforts, he himself was not sure afterward that he had achieved much in the Far East, at least so far as benefits to the United States were concerned. His intervention in the troubles of Europe was also of doubtful value, although it may have served to help postpone World War I. Whatever the results of his policies, he led America into arenas of international conflict on both continents.

American policy in China was formed in the time of McKinley by John Hay and was chiefly directed toward preserving and enhancing opportunities for American trade. It also called for the maintenance of the territorial and political integrity of the Manchu Empire, not so much for the sake of the Chinese as for the furtherance of trade with them. Seduced into seeking concessions from China, the United States did not really desire them, being interested only if China was to be partitioned among the Great Powers. Even should the partition occur, neither Hay nor Roosevelt keenly desired any concessions. It was decidedly otherwise with Russia and Japan, the most aggressive of the powers in the Far East early in the twentieth century. Firmly occupying Siberia and building a naval base at Vladivostok in the course of the preceding century, Russia had secured concessions in Manchuria, which was then attached to China. Because Vladivostok was icebound part of the year, Russia also wanted control of Port Arthur at the southern tip of Manchuria, and cast covetous eyes upon Korea.

THE RUSSO-JAPANESE WAR

The Russian ambitions directly clashed with those of Japan. Rather than be subjected to the demands of the Western powers, Japanese states-

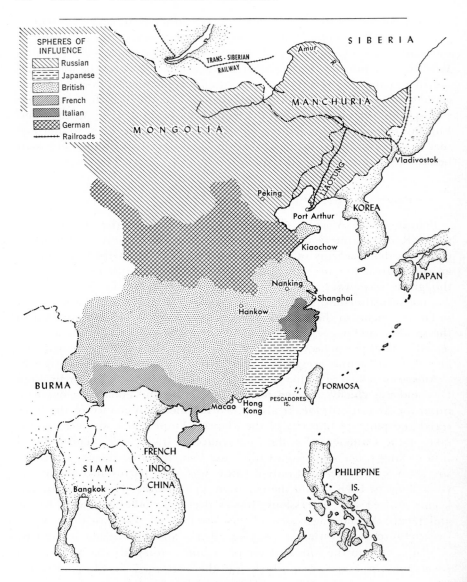

THE GREAT POWERS IN CHINA

men had successfully undertaken to westernize her economy, her army and navy, and even, to a degree, her political institutions. The parliamentary monarchy of Japan won a war with China in 1894 and 1895. In the Treaty of Shimonoseki that followed it, China was compelled to cede Formosa, the Pescadores Islands, and the Liaotung Peninsula, on which Port Arthur is located, to Japan. China was also forced to abandon a protectorate over Korea, to make easier Japanese penetration of the "hermit kingdom." Because Russia, Germany, and France insisted that Japan return the Liaotung Peninsula to China in return for a large increase in the indemnity that had also been exacted, the island monarchy was unable to keep Port Arthur at that time. However, Japan could and did move toward seizing control over Korea. Gaining strength at home and bolstered by their alliance with England of 1902, the Japanese determined that they must have Port Arthur, leased by China to Russia for twenty-five years in 1898. On February 8, 1904, the Japanese made a surprise attack upon Port Arthur, opening the Russo-Japanese War. They dealt effectively with the Russian war vessels in the Pacific, captured Port Arthur, and drove on northward into Manchuria. European Russia was connected with the scene of conflict only by the uncompleted one-track Trans-Siberian railroad, and it was difficult for Russia to bring her strength to bear. Moreover, the Tsarist regime was distressed for lack of money, and was threatened by a revolution at home. A desperate Russian attempt to retrieve victory from defeat failed. The Russian Baltic fleet was sent to Asian waters by way of the Suez Canal, but was destroyed by the Japanese in the battle of the Straits of Tsushima. The ministers of Tsar Nicholas II concluded that the war could not be effectively continued. The Japanese, almost exhausted and having little prospect of further military triumphs, also became willing to make peace. The negotiations were arranged by Roosevelt.

During the Russo-Japanese War the sympathies of the Americans, like those of the British, rested with the "little yellow men." Their love of fair play did not lead them to condemn the Japanese for making a surprise attack before declaring war. The empire of the Tsars was then unpopular in the United States because of its persecution of the Jews, against which America had several times protested. Moreover, it was conceived that Japan was the underdog, attacking the Russian colossus for good reason. The American public was hardly conscious that the war on land was fought on Chinese soil. Roosevelt also looked with favor upon the Japanese. Afterward, he even recalled, incorrectly, that he had warned Germany and France not to intervene on the side of Russia, for such a step would compel the United States to come to the support of Japan. Actually, he desired victory for the Japanese, but not one so decisive that Russia would be forced out of Manchuria. He preferred that some sort of balance of power continue between the two nations in the Far East. Such a balance, he believed, would best serve American trading interests in Manchuria in particular, and in China in general. Soon after the beginning of the war Roosevelt began efforts to persuade the combatants to bargain, urging them to pledge their allegiance to the principle of the Open Door policy.

Neither Russia nor Japan would subscribe to the Open Door, but exhaustion led them to accept his services as an intermediary. As a result, Japanese and Russian representatives met at Portsmouth, New Hampshire, in the summer of 1905 and signed a peace treaty. By its terms Russia recognized the "paramount" interest of Japan in Korea, and abandoned the lease on the Liaotung Peninsula to Japan, subject to the approval of China. Russia retained economic privileges in northern Manchuria. Japan also obtained the southern half of the Island of Sakhalin. Roosevelt was pleased by the outcome, although the Open Door in Manchuria was pretty well shut.

IMMIGRATION

The leaders of Japan were satisfied with the Treaty of Portsmouth, especially because, during the bargaining the United States conceded the Japanese right to take over Korea in return for a Japanese promise to do nothing that would imperil the American hold upon the Philippines. Japanese public opinion, however, became less friendly toward America, because Japan had failed to secure a hoped-for vast war indemnity. More serious as a cause for anti-American sentiment in Japan was the treatment given to Nipponese immigrants in California, Oregon, and Washington. After 1890 thousands of Japanese crossed the Pacific. Feeling in California rose high against them, and the governor of that state spoke out publicly of a Japanese "menace" as early as 1900. To prevent more serious trouble, the Japanese government promised in that year to grant no more passports to laborers seeking to enter the United States. However, they continued to come, using forged passports, also entering the Pacific coastal states by way of Hawaii, Canada, and Mexico. Talk of a Japanese "Yellow Peril" swelled, especially in California. In 1905 its legislature considered a bill to exclude all Orientals. The following year the school board of San Francisco placed the few Japanese, Chinese, and Korean children in the city in segregated schools; and in 1907 there were anti-Oriental riots all along the coast, extending even into British Columbia. Japan protested sharply against the action of the San Francisco school board. Condemning the discrimination of California against the Japanese, the President invited the school board to the White House and persuaded it to drop its segregation policy. Toward settling the larger problem, he sought more effective means to prevent the immigration of the Japanese. It was not possible to do this directly by a discriminatory law, for the Japanese government declared unacceptable any measure suggesting the inferiority of the Japanese to the other peoples of the world. At least, a discriminatory law could not be passed without causing serious offense in Tokyo. However, a solution was found by the so-called Gentlemen's Agreement of 1907, by which Japan and America promised to prevent unwanted immigration between the two countries.

Despite Roosevelt's efforts to soothe the Japanese, the "Yellow Peril" continued to receive stress in the United States, especially in the newspapers. Roosevelt himself became somewhat concerned and came to wish that America had not become committed to the defense of the Philippines. He expressed alarm, partly no doubt to persuade Congress to enlarge the navy. In the summer of 1907 he decided to send a fleet around the world to offer a demonstration of American power, despite heavy opposition in Congress. The fleet was welcomed in Japan. The advisers of the Japanese Emperor continued to act prudently. In 1908 Japan signed the Root-Takahira Agreement with the United States. Both parties promised to respect each other's territory and that of China, and also to respect the principle of the Open Door. It should be observed that the United States, in 1908 as in 1905, consented to Japanese control of Korea. After the beginning of the Russo-Japanese War, the Nipponese tightly gripped Korea, despite the opposition of Korean patriots such as Syngman Rhee. To be sure, it was impractical to do anything in behalf of Korea.

THE MOROCCAN CRISIS OF 1905

The fighting in Manchuria had not yet ended when Roosevelt became involved, even more deeply than he realized, in an attempt to secure a peaceful solution of the great European crisis of 1905. The immediate reason for the troubled state of European affairs was a quarrel over Morocco, a country which had earlier attracted Roosevelt's interest. In May, 1904, a Moroccan chief named Raisuli had kidnapped one Ion Perdicaris, who claimed to be an American citizen. Hay and Roosevelt responded energetically, demanding the release of Perdicaris, while American warships made their appearance at Tangier. Not quite sure that the captive was an American citizen, they nevertheless sent a cable to the American consul at Tangier, "Perdicaris alive or Raisuli dead." It was not necessary to send marines after the Moroccan chieftain.

The crisis of 1905 was a very different matter, one not susceptible to such a swift and simple solution. It arose from an effort by France to secure control of most of Morocco and to add it to her far-spreading African empire, an effort that had the approval of Britain and of Spain, for Spain had been promised a small slice of Morocco. The French would hardly have dared to try to assert sway over the bulk of Morocco, had they not been assured of English support, since the German Empire was almost certain to oppose the scheme. The support had been promised. France, badly defeated in the Franco-German War of 1870–1871, was thereafter on uneasy terms with Germany. There was hope in Paris of a successful war for revenge and for regaining the provinces of Alsace and Lorraine, taken from France at the end of the Franco-German War. In 1894 and 1895 France entered into a military alliance with Russia, to strengthen the position of both. However, France and Britain continued to be unfriendly until the early years of the twentieth century. Then, both fearing the rising power of Germany, they entered into the Entente Cordiale of April, 1904. By that agreement the French agreed to recognize the paramount interest of England in Egypt, and the English in return promised diplomatic support for French designs upon Morocco. By 1905 the French were bringing pressure upon Morocco, and their intent had become obvious. The advisers of Kaiser Wilhelm II persuaded him to land from a warship at Tangier and to make a speech warning that Germany was seriously displeased. Excitement mounted, and fear arose that a general European war would be the result.

Roosevelt helped, to a degree, to resolve the crisis. The Kaiser asked him to intervene because the United States had signed in 1880 a treaty at Madrid guaranteeing equality in trade with Morocco, establishing an Open Door there. Roosevelt consented, despite criticism at home, chiefly because he believed that a great European war must be prevented. He brought official pressure to bear in Paris. France, unable to rely on British military help and conscious of the weakness of Russia, then mired down by war with Japan and threatened by revolution, responded to his pressure. A conference of all the nations that had signed the Treaty of Madrid was called at Algeciras in Spain to consider the situation and to try to find a settlement, which was definitely a diplomatic victory for Germany. However, Roosevelt was pro-French, and pro-English as well. At the conference the American delegation steadily voted with the British and the French. By the Act of Algeciras, signed early in 1906, the integrity of Morocco was proclaimed, but France was given certain privileges that could be used to extend control over it. A war over Morocco was thus averted, but the settlement was a keen disappointment to Germany. Eight years later, when Europe was again threatened by a great war, another conference was proposed, but Germany refused to take part. Roosevelt's performance in the crisis of 1905 was not quite so brilliant as it seemed to his admirers at the time.

44 THE TRIUMPH OF PROGRESSIVISM

The tide of progressivism continued to rise after Roosevelt left the Presidency, and it won an impressive victory in the election of 1912. Believing that William Howard Taft would continue in the course he himself had charted, Roosevelt was largely responsible for the choice of Taft as President in 1908. Taft turned out to be an opponent rather than a disciple of progressivism. As chief executive he behaved as a moderate conservative. Roosevelt and Taft became bitter political enemies, and Roosevelt played a most important part in Taft's defeat at the polls when he sought reelection. However, the Democrat Woodrow Wilson, not Roosevelt, won the Presidency in 1912. In consequence, by one of those curious turns not uncommon in political affairs, Wilson and his party were given the opportunity to put the principles of progressivism into fuller effect.

There is little doubt that Roosevelt could have won another term in 1908, had he chosen to seek it, this despite his self-denying declaration four years earlier. The voters would hardly have held it against him that he had changed his mind. He felt bound by his statement, and he thought it unhealthy for the nation that he or anyone else should be President for eleven successive years. Convinced that the President must supply leadership, Roosevelt saw danger in a concentration of power, even in his own reliable hands, for too long a period. He was only 50 years of age in 1908; he possessed ample physical vigor, and would have enjoyed staying on in the executive mansion. Since he felt that he could not prudently and honorably do so, he searched about for a suitable successor. The ablest man in his official family was Elihu Root, but Root was not physically strong and was too conservative for Roosevelt's taste. Nor did any of the avowed progressives in his party have much appeal for him when he made his tentative choice, in 1906. It would seem that he misjudged Taft seriously when he made him his heir apparent, for Taft was not so much of a reformer as Roosevelt in 1906, and afterward lagged farther behind him. He liked Taft personally, and he failed to perceive that Taft, friendly and loyal as a Secretary of War, might behave differently as President.

ROOSEVELT PICKS HIS SUCCESSOR

Even had Roosevelt striven to secure the nomination by his party of an out-and-out progressive, such as Albert J. Beveridge, he might not have succeeded. Many of the members of the Republican national convention were under political obligation to Roosevelt, and it accepted Taft as its Presidential candidate with little resistance. Otherwise, dominated by more conservative elements, it made no great effort to please either Roosevelt or Taft. It named a conservative for the Vice-Presidency, and refused to insert some progressive planks in the party platform. It denied a special plea from Taft for a pledge to lower tariffs, but instead declared ambiguously for tariff revision. The only gestures made to please the progressives were statements in favor of conservation and anti-trust prosecutions. Progressives from the regions west of the Alleghenies were deeply disappointed with the platform, and they had their doubts about Taft.

Had the Democrats had a new and appealing candidate for the Presidency, the campaign that followed might have been a very uncomfortable one for the Republicans. As it was, the Democrats had little choice but to turn once more to Bryan, who was still popular in the South and the West. They forthrightly condemned monopolies; called for the revision of tariff rates downward until protection was destroyed; and proposed a measure that became extraordinarily popular a quarter of a century later, a federal guarantee of bank deposits. In the campaign Bryan urged that the great interstate railroads be nationalized, and asked the voters to support him on the ground that he, rather than Taft, would continue the policies of Roosevelt. He secured the endorsement of the American Federation of Labor, in part because he denounced the use of injunctions in struggles between capital and labor. Taft disliked politicking, campaigned half-heartedly, and aroused little enthusiasm; he too claimed to be the logical heir to Roosevelt. Bryan did not win the voters' confidence, and Roosevelt's campaigning in behalf of Taft was fruitful. Taft won rather easily, but by a much smaller margin than Roosevelt four years earlier. His popular vote was 7,679,006 to 6,409,106 for Bryan; his electoral majority was 321 to 162. Socialist Eugene V. Debs obtained 420,000 popular votes. Conservative Republicans had seemingly little reason to rejoice over the results of the election. Although their party retained control of both houses of Congress, the progressive Republicans and the Democrats made impressive gains. It was evident that both independent voting and the spirit of progressivism were gaining strength. Roosevelt, traveling to Africa to hunt big game after Taft's inauguration, was not dissatisfied. However, the conservative Republicans were happy to learn that Taft was largely their man and not a copy of Roosevelt. Roosevelt did not share their joy.

William Howard Taft, slightly older than Roosevelt, was born into a respected and well-to-do family in Ohio. Unlike Roosevelt, he was a superior scholar who graduated second in his class at Yale. After studying law in Cincinnati, he quickly entered upon a public career, interrupted only by service as a professor and dean in the Law School at the University of Cincinnati. Before he became Secretary of War under Roosevelt, he was an assistant prosecuting attorney, an internal revenue collector, a judge of the Superior Court of Ohio, Solicitor General of the United States, a judge on the Federal Circuit Court of Appeals, chairman of McKinley's Philippine Commission, and Governor of the Philippines. He had also been something of a "trouble shooter" for Roosevelt. He had never run for political office, and he would have preferred a place on the Supreme Court to the Presidency. He would later perform quite respectably as its Chief Justice. He was a large, fat man, weighing over 300 pounds and not fond of fighting. He was witty, good-humored, kindly, amiable, well-intentioned, and thoroughly honest. He was modest enough to believe that the election of Bryan in 1908 would not be fatal to the nation. Roosevelt, shifting rapidly toward the left during his second term, misread Taft when he assumed that his successor would of his own volition do likewise. Taft was not too seriously discontented with a world that had been comfortable enough for him; he did not yearn to be a master of men or of events; his circle of associates did not include progressives from the Midwest and the West; and he considered Gifford Pinchot to be a zealot. Moreover, Taft was never as friendly as Roosevelt toward labor, against which he had made use of the injunction in the courts. Besides, as a lawyer and a judge, he had great respect for principles from the past, and was temperamentally opposed to swift and great change. In the end, he quite logically came forth as a conservative, though a moderate one.

During his first weeks in office Taft did appear to be in the progressive camp. He announced that he favored a graduated inheritance tax, surely a potent weapon for reducing economic inequality. He also favored a postal savings bank system, much desired by the progressives because they disliked rich private bankers, and changes in tariffs so that they would give protection no more than equal to the difference between the cost of production in America and abroad. He urged enactment of other measures that had earlier been proposed by Roosevelt and opened an attack upon Speaker Joseph Cannon, trying to deprive Cannon of his dictatorial authority over the House of Representatives. In fact, continuing to seek this reform and that, and accepting others that he did not initiate, Taft might later have claimed that he had taken up Roosevelt's "Square Deal" and that he had done much more toward putting it into practice than had his predecessor.

Unfortunately for Taft, he quickly made serious political mistakes that could not be retrieved. He believed that his task was largely to lead in translating consensus of opinion in favor of reforms into law and practice. He made no effort toward establishing cordial relations with the progressives. Choosing for the bulk of his Cabinet corporation lawyers, men he thought most suitable for consolidating reforms generally approved, he failed to keep Roosevelt's friends in the highest places. He did not even ask Roosevelt for advice about the Cabinet. Disliking and distrusting Gifford Pinchot, he was soon involved in a bitter controversy with that loyal supporter of Roosevelt. Abandoning his campaign against Speaker Cannon in the hope of getting Cannon's help toward tariff revision, he further exasperated the progressives. Then, in curious fashion, after Nelson Aldrich and his allies had altered the tariff schedules to please themselves and not Taft, the President, having found Aldrich a congenial companion, came forth as a defender of a tariff law that was quite incompatible with the views he had earlier expressed. It may be doubted that Taft could in any event have pleased Roosevelt and his intimates; he might have gained the good will, or avoided the intense hostility of other progressive Republicans.

TAFT VERSUS THE PROGRESSIVES

Roosevelt had more than once considered an attack upon tariff protection, but had prudently refrained. Taft, since youth a believer in low rates, boldly or rashly called Congress into special session immediately after his inauguration, urging it to reduce the Dingley duties enacted in 1897. He promptly became enmeshed in difficulties, for Cannon and Aldrich refused to support him. Nor did Taft's withdrawal from his attempt to curtail Cannon's power persuade the Speaker to change his mind. Aldrich not only successfully insisted in the Senate that high duties be continued upon manufactured goods, but also convinced Taft that his approach toward the tariff was intelligent and sensible. Taft found much to like in Aldrich, and was converted by him, to a degree, into a protectionist. The President did secure some reductions, chiefly upon foreign products that competed with those of the Midwest and the South. In consequence, the Payne-Aldrich Act of 1909 substantially maintained the high level of protection given to Eastern industry by the Dingley law, but failed to do as much for the interests of the Midwest and the South. Both the progressive Republicans of the Mississippi Valley and of the West and the Democrats were exasperated. Taft made no effort to placate the progressive Republicans, for several of whom he entertained an increasing personal dislike. On a speaking tour that took him through the Midwest in the fall of the year he made evident his disapproval of several of them, refusing to appear with them before the public. Finally, and quite unnecessarily, he offered a thoroughgoing endorsement of the Payne-Aldrich law. At Winona, Minnesota he made a speech in which he described it as "the best tariff act" that had ever been passed. So he identified himself with Aldrich and appeared as an ardent champion of the protective tariff, considered by the progressives to be the "mother of trusts."

GRADUATED INCOME TAX

During the debates over the tariff Taft also clashed with the progressives over graduated income and inheritance taxes, the progressives pushing for both as means by which economic inequality might be reduced. The future importance of such levies was obvious to all; through them might well come the most stringent restrictions upon the American capitalistic system. Both were anathema to the conservative Republicans. Having committed himself to the graduated inheritance tax in his inaugural address, Taft was at first willing that such a measure be inserted in the Payne-Aldrich Act. However, the tax was set aside through the efforts of conservative Republicans in the Senate. Then Senator William E. Borah, Republican of Idaho, and Senator Joseph W. Bailey, Democrat of Texas, introduced a bill that would have imposed a graduated tax upon incomes over $5000 per annum. Since the measure was essentially similar to the levy found unconstitutional by the Supreme Court in 1895, it was certain, if enacted, to be challenged in the courts. Nevertheless, the progressives rallied in its behalf and accumulated enough votes to pass it. They could hope that the Supreme Court would reverse itself; if it did not, they would gain ammunition to be used against that body, which was already unpopular among them because the majority of the judges had displayed solicitude for property interests and hostility toward progressive economic regulation. Taft refused to bring pressure upon Congress to force the inheritance tax through, for he believed he should work with that body rather than try to lead it. He was averse to the income tax, and was convinced that it ought to be used only in wartime. He did not wish the Supreme Court to be embarrassed or assailed. Accordingly, he suggested a compromise calling for a tax on corporations engaged in interstate trade, together with the passage of a constitutional amendment placing Congress' power to levy an income tax beyond doubt. Since the progressives did not have votes enough to do what they wanted over his veto, they had to accept the bargain he offered. The imposition of the tax on incomes was thus delayed, and Taft was accused, not entirely without reason, of favoring the rich. Nevertheless, it should be observed that the President, having made an agreement, kept it in the spirit as well as in the letter, and that he personally urged members of the Ohio legislature to vote for the amendment, which was ratified as the Sixteenth to the Constitution in February, 1913, before Taft departed from the Presidency.

CONSERVATION

Far less important as a fundamental issue, but remarkably productive of public controversy and leading directly to a personal break between Taft and Roosevelt, was a bitter conflict waged by Gifford Pinchot and Taft over conservation policy. Not an enemy of the preservation of natural resources, Taft named as Secretary of the Interior Richard A. Ballinger of Seattle, whose views about conservation the new President considered "reasonable." Ballinger replaced Roosevelt's intimate friend, James R. Garfield. Perhaps Taft believed that the appointment of Ballinger would bring a softening of the strife between the champions of conservation and those in the West who sought to exploit its natural resources. Actually, Ballinger was committed to reducing the public domain rather than enlarging it. Soon after taking his post he denounced the wholesale withdrawal of water power sites that Garfield and Pinchot had executed, on the ground that they were suitable for ranger stations. He told Taft that the action was illegal, and that the sites ought to be returned to the public domain. Almost simultaneously Ballinger informed the President that the Bureau of Reclamation had far exceeded its authority, that it had committed funds to public works not authorized by Congress. The President, always deeply concerned for legality, accepted Ballinger's opinions and permitted the Secretary to transfer more than a million acres of land back to the public domain and to check spending for reclamation. Still head of the Bureau of Forestry, and almost fanatically devoted to the cause of conservation, Pinchot resented Ballinger's censure of his behavior. He learned from one Louis R. Glavis, an investigator in the General Land Office, that as its commissioner in 1907, Ballinger had improperly favored entrepreneurs seeking to secure control of coal fields in Alaska, among them J. P. Morgan and David Guggenheim. Pinchot accepted the charge made by Glavis as true and sent him to the President. It has not been shown that Ballinger was guilty of more than impropriety. Taft, thinking of Pinchot as "a radical and a crank," exonerated Ballinger, defended him as a friend of conservation, and ordered the discharge of Glavis. Pinchot then began to attack Ballinger both privately and publicly as an enemy of conservation, even supplying to popular magazines confidential anti-Ballinger documents from official files. Aware that dismissal of the forester was likely to arouse the wrath of Roosevelt, Taft nevertheless felt forced to put him out of office. A Congressional investigation of Ballinger disclosed no evidence that he had been guilty of fraud or corruption, and the committee making it praised the Secretary's conduct. Public opinion ran to the contrary, and Ballinger resigned, as he said, to reduce Taft's embarrassment. In his stead the President appointed Walter Fisher, a friend of Pinchot, who was unquestionably devoted to conservation. Moreover, Taft persuaded Congress to give him the power to reserve public lands that it had denied to Roosevelt. He and Fisher used that power, saving more lands for public use than had Roosevelt, Garfield, and Pinchot.

THE I.C.C.

Taft also quarreled with the progressives over increasing the authority of the Interstate Commerce Commission. The President desired further curbs on the railroads, but not enough to please the progressives. Early in 1910 Congress passed the Mann-Elkins Act, which gave the commission authority to change rail rates without waiting for a complaint, and also placed telegraph companies under its control. A new Commerce Court was created, through which appeals could be made against the decisions of the commission, but the rules laid down in connection with appeals made a reversal rather unlikely. Thus the commission was given massive authority which it never lost. Nevertheless, the progressives were dissatisfied because they had failed to get into the law a provision declaring that physical evaluation was to be the basis for setting rates. On the other hand, Taft was unhappy because they had successfully fought against some of his recommendations.

TAFT AND CANNON

Nor were the progressives pleased with the behavior of the President with respect to Speaker Cannon. After Taft abandoned his campaign to reduce the power of the Speaker, they went ahead without his help and finally brought Cannon down. Progressive Republicans led by George W. Norris of Nebraska made an alliance with the Democrats in the House of

Representatives. Possessing a majority in that body, in March, 1910, the combination sharply reduced the power of Cannon and of future Speakers as well. Cannon had very effectively used the House Committee on Rules to dominate the whole body. A bill could hardly reach the floor without the consent of that committee, and he had appointed its five members, of whom he was himself one. The committee was enlarged to fifteen, the Speaker was excluded from it, and the members were thenceforth chosen by the entire House. In effect, they were to be named in the future by party caucuses, each of the parties choosing members in proportion to its strength in the House. Later the power to name the members of other committees was similarly taken from the Speaker. These changes were widely acclaimed by the public, in the belief that "bossism" had been destroyed in the House of Representatives. Actually, both power and influence was distributed among the senior representatives, including the Speaker. Nevertheless, Cannon and the conservative Republicans who had supported him, resented their defeat and sought revenge. They urged Taft to withhold patronage from the "insurgent Republicans," and he did so.

THE SPLIT BETWEEN TAFT AND ROOSEVELT

Taft's concern lest Roosevelt join the progressive Republicans was well founded. Energetically hunting tigers and other big game in Africa, Roosevelt before long began to receive complaints against Taft. Pinchot hastened off to Europe to meet him immediately after his return from the jungle. Roosevelt listened sympathetically to Pinchot's tale of Taft's "desertion." Given his continuing desire to play a great role in the world, it could hardly have been otherwise. Having been lionized by the crowned heads of Europe, he returned home as restless and aggressive as ever. Rejecting Taft's efforts to justify himself, he refused for more than a year an invitation to visit the White House. He announced that he would undertake to reconcile the warring factions within his party, at the same time declaring anew his devotion to progressivism. In speeches at Denver and at Osawatomie, Kansas, in the late summer of 1910 he was militant, laying down the doctrines of the "New Nationalism." He urged a drastic remodeling of the American governmental system. Denouncing the federal courts for preventing effective action against economic injustice, he charged that they had created an area in which neither the nation nor the states had power. He held it against the federal judges not only that they had ruled the national income tax unconstitutional, but that by broad construction of the due process clauses of the Fifth and Fourteenth Amendments they had made it difficult to regulate hours of work, wages, and child labor. He urged that the authority of the federal tribunals, especially that of the Supreme Court, be limited, and that the capacities of Congress and

the President to govern be correspondingly augmented. The chief executive, he asserted, ought to be the "steward of the public welfare." Contending that property rights had been too much protected, he proclaimed that
the community ought to be able to regulate property "to whatever degree
the public welfare may require." To Taft the New Nationalism was completely detestable and he found it impossible to accept its author as a
mediator. Instead, finding socialistic "tendencies" in Roosevelt, the President attacked the progressives and Roosevelt ever more sharply. Many
progressive Republicans were already urging the nomination of Roosevelt
for the Presidency in 1912, to Taft's vexation. Nevertheless, the Rough
Rider declined for many months either to come forth as their leader, or
even to identify himself positively with them in their struggle with Taft.

Discovering that neither the progressives nor the regular Republicans
desired his services as a peacemaker, Roosevelt refrained from taking an
active part in the election of 1910. In alliance with the regulars, Taft
waged a furious battle against the party progressives, both at conventions
and in the primaries. The result was a long series of progressive victories
that made evident the unpopularity of Taft and the conservative Republicans. They were dealt further heavy blows when they faced the Democrats at the polls. Led by new and attractive men, the Democrats won a
majority in the House of Representatives, for the first time in 16 years.
Because only one-third of the Senate had to be chosen, they failed to secure
control of that body, which remained nominally in Republican hands.
There was little consolation for Taft in that fact, since progressive Republican senators actually held the balance of power and were as hostile
toward the President as were the Democrats. Nor could Taft find comfort by reflecting that he and his allies were firmly entrenched at the state
capitals. In several Eastern states progressive-minded Democrats won governorships, among them Woodrow Wilson of New Jersey, whose star was
rising rapidly.

Denied the leadership of Roosevelt, immediately after the election of
1910 many of the progressive Republicans determined nevertheless to try
to wrest the 1912 Republican nomination from Taft. Early in 1911 they
formed the National Progressive Republican League, and began to solicit
support for Senator Robert LaFollette. Many would have much preferred
to rally behind Roosevelt, but he insisted that he did not wish to oppose
Taft and refused to have anything to do with the League. He then believed
that Taft could not be prevented from securing the Republican nomination and also that he would be defeated by a Democrat. In June Roosevelt
announced that he would neither seek the leadership of his party nor endorse any other person for it. Then he changed his mind. Taft instigated
a suit under the Sherman Act against the United States Steel Corporation
in which it was charged, among other things, that the acquisition by that

company of the Tennessee Coal and Iron Company in 1907 proved that the giant corporation sought a monopoly. Severe criticism of Roosevelt was implicit in the charge, for Roosevelt, as Taft well knew, had approved the transaction as a measure to help relieve the panic of that year. Roosevelt recalled that Taft himself had been consulted and had not objected to it. As soon as the suit was announced, the furious Roosevelt let it be known that he could be persuaded to run against Taft. Progressive Republicans promptly began to work for him with enthusiasm. In February, 1912, Roosevelt declared that his hat was in the ring. Thereafter there were three contenders for the Republican nomination.

TAFT'S ACCOMPLISHMENTS

Rather strangely, the inevitable jockeying for advantage of parties, factions, and individuals in the election of 1912 did not prevent some solid accomplishments in the later years of Taft's term. Taft worked with liberal-minded men in both parties to carry through several minor social reforms, including a law firmly establishing the eight-hour day for federal workers that replaced an earlier one weakened by Supreme Court decisions. More important was the passage by Congress in May, 1912, of the Seventeenth Amendment, which provided for popular election of United States Senators and was ratified by the states in the following year. Even before its adoption no fewer than twenty-nine states followed the principle of popular choice, stipulating that their legislatures should choose the winner of a contest at the polls. Nevertheless, the passage of the amendment made sure that fewer millionaires would make their way into the Senate in the future. The measure probably did not raise the level of competence in that body, but it became far more responsive to public opinion. Taft neither advocated nor fought against the change, and of course his approval was not necessary.

Nevertheless, the President remained on bad terms with the progressives in both parties. In 1911 the territory of Arizona applied for admission as a state, offering a constitution calling for the use of the initiative, the referendum, and the recall. The recall was to be permitted with respect to judges as well as political officers. The constitution pleased the progressive Republicans and the Democrats, and they forced its approval by Congress. Taft, always a believer in a strong and independent judiciary, and opposed to swift action by mere majority vote, interposed his veto. Like many lawyers, he disapproved of election as a method of selecting judges. He believed it would be unwise to allow their recall in Arizona, for they would, in his view, be too much affected by the shifting tides of public opinion. In addition, he was much concerned because the federal judiciary was under heavy fire. His veto won for him only the increased hostility of his political enemies, who inveighed against him as a foe of democracy, a word that was becoming more popular than in the past. Arizona submitted a new constitution that omitted the provision for the recall of judges; it was sanctioned by the Congress and the President; and then Arizona, as a state, promptly inserted judicial recall in its basic document. Taft was not only attacked because of his stand, but was ultimately defeated on the specific issue.

At times during his Presidency the honest and often inept Taft must have felt that it was impossible to please anyone for very long. During his last three years in office, when he was frequently portrayed as a friend of privilege, he carried on a long campaign against the "trusts" that won acclaim neither from his conservative associates nor from his progressive critics. Sincerely believing in "trust-busting," he was responsible for more suits under the Sherman Act than Roosevelt had been. While the United States Steel Corporation survived an assault in the courts, other giant combinations were destroyed. The Department of Justice, under Taft, secured a decision from the Supreme Court which compelled the dissolution of the "tobacco trust" formed by James B. Duke. It had largely controlled both the manufacturing and the retailing of tobacco products throughout the nation. Under legal direction Duke dissolved it so as to restore competition. Also in 1911, a ruling was secured from the Supreme Court that forced the division of the Standard Oil Company into several geographical parts, these competing with each other to a degree. It cannot be denied that the prosecutions initiated by Taft not only reduced the size of corporate enterprises but stimulated competition. Yet the rulings of the Supreme Court exposed Taft, its defender, to criticism. In the Standard Oil Company and American Tobacco Company cases the Court announced that it would follow a "rule of reason," that it would not rule against all combinations restraining interstate trade, but only against those that did it unreasonably. The Court made the point that any such combination must interfere to some degree with the activities of competitors. There was much to be said for this view, and it did not vitally affect prosecution of the trusts. Nevertheless, the progressives cried that the "rule of reason" was another judicial usurpation of legislative power, with the President backing such behavior by the Court.

DOLLAR DIPLOMACY

Gaining few stout friends through his domestic policies, Taft failed to win laurels in foreign affairs as Roosevelt had. Following in the wake of Roosevelt, he exerted the influence of the United States to foster and protect American commerce and investments. He supported American investments in China and, more vigorously, in Latin America. Toward solving the financial troubles of Honduras and Nicaragua, both of which had failed to meet their obligations to European creditors, the Taft regime imposed upon them treaties placing their finances in American hands. The agreement with Nicaragua also would have given the United States the right to intervene in its affairs in whatever degree was necessary to preserve order and to prevent European intervention. The treaties were not endorsed by the Senate, but marines were sent to Nicaragua to maintain order. Taft also sent a contingent of them to the Dominican Republic for the same purpose. His so-called "dollar diplomacy" in the Caribbean world, sometimes condemned as calling for the use of both diplomatic pressure and the marines to make profits for American investors, was hardly new and was not utterly indefensible. Taft was not eager to intervene in Latin America. When the dictator Porfirio Díaz was overthrown in Mexico in 1910, Taft was urged by American investors in that country and by citizens endangered by the shooting of Mexican revolutionaries along the border to restore order in that troubled country. The President had approved of the Díaz regime, but he prudently refused to become embroiled in Mexico.

Taft was ardently devoted to peace, and he negotiated treaties with England and France in 1911 that called for arbitration even of disputes involving national honor and territory. They won public applause, but the Senate amended them to death. A trade reciprocity treaty made with Canada in the same year, also eagerly pushed by Taft, encountered no better fate. It provided for mutual lowering of tariffs, toward increasing Canadian-American trade. It would have opened Canadian markets to some American manufactured goods; on the other hand, it would have helped the Canadians to sell agricultural products in the United States. With the help of the Democrats, Taft managed to secure the approval of Congress. In the end, the agreement collapsed because of Canadian fears that American economic penetration of the Dominion would lead toward political union, desired by few Canadians. Those fears were enhanced by American expressions of opinion in favor of union—by an untimely declaration from Speaker of the House of Representatives Beauchamp (Champ) Clark that it must follow, and by another from Taft that Canada was "at the parting of the way." The Canadian Parliament refused its consent to the agreement. It had been strenuously opposed by the progressive Republicans of the Midwest, who did not fail to accuse the President of working to help Eastern manufacturers at the expense of Wisconsin and Iowa farmers.

THE ELECTION OF 1912

In the early months of the campaign year of 1912 there were three principal candidates for the Republican Presidential nomination, Taft, La-

Follette, and Roosevelt; then there were two, Taft and Roosevelt; and the less popular of the two won the prize. With Roosevelt's entrance into the race, LaFollette's chances for success swiftly faded. Beginning his career as an orthodox Republican, he had been converted to progressivism and had remodeled his native state of Wisconsin in accordance with its tenets. Able, determined, fond of his role as a tribune of the people, and sectional in his outlook, LaFollette was the leader of the progressive Republicans in the Midwest. He did not have the appeal of a Roosevelt, and many of his followers left him as soon as the former President entered the contest. When LaFollette collapsed while making a speech, thus raising doubt about his health, the flow of supporters to Roosevelt gained velocity. Roosevelt, with the backing of most of the progressives in his party, opened a furious attack upon Taft. He triumphed over the President in the Republican primaries, and he even won the delegates to the Republican national convention from Taft's own state of Ohio. It was apparent before it met at Chicago that he was more popular than Taft among the Republicans. Thanks to the manner in which Presidential candidates of the major parties are chosen, Taft was nevertheless named for the Presidency. A President controls the machinery of his party and can almost always compel his nomination for a second term. Delegates in the convention selected by the party workers stood by the President, and they were more numerous than those who clamored for Roosevelt. Many choices of delegates were contested between friends of Roosevelt and Taft. The dominant orthodox Republicans settled almost all of the contests in favor of the President, and Taft was then assured of an easy majority. He was nominated upon a platform calling for moderate reform.

One of the most dramatic events in American political history followed. The adherents of Roosevelt, utterly devoted to progressivism and convinced both that he had been cheated of the nomination and that they could expect little or nothing from Taft, were bitterly disappointed. Roosevelt himself was enraged. Many hundreds of his followers attended a second convention at Chicago, formed the Progressive Party, and named Roosevelt for the Presidency and Senator Hiram Johnson of California for the Vice-Presidency. Amidst wild enthusiasm the "Bull Moose" convention also gave an unqualified endorsement to the New Nationalism. As a platform the Progressives offered "A Contract with the People" calling for far-reaching reforms. Among them were preferential primaries for the Presidency; the direct election of United States senators; the initiative, referendum, and recall; the suffrage for women; prohibition of child labor; minimum wages for women; tariff revision; stringent regulation of Big Business; and the reversal of judicial decisions by legislative action. The crusading spirit of the Progressive convention was fully shared by Roosevelt, who quickly accepted its nomination.

With the Republicans so utterly divided and with public sentiment obviously shifting to the left, the Democrats could lose the election only through folly or extraordinary mischance. They made the most of their opportunity. Bryan could no longer be considered for the Presidency, as he himself admitted. A variety of new names was brought forward for the Democratic nomination, including those of Speaker Champ Clark of Missouri and Woodrow Wilson, Governor of New Jersey. In the national convention at Baltimore, Clark, supported by the officeholders of the party, and by William Randolph Hearst, was the leading contender. He even obtained a majority in the early balloting, but he could not secure the two-thirds vote then necessary for a choice by a Democratic convention. The friends of Wilson, Oscar W. Underwood of Alabama, and other seekers of the prize combined successfully to stop Clark. The delegates, among them Bryan, then turned toward Wilson. He was chosen, and the Democrats adopted a platform that called for reforms more impressive than those pledged by the Republicans, but less drastic than those urged by the Progressives.

The three-cornered contest between Taft, Roosevelt, and Wilson was actually a struggle between Roosevelt and Wilson, for Taft soon recognized that he had no chance to win and ceased to campaign. Roosevelt took the field with his customary vigor. He and his followers ringingly denounced economic privilege, political and judicial usurpation, and social inequities. So vehement was the language of Roosevelt that he almost seemed to be an Old Testament prophet. Wilson, much milder in manner, as befitted a former college professor, laid down the principles of a "New Freedom." Agreeing with Roosevelt that further reforms were badly needed, he stood forth as a moderate progressive. He agreed with Taft that business empires should be destroyed, and that it was unwise to expand the powers of the federal government more than was necessary for that purpose. He favored tariffs for revenue only and currency reform, as well as energetic action against concentration of economic power. Although his demeanor was conciliatory, some of the progressives of Republican heritage were inclined to believe that he was more likely to act than was Roosevelt. Roosevelt had only a hastily contrived party machine to help him, and the traditional Democrats were loyal as usual. Wilson received nearly 6,300,000 popular votes, Roosevelt more than 4,100,000, and Taft nearly 3,500,000. Socialist Eugene Debs received more than 900,000 popular votes. Wilson won an overwhelming victory in the electoral college, where the count was: Wilson, 435; Roosevelt, 88; Taft, 8. Taft carried only Vermont and Utah. Roosevelt, although he won only five states and a part of the electoral votes of California, had demonstrated both his own popularity and that of progressivism. The Democrats secured control of both houses of Congress. That the nation was moving to the left, and that the triumph of the

Democrats came from the split among the Republicans is evident. Wilson, winning by a plurality, obtained fewer ballots than had Bryan four years earlier; and the popular votes cast for Roosevelt and Taft together were fewer than Taft had received in 1908.

The election returns of 1912, seemingly indicating that thoroughgoing progressivism had been temporarily defeated, actually marked a victory for it. Its Republican leaders for several years were not given opportunity to play major roles toward putting it into effect, because of the party system. However, Wilson in office and carrying his party with him, more and more forcefully adhered to the ideals of progressivism and translated many of them into practice.

45 A NEWER FREEDOM

A SCHOLAR IN THE WHITE HOUSE

In American lore the worldly success of the progeny of clergymen has been so common that success seems almost as much assured to them as to children of the poorest of immigrants. One such was Thomas Woodrow Wilson, the son of a Presbyterian clergyman, born at Staunton, Virginia, in 1856. Wilson was of the Scotch-Irish stock that has supplied so many Presidents and that has been peculiarly addicted to education, formal and otherwise. Southern by birth and rearing, he attended Davidson College and, like so many other Southern Presbyterians, received his bachelor's degree at Princeton. After studying law at the University of Virginia and practicing it briefly in Atlanta, he forsook it for a career as a historian and political scientist. The South seemed to have little to offer a bright young man at the time. At The Johns Hopkins University he wrote a dissertation upon *Congressional Government* and received the degree of Doctor of Philosophy in 1885. Teaching briefly at Bryn Mawr and Wesleyan, Wilson secured a professorship at Princeton, made a reputation for himself as a scholar and a speaker, and served as President of the University from 1902 to 1910. He was imaginative and energetic, instilling vigor into that institution but in consequence he made enemies in the faculty, and campus life became uncomfortable for him. He left it when Roger Smith, Jr., the foremost Democratic "boss" in New Jersey, arranged for his nomination for the governorship in order to make the Democratic ticket look more respectable. Making it clear that he was not Smith's minion, Wilson campaigned as a reformer and was elected. As Governor he performed very well in a moderately progressive style, and so became a contender for the Presidency.

A lean, long-faced, almost handsome man, Wilson was much better fitted for a high station in public life than might be supposed from a casual inspection of his career. He was not a profound scholar, delving deeply into a small and seemingly esoteric area of learning, but a faithful student who read and wrote widely. His historical works were better than those of Theodore Roosevelt, but not very much better. He had learned about men and things from books, and he was truly a liberally educated man. A clear and able speaker, he could appeal effectively to reason, but he was also a maker of phrases that touched the emotions. An idealist, he was by no means ignorant of the ways of practical politics. As a minister's son, a professor, and a college president, he had plumbed the springs of human behavior. He had confidence in himself, and his will was resolute. When he came to the Presidency, he was much better fitted for it than had been most of his predecessors. He had his defects, among them an inability to perceive that an opponent might be partly right. Like Roosevelt, he was apt to ascribe sinister motives to those with whom he differed. He was reserved and imperious; he was to win many admirers, but he was to make and keep few friends.

After Taft left the Presidency and went on the Chautauqua circuit, where he was most successful and made some needed money, there was again energetic leadership in the White House. Unlike the modest Taft, who had sought to work with rather than to dominate Congress, but like Roosevelt and other "strong" Presidents, Wilson believed that the chief executive should play the principal role in the making of laws. In his doctoral dissertation he had found serious faults in the political system in Washington, especially in the division between the legislative and the executive branches so carefully made by the framers of the Constitution. Wilson would have preferred the English parliamentary system because of its concentration of power in the Prime Minister. However, as President he found many ways by which to assert his will, and Congress followed him during most of his period in office. A variety of laws of basic importance was enacted under his leadership. In some measure his success is explained by the fact that his wishes and those of the nation in general coincided. Even so, he supplied a driving force that went far toward translating desires and political opinions into laws and practices. He made the most of his power and influence as the head of the Democratic party, which had a majority in both Houses of Congress until 1917. He used the patronage potently, giving offices to Democrats long hungry for them, in return for support by their friends in Congress. He consulted and worked with influential men in the two legislative bodies. By means of the caucus the Democrats were mobilized when necessary. Wilson also made use of his ability as a speaker to influence Congress. Ever since the time of Jefferson, presidential messages to it had been put in writing; Wilson delivered them personally and persuasively. He further brought pressure upon the lawmakers by stimulating public opinion in favor of his proposals. Before the United States entered World War I the bulk of the progressive program had been achieved at the national level.

It has been well said, but not very accurately, that the English Prime Minister is *primus inter pares,* the first among equals, in his Cabinet. For all his admiration of the political order in England, Wilson did not conceive that the members of his Cabinet had anything approaching equality with him. They were his men, and they must work under his direction; he might or might not take their advice; and he sought counsel outside as well as within it. It had a Southern and Western flavor. The most conspicuous member of it, until he came to a parting of the ways with Wilson, was William Jennings Bryan, whom Wilson chose as Secretary of State in recognition of his standing in the Democratic party. The appointment was not popular among foreign diplomats stationed in Washington, if for no other reason than because Bryan was a prohibitionist and refused to serve liquor at public functions. He was intemperate with respect to food rather than alcohol. Perhaps the ablest man in the Cabinet was Secretary of the Treasury William G. McAdoo, who became Wilson's son-in-law. The man whose advice in foreign affairs carried most weight with Wilson, Colonel Edward M. House of Texas, was not a member. Until 1919, when their friendship collapsed, the President earnestly sought the opinion of House. Louis D. Brandeis, a distinguished lawyer and social philosopher, was Wilson's principal adviser on domestic questions during the campaign of 1912 and played an important part in the making of laws until he was appointed to the Supreme Court in 1916. In Congress Wilson had the help of many able men, including Senators Thomas J. Walsh of Montana and Robert L. Owen of Oklahoma, and Representative Carter Glass of Virginia.

WILSON AND THE NEW FREEDOM

Many progressives, both Democrats and Republicans, doubted that Wilson was one of themselves during the campaign of 1912 and for two or three years thereafter. When he spoke of ideals, he seemed to be one of the most thoroughgoing of progressives. Discussing specific questions, he was much less forthright. Many progressives were concerned because his thinking with respect to the bigness of business resembled that of Taft rather than that of Roosevelt. As a Democrat of Southern background, would he not be reluctant to use and expand the federal power? They were disappointed when he failed to put Brandeis in his Cabinet, and they feared that he would give too much heed to states' rights Democrats in Congress and out. They had reason to be concerned. Wilson was a latecomer to progressivism, having been quite conservative before his entrance into politics. His New Freedom was correctly construed to mean that he was averse to massive exercise of federal power. However, his goals altered during his first term, and his New Freedom ultimately had a close likeness to the New Nationalism. By 1916 Wilson was firmly committed to a vast exercise of federal authority in behalf of social justice. To one of the reforms urged by the New Nationalists, women's suffrage, he long refused to subscribe, bringing upon himself strenuous attacks by the female suffragettes. Nor did he agree with some ardent progressives who turned their guns against racial segregation; he not only permitted but defended the separation of whites and Negroes in federal offices. The status of the Negro in national service was lower when he left the Presidency than it had been when he entered it.

TARIFF AND TAXES

Among the many domestic measures for which Wilson was largely responsible was the Underwood-Simmons Law of 1913, which was extraordinary in two ways, for it both lowered tariffs substantially and made the graduated income tax a standard part of the federal revenue system. Despite Taft's sad experience in his attempt to revise tariffs, Wilson called a special session of Congress on inaugural day to reduce them. Going to Capitol Hill personally, he urged the lawmakers to act, both in a formal address and in private conferences with Democratic leaders. With the help and encouragement of the President, Oscar W. Underwood prepared and presented an unusual tariff bill to the House of Representatives. It contained no tricky rates, for all were based upon the value of the goods imported. It was honestly prepared to remove unnecessary protection that had been so long given to many American products. It was not a free trade measure. Iron and steel wares, agricultural machinery, clothing, shoes, sugar, wool, and other materials and goods were made duty-free. The rates were brought down from an average of more than 40 percent to one of 29 percent. The spirit of fairness with which the bill was drawn appears clearly in the provisions regarding sugar and wool, which inevitably aroused antagonism among the Democrats of Louisiana and of the Rocky Mountain states. Their votes were seemingly necessary to assure the passage of the bill, but Wilson and Underwood would not cater to their wishes.

Since the reduction of tariff rates would lead to a loss of revenue, perhaps as much as $100,000,000 per annum, advocates of the graduated income tax, led by Representative Cordell Hull of Tennessee, were able to add the tax to the bill. The Sixteenth Amendment having recently been added to the Constitution, there could no longer be any question regarding the power of Congress to levy the tax. The rates, contrasted with those that afterward prevailed, were very low. The bill introduced by Underwood fairly easily secured the approval of the House of Representatives, but was stiffly fought in the Senate. Democratic sugar and wool senators clamored against it, and progressives in both parties insisted that taxes on incomes be increased. Wilson exerted heavy pressure upon the Democratic senators who sought protection for the products of their states, demanding that they support the bill as a party measure, and threatening to withdraw patronage from them if they did not. His tactics were largely successful. He consented to raising the income tax. He countered the opposition of conservative Republicans and lobbyists with a sharp denunciation of "industrious and insidious" lobbyists. He denounced them as "great bodies of astute men" who sought "to create an artificial opinion and to overcome the interest of the public for their private profit." A Senate investigation that followed disclosed not only very extensive lobbying, but economic interests of various members of that body. In the end the Senate revised the Underwood Bill under the leadership of Furnifold Simmons of North Carolina, and came forth with one that delighted the President and became law in the autumn of 1913. The Underwood-Simmons Act reduced tariff rates to an average of 26 percent and imposed a tax of 1 percent on all incomes over $4000 per annum, together with surtaxes ranging from 1 percent to 6 percent on incomes larger than $20,000. An income of $500,000 was taxed at the rate of 7 percent.

THE FEDERAL RESERVE SYSTEM

Wilson had hardly won his battle for a "scientific" tariff when he became involved in a second bitter struggle, over currency and banking reform, that ended with the creation of the Federal Reserve System. It had long been apparent that the currency of the nation was seriously defective, not only because it was commonly insufficient for a growing country, but especially because it was inelastic. A second problem arose because control of credit was largely concentrated in New York City, and because it was often scanty where it was most needed. There was general agreement that Congress ought to face the problems, but little agreement regarding remedies. One was offered by the competent Monetary Commission—actually prepared by the able banker Paul M. Warburg—in 1912. His plan, warmly endorsed by the American Bankers Association, called for a powerful central bank, with branches in all parts of the nation. It was to be managed privately, issue currency upon its own authority, control in some part the reserves of member banks, and hold federal deposits. In essence, the plan urged the creation of a spiritual descendant of Alexander Hamilton's Bank of the United States. It contained very useful provisions, including a proposal that currency be based in part upon commercial notes held by the member banks. Wilson, before he took office, after consulting with Carter Glass and banking expert H. Parker Willis, gave it approval, except that he wished power in the system to be somewhat more diffused. However, a bill prepared by Glass and Willis encountered bitter opposition from progressive Democrats led by Bryan, who declared that it would surrender control both of banking and of currency to private interests. Threatened by a revolt in his party, Wilson, who apparently had not thoroughly studied either the problems or their proposed solutions, sought the advice of Louis D. Brandeis. The counsel of Brandeis was that the federal government must control both banking and currency. Wilson then took his stand substantially with Bryan and Brandeis. The result was the passage, over angry protests from the banking community, of the Glass-Owen, or Federal Reserve Act, in December, 1913. It established the Federal Reserve Board, its members nominated by the President, to supervise the operations of twelve Federal Reserve banks established in as many districts covering the nation. These district banks were to be run by men chosen by private banks that joined the system. National banks were required to become parts of it, and others were permitted to do so. Their reserves were held in part by the federal district banks. These were also authorized to issue currency supported by commercial paper. The founding of the Federal Reserve System was a great achievement. It assured a sound and elastic currency; made credit more available in those parts of the nation where it was needed; and neatly combined private control in the district banks with public authority over the whole system.

THE CLAYTON ANTI-TRUST ACT

In 1914 Wilson declined to go along with the advanced progressives on revision of federal policy regarding the trusts in much the same fashion that he refused to adopt their concept of a satisfactory Federal Reserve System. He was, however, largely responsible for the Clayton Anti-Trust Act of that year. A report to the House of Representatives in 1913 prepared by a committee under Arsène Pujot of Louisiana made it clear that consolidation in industry, commerce, and banking continued despite prosecutions under the Sherman Law. The Pujot Report laid stress upon the increasing control of railroads, insurance companies, public utilities, and industry by the great banking houses, especially those of New York. Among other evils it denounced interlocking directorates and the purchase of stock in competing companies as devices leading to monopoly and unhealthy concentration. The advanced progressives were disposed to deal harshly with the trusts, proposing such drastic regulation as a graduated tax upon corporations that would seize a large part of the earnings of the biggest ones. Wilson adopted a more moderate course, urging that the Sherman Law be revised so that it would become more effective, also so that labor unions would be protected against suits under it. In addition, he recommended the establishment of an agency to replace the Bureau of Corporations and to offer preventive medicine against monopoly.

In the fall of 1914 Congress substantially adopted Wilson's proposals, creating the Federal Trade Commission and passing the Clayton Anti-Trust Act. The new commission was a bipartisan body of five members. It was given authority to investigate the behavior of corporations, except for banks and others regulated by the Interstate Commerce Commission. Subject to review by the federal courts, it was empowered to issue orders preventing unfair business practices. Thus it became possible to issue warnings and to secure the cessation of such practices without resorting to the more drastic step of prosecution under the Sherman and Clayton Laws. Supplementing and strengthening the Sherman Act, the Clayton measure declared illegal interlocking directorates in industrial combinations capitalized at $1,000,000 or more; acquisition of stock in competitive companies to reduce competition; contracts demanding that a purchaser refrain from buying the products of a competitor; and price discriminations tending to create a monopoly. Officers of corporations were made personally responsible for their behavior. To protect both labor unions and agricultural societies, the law declared that "the labor of a human being is not a commodity or article of commerce," and that such groups were not to "be held or construed to be illegal combinations in restraint of trade under the antitrust laws." It also forbade the use of the injunction in labor disputes except to prevent irreparable injury to property; provided for trial by jury in cases where it was charged that an injunction had been violated; and declared that strikes, peaceful picketing, and boycotts were legal, so far as the federal government was concerned. With good reason organized labor hailed these provisions as its "Magna Carta," although they did not go so far as Samuel Gompers and other leaders had hoped. It should be observed that use of the injunction as a weapon against labor was actually not very seriously limited, since the court issuing it would decide whether or not there was danger of irreparable damage to property. Judges hostile to labor were to find quite frequently that the danger existed. Even so, the Clayton Act was a great landmark, for it gave to labor a special protection that had hitherto been denied. Something was achieved toward establishing a balance between labor and corporative power.

Two other measures passed by Congress and approved by Wilson during his first two years in office deserve mention, especially because they foreshadowed the future. One of these was the LaFollette Seamen's Act, by which sailors in the merchant marine received long-sought help against exploitation. Provision for their safety on American shipping was required, and contracts by which employers held sailors almost in bondage during long voyages were outlawed. The Smith-Lever Act had nothing to do with the sea. It provided for agricultural extension work to be carried on through the landgrant colleges, with the federal government matching sums supplied by the states for the purpose. The Seamen's Act was inspired by compassion. The principle of matching, used importantly for the first time in the Smith-Lever Act, was to come into common use as a means by which the national government would persuade or compel the states to adopt its educational and social policies.

WILSON THE PROGRESSIVE

In 1914, the tide of progressivism seemed more likely to drop than to rise. The approach and the beginning of World War I in Europe were accompanied by an economic downturn that affected the United States as well as the rest of the world. The depression, which was to vanish as soon as the Allies began to order vast quantities of foodstuffs and war material, was said by business interests to be the result of wanton attacks upon them. Wilson was embarrassed, and he may have become more cautious as a result. He sought to make friends with potent bankers, inviting them to visit him at the White House. The election of that year also seemingly dealt a blow to progressivism, for the followers of Wilson and Roosevelt did not fare well, although the Democrats retained narrow majorities in both Houses of Congress. In 1915 little was done toward internal reform, only in part because the President and the nation were preoccupied with foreign affairs. Then Wilson, and with him the Congress, changed course and enacted a series of far-reaching measures. In 1916 Wilson appeared as a thoroughgoing progressive. It is to be suspected that his shift to the left was made in part as a means toward securing reelection; doubtless his sympathies and his views had also altered as he became more familiar with the problems of the nation.

Wilson the aggressive progressive came forth positively in 1916 when he named for the Supreme Court Louis D. Brandeis, whose name was detested in conservative quarters. There was no doubt about his ability, but he was known as such an arch-reformer that Wilson had not quite dared to appoint him to his Cabinet in 1913. Three years later, despite heavy opposition, he successfully exerted pressure upon the Senate to secure its approval of Brandeis for the high court. As expected, on the bench Brandeis steadily and ardently defended progressive laws against charges that they violated the Constitution, and his opinions became famous for their sociological content. Recognizing that the Supreme Court makes law, Brandeis insisted upon supplying vast quantities of information to obtain the kind of law he desired. His influence as a judge was increased because he was commonly in agreement with his distinguished colleague Oliver Wendell Holmes, Jr., who had no love for disquisitions, sociology, or statistics. Except when defending personal rights, Holmes was reluctant to strike down laws made by elected lawmakers.

Beginning in the summer of 1916 and continuing until February of the following year, Wilson and the progressives carried through a series of measures of benefit to the farmers and labor, and changed federal taxes so that the burden of them was shifted toward the more prosperous. The farmers, who had found it difficult to borrow money except at high interest rates, received assistance through the Farm Loan Act. It set up a Farm Loan Bank in each of twelve districts under the direction of a national board. Farmers who belonged to cooperative associations that had membership in the banks could borrow money from them on mortgage for as long as forty years at interest rates lower than were ordinarily available. The farmers were also helped by the Warehouse Act, which made it possible for them to borrow money upon grain, cotton, tobacco, wool, and other products stored in warehouses; thus they could wait for more favorable opportunity to sell their crops. Both they and labor were benefited by the Smith-Hughes law, by which the federal government undertook to match expenditures by the states for instruction in farming, domestic science, and the trades.

Labor was also especially favored by the Adamson Act. When a railway strike was threatened in 1916, the President intervened to prevent a general stop in transportation that the nation could ill afford at the time of World War I emergency. The railway brotherhoods wanted an eight-hour day, with pay for overtime. The railroad presidents rejected the demand. Both they and the leaders of the unions refused to make concessions at a conference presided over by Wilson in the White House, despite an appeal from him that they do so for the safety and welfare of the nation. Concluding that the eight-hour day was proper, Wilson then asked both sides to approve it; wages for overtime could be determined later. The union leaders agreed to accept his compromise, but a group of railway presidents would not. Furious, Wilson said to the group, "I pray God to forgive you, I never can." After a call for a strike had been issued, Wilson swiftly obtained the passage of the Adamson Act, which imposed the eight-hour day upon railroads engaged in interstate commerce after January 1, 1917, and provided for a commission to study the wage problem.

Wilson was also personally responsible for the passage of the Keating-

Owen law, an attempt to strike at child labor, a problem that the states had failed to solve. The law forbade the shipment in interstate commerce of goods or products manufactured or mined by exploited children. Wilson drove it through despite strong opposition in his own party—from farmers who feared that they would lose the help of their children, from many who felt that the measure threatened parental control, and from businessmen who saw the law as an entering wedge for all sorts of regulation through the exercise of federal power over interstate commerce. Challenged in the courts, the Keating-Owen Act was declared unconstitutional by the Supreme Court in the case of *Hammer* v. *Dagenhart* in 1918, on the ground that its purpose was to regulate child labor rather than interstate commerce. In 1919, it may be added, Congress again tried to strike at the exploitation of child labor, imposing a tax of 10 percent upon the profits of the exploiters. The Supreme Court, in the case of *Bailey* v. *Drexel Furniture Company* in 1922, ruled that the tax was also unconstitutional because the intent of it was not to collect revenue, but to legislate in an area reserved to the states. Effective federal action against child labor was postponed until the Great Depression. Boys continued to work in Northern coal mines and girls in Southern cotton mills.

One very important measure favored by labor and most of the progressives Wilson refused to approve, but it was passed over his veto. By 1915 sentiment for curbing European immigration had become powerful, being shared with organized labor by anti-Catholic and anti-Jewish elements, sociologists, social workers, and others who feared that American institutions were strained by continuing massive additions of ignorant and illiterate people to the body politic. Many would have liked to put a stop to the "New Immigration" entirely; others favored its restriction. Early in 1915 Wilson vetoed the Burnett Bill, because it barred the entry of illiterates. He pointed out that the purpose of the requirement was not to select from among immigrants so as to secure superior people, but to lessen their number. In the campaign of 1912 he had promised to "fellow-citizens of foreign extraction" that he would not discriminate against the would-be Americans from southern and eastern Europe. He kept his word, and he again vetoed the bill in January, 1917. It became law nevertheless, for Congress then enacted it over his veto. It was evident that a demand for further restrictions would soon come.

TAX REFORM, 1916

The most momentous of all the reforms of 1916 was contained in the revenue act of that year. It set up a Tariff Commission, an independent body that was intended to study tariff rates and to supply objective reports that would enable Congress to raise and lower rates as needed to foster fair competition. Of far greater consequence were the taxes it imposed in order to pay for a national defense program adopted to meet the dangers arising from World War I. Its cost was about $250,000,000 per annum. Who should bear the burden of it? Levies upon individual and corporate income after 1913 brought into the Treasury little more than one-tenth of its tax receipts, the bulk of which came from import and excise duties. It was apparent that persons with large incomes were still paying a relatively small part of the costs of the federal government. The progressives insisted that they must shoulder a larger share of the burden. Driven on by Senators George W. Norris and Robert LaFollette, Congress was even more determined to "soak the rich" than were the President and Secretary of the Treasury McAdoo. The basic tax on income was raised to 4 percent; the surtax on incomes over $20,000 was increased so that the maximum rate was 15 percent; a levy was placed on corporation surplus and undivided profits; the gross receipts of munitions industries were taxed at the rate of 12½ percent; and a hitherto light tax upon inheritances was sharply increased so that a rate of 10 percent was imposed on very large estates. Essentially the progressives did what the English Liberals had done a few years earlier under the leadership of Herbert Asquith and David Lloyd George. The future would bring much greater shifting of the load of taxation in America.

With the entrance of the United States into World War I the progressive movement was interrupted. The energies of the nation were directed toward the battlefield, and political democracy was to a degree a temporary sacrifice. Nevertheless, the idealism that arose from the war hastened the coming of two massive reforms, the one not remarkably a measure of the progressives, the other favored by most of them, national prohibition and universal female suffrage.

PROHIBITION

Prohibition, even on the state level, made little headway before the opening of the twentieth century, despite the obvious evils of alcoholism. There were in 1900 only five "dry" states, with others offering local option. Thereafter, however, "John Barleycorn" suffered blow after blow, many of them being directed at him by the Anti-Saloon League. By 1916 no fewer than 19 states were no longer alcoholically wet, and elections under local option had put an end to the legal sale of liquor in hundreds of cities and counties in other states. Wartime fervor enabled the Anti-Saloon League, the Protestant clergy, and women to do "John Barleycorn" to death—at least according to law. It permitted Assistant Secretary of the Navy Franklin D. Roosevelt, supported by the Secretary, Josephus Daniels, to bar liquor from American warships, toward more accurate aiming of

6-inch and 16-inch guns. Moreover, Congress adopted national prohibition before the close of 1917 for the duration of the military emergency, to save calories, and also passed the Eighteenth Amendment, which forbade the manufacture, sale, and transport of alcoholic liquors. The Amendment was ratified early in 1919, before the soldiers reached home from France, as its enemies did not fail to point out. In the same year the Volstead Act for its enforcement became law. It should be observed that the Amendment was remarkable in two ways. It is strange that an intemperate attempt should have been made entirely to deprive tens of millions of people of the solace of alcohol. It is also noteworthy that the Amendment did not give Congress power to deal with the liquor problem, but placed prohibition in the Constitution itself, thus making repeal impossible except by the adoption of another amendment. Wayne Wheeler, lobbyist for the Anti-Saloon League, and other dry champions hoped that the friends of alcohol would never be able to muster the votes of three-fourths of the states for repeal. He and they miscalculated. It would have been more prudent and more consistent with the practices of good government to invest Congress with authority to limit the making, transport, and use of alcohol as time, the wishes of the public, and wisdom should indicate.

WOMEN'S SUFFRAGE

Women's suffrage attained more enduring success in much the same fashion as prohibition. The ranchers and farmers of the territory of Wyoming gave women the vote as early as 1869, but only four states had followed the example of the manly Westerners before the turn of the century. Men and some women felt that political questions were too complex and too much entwined with inevitable corruption for innocent and sheltered females. After 1900 the ladies were admitted to the polling places in several additional states. As Theodore Roosevelt had in 1912, Charles Evans Hughes urged women's suffrage in 1916. Wilson was personally opposed to it, although the Democratic platform of 1916 recommended that the states take action toward giving women the ballot. In 1918, however, when they had replaced men in factories and had otherwise shown that they could be much more than mere housewives, Wilson appeared before Congress and pleaded for their enfranchisement. When the legislators hesitated, suffragettes paraded and went on hunger strikes in Washington. The Nineteenth Amendment, declaring that the right of American citizens was to be neither "denied or abridged" by the United States or any state "on account of sex," was approved by Congress in 1919 and by the states in 1920. It was hoped that female suffrage would serve as a cleansing force in politics. It did double the size of the popular vote. The day when women would serve in large numbers in legislatures was still distant, and various legal and economic discriminations against them continued. They retained the weapons with which they had exerted profound influence over men since time beyond memory.

Submerged in the crisis of World War I, and in a postwar reaction, progressivism reappeared in new guises. The progressives might call themselves liberal Democrats or Progressive Republicans, but their goal continued to be a democratic society in which a regulated capitalism was basic. Among the heirs of the progressives of the first two decades of the twentieth century was Franklin D. Roosevelt, with his "New Deal," to be followed by Harry S Truman with his "Fair Deal."

46 AMERICAN LIFE BEFORE 1918

Although the Americans early in the twentieth century became increasingly conscious of frailty in their body political and social, although they learned more about troubles in other lands, and although they became vaguely aware that they were no longer totally secure between the oceans, relatively few of them felt weighed down by fundamental anxieties about the future. Some intellectuals, such as the brothers Henry and Brooks Adams, saw a darkening scene and were doomstruck. But they were exceptions and their pessimism was not fully shared even by the poverty-stricken, who were not commonly given to despair. Belief continued that American natural resources were either inexhaustible or replaceable. The lowly could reasonably hope to secure a larger part of the dividends of American prosperity, and if such hope faltered they could console themselves with the thought that they were richer than the poor of other countries. The discontents of the Americans remained relatively minor, and few Americans fancied that there was need for social revolution. Only the most heated partisans felt that the issues in politics were matters of life and death. Political questions were not actually of the black-or-white and now-or-never variety, but of the more-or-less and sooner-or-later sort. There was commotion enough as the nation moved from laissez-faire to a regulated capitalism, but the transition had not proceeded far at the time of America's entrance into World War I. The American economy was still largely free; government was not very expensive in terms of the national income; individual incomes and inheritances were lightly taxed if they were taxed at all; and national and state debts were not oppressive burdens. Even World War I, shocking as it was, did not convince most Americans that there were fundamental flaws in their special world.

MATERIAL ADVANCES

Life remained physically good for the mass of the Americans, better in comparison with life for other peoples than they realized. The economic troubles of the last decade of the nineteenth century diminished in the early years of the twentieth. Life was increasingly comfortable and it would later become even more so, as the products of a burgeoning industry were more widely distributed. Not usually in want of food, shelter, or educational opportunities, the Americans did not suffer much, either materially or mentally. The farmer strolling through his quiet pasture on a Sunday afternoon in August could contentedly consider the approaching harvest and the market for it; the worker at a factory bench was not constantly concerned lest he be laid off; the man who sold furniture and doubled as an undertaker was likely to profit from both of his occupations; the smaller industrialist might reasonably hope to become a bigger one. If worldly hopes did not prosper, it was consoling that the children, healthier and better educated than their parents, would very likely do better.

Material advance was everywhere evident, but especially in the towns and cities. Urban homes were much more comfortable than they had ever been. The coal stove had replaced the hearth fire as a means of heating long before 1900; after the turn of the century the hot-air furnace began to supersede the stove and every room in a house could be warmed. This luxury was matched in lighting. In the nineteenth century the whale oil and kerosene lamp were substituted for candlelight, the latter being more and more reserved for romantic social occasions. In the twentieth century gaslight was substituted for the kerosene lamp, then electric lights for gas. The cast-iron cookstove in the kitchen was replaced by a more efficient one using gas or electricity. The children's Saturday night weekly bath in a washtub became for middle-class Americans three or four baths in a bathtub each week, a change not entirely pleasing to adolescents. The telephone—10,000,000 of them were in use by 1915, some of them too constantly—was becoming a standard fixture. Over-stuffed furniture, comfortable if not always esthetically pleasing, made its appearance. Chlorinated municipal water robbed the family well of its importance and of its opportunity to spread disease. The family outhouse, which had often been placed near the well, moved indoors and assumed a more luxurious guise.

HOUSING

The interior of the American home of that era was hardly distinguished for beauty but it was likely to be snug. The prints to be found on its walls were almost invariably commonplace; Mr. Thomas Edison's talking machine was threatening to usurp the place of the piano; and the family library consisted of little more than the Bible, used schoolbooks, a volume or two offering medical advice, and a few cheaply printed novels. However, the public library made books available as they had never been before, and magazines were purchased freely. If art and classical music did not receive the attention they deserved, it cannot be said that American intellectual pursuits were confined solely to the classroom.

If charm and beauty were ordinarily lacking in the American home, its occupants were better sheltered from the caprices of nature than were families of similar social strata in other countries. To be sure, not all the Americans were well housed. In New York City tens of thousands lived in sunless tenements, notoriously on the East Side; on the Bowery, once the fruitful farm of Peter Stuyvesant, sojourned men who were utterly broken and who subsisted upon charity and their powers of endurance. In the slums and near-slums crime flourished; even so, many an Irish immigrant and many a Jew from the western borderlands of Russia rose from it to fame and fortune. On the land, especially in the South, were shacks and cabins that were as bare within as they were ugly without. Nor were villages and towns lacking in barren and cheerless homes; those of the workers in company towns were often monotonously alike and ugly. The bungalow, then becoming popular, was not a thing of beauty—the Americans were only comparatively well housed.

When in 1911 Katherine Lee Bates published her "America the Beautiful," she could fittingly sing of "the spacious skies" of Nebraska, "the amber waves of grain" of Kansas, and "the majesty of purple mountains" in North Carolina and Arizona. But her hymn could not glorify the structures placed by man on the landscapes that she extolled. One might still find distinction and charm in the clapboard houses of quiet New England villages; here and there in the South were to be found Georgian mansions that possessed both dignity and grace; mercantile buildings were occasionally both handsome and stylistically consistent; and the skyscraper soaring toward the heavens in New York City and Chicago was more than proof that space had become expensive in metropolitan America. Seen from its harbor or the adjacent heights of Long Island, the turreted magnificence of New York City was even then extraordinarily impressive. Many a college town was gracious to the senses. State capitols and city libraries were often stately and comely, even if copied from European structures. Not every railroad station was drab, despite the demands of function and billowing smoke from engines; the Pennsylvania and Grand Central Stations in New York City were handsome and imposing. Even so, middle-class American homes were usually nondescript in external style, and not distinguished for symmetry, elegance, or pleasing simplicity. The standard American house was a two-story box. Public and commercial buildings were often as lacking in refinement as were the ugly factories. Peculiarly offensive were false fronts that supposedly made buildings seem taller than they were but that deceived no one. Let it not be argued that the uncomfortable, quaint cottage of the European tenant was to be preferred to the plain American bungalow.

TRANSPORTATION

Whatever were the faults of American buildings, travel had become relatively easy. Well before 1900 the steamboat, and more especially the railroad, had made long journeys swift, and even delightful. In the early part of the century train service between cities was frequent, safe, and restful. For those who could afford it, Pullman berths and bedrooms were available. Those who could not afford such luxuries might sit up all night in coaches and slumber only fitfully, but they could eat as palatable meals in a dining car as those they had at home. In all cities the electric trolley car was becoming standard. New York and Boston had the doubtful boon of the subway, and both New York and Chicago benefited even more dubiously from the elevated train. For a time "suburban" electric cars threatened to replace those propelled by steam. Far more dangerous competitors for the railroads were beginning to appear; eventually they would deprive the railroads of much of their traffic in people, and part of it in goods. The bicycle, even the two-seated variety, common as it had become, was a serious rival neither to the street railway nor the railroad, since it was largely used for pleasure. But those who made and repaired bicycles and wagons, were turning, with increasing success, to the production of automobiles. The nation was beginning slowly to "get out of the mud" by means of gravel, brick, macadam, and cement roads. The airplane had just begun to fly.

Just when the automobile was "invented" it is difficult to say. A vehicle that moved by its own steam power without using tracks was actually made in the eighteenth century. As early as 1877 George B. Selden, a New York state engineer and patent lawyer, designed a "horseless carriage," to be propelled by a gasoline engine. However, the early development of the automobile, generally considered in America to be a peculiarly American product, took place chiefly in Europe, and especially in France. At the opening of the twentieth century there were more motor cars in England than there were in the United States. In 1897 a French automobile in a race from Paris to Dieppe reached an amazing average speed of 25 miles an hour. Following the European car makers, the American ones became both very active and successful in the 1890s. The body of the car seemed to present no great difficulty, for carriages and wagons served as models—at least one early automobile had a whip receptacle. Nor were tires a fundamental problem, for rubbor ones were already in use on bicycles. How to secure power and transmit it to the wheels offered a greater challenge to ingenuity. Several methods were tried. For a time the Stanley Steamer and automobiles driven by electric batteries competed more or less successfully with those propelled by internal combustion gasoline engines. But the latter gained an easy superiority over the Steamer because of its lighter weight and its lighter fuel, and over the electric vehicle with a battery requiring frequent charging. Before the end of the century Charles E. Duryea, Henry Ford, Ranson E. Olds, and Elwood Haynes had constructed automobiles that moved with some consistency under expert direction.

At first the automobile was a "one-lunger," the property of a mechanic or of a wealthy man who fancied himself as a mechanic. Then, in the early years of the twentieth century, the automobile was swiftly improved, and fairly reliable 4-, 6-, and 8-cylinder engines made their appearance. It was sufficiently developed so that a man and even an occasional woman might reach the doubtful conclusion that it was safe to drive one. Also came mass production, of which Olds was the pioneer and Ford the master. Automobiles were at first far too expensive to be owned by any but the wealthy. Mass production, based upon the principle of interchangeable parts, brought down the price, and after 1908 Ford's cheap car for the masses, his famous Model T, succeeded brilliantly. Ford made more than a quarter-million of chugging, funereal black, simple, and reliable automobiles during 1914. In the following year more than 2,500,000 cars were registered. It was then evident that the day of the horse was passing; already the car was being used for journeys that would earlier have been made by train; and the automotive truck was soon to be widely used. That the average man or woman was truly qualified to drive automobiles remained rather doubtful, for the gruesome slaughter on American streets and highways had begun. In 1945, at the close of World War II, despite its heavy casualties, it was estimated that automobiles and trucks had been responsible for far more deaths and injuries than all of America's wars combined.

The coming of the automobile brought with it a revolution no less impressive than that which resulted from the building of the railroads, and an even vaster one began while the automobile industry was still in its infancy. In December, 1903, at Kitty Hawk on the seacoast of North Carolina, a former bicycle mechanic named Orville Wright took off from the ground in an airplane, flew it for twelve seconds, and landed it safely. For many centuries man had imagined himself flying through the air, and Wright was by no means the first person to move through the atmosphere under power. Immediately after the War of Independence a Frenchman had gone into the air and returned in a balloon; and another one had managed to push a balloon through air by means of a motor as early as 1851. In 1900 the German Count Zeppelin made the first of the airships known by his name, one that could be steered and otherwise controlled with some assurance. Other inventors had created craft with wings or vanes and motors that flew briefly without a pilot. However, the lighter-than-air ships of Zeppelin and his successors never became sufficiently safe and manageable to rival the heavier-than-air craft constructed by Orville Wright and his brother Wilbur, and by other inventors. Until the Wright brothers made their first flights—Wilbur flew for nine seconds the day after Orville had completed his flight—and for some years thereafter, it was generally believed that a vehicle weighing more than the atmosphere could not remain aloft more than very briefly. The law of gravity was cited, as well as failures of airplanes before and after the Kitty Hawk flights. Before the Wright brothers' success, an airplane made by Samuel Langley had been sent into the air near the Potomac River and had dived into it. The fact that Langley's machine had moved from the ground attracted little attention; that it had fallen into the water aroused laughter. It was suggested that Langley should leave flying to the angels, and that he ought to turn his efforts toward constructing a better submarine. Not eager to be the butt of misplaced public humor, the Wright brothers quietly continued their experiments until 1908, when they were able to exhibit an unquestionably successful airplane. The following year Louis Bleriot flew from France across the English Channel. At the beginning of World War I men were already conceiving of trans-Atlantic flight.

The automobile was to shrink nations; the airplane would contract both nations and the globe. It inevitably became a military device, and was used as such in World War I, although it was far less important than it would be in World War II. In the "dogfighting" on the Western Front pilots fired pistols and threw wrenches at each other until the machine gun firing between propeller blades was perfected. The Germans employed both Zeppelins and airplanes to bomb England, and the English late in the war dropped bombs on German cities. In the main airplanes were used for scouting, strafing, and bombing over the battle lines in France. The Germans were generally superior in the air, but their power there was not great enough to achieve a decisive result.

ENTERTAINMENT

The shape of things to come was also being discerned by the farsighted in the motion pictures that became a basic part of American civilization before the end of World War I. Before 1900 theaters offered plays, musical comedy, and vaudeville. Animated picture films were not thrown on the screen commercially until 1894. A decade later movie theaters and halls were playing to throngs and by 1908 it was estimated that they offered amusement daily to between two and three million persons. The early movies were crude and in no way comparable to the plays and musical shows available in the large cities. They had little in common with "The Merry Widow" of Franz Lehar, played on the New York stage in 1907, or "The Chocolate Soldier" of Oscar Strauss, offered two years later. Nor was their quality up to that of Victor Herbert's "Babes in Toyland" or "The Red Mill." The first movies were often shown in a vacant store or hall at an admission price of five cents. Photographic skill and technical knowledge did not, as they afterward did, compensate for lack of content. On the other hand, the early movies had a wondrous novelty. After 1905 studios appeared in and about New York City, a little later in Hollywood, with its helpful sunshine. With the better equipped studio came the movie theater in every city and town. A new dimension was given to American amusement, scores or hundreds of people sitting in the half-dark and watching slapstick comedy and Westerns, with music supplied by a small orchestra or a local pianist. Gradually both plots and acting became more sophisticated, and the pie-throwing of the comedians, alas, was abandoned. The Western never lost its popularity; instead it gradually became standard movie fare, even in remote villages of the Yukon and Patagonia. The brave cowboy, the heroine from the East, the sinister villain, the hostile Indians, and scenes of the Wild West photographed in the hills of Hollywood enchanted the public in 1914 and still did a half-century later.

The movie-makers did not confine themselves to "horse operas" and the antics of custard-hurlers, for some took their art seriously. In 1914 David Griffith produced "The Birth of a Nation," a dramatic and classic film that dealt with Radical Reconstruction and the Ku Klux Klan. Actors and actresses of the stage long despised moving pictures and refused to take part in them. However, as the movies acquired technical proficiency and such stars as Mary Pickford began to amass fortunes, trains started to carry people of the "legitimate" theater from Broadway to Beverly Hills. This westward trek did not become commonplace until after World War I. Before the war ended, the romance of the movies had firmly clutched the American imagination and no other amusement or sport had such insistent appeal. Movies might be looked upon with patrician disapproval by "intellectuals," but they were dear to the hearts of practically everybody else.

Although the movies quickly attracted more watchers than any other form of mass entertainment, sports also drew larger and larger crowds. Unquestionably the "national pastime," at least out-of-doors, baseball flourished in the first part of the century. Many a village had its team, and the game was played everywhere on sandlots. Soon after 1900 the American League joined the National one as a fixture, and the World Series made its appearance. An attempt to form a third Federal League in 1914 failed. The New York Giants, the Chicago Cubs, the Philadelphia Athletics, and the Detroit Tigers were among the clubs that became immensely popular, together with players such as Ty Cobb, Christy Mathewson, and "Home Run" Frank Baker.

Not yet a rival of baseball, football was winning its way into public favor. It was seldom played as a professional game until after World War I, but almost every college with male students had a team. At the turn of the century football was less spectacular than it afterward became, for the forward pass did not become legal until 1906 and was little used until 1913. Nevertheless, the crowds at college contests rapidly became larger, and the stadium for 30,000 or 40,000 spectators dwarfing the college library became important at major institutions of advanced learning and at some not so renowned for academic achievement. The paid coach made his way into the headlines of the sports section in the newspapers; among the most famed were Walter Camp, Percy Haughton, Fielding "Hurry Up" Yost, and Glenn "Pop" Warner. Harvard, Yale, Princeton, and Pennsylvania had great days in football, being replaced by Michigan, Chicago, and Minnesota. "All American" teams were avidly inspected in the magazines by sports lovers, and the merits of one formation and another were carefully canvassed. As football proficiency and crowds increased, players became more valuable and they had less time and energy for their studies; the semi-professional, paid in one way or another, was a conspicuous figure on campus at wealthy colleges and at others not rich in books or laboratories. Their Presidents might feel that such institutions should strive to develop many sound minds in many sound bodies, but alumni and pseudo-alumni often assumed that the hallmark of a superior collegiate institution was the presence of a winning team. The time when the college athlete was openly paid was yet to come, but thoughtful men in the halls of learning doubted that educational institutions should devote part of their energies to public entertainment.

EDUCATION

In part, mass entertainment flourished simply because America was the home of masses of people, and it was hardly a sure sign either of bad taste or decadence. Offering entertainment to the public—high schools as well as colleges acquired football teams—educational institutions also purveyed instruction on an ever vaster scale. Elementary education at public expense became available to almost all early in the twentieth century, and the public high school came within the reach of many adolescents. It was generally believed that possession of a diploma from one gave its owner economic as well as cultural advantages. Before World War I the high school usually placed before the student only a four-year procession of courses in the liberal arts and science. They were thinner versions of similar courses presented on college campuses. However, change was in the educational air. In the muddy prose of the philosopher John Dewey, whose mind was clearer than his language, inspiration was found for a new method in elementary and secondary teaching. The concept that education should be "child-centered" was rapidly gaining adherents, and with it the belief that there should be "practical" learning. To some degree these notions helped start the junior high school, divided from the senior one. Hence also came courses in the senior high school directed toward "preparation for life" rather than for college. The change was healthy for many students, especially those who were not of college caliber; carried to an extreme, the principle of "life-adjustment" led to the substitution of trivia for learning fundamentally useful both to society and to the individual. More and more high school graduates, sometimes ill-prepared for higher education, made their way to the colleges. Secondary instruction was gradually improving, if for no other reason than because the number of high schools was growing swiftly.

On the college level, too, there was improvement, readily observable in the quantity of students but not quite so evident in their quality. Oddly, the salary and status of the professor diminished as his clientele grew. His condition was comparable to that of the physician at the opening of the century but it was not so two decades later. Even so, American graduate and professional schools made steady progress, and with them research in pure and applied science, in medicine, in history, and in the humanities and the "social sciences." There were those at the end of World War I who feared that the kindergarten, widely introduced during the preceding decade, was being extended into the senior year of high school. Such alarmists would later become numerous. There was no reason to be smug about the progress of American education; the staggering dimensions of the task of mass instruction were not always appreciated, and there remained critics who narrowly or snobbishly believed that advanced instruction should be confined to a privileged and qualified few.

THE PUBLIC LIBRARY

Learning has never been confined within the walls of schools, and it was powerfully fostered by the free libraries, usually tax-supported, that were springing up all over the nation at the end of the nineteenth century. There were at that time more than 1700 of them that possessed at least 5000 volumes; by the beginning of World War I the doors of 3000 such libraries had been opened. In many communities it was properly felt that a library was almost as essential as schools. Red brick buildings housing books and magazines, the gift of Andrew Carnegie, appeared all over the country, about one thousand of them being built between 1906 and 1916. The Carnegie structures might be externally undistinguished—they were much the same from city to town—but within them were treasures. From their shelves came amusement for idle hours and solid learning for those who were determined to have it with or without formal schooling. It is hardly possible to assess the influence of the free library; its importance can best be understood by contemplating the city, the town, the village without one. They offered vicarious romance to both spinster and housewife, while books for boys by G. A. Henty led many a boy into a career as an historian. There were the novels and poetry of eminent authors, and tomes of history, government, philosophy, and science sufficient for the determined student to acquire a liberal education. Compared with the majestic New York Public Library, the Library of Congress, or with those of universities like Harvard, Illinois, and Michigan, the Carnegie libraries were humble indeed; collectively they were of great importance.

It could be contended with some cogency, especially by Europeans, that America was still intellectually and culturally backward at the beginning of World War I. It had to be conceded that the Americans were doing very well in things material, and also that they managed to maintain a respectable political order. But was not the western republic arid, or nearly so, with respect to literature, music, and the arts? The shortsighted European sophisticate might believe that American civilization was and would remain a pale copy of the European. More astute observers from London and Paris saw in America a rising Rome compared with a European Greece and were not so sure that the New World Romans would excel only in things material. A few European well-wishers to America dared to hope that the glory of Greece would be mingled with the grandeur of Rome in a new and better order west of the Atlantic. A half-century later, when Americanization was progressing rapidly in Western Europe, room remained for speculation about the American cultural contribution.

LITERATURE AND MUSIC

It is not at all difficult to draw up a formidable indictment of the collective American mind as it was early in the century. The reading habits of the Americans continued to be particularly vulnerable to assault, for they bought in large quantities shallow and sugary romances such as *The Trail of the Lonesome Pine* by John Fox, Jr., and *The Shepherd of the Hills* by Harold Bell Wright. They wept over the saccharine stories of Gene Stratton Porter, and fancied that Zane Grey's Western novels, good of their kind, were great books. The disgusted critic might forget that poorer books sold more than better ones in England and France, and that the handsome sales of inferior ones in America arose in part from American prosperity. The European counterparts of the Americans who read poor books often read none. Critics have expressed disgust because Theodore Dreiser found it difficult to secure the publication of his naturalistic novels; had they not been so clumsily written, they might more readily have reached the public. It is also easy to criticize the presumably well-educated Americans who believed that *An Economic Interpretation of the Constitution* by Charles Beard, published in 1913, was both erroneous and unpatriotic. Professor Beard's contention that the Constitution was made and ratified through the efforts of a class of men of wealth principally concerned for their own good was a horrifying thesis. Even more disconcerting is the fact that presumably informed Americans were reluctant to admit that the Founding Fathers concerned themselves with the economic effects of their work, although it was well known that they had discussed economic matters at length in the federal convention. However, the book is in itself testimony of the growth toward maturity of American scholarship; and the fact that it was received with both praise and caution bears even better witness to the competence of American historians of that day.

There were other bright spots upon the intellectual and cultural scene. Greenwich Village in New York City afforded a home to hundreds of creative and would-be creative spirits. Like Theodore Dreiser, Frank Norris excelled in the naturalistic novel, trying with success to depict the seamier side of American life in *The Octopus* and *The Pit*. Even before the close of the century he had published *McTeague,* a powerful book that portrayed a man breaking under economic pressure. In lumbering prose that achieved power because it conveyed a sense of reality, Dreiser himself limned with almost painful exactness in *Sister Carrie, Jennie Gerhardt, The Financier,* and other works, the tragedies of "fallen women," business magnates, and artists. Far more popular at the time was Jack London, whose flood of books described harsh realities, of which he had had biting experience. Ironically, London, not quite a genius, was afterward remembered in his own country as the author of *The Call of the Wild,* a dog story; on the other hand, he was much read in the Soviet Union because the American society he depicted was in dark colors. Willa Cather, possessing a surer talent than London, saw a more generous America than he. In *O Pioneers!* (1913) and *The Song of the Lark* (1915), followed by other distinguished novels, she wrote with grace about pioneers in Nebraska whom she did not portray as mere mean victims of a harsh fate. New and distinguished poets made their appearance, including the cigar-smoking Amy Lowell, whose free verse was avant-garde; Edgar Lee Masters, whose *Spoon River Anthology* offered brilliant, bitter, and poignant comment, in the form of epitaphs, upon Midwestern town life; and Robert Frost, who was later to win a wide reputation based upon spare, dignified, and powerful phrasing suffused with restrained emotion. The founding of *Poetry* magazine in 1912 offered sharp stimulus to American verse.

Less attractive than the literary landscape was the musical vista immediately before America's plunge into World War I, for native talent and themes had not yet been much developed in the classical tradition. The symphony orchestra had made its appearance in the very largest American cities well before 1900, and such cities as Cincinnati, Pittsburgh, St. Louis, and Minneapolis acquired one before or soon after that year, thanks in considerable part to the love of music among the German-Americans. But ragtime and blues music was far more popular. Dear to the heart of the average American were "Sweet Adeline," "Take Me Out to the Ballgame," Carrie Jacobs Bond's "A Perfect Day," and "When Irish Eyes Are Smiling," all of which were composed between 1903 and 1910. The fabulous blues song that would be played and sung from Paris to Singapore, W. C. Handy's "St. Louis Blues," was composed in 1914. Immediately thereafter jazz reached Chicago and New York from New Orleans, soon securing an overwhelming popularity. But opera and concert performers continued to be European rather than American. Nor did the Americans excel in the composition of classical music. Edward McDowell and Charles Wakefield Cadman sought inspiration and vitality in American Indian themes with some success, and others tried to find native power and beauty in the culture of the American Negro, with less success. At the close of World War I there were those who mistakenly felt that classical music in America was dying; its growth had only begun.

To many thoughtful Americans the intellectual and cultural panorama early in the century was not at all attractive. The frontier was gone; it was no longer necessary to fight the Indian; the log cabin had become almost a relic; and America had a stable and relatively healthy society. Was it not time that the republic equal if not surpass Europe in more than material achievement? It seemed that the westward march of the Americans from Jamestown to the Pacific was theme grand enough for an epic, but no Yankee Vrigil had done justice to the magnificent chronicle. Among the many estimable American historians, why was there no Edward Gibbon describing the mighty progress of a great people in mature reflection? Equivalents of Shakespeare, Shelley, and Charles Dickens were not seen. Where was an American Mozart or Caruso? A cynical and witty American architect, Frank Lloyd Wright, was afterward to say that his country was the only one that had gone from barbarism directly to decadence. His assessment was not quite so ridiculous in fact in 1914 as it was 40 years later. A more prudent appraisal of American intellectual and cultural progress at the beginning of World War I, or even at the beginning of the Great Depression, would take into account the short and simple annals of the busily prosperous, the brevity of the American time span, the American isolation drawing to an end, and an easy American optimism that must fade. The maturity of the nation was rapidly approaching.

47 THE COMING OF WORLD WAR I

In the 1950s there was a facetious Republican explanation for "the fix we are in" that was simple and gained some currency. Dean Andrew West was responsible. Since West in life was famed only in academic circles, the thesis that he was so vitally important in the affairs of men and nations was at least novel. The argument ran thus: as a dean at Princeton University West made life so uncomfortable for Woodrow Wilson that he went from the campus to the governorship of New Jersey; the governorship led Wilson to the White House; as President Wilson dragged the nation into World War I; the Great Depression of 1929 grew out of World War I; World War II proceeded from the Great Depression; and the perilous conditions of the 1950s developed from the second global conflict. This semi-humorous thesis places a heavy burden upon Wilson, even though it was sometimes modified by a statement that Wilson received decisive assistance from Franklin D. Roosevelt. Wisdom requires skepticism regarding the vast consequences of all the deeds of heroes; it also demands that great events be not casually and hastily ascribed to the deeds, or lack of them, of weak or vicious men. Besides, Wilson was neither feeble nor wicked. On the other hand, was Wilson the greatest of mankind in his generation, as many of his admirers believed? Was his behavior with respect to America's entrance into World War I beyond criticism and above reproach? The Wilson record in foreign affairs, like almost any other one, is mixed. It is appropriate to think of him as a well-intentioned and able man doing as well as he could. It is not too much to say he exhibited naiveté in his dealings with other nations during the early months of his Presidency. Like most occupants of the White House, he had to educate himself about them after taking office. Again among the majority, he was more familiar with things domestic than he was with the intricacies of the policies of other nations. Nor was he very well versed in international law. It has frequently been said against him that he was too idealistic and unrealistic; at least eventually, his idealism became realism. Confronted by the convulsion of World War I, it is doubtful that any other American leader of his time would have done better.

WILSON AND LATIN AMERICA

Certainly Wilson behaved both honorably and sensibly in dealing with one foreign question that he had to face soon after he became President, that of the Panama Canal tolls. Despite the Hay-Pauncefote Treaty's unequivocal statement that the ships of all nations were to use the Canal on terms of "perfect equality" and that charges by the United States would not discriminate against the ships of other nations, Congress had by a law of 1912 given special favor to American shipping. American vessels using the waterway on voyages between the East and West Coasts had been exempted from tolls on the excuse that they were engaged in coastal commerce rather than foreign, and that the treaty did not cover such traffic. The law had been endorsed by the Progressives, the Democrats, and by Wilson himself in the campaign of that year. Reconsidering the situation after his election, Wilson changed his mind and concluded that a British protest that the law violated the treaty was well founded. When Britain again complained in 1913, the President confidentially conceded that America had failed to keep faith and requested time so that he might be able to ask for repeal when it could be secured with less damage to his party and his program for domestic reform. To repudiate the Democratic platform was embarrassing. Anti-British elements, including the Irish-Americans so important among the Democrats, could be expected to fight hard against repeal. Early in 1914 Wilson kept his word to the British, first quietly urging repeal before a committee of Congress and then publicly calling for it. Some principal Democrats preferred to keep a campaign promise rather than a prior one to Britain, while others hostile to that country fought a long and rhetorical battle against repeal. Finally, with the help of many Republicans, Wilson secured the revocation of the special privilege in the spring of 1914.

It was one thing to insist upon honorable dealing with the relatively responsible British and quite another to manage American interests in the Caribbean world. It was generally assumed in 1913 that the Democrats, having forthrightly condemned the Republicans for undertaking political, economic, and military adventures in Central America and the Caribbean Islands, would adopt a policy of non-intervention in Latin America. So far as words went, the expectation proved to be correct, for Wilson's Secretary of State Bryan and Bryan's successor, Robert Lansing, again and again declared that they were opposed to both European and North American meddling. Wilson most emphatically asserted the equality of the republics of the Western Hemisphere. Denouncing dollar diplomacy, Bryan urged that the American government offer to the Latin American nations whatever financial help they needed, without strings. Under their leadership, the United States proposed that all the American republics combine as equals for their common defense. Here were all the elements of the later "Good Neighbor" policy of Franklin D. Roosevelt. These were largely idealistic utterances, sincere enough, but hardly consistent with practice. Wilson continued to claim for the United States the exclusive right to execute the Monroe Doctrine; he would not accept hemispherical enforcement of its principles as a substitute. Moreover, Bryan could not get support for his proposal that American public rather than private money be invested in Latin America.

Despite the best intentions on the part of both Wilson and Bryan, the United States intervened vigorously in the Caribbean world after 1913. As it turned out, the danger of European political and military action for the real or pretended purpose of collecting debts faded away, largely because Europeans had little money to lend in the New World after the outbreak of World War I. Nevertheless, Wilson and Bryan felt forced to use military power in several Caribbean republics in order to maintain internal peace within them. Neither the President nor the Secretary of State knowingly lent help to unscrupulous American investors, but some of their subordinates, too much trusted, were not quite so high-minded. The need to protect the northern approaches to the Panama Canal also stimulated armed intervention, because American admirals wished to make sure that nothing would impede the passage of warships through the canal, especially during the critical years of World War I. Besides, commitments made before 1913 made it difficult for Wilson and Bryan to avoid intervention. Bryan, to whom Wilson gave a free hand in the Caribbean, was remarkably naive. In consequence, to prevent anarchy, as Bryan and Wilson thought, American marines landed in Nicaragua in 1912, helped to suppress a revolt, and remained there for thirteen years. After 1913 there was utter confusion in the Dominican Republic, dictators and would-be dictators struggling for supremacy and the receipts of the customs houses. The situation was exacerbated by the conduct of the American minister to the republic, James M. Sullivan, who misused his influence in support of one political faction against another. A civil war that broke out in 1913 continued intermittently for three years, as Wilson's efforts to persuade the contending parties peaceably to accept a new regime failed. The President then established American military rule over the republic, before the end of 1916.

Meanwhile, America had become thoroughly enmeshed in the troubles of neighboring Haiti, which also underwent commotion, civil war, and anarchy after 1913. Bloody clashes for power were not reduced by American diplomatic pressure, which included a request that the Haitians abandon the control of public finances to American managers. In 1915, after the Haitians had indulged in a singularly sanguinary series of struggles, American sailors and marines went ashore. A new government under American influence was formed, and it was compelled to sign a treaty that provided for American control of finances and police. Thus Haiti, like Nicaragua and Santo Domingo, became, in effect, an American protectorate. This was not done without cost to the marines. Haitian soldiers, fighting desperately against American domination, fled to the mountains of the little country and carried on guerrilla warfare for many months. About 2000 of them were killed before quiet came to Haiti. Only those who fancy that peace, order, and a popular government could have been maintained in the three republics without American interference will condemn either Wilson or Bryan.

TROUBLES IN MEXICO

Of far greater importance to the United States, and also of much deeper concern, was Mexico, swept by tides of revolution and war. Innocence, idealism, and inexperience again added to troubles that Wilson had to face, they being sufficient to vex the most astute and veteran statesman. The Mexican revolution that began in 1911 was extraordinary. Mexico had been shaken and rent by many conspiracies, revolts, and political overturns before Porfirio Díaz became its dictator in 1876. Which politician or which general triumphed had mattered little to the Mexican masses, for except for Benito Juarez, none sincerely sought to better the hard lot of the poor. A landed aristocracy, self-seeking politicians, and ambitious army officers had dominated Mexico, whether in peace or disorder, except for the brief rule of Juarez. Porfirio Díaz sat firmly in the saddle for 35 years. He prevented the rise of rivals, preserved order, and did not disturb the aristocracy or the church. He was little concerned for the welfare of the illiterate peons who formed the bulk of the Mexican people, and he was gracious to foreigners who wanted mining and ranch properties. At last, when Díaz had become old and less vigorous, discontent flowered into a formidable rebellion that he was unable to suppress.

He went into exile; the revolutionists, under the leadership of Francisco I. Madero, attained power, and Mexico entered upon a decade of disturbance. Counterrevolution was attempted in behalf of privilege, while the leaders of the revolution struggled among themselves for ascendancy. Gradually, amidst all this ferment and uproar, men more or less sincerely devoted to uplifting the Mexican masses obtained sway. Wilson gave them his blessing and tried to help, but not very successfully. Twice he sent American military forces into Mexico, narrowly escaping a war with the revolutionists and winning the distrust and enmity of their more altruistic leaders. His good intentions were vitiated by a lack of information.

Actually, by employing the influence of the United States toward preventing a successful counterrevolution Wilson demonstrated during his early months in the Presidency that he favored the revolutionists. Early in 1913 reactionary forces rallied under General Victoriano Huerta, seized control of Mexico City, and captured Madero. Scion of a wealthy family but utterly devoted to the welfare of the poor, Madero was murdered by the Huertistas, who announced that he had been killed while attempting to escape. Huerta himself was at least indirectly responsible for the crime. Nevertheless, when he proclaimed himself President, Americans living in Mexico, including the ambassador, Henry Lane Wilson, urged that the Huerta regime be officially recognized. State Department officers and American business interests that had a stake in Mexico also pressed for recognition of the reactionary regime, claiming not only that it was the Mexican government in fact, but also that it offered the only hope for the maintenance of order south of the Rio Grande. To them the murder of Madero and Huerta's seizure of power were internal matters of no direct concern to the United States. Taft would have extended recognition to Huerta, except for the fact that he did not wish to act hastily; he assumed that Wilson would do so. Wilson and Bryan saw Mexico with the eyes of moralists rather than of legalists. Wilson high-mindedly resolved that the United States must officially ignore the existence of a "government of butchers" that had overthrown a constitutional and popular one. When Madero's followers, especially General Venustiano Carranza, took up arms against Huerta outside Mexico City, Wilson was pleased. He tried vainly to persuade Huerta to abandon his authority and to permit a free election of a new President and congress. Huerta managed to maintain himself in Mexico City and its vicinity for two years. Had he secured American recognition, he might well have been able to crush his enemies, who were divided among themselves by personal rivalries and hostility. Wilson helped to bring down Huerta by permitting his enemies to buy arms north of the Rio Grande, and by putting heavy pressure on Britain to withdraw recognition that she had given to his government.

Striking hard at Huerta, Wilson came close to declared warfare against his regime. In April, 1914, American sailors who went ashore at Tampico were arrested by Huertistas for landing without permission. They were quickly released, and an apology was sent to Admiral Henry T. Mayo, who commanded an American naval squadron stationed off Vera Cruz. Mayo considered the apology to be insufficient and demanded that the Huertistas offer a 21-gun salute to the American flag. It was a little odd that a salute should be required from a regime that America did not recognize, but Wilson backed Mayo. Huerta was willing to give the salute only if it were returned by the American Navy. Wilson insisted that he offer the salute without return or take the military consequences. War was threatening when a German steamer carrying ammunition for the Huertistas approached Vera Cruz, for Wilson did not intend to let it be used against American forces. To prevent its landing he ordered the Navy to occupy the port, which was seized despite resistance by Mexican cadets and civilians: 19 Americans and 126 Mexicans were killed. Even Carranza's followers were made unhappy by seizure of the port. Brazil, Argentina, and Chile helped to preserve peace. Offering mediation, they arranged a conference at Niagara Falls between representatives of the United States, Huerta, and Carranza. The discussion continued until Huerta lost Mexico City and fled into exile.

When the followers of Madero regained hegemony in Mexico, Wilson might prudently have withdrawn his burnt fingers from that country. However, the revolutionists turned against each other, with one Doroteo Arango, better known as Francisco "Pancho" Villa, challenging Carranza for supremacy in a new civil war. Wilson and Bryan, disgusted with Carranza, tried to persuade him to retire and to permit the free election of his successor. In effect, they favored the illiterate but able bandit Villa, a passionate, violent, and cruel man who was quite unfit to rule, but who pretended to be friendly toward the United States. After Carranza had crushed Villa's army and had driven him into hiding in northern Mexico, Wilson, well advised by Robert Lansing, Bryan's successor, sensibly arranged for a general foreign recognition of Carranza. All might then have been well, at least so far as the United States was concerned, had not Villa been possessed by dreams of grandeur and hot for revenge against all and sundry. The bandit killed 17 Americans in northern Mexico in January, 1916. Two months later he raided Columbus, New Mexico, burning the town and murdering 19 more Americans. Since Carranza seemed unable to destroy Villa, Wilson felt forced to send a punitive expedition into northern Mexico under General John J. Pershing to find and crush the elusive and bloody outlaw. Pershing never could quite catch him, although he marched 300 miles into Mexico and dispersed Villa's followers. Moreover, clashes came between the American troops and those of Carranza, who feared that the Americans had come to stay. He demanded their withdrawal, and war between the United States and Mexico again threatened. Wilson saw that one would gain nothing and withstood heavy pressure at home for a declaration of war. Even though Villa and a few of his follow- ers were still at large early in 1917, Wilson ordered Pershing to retire across the Rio Grande. The Mexican revolution continued; Villa escaped punishment for some years, finally meeting death at the hands of an un- known assailant. Wilson was especially eager to avoid war with Mexico because a more important one with Germany seemed in the offing.

WAR IN EUROPE

On June 27, 1914, not one American in a thousand could have located the town of Sarajevo in the province of Bosnia of the Habsburg Austro- Hungarian empire. For that matter, the province was equally unknown in America, and knowledge of the empire was neither profound nor wide- spread. On the following day Gavrilo Prinzip, a tubercular student who passionately wanted to free Bosnia and the neighboring province of Herzo- govina from Austrian rule and to unite them with the kingdom of Serbia, murdered the Archduke Franz Ferdinand, heir to the Habsburg throne, in the streets of Sarajevo. He believed that the shooting of the Archduke would advance his cause. Four years later the kingdom of Yugoslavia was born with Serbia as its nucleus. Dying in prison, Gavrilo Prinzip had achieved his purpose; but Yugoslavia made its appearance only after the convulsion of World War I had shaken the world. American newspapers reported the killing; some editors expressed concern lest it lead to a European crisis, but the affair was crowded off front pages by stories of more immediate interest for the next several weeks. Then suddenly a large part of Europe went to war. The conflict continued and spread, becom- ing the most destructive that mankind had known. America ultimately be- came one of the principal antagonists.

Before and immediately after the shooting of the Archduke, it was widely felt in Europe and elsewhere that even a continental war was "un- thinkable." There had been no armed struggle involving most of Europe since the downfall of Napoleon a century earlier. There had been wars, but they had been confined in area and short in duration. Optimists who saw a progressing and improving world fancied that those wars were passing shadows. Many believed that weapons had become so destructive that governments would not resort to them. Surely, the informed and so- phisticated heads of the European states were aware that no nation could reasonably expect permanent profit from a major conflict.

Nevertheless, the powers of Europe were heavily armed in 1914, and they had made political as well as military preparations for the day of battle. Ancient jealousies and enmities persisted and rivalry for wealth and empire had created new ones. Entangling alliances and other agreements made it difficult to confine any outbreak of hostilities. The powerful nations of Europe were divided into two armed camps. Germany and Austria-Hungary were tightly linked; the preservation of the Habsburg empire was considered essential in German policy. France and Russia were as closely allied, and England, entering into an Entente Cordiale with France in 1904, had patched up her quarrels with Russia in 1907 and afterward. In the event of war several of the weaker nations must be involved, in part because of treaty obligations. Fear that one nation or another might strike a crippling blow by a swift stroke against the unprepared hastened both diplomatic and military decisions. In late July and early August ultimata and declarations of war came in hasty succession. Austria-Hungary, its existence threatened by Slavic nationalist movements among its peoples, blamed Serbia for Prinzip's crime and demanded important concessions. Encouraged by Russia, a Slavic "Big Brother," Serbia refused to do all that the Habsburg empire required. Then came a chain reaction. When Russia began to mobilize despite a warning against it from Berlin, negotiation became almost impossible. Germany soon fell to blows with both Russia and France, for France would not guarantee to remain neutral. Although the German Empire had promised not to violate Belgian territory, German troops promptly began to move through Belgium toward Paris. The violation of Belgian neutrality gave Britain a reason to declare war upon Germany, although she was not pledged to come to Belgium's defense. In any case, England was more or less morally pledged to the assistance of France. By August 4, Serbia, Russia, France, Belgium, and England were engaged against Germany and Austria-Hungary. Turkey and Bulgaria later joined the Central Powers. Many other nations joined their opponents, the Allies eventually including Italy, Rumania, Japan, China, and the United States.

Enduring for more than four years, World War I shook the earth. Hundreds of millions of people took part in, or were directly affected by it, and few human beings were unaffected. The dead numbered in the millions, and the economic and social costs were so vast that they could hardly be computed. There was fighting on the sands of Arabia, in the jungles of fever-ridden Africa, and off the coral reefs surrounding South Pacific islands. However, the principal theaters of combat were in Europe and on its sea approaches. There was fighting in the Balkan Mountains, in the Straits of Constantinople, and in the river valleys of northeastern Italy. Greatest of all theaters of conflict on land were the Western and Eastern Fronts; on the Eastern Front Russia, with later and minor help from Rumania, wrestled with the Habsburg and Hohenzollern empires; on the Western one, the Germans fought the French, British, Belgians, Portuguese, and eventually, the Americans. Less gory, but also of profound importance, was encounter at sea, for control of the shipping lanes of the Atlantic could have brought victory to either side.

STALEMATE ON LAND

There were those on both sides who hoped for early victory. This was especially true among the Germans, who as military strategists had laid plans for a swift and decisive finish of France. Germany had the most powerful army in the world, and hoped that France might be driven from the war before Britain could mobilize and send many divisions to her assistance. The more quickly to paralyze French resistance, the Germans swept through neutral Belgium and advanced rapidly toward Paris. However, with the help of a small British expeditionary force, the French checked the German thrust at the Marne River. Both sides hastily dug in along a line stretching from the Alps to the North Sea, and settled down to trench warfare. The history of the Eastern Front in 1914 was somewhat similar; a massive Russian attack upon German East Prussia was repelled, and a long fighting line was established, stretching southward from the Baltic Sea to the border of Rumania. In 1915 the Germans concentrated their efforts against Russia, and drove the troops of the Tsar back through Russian Poland. In the following year they strove again to break through to victory in the West, vainly trying to take the massive French fortress of Verdun. A mighty offensive undertaken almost simultaneously by the British on the Somme River also failed dismally. By the spring of 1917 the losses on both sides had become enormous, and the Russian empire was tottering. Rumania had come into the war in 1916 as one of the Allies, but had been quickly crushed. Germany made an immense effort to win the war on land before American troops came in great force to the help of the Allies in the West. While the German armies in France fell back into the powerfully fortified Hindenburg Line and successfully defended it, those on the Eastern Front moved forward, sweeping through the Baltic provinces of Russia, White Russia, and the Ukraine. Before the end of the year the empire of the Tsars fell, and Russian resistance virtually came to an end. In March, 1918, the Communists, who seized authority in St. Petersburg and Moscow, signed a treaty of peace with Germany at Brest-Litovsk. Germany was then able to mount a last great offensive in the West. It came too late, for the Americans had arrived in France. The throne of the German Hohenzollerns endured only one year longer than that of the Russian Romanovs.

There is little romantic allure in World War I; cavalry did not dash to brilliant triumphs; genius did not compensate for physical weakness; armies seldom moved rapidly; the airplane and the tank were not yet the military instruments they afterward became; and personal exploits were obscured in mass combat. It was a war of attrition, one in which the de-

- → German Advances, August 1914
- •••••••• Line of Trench Warfare, 1914-1917
- ━ ━ ━ Limit of German Advance, 1914

THE WESTERN FRONT, WORLD WAR I

fense had such a great advantage that stalemate continued until one party or the other sank in exhaustion. Trenches, barbed wire, machine guns, and artillery prevented sudden advances, breakthroughs, or a war of movement. Artillery could bombard the front lines of the enemy and open a way for infantry, but the pounding of the big guns gave warning of attack and permitted the enemy to dig new entrenchments and to bring up fresh troops. Poison gas might have served as a means to break down the defense, but its efficacy was soon diminished by the invention of the gas mask. During four years of fighting, generals on both sides tried to break through on the Western Front, without success. The losses suffered as a result were almost unbelievable. The slain were counted by tens of thousands; the valley of the Somme and the hills about Verdun were drenched with blood.

Nor was the war at sea one of splendor and derring-do. There were a few splendid exploits of mariners and single ships, and one might romance

WORLD WAR I

about them, just as one could about the deeds of Colonel Lawrence of Arabia on land. In the main, however, the fighting on water was grim and grinding. With French and Italian assistance the British navy soon swept the ocean surfaces of German vessels, and the German colonies became fair prey for the Allies. In the home waters of the North Sea there was no titanic battle to the death between the British and German fleets. The British, establishing a naval blockade to sap the strength of the Central Powers, prudently refrained from attacking the strong German fleet stationed on the eastern side of the North Sea, for defeat might be ruinous. On the other hand, although Germany had more to gain and less to lose in a major encounter, her fleet was sufficiently inferior in strength to suggest the wisdom of keeping it in sanctuary. In 1916 it came forth as if to engage in a vital struggle, but after achieving success in the opening clashes at the Battle of Jutland, it withdrew in the face of gathering British might. Germany chose instead to rely upon the submarine, hoping to blockade Britain and France by means of underwater craft. So the war at sea, like that on land, was primarily one of endurance.

AMERICAN NEUTRALITY

Much has been said about the reasons why America entered World War I. Haunted by a feeling that the sacrifices made in the seemingly hallowed cause had been merely wasted, many Americans were afterward disposed to accept the argument that the nation had been seduced into a conflict in which it had little at stake. The makers of munitions were blamed as "merchants of death," indirectly or even directly responsible for the fateful decision. Sinister British propaganda that lied and deceived an innocent and well-meaning people was another simple explanation. Many would have had it that the sale of vast quantities of Allied bonds in the United States created an economic interest that demanded victory for the Allies, hence that Wall Street bankers had been demonic agents. Such contentions assumed that Wilson and all those who had a part in the making of American policy were incompetent and trapped into doing what they ought not to have done. Actually, Wilson, well advised from the beginning of the war by Colonel House, was much better informed about things European than he was about those Latin American. A simple and clear explanation for the taking up of arms by America is not to be found. When all is said and considered, it would seem that the Americans were pro-Ally from the beginning; that they became more positively anti-German as it progressed; that German submarine warfare profoundly affected American sentiment and policy; and that fear lest a militaristic and triumphant Germany dominate Europe and threaten America was vital in forming the resolution to fight. If one must offer a cause for that resolution in few words, it should be that America, not afraid of British or French attack, became profoundly concerned lest Kaiser Wilhelm II and the German militarists destroy the balance of power in Europe and become a menace to the United States.

The image of imperial Germany in American minds before the shooting began, in so far as one existed, was commonly that of an aggressive, warlike, and undemocratic nation. In Washington the Kaiser was distrusted and disliked. Although scholars appraising the conduct of the nations in the crisis that led to the war have apportioned responsibility for it quite widely, it seemed to American observers at the time that Germany and Austria-Hungary were the major culprits. The invasion of the small and neutral country of Belgium by the goose-stepping troops of the Kaiser deeply offended American sentiment. As the struggle continued, American feeling against Germany became more intense. When it began, Wilson not only formally declared American neutrality, but adjured his countrymen to avoid taking the part of one side or the other, even in thought. They could not do so. Some were anti-British because of hostility inherited from the distant past; Irish-Americans were affected by ancestral and current grievances of the Irish against Britain; and German-Americans tended to dislike England, many inevitably favoring their former homeland. In the main, however, it was sympathy for the Allies that made it impossible to be neutral in thought. The ties of blood, culture, and sentiment were strong between America and England, and France was romantically remembered as an ancient ally in the War of Independence. American feeling swung heavily against Germany because submarine warfare took the lives of many Americans on the Atlantic and because it was conceivable that Germany might conquer the Allies.

THE SUBMARINE ENTERS WARFARE

Resorting to naval blockade, toward choking Germany and the other Central Powers into submission, the Allies, especially Britain, injured the maritime commerce of the United States. Once again America became the champion of neutrals on the oceans. As the war progressed, the British blockaded Germany even more tightly, at length undertaking to prevent every sort of goods from reaching Germany by way of the Atlantic, whether directly or indirectly through neutral countries such as Holland and Denmark. Again and again America protested against search and seizure of American vessels, British contraband lists, and "rationing" of American shipping to neutral nations. At times in 1915 and 1916 relations between Washington and London were strained, in much the same fashion they had been during the wars of the French Revolution and Napoleon. However, no American lives were taken by the British blockaders. Reparation for economic losses could be secured from Britain after the war, if she were among the victors, so American exasperation was not deep enough to lead to military action, or the threat of it in defense of the rights of neutrals on the sea. It was otherwise with submarine warfare, which took both American property and lives.

In modern warfare nations use any weapon at hand, unless its employment seems likely to be unprofitable. Having dozens of undersea craft, Germany determined to send them out to do as much damage as possible. In February, 1915, Germany declared that the British Isles were under submarine blockade; that all enemy ships within a zone circumscribing Britain would be sunk; and that neutral vessels would be endangered because the British hoisted neutral flags to hide their identity. America quickly protested. Under international law as it then was, Germany could legally neither sink American vessels nor Allied merchantmen carrying American citizens without warning. Provision had not been made to cover the use of the submarine, which had to fire its torpedoes without warning because it was vulnerable to counterattack. America asserted Germany would be held to a "strict accountability" for the loss of American ships

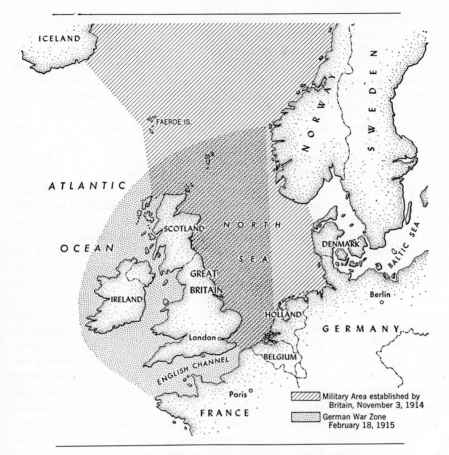

Military Area established by Britain, November 3, 1914

German War Zone February 18, 1915

THE SUBMARINE ENTERS MODERN WARFARE

and people, and that whatever was necessary to defend American rights would be done. Germany then indicated that care would be taken to prevent the torpedoing of American vessels, but refused to guarantee the safety of American citizens traveling on Allied merchant ships.

In March, 1915 a German submarine sank a British steamer without parley, and an American life was lost. On May 7, again without warning, the British liner *Lusitania* was sent to the bottom. Among the nearly 1200 civilians who lost their lives were 128 Americans. They had boarded the ship at New York despite a newspaper notice from the German embassy in Washington that the *Lusitania* might be torpedoed. They did not believe that the Germans would actually try to destroy the liner. The news that the *Lusitania* had been sunk shocked the American people, and some of them, including Theodore Roosevelt, vehemently cried out for an immediate declaration of war. Wilson and most Americans were not ready to take up weapons quite so quickly. He was praised when he said that "There is such a thing as a man being too proud to fight." Instead, the President demanded from Germany that a stop be put to the sinking of merchant vessels without warning. The torpedoing of another ship such as the *Lusitania* would be looked upon as a "deliberately unfriendly" act. It would, in effect, bring the breaking of diplomatic relations with Germany, and perhaps war. Wilson could hardly decently do less, but Bryan, eager to maintain peace with Germany, believed that the President had gone too far, and resigned as Secretary of State, being succeeded by Robert Lansing. Germany did not promptly reply in such a way as to satisfy Wilson, and two more Americans were lost in August when the British liner *Arabic* went down under a surprise torpedo assault. Then, concerned lest America enter the war, Germany went so far as to promise that unarmed passenger ships, provided they did not try to escape, would not be sunk without provision for the safety of civilians aboard. Early in 1916, while not admitting that the attack upon the *Lusitania* had been unlawful, the German empire also undertook to offer indemnity for the American lives taken in her sinking. Soon afterward, however, the Kaiser's submarines began an unrestricted warfare against Allied merchant vessels, and American lives were again endangered. In April Wilson peremptorily demanded that such attacks cease; if they did not, the United States must break diplomatic relations with Germany. In the following month the German government a second time gave way, promising that no merchant vessel anywhere would be attacked without warning. Thereafter, for more than six months, there was no threat of a complete rupture between Berlin and Washington. In the fall of 1916 Wilson was almost as angry about vexing British measures, such as an economic blacklist of Americans who did business with Germany and the opening of American mail, as he was about German misbehavior. This, even though sabotage by German and Austrian agents of factories making munitions for the Allies created much public excitement.

Wilson did all that might reasonably be expected toward keeping America out of the great war, and also toward getting ready to fight, in the event that involvement became necessary. In the end, America could have remained aloof only by keeping her ships and her people at home, a measure that appealed only to a minority in Congress and the nation. With the help of hindsight, one may censure the President because he did not urge that step; at the time it was not remarkable for him to insist upon American rights under international law. It should also be said in his behalf that he managed to protect them during many months without resort to the use of weapons. It should also be recalled that Wilson tried to persuade the Allies and Central Powers to abandon their struggle. He twice sent Colonel House across the Atlantic for that purpose; the House missions failed, for the Allies were not disposed to make concessions, and Germany insisted upon territorial and military gains commensurate with her early military triumphs. Wilson's record with respect to preparing for war is more obviously defensible. In 1916, following his leadership, Congress passed a series of laws providing for the building of a navy second to none; doubling the army; bringing the state national guards under federal control; and offering a huge subsidy for the building of a great American merchant marine.

"HE KEPT US OUT OF WAR"

Rather strangely, the Wilson who afterward seemed to some of his countrymen to have been overly aggressive in asserting American rights on the oceans was in 1916 elected to the Presidency a second time principally because "he has kept us out of war." As the campaign approached, it seemed doubtful that he could win again, for Theodore Roosevelt had decided that his "Bull Moose" movement had no future and that he would rejoin the Republicans. It seemed likely that they would regain their dominance at the polls. The Progressive Party held a convention and nominated him for the Presidency, but he refused to lead it and so destroyed it. Instead, he sought the support of a solid Republican Party. Leaders of the orthodox Republicans wanted the votes they had lost to Roosevelt four years earlier, but they did not want to nominate him. Besides, many Republicans were opposed to him because he had favored a declaration of war against Germany. The Republican national convention, managed by men who tried to find the happy medium, named for the Presidency Charles Evans Hughes, Associate Justice of the Supreme Court, who had not taken part in the bitter fighting of 1912 and who had earned a reputation as a reformer when he was governor of New York, before he was appointed to the high court. Able, highly respected, and bearded, Hughes had won early fame by exposing vicious practices in the insurance business in New York and by helping to establish a model remedial code for it in that state. He had performed well both as a lawyer and as a judge. Calling for "a straight and honest" neutrality, and for moderate domestic reform, the Republican platform was unusually unimportant. The party leaders hoped to avoid taking decisive stands on important issues and to obtain the votes of all those dissatisfied with Wilson, for whatever reasons. The Democrats, on the other hand, aggressively bid for votes. Wilson was renominated without a struggle, and personally drafted their platform. It pledged them to a thoroughgoing progressivism, partly because the Democrats needed the help of some Bull Moose people to win. Endorsing the party record with respect to neutrality, the platform also urged that after the war America enter a society of nations to prevent future conflicts. Both in their convention and in the campaign that followed, the Democrats claimed that they were utterly devoted to the preservation of peace. Thus they appealed not only to the progressive-minded, but to Socialists, to pacifists, and to the isolationists of the Midwest and the West.

The campaign of 1916 was remarkable in that the conservative and progressive elements were quite clearly aligned against each other. Only some of the Irish-Americans and German-Americans failed to vote as conservatives or progressives. The Republicans, including Hughes, eagerly sought the support of those "hyphenated" groups, portraying Wilson as pro-British and anti-German. Roosevelt, who made speeches insisting that Germany was an enemy, robbed this claim of some of its force. Nevertheless, it was effective among the Irish-Americans, less so among the German-Americans, many of whose ancestors had fled across the Atlantic to escape from an autocratic and militaristic Germany. In general, however, Hughes had little talent for politicking. He neglected to appeal to the Bull Moose leaders, many of whom refused to follow Roosevelt back into the Republican Party and rallied to Wilson. On election night, newspaper extras proclaimed victory for Hughes because the Republicans had triumphed in the Eastern states, and Wilson went to bed believing that he had lost. Late returns, especially from the West, reversed the Republican tide. Wilson carried New Hampshire, Ohio, the Border States, the South, and almost all of the states west of the Missouri River. His popular vote was nearly 600,000 larger than that of Hughes, 9,128,606 to 8,538,221, although his margin in the electoral college was very narrow, 277 to 254. The election was so close that a handful of Progressives and Independents gained the balance of power in the House of Representatives, the Democrats retaining a small majority in the Senate. It is clear that the votes of women, Socialists (their party had 300,000 fewer ballots in 1916 than in 1912), and former Bull Moose people had brought victory to Wilson. His ardent admirers believed that peace, prosperity, and progressivism were at least temporarily safe. Six months later America was at war; it would hardly have been otherwise had Hughes defeated Wilson.

After his second triumph at the polls Wilson made his second attempt to persuade the Central and Allied Powers to make peace. But neither side would consider a settlement that did not badly injure the other; both were still determined to win and to use whatever weapons were necessary. In consequence, in the belief that unrestricted use of submarines would bring Britain to her knees and force the collapse of the Allies, Germany announced in January, 1917, that after February 1 the U-boats would sink without warning all ships, Allied or neutral, armed or unarmed, in a zone about Britain, France, and Italy. One American passenger ship might safely sail from New York to England each week, provided that it carried no contraband and was painted with red and white stripes. It was assumed in Berlin that such merciless submarine warfare would bring an American declaration of war, but it was believed that with full use of undersea striking power victory could be achieved before American strength could be mobilized.

Wilson, unwilling meekly or prudently to undertake keeping American citizens and ships out of that zone, sadly determined to sever diplomatic relations with Germany. On February 3 he announced his decision to a joint session of Congress. Hope continued that Germany would not actually use submarines so ruthlessly, and that if she did, America could wage a limited war on the sea. However, war fever rose in the United States when the contents of the Zimmerman Note were made public by Wilson at the end of March. Alfred Zimmerman, the German Foreign Secretary, had sent a message to the German minister to Mexico, proposing that Mexico ally herself with Germany in the event that America went to war. The message was intercepted and turned over to Wilson. In return for Mexican help against the United States, that country was to receive Texas, New Mexico, and Arizona, if Germany should triumph. Moreover, Mexico was to be urged to try to persuade Japan to change sides. A filibuster in the Senate before March 4, was all that prevented the passage of a bill that would have given the President authority to wage an undeclared naval war. Soon afterward, under an old law, Wilson undertook to arm American merchant vessels, and orders were issued that gun crews upon such ships were to attack submarines that threatened them. At last war could no longer be avoided. On March 18 submarines sank three American ships without warning, taking many American lives. Immediately thereafter Wilson called Congress into a special session and on April 2 he asked it to declare war upon Germany. He said that neutrality was not possible. Painfully aware that entrance into the war would require immense sacrifice and that the consequences of the conflict must be shattering, he asserted that Germany had permitted no other choice. Because Tsarist Russia, staggering under German blows, had recently become a constitutional monarchy, he was able to assert that "The world must be made safe for democracy." "It is a dreadful thing," he declared, "to lead this great peaceful people to war, and to the most terrible and senseless of all wars. Civilization itself seems to be in the balance. But . . . we shall fight . . . for democracy, . . . for the rights and liberties of small nations, for a universal dominion of right by such a concert of free peoples as shall bring peace and safety to all nations and make the world itself at last free." The Congress promptly passed a resolution declaring war on Germany, the Senate by a vote of 82 to 6, and the House of Representatives by a tally of 373 to 50 two days later. The news quickly flashed around the world that America had joined the Allies.

48 WORLD WAR I

It may be denied that the United States entered World War I because of its fear of Imperial Germany—in other words, to preserve a balance of power—but not that America contributed powerfully, or even decisively, to Allied victory. In the spring of 1917 the Allies were staggering under their heavy losses, while the Germans, despite enormous casualties, remained confident of final success. Russia was weakening rapidly; there was a gloomy spirit in the French army; and the British reported that the German submarines had reduced their foodstuffs to a six-weeks' supply. An immense American effort was required, and it was made. Men, equipment, and food poured into France and England, and Germany at last collapsed in the fall of 1918. Before the Kaiser fled into exile in Holland, American "doughboys" faced the Germans on a large segment of the Western Front.

MOBILIZING FOR WAR

No better testimony to the earnestness and vigor of America in waging World War I can be found than the nation's swift and massive resort to the draft. The ranks of the Navy and of the Marine Corps were swelled as in past emergencies, by enlistment, and it was expected by the majority of

Americans that the land forces would also be filled by volunteers. However, even before the declaration of war, President Wilson had reached
the conclusion that conscription would be necessary and had begun to lay
plans for it. Many men had already enlisted for military duty, and not a
few had long since hurried off to Canada to pose as British subjects and to
serve with the British army. There was widespread feeling in the spring
of 1917, in Congress and out, that volunteers would come forward in such
numbers that it would not be necessary to compel men to put on uniforms. Many believed that use of the draft would be disgraceful and that
troops collected by such means would not be reliable. Some would have it
that conscription was a most tyrannical measure, acceptable only in the
countries of the enemy; it was also inaccurately assailed as a violation of
personal rights under the Constitution. Wilson knew that American troops
would be badly needed in France, and that it was unsafe to rely upon enlistments. It was well known that the casualties of the Allies had long since
passed beyond 3 millions. Moreover, drafting was fairer, and more systematic as well. Accordingly, the President asked Congress to make all
men aged 21 through 30 subject to military call. After a brief delay, Congress passed a Draft Act in May. In the summer of 1918 a second draft law
required all men aged 18 through 45 to register for possible military
service.

There was only trifling resistance to forced enlistment; there were some
hundreds of draft evaders, and some North Carolina mountain men at first
refused to register because they did not know the United States was at war
with Germany. A special reason for the success of compulsory soldiering
was the manner in which President Wilson and Secretary of War Newton
D. Baker arranged for it. Recalling the draft riots in New York City during
the Civil War, they substituted the term "selective service" for the unpopular word "draft." They also arranged that local civilian boards should
choose the men to be selected from lists of all those subject to call. In addition, they carried on an extraordinarily successful campaign of propaganda
to persuade the draftees that they possessed the esteem and affection of
their fellow citizens. Before the war ended, more than 24,000,000 men were
registered for service and 2,700,000 had put on khaki uniforms. More than
2,000,000 soldiers landed in French ports, and about half of them saw duty
in the trenches. Hundreds of thousands were in training camps when the
war came to its close.

SUPPLIES AND THE "BRIDGE TO FRANCE"

The rapidly increasing strength of the regular United States Army, the
Army of the United States, the Navy, and the Marine Corps was matched
by a massive industrial effort. Weapons, uniforms, gas masks, trucks, and a
host of other military materials were made in vast quantities. A Council

of National Defense, composed chiefly of Cabinet members and advised by a committee of business executives had been established in 1916 and had laid the groundwork for concerted production efforts. Among those engaged in the planning was Bernard M. Baruch, who became a "czar" over American factories and mines. Baruch was splendidly fitted for his part. He was independently rich, having made a fortune on the New York stock market. Shrewd, enthusiastic, tactful, and endowed with an infectious humor, he persuaded rather than compelled the leaders of industry to devote their men and machines to the making of war materials. He was helped by experts in industrial processes whom he chose for their ability rather than their prominence; these commonly served at a salary of $1.00 per annum. Filling British and French orders for weapons and supplies, American factories also largely met the needs of the American armed forces and production had by no means reached its maximum capacity when the war came to an end. The tanks, airplanes, and heavy artillery used by the Allies were mostly made in England and France. In World War I America was not the arsenal of the Allies that it was to be in World War II, but the American contribution was essential to victory.

Of paramount value to the Allied cause was the food sent across the Atlantic. Britain needed it especially, since the British Isles did not produce enough to feed their people, even in time of peace. Under the Lever Act of August, 1917, President Wilson was given vast authority for the purposes of increasing and preserving supplies of foodstuffs and fuels. To wield it under his direction the President chose Herbert Clark Hoover, a Quaker mining engineer who had performed magnificently at the head of a commission that had brought relief to starved Belgium early in the war. Under Hoover's supervision farmers and ranchers produced grain and cattle, as never before—what the Allies wanted so badly and could be carried across the Atlantic. To increase further the flow of food, Hoover called upon those who remained at home to save it. Like Baruch, he relied largely upon persuasion rather than force. Tuesdays on which no meat was eaten and Thursdays and Saturdays when no pork was consumed, conserved proteins and fats so needed in France and Belgium. Eating oatmeal bread that was actually better than white bread made it possible to heighten the flood of wheat into bins in England and France. Waste of food, an American habit, was discouraged. Toward the end of the war each person was allowed two pounds of sugar per month. Children were ordered to finish their food in more emphatic language than parents had been accustomed to employ; a boy eating an apple was told that he must be patriotic to the core. The result was spectacular. Shipments of grain, meat, fats, and sugar from the United States and the West Indies were almost three times as great in 1918 as they had ever been.

It mattered little that soldiers, guns, and food, in great numbers and quantities were accumulated in North America, if they did not reach Europe. When the United States went to war, the forty or fifty submarines that Germany could keep at sea were sinking Allied merchant vessels twice as fast as they could be built. The European Allies could not increase the rate of launchings, and the need for ships became imperative, since an American army and everything necessary for its support had to be sent to France. The American merchant marine had long languished and was comparatively small; nevertheless, a "Bridge to France" had to be constructed. America made a spectacular effort to secure ships. Many German merchant vessels that had sought safety in American ports and had been interned were seized and converted into American ones, while others belonging to neutrals were commandeered. Ships accustomed to ply the waters of the Great Lakes were taken apart, carried to the Atlantic seaboard, put together again, and sent across the Atlantic. A vast building program was started, under Charles M. Schwab, who was made head of the Emergency Fleet Corporation in April, 1918. Shipyards sprang up on the Atlantic and Pacific coasts, 341 of them being completed before the end of the war. Their workers were excused from military service, or "deferred." At the time of the Armistice in 1918 there were 350,000 persons engaged in the construction of ships. Even mass production use of interchangeable parts, something utterly new in the making of ships, was attempted. There was also an effort to make them out of concrete. The result was impressive; 533 vessels, or more than 3,000,000 tons of shipping were launched in 1918—95 craft being sent down the ways to celebrate the Fourth of July. Impressive to the scholar afterward was the fact that shipbuilding did not reach its peak until the war had ended—it was disconcerting to learn that half of the American troops who went to France were carried in British vessels. Helpful as it was, American shipbuilding on the great scale by no means accomplished all that had been hoped from it.

Although the American war effort was not total, new and extraordinary measures were taken to insure victory. There was some price-fixing as well as rationing; foodstuffs could not be used to make alcoholic liquors; and all railways were governmentally managed by Secretary of the Treasury William G. McAdoo after December, 1917. A giant War Finance Corporation with a capital of $500,000,000 was established in April, 1918, to extend credit to financial institutions that in turn lent money for the building of factories and the making of war materials. The following month Congress passed the Overman Act, which authorized the President to do what he would with the executive branch of government to secure efficiency and economy. The Espionage Act of June, 1917, struck heavily at persons guilty of helping the enemy, of discouraging enlistment in the armed forces, or of causing disloyalty or disobedience among the nation's fighting men. Such treason and disloyalty could be punished by a heavy fine or imprisonment for as long as twenty years. The law also gave the Postmaster General authority to bar from the mails printed materials that were treasonable or seditious. The Sedition Act of May, 1918, placed further restrictions upon individuals. It imposed heavy penalties upon persons guilty of making or spreading lies that injured the war effort; those who willfully used "disloyal, profane, scurrilous, or abusive language" against the American government, the Constitution, the flag, or the armed services; persons who tried to persuade others to slow down in the production of war materials; and all those who urged, taught, defended, or suggested such practices. A memorable and afterward somewhat disquieting novelty was a Committee on Public Information, created by Wilson to spread propaganda both at home and abroad.

Money had to be raised, and in huge sums. Excise levies on liquor, tobacco, luxuries, and amusements were heavily increased in the War Revenue Act of October, 1917. Far more important toward getting money were raises of income and corporation taxes. A minimum tax of 4 percent was placed on income above $1000 per annum, and the basic tax upon corporations was set at 6 percent. A graduated excess profits levy of 20 percent to 60 percent upon the income of corporations and persons both brought in a revenue and limited profiteering. But it was necessary, as it had been in all of America's greater wars, to borrow much more money than could be obtained through taxes. Five arduous campaigns to sell Liberty Bonds, the last of them in early 1919, were almost astonishingly successful. So well conducted were they that nearly every adult American was asked to subscribe, and more than half did. Altogether, $20,500,000,000 worth of the bonds was bought. They not only nourished the war machine, but proved to be an excellent investment.

PROPAGANDA AND MORALE

The most original contribution toward winning the war was that of George Creel, who conceived the Committee on Public Information and directed it until the close of hostilities. Generously given funds by Wilson, Creel undertook to educate the American people concerning the conflict and at the same time to excite enthusiasm. Toward those ends he made use of newspaper and magazine articles, pamphlets, posters by distinguished artists, speeches by war heroes and movie stars, and every other means that occurred to him. In effect, Creel ran a potent bureau of propaganda, something new in America. He undoubtedly stirred the nation to greater effort. On the other hand, although he was opposed to a strict censorship, he could not and did not fail to color the news and comment upon it. While Creel refrained from making the most vicious use of his influence over the minds of his fellow citizens, he was to a degree responsible for war hysteria as well as enthusiasm and will to win. Hate of Germany and everything German reached such a height that a Beethoven

symphony could not be played in American cities, sauerkraut was renamed
"liberty cabbage," and the loyalty of persons of German descent was questioned by their neighbors. The tiny village of Berlin in Michigan became
Marne. The superb musician Fritz Kreisler was not permitted to offer a
performance upon the violin because he had once been a lieutenant in the
Austro-Hungarian army—this despite the fact that his homeland was only
a secondary enemy, against whom the United States did not declare war
until many months after the conflict with Germany had begun. Americans
of Danish and Swedish stock were persecuted by super-patriots, because
Denmark and Sweden were neutral and near Germany. Even the teaching
of the German language was largely abandoned, because of the pressure
of public opinion, but also because of hostile laws. The state of Nebraska
forbade instruction in any foreign language in its schools, even in private
ones, so exceeding its constitutional authority. Many Socialists and anarchists were arrested and sent to prison, some for expressing views that were
obnoxious but not really dangerous.

Creel did not confine himself to convincing the American people of the
justice of the cause. He also carried on campaigns "for the verdict of mankind," trying to "sell" America's war aims to the world and at the same
time to sap the morale of the Central Powers. He waged ideological warfare in Europe, making especially persuasive use of speeches and statements
by Wilson. In fact, Creel and the President were a singularly efficient propaganda team that weakened the will to fight of the Germans and their
comrades in arms. Wilson declared that the Americans were not enemies
of the German people, but their friends; America was fighting only against
"the ruthless master" and the "ruling classes." He said "This is a People's
War," fought "to make the world safe" for all, including the downtrodden
masses of Middle Europe. He assailed the "military masters" in Berlin as
oppressors alike of Germans, Slavs, and the "indomitable Turks." Wilson
undertook to drive a wedge between governments and governed in the
enemy nations, and extended a promise of a better and democratic world,
including freedom for oppressed nationalities. Creel saw to it that these
declarations and promises were spread behind the lines of the Central
Powers. Leaflets dropped in Germany had such effect that German officers
forbade their men to take them from the ground. There is no doubt that
this American propaganda weakened the Central Powers, that it appealed
to their war-weary and discontented subjects. When the struggle ended,
Wilson, who had carefully refrained from describing the United States as
one of the Allies but had consistently referred to America as a nation "associated" with them, was looked upon by the humble and the oppressed
everywhere in Europe as one who would lead toward a happier time. It
had then become apparent that America sought neither territorial nor
commercial gains from the war.

Let it not be assumed that the American propaganda, seductive because it sincerely promised that the President would work in behalf of national freedom and democracy, had decisive effect before the tide of battle turned in favor of the Allies. So long as the Central Powers seemed likely to be victorious, the words had relatively little influence. Only when their military position became doubtful did Wilson's arguments find widespread acceptance in the minds of the Germans. Until the late summer of 1918 the military advantage was held by Germany and her partners rather than by the Allies. In the early summer of that year, the Germans came close to crushing Allied resistance on the Western Front.

PROGRESS OF THE WAR: 1917

The news from the battle lines was almost uniformly bad for the Allies throughout 1917. Offensives undertaken by the French and British in France brought small gains and heavy casualties. So shaken was the morale of the French army by its losses and lack of achievement that there were minor mutinies in it. These so seriously threatened to spread that its commander was removed and replaced by Marshal Henri-Philippe Pétain, who believed that the Allies had to remain on the defensive until the Americans should arrive in France in great force. The Germans on the Western Front retreated, but only to the Hindenburg Line, which had been so strongly fortified that it could be held with fewer troops, thus making it possible to strengthen the German forces on the Eastern Front, and also to strike heavily against Italy. In consequence, the German armies were able to erase vestiges of resistance in Rumania and to compel both Rumania and Russia to make peace; and Italy almost collapsed. The Germans and Austro-Hungarians advanced steadily through the Russian Baltic provinces and also into the Ukraine.

The war losses and sufferings of the Russians had become immense, and the Romanov dynasty fell in May. During the next six months a republican regime in which Alexander Kerensky was the dominant figure tried to carry on the struggle, but both the spirit and the means needed to hold back the Germans were lacking. In the fall came a second revolution, a Communist one under the leadership of Nicolai Lenin and Leon Trotsky. The Communists swiftly asked for peace terms. So much was asked by Germany that the Communists balked. They had no real choice but to submit, and in March, 1918, the new Soviet Russia signed the treaty of Brest-Litovsk, by which 60,000,000 people in Russia's western and southern borderlands, including Lithuanians, Poles, Ukrainians, and Armenians, came under German hegemony. Attempts on the part of Russia's former allies in 1918 to rebuild some sort of eastern line against the Germans, by sending troops and ships to Archangel, the Crimea, and Vladivostok, and by supporting counterrevolutionary movements in Russia, gained only the hostility of the Communists. The kingdom of Italy, engaged on its north-eastern frontier with part of the armies of Austria-Hungary, barely managed to maintain an effective defense in 1917. The Austro-Hungarian forces, stiffened by six German divisions, almost routed the Italians in the campaign of Caporetto. The enfeebled Italians barely held their enemies away from the open plains of Lombardy, and Allied leaders felt it necessary to send troops from France to their assistance. The only really good news of the fighting on land in that year for the Allies was the capture of Jerusalem from the Turks by British soldiers and Arab auxiliaries, advancing from Egypt under General Edmund Allenby. The stage was ready for a mighty German effort to drive France, and perhaps England, out of the war in 1918, before American troops could arrive in strength.

The Allies were also staggered at sea in 1917, but gradually overcame the menace of the German submarines. As suggested above, men, military materials, and food gathered in America would be of no help if they remained there or found their way to the bottom of the ocean. For many months after the American entrance into the war it was doubtful that they would reach England and France in any great quantity. The few dozens of U-boats that the Germans were able to keep under the sea were truly formidable. During the six months from February to July they sank, on the average, about 100 Allied vessels every 30 days. Many other merchant ships were damaged and crippled. Had the submarines continued at this rate, Germany indeed might have been the victor. American shipbuilding in 1918—it will be recalled that it did not reach its peak until the end of the war—would have replaced only half of such losses. Important as was this contribution, the Allies had to rely heavily upon British vessels, which carried tens of thousands of seasick American troops to France. Fortunately for the Allies, America had a navy that could offer essential service. Its destroyers and smaller submarine chasers, added to those of the British and French, made possible an energetic and continuous campaign against the U-boats in the Atlantic. The Allies were able to set up a convoy system. The German sinkings were cut in half by the end of 1917, and to one-third in 1918, when Allied losses in merchant vessels were replaced. The convoy system was so sound that only 100 American soldiers en route to France were drowned because of German torpedoes. Germany lost the war at sea.

"OVER THERE"

On August 15, 1917 there was an extraordinary sight in London, a parade of American troops amidst wild cheering by the inhabitants of that old city. The Yanks were arriving "Over There." But the Americans did not reach France in large numbers before the close of the year. The first of them entered the trenches in October, 1917, but they were not engaged in large-scale fighting with the Germans before April 24, 1918, when "doughboys" helped to check an offensive by the "Huns." Large numbers reached France in 1918; by July 1 there were one million of them; by the end of October two millions. However, they could not prudently be thrown into combat against German veterans immediately. Usually they had had only six months of training at home. Accordingly, they were commonly given two months more of instruction in France and sent into a relatively quiet section of the Western Front for another month before they were placed in vital areas on the lines. About 1,400,000 did serve in the lines, but the Americans did not hold a large part of them until the summer of 1918. They arrived just in time. Most of them, before moving up to the trenches, had enough leisure to learn to sing "Tipperary" and especially "Mademoiselle from Armentières" which was, with many verses, the favorite song of the men in khaki. One verse ran:

> Oh, the General got the Croix de Guerre; parley-vous?
> Oh, the General got the Croix de Guerre; parley-vous?
> Oh, the General got the Croix de Guerre,
> But the son-of-a-gun was never there!
> Hinky Dinky, parley-vous?

Another verse declared that:

> Mademoiselle from Armentières
> She hasn't been kissed in forty year.

Meanwhile for many weeks the news from the trenches was bad.

The Allies knew that Imperial Germany must take the offensive in the spring of 1918 in northeastern France in a last mighty effort to win the war before American strength should make itself felt, but they were not so ready for the onslaught of the Germans as they might have been. By July German troops were again on the Marne River, only 37 miles from Paris and probable victory. The skillful generals Paul von Hindenburg and Erich von Ludendorff collected men and materials in the early weeks of 1918 until they had secured superiority in both. The French were so weakened by their losses that the British had to take over areas formerly defended by the *poilus;* at the same time, David Lloyd George, the British Prime Minister, kept several hundred thousand soldiers at home to prevent Marshal Douglas Haig, commander of the British troops in France, from ordering expensive attacks. In March the Germans surprised the French and British with a great assault at the point where their armies met, and almost drove them apart. A yawning gap between them was closed barely in time to prevent the Germans from pouring through. The British lost 150,000 men, including 19,000 prisoners. The near-disaster did bring one improvement for the Allies. To make sure that the French and British armies would henceforth work together more closely, Marshal Ferdinand Foch was made commander in chief of all the Allied forces in France and Belgium. But this change was not made immediately and did not win the war. In April the Germans again pushed back the British near Ypres. In May, June, and early July they struck thrice against the French, driving them back toward their capital. The Germans did not reach it. They had inflicted one million casualties upon the Allies, but they themselves had suffered as many. The Americans under General John J. Pershing were moving into the front lines in force, taking over a sector at Chateau-Thierry. They helped to contain the Germans, and their presence gave the Allies superiority in numbers by August 1.

COLLAPSE OF THE CENTRAL POWERS

Then came the final turning of the military tide. On July 18, with the equivalent of 18 American divisions at the front and others moving up, Marshal Foch ordered a counteroffensive that was successful. The relatively inexperienced American troops performed brilliantly, not only at Chateau-Thierry but at Belleau Wood, in the Argonne Forest, and in the reduction of the St. Mihiel salient. They drove forward despite heavy losses. The Allies had finally begun to produce tanks in quantity, and they were very effectively used by the British army. On August 8 a British attack supported by more than 400 of these land battleships broke through the German lines. It was, said Ludendorff, the "Black Day of the German Army." Foreseeing final defeat, he fell into a panic, and urged his masters in Berlin to sue for peace while German troops were still on French soil. However, he soon recovered his poise and managed to put up a stiff resistance against continuing Allied attacks, although he was steadily forced back across both France and Belgium. Meanwhile, the news that he had given up hope of victory leaked out among both civilians and soldiers of the Central Powers and undermined their morale. While the Germans fell back toward the Rhine in the fall of 1918, their partners collapsed. An Allied army that had landed at Salonika on the Aegean Sea compelled Bulgaria to lay down arms on September 30. A month later Turkey dropped out of the war. Taking advantage of the exhaustion of Austria-Hungary in both body and spirit, the Italian army under General Diaz opened a final offensive that led to the easy triumph of Vittorio Veneto. On November 3 the Habsburg emperor signed an armistice, soon afterward abdicating his throne. Eight days later representatives of a new German republic put their names on another armistice in a railway car in the forest of Compiègne and ended hostilities on the Western Front.

Afterward there were those in Germany, especially Adolf Hitler and other National Socialists, who would not accept the fact that Germany

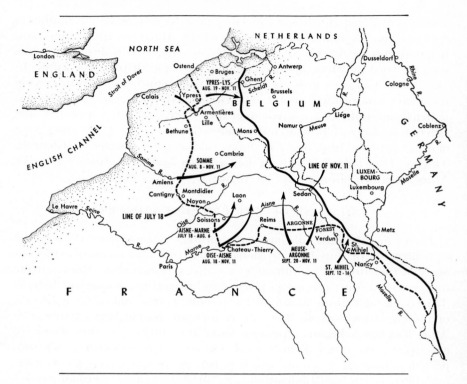

AMERICANS ON THE WESTERN FRONT, 1918

had been beaten in battle and who claimed that their country had been tricked into surrender and then betrayed by the Allies, especially by Woodrow Wilson. They claimed that Germany, still fighting on French and Belgian territory and able to resist indefinitely, had agreed to end the struggle and to work with the Allies toward making a better Europe on the basis of Wilson's Fourteen Points and other later declarations of war aims. There was an element of truth in the claim. However, the Allies could unquestionably have marched into Berlin, however desperate might have been German resistance. Moreover, while Wilson had made promises to work for democracy, self-determination, freedom of the seas, and a just and lasting peace, the Allies in general had not endorsed his views. When Germany asked for an armistice with the understanding that Wilson's pronouncements would be the basis for the terms of peace, the Allied War Council in Paris merely offered specific provisions for an armistice that contained no pledge concerning final settlements in consonance with Wilson's declarations. The armistice of November 11, 1918, was signed because German defeat had become inevitable.

Wilson's plans for a brighter future sapped the strength of the Central Powers after the tide of war had already turned. They hastened the end of the conflict only because the Germans and the other peoples of Central Europe who fought at their side refused to make further sacrifices in a doomed cause, or in behalf of rulers whom they disliked and even hated. Revolution was in progress everywhere between the North Sea and the Caspian in the fall of 1918. The Czechs, Slovaks, Slovenes, Croats and other peoples long held in subjection by the German Austrians and the ancient dynasty of the Habsburgs were in successful revolt, seeking independence. The Habsburg monarchy collapsed in Austria, and was only nominally maintained in an independent Hungary. There was civil strife in Bulgaria and Turkey. The Poles took up arms against all their oppressors, German, Austrian, and Russian. Nor could the Hohenzollern family or any of the Serene Highnesses of the German Empire cling to their thrones. As the military fortunes of Germany sagged, Kaiser Wilhelm too late sought to appease discontent by appointing as Imperial Chancellor Prince Max von Baden, a liberal-minded man who was no friend to the Junker aristocrats and industrialists who had shared power with the Hohenzollerns. The concession was useless; Wilson refused even to bargain with a Germany that remained imperial, even though her Chancellor was not a militarist. Early in November there were mutinies in the German navy; its admirals wished to take the fleet out into the North Sea on a "deathride." With revolution spreading, Prince Max and others urged the Kaiser to resign his crown. Had he done so, he might have preserved it for one of his grandsons. He refused, and Prince Max announced on November 9, without Wilhelm's consent, that the Emperor had abdicated. The declaration was received with pleasure, and the Kaiser prudently fled into exile in Holland and entered oblivion. Within hours of his flight republicans seized a shaky control of Germany.

Wonderstruck by the silence that came along the lines in France on November 11, the American soldiers gratefully and wearily began to think of going home. They were most joyously welcomed back in the New World, where neither cities nor countryside displayed the scars of war. Forty-nine thousand did not return, for they had been killed in Europe, and 230,000 more had been wounded. Altogether about 112,000 soldiers, sailors, and marines lost their lives in World War I, disease taking a somewhat heavier toll than the weapons of the enemy. Many thousands in the armed services had died of influenza, which also carried off several hundred thousand American civilians during the last year of the war. There were too many Gold Star mothers and too many permanently disabled veterans, but for most Americans their landscapes were still smiling ones. It was otherwise in Europe. Among its peoples the casualties in warfare were immense, the slain numbering about 8,400,000, including almost

1,800,000 Germans, perhaps as many Russians, more than 1,350,000 Frenchmen, about 1,200,000 Austro-Hungarians, and slightly above 900,000 soldiers of Britain and her Commonwealth. The youth of Europe had been
decimated, and as many civilians and soldiers may have died of hardships
and disease. In Eastern and Central Europe after the end of the war there
was confusion, starvation, and anarchy as well as revolution. The task of
reconstruction was awesome. Britain, France, Italy, and the other European
nations among the Allies were also badly shaken. In 1914 Sir Edward Grey,
the English Foreign Secretary, had commented that the lamps were going
out over Europe, and had wondered if and when they would come on
again. They came on again when the war ceased, but they only flickered
for some time.

49 THE RETURN TO ISOLATION

The design for a better world announced by Wilson in the Fourteen Points in January, 1918, and in six other points he later added, was suffused by novelty and idealism. It contained special concessions for two of the Allies, Serbia being promised free access to the Adriatic Sea and France the provinces of Alsace and Lorraine, which she had been forced to cede to the German Empire after her defeat in the Franco-German war of 1870 and 1871. Wilson thus in advance put a limit to Italian claims to the eastern shore of the Adriatic, and denied that Germany had a legitimate right to Alsace and Lorraine. Nor were the people in either of the disputed areas to be permitted to voice their wishes. Doubtless unwisely, the President promised to an independent Poland "free and secure access" to the Baltic Sea. In general, however, Wilson laid down broad and consistent principles toward securing justice and peace for all; in addition, he urged the forming of a society of nations. He desired that the treaties ending the war should insofar as possible correct past wrongs, and that future disputes be resolved without recourse to war, by an international government. Wilson called for: "Open covenants of peace openly arrived at"; complete freedom of the seas, except that they might be closed by his League of

Nations; removal of all economic barriers; reduction of armaments to the lowest point consistent with domestic safety; a just settlement of all colonial claims, taking into account the welfare of the colonial peoples; redrawing of boundaries and changing governments in Europe and the Near East in accordance with the principle of nationality; free passage of ships of all nations under international guarantee through the Straits of Constantinople; and, above all, the forming of a League of Nations that would guarantee independence and territorial integrity to great and small states alike. As the war drew to its close, there was high hope in the New World as well as the Old that Wilson's plan would be largely carried out. However, many parts of it encountered bitter resistance in Europe, and Wilson's own country refused to join the League of Nations. The peace treaties mingled idealism with punishment of the Central Powers and rewards for the Allies. In the end, America not only declined to join the League of Nations, but resolved to go back to the tradition of avoiding permanent foreign alliances and entanglements.

THE PARIS PEACE CONFERENCE

Determined to do all he could toward creating a peaceful, prosperous, and free world, Wilson undertook personally to lead a crusade for it at Paris, which had been chosen by the Allies as the place where World War I should be officially and finally terminated. He embarked on the *George Washington* for France in early December, 1918. His mission was extraordinary, and it was not undertaken with the unanimous approval of the American people. He went with the enthusiastic endorsement of idealists and of people saddened by war who were at least temporarily disposed to take the most drastic steps toward preventing another great conflict. However, there were many Americans then, and there would be more later as memory of the war receded, who feared that the United States would lose rather than gain by lowering tariffs and by entering the League of Nations. They believed that once the German menace had been removed, their country could turn back toward political isolation. Although some prominent Republicans, including William Howard Taft, had spoken for a society of nations, others, especially those like LaFollette of the progressive persuasion, were bitterly opposed. Republicans were inevitably tempted to oppose the Wilsonian program because it was a Democratic one. Nor were all of the leaders in Wilson's own party convinced that it was necessary for America to be committed to help mend global wrongs and to accept world government.

It was rather ominous for Wilson that he had suffered a setback at the polls a month before he took ship. Before the off-year election of 1918 he had urged the voters to show their confidence in him by casting Democratic ballots. Instead, not carried away by wartime enthusiasm for the President, they had given the Republicans a majority in both houses of Congress. After the defeat of his party prudence dictated that he seek the support of powerful Republicans, especially in the Senate, who would help secure approval of any treaty or treaties that he might sign at Paris. The President injured his chances of success by failing to do so. The man who could have been most helpful to Wilson's cause was Henry Cabot Lodge, Senator from Massachusetts, soon to become chairman of the Committee on Foreign Relations in the upper house. Lodge had committed himself to some sort of union of the nations, and he would have a profound influence on the course of the Senate with respect to any agreement that Wilson might want to make. However, Wilson and Lodge disliked and distrusted each other, and Wilson would not have Lodge among the commissioners who accompanied him. Nor, for one reason or another, did he find any other Republican senator to be suitable. From the party that opposed him he took with him only Henry White, who was well informed about international affairs, but who had never carried great weight among the Republicans. The other members of Wilson's commission were Colonel House, Secretary of State Lansing, and General Tasker Bliss. To help him Wilson also selected various "experts," especially university professors familiar with European problems. Intending to make a basic change in American foreign policy, Wilson chose as his counselors men who had largely been inactive in political life; he erred, for he should have had a bipartisan commission. After nearly six strenuous years in the Presidency, he was tired.

Arriving in France before the peace conference began, Wilson journeyed through France and Italy, and was everywhere acclaimed as the symbol of an America that had come to a military rescue and that would lead the way toward a shining future. Humble folk saw him as a Messiah from a fresh and happy New World who would mend the gaping wounds of Europe. Nor was Wilson welcomed joyously only by the French and Italians, for he was seen as a savior by peoples who had been oppressed since time beyond memory, Estonians, Ruthenians, Slovenes, Armenians, and others. Men wearing strange costumes and speaking obscure tongues came to see Wilson and to plead for his help toward securing independence and democracy. There was hope even among the defeated Germans that their welfare would not be ignored, and that they too would find in Wilson a good and disinterested friend. Much was hoped and expected from Wilson.

It was, however, doubtful from the first that Wilson would readily be allowed to lead in the reconstruction of Europe and the world. The enthusiasm voiced for him had a desperate note. Europe had been bled white. Warfare still continued, and new wars were about to begin—Russians against Russians, Poles against Russians, Hungarians against Hungarians,

Greeks against Turks. Want and privation reigned in Central Europe, in part because the Allied blockade was not abandoned at the armistices. There was despair as well as hope, and Western Europe was both exhausted and languid. Old national hatreds continued, and new ones were blossoming. The Germans resented the continuance of the Allied blockade after they had laid down their arms. There was determination in Belgium and France that their ruined lands and cities, some devastated almost beyond belief, must be restored at German expense. David Lloyd George, Prime Minister and chief British spokesman at Paris, had hastily called a general election as soon as German resistance had ceased, in order to take political advantage of wartime fervor. He had won with a promise that he would do everything possible to make Germany pay the entire cost of the conflict. Some of his adherents had cried, "Hang the Kaiser!" A shrewd and artful politician, the British Prime Minister did not intend to rely upon a League of Nations for British security. Counting on the friendship of the United States, he sought to provide for the safety of Britain by maintaining her navy and by a balance of power policy for Europe—he was concerned lest France dominate the Continent. Georges Clemenceau, the French premier known as "The Tiger," who had dauntlessly driven his country on to victory, was just as obstinately determined that its fruits be realistically reaped. An old man who had learned to hate the Germans in his youth, he was utterly unwilling to put faith in any international assembly. He wanted as absolute guarantees of the safety of France against future German aggression as he could get, including an Anglo-French-American military alliance that would require Britain and the United States to come to France's aid in the event of another German attack. Nor was Vittorio Orlando, the Italian premier and chief representative from Rome, much given to thoughts about the brotherhood of man. He was primarily interested in securing territorial gains for his country, including German districts in the Alps, which would give Italy a frontier easier to defend. Another obstacle in Wilson's path were secret treaties signed by the Allies before the entrance of the United States into the war; these contained solemn promises of territorial and other gains in the event of triumph. Such pledges made by Britain, France, and Italy to each other could not lightly be pushed aside.

Wilson was quite unable to dominate the Peace Conference, and he was compelled to accept compromises. He was one of a Council of Ten that directed the work of the dozens of delegates, and with Clemenceau, Lloyd George, and Orlando, he was also one of the "Big Four" that guided the Council of Ten. In Asian and Pacific questions Japan also had a major voice. The Allies had not promised to labor toward an enduring and fraternal peace at the time of the Armistice, nor had they committed themselves to the Fourteen Points. Britain had offered a specific reservation with respect to freedom of the seas, and a demand for reparations had also been made. That Wilson would be forced to bargain with Clemenceau, Lloyd George, Orlando, and others, and to offer further concessions was evident even in the structure of the Peace Conference, for the Central Powers were not permitted to send delegates. In the past, the vanquished had been permitted to take part in the negotiations following European wars. They had done what they could to moderate the demands of their enemies, and even to profit from divisions among the victors. The Allies were determined to impose a treaty upon Germany without such interference, and their delegates drew up a series of treaties which the defeated were forced to sign without much ado. Wilson himself believed that Germany was specially responsible for the war and deserved no very gentle treatment. The treaties, signed at and near Paris, removed ancient wrongs, created some new ones, and founded the League of Nations, which offered a brighter hope for the future.

THE TREATY OF VERSAILLES

The political map of Europe was much improved at Paris. The profound desires of several peoples for nationhood were properly satisfied. Indeed, not entirely because of the efforts of the peacemakers, the map of Europe in 1920 more closely followed the principle of nationality than ever before. There was much to be said for the creation or recreation of Finland, the Baltic States, Poland, Czechoslovakia, and Yugoslavia. However, the new nations, like the old, were permitted to erect economic barriers, which they did to their common loss, especially in the valley of the Danube. Besides, boundaries were not drawn as nearly as possible in conformity with the principle of nationality. Exceptions were made on economic and military grounds in favor of the Allies, and areas in which two or more peoples were mingled were commonly taken from the Central Powers (the new countries of Austria and Hungary were punished for the sins of the Austro-Hungarian Empire). So Austrians came under the Italian flag, Germans under the Polish, and Hungarians under the Rumanian.

The Treaty of Versailles, signed by representatives of the new German republic in the Hall of Mirrors on June 28, 1919, contained many seeds for future trouble, and at no distant time. Two of several territorial changes required of Germany deeply injured German national sentiment. On the west Germany had to cede Alsace and Lorraine, as was to be expected, but more important, she was forced to abandon the German-populated Saar Valley and its mines to French exploitation for a period of years. A plebiscite was then to determine the fate of the Saar in accordance with the wishes of its people. Far more productive of German discontent was the creation of a Polish Corridor to Danzig on the Baltic Sea that separated

East Prussia from the remainder of Germany. The Allies felt that a free Poland had to have an outlet to the Baltic; the Germans were to feel that they had on the east "bleeding frontiers." The principle of nationality was not applied to the Germans; had it been, they might have become more dominant in Central Europe than they had been in the past, for Austria would logically have been annexed to Germany. Moreover, the territories which Germany was to lose either permanently or temporarily deprived her of a large part of the mineral wealth upon which her prosperity and military potence had been based. Germany was also compelled to sign a so-called "war-guilt" clause, which declared that Germany (together with Austria-Hungary) had been the aggressor in the Sarajevo crisis of 1914. Germany was therefore compelled to pay reparations for war damages, which were tentatively set by the Allies in 1921 at the then vast figure of $31 billion. Germany was also deprived of all her colonies, which came under the control of one or another of the Allies. To make sure that the treaty would be honored, the Allies insisted upon the reduction of the German army and navy to very small forces, and they also required Germany to accept armed occupation of the Rhineland by the Allies for fifteen years. The treaty, especially in its economic terms, was too harsh; alternatively, for the prevention of future wars, it was too easy. From the commission of one injustice the Allies were saved by the Dutch government, which refused to turn over Kaiser Wilhelm II to be tried as a "war criminal."

THE LEAGUE OF NATIONS

Wilson knew that the Treaty of Versailles was severe upon Germany and likely to cause bitter resentment among her people, although he did not foresee how profoundly they would detest it. He accepted many of its onerous provisions because Clemenceau, and to a lesser extent, Lloyd George, insisted upon them. He bent toward Clemenceau's wishes in order to get French consent to the inclusion of the Covenant of the League of Nations in the treaty. To persuade the French premier to support the League he even, with Lloyd George, went so far as to sign a military alliance by which the United States and Britain promised to come to the aid of France in the event of an "unprovoked" attack upon her by Germany—a treaty that was not ratified by the Senate. Wilson believed that the League, serving for the prevention of war generally, would be used to rectify mistakes and wrongs committed in the Versailles document. Although Germany was not to be accepted immediately as a member of the League, he hoped that membership would not long be withheld. To Wilson, more than ever the League represented the hope for the future. The Covenant provided for an Assembly in which all the nations of the League had a

CENTRAL EUROPE AFTER WORLD WAR I

vote, and for a Council composed of delegates from nine countries, among them the United States, Britain, France, Italy, and Japan. All nations joining the League promised to submit for its consideration all disputes that threatened to end in war, to reduce their armaments, and to help to form a Permanent Court of International Justice. They also pledged themselves to respect and preserve against aggressors the territorial integrity and independence of all members, and to join in economic and military sanctions against military aggressors. Geneva in Switzerland became the capital of the League. The League, it should be observed, was intended to exert far larger authority than was the later United Nations.

How much the League might have achieved with the sturdy support of the United States no one can say; had America joined it, it must have been more useful than it was. The Senate refused its consent to the Covenant, thus destroying Wilson's dream.

THE LEAGUE AT HOME

Whether or not America should enter the League became a burning question at home long before Wilson wrote his name upon the Treaty of Versailles. When the President returned to Washington for a visit during February and March, 1919, a draft of the Covenant which he and others had prepared was denounced by many Republicans and some Democrats. On March 2, 37 Republican Senators and two Republican Senators-elect signed a "round-robin" which declared Wilson's proposals were quite unacceptable and that a decision regarding the Covenant should not be taken until after peace had been officially made with Germany, Austria, and Hungary. Sentiment in the United States was divided, mixed, and confused, and it was to remain so. Editorial opinion in the press was rather generally in favor of some sort of society of nations, and voters who told their senators what they wanted commonly said that they favored one. However, the progressive Republicans in the Senate were devout isolationists and completely against any sort of international regime. They and their followers of the Midwest and West convinced themselves that the troubles of the world, especially those of Europe, could be kept far away. They were formidable enemies of the League. Conservative Republicans were divided, most of them in the Senate taking the position that Wilson's League might be satisfactory if they were permitted to amend it suitably— care should be taken to prevent Democratic mistakes and too great concentration of power in international government. The Democrats, not without partisan zeal, tended to rally behind the President, although some of them were also solicitous lest America cede too great power to an external authority. One Democratic Senator, James A. Reed of Missouri, was a determined enemy to any kind of international association. On the whole, in the early months of 1919 it seemed likely that the Senate would ratify the peace treaty with Germany, including the Covenant, but with amendments. The majority of Americans then seemed to desire such action. No fewer than 32 state legislatures and 33 governors declared that they endorsed the League of Nations.

Had the Democrats controlled the Senate when Wilson presented the Treaty of Versailles for approval, the Senate probably would have given basic consent. As it happened, the Republicans had a majority of 49 to 47 and dominated its committees, including that on foreign relations, to which the treaty had to be referred. They were able to delay a decision, and to compel a careful analysis of the treaty. Meanwhile, reaction from wartime idealism spread, and American willingness to accept great innovations that there should be "no more wars," weakened. It was further sapped by the propaganda of the enemies of Wilson's League, who made use of the time granted by the Senate. Two rich Republicans, Henry Clay Frick and Andrew Mellon, contributed funds for a campaign against unnecessary involvement in world affairs; money played its part in the making of speeches and the writing of papers demanding that the treaty be much modified or defeated. Had not Washington, Jefferson, and many another American statesman solemnly warned against foreign entanglements? Did the American people wish to send soldiers to enforce the dictates of a government beyond their control, send marines to Europe, Asia, or Africa? Fire was directed not only against the Covenant, but also against the other provisions of the treaty. Criticisms on the ground that it dealt cruelly and unwisely with Germany had effect among the Americans of German descent. Those of Irish ancestry were only too acutely aware that the treaty would place German colonies under British control, and that it did not free Ireland. Propaganda against the Treaty outside the Senate was accompanied by lengthy meetings of its Committee on Foreign Relations in which every opportunity was given to bring forth all the possible objections to it. Senator Henry Cabot Lodge, who said that the treaty would be acceptable if drastically amended, used his power as chairman of the committee to present the treaty in a very unfavorable light. It has frequently been charged that he was actually opposed to the Covenant, that he merely pretended to be for it with amendments, and also that he was hostile to it because he had not had a part in making it. His intent remains disputed. In any event, the Republican majority of the committee on September 10 asked the Senate to endorse 45 amendments and four reservations to the treaty. Since it was unlikely that the consent of the signers of the treaty to so many changes could be secured, the report of the committee virtually asked the Senate to turn down the Covenant.

Conscious that the Covenant would encounter tenacious resistance in the Senate and that public sentiment for the League was waning, Wilson had decided a week earlier that he must strive to turn the tide of opinion and so to put heavy pressure upon the Senate to ratify. His health was precarious, and his physicians warned him not to do it, but he undertook to make a personal appeal to the voters. He stubbornly went by train on a speaking tour that took him to the Pacific Coast and that exhausted his failing energies. He now defended the treaty almost as intemperately as its enemies attacked it. He praised its boundary provisions, along with the

Covenant, and he portrayed Lloyd George and Clemenceau as great and altruistic men. His many speeches aroused some enthusiasm in the West, but he fought against heavy odds. Senators William E. Borah of Idaho and Hiram Johnson of California, progressive Republicans who were hostile to the Covenant, followed Wilson and successfully counterattacked in city after city where the President had spoken. Turning eastward, Wilson planned to make speeches on a route that would take him all the way to Boston. Suddenly, at Pueblo, Colorado, his tour came to an end when he suffered a slight stroke. Brought back to Washington, he failed to recover, and a second and more damaging stroke soon made him an invalid. He carried on the struggle as best he could. Earlier he had indicated that approval of the treaty with some reservations would be acceptable; he now insisted that it must be endorsed completely. He had hitherto been able to give way about details in order to win support on major questions, but after his illness he was unwilling to make any compromises. He was a broken man, unable for many months to do even the lesser tasks of the Presidency. His wife, Edith Bolling Wilson, helped by Admiral Cary Grayson, the President's physician, saw to it that routine duties were performed until he had partly recovered. Ill or half-well, he would not permit his Cabinet to act for him, and he forced Secretary of State Lansing out of it when Lansing displayed a willingness to assume authority. He was perhaps the more determined to have his way because of his failing health.

The United States did not ratify the Treaty of Versailles. In the winter of 1919–1920, a majority in the Senate was willing to endorse it, subject to reservations, including the maintenance of the Monroe Doctrine and a proviso limiting the power of the League of Nations to commit America to military action. However, the will of the majority was defeated by two very determined minorities. The "Irreconcilables," chiefly Republicans, were passionately against any kind of world government, while a few Democrats who followed the leadership of Wilson and were ardent believers in the League of Nations insisted that the treaty be approved without hedging statements. In November, 1919, the Senate rejected the amendments submitted by its Committee on Foreign Affairs, since the amendments would doubtless destroy the Covenant; on the other hand, it refused to ratify the treaty in its original form by a vote of 53 to 38. Many Democratic Senators might then have combined with many Republican ones to ratify the treaty subject to fourteen "reservations" prepared under Lodge's leadership, but Wilson insisted that they support him, and most of them did. The compromise was defeated by a vote of 55 to 39. An outcry followed, as teachers, preachers, editors, and writers demanded that the League of Nations not be crippled by American refusal to join it. Petitions and appeals flooded into the Senate. The issue was tried again, in March of 1920. A second time Wilson and the Irreconcilables joined to prevent endorsement of the treaty with reservations. He stubbornly entreated the Democratic Senators to stand for the treaty as it came from Paris. About half of them, aware that the choice lay between the treaty with some reservations and no treaty at all, resolved to vote for compromise despite Wilson's plea. Enough of them stood by the President so that the treaty with reservations was lost by a vote of 49 yeas to 35 nays. Had seven more Democrats deserted Wilson, the compromise would have been carried. So close did America come to joining the League of Nations. While the reservations demanded by the majority of the Republicans were not all easily defended—one of them declared that America favored the independence of Ireland—Wilson would have done well to accept a bargain. He mistakenly believed that the election of 1920 would bring both to the Presidency and to the Senate people of his way of thinking.

THE FIRST POSTWAR ELECTION

In seclusion in the White House and without sound information about the mood of the American people in the early months of 1920, the ill and weary Wilson believed that his party could make adherence to the League the great issue in the approaching campaign and thus win the election. Hoping to regain his strength, he might even consider seeking a third term for himself. Actually, only a few devoted admirers were clinging to him. Their number diminished in part because of his own behavior—he refused to have anything more to do with Colonel House because House advised him to accept reservations to the Treaty of Versailles. The President could still exert influence in his own party, but it had to find a new leader if it wanted to have any chance in the campaign. He was steadily losing popularity, and his party with him. Indeed, it is difficult to conceive of any combination of candidate and issues that would have permitted the Democrats to make a good fight. The League was perhaps their best issue, despite the doubtfulness of its appeal. The country had tired of domestic reform, and the progressive Republicans who favored it and had supported Wilson in 1916 had turned against him and his party. Isolationists, the progressive Republicans would stand stoutly with the orthodox Republicans.

Labor had also lost its enthusiasm for the Democrats. The war years had been prosperous ones for the factory worker and miner. In 1914 Henry Ford had shocked the nation by establishing five dollars per day as a minimum wage for those employed by the Ford Motor Company. As the conflict continued, the wages of war workers soared far above that figure, and they were better off than they had ever been before. However, they lost their gains in an inflation of prices that continued through 1919 and 1920. More than 2,000,000 workers went on strike in the former year, and there were massive walkouts from coal mines and the steel industry that failed to achieve their purposes. The strikes were accompanied by violence. There was commotion in Boston, where a strike by underpaid police seeking to affiliate with the American Federation of Labor continued until it was broken by National Guards and volunteer patrolmen. Labor, so friendly to Wilson and the Democrats in 1916, was not enthusiastically devoted to Wilson's party in 1920.

Moreover, the Democrats had lost favor as a result of the "Great Red Scare," during the later months of World War I and immediately afterward. The Department of Justice had seen to it that many Socialists and anarchists were behind bars for violations of the Espionage and the Sedition Acts. The jailing of some of those persons, including Eugene V. Debs, for offenses that were hardly serious had offended liberal-minded men. But the postwar "red" menace was more than trifling. Communists, anarchists, and syndicalists were actively inciting industrial unrest. The Industrial Workers of the World, syndicalists led by William Haywood, created disorder in the West. Spurred on by the Russian Bolsheviks, American Communists formed a Workers Party. Attempts were made to assassinate various public officers, chiefly by anarchists. Mitchell Palmer, Wilson's Attorney General, took the lead in suppressing the would-be revolutionaries. Under his direction thousands of Communists, real and alleged, were arrested, and a few were deported to Russia. The "Great Red Scare" was both a symptom and a cause of a political swing to the right that could not fail to injure the chances of the Democrats. Indicative of the force of that swing was the imposition of special oaths of allegiance upon professors and teachers by several states, and a swift growth of the Ku Klux Klan, revived in 1915 and made into an efficient and profitable machine by its national officers in 1920. The Klan did not flourish on the north Atlantic seaboard, but it should not be thought that the shift to the right did not manifest itself there. In April, 1920 the New York Assembly expelled five Socialists as "traitors," despite the protests of Theodore Roosevelt, Jr., and Charles Evans Hughes.

"SAFE" CANDIDATES

Scenting victory at the polls in 1920, the Republicans happily observed the change in public sentiment, became more and more convinced that the need for the League of Nations was less than urgent, and named for the Presidency a "safe" man who was singularly unfitted for the job. Their choice was limited by a dearth of talented and well-known men, and they made a poor selection from those that were available. They might have rallied behind Theodore Roosevelt, but he had died in January, 1918. Charles Evans Hughes must have been the Republican candidate, had proven merit dictated the decision. As it happened, Hughes, saddened by the death of a beloved daughter, had no heart for the flummery and mum-

mery of politics, and declined to seek the support of delegates to the national convention. Thus less distinguished men were able to push forward,
among them, General Leonard Wood, Governor Frank O. Lowden of
Illinois, Senator Hiram Johnson, President Nicholas Murray Butler of
Columbia University, Senator Robert LaFollette, Senator Warren G. Harding, of Ohio, and Governor Calvin Coolidge of Massachusetts. Noteworthy
among the seekers of the nomination was the outsider Herbert Hoover,
who had never been an enthusiastic Republican.

General Wood and Governor Lowden were respected public servants,
and they led in the early ballots at the national convention in Chicago.
However, neither was able to secure a majority. As the former commander
of the Rough Riders, Wood had the allegiance of many of the followers of
Theodore Roosevelt, but he had injured his chances by announcing that he
favored universal military service. Lowden was hurt because two of his
supporters in Missouri used money that he sent to them for campaign purposes to secure their own election as delegates to the convention. Wood and
Lowden tried to form an alliance, but failed because they could not agree
which should have the Presidency and which the Vice-Presidency. They
cancelled each other out, and Senator Harding, an amiable man who had
no enemies and who was pleasing to the more conservative wing of the
party, moved forward. It has often been dramatically said that the choice of
Harding was determined by a gathering of politicians in "a smoke-filled
room." Actually, after many conferences in that room and others—tobacco
smoke was doubtless present in all of them—he was named on the tenth
ballot as the man most acceptable to all. Those who knew him were aware
that he was neither particularly able nor strong-willed, but they nevertheless hoped for the best. To balance their ticket, the Republicans joyfully
designated for the Vice-Presidency Governor Coolidge, who was no great
man and who did not pretend to be one. He had won national fame by
declaring toward the end of the Boston police strike: "There is no right to
strike against the public safety, by anybody, anywhere, any time." Choosing
inoffensive candidates, the convention also sought to avert a quarrel within
the party over the League of Nations; the Republican platform came out
against the Covenant, but declared that the party desired an "agreement
among the nations to preserve the peace of the world."

The Democrats in convention at San Francisco did somewhat better than
the Republicans. They too had to choose among many aspirants to the
Presidency, no one of them obviously superior to the others. Wilson overshadowed them all, but he could not be named for a third term. In the end,
the contest was between Attorney General Palmer, a Quaker both admired
and disliked for his Red-hunting; William G. McAdoo, who had displayed
competence in national office, but had inherited Wilson's enemies by marrying one of his daughters; and James M. Cox, who had performed well as

Governor of Ohio. No fewer than 44 ballots were required to select the candidate; in the end, the Democrats did what the Republicans had done. They selected Cox, because he had few enemies and might carry Ohio. Like Harding, Cox was by calling a newspaper editor; he was a respectable man, decidedly superior to Harding in character and ability. He was not a towering figure, and he lacked color. For the Vice-Presidency, the Democrats put forward handsome young Franklin D. Roosevelt of New York, who had made a decent record as Assistant Secretary of the Navy. It was hoped that the name Roosevelt would attract voters. A distant cousin of Theodore Roosevelt, Franklin was considered to be suitable rather than greatly gifted. The Democrats forthrightly endorsed the Treaty of Versailles, but declared that they were not opposed to reasonable reservations. They would no longer follow Wilson in his demand for ratification of the treaty without change.

RETURN TO "NORMALCY"

In the campaign that followed, Cox and Roosevelt made the League of Nations the first issue, partly in deference to the wishes of Wilson. They spoke for it with frequence and energy, but aroused little enthusiasm. Their arguments won them few votes, partly because Republicans, including Hughes and Taft, declared that the cause of the League would be safer in Republican hands. Copying McKinley, Harding spoke only from his front porch. He said nothing that would be offensive. He carefully placated the friends of the League in his party and among the independent-minded by saying that he was against the League of Nations, but for an Association of Nations, presumably a better formed body. What he said did not profoundly disturb the Irreconcilables. Harding had earlier announced that the country needed "normalcy," a rest from international and domestic adventures. The voters agreed with him. They had had enough of Wilson, and they turned against Cox. Harding was elected by a crushing majority, 16,152,200 to only 9,147,353 for Cox. Eugene V. Debs, in a federal prison at Atlanta, obtained 919,799 votes. In the electoral college also Harding's victory was overwhelming. Winning little more than the Solid South, Cox had only 127 votes to 404 for Harding. Congress became more heavily Republican. Going into quiet retirement in Washington, Wilson declared that he would show the new President how a former one should act. More sorely needed by Harding was instruction on how the chief executive should behave in office.

The bitter fight over the League of Nations had ended. Soon after he had become established in the White House, President Harding made it clear that he would do nothing toward creating the Association of Nations which he had offered as a hazy substitute. America was not to be deeply involved in the troubles of Europe. Before Wilson retired, the United States had made some contribution toward relieving the political sicknesses of that continent. Besides, America had lent several billion dollars to her former Allies and even to the defeated people of Europe toward their economic recovery. Further American help, further American "interference" in the affairs of Europe, would be severely limited for many years.

50 THE HARDING REGIME

Regaining control of the White House in 1921, the Republicans easily secured two renewals of their lease upon it, and they clung to it until 1933. During more than half of that twelve-year period they were also easily dominant on Capitol Hill. To the orthodox in the G.O.P., all was almost well with the world again, and they did what they might toward restoring "the good old days" of the beginning of the century. They offered a striking exception to the famous maxim of Lord Acton, so often quoted with solemn approval, that "power corrupts, and absolute power corrupts absolutely." The American nation had become the strongest and the richest in the world; its industrial might was unchallenged; New York had taken the place of London as the banking center of the globe; and Washington could have been made its chief political rendezvous. But the Republicans did not yearn to direct the destinies of all men and were reluctant to engage in adventures in foreign affairs, even toward the maintenance of peace. At home they desired economy both in public expenditures and the use of governmental authority. There was rottenness enough in federal offices during the first two years of Republican ascendancy after 1921, but though spectacular, it was relatively minor and temporary, a consequence in some part of a postwar reaction from the idealism of 1917 and 1918. The behavior of the Republicans in the "Reckless Twenties" may be more open to criticism for acts of omission than for those of commission. They displayed little vision; the Democrats did not see much more clearly. For almost a decade the United States enjoyed an Indian Summer, both in foreign and domestic affairs, that was followed by an extraordinarily harsh blast of winter.

Afterward, most of those who described the American scene as it was when Warren G. Harding occupied the Presidency, saw a carnival of graft and incompetence that stimulated almost as much wit as pain; and Harding himself was the frequent target of much satire. It has been debated whether he or Ulysses S. Grant was the worst American President. Yet there were also many, including some who later made him the butt of their wit, who believed that Harding had splendid qualifications for his high office when he entered it. He was handsome, and at first glance imposing, a little like Washington in external appearance. He also had one of the great qualities of Lincoln, for he was truly and generously kind—soon after assuming his duties he pardoned Eugene V. Debs, releasing him as soon as possible from the Atlanta penitentiary. He was socially democratic, and the silence and austerity that had reigned in the executive mansion during the last years of Wilson's residence were replaced by cheer and good humor. Even so, Harding was quite unfitted for his tasks; he had grave defects that led to his ruin. Despite his long political experience, he understood no public question containing complexities. His intellectual endowment, despite his fine brow, was moderate; and he had never made much use of it. He had somehow been a successful editor and publisher of a newspaper in Marion, Ohio, and the holder of various offices, including a seat in the United States Senate, without learning much about either the troubles or wickednesses of his fellow men. He had not learned to distinguish between an honest man and a thief. Remaining in Marion, he would have been liked and respected to the end of his days. However, Harding looked well on the platform, and he spoke smoothly, although not pointedly. No one could hate him. His ambitious wife, with the assistance of his good friend and political adviser, Harry M. Daugherty, pushed him up the ladder of public preferment in Ohio. He was sufficiently aware of his shortcomings not to be avid for the Presidency, but Fate, his wife, and Daugherty led him to it. He was happiest when he was enjoying a glass of whiskey and a hand of poker with the boys.

GOVERNMENT BY FRIENDSHIP

That Harding meant well, according to his lights, and that he was quite unequal to his tasks is readily evident in his selection of Cabinet members and other high officials. He appointed Charles Evans Hughes Secretary of

714   RISE OF THE AMERICAN REPUBLIC

State; the able business tycoon Andrew Mellon of Pittsburgh to the Treasury; and the honest and gifted manager, Herbert Hoover, who had definitely decided that he was a Republican, to be Secretary of Commerce. Having thus made some attempt to care for the needs of the nation, he rather casually chose various other rich men for one post or another, and bestowed offices upon his personal and political friends and acquaintances without bothering to weigh their characters or capabilities. The selection of Will H. Hays as Postmaster General and that of Edwin Denby as Secretary of the Navy were not inspired. Albert E. Fall, appointed Secretary of the Interior, acquired that office because he had been friendly to Harding in the Senate; he was not known as a champion of conservation, and he was to be unfaithful to the trust Harding reposed in him. The shortcomings of Denby and Fall were not generally known when they were appointed, but the choice of Harry M. Daugherty as Attorney General, made to reward a loyal but unqualified friend, was obviously a bad one. Daugherty was distinguished, not as a lawyer or judge, but as a political manipulator; he was to win enduring fame as the head of "the Ohio gang." Other appointments by Harding were shabby and ill-advised. He chose his brother-in-law, who had been a Seventh Day Adventist missionary in Southeast Asia, as commissioner of the federal prisons. For his official physician the President selected a homeopathic practitioner from Marion, giving him the rank of brigadier general. Placed over the important new Veterans Bureau was Charles R. Forbes, whom Harding had met on a vacation trip in Hawaii; the President had taken a fancy to Forbes, an extrovert who seemed to be a friendly sort. He would also betray Harding's thoughtless trust. Unscrupulous men found it only too easy to attach themselves to the easygoing Harding. Harding entertained respect for Hughes, intelligent and incorruptible, and for Mellon, the man of much money; he liked Daugherty and Forbes.

After Harding's death all sorts of scandalous revelations about him and his associates were offered to an eager public, some of them only too true, others being largely fabricated. A ghost-written memoir entitled *The President's Daughter,* supposedly written by one Nan Britton, related in mawkish phrases that Harding as a Senator was the father of a child by Miss Britton, and that she quietly made visits to the White House. The established facts were startling enough. However, they were not widely known until Harding's Presidency was near its end. The well-informed of Washington became aware rather soon that a certain raffishness had entered the executive mansion with Harding, and that on its second floor liquor flowed rather freely, despite the Volstead Law. A few knew that the President enjoyed playing cards with cronies of an evening in a little house on "K" Street. On the surface, Harding was devoting himself to his duties; indeed, he did his best to deal with the public questions he had to face.

INTERNATIONAL RELATIONS

The Harding record in international affairs was better than it might have been, thanks to the efforts of Secretary of State Hughes, who was to Harding as Hamilton Fish had been to Ulysses S. Grant. The President harbored no desire to reform the world, in fact no wish to be aggressive about anything. He had said so in pretentious and clumsy phrases in a speech in Boston before his party named him for the Presidency. He had then declared that the nation needed "not heroism but healing, not nostrums but normalcy, not revolution but restoration, not agitation but adjustment, not surgery but serenity, not the dramatic but the dispassionate, not experiment but equipoise, not submergence in internationality but sustainment in triumphant nationality." Nevertheless, many voters in 1920 had managed to persuade themselves that Harding's advocacy of an Association of Nations as opposed to Wilson's League of Nations was sincere and that he would do something about it. There is little doubt that they wished to be deceived; in their defense, it should be recalled that such a one as Herbert Hoover had declared during the campaign that Harding and his followers were solemnly pledged to a satisfactory substitute for the League. Hoover had declared, "The carrying out of this promise is the test of the entire sincerity, integrity, and statesmanship of the Republican party." Hughes had also permitted himself to believe that a better and broader society of nations could and would be created under Republican auspices. But once in office, Hughes and Hoover did not insist that the President act. In his inaugural address Harding made it clear enough that the campaign had ended and that his Association of Nations was also finished; "Confident of our ability to work out our own destiny and jealously guarding our right to do so, we seek no part in directing the destinies of the Old World. We do not mean to be entangled. We will accept no responsibility except as our own conscience and judgment may determine." Hughes did not fight; he respected the Presidential office, if not its holder. Besides, it was doubtful that any scheme of world government would succeed in the Senate, at least not without a harassing struggle within the Republican party, for its Irreconcilables were as ardently isolationist as ever. The toil was not worth his effort; nor was he eager to make it. In the summer of 1921 Congress by a joint resolution officially declared that the war with Germany, Austria, and Hungary was ended. Wilson had vetoed an earlier resolution to the same effect, but Harding signed his name without further ado. During twenty years thereafter those Americans who urged the necessity, or even the wisdom, of joining the League of Nations were decidedly in a minority. Chief among them were clergymen, professors, and teachers.

In the light of later events, one meditating upon the affairs of men might well conclude that it would have been wise for America to take her part in the League. A principal argument in defense of that conclusion is that the procession of world events for the next quarter-century could hardly have been more woeful than it was, and that the League would have achieved more than it did if it had been buttressed by American support. The League, with its Council and Assembly meeting at Geneva, was to be useful in the solution of mankind's troubles, but far from useful enough. After America had substantially withdrawn from it, the European scene darkened rather than brightened. France and Britain, quite understandably, sought to squeeze as large reparations as possible from Germany. They were able to exact only a few billion dollars in cash and goods, but their demands for more weighed heavily upon a German economy injured by war. Even before Harding's death in 1923, the new German Republic, from its beginning threatened by Communists and monarchists, was badly shaken by currency inflation resulting in part from Allied attempts to collect reparations. The German mark became worthless before the end of 1923, its value not being increased by French occupation of the Ruhr valley in an attempt to force continued payment of reparations. That inflation, enriching a few industrialists who were able to take advantage of it, reduced many Germans to poverty; they blamed the Allies and the German Republic for their wretchedness. Some listened to a fanatical ex-painter and ex-soldier, the Austrian-born Adolf Hitler, who told all who would listen that the miseries of Germany arose from no German fault. He would have it that imperial Germany would have won World War I except for treachery on the part of Jewish bankers, that Germany was not actually defeated but perfidiously induced to lay down arms on the basis of the Fourteen Points, and that the Allies, dishonoring their promises, imposed upon Germany the unjust, the vindictive, dictated peace of Versailles. Preaching both German nationalism and socialism, he tried to foment an insurrection in Munich in 1923. His "beer-hall putsch" was suppressed by police, and Hitler went to prison for a few months. His gruesome time had not yet come, but it would.

There were other shadows of coming European events to disturb Americans who believed that their country ran greater risks by withdrawing from the Old World than by entering actively into its affairs. Hostility toward the United States solidified in Russia, for Harding, like Wilson, refused to recognize the Soviet Union, partly because its Communist masters refused to repay approximately $200,000,000 borrowed from the United States by their predecessors. The American government also discouraged trade with the Soviet Union, and obviously hoped it would go away. In Russia the belief that America was an enemy, proceeding from American behavior during the Russian civil wars of 1918 to 1920, became stronger. Friendly relationships between the United States and Russia might have been impossible in any case, because of Communist adherence to and action in behalf of the Marxian doctrine of world revolution. At the time Russia posed no military danger.

Untoward also was the rise to power in Italy of Benito Mussolini, who as "Il Duce" imposed Fascism upon his king and country in 1922. The strutting of that new Caesar aroused admiration as well as amusement outside Italy; to the thoughtful, his denunciations of democracy, his "corporate" state, his blackshirted militia, and his avowed intention to revive the Roman empire were disquieting. Nor was there cause for comfort in the emergence of Marshal Pilsudski as a dictator in Poland, for dictators are never the most reliable champions of peace. Nor was it altogether pleasing news that France, in order to attain security, turned toward alignment with Poland and the "Little Entente," Rumania, Czechoslovakia, and Yugoslavia. The Europe that Wilson had envisioned seemed increasingly remote. Moreover, the economic recovery of the continent from World War I was neither swift nor certain, the Germans having the most difficult time, except for the Russians.

It was impossible, of course, for America to be entirely unconcerned with Europe—some of the most bitter isolationists were quite willing, or even eager, to bargain with European nations about the reduction of navies. Nevertheless, fear of unnecessary involvement in international disputes, together with fear lest there be foreign interference in American affairs, made it impossible for the United States to join in setting up and making use of the Permanent Court for International Peace, commonly known as the World Court. That tribunal, because it was linked with the League of Nations, was disliked by the isolationists in the Senate. Harding—and Coolidge, Hoover, and Franklin Roosevelt after him—urged that the United States officially support the World Court, but the Senate demurred.

REPARATIONS AND WAR DEBTS

Nor would America permit the payment of Allied debts to be tied to the payment of reparations by the defeated powers. The Harding Congress insisted that the so-called "war debts" must be paid, and with good interest, regardless of difficulties and consequences. America's former Allies were reluctant; there was a feeling among them that America ought to cancel the debts, which had been incurred in a common cause to which the United States had contributed late and minor military help. There was a disposition among them to forget that part of the money had been lent for reconstruction rather than for waging war. England, having lent even larger sums to the Allies on the continent, suggested a general writing-off of inter-

Allied debts. It was also urged from London, Paris, Brussels, and Rome that payment to the United States could not be made without ruinous effects to the Allies, except by collecting reparations in proportion. In effect, the politicians at those capitals proposed that they pass on to the United States monies received from Germany, Austria, and Hungary. In what other way could they meet their obligations without severe injury to their own countries? The United States had more than half of the world's gold supply, and would hardly accept goods in lieu of cash. How Germany could pay the Allied nations without severe additional damage to herself, those politicians did not indicate. In the end, refusing to admit that there was any connection between reparations and Allied debts, America reduced her demands. A War Debts Commission established at Washington was allowed in 1923 to make a bargain with Britain by which that country would repay over a period of 62 years, with 3.3 percent interest. Other agreements afterward made with the European borrowers were much more generous to them, both principal and interest being reduced. The scaling down of the obligations was not enthusiastically applauded in the United States, where feeling was well if inelegantly expressed by President Coolidge: "They hired the money, didn't they?" On the other hand, in England, France, Belgium, and Italy "Uncle Sam" was often called "Uncle Shylock." Eventually a large part of the debts was repaid—indirectly with American money. The bickering over them strengthened isolationist sentiment in America, where it was widely felt that American generosity was not properly appreciated. Another consequence was a softening of American feeling against Germany.

DISARMAMENT

The American retreat from a world society of nations and from Europe in the early 1920s was accompanied by a military withdrawal in the Pacific and by reduction of the armed forces. At the close of World War I the army was routinely thinned to its customary meager ranks. There was no keen desire to increase the infant air power of the nation, except in a few deluded individuals such as General William Mitchell, who was later court-martialed for excessive zeal in behalf of the development of bombing airplanes. Rather surprisingly, however, the naval building program under the law of 1916, which would have made the navy more powerful than any other in the world by 1924, was largely abandoned, even though it continued to be looked upon as the "first line of defense." Several arguments were adduced against continuing to expand American power on the surfaces of the oceans. It was pointed out that there was no longer any danger from the dismantled German navy; that the British one could be expected to assist in rather than to threaten the defense of the United States; that the building program was expensive; and that, if it proceeded,

Britain and Japan would be challenged to a naval race. The most persuasive reason for continuing to build was the rising power of Japan in Asia and in the western Pacific. The question of naval "disarmament" was therefore tightly linked with difficulties in the Far East and the Pacific. Disarmament would hardly be possible without reaching agreement with Japan, not only with respect to the Japanese navy but with regard to various other problems. Nor could Britain prudently weaken her forces on the water, despite economic strain at home, unless her possessions and interests in the Orient were somehow safeguarded.

Although the Japanese Empire was one of the Allies during World War I, America and Britain were not on the best of terms with that rising Asian power at its close. There was in both of the Western countries a feeling that the Japanese might have done more for the common cause, and that they had devoted themselves to the expansion of their own empire while the Western nations were engaged in Europe and unable effectively to check Japanese ambitions. Besides, after the war had ended it was evident that the Japanese were moved by a desire for expansion. During the conflict Japan had captured Kiaochow and the Shantung peninsula in China from the Germans, and had clung to them. Japanese troops that had entered eastern Siberia with other Allied forces in the vain attempt to overthrow the Russian Communists were still there in 1921. There was concern in the United States because in the Treaty of Versailles Japan had obtained a mandate under the League of Nations over the islands formerly possessed by Germany in the central Pacific; that mandate was virtually equivalent to ownership. There was also resentment in Washington because Japan had begun a drive during the war to secure a paramount influence over all of China, which, weak and riven by dissension, had become a republic in 1912. In the Twenty-one Demands made upon China in 1915 Japan had sought to require from the new republic, not only recognition of Japanese rights and privileges in those parts of it where the Japanese were already established, but also of something very like a protectorate. While forced to make new concessions to Japan, China had been able to deny a paramount influence in her affairs to the island empire, thanks in part to diplomatic support from the United States. There was no reason to believe that Japan had permanently abandoned the design to bring China within a Japanese sphere of control.

It may well be believed that isolationism and military weakness could not be reconciled in 1921, but Senator William E. Borah did not fear the consequences of linking them. At his insistence Congress urged President Harding to call an international meeting to limit the major navies of the world. Harding complied, inviting the Great Powers (except for Russia) and several smaller ones to send delegates to Washington to consider Pacific and Asian questions as well as naval ones. The result was the Washington

Armament Conference of 1921–1922, at which Secretary of State Hughes displayed far more energy than he had shown with respect to an association of nations. As chairman of the gathering Hughes ardently insisted that there must be no race for naval power; for one reason and another, he largely had his way. The United States, Britain, Japan, France, and Italy signed a treaty by which they agreed to build no new battleships for a period of ten years; they were to maintain their battleships respectively in the ratio of 5–5–3–1.67–1.67; and vessels under construction were to be destroyed as necessary to reach the ratio. It was not possible to agree to limits on cruisers, destroyers, or submarines. In a series of other treaties and agreements the Anglo-Japanese alliance of 1902 was cancelled; the Japanese withdrew from Siberia, Kiaochow, and Shantung; the Great Powers represented at Washington promised to seek no further special privileges in China; and America, Britain, and Japan pledged each other not to build additional fortifications at various strategic spots in the Pacific and on its fringes. The result was military gain for Japan. America, Britain, and Japan were relieved of expense for naval construction that only America could really afford. The powers most concerned also promised to consult each other when serious trouble threatened in East Asia. The pledge was not worth very much.

It was widely believed in the United States at the time that Hughes had won a great diplomatic victory, that the gathering at Washington was actually a successful peace conference. It was hardly observed in the United States, except by American naval officers, that Japan had profited more than Britain and America. The nation at large was even less interested in watching to the westward than it was to the eastward. So eager for economy and so complacent were most Americans that very few smaller naval craft were built in American shipyards during the following decade. Abandoning collective security—except in the Far East—America also permitted her military strength to dwindle. It has been suggested that Hughes ought to have insisted upon a wiser course; he was not omniscient and he was cramped by a careless public opinion.

The Harding regime, drawing inward from Europe and Asia, also moved with restraint in its dealings with Latin America. Hughes pursued a middle-of-the-road policy, cautiously avoided taking extreme stands in several disputes that arose. In particular, when Mexico turned toward expropriation of foreign oil rights and properties, Hughes undertook, with some success, to reconcile the conflicting interests of Mexico and American investors. His department did what it could decently do to foster the expansionist activities of American oil companies in Latin America, including negotiation of the treaty with Colombia of 1921 that finally settled the Panama Canal controversy. In fact, Hughes generally encouraged the development of trade with and investment in Spanish and Portuguese America. Believing, like his predecessors, that it was necessary to keep reasonable order in the Caribbean, he did not urge removal of American forces from the republics that lay within that sea and upon its shores.

BARRIERS AGAINST ALIENS: PEOPLES AND GOODS

Seeking to escape political and military entrapment in the troubles of the peoples of the outside world after World War I, America undertook to limit severely the numbers and kinds of people who might seek new homes as immigrants within her boundaries. The war had stopped the tide of Europeans flowing into the Republic, but it would resume unless stout dikes were built against it. Among many Americans the feeling that the nation was already crowded had become a conviction. Some were alarmed because a few recent immigrants had been less than loyal during the war. It was commonly believed that America had not digested, and perhaps could not digest, the diverse elements that had entered her ports. Feeling against the New Immigration, if it had changed, was stronger than it had been before 1914. In a slump that followed the war, labor was keenly against bringing in competitors for jobs; on the other hand, employers considered the existing stock of skills and muscles to be ample. The Ku Klux Klan disliked foreigners as well as Negroes, Roman Catholics, and Jews; its 100 percent Americanism could not be achieved by an American born abroad. Sentiment for more drastic restriction of immigration was overwhelming, although there was disagreement regarding both the number and nature of persons to be admitted in the future. In May, 1921, Congress passed an Emergency Quota Act that added a special restriction to those imposed in the past. It declared that the number of aliens of any nationality admitted per annum should not exceed 3 percent of the foreign-born persons of that nationality resident in the United States in 1910. Wilson had vetoed a similar measure in 1920, but Harding signed the law. It remained in force until 1924, although it was intended to be a temporary one. It permitted the entrance of somewhat more than 350,000 persons per annum from Europe, about five-ninths of whom could come from the northwestern part of the continent, four-ninths from its southeastern regions. The discrimination between the two divisions of Europe and also between the European nations made it impossible to secure the passage of a "permanent" limit on numbers for several years. However, the nation was definitely committed to a policy of substantial exclusion, and almost as positively engaged to distinguish between the Old and New Immigrations.

The raising of the walls against "foreigners" was matched by the erection of higher ramparts against their goods. Sentiment for lofty and sturdy tariff barriers ran so high after World War I that it seemed almost unpatriotic to speak out for international free trade, or even for maintaining the Underwood-Simmons rates of 1913. It was to be expected that Harding and his Cabinet, composed chiefly of orthodox and wealthy Republicans, would favor the raising of tariffs, and that the orthodox Republican majorities in Congress would do likewise. Revision upward was therefore almost inevitable; but it went much too far, for neither the Democrats nor the progressive Republicans from the farm states ardently fought against it. Manufacturing was moving into the South, and Southern industry was seeking safeguards against European and Japanese competition. Nor did a so-called "Farm Bloc" composed of progressive Republicans of the Midwest and West rail against high tariff barriers. In May, 1921, when the farmer, having overexpanded production and mortgages during World War I, was going through a financial wringer, the Bloc secured the passage of an emergency tariff law. It placed almost prohibitive rates upon 28 agricultural products. As might have been expected, the benefits that the farmer was supposed to receive turned out to be small. Since the Bloc had ardently espoused the principle of high protection for the farmer, it could not easily deny the validity of it for the manufacturer. The result was the Fordney-McCumber Tariff Act of 1922, which was opposed chiefly by Democrats who had already done what they could to defend the interests of their agricultural and industrial constituents. It continued to offer the help, such as it was, that the farmers had received in the preceding year; it also, and more effectively, shielded the manufacturer.

The Fordney-McCumber rates were on the average higher than ever before in American history. Duties placed on dye stuffs, chemicals, china, cutlery, toys, and silk and rayon textiles were prohibitive or nearly so. "Cheap" articles from Germany and Japan were not wanted. There was little concern that Germany, if limited in sales to the United States, might not be able to buy American goods and to pay reparations. Nor was there alarm lest Britain, America's best customer, might be unable readily to buy American products and to pay her war debt with her American market limited. The law gave lip service only to the principle of equalizing the cost of production at home and abroad. Moreover, although the Tariff Commission was continued, with authority both to raise and to lower rates with the President's consent, that body would do little lowering and some raising. Harding and his immediate successors appointed to it devout protectionists. Few economists have argued in behalf of the Fordney-McCumber Act or praised the behavior of the Tariff Commission in the 1920s. Other nations retaliated as best they might; the immediate effects were not obviously or remarkably injurious to America, but its long-range consequences were less happy.

BUSINESS AND PROSPERITY

The solicitude for the interests of the business community so evident in the Fordney-McCumber Act, it is almost unnecessary to say, was characteristic of Washington in the Harding time. From the viewpoint of the banker and the merchant, the Washington scene was as attractive as it was to the manufacturer. All of them would feel some misgiving when it was revealed that graft had permeated the executive branch of the government, but they could be philosophical and conclude that every gem must have at least a minor flaw. Many good things came to the business community. It was especially happy because Secretary of the Treasury Mellon, a man after its own heart, led the way in the reduction of both the national debt and taxes. After 1921 national expenditures ran annually somewhat over $3,000,000,000, receipts in Washington about $4,000,000,000. The surplus was applied to the nation's debt, which shrank from approximately $24,000,000,000 in 1921 to about $16,000,000,000 in 1930. Moreover, the burden of federal taxation was much reduced, especially for the wealthy. The Pittsburgh industrialist, who earned in the business community a reputation as "the greatest secretary of the treasury since Alexander Hamilton," sincerely believed that great incomes ought not be so heavily taxed that the rich would put their money into "safe but unproductive forms of investment." His economic philosophy happened to coincide with his own interests and those of his wealthy fellows. Had Mellon had his wish, in 1921 the wartime excess profits tax would have been repealed; the maximum surtax rate upon income would have been reduced from 65 to 40 percent, and the revenue lost would have been made up through excise levies and an increase in postal rates. Congress would not quite give Mellon all that he wanted. However, in the Revenue Act of that year, the excess profits tax was removed and the maximum surtax was set at 50 percent. The tax on corporation profits was raised from 10 percent to 12½ percent; income tax exemptions were raised so that many poor Americans paid nothing whatever; and excise levies were reduced. Even so, the affluent had special reason to be pleased. Further reductions especially favoring them would come.

The business community was pleased in various other ways. It could not find serious fault in Secretary of State Hughes, whose department did what it could to help in the investment of money and the finding of markets abroad. Secretary of Commerce Hoover fostered trade associations within the country, supplied technical information to business, and put some Quaker idealism and common sense into it. Harding and his advisers fought off a demand from the veterans of World War I for a Soldier's

Bonus. Some veterans contended that they had been poorly paid in service while profiteers flourished in civil life, and that they deserved special compensation. The newly formed American Legion, to which many of them belonged, campaigned for them in Washington. Responding to its pressure, Congress in 1922 passed a bill that would have given each veteran a paid-up insurance policy of a value determined by the length of his service at home and abroad. Manifesting unusual resolution, Harding vetoed the bill, putting a temporary end to the "Bonus" drive.

Nor was the satisfaction of the business community confined to the behavior of the executive and legislative branches of the federal government. Attorney General Daugherty was not averse to the use of the injunction against strikers. The Supreme Court having ruled that the Clayton Act recognized generous authority in the courts to avert "irreparable" injury in labor disputes, the employment of that weapon was not seriously limited. In 1922 Federal Judge James Wilkerson, at the request of Daugherty, invoked it to break a strike of railroad shopmen. It will be recalled that in 1922 the Supreme Court held the second Federal Child Labor Law of 1919 to be unconstitutional, so helping to put off the day when the continuing abuse of child labor could be substantially ended. (In 1924 Congress passed a constitutional amendment which would have given it unquestionable power to act, but the state legislatures did not ratify.) The Supreme Court, in 1923, also asserted that a District of Columbia law establishing minimum wages for women violated the Constitution. Its decision, in *Adkins* v. *Children's Hospital,* by implication denied the power to set such minimum wages not only to the federal government but to the states. William Howard Taft, who had become Chief Justice upon the nomination of Harding and who was not a devout Socialist, refused to subscribe to that decision. He could not believe that the "due process" clauses of the Constitution were intended to prevent Congress and the state legislatures from making laws that their members obviously and reasonably considered to be in the public interest. The federal tribunals reflected the spirit of that time.

There was one businessman, Henry Ford, who failed to get all that he wanted in Washington. During and immediately after World War I two factories had been built at federal expense at Muscle Shoals in the Tennessee River valley to extract nitrogen from the air, nitrogen being useful for military purposes. Congress had also authorized the construction of a series of dams on the river to supply power for the two factories, and one dam had been partly completed in 1921. The Harding regime stopped all federal activity in the project, and offered to sell the public property and the right to make use of it to private investors. Henry Ford was the only active bidder. He proposed to finish the dams, produce nitrogen for cheap fertilizer for the farmers in time of peace, and provide it for the federal government in wartime. He intended to use any generated power not necessary for that purpose in his own various industrial and mining enterprises. He offered to pay some cash, but wanted a long-term lease and federal financial help in the form of a large loan. Farmers enthusiastically supported Ford's scheme, but it finally came to nought. Ford was a "maverick" in the business community, which did not rally behind him. Moreover, Senator George W. Norris, chairman of the Senate Committee on Agriculture, persistently and successfully fought against private exploitation of the Muscle Shoals complex. He envisaged completion of the dams at public expense, the sale of large quantities of cheap electric power in the valley by the federal government, and indeed a vast development of the valley under federal auspices. Eventually, he would have his way.

The help and sympathy extended to commerce and industry in the Harding era were extraordinary enough. Another instance of it was the return, under the Esch-Cummins law of 1920, of the railroads to private hands, in better shape than the railroads were when they were taken over by McAdoo during World War I. But the Americans as a whole gained from tax reduction. They also benefited from more stringent regulation of the meat packing business, and from road-building, stimulated by matching grants made to the states by the federal government. Moreover, despite federal hostility toward both strikes and unions, labor was offered a measure of favor. Partly because of this hostility, the unions, except for the "company" variety, actually lost members in the 1920s. However, another reason why they made no headway was that the workmen, except for the coal miner, shared in the prosperity that was again favoring the Americans by 1922. Hours of work were shortened, and pay was increased; enlightened employers were willing to agree to such changes. To his credit, President Harding successfully urged leaders of the great corporations to be more generous to their employees. Like McKinley, Harding believed in the "full dinner pail." Which is not to say that the workman received his due in the division of the proceeds of the American economy.

Thanks to the efforts of the Farm Bloc, even the farmer was offered boons in the Harding period. Given little help by the Fordney-McCumber law, the farmer benefited to some degree from a grant of $1,000,000,000 by Congress to the War Finance Corporation to help transport and export farm products. The sum was quite handsome in view of the fact that a Bureau of the Budget was established almost simultaneously toward achieving economy. Unfortunately, such measures as were taken to assist the farmer were not of much avail. He produced much more than was consumed in the domestic market, while his foreign ones, vast during World War I, had shrunk. The result was surpluses. Moreover, entranced by the results of large crops and the very high prices that they had brought during World War I, many farmers had mortgaged themselves to buy more land.

Foreclosures were only too common immediately after 1920. The condition of the farmer improved somewhat as the 1920s continued, but relatively agriculture remained depressed.

CORRUPTION IN HIGH PLACES

For what is the Harding regime most remembered? A Saturnalia of corruption in high and medium places. In the early summer of 1923 the President, accompanied by officials and reporters, traveled to Alaska, making speeches as he went. He had made his will before leaving Washington; his talks were without gusto, and those who journeyed with him observed that he was nervous and worried. He hinted to reporters that his trust in some officers whom he had appointed had been betrayed. Returning from Alaska, Harding suffered a heart attack in Seattle. Proceeding to San Francisco, he died there on August 2, the immediate cause of his death being a stroke of apoplexy. Afterward it was widely believed that he had been murdered, that he had committed suicide, or that grief over the behavior of his friends had weakened his will to live, and so contributed to an untimely death. Actually, it was not remarkable that a man 57 years of age who had enjoyed himself generously, as Harding had, should suffer a fatal stroke. The strain under which the President had been laboring may have hastened his end. Rumors, and some evidence of grave misconduct in Washington existed before Harding died. Afterward, with Calvin Coolidge in the White House, it was gradually revealed that embezzlement, fraud, and bribery had flourished amazingly in the executive branch while it was under Harding's guidance.

Juicy revelations continued to be made during several years after Harding's death. Charles B. Forbes, as head of the Veterans Bureau, cheated the nation of almost fantastic sums; he went to Leavenworth penitentiary for committing fraud. Charles E. Cramer, second in command to Forbes, committed suicide before the affairs of the Bureau were investigated. Thomas W. Miller, the Alien Property Custodian, accepted a bribe of $50,000 from a claimant of $6,500,000 worth of Liberty Bonds in his care; the claimant secured the bonds, part of which went to Jess Smith, Harry M. Daugherty's friend; Miller finally went to prison. Bonds received by Smith were turned into cash that found its way into a bank account in Ohio used for political purposes by Daugherty. Before that fact and other disquieting ones came forth, Smith put an end to his life. Dismissed by Coolidge, Daugherty was twice tried for committing fraud. The former Attorney General of the United States claimed the protection of the Fifth Amendment, refusing to testify on the ground that he might be incriminated. He hinted that, were he to speak, Harding's reputation and that of his wife might suffer. Two juries disagreed about his conduct, and he was not convicted. It also came out that a combination of four executives of oil companies, including Harry F. Sinclair, had bought oil at $1.50 a barrel and had sold it to their own companies at $1.75—and that part of the profit had gone through Sinclair in the form of a loan and a gift to the Republican National Committee. Part of it went into the hands of Albert B. Fall, who was the central figure in the most notorious of the scandals.

Austere, eagle-eyed, masculinely Western, Fall wore the appearance of an honest man. He succumbed to temptation of much money. He was in financial distress when he became Secretary of the Interior and had not paid the taxes on a ranch he owned in New Mexico for almost a decade. Not long afterward, expensive blooded stock and other indications of wealth appeared on the ranch. Those evidences of sudden affluence aroused curiosity in Washington, especially because Fall had gone out of his way to please oilmen Edward L. Doheny and Sinclair. Great oil reserves had been set aside by the federal government before 1921 to make sure of a sufficient supply for the navy in the future, for it had been feared that the American oil fields would be exhausted. The reserves were under the care of the Secretary of the Navy Edwin Denby. Soon after taking office, Fall asked Denby to permit their transfer to the Department of the Interior, and Denby unwisely consented, although the legality of the transaction was doubtful. Harding also agreed to it, although he is said to have remarked, "I guess there will be hell to pay." Fall then promptly gave a lease to exploit a reserved area in California called Elk Hills to Doheny, and a similar one to Sinclair to take oil from a reserved area named Teapot Dome in Wyoming. The leases could be and were defended on the score that they were to the public benefit. It was truly said in their behalf that oil wells nearby were drawing away petroleum from the reserves. However, suspicious members of the Senate insisted upon finding out whether there was any connection between the leases and Fall's recent opulence. Democratic Senator Thomas J. Walsh of Montana conducted a searching investigation despite charges that he was guilty of character assassination. The facts that gradually emerged were shocking. Doheny had made a "loan" of $100,000 in currency to Fall, and a much larger sum had come to Fall from the hands of Sinclair. Fall was forced to resign his post, was convicted of accepting a bribe, fined $100,000 and sent to jail for a year. Sinclair and Doheny, rather curiously, were not convicted on charges of bribery and conspiracy to defraud the federal government. Sinclair did not entirely escape imprisonment. Declining to testify before a Senate committee, he was fined $1000 and sent to jail for three months for contempt of the Senate. He was also sentenced for another six months because his detectives tampered with the jury during his trial for bribery and conspiracy. Doheny and Sinclair had hoped to reap immense profits for their companies, as much as $100,000,000 from each of the reserves. The Teapot Dome and Elk Hills leases were cancelled, but otherwise the two men were not heavily punished, even in public opinion. Innocent Denby had to retire to private life; and Fall was ruined. Such was the state of American morality at the time that the two businessmen could be excused by many.

Harding was perhaps fortunate not to have lived to see the disgrace of his friends and his associates. Had he lived longer, the nation might have learned to know a different, a more mature Harding. It should be remembered that politicians and voters had not demanded the election of a better man in 1920, and it is questionable whether the public deserved anything better.

51 INDIAN SUMMER

"SILENT CAL" COOLIDGE

Calvin Coolidge was 51 years old when the news of Harding's death reached him in Vermont. Characteristically, by the light of a kerosene lamp, he took the oath of office before his father, who was a justice of the peace, in his father's home. In his person the American business community secured a President after its own political and commercial heart. It had been well satisfied by Harding, despite his unregulated generosity to his associates and his willingness to spend money on the farmers. It could find no fault in his successor, a plain, honest man who had no erratic penchant for ideas, who desired to embark upon no adventures, who had no lust for power, and who did not seek to impose his will upon the world of business. Coolidge was a man of simple tastes, thrifty and self-reliant. He was thin-faced, cautious, and shrewd, of a type not uncommon in the villages of New England. He was not born in a log cabin, but his parents were merely very respectable folk. By the record, he was well-educated, being a graduate of Amherst College and a lawyer by profession. He was a politician by inclination, and he climbed slowly but steadily up a chain of public offices in Massachusetts until he reached the governorship and achieved national fame for breaking the Boston police strike, for which achievement he was only partly responsible. Loquacious enough in private, he was taciturn as well as conscientious and modest in public life. He had a charming wife, Grace, who helped him up the political ladder. He was also assisted by rivals whom he overcame; he prudently made it appear that he performed only a little bit better than they did; he made no bitter enemies. Coolidge had never had to meet a private payroll, but he was averse to expanding public ones. He was rather well informed about American history, but he knew and cared less about European and Asian history. He had no desire to make any history himself. Prosperity and business reigned during his 67 months in office, and he acquired the trust and respect, if not the affection, of the bulk of the American people. They came to believe, with some reason, that the man from Plymouth, Vermont, brought to Washington the character and principles they associated with Plymouth Rock. The famous Kansas journalist, William Allen White, saw Coolidge's situation in Washington somewhat differently; to a book he wrote about Coolidge he affixed the title *Puritan in Babylon*. Time had to pass before it became apparent that Coolidge's horizons, like those of many Americans, were too close and too narrow; his wisdom, like that of so many of his fellows, was parochial. In essence, Coolidge was a worthy, responsible, and less likeable Harding.

To many observers of the American scene in the later months of 1923 and the early ones of 1924 it seemed that Coolidge might be only a "caretaker" President, that he would merely finish the term for which Harding had been elected. His party was riven by dissension, and continuing revelations of gross misconduct on the part of men in high places under Harding seemed to offer plentiful ammunition to the Democrats. "Silent Cal" was not even assured of the Republican nomination in 1924. Farm and labor elements were restless, dissatisfied with a regime that so specially favored industry and commerce. In the off-year election of 1922 progressive Republicans had done very well at the polls in the Midwest, and the Democrats had also gained at the expense of the orthodox Republicans. The "Sons of the Wild Jackass," as Senator George H. Moses, conservative Republican of New Hampshire, called his progressive brethren, were so numerous in Congress after that election that they held a balance of power in both houses. They had no affection for Coolidge. Alfred E. Smith, Democrat, had been elected Governor of New York. Enforcement of the Volstead Act was making no friends for the Republicans; while they really made no great effort to execute it, they were too vigorous to please the many Americans who desired access to alcoholic liquors. Disturbing for Coolidge and regular Republicans was the rising influence of the Conference for Progressive Political Action, formed in 1922. Supported by farmers and by railway labor, it looked like the nucleus of a new Progressive Republican party. It seemed quite possible that the campaign of 1924 would follow the pattern of 1912, the Democrats winning because of the division among their rivals.

ELECTION OF 1924

If Coolidge was worried by the political situation as the campaign of 1924 approached, he gave no outward sign of it. He kept in office the able and respectable men in Harding's Cabinet, including Hughes, Hoover, and Mellon. He might have posed as an outraged cleanser of the Temple in dealing with the men who had betrayed Harding and their public trusts; he might also have tried to draw veils over their crimes and sins. Instead, without making any great fuss, he quietly did his duty toward driving them from their posts and into jail. Nor did he raise a new issue or issues to distract attention from the scandals; he cleaned the Republican house, but he did and said nothing about remodeling it. He sought the Republican nomination for the Presidency and easily secured it. The orthodox Republicans of the East gladly rallied behind him, and the presidential patronage, together with shrewd manipulation by his veteran political adviser C. Bascom Slemp, brought him the support of the Southern Republicans. His only serious rivals were Hiram Johnson and Robert LaFollette. Except in progressive Republican strongholds they could not challenge him effectively, for Coolidge controlled the party machinery. When the delegates to the Republican national convention assembled at Cleveland, the nomination of Coolidge was inevitable. He received 1065 votes on the first ballot, LaFollette, 34, and Johnson, 10. Toward placating the dissatisfied progressives, Coolidge had tried to persuade Frank Lowden and Senator Borah to run for the Vice-Presidency, but both refused. The choice then fell upon Charles G. Dawes, former Director of the Budget, able businessman and banker, who had the merit of residing in the Midwest. Dawes was no Robert LaFollette. He was colorful, flamboyant, and as regular a Republican as Coolidge. The Republican platform, like the candidates, offered no real concession to the progressives. It recounted the recent Republican record with pride and promised that it would be continued, except for plundering the Treasury and the nation's natural resources.

Many progressive Republicans, stung by the rebuff given them at Cleveland, promptly proclaimed their desire for a third party. LaFollette urged instead that they merely name candidates for the Presidency and the Vice-Presidency. He pointed out that the ranks of the "Sons of the Wild Jackass" in Congress would probably be thinned if they abandoned their places on the Republican ticket—or the Democratic one. His advice was followed. The Conference for Progressive Political Action called another convention at Cleveland that put forward LaFollette as a Progressive candidate for the Presidency. He was given an extraordinary platform, especially with reference to questions of war and peace. It denounced "monopoly" and called for a return to competition; urged public ownership of water power and eventually of the railroads; demanded that an end be put to the use of injunctions in labor disputes; and backed labor's right to bargain collectively. It condemned favoritism for the rich in Washington. The federal courts were also assailed. A ten-year term was advocated for their judges, and a limit upon the "judicial veto" was asserted to be necessary. The platform also castigated conscription, and urged that war be outlawed, armaments be reduced, and declarations of war be subject to approval by public referendum. It was so attractive to the Socialists and the Farmer-Laborites that they rallied behind LaFollette. Senator Burton K. Wheeler of Montana, a Democrat who had won fame for prosecuting Harry Daugherty and who had refused to support his party's presidential candidate, accepted the Progressive nomination for the Vice-Presidency. It was hoped that he would bring Democratic votes with him. Moreover, the American Federation of Labor, turning against the major parties, endorsed LaFollette and Wheeler. It seemed that they would take many votes from Coolidge and Dawes.

The emergence of LaFollette as a Progressive candidate disturbed the regular Republicans, but the behavior of the Democrats gave them reason both to rejoice and to be amused. In 1924 the Democrats gave every appearance of wishing to lose the election. They assailed each other ferociously, and then named for the Presidency a "me-too" candidate. Quite fittingly, they held their convention in Madison Square Garden in New York City, an arena renowned for boxing contests. Many of them called themselves liberals, but the Wilsonian spirit in the convention was weak. There were two principal seekers of the nomination for the Presidency, William G. McAdoo and Alfred E. Smith, neither a flaming reformer. Smith, a Roman Catholic, was the favorite of Tammany Hall, through which he had risen to eminence, and of other Democratic political machines entrenched in the Eastern cities. He was ardently supported by Roman Catholics, Jews, "wets," and other urban elements. McAdoo had a somewhat larger following that was Southern and Western, Protestant, rural, "dry," and nativist. He had lost face by accepting a lawyer's retainer from Edward Doheny, before Doheny's dealings with Albert Fall had been revealed; learning about them, McAdoo had promptly severed his connection with Doheny, but he had incurred "guilt by association." The rivalry between McAdoo and Smith was the more bitter because Smith's friends insisted that the party platform specifically condemn the Ku Klux Klan. Then at the height of its influence, the Klan had about 4,000,000 members and was indulging in virulent attacks upon Roman Catholics, Jews, other "foreigners," and Negroes. It was especially potent and feared in the South and the Midwest, and many a man in public life had felt compelled to join it in order to obtain political advancement. Klansmen and McAdoo-men looked alike to the Smith following. Amid great excitement a resolution condemning the Klan by name was lost by less than 5 votes. The clash over it was succeeded by an astonishingly long fight between the forces of McAdoo and Smith. While New York City provincials in the galleries announced their dislike of Southern backwardness, the balloting went on day after day. McAdoo steadily obtained more votes than Smith, but he could not get a majority, much less the two-thirds of the delegates required. The two men were stalemated for more than 90 ballots, each refusing to give way to the other. At last, from sheer weariness, the convention turned away from both. On the 103rd roll call, after 16 days in session, it named for the Presidency John W. Davis, a West Virginian, corporation lawyer, and moderate conservative. For the Vice-Presidency the Democrats put forward Governor Charles Bryan of Nebraska, known to fame only as a younger brother of William Jennings Bryan. They offered a middle-of-the-road platform, one that curiously equivocated concerning the League of Nations. They were for it as the best means of attaining peace, but they favored entrance into it only after that step had been endorsed by a popular referendum.

The spectacular performance of the Democrats in Madison Square Garden, described in detail over the radio to tens of thousands of listeners, hurt their chances, for they seemed to be quite irresponsible. Nor could Davis offer anything distinctive and attractive to the voters. In the campaign the Republicans claimed credit for the prosperity of the nation, urging that nothing be done to interrupt it. Their plea was seductive, especially since the condition of the farmers was temporarily improved in the fall of 1924. Moreover, Davis spent much energy in attacking La-Follette and the Progressives. Since the Republicans also concentrated their fire against LaFollette, Davis, the Wall Street lawyer, appeared to be only a handsomer copy of Coolidge. They warned that votes for LaFollette might throw the election into the electoral college; it was "Coolidge or Chaos." They had little cause for alarm. The whole story of the Harding scandals was not yet known. LaFollette, 69 years of age, campaigned as best he could, speaking at many places. He did surprisingly well at the polls, chiefly at the expense of the Democrats. He had 4,822,856 popular votes, Davis, 8,385,586, and Coolidge, 15,725,016. In the electoral college LaFollette had only thirteen votes, all from his home state of Wisconsin; Davis, with 136, carried little more than the Solid South; and Coolidge had 382. The nation had decided to "Keep Cool with Coolidge" and to continue to be prosperous. Coolidge's easy victory was accompanied by the election of Republican majorities in both houses of Congress. The Conference for Progressive Political Action discouragedly disbanded. La-Follette died in 1925 but he had outlived his embryo Progressive party.

"THE BUSINESS OF THE UNITED STATES IS BUSINESS"

The voters could not afterward fairly say that candidate Coolidge deceived them. He went on in the fashion he had begun, in the way he said he would. Nor did the constant good fortune that he had encountered in his rise to the Presidency desert him. The prosperity that assured his victory over Davis and LaFollette persisted until after he had retired to private life. In fact, the nation flourished economically as never before. Under Coolidge's leadership the national debt, federal expenses, and federal taxes continued to be reduced. It was a happy time for most Americans, and their economic advance encouraged the recovery of the world from World War I. A consequence of that recovery was an improvement in the political state of Europe. At home, nevertheless, the farmers did not overcome their difficulties. Nor was Coolidge willing to do very much to help them. Within the wall of the Fordney-McCumber tariff he earnestly desired that the American economy be as free as possible, even where it hurt. Nor did he become alarmed and eager to act because some tens of thousands of coal miners had little share in the general well-being. He was devoted to laissez-faire, within limits satisfactory to the banker, the industrialist, and the merchant. He was censured at the time because he was unwilling to exert federal power or to spend money to help the farmers. It was later contended that agricultural distress in the 1920s finally had its effect upon commerce and industry, so contributing forcefully to the onset of the Great Depression at the end of the decade.

If doubt must prevail regarding the ultimate wisdom of Coolidge's Republicanism, it is not possible to deny that it existed in deed as well as word. Its verbal commitment to commerce and industry, especially Big Commerce and Big Industry, was expressed in the Coolidge aphorism: "The business of the United States is business." That saying later was often quoted with contempt, for the eternal verities of one decade may turn out to be verbal temerities in the next. At the time when it was uttered, it seemed to many Americans to be accurate enough. There was at least as much solicitude for the needs and desires of industry and commerce in Washington in the Coolidge years as there was during the Harding time. The Fordney-McCumber Act was not altered; men appointed to federal regulating agencies were sympathetic to the interests of those whose activities they regulated; the Department of Commerce continued gladly to serve business at home, while the Department of State advanced its cause abroad; an "easy money" policy stimulated economic expansion.

Not the least pleasing of the beneficences of the Coolidge regime to better and bigger business was tax reduction. In 1924, with federal revenue continuing to run well above expenses, it was possible to lessen the flow of money into the Treasury, to lighten the burden of taxes as they had been set in 1921. Andrew Mellon then did all he could toward securing favor for the larger taxpayers, but he was not too successful. It was a campaign year, and progressive Republicans combined with Democrats to revise a new tax plan proposed by the Secretary of the Treasury. The result was a compromise revenue law that reduced the tax on small incomes by 50 percent, that on somewhat larger incomes by 25 percent. Surtaxes that Mellon wanted to slice were cut only moderately. Moreover, the maximum inheritance rate was increased from 25 percent to 40 percent, and a levy was put upon gifts, in an attempt to prevent evasion of the duty upon estates. Further, individual returns could be published by the Treasury. Two years later, however, Mellon had his way. Surplus receipts persisted. Backed by Coolidge, Mellon was then able to secure a revenue law much nearer to his heart's desire. The maximum surtax on income was reduced from 40 to 20 percent, and the highest rates on inheritances were similarly diminished. The levy on gifts was repealed, together with the provision for publicity concerning personal income tax returns. Various excise levies were also abandoned. The law was unsatisfactory to the wealthy in only one way: it raised the corporation tax rate from 12 percent to 12½ percent for 1927 and 13 percent for 1928. Under the law the citizen kept more than four-fifths of a taxable income of $1,000,000 per annum. Two years later, the corporation tax was put back to 12 percent and Coolidge was able to say to Congress regarding the national finances:

Four times we have made a drastic revision of our internal revenue system, abolishing many taxes and substantially reducing almost all others. Each time the resulting stimulation to business has so increased taxable incomes and profits that a surplus has been produced. One-third of the national debt has been paid, while much of the other two-thirds has been refunded at lower rates, and these savings of interest and constant economies have enabled us to repeat the satisfying process of more tax reductions.

The President's prose was not magnificent, but its message comforted even those who did not benefit very much from tax reduction.

The orthodox Republicanism of the Coolidge era displayed its allegiance to industrial and commercial interests in various other ways. After 1922, under the direction of a Shipping Board, the merchant vessels built by the federal government for military purposes during and immediately after World War I were either scrapped or sold at low prices. It was hoped that the American merchant marine, temporarily revived as a result of the war, would continue to flourish. It did not, and it was therefore offered assistance by a law of 1928 that subsidized it with generous long-term contracts for carrying mail and made available a loan fund for the construction of new ships. The merchant marine continued to languish, but not because government was indifferent to its fate. Coolidge, like Harding, favored the St. Lawrence Seaway project to improve commerce and it was not his fault that its completion was long delayed. In 1928 he signed a law providing for a long-range program to control floods in the Mississippi Valley and to stimulate water traffic within it. In the same year he approved another authorizing the Boulder Canyon dam project, to provide water in the lower Colorado River Valley and adjacent southern California. Senator Hiram Johnson, with Herbert Hoover a driving force behind that great enterprise, desired that the electric power resulting be sold by the federal government, but he was not permitted to insert in the law a stipulation to that effect. Nor did Senator George Norris get approval for public manufacture and distribution of electric power in the Tennessee River Valley. Johnson and Norris might think that such operations would supply a "yardstick" against which the rates of private power companies, which they considered to be excessive, might be measured. Coolidge was opposed to public competition with private enterprise.

ECONOMY AND PROSPERITY

Coolidge's devotion to economy and laissez-faire is strikingly shown by the manner in which he dealt with the demand of the American Legion for a Soldier's Bonus and that of the farmers for massive federal assistance. Like Harding, he did not find merit in the theory that the difference between the pay of the man in service and that of the civilian workman was unjust and required remedy. The cost of it disturbed him, and in 1924 he vetoed a bill giving a twenty-year endowment insurance policy to every veteran below the rank of major. The measure was passed over his veto by a Congress more desirous to do justice to and to please the veterans— and also more liberal with public money than he was. But Coolidge had his way when agricultural groups, including the American Farm Bureau Federation, sought to secure passage of the McNary-Haugen bill. Surpluses and consequent low prices continued to plague the farmer, and he insisted that Washington do something about the surpluses. There was no easy answer, and there would be none during several decades to come. The American farmer then and afterward produced more than could be consumed at home and sold abroad, except when war or other distress enlarged his foreign market. Additions to the amount of tillable soil by irrigation, improved machinery, advances in agricultural methods, and other changes constantly increased the yield of the American farm. The McNary-Haugen remedy was to set up a federal farm board that would purchase the surpluses of certain products, keep them off the domestic market until prices were satisfactory, or sell them abroad at whatever prices they would bring. The producers of the commodities handled in this way were to pay an equalization fee, if the board incurred losses by selling cheaply in foreign markets. The bill in one form or another confronted Congress session by session after 1924. Passed in 1927 and again in 1928, it was twice vetoed by Coolidge. He did not like price-fixing upon the produce of the land; he looked upon the equalization fee as an unconstitutional tax; and he was solicitous lest the feelings of foreign farmers and nations be injured. He did not make the American farmer happy.

If the contribution of Republican orthodoxy to prosperity in the 1920s cannot be accurately assayed, it cannot be said that prosperity did not exist. The tillers of the soil in the Missouri Valley were distressed; New England suffered because its cotton mills went south in search of cheaper labor; coal miners in West Virginia were often unemployed; and Florida suffered from the collapse of a resort boom and from a hurricane in 1926. But the national income and buying power rose almost steadily. Before the end of the decade there were 13 corporations capitalized at more than one billion dollars, and there were nearly 300 persons who enjoyed annual incomes of one million dollars or more. It was not merely that the rich became richer. Wages advanced, those of labor purchasing 2 percent more each year in the middle and later 1920s. The number of Americans increased by more than fifteen millions between 1920 and 1930, approaching 123 millions in the latter year. The national income rose even more rapidly and the American physical standard of living moved upward with it. Such prosperity had never before been known. By 1929 most American families had a car and a radio, and about half of them owned or partly owned their own homes. It seemed to all but those of little faith that the United States was moving with rapid strides toward an economic millennium.

FOREIGN AFFAIRS: OUTLAWING WAR

The economic scene at home was all the more cheerful because it brightened abroad during the second half of the decade. In 1924, with the help of American financial experts headed by Charles G. Dawes, Germany reached agreements with the Western Allies which made it possible for that nation to get back on its feet. Under the so-called Dawes Plan, Germany was enabled to borrow through an international loan a vast sum toward the support of a new currency; moreover, her reparations payments were adjusted so that they could be borne without excessive strain. It was simultaneously arranged that French troops should be withdrawn from the Ruhr Valley. The result was that the German Republic swiftly acquired a stable currency and became relatively prosperous. By 1925 European sentiment had changed so much that it was possible for Germany and her former enemies to share "the spirit of Locarno." At that little town in Switzerland, Germany, Belgium, and France signed a treaty in which they promised not to attack each other. There the three nations and others also guaranteed the western frontiers of Germany. The good will so much in evidence at Locarno continued. In 1926 Germany became a member of the League of Nations, and three years later, under a plan prepared under the leadership of Owen D. Young, the burden of her reparations was again reduced. Meanwhile, American investments in Germany gave some strength to that nation's economy. In 1929 western and central Europe seemed stable and pacific. True, France and Italy had done all they could to prevent the success of a second effort to reduce naval armaments initiated by the United States in 1927, and a conference held for that purpose at Geneva failed to apply the Washington naval ratio for capital ships to cruisers and other smaller war vessels. In consequence, Coolidge and Congress felt forced in 1928 to strengthen the American navy. Even so, a major conflict then seemed unlikely, either in Europe or Asia. There was resentment in Japan because the United States had specifically excluded Japanese immigrants by law, but Japan was not particularly aggressive at the time. The Chinese republic was in semi-anarchy, with warlords fighting each other for primacy. What happened in China did not seem to be of the first importance.

Nor were there alarming troubles in Latin America, although existing difficulties survived and new ones appeared. In 1924 the marines came home from the Dominican Republic and the small American force keeping order in Nicaragua was withdrawn the next year. However, that country promptly slipped toward anarchy, and two years later the marines were back again to restore order. They accomplished their mission, except that they could not catch the liberal bandit leader General Augusto Sandino, who would not accept a regime satisfactory to the heads of other factions and who carried on guerrilla warfare until his death in 1934. There was also a near-crisis in 1927 in American-Mexican relations. Mexican policy limiting the rights of foreign oil companies and pointing toward ultimate expropriation of American-owned wells aroused concern in the United States. A campaign of the Mexican Revolutionary Party against the Roman Catholic Church aroused the resentment of Catholics north of the Rio Grande and increased tension between the two countries. It was relieved by the efforts of banker J. P. Morgan and his partner, Dwight Morrow, who was sent to Mexico City as ambassador. Morrow persuaded the Mexican government to proceed slowly with respect to the oil wells, and it also adopted a softer attitude toward the Church. Latin American enemies of "Yankee imperialism" were soothed a little in 1928 by the issuance of the Clark Memorandum, in which the United States renounced future resort to the Roosevelt Corollary.

The international scene was bright enough in 1927 so that American idealists fancied that warfare might be prevented by outlawing it. Chicago lawyer Salmon Levinson, Professor James T. Shotwell of Columbia University, and Senator William E. Borah believed that much was to be gained by an international declaration that war was illegal. Frank B. Kellogg, Secretary of State after 1925, with the French Foreign Minister, Aristide Briand, adopted the proposal. Briand urged that the United States and France assert the unlawfulness of war between them. Kellogg successfully insisted that other nations accept the scheme. The result was the Kellogg-Briand Pact, signed by 15 nations in August, 1928, and later by 49 more. All of the more powerful countries subscribed to it and all 64 nations renounced war "as an instrument of national policy," pledging themselves to settle all quarrels of "whatever nature or whatever origin" peacefully. Since the treaty did not commit America to any use of force, it was readily endorsed by the Senate. It was obviously harmless. Perhaps there was some value in the pact because it displayed the better nature of mankind. The cynical were sure that it would do no good and they quite correctly predicted that outlawing war was not likely to deter nations from waging it in the near future.

To those Republicans who believed that freedom of enterprise ought not be permitted to aliens seeking to enter the United States, the Coolidge regime had something still more to offer. In 1924, with the help of like-minded Democrats, they secured the passage of a law that reduced the flow of the New Immigration to not much more than a trickle. Indeed, setting up quotas like that of 1921, it severely limited immigration from all of Europe and barred it from Japan. It reduced the quotas for the next three years by about one-half, establishing proportions in accordance with the numbers of persons of European nationalities in the United States in 1890. Thereafter, no more than 150,000 persons were to be admitted in any one year, new quotas being established in proportion to the number of individuals in the United States in 1920 associated with a given European area by birth or ancestry. This provision did not go into effect until 1929, partly because it was difficult to interpret, and partly because it was opposed by New Immigrants, their progeny, and others who believed the restriction to be unjust and ungenerous. In 1929, however, it became a cornerstone of American immigration policy. Thenceforward the relatively few people from northwestern Europe who desired to settle in America could ordinarily do so; it was otherwise for the peoples of southeastern Europe. In the Great Depression, partly for economic reasons, immigration sank as low as 50,000 persons per year, and during the fourth decade of the century came the novel spectacle of an excess of emigrants to Europe over immigrants from that continent. The law of 1924, if it could be justified with respect to the limits it placed upon such immigrants, (which was debatable), could not be defended insofar as it applied to immigration from Asia. It forbade the entrance of persons who could not become citizens—and Japanese could not become citizens. Since the "Gentleman's Agreement" made with Japan by Theodore Roosevelt effectively prevented the entrance of a Japanese, the legal bar was unnecessary. It was considered an insult in Japan and led to a "hate America" fever in that country. A formal protest from the Japanese merely insured the law's passage. Coolidge might have vetoed it, but he did not. Making no friends for America in Japan, it did not do all that the exclusionists hoped it would do. It did not restrict immigration from the nations of the New World, nor from Puerto Rico. Mexicans, French Canadians, and Puerto Ricans continued to settle on the mainland of the United States in large numbers.

"I DO NOT CHOOSE TO RUN"

Although Protestant nativist Republicans devoted to laissez-faire gladly kept cool with Coolidge, it ought not be assumed that their satisfaction was universal. So ardent was feeling on the farm against the laissez-faire Republicans that progressives running on the Republican ticket, such as Robert LaFollette, Jr., of Wisconsin and Smith Brookhart of Iowa, gained a balance of power in the Senate in the off-year election of 1926. The "Sons of the Wild Jackass" bitterly resented the hostility of Coolidge and regular Republicans to the McNary-Haugen bill. Moreover, the Democratic party was obviously gaining strength in the cities of the northeast, where the Roman Catholic vote was becoming increasingly important, and where that party had a special appeal because its regional leaders were enemies of prohibition. The Republicans continued to be at least officially committed to executing the Volstead Act, and prohibition was particularly unpopular in the northeastern cities. They were growing rapidly, and the entrance into the Senate of Roman Catholic David I. Walsh of Massachusetts as a result of the election of 1926 was a harbinger of Democratic victories in New England to come. Nor did labor gaze at Coolidge Republicanism with fond eyes. As the campaign of 1928 approached, it seemed possible that a combination of its enemies, coupled with an economic downturn, would put at least a temporary end to it. Instead, prosperity and the orthodox Republicans won another triumph. The stock market was booming.

There is little doubt that Coolidge could have had the Republican nomination in 1928 for the asking, or that he could have been elected for another term. There is some reason to believe that he would have responded to a "draft" by his fellow Republicans, but he refused to lift a finger toward getting his party's support. In 1927, while vacationing in the Black Hills of South Dakota, he announced that "I do not choose to run for President in 1928." Thereafter, he declined to explain or alter that curious declaration; without at least an encouraging phrase or nod from him there could be no "draft," and various ambitious Republicans made known their wishes to be his successor. Chief among them was Secretary of Commerce Herbert Hoover, who was every whit as loyal to laissez-faire as Coolidge. He was pleasing to the business community because he had been a member of it, although there was some fear within it that he was too idealistic. A Quaker born into a family in ordinary circumstances in Iowa, he had been orphaned early in life, had been helped by uncles and aunts, had worked his way through Stanford University, and had made a fortune as a mining engineer and promoter. He was an almost perfect example of the "rags to riches" American dream come true. He was opposed by Pennsylvania Republicans led by Andrew Mellon and "Boss" William Vare. However, Mellon, who was suffering from "White House fever," was too rich and too cold to win the affection of many Republicans. Hoover's most dangerous rival in his party was Frank Lowden. Otherwise conservative in his views, Lowden appealed to Republicans of the Midwestern farm belt because he favored the McNary-Haugen bill—Hoover liked that measure no better than did Coolidge. Ultimately, Mellon and Vare, realizing that they could hardly stop Hoover, rallied to his support. In their national convention at Kansas City the Republicans named Hoover on their first ballot; as a gesture toward abating farm discontent they selected for the Vice-Presidency Senator Charles Curtis of Kansas, formerly but no longer a champion of the man on the land. They put Hoover and Curtis upon a platform which softly suggested that the farmers take collective action toward improving their own lot, but without the help of an equalization fee, without excessive federal interference. They also hinted that injunctions against labor possibly required curbing. Otherwise, they indicated their satisfaction with and their pride in things as they were, including even prohibtion.

CAMPAIGN OF 1928: RELIGION AND PROHIBITION

Gathering behind Hoover, Republican leaders were confident that he would win. After their convention in Houston, Texas, thoughtful Democrats conceded victory to Hoover, and not without reason. Had their party appealed to all those who were discontented with Harding-Coolidge-Hoover Republicanism, and had it found a progressive, able, and otherwise unobjectionable candidate, the outcome might not have been so certain. But Alfred E. Smith had not abandoned his presidential ambition; and his Roman Catholic admirers insisted that his party, having set him aside in 1924, must name him for the Presidency in 1928. They would accept no other person; there was no Protestant candidate for the Democratic nomination who had a large and devoted following, and Smith easily won it at Houston. With him the Democrats offered Protestant and "dry" Senator

Joseph P. Robinson of Arkansas for the Vice-Presidency, and a platform not remarkably different from the Republican. It endorsed the McNary-Haugen bill in principle and urged that independence be given to the restless Filipinos. Also, the Democrats did use stronger language in condemning the abuse of the power of injunction in labor disputes, and they did say that their rivals had favored the rich with respect to the income tax. They once more called for tariffs to redress the balance between the costs of production abroad and at home. They were most vehement when they condemned corruption in Washington under Republican rule.

The party platforms were quite unimportant in the campaign, which swiftly developed into a struggle between big city elements, "wets," and Roman Catholics ardently backing Smith, and Big Business, small-town rural folk, Protestants, and "dries" supporting Hoover. Smith made prohibition an issue, indicating that he desired a repeal of the Eighteenth Amendment, although his party had pledged an "honest effort" to enforce the Volstead Act. Hoover, who cautiously described prohibition as "a great social and economic experiment, noble in motive and far-reaching in purpose," easily won the favor of the "dries." Otherwise, Smith made no great effort to distinguish his views from those of Hoover. He hedged upon the McNary-Haugen equalization fee. Nor did he denounce Republican allegiance to business and laissez-faire. Hoover flatly and plainly committed himself to "rugged individualism," claimed that adherence to that doctrine had brought prosperity, and said that loyalty to it would bring a rosy future. "We in America today are nearer to the final triumph over poverty than ever before in the history of any land. The poorhouse is vanishing from among us. We have not reached the goal, but, given a chance to go forward with the policies of the last eight years, we shall soon with the help of God be in sight of the day when poverty will be banished from this nation." Smith bid for support in the business community by securing the appointment of his friend John J. Raskob, a high officer in the General Motors Corporation, as chairman of the Democratic National Committee; Raskob, who was a Roman Catholic and who had been a Republican, let it be known in the business world that Smith would not seriously disturb it.

Condemning national prohibition as "unworkable," Smith raised an issue that aroused passion. It undoubtedly brought him votes, but it also cost him many. By 1928 it was apparent that rigid country-wide enforcement of prohibition was impossible. Too many Americans desired the solace of alcohol, too many enterprising individuals had found it profitable to gratify this thirst, and the combined efforts of federal and state enforcement officers had prevented neither the manufacture nor the transportation nor the sale of intoxicating beverages. "Bootlegging" had become a major private enterprise in American cities and a rather common occupation almost everywhere. The "bootlegger" had frequently corrupted police officers; illegal traffic in "booze," especially beer, had brought profits and power to big city gangsters, notoriously in Chicago. While the flow of liquor diminished during the decade after 1918, the evils resulting from immoderate drinking had not vanished, and the "dries" hoped that time and stern enforcement of prohibition would destroy this social menace. The "dries" were especially strong in small-town and rural America, which also held it against Smith that he was a New Yorker and a Tammanyite. His variety of the American language, learned on the sidewalks of New York City's East Side, seemed "foreign" on the radio (Smith called it "raddio"). But above all it turned against him because of his religion. He said as plainly as might be that he believed in the principle of separation of church and state, but he could not overcome religious prejudice. It was widely believed that he would take orders from the papacy. Protestant clergymen thundered against him in the South, and many lifelong and devoted Democrats, especially in the South, refused to vote for him. It mattered little to them that "Al" was truly able and had made a fine record. Beginning as a poor boy with little formal education, he had indeed been helped up in the world by Tammany Hall. However, his own gift for good government, his unquestioned honesty, and his sympathy for the poor from whom he sprang had four times brought him election to the governorship of New York.

Seemingly assured of victory, Hoover campaigned very little. He did not attack Smith—he never mentioned him. Hoover's confidence in the outcome was thoroughly justified. Smith obtained 15,016,433 popular votes, more than any Democratic contestant for the Presidency before him had ever received. Roman Catholics, along with the "wets," voted for him in large numbers; he carried two states in New England where members of his faith were proportionately numerous, Massachusetts and Rhode Island. Because he had taken no positive stand for the workingman, he was not endorsed by the American Federation of Labor, which could not easily distinguish between him and Hoover. Even so, he ran ahead of his rival in the great Northern cities, a portent of Democratic power to come. He made a fair showing in the Farm Belt, where Hoover was not at all popular. But most voters went to the polls for Hoover, 21,392,190 of them. They were for Protestantism, prohibition, and prosperity. So many Protestant and "dry" Democrats deserted their party's leader that Smith carried only six states outside New England, those being Southern ones where the habit of voting Democratic was almost unshakable. Hoover carried Virginia, North Carolina, Florida, Tennessee, and Texas. Smith had only 87 electoral votes, Hoover 444. Hoover's overwhelming victory brought with it easy Republican majorities in both houses of Congress.

All considered, it was not surprising that the voters poured out of their homes and offices, nor that they gave their blessing to Old America. What is strange is that there was no real fighting over things economic or questions of foreign policy in the year 1928. Its tumult and shouting seemed to have little to do with pocketbooks or national safety.

52 CONTENT AND DISSENT

Looking back at the American scene in the third decade of the twentieth century, social and literary historians saw it as "The Roaring Twenties," "The Reckless Twenties," and "The Jazz Age." All three of those terms have some validity, but all three taken together do not fully describe the panorama of the time. There was roaring enough, especially on the stock market, and there was sufficient recklessness—economic, moral, and political. But such terms suggest that the decade was merely a frothy and sensational one, and two of them hint that the American economy was flashy rather than sound. Actually, America made solid material progress. The lives of most Americans became easier and more comfortable than they had been, and the decade was remarkable for a cultural flowering. Many an American intellectual, disliking intensely what he saw, sought sanctuary across the Atlantic. Many an observer less solicitous for freedom of expression discerned moral collapse; and many an examiner of the ways of men and things failed to see that the Americans were, on the whole, perhaps as content as a people may be. Moreover, after the decade ended in economic catastrophe, the seamier and shiny facets of the Twenties continued for some years to draw more attention than its true brilliances, its basic achievements. One would not easily learn from Frederick Lewis Allen's colorful and entrancing description of that decade in *Only Yesterday* that it was a good time for most of his countrymen, even for the intellectuals.

MATERIAL PROSPERITY

That material prosperity reigned in the Twenties cannot be seriously questioned. The national income rose remarkably; it was $74.3 billions in 1923, then an astonishing $89 billions in 1929. Corporation income increased handsomely; life insurance in force soared; and personal savings mounted steadily. The rich became richer, but so did the not-so-wealthy and the poor, with notable exceptions on farms and in mines. It has been estimated that the wealthiest one percent of the American population had 20 percent of its income. However, the purchasing power of industrial workers grew by 26 percent between 1919 and 1929, while their average hours of work per week dropped from 47.3 to 45.7. Mass production, adopted far more widely, brought an extraordinary flow of machines and goods. More and more they were sold according to the Henry Ford formula of small profit per item and mass consumption. In 1920 the number of automobiles registered in the nation was substantially above 8,000,000; ten years later it was over 23,000,000. Commercial radio broadcasting did not begin until November, 1920, when station KDKA of Pittsburgh sent out election returns over the air waves; ten years later there were more than 600 stations, and 12,000,000 families had at least one receiving set. In the middle Twenties new homes were built in unprecedented numbers, especially in the suburbs. Indicative of the rise of commercial structures was the Empire State Building, finished in 1931, which thrust upward nearly one quarter of a mile through the fumed air of Manhattan. Also significant of American economic progress was a rapidly rising use of electric power; generating stations could produce more than 43 million horsepower in 1930, double their capacity ten years earlier. Despite distress on the land, farmers bought vast quantities of new and improved machinery, for the use of engines was obviously the way to personal, if not collective, prosperity. The efficient use of constantly better machines and techniques was beginning to threaten the American people as a whole with comfort and even luxury.

Love of money is not the root of all evil, nor is the possession of wealth merely pernicious. It must be doubted that prosperity injures either nations or individuals more than poverty does. The thoughtful student will not deny that American material progress in the Twenties had its dark side, but it is not unimportant that many tens of millions of people should be as nearly content as men may be. Most Americans were basically satisfied with their lot in the Twenties. They wore better clothes (if they were less fully covered than in the past); they ate more and better food, thanks in part to the coming of the chain stores; they were also better if not more beautifully housed. Amusement, largely innocent if not elevating, entered the home through the radio. Toward the end of the decade millions followed the humorous adventures of Amos 'n Andy in Harlem harmlessly and pleasantly in their living rooms. The automobile increasingly brought pleasure outside the home, especially because it made possible the visiting of new scenes, relieving the monotony of daily life. It came within the financial reach of most families, in no small part because of the policies of Henry Ford, who became one of the most popular men in the nation. With the introduction of the closed car—sedans and coupés —in 1922, the automobile could be used even in winter. After 1927 the American could choose among no fewer than three low-priced, sound, and comfortable cars, the Chevrolet of General Motors, the Model A of Ford, and the Plymouth of the Chrysler Corporation. Touring became a pastime; the gasoline station became a common sight, and the "tourist home" was for some years ubiquitous proof that the spirit of private enterprise had not vanished. The neighborhood movie flourished, offering romantic entertainment, generally harmless enough, near the home; it brought much happiness, however transient, to young and old. Playgrounds, parks, and golf courses thrived. There was more money for magazines. The schools flourished; the high school diploma came within reach of nearly all white Americans, and college education became attainable even for the children of relatively poor whites. Money and depreciated European currencies made it possible for Americans in far larger numbers than ever before to travel and to sojourn in Europe. Prosperity brought opportunity as well as innocent pleasure.

THE CULT OF THE BUSINESSMAN

If only a romantic could claim that poverty would have been preferable to prosperity in the decade that followed World War I, it is only too evident that its material progress was attended by several ills. One of them was the rise of a business cult, the first tenet of which was that businessmen were the priests of a new civilization. Men of economic affairs, both to themselves and to others, seemed to be finding the solutions to all of mankind's problems and fulfillment of all its desires. The businessman became a knight as well as a priest, for he was successfully fighting the good fight for a better world. He was engaged in the service of mankind, hence in part the astonishingly swift growth during the decade of the "service" clubs, Rotary International, Kiwanis, Lions, and Exchange. If membership in such clubs brought status and economic opportunity, the idealism to which they subscribed was very real, though too often misguided. So pervasive was the influence of the cult of business that clergymen, teachers, and politicians adopted the views, the methods, and the language of the salesman. Sometimes the man in the pulpit and the professor thus acquired a dubious repute. But the politician found it difficult to win respect. The famous newspaper columnist Will Rogers won chuckling approval whenever he suggested—and he did it many times during the decade—that the best thing Congress could do was to adjourn. In a best-selling book the advertising agency executive Bruce Barton asserted that Christ, *The Man Nobody Knows,* was a great organizer and a superb salesman. The merchant, the industrialist, the advertising man, and the salesman, having no reason to be ashamed of their worthy occupations, only too commonly claimed for themselves wisdom and even sanctity that their fellow citizens might or might not possess. Their fumbling platitudes, the more because they were often given to stand-pattitudes, exposed them at the time and later to ridicule.

The reign of business brought with it other phenomena that were disconcerting and ultimately even disastrous. The "hard sell" of the salesmen and of advertisers acquired vogue. To too many of them it became a duty to sell goods to the consumer, whether he wanted them or not, for his own benefit. Moreover, the good end justified the doubtful means so that attractive but misleading claims for one's product were justifiable. Toothpastes, mouthwashes, and soaps were sold by appeals to the social fears of adolescents and supposedly more mature people. Young men learned that greasing their hair would make them irresistible to young ladies, who in turn learned that male youth, certain to be drawn to them in any case, would be even more enticed by certain brands of lipstick. The public was more exposed to advertising than in the past, for advertising increasingly financed the radio stations; their commercials were unquestionably effective.

Almost inevitably, because government did not seriously interfere, the speculative spirit became overbold. Toward the end of the reign of business, stock market gambling became very nearly a mania. The collapse of the great "bull market" of the Twenties was to usher in the Great Depression. Banking practices became remarkably careless; they later became extraordinarily costly. The building of holding company empires, layer upon layer of companies managed through one or two at or near the top of a pyramid, made possible "inside" manipulation to the disadvantage of innocent and uninformed stockholders. Such an empire erected in public utilities by the brilliant Samuel Insull became so complicated that even he did not fully understand its workings. It is almost needless to say that greed was not inconspicuous in a society that blessed the acquisition of money with unusual fervor. In such a milieu the temptations associated with the chance to get-rich-quick were unusually alluring.

MORALS AND CULTURE

Associated with emphasis on material advance were distaste and dislike for things intellectual and cultural. Classical music was for Europeans and long-haired aesthetes. Poets were unpopular and unworldly, unless, like Edgar Guest, who could compose a poem every day, they sang of simple things in homely language and unfailing rhyme. "Fundamentalism" flourished in the Protestant churches, challenging "Modernists" who strove to reconcile the Christian faith with the onward march of learning. To the Fundamentalist, the findings of Biblical and scientific scholarship were heretical and dangerous insofar as they conflicted with literal interpretation of the Holy Scriptures in the King James Version. "Back to God" was an appealing battle cry, especially in the regions west of the Appalachians and south of the Mason-Dixon Line. Historians enjoyed only modest acclaim, unless they concentrated upon the weaknesses and the foibles, real or otherwise, of the great. "History," said Henry Ford, to the applause of many, "is bunk." Who could doubt that the Great Mechanic knew whereof he spoke, whether about piston rings or the ways of consuls and kings? The prestige of learning, at least of learning that seemed irrelevant to economic progress, was at low ebb.

Of such low estate was learning that it was coupled in the minds of many Americans with "foreigners" and a lack of patriotism. Such was their ignorance and their intolerance, such was the climate of opinion, that the Ku Klux Klan could parade before the Capitol in Washington in full "uniform," with lifted masks, to be sure. The states of Wisconsin and Oregon required by law that teachers do justice to American heroism in the War of Independence and the War of 1812. In Chicago William "Big Bill" Thompson, a political boss, ran for mayor with a slogan: "Bust King George on the snoot!" Thompson was unable to demonstrate that George III or the reigning George V had anything to do with the government of Chicago, but he was not promptly hustled back into private life by the voters. Attempts to curb scholarship were not confined to the field of history. State legislators undertook by statute to repeal the law of evolution. In 1925 those of Tennessee set an example that was later followed by their fellows in a few other states. They made it unlawful for any teacher or professor in any public school, normal college, or university in the state of Tennessee "to teach any theory that denies the story of the Divine Creation of man as taught in the Bible, and to teach instead that man has descended from a lower order of animals."

Passage of the Tennessee law speedily led to the singular Scopes Trial, a judicial carnival that drew the attention of the whole civilized world. Tennessee officials would gladly have let the law become a dead letter, but John Thomas Scopes, a high school teacher in the small town of Dayton, and George Rappelyea, a mining engineer with a sense of humor, arranged to challenge it in the courts. Scopes continued to teach about evolution, using a textbook approved by the Tennessee State Board of Education, and his friend Rappelyea secured a warrant for his arrest for doing it. The trial that followed was a spectacular struggle that attracted thousands of the curious to Dayton. It was widely and thoroughly reported, and ultimately served the cause of education. The distinguished lawyers Clarence Darrow and Arthur Garfield Hays defended Scopes; William Jennings Bryan, who had reached the erroneous conclusion that he was a Biblical expert, assisted the prosecution. The case reached its climax when Bryan took the stand as a witness and was cross-examined by Darrow, a religious agnostic, and a brilliant and probing lawyer. As a champion of absolutely literal interpretation of the book of Genesis, Bryan was made to look ridiculous. He testified that the earth was made before the sun, and he was trapped into saying that fish drowned—in the ordinary meaning of that word—in the Flood. Scopes was found guilty, but the outcome of the trial was humiliating to Bryan and those who were enemies of intellectual freedom.

Bryan and Fundamentalists like him were as unhappy about the evolution of American morals as they were about the descent or rise of mankind, and with better reason. They stoutly supported prohibition; at one time Bryan even urged that a thirsty American imbibing alcoholic liquor in a foreign country should be criminally prosecuted. To the middle-aged and the elderly, morals are commonly in decay. In the Twenties evidence that those of the Americans were deteriorating piled high. Corruption and gangsterism bloomed in the great cities, notoriously in Chicago. They thrived long after the federal government had been cleansed of Harding's ignoble associates. Even more disturbing to many observers were a general increase in crime, the flouting of law by "respectable" citizens, an increase in divorces, and sexual laxity. To a degree these are to be explained as parts of a letdown from, a reaction to the idealism of World War I. There were, however, other causes, including the desire of women for equality with men and social freedom; materialism; the mobility and the privacy offered by the motor car; the influence of Sigmund Freud and other psychoanalysts; and the disconcerting effects of total prohibition.

CHANGING SOCIAL STANDARDS

It was apparent in the Twenties to alarmed viewers that the institution of marriage was breaking down and that sexual chastity was gravely threatened. Widespread and urgent demands for greater social freedom led to a softening of divorce laws and a startling increase in the divorce rate. In several states "mental cruelty" and even "incompatibility" were made grounds for divorce; where it was permitted only for adultery, as in New York, the courts accepted faked evidence to free unhappy mates from their marriage bonds. When Nevada began to offer easy divorce after short residence, Reno became a Mecca for the unfaithful to their marriage vows. For every one hundred marriages in 1910 there were 8.8 divorces; twenty years later, there was one divorce for every six marriages. Persons whose matrimonial bonds had been dissolved were not considered quite respectable before World War I; after it they were more and more accepted as individuals who had simply encountered misfortune, which was indeed often the case. "Until death do you part" came to mean to irresponsibles, "Until you have had enough of it." The "broken homes" that resulted, especially those in which there were children, were socially costly. A mitigating fact that gradually emerged was that divorced persons frequently remarried successfully. For them, the first union was a trial one; matured and sobered by its collapse, they did better the second time.

Concern over the behavior of the married was, as usual, overmatched by anxiety over the conduct of the young and unmarried, with good cause in the Twenties. They were the years of "Flaming Youth," of heavy emphasis upon the possession of "It," and of a supposed discovery of "necking" and "petting." In the past it had not been thought remarkable, under a double standard, that a young man would sow wild oats. After World War I young women and girls demanded that they be permitted at least some of the premarital freedom accorded to males, and they had their way. The "flapper" made her appearance as a young "modern." Girls in their late and delayed 'teens, even when they did not quite arrive at the status of flapper, changed swiftly and strikingly from what they had been before World War I. They had their "crowning glory" bobbed; they resorted to lipstick and rouge; they wore silk instead of cotton stockings; and their clothing weighed and covered less and less. It seemed that corsets and petticoats were on the road to extinction. Skirts became shorter and shorter until they reached knee-length; and when they became a trifle longer again, their more daring wearers for a time "rolled" their stockings below the knee. Bathing suits that had protected feminine modesty to the wrists and ankles shrank fast and far. The new freedom and frankness displayed in milady's clothing, or lack of it, also appeared in her speech, her manners, and her tastes. Ladies began to smoke cigarettes and to imbibe cocktails, at least in private. If fathers and older men were dismayed by the change, the young males were not displeased. They too gained freedom; they did not complain bitterly against the making of a single standard, so long as it was not a high one. They threw off their stiff collars for soft ones, abandoned long underwear and garters, gladly joined in substituting the foxtrot and the Charleston for the waltz, danced to the music of sensuous saxophones, and happily did their courting in automobiles instead of front parlors and buggies. Judge Ben Lindsay of the Juvenile Court of Denver, aware or perhaps overaware of sexual laxity among the young, urged that society change its rules to fit the new standards; he proposed that trial marriage, not unknown among primitive peoples, be legally recognized. His remedy was too sophisticated to be acceptable. Critics of American youth often failed to see that it had changed little fundamentally, that it was as wholesome and as young as of yore.

PROHIBITION

Most disconcerting was the failure of national prohibition. Its friends were vexed because it was not enforced; its enemies were alarmed because it was enforced and because it could not be enforced successfully. Although the consumption of alcoholic liquors was undoubtedly less than it had been in the preceding decade, so many Americans continued to thirst for them that it proved impossible to prevent their manufacture, transportation, or sale. This even though 46 of the 48 states had laws against the traffic in liquors after 1923 (in that year New York repealed its prohibition law; Maryland never passed one). The "dries" liked to think that the Volstead Act was a death blow, to the saloon in particular and the liquor business in general, despite evidence to the contrary. But a large fraction of the people, not necessarily hostile to temperance nor even to rigid control by local option, insisted that the use of alcohol was neither sinful nor, in moderation, injurious. Nor was there an overwhelming majority satisfied that making and selling of liquor should be a crime; there was not the same willingness to punish a violator of the Volstead Act as there was to execute or imprison a murderer. This even though the drunken driver was killing and would continue to kill on the highways. Those who wanted the solace and the confidence engendered by alcohol continued to get it, though not so easily as in the past. It was brought in from abroad by "rum-runners" that slipped past federal revenue craft; it was manufactured in vast quantities in big city distilleries; and it was made in tens of thousands of smaller "stills" located in city, town, and country. The bootlegger became to many citizens the equivalent of the milkman or the postman. The liquids that he sold were often dangerous, for the makers of illegal liquor were frequently careless about both its ingredients and their methods of distilling. Some consumers were racked by pain, blinded, and even poisoned to death. The drinker often made his own tipple, concocting "bathtub gin" from unhappy combinations of uncertain fluids, or making a batch of "home brew" beer in his basement.

Those who were satisfied with any kind of whiskey or beer could secure it. The young in age or heart enjoyed the game of getting them because it was forbidden. Since it was not illegal to drink liquor, the pocket flask, assuring the owner a temporary supply of it, became for many Americans as important as the billfold. However, the consumer did not need to carry his supply everywhere. "Speakeasies," nightclubs, and "beer joints" cautiously opened their doors in the cities and just outside the limits of towns and villages. In Detroit and Chicago beer was openly sold over bars.

The enemy of total prohibition was often as concerned about its failure as were its champions, but for different reasons. Profoundly disturbing to the thoughtful was the stimulation that prohibition gave to gangsterism, corruption of police officers, and disregard for law. Police and politicians, commonly not eager in any case to do anything against liquor, learned that winking at illegal traffickers in it was profitable. What was worse, gangsters quickly discovered that the business was enormously lucrative. They assumed control of it in the big cities and gangsterism flourished as never before in America. Leaders of gangs in Chicago acquired so much money and so great power through control of the unlawful beer business that they could not be touched by honest police. They waged "wars" among themselves for the profits on such a scale that "rubbed out" and "taken for a ride" became standard American—and English—phrases. Gang murders mounted into the hundreds in Chicago before a syndicate headed by Alphonse (Al) Capone secured dominance. Its sensational "execution" of seven members of an opposing gang on St. Valentine's Day in 1929 made it clear that Capone was boss over much of the life of the city. That sinister individual went on his unhindered way until the Federal Bureau of Investigation, which had been made into an effective national police unit by J. Edgar Hoover, proceeded against him. It brought down Capone, but not for the numerous murders for which he was responsible. He had failed to pay enough income tax upon his illegal gains. He was sentenced to eleven years imprisonment in 1931, but his syndicate was not dissolved. If total legal prohibition diminished the flow of liquor, it also grievously injured American public, if not private, morals. The corruption it encouraged touched the gay nightclubbing Mayor "Jimmy" Walker and several judges of New York City as well as ward leaders in Chicago.

EDUCATION

It has been said that the social scene in the Twenties was, on the whole, attractive. So was the intellectual and cultural vista, despite the presence in it of materialism, cynicism, and despair. In that decade elementary education was denied to almost no American; the high school diploma, within the easy reach of nearly everyone save the Southern Negro, was looked upon as an economic necessity. Precollege instruction was not only made available, but was required. Most of the states had come to demand that children be exposed to formal learning of one sort or another until they reached the age of sixteen or seventeen. Consolidated schools, made possible by the building of better roads, automobiles, and buses, tended to replace the "little red schoolhouse," an improvement despite the nostalgic recollections of such one-room establishments by the middle-aged and the elderly. The professional quality of the teacher was heavily emphasized, and not without good results, although her pay hardly matched the dignity claimed for her. (The feminine pronoun must be used, for men tended to leave the classroom for the salesroom and the office.) The level of achievement by the average student probably did not rise very much, for the problem of coping with numbers made difficult the task of raising, or even maintaining, the quality of teaching. Also impressive was the growth of the college and university population. Well before the end of the decade one of every eight Americans between the ages of eighteen and twenty-one was enrolled in an institution of higher learning, at a time when the proportion was one to forty or fifty in western European nations. It had become widely known that an A.B. or a B.Sc. was worth more in money than was a high school diploma. Prudent fathers as well as indulgent ones, richer than in the past, sent their sons to the campus—also daughters who desired careers, suitable mates, or both. Prosperity also made it easier for a young man, or even a young woman, to earn part or all of the expense of attending college. Many a bright young man "worked his way," especially in the state institutions, where tuition fees were low. He might be a gasoline station attendant or a stevedore in the summer. During the remainder of the year he might wait table or wash dishes before and after classes. Such worthy and humdrum tasks were combined with the fascinations of constitutional law, Voltaire's *Candide,* and Thorstein Veblen's *Theory of the Leisure Class.* He might wish he could have some of the leisure enjoyed by his classmates, but at least he could get his sheepskin. More and bigger colleges and universities offered opportunity to more and more young people.

The flood of students into institutions of advanced learning, even though it did not reach so high as later ones in the 1940s and 1960s, strained their resources, especially those of the universities. They resorted increasingly to large lecture classes for undergraduates, thereby requiring the student to shoulder a larger share of the burden of his education. It was not entirely bad that he was forced to become the adult he claimed to be. Another result was the rise of professional and technical specialization among undergraduates, for they now sought training that would help them to secure specific employment or to serve as the basis for advanced study in graduate and professional schools. The college of business administration made its appearance, and the major in chemistry studied more chemistry. If the education of the undergraduate became too vocational, no injury was done to graduate studies or professional instruction. American medical colleges became as good as any in the world, and American dentists excelled all others. The colleges of engineering were commonly excellent. One undoubtedly learned much about economics and accounting in those of business administration; and an introduction of sorts to teaching could be obtained in the college of education. The American Ph.D. became the equal of any; the American scholar could hold his own with those of other lands. The universities became the principal centers of intellectual and scientific advance in the nation; they were aided by liberal arts colleges, institutions for teacher training, and a variety of other educational corporations. So massive was the company of scholars and scientists that the singling out of individuals must do injustice to hundreds of others. Among the more conspicuous of the learned were physicists Robert A. Millikan and Arthur H. Compton; sociologists Robert S. and Helen M. Lynd, whose study of the people of Muncie, Indiana, *Middletown,* created excitement in 1929; the brilliant and facile Vernon Louis Parrington, whose *Main Currents in American Thought* stimulated the study of American intellectual history; and James H. Breasted, Claude H. Van Tyne, and Carl Becker, historians who wrote profoundly and gracefully about Egyptian dynasties, the American Revolution, and eighteenth century thought respectively.

Too many college students of that decade cared little for earnest study, although the majority, as always, was serious-minded. College sports were an ever greater distraction, for the Twenties was the age of the "Four Horsemen of Notre Dame," of Harold "Red" Grange, who ran for five touchdowns against a fine Michigan football team in one afternoon, and of Albie Booth, whose exploits revived gridiron glory at Yale. (It was also the decade of such superb professional athletes, as "Big Bill" Tilden, the tennis champion, George Herman "Babe" Ruth, the tremendous baseball slugger, and Jack Dempsey, the extraordinary heavyweight fighter.) In 1927 the University of Michigan dedicated a football stadium that would hold 87,500 people. The pervasive materialism of the time had its effect on the student, as did his possession of money and the feeling of disillusion that followed World War I. Not a few students felt it their duty to challenge prohibition. Intellectuals in the body collegiate, excessively aware of the fleetingness of youth, turned to hedonism; they memorized Edward Fitzgerald's sadly beautiful translation of the quatrains of Omar Khayyám. With Fitzgerald and the Persian tentmaker they lamented that they were no more than chess pieces moved without seeming purpose by an inscrutable and indifferent Player. They must be as happy as they might be, before it was too late, with food, wine, song, and a member of the opposite sex. With Edna St. Vincent Millay, an appealing poet of their own time, they felt self-pity mingled with joy. With her they burned the candle at both ends. It would not endure, but it gave a lovely light. To many of them the Great Depression brought tragedy they had not really expected.

WRITERS OF THE TWENTIES

The world-weary campus intellectual reflected the moods and discontents of American writers and poets, who passionately denounced a "business civilization" and sought to escape it, fleeing to alcohol, Greenwich Village, and Paris. To be sure, not every gifted novelist or poet took evasive action. One idol of the campus, Henry Louis Mencken, occupied a comfortable lair in Baltimore from which he waged ferocious war against ignorance, obscurantism, mediocrity, and folly. In the *American Mercury,* a magazine beloved of the sophisticates, he unmercifully belabored the Ku Klux Klan, Fundamentalists, Rotarians, and anyone else who stirred his ire. He savagely scored *Americanus Boobensis,* the uninformed and narrow-minded American of the "hinterland" who sought to impose his standards upon his country. A wit, a scholar, a stylist, Mencken was a sturdy knight for intellectual freedom. He was also something of an intellectual snob, feeling no pity for the "booboisie" that he stabbed so adroitly. More typical of the behavior of the more distinguished writers and poets were Ernest Hemingway, F. Scott Fitzgerald, Ezra Pound, and Thomas Stearns Eliot, who sought freedom and inspiration through flight.

If Mencken did not quite deserve the worship that was offered him, there were other literary gods, novelists and poets of the postwar decade who richly deserved acclaim, for it was a flowering time in American literature. Afterward it could not be said that the American novel was a pale, even if worthy, copy of European ones; Ernest Hemingway and William Faulkner became deities before whom Old World intelligentsia bowed in praise. Two of the established American novelists, Edith Wharton and Willa Cather, tended to fade; the former had perhaps exhausted her talent, while the latter turned away from the Nebraska scene she knew so well and treated so imaginatively. However, two other older writers, Ellen Glasgow and Theodore Dreiser, reached their summits. Continuing a series of novels upon the theme of Virginia society from the Civil War into the twentieth century, Miss Glasgow, making perceptive and witty comment, struck heavily at Southern sentimentalism that glorified a dead past. In 1925 Dreiser published *An American Tragedy,* commonly assayed as his finest work. In massive detail he described the pitiful life of Clyde

Griffiths, a young man overwhelmed and destroyed by an American society that stressed money and what it could buy. Clyde was executed for slaying his pathetic and pregnant sweetheart, for a murder he committed only in thought. Despite Dreiser's continuing, though lessening, crudities, *An American Tragedy* had a disconcerting power. But new and far more skillful writers were rapidly appearing to thrust Dreiser into the background. Sherwood Anderson, whose *Winesburg, Ohio* was published in 1919, depicted the inner lives of the people of that town in a series of short stories that described personal turmoil and frustration beneath outward calm. In those stories and in later novels he passionately expressed revolt against imprisoning Midwestern conformity. The civilized had to flee from it. Sinclair Lewis, after publishing several rather mediocre novels, achieved sudden fame in 1920 with his *Main Street.* In it, in *Babbitt,* and in *The Man Who Knew Coolidge,* and in other less important works, Lewis marvelously reproduced the speech, the folkways, and the intellectual poverty of the middle class Midwesterner. Because he could not burlesque the distinguished scholars, lawyers, and public servants of that region as he did real estate man Babbitt, he gave the impression that the region was a wasteland. Lewis wrote brilliant parody. He, Anderson, and other writers, such as Floyd Dell, whose *Mooncalf* and *The Briarybush* spiritually chronicled his own flight from the Mississippi Valley to Greenwich Village and preached the merits of free love, combined to strengthen an Eastern provincial persuasion that the western boundary of American civilization ran along the Allegheny divide.

Nevertheless, it was from that desert of corn and fat pigs and from the backward South that Anderson, Lewis, and the great majority of the most distinguished American novelists of that and later decades came. From St. Paul, Minnesota, F. Scott Fitzgerald went to Princeton and thence swiftly to fame. He was a spokesman extraordinary for the postwar "Lost Generation." Not profound, he wrote with an evident sincerity, in bittersweet phrases, about the "fast set" of metropolitan New York. He personally burned the candle at both ends. Achieving startling success as a writer almost immediately after leaving college, he married a beautiful girl, wrote prolifically, partied gayly, became an alcoholic, and ended a too brief life as a scenario writer in Hollywood. Even so, his novels and his romantic and pathetic personal history will not let his name die. *The Beautiful and Damned, This Side of Paradise, The Great Gatsby,* and his other works, tell very well part of the tale of an era. Of tougher stuff than the goodlooking young Fitzgerald was Ernest Hemingway, from Oak Park, Illinois, who turned from journalism to writing novels in Paris soon after World War I. He too made much of the "Lost Generation," but saw a harsher reality than Fitzgerald. Developing a lean, economical style that was deeply to influence American writing, he dwelt upon the ugliness and cruelty of war, and he saw the bravest of men as creatures of stern fate. His disillusionment appears in *The Sun Also Rises* (1928) and *A Farewell to Arms* (1929). In later books that added little to his reputation he could only advise that the male be virile in a hostile universe. His stoicism, tinged by an affinity for cruelty, is not impressive; but he excelled as a craftsman with words.

The year 1929 was memorable for *Look Homeward, Angel* as well as for *A Farewell to Arms*. Its author, North Carolinian Thomas Wolfe, for some years was a literary giant. He had only one story to tell, his own, but he told it with astonishing gusto in several sprawling novels. His talent was undisciplined, and he rhapsodized lengthily and rhetorically about trifles, but his Gant family is unforgettable, and he wrote passages that had a lyric quality. A far greater figure from the South was William Faulkner of Mississippi. World War I veteran, graduate of the University of Mississippi, and a brilliant chronicler of a deadly conflict between the aristocrats and poor whites in his native state. He displayed power and passion; like Wolfe, he was fond of rhetoric, but he could keep it within bounds. Decay and despair dominated his narratives, and they were studded with crime and ugly incident. Even so, after the appearance of *The Sound and the Fury* in 1929 it gradually became apparent that one of the very greatest of American novelists was creating fabulously, not in New York City or Paris, but in Oxford, Mississippi.

American poets and playwrights in the Twenties were hardly less impressive. Ezra Pound in his *Cantos* might use several languages and indulge in obscurity, but he also had poetic genius and he ably taught the mission of the poet. Greater than Pound was T. S. Eliot, who distinguished himself for both criticism and verse. Like Pound, he was a trenchant foe of America's business civilization, which he considered to be uncivilized. Born in St. Louis, he had fled eastward, then to England, becoming a British citizen in 1927. He found consolation and reassurance in British royalism, British autocracy, British classical tradition, and Anglo-Catholicism. In *The Waste Land, The Hollow Men,* and other poems published in that decade he bitingly described American life as empty, vulgar, and purposeless. He erected a standard of literary excellence that would attract admirers and disciples for many years. In the world of the stage Eugene O'Neill began a reign as absolute as that of Eliot in criticism. With the starkest realism he portrayed man in tragic struggle with evil impulses and forces largely beyond his control. His plays were not prettily written and were not easily produced in the theater. They had a somber and sometimes poetic power; they disturbed, shocked, and forced thought about the fundamental nature of man. After the appearance on the stage of *Desire Under the Elms* in 1924 there could be no doubt that, despite crudities, O'Neill had magnificence.

There were many other indications that the American "business civilization" of the Twenties, so bitterly assailed from the domain of letters, was astonishingly productive of literary and artistic genius, even if revolt against it was not only fashionable but deeply felt among all the intelligentsia. At least indirectly its money, ironically, supported their efforts, however shabbily. The inhospitable cultural climate of the United States was singularly productive; its stony soil gave forth rich seedlings, not all of which went abroad to bloom. The story was the same in the arts. Frank Lloyd Wright heartily condemned an America that did not care for his functional architecture—but his buildings arose from, or rather clung to, the American landscape. The movies were frivolous, inane, and made almost entirely for profit, yet they offered to tens of millions the artistry of Charles Chaplin and of the hauntingly beautiful Greta Garbo. If the Twenties were the worst of times, they were also assuredly the best of times.

53 THE GREAT DEPRESSION

Herbert Hoover, often said to be one of the architects of the New Deal, was, when he succeeded Coolidge, the very model of the rugged individualist—except, perhaps, that he was also something of an idealist. Mature when he took office, he changed little during the four years that followed. As a Friend, he was taught in youth the virtues of toil and thrift, of self-help, of private generosity to the poor and the distressed. His Quakerism dovetailed neatly enough with the cult of laissez-faire. He was no "robber baron," nor was he a commercial feudalist; though a self-made man, he was shy rather than aggressive when he became President; he had risen in the world without violating either his religious or economic tenets. Faithfully and honorably clinging to them in prosperity, he did not abandon them in adversity. On March 4, 1929, he saw before the American people an almost unclouded sky. A few months later that sky was swiftly darkened by a tremendous stock market crash, and thereafter America and the world went into an economic downspin that proved to be catastrophic. Within the limits of his political philosophy, Hoover did everything possible both to bring the Great Depression to a halt and also to relieve the suffering that came from it. It may even be said that he set aside that philosophy to a degree, in order to fight against ever-increasing troubles. His efforts were largely in vain, and he was a bitterly abused man when he retired to private life, for within four years the American nation had slipped from a peak of material progress to an economic nadir. Nor were these afflictions merely domestic. The Great Depression was world-wide. It enabled Adolf Hitler and his Nazis to seize power in Germany; Fascism and Communism also flourished; and Japanese expansionists were encouraged and stimulated to action. In the early months of 1933 pessimistic intellectuals found ample evidence that German science teacher Oswald Spengler was a prophet, for he had predicted in *The Decline of the West* in 1918 that liberalism, democracy, and humanitarianism would give way to brutal dictatorship.

"THE GREAT ENGINEER"

On his inaugural day in 1929 Hoover did not sense impending disaster. He and his advisers were disturbed because the New York stock market threatened to become wildly speculative, but they did not doubt that the nation was economically healthy. It was widely believed that he would supply leadership toward a greater prosperity, the benefits of which would be received by almost all. Such was his purpose, he said, indicating confidence that it could be achieved. He declared that contempt for and disobedience of law—referring to prohibition and gangsterism—was "the most malign of all the dangers" on the domestic scene. He hinted that the fates of the United States and other nations were intertwined, and that all was not so well as it might be abroad, but he did not express alarm.

The public expected from Hoover business efficiency, and received it. He was not able to get all the talent he desired to assist him, and some of his Cabinet members were mediocre. He found a truly able Secretary of State in Henry L. Stimson and he kept Andrew Mellon at the Treasury until 1932, when Mellon resigned and was replaced by the skillful financier Ogden Mills. At the head of the Department of Interior he placed his good friend Ray Lyman Wilbur, President of Stanford University, who carefully protected the public domain, including its oil reserves. Hoover himself worked long hours, setting an example that many of his subordinates followed. During his Presidency, and afterward, he continued to be a "Great Engineer."

More, much more, has been demanded of an American President in the twentieth century than efficiency in management. He must supply leadership in the large things as well as the small. In other words, he must be a politician, in the better sense of that term. It is, in fact, far more difficult to be wise in the making of policy and astute in executing it than it is to direct a bureaucracy, whether private or public. Afterward, when Hoover failed to solve this problem or that, it was said in his defense that "He is not a politician." His duties required that he be one. It may properly be said that he had some of the qualities of the politician-statesman—honesty, energy, wide experience, broad sympathies, and a desire for peace. It is also true that he was hampered by partisan and factional enemies, almost from his first day in office; to be sure, such is commonly the lot of a President. It must nevertheless be admitted that the alliance of Democrats and progressive Republicans which dominated Congress after 1930 did not gladly work with the President to solve every public question. As early as February of that year this alliance tried to prevent the confirmation in the Senate of Hoover's appointment of Charles Evans Hughes as Chief Justice of the Supreme Court to replace Taft. Hughes was endorsed by the Senate, but twenty-six of its members voted against him, ostensibly because he was a conservative. Some weeks later the nomination of John J. Parker of North Carolina to be an Associate Justice of the high court was actually defeated in the Senate, principally because he also was thought to be too conservative. After the election of 1930 Hoover's troubles with Congress increased, for the Democrats secured control of the House of Representatives. Be that as it may, there was little that Hoover really wanted to do that was checked by his political enemies. Insofar as he failed, it was because he did not wish to do enough quickly enough. One may speculate whether "Al" Smith in the same circumstances would have performed better.

FARM PROBLEMS AND THE TARIFF

There is no question that Hoover was more concerned than Coolidge over the lot of the American farmer in the 1920s. Moreover, he and other Republicans whose economic interests were primarily those of business knew that long-continued economic trouble among the farmers could hardly fail to spread. In April, 1929 he called Congress into special session to create a "great instrumentality"—like several New Dealers after him, Hoover had a fondness for big words—that would help the man on the soil to market profitably. He also called for tariff increases on agricultural goods. He secured his "instrumentality." The Senate, dominated by Farm Bloc progressive Republicans and Democrats, had its own remedy for farm ills, an export debenture plan. This would have required the payment of bounties on basic farm commodities sent abroad, equal to one half of the American tariff duties on the same commodities. Payment was to be in the form of certificates that could be used in payment of import duties. By this arrangement the difference between domestic and world prices upon those commodities would be paid to the producers out of customs receipts. Hoover was utterly opposed to such subsidies. Threatening a veto of the Senate plan and securing the help of the House of Representatives, he was able to force passage of the Agricultural Marketing Act in June. This established a Federal Farm Board with a fund of $500,000,000 to make loans to agricultural cooperatives and other special agencies toward planned and more efficient selling of surplus commodities, including cotton, grain, and livestock. Had the scheme been put into effect earlier, it would have been more useful. The Board established several "stabilizing" corporations in 1930 and lent money to them. By that time, however, the Great Depression was under way, and world prices were falling steadily and sharply. The Board was able only to delay the fall of American farm income. Ever lower prices merely led farmers to increase production. In 1931, after it had lost $180,000,000, the Board abandoned its purchases of surplus commodities as both useless and expensive. It vainly advised farmers to produce less. They became steadily more desperate. The farm price of wheat slipped from $1.05 per bushel in 1929 to less than 39¢ in 1932; cotton worth 17¢ per pound in 1929, brought only 6½¢ in 1932. Mortgage foreclosures became ever more common across the land.

Nor was the farmer much assisted by tariff reform. On the contrary, the whole nation suffered from it. There was little objection in Congress to raising rates on imported farm products, but believers in generous protection for industry, led by Republican Senator Joseph Grundy of Pennsylvania, insisted that industry deserved and needed shielding against foreign competition as much as agriculture did. In consequence, there was a long and sharp struggle over rates that endured until the early summer of 1930. Meanwhile, the Great Depression was well under way. Professional economists became more and more alarmed lest rates be raised generally. More than one thousand of them, in astonishing agreement, signed a trenchant protest when the will of Congress finally appeared in the Hawley-Smoot bill. It was the result of much bargaining over special interests rather than those of the nation as a whole. Those who wanted high barriers against foreign raw materials, had to vote for high walls against foreign manufactures in order to get it. The bill provided for rate increases on agricultural products from 38 percent to 49 percent; it added about one-third to the duties upon manufactured goods. Professional and professorial economists asserted that the bill had hardly a saving grace; it would hurt the consumer; it would do little for the farmer; it would discourage the sale of American things in foreign nations that could not sell in America; it would provoke retaliatory tariffs; it would add to unemployment; and it must make enemies in foreign countries. About all that could be said in defense of the bill was that it continued the Tariff Commission, giving it ample authority to investigate the results of tariff rates. In accordance with findings of the Commission, the President was given the power to lower or raise rates by as much as 50 percent. In view of past experience, the economists doubted that the Commission and the President would undo the damage done by Congress. Hoover managed to satisfy himself that errors in the bill could be rectified, and he put his name to it. The predictions of the economists were only too correct. The Hawley-Smoot Act encouraged economic decline on both sides of its barriers. It won no friends for America, and it provoked foreign retaliation. The reputation Hoover had won in the business community for economic statesmanship sank. It was already under savage attack for other reasons.

THE CRASH

In October, 1929, came *the* stock market crash, easily the most devastating one in American history. It was not unforeseen by a prudent few, but it profoundly shocked the many, and it started a chain of economic disaster that grievously affected both the careful and the careless, in America and around the world. Stock prices had begun to rise in 1924, not unreasonably, in view of the national prosperity. However, toward the end of 1927 they began to advance with great rapidity, partly because the Federal Reserve Board had made money easier to obtain in order to help European governments struggling toward recovery from World War I. Before the close of the year thoughtful bankers were worried because the speculative spirit of the American people was running high. They were especially concerned because large quantities of stock were being purchased on margin in the expectation of making quick and large profit, for it was then possible to buy stock with as little as 10 percent of its cost, the remainder being borrowed by brokers. At that time brokers had borrowed more than $3,500,000,000. In January, 1928, President Coolidge announced officially that he saw no cause for alarm, and prices of stocks surged upward in the following March. The "Big Bull Market" was under way. The Federal Reserve Board then began to try to restrict the supply of money for gambling in the market, without success. Soon after Hoover became President, Secretary of the Treasury Mellon issued a statement advising investors to buy bonds rather than stocks, but his counsel went largely unheeded. New York banks continued to lend money for the use of speculators, despite his warning, and despite pressure from the Federal Reserve Board. By the late summer of 1929 they had the use of seven billion dollars and gambled that stocks would go up and up and up. Despite "breaks" in the market, so many get-rich-quick investors had so much faith that it recovered from every one and went on to higher levels, until the fall of 1929. By that time the prices of stocks were about double what they had been two years earlier; in many cases they were triple and quadruple. Perhaps as many as a million Americans were then "in the market," many of them harboring dreams of easy wealth. In many cases stock prices bore almost no relation to earnings. In September they began to drift downward in New York; they also slipped in London. On Wednesday, October 23, the storm broke; fifty leading stocks had an average loss of 18 points on the New York Exchange. The following day was even worse, as speculators strove to sell, and as brokers sold the shares of investors whose margins had vanished. Powerful bankers tried to arrest the panic, but they failed. On the following Monday and Tuesday prices continued to fall swiftly. Reassuring statements by John D. Rockefeller, Jr., John J. Raskob, and other financiers finally succeeded in checking the panic, but prices continued to fall. In mid-November, when they seemed to have reached bottom, "sound" stocks could be bought at about 50 percent of their cost in September—if one had money to buy. General Motors had sunk from 72 to 36, General Electric from 196 to 168, and Radio Corporation of America from 101 to 28. Weaker stocks had fared even worse. Billions of dollars of values, many of them only in paper, had vanished.

Humpty Dumpty had fallen, but did it matter, except to those who held or had held stocks? Although brokerage offices had been opened in almost every considerable city in the nation, gambling in stocks had been confined to relatively few persons. Most Americans knew little if anything about the "Big Bull Market." They were, however, conscious of its crash, for that was chronicled in heavy headlines in the newspapers, together with many sensational reports of suicides by "ruined" speculators who jumped to their deaths from New York City skyscrapers, shot themselves, or otherwise put an end to their troubles. It was widely believed, or at least hoped, that the tragedy of the stock exchange would not affect those who had owned none of the collapsing shares. Business and political leaders said that the crash was an unfortunate incident, that people should not become panicky, that there was no good reason why production, selling, and buying should not continue as in the past. Hoover and well-informed economists knew better, for they were well aware that a deranged economy would require painful readjustment. Leaner years must follow the fat ones. Neither they nor any "sensible" person saw the crash as a catastrophe. But business promptly slackened, and men and women began to lose their jobs.

FROM PANIC TO WORLD-WIDE DEPRESSION

Had the American economy been without basic weaknesses, the shock of the stock market crash might have been sustained without deep injury. Instead, it served as a trigger; it destroyed confidence among those directly affected, and their loss of faith spread in ever widening circles. Why, it is not easily said. It may be observed, however, that the frailty of the European economy hurt the American one. Continuing agricultural distress was shrinking the American market for finished goods, while income had not been sufficiently diffused to maintain purchasing power and to soften the effects of unemployment. Personal debts had risen, thanks in part to the growing popularity of installment buying. Technological unemployment had made its appearance. Recently formed and jerry-built holding company empires in the field of public utilities could not withstand attack, while reckless banking practices injured the economy profoundly—this last was perhaps the most serious weakness in the economic structure. During the prosperous years 1927–1929 no fewer than 1600 American banks failed. Many more were vulnerable, and during the years 1930–1932, 4377 bands holding two billion dollars in deposits would close their doors.

Hoover moved swiftly to soften the effects of the stock market crash and to prevent repercussions. The Federal Reserve system sought to pump out credit. In November, 1929, the President held a series of conferences with industrial and commercial magnates who agreed at his urging to maintain employment, wages, and building programs. He asked Congress to cut income taxes and to approve a program of increased public works, including the erection of Boulder Dam. That body readily complied. He likewise requested the states and the cities to spend more money for public improvements. He hoped to hold unemployment in industry and commerce, which he knew would increase, to a minimum, and to provide new jobs through public expenditures. Hoover was convinced that these measures would restore confidence.

For some weeks there seemed to be reason to believe that the nation had turned an awkward corner. Toward the end of 1929 there were about three million persons unemployed, but that figure shrank early in 1930 and, in March Hoover said that another two months would bring an end to joblessness. By spring about half of the losses suffered on the stock market had been regained. In May Hoover said that "we have now passed the worst and with continued unity of effort we shall rapidly recover." A little later in the same month he declared that business would be normal by autumn. But alas, conditions had already taken a turn for the worse. Cutting income taxes, which were already low, did not do much to increase purchasing power. Hoover's public works programs provided jobs for relatively few, and industry laid off men rather than produce goods that could not be sold. Continuing failures of brokerage houses and especially of banks almost continuously added to uneasiness. The number of unemployed mounted higher than before in the late spring of 1930; the stock market sagged again; during the summer a drouth struck heavily in the lower Mississippi Valley. By the fall of 1930 the nation—and the world—was unquestionably in the throes of a major depression.

The American people as a whole were not quite desperate that autumn, and they did not violently turn against the Republican party in the election of 1930. By that time many Democrats were calling for direct federal aid to the unemployed, and all of them hoped that the voters would cast their ballots against hard times. Charles Michelson, publicity agent for the Democratic National Committee, opened a long campaign against Hoover and the Republicans. They claimed credit for prosperity, he said, and they must accept the blame for adversity. He and Democratic politicians denounced Hoover for empty optimism and inaction. Hoover defended himself and his party, saying in October that there was only "a temporary halt in the prosperity of a great nation." The voters, as was expected, expressed their unhappiness, but rather mildly. The election results gave the Democrats control of the House of Representatives by a small margin and enabled them to make John N. Garner of Texas its Speaker. The Senate remained under technical Republican management, with 48 Republicans, 47 Democrats, and 1 Farmer-Laborite. Actually, it was easily dominated by an alliance of Democrats and progressive Republicans. After 1930 Hoover had to deal with an increasingly hostile Congress that urged more drastic measures against the depression.

The depression continued to deepen. In December, 1930 the Bank of the United States, an old, private, and large one in New York City, sensationally failed. At that time there were about five million persons unemployed in the nation. During some weeks early in 1931 the bottom seemed again to have been reached, and optimists again fancied that an upward trend would soon begin. Instead, a new downward impulse came from abroad. Withdrawals from the United States of European gold and money adversely affected America. What was worse, economic strain in central Europe was such that banks and government staggered. In May, 1931, the Kredit Anstalt, the largest bank in Austria, announced that it must go down unless it received prompt aid from other countries. The help was given, but actual bank closings in Germany soon followed. Hoover rapidly moved toward restoring confidence in Europe by proposing a one-year moratorium upon all intergovernmental debts. That statesmanlike step, unfortunately, came too late. In September, Britain was forced off the gold standard. Other nations soon followed her example. Economic warfare in which devalued currencies as well as tariffs were used as weapons increased among the nations. At last, in 1932, the Allies signed an agreement with Germany at Lausanne by which reparations were virtually cancelled, provided that the United States dealt generously with them by scaling down their war debts. Reparations then came to an end, for Germany refused to make any further payments, even though the United States declined to cancel the war debts. Several nations, including France, failed to make any payment on them in 1932. After that year Britain paid only token sums and only Finland made payments in full. So the question of the war debts faded away without much financial benefit to the United States.

The European economic crisis of 1931 drove the prices of stocks on the New York Exchange down again, to a point far below that reached in the crash of 1929. Wage cuts became numerous, unemployment figures swept upward, and bank failures mounted again. Currency hoarding came into vogue. Under Hoover's leadership an association of great bankers was formed to defend the solvency of banks under attack. It worked for a time only. The national debt was climbing—it went from $16.2 billions in 1930 to $22.5 billions in 1933—since Congress could not increase taxes to match increased expenditures. At the beginning of 1932 the American gold standard was threatened. To meet the crisis the President and Congress created the Reconstruction Finance Corporation in January and passed the Glass-Steagall Act in February. The latter made it possible to use more securities and less gold in support of currency, so protecting the gold standard. The RFC, given a capital stock of $500 millions and the right to borrow three times that sum, was empowered to lend to banks, trust and insurance companies, farm credit associations, and, with the sanction of the Interstate Commerce Commission, to railroads. In the following summer, the RFC was given a much larger capital and was authorized to lend as much as $300 millions to the states to be spent for the relief of the needy. Many Democrats clamored louder than before for direct federal grants to those in distress. Hoover had long contended that there should be no national "dole" until the resources of private charity and of the cities and states had been exhausted. The loans to the states came close to direct federal relief, and they helped. The RFC, well managed, saved many banks and trust and mortgage loan companies, at least temporarily. Several railroads and insurance companies were also helped. The RFC proved to be so useful that it was continued for more than a decade.

THE HUMAN SIDE OF DEPRESSION

The vigorous measures taken by Hoover and the Congress did not bring the depression to a halt. Toward the end of 1932 the official number of unemployed was more than 10 million, and it may actually have been as high as 17 million. By that time the national income had shrunk by 40 percent. The suffering caused by the depression continued, and it was tragic. Volumes could be written about personal and family catastrophe during the grinding years after the collapse of the stock market. Men who were "laid off" or discharged often became permanently idle. City families were evicted from apartments or lost their homes because they could not make mortgage payments. When they fled to the countryside, as many of them did, they saw farms sold under the hammer because of default in paying mortgages or taxes. The young graduated from high school and college into unemployment, or stayed on in school for lack of something better to do. Young and old, helpless and discouraged at home, took to the roads and the railroads; tens of thousands wandered about aimlessly. Those who had jobs feared the day of discharge. "Runs" on banks were a too frequent and sad sight. Factories and offices darkened, and empty stores appeared on innumerable city streets. Bread lines and soup kitchens offered melancholy scenes. Men were seen trying to scavenge food from garbage pails behind city restaurants, a dismal spectacle. The great efforts of private charity, of the cities, and of the states to relieve distress were insufficient.

Strangely enough, the American people, not generally given credit for patience, underwent the trials of the depression with little commotion until 1932. Then came signs that despair might lead to serious violence. In the spring of that year Iowa farmers under the leadership of Milo Reno began a "Farm Holiday." Of what avail to raise and carry to markets foodstuffs that commanded prices so low it was not worthwhile? Masses of farmers decided to "Stay at Home—Buy Nothing—Sell Nothing," hoping that their "strike" would somehow improve their lot. Mobs of farmers would not let nonparticipants in the "strike" carry milk to town; they spilled milk on the roads rather than let it go to the creamery. They also forcibly prevented the sale of farms upon which mortgages had been foreclosed. The Farm Holiday ended only because it was useless. The summer of 1932 brought violence in Washington, too. It came as the result of the march upon the capital of the "Bonus Army." Almost from the beginning of the depression the American Legion sought special help for military veterans. Responding to its pressure, and overriding Hoover's veto, Congress in 1931 enacted a law permitting veterans to borrow as much as 50 percent of the value of the endowment policies they had received in 1924. Soon the former soldiers, sailors, and marines were asking for full payment. To support that demand, 10,000 or more veterans converged upon Washington in the late spring of 1932. They moved into empty government buildings and threw up shacks on the Potomac. A bill giving them what they wanted was defeated in the Senate. Hoover, who was also against the measure, asked Congress to supply money for the "Bonus Expeditionary Force" to go home, and this was done. However, about 2000 veterans obstinately stayed on, some of them continuing to live in federal buildings. The President finally ordered the Washington police to clear the buildings, and the veterans were forcibly ejected on July 28. Two of them were killed. Then Hoover called upon the army to drive the remainder of the Bonus Army from the District of Columbia. General Douglas MacArthur saw to it that the removal was as painless as possible, and the army did no killing. Whether the use of force was truly necessary has been questioned;

there was something ominous in the presence of the veterans in the nation's capital. Certainly Hoover did not win many friends in the American Legion.

Things had a way of going perversely for Hoover. In 1929, facing up to an awkward problem that with most other politicians he had tried to dodge, he appointed a commission headed by George W. Wickersham to study prohibition and to recommend action in accordance with its findings. Early in 1931 the eleven men who composed it brought in a report that aroused whatever humor still remained in the nation. It said that national prohibition was a failure and that it had corrupted police and courts— also that it had enhanced chronic American disrespect for law. But the commission could not agree about what should be done. Two of its members favored the continuation of the Great Experiment, while two others urged repeal of the Eighteenth Amendment. The majority seemed to desire that the Constitution be again altered so that Congress would have the power to do whatever it willed about the manufacture, transportation, and sale of intoxicating liquors. The mammoth report of the commission confused as well as amused the public.

INTERNATIONAL SCENE

As the election of 1932 approached, the international scene had a look almost as ugly as the domestic one, and there was little that Hoover or the nation could reasonably do about it. In 1930, with the help of Prime Minister J. Ramsay MacDonald of Britain, Hoover won a doubtful triumph by means of the London Naval Conference. Japan, France, and Italy were persuaded to send delegates to it to work with those of the United States and Britain toward further reduction of sea forces. The result was a treaty by which America, Britain and Japan agreed to a ratio of 10:10:6.5 for cruisers and one of 10:10:7 with regard to destroyers. Also, the three powers undertook to scrap several battleships immediately and to build no more before 1936. Still further, they accepted the principle of equality for the three nations in submarine tonnage. The treaty strengthened Japan in western Pacific waters. Since she proceeded to build to the limits set by the treaty and Britain and America did not, she gained further advantage during the following six years. What was worse, this improving military position in the western Pacific, together with the economic difficulties of America and Britain, encouraged the Japanese to use force to settle the contest between them and the Chinese over Manchuria. China was badly disorganized, but undertook to challenge Japanese economic and police rights in that huge and rich province. Japanese troops overran Manchuria between September, 1931, and January, 1932, and it was promptly made into the "independent" state of Manchukuo, under Japanese guidance. China responded in part by a boycott of Japanese goods, which was abandoned only after an attack by Japanese upon Chinese soldiers at Shanghai. Since Japan, whatever the provocation, had broken two formal promises of nonaggression, Secretary of State Henry L. Stimson at length proposed that the United States, with the League of Nations, impose economic sanctions upon Japan. Hoover would not go so far, nor would the League of Nations, for such sanctions might well lead to war. However, both the United States and the League condemned the behavior of Japan. While recognition was refused to Manchukuo, Japan clung to control of it and made it into a puppet state under an emperor, Henry P'u-Yi, a descendant of the Manchu dynasty. Moreover, Japanese militarists took advantage of aroused Japanese feelings against the Western nations to lead their country toward further adventures. In Germany, too, the course of events presaged trouble to come, for the desperate Germans were turning toward the fanatical and half-mad Adolf Hitler. Only President von Hindenburg stood between him and mastery of Germany. In January, 1933, the old President appointed the former Austrian painter Chancellor. Before Hoover left office in America, Hitler was tightening his grip upon Germany.

DOWNFALL OF THE REPUBLICANS

At Chicago in mid-June, 1932, the Republicans renominated Hoover and Charles Curtis. They could hardly do otherwise. In an atmosphere of gloom they stood almost desperately by their record, calling for governmental economy, a balanced budget, maintenance of the gold standard, and high protective tariffs. They came out for revision of the Eighteenth Amendment, proposing that the liquor problem be returned to the states, with the federal government helping any state that desired to be "dry" by preventing the shipment of alcoholic beverages into it. The Republican strategy was to portray Hoover as one who had dauntlessly and imaginatively fought against the Depression. If his efforts and those of his party had not yet turned the economic tide, they had checked it somewhat; given more time, they must be successful. The voters were asked to express their gratitude to and their faith in Hoover the hero and the humanitarian.

Democratic politicians, like the Republican ones, knew that Hoover—and his party—would not profit much from gratitude at the polls. It was clear when the Democratic national convention met at Chicago late in June that the voters would cast their ballots against the Depression, against Hoover, and against the Republicans. Unless the Democratic candidate made some extraordinary mistake, he must triumph in November. Norman Thomas was already campaigning as the leader of the Socialists, but it was obvious that most of those tempted to support him would vote for the Democratic candidate in order to make sure the defeat of Hoover. The

Democratic nomination was therefore a prize eagerly sought, this despite the oppressive burden that would fall upon Hoover's successor. Governors Albert Ritchie of Maryland and William "Alfalfa Bill" Murray of Oklahoma sought it. Newton D. Baker, Wilson's Secretary of War, was pushed by some. The principal aspirants for the nomination were Franklin D. Roosevelt, John N. Garner, and Al Smith. Roosevelt had put the name of Smith before the Democratic convention in 1924 and again in 1928. In 1928 he had been elected Governor of New York by a small majority; in 1930 he had been reelected by a large majority. He had performed respectably at Albany. He was not generally thought to be a great man; the columnist Walter Lippman had written, "He is a pleasant man, who without any important qualifications for the office, would very much like to be President." However, Roosevelt was otherwise highly suitable, and his political managers, notably James A. Farley, had obtained promises of support from more than half of the delegates. Garner, Speaker of the House of Representatives, had the backing of William G. McAdoo and William Randolph Hearst, and the delegates from California and Texas. Many Eastern Democrats rallied behind Smith, who was Roosevelt's most potent rival. For the first three ballots for the nomination Roosevelt had a majority, but not the two-thirds required. When it seemed that his following would wither and that Smith might come forward, McAdoo and Hearst, neither of whom had reason to be fond of Smith, carried the Garner following into the Roosevelt camp. The New York Governor was then swiftly nominated, with Garner, rewarded for his compliance, as a running mate. The Democrats, in a remarkably brief platform, flatly declared for the repeal of the Eighteenth Amendment and for a 25 percent cut in the federal budget, which they promised to put back in balance. Otherwise, it was not more precise in few words than that of the Republicans in many. It hinted that the Democrats were determined to do something decisive toward helping the farmers and that tariffs might be lowered. Flying from Albany to Chicago, Roosevelt went before the convention and promised a "New Deal." He displayed energy but made no specific promises.

In the campaign of 1932 all sorts of charges were leveled against Hoover and the Republicans, and many and diverse remedies for the ills of the nation were urged. Hoover was a target for unusually vicious slander; he was portrayed as a selfish, unscrupulous, and heartless money-grabber. The recent record of the Republicans was bitterly attacked, with more justification. Despair and frustration induced a belief in the wildest charges and in exotic cures for the nation's woes. The Communist Party, hitherto feeble, was acquiring recruits among intellectuals. Howard Scott, an engineer, appeared as a savior to some. His "Technocracy" called for a scientific system of government, his grand panacea being a currency based upon units of energy. Just how his money would be different, and exactly how it would help, he could not quite explain. Radio orator Father Charles Coughlin of Royal Oak, Michigan, passionate and fluent, berated bankers, to the great satisfaction of millions of listeners. It was not clear what he wanted for the future; he urged the election of Roosevelt. Dr. Francis Townsend, elderly and impoverished, fancied that national pensions to the aged would solve many troubles.

Attacked from every quarter, Hoover struck back as best he might, defending his deeds of omission and commission, and warning against the Democrats as irresponsibles. His speeches had little effect. Roosevelt would doubtless have won without making any effort. However, he too campaigned energetically, in part, no doubt, to demonstrate that, though a cripple, he was healthy and sturdy. It was unnecessary for him to commit himself upon many public questions, and he avoided making specific promises, with two important exceptions. He delighted the Midwestern farmers with a pledge to pay out federal money for reducing crops, and he announced his personal allegiance to economy and a balanced budget. Hoover was sober and rather depressed; Roosevelt was buoyant and vigorous, although the qualities of leadership that he afterward displayed to such a remarkable degree were not yet evident. It was quite unnecessary for him to exhibit transcendent abilities, for many millions of Americans were already determined upon political change. Roosevelt and the Democrats won an overwhelming victory. Roosevelt had 27,821,857 popular votes, Hoover only 15,761,841, while Socialist Norman Thomas had 884,781, and Communist William Z. Foster 102,991. A prohibitionist candidate ran about 20,000 votes behind Foster, and others fared even worse. Hoover carried only New England, except for Massachusetts, together with Pennsylvania and Delaware; Roosevelt won in 42 states. He secured 472 electoral votes, Hoover only 59. The Democrats obtained large majorities in both houses of Congress, more than two-thirds in the House of Representatives. In the Senate there were to be 59 Democrats, 36 Republicans, and one Farmer-Laborite.

Hoover's travail was not yet ended. The Twentieth Amendment, by which the Congress begins on January 3 and the President takes office on January 20, was not approved by the states until February, 1933. Accordingly, Hoover and the last "lame-duck" Congress did the best they could until the following March 4. The Twenty-first Amendment, repealing the Eighteenth, was sent to the states. Hoover and his followers could undertake little more without assurance by Roosevelt and the Democrats that they would continue measures already begun; on the other hand, Roosevelt and his party were reluctant to pledge adherence to policies they could not initiate. Seeking to retain freedom of action, Roosevelt declined invitations from Hoover toward concerted efforts. During the four months after the election of 1932 the affairs of the nation went from very bad to worse. Panic came in February, when Governor William Comstock of Michigan proclaimed an eight-day bank holiday for his state. Comstock's proclamation began an epidemic of such closings, and the banks in 22 states were shut on March 4. In retirement, Hoover very gradually regained public esteem. Roosevelt and the triumphant Democrats faced a crisis.

54 THE NEW DEAL MEASURES

Franklin D. Roosevelt, like his fifth cousin Theodore, came into the world as the son of a country magnate. Born in 1882, he was sent, like his cousin, to Groton School and thence to Harvard. He also studied law at Columbia University and practiced it briefly. Marrying Anna Eleanor Roosevelt, a niece of Theodore, he entered politics in 1910, when he was elected to the Senate of New York. A scion of the Roosevelts of Hyde Park, reared as a Democrat, he stood out among his Republican neighbors and was early marked for distinction in his party. As Assistant Secretary of the Navy and as a candidate for the Vice-Presidency in 1920, he offered no striking evidence that he was particularly gifted. A turning point in his life came in 1921 when he was stricken by infantile paralysis. He was never thereafter able to walk, even for a few steps, except with the help of braces and of canes. But his illness reduced him to elementals, stimulated the hereditary Roosevelt stubbornness and courage, and broadened his sympathies. As Governor of New York he still seemed to be no more than competent, partly, no doubt, because his eyes frequently strayed from Albany toward Washington after 1930. Had he had a long and brilliant record, he might not have been the choice of the Democratic party, since such records are not made without accumulating enemies. In many ways he was peculiarly fitted for the awesome burdens that fell upon him. Except for his legs, he was physically powerful. He was brave, confident, cheerful, tactful, and charming. He was a superb speaker, and he was adept in the art of politics. He was not a devoted scholar, but he possessed mental ingenuity. He knew little about economics, and he was no profound political philosopher. He was pragmatic, inventive, and adaptable. Roosevelt conceived that the President must supply leadership in ample quantity, and he gladly gave it. He made a host of enemies, and he acquired a myriad of admirers. At the head of the American republic during more than twelve years, Roosevelt led vigorously in both peace and war. Under his guidance America was internally remodeled, becoming a democracy with a regulated capitalistic system and provision for social security. He also directed the national effort toward victory in World War II, dying just before it was achieved.

When Roosevelt was elected in 1932, there seemed to be little reason to expect profound domestic change. He had announced his concern for "the forgotten man," but had offered only strong hints about his New Deal. It was hardly to be expected that he would seek to alter in any essentials an economic order that had been so generous to him and his. Nor did his Cabinet selections suggest anything earthshaking to come. He appointed William H. Woodin, industrialist, to the Treasury; when he soon had to find a successor to Woodin, he choose Henry Morgenthau, a country gentleman and Hyde Park neighbor. Cordell Hull, his Secretary of State for many years, was a liberal Tennesseean, no firebrand. Frances Perkins, made Secretary of Labor, was competent but was remarkable chiefly because she was the first of her sex to achieve Cabinet rank. Impetus toward any large change could be expected only from Harold L. Ickes, a veteran progressive Republican placed at the head of the Department of the Interior, and Henry A. Wallace, Secretary of Agriculture, a man fond of the farmer and fertile in ideas.

NOTHING TO FEAR

It could reasonably be conjectured on March 4, 1933, that Roosevelt's New Deal would strongly resemble Woodrow Wilson's New Freedom, with some added exertions of federal power to meet the national emergency that existed. Actually, ever since his election, Roosevelt had been considering action on a wider front, and he had begun to assemble a corps of special advisers, the so-called "Brain Trust," composed of young and vigorous men, including professors and recent law school graduates. Moreover, the crisis that he faced upon taking office persuaded him that he must move both drastically and speedily. In his inaugural address he made it clear that he intended to fight against the national emergency as if the nation were at war, and that the "direct, vigorous action" wished for by his listeners would be supplied. Confidently asserting that "the only thing we have to fear is fear itself," he assured them the nation would endure in democracy, revive, and prosper. It must behave as a "Good Neighbor" abroad. But he stressed again and again the need for action at home. The country breathed easier. In the large he was as good as his word. One specific need that he stressed, that of making federal income match outgo, he never quite met.

Roosevelt and the New Dealers dealt swiftly with the banking crisis. On March 5 he proclaimed a national banking holiday, and called the Congress into special session. Four days later the Congress convened and gave its approval to the holiday. On March 11 the President announced that most of the nation's banks were sound and that they would be open again the following week. About one in ten of them was kept at least temporarily closed. Placed under the control of "conservators," many of them eventually resumed business. Just how the Treasury decided within one week which banks were sound and which were not, the public did not know. But it accepted the opinion of government, and there were no runs on reopened banks. In a "fireside chat"—one of many speeches Roosevelt was to make over the radio—the President had assured the nation that it could trust the judgment of Treasury officers. It gave full faith; perhaps it could not do otherwise.

THE HUNDRED DAYS

Following Roosevelt's lead, the New Dealers continued to move with extraordinary, even feverish, speed in the spring of 1933. Amid popular acclaim the President and his advisers, Cabinet members and Brain Trusters, thrust measure after measure through a willing and often bewildered Congress. To enforce them new agency after new agency sprang up in confusing profusion. Hastily drawn laws were passed that were even more hastily read, if read at all, by the lawmakers. During the Hundred Days that followed the convening of the special session called to meet the banking crisis on March 9, Washington seemed almost to be at war. All of what was done cannot possibly be chronicled in brief space. It may be said, however, that the New Dealers aimed at relief and recovery, secondarily at reform, and that they went beyond the New Freedom to a Newer Nationalism. In fact, it is appropriate to say that Roosevelt II acted in the spirit of the Roosevelt I of 1912 during his first two years in office.

During the Hundred Days federal salaries and military pensions were cut, for Roosevelt, thrifty in his private affairs, sincerely believed in economy in public ones. The Volstead Act was amended so that light wines and beer became legal. Endorsing the purpose of the London Economic

Conference, arranged by Hoover and the leaders of the other great nations for the purpose of stabilizing currencies, Roosevelt changed his mind and undertook to stimulate recovery at home by manipulation of the American currency. As usual, Congress followed his lead, and the nation went off the gold standard. Stringent federal controls were established over banking and credit. By the Glass-Steagall Banking Act individual deposits under $5000—later raised to $10,000—in approved banking institutions were guaranteed through the Federal Bank Deposit Insurance Corporation. The Home Owners Loan Corporation was created to help homeowners burdened by mortgages to refinance them at lower rates and also to lend money for taxes and repairs to homeowners who were not staggering under mortgages. A Farm Credit Act similarly to help farmers refinance their mortgages was passed. A great effort to help the destitute and the unemployed began. The Civilian Conservation Corps was established to give work to jobless young men and to help their families. Under the direction of the army they were given tasks in the national forests, and in road construction, flood control, and other useful public services. Nor did the New Dealers hesitate to offer help toward direct relief of distressed families. They created the Federal Emergency Relief Administration with a capital of $500,000,000 and authority to give as much as half of that sum to states and cities for relief. Another $250,000,000 was made available to the states and cities on a matching basis.

Another great departure from the past was the creation of the Tennessee Valley Authority. Both Coolidge and Hoover had successfully vetoed bills calling for federal operations at Muscle Shoals; both wanted as little competition as possible between government and private enterprise. Roosevelt gladly accepted and in fact expanded Senator George W. Norris's scheme for making and selling public power in the valley of the Tennessee. Three directors of the TVA were given money and vast power, not only to make and sell electricity, but to control floods, restore forests, and to improve lands—indeed, to develop the entire valley of the Tennessee River.

Two more far-reaching measures were enacted during the Hundred Days. They were intended to bring both order and at least a degree of prosperity to agriculture, commerce, and industry. The Agricultural Adjustment Act proposed to bring "parity" to the producers of basic farm commodities, corn, cotton, wheat, hogs, rice, and dairy stuffs and liquids. It was believed that the farmers had received fair prices for these products in relation to other prices, during the period from 1909 to 1914. To achieve "parity" meant to restore that relationship. This was to be done by paying farmers for reducing their output, the necessary funds being obtained from a tax levied upon the processors of farm commodities. Presumably the farmers would raise less and would get more money for what they raised

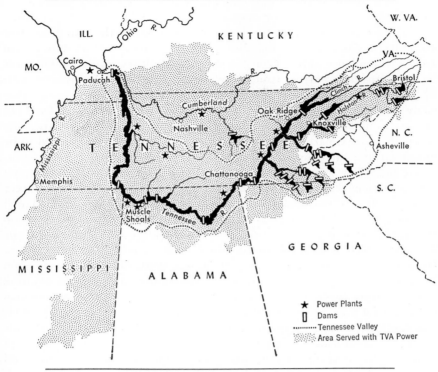

THE TVA

(or did not raise) until they were on a satisfactory economic level with respect to other citizens.

Commerce and industry were to be supported, revived, and cleansed of bad labor practices through the National Industrial Recovery Act. It called for the establishment of codes of behavior for many lines of business, prepared by persons engaged in those fields, under the guidance of a National Recovery Administration. It was required of all subscribers to the codes that they recognize the right of workmen to bargain through persons "of their own choosing," and child labor was outlawed. Under each code hours of labor, prices, and trade practices could be regulated. It was hoped that provision for shorter hours would increase employment. To create jobs and purchasing power until the NRA reached its goals of order and prosperity, the same law established the Public Works Administration under the direction of Secretary of the Interior Ickes and gave it $3,300,-000,000 to build roads, post offices, and other public structures. The spending of that vast sum was to prime the economic pump. It was then

Roosevelt's intention to rebuild America with the help of the farmer, the businessman, and the working man.

It is obvious enough that the Roosevelt program of the Hundred Days had defects. There was contradiction in it; the AAA aimed at scarcity, the TVA at abundance. NRA gave vast power to industry, while banking was rigidly controlled. Further trouble was to arise because agencies were hastily given overlapping authority. Another difficulty lay in the fact that many parts of the program were of doubtful constitutionality. Even so, national confidence revived. Industrial production moved upward rapidly, and with it stock market prices. An almost complete recovery seemed to be in sight in the early summer of 1933.

But the NRA was largely a failure. The Hearst newspapers were not entirely wrong when they asserted that the letters meant, "No Recovery Allowed." It was managed with almost ferocious energy by General Hugh Johnson, and it had some good results. It virtually ended the exploitation of child labor, and it lessened the hours of work for adults. However, the stimulus which it gave to production was shortlived. Management and labor did not work as a team with government; the codes were soon broken; strikes became frequent, in part because labor's right to organize was sabotaged through the forming of company unions. The businessman did not want a Newer Nationalism. The farmers received no subsidies before the fall of 1933. Especially disturbing was the fact that NRA made few jobs, partly because machines were increasingly taking the place of men. By that time the nation was again in an economic downturn and was losing faith in the New Deal.

PRIMING THE PUMP

With businessmen—and Republicans—becoming increasingly critical of the New Deal, especially on the score that it imposed an economic "dictatorship," with thunder on the left from many who said that Roosevelt was tinkering with but not attacking America's fundamental troubles, the President drove on along many fronts from the autumn of 1933 to that of 1934. Given the necessary power by Congress, he reduced the gold content of the dollar to 59.06 and bought gold at high prices in the market in the hope that cheapening the dollar in terms of gold would induce people to spend it more freely. So Roosevelt thought he might get the benefits of inflation without inflating the currency. That psychological weapon failed to hit its mark, and the dollar continued to be held in high esteem. Moreover, the President exposed himself to the charge that he had turned it into "baloney" and "rubber," although billions of dollars in gold that could be used to support it piled up in federal vaults. Nor did the repeal of prohibition by the Twenty-first Amendment in December, 1933 do very much toward stimulating industrial activity. By that time, in fact, Roosevelt had resolved to do more pump-priming, and the Civil Works Administration, under the direction of Harry L. Hopkins, had been formed. Created by Congress in the preceding month, it spent more than $900,000,000 during the winter of 1933–1934 upon local made-work. In February Congress supplied another $950,000,000 for such work and also for direct relief through the Federal Emergency Relief Act. More than 2,000,000 persons were soon employed in the made-work programs. Enough money was poured out by government to relieve the worst distresses in the cities and to bring another rising economic trend.

During the same period there were many more remedial laws. Several of these, including the Frazier-Lemke Farm Bankruptcy Act of 1934, were intended to help the farmers. Of basic importance was the Security Exchange Act, which placed control of stock exchanges and trading in most securities in the Securities and Exchange Commission. The law also authorized the Federal Reserve Board to set limits upon borrowing by speculators and brokers for the purpose of buying stocks upon margin. A Federal Communications Commission was established to regulate radio broadcasting, together with telegraph and cable systems. A series of laws was passed toward stopping the national "crime wave," among them one which made the carrying of a kidnap victim across a state boundary a federal crime punishable by death. Not quite so obviously beneficial to the nation as a whole was legislation compelling federal purchase of silver at generous prices, restoring the cuts made in federal pay in 1933, and full payment of the soldier's bonus. Congress overrode the President's veto to help federal workers and the veterans.

In the fall of 1934 the New Deal had to stand scrutiny by the voters. It was under fire both because it went too far and because it did not go far enough. It was already becoming apparent that Roosevelt and his followers had no magic formula which would bring an early return to a genuine prosperity. On the other hand, it was equally obvious that they were striving mightily to better the lot of the nation. The voters could not believe that the Republicans would do as much or do it any better. Nor would they listen to siren voices of extremists and cranks, whether of the left or the right, who urged remedies even more novel and more drastic than those of the New Dealers. The Democrats won an overwhelming victory at the polls, gaining ten seats in the Senate, and adding another ten to their already overwhelming majority in the House of Representatives.

THE SECOND NEW DEAL

It was comforting to Roosevelt that the voters endorsed the New Deal in the election of 1934, but it had become evident that NRA was a failure.

Industrial and commercial activity seemed to depend upon the putting of federal money into the hands of consumers. Old businesses failed to expand and new ones did not appear in quantity. The troubles of the farmers of the Midwest were somewhat reduced by money received for not producing grain and pigs, but they were increased by the vagaries of Nature, for drought struck savagely in the Mississippi Valley in 1934 and after. There farmers often had no income beyond what they received for not raising the crops and animals they longed to raise. The federal budget was seriously unbalanced; receipts were more than $3,500,000,000 under expenditures in the fiscal year 1933–1934, and the deficit would be about $3,000,000,000 in that of 1934–1935. Various New Deal measures were under attack in the courts, including NRA, and it was likely that the Supreme Court would find several major ones unconstitutional. Attacks upon the New Deal continued because it did too much and because it did not do enough. What to do? Roosevelt undertook to spend even more money to relieve distress and to prime the pump, and he sought and secured more basic reforms that were far-reaching. Unable to work in partnership with the business world, he made less and less effort to please it. Early in 1935 Roosevelt began what has often been called the "Second" New Deal, a revised version of the first one. It called for putting several millions of the unemployed to work at federal jobs until such time as private employment became available; continued help to the farmer, and more of it to labor; a permanent social security system; better housing and slum clearance; and rigid regulation of holding companies. The first New Deal had harked back to Theodore Roosevelt's New Nationalism; the second one bore more resemblance to Wilson's New Freedom.

EMPLOYMENT AND SOCIAL SECURITY

At the beginning of 1935 there were still something like 9,000,000 persons unemployed in the United States. Hitherto Roosevelt had sought to help the distressed both through made-work and supplying money for doles. But he had reached the conclusion that as many as possible of those who could work should be given tasks to perform. Those who could not should receive doles from the states and the cities. It would have been far cheaper merely to pay for the subsistence of the needy, but the President— and Harry Hopkins—was convinced that the much higher costs of made-work were counterbalanced by its usefulness. It was far better for the individual who could work that he do so, and the product of his labors would have value for the nation. Following Roosevelt's leadership, Congress voted $4,800,000,000 in April of 1935 to supply emergency employment, most of which money went to a new Works Progress (later Projects) Administration, placed under the direction of Hopkins. Some money went to the PWA of Harold Ickes, who was engaged in the building of dams and other permanent improvements in the valleys of the Tennessee, Missouri, Columbia, and Colorado Rivers.

Hopkins, a cynical idealist and an excellent manager, brilliantly performed his novel duty, whatever may be said about the merits of the philosophy of WPA. He promptly put under way work projects in amazing numbers, and had as many as 3,400,000 people on his payroll within a year, all of them receiving low "security" wages. Most of the people he employed did manual labor, building or repairing roads, bridges, airport landing fields, public buildings, parks, and streets. However, jobs were also given to "white-collar" workers, teachers, actors, artists, writers, and musicians. Because private employment did not increase very substantially, WPA continued until World War II was under way, and about $11,000,-000,000 was eventually spent on it. It was not an unqualified success, aside from its cost. Some of the tasks assigned to those upon its rolls were not worthwhile, and not all of those employed by the WPA needed the pay they received. Critics of it, usually Republicans, gravely doubted that actors and artists ought to be federally paid for their endeavors. Another serious charge was that its executives used their influence in behalf of the Democratic party. On the whole, however, Hopkins did very well what he was assigned to do. The WPA, with the CCC, PWA, and other agencies that offered federal work, did supply it on a grand scale until World War II put an end to the Great Depression.

The WPA seemed permanent as the depression continued, but was not; the Wagner Labor Relations Act of 1935 did endure. It replaced the provisions of the NIRA requiring honest collective bargaining, that law having been declared unconstitutional by the Supreme Court. It established a Board to compel such bargaining by firms engaged in interstate and foreign commerce. The Wagner Act, rather than the Clayton Act of 1914, proved to be the Magna Carta of organized labor, for it gave powerful support to unions.

The Social Security Act, passed in August, 1935, also became a part of the new order. It provided for both unemployment and old age insurance. It levied a tax upon employers of eight or more persons, with the bulk of the proceeds being distributed among the states so that they could make payments during many weeks to men and women who were laid off or who lost their jobs. The suffering caused by unemployment was thus, to a degree, lessened. Far more important was the old age insurance plan established by the law. Until 1935 the elderly had had to live upon their savings, private pensions, their relatives, or public alms; or they had to toil until the end of their days. In 1935 there were many tens of thousands of the aged who were destitute, or almost so, through no fault of their own. The law provided for grants of money to them, with the national government and the states sharing the burden. Of much greater significance was insurance arranged for the old of the future. Taxes were levied upon the earnings of workers and also upon their employers, at first one percent of the employee's wages, but later increased. The proceeds were used to pay pensions to workers, beginning at age 65, or to care for their dependents. The old age insurance system was later several times revised, and its benefits were offered to more and more persons. The possession of a Social Security card came to mean to its holder that he or she would have at least a modest income when in advanced years.

Other laws pushed through by the New Dealers in 1935 further increased the powers of the Federal Reserve Board. It was declared illegal for holding companies in public utilities to own holding companies or to control operating companies engaged in different lines of business or widely separated in location, the holding companies being given five years in which to comply. The principle of high tax rates upon very large incomes was restored. Roosevelt sought to "soak the rich," as they thought. He wanted a heavy inheritance tax and an even higher rate upon very large incomes, "to prevent an unjust concentration of wealth and economic power." Congress would not go so far. However, the maximum income tax rate reached 75 percent, gift and estate taxes were increased, and large corporations had to pay heavier taxes upon their profits than did small ones. In 1936 Congress also levied a tax upon undistributed corporation profits. Because the AAA had been ruled unconstitutional by the Supreme Court, that year brought in addition a Soil Conservation Act, which authorized payments to farmers for saving their soil, principally by not growing crops upon it. It was a stopgap measure, but it indicated a continuing determination to help the farmers.

ALTERNATE PLANS AND ATTACKS ON THE NEW DEAL

Although the Second New Deal contained several measures of fundamental and permanent importance, it was shaped in part to counter attacks on the New Deal from the left, in part to meet assaults from the right, and in part to solve constitutional difficulties raised by the Supreme Court. By 1935 Roosevelt was under heavy fire on the ground that he was not doing enough to cure economic and social ills of the nation. By that time Dr. Francis Townsend had won a vast following among older Americans with his Old Age Revolving Pensions plan, which presumably would not only assure a comfortable retirement to every American but assure prosperity to all the others. His scheme proposed a pension of $200 per month to every citizen reaching the age of 60, the necessary funds to be obtained through a sales tax. Every pensioner had to spend his allowance within thirty days. Thus, Townsend would have it, purchasing power would be permanently enhanced, and the sales tax would not really hurt. That elderly physician's panacea was preached in thousands of Townsend Clubs containing several million members. Senator Huey "Kingfish" Long, who had made himself the virtual dictator of his native Louisiana, presented a very different approach. A ruthless and intelligent demagogue, he had given its people good roads, good schools, a large and fine state university, and a balanced budget. Long had a "Share Our Wealth" scheme by which every American family was to be guaranteed an income of at least $5000 per annum. The necessary funds for it, he said, would be obtained by shrinking "swollen fortunes" of the rich. Despite his rather obvious desire to be a dictator over the whole nation, Long had a large following. So too did Father Charles Coughlin, whose magnetic radio voice was calling for "a living annual wage," together with "nationalization" of banking and natural resources. Coughlin, having turned against Roosevelt, talked persuasively, though vaguely, failing to tell just what sort of regime could do what he wanted done. The creation of WPA and of the Social Security system, with other measures of the Second New Deal, deprived Townsend, Long, and Coughlin of much of their ammunition. It also dealt a blow to communism, which was winning adherents, notably among professors and students in the eastern colleges and universities. "Share Our Wealth," also described as "Every Man a King," died when Huey Long was assassinated by one of his Louisiana enemies.

The Wagner Labor Relations Act and other pieces of the Second New Deal were necessary, as Roosevelt saw it, to replace segments of the First New Deal destroyed by the Supreme Court. By the summer of 1934 most conservatives, Republicans and Democrats, were making violent charges against Roosevelt and almost all of his works. They looked upon him as a collectivist, a spendthrift, and a threat to freedom. They condemned many of his early ventures as unconstitutional. Former President Hoover declared that the American way of life was endangered, and the Liberty League, founded and nourished by Du Ponts and other rich industrialists, began a campaign against the novel and dangerous "regimentation" to which the President was addicted. Even Al Smith, embittered because Roosevelt had secured a prize denied to him, gave support to the League and denounced the man who had twice placed his own name in nomination for the Presidency.

THE SUPREME COURT

The views and feelings of the conservatives extended into the Supreme Court. During his last days on the bench the venerable Justice Oliver Wendell Holmes had advised Roosevelt to fight the depression as he would a war. But Holmes was gone when the enemies of the New Deal, in traditional American fashion, aggressively attacked its major and minor laws in the federal courts, asking that they be declared unconstitutional.

When cases challenging the validity of the first New Deal laws reached the supreme tribunal through appeals, the Court contained a majority unsympathetic to the New Deal. Although many of its early measures reached to, if not beyond the limits of federal power under the Constitution as interpreted before 1933, and although they were not carefully enough worded to increase their chances of acceptance by the justices, three of the judges were disposed to rule that most of the laws were constitutional. Four others looked with disfavor upon almost every phase of the New Deal. In the middle were Chief Justice Hughes and Justice Owen J. Roberts, who were less hostile. In January, 1935, the Supreme Court first reviewed a questioned New Deal statute. During the 18 months following, with Roberts and Hughes commonly joining the four conservative justices, eight important decisions out of ten were handed down against New Deal laws. Several of them were made by votes of five to four. A large part of the First New Deal was destroyed by the Court. It did not rule against the currency laws of 1933 which set aside the gold standard, nor against the Tennessee Valley Authority. However, it struck down NIRA, AAA, and a string of less basic laws. The decision of the Court against the NIRA, in May, 1935, was unanimous. Several of the justices asserted that federal authority over interstate and foreign commerce had been extended unconstitutionally into intrastate commerce and production by the NIRA; all of them, in one way or another, found that power had been unconstitutionally delegated, Congress to President to federal executives, even to private persons. That decision was obviously defensible, but others made by the Court by votes of five to four were as obviously dubious. In *United States* v. *Butler,* decided by a vote of six to three in January, 1936, the majority clearly went out of its way to rule against the AAA. As Justice Harlan F. Stone pointed out in a strong dissenting opinion, it unnecessarily ruled that the AAA, with its processing taxes, was an unconstitutional effort to regulate agriculture.

It was evident by the spring of 1935 that a majority of the Supreme Court justices was prepared to do strenuous battle against Roosevelt and his followers. Roosevelt was somewhat relieved by the destruction of NIRA, which had already largely failed. Nevertheless, he was at first inclined to accept the challenge of the Court, and to undertake to alter it by enlarging it, adding to it judges who would define federal powers in more generous terms. Attorney General Homer Cummings urged the President to attack the Court. Roosevelt angrily asserted that the judgment of the Court in invalidating the NIRA contained a "horse-and-buggy definition of interstate commerce." He might have tried either to enlarge the Court or to secure the passage of a constitutional amendment that would unquestionably give Congress all the powers it had attempted to exercise. For the time being, rather than become enmeshed immediately in a struggle over the judiciary or put off his reforms until the Constitution could be amended (if it could be), he chose to try to recast some of his basic reforms in new laws in such fashion that the Court would be compelled to accept them. Thus the Wagner Labor Relations Act replaced the provision in NIRA concerning the right of labor to bargain collectively, and the Soil Conservation Act, without processing taxes and ostensibly devoted to protection of natural resources, were devised. Roosevelt offered the Court a chance to change its collective mind. He could reasonably hope that one or more of the conservative justices, most of whom were elderly, would soon resign or die; the appointment of even one judge after the President's own heart would probably persuade the Court to look with favor upon his measures.

Roosevelt postponed a day of reckoning with the Supreme Court, but he could not delay the election of 1936. He had to get the endorsement of the voters as well as the high court before his New Deal could achieve any sort of permanence. He obtained both.

55 MEASURING THE NEW DEAL

There might even have been a third New Deal, had Franklin Roosevelt had his way in the second half of the Thirties, for he and his advisers remained fertile in ideas. He was acclaimed by the voters in 1936, and the Supreme Court ceased to oppose his measures the following year. However, a coalition of conservative Democrats and Republicans in Congress compelled him to settle for the Second New Deal. Prosperity did not return until World War II was under way; unemployment, the WPA, and national deficits continued. The American people in the late Thirties felt uneasy about the future. Communism, Nazism, and Fascism gained adherents. American writers expressed the lack of confidence of their fellows. In the main, however, most of the intelligentsia and Americans as a whole found *the* New Deal to be generally satisfactory. There was no serious doubt by 1940 that it had come to stay, assuming that World War II would not fundamentally alter the domestic course of the nation.

THE NEW DEAL—HERE TO STAY

If the Second New Deal looked somewhat more like the New Freedom than the New Nationalism in 1936, the change meant little to the voters, who had to decide whether it was to continue. So subtle a difference, if they were aware of it, concerned them little. They had to choose among Roosevelt and the New Deal, Republican Alfred M. Landon and a modified New Deal, William Lemke and Long-Coughlinism, Norman Thomas and socialism, and Earl Browder and communism—unless they still fancied that prohibition was the most important issue before the nation.

As usual, the Republicans offered the only serious challenge to the Democrats. Many were bitter enemies of the New Deal, condemning "that man" Roosevelt and all his works. The wealthier among them, and some that were not so rich, damned him as "a traitor to his class," showing that they themselves felt superior. Roosevelt was an exceedingly unpopular name in New York City clubs, banking and industrial circles, and Chambers of Commerce. More moderate Republicans conceded that the New Deal contained some things of merit along with others of little or no worth; both were convinced that the Democrats were bad administrators. Hence, they argued they should be given a mandate to execute a modified New Deal. Nearly all Republicans agreed that Roosevelt was wasteful of public money and censured him for his deficits of the past and for those to come. They also believed quite generally that the Supreme Court was performing nobly by knocking down New Deal laws like tenpins. At Cleveland the Republicans drew up a platform strongly resembling that made by the Democrats shortly afterward, and named for the Presidency a man not distinguished as a hater of Roosevelt. There was a suspicion among the delegates that the New Deal had a certain popularity; besides, those Republicans who felt scorn for the President and everything about him obviously would not desert their party. Herbert Hoover wished to try again, to seek vindication, but it could not be hoped that he would win against the Democratic charmer who had defeated him four years earlier. There was some talk of naming Senator Borah, or Senator Arthur Vandenberg of Michigan, or Frank Knox, a Chicago newspaper executive. Without any real contest the nomination went to Governor Alfred M. Landon of Kansas, an oil producer who had performed well at Topeka and had the backing of William Randolph Hearst. Known as a "Kansas Coolidge," he had been a Bull Mooser in 1912, and he was a liberal Republican whose views fitted his party's platform. Knox, whose political history and approach resembled those of Landon, was put forward for the Vice-Presidency.

The Republican delegates had hardly reached home when William Lemke announced that he would seek the Presidency as the head of a Union party. A doughty champion of the farmers, he had striven mightily to free them from their mortgage burdens, but more than one law he had pushed through Congress for that purpose had been struck down by the Supreme Court. He wanted currency inflation, and he had the support of

Father Coughlin and the Reverend Gerald K. Smith, a disciple of Huey Long. Lemke was popular among the farmers of the Midwest, and Coughlin among the Roman Catholics of its cities. It seemed that Lemke would draw away votes from Roosevelt in the Mississippi Valley, and also that the President would suffer from Democratic defections in the East, for Al Smith, John W. Davis, and Bainbridge Colby, once Woodrow Wilson's Secretary of State, had deserted their party and come out for Landon. It was small encouragement to the loyal Democrats that they obtained the unwelcome help of the Communists, who were then committed to a "Popular Front" around the world. Late in the summer, after Roosevelt had been renominated, the Communists named Earl Browder for the Presidency, but their fire was concentrated upon Landon as a "fascist," and some of their few votes went to Roosevelt.

Names and newspapers were largely against Roosevelt, but he and Garner were enthusiastically renominated by the Democratic national convention at Philadelphia in late June. Many delegates, especially from the South, were inclined to believe that the New Deal was going too far, but none of them were disposed to leave their party. Most of the delegates were fervent admirers of the President. Appearing before them, Roosevelt opened his campaign by assailing "economic royalists" who, he said, had "created a new despotism and wrapped it in the robes of legal sanction." He offered no clue as to what he would do about the Supreme Court, nor did the Democratic platform, which suggested that a "clarifying" constitutional amendment might be necessary to redefine the powers of the federal government and of the states.

Throughout the fall of 1936 the *Literary Digest,* a magazine that conducted a straw vote, steadily predicted a Republican victory and the election of Landon. By every other indication the election of Roosevelt became more and more certain. Lemke made little impression, and Landon proved to be a very poor speaker as well as a modest man. Roosevelt was at the height of his powers; he was aggressive, dominating, confident, and even gay. Traveling across the nation, he ignored Landon and his speeches and continued to attack the "economic royalists," the big business men of the Republican party, as if they owned it. Immense, almost unbelievably large, crowds gathered to hear him. Veteran political observers could not believe that Roosevelt would be defeated. It seemed to them that Roosevelt had won the devotion of millions of "common men." As election day grew near, the Democratic campaign manager, James Farley, predicted that Roosevelt would carry every state except Maine and Vermont. It was his duty to claim victory, but wasn't his prophecy extravagant?

Farley was precisely right, and the *Literary Digest,* hopelessly wrong, died away soon afterward (its reputation was ruined, but the straw polling game went on, since it fascinated the public, even though actual voting somehow refused reliably to follow the patterns seen by the pollsters). The many who profited directly from the New Deal—organized labor, farmers, Negroes, WPA workers—rallied behind the President. So did many who were not so directly benefited by the New Deal. Roosevelt did carry every state except Maine and Vermont, he and his party winning a stunning triumph. He had 27,751,612 popular votes, Landon 16,681,913, and Lemke 891,858. The electoral count was Roosevelt 523, Landon 8. The tide of Democratic ballots ran so high that the Republicans numbered only 19 in the Senate and 107 in the House of Representatives. The Republicans had been dealt a defeat such as no major party had ever before encountered.

It was an ebullient Roosevelt that called for expansion of the New Deal in his second inaugural address in January, 1937. He saw "one-third of a nation ill-housed, ill-clad, ill-nourished," and he wanted to move further toward bettering the lot of that one-third. He had reason to believe that he could do it. His party had tremendous majorities in both houses of Congress. Besides, at that time his pump-priming seemed to be reaching success, for industrial production was approaching the level it had attained in 1929. He even had some hope of balancing the budget within a year or two. The international situation, while somber, was not yet alarming. He had one immediate worry, that the Supreme Court would strike at his Second New Deal as it had at the first one. He opened an attack upon the Court and was defeated, while he lost the loyalty of a part of his party upon domestic questions. Although he was not able to carry through major new reforms at home, he was able to rivet down those of the Second New Deal. A recession in the latter part of 1937 persuaded him to abandon his dream of a balanced budget and to resume pump-priming. Full economic recovery did not come until World War II stimulated industry, agriculture, and commerce.

ROOSEVELT AND "PACKING" THE COURT

The Supreme Court vexed not only Roosevelt but Landon just as the campaign of 1936 was about to begin. Having earlier ruled that the federal government could not regulate wages and hours, that tribunal had further declared, in *Morehead* v. *Tipaldo,* by a vote of five to four, that the state of New York could not establish minimum wages for women. Its decision, in effect, meant that the national government and the states as well were almost powerless to control wages and hours. It infuriated Roosevelt, who was given good reason to fear that the Court would continue to rule against his measures. In February, 1937, he resolved to "pack" the Court so as to change its attitude.

Roosevelt felt that the affairs of the nation could not wait for the passage of a constitutional amendment—if, indeed, one could be secured—enlarging federal powers; nor did he believe they could wait until one or more of the old and conservative justices of the Court should die or resign. Pretending that all of the federal courts were behind in their work, he asked Congress to permit the appointment of many additional judges. He wanted power to augment the Supreme Court by the addition of one judge, up to a total of 15, for every member who was 70 years of age or older. Had the bill prepared for his purposes been passed, Roosevelt would quickly have been able to appoint as many as six justices of his own views and so to obtain decisions satisfactory to himself. It would have been quite legal to add to the membership of, or "pack" the Supreme Court. But the reason given for doing it, delays in the handling of cases, supposedly caused in part by the feebleness of old judges, was not an honest one. The President's lack of frankness strengthened the opposition to his scheme, which would have been formidable in any case. Many Democrats who had gone along more or less reluctantly with the New Deal now turned against Roosevelt. The bill was long kept in committee in the House of Representatives. Led by Burton K. Wheeler, with the help of all the Republicans, they fought hard against it in the Senate. Although Roosevelt exerted heavy pressure, including the seeking of public support through a "fireside chat," it was doubtful from the beginning that his bill would pass. Chief Justice Hughes undertook to do what he could to save the Court from "packing." He informed the Congress that the Court was not behind in its work. Much more important, with the help of Justice Owen Roberts, he changed the attitude of the Court in the spring of 1937. Joining the three justices who had quite steadily voted in favor of New Deal measures, they formed a new majority, which endorsed the constitutionality of a string of New Deal laws, including the Wagner Labor Relations Act and the Social Security Act. Thus Hughes and Roberts made the President's bill unnecessary. The struggle over it ended with a "compromise" which permitted federal judges to retire, after ten years' service, at the age of 70, upon full pay. Roosevelt had lost the battle. However, it is often said that he won a war, for with its composition rapidly changing because of retirements and new appointments, the Supreme Court thereafter ceased to find that his measures violated the Constitution.

LATER NEW DEAL MEASURES

Actually, Roosevelt won over the judiciary, but was checked politically. After the struggle over the Supreme Court, he no longer commanded a reliable majority in Congress on domestic issues. Conservative Democrats, especially from the South, combined with the Republicans to curb further expansion of the New Deal. New Dealers vainly pushed for a Missouri Valley Authority like that in the watershed of the Tennessee River; a ship canal across northern Florida; and an attempt to harness for power the high tides of Passamaquoddy on the coast of Maine. Seeking to secure control over his party, Roosevelt personally intervened in its primaries in 1938, trying to "purge" it of his opponents. He failed in almost every instance, for those whom he sought to purge, with one exception, successfully appealed to the Democratic voters for help against "dictatorial interference." Besides, in the election of 1938 the Republicans made something of a comeback, gaining 7 seats in the Senate and 80 in the House of Representatives. However, Roosevelt continued to enjoy a vast personal popularity—and to retain the intense dislike and distrust of a minority.

Although the further advance of the New Deal was checked by 1938, several of its older measures acquired permanence in that year. A balky Congress revised the corporation tax rates of 1936 in favor of big business, passing a law which Roosevelt disdained to sign. However, the Congress also passed a new Agricultural Adjustment Act which was basically like the law of 1933 that had been invalidated by the Supreme Court, except that its processing taxes were omitted, payments to farmers being made from the general funds of the Treasury. When two-thirds of the farmers raising an exportable crop consented, acreages devoted to them could be reduced by the Department of Agriculture. Arrangements were also made to handle all surpluses remaining so that farmers would receive "parity payment" (based on prices during the period 1909–1914) and the federal government would market the surpluses in such fashion as to maintain an "ever-normal granary." Thus a solid platform was placed under the prices of the basic farm commodities. Of fundamental and permanent importance also was the Fair Labor Standards Act, applying to all workers in enterprises engaged in or affecting interstate and foreign commerce. It set minimum wages for them and severely limited labor by children under sixteen. The Fair Labor Standards Act was challenged in the Federal courts, but its constitutionality was upheld by the Supreme Court in 1941. So the exploitation of child labor came legally to an end; and so the federal government acquired a vast and unquestioned power to reduce hours of work and to increase wages toward preventing the exploitation of adults.

Although the New Deal ceased to expand before the coming of World War II, it had gone far. The authority of the federal government had been greatly increased, and it had become accepted that this power should be exerted for all sorts of economic and social purposes. The New Deal had obviously come to stay, and it could safely be predicted that the future would bring some sort of general welfare state. His enemies continued to attack Roosevelt as a Socialist and even as a Communist. He thought of himself as a true conservative, trying to cleanse and strengthen a democratic and capitalistic society. He was right. His foes could censure him because America's economic machinery did not move with the rapidity it had achieved in 1929, until World War II compelled the fullest possible production. He could reply, as Hoover had, that he had done his best. They could point out that he had consistently failed to balance the federal budget, and that the national debt doubled (reaching about 45 billion dollars) between 1933 and the coming of World War II. He could and did defend his financial record fundamentally on the ground that he had placed people before money. Afterward, in view of the vast deficits incurred during World War II, those of the Thirties seemed small.

Be all these things as they may, the confidence of the American people was not fully restored. Even Nature contributed savagely to the anxieties of the mid-Thirties. Frightening and disheartening dust storms accompanying drouth and heat swept eastward across the Great Plains, especially in 1934 and 1936. Flying dirt filled the skies for hours and days, even turning days into nights. Parts of Oklahoma, western Kansas, and eastern Colorado were carried as far as the middle of the Atlantic Ocean. Tens of thousands fled from a region that God seemed to have deserted, making their way westward to California, which did not want them and unlawfully tried to stop them at the state boundary. Drouths and searing heat did reduce surplus crops and livestock. Stingy with water on the western reaches of the Great Plains, Nature gave it too bountifully on the eastern branches of the Mississippi in 1937, causing violent floods in the valley of the Ohio, the waters of the once "Beautiful River" rising to unprecedented heights and doing immense damage.

LABOR AND UNIONS

Also profoundly disturbing was strife between employers (or their managers) and employees. When Franklin Roosevelt became President in 1933, the labor unions—excluding the company variety—had in all fewer than three million members. Under the NIRA they grew amazingly, for their leaders could say to workers, "The President wants you to join the union." The Wagner Labor Relations Act was even more helpful to the cause of unionism. By 1941 no fewer than 10,500,000 men and women had joined one union or another. Because the American Federation of Labor continued for some time to enlist recruits only in terms of crafts, President John L. Lewis of the United Mine Workers and other leaders formed a Committee for Industrial Organization in 1935. The CIO (after 1938 the Congress of Industrial Organization) enlisted workers in accordance with the industries in which they were employed rather than in accordance with their skills or lack of them. It was immensely successful, for it had a place for most workers, and it could carry on collective bargaining on a regional and even national basis.

During the eight years after 1933 the General Motors Corporation, almost all of the steel companies, and many others recognized and signed contracts with labor unions. But the great change was by no means smoothly accomplished, for many Americans still believed that it was proper to combine capital but not workers. Employers continued to form company unions and to claim that they genuinely represented labor; and for some time they violated the Wagner Act in the mistaken belief that it would be found unconstitutional. There was commotion, too, because the AFL and the CIO waged jurisdictional wars and strikes, each trying to crowd out the other. Peculiarly productive of strife was the use by employers of private armed "service" men to coerce their workers, and resort to the "sit-down" strike by the unions to constrain management. The beating of Ford Motor Company workers by service men led by Harry Bennett— Henry Ford being bitterly against collective bargaining—aroused public feeling. So did the sit-down strike which the United Automobile Workers (UAW) waged against General Motors, beginning on December 31, 1936 and lasting until mid-February, 1937. Earlier tried on a small scale, the sit-down strike was unquestionably illegal, a fact which the Supreme Court afterward asserted. However, General Motors could not break the strike, unless its workers were driven from its plants. Governor Frank Murphy of Michigan declined to use state troops to drive them out, instead urging General Motors to recognize the union. In the end, General Motors capitulated. The United States Steel Corporation signed a contract with the steel workers union soon afterward, but several of the smaller steel companies fought desperately against it. Tom M. Girdler, head of the Republic Steel Company, said he would not bargain with "an irresponsible, racketeering, violent, communistic body like the CIO." He broke a strike at Republic's plant in South Chicago with the help of "loyal workers," company guards, and the police, but not until the police, reinforced by special deputies, had forcibly destroyed a picket line, killing ten strikers and wounding ninety more. Distressed by the behavior of both capital and labor, Roosevelt said, "A plague on both your houses." Both the AFL and the CIO flourished, but amidst bitterness that was to lessen but slowly.

THE END OF OPTIMISM

A sobered people, the American people were not in the Thirties what they had been in the Twenties. Gone was the easy optimism that had been so pervasive before October, 1929. Gone, too, alas, was assurance that at least eventually all would be right in the American world. The bruising realities of the Thirties induced instead skepticism, cynicism, and despair, a pessimism that survived the coming of the New Deal. Even those whose personal fortunes were not directly damaged, if they looked about, saw the weakness of man and his things. The casual observer could not fail to descry both deepseated troubles at home and coming wars in Europe and Asia. The American poor, like the poor everywhere, had commonly been accustomed to calamity and had learned to accept it, even if rebelliously, as a part of their lives. Those who were most shaken by the shocks and alarms of the Great Depression were, as might be expected, the sensitive intellectuals, especially those who had and could make little money. Such sensitive persons, always responsive to schemes for thoroughgoing reconstruction of human society, were tempted to believe that Karl Marx and others hitherto little known in America had found a formula for it. Most of the intellectuals gladly rallied behind Roosevelt. So, too, did a host of less informed Americans who were tempted by native panaceas simpler than Marxism, but who gladly learned that their nation possessed the desire and power to help them solve their problems without resort to untried and exotic remedies. It was the wish and belief, often shakily held, of most Americans that the New Deal or something approaching it, must continue in America. Somehow, the nation must again attain economic order and prosperity. Meanwhile, life went on.

Willy-nilly, the American people had time in the Thirties to meditate about their common fortune as well as their individual misfortunes. They had never had so much freedom from toil, a liberty only too often enforced. But those who were employed also spent less time at the factory and the counter, for NRA codes, later restrictive laws, the constantly stronger labor unions, more efficient machines, shrunken demands for goods and services, and other circumstances shortened both the working day and week. Saturday tended to become a day of rest and eight hours steadily gained popularity as the proper length of the working day. What to do with free hours became more acute with the passing years and the growing power and subtlety of machines.

LEISURE AND ENTERTAINMENT

No one familiar with human vagaries and infirmities would expect that the increased leisure of the Thirties would be entirely devoted to spiritual, intellectual, and artistic pursuits; nor was it. It nourished both juvenile and adult delinquency. Much of it was devoted to play, healthy and otherwise. Contract bridge, introduced in 1925, became a popular pastime, with hundreds of thousands studying the delicacies of bids and end-plays; expertness in bridge almost seemed to replace proficiency in billiards as the sign of a misspent youth—also offering evidence of an idle middle age. Golf likewise became popular, with private courses opening to those who could afford the fees, and with municipal courses appearing everywhere. It can be said in behalf of contract bridge that it induces some cerebration, for golf that it leads to exercise and the inhalation of fresh air. Not quite so socially beneficial was the continued growth of spectator sports, including professional football, which came into its own in the Thirties. Much more disturbing was the acceptance as normal of "athletic scholarships," toward producing better teams in the colleges and universities, for it enhanced the role of educational institutions in the area of entertainment, diverting them from their true purposes. The tens of thousands watching baseball, football, and other games made the Americans resemble somewhat those Romans who thronged into the Colosseum to watch gladiatorial combat. Nor was radio-listening, a diversion that attracted almost all in the Thirties, entirely profitable. The "horse-operas" offered on the radio in the evening were only a trifle less obnoxious than the "soap-operas" purveyed in the mornings and afternoons.

Nevertheless, the new leisure had other good uses. Camping and automobile touring thrived along with golf and softball teams. Reading increased, and it was not uniformly of the escapist variety. Record playing had an astonishing revival, the more remarkable because its devotees very often listened to classical music. One startling and heartening development in the Thirties was a sharp rise to popularity of Bach and Beethoven. Symphony orchestras flourished as never before, and it can be said that America was becoming mature in the realm of music. American singers such as Grace Moore, Gladys Swarthout, and Marian Anderson achieved international fame. Radio broadcasting was steadily improving. It carried Metropolitan Opera performances and symphonies as well as pleas to smoke manly cigarettes and to use enticing lotions. Radio also carried news almost everywhere throughout the nation, especially because most farms and ranches were electrified by the end of the decade, thanks to a New Deal rural electrical program that carried power into areas where private companies could not profitably function.

In idle hours the Americans of the Thirties also fled into the past, making Margaret Mitchell's *Gone With the Wind,* a Civil War saga, an all-time best-seller. When it was put upon the movie screen millions went to see the burning of Atlanta, together with the adventures and misadventures of Southern ladies, heroes, vixens, and profiteers. Also amazingly popular, both as a book and as a play, was Clarence Day's *Life with Father,* which nostalgically portrayed with humor a secure and confident American family before World War I. Attractive also to the public were novels dealing with the more distant past of the eighteenth century, such as Hervey Allen's *Anthony Adverse,* a chronicle of the picaresque career of a gallant wanderer who fought and loved freely. The romances of Kenneth Roberts, splendid of their kind, who used the French and Indian War and the War of Independence for historical backgrounds, were widely read. The Midwestern painting of Thomas Hart Benton, Grant Wood, and John Steuart Curry won popularity in part because, like *Gone With the Wind,* they dealt with themes peculiarly American.

Reality could not be permanently set aside, nor could speculation concerning the future be eschewed. Even if the observer managed to look only at things domestic, he did not see the perpetual progress envisioned by the business philosophers of the Twenties. Toward the close of the Thirties, indeed, many fancied that America had reached a maturity in which a large part of her people would continue to feel the anxieties and sufferings of poverty. Sociologists, taking note of a sharply falling birth rate, were tempted to predict that the American population would become stationary within a generation at about 160,000,000. While rising numbers had already raised the fear that they would overstrain the nation's natural resources, which were obviously being exploited with great rapidity, it was also true that more people tended to make for larger demands for goods. It was argued that America had enjoyed a boom for centuries arising fundamentally from the riches of Nature in the New World, and that the boom had reached, or was approaching its end. Must, then, the American standard of living sink to the level of that of Western Europe, or even below it? There were those who believed so.

THE AMERICAN AND FOREIGN ISMS

Mulling over the condition of men and things, many intellectuals began to consider the teachings of Karl Marx with greater sympathy, for precocity in learning may be accompanied by ferocity in opinion. Did he, after all, point the way toward an ideal and happier society? Or, if the course which he had laid out was impossible, did he not have fruitful concepts that deserved to be tried? There was some wishful thinking that the foundations of Paradise had been laid in the Soviet Union, or that they would be laid there. Such intellectuals were disposed to gloss over the failures and rather obvious shortcomings of the Soviet Union, over which Josef Stalin had gained dictatorial control. They were tempted to overlook the tyranny, the brutalities, and the poverty, and to excuse its abuse of humanity on the ground that humanity would ultimately profit. As Fascism and Nazism achieved strength in Europe, Communism acquired an even stronger appeal among American intellectuals, for Stalin and Communist apologists throughout the world proclaimed the Soviet Union to be the only great and sure bulwark against dictatorship from the Right. When Stalin called for a Popular Front in 1935 to check the advance of Fascism, the idealistic and naive, such being the persons most attracted by Communism, found added reason to look upon it with friendlier eyes. Stalin intended that all the enemies of the Fascists and Nazis combine, but destruction of all capitalistic society remained his ultimate goal; he did not consider defenders of political democracy, whether capitalists or socialists, to be his brethren. Nevertheless, there were those in America as well as in Europe, who persuaded themselves that he was an ally, if not the principal leader, in a common cause, which was the betterment of the lot of mankind. The Communist party "cells" grew and acquired adherents in America, notably on college and university campuses. "Fellow travelers" also made their appearance in numbers; both they and the few committed Communists gained a small measure of influence in Washington. Afterward the members of campus Communist cells were surprised to find that they were suspected of being disloyal to their country. To be sure, the professor who was converted to Communism was a rarity, if for no other reason than because teachers, if they were employed at all, were better off economically than they had been, and better off than they would be for the next two decades. Moreover, whatever the Soviet Union might seem to be in the minds of its inhabitants, it then looked like an ugly Hades to most Western eyes.

Totalitarianism was preached in the United States by Fascists and Nazis as well as by Communists. Toward the end of the Thirties Father Coughlin headed a Christian Front; Lawrence Dennis openly proclaimed himself the leader of an American Fascist movement that would put the nation to rights; and William Dudley Pelley recruited Silver Shirts with the avowed purpose of emulating Mussolini and Hitler. Like Hitler, Pelley proposed to purge the Jews. Most remarkable of all those who would cure America's troubles by dictatorship were the members of the German-American Bund, led by Fritz Kuhn. Mostly of German blood, they carried out military drills, wore Nazi-style uniforms at public meetings in New York City, and brazenly let it be known that they were disciples of Hitler.

THE LITERATURE OF DEPRESSION

It is not surprising that American writers, not content with the American scene in the Twenties gazed upon it unhappily in the Thirties, though not precisely for the same reasons. One could find grievous conditions enough, even if one were not convinced that capitalistic society was rapidly moving toward its inexorable doom. Only a handful of writers followed Theodore Dreiser into the Communist camp, but realism and naturalism acquired vogue. Most of the bright stars of the literary firmament of the Twenties continued to shine through the Thirties and beyond, including Faulkner, Hemingway, Frost, and Eliot. They were joined by new and decidedly lesser luminaries who wrote "proletarian" novels that had Communist strikers for heroes or bourgeois that learned to see the Communist way and truth. Their books were didactic treatises rather than novels. It seemed almost as difficult to write an appealing odyssey of a labor leader as to relate dramatically the saga of a professor. Novelists who did not hew to the Communist party line, but whose approach was realistic-naturalistic, had much more to offer. Foremost of them was John Dos Passos, who had begun to make a reputation with his *Manhattan Transfer*, published in 1925. Between 1930 and 1936 he published his massive trilogy *U.S.A.*, consisting of *The Forty-Second Parallel, Nineteen-Nineteen,* and *The Big Money.* In *U.S.A.* Dos Passos offered a fictional history of America during the first three decades of the twentieth century. Studded with vignettes of public figures (heroic, if they were champions of the underdog) that offered a sense of reality and immediacy, his narrative portrays the crushing of all sorts of individuals by a corrupt, materialistic, and dismal society. *U.S.A.* belongs to the genre of the "collectivist novel," having no true heroes or heroines, but diverse creatures fated to fail and to fall. Dos Passos brilliantly reported the seamier side of American life; it is unfortunate that his characters were merely wooden puppets. Certainly he offered a potent antidote to an optimistic view of American progress.

So, too, did James T. Farrell, whose talent was somewhat more restricted, but valid enough. In a trilogy about Studs Lonigan that came off the press between 1932 and 1935 Farrell portrayed the collapse of lower middle-class people in Chicago under heavy social and economic pressures. Young Lonigan learned more in the poolroom and on the streets than he did in school or in church, dying young and leaving his fiancée pregnant. Farrell reproduced the speech and notions of his youthful Chicagoans, vulgar, dull, and profane, with astonishing accuracy. The honest critic had to admit that boys and young men in American cities only too often spoke and behaved as did Studs and his friends. In later novels Farrell offered at least a fighting chance, through advanced education, to his Chicago boys. Both Dos Passos and Farrell somehow lost vitality when they ventured to depict the brighter side of American life, and John Steinbeck similarly failed. But Steinbeck did write *The Grapes of Wrath* (1939), a realistic tale of "Okies" migrating westward to California. When Steinbeck tried to wax philosophical and to introduce symbolism in his narrative, he struck jarring notes, but his description of the trek of the Joads from the parched Great Plains to a doubtful Eden in California is almost epic.

Every generation has a rendezvous with destiny. That of the Thirties, shaken by the course of events at home, was confronted by growing menaces from both Europe and Asia. What to do about them perplexed a troubled people who lacked the confidence that Americans once had. It was their fate to face the threats of aggressive dictators from the east and of militaristic Japanese from the west. They were tempted to believe that they could and ought to let peoples outside the western hemisphere settle their affairs as they might, that the Americans could live to themselves in safety. Why would not Europeans and Asians leave the Americans in peace? But they went into the greatest of all wars and came forth triumphant.

56 THE APPROACH OF WORLD WAR II

Announcing in 1933 his intention that the United States be a "Good Neighbor," Franklin Roosevelt strove to foster peace and international prosperity by removing trade barriers. After the London Economic Congress he also worked with the heads of other nations to solve their common currency difficulties. He made a great and successful effort to win friends for the United States in Latin America. But he could do little to prevent conflicts in Europe that ultimately led to World War II, nor was he able to persuade Japan to abandon her dream of securing hegemony in the Far East. The isolationist sentiment that pervaded America in the Twenties continued into the Thirties, even gaining strength at the middle of the decade. Roosevelt joined Congress in making laws intended to save America from being drawn into the threatened conflict in Europe. By 1937, however, he began to look upon Nazi Germany, Fascist Italy, and imperial Japan as growing menaces to American security. When the Japanese invaded China in 1937, he indicated that America opposed Japanese territorial expansion. After the outbreak of war in Europe in 1939 he did not try to hide his hope that Hitlerian Germany and her allies would encounter defeat. After the fall of France, in the spring of 1940, he success-fully urged that America do all within her power short of war to help Britain against Germany and Italy. When the Nazis and their allies in-vaded Soviet Russia, help was similarly extended. By the autumn of 1941 Americans and Germans were exchanging blows in the Atlantic. Mean-while, Japanese militarists decided that the time was ripe to expand the Japanese Empire. A Japanese attack upon Pearl Harbor in Hawaii on December 7 of that year swiftly led to a global conflict.

A GOOD NEIGHBOR

In his first inaugural address Roosevelt asserted that America desired to be a Good Neighbor in the community of nations. Then and for several years afterward he expressed no wish for a government over that com-munity. In May, 1933, he sent a message to the heads of 54 countries urging disarmament. His plea for a reduction in weapons went almost un-heeded, and the next year he found it necessary to ask Congress to supply funds to modernize the American navy, a request that Congress approved. This was necessary because in that year Japan announced that the naval ratios established by the Washington and London Conferences would be entirely unacceptable to her after 1936. The Japanese insisted upon parity with Britain and America, which they would not grant. The result was that all three nations were free to enlarge their navies after 1936; the Japanese promptly took advantage of their new freedom. To keep pace with them Congress voted one billion dollars toward increasing American naval power in 1938. Land armaments were actually much increased dur-ing the Thirties, notably in Germany, Italy, Russia, and Japan. By 1934 Adolf Hitler was absolute master of Germany. Declaring that the Treaty of Versailles was void, he soon began to build a massive army, later equipping it generously with tanks. By 1939 Germany once more had the most pow-erful land forces in Europe, and probably in the world. By that time Hitler was also engaged in developing both air and sea power. With smaller means, the Japanese also built an efficient and well-rounded military ma-chine during the late Thirties. Britain and France, America's allies in World War I and allies-to-be in World War II, lagged behind, and Ameri-ca's ground forces were almost pitifully small at the beginning of World War II. America remained almost unarmed on land until the great conflict actually began.

Nor was it possible to persuade the Soviet Union to behave as a friendly neighbor. Believing that nothing was to be gained by continuing refusal to recognize Soviet Russia, Roosevelt in 1933 made a bargain with the Reds by which, in exchange for recognition by the United States, the Soviet Union promised to negotiate concerning debts to America incurred by early Russian governments, and to refrain from meddling in American internal affairs. The two countries accordingly resumed diplomatic relations, but without cordiality. American hope for trade with Russia was disappointed. Moreover, the Communists neither paid the debts of Tsarist and Kerensky Russia, nor refrained from subversive activities in the United States. The Stalinist regime did not abandon its determination to foster the world revolution from which would come Communism triumphant over the globe. Communist efforts to win converts in America continued, even while Moscow was forcefully urging the Popular Front, not without some success.

Roosevelt and Secretary of State Cordell Hull did make some progress toward economic disarmament. Hull, a longtime champion of tariff reduction, was convinced that economic warfare brought no ultimate advantage and few immediate ones to the United States. Sturdily backed by Roosevelt, he secured, despite strong opposition, the passage by Congress of the Trade Agreements Act in 1934. Renewed several times, it authorized the President to make bargains with other nations for reciprocal reductions in tariff rates as high as 50 percent. Since such lowering of rates was automatically extended by existing most-favored nation treaties, the President was given vast authority. It was used. By 1941 such agreements had been made with 26 nations, with which the United States carried on two-thirds of its foreign commerce. That trade, particularly with Latin America, increased strikingly in the late Thirties.

LATIN AMERICA

Although it was impossible to make comfortable neighbors of Germany, Italy, Japan, and Russia, Roosevelt won many friends for the United States in Latin America. At Montevideo in 1933 the United States joined with the Latin American republics in signing a statement which denied the right of any of them to intervene in the "internal or external affairs of another." Roosevelt and Hull took the pledge sincerely, and "Dollar Diplomacy" definitely came to an end. Their acts were as good as their words. They carefully refrained from interference in a Cuba racked by revolution during 1933–1934. Moreover, when a new and stable government dominated by Sergeant Fulgencio Batista made its appearance, they agreed to cancel the Platt Amendment. The result was a treaty of 1934 by which the United States abandoned its protectorate over the island republic, retaining only its right to maintain its naval base at Guantanamo Bay. Cuba was also given financial help through a reciprocal trade agreement which lowered American duties upon Cuban sugar. Other island nations in the West Indies discovered that Yankee imperialism was at least temporarily dead. In January, 1935, the marines came home from Haiti, and three years later the United States guaranteed a loan of five million dollars to that country for the building of public works. In 1939 the United States acknowledged the sovereignty of Panama over the Canal Zone, and in the following year the American customs receivership in the Dominican Republic was brought to an end.

America was a good, even a generous neighbor to Mexico, carefully avoiding interference when Mexico again embarked upon expropriation of foreign properties after 1936. When Mexico declared, in 1938, that all such properties belonged to the Mexican people, America struck back by ceasing to buy Mexican silver, which it had been buying at generous prices. However, Hull conceded that such seizure was legal, provided that the Mexican government compensated the foreign investors. When it failed to promise to pay, Hull patiently proposed arbitration. He was told that Mexico would reimburse the foreigners in her own way and at her own convenience. The Secretary of State, however, knew that Mexico must yield to his just demand and continued to be patient. Mexico needed financial help, and finally agreed in 1941 to compensate American investors for their losses. Eventually they received about $73,500,000. But Mexico secured in exchange a resumption of American purchasing of Mexican silver, American support of the Mexican peso, and also a $30,000,000 credit to build roads. Thereafter, there was less declaiming in Mexico against Yankee imperialism.

The Good Neighbor policy was also successful in that it checked Nazi, Fascist, and Communist infiltration south of the Rio Grande. Only in Argentina, which had an economy competitive with that of the United States and which aspired to political leadership in Latin America, did the Nazis and Fascists win many friends. At Buenos Aires in 1936, all the republics of the Americas signed a pact pledging themselves to consultation regarding common measures to be taken if war threatened. Two years later, at Lima, they subscribed to a stronger statement announcing their common intention to resist "all foreign intervention or activities that may threaten them." In 1939, after the outbreak of World War II, they proclaimed a neutral zone extending out to sea three hundred miles from their shores. In July, 1940 the Latin American republics with the United States announced at a conference held in Havana that an act of aggression against any of them was an attack upon all of them. During World War II all of them eventually declared war against America's Axis enemies, and Brazil sent troops into the struggle.

PHILIPPINE INDEPENDENCE

The generous spirit of the Good Neighbor policy extended also to the "little brown brothers" in the American household. In January, 1933 the Democrats in Congress had passed over President Hoover's veto the Hawes-Cutting Act, which would have established the independence of the

Philippine Islands in 1945. That law displeased the Filipinos, because it called for the continuance of American land and sea bases in the islands and because it raised tariff barriers against the products of the free Philippine republic-to-be. Motivated by idealism, Congress insisted that the Filipinos be turned into good neighbors. But Philippine independence was favored for other reasons. American farmers hoped that independence would at least eventually give them tariff protection against Filipino competitors. Besides, many in Congress hoped that political withdrawal from the islands would eventually permit the United States to escape responsibility for their defense. They were eager to reduce the commitments of the nation beyond seas. In consequence, in March, 1934 Congress passed the Tydings-McDuffie Act, which modified the Hawes-Cutting law so as to satisfy the Filipinos. It provided for the removal of land bases in the islands and for a future decision concerning the naval ones. The Philippine legislature promptly accepted the American offer of independence, which was accompanied by an American promise that tariff preferences given to Philippine products would be only gradually withdrawn. Accordingly, Filipino President Manuel Quezon replaced an American governor in 1935, and complete independence was scheduled to take place on July 4, 1946. It would prove to be most difficult for the United States to place the entire burden for their defense upon the Filipinos. The attempt to withdraw from the archipelago encouraged the Japanese to try to expand their empire, and they invaded it even before the American commitment formally expired.

THE PERIOD OF NEUTRALITY

Whatever may have been the merits of American foreign policy between 1933 and the outbreak of World War II, there can be no doubt that it pleased aggressors in Europe as well as in Asia. Thoughtful Americans feared as early as Hitler's first year in power that another world conflict would come. By 1934 it was already evident that he would seek not only to reverse the verdict against Germany of World War I, but to assert German hegemony over Europe, or even over the globe. For all his strutting, Mussolini had not caused and would not cause much alarm. There was in Italy neither the potential strength nor the desire for vast adventures, and Mussolini was correctly considered a "Sawdust Caesar" whose dream of resurrecting the Roman Empire was beyond hard realities. Hitlerian Germany was something else, from its beginning a potent menace. Germany could build and maintain a great military machine, and Hitler immediately infused a startling vigor into the whole nation. He was very badly educated, not gifted intellectually, and emotionally unbalanced. To some the "paperhanger" seemed as ridiculous as Mussolini. But Hitler was a courageous fanatic, a vehement orator who had a singular appeal to the Germans, a cunning and unscrupulous man, and one of iron will. He gave Germany a vicious purpose as well as strength. Believing that the Aryan race was superior to all others and that the Germans were the best, if not the only true Aryans, he conceived that it was the duty and the right of the Germans to dominate Europe and the world. Immediately after becoming master of Germany he began a wicked persecution of the Jews, and he bloodily wiped out any other Germans whom he recognized as enemies. His rise to supreme authority encouraged and emboldened Mussolini to try to make his own dream of empire a reality. The two dictators posed as defenders of Europe against Communism, but it was apparent by 1934 that they were as likely to wage war against France and Britain as against the Soviet Union. Nazi Germany, Fascist Italy, and imperial Japan—and for that matter Soviet Russia—had to be looked upon in America as both likely and dangerous aggressors.

What America did as a result of mounting threats of war in Europe and Asia was to try to avoid entanglement in struggles to come. The majority of Americans believed in the spring of 1934 that their participation in World War I had been a mistake and that they had been seduced into it by British propaganda, by sinister economic interests, and by an unwise defense of the rights of neutrals on the sea. The same sentiment pervaded Congress. Loans to the Allies of World War I were believed to have helped drag the United States into that conflict. Accordingly, in April of that year, Congress passed the Johnson Debt Default Act, which forbade new loans to any foreign country that failed to make payment upon obligations incurred in consequence of World War I. Thus Britain and France were among the nations prevented from borrowing money in America.

Other drastic steps followed. From 1934 to 1936 a Senate committee headed by Gerald P. Nye, a stout isolationist from North Dakota, studied the manufacture and sale of arms. It found evidence that World War I had brought handsome profits to the makers of munitions and to bankers who trafficked in them. The committee also "discovered," without evidence, that those "merchants of death" somehow helped to entice America into a war from which the nation could gain nothing. The "revelations" of the committee enhanced isolationist feeling. When Mussolini successfully undertook the conquest of Ethiopia in 1935, Congress by resolution gave power to the President, after he had proclaimed the existence of a foreign war, to stop shipment of arms to all the belligerents, and also to announce that Americans traveling on vessels belonging to the nations at war did so at their own peril. Roosevelt disliked the measure; he wished to have authority to prevent the shipment of arms to aggressors while permitting it to those attacked. He said that the resolution was likely to "drag us into war instead of keeping us out," but he signed it. That same year Hitler announced that Germany would rearm despite the Treaty of Versailles. Nevertheless, in February, 1936 the resolution, enlarged to forbid loans or credits to all nations at war, was extended to 1937. Before it expired, Hitler sent troops into the Rhineland in violation of the Treaty of Versailles. Then came the Spanish Civil War. Although the Neutrality Acts did not apply to internal conflicts, Congress requested the President to put them into effect with respect to Spain, and he did so. The effect was to lessen the chances of survival of the lawful government of Spain, supported by republicans, socialists, and Communists. The rebels, led by General Francisco Franco, were receiving arms from Italy and Germany. The Loyalists, given help by Russia but denied it by Britain and France, were at last crushed after long and bloody fighting, and Franco became a Spanish-style Fascist dictator. American determination not to become involved in foreign wars continued. In May, 1937 Congress passed an even more comprehensive neutrality act, and the President signed it. It repeated earlier restrictions with respect to munitions and loans, and declared it unlawful for an American to travel on a vessel belonging to a belligerent. The safeguards were applied to "civil strife" as well as to war between nations. It was also stipulated that raw materials useful to those at war must be paid for in the United States and carried away by the buyers. This "cash and carry" clause was to be enforced for only two years. America could hardly have served any more emphatic notice of her intent not to be seduced into European or Asian struggles.

The neutrality laws were only a partial approach to the fundamental question that faced the American people, one that many of them failed to consider carefully—how could they best provide for their own safety? It was not a new question, and it was not one that could be easily and finally answered. The neutrality laws were consistent with a belief that events in Europe and Asia did not vitally affect American security, with a hope that they would not be dominated by aggressive enemies, and a belief that in the last analysis the Americans could protect themselves and prosper in the New World, no matter the number and powers of their foes. Americans devoutly wanted peace, but were they willing to let happen in Europe and Asia whatever might happen? When put to the test, most of them were not willing.

WAR IN ASIA

The testing began in Asia in the summer of 1937, when World War II commenced in the form of undeclared hostilities between Japan and China. Seeking to impose a New Order in which Japan would be dominant in East Asia, the Japanese were confronted by a Chinese boycott of their goods. The Japanese invaded China, opening hostilities that endured for eight years. Divided among themselves, the Chinese resisted as best they could. A government headed by Generalissimo Chiang K'ai-shek slowly withdrew its armies into the distant interior as the Japanese advanced. Meanwhile, small bodies of Chinese Communists carried on guerrilla warfare behind the Japanese lines. The vast distances in China tended to counterbalance the superiority of the Japanese army, and Chiang K'ai-shek was able to maintain a temporary capital at Chungking. In October, 1937, with Japan committed to imperialist expansion by force, and Hitler and Mussolini threatening aggression in Europe, Roosevelt suggested in a speech at Chicago that something be done to "quarantine" them. He said that one-tenth of the world's peoples ought not to be allowed to endanger the peace and security of the other nine-tenths. But the speech was condemned rather than praised. Those Americans who felt any sympathy in the war in the Far East generally extended it to China, but most of them preferred to abandon all American rights in China rather than become involved in the conflict. Indignities inflicted upon Americans by Japanese troops in China made little difference. Nor did the sinking of three Standard Oil tankers and a bombing attack on the American gunboat *Panay* in Chinese waters in December, 1937. Two members of the crew of the *Panay* were killed and thirty more were wounded. A prompt apology and promise of reparations from Tokyo were sufficient to soothe American resentment. In January, 1938, isolationism was so potent that a proposed amendment to the Constitution, which would have required that no declaration of war be made without the consent of the voters ascertained by referendum (except in the event of actual invasion), was narrowly beaten in the House of Representatives. Roosevelt had to exert heavy pressure to prevent its passage.

Despite the strength of isolationism, Roosevelt and Hull insisted that Japan continue to recognize American treaty rights in China, a demand that Japan rejected. Before the end of 1938 the Japanese were firmly committed to creation of their New Order in East Asia, and relations between the United States and Japan continued to deteriorate.

FAILURE OF APPEASEMENT

Meanwhile, for the United States, things went from bad to worse in Europe. So long as France and Britain were stronger than Germany and Italy, so long as there was something like a balance of military power in Europe, America was quite safe against attack from the east. However, by 1938 Hitler had developed a new German war machine that was formidable. In March he annexed Austria to his Third Reich; the British and the French, no more eager for war than were the Americans, made no effort to stop him. A hope that the League of Nations would check Hitler proved vain, for he despised it, and it was dying. With every success both Hitler's strength and demands grew. In the fall of 1938 he insisted upon taking

THE NEW ORDER IN ASIA TO 1941

parts of Czechoslovakia where German-speaking people lived, and in a
conference held at Munich Britain and France gave their consent. They
sought to appease the German dictator, earning only his contempt. The following March he brazenly seized control of most of the remainder of
Czechoslovakia, turning it into a German protectorate. There could be no
decent, peaceful end to his demands. At last Britain and France declared
that they would go to war against Germany rather than permit Hitler to
despoil Poland. A few days later Mussolini invaded and conquered Al-
bania. During the spring and summer of 1939 Britain and France tardily
sought to make a defensive alliance with the Soviet Union, but failed.
Hitler, disregarding appeals from Roosevelt and others to preserve peace,
prepared for war. On August 22 he hoodwinked Stalin into signing a pact
assuring the neutrality of the Soviet Union (he intended to deal with it
later) while he was engaged in warfare with Britain and France. He then

sent an ultimatum to Poland, and his troops crossed her borders before she had time to reply. Britain and France kept their word, and World War II began in Europe on September 3.

Americans were shocked when the Nazis, making use of many tanks and airplanes, destroyed Polish resistance in a "Blitzkrieg" that lasted only three weeks. Their alarm abated, however, as month after month passed without serious fighting on the frontier between France and Germany. They vainly hoped that Stalin, who countered Hitler's thrust into Poland by seizing other parts of that country, strategic spots from Finland, and the Baltic states, would become embroiled with Hitler. They even hoped that the German dictator would somehow or other make peace with France and Britain and turn his attention against Soviet Russia. Thinking in terms of World War I, they expected a continuing stalemate on a Western Front, with Germany eventually blockaded into submission. During the fall and winter of 1939 most Americans came to realize that they desired victory for Britain and France. Revising the Neutrality Act of 1937, Congress made it possible for them to purchase munitions in the United States on the "cash-and-carry" basis.

BLITZKRIEG

Then Hitler suddenly struck again with paralyzing power. In April, 1940 his forces invaded and conquered Denmark and Norway within a few days. Starting May 10, the Nazis within 20 days went around the fortified Maginot Line of the French, overran Holland, Belgium, and Luxembourg, split apart the British and French armies, and forced the British to withdraw the remains of their army from Dunkirk to England. Their tanks and bombing airplanes were extraordinarily effective. On June 10, with France falling under the blows of the Nazis, Mussolini entered the war to extort what he could from France. On June 22 France was compelled to sign an armistice, by the terms of which the northern part of the country and all her Atlantic ports were occupied by Germany. A new French government established at Vichy collaborated with Hitler. In the summer only Britain, the Commonwealth, and small forces of Free French, Dutch, Norwegians, and Poles continued the struggle against Hitler and Mussolini. There was but one small comfort for the Americans. As the Germans swept through the Low Countries toward France, Britain called into service as Prime Minister the doughty Winston Churchill, brilliant orator and tenacious and resourceful warrior.

During many months after the collapse of France it seemed likely that Britain, and perhaps the British fleet, would be seized by the Germans. If Britain fell, America would indeed be exposed to attack, both from the east and from the west, for it was to be expected that Japan would move in the Pacific when the insatiable Hitler should strike across the Atlantic.

Map legend:
- Axis Countries, 1939
- Occupied in First Year of War

BLITZKRIEG

Were Britain subjugated, America could hope for help only from the Soviet Union, and there was no assurance either that Russia possessed great military power or would use it. Americans became suddenly alarmed and Congress voted $17,000,000,000 in the summer of 1940 toward building a two-ocean navy, a stronger army, and a powerful air force. In September it passed a conscription act, America's first resort to the draft at a time when the nation was at peace.

THE DRIFT AWAY FROM NEUTRALITY

But America went further than to begin to prepare for a mighty conflict. Isolationism, although it remained potent, lost some of its vigor. With Roosevelt leading the way, American sentiment swung toward giving Britain all possible aid short of entering the war as her open ally. Even before the fall of France, the President made arrangements by which 600,000 rifles, together with machine guns, light artillery, and ammunition to match went from American arsenals through private hands to England, then in desperate need of arms. The United States disposed of the guns and ammunition as antiquated, later selling airplanes and tanks in similar fashion. Out-of-date the equipment might be, but it was useful to Britain. As early as June it was obvious that the President would no longer even pretend to be neutral. Describing Mussolini's attack upon France, Roosevelt publicly declared that "the hand that held the dagger has struck it into the back of its neighbor." The following September the President broke both domestic and international law to give the British further badly needed help. Britain and Germany were striving to strangle each other by sea blockades, as in World War I, and German submarines were taking a heavy toll of British shipping. Roosevelt made a bargain with Britain by which America acquired bases by gift and lease on British territories between Newfoundland and British Guiana, in return for fifty older American destroyers. The destroyers were by no means so ancient that they could not hunt German submarines. Passionate isolationists and experts in international law pointed out that the bargain should have been made by treaty and that it was hopelessly unneutral. However, most Americans were no more interested in legal technicalities than was the President. It was obvious that Germany had ignored international law at will, and the trade was heartily approved as a measure to help meet a national emergency.

While the destroyer deal was in process, America received some comfort from a promise by Winston Churchill that the British fleet would neither be surrendered nor sunk to escape capture by the Germans. But the British situation continued to be perilous. In the late summer and early fall of 1940, Britain won a long battle for control of the air over her islands, her new Spitfire airplanes inflicting heavy losses upon the German *Luftwaffe* and preventing a Nazi invasion. Nevertheless, the Germans continued to bomb London and other English cities and to keep Britain under siege. Hungary, Rumania, and Bulgaria aligned themselves with Germany, and Mussolini invaded Greece in October. Even more ominous was the signing in September of a treaty between Germany, Italy, and Japan which created the Berlin-Rome-Tokyo Axis. By its provisions, if any nation other than Russia came to blows with any one of the three partners, all of them would wage war against it. The pact was obviously aimed at America. Also ominous was a southward advance by the Japanese on the Asian continent into French Indo-China. They had extorted permission from the Vichy government to occupy bases there. So concerned was Roosevelt by this southward drive that, toward weakening the Japanese, who had relatively small stores of iron, he forbade the shipment of scrap iron across the oceans, except to Britain. The Japanese described his embargo as an "unfriendly act." The world situation tempted the Japanese to seize Southeast Asia and British, Dutch, and American possessions in the western Pacific. The Japanese were prepared to risk the results of war with the United States; they did not yet dare to attack, for they feared they might also become involved in a conflict with Russia.

ROOSEVELT'S THIRD TERM

Crisis or not, the election of 1940 had to take place. Until the Republican convention met in Philadelphia the most popular Republicans seeking to lead their party were Thomas E. Dewey, a young district attorney of New York who had won fame by sending racketeers off to prison, and Senator Robert A. Taft of Ohio, a son of William Howard Taft, who was a leader among the isolationists. But influential eastern Republicans rallied to Wendell L. Willkie, who had once been a Democrat. As president of Commonwealth and Southern, he was the guiding hand of a public utilities empire. On the sixth ballot, the convention turned from Dewey and Taft and named Willkie for the Presidency. It then nominated Senator Charles L. McNary of Oregon for the Vice-Presidency. It called for an improved New Deal under Republican management, declared against "involving this nation in foreign war," and promised aid to "all peoples fighting for liberty." The G.O.P. also called for a constitutional amendment limiting a President to two terms, a hit against Roosevelt.

For Roosevelt was certain to be the Democratic candidate for the Presidency and a third term. There was talk among the Democrats in the spring of 1940 of naming Cordell Hull, while Postmaster General Farley, Vice-President Garner, and others sought to succeed Roosevelt. By remaining silent he indicated that he was willing to run again, and Harry Hopkins and other New Dealers labored to secure the nomination for him. When the convention met at Chicago in July, many of its delegates were pledged to Roosevelt and there was no doubt that he would be renamed unless he resolutely refused to accept the nomination. After the convention had begun, he let it be known that he was not actively seeking it and that delegates who had promised to support him were free to do as they wished. It was also apparent that he would not refuse to run, and he was named with enthusiasm on the first ballot. For the Vice-Presidency the Democrats offered, not Garner, who had found the New Deal to be too thoroughgoing, but Henry A. Wallace, one of its ardent champions. In their platform the Democrats said the New Deal ought to be continued under its originators, that they would not join "in foreign wars," that they would not send the armed forces abroad to fight, "except in case of attack."

Roosevelt would have preferred to stay on in the Presidency as the head of a bipartisan government. Before the Republicans met in national convention, he brought two of them into his Cabinet, Henry L. Stimson as Secretary of War and Frank Knox as Secretary of the Navy. Accepting the Democratic nomination, he announced that he would not campaign. However he soon found it necessary to appeal for votes, for Willkie spoke and shook hands with remarkable energy and made a splendid impression. Coming from an Indiana family in modest circumstances, he had risen far; when he contended that the New Deal was badly run and that it cramped both individual freedom and the American economy, he secured a respectful hearing. Harold Ickes called him "the barefoot boy of Wall Street," but Willkie was obviously sincere. No isolationist, he promised to extend even more aid than Roosevelt to those fighting the Nazis and Fascists. Meanwhile, other Republicans accused the President of trying to drag the nation into the war. They also charged him with seeking to be dictator, pointing out that no other man had been permitted a third term. It became increasingly doubtful that Roosevelt could be elected a third time, and he took the field, defending his record and asking that he be returned to office as the man best qualified to lead in a great emergency. Toward the end of a very heated campaign, both Willkie and Roosevelt behaved irresponsibly. Willkie said America would be fighting within five months if Roosevelt won. Roosevelt declared, "I have said this before, but I shall say it again and again and again. Your boys are not going to be sent into any foreign war."

The outcome was a precedent-breaking triumph for Roosevelt. Independent voters who might have gone either way thought it more important that the vigorous and experienced Roosevelt continue in office than that the tradition against a third term be followed. He won handily, but not overwhelmingly, by a popular vote of 27,244,160 to 22,305,198. Willkie carried ten states, located, except for Maine and Vermont, in the traditionally Republican and isolationist Midwest. He had only 82 votes in the electoral college, Roosevelt 449. The Democrats easily retained control over Congress as well as the Presidency.

Isolationists, especially an "America First Committee," strove bitterly to reverse the verdict of the election with respect to the war. Charles Lindbergh, who had won fame in 1927 by flying from New York to Paris in a single-motored airplane, was the most effective enemy of intervention. But the America First Committee was counterbalanced by another, formed by William Allen White, that urged all possible aid short of war to Britain and her few allies. More and more help was extended to them, and the United States became more and more identified with them, including Russia, after June, 1941.

BRITAIN GETS ALLIES

Standing up sturdily under German assaults from the air in the early months of 1941, Britain carried on as best she might. British forces, having overrun Ethiopia, clung to Egypt and to Malta and checked the Italian fleet in the Mediterranean Sea. But the British in Egypt were soon gravely threatened by a German-Italian army that advanced against them from the west under "The Desert Fox," General Erwin Rommel. Moreover, the Italian attack upon Greece being halted, Hitler's armies went to Musso-lini's help and rapidly conquered both Yugoslavia and Greece in the spring. British troops who moved from Egypt to help the Greeks were swiftly driven back, and the Germans occupied even the island of Crete. Meanwhile, German submarines continued to sink British shipping, and Britain's finances became badly strained. In March America moved more positively to the rescue. A Lend-Lease bill, cleverly conceived by Roose-velt so as to avoid conflict with the Neutrality Act of 1937, was heartily supported by Wendell Willkie and passed by Congress. Theoretically, it provided for lending war materials to the enemies of the Axis, to be re-turned at some future time. Roosevelt immediately made arrangements to send billions of dollars' worth of arms and other war materials to Britain.

Although Churchill had said, "Give us the tools, and we will finish the job," the British could do little on the continent of Europe without powerful allies. They secured one on June 22, 1941, when Hitler, joined by Finland, Hungary, and Rumania, suddenly attacked Russia without warning. Britain promptly signed an alliance with the Soviet Union, and Roosevelt quickly undertook to extend Lend-Lease help to Stalin. It seemed doubtful at first that Russia could long withstand the assaults of the Nazis. It was commonly believed that the Germans would be in Moscow within six weeks. Had Russia fallen, Hitler might indeed have been able to make good his boast that he would create a German empire that would last for a thousand years. However, Stalin sacrificed vast num-bers of Russian troops to hold off the Germans and their allies until winter came. His strategy worked. When snow flew, forcing Hitler's armies to halt, the Red armies still held Leningrad, Moscow, and Rostov on the Black Sea. Hitler had taken on an immense task by creating an Eastern Front.

Meanwhile, America steadily moved toward war with Germany. Amer-ican troops occupied Greenland and Iceland to keep them out of Nazi hands. Roosevelt closed German and Italian consulates in the United States. In May, 1941 a German submarine sank an American merchant vessel, the *Robin Moor*, in the south Atlantic, after those aboard it had been forced to take to small boats hundreds of miles from land. In August Roosevelt and Churchill met at sea off Newfoundland and signed the Atlantic Charter, in which they laid down a program for a satisfactory peace. It called for self-determination of peoples; free access for all of them to trade and raw materials; international action for economic advance and social security; permanent peace with freedom from fear and want; freedom of the seas; disarmament of aggressors; and the formation of some sort of world government. By that time American destroyers were already convoying Lend-Lease materials as far as Iceland, this to help the British keep open their sea lanes. Early in September the American destroyer *Greer,* following a German submarine and broadcasting its position off the coast of Iceland, became the target of two torpedoes from it. They missed, and the *Greer* retaliated by dropping depth charges against the U-boat. On September 11, Roosevelt announced that American war vessels would sink German submarines upon sight in American defensive zones in the western Atlantic. On October 17 the destroyer *Kearny* engaged a German submarine or submarines southwest of Iceland, eleven of her sailors being killed by the Germans. Thirteen days later the destroyer *Reuben James* was torpedoed and sunk off Iceland, with a loss of about one hundred men. Congress then repealed most of the Neutrality Act, but continued to forbid loans to nations at war and travel on the ships of belligerents by American citizens. America was on the verge of full war with Germany.

TO PEARL HARBOR

But that all-out war began in the Pacific. The German invasion of Russia tempted Japan to take a great gamble. Even if Russia did not go down under the assaults of Hitler, she would be unable for some time to do anything toward checking the Japanese. Aggressive imperialists in Tokyo saw a heaven-sent opportunity to expand southward. In July, 1941, Japan demanded and obtained bases from the Vichy government in southern French Indo-China. Roosevelt promptly took actions that virtually ended trade between the United States and Japan. This economic boycott, coupled with continued American support of the Chinese government at Chungking, exasperated the Japanese, bogged down in their Chinese war. It was apparent that America was opposed to any Japanese expansion. In October Japanese militarists under General Tojo assumed power in Tokyo. The following month they sent a special envoy, Saburo Kurusu, to Washington to join the Japanese Ambassador Nomura, in making a final offer to the United States. Should it not be accepted, Premier Tojo planned to begin hostilities immediately. He and other Japanese imperialists believed that they could conquer Southeast Asia and most, if not all, of the islands in the western Pacific before the full weight of American strength could be asserted. If Japan went to war with the United States, so would Germany and Italy. If and when America should be able to take the offensive in the western Pacific, the Japanese imperialists hoped to be so well entrenched that they could stave off attacks and tire America and her allies into accepting an accomplished fact. Tojo was prepared for a huge gamble.

On November 20 Kurusu and Nomura presented the final offer to Secretary of State Hull. What they proposed was a temporary agreement that would presumably lead toward a lasting peace. If the United States would cease to help China, reopen trade with and supply oil to Japan, and help Japan to obtain raw materials from the Netherlands East Indies, Japan would cease to advance southward and would abandon the bases she had occupied in French Indo-China—after peace had been made with China. In effect, America was asked to give its blessing to the Japanese attempt to subjugate China in return for a promise that Japan would not expand southward. On the following day Roosevelt and Hull gave their answer. Both the British and the Nationalist Chinese were insisting that there be no appeasement of Japan. Roosevelt and Hull knew, through the interception of Japanese messages in a code that had been broken by American cryptographers, that Japanese forces were about to move, if they had not already done so. Hull told the two envoys that the way to peace for Japan was to evacuate both China and French Indo-China and to abandon all schemes for expansion. In return, the United States would reopen trade with and give economic help to Japan. Neither Roosevelt nor Hull entertained any hope that these terms would be accepted. Rather, they believed that Japanese troops would advance into Thailand or British Malaya and that war between Japan and America had become inevitable. On December 1 the Japanese Foreign Minister denounced the American terms as "fantastic," but his government nevertheless urged that negotiations be continued. A Japanese task force was already moving across the Pacific to attack Pearl Harbor. On December 6 Roosevelt personally appealed to the Emperor Hirohito to prevent war, asking him to withdraw the Japanese troops in French Indo-China. Nomura and Kurusu presented the Japanese answer to the American proposals on December 7. It was a flat rejection. Actually, Japan replied an hour earlier, when Japanese planes began to rain death and destruction at Pearl Harbor. The American fleet, concentrated there because of the emergency, was badly damaged.

The news of the Japanese assault shocked the American people early in the afternoon of December 7. There could then be no question that the United States was fully engaged in World War II. On the following day, describing December 7 as "a date which will live in infamy" and denouncing the Japanese attack as "unprovoked and dastardly," Roosevelt asked the Congress to declare that a state of war existed with Japan. It did so immediately, unanimously, except for Representative Jeannette Rankin of Montana. Three days later Germany and Italy, in accordance with the Axis treaty of 1940, announced that they were at war with America. Congress unanimously agreed that such was the fact.

Many hundreds of American fighting men were killed on December 7, and all effort to avoid total war ceased. The Japanese attack upon Pearl Harbor was startlingly successful, partly because American commanders in Hawaii had not been warned in time with sufficient emphasis from Washington to be on the alert, and partly because they could not quite believe that the Japanese would strike against Hawaii. Had the Japanese moved instead in Southeast Asia, there must have been a debate in the United States regarding the course to take. On the basis of these facts it was afterward contended that Roosevelt had not only deliberately provoked the Japanese to assail Pearl Harbor, but had intentionally neglected to warn the American forces there, so that a heavy Japanese blow would create American unanimity for war. No evidence in support of either charge has been brought forward. It is to be believed that Roosevelt, like the American commanders in Hawaii, had not yet abandoned the psychology of peace for that of war. He too was surprised that the Japanese attacked where they did. It was they who decided when and where the decisive struggle would begin.

57 WORLD WAR II:
DEFENDING AND PREPARING

Within a month after Pearl Harbor, America, Britain, Russia, and the many weaker foes of the European Axis formed an alliance to destroy it. Many of them also joined in a common effort to defeat Japan, Russia being an important exception. Reeling under the blows of the Nazis, the Soviet Union did not wish to engage in a two-front war. The Allied nations suffered many defeats in 1942, and they were kept on the defensive during most of that year. Americans overseas did not take the offensive until August, and then only on a small scale. But by November the Allies had checked the advances of the Axis powers. Meanwhile, America prepared prodigiously, mobilizing vast forces.

JAPANESE ADVANCES

The war in the Pacific went very badly until June, 1942, in large part because the attack of the Japanese upon Hawaii was successful beyond the dreams of their military planners. They wished to conquer quickly French

Indo-China, Thailand, British Malaya, the Philippines, and the Dutch East Indies, as those regions contained rice, oil, tin, and rubber that Japan needed to fight a long war. Controlling those areas, they hoped to entrench themselves so thoroughly that they could withstand eventual massive attacks from America and weary her into accepting a great Nipponese empire as inevitable. But could the Japanese strike southward rapidly with the American fleet stationed at Pearl Harbor and strong enough to challenge them in the western Pacific? Before December 7, 1941 that fleet was a menace, although it was hardly strong enough to battle the Japanese navy on equal terms in its home waters. The Japanese planners hoped that their surprise attack would inflict damage enough so that they could thrust southward for a few months without serious interference by the American navy.

Executing their plan, the Japanese sent against Hawaii the greatest airplane carrier task force ever assembled. It contained no fewer than 6 aircraft carriers (Japan had only 10 in all), with 425 planes, together with protecting battleships, cruisers, and destroyers. If the American fleet was at anchor in Pearl Harbor, as the Japanese expected, this force was to bomb it from the north and drive it out to sea. There it was to be attacked by 30 Japanese submarines. The underwater craft accomplished little, for only a small part of the American fleet was able to put to sea. But the bulk of it was in the harbor. Japanese bombers took off from the carriers 200 miles north of Hawaii just before dawn. Their coming was a complete surprise. They found the American fleet at anchor in the harbor on a quiet Sunday morning, and they struck savagely at it, also at airfields and other targets. A second wave of Japanese bombers added to the destruction. The Americans were completely unready, naval crews being ashore for the weekend. In less than two hours, losing only about 30 planes and 1 submarine, the Japanese sank or damaged 19 war craft, including 8 battleships. They destroyed almost 200 airplanes; they killed about 2400 Americans and wounded another 1400. They might have inflicted even greater damage had they persisted in their attacks. But the task force had accomplished far more than had been expected, and it returned to Japan in exultation. Pearl Harbor was an American disaster, and the Japanese were able to carry out their plan to advance rapidly southward for many months without interference from Hawaii.

In the long run, the losses of the fleet at Pearl Harbor were less serious than they seemed to be at the time. As it happened, the two American aircraft carriers stationed there, the *Lexington* and the *Enterprise,* were away on missions when the Japanese struck. Moreover, the overwhelming victory of the Japanese brutally settled a debate among the Americans over the merits of the aircraft carrier as against those of the battleship. After Pearl Harbor there could be no doubt that the carrier was the more im-

portant. Then building a new navy, America laid the keels for many carriers as well as battleships, cruisers, and destroyers. That new navy would
not be ready for action until 1943. Meanwhile the American carriers in
service on December 7 were used efficiently against the Japanese.

For the time being, however, there was no stopping the Japanese. Manila
was attacked from the air on the same day as Pearl Harbor. Within ten days
no fewer than 21 Japanese forces moved southward and eastward with an
astonishing display of efficiency. Before the end of 1941 the little yellow
men who had often been foolishly underestimated took Guam and Wake
Island from the Americans and Hong Kong from the British. Thailand fell
to them without a struggle. The Japanese also invaded British Malaya and
the Philippines before the close of the year. The sinking by Japanese
torpedo planes of the British battleship *Prince of Wales* and battle cruiser
Repulse on December 10 in the South China Sea enabled the Japanese to
land detachments behind weak British forces trying to defend Malaya. By
the end of January that peninsula was in Japanese hands, and they seized
the great British naval base at Singapore off its southern tip on February
15. The forces of Nippon swept on into Burma, driving to the border of
India and cutting the Burma Road, by which Chiang K'ai-shek had received important help. They also quickly overran most of the Dutch East
Indian islands.

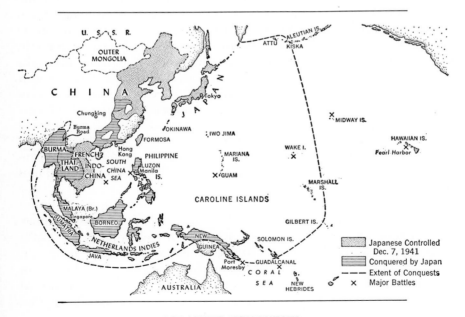

JAPANESE CONQUESTS

BATAAN TO GUADALCANAL

The Philippines likewise fell to the Japanese. General Douglas Mac-Arthur, a veteran American officer who had retired to train a Filipino army, was charged with the defense of the islands. Having returned to the American service in the summer of 1941, he commanded the American and Filipino forces, both small. Nearly 62 years old when the Japanese began to flood over the island of Luzon, MacArthur was one of the two best American generals, the other being George Marshall, the Chief of Staff. Imperious and given to flowery speech, MacArthur was experienced, dauntless, brilliant, and determined to win. But he had to wait for his greatest glory. With the meager forces he had, he could only hold out as long as possible. Without hope of relief, he defended Manila briefly, then executed a preconceived plan to retreat to the Bataan Peninsula, where the Americans and Filipinos resisted desperately for many weeks. Because that resistance could not continue indefinitely and because the services of MacArthur were badly needed, he was appointed commander of the Allied forces in the Southwest Pacific in February, 1942, and ordered to try to escape. Assuring the Filipinos "I shall return," he successfully made his way to Australia and assumed his new duties. His successor, General Jonathan Wainwright, managed to defend Bataan until April 9, then retreated to a fortress on the island of Corregidor. Weary and worn, hungry and stricken by malaria, the defenders of Corregidor were bombed day and night. Finally, on May 6 Wainwright had to surrender. The Japanese celebrated their triumph by forcing their captives to make a "Death March" across Bataan en route to prison camps. Forced to walk when they were not able, many hundreds died or were killed by the Japanese on that cruel march. The Japanese won a reputation for brutal treatment of prisoners which they afterward sedulously maintained; they were also valiant soldiers. After the fall of Corregidor they quickly occupied all of the Philippines. Thereafter, for many long months, opposed only by guerrilla fighters, they firmly gripped the islands. Pretending that they came as friends to the Filipinos, they managed to win the support of the aging Aguinaldo. To most of the Filipinos they were anything but friends.

The desperate defense of Luzon did not delay the southward advance elsewhere of the Japanese, who landed on the north coast of New Guinea on March 8. Then the forces of the Rising Sun had to pause and make ready for further penetration. Australia seemed to be in grave danger in the spring of 1942. Until that time the only offensive gesture on the part of the American navy was a bombardment in January of the Japanese-held Marshall and Gilbert Islands. On April 18, the Americans made another gesture. Army bombers under the command of General James H. Doolittle, taking off from aircraft carriers, raided Tokyo. They did not do much

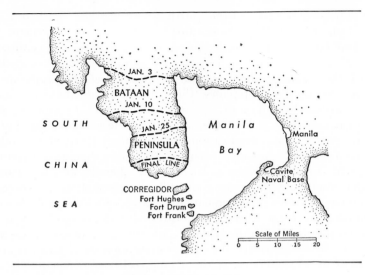

JAN. 3

BATAAN

JAN. 10

SOUTH

JAN. 25   *Manila*

PENINSULA   *Bay*

CHINA

FINAL LINE

Manila

Cavite
Naval Base

CORREGIDOR
Fort Hughes
SEA   Fort Drum
Fort Frank

Scale of Miles
0   5   10   15   20

THE END IN BATAAN

damage, but their appearance over the capital of Nippon was a harbinger of things to come. At last, however, the Japanese movement toward Australia was checked. A Japanese squadron seeking to open the way for the capture of Port Moresby on the southern coast of New Guinea was challenged by an American one on May 4 in the Coral Sea. In the battle that followed the aircraft carrier *Lexington* was sunk and the *Yorktown* was badly damaged, but the Japanese lost a carrier and several other large ships and were forced to withdraw. Moreover, when they sought to reach Port Moresby by land from the north coast of New Guinea, they were stopped by jungles, mountains, and Australian troops under MacArthur. Australia was at least temporarily safe.

Early in June, 1942 the war in the Pacific reached a more definite turning point. The Japanese finally dared too much. Bombarding the coast of Alaska, they seized the Aleutian islands of Attu and Kiska. However, a simultaneous attack upon Midway, guarding the western approaches to Hawaii, brought disaster to them. They were still using that secret code that had been deciphered by the Americans before Pearl Harbor. Intercepting their messages, the Americans learned that a Japanese task force was moving toward Midway. On June 3 over 100 of Hirohito's ships, including four aircraft carriers and carrying troops to garrison Midway after it had been captured, advanced toward the island. The Americans had gathered all possible strength to meet the attack, including land-based and naval bombers. During the following three days they inflicted a smashing defeat upon the Japanese. American naval bombers sank three of the enemy aircraft carriers and damaged the fourth, which was afterward sunk by an American submarine. The Americans lost the carrier *Yorktown,* a destroyer, and 150 airplanes; the Japanese, losing all their carriers, airplanes, pilots, and a cruiser, encountered disaster as well. When they withdrew westward, the balance of seapower in the Pacific had been restored.

Another major forward Japanese thrust in the Pacific, however, was not checked until the beginning of November. Advancing through the islands lying to the eastward of New Guinea during the summer, the Japanese threatened to cut off communications between the United States and Australia. To stop them American marines began on August 7 to land on Guadalcanal and other Solomon Islands. The marines and naval detachments that supported them were immediately assailed by Japanese land and sea forces. In sharp engagements the marines had to fight desperately to maintain their foothold on Guadalcanal. They managed both to seize and to hold the air field on the island. Gradually, with some help from Australians and New Zealanders, the Americans gained control of the air and of the water in the Solomons. Without powerful reinforcements, the Japanese on Guadalcanal were driven back in November. The Japanese onslaught was at last brought to a halt.

WAR IN THE WEST

At length contained, the Japanese had conquered almost all that they had hoped to conquer. Would they be able to keep this vast empire they had won so easily? The counteroffensives came sooner and more powerfully than Tojo had expected, even though the Allies decided that they must first overthrow the Axis in Europe, then deal with Japan. Soon after Pearl Harbor Winston Churchill came to Washington to confer with Roosevelt. Arranging for concerted action, they and their advisers concluded that the Axis powers in Europe must be brought down first because they were more powerful and potentially more dangerous. Therefore the war with Japan had to be secondary and even defensive until Hitler and Mussolini had been destroyed. This strategy, of course, pleased Stalin, since the Soviet Union was mortally menaced on the west and in no immediate danger on the east.

In 1942 Stalin wanted much more from Churchill and Roosevelt than satisfactory strategy. He insisted that they create a Western Front to relieve pressure upon Russia. But it was not possible for them to do it, for they had neither the men nor the means to make a breach in the fortifications the Germans were building on the coasts of occupied France and Belgium. Despite bitter complaints from Stalin, Britain and America necessarily spent most of 1942 preparing to open a second front. In fact, except for commando raids upon France and air strikes against Germany, they remained on the defensive until November. The commando raids brought heavy casualties and no remarkable profits. But the Allies began to hit hard at Germany from the sky. Convinced that they would win the war in Russia, the Nazis neglected to do all within their power in 1941 and 1942 to make airplanes. They lost superiority in the air over western Europe and never regained it. By the spring of 1942 the Royal Air Force had grown so powerful that it could bombard German military and industrial centers on a large scale. In May 1000 British bombers rained destruction from the skies upon Cologne, and an equally large fleet of aircraft struck at the industrial Ruhr Valley the very next day. Thereafter, tremendous raids upon Germany, by American Flying Fortresses as well as British bombers, became ever more frequent. The war began to come home to the Germans as their cities suffered increasingly, although Germany was able to maintain her military machine on land effectively until 1944.

Making ready to attack the European Axis, Britain and America, in World War II as in World War I, had to meet a German submarine menace. They had to win the Battle of the Atlantic before they could engage the Axis on land in Europe. Early in the war the British had either sunk or driven into port almost all of the larger German war ships that Hitler had collected and built. But his submarines, even more deadly than in World War I, for a time exacted a very heavy toll of Allied merchant shipping. Fortunately, the British had developed radar, which made it possible to locate submarines far under water; and depth bombs had become very effective. Moreover, submarines were vulnerable to attack from the air. Using convoys and patrolling the Atlantic with airplanes and scores of destroyers and submarine chasers, the Anglo-American forces secured control of the Atlantic before the end of 1942. During that year the Germans sank more than 8,000,000 tons of Allied shipping, but only half so much in 1943. The submarines continued to be dangerous through 1944, but the Allies were able to replace their losses with new ships.

PINCERS ON THE NEAR EAST

Meanwhile the Axis partners in Europe used the first ten months in 1942 in almost successful efforts to seize the Suez Canal and to overwhelm the Soviet Union. In January the British Eighth Army was well advanced from Egypt into Libya. Suddenly Erwin Rommel, the Desert Fox, with his German Afrika Corps and Italian auxiliaries, opened a crushing attack that drove the British into retreat. In May, using tanks and heavy mobile artillery, Rommel resumed his drive eastward, pushing the British back toward the Nile. By the end of June he had reached El Alamein, only 70 miles from Alexandria. Checked there, he waited for reinforcements that would permit him to sweep on through Egypt. Until October the Canal seemed to be within his easy grasp. The story of the Eastern Front was

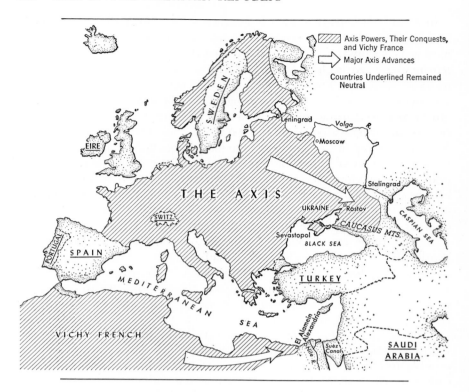

GREATEST AXIS ADVANCES, 1942

similar, although the fighting was on a far larger scale and took place in dirt and mud rather than on desert sands. After checking a small Russian offensive in the spring of 1942, the Germans and their Axis allies began a series of massive attacks in southern Russia in June. Hitler believed that he could triumph by securing firm control of the Ukraine with its wheat and the Russian Caucasus with its oil. While maintaining pressure upon Leningrad and Moscow, he directed his main attack north and east of the Black Sea. The Russian fortress of Sevastopol fell, and Hitler's men pushed on into the Caucasus, being ultimately stopped by distance, rough terrain, and Soviet troops. Moreover, they drove on to the Volga River, entering the city of Stalingrad on its west bank before the middle of September. Hitler then seemed to be well on the way to achieving his goal. Ukrainians, long restive under Soviet rule, had rallied by tens of thousands as allies to his standard and mastery of the lower Volga was all but in his grasp. He never gained it. A Russian garrison in Stalingrad, supported by Red artillery firing from the eastern bank of the river, fought on and on in the ruins of the city until winter began to approach.

In November, 1942 the tides of war finally turned against the European Axis, more violently than they did against the Japanese. On the fourth day of that month Rommel was driven into disastrous retreat; four days later an Anglo-American army began to land upon the northwestern shores of Africa; and on November 19 the Russians began a series of offensives that would grievously injure the Hitlerian forces. The long roads to Berlin were slowly opening; the sea lanes to Tokyo, also long, would not always remain closed to advancing American forces.

THE HOME FRONT: MOBILIZATION

While the Axis forces advanced both in Europe and in the Pacific, America mobilized for a titanic struggle. All doubts and uncertainties were resolved by the Japanese attack on Pearl Harbor. Plunged into the war, the isolationists were as determined as the interventionists to win it. There was panic on the Pacific Coast after Pearl Harbor, shared to a degree in other parts of the nation, lest the Japanese invade. In consequence, more than 100,000 persons of Japanese descent, whether citizens or no, were transported from California, Oregon, and Washington to concentration camps in the Midwest, where most of them were kept long after fear of a Japanese invasion had vanished. Confidence of victory came only slowly, for Axis boasts of overwhelming power had impressed the Americans, along with other peoples of the world. Because the war had long been coming on, America was better prepared for it than the nation had been for World War I. It was therefore possible to gird more rapidly for conflict than it had been in 1917. Even so, American strength could not reach its peak abroad until 1944. Fortunately, her allies, with such help as America was able to send, managed to hold on until powerful forces came to their assistance from the New World.

Although all the energies of the United States were not employed, since it proved unnecessary to wage a total war, the American effort was nevertheless prodigious. Before the conflict ended more than 15 million men were in military uniform, together with many thousands of women who served as noncombatant volunteers. The draft, in effect after 1940, was used far more drastically than in World War I. During a few weeks early in 1942 all men between the ages of 19 and 45 were eligible for immediate service. In the spring of that year males 38 years of age and older were exempted from the draft, but in the following November youths aged 18 became subject to call. Moreover, after that time the ranks of the navy and the Marine Corps, which had hitherto been filled by volunteers, were supplied by selective service. Deferment was limited to the clergy, those having dependents, and those engaged in vital work in industry, agriculture, or government. The number of Americans in uniform in World War II was three times that of those mustered in during World War I.

American production toward winning the war was also impressive, even astounding. The unemployment problem vanished before the war was well under way, and American industry accomplished the miracles its ardent admirers said it could. Roosevelt proclaimed that America must become the "Arsenal of Democracy," and it did. By 1943 the United States was making more materials for war than Germany and Japan combined. While those enemy nations continued to increase their military production into 1944, they fell farther and farther behind the United States.

The magnitude of the output of American industry cannot be fully described. So vast was the building of ships that the United States and Canada during the war put into the water more than 20,000,000 tons of carrying craft, notably the so-called Liberty ships. Combat vessels went down the ways from American shipyards in almost unbelievable numbers and variety. By 1943 26 fast airplane carriers had been commissioned, 8 new battleships, dozens of cruisers, hundreds of destroyers, and tens of thousands of smaller craft. That same year, more than two hundred American submarines were ready for sea duty. The story was much the same with respect to airplanes. When Roosevelt set a goal of 50,000 planes per annum, he was jeered. After America was fully committed to the war, he doubled the figure, and it was actually exceeded before the end of the war. American industry also put forth many thousands of tanks, trucks by hundreds of thousands, guns in the millions, and an infinite variety of other military equipment. It armed America and helped to arm America's allies.

The achievements of industry were matched by those of the farmers. They were called upon to raise foodstuffs to the best of their ability rather than to limit their output, and they were glad to do it. Handicapped by lack of young and strong hands and of new machinery, but favored by good weather, they broke agricultural records. In 1942, 1943, and 1944 they produced annually more than three billion bushels of corn. In 1944 they harvested more than a billion bushels of wheat. Every year after 1942 more than 20 billion pounds of meat came from American farms and ranches. Enough food was supplied to nourish people at home, the American armed forces, and many of the civilians and fighting men of the Allies.

FINANCING THE WAR

As usual in wartime, America spent lavishly, over $300 billion in all, or nearly ten times as much as had been expended in World War I. Since the conflict could not be financed from income, the national debt climbed to $270 billion. Huge annual deficits caused less concern than the relatively small ones of New Deal days. However, the American people knew that victory was beyond price. They also cheerfully accepted high taxes in order to win the war. More of its cost was paid from current federal income, about 37 percent, than in any of America's earlier wars. In October, 1942 income taxes were raised sharply. Thereafter a single person had an exemption of only $500, a married taxpayer of only $1200. The basic rate was set at 6 percent, with surtaxes moving upward from 13 percent on the first $2000 of income taxed to a maximum of 82 percent. Besides, a special "Victory Tax" of 5 percent was imposed. Levies upon corporations were pushed as high as 40 percent; excess profits were taxed at the rate of 90 percent; and excise levies were either increased or placed upon theater and travel tickets, telephone service and telegrams, and alcoholic beverages. In 1944 Roosevelt urged that income and corporation taxes be raised even further. There was then some grumbling, and Congress refused to follow his leadership. It passed a law over his veto that increased the excess profits tax to about 95 percent and raised the excise levies. Immense sums from taxes flowed into the Treasury, more than $46 billion between June 30, 1944 and June 30, 1945.

Nor did the federal government have difficulty in borrowing the money it needed to meet its deficits. A wartime prosperity made it possible for the Treasury to sell bonds of various sorts in vast quantities. Among them were the "E" bonds, about $40 billion worth being sold to individuals, who commonly purchased them through payroll deductions.

LABOR, PRICES, AND RATIONING

Labor and management did not perform quite so well in their relations with each other. So many women took jobs that the number of employed persons soared to 60 million during the war. Their presence did not soften bargaining between unions and "bosses," nor did the peril of the nation prevent labor disputes. Soon after Pearl Harbor industrial and union leaders announced that there would be no stopping of essential production, and that any dispute not settled through peacetime methods would be referred for decision to the National War Labor Board. That body, containing representatives of employers, workers, and the public, was appointed by Roosevelt in January, 1942. The system worked well until 1943. The board pleased labor by allowing, in 1942, raises up to 15 percent to match a rise in living costs. But prices continued to advance, and workers sought further increases. There was a rash of strikes in 1943, the most serious one being called by John L. Lewis for the United Mine Workers. Lewis secured better pay for his men, but the interruption in coal mining and his successful defiance of the board caused much bitterness. An angry Congress, subscribing to a work-or-fight formula, decided that employers, and especially unions, needed further coercion. Over the protests of the unions and over a veto by Roosevelt, it passed the Smith-

Connally War Labor Disputes Act. Enlarging the powers of the board, it sanctioned seizure and operation by the President of war industries that were not functioning because of labor disputes. The law also made it a crime to foment or direct a strike after the President had replaced private management. Thereafter there were fewer strikes and labor unrest did not seriously affect the war effort. However, as late as 1944 Roosevelt had to take control of the railroads temporarily in order to prevent a strike.

The basic cause for unrest among workers, as might be expected, was rising prices. The consumer paid 31 percent more for what he bought in 1945 than he did in 1941. Labor disputes would have been more disturbing than they actually were, had price rises not been checked—during World War I they rose 62 percent. An Office of Price Administration, created in 1941, managed in succession by Leon Henderson, Prentiss M. Brown, and Chester Bowles, was given authority to set ceilings over the prices of all goods, except agricultural ones, and also to limit raises in rents in areas critical for the national defense. OPA, successfully executing hold-the-line orders in the spring of 1943, stemmed the tide of inflation. But it was not possible to check it absolutely. The rulings of OPA were often evaded through "black marketing." Rationing was even more necessary in World War II than it was in World War I, and machinery and raw materials were carefully apportioned among the war industries. It was imposed upon consumers by OPA, which never attained popularity beyond that of a necessary evil. Automobile tires were rationed less than three weeks after Pearl Harbor and remained in very short supply for civilians until after the war had ended. Vast quantities of rubber fell into Japanese hands early in the conflict, and a vigorous attempt to make synthetic rubber was not very successful. Gasoline was rationed soon after rubber, as was coffee. Early in 1943 wheat, butter, cheese, and other foods were rationed, and later, shoes. Such scarce commodities could be obtained only through coupons, the number of these being strictly limited for every consumer. Despite black marketing, immense quantities of food, gasoline, rubber, and other materials were thus saved to nourish the armed forces. Rationing also resulted in more equitable distribution at home. The Americans continued to be better fed and clothed than any other people. Unable to buy automobiles (the automobile factories quickly turned to making trucks and tanks for military use), limited by shortages, protected by price-fixing, they saved vast sums during the war. Savings banks were embarrassingly full of money by 1945.

REGIMENTATION

Inevitably there was also censorship and repression of disloyalty. However, internal censorship was relatively mild, being voluntary for newspapers and radio broadcasters, and the treatment of seditious persons was less of a problem than it had been in World War I. Several native American Fascists were arrested for putting forth propaganda favorable to Hitler and Mussolini and injurious to the war effort. A few of them were sent to prison, but a mass trial of 26 such persons accused of sedition ended without a verdict. Father Charles Coughlin's newspaper *Social Justice* was kept from the mails. The difficulties raised by Communists and Socialists during World War I were not repeated. The Reds denounced the war as a capitalist contrivance until June 22, 1941; the day after Germany attacked the Soviet Union they suddenly discovered that the Allies were fighting for democracy. Thereafter they could hardly be enthusiastic enough about a war against the brutal Fascists. Nor could Socialists condemn it as a vicious product of capitalism, in view of the fact that Russia was engaged in it. Very few acts of disloyalty were committed by Americans of German or Italian descent; the German-American Bund vanished when America became the enemy of Germany. Although all enemy aliens above the age of 14 were required to register, few were put in prison, somewhat more than 1200 Germans and about 200 Italians. Defenders of personal freedom in the United States were seriously offended only by the treatment accorded to the Japanese-Americans. Their removal from the Pacific Coast could be justified only by military emergency. The assumption that persons of Japanese descent would be less loyal to the United States than those of European or African ancestry proved to be utterly unjustified. Not a single one of the Japanese-Americans was found guilty of sedition, and more than 17,000 of them served in the American armed forces. In 1944 the Supreme Court declared that their removal from the Pacific Coast was, under the circumstances, legal, but that their detention in concentration camps violated the Constitution. Even after the court had spoken, defenders of personal rights continued to assail the removal as unnecessary, insulting, injurious, and unlawful.

Although American thought and its expression remained almost surprisingly free, partly because Roosevelt opposed unnecessary restrictions upon personal liberty, there was so much regimenting in things economic and military that the federal government contained agencies of which the average citizen was quite ignorant. One of those agencies, an extraordinary one, was known to very few until the end of the war. The Manhattan District was created by Roosevelt and placed under the command of Brigadier General Leslie R. Groves in August, 1942. Advised by the great physicist Albert Einstein that it was possible to make a nuclear bomb having an explosive power immensely greater than that of any other bomb hitherto developed, the President risked $2 billion through the Manhattan District to find out whether such a terrible weapon could be manufactured. Hitler was fond of boasting of "secret weapons," but German physicists trying to manufacture a nuclear bomb at the time decided that it could not be done.

Their experiments in laboratories beside the Baltic Sea were hindered by Allied air attacks and by their inability to get the help of non-German scientists. The Manhattan District, establishing its principal units at Oak Ridge, Tennessee, Hanford, Washington, and Los Alamos, New Mexico, had the help of both native and foreign-born scientists. It achieved an astounding success. On December 2, 1942 scholars and technicians employed on the Argonne Project at the University of Chicago set off the first self-sustaining nuclear reaction. Thirty-one months later the first atomic bomb was exploded. Eighteen days more, and the weapon was ready for use against the enemy.

So obvious was the need for regimentation that American civilians accepted it without much grumbling. Nor was there disaffection in the armed services, exposed to hardship and the dangers of a war in which weapons were more effective and terrible than ever before. The sense of uncertainty that pervaded America in the Thirties diminished; in the last years of the war the birth rate moved rapidly upward. To be sure, political fighting did not cease. In the election of 1942 Democrats and Republicans threw words at each other as usual. Both parties claimed they would supply better leadership toward victory. The Democrats retained majorities in both houses of Congress, though not large margins. Before another national election, victory in Europe was in sight.

58 WORLD WAR II: THE VICTORIES

Although the Axis nations first lost ground irrecoverably at the beginning of November, 1942, they remained truly formidable. They had the great advantage of interior lines in Europe, and so long as Russia was not involved in the Asian war, Japan was protected by immense distances. During and after 1942 America sent through Lend-Lease vast numbers of trucks, airplanes, tanks, and other military materials to Russia. Thus helped, the troops of the Soviet Union gradually forced their way westward into Germany. Meanwhile, Allied armies chiefly composed of American and British soldiers drove the Germans and Italians from Africa, forced Italy out of the war, and opened a Western Front. In early May, 1945 the Nazi regime at last collapsed. Meanwhile, America waged a "left-handed" war against Japan, moving against Tokyo from the south and the east. A little more than three months after the downfall of Nazi Germany imperial Japan submitted to defeat. Mussolini was slain, Hitler took his own life, and Emperor Hirohito became less than a god in Japan. But the Axis aggressors were conquered only after the Allies had made almost immeasurable sacrifices.

CAMPAIGNS OF 1942–1943

AFRICA

During many months in 1942 Churchill and Roosevelt were deeply concerned lest Rommel reach the Nile River and the Red Sea. Had he broken through, all the Near East seemed likely to pass into German hands; it was even possible that European Axis forces would enter the Indian Ocean from the west while Japanese ones came into it from the east. Checked at El Alamein, Rommel did not receive the reinforcements he needed to push on to Alexandria. On the other hand, America and Britain sent important aid, especially by means of ships that went around Africa, to the hard-pressed British defenders in Egypt. American tanks reached them in surprising numbers, making it possible for them to take the offensive. Under General Bernard L. Montgomery the British Eighth Army, a magnificent body of well-equipped veterans, assailed Rommel's lines at El Alamein on October 23. Rommel could not withstand Montgomery's tanks and artillery, and had to fall back. Montgomery pursued him relentlessly for many hundreds of miles, taking Tripoli in Libya on January 24, 1943. The Nazi threat to the Near East was ended.

But Roosevelt and Churchill undertook to do more in Africa than to check Rommel. Without sufficient strength to open a Western Front in Europe, they decided they had enough to drive the Axis out of Africa. Except for Tunisia, occupied by the Germans and Italians, French North Africa was under the control of Vichy France. The two Allied leaders could hope that the Vichy French officers there would not seriously oppose an Allied invasion. With the Mediterranean serving as a shield against strong Axis counterthrusts, Roosevelt and Churchill believed that Anglo-American forces, with the help of the Free French, could take Morocco and Algeria. Then, if fortune favored, Tunisia could be wrested from the Axis, with the help of Montgomery. Early in November, 1942, an Allied armada moved toward French North Africa from the west. Battleships that were part of it bombarded ports of Morocco and Algeria on the 8th of that month, and Anglo-American troops under the command of General Dwight D. Eisenhower made several landings on the same day. After a brief resistance Admiral Jean-François Darlan, commander of the Vichy French in North Africa, signed an armistice on November 11. The Allies continued to land until Eisenhower had 400,-000 men, the majority of them Americans, under his command. Morocco and Algeria came under the control of the Free French, and Eisenhower began an advance toward Tunisia.

Tunisia did not fall easily. Hitler struck back rapidly, quickly sending troops through unoccupied France to the Mediterranean. He hoped to

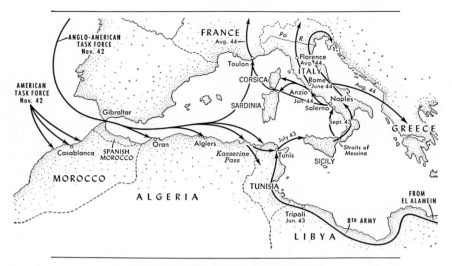

EUROPE'S "SOFT UNDERBELLY"

seize a part of the French fleet, gathered at Toulon, but its crews scuttled it rather than let it fall into the hands of the Germans. Hitler and Mussolini also sent reinforcements to Tunisia, where Rommel was making a stand against the Allies advancing from both the west and the east. In mid-February, 1943 Americans advancing from Algeria were temporarily checked in the battle of the Kasserine Pass, but soon pushed forward again under the command of Major General George S. Patton, Jr. In the following month, Montgomery broke through the Axis lines in southern Tunisia, and in April the combined Anglo-American forces penned the Axis ones against the Mediterranean. Unable to send sufficient reinforcements to enable him to hold out, Hitler recalled the useful Rommel for service elsewhere. In May what was left of the German and Italian contingents in Africa, 250,000 men, mostly Italian, surrendered. One continent had been cleansed of the Axis. The Americans had sustained 18,500 casualties.

ITALY

The pattern of the war in Europe in 1943 was much like that of 1942. Again Stalin demanded that his allies open a Western Front, and Roosevelt and Churchill again declined to try it. Meeting at Casablanca in Morocco in January, they agreed that they did not yet have enough strength to strike across the Channel and to invade France. A repulse, not at all unlikely, would be extremely costly. Instead, they ordered ever more massive attacks on Germany from the air, and undertook to drive Italy from the war.

In May the Allied forces in North Africa, under General Eisenhower, began the conquest of the Italian Fascists. Italian garrisons on the islands between Sicily and Africa were bombarded from the air and sea until they surrendered and the Mediterranean opened to Allied traffic. From bases in Africa air forces under Eisenhower then struck hard at Sicily and the Italian peninsula. On July 9 American parachute troops landed on Sicily, quickly followed by 150,000 infantry, well supported by tanks and artillery. American tank forces under General Patton swept through and around the defenses, and the British Eighth Army under Montgomery was efficient as usual. After more than a month of hard fighting the resistance of the Axis collapsed. It lost 150,000 men in Sicily, the Allies about 25,000.

Meanwhile, the Allies bombed and threw artillery shells at ports and military places on the Italian peninsula to soften it for invasion by land forces. Never eager for the war and discouraged by the heavy losses they had suffered, the Italians turned against Mussolini. When Hitler told Mussolini that he could not immediately send him further help, and that Italy south of the Po River had to be given up to the Allies, Marshal Pietro Badoglio, with the help of the Italian king, overthrew Mussolini and made him a prisoner. Announcing that Italy would continue to fight, Badoglio secretly sought to make peace before Hitler could interfere. On September 3 Montgomery crossed the Straits of Messina, landed upon the toe of the Italian peninsula, and began to push northward. Five days later, Badoglio unconditionally surrendered to the Allies. The following day American troops under General Mark Clark landed at Salerno on the Bay of Naples. But a bitter struggle ensued. German paratroopers rescued Mussolini, who established an Italian Fascist republic under German protection. The German troops in southern Italy continued to fight, and Hitler sent aid to them. They fell back gradually, while Eisenhower landed more and more troops. Naples was surrendered on October 1, but the Germans built the Gustav Line across the narrow peninsula south of Rome and held it during many weeks. With what little help they received from Mussolini they still controlled most of Italy at the end of 1943. However, they had lost the islands of Sardinia and Corsica.

RUSSIAN FRONT

The triumph of the Allies in Africa was of great importance, and it broke Mussolini's grip upon Italy. However, it did not injure the European Axis so grievously as did Russian counterattacks on the Eastern Front that began on November 19, 1942. The flanks of the German army at Stalingrad were then badly exposed on both the north and the south, and the Russians assailed them. Threatened with encirclement, its commander, General Friedrich von Paulus, asked permission from Hitler to retreat. The German dictator insisted that von Paulus hold fast; he said that "not one square yard of ground will be given up." Whoever was responsible for the strategy of the Russians—credit for it was given to Stalin, at the time, but Nikita Khrushchev was the chief political officer with the Soviet troops on that front—it was brilliantly successful. The Russian flank attacks cut off retreat by von Paulus, and he was forced to surrender the remains of his army on February 2, 1943. The result was disastrous for Hitler, and the Russians won several other victories in the winter of 1942–1943. They drove his armies from the Caucasus, regained control of part of the Ukraine, and put an end to the siege of Leningrad. The losses of the Russians, as well as those of the Germans and their partners were immense; Hitler could not afford them.

By 1943 Russia was receiving major assistance in weapons and military materials of all sorts from America, this despite the fact that German surface raiders and submarines sank many Allied ships on the Murmansk route. Both by way of the Arctic and through Iran Russia continued to receive machines and arms, so that by 1943 the Russians probably surpassed the Axis forces on the Eastern Front in fire power. On that long battle line something like 5,500,000 Russians struggled with about 4,000,-000 Axis troops, chiefly German. The heavy, grinding fighting of 1941 and 1942 went on. At Kursk in the spring of 1943 the Germans staged a last great offensive, using masses of tanks. Expecting it, the Russians checked it by means of defenses prepared in great depth, and swiftly counter-attacked elsewhere. Hitler's men again swayed backward; many of them were forced to surrender because the German dictator again insisted that they hold their ground at all costs. The Russians drove on westward and were approaching their 1938 boundary when winter brought the campaign to an end.

CAMPAIGN OF 1944

Deciding against a Western Front in 1943, Roosevelt and Churchill met at Washington with their Combined Chiefs of Staff in May and determined to make an attempt at the beginning of May, 1944. Churchill had earlier preferred to avoid an assault across the English Channel and had urged instead powerful thrusts from the south at the "soft underbelly" of the European Axis, but at Washington he agreed to strike at its hard chest and head. At another conference in Quebec in August Roosevelt and Churchill decided not only that there must be a massive attack upon the coast of Normandy, but that it should be accompanied by an Allied landing in southern France from the Mediterranean. These decisions pleased Stalin. At Moscow in October he promised that Russia would declare war on Japan as soon as the struggle in Europe ended, and that when a general peace came, Russia would help to form an international body to preserve it. A month later he met Churchill and Roosevelt at Teheran in Iran and confirmed the two promises. The three set dates for offensives against Hitler from the east, west, and south in 1944.

At Teheran Stalin told Roosevelt and Churchill that he had 60 divisions more than Hitler on the Eastern Front and that the Russians could make a series of attacks which Hitler would not be able to stop. Such proved to be the fact. The Soviet army opened ten offensives, one after another, in 1944. It drove westward along the northern shores of the Black Sea, and swept on into the Balkans. The Germans withdrew from Greece; Axis Bulgaria collapsed; and Hitler had to kidnap the leaders of Axis Hungary to prevent their surrender. With the help of Communist guerrillas led by Marshal Tito, the Russians captured Belgrade on October 20 and on December 29 Budapest fell to them. Meanwhile, to the north the Russians made slower progress, although they entered East Prussia and were threatening Warsaw before the end of 1944. The Nazi empire was crumbling on the east and southeast.

When Churchill urged that the western Allies concentrate their forces for an assault upon Axis Europe from the Mediterranean, he undoubtedly had in mind conditions as they should be at the end of the war. Anticipating expansion of Soviet territory and influence, he saw that the presence of Anglo-American troops in Austria and the western Balkans would check it. He was a superb civilian leader rather than a military strategist. The mountains of southern Europe were a formidable obstacle to powerful Allied offensives from the Mediterranean. General Mark Clark, commander of the Allies in Italy, was able to push forward only very slowly and at heavy cost, for the German forces took full advantage of the Italian mountains and the narrowness of the peninsula. An Allied landing in January at Anzio, behind the Gustav Line, did not immediately force a German retreat, and Clark's men suffered very heavy losses on the Anzio beachhead. They were contained there for many weeks, and the Gustav Line, anchored by Monte Cassino, was held by the Germans until May. At last the Germans had to fall back, and Allied progress northward became somewhat easier. Americans took Rome on June 4, and the British captured Florence on August 12. Then the Germans fell back to a Gothic Line in northern Italy, which they were able to defend until the war in Europe was almost ended.

THE SECOND FRONT

The western Allies were unable to open the Western Front on May 1, as they had planned. To attack across the Channel was an immense and risky undertaking, and General Eisenhower, who had been placed in charge of the operation in December, 1943, was unable to put his forces in motion until early June. Conditions were then far more favorable than they had earlier been. Massive bombings of German industrial and railroad centers by British fliers at night and American bombers by day had reduced the ability of the Nazis to resist, and the Germans were no longer confident of victory. Eisenhower was able to accumulate a powerful and well-equipped army as well as a vast quantity of shipping. He also had overwhelming air power at his command. The American and British troops that he collected in England were highly mechanized. Nevertheless, the Germans had mined and blocked the harbors of France, strung entrenchments along the French coast, and otherwise thoroughly prepared for an Allied landing. They had all the advantages of terrain, and it was to be feared that a landing, even in great force, might be bloodily repulsed. Doing everything possible to assure success, Eisenhower finally sent his forces across the Channel on June 6 to seize a 6o-mile wide beachhead in Normandy. Preceded by Anglo-American airborne troops, an Allied armada such as the world had never seen streamed toward France. An army of about 175,000 men was carried in 4000 landing craft protected by an air cover of 12,000 planes and by 600 warships. The assault was not a surprise, although the Germans did not know precisely where

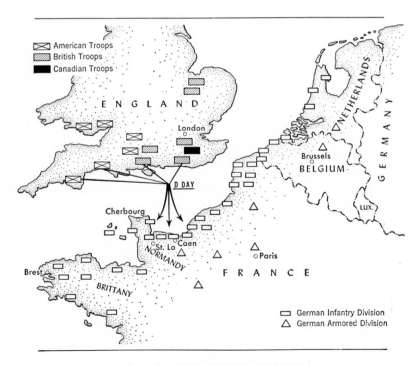

D-DAY—THE SECOND FRONT

the Allies would strike. They resisted strenuously. Many of the Allied soldiers did not reach the French shore, and those who did suffered heavy losses when they tried to push inland. However, the beachhead was established. Then Eisenhower, using "artificial harbors" towed across the Channel to substitute for natural ones, brought up more and more of his army. The beachhead was gradually expanded northward and southward; Cherbourg was captured by American troops on June 27, St. Lô on July 18, and Anglo-Canadian forces seized Caen on July 9. The Allies had won the Battle of Normandy. The Battle of France soon followed.

The opening of the Western Front in Normandy was disastrous for Nazi Germany. Hitler changed generals, and resumed his bombardment of London, using the V1, a jet-propelled pilotless aircraft launched from the coasts of Belgium and northern France. Exchanging one general for another made little difference, and the V1 bombings, although accurate enough, came too late to destroy the British will to fight. It had become evident to sensible men in Germany that the war could end only in defeat, but Hitler believed that victory could still be won. If Germany must fall, he was fanatically determined to fight to the death. The full enormity of his crimes, including the murder of millions of Jews, was not yet known, but on July 20 desperate German army officers and others undertook to kill him and to destroy the Nazi regime. However, the plot failed. A bomb attack on Hitler only injured his arm; the conspirators were unable to seize control of Berlin; and most of them were captured and executed in barbaric fashion. Rommel, privy to the plot, was allowed to commit suicide.

A few days later Eisenhower began the Battle of France. He had already accumulated in Normandy more than a million men, with powerful tank forces. The Allies easily controlled the air. With far fewer tanks, the Germans could not withstand an Allied Blitzkrieg. On July 25 an American armored column under General Patton broke through the Germans at St. Lô and drove southward and eastward. Penetrating far into the rear of the Germans, Patton surrounded and forced the surrender of many of them. Compelled to fall back, the Germans were rapidly pursued. Paris was liberated on August 25, and British troops captured Brussels and Antwerp ten days later. Their advance came just in time to prevent Hitler from making effective use of another secret weapon, the V2, a long-range rocket carrying explosives, that his men began to fire at London on September 12. That menace was ended by the capture of the launching places for the V2. Meanwhile, the American Seventh Army under General Alexander M. Patch landed in southern France, in mid-August, and pushed northward. By September 12 Allied troops had reached German soil and the Battle of France was over.

Then began the Battle for Germany. Hitler hoped to hold the Allies at the Siegfried Line, planned and built before the war to protect Germany's western frontier. During the last two weeks of September the Allies tried to outflank it and to secure a bridgehead on the Rhine, landing more than 30,000 airborne troops in Holland. That daring venture was a costly failure, but American troops broke through the Siegfried Line in October. Between November 21 and November 23 the Americans captured Aachen, Metz, and Strasbourg. It then seemed to optimists among the Allies that Germany must soon succumb.

ROOSEVELT'S FOURTH TERM

While the Allies were advancing in Europe and in the Pacific in 1944, Roosevelt waged his last battle for the Presidency. For the first time since 1864 the Americans had to choose a President while the nation was at war. The campaign at home was hard-fought. Wendell Willkie, who had become a devout internationalist and whose book *One World* had made a deep impression, was for a long time looked upon as the probable Republican candidate. However, Willkie rashly challenged isolationism in Wisconsin, and was defeated in its Republican primary. His chances then faded, and Thomas E. Dewey, who had been chosen Governor of New York in 1942, was nominated on the first ballot at the Republican convention in Chicago. Senator John Bricker of Ohio was named for the Vice-Presidency. Dewey was not an isolationist, nor was his party. The Republicans pledged themselves to "a postwar organization among sovereign nations to prevent military aggression and to obtain permanent peace." They promised to prosecute the war to a successful finish, and then to try to restore "liberty at home."

There could be no doubt that Roosevelt would run for a fourth term, if he were asked to do so. Conservative Southern Democrats were not entirely satisfied with him, partly because he was friendly toward labor unions and toward the Negroes. Nevertheless he was named for the Presidency on the first ballot at the Democratic convention. There was a struggle over the nomination for the Vice-Presidency, many Southerners denouncing Henry Wallace and championing James F. Byrnes of South Carolina. Toward alienating as few voters as possible, Roosevelt finally gave his blessing to Senator Harry S Truman of Missouri, who then had only a modest reputation in public affairs but who had accumulated few enemies. As usual, it was assumed that Truman, if elected, would not succeed to the Presidency.

In the political campaign Dewey urged that Roosevelt and other "tired old men" be replaced by younger and more vigorous ones, like himself. The strain of war and the irritations of wartime controls favored Dewey and the Republicans. They received some help from Congress, which passed a law permitting persons in the armed services to vote, but did not make it easy for them to do so. Roosevelt was powerfully assisted by the Political Action Committee of the CIO, which arranged political rallies and a house-to-house canvass in his behalf. The burden of office had told upon him, and his appearance gave color to Dewey's charge that he was a tired old man. However, Roosevelt struck back with his customary vigor in a series of speeches in the last days of the campaign. The voters again decided in his favor—that it was not prudent to "change horses in the middle of the stream." He won an easy victory in the electoral college, 432 to 99. The popular balloting was closer, Roosevelt winning by 25,602,505 to 22,600,278. The Democrats retained their majority in the Senate and secured a firmer grip upon the House of Representatives.

THE END IN EUROPE

It was hoped in America that the war in Europe would end soon after the political campaign, possibly before Christmas. That hope was ill-founded. Retreating across France, the Germans occupied shorter and partly fortified lines; and the pursuing Allies had to regroup and prepare for new thrusts. During ten days in December it seemed that the collapse of Germany might be very long delayed. Collecting men and all the tanks possible, Hitler ordered General Karl von Rundstedt, one of his ablest commanders, to counterattack in the Ardennes, where the Allies were weakest. He believed that a sudden massive advance might reach Antwerp and split the Allied armies. Thus, he thought, defeat in the West might be staved off indefinitely. Eisenhower was surprised, and the Germans drove forward for 50 miles, inflicting many casualties upon American infantry. However, von Rundstedt's drive was checked before he reached his objective, and he was forced to fall back. Hitler did not win this Battle of the Bulge. His losses were also heavy; he spent men and machines that would have been useful in checking Allied thrusts into Germany.

In the early months of 1945 the Allies put an end to the Hitlerian empire. They did not rest until spring. In January the Russians smashed forward in Poland, capturing Warsaw, and reached the Oder River. In February and early March the British and Americans drove the Germans to the Rhine River. On March 7 the Americans began to pour over the Remagen bridge across the Rhine, which the Germans had neglected to destroy, and two weeks later they crossed at other points. The Germans no longer had any significant numbers of airplanes or tanks. In April 325,000 of them were surrounded and forced to surrender in the Ruhr.

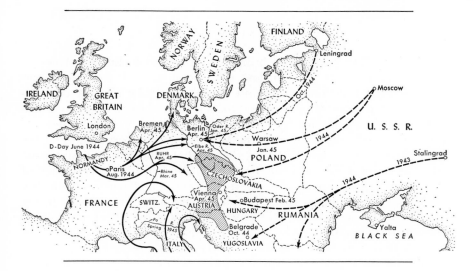

COLLAPSE OF GERMANY

American troops reached the Elbe River on April 11; British forces captured Bremen two weeks later. Meanwhile, the Russians crossed the Oder,
and fought their way into Berlin. During the last week of April the Germans ceased to resist in northern Italy, and Mussolini was captured and
killed by Italian guerrilla fighters. Not many hours later Hitler committed
suicide in an underground bunker in Berlin. The German capital was
surrendered to the Russians on May 2, and within the next six days all
the German forces unconditionally laid down their arms. Officially the
European war ended upon May 8.

    Roosevelt did not live to share the joy of the victory in Europe. In
February he met with Stalin and Churchill at Yalta in the Crimea. There,
to secure the help of the Russian dictator in the war against Japan and
in postwar reconstruction of the world, he and Churchill promised large
concessions to the Soviet Union in both Europe and Asia. Wearily returning home, he went for a rest to a cottage he owned at Warm Springs in
Georgia. He died there on April 12 of a cerebral hemorrhage. Vice-President Truman, shocked with the rest of the nation, took up Roosevelt's
burdens. Like most Americans, he had not expected that the responsibilities of the President would be thrust upon him. He was at first awed
by his tasks, which were great enough to daunt a man far less modest than
Truman. Fortunately, although he did not know it, the war in the Pacific
was moving toward its end along with that in Europe. Before Japan fell,
Truman had to make a momentous decision.

CONQUEST OF JAPAN

While the Allies struggled to bring down the Axis in Europe, America, with what help China, Britain, and the Commonwealth could give, carried on left-handed offensives against Japan. It will be recalled that, despite their defeat at Midway, the Japanese had accomplished as much as they dared to hope for by late 1942. The Japanese empire then extended from India on the west to the Marshall and Gilbert Islands on the east, and from Attu and Kiska on the north to the Dutch East Indies, New Guinea, and the Solomon Islands on the south. The perimeter of that empire lay thousands of miles from Tokyo. If Japan's oceanic empire had to be conquered island by island, and then the Japanese homeland had to be reduced, a left-handed effort was by no means enough. However, the successes of the Japanese had made it clear that much could be accomplished in the Pacific arena by the exercise of superior power in the air and on the water. America achieved such superiority in 1943. Moreover, American submarines, eventually even more potent than those of the Germans, were putting to sea.

America and her allies made the most of their strength. Seeking to help Generalissimo Chiang K'ai-shek, they sent him what supplies they could by air over the Himalayas from India. They also undertook to reconquer Burma and to reopen the Burma Road to Chungking. They finally succeeded in the summer of 1944, despite stubborn Japanese resistance in the jungles of Burma. With the Japanese concentrating their efforts elsewhere, Chiang K'ai-shek managed to hang on. Meanwhile, the American "silent service," the submarines, struck ever more decisively at Japanese shipping. Cruising in the South China Sea and in the home waters of Japan, the undersea craft torpedoed more and more enemy vessels as the war went on. They made it difficult for Japan to send out reinforcements, and they also prevented the Japanese from making full use of the raw materials of the territories they had won. Before the end of the war the Japanese merchant marine was so reduced that the submarines had difficulty in finding worthy targets. The exploits of the Allies on and above the surface of the Pacific were spectacular. The American navy and Marine Corps, under the command of Admiral Chester Nimitz, moved toward Japan from the southeast. General MacArthur, with land, sea, and air forces that were chiefly American but included contingents from Australia and New Zealand, advanced against it from the south. Under Nimitz the navy used Pacific islands as stepping-stones to get within bombing reach of Japan. In the wake of its advance Japanese garrisons, cut off from reinforcement, were left on various islands "to wither on the vine." MacArthur also leapfrogged to the Philippines, bypassing large numbers of Japanese troops, especially in the Dutch East Indies.

If the northward drive of MacArthur was spectacular, it also included much bitter fighting under cruel conditions. By 1943 he had acquired sufficient strength to undertake the reconquest of northern New Guinea. Making effective use of air and sea power, he seized the principal Japanese bases there. But his successes were not easily won, for the Japanese, the heat, and the jungle were formidable foes. In the jungle the Japanese went on fighting for many months after their bases had been captured. Nor were they readily driven from the Solomon Islands and others east of New Guinea. They evacuated Guadalcanal in February, 1943, but they fought desperately to hold on to the central and northern Solomons. However, superior Allied strength in the air and on the water began to tell increasingly in the summer of 1943. That summer—it was really always summer in those parts of the world—American troops landed on New Georgia, and in November marines went ashore at Bougainville. In a series of engagements the American navy defeated and drove back squadrons sent to relieve and reinforce the Japanese garrisons. Rabaul, Japan's principal military and naval base in the Southwest Pacific, was bypassed. In December, 1943 American forces landed on New Britain. The way was opening for MacArthur to push on into the Philippines.

The navy was strong enough in the spring of 1943 not only to take the

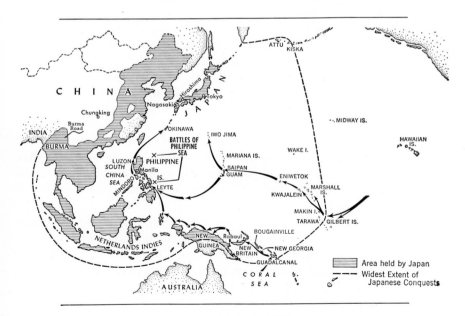

DEFEAT OF JAPAN

offensive in the Southwest Pacific, but to help expel the Japanese from the Aleutian Islands. It drove away Japanese war vessels supporting the garrisons on Attu and Kiska, and opened the way for an attack upon Attu by ground troops in May. After three weeks of hard fighting in cold, fog, and high winds, the island was recaptured. Two months later the Japanese evacuated Kiska; American and Canadian soldiers occupied it without a struggle on August 15.

The navy did not move against Tokyo from the southeast until November, 1943. By that time Admiral Nimitz had under his command forces that were superior to those of the Japanese, and he was steadily gaining strength—before 1944 was far advanced the Japanese navy was comparatively much weaker. On November 21 the Pacific fleet bombarded Japanese-held Tarawa and Makin in the Gilbert Islands, and landed marines. They suffered heavy losses on Tarawa, but they captured the islands. In February, 1944 key points in the Marshall Islands were similarly taken, with airplanes and naval guns isolating and bombarding the Japanese garrisons and clearing the way. In the following summer Saipan and Guam in the Marianas were taken despite fierce Japanese resistance. So threatening was the American advance into the Marianas that a Japanese fleet was sent to the rescue of the garrisons. It challenged the American fleet under Admiral Raymond A. Spruance on June 19–20. In the First Battle of the Philippine Sea, basically a struggle between carrier-based airplanes, Spruance inflicted a smashing defeat upon the Japanese. Of nine Japanese carriers brought into the action, six were sunk by American bombers and submarines, and the other three were damaged. The Japanese lost more than 400 airplanes, a battleship, and several other smaller vessels. Spruance lost only 130 airplanes and 76 pilots.

The Japanese navy was so badly hurt in the First Battle of the Philippine Sea that Emperor Hirohito abandoned hope that Japan could hold out indefinitely against the Allies. Premier Tojo was forced out of office, and Japan thereafter sought a negotiated peace. But the Allies could not permit the war to end with Japan keeping any part of the territories seized from them. In fact, Roosevelt and Churchill had declared at their conference in Casablanca that the Axis powers must surrender unconditionally, and Stalin had subscribed to that declaration. The war had to continue.

In the fall of 1944 the reconquest of the Philippines became the principal Allied objective. Marines landed in the Palau Islands in September, and General MacArthur waded ashore to the Philippine island of Leyte on October 20. Leaving the Philippines in February, 1942, he had made good his promise, "I shall return." The Japanese quickly responded with a determined effort to smash his beachhead. Their navy offered a last desperate challenge that led to the Second Battle of the Philippine Sea from October 23 to 25. It actually consisted of three separate engagements, widely separated in space, the principal American force being under the command of Admiral William Halsey. The Japanese, losing more than 30 ships, were so thoroughly beaten that their navy was no longer formidable. The American losses were small. MacArthur was able to take Leyte, to jump to Mindoro, and then, in January, 1945, to Luzon. He captured Manila in February, and Japanese resistance in the Philippines ended in the following July.

In the early months of 1945, although some of America's strategists believed that Japan could be forced to submit by naval blockade and bombing, the dominant opinion among them was that it would be necessary to invade Japan. This opinion was partly responsible for Roosevelt's concessions to Stalin at Yalta, toward insuring that Russia would join in the attack upon Japan. By that time American bombers were hitting at Japan from bases in both China and the Marianas, but the distances they had to cover limited their efforts. In February, to help the bombers from the Marianas, the marines landed on the island of Iwo Jima, only 750 miles from Tokyo. They completed its capture, but only after the most bitter fighting, in which they suffered 20,000 casualties in a month. Two weeks after the fall of Iwo Jima an American army landed on Okinawa, only 360 miles southwest of Japan. There too the Japanese fought almost to the death, resisting for nearly three months without hope of rescue. Very costly to the American fleet covering the invasion of Okinawa were "Kamikaze" attacks by Japanese fliers who directed bombing planes directly at American ships. These suicide assaults were difficult to stop, and the navy suffered more damage and lost more sailors than in any other engagement during the war.

In the late spring of 1945 an Allied army drove the Japanese backward in Southeast Asia, and Japan proper was exposed to heavy bombing attacks from bases on Okinawa, Saipan, and China. From them and from aircraft carriers explosives fell more and more frequently on Tokyo and other Japanese cities. Preparations were made for an invasion, which could be expected to succeed only at very heavy costs. Invasion, happily, proved to be unnecessary. The bombing, carried on by both American and British fliers and accompanied by shelling of Japanese ports from the sea, daunted the will of the Japanese to fight on. On certain days there were as many as 2000 Allied fliers over Japanese cities. On July 26 from Potsdam in Germany Truman and Clement Attlee, who had succeeded Churchill as Prime Minister of Britain, demanded immediate and unconditional surrender. Otherwise, Japan would be destroyed. Militarists in Tokyo insisted that the war continue. To save American lives and to bring the conflict to a swift end Truman resolved to make use of the atomic bomb, and at his order an American bomber dropped one on Hiroshima on August 6. The

American "secret weapon" was a terrible one. It struck with the force of 20,000 tons of TNT, and it killed or injured about 160,000 people. Russian troops attacked the Japanese army in Manchuria two days later and on the ninth another atomic bomb hit Nagasaki, inflicting losses similar to those suffered at Hiroshima.

The Japanese war then quickly came to an end. Japan still had a powerful army, but Emperor Hirohito knew that it was useless to fight on. On August 10, at his command, Japan offered to lay down arms, provided that the Emperor retain his sovereign power. Truman's answer was that Hirohito and the Japanese government had to accept the authority of the commander of Allied forces that would occupy Japan. His terms were accepted on August 14, and MacArthur formally received the Japanese surrender on board the battleship *Missouri* in Tokyo Bay on September 2.

The greatest war in human history had ended. How many lives it took can hardly be estimated, but tens of millions were dead. America had 322,000 killed and about 700,000 wounded, losses far greater than in World War I. Had it not been for the use of penicillin, sulfa drugs, and blood plasma, American casualties must have been even larger. Nearly two million Japanese were slain. How many Chinese and South Sea islanders died at the hands of the Japanese, no one can say. Germany had about 3,500,000 military dead, and more than a half million civilians killed, exclusive of Jews who were exterminated by the Nazis. Altogether, possibly 20,000,000 Russians lost their lives. Perhaps a tenth of the people in eastern and southeastern Europe were dead. Britain and France suffered far fewer casualties than in World War I, but many cities in western Europe were half destroyed. London was badly injured, as was Coventry, and Rotterdam in Holland. Berlin and several other German cities were shambles. Japan and Germany were reduced to poverty; Britain was exhausted by her immense war effort. Much of western Russia was desolated. To some the wounds of the world seemed almost beyond healing. And could another such conflict be prevented?

59 THE COMING OF THE COLD WAR

THE MAN FROM MISSOURI

Reaching the Presidency only because of the death of the preeminent Roosevelt, Harry S Truman also inherited many great troubles. It became his duty to make momentous decisions. The opinion that he was not equal to the tasks of the Presidency when he succeeded to it was not confined to Republican partisans. Born at Lamar, Missouri in 1884, he was nearly 61 years of age when he entered the White House. Short, nearsighted, plain in speech, he did not have the commanding presence of Roosevelt. Nor did he seem to be qualified by education or experience to wield the vast authority that fell to him. Formal instruction that he received in Missouri as a boy was limited. He was a farmer for a decade, and then served as an artillery officer in World War I. Returning home, he and a partner opened a haberdashery in Kansas City, but the venture ended in bankruptcy. In 1922, with the support of the notorious "Boss" Tom Pendergast of Kansas City, Truman became a member of the Jackson County Court. As such he was the equivalent of a county commissioner. He remained a member of the court until 1934. During the early months of his service on it he studied law at night in Kansas City, but he was not

called to the bar. In 1934, again with the help of Pendergast, Truman secured the Democratic nomination for the Senate, was elected, and entered
upon the national political scene. There he was inconspicuous for some
years, being looked upon by many as a mere tool of Pendergast. But he
was reelected to the Senate in 1940, and he quietly made a reputation for
reliability during World War II as the chairman of a Senate committee
appointed to investigate waste and inefficiency in the production of military materials. He then was looked upon in Washington as a useful man,
equal to the dignity of the Vice-Presidency. He had made few enemies;
hence, to his own surprise, he was selected by Roosevelt as a running mate.
He was better fitted for the Presidency than he at first seemed to be. Over
the years he had read extensively in American history, although his knowledge of it was less thorough than he thought it was. No wardheeler, he was
never subservient to Pendergast. He had the prime requisite for success
in the Presidency, courage. He was not given to evading thorny questions;
he was well-schooled in the art of partisan politics; and he could speak
clearly, if plainly and sometimes profanely. A moderate New Dealer, Truman liked to call himself a liberal. His most obvious fault was excessive
loyalty to unworthy friends who took advantage of their relationship to
him. He was impulsive. If he did not perform as one of the greatest Presidents, he was far from being one of the worst of them.

During many long months after he succeeded Roosevelt, Truman suspected that his role in American history would be like that of Andrew
Johnson, that he would be to Roosevelt as Johnson had been to Lincoln.
He found himself in a sea of troubles; he and his domestic policies were
bitterly attacked by many Republicans, and he acquired enemies in his
own party. But Truman escaped the political fate of Johnson. Unlike
Johnson, he successfully asserted dominion over the Cabinet that he had
inherited. Only three of those appointed to it by Roosevelt were still in
office at the end of 1945, and those three did not long remain. Harold Ickes
and Henry A. Wallace, quarreling with the President over policy, resigned.
The new men brought into the Cabinet, whatever might be their merits,
had to be Truman's own. Trying to continue the New Deal in what he
later called the "Fair Deal," Truman was not very successful. He led vigorously in foreign affairs, in which he had the support of many Republicans.
In the election of 1948, largely fought over domestic issues, he won a surprising victory. Fortunately, there was no major depression after World
War II; had there been one, Truman's tale might indeed have been like
that of Andrew Johnson.

THE FAIR DEAL

It was commonly assumed at the end of World War II that a depression
must soon come. It was feared that the demobilization of industry would

create a large body of unemployed, and that it would be swelled by returning veterans. To the pleased surprise of all, the return of the "boys"—and
girls—to civil life was a return to school and to work rather than to idleness. So great was the popular demand for release from service that about
13,000,000 of them put off their uniforms in the years 1945 and 1946. However, provision had been made for them by the "GI" Bill of Rights passed
by Congress in June, 1944, as well as by other means. Veterans received
allowances for a fixed period after discharge, or until they secured employment. Tens of thousands of them, offered financial help in proportion to
length of service in order to go back to school, flooded into colleges, universities, and other educational institutions. Air Force colonels went to
classes with rank-and-file soldiers. When they finished their schooling, they
could find jobs, for there was a vast demand for the housing, automobiles,
refrigerators, and clothing, and all the goods and services that had not
been available during the war; and money saved during the war could be
used to buy them. In the spring of 1946 unemployment reappeared, but
not much of it. After 1947, despite occasional economic lulls, the American
people were again afflicted by a general prosperity. It was not attained
without hard-fought contests in Washington and strife between management and labor that tried the patience of the nation. It was accompanied
by inflation that discriminated seriously against those who had relatively
fixed salaries, and especially against those who had retired or would soon
retire upon pensions.

In September, 1945 Truman sent to Congress his blueprint for future
domestic policy. He urged that selective service and controls over prices
and wages be temporarily continued for the years ahead. Truman envisaged a peacetime economy which would produce on something like the
level achieved during the war. Toward that obviously desirable end, he
proposed that "full employment" be a great goal of the nation, with government assuming responsibility for its attainment. This accorded with
the thought of the English economist Maynard Keynes, that whenever the
economy faltered, government should spend to stimulate it, regardless of
deficits. Truman also called for social reforms, including a raise in the
federal minimum wage, national health insurance, and a federal housing
program. During the war Roosevelt had taken action toward refusing government contracts to those who refused to hire Negroes. Truman asked
that a commission be established by law to see to it that industries receiving federal contracts employed men and women without respect to race
or color.

To Republicans and to conservative Democrats, especially Southerners,
in Congress, much of what Truman asked was highly distasteful. It reluctantly extended selective service until March, 1947, largely because General Eisenhower, as Chief of Staff of the army, insisted that it was necessary.
But Truman's economic and social plans, amounting to a permanent and

enlarged New Deal, were hotly opposed on Capitol Hill. Southerners there did not want federal power to be used against racial discrimination. With Truman and the Republicans they agreed that production and employment must be kept at a high level. If they were not, how could a national debt of $270 billion be carried, and how could the running expenses of government, vastly increased by new responsibilities abroad, be met? However, neither the Southern Democrats nor the Republicans desired more of the New Deal; they denounced regimentation, deficit spending, and Keynesian economics. They believed that lower taxes, relaxation of federal controls, and the prospect of profits would bring genuine prosperity. Accordingly, Congress reduced corporation and income taxes before the end of 1945 and passed an act early in 1946 that ambiguously endorsed maximum employment without positively pledging governmental action to secure it. Truman had to accept this watered-down version of his full employment.

WAGE AND PRICE CONTROLS

Truman's request that wartime wage and price controls be continued until scarcities ended, was also sharply opposed in Congress. Indeed, when and how to remove controls were questions that created ugly controversies throughout the nation. Landlords wanted "ceilings" on rents lifted immediately and tenants wished them to be preserved indefinitely. Industry wanted freedom to charge as much as it could for its products, but was not eager to raise wages. Labor leaders insisted that prices, including rents, be restricted, but that wages be raised. They claimed that profits had risen more rapidly than wages during the war, and that management could afford to give higher pay without increasing prices. Truman was eager to prevent a runaway inflation such as had occurred immediately after World War I. On the other hand, staunch champions of laissez-faire in and out of Congress declared that shortages which might lead to inflation would quickly end, if price controls were destroyed and profits were more or less assured.

While the issue of controls was before Congress, the nation was troubled by a series of great strikes. Workmen, foreseeing the end of wartime overtime pay and a reduction in take-home pay, wanted raises so that they would receive as much in the future for a forty-hour week as they had for one of forty-eight hours. Management commonly claimed that it could not afford to raise wages so far unless price controls were removed. The unions had grown powerful; they had 14,500,000 members in 1945, and their leaders insisted that the request of the workers could be met without price increases. Strikes followed, one after another, in 1945 and 1946, the United Automobile Workers against the General Motors Company, a railroad strike, another in steel, and one waged by John L. Lewis and the United Mine Workers against the coal industry. The unions sought increases of approximately 30¢ per hour. After much turmoil they secured about two-thirds of their demands in accordance with a formula worked out by federal mediators. Before the strikes were settled, Truman temporarily had to take over both the railroads and the coal mines. He was also forced to accept a raise in the price of steel, thus creating what he called a "bulge" in controls.

More bulges came rapidly. The OPA would expire in June, 1946, unless Congress renewed it. Sentiment in Congress was divided, with some favoring extension of OPA, some demanding that it be permitted to die, and some taking the view that it should be maintained with reduced authority. Congress finally passed a measure extending OPA, but limited its powers. Truman vetoed it on June 29, and there were no controls for a period of three weeks. Prices immediately soared. Congress then voted another compromise measure, which the President did sign. It contained several great bulges, so many that Truman became convinced, in October, 1946, that it was not worthwhile to try to hold any economic line except that concerned with rents. With the exception of the "ceiling" on rents, the American economy became free of wartime controls. The inflation that came with that freedom lessened the burden of the national debt; it also diminished the purchasing power of government bonds, and grievously hurt the elderly, who benefited little, if at all, from higher wages. Prices moved upward, then wages, then prices again and wages.

A REPUBLICAN CONGRESS

The election of 1946 came in the midst of social and economic turmoil. The Republicans had been gaining strength for a decade, but they had been checked by the popularity of Roosevelt and by his adept political maneuvering, which loosely kept together clashing elements among the Democrats. Truman had no great personal following. The many dissatisfactions of the postwar era injured the Democrats; they were divided and defensive. "Had enough? Vote Republican!" was an appealing battlecry. Foreign affairs offered no great issue, but a doubtful world outlook favored the party out of power. The Republicans decisively won the election, gaining a majority of more than 50 in the House of Representatives and also securing dominance in the Senate by 51 to 45. Did the election mean to Truman what that of 1866 had meant to Andrew Johnson? Senator James Fulbright, Democrat from Arkansas, thought so. He declared that Truman had been repudiated, and that he and other Democratic dignitaries should resign in such fashion as to bring a Republican into the Presidency, a person who could work smoothly with a Republican Congress. Truman ridiculed the proposal; other Presidents had had to deal with a politically hostile Congress; if he must fight Congress, he would.

He did, on domestic issues, without remarkable success. The Republicans worked with Truman to strengthen the military forces by the National Security Act of 1947, which placed all of them under a new Secretary of Defense. Toward the same end selective service was revived in the following year. The Republicans agreed with Truman that arrangements for succession to the Presidency needed to be changed. Under a law made in 1886 Cabinet members would succeed after the Vice-President. In 1947 the law was revised so that men elected to office, the Speaker of the House of Representatives, and the presiding officer of the Senate, would follow the Vice-President. However, the Eightieth Congress wanted little of Truman's Fair Deal. It deprived some persons of the benefits of Social Security, and it reduced income taxes by its own formula, despite Presidential disapproval. Such was the prosperity of the nation that the federal budget was balanced during 1946–1947 and 1947–1948 at approximately $35,000,000,000 per annum. The Republicans wanted to do what they had done in the Twenties: cut taxes below the wartime level, increase private income, and pay part of the national debt. Truman vetoed three tax reduction bills passed by them, saying that they favored the wealthy. In 1948, with the support of many Democrats, the Republicans overrode his veto. The Eightieth Congress hit at Roosevelt as well as Truman. In 1947 it proposed the Twenty-second Amendment, which was ratified four years later. It declared that no person should be elected to the Presidency more than twice, and that anyone inheriting and occupying the Presidency for as much as two years should be restricted to one elective term. The amendment did not apply to Truman; it did afterward apply to Dwight Eisenhower, to the regret of many Republicans.

One partisan issue raised by the Republicans, that of Communists in government, led to a warm dispute between them and Truman. In 1938 the House of Representatives had established a committee to investigate un-American activities. Making use of it at a time when communism was becoming a serious menace, they charged that the Democrats had allowed Reds to seep into federal offices. Truman asserted that the charge was false and insincere, but ordered a "loyalty check" in 1947 that forced some persons from office. He did not do enough to satisfy the Republicans. The issue acquired drama in the summer of 1948 when Whittaker Chambers, once a Communist courier, declared that Alger Hiss, who had been a federal official of some importance, had also been a Communist before World War II.

Most important of all the laws passed by the Eightieth Congress was the Taft-Hartley Act, which the Republicans enacted over Truman's veto in June, 1947 with the help of some Democrats. Attaining power as great as that of industrial tycoons, labor leaders—some of them—abused it. Public opinion put much of the blame for postwar industrial unrest upon the labor unions. A walkout of the coal miners under the direction of John L. Lewis in the winter of 1946–1947, executed despite a restraining order from a federal court, increased feeling against the unions. The Taft-Hartley law imposed severe restrictions upon them and their officers. It prohibited the closed shop—forcing workers to join a union before being employed—although it permitted the union shop—compelling them to join after being hired. Jurisdictional strikes and secondary boycotts were barred. Unions were not allowed to make political contributions, and they were forced to publish financial statements. Their officers, but not employers, were compelled to sign an affidavit declaring that they were neither Communist nor affiliated with any organization seeking the overthrow of the American government. The inequity of that provision, even though a Communist employer was a most unlikely person, is obvious. Of special importance was a "cooling-off" period of 60 days, required before one or the other party to a labor contract could denounce it. Even more important to the public, the federal government could through injunction stop a strike threatening the nation's health or safety for 80 days. As Senator Robert Taft, one of the sponsors of the law, admitted, parts of it were unnecessarily harsh. The bulk of it endured.

BIPARTISAN FOREIGN AFFAIRS

There was much less partisan conflict over foreign affairs after World War II, partly because Truman, like Roosevelt, carefully included Republicans in the making of foreign policy. Republicans joined Democrats to continue the program of tariff reduction through reciprocal trade agreements. Isolationism, in the form it had in the Thirties, virtually died with the war. It was obvious that America could not hope to live in seclusion and peace in the western hemisphere. There was a general determination among both Democrats and Republicans that the world must have some sort of society of nations and the two parties worked together to transform the United Nations into a world body. It did not solve all international difficulties. Relations between the United States and the Soviet Union became increasingly strained. In 1947 America undertook to help the countries of western Europe toward prosperity and political stability, and also to contain Communist expansion. The Communists were checked in Europe, but not in Asia.

In the spring and early summer of 1945 a charter was made and signed for the United Nations at a gathering of delegates from 50 countries in San Francisco. Republicans, especially Senator Arthur Vandenburg of Michigan, shared with Democrats in the making of the charter, and it was quickly ratified in the Senate by a vote of 89 to 2. It had been carefully drawn to avert a struggle over ratification. Roosevelt had seen to it that the UN had less authority than the League of Nations, to satisfy both the Soviet Union and American nationalist sentiment. Complex machinery was set up for the UN. Basic in it was a General Assembly, a policy-making body, in which each country had one vote (except that, as a result of an effort by Roosevelt and Churchill to please Stalin, the Soviet Union was given three, two of them for republics belonging to that Union). Also of the first importance was a Security Council of eleven members, in which America, Russia, Britain, France, and China were given permanent seats. The Council was tendered power to deal with political and military troubles, seven votes being necessary to take any action. While the Council could resort to both economic and military sanctions, the unanimous consent of the Big Five was required. A Secretary-General was made the principal executive officer. The UN charter also called for an international court at The Hague; an international body, UNESCO, to foster educational, scientific, and cultural exchange; and other bodies to assert human rights and to control troubled colonial areas.

Established in New York City in modernistic quarters beside the East River, the UN was useful from its beginning in settling international disputes and in various other minor ways. It soon proved its value by mediating a dispute between the Netherlands and the new Republic of Indonesia, and another between the new Zionist state of Israel and the neighboring Arab countries. However, the UN also quickly became the scene of political conflict between America and Russia, each receiving support from other countries. Of profound importance was their inability to agree upon disarmament, and especially a plan to prevent the use of nuclear weapons in the future. America proposed one by which the UN would be given full power toward that end, including the right to make inspections in all countries to make sure that no one of them independently and secretly manufactured nuclear bombs. Russia insisted upon having a veto over inspection, and that nothing be done toward controlling nuclear weapons without her consent at every step. America would not accept less than thorough and unrestrained inspection. By 1947 the two countries were deadlocked over the issue, and they remained so for many years. Meanwhile, America continued to make atomic bombs. Russia, securing information through espionage, rapidly searched out the secrets of nuclear explosion.

As the war receded into the background, the Allies continued to agree that war criminals should be punished. Russia, America, Britain, and France set up an international tribunal at Nuremberg in November, 1945 to try more than a score of captured Nazi leaders for waging aggressive war and for committing atrocities. Several of the principal Nazis were already dead by their own hand, including Hitler, Josef Goebbels, Nazi propaganda chief, and Heinrich Himmler, head of the German secret police.

Hermann Goering, head of the German air force, however, was among the defendants. Trials of the vanquished by the victors can hardly be impartial, and it was very doubtful that the Nazis had broken any generally recognized law when they helped Hitler plot and execute his aggressions. There was no question that they were morally guilty of many atrocities, especially against the Jews. Eleven of the defendants, including Goering, were found guilty and ordered to be hanged. They were, except for Goering, who managed to take his own life by poison. The remaining eight Nazis were given long prison terms. Few will say that they did not deserve their fate. Many more Nazis were tried in Allied military courts for murdering prisoners and for almost unbelievable atrocities; the American army executed nearly 300, the Russian army perhaps many more. German civil authorities afterward punished tens of thousands of Nazis in various ways. Meanwhile, former Japanese Premier Tojo and six other Japanese leaders were found guilty of conspiring to wage aggressive war by an international court sitting at Tokyo. They were executed, and 14 other Japanese found guilty with them were sentenced to life imprisonment. American military courts tried many Japanese officers accused of violations of the laws of war. At least 420 of them were executed for committing atrocities, and many more were imprisoned, for they had too often murdered prisoners in cold blood.

THE IRON CURTAIN IN EUROPE

Choosing to try to settle European territorial and other related problems piecemeal rather than in a general peace conference, the Allies soon quarreled over eastern Europe. At Yalta a way had been found to solve many of these difficulties, or at least Roosevelt so believed. He, Churchill, and Stalin had agreed that the countries in that region freed from the Nazis should have their own governments chosen by free elections. They also decided that two Polish governments-in-exile, one democratic and the other Communist, should merge peacefully and equally to control Poland. To his joy, Roosevelt found Stalin to be almost astonishingly amenable. To satisfy Stalin, Truman and Clement Attlee at Potsdam in the following summer consented to the inclusion of part of East Prussia and much of prewar Poland within the Soviet Union, Poland being compensated at the expense of Germany. Nor did the western Allies strongly object to the terms of treaties signed in 1946 by which Finland and Rumania made territorial concessions to Russia, although they believed that reparations exacted from Finland were excessive.

However, Stalin broke the agreement made at Yalta. Russian armies occupying eastern Europe supported Communists, and such elections as were held were not at all free. Reds swiftly assumed power in Yugoslavia, Bulgaria, Rumania, Hungary, and Poland. Receiving help through Yugoslavia, the Communists failed to take over Greece only because Britain sent armed forces to the help of the Greek monarchy. Aware that the Russians feared a revival of Germany and that they therefore wished to push their military defenses westward, Truman and his advisers tried to be patient. However, it became increasingly apparent that the behavior of the Russians was to be explained by Communist imperialism rather than by Russian needs for defense, however exaggerated they might be in the mind of Stalin. At Fulton, Missouri, in the spring of 1946 Winston Churchill declared that Russia had let fall an "iron curtain" from the Baltic Sea to the Adriatic. Truman did not comment on Churchill's phrases, but he obviously agreed with the former Prime Minister.

In central Europe, too, there was a sharp division between the western Allies and Russia that gradually worsened. They quarreled over the future of Austria. Eventually, in 1955, Russian occupation troops withdrew, and Austria became a western-style republic. Czechoslovakia was also revived, but, under Russian pressure, it became Communist-dominated. What to do about Germany was a great source of discord. The Russians occupied the eastern part of the country; France, Britain, and America the western part, while Berlin was divided among the four. Many troubles followed. The western nations proposed that Germany be eventually made into a federal republic and that the Germans be permitted to rebuild their economy, except for military purposes. The Russians urged that power be concentrated in the German nation, at the same time insisting upon reparations in such kind and quantity that its highly centralized regime would be disliked by the Germans and susceptible to overthrow. As a result, the western Allies concluded that Russia did not desire a weak Germany to assure her own safety, but one that could be made into a Communist satellite, like Poland and other eastern European states. Observing that the Russians encouraged German Communists in their zones of occupation, they resolved that Germany as a whole must not fall into hands controlled by Russia.

Early in 1947, in view of Communist activity in both Europe and Asia, Truman and his advisers moved toward a momentous change in American foreign policy. The aggressiveness of the Reds was not limited to eastern and central Europe. In both France and Italy, reconstituted as republics after the war, a Communist party thrived. Moreover, recovery of all the nations in western Europe, including Britain, was as yet slow and uncertain. Greece was gravely threatened by Communist revolutionaries, and Turkey was under heavy pressure from Russia. Communists were aggressive in Japan, Korea, and China. On February 21 came a great turning point. Britain had undertaken after the war to support Greece and Turkey against Communist imperialism. On that day Britain, exhausted, informed the American government that it was no longer within her strength to help those two countries. If they were to be saved from the Communists, it must be chiefly by American power. Truman rapidly accepted the challenge. On March 12 he addressed Congress in joint session, asking it to recognize that "totalitarian regimes imposed on free peoples, by direct or indirect aggression, undermined the foundations of international peace and hence the security of the United States." To halt the advances of the Communists, he urged that America extend massive economic help to free peoples threatened by them—and added that more than economic aid might be necessary. To thwart their designs upon Greece and Turkey, he asked Congress to vote $400,000,000 to support the governments of the two countries and also to authorize the sending of American officers to train and advise their armies. Hesitating only briefly, Congress voted by large majorities to help Greece and Turkey. With American support the two countries retained their independence.

THE MARSHALL PLAN

But was America prepared to follow a policy of containment everywhere on the globe? In June, 1947 General George Marshall, then Secretary of State, in a speech made at Harvard University, urged that America extend major economic help to Europe as a whole. The United States had already made loans to Britain and France, but they had been insufficient to stimulate economic revival. Marshall suggested that the European nations, including the Communist ones, develop together a plan to achieve their common prosperity and that they ask the United States for necessary financial aid. The Soviet Union and its satellites declined to participate— the Communists desired neither to see the capitalistic part of Europe prosper nor to accept capitalistic money from America—but representatives of sixteen other European countries gathered at Paris, drew up a four-year program for recovery, and asked the United States to contribute $15 billion to insure its success. The Marshall Plan was by no means universally acclaimed at home. Senator Robert Taft doubted that America could afford to spend the huge sums that would be necessary—far more than $15 billion —to execute it and to apply its principle wherever Communism threatened. Henry Wallace, who had urged that America deal softly with Russia and had resigned from Truman's Cabinet, sharply attacked the plan, but for different reasons. However, a complete seizure of power by the Communists in Czechoslovakia early in 1948 gave new evidence of Red aggressiveness. Congress undertook not only to execute the Marshall Plan, but to supply funds to the government of Chiang K'ai-shek, assailed by the Chinese Communists.

The carrying through of the Marshall Plan effectively stimulated the recovery of non-Communist Europe, which began a steady advance toward prosperity. The Communist parties in France and Italy began to lose rather than to gain ground. In the spring of 1948, to assure European revival, Britain, France, and America merged their occupation zones in Germany. Considering the restoration of civil government and of German industry essential to the prosperity of western Europe, they helped to build a German civilian regime within their common zone. At the same time Britain, France, the Netherlands, Belgium, and Luxembourg entered into a defensive military alliance directed against the Communists.

The decisive measures taken by the United States and its Marshall Plan friends in western Europe were resented in Moscow. Stalin hit back, notably by placing Allied zones in Berlin under blockade. The zones were 100 miles within the German territory controlled by the Russian army. In April, 1948 the Reds began to interfere with traffic through that area, and in June they stopped it entirely. Apparently they hoped thus to gain complete authority over Berlin, and perhaps even to compel America, Britain, and France to abandon their plan for a west German republic. They had no specific right by treaty to maintain surface traffic into and from Berlin. Without supplies the western area in Berlin must starve. Some Americans urged that they be sent through the Russian zone, nevertheless; they were willing to risk war. Instead, the Western powers ingeniously resorted to an airlift into Berlin. To the general astonishment it was successful and the Russians refrained from serious interference. Western planes made more than a quarter of a million flights into the city, carrying food and supplies. In the spring of 1949 the Russians finally abandoned the blockade, having gained nothing from it.

By the spring of 1948, with America and Russia as the principal antagonists, a "Cold War" was in progress. It would not be a brief contest. By that time it had become apparent that America could not halt Communist imperialism merely by giving economic help to governments and peoples threatened by the Reds. In June the Senate took a historic step toward meeting the Communist challenge; it announced its readiness to endorse permanent entangling alliances. At the instance of Senator Vandenberg, by a vote of 64 to 4, the Senate declared that it was ready to ratify treaties committing America to the defense of regions menaced by the Communist advance.

COMMUNISM IN ASIA

America's postwar problems in foreign policy were not confined to Europe. Asia posed many difficulties. There was one bright spot in the Orient, for the Philippine Republic joined the family of nations in 1946, with hearty American approval. Acquiring independence, the Filipinos, except for a small Communist minority, cherished American friendship and sought American protection. After World War II they wanted American military bases in their country. Accordingly, the Philippine Republic agreed to 99-year American leases upon several such bases. But it was otherwise on the Asian continent. The European colonies on the coast of China and in southeast Asia reappeared at the end of the war. In accordance with agreements reached by the Allies during the conflict, China obtained Formosa and other islands from Japan; Korea became independent; and Russia made various gains, acquiring the Kurile Islands, the southern half of Sakhalin Island, and special rights in Manchuria, the Liaotung Peninsula, and Outer Mongolia. In consonance with bargains made at Yalta, the Russians also occupied the northern half of Korea. The Americans occupied southern Korea, together with the home islands of Japan and those to the eastward that Japan had controlled before Pearl Harbor. Several major conflicts of interest between Russia and America soon developed. Although the Russians had made only a token contribution to the Allied victory over Japan, the Soviet Union secured handsome gains at the expense of Japan and China. Moreover, disarming Japanese armies on the Asian mainland, the Russians turned over large quantities of weapons taken from the Japanese to the Chinese Communists. They also fostered Communism in North Korea and did what they could to spread it in Japan.

The expansion of Russian power and influence in the Far East at such small expense soon created concern in Washington. In consequence, America insisted that Russia should have no more than a nominal share in the management of postwar Japan. While he was technically responsible to supervisory bodies composed of representatives of Russia and others of the Allies, General MacArthur ruled Japan through the Emperor Hirohito, who executed his commands, until a peace treaty was made with Japan in 1951. Under the direction of MacArthur, the nation underwent swift change. The Japanese accepted MacArthur with good grace, despite the memory of the nuclear bombings of Hiroshima and Nagasaki and executions of Nipponese war criminals. Under his guidance the Japanese adopted in 1946 a new constitution and created a democratic system of government, Emperor Hirohito being made responsible to the will of his people. In it the Japanese also renounced war and declared that they would maintain no armed forces. Impoverished, they sought to restore their shattered economy. At least temporarily reduced to the status of a minor power, the future of Japan remained uncertain.

Communism made little headway in Japan immediately after the war, but such was not the case in Korea. It flourished in the northern part of the country under the protection of Russian troops. America declared that Korea must be united, free, and independent, but the Russians wanted something different. With their blessing, in May, 1948, Communists in North Korea established a People's Democratic Republic of Korea. In August a Republic of Korea was proclaimed, with the veteran patriot Syngman Rhee as President, at Seoul in the American zone of occupation. Both governments claimed dominion over the entire nation. That of the Communists began to prepare for war, and after 1948 threatened an invasion of southern Korea.

The Communist advance into South Korea immediately after the war was checked by the presence of American troops. There were no American forces in China, and that country fell to the Communists. Even during the war against Japan the Chinese Nationalists under Chiang K'ai-shek and the Chinese Communists under Mao Tse-tung clashed with each other. After the withdrawal of the Japanese, General Marshall tried to persuade the two factions to make peace and to unite in forming a coalition government, but neither side would listen to him. If the Chinese Communists were to be checked, America then had to do whatever was necessary to uphold Chiang K'ai-shek. He was sent arms and supplies at a cost of $3,000,000,000. However, the Chiang K'ai-shek regime was corrupt, inefficient, and arbitrary, and he declined to listen to American pleas to reform it. Arms furnished at American expense often found their way into the hands of Communist troops. The Chinese people, suffering from war and inflation as well as corruption, did not warmly support Chiang's Kuomintang. The Communists were firmly entrenched in western China. Chiang might have been able to hold on indefinitely in the south, but he dissipated much of his strength upon an unsuccessful drive into Manchuria. When it failed, only full-scale use of American military force could have saved him. Unwilling to commit America so heavily, Truman and his advisers declined to supply it, especially because they continued to hope that Chiang would manage to keep control of at least part of the Chinese mainland. However, the Communists swept rapidly southward during 1948 and early 1949, and finally forced the Generalissimo to seek refuge on the island of Formosa. There his regime was temporarily safe, although communism had won China. Checked in Europe by 1948, it had achieved a great triumph in Asia.

ELECTION OF 1948

In the midst of a host of vexations at home and abroad, Truman had to face the voters in 1948. Sensing victory at the polls, the Republicans almost gaily held their national convention at Philadelphia in June. They had reason to believe that they would both keep control of Congress and win the Presidency, the more so because the Democratic party was rent by bitter internal quarrels. The Republican nomination for the Presidency was therefore a prize, and it was eagerly sought by Thomas E. Dewey, Senator Robert Taft, former Governor Harold Stassen of Minnesota, and others. Dewey, reelected governor of New York by a majority of 600,000 in 1946, was stoutly supported by Eastern Republicans. His rivals were unable to combine against him, and he was named on the third ballot. For the Vice-Presidency the Republicans chose Earl Warren, popular Governor of California. They had little difficulty in drawing up an appealing platform. They were for the UN and the Marshall Plan, but they were also for cutting expenses and taxes. They did not explain how they would lower taxes and expenses and at the same time spend the huge sums required to bolster America's friends abroad. The Republicans also said they would curb inflation and do something toward advancing civil rights for the Negroes. Further, they would curb communism within the United States.

There was little enthusiasm in the Democratic convention, also held in Philadelphia, a month later. Henry Wallace was condemning Truman because he was not enough of a New Dealer, and because he had challenged Russia. Wallace was about to take the field at the head of a new Progressive Party. On the other hand, many conservative Southern Democrats were saying that they also would bolt their party if the convention took a strong stand against the segregation of Negroes. In the convention some of them joined with a few ardent disciples of Roosevelt in an attempt to deny the nomination to Truman and to offer it to Dwight Eisenhower or Supreme Court Justice William O. Douglas. Neither Eisenhower, who was, if anything, a Republican, nor Douglas wanted the nomination. Truman did want it, and he forced the convention to name him. To indicate their respect and liking for Senator Alben W. Barkley of Kentucky the Democrats put him forward for the Vice-Presidency, although they had little hope that he would preside over the Senate. Disappointed when Northern big city Democrats insisted that the party forthrightly endorse civil rights for the Negroes, many conservative Southerners went home. Those Democrats who remained gloomily declared their support of the Fair Deal and of Truman's foreign policy.

Truman's chances of reelection seemed slight throughout the campaign that followed. Henry Wallace, with his Progressive Party, supported by the Communists, was certain to draw votes from Truman in several Northern states. A States' Rights party formed by Southern conservatives known as "Dixiecrats" named Governor J. Strom Thurmond of South Carolina for the Presidency and threatened Truman below the Mason-Dixon Line. National straw votes indicated that Dewey would win easily. Accordingly he campaigned gently, avoiding issues and calling for national unity. Truman fought hard. Saying that Republican pledges made at Philadelphia were insincere, he called the Eightieth Congress into special session to give them a chance to fulfill their promises. The Congress did little and went home quickly. Truman's maneuver probably had some effect, although voters were not accustomed to take party platforms too seriously. Truman certainly made headway when he climbed on speaking platforms all over the nation, day after day, to denounce both Congress and the Republican Party in plain language. Large crowds listened intently to him. The labor unions rallied to him, as did Negro voters, and farmers, for he convinced them that he was a good friend to agriculture.

Although Truman claimed throughout the campaign that he would win, very few political observers agreed with him. Thurmond secured 1,169,312 popular votes and 39 votes in the electoral college; Wallace, while obtaining no electoral votes, was named on 1,157,172 popular ballots. Dewey ran well ahead of Truman in the East. Nevertheless, Truman triumphed. Most of the South, the Midwest, and the West favored him. His margin over Dewey was very thin in several states that he carried, but he secured 24,104,836 popular votes to 21,969,500 for Dewey. Truman had 303 electoral votes, Dewey 189. To a degree, Truman's stunning victory is to be explained by the fact that the Democratic party had become far stronger than the Republican one. It won easy majorities in both houses of Congress, and in many cases Truman did not do so well as other Democratic candidates. It is also clear that Dewey lost ground because he declined to make a contest. The attacks of Wallace and of Thurmond upon Truman undoubtedly made many friends for him among independent voters. It would seem that many Republicans, assured that Dewey would win, did not bother to vote. Whatever the reason for it, Truman's victory so confounded the political experts that the nation enjoyed a hearty laugh. Even so, Truman underwent four more grim years in the Presidency.

60 THE STRUGGLE FOR KOREA

After the election of 1948, Harry S Truman, who learned of his victory in the solitude of a hotel room in Kansas City, returned to Washington, where he received an ovation. He was briefly idolized. But he and the Democrats who stood for the Fair Deal had not secured control over Congress. Southern Democrats and Republicans combined, as they so often did after 1938, to prevent the consummation of the Fair Deal. Parts of it were translated into law, most of it not. In the election of 1950 the Fair Dealers lost ground, although the Democratic party retained nominal control over Congress. Communism in government became a burning and ugly issue. Corruption in public life made headlines. Meanwhile, America moved more and more forcefully to check international Communism, eventually going to war to prevent its spread into South Korea. After two years of hard fighting South Korea was cleansed of Korean and Chinese Communists by UN forces, chiefly American, at heavy cost. The "Hot War" in Korea helped to bring the Republicans back into power in Washington, and so ultimately to soften domestic discord. The Cold War, or at least a Cold Peace, continued.

Early in 1949, in the flush of his victory, Truman renewed his efforts in behalf of the Fair Deal. He asked for legislation to remove discrimination against the Negroes; Southern Democrats prevented it by threatening to filibuster. He wanted to add a health insurance system to Social Security; his plan was assailed as socialized medicine, and Congress declined to act upon it. He asked for repeal of the Taft-Hartley law, but did not get it. Maintaining price supports for agriculture—not in desperate straits just after World War II—the lawmakers set aside a scheme to revise them prepared by Truman's Secretary of Agriculture, Charles F. Brannan. Congress did join with Truman in making some changes. It raised the federal minimum wage from 40 cents to 75 cents an hour; it provided funds for more than 800,000 units of public housing; it enlarged the benefits offered by Social Security and extended them to college professors, servants, farm labor, and self-employed persons; and it worked with the President to streamline the executive departments. The lawmakers also joined Truman to revise immigration policy. More than 800,000 "displaced persons" who had been rendered homeless by Nazi and Communist aggression sought asylum after 1945. In 1948 Congress had especially authorized the entrance into the United States of 205,000 such people, but had imposed restrictions that kept many of them away from American shores. By a law of 1950 provision was made to accept more than 400,000 of them. However, with that temporary though important exception, the immigration policy established by the United States in the 1920s remained unchanged. It was reasserted in the McCarran-Walter Act of 1952, which continued the quota system of 1929. The new law offered one improvement, in that it did not specifically bar immigrants from Asia.

SPIES AND "SUBVERSIVES"

Upon one matter Truman and the Congress had been and remained united. They were determined to carry on research in nuclear weapons with Britain as a partner, and also to produce them if genuine and effective international control of military nuclear science could not be secured. Since Russia steadily refused to accept any plan that would give the UN power of inspection to prevent secret violation of a ban upon such arms, America tried out nuclear bombs at Bikini in the Pacific in 1946 under the direction of the newly created Atomic Energy Commission, and exploded more powerful ones at Eniwetok in the Pacific in 1948. Moreover, America stored such weapons. The fact that no other nation had any during the early years of the Cold War was a source of disquieting comfort. However, in September, 1949 American surveillance revealed that an atomic explosion had taken place in the Soviet Union. Some atomic scientists, pacifists, and others urged that America decline to make more nuclear bombs and refuse to compete with the Russians. Truman and the Congress determined instead that America must retain, if possible, superiority in nuclear weapons. Early in 1950 he personally ordered researches toward making the hydrogen bomb, many times more devastating than the bombs exploded over Japan in 1945. One was detonated at Eniwetok in November, 1952. America held superiority in nuclear weapons for some years.

But the news that Russia had the "secret" of the nuclear bomb, and that she had acquired information about it through spies, created a profound disturbance in America and supplied ammunition to those who claimed that Roosevelt and Truman had permitted infiltration of the federal government by Communists and Red sympathizers. It came out that Dr. Klaus Fuchs, a German-born physicist in British service, a secret Communist for many years, had obtained important atomic information at Los Alamos and had conveyed it to Russia. Moreover, sensational announcements of the arrest and trial of Soviet agents in the United States followed. Five Americans, Harry Gold, Julius Rosenberg, Ethel Rosenberg, David Greenglass, and Morton Sobell were found guilty of atomic espionage in behalf of Russia, the Rosenbergs being executed for that crime. There could be no doubt that atomic spies had hurt the United States, even though Russia would have been able sooner or later to make atomic weapons by using her own scientists. Defenders of Roosevelt and Truman said that spying in behalf of Russia was to be expected, and that checking it ought to be left in the hands of those best qualified to meet the threat, agents of the FBI and other counterintelligence officers; but the fact of Communist infiltration could not be denied. Congressional hunters of Communists in government, with a show of reason, claimed that not enough had been done to halt Communist conspirators, and that congressional committees must search them out and prepare laws to curb them.

Accused of doing less than it should have done to check Communism within America, the Department of Justice was able to point out that it had brought to trial and secured the conviction and imprisonment of eleven leaders of the Communist party in the United States. They had been successfully prosecuted under the Smith Act of 1940, which made it unlawful to advocate overthrow of the American government by force or to form or to be a member of any group dedicated to that end. Enforcement of the Smith Act damaged the Communist party, which was obviously directed from Moscow. That party was also hit hard by the FBI under J. Edgar Hoover; its agents penetrated into many Communist cells. Congressional seekers of Communists in government continued to insist that they had much work to do, that Communists and fellow travelers had penetrated into labor unions, federal offices, and colleges and universities as well as defense plants.

That persons who were, or had been, Communists were to be found among the officials of labor unions and among college professors was generally admitted by 1949. Making much use of FBI files, the Un-American

Activities Committee of the House of Representatives had helped to expose such persons; and it continued to search them out. Its public hearings were often conducted as if witnesses were on trial; if a Mr. Smith was compelled to testify before it, newspapers were apt to report about the Smith "case." The committee pilloried both dedicated Communists and individuals who had once been Reds but had left the Communist party. Most such persons had joined in the innocence of youth, leaving the party when they learned it was merely a part of the Red international network spun in Moscow. They often found publicity given to their youthful indiscretion embarrassing and humiliating; moreover, they were forced to reveal the names of associates and friends who had made the same mistake; if they declined to do it, they were subject to punishment for contempt of Congress. What was worse, some people who had never been Communists were accused without good reason, and were "grilled" by the committee. Only too often innocent people acquired a reputation for disloyalty on the basis of "guilt by association." Defenders of personal freedom frequently condemned the behavior of the committee; they pointed out that the great majority of labor leaders and of professors had been and were unquestionably loyal, and they accused the committee of seeking to get favorable publicity for its members rather than information upon which to prepare laws.

Were there Communists in important federal offices? A few persons were accused by name, without conclusive proof. However, substantial evidence appeared that Alger Hiss, once a brilliant young New Dealer in the Department of State, had conveyed secret public documents to a Communist courier in 1937 and 1938. Appearing before a federal grand jury, Hiss denied that he had done so, denied also that he had ever met the courier, Whittaker Chambers. But Chambers, a repentant Communist, swore that Hiss had given him the documents for transmission. Because of the passage of time, Hiss could not be tried for betraying his trust. He was indicted for perjury because Chambers could produce some secret Department of State documents copied on a typewriter that had been in the possession of Hiss. Tried in the summer of 1949, Hiss was described as a man of high principles by several honored witnesses, and the jury could not reach a verdict. In January, 1950, after a second trial, he was found guilty of perjury and sentenced to imprisonment for five years.

The search for "subversives" spread from Washington to the state capitals, where it became fashionable to impose special oaths of loyalty upon teachers and professors, this despite the fact that Communists were well known to have no respect for oaths that hampered their cause. Bitter protests came from those who were entrusted with the teaching of the young; they were indignant because they were singled out for repression. An attempt to impose a special oath upon its professors shook the University of California to its foundations. A few teachers who were, or had been,

Communists were discharged from their posts. Some whose political opinions were orthodox suffered harassment and embarrassment. It is doubtful that Red revolution was thus prevented.

Most reckless of all those who made subversives their quarry was Republican Joseph R. McCarthy, who was elected to the United States Senate in Wisconsin in 1946. He took the view that Communist fire must be fought with fire, and that injury to some innocent individuals must not prevent the harrying of Reds. In February, 1950, at Wheeling, West Virginia, McCarthy declared that there were at least 57 Communists in the Department of State. His charge created a sensation. The triumph of the Chinese Communists was seen as a defeat for the United States; the news that Russia had the secret of atomic explosion had created alarm, and the Hiss and Soviet espionage cases had increased it. Finding ready listeners and newspaper headlines, McCarthy later said there were, or had been, 81 persons in the Department of State who were security risks. He then developed a theory that the department was responsible for a betrayal of Nationalist China, and he named Professor Owen Lattimore of The Johns Hopkins University as the principal agent of Soviet Russia in America and the architect of American policy that had led to the downfall of Chiang K'ai-shek. Challenged to produce evidence of these charges before a Senate committee, he was unable to give the name of any Communist in the Department of State, or to offer evidence that Professor Lattimore had a role in the making of American policy. Lattimore emphatically denied the charge made against him. The Democratic majority of the committee signed a report condemning McCarthy for making false and unfounded accusations, while committee Republicans were not so sure that McCarthy was entirely wrong. McCarthy was not at all daunted by Democratic disapproval.

CONTAINMENT IN EUROPE—NATO

Assailed by charges that they had not done enough to check Communism in China or at home, Truman and his advisers continued to take steps sufficiently forthright toward stopping their progress in Europe. In 1949 America assumed responsibility for the defense of several western European countries. It seemed prudent to warn Russia that military attack upon any one of them would compel the United States to take up arms. In April at Washington representatives of America, Britain, Canada, France, Belgium, the Netherlands, Luxembourg, Italy, Denmark, Norway, Iceland, and Portugal signed the North Atlantic Treaty. It declared that an attack upon any one of those countries would be considered as an attack upon all of them. It will be recalled that in 1948 the Senate had announced its willingness to enter into such engagements. In July, 1949 it ratified the treaty by a vote of 82 to 13. By its terms a North Atlantic Treaty Organization (NATO) was formed to assure effective common military action. Joined by Greece and Turkey in 1952, NATO became a barrier against Russian expansion. America, Britain, and France established another barrier that same year by helping the Germans who lived in the territory they controlled form a West German Republic with a capital at Bonn. Russia retaliated, setting up a German Democratic Republic, with a capital in the Russian zone of Berlin. Communist East Germany failed to prosper; democratic West Germany flourished and gave economic strength to western Europe generally. It seemed before the end of 1949 that means had been found to contain Communism in Europe. There was even a hint that it might recede there. In 1948 Marshal Tito had quarreled with the Moscow Communists and had been denounced by them. Remaining a Communist, he was determined to be master of Yugoslavia. He looked westward for help and received it. Conscious that an attack upon any of the NATO countries must lead to war and that the air fleets of America's Strategic Air Command would, in the event of such hostilities, in all likelihood drop nuclear bombs upon Russian cities, Stalin refrained from major adventures in Europe for several years.

CONTAINMENT IN ASIA

However, stubbornly blocked in Europe, the Communists aggressively undertook by force of arms to bring all of Korea under their control in 1950, and this precipitated the hard-fought Korean War. Its basic cause was, of course, Communist imperialism. It was steadily assumed in Moscow and other Communist capitals that the Red world revolution must come, and that it was entirely proper for Communists ruling over "peace-loving peoples" to use any and all means to bring it about. But why did the Communists venture to attack the Republic of Korea? They hoped to destroy that weak nation without any military challenge by America and the UN. That hope was based upon a grave miscalculation. It, in turn, seems to have been founded to a degree upon another miscalculation, by Dean G. Acheson, Secretary of State after George Marshall. Acheson believed immediately after 1949 that it was possible to restore the "historic friendship" between the United States and China by recognizing the Chinese Reds, and also that South Korea was not gravely endangered. The American troops occupying South Korea were withdrawn in 1949. Describing a perimeter of American defense in Asia that included Japan and Okinawa, Acheson publicly warned the Communists against attempting to cross it. However, he did not say that America would come to the aid of the Republic of Korea or of the Chinese Nationalists on Formosa. The American army in the Far East was weak, and he was anxious to avoid a ground war there, partly because American strength was heavily committed to the defense of Europe. He also believed that Communist China and Russia must sooner or later quarrel, because the Russians controlled several Chinese provinces, and because Chinese Communist leaders must eventually resent dictation from Moscow. He therefore thought that America should officially recognize Communist China and seek its friendship. Then the inevitable rift he foresaw between Peiping and Moscow would widen more rapidly, and Russia in consequence would be halted in Asia.

Whatever the validity of Acheson's thought for the long run in Asia, it did not accurately envisage the short run. The Chinese Communists did not seek an understanding with the United States immediately after their triumph over Chiang K'ai-shek. "The historic friendship" between China and America meant nothing to them except that America was an enemy of socialism. They furiously assailed "imperialistic. warmongering" America; Mao Tse-tung did not quickly display a desire to be a Chinese Marshal Tito. In February, 1950 the Russian and Chinese Reds signed an alliance by which the Soviet Union promised military aid to Communist China in the event that it was attacked by Japan or by any other nation (obviously America) supporting Japan. Moreover, the conclusion was reached in Moscow that neither America nor the UN would wish to fight a war in defense of South Korea against masses of Asian troops and to risk a nuclear conflict for such small cause. On June 25 the North Korean army, which had been trained and equipped by the Russians, crossed the 38th parallel, the line between North and South Korea, and rapidly pushed forward, easily overcoming weak resistance.

MILITARY CAMPAIGN IN KOREA

The invasion of South Korea, obviously begun with the approval of Communist China and Russia, was naked aggression. Its President, Syngman Rhee, begged that help be sent before it was too late. It was only too clear that the Communists were flouting the UN and challenging the United States. Were America to fail to come to the rescue of South Korea, faith in American promises to help stop the Communists must diminish everywhere. Both America and the UN moved with speed and decision. As it happened, Russia was then boycotting the Security Council, because the UN had refused to recognize Communist China in place of Nationalist China. There was no Russian delegate on hand to veto action by the Council. On the very day the invasion began the Council condemned it and demanded that the North Korean army withdraw. Two days later Truman ordered General MacArthur to send air and sea forces to the help of South Korea. It was clear that South Korea would soon fall completely into the hands of the Communists unless military action was swiftly taken. Truman's decision was firmly endorsed by Democrats and Republicans alike. It was accompanied by the passage of a resolution in the Security Council that called upon all UN members to furnish military forces to drive back the invaders. Thus the war became an international police action against aggression—America never formally declared war as a nation. Eventually sixteen members of the UN, including Canada and Turkey, sent troops to Korea. However, the burden of helping South Korea fell largely upon the United States, and the UN police action was also for America a war, though undeclared. It was, in fact, a very costly one. Five days after the North Koreans crossed the 38th parallel Truman had to tell MacArthur to use ground troops as well as airplanes and ships. Fighting on the ground continued for more than two years, and American losses were heavy.

Despite the celerity with which America and the UN reacted, the Communists seized most of South Korea, taking its capital, Seoul, on June 28, before MacArthur could scrape together enough strength to bring them to a halt. His garrison forces in Japan were thin. Moving with his usual energy, he managed to form a line of defense about the port of Pusan on the southeastern coast of Korea. During August and early September, with heterogeneous forces of South Koreans and Americans, he repelled massive Communist attacks. He inflicted very heavy casualties upon the Reds, and he established a firm beachhead for the gathering UN army. Entrusted with the task of executing the UN police action, after July, 1950, MacArthur was eager to finish his work quickly. Rapidly reinforced by sea and air, he took the offensive in mid-September. He boldly made a successful amphibious assault upon Inchon, far behind the Communist lines, and then ordered an advance from his beachhead. He scored a brilliant success. Heavily outnumbered but much better equipped than their enemies, his men drove the Communists back, recaptured Seoul on September 26, and reached the 38th parallel a few days later.

With the flight of the Reds beyond the 38th parallel America and the UN might have been able to put an end to hostilities. It was possible that the Korean Communists had been taught such a lesson that they would agree to stay to the north of the line. However, the UN Assembly, which had acquired power to act in the absence of decision by the Security Council, overwhelmingly voted on October 7 for the establishment of a united and democratically governed Korea. The UN desired that MacArthur crush the Communists in that country to settle its troubles permanently. The Assembly so acted despite a roundabout warning from Communist China that it would intervene to prevent the destruction of Communist North Korea. The war therefore continued. MacArthur's troops swept on from the 38th parallel, seized Pyongyang, the Communist capital, and moved forward toward Chinese Manchuria. On October 24, MacArthur began an all-out offensive in the hope of bringing the war to a swift conclusion.

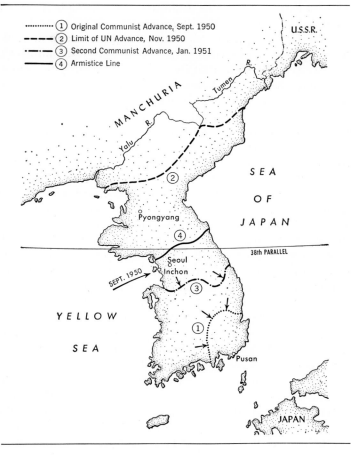

··········—① Original Communist Advance, Sept. 1950
— — —② Limit of UN Advance, Nov. 1950
—·—·—③ Second Communist Advance, Jan. 1951
————④ Armistice Line

WAR IN KOREA

Two days later tens of thousands of Chinese Communist "volunteers" who
had quietly advanced from Manchuria into the mountains of North Korea
counterattacked, along with the Korean Communists. Unprepared for such
a massive onslaught, MacArthur's forces were driven apart and backward.
Only the most desperate and resourceful fighting by them prevented a
disaster. Seoul and Inchon were again in the hands of the Communists
before they were checked.

TRUMAN AND MACARTHUR

The intervention of the Chinese Communists in behalf of the "peace-
loving" North Korean army posed far more than a serious military question
for the United States. General MacArthur knew that it would be difficult

and expensive, if it were possible at all, to drive the Chinese "volunteers" out of Korea so long as they could be supplied and reinforced indefinitely from Manchuria. There was no shortage of Chinese manpower. Believing in the necessity of decisive victory, he urged that Communist China be subjected to a naval blockade, that its bases in Manchuria be bombed from the air, and that Chiang K'ai-shek invade from Formosa. His opinion that counterblows be struck at Red China was shared by many at home. On the other hand, America's friends in the UN feared that they would lead to a total war with Red China and with Russia. They were reluctant even to declare Communist China to be an aggressor, and the UN Assembly did not do so until February, 1951. After much consulting with military and diplomatic experts, Truman chose to try to confine the war to Korea. At the beginning of the conflict he had ordered the navy to prevent a Communist attack upon Formosa and an attack by Chiang K'ai-shek upon the mainland of China. He knew that Chiang K'ai-shek was militarily weak. He was not at all sure that Russia would not come to the aid of Red China. To him it did not seem worthwhile to risk a general war. Instead, he chose merely to drive back the Communists in Korea and to inflict such heavy losses upon them that they would abandon the struggle.

Despite MacArthur's continuing opposition to it, Truman executed his plan to seek a limited victory. Greatly strengthened, the UN forces took the offensive again in the early months of 1951 and drove the Reds back to a line that crossed the 38th parallel. In the following June, after the Chinese and North Koreans had sustained immense losses, Soviet Russia suggested that they might accept an armistice, both sides withdrawing from the 38th parallel. Negotiations soon followed in Korea toward such an armistice. They were abandoned briefly, then resumed and carried on during many months. It seemed almost impossible to reach an agreement. Meanwhile fighting continued, gradually diminishing in violence, without any great gain by either side. An armistice was finally signed in 1953 by which South Korea was at least temporarily relieved from the threat of Red aggression. Before it was signed, Truman had left the Presidency.

The military career of Douglas MacArthur came to a swift close more than two years before the end of the Korean War. Disagreeing with his superiors regarding policy in 1950 and 1951, he did not hesitate to make public his own views. In October, 1950 Truman flew to Wake Island to meet the General and to try to eliminate the discord. It continued. Ordered to make no more public statements contradictory to positions taken by the President, MacArthur persisted. The great soldier would not be bridled, for he was sure that his superiors erred. On April 11, 1951, in accordance with the advice of his highest military and civilian officials, Truman exerted his authority as commander in chief and removed MacArthur from all his commands in the Far East. MacArthur came home to receive a hero's welcome; the nation was grateful to him for his great services.

America was militarily unprepared for the Korean War, and was even less ready in 1950 to carry all the military responsibilities entailed by the policy of containment. The outbreak of hostilities in the Far East stimulated American rearming. Truman undertook to increase the number of men in the nation's armed forces to 3,500,000; selective service was not only used, but became more or less permanent; and military production was vastly increased. Congress voted $35 billion in 1950 for national defense, of which some $10 billion was used to strengthen America's friends. In 1951 and 1952 much larger amounts were spent upon the armed forces, together with billions of dollars for foreign aid. So great was the effort of the nation that it spent $65 billion in 1952 and $75 billion in 1953. Although the Korean War was never a declared one—Truman did proclaim a state of emergency in December, 1950—the crisis of which it was the principal part was so great that many governmental controls were necessary. The Defense Production Act of September, 1950 gave the President authority not only to divert industry to the making of arms but, if necessary, to fix prices and wages. Under the direction of Charles E. Wilson, former president of the General Electric Company, industry did its job well—the American forces in Korea were far better equipped than their Communist adversaries. However, inflation, almost unchecked after 1946 and stimulated by the war, posed a difficult problem. Truman urged voluntary maintenance of prices and wages, but unsuccessfully. In January, 1951 controls were imposed upon both. They were only partly effective, largely because the public did not feel that the country was in great danger. Softened by Congress in the summer of 1951, controls slowed down the inflationary spiral, but did not stop it.

POLITICS AT HOME

The Korean War inevitably affected politics at home. It hurt the Democrats in the election of 1950, in which they suffered losses, although they managed to retain a majority in both houses of Congress. As the conflict continued, they were blamed for accumulating grievances. Inflation and wartime controls exasperated many. There was a feeling of frustration because the war was not quickly and easily won, and doubt increased that it was worthwhile to make sacrifices to stop the Reds in Korea. Republicans charged that Truman and Acheson had erred in their Far Eastern policy; they said not only that Nationalist China should have been supported and saved from the Reds, but that the Reds would not have invaded South Korea, had it been made clear that America would use force to stop them.

Senator McCarthy went further. In June, 1951 he suggested that the Democrats had been worse than incompetent in dealing with the Far East. He connected General George Marshall, a whole-souled patriot, with "a conspiracy so immense, an infamy so black, as to dwarf any in the history of man." Hurt by accusations that they harbored Communists in executive offices, the Democrats were also injured by scandals of a traditional kind. Graft and corruption in federal office were uncommon during the quarter century after the exposure of the misdeeds committed in Harding's Presidency. After 1949 evidence accumulated of "influence-peddling" and other forms of graft and misconduct in Washington, especially in the Internal Revenue Service. Corruption also was found in the Reconstruction Finance Corporation and in the Department of Justice. More than 200 members of the bureau of Internal Revenue, some of them in important posts, either resigned or were dismissed, and a few of them went to prison for accepting bribes. Truman was censured for permitting dishonesty and negligence in office; some of the delinquents were his personal acquaintances. He did not move rapidly enough against them to satisfy the public, and he was held responsible for the "mess in Washington."

ELECTION OF 1952

As the election of 1952 approached, it was apparent that the Republicans had an excellent opportunity to regain the supremacy in Washington they had lost in the Great Depression. The Republican nomination for the Presidency was therefore eagerly sought. General MacArthur wanted it, and was supported by some of the more conservative Republicans. Governor Earl Warren of California, able and so moderate as a Republican that he pleased many Democrats, desired it. Harold Stassen continued to long for the Presidency. However, the principal candidates for the nomination turned out to be Senator Robert Taft and General Eisenhower. Taft, honest and industrious, was the idol of many Midwestern Republicans, the man favored by party "wheelhorses." Taft's friends wanted, so far as possible, a return to "the good old days." They rejected the Fair Deal and still disliked important parts of the New Deal. They wished to reduce America's commitments abroad, except in Asia, although they were strongly anti-Communistic. Eisenhower was the favorite of Eastern Republicans, of those who gave allegiance to the UN and who did not shy away from commitments abroad, of those who believed that valuable parts of the New and Fair Deals should be retained and improved, and of those who desired to make a Republican victory as certain as possible. It was doubtful that Taft could be elected. That fact in the end gave the nomination to Eisenhower. He was easily the most popular of America's generals in World War II, and he could hardly fail to win. Persuaded that it was his duty to fight against Republican isolationist tendencies and Democratic corruption, he reluctantly entered politics. At the Republican convention in Chicago a very large minority of the delegates favored Taft, although the convention named Eisenhower on the first ballot, and with him Richard M. Nixon for the Vice-Presidency.

Several men were eager to lead the Democratic party, despite its liabilities, in the campaign. Truman was constitutionally available. He could not hope to repeat the "miracle" of 1948, had he wished to try. He announced that almost eight years in the Presidency would be enough for him, but he exerted influence in the selection of the Democratic candidate. Most active of all the Democratic aspirants was Senator Estes Kefauver of Tennessee, who had gained reputation as the head of a Senate committee that investigated crime and corruption. Kefauver ran well in several of his party's primaries; wearing a coonskin cap, he sought support as a homespun man. Truman opposed him. Another principal contestant for the nomination was Vice-President Alben W. Barkley, much loved in his party. However, as the convention gathered in Chicago, labor leaders came out against him on the ground that he was too old. Truman and many other politicians then rallied behind Governor Adlai E. Stevenson of Illinois, although he was not at all eager to do battle against Eisenhower. After Kefauver had led on two ballots, Stevenson was named. For the Vice-Presidency the Democrats chose Senator John J. Sparkman of Alabama. They forthrightly stood by the Truman record and pledges.

There was nothing homespun about Stevenson. Of a family long prominent among the Democrats, he was a man of means, a graduate of Princeton and of the law school of Northwestern University, a veteran public servant, a polished and witty speaker. He was an effective campaigner, making a series of eloquent and pungent speeches in which he incisively discussed the issues. He quickly won ardent followers among intellectuals, and he secured the enduring esteem of many independent-minded men and women. He had no remarkably new ideas to offer; he was a devout internationalist; and he proposed to consolidate the domestic reforms of the past rather than to urge added ones.

Eisenhower proved to be neither sophisticated nor adept in oratory. However, he displayed a warm, friendly, and magnetic personality, and overcame fear that as a military man he would be dictatorial in the White House. He persuaded Senator Taft that he was a true and sound Republican. In mid-campaign he and other Republican leaders became alarmed because of a revelation that Richard Nixon had accepted gifts amounting to $18,000 from various California Republicans. Why were gifts made to him? Perhaps he should be asked to resign as a Vice-Presidential candidate. Nixon explained that the money was a fund to enable him to fight against Communists and fellow travelers. Eisenhower felt the explanation was quite acceptable. The gifts did not become a major issue, particularly since it soon became known that as governor of Illinois Stevenson had quietly added private money to public salaries in order to persuade able state officials to remain at their posts. Eisenhower scored by denouncing "the mess in Washington," although Stevenson was hardly responsible for it. He satisfied many farmers by a promise that they would receive parity "in the market place," whatever that phrase meant. He pleased many by pledging a great effort to balance the federal budget and to put an end to inflation. He also won favor by his stand on foreign affairs. Endorsing the Truman foreign policy, he felt that it had been badly executed. He asserted that under his leadership America would take the aggressive diplomatically, and he indicated that something would be done to liberate peoples captive behind the Iron Curtain in Europe. Toward the end of the campaign he made an especially potent appeal to the voters, saying that, if he were elected, he would immediately go to Korea to try to find means to bring the Korean War to an end.

Eisenhower was an easy victor. Stevenson received 27,314,992 popular votes, more than any earlier Democratic candidate had ever obtained, but Eisenhower had 33,936,252, and he won overwhelmingly in the electoral college, 442 to 89. So disliked in the South was the stand of the Democratic party in behalf of the Negroes, and so well liked was Eisenhower, that he carried Virginia, Tennessee, Florida, and Texas. Eisenhower's popularity was such that his party, much less esteemed than he, won control of both houses of Congress by narrow majorities. It was apparent that the Republicans, returning to power in Washington, had not been given a mandate to destroy all the works of their rivals. Eisenhower did not intend to try.

61 EISENHOWER THE PACIFIER

A MODERATE IN WASHINGTON

Born in Texas and reared in Kansas, Dwight D. Eisenhower was 62 years old when he became President. A graduate of West Point, he had spent all of his mature years in military service, except for a brief period after World War II when he was uncongenially president of Columbia University, before he entered politics. He was a conscientious and competent professional soldier rather than a great one; he won renown neither as a strategist nor as a leader of troops in battle. He excelled as the director of a great war machine in Europe by making the best use of the talents of the officers who served under him. He displayed a remarkable gift for securing harmony among them. As a general, he was a good politician; as a politician, he remained something of a general. He believed in teamwork, each person having and performing precise duties. Entering the Presidency, he expected to work with rather than to dominate Congress, to leave smaller decisions to subordinates, and to make important ones collectively. Not an ardent party man—it was doubtful before 1952 whether he was a Democrat or a Republican—he hoped to work in concert with Democrats as well as Republicans. He did not get all the har-

879

mony he desired, nor could he avoid partisan combat. He discovered to his vexation that a President must be concerned with small as well as great matters. Nevertheless, as a moderate, or progressive, conservative, he dealt quite successfully with domestic questions and his popularity increased rather than diminished. His party did not gain strength with him, but he was often able to secure the help of many Democrats. "Ike" neither spoke nor wrote well, but he was friendly, almost always good-humored, and socially democratic. Whatever historians in the light of perspective may say about the Eisenhower record in foreign affairs, none will deny that he softened political and social antagonism at home.

Democrats who doubted that Eisenhower would be a moderate conservative, and feared that the President would provide a front for control of the nation by business interests, found confirmation for their alarm in the choices Eisenhower made for his Cabinet. It was largely one of businessmen, containing, critics of the President said, "eight millionaires and a plumber." The "plumber," Martin Durkin, a labor union leader chosen to show that Eisenhower was not hostile to labor, soon resigned. The eight millionaires were not all actually such, but Eisenhower's Cabinet did resemble that of Warren G. Harding, except that there was no Albert Fall or Harry Daugherty in it. John Foster Dulles, a veteran student of foreign affairs, was made Secretary of State; he was a corporation lawyer as well as a diplomat. Eisenhower's chief financial adviser was Secretary of the Treasury George Humphrey, a rich Ohio industrialist. At the head of the Department of Defense Eisenhower placed Charles E. Wilson, who had been president of General Motors. Had Eisenhower steadily followed the advice of Humphrey, Wilson, and others like them, he might indeed have tried to lead the nation, with respect to domestic questions, back to the Twenties. However, the President had advisers of varying complexions, including his brother, Milton Eisenhower, president of Pennsylvania State University and later of Johns Hopkins. Eisenhower the President behaved very much like Eisenhower the General. Listening as patiently as he could to all sorts of counsel, including that of congressional leaders, he sought above all to reconcile conflicting views and interests. He was surprisingly successful. His course was somewhat erratic, but in general it followed a middle way.

INFLUENCE AND COMMUNISTS IN GOVERNMENT

Eisenhower cleaned up the mess in Washington, so far as graft and influence peddling were concerned, although the problem of the mess posed unexpected difficulties for him. Most of the Democratic delinquents had been driven from office before he was inaugurated. To his vexation he discovered that Republicans were as likely as Democrats to violate public trusts, and that some members of his team did not live up to his own standard of morality. His first Secretary of the Air Force, Harold E. Talbott, was forced to resign when it was learned that he had used his official position to foster his private business interests. Later Sherman Adams, Eisenhower's principal assistant in the White House, was also driven to resign. He had incautiously accepted gifts and loans from businessman Bernard Goldfine, who sought to buy his influence. Adams had to go, even though he had done very little to help his would-be corruptor; he had been indiscreet rather than dishonest. Some other minor figures who entered office with the President also were driven out. Eisenhower insisted that his people be "as clean as a hound's tooth," and sadly learned that the line between proper and improper conduct in office is often a thin one, and that Democrats as well as Republicans could cry "corruption." It remained a problem and a political issue, as of yore; the ever-growing power of the federal government, exerted in innumerable ways, made abuse of it only too likely.

Eisenhower also encountered trouble when he sought to settle the issue of Communists in government. Soon after taking office, he ordered a thorough cleansing of the executive branch of security risks. He gave authority to the heads of all government agencies, whether or not they were concerned with national security, to discharge employees, after a proper hearing, for various reasons, indicating lack of reliability. Association with Communists could be a ground for dismissal. Immoral conduct, habitual drunkenness, and addiction to drugs were others, since individuals beset by personal weakness would be subject to Communist blackmail. More than 6000 people either were discharged or resigned from federal service before the end of 1954. Injustice was undoubtedly done to some innocent and harmless folk who resigned rather than subject themselves to inquiries they considered humiliating. Democrats contended that it was illegal to remove persons who worked in offices that had nothing directly to do with the national safety on such grounds, a view later taken by the Supreme Court. They assailed witchhunting. Nor did the decisive action taken by Eisenhower satisfy those in Congress who had busied themselves in committees hunting Reds. Senator Joseph McCarthy, searching for Communists, claimed that he found evidence of Red infiltration in books and broadcasts sent overseas to win friends for America, in the army, and even in the Central Intelligence Agency, which was charged with the major responsibility for American espionage and counterintelligence. Exasperated, the President at length struck back. The Department of the Army accused McCarthy of using his influence to get special privileges for David Schine, who had helped McCarthy in his investigations and who had been drafted into service. A Senate hearing of McCarthy's charges against the Army and the Army's charges against McCarthy went on for weeks during the spring of 1954. Nationally televised, it brought no credit to the antagonists. However, McCarthy had overreached himself. Many Republicans who had not objected to his efforts to embarrass the Truman regime would not countenance his attacks upon Eisenhower's. A Senate committee presided over by conservative Republican Arthur Watkins of Utah reported that McCarthy had twice displayed contempt for the Senate, and that body then voted to condemn McCarthy. McCarthy's influence then rapidly faded. He died in 1957, but charges of communism in government, though muted for a time, persisted.

RESISTING "CREEPING SOCIALISM"

Although some of the more conservative Republicans found fault with Eisenhower because he turned against Senator McCarthy and because he was too much of an internationalist, most Republicans in the business community were pleased by his economic policies. As he had said he would, he sought to check inflation, balance the budget, and reduce taxes. Partly because Secretary of the Treasury Humphrey, with the help of the Federal Reserve Board, followed a "tight money" policy—Humphrey raised the interest rate on government bonds to attract capital from private enterprise—inflation was halted for about three years. When it resumed, it proceeded at a slower pace. Eisenhower did not succeed in balancing the budget for all of the eight years he spent in office, but he managed it for three of them and kept down deficits in the others. Although the national debt continued to rise, its growth was annoying rather than alarming, for the income of the American people rose much more rapidly. Moreover, although taxes were not cut several times, as they had been in the Twenties, they were reduced once, in 1954. If Republicans of the business community did not get all they wanted, they had reason to be pleased. They were the more satisfied because Secretary of the Treasury Humphrey was one of themselves and presumably did his best to execute their wishes. What discontent they felt was submerged in waves of prosperity. The total personal income of the American people moved steadily upward during the Eisenhower era. Estimated at $228 billion in 1950, it soared to $310 billion in 1955, and to $383 billion in 1959.

Eisenhower also did something toward stopping what he called "creeping socialism," thereby pleasing Southern Democrats as well as Republicans. He favored private production of electricity as against public, and opposed expansion of the power-making facilities of the Tennessee Valley Authority. If power had to be publicly produced, he preferred that it be done under state or local control, with the federal government acting only when it alone was competent. He spoke of a partnership between government and private persons in the development of both electric and atomic power. With reference to offshore oil, he desired no partnership. After World War II, the exploitation of deposits of petroleum beneath waters adjacent to the shores of California, Texas, Louisiana, and Florida created a burning question. President Truman twice vetoed bills passed by Congress to vest ownership of it in the adjacent states. The deposits were especially rich on the shores of the Gulf of Mexico, and Southern Democrats, because they wished the oil to be privately exploited and because they were champions of states' rights, angrily condemned Truman. They were made happy by Eisenhower, who in 1953 gladly signed a law that transferred control of the deposits within a three-mile limit (ten and one-half miles for Texas and Florida because of treaty stipulations) to the adjacent states.

The least happy of those who had voted for Eisenhower in 1952 were farmers who had been comforted by his assurance that he stood for agricultural parity "in the market place." Farmers who interpreted this pledge made to mean that he would favor any and all steps necessary, as New and Fair Dealers had, to give them the parity of 1909–1914, were disappointed. Americans who lived on the land did not share equally with others in the general prosperity of the Eisenhower era. Farm population was declining steadily, while cities and suburbs were growing rapidly. Nevertheless, and despite acreage controls, farmers raised more of several basic products than they could sell. American efficiency in agriculture was such that a farmer could raise four times as many potatoes per acre in 1955 as he had been able to in 1925. If farmers were to have the ideal parity so many of them desired, subsidies and controls were necessary. Eisenhower disliked both, and his Secretary of Agriculture, Ezra Taft Benson of Utah, was even more hostile to them. Between 1949 and 1954 the producers of basic crops were assured of prices equivalent to 90 percent. Benson declared that such price supports encouraged surpluses and that they ought to be made flexible under his direction. Flexibility meant lowering the supports so as to persuade farmers to reduce their output where surpluses existed. Eisenhower backed Benson and secured for him the authority he desired in the Agricultural Act of 1954. However, the Democrats gained so many friends among the farmers by demanding that 90 percent parity be maintained that Benson made little use of the power vested in him. Controls, price supports, and surpluses continued. A law of 1956 by which $1,200,000,000 was given to farmers who turned croplands into pasturage or forest made little difference. The farm problem persisted. It is doubtful that Eisenhower became seriously unpopular among the farmers as a consequence; they shared to a degree in the general American prosperity of the 1950s.

LABOR AND SOCIAL PROGRESS

It was not to be expected that Eisenhower would entirely please organized labor, and he did not. Union officers charged that he packed the National Labor Relations Board in favor of management. They were also unhappy because he made no great effort to revise the Taft-Hartley law. However, James P. Mitchell, who succeeded the "plumber" as Secretary of Labor, proved to be satisfactory to workmen. He, Eisenhower, and a Democratic Congress raised the federal minimum wage to $1.00 per hour in 1956. Workmen received steadily improved pay, together with "fringe benefits" such as vacations on pay and health insurance, while "Ike" was in office. It is to be suspected that he was better liked by labor than by its leaders. Be that as it may, the power of the unions continued to grow. In 1955 the AFL and the CIO combined to form the AFL-CIO with something like 15,000,000 members. The men at the head of the new federation were able and responsible. One of them, Walter Reuther, devised an ingenious plan to promote industrial peace and persuaded the General Motors Company to accept it in 1955. It called for contracts between management and unions lasting several years, with wages adjusted annually in accordance with the cost of living. The scheme was soon generally adopted in the automobile industry and in others as well. Strikes were uncommon while Eisenhower was in the Presidency. Neither he nor anyone else found an easy answer to one problem that became acute in the later 1950s, corruption among union "bosses." Several such bosses controlled unions so tightly that they were able, almost with impunity, to misappropriate union funds.

Hostile to the Fair Deal, Eisenhower nevertheless favored federal action toward social reform. In 1953 he signed a bill that created the Department of Health, Education, and Welfare, and appointed as its head a woman, Mrs. Oveta Culp Hobby. In 1954, under his leadership, Congress increased the benefits paid to the aged under the Social Security Act and made clergymen, farmers, and state and local employees eligible to receive them; and two years later he accepted further changes in the Social Security Act proposed by a Democratic Congress that permitted women to receive retirement pensions at the age of 62. In 1954 Eisenhower secured the passage of a housing act which made it possible to buy or build a home for those who had little cash. After 1955 the President also urged Congress to supply funds to help build schools—he was unsuccessful, although classrooms were becoming increasingly crowded because of a rapidly growing population. Eisenhower likewise used his authority against the segregation of Negroes.

Conservative Republicans, together with Southern Democrats, checked some of Eisenhower's proposals for social reform, but he secured their consent to the building of the St. Lawrence Seaway and of a vast network of federal highways. The Seaway had been blocked in Congress for a quarter of a century. At last Canada insisted that it be built, preferably by Canada and the United States, but if necessary by Canada alone. American steel interests that desired easier access to iron ore in Labrador urged that the Seaway be constructed. In 1954 Eisenhower obtained the approval of Congress. Under joint Canadian-American control the Seaway was largely completed by 1960. As early as 1959 oceangoing vessels docked at Chicago and Duluth. By that time construction crews were busily engaged in carrying out the President's highway program, endorsed by Congress in 1956. It called for the building of more than 40,000 miles of "superhighways" over a period of 16 years at an estimated expense of more than $33 billion. Nine-tenths of the cost was to be borne by the federal government, the states paying the remainder and managing construction. Expensive though the program was, it could be justified, because the nation's roads had become quite inadequate for an ever-growing traffic.

However well they might be built, the new superhighways could not offer easy access to all of the states, for Eisenhower also signed bills by which Alaska and Hawaii, long refused entrance into the Union, became states, in 1959 and 1960 respectively. The fact that they were not contiguous to the "heartland" of America, the fewness of the Alaskans, and the heterogeneous population of Hawaii had served as arguments against their admission. In the 1950s these arguments no longer carried conviction. Considerations of partisan advantage caused further delay, but the wishes of the inhabitants of the two territories, national pride, and a desire to assert beyond question that Alaska and Hawaii must remain American soil had their effect. Completely abandoning their colonial character, Alaska and Hawaii were the 49th and 50th states to be admitted.

REELECTION

So near to the middle, so sensitive to opinion upon both domestic and foreign policy was the Eisenhower regime that it made few bitter enemies. It did not entirely satisfy the most conservative of the Republicans, nor did it please ardent Northern Democrats. However, Eisenhower was able to work amicably with conservative Democrats and with moderate ones such as Samuel Rayburn and Lyndon Johnson, party leaders in the House of Representatives and the Senate respectively. The effects of Eisenhower moderation and prosperity upon the voters were rather curious. He became more popular, but his party did not. The voters favored the Democrats and the President. They elected Democratic majorities in both houses of Congress in 1954, 1956, and 1958, but they kept Republican Eisenhower in the executive mansion as long as they could.

In 1956 the Democrats again put forward Adlai Stevenson for the Presidency. He had lost favor with former President Truman, who endorsed Governor Averell Harriman, a devoted disciple of Franklin Roosevelt. Truman had reached the conclusion that Stevenson was too near the middle with respect to domestic questions. However, Stevenson had acquired a great personal following, and he was more acceptable to the Southern Democrats than any other Northern Democrat of stature. After Stevenson defeated Senator Estes Kefauver in a party primary in California, his nomination was assured. At the Democratic national convention in Chicago he was named on the first ballot, and Kefauver was selected for the Vice-Presidency. Shortly afterward, the Republicans enthusiastically put forward Eisenhower for a second term and renominated Richard Nixon with less heartiness. In the campaign Stevenson again demonstrated his remarkable ability as a speaker, displaying both a grasp of the issues and the wit for which he had become renowned. He proved again that he was a much more sophisticated man than Eisenhower. More friendly to the Fair Deal than was the President, he offered no clearcut distinction between himself and Eisenhower on matters of foreign policy. In the main he contended that he would do better what the President was already doing. His argument gained strength because Eisenhower had suffered a heart attack in 1955 and had undergone an emergency operation to remove an intestinal obstruction in 1956. Neither the state of Eisenhower's health nor his lack of verbal ingenuity affected the result. While Stevenson was liked and esteemed, Eisenhower was reelected by a larger margin than in 1952. He secured 35,585,316 popular votes to 26,031,322 for Stevenson; he carried 41 states, including five in the South, which threatened to abandon its Democratic solidity; and he won an overwhelming victory in the electoral college, 457 to 73. Despite his age and his physical difficulties Eisenhower was able to continue through his second term as he had in his first.

PROSPERITY AND GROWTH

An important ingredient in the enduring popularity of Eisenhower was the economic progress of the nation. He and his advisers struggled against both inflation and depression. At times it seemed that it would be almost impossible to avoid both. In the large, however, they won both battles. Prices rose again after Eisenhower's reelection, though not very rapidly; there were recessions, but they were so mild that they hardly deserved the name. When the number of unemployed reached 4,000,000, there was alarm, even though the number of those at work remained steadily above 62,000,000 during the late 1950s. The recessions proved to be slight dips between rising waves of prosperity. In the late 1950s the national debt moved upward toward $300 billion and the federal budget threatened to reach $100 billion. But such figures did not seem quite so staggering as they might have in the past, since the personal income of the American people rapidly advanced toward $400 billion per annum. It was often suggested in the 1930s, and even in the 1940s, that a nation could not have both guns and butter. In the 1950s America spent vast sums for defense, foreign aid, and internal improvements, but most Americans could buy more than butter. As the decade ended, they were better fed, better housed, and better clothed than they had ever been before. Many families owned—or were making payments upon—two automobiles, and the number of those that owned a boat was soaring. Homes without a radio or a television set had become unusual. In most of them electric lighting, the refrigerator, central heating, and all sorts of gadgets that put an end to drudgery were taken as a matter of course. Long strides had been taken toward the attainment of social security. Regarded as a whole, the economic scene seemed bright.

Marxist predictions that American capitalism, like all other forms of capitalism, must collapse, did not come true in the 1950s. Instead, it stimulated an almost astonishing economic revival in western Europe, where American gifts, loans, machines, and techniques were employed with great success. Moreover, the western European peoples helped themselves remarkably. As early as 1953 they formed a steel community, and in 1957 France, West Germany, Italy, the Netherlands, Belgium, and Luxembourg, tearing down tariff barriers, created the European Common Market. Industry grew swiftly in the Common Market countries. To be sure, as the decade drew to an end, the American economic outlook was comparatively less favorable than it had been in the past. The Soviet Union threatened to catch up with the United States in the production of steel, and the rate of economic growth was higher both in Russia and western Europe than it was in America. There was concern among American economists because the nation was becoming more and more dependent upon foreign sources of raw materials, and because the American system laid such heavy emphasis upon consumption. A steady drain upon the American gold reserve caused by huge expenditures abroad—America spent more than $50 billion for economic and military aid to Europe between 1945 and 1960—aroused concern. On the whole, however, the economic condition of the Americans remained enviable to other peoples.

Associated with the massive growth of the American economy, and in part a cause of it, was a rapid increase in the number of Americans after World War II. During the Great Depression the number enlarged slowly. In 1940 the census count was 131,669,275, a figure which indicated that population had grown by less than 9,000,000 during the preceding decade. In 1950, however, census gatherers found in America no fewer than 150,-

697,361 persons, and there were more than 180 million by the early 1960s. After 1943 there were proportionately more marriages, more children per marriage, and more Americans living longer lives. In the 1930s, noting that the Americans were reproducing less rapidly than other peoples, a pessimistic observer might reasonably suggest that they were in some danger of committing national suicide. A generation later American students of population were not alarmed lest there be too few Americans; many of them were worried lest the whole human race breed beyond its living space. At the end of the sixth decade of the century the earth supplied a home of some sort to almost 3,000,000,000 people. If it remained at peace and if births were not controlled, it was feared that humanity would place too great a burden upon its natural and scientific resources.

Although augmenting numbers supplied economic stimulus, they posed immediate domestic problems as well as global questions. The Americans were becoming an urban and suburban people, and the impact of added bodies was particularly felt in cities and towns. By 1960 less than one American in ten was engaged in agriculture. The center of American population was still moving westward, but toward the cities of the Pacific Coast—it was expected that California would pass New York in population in 1962 or 1963—rather than toward mines and farms. Concentration in metropolitan areas aggravated traffic difficulties, social tensions, and crime. In 1960 the city dweller became a criminal three times as often as a rural inhabitant. At that time the number of major crimes committed per annum was reaching toward 2,000,000. Cities encountered economic as well as social distress; flight to the suburbs deprived them of hundreds of thousands of prosperous families and of tax revenues as well. By 1960 it was being suggested that the federal government must help the cities solve their transportation as well as their housing problems; some would have it that a Secretary for Urban Affairs was needed in the President's Cabinet.

A CHANGING SOCIETY

That crime flourished after the mid-century indicates that all was not well in the family, despite prosperity and a relatively high birth rate, and such was the case. After World War II there was approximately one divorce for every four marriages, and broken homes nourished juvenile delinquency, which all too often blossomed into adult misconduct. Another source of juvenile delinquency was the neglected home. While it was gratifying that the number of the employed remained high during the late 1950s, it was not quite so pleasing that one-third of them were females. Both parents went out to work from many homes, and the young in them were frequently neglected. Too often adults had too much work to do, and children not enough. The teen-aged, deprived of parental affection, discipline, and the benefits of healthy work, misbehaved more frequently than had American youth in the past. That juvenile delinquency prevailed in other countries at the same time—it was to be found in Moscow as well as in New York—was not very comforting. America proportionately had more of it. Teen-aged gangster killings in New York City frequently made headlines, and the number of major crimes committed by persons under 20 years of age disturbed the thoughtful.

Pessimists—or realists—who saw a decline in the morals of youth in the 1950s found causes for it other than parental neglect. They cited television as a special instrument of Satan, receiving assistance from the movies, "paperbacks," and magazines. Censorship had been discouraged by judicial tribunals, especially the United States Supreme Court, and writings and pictures circulated freely that would at an earlier time have been generally condemned as obscene or pornographic. "Girlie" magazines and cheap paperback books luridly dealing with sex and violence could be bought in thousands of drug stores. The movies less stridently stressed the same themes, but nudity upon the screen shocked many older people. They might derive consolation from the fact that the movies tended to lose rather than to gain customers. They could not find comfort from any loss in the popularity of television. It was a major industry after 1951, when it became possible to transmit its programs across the continent. Thereafter commercial television stations sprang up rapidly; organized in chains, there were 653 of them in 1960. By that time houses without a television mast were in the minority; there were more than 50 million receiving sets in America. What they received was commonly not very edifying. Financed by advertising, television offered principally soap opera, light comedy, Westerns, detective stories, and old movies. Much of what television purveyed was banal; too often it portrayed sadistic violence. Critics charged that television, in order to attract as many viewers as possible, was aimed at "the lowest common denominator." They saw it as a "wasteland," also as a potent vehicle of sinister suggestion. Commercial television had its brighter side, for it offered news broadcasts, opera, symphony orchestras, weather reports, and much innocent entertainment. How to make it more beneficial socially posed an awkward problem.

Were the American people "going to the dogs"? They were still going to church. In fact, if church membership is any measure of the level of public morality, the Americans were becoming ethically superior. At the beginning of the century hardly more than a third of them officially belonged to a church; in 1960 almost two-thirds were reported to be members. While religious statistics are highly untrustworthy, it is apparent that church affiliation had become more popular. There is reason to believe that the Roman Catholic and the evangelical Protestant sects especially had grown in numbers. Whatever might be the facts about religious connection, it would appear that membership was not matched by attendance and fervor. It is probable that the churches had less moral influence than they had had in the past.

EDUCATION AND THE ARTS

No institution felt the burdens and strains of postwar life more than did the schools. In 1960 the public elementary and secondary schools had about 35,000,000 students enrolled, and there were approximately 125,000 such schools in the United States. Merely to provide buildings, teachers, and equipment was a staggering task, one that the states and school districts found increasingly difficult to bear, so much so that demands for federal aid to education became ever more vigorous. Parochial and other private schools also felt the weight of sheer numbers. Double shifts were not uncommon in congested areas. But the problems of the schools were not confined to the physical. In an increasingly complex world it was necessary to raise the standard of instruction, which was done amidst much discussion regarding its aims and methods. A happy change was increased emphasis on science, mathematics, and foreign languages.

The colleges and universities also suffered a physical strain after World War II. By 1960 there were some 3,500,000 students enrolled in institutions of higher learning and it was estimated that the figure would double by 1970. Professors and deans managed as best they could on the campus, while the president more frequently than ever scurried off to solicit funds to build more classrooms, throw up more dormitories, and employ more professors. Sometimes it was necessary for a professor to lecture to two bodies of students simultaneously, one being in contact only by radio. During the decade after World War II the state institutions, because they were able to get additional funds from the public, were better able to do their work. Private colleges and universities, dependent largely on tuition for their support, were often hard-pressed financially. However, their situation improved rapidly after 1955, for they were able at the same time to raise tuition, lift admission standards, and restrict enrollment in accordance with their facilities. Toward the end of the 1950s the universities and colleges began to lay plans for the following decade. They had largely solved their physical problems, and they had even raised the salaries of professors to respectable levels. What would they do when still larger waves of students struck them in the 1960s? To many more federal aid— they were already receiving handsome help in one way and another— seemed indispensable.

Congestion on the campus, despite the difficulties it raised, was a sign of intellectual and cultural progress. This was evident in many other ways, although in short perspective the world of letters and the arts seemed to be in transition rather than in flower at the middle of the century. At the end of the 1950s the literary gods Robert Frost, William Faulkner, T. S. Eliot, Ernest Hemingway, and John Dos Passos of the Twenties and Thirties were still alive, and at least Frost and Faulkner remained significantly productive. But their successors as literary lights had not yet clearly emerged. Among the more conspicuous novelists were Norman Mailer, John O'Hara, Herman Wouk, Robert Penn Warren, and James Gould Cozzens. Whether they or any other novelists of their generation would reach the stature of Faulkner remained doubtful. The reputation and influence of playwright Tennessee Williams seemed more firmly established; dealing with the sordid and the decadent, he displayed power, and appeared to be a not unworthy successor to Eugene O'Neill. At least in terms of technique the literary future was bright, for criticism had become sophisticated. Expertise in art and music was also widespread by the end of the 1950s. Abstract art was in almost undisputed ascendancy, although it remained a compound of mysteries to the layman, who found it perplexing and amusing rather than appealing. "Modern" music, which had not displaced Bach and Beethoven as abstract painting had replaced Rubens and Rembrandt, also puzzled the unsophisticated. If the world of music was in transition, symphonies and operas hallowed by tradition were more popular than ever. However one might assess the condition of literature, the arts, and music in America in 1960, the nation was not a cultural wasteland, and it was obviously unnecessary for American genius and talent in such pursuits to seek a comfortable and inspiring environment abroad.

EMPHASIS ON SCIENCE

In 1960 there could be no question about the achievement of American science and engineering. In fact, after World War II science and engineering made great strides throughout the civilized world, and man began to move into space. Advances in medicine were remarkable. The making of a vaccine by Dr. Jonas Salk in 1953 that effectively checked poliomyelitis (infantile paralysis) astonished a public that was rapidly becoming accustomed to wondrous discoveries. Extraordinary results came from new methods in brain and heart surgery. It became possible by surgery to help some of those who suffered from Parkinson's Disease, as well as some of the mentally deranged. Defective and damaged hearts were repaired. Progress was made in the treatment of cancers, and hope blossomed that something might even be done to relieve the distress of the common cold. Scientists delved into the secrets of the infinitely small and the vastly large. The origin of life as the human being knows it no longer seemed to be utterly beyond understanding, and the use of atomic power was spreading. American submarines propelled by it made their way under the North Pole, and an American craft circumnavigated the globe without rising to the surface. No one could safely predict all the uses to which atomic energy might be put. While it was feared by many that man would use it to destroy himself, it could be hoped that he would decline to use hydrogen bombs as he had refused to resort to poison gas and germ weapons in World War II.

Like the science of atoms, that of rocketry as it developed in the 1950s was at least two-edged. The rocket was by no means new. It had been used as a weapon for centuries, and its potentiality as a means to penetrate beyond the earth's atmosphere had been pointed out as early as 1915 by the American scientist Dr. Robert H. Goddard, who proved that a rocket could move in a vacuum. German scientists, learning how to propel rockets by means of liquid fuel, not only gave Hitler a powerful weapon in the form of the V2, but opened the way for the exploration of space. With the assistance of captured German scientists, both Soviet Russia and the United States sought to make rockets that could be propelled and controlled over vast distances. Both nations were successful, Russia scoring a series of remarkable "firsts." In October, 1957, the Russians used a rocket to place the satellite Sputnik I in orbit, to be followed a month later by their Sputnik II. The following January America's Explorer I took its place as a satellite. Thereafter both countries created many satellites, using them to secure information about space. In October, 1959, the Russian Lunik III circled the moon and sent back a photograph of its far side, never before seen by man. His own entrance into space followed swiftly. After animals had been sent into it and safely brought back to earth in capsules, it became clear that human beings could do likewise. In April, 1961, Russia's Yuri Gagarin went around the earth three times in a capsule and returned safely, and in August the Soviet astronaut Gherman Titov spent more than 24 hours in orbit about the earth, also returning safely. In the spring of 1962 the American astronaut John H. Glenn, Jr. successfully completed a journey similar to that of Gagarin. By that time it seemed quite possible that human beings making use of spacecraft would reach and return from the moon within a decade. From a space-station on the moon exploration of the solar system of which the earth is a part would become feasible. The highly imaginative conceived —what seemed to be an impossibility—that man would some day travel to planets in other solar systems.

WITH ALL DELIBERATE SPEED

Science was opening seemingly endless vistas, but it could provide no immediate answer to many human problems. One of them was that of the relationship between whites and Negroes in America. The Negro forged steadily ahead in the 1940s and 1950s. Especially noteworthy was his progress in the South, where he was still not much more than a second-class citizen at the end of World War II. A great turning point for the Southern Negro was a Supreme Court decision in May, 1954, in the case of *Brown* v. *Topeka,* which declared that racial segregation in public schools deprived Negroes of the "equal protection" guaranteed by the Fourteenth Amendment. A year later the Court announced that such segregation must be ended with "deliberate speed." The Court was assailed because it overturned its own earlier decisions approving separate —and equal—facilities in education, and its order that segregation in the schools be ended with "deliberate speed" was strenuously resisted. It was rapidly obeyed in states such as Kentucky and Kansas that had legally required racial separation; in the Upper South "token" integration came rather promptly; in the Lower South there was no integration whatever as late as 1960. By that time it seemed that school segregation on the basis of race or color was moving toward its end with "deliberate speed." Threats to close the public schools rather than obey the rulings of the court had commonly been made in the South, but were followed by action in only one county of Virginia. The change did not come without commotion. In 1957 President Eisenhower found it necessary to send troops to protect nine Negro students enrolled by a federal court order in the Central High School of Little Rock, Arkansas. By 1960 private schools, colleges, and universities in the South were beginning to open their doors to Negroes. In the late 1950s racial separation on trains and buses in the South was also rapidly decreasing, in part because of a ruling against it by the Interstate Commerce Commission. Also, federal pressure to help the Negroes to register and to vote in the South was having an effect.

Amidst turbulence, and not without violence, the Negro was achieving in the South the political and social status he had long had in the Northern states. Indeed, the problem of race relations, so long peculiar to the South, was rapidly becoming a question uniformly the same throughout the nation. So many Negroes were moving from the South to Northern and Western cities that the question was becoming less acute in the South and more vital in other parts of the nation. That the status of the Negro tended to become the same throughout America did not mean that racial discrimination was swiftly drawing to an end. Outside the South there was school segregation based upon residence. Negroes were confined to poorer sections of the cities of the North and the West. Many labor unions did not welcome them, and they found it difficult to obtain employment commensurate with their talents. Subtle—and even illegal—discrimination outside the South often had the same effect as open discrimination within it. However, the National Association for the Advancement of Colored People was a potent force, and the condition of the Negro was improving everywhere. Negro voters were so numerous in Northern cities that they often held a balance of power between Democrats and Republicans in city, state, and Presidential elections. They could extort promises of help from white office-seekers, and such promises were frequently kept. International politics added some strength to the cause of the Negro. The Communist charge that America stood for racial discrimination was embarrassing, especially in Asia and Africa, where nonwhites were achieving independence, power, and influence. Although much could be achieved by political pressure, what the Negroes most needed was economic and educational opportunity. While this could not be completely assured by law, by 1960 Negroes were finding their way in ever larger numbers into the colleges and universities and into the professions, also into public office. The fields in which the Negro might achieve success now included more than teaching, sports, and entertainment.

62 EISENHOWER AND THE COLD WAR

Soothing discord at home by following a middle way, Eisenhower was also basically moderate with respect to foreign policy, although he found it difficult to check the advance of communism, to maintain peace, and foster harmony among the nations. During his Presidency Communist imperialism made further progress in Asia and became a force with which to reckon in Africa and Latin America. Cuba became a Communist state. Declarations by the Republicans in the campaign of 1952 that they would both secure peace and "roll back" communism were not, nor hardly could be, made good. John Foster Dulles, who continued to serve as Eisenhower's Secretary of State until 1959, was astonishingly energetic, confident in manner, and sufficiently positive in language. Eisenhower placed great trust in him, and Dulles was for six years the principal maker of American foreign policy. He was less aggressive than he sometimes appeared to be. In essence, Eisenhower and Dulles, like Truman and Acheson, sought to contain communism without resorting to force. Like their predecessors, they hoped that Red imperialism would sooner or later develop serious internal schisms and lose its crusading vigor. Toward the end of the 1950s there was some reason to believe that the Russian Communists were becoming somewhat more cautious, although the Chinese Reds remained aggressive. The Cold War, it seemed, might become a Cold Peace, even eventually a warmer peace. However, the race in nuclear arms continued. Eisenhower's successor, John F. Kennedy, inherited immense responsibilities and in 1961 the existence of civilization, even of man, seemed to many to be at stake. It was obvious to all that mankind was passing through a period of extraordinary change.

ARMISTICE IN KOREA

Eisenhower and Dulles did manage to bring the Korean War to an end, in the summer of 1953. Visiting Korea the previous December in accordance with his campaign promise, Eisenhower found no formula by which the war could be triumphantly and cheaply brought to a close. As President he resolved to accept a divided Korea; he would make no effort to "liberate" the people of the northern half of that unhappy country—if the Communists would abandon their efforts to seize the southern part of it. Exerting pressure toward forcing the Chinese Reds to agree to an armistice, he announced that the American Seventh Fleet, commanding the waters between Formosa and the Chinese mainland, would no longer shield the Reds against attacks by Chiang K'ai-shek. The unleashed Chiang K'ai-shek lacked strength to invade the mainland, but the Chinese Communists were given some food for thought, since they could not be sure that American forces would not assist the Generalissimo. The Chinese Communists were not enough impressed by the threat to declare themselves ready to sign an armistice satisfactory to America and the UN. In the spring of 1953, however, Eisenhower and Dulles menaced Red China more seriously. Through Prime Minister Jawaharlal Nehru of India Dulles sent word to Peiping that, failing an armistice in Korea, American forces would blockade Red China, bomb its military and industrial bases from the air, and possibly even make use of smaller atomic weapons in Korea. The threat was made at an opportune time, for Stalin had recently died and his successor had not yet emerged. While they contested among themselves for supremacy, Russian leaders called for "peaceful co-existence." In early June the Chinese Reds yielded, agreeing to resume negotiations for an armistice, and one was finally signed late in July. By its terms North and South Korea were separated by a military line running across the 38th parallel, one which gave South Korea a somewhat more favorable boundary than it had at the beginning of the war. The Communists not only accepted that line, but agreed to let all prisoners decide whether they desired "repatriation" (to return to their military duty) or to remain with their captors, an arrangement upon which the UN insisted.

Repatriation disclosed the unpopularity of the Communist regimes in North Korea and China. Twenty-odd Americans who had been captured by the Reds and exposed to their propaganda chose to remain with them; almost all of them later regretted their decision and returned to their duty. No fewer than 26,000 Red troops preferred to stay in South Korea. Nevertheless, Communist North Korea endured and continued to claim to be the lawful government for all of Korea. The armistice brought an uneasy peace, for it seemed quite possible that the Reds would again seek to overrun South Korea when opportunity should offer. However, the peace was buttressed by a declaration from the sixteen countries which had engaged the Communists that hostilities could hardly be confined to Korea in case of a second attack. More importantly, in August, 1953, America promised to come to the aid of South Korea in the event of another attack.

Although the armistice brought a shaky peace to Korea, tension continued in Asia. The Communists looked upon their defeat as a temporary check to a holy cause that must eventually triumph. Peaceful co-existence as defined by the Russians in 1953 and during the remainder of the 1950s did not mean that the Communists would cease their efforts to expand their sway. It was assumed that attempts to win recruits for their cause would continue, and that Communists in colonial areas dominated by the capitalists would seek to overthrow their rulers. Communists also assumed their own right to encourage colonial peoples to seek independence, to supply them with arms, and to give them military advice. After the Korean War, the Russian and Chinese Reds continued to gain recruits in Japan, the Philippines, and in Southern Asia. They made slow progress in Japan and in the Philippines, where a "Huk" revolt among the Filipinos was effectively suppressed. Nor did they gain much ground in Pakistan, India, Ceylon, or Burma, new nations created in and after 1947. Made independent by Britain, those countries, at least in their early years of independence, found little in communism to attract them. The Reds also lost a guerrilla war they waged against the British in Malaya. However, they overran part of French Indo-China and threatened to extend their net over all of Southeast Asia.

INDO-CHINA

Even before the end of the Korean War French Indo-China posed an international question; by 1954 that part of it adjacent to the South China Sea seemed about to pass under Communist control. Only America had the strength to prevent it, and America was confronted by a situation much like that which had existed in Korea in 1950. Reestablishing themselves in Indo-China after World War II, the French were faced by demands for independence. At first they refused to make any concessions, and nationalists in northern Indo-China rose in revolt. At length the French reorganized their possessions. To the existing kingdoms of Cambodia and Laos they added an empire of Vietnam, over which they placed a native ruler. However, they abandoned very little of their authority. Nationalists in northern Vietnam continued to fight against the French, fell under Communist domination, and obtained arms through Red China. Although unwilling to abandon Indo-China, the Fourth French Republic was unable to defend it. The French army in northern Vietnam could not withstand the guerrilla attacks of the Communists, who in the spring of 1954 seemed about to engulf Laos as well as Vietnam. Then a new French Cabinet decided to withdraw from Indo-China. America had helped France with money and arms to fight the Communists; now it appeared that America must send an army to Indo-China if the Communists were to be stopped there. Alternatively, the United States could threaten war and demand that Red China cease to help the Communists in Vietnam.

Put to the test, Eisenhower and Dulles did not counter Red Chinese intervention in Indo-China with force. Eisenhower had said that its fate was of "transcendent importance" to America, and Dulles had asserted that Red Chinese interference would cause "grave consequences which might not be confined to Indo-China." In mid-April, 1954, they decided to send troops—if France granted independence to that region and if Britain, Australia, and New Zealand would support the American action. Britain preferred to negotiate with the Reds, and Eisenhower and Dulles were not at all eager to wage another Korean war, for which America was not prepared. Nor were they disposed to risk all by striking directly at Communist China. At length, in July Dulles agreed to accept an armistice by which Vietnam north of the 17th parallel would remain in the hands of the Communists. That solution was also endorsed by Red China, and it was formally approved by an international conference at Geneva on July 21, 1954. The result was the appearance of four states in which had been Indo-China, Laos, Cambodia, South Vietnam, and Communist North Vietnam.

The settlement reached at Geneva obviously was not a permanent one, for it was certain that the Communists would resume their attempt to infiltrate and overrun Southeast Asia. To forestall them Dulles persuaded Britain, France, Australia, New Zealand, the Philippines, Thailand, and Pakistan to join with the United States in the Southeast Asia Treaty Organization (SEATO). Formed in September, 1954, SEATO was intended "to prevent and counter subversive activities directed from without" against its members, Laos, Cambodia, and South Vietnam. The SEATO nations also declared that they favored self-determination for all peoples.

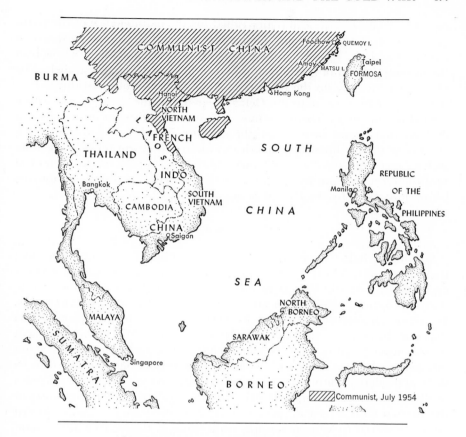

SOUTHEAST ASIA AND THE COLD WAR

Dulles described SEATO as a Monroe Doctrine for Southeast Asia. Toward checking the Communists there, the United States also supplied economic aid to South Vietnam, Laos, and Cambodia. However, it remained doubtful that the Communists could permanently be held back without the exercise of American military force and by the late 1950s Communist infiltration into South Vietnam and Laos posed new challenges. Tension in Southeast Asia continued, and the outcome of the clash with the Communists in that region remained doubtful.

Tension in the Far East after the Korean War was not confined to its southeastern part. America steadily refused to recognize Red China, successfully exerted influence to prevent it from securing membership in the UN, and firmly supported the regime of Chiang K'ai-shek on Formosa. On the other hand, America would not permit the Generalissimo to undertake adventures on the Chinese mainland, which at the time could not possibly succeed. In effect, American policy called for the maintenance of the status quo between the two Chinas. That policy was put to an awkward test in 1954 and again in 1958 when the Communists directed artillery fire against the offshore islands of Quemoy and Matsu, held by Chiang K'ai-shek. The two islands lie close to the harbors of Amoy and Foochow. In themselves, they were of little value to the Generalissimo, but the shelling was accompanied by threats to invade Formosa. The Communists on both occasions decided that actual invasion of the offshore islands was too dangerous, because of the likelihood of American military intervention. Chiang K'ai-shek's forces continued to hold them, with the support of the American Seventh Fleet. An uneasy stalemate between Red China and Nationalist China buttressed by the United States endured.

THE NEAR EAST

Striving to halt the spread of communism, Eisenhower and Dulles had to meet Russian thrusts in the Near East as well as the Far East. For many decades before World War II Britain had checked Russian expansion into that region, but was no longer able to hold off the Communists after 1947. It will be recalled that America intervened directly in the Near East in that year by going to the rescue of the Turkish republic, strengthening it against heavy pressure from the Soviet Union. Thereafter the United States increasingly became the chief bulwark in that region, one that was torn by strife and offered tempting opportunity to the Communists. Vast oil fields in the sands of Arabia, in the Tigris-Euphrates valley, and on the shores of the Persian Gulf served as special magnets to the Russians. Near Eastern oil was essential to western Europe; controlling it, the Soviet Union could seriously embarrass its enemies, especially Britain and France. Also inviting to Russia was the fact that governments and peoples in the Near East could be manipulated against each other and against "exploiting imperialists." The entire region, between Iran on the east and Egypt on the west, was in upheaval. Most of its peoples were Arabs, but their rulers, some of them very new, were at odds with each other. The Near Eastern scene was still further complicated by the appearance of the Republic of Israel in 1948. It was created by passionate Zionists who went to Palestine, under British mandate until 1948, to restore the ancient Jewish nation. When the British departed, the Zionists not only proclaimed the independence of Israel but defeated armies sent against it by the neighboring Arab rulers. These rulers were forced to sign an armistice with the Jews, although they refused to admit that the Jews had a right to return to Palestine; they would not recognize the independence of Israel; and they vowed to destroy it. Border incidents were common between Israel and her Arab neighbors after 1949. Still another cause of disturbance in the Near East was a rising wave of

Arab nationalism. The Arab who rode it might be able to make himself master of most of the region.

To form a solid front against communism in the Near East was a task almost beyond the wisdom of Solomon, but Dulles tried to do it. In 1955, with his blessing Turkey, Iraq, Iran, Pakistan, and Britain signed a defensive alliance directed against the Soviet Union. It was intended to check the Russians in Southern Asia generally as well as the Near East. However, only one Arab state—Iraq—was a party to it. It was a dike of sorts against communism, but troubled waters remained far behind it for Russian fishing. Dulles found it impossible to erect an impregnable bulwark against the Communists, and America became involved in quarrels with Egypt, Britain, and France over Near Eastern questions. America won few friends among the Arabs, partly because of American friendship with Israel, which was bolstered by money from American Zionists and both money and diplomatic support from Washington. In 1958 America resorted to force to check the spread of a United Arab Republic. Russian influence became important among the Arabs, although the Communists failed to secure control of any of the Arab states during the 1950s.

THE SUEZ CRISIS

Negotiating with Colonel Gamal Abdel Nasser, after 1954 master of a newly created Egyptian republic, with the intention of securing Egyptian good will by supplying funds for a great dam at Assuan, Dulles became enmeshed in difficulties that led to an international crisis. Nasser dreamed of uniting all the Arabs under his rule and sought to play the Soviet Union against America. While the negotiations were in progress in 1955, he signed an agreement with Communist Czechoslovakia by which he obtained arms, and he also laid plans to attack Israel. Dulles responded by declining to supply funds for the dam. Nasser struck back swiftly; in July, 1956 he announced that Egypt was "nationalizing" the Suez Canal, owned chiefly by British and French investors. He would reimburse them from tolls collected on the Canal and would use part of the tolls to build his dam.

Nasser's action caused dismay in the United States and anger in Britain, France, and Israel, since free use of the Canal was most important to them. There was much talk in the UN and outside it of operating the Canal under international auspices, but Nasser insisted that it was Egyptian property. Suddenly, on October 29, Israel, depending upon French and British support, began a "preventive war" against Egypt. Israeli mechanized forces crushed Egyptian resistance and swept on toward the Canal. On the following day France and Britain—France by prearrangement with Israel—demanded that both Egyptians and Israeli withdraw from the region of the Canal and permit occupation of key points within it by French and

British troops. Nasser rejected their ultimatum, and French and British forces landed near the Canal, overcoming Egyptian resistance. The outbreak of the war surprised and embarrassed Dulles, who promptly urged the Assembly of the UN to call upon Israel, France, and Britain to withdraw their troops. The Assembly did so, and France and Britain complied quickly, Israel later. However, before the seven-day war came to an end, Russia, supporting Dulles, bluntly threatened to use force, including nuclear weapons, "to crush the aggressors," if they did not withdraw. Nasser retained control of the Canal; the Russians boasted that their menaces had checked the "imperialists"; and America, getting little credit among the Arabs, lost some friends in Britain and France.

Although his army was routed in the seven-day war, Nasser emerged from the Suez crisis as a triumphant hero, not only in Egypt but in other Arab lands. With Russian diplomatic support he undertook to extend his sway to the borders of Turkey and Iran, striving to foment revolutions in his favor against the governments of all the Arab states in the Near East. Early in 1958 he was able to form the United Arab Republic, including Egypt, Syria, and Yemen. However, he was checked in seeking to subvert Iraq, Jordan, and Lebanon. A revolution that he inspired in Iraq led only to the appearance of a local military dictator, while he was successfully defied by King Hussein of Jordan, supported by British troops. His designs upon Lebanon led to the most drastic American action. Gravely threatened by Nasser, the partly Christian Lebanese republic appealed for help. Despite Russian protests, Eisenhower sent the Sixth Fleet and contingents of marines to the rescue. The marines remained in Lebanon during many weeks, until that republic was at least temporarily safe from Nasserism. Nasser's star then seemed to fade, but no one could say that it would not rise again. The Near East remained troubled. America was still struggling to check Communism and to find friends and allies among the Arabs as the 1950s came to an end.

KHRUSHCHEV AND WEST BERLIN

Spreading elsewhere, the Cold War persisted in Europe. The fate of the Germans, above all those of West Berlin, remained the great issue there. The Soviet Union withdrew its occupation troops from Austria in 1955, but was determined that East Germany remain Communist and that West Berlin become a part of it. On the other hand, America, Britain, and France steadfastly declared that they would neither abandon West Berlin nor recognize East Germany. In 1955 they strengthened the military forces of NATO by adding to them West German troops (West Germany did not become a member of NATO, but supplied the men as a partner in the European Defense Community, organized under the leadership of Prime

THE TWO GERMANYS

Minister Anthony Eden). At the same time West Germany was officially recognized by America and her allies in Europe. The Russians responded by tightening their ties with their own allies behind the Iron Curtain, in the Warsaw Pact.

After the death of Stalin the Soviet Union had its own troubles behind that Curtain, but surmounted them. In the Union itself there was a struggle for Stalin's power. However, it was resolved without any serious internal struggle—to the disappointment of those who cherished a hope that such a conflict would weaken the Soviet Union. There was little violence after the ambitions of Lavrenti P. Beria, the chief of Stalin's secret police, were terminated by his execution. Thereafter, Nikita Khrushchev, secretary of the Communist party, gradually took control in its councils. By 1958 he was firmly in the saddle. Under his direction the Communist machine ran quite smoothly in Russia, although it had become apparent by the middle 1950s that Russian communism was detested in the "satellite" countries. In the spring of 1953 there was rioting against the Red regime in Rumania and also against that of East Germany. There was a general strike in East Germany, and its government would have fallen had not Russian troops come to its rescue. In 1956 unrest was so great in Poland that the Reds granted a measure of economic and personal freedom to soothe discontent. In the same year the Communist regime in Hungary was actually overthrown by a sudden revolt in which students were leaders. It was restored by the Russian army. Such uprisings were doomed to failure without outside help, which was not forthcoming. But they demonstrated beyond doubt that the "peace-loving" Communists were hated in the satellite countries and that Red democracy still included suppression of freedom by force.

Khrushchev's rise to power made little, if any, immediate difference, so far as the German question was concerned. In November, 1958, he announced that Russia would declare the military occupation of Berlin to be ended within six months and that Russia would place control of the routes leading into West Berlin in the hands of the East German Communists. America, Britain, and France asserted that Russia could not terminate the occupation without their consent, and that they would not deal with East Germany. Khrushchev did not make good his threat, but he continued to demand that the American, British, and French troops in West Berlin be withdrawn. At conference after international conference the question of West Berlin was discussed, but the impasse remained.

NEW NATIONS IN AFRICA

In the 1950s Africa also became a battleground between communism and democracy. Communist agents found fertile fields to till on the Dark Continent. Western-style colonialism was passing in Africa, and new and independent African nations appeared upon the map in numbers after World War II. The Italian empire in Africa was liquidated in 1945; all the French possessions, except for Algeria, were granted independence by 1960; Belgium relinquished her Congo; and Britain gave independence to some of her colonies and self-government to others. However, Portugal clung to her possessions, and the withdrawal of European authority elsewhere was not always sufficiently rapid to please the natives, the Russians, and American idealists. Communist propaganda about imperialistic exploitation found ready listeners in Africa. The Western democracies were also embarrassed by the behavior of the Afrikaners of the Union of South Africa, who were determined to maintain their supremacy and who adopted the harsh policy of *apartheid* toward those ends. *Apartheid* meant segregation of and severe discrimination against non-Europeans in the Union.

Under pressure, European authority was often withdrawn before the natives were competent to govern themselves. This happened in the Belgian Congo, which became the Republic of Congo in 1960. The new nation was swiftly torn by internal strife. Premier Moise Tshombe of its Katanga province, backed by European mining interests, promptly proclaimed Katanga's independence. Fighting broke out between Tshombe and the new Congolese government; tribal conflicts flared into violence; Europeans were attacked and killed; and Khrushchev tried to secure a communist regime, or at least one friendly to Russia. The UN had to send troops to restore order. After some fighting and amidst much confusion they finally accomplished their task, but the future of the equatorial republic remained doubtful. It could be predicted with some assurance, if the Communists continued to be aggressive in Africa, that the history of that continent would be troubled indeed in the 1960s. Algeria was a likely field for Communist activity. In revolt against France after 1954, Arab nationalists in Algeria had at least the propaganda support of Soviet Russia. And an Algeria that gained independence in July, 1962, would not be ignored by Russia.

COMMUNIST CUBA

It was not to be expected that the Communists, working energetically in Europe, Asia, and Africa, would neglect the New World. Latin America, poor, undeveloped, afflicted by ignorance, burdened by dictators and aristocracies, and sensitive about "Yankee imperialism," offered tempting possibilities. The Reds did not fail to take advantage of them. They fomented discontent and anti-American feeling everywhere in the southern half of the New World in the 1950s. As the decade drew toward its close, they won a stunning triumph in Cuba. In 1956 a revolt began in the mountains of eastern Cuba against the Batista regime, which had become both corrupt and brutal after nearly a quarter-century of power. The leader of the uprising was a bearded young lawyer named Fidel Castro who became a heroic and unconventional figure in American newspapers. Toward the end of 1958 the Batista dictatorship collapsed, because of its unpopularity rather than Castro's military prowess, and Castro became the master of Cuba. Optimists in the United States hoped and believed that Castro was a champion of democracy; others more familiar with the ways of Latin America predicted that he, like Batista, would become just another dictator. For a time he behaved like the usual despot, a bloodthirsty one who joyously executed dozens of Batista's followers. Serious doubt arose in the

United States regarding his benevolent intentions when he expropriated, without promising to pay for them, sugar mills and plantations, mines, and factories owned by foreigners, who were chiefly American. When the American government declared that Cuba ought to pay for property taken from Americans, estimated to be worth between $500 million and $1 billion, he said that Washington was insolently interfering in Cuban affairs. In January, 1960, President Eisenhower declared that there would be no American reprisal or intervention in Cuba. However, Castro proclaimed himself to be a Marxist, then announced himself to be a Communist, and it became increasingly apparent that he intended not only to fasten communism upon Cuba but to spread it to other Latin American nations. It also became clear that he had the support of both Russia and Red China. Relations between America and Cuba went from bad to worse, for it was only too obvious that communism had acquired a strong outpost in the western hemisphere.

THE COLD WAR CONTINUES

As friction with the Communists persisted in so many parts of the world, so did the danger that mankind might engage in a third global war. This danger was so great that America's Strategic Air Command remained constantly on the alert, prepared almost instantly to make nuclear bomb attacks from all directions upon Russia, if the Communists resorted to all-out war. Men everywhere feared that such a conflict might mean the destruction of a large part of the human race and of civilization. At meetings of the UN and in many international conferences in the 1950s proposals for disarmament continued to be discussed, but without result. Instead, an ever more deadly nuclear arms race added to the alarm. The Russians exploded a hydrogen bomb in August, 1953, less than a year after the Americans had developed that awesome weapon. Britain, exploding her first atomic bomb in 1952, detonated one of the hydrogen variety in 1957, and France set off her first atomic bomb in 1960 in the Sahara Desert. By that time bombs far more powerful than the hydrogen kind were in the making. Both America and Russia had a stockpile of nuclear weapons. Attempts to reach an enduring international agreement to ban tests of nuclear bombs remained unsuccessful. America was willing to stop testing; Russia was not, at least not until her ability to drop bombs equalled that of the United States. As the decade drew to its close, the arms race became even more intense because of the rapid development of the rocket, for it could be used as a missile as well as a means of penetrating into space. Missiles with nuclear warheads that could hit a target at a great distance had been made, and were ready for use.

Hope remained in 1960—and was increasing somewhat—that effective defenses would be found against nuclear weapons, as they had been found against other weapons in the past. Both America and Russia were striving to make, and with increasing success, missiles that would find and destroy other missiles, and manned airplanes as well. It also remained possible that nations would not resort to the use of major atomic weapons because of fear of retaliation.

Was there any chance to avert the catastrophe of war that was less than totally destructive? There was evidence toward the close of the decade that the Russian attitude toward the West was softening somewhat. The remarkable achievements of the Russians in nuclear and rocket science soothed irritation and suspicion in a country which had been looked upon by Europeans and Americans as a poor relation, even an illegitimate one. Air bases established by America and her allies near the frontiers of the Soviet Union no longer seemed so menacing. Also the Russians could take pride in swift progress in education, the arts, engineering, and even in sports. Life was easier and more comfortable for them than it had earlier been; they had much more to lose now than they had had. It was inevitable that Russian intellectuals should eventually question rigid Communist dogmas, however cautiously. Another reason for turning toward the West was a growing rift between Russia and Red China, with Mao Tse-tung challenging Khrushchev for leadership among the Communists of the world. The Russians did not tell the Red Chinese how to make atomic weapons. On the other hand, they were less truculent in their dealings with the West, and it seemed possible that the Russians would come to see themselves as a part of that West. It also seemed not unlikely that better acquaintance with the Americans would improve the Russian opinion of them. When President Eisenhower with other European leaders met the Russians in a "summit" meeting at Geneva in 1955, hope was nourished in America that it would allay Russian fears and reduce Russian hostility. More was probably accomplished by a visit to America by Khrushchev in 1959. When airman Francis Gary Powers, in the employ of the Central Intelligence Agency, was shot down and captured while taking photographs of Russia from high altitude in the spring of 1960, he was sentenced to ten years' imprisonment rather than death. Later the Russians exchanged him for one of their spies captured in the United States. However, there was no assurance that the Russians would change greatly and soon. There was no positive sign of a thaw in the Cold War.

THE ELECTION OF 1960

Because the Cold War had abated little, if at all, the election of 1960 took place in an atmosphere of continuing crisis. Despite the age of Eisenhower—he reached his seventieth birthday in October, 1960—and his physical difficulties, many Republicans would have urged him to seek a third term, had it been constitutionally possible. It is to be suspected that he could have won a third time. As it was, Vice-President Richard Nixon secured the Republican nomination almost without a struggle. In 1959 Nelson Rockefeller, a grandson of John D. Rockefeller, who had been chosen Governor of New York in the preceding year, challenged Nixon for the leadership of their party. Rockefeller claimed that he was less conservative than Nixon, that he could guide the party to victory, and that Nixon could not. However, Rockefeller discovered that Nixon was the choice of Republican "wheelhorses," and that he had little chance in a contest with the Vice-President. In December, 1959, he announced his withdrawal from the race. In the following March Eisenhower declared that he wished Nixon to be his successor. There was little enthusiasm for him among independent voters, and none at all among those Democrats who had supported Eisenhower. The hopes of Rockefeller afterward revived, and he declared that he would not mind being "drafted." Some of the most conservative Republicans opposed the Vice-President because they thought he was not forthright enough in attacking the Democrats; they favored Senator Barry Goldwater of Arizona. There was no stopping Nixon. He conferred with Rockefeller and satisfied him that they were not far apart on policy. At the Republican convention in Chicago only Nixon and Goldwater were officially considered, and Nixon was nominated by acclamation. For the Vice-Presidency the Republicans named Henry Cabot Lodge, the American ambassador to the UN. In their platform they heaped praise upon themselves for the achievements of the Eisenhower regime and asserted that more of the same could be expected from one presided over by Nixon.

The Republican nomination went to Nixon largely because he began to seek friends and delegates long before 1960, and Senator John F. Kennedy similarly secured the endorsement of the Democrats well in advance of the Democratic convention. Adlai Stevenson was undoubtedly the most respected and most popular Democrat as the election of 1960 approached, but he would not fight for the Presidential nomination. He would respond only to a "draft," and he would do nothing to stimulate one. Kennedy, entering his party's primaries, was challenged only by Senator Hubert H. Humphrey of Minnesota, whom he easily defeated. At the Democratic convention in Los Angeles Senator Lyndon B. Johnson of Texas was supported by almost all the Southern delegates, but he had far less strength than Kennedy. An attempt to "stampede" the convention for Stevenson failed and Kennedy was named on the first ballot. At his request Senator Johnson was put forward for the Vice-Presidency.

In the campaign of 1960 Kennedy had a great advantage in that there were more Democrats than there were Republicans. If party lines held, he would win—the Democrats had won an easy control of Congress in 1958. He also had more personal appeal than Nixon. Only 43, a son of Joseph P. Kennedy, a rich Boston businessman who had been ambassador to Britain, he was a World War II hero, a photogenic and witty extrovert. Nixon, also a veteran, was 47 years of age, less forthright and not favored by the camera. Kennedy made a better impression than his rival in a series of four novel television debates. Kennedy's political record, or lack of it, was likewise in his favor. He had not been a conspicuous member of the Senate, and had not taken strong stands on burning issues. He had said nothing for or against Senator Joseph McCarthy. On the other hand, Nixon had been an extremely vigorous Republican partisan and had long been in the public eye. He had acquired many enemies by pounding at the issue of Communists in government. Both men were well educated, Kennedy being a graduate of Harvard University, Nixon of Whittier College and of the Duke University Law School. Both men were skillful in handling public questions, both avoided extreme positions, and both courted the votes of special interest groups. Kennedy declared that the American economy was not growing as rapidly as it should, that the nation should move toward "New Frontiers." Nixon, defending the Eisenhower record, charged that the Democrats were too careless with public money, as did Eisenhower, who also assailed the "spenders." On questions of military and foreign policy Kennedy said he could do better than the Republicans had; Nixon said he could not. One issue in the campaign, which Nixon said was not an issue, was that of the relationship between church and state. A Roman Catholic, Kennedy asserted that he believed in separation of church and state and that his religious faith ought not be held against him. Nixon agreed, but many Americans who were not of Kennedy's faith were not satisfied by his assurance.

Throughout the campaign Kennedy seemed to be in the lead, and he led when the ballots were counted, but by an astonishingly narrow margin. He did not get a majority in the popular vote, which totaled about 68,800,-000, but he won a plurality over Nixon of 112,881. In the electoral college Kennedy had 303 votes, Nixon 219, Senator Harry F. Byrd of Virginia 15. The election results were so close in several states in which Kennedy won that Republicans challenged them, without success. They had to accept his "paper thin" popular plurality and electoral majority. It was apparent that religion had powerfully affected the decision of the voters. The Democrats kept control of both houses of Congress, although they did not do so well as they had in 1958. Kennedy ran behind his fellow Democratic office-seekers. He easily defeated Nixon in Eastern and Northern cities where Roman Catholics were numerous, but he was far less popular in areas that were Protestant. Nixon carried more states, including several Southern ones, than Kennedy. Kennedy's selection of Lyndon Johnson as his Vice-Presidential candidate proved to be a master stroke. Except for his presence on the Democratic ticket and his efforts in behalf of it, Kennedy would doubtless have been defeated through the loss of Texas and other Southern states that he managed to carry.

In January, 1961 John F. Kennedy was duly inaugurated. Precisely where his "New Frontiers" were remained somewhat uncertain. There could be no doubt that he was cool-headed, realistic, gifted in the art of politics, and courageous. An immense burden fell upon him. Only the future could tell how well he would bear it.

SUGGESTIONS FOR FURTHER READING*

GENERAL

Richard Bardolph, *The Negro Vanguard* (1959); Loren Barity, "The Idea of the West," *American Historical Review,* 66 (April, 1961), 618–640; Samuel F. Bemis (ed.), *The American Secretaries of State and Their Diplomacy,* 10 vols. (1927–1929); Samuel F. Bemis, *The Latin American Policy of the United States* (1943); William C. Binkley, "The South and the West," *Journal of Southern History,* 17 (February, 1951), 5–22; Herbert E. Bolton, *The Spanish Borderlands* (1921); Beverly W. Bond, Jr., *The Civilization of the Old Northwest* (1934); Edward G. Bourne, *Spain in America, 1450–1580* (1905); Van Wyck Brooks, *Makers and Finders: a History of the Writer in America, 1800–1915,* 5 vols. (1936–1952); Arthur W. Calhoun, *A Social History of the American Family,* 3 vols. (1917–1919); Lester J. Cappon, "The Provincial South," *Journal of Southern History,* 15 (February, 1950), 5–24; Robert K. Carr, *The Supreme Court and Judicial Review* (1942); Wilbur J. Cash, *The Mind of the South* (1941); Zachariah Chafee, *The Blessing of Liberty* (1956); Thomas D. Clark, "The Great Visitation to American Democracy," *Mississippi Valley Historical Review,* 44 (June, 1957), 3–28; Paul Clyde, *The Far East, a History of the Impact of the West on Eastern Asia* (2nd ed. 1952); Henry S. Commager and Richard B. Morris (eds.), *New American Nation Series* (1954–); John R. Commons *et al., History of Labor in the United States,* 4 vols. (1918–1935); Lawrence A. Cremin, *The Transformation of the School: Progressivism in American Education, 1876–1957* (1961); Merle Curti, *The Growth of American Thought* (2nd ed. 1951); Bailey W. Diffie, *Latin American Civilization: Colonial Period* (1945); Joseph Dorfman, *The Economic Mind in American Civilization,* 3 vols. (1946–1949); Foster Rhea Dulles, *Labor in America* (1949); Henry P. Fairchild, *Immigration* (1925); John Hope Franklin, *From Slavery to Freedom: A History of American Negroes* (1947); John Hope Franklin, *The Militant South, 1800–1861* (1956); Ralph H. Gabriel, *The Course of American Democratic Thought* (1940); Doris A. Graber, *Crisis Diplomacy: A History of U.S. International Policies and Practices* (1959); Fletcher M. Green, "Cycles of American Democracy," *Mississippi Valley Historical Review,* 48 (June, 1961), 3–23; Alfred W. Griswold, *The Far Eastern Policy of the United States* (1938); Bray Hammond, *Banks and Politics in America, from the Revolution to the Civil War* (1957); Oscar Handlin, *The Uprooted: the Epic Story of the Great Migrations that Made the American People* (1951); Oscar Handlin (ed.), *Library of American Biography,* 19 vols. (1954–); Marcus L. Hansen, *The Atlantic Migration, 1607–1860* (1940); Frederick E. Haynes, *Third Party Movements Since the Civil War* (1916); John

---

* The instructor is the best guide to additional study and reading. Only a sampling of the vast quantity of writings about American history is offered here. For more help toward finding books and articles see Oscar Handlin *et al.* (eds.), *Harvard Guide to American History* (1954); Donald H. Mugridge and Blanche P. McCrum (eds.), *A Guide to the Study of the United States of America: Representative Books* (1960); George Howe *et al.* (eds.), *The American Historical Association's Guide to Historical Literature* (1961); and William H. Cartwright and Richard L. Watson (eds.), *Interpreting and Teaching American History, Thirty-First Yearbook, National Council for the Social Studies* (1961).

Higham, "The Rise of American Intellectual History," *American Historical Review*, 56 (April, 1951), 453–471; Richard Hofstadter, *The American Political Tradition and the Men Who Made It* (1948); Richard Hofstadter and Walter P. Metzger, *The Development of Academic Freedom in the United States* (1955); W. Eugene Hollon, *The Southwest: Old and New* (1961); W. Stull Holt, "Some Consequences of the Urban Movement in American History," *Pacific Historical Review*, 22 (November, 1953), 337–352; Jay B. Hubbell, *The South in American Literature, 1607–1900* (1954); James W. Hurst, *Law and Social Process in United States History* (1960); Samuel Isham, *The History of American Painting* (1927); Allen Johnson and Allan Nevins (eds.), *The Chronicles of America*, 56 vols. (1918–1921, 1950–1951); Maldwyn A. Jones, *American Immigration* (1960); Hugh L. Keenleyside, *Canada and the United States: Some Aspects of Their Historical Relations* (1952); S. Fiske Kimball, *American Architecture* (1928); Edward C. Kirkland, *A History of American Economic Life* (1951); Dudley W. Knox, *A History of the United States Navy* (1948); Oliver W. Larkin, *Art and Life in America* (1949); Leon F. Litwack, *North of Slavery: The Negro in the Free States, 1790–1860* (1961); Richard P. Longaker, *The Presidency and Individual Liberties* (1961); Reinhard H. Luthin, "Some Demagogues in American History," *American Historical Review*, 57 (October, 1951), 22–46; Charles A. Madison, *Leaders and Liberals in 20th Century America* (1961); Malcolm C. Moos, *The Republicans: A History of Their Party* (1956); Douglass C. North, *The Economic Growth of the United States, 1790–1860* (1961); Gilman Ostrander, *The Rights of Man in America, 1606–1861* (1960); Vernon L. Parrington, *Main Currents in American Thought*, 3 vols. (1927–1930); Dexter Perkins *et al.*, *The Education of Historians in the United States* (1962); Walter B. Posey, "The Protestant Episcopal Church: An American Adaptation," *Journal of Southern History*, 25 (February, 1959), 3–30; David Potter, *People of Plenty: Economic Abundance and the American Character* (1954); Arthur Hobson Quinn, *A History of the American Drama* (1943); Sidney Ratner, *American Taxation* (1942); Joseph G. Rayback, *A History of American Labor* (1959); Roy M. Robbins, *Our Landed Heritage, the Public Domain, 1776–1936* (1942); Clinton L. Rossiter, "The Shaping of the American Tradition," *William and Mary Quarterly*, Third Series, 11 (October, 1954), 519–535; Clinton L. Rossiter, *Conservatism in America* (1955); Walter N. Sage, "Canada: The Neighbor to the North," *Pacific Historical Review*, 20 (May, 1951), 111–122; Arthur M. Schlesinger and Dixon Ryan Fox (eds.), *A History of American Life*, 13 vols. (1927–1948); Boyd C. Shafer, "The American Heritage of Hope, 1865–1940," *Mississippi Valley Historical Review*, 37 (December, 1950), 427–450; Fred A. Shannon, "Culture and Agriculture in America," *Mississippi Valley Historical Review*, 41 (June, 1954), 3–20; Paul F. Sharp, "The Northern Great Plains: A Study in Canadian-American Regionalism," *Mississippi Valley Historical Review*, 39 (June, 1952), 61–76; Richard H. Shryock, *The Development of Modern Medicine* (1947); Henry N. Smith, *Virgin Land: The American West As Symbol and Myth* (1950); James W. Smith and A. Leland Jamison (eds.), *Religion in American Life*, Vols. I, II, and IV (1961); Oliver L. Spaulding, *The United States Army in War and Peace* (1937); Robert E. Spiller *et al.*, *Literary History of the United States*, 3 vols. (1948); Maurice P. Stein, *The Eclipse of Community: an Interpretation of American Studies* (1960); Wendell H. Stephenson and E. Merton Coulter (eds.), *A His-*

tory of the South (1948–); Frederick J. Turner, *The Frontier in American History* (1950); Walter Prescott Webb, *The Great Frontier* (1952); William H. Werkmeister, *A History of Philosophical Ideas in America* (1949); William A. Williams, *American-Russian Relations, 1781–1947* (1952); William A. Williams, "The Frontier Thesis and American Foreign Policy," *Pacific Historical Review*, 24 (November, 1955), 379–396; Chilton Williamson, *American Suffrage from Property to Democracy, 1760–1860* (1960); Oscar O. Winther, *The Great Northwest* (1947); Harvey Wish, *Society and Thought in America*, 2 vols. (1950–1952); Clark Wissler, *Indians of the United States* (1960); Carl F. Wittke, *We Who Built America: the Saga of the Immigrant* (1939); Carl F. Wittke, *The Irish in America* (1956).

THE COLONIAL PERIOD

James T. Adams, *The Founding of New England* (1921); James T. Adams, *Revolutionary New England, 1691–1776* (1923); Charles M. Andrews, *Colonial Background of the American Revolution* (1924); Charles M. Andrews, *The Colonial Period of American History*, 4 vols. (1934–1938); Bernard Bailyn, *Education in the Forming of American Society: Needs and Opportunities for Study* (1960); Daniel J. Boorstin, *The Americans: the Colonial Experience* (1958); Carl Bridenbaugh, *Myths and Realities: Societies of the Colonial South* (1952); Samuel H. Brockunier, *The Irrepressible Democrat: Roger Williams* (1940); Vincent Buranelli, "Colonial Philosophy," *William and Mary Quarterly*, Third Series, 16 (July, 1959), 343–362; Dora M. Clark, *The Rise of the British Treasury: Colonial Administration in the Eighteenth Century* (1960); Cyclone Covey, "Puritanism and Music in Colonial America," *William and Mary Quarterly*, Third Series, 8 (July, 1951), 378–388; Catherine S. Crary, "The Humble Immigrant and the American Dream: Some Case Histories, 1746–1776," *Mississippi Valley Historical Review*, 46 (June, 1959), 46–66; Verner W. Crane, *The Southern Frontier, 1670–1732* (1929); Wesley F. Craven, *The Southern Colonies in the Seventeenth Century, 1607–1689* (1949); John R. Cuneo, *Robert Rogers of the Rangers* (1959); John Duffy, "The Passage to the Colonies," *Mississippi Valley Historical Review*, 38 (June, 1951), 3–20; Douglas J. Elwood, *The Philosophical Theology of Jonathan Edwards* (1960); E. James Ferguson, "Currency Finance: An Interpretation of Colonial Monetary Practices," *William and Mary Quarterly*, Third Series, 10 (April, 1953), 153–180; James T. Flexner, *Mohawk Baronet: Sir William Johnson of New York* (1959); David H. Fowler, "Connecticut's Freemen: The First Forty Years," *William and Mary Quarterly*, Third Series, 15 (July, 1958), 312–333; W. Nelson Francis, "Hakluyt's Voyages: An Epic of Discovery," *William and Mary Quarterly*, Third Series, 12 (July, 1955), 449–455; Malcolm Freiberg, "Thomas Hutchinson: The First Fifty Years (1711–1761)," *William and Mary Quarterly*, Third Series, 15 (January, 1958), 35–55; George F. Frick and Raymond P. Stearns, *Mark Catesby: The Colonial Audubon* (1961); Edwin S. Gaustad, "Society and the Great Awakening in New England," *William and Mary Quarterly*, Third Series, 11 (1954), 566–577; Marcel Giraud, "France and Louisiana in the Early Eighteenth Century," *Mississippi Valley Historical Review*, 36 (March, 1950), 657–674; Jack P. Greene, "Foundations of Political Power in the Virginia House of Burgesses, 1720–1776," *William and Mary Quarterly*, Third Series, 16 (October, 1959), 485–506; Jack P. Greene, "The Role of The Lower Houses of Assembly in Eighteenth-Century Politics," *Journal of Southern History,* 27 (November, 1961), 451–474; Philip S. Haffenden, "The Crown and the Colonial Charters, 1675–1688: Part I," *William and Mary Quarterly,* Third Series, 15 (July, 1958), 297–311; Philip S. Haffenden, "The Crown and Colonial Charters, 1675–1688: Part II," *William and Mary Quarterly,* Third Series, 15 (October, 1958), 452–466; Albert Harkness, Jr., "Americanism and Jenkins' Ear," *Mississippi Valley Historical Review,* 37 (June, 1950), 61–90; Lawrence A. Harper, *The English Navigation Laws* (1939); Einar Haugen (ed.), *Voyages to Vinland* (1941); Brooke Hindle, "Cadwalladen Colden's Extension of the Newtonian Principles," *William and Mary Quarterly,* Third Series, 13 (October, 1956), 459–475; Keach Johnson, "The Baltimore Company Seeks English Markets: A Study of the Anglo-American Iron Trade, 1731–1755," *William and Mary Quarterly,* Third Series, 16 (January, 1959), 37–60; Leonard W. Labaree, *Royal Government in America* (1930); Lawrence H. Leder, *Robert Livingston, 1654–1728, and the Politics of Colonial New York* (1961); Sister Joan Leonard, "Elections in Colonial Pennsylvania," *William and Mary Quarterly,* Third Series, 11 (July, 1954), 385–401; Beverly McAnear, "College Founding in the American Colonies, 1745–1775," *Mississippi Valley Historical Review,* 42 (June, 1955), 24–44; James F. Maclear, " 'The Heart of New England Rent': The Mystical Element in Early Puritan History," *Mississippi Valley Historical Review,* 42 (March, 1956), 621–652; John K. Mahon, "Anglo-American Methods of Indian Warfare, 1676–1794," *Mississippi Valley Historical Review,* 45 (September, 1958), 254–275; Robert Middlekauff, "A Persistent Tradition: The Classical Curriculum in Eighteenth-Century New England," *William and Mary Quarterly,* Third Series, 18 (January, 1961), 54–67; Genevieve Miller, "Smallpox Inoculation in England and America: A Reappraisal," *William and Mary Quarterly,* Third Series, 13 (October, 1956), 476–492; Perry Miller, *The New England Mind* (1939); Edmund S. Morgan, *Virginians at Home: Family Life in the Eighteenth Century* (1952); Samuel E. Morison, *Admiral of the Ocean Sea,* 2 vols. (1942); Richard L. Morton, *Colonial Virginia, 1607–1763,* 2 vols. (1960); George L. Mosse, "Puritanism and Reason of State in Old and New England," *William and Mary Quarterly,* Third Series, 9 (January, 1952), 67–80; Wallace Notestein, *The English People on the Eve of Colonization, 1603–1630* (1954); Emil Oberholzer, *Delinquent Saints: Disciplinary Action in the Early Congregational Churches of Massachusetts* (1955); Alison G. Olson, "William Penn, Parliament, and Proprietary Government," *William and Mary Quarterly,* Third Series, 18 (April, 1961), 176–195; Richard Pares, *Yankees and Creoles: the Trade between North America and the West Indies before the American Revolution* (1956); Francis Parkman, *France and England in North America,* 9 vols. (1865–1892); Catherine O. Peare, *William Penn: A Biography* (1957); Howard H. Peckham, *Pontiac and the Indian Uprising* (1947); W. H. Prescott, *History of the Conquest of Mexico,* 3 vols. (1843); W. H. Prescott, *History of the Conquest of Peru,* 2 vols. (1847); Edgar Prestage, *The Portuguese Pioneers* (1933); Benjamin Quarles, "The Colonial Militia and Negro Manpower," *Mississippi Valley Historical Review,* 45 (March, 1959), 643–652; Edward M. Riley, "The Town Acts of Colonial Virginia," *Journal of Modern History,* 16 (August, 1950), 306–323; Charles R. Ritcheson, "The Preparation of the Stamp Act," *William and Mary Quarterly,* Third Series, 10 (October, 1953), 543–559; A. L. Rowse, *Sir Richard Grenville* (1937); A. L. Rowse, *The England of Elizabeth* (1950); Edwin C.

Rozwenc, "Captain John Smith's Image of America," *William and Mary Quarterly,* Third Series, 16 (January, 1959), 27–36; Max Savelle, *Seeds of Liberty* (1948); Robert L. Schuyler *Parliament and the British Empire* (1929); William H. Seiler, "The Anglican Parish Vestry in Colonial Virginia," *Journal of Southern History,* 22 (August, 1956), 310–337; Alan Simpson, "How Democratic Was Roger Williams?" *William and Mary Quarterly,* Third Series, 13 (January, 1956), 53–68; Bradford Smith, *Bradford of Plymouth* (1951); Bradford Smith, *Captain John Smith, His Life and Legend* (1953); James M. Smith, *Seventeenth Century America: Essays in Colonial History* (1959); Harold C. Syrett, "Private Enterprise in New Amsterdam," *William and Mary Quarterly,* Third Series, 11 (October, 1954), 536–550; Frederick B. Tolles, *James Logan and the Culture of Provincial America* (1957); Willard M. Wallace, *Sir Walter Raleigh* (1959); Harry M. Ward, *The United Colonies of New England, 1643–1690* (1961); Wilcomb E. Washburn, *The Governor and the Rebel: a History of Bacon's Rebellion in Virginia* (1957); Glenn Weaver, "Benjamin Franklin and the Pennsylvania Germans," *William and Mary Quarterly,* Third Series, 14 (October, 1957), 536–559; Thomas J. Wertenbaker, *The Founding of American Civilization, The Middle Colonies* (1938); Thomas J. Wertenbaker, *Torchbearer of the Revolution* (1940); James A. Williamson, *The Voyages of the Cabots and the English Discovery of North America* (1929); Ola E. Winslow, *Meetinghouse Hill, 1630–1783* (1952); Ola E. Winslow, *Master Roger Williams, A Biography* (1957); Louis B. Wright, *The First Gentlemen of Virginia* (1940); Louis B. Wright, *The Cultural Life of the American Colonies, 1607–1763* (1957); Louis B. Wright, "Intellectual History and the Colonial South," *William and Mary Quarterly,* Third Series, 16 (April, 1959), 214–227; George M. Wrong, *The Rise and Fall of New France,* 2 vols. (1928); Silvio Zavala, "A General View of the Colonial History of the New World," *American Historical Review,* 66 (July, 1961), 913–929.

THE ERA OF THE REVOLUTION (1763–1789)

Randolph G. Adams, *Political Ideas of the American Revolution* (1922); John R. Alden, *General Gage in America* (1948); John R. Alden, *The American Revolution, 1775–1783* (1954); John R. Alden, *The South in the Revolution, 1763–1789* (1957); Herbert Aptheker, *The American Revolution, 1763–1783* (1960); John E. Bakeless, *Background to Glory: the Life of George Rogers Clark* (1957); Alice M. Baldwin, *The New England Clergy and the American Revolution* (1928); John D. Barnhart (ed.), *Henry Hamilton and George Rogers Clark in the American Revolution* (1951); Charles A. Beard, *An Economic Interpretation of the Constitution of the United States* (1913); Carl L. Becker, *The Eve of the Revolution* (1918); Carl L. Becker, *The Declaration of Independence* (1922); George L. Beer, *British Colonial Policy, 1754–65* (1907); George A. Billias, *General John Glover and his Marblehead Marines* (1960); Robert E. Brown, *Middle-Class Democracy and the Revolution in Massachusetts, 1691–1780* (1955); Robert E. Brown, *Charles Beard and the Constitution, a Critical Analysis of "An Economic Interpretation of the Constitution"* (1956); William A. Bryan, "George Washington: Symbolic Guardian of the Republic, 1850–1861," *William and Mary Quarterly,* Third Series, 7 (January, 1950), 53–63; Herbert Butterfield, *George III and the Historians* (1957); John H. Cary, *Joseph Warren: Physician, Politician, Patriot* (1961); Moncure D. Conway, *The Life of Thomas Paine*, 2 vols. (1892); Verner W. Crane, *Benjamin Franklin and a Rising People* (1954); Oliver M. Dickerson, *The Navigation Acts and the American Revolution* (1951); Elisha P. Douglass, *Rebels and Democrats: the Struggle for Equal Political Rights and Majority Rule during the American Revolution* (1955); E. James Ferguson, "Business, Government, and Congressional Investigation in the Revolution," *William and Mary Quarterly*, Third Series, 16 (July, 1959), 293–318; E. James Ferguson, "State Assumption of the Federal Debt During the Confederation," *Mississippi Valley Historical Review*, 38 (December, 1951), 403–424; Douglas S. Freeman *et al.*, *George Washington: A Biography*, 7 vols. (1948–1957); Bruce I. Granger, *Political Satire in the American Revolution, 1763–1783* (1960); Charles S. Grant, *Democracy on the Connecticut Frontier* (1961); Evarts B. Greene, *The Revolutionary Generation, 1763–1700* (1943); Jack P. Greene and Richard M. Jellison, "The Currency Act of 1764 in Imperial-Colonial Relations, 1764–1776," *William and Mary Quarterly*, Third Series, 18 (October, 1961), 485–518; R. Don Higginbotham, *Daniel Morgan, Revolutionary Rifleman* (1961); Wilbur S. Howell, "The Declaration of Independence and Eighteenth-Century Logic," *William and Mary Quarterly*, Third Series, 18 (October, 1961), 463–484; Merrill Jensen, *The Articles of Confederation* (1948); Merrill Jensen, *The New Nation* (1950); Allen S. Johnson, "The Passage of the Sugar Act," *William and Mary Quarterly*, Third Series, 16 (October, 1959), 507–513; Sidney Kaplan, "Veteran Officers and Politics in Massachusetts, 1783–1787," *William and Mary Quarterly*, 9 (January, 1952), 29–58; Cecelia M. Kenyon, "Men of Little Faith: The Anti-Federalists on the Nature of Representative Government," *William and Mary Quarterly*, Third Series, 12 (January, 1955), 3–43; Marie Kimball, *Jefferson: The Scene of Europe, 1784 to 1789* (1950); Bernhard Knollenberg, *Washington and the Revolution* (1940); Bernhard Knollenberg, "General Amherst and Germ Warfare," *Mississippi Valley Historical Review*, 41 (December, 1954), 489–494; Bernhard Knollenberg, *Origin of the American Revolution* (1960); Adrienne Koch, "Pragmatic Wisdom and the American Enlightenment," *William and Mary Quarterly*, Third Series, 18 (July, 1961), 313–329; Harold Larson, "Alexander Hamilton: The Fact and Fiction of His Early Years," *William and Mary Quarterly*, Third Series, 9 (April, 1952), 139–151; Murray T. Lawson, "Canada and the Articles of Confederation," *American Historical Review* (October, 1952), 39–54; William R. Leslie, "The Gaspee Affair: A Study of Its Constitutional Significance," *Mississippi Valley Historical Review*, 39 (September, 1952), 233–256; David S. Lovejoy, "Rights Imply Equality: The Case Against Admiralty Jurisdiction in America, 1764–1776," *William and Mary Quarterly*, Third Series, 16 (October, 1959), 459–484; William L. Lumpkin, *Baptist Foundations in the South: Tracing through the Separates the Influence of the Great Awakening, 1754–1787* (1961); Forest McDonald, *We The People: The Economic Origins of the Constitution* (1958); Andrew C. McLaughlin, *The Confederation and the Constitution, 1783–1789* (1905); Jackson T. Main, *The Anti-Federalists: Critics of the Constitution, 1781–1788* (1961); Robert D. Meade, *Patrick Henry: Patriot in the Making* (1957); John C. Miller, *Origins of the American Revolution* (1943); Ralph N. Miller, "American Nationalism as a Theory of Nature," *William and Mary Quarterly*, Third Series, 12 (January, 1955), 74–95; Edmund S. and Helen M. Morgan, *The Stamp Act Crisis: Prologue to Revolution* (1953); Edmund S.

Morgan, *The Birth of the Republic, 1763–1789* (1956); Samuel E. Morison, *John Paul Jones, a Sailor's Biography* (1959); Samuel E. Morison, "Prelude to Independence: The Virginia Resolutions of May 15, 1776," *William and Mary Quarterly,* Third Series, 8 (October, 1951), 483–492; Russel B. Nye, *The Cultural Life of the New Nation: 1776–1830* (1960); Howard H. Peckham, *The War for Independence, a Military History* (1958); J. R. Pole, "Representation and Authority in Virginia from the Revolution to Reform," *Journal of Southern History,* 24 (February, 1958), 16–50; Robert C. Pugh, "The Revolutionary Militia in the Southern Campaign, 1780–1781," *William and Mary Quarterly,* Third Series, 14 (April, 1957), 154–175; Blackwell P. Robinson, *William R. Davie* (1957); Clinton L. Rossiter, *Seedtime of the Republic: the Origin of the American Tradition of Political Liberty* (1953); Kenneth R. Rossman, *Thomas Mifflin and the Politics of the American Revolution* (1952); Robert A. Rutland, *The Birth of the Bill of Rights, 1776–1791* (1955); Arthur M. Schlesinger, *The Colonial Merchants and the American Revolution, 1763–1776* (1918); Arthur M. Schlesinger, *Prelude to Independence: the Newspaper War on Britain, 1764–1776* (1957); Charles P. Smith, *James Wilson, Founding Father, 1742–1798* (1956); Albert B. Southwick, "The Molasses Act—A Source of Precedents," *William and Mary Quarterly,* Third Series, 8 (July, 1951), 389–405; Charles S. Sydnor, *Gentlemen Freeholders: Political Practices in Washington's Virginia* (1952); Theodore G. Thayer, *Nathanael Greene: Strategist of the American Revolution* (1960); Frederick B. Tolles, "The American Revolution Considered as a Social Movement: A Reevaluation," *American Historical Review,* 60 (October, 1954), 1–12; Roland G. Usher, Jr., "Royal Navy Impressment During the American Revolution," *Mississippi Valley Historical Review,* 37 (March, 1951), 673–688; Carl C. Van Doren, *Benjamin Franklin* (1938); Carl C. Van Doren, *Secret History of the American Revolution* (1941); Claude H. Van Tyne, *The Loyalists in the American Revolution* (1902); Claude H. Van Tyne, *The Causes of the War of Independence* (1922); Willard M. Wallace, *Appeal to Arms: a Military History of the American Revolution* (1951); Willard M. Wallace, *Traitorous Hero: the Life and Fortunes of Benedict Arnold* (1954); Christopher Ward, *The War of the Revolution,* ed., John R. Alden, 2 vols. (1952); William A. Williams, "The Age of Mercantilism: An Interpretation of the American Political Economy, 1763 to 1828," *William and Mary Quarterly,* Third Series, 15 (October, 1958), 419–437; Esmond Wright, *Fabric of Freedom, 1763–1800* (1961).

FEDERALISTS AND REPUBLICANS (1789–1815)

Thomas P. Abernethy, *The Burr Conspiracy* (1954); Henry Adams, *History of the United States of America,* 9 vols. (1889–1891); Mary P. Adams, "Jefferson's Reaction to the Treaty of San Ildefonso," *Journal of Southern History,* 21 (May, 1955), 173–186; Harry Ammon, "The Formation of the Republican Party in Virginia, 1789–1796," *Journal of Southern History,* 19 (August, 1953); 283–310; John D. Barnhart, *Valley of Democracy: The Frontier versus the Plantation in the Ohio Valley, 1775–1818* (1953); Charles A. Beard, *Economic Origins of Jeffersonian Democracy* (1915); Francis F. Beirne, *The War of 1812* (1949); Albert J. Beveridge, *The Life of John Marshall,* 4 vols. (1916–1919); Irving Brant, "Edmund Randolph, Not Guilty," *William and Mary Quarterly,* Third Series, 7 (April, 1950), 179–198; Irving Brant, "James Madison and His Times," *American Historical Review,* 57

(July, 1952), 853–870; Irving Brant, "Madison: On the Separation of Church and State," *William and Mary Quarterly,* Third Series, 8 (January, 1951), 3–24; Edward H. Cameron, *Samuel Slater, Father of American Manufactures* (1960); Joseph E. Charles, *The Origins of the American Party System; Three Essays* (1956); Edward S. Corwin, *John Marshall and the Constitution* (1919); Marcus Cunliffe, *The Nation Takes Shape, 1789–1837* (1959); Noble E. Cunningham, *The Jeffersonian Republicans: the Formation of Party Organization, 1789–1801* (1957); George Dangerfield, *Chancellor Robert R. Livingston of New York, 1746–1813* (1960); David B. Davis, "The Movement to Abolish Capital Punishment in America, 1787–1861," *American Historical Review,* 63 (January, 1957), 23–46; Alexander DeConde, *Entangling Alliance: Politics and Diplomacy under George Washington* (1958); Jane Lucas DeGrummond, *The Baratarians and the Battle of New Orleans* (1961); Clement Eaton, *The Growth of Southern Civilization, 1790–1860* (1961); Clement Eaton, "Southern Senators and the Right of Instruction, 1789–1860," *Journal of Southern History,* 18 (August, 1952), 303–319; William O. Foster, *James Jackson: Duelist and Militant Statesman, 1757–1806* (1960); Felix Gilbert, *To the Farewell Address: Ideas of Early American Foreign Policy* (1961); Jay C. Heinlein, "Albert Gallatin: A Pioneer in Public Administration," *William and Mary Quarterly,* Third Series, 7 (January, 1950), 64–94; Reginald Horsman, "American Indian Policy in the Old Northwest, 1783–1812," *William and Mary Quarterly,* Third Series, 18 (January, 1961), 35–53; Reginald Horsman, "British Indian Policy in the Northwest, 1807–1812," *Mississippi Valley Historical Review,* 45 (June, 1958), 51–66; Maud M. Hutcheson, "Mercy Warren, 1728–1814," *William and Mary Quarterly,* Third Series, 10 (July, 1953), 378–402; William T. Hutchinson, "Unite to Divide: Divide to Unite: The Shaping of American Federalism," *Mississippi Valley Historical Review,* 46 (June, 1959); 3–18; Wilbur D. Jones (ed.), "A British View of the War of 1812 and the Peace Negotiations," *Mississippi Valley Historical Review,* 45 (December, 1958), 481–487; Lawrence S. Kaplan, "Jefferson, the Napoleonic Wars, and the Balance of Power," *William and Mary Quarterly,* Third Series, 14 (April, 1957), 196–217; Adrienne Koch, *Jefferson and Madison: The Great Collaboration* (1950); Dumas Malone, *Jefferson and His Time,* 2 vols. (1948, 1953); Alpheus T. Mason, "The Federalist—A Split Personality," *American Historical Review,* 57 (April, 1952), 625–643; John C. Miller, *Crisis In Freedom: The Alien and Sedition Acts* (1951); John C. Miller, *Alexander Hamilton: Portrait in Paradox* (1959); John C. Miller, *The Federalist Era, 1789–1801* (1960); Nathan Miller, *The Enterprise of a Free People* (1962); Broadus Mitchell, *Alexander Hamilton,* 2 vols. (1957–1961); Donald G. Morgan, "The Origin of Supreme Court Dissent," *William and Mary Quarterly,* Third Series, 10 (July, 1953), 353–377; Curtis P. Nettels, *The Emergence of a National Economy, 1775–1815* (1962); Allan Nevins and Jeannette Mirsky, *The World of Eli Whitney* (1952); John S. Pancake, "Aaron Burr: Would-Be Usurper," *William and Mary Quarterly,* Third Series, 8 (April, 1951), 204–213; John S. Pancake, "The 'Invisibles': A Chapter in the Opposition to President Madison," *Journal of Southern History,* 21 (February, 1955), 17–37; Bradford Perkins, "George Canning, Great Britain and the United States, 1807–1809," *American Historical Review,* 63 (October, 1957), 1–22; Norman K. Risjord, "1812: Conservatives, War Hawks, and the Nation's Honor," *William and Mary Quarterly*, Third Series, 18 (April, 1961), 196–210; Marshall Smelser, "George Washington and the Alien and Sedition Acts," *American Historical Review*, 59 (January, 1954), 322–334; James M. Smith, *Freedom's Fetters: The Alien and Sedition Laws and American Civil Liberties* (1956); Anthony Steel, "Impressment in the Monroe-Pinkney Negotiations, 1806–1807," *American Historical Review*, 57 (January, 1952), 352–369; Leonard D. White, *The Jeffersonians: A Study in Administrative History, 1801–1829* (1951); Raymond Walters, Jr., *Albert Gallatin: Jeffersonian Financier and Diplomat* (1957); Leonard D. White, *The Federalists* (1948).

SECTIONALISM, JACKSONIAN DEMOCRACY, AND SLAVERY (1815–1841)

Gilbert H. Barnes, *The Anti-Slavery Impulse, 1830–1844* (1933); Samuel F. Bemis, *John Quincy Adams and the Foundations of American Foreign Policy* (1949); Samuel F. Bemis, *John Quincy Adams and the Union* (1956); Arthur E. Bestor, *Backwoods Utopias* (1950); Chauncey S. Boucher, *The Nullification Controversy in South Carolina* (1916); R. C. Buley, *The Old Northwest: Pioneer Period, 1815–1840*, 2 vols. (1950); Gerald M. Capers, *John C. Calhoun, Opportunist: A Reappraisal* (1960); E. Malcolm Carroll, *Origins of the Whig Party* (1925); Margaret L. Coit, *John C. Calhoun, American Portrait* (1950); Richard N. Current, *Daniel Webster and the Rise of National Conservatism* (1955); George Dangerfield, *The Era of Good Feelings* (1952); Margaret B. DesChamps, "Union or Division? South Atlantic Presbyterians and Southern Nationalism, 1820–1861," *Journal of Southern History* 20 (November, 1954), 484–498; John Duffy, "Medical Practice in the Ante-Bellum South," *Journal of Southern History*, 25 (February, 1959), 53–72; Dwight L. Dumond, *Anti-Slavery Origins of the Civil War in the United States* (1939); Clement Eaton, *Henry Clay and the Art of American Politics* (1957); Clement Eaton, "Slave-Hiring in the Upper South: A Step Toward Freedom," *Mississippi Valley Historical Review* 46 (March, 1960), 663–678; Stanley M. Elkins, *Slavery: A Problem in American Institutional and Intellectual Life* (1959); Claude M. Fuess, *Daniel Webster*, 2 vols. (1930); Paul W. Gates, *The Farmer's Age: Agriculture, 1815–1860* (1960); Constance M. Green, "The Jacksonian Revolution in the District of Columbia," *Mississippi Valley Historical Review*, 45 (March, 1959), 591–605; Clifford S. Griffin, "Religious Benevolence as Social Control, 1815–1860," *Mississippi Valley Historical Review*, 44 (December, 1957), 423–444; Oscar and Mary F. Handlin, "Origins of the Southern Labor System," *William and Mary Quarterly*, Third Series, 7 (April, 1950), 199–222; Joseph H. Harrison, Jr., "Martin Van Buren and His Southern Supporters," *Journal of Southern History*, 22 (November, 1956), 438–458; Charles A. Johnson, "The Frontier Camp Meeting: Contemporary and Historical Appraisals, 1805–1840," *Mississippi Valley Historical Review*, 37 (June, 1950), 91–110; Louis C. Hunter, *Steamboats on the Western Rivers* (1949); Marquis James, *The Raven, a Biography of Sam Houston* (1929); Marquis James, *Andrew Jackson*, 2 vols. (1933–1937); Lawrence Lader, *The Bold Brahmins: New England's War against Slavery, 1831–1863* (1961); Richard P. Longaker, "Was Jackson's Kitchen Cabinet a Cabinet?" *Mississippi Valley Historical Review*, 44 (June, 1957), 94–108; Richard D. Mc-

Cormick, "New Perspectives on Jacksonian Politics," *American Historical Review,* 65 (January, 1960), 288–301; Gale W. McGee, "The Monroe Doctrine—A Stopgap Measure," *Mississippi Valley Historical Review,* 38 (September, 1951), 233–250; Douglas H. Maynard, "The World's Anti-Slavery Convention of 1840," *Mississippi Valley Historical Review,* 47 (December, 1960), 452–471; Bernard Mayo, *Henry Clay* (1937); Hugo A. Meier, "Technology and Democracy, 1800–1860," *Mississippi Valley Historical Review,* 43 (March, 1957), 618–640; Chase C. Mooney, *Slavery in Tennessee* (1959); Glover Moore, *The Missouri Controversy, 1819–1821* (1953); Richard B. Morris, "The Measure of Bondage in the Slave States," *Mississippi Valley Historical Review,* 41 (September, 1954), 219–240; Ralph E. Morrow, "The Proslavery Argument Revisited," *Mississippi Valley Historical Review,* 48 (June, 1961), 79–94; Russel B. Nye, *William Lloyd Garrison and the Humanitarian Reformers* (1955); Robert A. Parker, *A Yankee Saint: John Humphrey Noyes and the Oneida Community* (1935); Howard H. Peckham, "Books and Reading on the Ohio Valley Frontier," *Mississippi Valley Historical Review,* 44 (March, 1958), 649–663; Dexter Perkins, *The Monroe Doctrine, 1823–1826* (1927); Dexter Perkins, *Hands Off: a History of the Monroe Doctrine* (1941); Edward Pessen, "The Workingmen's Movement of the Jacksonian Era," *Mississippi Valley Historical Review,* 43 (December, 1956), 428–443; Ulrich B. Phillips, *American Negro Slavery* (1918); Ulrich B. Phillips, *Life and Labor in the Old South* (1929); Norris W. Preyer, "Southern Support of the Tariff of 1816—A Reappraisal," *Journal of Southern History,* 25 (August, 1959), 306–322; Arthur H. Quinn, *Edgar Allan Poe* (1941); Arthur M. Schlesinger, Jr., *The Age of Jackson* (1945); Charles G. Sellers, "Jackson Men with Feet of Clay," *American Historical Review,* 62 (April, 1956), 537–551; Oscar Sherwin, *Prophet of Liberty: the Life and Times of Wendell Phillips* (1958); Charles W. Smith, *Roger B. Taney: Jacksonian Jurist* (1936); Elbert B. Smith, *Magnificent Missourian: The Life of Thomas Hart Benton* (1958); Kenneth M. Stampp, *The Peculiar Institution: Slavery in the Ante-Bellum South* (1956); P. J. Staudenhaus, *The African Colonization Movement, 1816–1865* (1961); Harry Stevens, *The Early Jacksonian Party in Ohio* (1957); Charles S. Sydnor, *The Development of Southern Sectionalism, 1819–1848* (1948); Benjamin P. Thomas, *Theodore Weld: Crusader for Freedom* (1950); Glyndon G. Van Deusen, *The Life of Henry Clay* (1937); Glyndon G. Van Deusen, "Some Aspects of Whig Thought and Theory in the Jacksonian Period," *American Historical Review,* 63 (January, 1958), 305–322; Glyndon G. Van Deusen, *The Jacksonian Era, 1828–1848* (1959); Richard C. Wade, "Urban Life in Western America, 1790–1830," *American Historical Review,* 64 (October, 1958), 14–30; Arthur P. Whitaker, *The United States and the Independence of Latin America, 1800–1830* (1941); Leonard D. White, *The Jacksonians: A Study in Administrative History, 1829–1861* (1954); Charles M. Wiltse, *The New Nation, 1800–1845* (1961); George R. Woolfolk, "Taxes and Slavery in the Ante-Bellum South," *Journal of Southern History,* 26 (May, 1960), 180–200; Paton Yoder, "Private Hospitality in the South, 1775–1850," *Mississippi Valley Historical Review,* 47 (December, 1960), 419–433; Mary E. Young, "The Creek Frauds: A Study in Conscience and Corruption," *Mississippi Valley Historical Review,* 42 (December, 1955), 411–437; Mary E. Young, "Indian Removal and Land Allotment: The Civilized Tribes and Jacksonian Justice," *American Historical Review,* 64 (October, 1958), 31–45.

EXPANSION AND INTERNAL CONFLICT (1841–1861)

Newton Arvin, *Herman Melville* (1950); Ray A. Billington, *The Far Western Frontier, 1830–1860* (1956); William C. Binkley, *The Texas Revolution* (1952); F. Brodie, *No Man Knows My History: The Life of Joseph Smith* (1945); Henry S. Canby, *Walt Whitman, an American* (1943); Gerald M. Capers, *Stephen A. Douglas, Defender of the Union* (1959); John A. Caruso, *The Great Lakes Frontier: an Epic of the Old Northwest* (1961); William N. Chambers, *Old Bullion Benton, Senator from the New West: Thomas Hart Benton, 1782–1858* (1956); Arthur Chapman, *The Pony Express* (1932); Freeman Cleaves, *Old Tippecanoe: William Henry Harrison and His Time* (1939); Robert G. Cleland, *This Reckless Breed of Men: the Trappers and Fur Traders of the Southwest* (1960); Henry S. Commager, *Theodore Parker* (1936); Avery O. Craven, *The Coming of the Civil War* (1942); Avery O. Craven, "The 1840's and the Democratic Process," *Journal of Southern History*, 15 (May, 1950), 161–176; Avery O. Craven, *The Growth of Southern Nationalism, 1848–1861* (1953); Avery O. Craven, *Civil War in the Making, 1815–1860* (1959); Granville D. Davis, "Arkansas and the Blood of Kansas," *Journal of Southern History*, 16 (November, 1950), 431–456; Philip F. Detweiler, "Congressional Debate on Slavery and the Declaration of Independence," *American Historical Review*, 63 (April, 1958), 598–616; Merton L. Dillon, "The Failure of the American Abolitionists," *Journal of Southern History*, 25 (May, 1959), 159–177; Dwight L. Dumond, *The Secession Movement* (1931); Robert F. Durden, "J. D. B. DeBow: Convolutions of a Slavery Expansionist," *Journal of Southern History*, 17 (November, 1951), 441–461; William H. Ellison, "San Juan to Cahuenga: The Experiences of Frémont's Battalion," *Pacific Historical Review*, 27 (August, 1958), 245–262; Don E. Fehrenbacher, "The Origin and Purposes of Lincoln's 'House-Divided' Speech," *Mississippi Valley Historical Review*, 46 (March, 1960), 615–643; D. E. Fehrenbacher, "Lincoln, Douglas, and the 'Freeport Question'," *American Historical Review*, 66 (April, 1961), 599–617; Louis Filler, *Crusaders for American Liberalism* (1950); Matthew A. Fitzsimons, "Calhoun's Bid for the Presidency, 1841–1844," *Mississippi Valley Historical Review*, 38 (June, 1951), 39–60; Betty L. Fladeland, *James Gillespie Birney: Slaveholder to Abolitionist* (1955); Joseph C. Furnas, *The Road to Harper's Ferry* (1959); John Hope Franklin, "The Southern Expansionists of 1846," *Journal of Southern History*, 25 (August, 1959), 323–338; Norman F. Furniss, *The Mormon Conflict, 1850–1859* (1960); Larry Gara, *The Liberty Line: The Legend of the Underground Railroad* (1961); Robert Gardner, "A Tenth-Hour Apology for Slavery," *Journal of Southern History*, 26 (August, 1960), 352–367; Paul W. Gates, *The Illinois Central Railroad and Its Colonization Work* (1934); Norman A. Graebner, *Empire on the Pacific: A Study in American Continental Expansion* (1955); Fletcher M. Green, "Northern Missionary Activities in the South, 1846–1861," *Journal of Southern History*, 21 (May, 1955), 147–172; Holman Hamilton, "Democratic Senate Leadership and the Compromise of 1850," *Mississippi Valley Historical Review*, 41 (December, 1954), 403–418; Holman Hamilton, "The 'Cave of Winds' and the Compromise of 1850," *Journal of Southern History*, 23 (August, 1957), 331–353; Lowell H. Harrison, "John Breckinridge: Western Statesman," *Journal of Southern History*, 18 (May, 1952), 137–151; Frank H. Heck, "John C. Breckinridge in the Crisis of 1860–1861," *Journal of Southern History*, 21 (August, 1955), 316–346; Robert S. Henry, *The Story of the Mexican War* (1950); Harry V. Jaffa, *Crisis of the House Divided: an Interpretation of the Lincoln-Douglas Debates* (1959); Robert W. Johannsen, "The Kansas-Nebraska Act and the Pacific Northwest Frontier," *Pacific Historical Review*, 22 (May, 1953), 129–142; Robert W. Johannsen, "Stephen A. Douglas, 'Harper's Magazine,' and Popular Sovereignty," *Mississippi Valley Historical Review*, 45 (March, 1959), 606–631; Wilbur D. Jones, "Lord Ashburton and the Maine Boundary Negotiations," *Mississippi Valley Historical Review*, 40 (December, 1953), 477–490; Wilbur D. Jones, and J. Chal Vinson, "British Preparedness and the Oregon Settlement," *Pacific Historical Review*, 22 (November, 1953), 353–364; Weymouth T. Jordan, "Cotton Planters' Conventions in the Old South," *Journal of Southern History*, 19 (August, 1953), 321–345; Ralph Korngold, *Two Friends of Man: The Story of William Lloyd Garrison and Wendell Phillips, and their Relationship with Abraham Lincoln* (1950); Ernest M. Lander, Jr., "Charleston: Manufacturing Center of the Old South," *Journal of Southern History*, 26 (August, 1960), 330–351; Harral E. Landry, "Slavery and the Slave Trade in Atlantic Diplomacy, 1850–1861," *Journal of Southern History*, 27 (May, 1961), 184–207; Alma Lutz, *Susan B. Anthony: Rebel, Crusader, Humanitarian* (1959); Helen E. Marshall, *Dorothea Dix: Forgotten Samaritan* (1937); Francis O. Matthiessen, *American Renaissance* (1941); Frederick Merk, "The Genesis of the Oregon Question," *Mississippi Valley Historical Review*, 36 (March, 1950), 583–612; Frederick Merk, "The Oregon Question in the Webster-Ashburton Negotiations," *Mississippi Valley Historical Review*, 43 (December, 1956), 379–404; Frederick Merk, "Presidential Fevers," *Mississippi Valley Historical Review*, 47 (June, 1960), 3–33; Edwin A. Miles, " 'Fifty-four Forty or Fight'—An American Political Legend," *Mississippi Valley Historical Review*, 44 (September, 1957), 291–309; George F. Milton, *The Eve of Conflict: Stephen A. Douglas and the Needless War* (1934); J. Preston Moore, "Pierre Soulé: Southern Expansionist and Promoter," *Journal of Southern History*, 21 (May, 1955), 203–223; Powell Moore, "James K. Polk, Tennessee Politician," *Journal of Southern History*, 17 (November, 1951), 493–516; Allan Nevins, *Frémont, the West's Greatest Adventurer*, 2 vols. (1928); Allan Nevins, *The Emergence of Lincoln* (1950); Roy F. Nichols, *Franklin Pierce* (1931); Roy F. Nichols, *The Disruption of American Democracy* (1948); Roy F. Nichols, *The Stakes of Power, 1845–1877* (1961); William L. Neumann, "Religion, Morality, and Freedom: The Ideological Background of the Perry Expedition," *Pacific Historical Review*, 23 (August, 1954), 247–258; James W. Patton, "Facets of the South in the 1850's," *Journal of Southern History* 23 (February, 1957), 3–24; Robert J. Rayback, *Millard Fillmore: Biography of a President* (1959); Joseph G. Rayback (ed.), "Martin Van Buren's Desire for Revenge in the Campaign of 1848," *Mississippi Valley Historical Review*, 40 (March, 1954), 707–716; Jesse S. Reeves, *American Diplomacy under Tyler and Polk* (1907); Edwin C. Rozwenc (ed.), *Slavery as a Cause of the Civil War* (1949); Robert R. Russel, "What Was the Compromise of 1850?" *Journal of Southern History*, 22 (August, 1956), 292–309; Charles G. Sellers, Jr., *James K. Polk: Jacksonian, 1795–1843* (1957); Charles G. Sellers, Jr., "Who Were the Southern Whigs?" *American Historical Review*, 59 (January, 1954), 335–346; Timothy L. Smith, *Revivalism and Social Reform in Mid-Nineteenth-Century America* (1957); C. P. Stacey, "The

Myth of the Unguarded Frontier, 1850–1871," *American Historical Review,* 56 (October, 1950), 1–18; Kenneth M. Stampp, *And the War Came: the North and the Secession Crisis, 1860–1861* (1950); Glyndon G. Van Deusen, *Thurlow Weed* (1947); Glyndon G. Van Deusen, *Horace Greeley, Nineteenth-Century Crusader* (1953); Mason Wade, *Francis Parkman, Heroic Historian* (1942); Rush Welter, "The Frontier West as Image of American Society: Conservative Attitudes before the Civil War," *Mississippi Valley Historical Review,* 46 (March, 1960), 593–614; Albert K. Weinberg, *Manifest Destiny* (1935); Frank B. Woodford, *Lewis Cass, the Last Jeffersonian* (1950).

THE CIVIL WAR

Ephraim D. Adams, *Great Britain and the American Civil War,* 2 vols. (1925); John G. Barrett, *Sherman's March Through the Carolinas* (1956); Edward C. Boykin, *Ghost Ship of the Confederacy: The Story of the Alabama and her Captain, Raphael Semmes* (1957); Gamaliel Bradford, *Union Portraits* (1916); Robert Carse, *Blockade: The Civil War at Sea* (1958); Bruce Catton, *Mr. Lincoln's Army* (1951); Bruce Catton, *Glory Road: the Bloody Route from Fredericksburg to Gettysburg* (1952); Bruce Catton, *A Stillness at Appomattox* (1953); Bruce Catton, *U. S. Grant and the American Military Tradition* (1954); Bruce Catton, *Grant Moves South* (1960); Freeman Cleaves, *Rock of Chickamauga, The Life of General George H. Thomas* (1948); Thomas C. Cochran, "Did the Civil War Retard Industrialization?" *Mississippi Valley Historical Review,* 48 (September, 1961), 197–210; Henry S. Commager (ed.), *The Blue and Gray: the Story of the Civil War as Told by Participants,* 2 vols. (1950); E. Merton Coulter, *The Confederate States of America, 1861–1865* (1950); Richard N. Current, *The Lincoln Nobody Knows* (1958); David H. Donald, "The Confederate as a Fighting Man," *Journal of Southern History,* 25 (May, 1959), 178–193; David H. Donald, *Lincoln Reconsidered: Essays on the Civil War Era* (1956); John P. Dyer, "Northern Relief for Savannah during Sherman's Occupation," *Journal of Southern History,* 19 (November, 1953), 457–472; Clement Eaton, *A History of the Southern Confederacy* (1954); Shelby Foote, *The Civil War, a Narrative* (1958); Seymour J. Frank, "The Conspiracy to Implicate the Confederate Leaders in Lincoln's Assassination," *Mississippi Valley Historical Review,* 40 (March, 1954), 629–656; Benjamin F. Gilbert, "French Warships on the Mexican West Coast, 1861–1866," *Pacific Historical Review,* 24 (February, 1955), 25–38; Wood Gray, *The Hidden Civil War* (1942); Bray Hammond, "The North's Empty Purse, 1861–1862," *American Historical Review,* 67 (October, 1961), 1–18; Burton J. Hendrick, *Statesmen of the Lost Cause* (1939); Robert S. Holzman, *Stormy Ben Butler* (1954); Ludwell H. Johnson, "Fort Sumter and Confederate Diplomacy," *Journal of Southern History,* 26 (November, 1960), 441–477; Donaldson Jordan and Edwin J. Pratt, *Europe and the American Civil War* (1931); Frank L. Klement, "Middle Western Copperheadism and the Genesis of the Granger Movement," *Mississippi Valley Historical Review,* 38 (March, 1952), 679–694; Basil H. Liddell Hart, *Sherman: Soldier, Realist, American* (1929); Douglas H. Maynard, "Plotting the Escape of the Alabama," *Journal of Southern History,* 20 (May, 1954), 197–209; Douglas H. Maynard, "Union Efforts to Prevent the Escape of the *Alabama*," *Mississippi Valley Historical Review,* 41 (June, 1954), 41–60; Earl S. Miers, *The Web of Victory:*

Grant at Vicksburg (1955); Jay Monaghan, *Civil War on the Western Border, 1854–1865* (1955); Allan Nevins, *Ordeal of the Union,* 2 vols. (1947); Allan Nevins, *The War for the Union,* 2 vols. (1959); Roy F. Nichols, "1860–1861: The American Civil War in Perspective," *Journal of Southern History,* 15 (May, 1950), 143–160; Roy F. Nichols, "The Operation of American Democracy, 1861–1865," *Journal of Southern History,* 25 (February, 1959), 31–52; Frank L. Owsley, *States Rights in the Confederacy* (1925); Frank L. Owsley, *King Cotton Diplomacy* (1931); Thomas J. Pressly, *Americans Interpret Their Civil War* (1954); Raoul S. Naroll, "Lincoln and the Sherman Peace Fiasco—Another Fable?" *Journal of Southern History,* 20 (November, 1954), 459–483; Fletcher Pratt, *Stanton, Lincoln's Secretary of War* (1953); Benjamin Quarles, *The Negro in the Civil War* (1953); James Z. Rabun, "Alexander H. Stephens and Jefferson Davis," *American Historical Review,* 58 (October, 1952), 290–321; James G. Randall, *The Civil War and Reconstruction* (1937); James G. Randall, *Lincoln, the President,* 4 vols. (1945–1955); Donald B. Sanger and Thomas R. Hay, *James Longstreet: Soldier, Politician, Officeholder, and Writer* (1952); Nathaniel W. Stephenson, *Abraham Lincoln and the Union* (1918); Philip V. Stern, *An End to Valor: The Last Days of the Civil War* (1958); William N. Still, Jr., "Confederate Naval Strategy: The Ironclad," *Journal of Southern History,* 27 (August, 1961), 330–343; Benjamin D. Thomas, *Abraham Lincoln, A Biography* (1952); Frank E. Vandiver, *Rebel Brass: The Confederate Command System* (1956); Frank E. Vandiver, *Mighty Stonewall* (1957); Paul P. Van Riper, and Harry N. Scheiber, "The Confederate Civil Service," *Journal of Southern History,* 25 (November, 1958), 448–470; Charles H. Wesley, *The Collapse of the Confederacy* (1937); Bell I. Wiley, *The Plain People of the Confederacy* (1943); Bell I. Wiley, *The Life of Johnny Reb, the Common Soldier of the Confederacy* (1943); Bell I. Wiley, "Southern Reaction to Northern Invasion," *Journal of Southern History,* 16 (November, 1950), 491–510; Bell I. Wiley, *The Life of Billy Yank, the Common Soldier of the Union* (1952); Bell I. Wiley, "A Time of Greatness," *Journal of Southern History,* 22 (February, 1956), 3–35; Kenneth D. Williams, *Lincoln Finds a General: A Military Study of the Civil War,* 5 vols. (1949–1959); T. Harry Williams, "Abraham Lincoln—Principle and Pragmatism in Politics," *Mississippi Valley Historical Review,* 40 (June, 1953), 89–106; Thomas H. Williams, *Lincoln and His Generals* (1952); Wilfred B. Yearns, *The Confederate Congress* (1960).

RECONSTRUCTION AND CONSTRUCTION (1865–1898)

Henry Adams, *The Education of Henry Adams* (1918); Thomas A. Bailey, "America's Emergence as a World Power: The Myth and the Verity," *Pacific Historical Review,* 30 (February, 1961), 1–16; Charles A. Barker, *Henry George* (1955); Harry Barnard, *Eagle Forgotten: The Life of John Peter Altgeld* (1938); Harry Barnard, *Rutherford B. Hayes and His America* (1954); Constantine G. Belissary, "The Rise of Industry and the Industrial Spirit in Tennessee, 1865–1885," *Journal of Southern History,* 19 (May, 1953), 193–215; Rowland T. Berthoff, "Southern Attitudes Toward Immigration, 1865–1914," *Journal of Southern History,* 17 (August, 1951), 328–360; John Berryman, *Stephen Crane* (1950); Allan G. Bogue, *Money at Interest: The Farm Mortgage on the Middle Border* (1955); Harold W. Bradley, *American Frontier in Hawaii* (1942); Solon J. Buck, *The Agrarian Cru-*

sade (1920); Paul H. Buck, *The Road to Reunion, 1865–1900* (1937); Jacqueline P. Bull, "The General Merchant in the Economic History of the New South," *Journal of Southern History,* 18 (February, 1952), 37–59; Gerald Carson, *The Old Country Store* (1954); Hodding Carter, *The Angry Scar: the Story of Reconstruction* (1959); J. Stanley Clark, *The Oil Century, from the Drake Well to the Conservation Era* (1958); Paolo E. Coletta, "Bryan, McKinley, and the Treaty of Paris," *Pacific Historical Review,* 26 (May, 1957), 131–146; Paolo E. Coletta, "McKinley, the Peace Negotiations, and the Acquisition of the Philippines," *Pacific Historical Review,* 30 (November, 1961), 341–350; Henry S. Commager, *The American Mind: An Interpretation of American Thought and Character Since the 1880's* (1950); Egon C. Corti, *Maximilian and Charlotte of Mexico,* 2 vols. (1928); Stanley Coben, "Northeastern Business and Radical Reconstruction: A Re-examination," *Mississippi Valley Historical Review,* 46 (June, 1959), 67–90; La Wanda Cox, "The Promise of Land for the Freedmen," *Mississippi Valley Historical Review,* 45 (December, 1958), 413–441; Merle Curti and Kendall Birr, "The Immigrant and the American Image in Europe, 1860–1914," *Mississippi Valley Historical Review,* 37 (September, 1950), 203–230; Edward E. Dale, *The Range Cattle Industry* (1930); Ethel M. Damon, *Sanford Ballard Dole and His Hawaii* (1957); William C. Darrah, *Powell of the Colorado* (1951); Henry David, *The History of the Haymarket Affair* (1936); Anna A. De Mille, *Henry George, Citizen of the World* (1950); Vincent P. De Santis, *Republicans Face the Southern Question: the New Departure Years, 1877–1897* (1959); Chester M. Destler, "The Opposition of American Businessmen to Social Control During the 'Gilded Age,'" *Mississippi Valley Historical Review,* 39 (March, 1953), 641–672; Herbert J. Doherty, Jr., "Voices of Protest from the New South, 1875–1910," *Mississippi Valley Historical Review,* 42 (June, 1955), 45–66; Henderson H. Donald, *The Negro Freedman: Life Conditions of the American Negro in the Early Years After Emancipation* (1952); Timothy P. Donovan, *Henry Adams and Brooks Adams: The Education of Two American Historians* (1961); Martin B. Duberman, *Charles Francis Adams, 1807–1886* (1961); William E. B. Du Bois, *Black Reconstruction* (1935); Robert F. Durden, *James Shephard Pike: Republicanism and the American Negro, 1850–1882* (1957); Gerald G. Eggert, "Richard Olney and the Income Tax Cases," *Mississippi Valley Historical Review,* 48 (June, 1961), 24–41; Harold U. Faulkner, *Politics, Reform, and Expansion, 1890–1900* (1959); Gilbert C. Fite, "Republican Strategy and the Farm Vote in the Presidential Campaign of 1896," *American Historical Review,* 64 (July, 1960), 787–806; Sidney Fine, "Richard T. Ely, Forerunner of Progressivism, 1880–1901," *Mississippi Valley Historical Review,* 37 (March, 1951), 599–624; Sidney Fine, *Laissez Faire and the General-Welfare State: A Study of Conflict in American Thought, 1865–1901* (1956); Leslie H. Fishel, Jr., "The Negro in Northern Politics, 1870–1900," *Mississippi Valley Historical Review,* 42 (December, 1955), 466–489; Joe B. Frantz and Julian E. Choate, *The American Cowboy: The Myth and the Reality* (1955); Wayne Gard, *The Great Buffalo Hunt* (1959); Ray Ginger, *Altgeld's America: The Lincoln Ideal versus Changing Realities* (1958); Dewey W. Grantham, *Hoke Smith and the Politics of the New South* (1958); Fletcher M. Green, "Origins of the Crédit Mobilier of America," *Mississippi Valley Historical Review,* 46 (September, 1959), 238–251; Gene M. Gressley, "The American Cattle Trust: A Study in Protest," *Pacific Historical Review,* 30

(February, 1961), 61–78; Le Roy R. Hafen and Carl C. Rister, *Western America* (1941); Rowland H. Harvey, *Samuel Gompers, Champion of the Toiling Masses* (1935); Paul L. Haworth, *The Hayes-Tilden Disputed Presidential Election of 1876* (1906); Burton J. Hendrick, *The Life of Andrew Carnegie*, 2 vols. (1932); Robert S. Henry, *The Story of Reconstruction* (1938); Paxton Hibben, *The Peerless Leader: William Jennings Bryan* (1929); John Higham, "The American Party, 1886–1891," *Pacific Historical Review,* 19 (February, 1950), 37–46; John Higham, *Strangers in the Land: Patterns of American Nativism, 1860–1925* (1955); John Higham, "Anti-Semitism in the Gilded Age: A Reinterpretation," *Mississippi Valley Historical Review,* 43 (March, 1957), 559–578; Mark D. Hirsch, "Samuel J. Tilden: The Story of a Lost Opportunity," *American Historical Review,* 56 (July, 1951), 788–802; Richard Hofstadter, *Social Darwinism in American Thought, 1860–1915* (1944); Ari Hoogenboom, "The Pendleton Act and the Civil Service," *American Historical Review,* 64 (January, 1959), 301–318; Emerson Hough, *The Story of the Cowboy* (1897); Joseph B. James, "Southern Reaction to the Proposal of the Fourteenth Amendment," *Journal of Southern History,* 22 (November, 1956), 477–497; Guion G. Johnson, "Southern Paternalism toward Negroes after Emancipation," *Journal of Southern History,* 23 (November, 1957), 483–509; Albert D. Kirwan, *Revolt of the Rednecks: Mississippi Politics, 1876–1925* (1951); Alfred H. Kelly, "The Congressional Controversy over School Segregation, 1867–1875," *American Historical Review,* 64 (April, 1959), 537–563; Edward C. Kirkland, *Dream and Thought in the Business Community, 1860–1900* (1956); Edward C. Kirkland, *Industry Comes of Age: Business, Labor, and Public Policy, 1860–1897* (1961); Oliver Knight, *Following the Indian Wars: the Story of the Newspaper Correspondents among the Indian Campaigners* (1960); George H. Knoles, *The Presidential Campaign and Election of 1892* (1942); Ralph Korngold, *Thaddeus Stevens: A Being Darkly Wise and Rudely Great* (1955); Margaret Leech, *In the Days of McKinley* (1959); Jacob C. Levenson, *The Mind and Art of Henry Adams* (1957); Elsie M. Lewis, "The Political Mind of the Negro, 1865–1900," *Journal of Southern History,* 21 (May, 1955), 189–202; Rayford W. Logan, *The Negro in American Life and Thought: The Nadir, 1877–1901* (1954); Milton Lomask, *Andrew Johnson: President on Trial* (1960); Clarence D. Long, *Wages and Earnings in the United States, 1860–1890* (1960); Denis T. Lynch, *The Wild Seventies* (1941); Eric L. McKitrick, *Andrew Johnson and Reconstruction* (1960); W. D. McIntyre, "Anglo-American Rivalry in the Pacific: The British Annexation of the Fiji Islands in 1874," *Pacific Historical Review,* 29 (November, 1960), 361–380; Percy F. Martin, *Maximilian in Mexico* (1914); Horace S. Merrill, *Bourbon Democracy of the Middle West, 1865–1896* (1953); Horace S. Merrill, *Bourbon Leader: Grover Cleveland and the Democratic Party* (1957); Arthur E. Morgan, *Edward Bellamy* (1944); Ralph E. Morrow, "Northern Methodism in the South During Reconstruction," *Mississippi Valley Historical Review,* 41 (September, 1954), 197–218; David S. Muzzey, *James G. Blaine* (1934); Allan Nevins, *The Emergence of Modern America, 1865–1878* (1928); Allan Nevins, *Grover Cleveland: a Study in Courage* (1932); Allan Nevins, *Hamilton Fish: the Inner Story of the Grant Administration* (1936); Allan Nevins, *Study in Power: John D. Rockefeller, Industrialist and Philanthropist,* 2 vols. (1953); Charles M. Oehler, *The Great Sioux Uprising* (1959); Ernest S. Osgood, *The Day of the Cattleman*

(1929); Richard C. Overton, *Burlington West* (1941); Frederic L. Paxson, *The Last American Frontier* (1910); Dexter Perkins, *The Monroe Doctrine, 1867–1907* (1937); Julius W. Pratt, *Expansionists of 1898* (1936); Samuel Rezneck, "Patterns of Thought and Action in an American Depression, 1882–1886," *American Historical Review*, 61 (January, 1956), 284–307; Robert E. Riegel, *The Story of the Western Railroads* (1926); Andrew F. Rolle, "California Filibustering and the Hawaiian Kingdom," *Pacific Historical Review*, 19 (August, 1950), 251–264; Margaret S. Royall, *Andrew Johnson—Presidential Scapegoat: a Biographical Reevaluation* (1958); William A. Russ, *The Hawaiian Revolution, 1893–1894* (1959); William A. Russ, *The Hawaiian Republic, 1894–1898, and Its Struggle to Win Annexation* (1961); James F. S. Russell, "The Railroads in the 'Conspiracy Theory' of the Fourteenth Amendment," *Mississippi Valley Historical Review*, 41 (March, 1955), 601–622; Theodore Saloutos, "The Grange in the South, 1870–1877," *Journal of Southern History*, 19 (November, 1953), 473–487; Ernest Samuels, *Henry Adams, the Middle Years* (1958); Edward N. Saveth, *American Historians and European Immigrants, 1875–1925* (1948); Roy V. Scott, "Milton George and the Farmer's Alliance Movement," *Mississippi Valley Historical Review*, 45 (June, 1958), 90–109; Jack B. Scroggs, "Carpetbagger Constitutional Reform in the South Atlantic States, 1867–1868," *Journal of Southern History*, 27 (November, 1961), 475–493; Jack B. Scroggs, "Southern Reconstruction: A Radical View," *Journal of Southern History*, 24 (November, 1958), 407–429; Robert Seager, II, "Ten Years Before Mahan: The Unofficial Case for the New Navy, 1880–1890," *Mississippi Valley Historical Review*, 40 (December, 1953), 491–512; Francis B. Simkins, *The Tillman Movement in South Carolina* (1926); John G. Sproat, "Blueprint for Radical Reconstruction," *Journal of Southern History*, 23 (February, 1957), 25–44; Sylvester K. Stevens, *American Expansion in Hawaii, 1842–1898* (1945); Harold C. Syrett (ed.), *The Gentleman and the Tiger: The Autobiography of George B. McClellan* (1956); Philip Taft, *The A.F. of L. in the Time of Gompers* (1957); George B. Tindall, *South Carolina Negroes, 1877–1900* (1952); Arlin Turner, *George W. Cable, A Biography* (1956); Stanley Vestal, *Sitting Bull, Champion of the Sioux* (1932); Walter Prescott Webb, *The Great Plains* (1931); Francis D. Weisenburger, *Ordeal of Faith: The Crisis of Church-Going America, 1865–1900* (1959); Clifford D. Westermeier, *Who Rush to Glory: The Cowboy Volunteers of 1898* (1958); Leonard D. White, *The Republican Era, 1869–1901: A Study in Administrative History* (1958); Marcus M. Wilkerson, *Public Opinion and the Spanish-American War* (1932); Harold F. Williamson and Arnold R. Daum, *American Petroleum Industry: the Age of Illumination, 1859–1899* (1959); George R. Woolfolk, *The Cotton Regency: Northern Merchants and Reconstruction, 1865–1880* (1958); C. Vann Woodward, *Tom Watson, Agrarian Rebel* (1938); C. Vann Woodward, *Reunion and Reaction: The Compromise of 1877 and the End of Reconstruction* (1951); C. Vann Woodward, *Origins of the New South, 1877–1913* (1951); C. Vann Woodward, *The Strange Career of Jim Crow* (1955).

THE RISE OF PROGRESSIVISM (1898–1914)

Frederick L. Allen, *The Great Pierpont Morgan* (1949); Frederick L. Allen, *The Big Change: America Transforms Itself, 1900–1950* (1952); George L. Anderson, *Issues and Conflicts: Studies in 20th Century American Diplomacy* (1959); Clarence

A. Bacote, "Negro Proscriptions, Protests, and Proposed Solutions in Georgia, 1880–1908," *Journal of Southern History,* 25 (November, 1959), 471–498; J. Leonard Bates, "Fulfilling American Democracy: The Conservation Movement, 1907 to 1921," *Mississippi Valley Historical Review,* 44 (June, 1957), 29–59; Lawrence H. Battistin, *The Rise of American Influence in Asia and the Pacific* (1960); Howard K. Beale, *Theodore Roosevelt and the Rise of America to World Power* (1956); Adolph A. Berle, Jr., *The 20th Century Capitalist Revolution* (1954); John M. Blum, *The Republican Roosevelt* (1954); Francis L. Broderick, *W. E. B. Du Bois, Negro Leader in a Time of Crisis* (1959); Eugene K. Chamberlin, "The Japanese Scare at Magdalena Bay," *Pacific Historical Review,* 24 (November, 1955), 345–360; Tyler Dennett, *Roosevelt and the Russo-Japanese War* (1925); Tyler Dennett, *John Hay: From Poetry to Politics* (1933); John A. De Novo, "Petroleum and the United States Navy before World War I," *Mississippi Valley Historical Review,* 41 (March, 1954), 641–656; Donald D. Egbert and Stow Persons (eds.), *Socialism and American Life,* 2 vols. (1952); Raymond A. Esthus, "The Changing Concept of the Open Door, 1899–1910," *Mississippi Valley Historical Review,* 46 (December, 1959), 435–454; Harold U. Faulkner, *The Quest for Social Justice, 1898–1914* (1931); Harold U. Faulkner, *The Decline of Laissez-Faire, 1897–1917* (1951); Sidney Fine, "Anarchism and the Assassination of McKinley," *American Historical Review,* 60 (July, 1955), 777–799; Sidney Fine, "The Eight-Hour Day Movement in the United States, 1888–1891," *Mississippi Valley Historical Review,* 40 (December, 1953), 441–462; Charles Forcey, *The Crossroads of Liberalism: Croly, Weyl, Lippmann, and the Progressive Era, 1900–1925* (1961); Felix Frankfurter (ed.), *Mr. Justice Holmes and the Constitution* (1927); Frank B. Freidel, *The Splendid Little War* (1958); Lionel M. Gelber, *The Rise of Anglo-American Friendship* (1938); Paul W. Glad, *The Trumpet Soundeth: William Jennings Bryan and His Democracy, 1896–1912* (1960); Allen J. Going, "The South and the Blair Education Bill," *Mississippi Valley Historical Review,* 44 (September, 1957), 267–290; William H. Gray, "The First Constitution of the Philippines," *Pacific Historical Review,* 26 (November, 1957), 341–352; Fred Greene, "The Military View of American National Policy, 1904–1940," *American Historical Review,* 66 (January, 1961), 354–377; J. A. S. Grenville, "Great Britain and the Isthmian Canal, 1898–1901," *American Historical Review,* 61 (October, 1955), 48–69; Paul Y. Hammond, *Organizing for Defense: The American Military Establishment in the Twentieth Century* (1961); John D. Hicks and Theodore Saloutos, *Agricultural Discontent in the Middle West, 1900–1939* (1951); Richard Hofstadter, *The Age of Reform: From Bryan to F.D.R.* (1955); Arthur M. Johnson, "Anti-trust Policy in Transition, 1908: Ideal and Reality," *Mississippi Valley Historical Review,* 48 (December, 1961), 415–434; Arthur M. Johnson, "Theodore Roosevelt and the Bureau of Corporations," *Mississippi Valley Historical Review,* 45 (March, 1959), 571–590; Matthew Josephson, *Edison: a Biography* (1959); Padriac C. Kennedy, "La Follette's Imperialist Flirtation," *Pacific Historical Review,* 29 (May, 1960), 131–135; Belle C. La Follette, and Fola La Follette, *Robert M. La Follette, June 14, 1855–June 18, 1925,* 2 vols. (1953); Christopher Lasch, "The Anti-Imperialists, the Philippines, and the Inequality of Man," *Journal of Southern History* (August, 1958), 319–331; Richard W. Leopold, *Elihu Root and the Conservative Tradition* (1954); Richard W. Leopold, "The Mississippi

Valley and American Foreign Policy, 1890–1941: An Assessment and an Appeal,"
Mississippi Valley Historical Review, 37 (March, 1951), 625–642; William E.
Leuchtenburg, "Progressivism and Imperialism: The Progressive Movement and
American Foreign Policy, 1898–1916," *Mississippi Valley Historical Review,* 39
(December, 1952), 483–504; A. Lincoln, "Theodore Roosevelt, Hiram Johnson,
and the Vice-Presidential Nomination of 1912," *Pacific Historical Review,* 28
(August, 1959), 267–284; Arthur S. Link, *American Epoch: a History of the
United States since the 1890's* (1955); Seward W. Livermore, "The American Navy
as a Factor in World Politics, 1903–1913," *American Historical Review,* 63 (July,
1958), 863–879; M. Nelson McGeary, *Gifford Pinchot, Forester—Politician* (1960);
William G. McLoughlin, *Billy Sunday Was His Real Name* (1955); Arthur Mann,
"British Social Thought and American Reformers of the Progressive Era," *Missis-
sippi Valley Historical Review,* 42 (March, 1956), 672–692; Arthur Mann, *Yankee
Reformers in the Urban Age* (1954); Francis O. Matthiessen, *Theodore Dreiser*
(1951); Henry F. May, *Protestant Churches and Industrial America* (1949); Ralph
E. Minger, "Taft's Missions to Japan: A Study in Personal Diplomacy," *Pacific
Historical Review,* 30 (August, 1961), 279–294; George E. Mowry, *The California
Progressives* (1951); George E. Mowry, *The Era of Theodore Roosevelt, 1900–1912*
(1958); David W. Noble, *The Paradox of Progressive Thought* (1958); Dexter
Perkins, *Charles Evans Hughes and American Democratic Statesmanship* (1956);
Amos R. E. Pinchot, *History of the Progressive Party, 1912–1916* (1958); Julius W.
Pratt, *America's Colonial Experiment: How the United States Gained, Governed,
and in Part Gave Away a Colonial Empire* (1950); Henry F. Pringle, *Theodore
Roosevelt* (1931); Henry F. Pringle, *The Life and Times of William Howard Taft,*
2 vols. (1939); William D. Puleston, *Mahan* (1939); Merlo J. Pusey, *Charles Evans
Hughes,* 2 vols. (1951); Edwin O. Reischauer, *United States and Japan* (1950);
David Riesman, *Thorsten Veblen, a Critical Interpretation* (1953); Carl C. Rister,
"The Oilman's Frontier," *Mississippi Valley Historical Review,* 37 (June, 1950),
3–16; Vernon W. Roelofs, "Justice William R. Day and Federal Regulation,"
Mississippi Valley Historical Review, 37 (June, 1950), 39–60; David A. Shannon,
The Socialist Party of America: A History (1955); Fred Shannon, "The Status of
the Midwestern Farmer in 1900," *Mississippi Valley Historical Review,* 37 (De-
cember, 1950), 491–510; Herbert W. Schneider, *Religion in 20th Century America*
(1952); Nathaniel W. Stephenson, *Nelson W. Aldrich, a Leader in American
Politics* (1930); Emma Lou Thornbrough, "The Brownsville Episode and the
Negro Vote," *Mississippi Valley Historical Review,* 44 (December, 1957), 469–493;
Emma Lou Thornbrough, "The National Afro-American League, 1887–1908,"
Journal of Southern History, 27 (November, 1961), 494–512; Florence C. Thorne,
Samuel Gompers, American Statesman (1957); Willard Thorp, *American Writing
in the Twentieth Century* (1960); Payson J. Treat, *Diplomatic Relations between
the United States and Japan, 1853–1905,* 3 vols. (1932–1938); Charles R. Van Hise,
The Conservation of Natural Resources in the United States (1910); Paul A. Varg,
*Missionaries, Chinese, and Diplomats: the American Protestant Missionary Move-
ment in China, 1890–1952* (1958); Charles Vevier, "The Open Door: An Idea in
Action, 1906–1913," *Pacific Historical Review,* 24 (February, 1955), 49–62; Edward
Wagenknecht, *The Seven Worlds of Theodore Roosevelt* (1958); Robert H.
Wiebe, "The Anthracite Strike of 1902: A Record of Confusion," *Mississippi*

Valley Historical Review, 48 (September, 1961), 229–251; Robert H. Wiebe, "Business Disunity and the Progressive Movement, 1901–1914," *Mississippi Valley Historical Review*, 44 (March, 1958), 664–685; Robert H. Wiebe, "The House of Morgan and the Executive, 1905–1913," *American Historical Review*, 65 (October, 1959), 49–60; Jane Zimmerman, "The Penal Reform Movement in the South during the Progressive Era, 1890–1917," *Journal of Southern History*, 17 (November, 1951), 462–492.

WORLD WAR I AND ITS AFTERMATH (1914–1933)

Richard M. Abrams, "Woodrow Wilson and the Southern Congressmen, 1913–1916," *Journal of Southern History*, 22 (November, 1956), 417–437; James T. Adams, *Our Business Civilization* (1929); Selig Adler, *The Isolationist Impulse: Its Twentieth Century Reaction* (1957); Herbert Asbury, *The Great Illusion: An Informal History of Prohibition* (1950); Lewis E. Atherton, *Main Street on the Middle Border* (1954); Wesley M. Bagby, "The 'Smoke Filled Room' and the Nomination of Warren G. Harding," *Mississippi Valley Historical Review*, 41 (March, 1954), 657–676; Ray S. Baker, *Woodrow Wilson, Life and Letters*, 8 vols. (1927–1939); Thomas A. Bailey, *Woodrow Wilson and the Lost Peace* (1944); Thomas A. Bailey, *Woodrow Wilson and the Great Betrayal* (1945); Bernard M. Baruch, *My Own Story*, 2 vols. (1957, 1960); J. Leonard Bates, "The Teapot Dome Scandal and the Election of 1924," *American Historical Review*, 60 (January, 1955), 303–322; Burton F. Beers, *Vain Endeavor: Robert Lansing's Attempts to End the American-Japanese Rivalry* (1962); Irving Bernstein, *The Lean Years: A History of the American Worker, 1920–1933* (1960); John M. Blum, *Joe Tumulty and the Wilson Era* (1951); Edward K. Brown and Leon Edel, *Willa Cather, a Critical Biography* (1953); Clarence C. Clendenen, *The United States and Pancho Villa* (1961); Margaret L. Coit, *Mr. Baruch* (1957); Clarence H. Cramer, *Newton D. Baker, a Biography* (1961); Richard N. Current, "The Stimson Doctrine and the Hoover Doctrine," *American Historical Review*, 59 (April, 1954), 513–542; Roy W. Curry, "Woodrow Wilson and Philippine Policy," *Mississippi Valley Historical Review*, 41 (December, 1954), 435–452; Virginius Dabney, *Dry Messiah: The Life of Bishop Cannon* (1949); Kenneth S. Davis, *The Hero: Charles A. Lindbergh and the American Dream* (1959); Alexander De Conde, "The South and Isolationism," *Journal of Southern History*, 24 (August, 1958), 332–346; Joseph Dorfman, *Thorstein Veblen and His America* (1934); L. Ethan Ellis, *Frank B. Kellogg and American Foreign Relations, 1925–1929* (1961); Harold U. Faulkner, *From Versailles to the New Deal: a Chronicle of the Harding-Coolidge-Hoover Era* (1950); Richard F. Fenno, *The President's Cabinet: an Analysis in the Period from Wilson to Eisenhower* (1959); Robert H. Ferrell, *Peace in Their Time: the Origins of the Kellogg-Briand Pact* (1952); Russell H. Fifield, "Secretary Hughes and the Shantung Question," *Pacific Historical Review*, 23 (November, 1954), 373–386; Russell H. Fifield, *Woodrow Wilson and the Far East: The Diplomacy of the Shantung Question* (1952); Gilbert C. Fite, "The Agricultural Issue in the Presidential Campaign of 1928," *Mississippi Valley Historical Review*, 37 (March, 1951), 653–672; John K. Galbraith, *The Great Crash, 1929* (1955); John A. Garraty, *Henry Cabot Lodge, a Biography* (1953); John A. Garraty, *Woodrow Wilson: a Great Life in Brief* (1956); Ray Ginger, *Six Days or Forever: Tennessee v. John*

Thomas Scopes (1958); Oscar Handlin, *Al Smith and His America* (1958); Fred H. Harrington, *God, Mammon, and the Japanese* (1944); Joseph R. Hayden, *The Philippines* (1942); Will H. Hays, *Memoirs* (1955); John D. Hicks, *Republican Ascendancy, 1921–1933* (1960); Sidney Hook (ed.), *John Dewey: Philosopher of Science and Freedom: A Symposium* (1950); Herbert C. Hoover, *The Cabinet and the Presidency, 1920–1933* (1952); Herbert C. Hoover, *The Memoirs of Herbert Hoover,* 3 vols. (1951–1952); Irving Howe, *Sherwood Anderson* (1951); Theodore G. Joslin, *Hoover Off the Record* (1934); Morton Keller, *In Defense of Yesterday: James M. Beck and the Politics of Conservatism, 1861–1936* (1958); George F. Kennan, *Russia Leaves the War* (1956); William E. Leuchtenburg, *The Perils of Prosperity, 1914–1932* (1958); Charles A. Lindbergh, *The Spirit of St. Louis* (1953); Arthur S. Link, *Wilson,* 3 vols. (1947–1960); Arthur S. Link, "What Happened to the Progressive Movement in the 1920's?" *American Historical Review,* 64 (July, 1959), 833–851; Arthur S. Link, *Woodrow Wilson and the Progressive Era, 1910–1917* (1954); Robert S. Lynd, *Middletown* (1959); William Manchester, *Disturber of Peace: the Life of H. L. Mencken* (1951); Laurence W. Martin, *Peace Without Victory: Woodrow Wilson and the British Liberals* (1958); Alpheus T. Mason, *Brandeis, a Free Man's Life* (1946); Ernest R. May, "American Policy and Japan's Entrance Into World War I," *Mississippi Valley Historical Review,* 40 (September, 1953), 279–290; Ernest R. May, *The World War and American Isolation, 1914–1917* (1959); Henry F. May, *The End of American Innocence: a Study of the First Years of Our Own Times, 1912–1917* (1959); Arno J. Mayer, *Political Origins of the New Diplomacy, 1917–1918* (1959); Charles Merz, *The Great American Band Wagon* (1928); Charles Merz, *The Dry Decade* (1931); Donald B. Meyer, *The Protestant Search for Political Realism, 1919–1941* (1960); Walter Millis, *Road to War: America, 1914–1917* (1935); Arthur Mizener, *The Far Side of Paradise: A Biography of F. Scott Fitzgerald* (1951); Edmund A. Moore, *A Catholic Runs for President: The Campaign of 1928* (1956); Elting E. Morison, *Admiral Sims and the Modern American Navy* (1942); Elting E. Morison, *Turmoil and Tradition: A Study of the Life and Times of Henry L. Stimson* (1960); Robert K. Murray, "Communism and the Great Steel Strike of 1919," *Mississippi Valley Historical Review,* 38 (December, 1951), 445–466; Robert K. Murray, *Red Scare: a Study in National Hysteria, 1919–1920* (1955); William S. Myers, *Foreign Policies of Herbert Hoover* (1940); Gerald D. Nash, "Herbert Hoover and the Origins of the Reconstruction Finance Corporation," *Mississippi Valley Historical Review,* 46 (December, 1959), 455–468; Allan Nevins and Frank E. Hill, *Ford: Expansion and Challenge, 1915–1933* (1957); Allan Nevins, *The United States in a Chaotic World: a Chronicle of International Affairs, 1918–1933* (1950); Burl Noggle, "The Origins of the Teapot Dome Investigation," *Mississippi Valley Historical Review,* 44 (September, 1957), 237–266; Russel B. Nye, *Midwestern Progressive Politics: A Historical Study of Its Origins and Development, 1870–1950* (1951); Horace C. Peterson and Gilbert C. Fite, *Opponents of War, 1917–1918* (1957); Henry F. Pringle, *Alfred E. Smith: a Critical Study* (1927); Elizabeth A. Rice, *The Diplomatic Relations between the United States and Mexico, 1925–1929* (1959); Charles Seymour (ed.), *The Intimate Papers of Colonel House,* 4 vols. (1926–1928); Charles Seymour, *American Neutrality, 1914–1917* (1935); James H. Shideler, "Herbert Hoover and the Federal Farm Board Project, 1921–1925," *Mississippi*

Valley Historical Review, 42 (March, 1956), 710–729; Daniel M. Smith, *Robert Lansing and American Neutrality, 1914–1917* (1958); Henry L. Stimson, *The Far Eastern Crisis* (1936); Philip Taft, *The A.F. of L. from the Death of Gompers to the Merger* (1959); Charles C. Tansill, *America Goes to War* (1938); Emma Lou Thornbrough, "Segregation in Indiana during the Klan Era of the 1920's," *Mississippi Valley Historical Review,* 47 (March, 1961), 594–618; Seth P. Tillman, *Anglo-American Relations at the Paris Peace Conference of 1919* (1961); Betty M. Unterberger, *America's Siberian Expedition, 1918–1920: a Study of National Policy* (1956); Richard W. Van Alstyne, *American Crisis Diplomacy: The Quest for Collective Security, 1918–1952* (1952); John C. Vinson, *The Parchment Peace: the United States Senate and the Washington Conference, 1921–1922* (1955); John C. Vinson, *William E. Borah and the Outlawry of War* (1957); Hoyt L. Warner, *The Life of Mr. Justice Clarke: a Testament to the Power of Liberal Dissent in America* (1959); Harris G. Warren, *Herbert Hoover and the Great Depression* (1959); Richard L. Watson, Jr. (ed.), *Bishop Cannon's Own Story* (1955); Gerald E. Wheeler, "Isolated Japan: Anglo-American Diplomatic Cooperation, 1927–1936," *Pacific Historical Review,* 30 (May, 1961), 165–178; Gerald E. Wheeler, "Republican Philippine Policy, 1921–1933," *Pacific Historical Review,* 28 (November, 1959), 377–390; William A. White, *A Puritan in Babylon* (1938); Kathleen L. Wolgemuth, "Woodrow Wilson's Appointment Policy and the Negro," *Journal of Southern History,* 24 (November, 1958), 457–471.

THE ERA OF FRANKLIN ROOSEVELT (1933–1945)

Frederick L. Allen, *Since Yesterday* (1940); Edward N. Barnhart, "The Individual Exclusion of Japanese Americans in World War II," *Pacific Historical Review,* 29 (May, 1960), 111–130; Charles A. Beard, *President Roosevelt and the Coming of War, 1941* (1948); Bernard Bellush, *Franklin D. Roosevelt as Governor of New York* (1955); John M. Blum, *From the Morganthau Diaries: Years of Crisis, 1928–1938* (1959); Omar N. Bradley, *A Soldier's Story* (1951); Denis W. Brogan, *The Era of Franklin D. Roosevelt: a Chronicle of the New Deal and Global War* (1950); Robert P. Browder, *The Origins of Soviet-American Diplomacy* (1953); James M. Burns, *Roosevelt: The Lion and the Fox* (1956); Robert J. C. Butow, *Japan's Decision to Surrender* (1954); Robert J. C. Butow, "The Hull-Nomura Conversations: A Fundamental Misconception," *American Historical Review,* 64 (July, 1960), 822–836; Sir Winston Churchill, *The Second World War,* 6 vols. (1948–1953); Paul K. Conkin, *Tomorrow a New World: The New Deal Community Program* (1959); Wayne S. Cole, *America First: The Battle Against Intervention, 1940–1941* (1953); Wayne S. Cole, "America First and the South, 1940–1941," *Journal of Southern History,* 22 (February, 1956), 36–47; Wayne S. Cole, "Senator Key Pittman and American Neutrality Policies, 1933–1940," *Mississippi Valley Historical Review,* 46 (March, 1960), 644–662; Stetson Conn and Byron Fairchild, *The Framework of Hemisphere Defense* (1960); Edward S. Corwin, *Court Over Constitution* (1938); Wesley F. Craven and James L. Cate (eds.), *The Army Air Forces in World War II,* 7 vols. (1948–1958); E. David Cronon, "A Southern Progressive Looks at the New Deal," *Journal of Southern History,* 24 (May, 1958), 151–176; Charles de Gaulle, *War Memoirs,* 2 vols. (1955–1959); Robert A. Divine, "Franklin D. Roosevelt and Collective

Security, 1933," *Mississippi Valley Historical Review,* 48 (June, 1961), 42–59; Donald M. Dozer, *Are We Good Neighbors? Three Decades of Inter-American Relations, 1930–1960* (1959); Theodore Draper, *American Communism and Soviet Russia, the Formative Period* (1960); Theodore Draper, *The Roots of American Communism* (1957); Donald F. Drummond, *The Passing of American Neutrality, 1937–1941* (1955); Dwight D. Eisenhower, *Crusade in Europe* (1948); Herbert Feis, *The China Tangle: The American Effort in China from Pearl Harbor to the Marshall Mission* (1953); Herbert Feis, *Churchill-Roosevelt-Stalin: The War They Waged and the Peace They Sought* (1957); Herbert Feis, *Japan Subdued: The Atomic Bomb and the End of the War in the Pacific* (1961); Herbert Feis, *The Road to Pearl Harbor: The Coming of the War Between the United States and Japan* (1950); Sidney Fine, "President Roosevelt and the Automobile Code," *Mississippi Valley Historical Review,* 45 (June, 1958), 23–50; John F. C. Fuller, *The Second World War, 1939–45* (1949); Daniel R. Fusfeld, *The Economic Thought of Franklin D. Roosevelt and the Origins of the New Deal* (1956); Frank B. Freidel, *Franklin D. Roosevelt* (1952–); Walter Galenson, *The C.I.O. Challenge to the A.F.L.: A History of the American Labor Movement, 1935–1941* (1960); Eric F. Goldman, *Rendezvous with Destiny: A History of Modern American Reform* (1953); Joseph C. Grew, *Ten Years in Japan* (1944); Edward O. Guerrant, *Roosevelt's Good Neighbor Policy* (1950); John Gunther, *Roosevelt in Retrospect, A Profile in History* (1950): Walter J. Heacock, "William B. Bankhead and the New Deal," *Journal of Southern History,* 21 (August, 1955), 347–359; Cordell Hull, *The Memoirs of Cordell Hull,* 2 vols. (1948); Harold L. Ickes, *The Secret Diary of Harold L. Ickes,* 3 vols. (1953–1954); Robert H. Jackson, *The Struggle for Judicial Supremacy* (1941); Donald B. Johnson, *The Republican Party and Wendell Willkie* (1960); Walter Johnson, *The Battle Against Isolationism* (1944); Walter Johnson, *1600 Pennsylvania Ave.: Presidents and the People, 1929–1959* (1960); Walter Johnson, *William Allen White's America* (1947); Harnett T. Kane, *Louisiana Hayride* (1941); George F. Kennan, *The Decision to Intervene* (1958); John M. Keynes, *The General Theory of Employment, Interest, and Money* (1936); Samuel J. Konefsky, *Chief Justice Stone and the Supreme Court* (1945); William L. Langer and S. Everett Gleason, *The Challenge to Isolation, 1937–1940* (1952); William L. Langer and S. Everett Gleason, *The Undeclared War, 1940–1941* (1953); Huey P. Long, *Every Man a King* (1933); Robert S. Lynd, *Middletown in Transition* (1937); Donald R. McCoy, *Angry Voices: Left of Center Politics in the New Deal Era* (1958); Donald R. McCoy, "The National Progressives of America, 1938," *Mississippi Valley Historical Review,* 44 (June, 1957), 75–93; Arthur Mann, *La Guardia: A Fighter against His Times, 1882–1933* (1959); Alpheus T. Mason, *Harlan Fiske Stone: Pillar of the Law* (1956); Alpheus T. Mason, *The Supreme Court from Taft to Warren* (1958); Ernest R. May, "The United States, the Soviet Union, and the Far Eastern War, 1941–1945," *Pacific Historical Review,* 24 (May, 1955), 153–174; Lewis Merriam, *Relief and Social Security* (1946); Walter Millis, *This is Pearl!* (1947); Samuel E. Morison, *History of United States Naval Operations in World War II,* 14 vols. (1947–1960); Jeannette P. Nichols, "Roosevelt's Monetary Policy in 1933," *American Historical Review,* 56 (January, 1951), 295–317; William L. Neumann, "Franklin D. Roosevelt and Japan, 1913–1933," *Pacific Historical Review,* 22 (May, 1953), 143–154;

Fletcher Pratt, *War for the World: a Chronicle of our Fighting Forces in World War II* (1950); Willard Range, *Franklin D. Roosevelt's World Order* (1959); Basil Rauch, *History of the New Deal, 1933–1938* (1944); Edgar E. Robinson, *The Roosevelt Leadership, 1933–1945* (1955); Frederick Rudolph, "The American Liberty League, 1934–1940," *American Historical Review,* 56 (October, 1950), 19–34; Arthur M. Schlesinger, Jr., *The Age of Roosevelt* (1957–); Paul W. Schroeder, *The Axis Alliance and Japanese-American Relations, 1941* (1958); Gertrude A. Slichter, "Franklin D. Roosevelt and the Farm Problem, 1929–1932," *Mississippi Valley Historical Review,* 43 (September, 1956), 238–258; Raymond J. Sontag, "Between the Wars," *Pacific Historical Review,* 29 (February, 1960), 1–18; Henry L. Stimson and McGeorge Bundy, *On Active Service in Peace and War* (1948); Charles C. Tansill, *Back Door to War: The Roosevelt Foreign Policy, 1933–1941* (1952); Helen S. Thomas, *Felix Frankfurter: Scholar on the Bench* (1960); Francis E. Townsend, *New Horizons* (1943); Hans L. Trefousse, "Failure of German Intelligence in the United States, 1935–1945," *Mississippi Valley Historical Review,* 42 (June, 1955), 84–100; Hans L. Trefousse (ed.), *What Happened at Pearl Harbor?* (1958); Rexford G. Tugwell, *The Democratic Roosevelt: a Biography of Franklin D. Roosevelt* (1957); T. Harry Williams, "The Gentleman from Louisiana: Demagogue or Democrat?" *Journal of Southern History,* 26 (February, 1960), 3–21.

THE NUCLEAR AGE (1945–   )

Herbert Agar, *The Price of Power: America Since 1945* (1957); Carlos H. Baker, *Hemingway: the Writer as Artist* (1952); William L. Baldwin, *Antitrust and the Changing Corporation* (1961); Alan Barth, *The Loyalty of Free Men* (1951); William F. Buckley, Jr., and L. Brent Bozell, *McCarthy and His Enemies: the Record and Its Meaning* (1954); James M. Burns, *John Kennedy: a Political Profile* (1960); Noel F. Busch, *Adlai E. Stevenson of Illinois, a Portrait* (1952); Robert K. Carr, *The House Committee on Un-American Activities, 1945–1950* (1952); Hodding Carter, *Southern Legacy* (1950); Marquis W. Childs, *Eisenhower, Captive Hero: a Critical Study of the General and the President* (1958); Lucius D. Clay, *Decision in Germany* (1950); Thomas C. Cochran, *The American Business System: A Historical Perspective, 1900–1955* (1957); Alistair Cooke, *A Generation on Trial: U.S.A. v. Alger Hiss* (1950); Jonathan Daniels, *The Man of Independence* (1950); Elmer H. Davis, *But We Were Born Free* (1954); Kenneth S. Davis, *A Prophet in His Own Country: The Triumphs and Defeats of Adlai E. Stevenson* (1957); Robert A. Divine, *American Immigration Policy, 1924–1952* (1957); Foster Rhea Dulles, *America's Rise to World Power, 1898–1954* (1955); John K. Galbraith, *The Affluent Society* (1958); John K. Galbraith, *American Capitalism: the Concept of Countervailing Power* (1952); Walter Gellhorn, *Security, Loyalty and Science* (1950); Charles G. Haines, *European Integration* (1957); Eric F. Goldman, *The Crucial Decade: America, 1945–1955* (1956); Norman A. Graebner, *The New Isolationism: A Study in Politics and Foreign Policy Since 1950* (1956); Herman Kahn, *On Thermonuclear War* (1960); George F. Kennan, *American Diplomacy, 1900–1950* (1951); George F. Kennan, *Realities of American Foreign Policy* (1954); V. O. Key, *Southern Politics in State and Nation* (1949); Henry A. Kissinger, *Nuclear Weapons and Foreign Policy* (1957); Klaus E. Knorr (ed.),

NATO and American Security (1959); John Norman, "MacArthur's Blockade Proposals against Red China," *Pacific Historical Review,* 26 (May, 1957), 161–174; Victor Lasky and Ralph de Toledano, *Seeds of Treason: the True Story of the Hiss-Chambers Tragedy* (1950); Harold D. Lasswell, *National Security and Individual Freedom* (1950); Samuel Lubell, *The Future of American Politics* (1952); Samuel Lubell, *Revolt of the Moderates* (1956); Earl Mazo, *Richard Nixon: a Political and Personal Portrait* (1959); Kevin McCann, *Man From Abilene* (1952); Joe A. Morris, *Nelson Rockefeller, a Biography* (1960); Lewis Mumford (ed.), *Roots of Contemporary American Architecture* (1952); Gunnar Myrdal, *An American Dilemma,* 2 vols. (1944); Hortense Powdermaker, *Hollywood, the Dream Factory: an Anthropologist Looks at the Movie-makers* (1950); Harry B. Price, *The Marshall Plan and Its Meaning* (1955); Merlo J. Pusey, *Eisenhower: the President* (1956); David Riesman, *The Lonely Crowd: a Study of Changing American Character* (1950); Arnold M. Rose, *The Negro in Postwar America* (1950); Richard H. Rovere and Arthur M. Schlesinger, Jr., *The General and the President* (1951); Richard H. Rovere, *Senator Joe McCarthy* (1959); John L. Snell (ed.), *The Meaning of Yalta: Big Three Diplomacy and the New Balance of Power* (1956); F. H. Soward, "The Changing Relations of Canada and the United States Since the Second World War," *Pacific Historical Review,* 22 (May, 1953), 155–168; John W. Spanier, *American Foreign Policy Since World War II* (1960); Robert E. Spiller et al. (eds.), *American Perspectives: The National Self-Image in the Twentieth Century* (1961); George R. Stewart, *The Year of the Oath: the Fight for Academic Freedom at the University of California* (1950); Kenneth W. Thompson, *Political Realism and the Crisis of World Politics: an American Approach to Foreign Policy* (1960); Harry S. Truman, *Mr. President* (1952); Nathaniel Weyl, *The Battle Against Disloyalty* (1951); William H. Whyte, Jr., *The Organization Man* (1956); Frank B. Williams, Jr., "The Poll Tax as a Suffrage Requirement in the South," *Journal of Southern History,* 18 (November, 1952), 469–496; William F. Zornow, *America at Mid-Century: the Truman Administration; the Eisenhower Administration* (1959).

APPENDIX

THE DECLARATION OF INDEPENDENCE
IN CONGRESS, JULY 4, 1776

THE UNANIMOUS DECLARATION OF THE THIRTEEN
UNITED STATES OF AMERICA

When in the Course of human events, it becomes necessary for one people to dissolve the political bands which have connected them with another, and to assume among the powers of the earth, the separate and equal station to which the Laws of Nature and of Nature's God entitle them, a decent respect to the opinions of mankind requires that they should declare the causes which impel them to the separation.——We hold these truths to be self-evident, that all men are created equal, that they are endowed by their Creator with certain unalienable Rights, that among these are Life, Liberty, and the pursuit of Happiness.——That to secure these rights, Governments are instituted among Men, deriving their just powers from the consent of the governed.——That whenever any Form of Government becomes destructive of these ends, it is the Right of the People to alter or to abolish it, and to institute new Government, laying its foundation on such principles and organizing its powers in such form, as to them shall seem most likely to effect their Safety and Happiness. Prudence, indeed, will dictate that Governments long established should not be changed for light and transient causes; and accordingly all experience hath shewn, that mankind are more disposed to suffer, while evils are sufferable, than to right themselves by abolishing the forms to which they are accustomed. But when a long train of abuses and usurpations, pursuing invariably the same Object evinces a design to reduce them under absolute Despotism, it is their right, it is their duty, to throw off such Government, and to provide new Guards for their future security.——Such has been the patient sufferance of these Colonies; and such is now the necessity which constrains them to alter their former Systems of Government. The history of the present King of Great Britain is a history of repeated injuries and usurpations, all having in direct object the establishment of an absolute Tyranny over these States. To prove this, let Facts be submitted to a candid world.——He has refused his Assent to Laws, the most wholesome and necessary for the public good.——He has forbidden his Governors to pass Laws of immediate and pressing importance, unless suspended in their operation till his Assent should be obtained; and when so suspended, he has utterly neglected to attend to them.——He has refused to pass other Laws for the accommodation of large districts of people, unless those people would relinquish the right of Representation in the Legislature, a right inestimable to them and formidable to tyrants only.——He has called together legislative bodies at places unusual, uncomfortable, and distant from the depository of their public Records, for the sole purpose of fatiguing them into compliance with his measures.——He has dissolved Representative Houses repeatedly, for opposing with manly firmness his invasions on the rights of the people.——He has refused for a long time, after such dissolutions, to cause others to be elected; whereby the Legislative powers, incapable of Annihilation, have returned to the People at large for their exercise; the State remaining in the mean time exposed to all the dangers of invasion from without, and convulsions within.——He has endeavoured to prevent the population of these States; for that purpose obstructing the Laws for Naturalization of Foreigners; refusing to pass others to encourage their migrations hither, and raising the conditions of new Appropriations of Lands.——He has obstructed the Administration of Justice, by refusing his Assent to Laws for establishing Judiciary powers.——He has made Judges dependent on his Will alone, for the tenure of their offices, and the amount and payment of their salaries. ——He has erected a multitude of New Offices, and sent hither swarms of Officers to harass our people, and eat out their substance.——He has kept among us, in times of peace, Standing Armies without the Consent of our legislatures.——He has affected to render the Military independent of and superior to the Civil power.——He has combined with others to subject us to a jurisdiction foreign to our constitution, and unacknowledged by our laws; giving his Assent to their Acts of pretended Legislation:——For quartering large bodies of armed troops among us:——For protecting them, by a mock Trial, from punishment for any Murders which they should commit on the Inhabitants of these States:——For cutting off our Trade with all parts of the world:——For imposing Taxes on us without our Consent:——For depriving us in many cases, of the benefits of Trial by Jury:——For transporting us beyond Seas to be tried for pretended offences: ——For abolishing the free System of English Laws in a neighbouring Province, establishing therein an Arbitrary government, and enlarging its Boundaries so as to render it at once an example and fit instrument for introducing the same absolute rule into these Colonies:——For taking away our Charters, abolishing our most valuable Laws, and altering fundamentally the Forms of our Governments: ——For suspending our own Legislatures, and declaring themselves invested with power to legislate for us in all cases whatsoever.——He has abdicated Government here, by declaring us out of his Protection and waging War against us.——He has plundered our seas, ravaged our Coasts, burnt our towns, and destroyed the lives of our people.——He is at this time transporting large Armies of foreign Mercenaries to compleat the works of death, desolation and tyranny, already begun with circumstances of Cruelty & perfidy scarcely paralleled in the most barbarous ages, and totally unworthy the Head of a civilized nation.——He has constrained our fellow Citizens taken Captive on the high Seas to bear Arms against their Country, to become the executioners of their friends and Brethren, or to fall themselves by their Hands.——He has excited domestic insurrections amongst us, and has endeavoured to bring on the inhabitants of our frontiers, the merciless Indian Savages, whose known rule of warfare, is an undistinguished destruction of all ages, sexes and conditions. In every stage of these Oppressions We have Petitioned for Redress in the most humble terms: Our repeated Petitions have been answered only by repeated injury. A Prince, whose character is thus marked by every act which may define a Tyrant, is unfit to be the ruler of a free people. Nor have We been wanting in attentions to our British brethren. We have warned them from time to time of attempts by their legislature to extend an unwarrantable jurisdiction over us. We have reminded them of the circumstances of our emigration and settlement here. We have appealed to their native justice and magnanimity, and we have conjured them by the ties of our common kindred to disavow these usurpations, which, would inevitably interrupt our connections and correspondence. They too have been deaf to the voice of justice and of consanguinity. We must, therefore, acquiesce in the necessity, which denounces our Separation, and hold them, as we hold the rest of mankind, Enemies in War, in Peace Friends.——

We, therefore, the Representatives of the united States of America, in General Congress, Assembled, appealing to the Supreme Judge of the world for the rectitude of our intentions, do, in the Name, and by Authority of the good People of these Colonies, solemnly publish and declare, That these United Colonies are, and of Right ought to be Free and Independent States; that they are Absolved from all Allegiance to the British Crown, and that all political connection between them and the State of Great Britain, is and ought to be totally dissolved; and that as Free and Independent States, they have full Power to levy War, conclude Peace, contract Alliances, establish Commerce, and to do all other Acts and Things which Independent States may of right do.——And for the support of this Declaration, with a firm reliance on the protection of Divine Providence, we mutually pledge to each other our Lives, our Fortunes and our sacred Honor.

JOHN HANCOCK

New Hampshire
Josiah Bartlett,
Wm. Whipple,
Matthew Thornton.

Massachusetts Bay
Saml. Adams,
John Adams,
Robt. Treat Paine,
Elbridge Gerry.

Rhode Island
Step. Hopkins,
William Ellery.

Connecticut
Roger Sherman,
Sam'el Huntington,
Wm. Williams,
Oliver Wolcott.

New Jersey
Richd. Stockton,
Jno. Witherspoon,
Fras. Hopkinson,
John Hart,
Abra. Clark.

Pennsylvania
Robt. Morris,
Benjamin Rush,
Benja. Franklin,
John Morton,
Geo. Clymer,
Jas. Smith,
Geo. Taylor,
James Wilson,
Geo. Ross.

Delaware
Caesar Rodney,
Geo. Read,
Tho. M'Kean.

Virginia
George Wythe,
Richard Henry Lee,
Th. Jefferson,
Benja. Harrison,
Ths. Nelson, Jr.,
Francis Lightfoot Lee,
Carter Braxton.

North Carolina
Wm. Hooper,
Joseph Hewes,
John Penn.

South Carolina
Edward Rutledge,
Thos. Heyward, Junr.,
Thomas Lynch, Junr.,
Arthur Middleton.

Georgia
Button Gwinnett,
Lyman Hall,
Geo. Walton.

New York
Wm. Floyd,
Phil. Livingston,
Frans. Lewis,
Lewis Morris.

Maryland
Samuel Chase
Wm. Paca,
Thos. Stone,
Charles Carroll of Carrollton.

THE CONSTITUTION OF THE UNITED STATES

PREAMBLE

We the People of the United States, in Order to form a more perfect Union, establish Justice, insure domestic Tranquility, provide for the common defence, promote the general Welfare, and secure the Blessings of Liberty to ourselves and our Posterity, do ordain and establish this Constitution for the United States of America.

ARTICLE I

Section 1. All legislative Powers herein granted shall be vested in a Congress of the United States, which shall consist of a Senate and House of Representatives.

Section 2. The House of Representatives shall be composed of Members chosen every second Year by the People of the several States, and the Electors in each State shall have the Qualifications requisite for Electors of the most numerous Branch of the State Legislature.

No Person shall be a Representative who shall not have attained to the Age of twenty five Years, and been seven Years a Citizen of the United States, and who shall not, when elected, be an inhabitant of that State in which he shall be chosen.

Representatives and direct Taxes shall be apportioned among the several States which may be included within this Union, according to their respective Numbers, [which shall be determined by adding to the whole Number of free Persons, including those bound to Service for a Term of Years, and excluding Indians not taxed, three fifths of all other Persons.][1] The actual Enumeration shall be made within three Years after the first Meeting of the Congress of the United States, and within every subsequent Term of ten Years, in such Manner as they shall by law direct. The Number of Representatives shall not exceed one for every thirty Thousand, but each State shall have at Least one Representative; and until such numeration shall be made, the State of New Hampshire shall be entitled to chuse three, Massachusetts eight, Rhode-Island and Providence Plantations one, Connecticut five, New York six, New Jersey four, Pennsylvania eight, Delaware one, Maryland six, Virginia ten, North Carolina five, South Carolina five, and Georgia three.

When vacancies happen in the Representation from any State, the Executive Authority thereof shall issue Writs of Election to fill such Vacancies.

The House of Representatives shall chuse their Speaker and other Officers; and shall have the sole Power of Impeachment.

Section 3. The Senate of the United States shall be composed of two Senators

[1] Superseded by the Fourteenth Amendment.

from each State, [chosen by the Legislature thereof,]² for six Years; and each Senator shall have one Vote.

Immediately after they shall be assembled in Consequence of the first Election, they shall be divided as equally as may be into three Classes. The Seats of the Senators of the first Class shall be vacated at the Expiration of the second Year, of the second Class at the Expiration of the fourth Year, and of the third Class at the Expiration of the sixth Year, so that one third may be chosen every second Year; [and if Vacancies happen by Resignation, or otherwise, during the Recess of the Legislature of any State, the Executive thereof may make temporary Appointments until the next Meeting of the Legislature, which shall then fill such Vacancies.]³

No Person shall be a Senator who shall not have attained to the Age of thirty Years, and been nine Years a Citizen of the United States, and who shall not, when elected, be an Inhabitant of that State for which he shall be chosen.

The Vice President of the United States shall be President of the Senate, but shall have no Vote, unless they be equally divided.

The Senate shall chuse their other Officers, and also a President pro tempore, in the Absence of the Vice President, or when he shall exercise the Office of President of the United States.

The Senate shall have the sole Power to try all Impeachments. When sitting for that Purpose, they shall be on Oath or Affirmation. When the President of the United States is tried, the Chief Justice shall preside: and no Person shall be convicted without the Concurrence of two thirds of the Members present.

Judgment in Cases of Impeachment shall not extend further than to removal from Office, and disqualification to hold and enjoy any Office of honor, Trust or Profit under the United States: but the Party convicted shall nevertheless be liable and subject to Indictment, Trial, Judgment and Punishment, according to Law.

Section 4. The Times, Places and Manner of holding Elections for Senators and Representatives, shall be prescribed in each State by the Legislature thereof; but the Congress may at any time by Law make or alter such Regulations, except as to the Places of chusing Senators.

[The Congress shall assemble at least once in every Year, and such Meeting shall be on the first Monday in December, unless they shall by Law appoint a different Day.]⁴

Section 5. Each House shall be the Judge of the Elections, Returns and Qualifications of its own Members, and a Majority of each shall constitute a Quorum to do Business; but a smaller Number may adjourn from day to day, and may be authorized to compel the Attendance of absent Members, in such Manner, and under such Penalties as each House may provide.

Each House may determine the Rules of its Proceedings, punish its Members for disorderly Behaviour, and, with the Concurrence of two thirds, expel a Member.

2 Superseded by the Seventeenth Amendment.
3 Modified by the Seventeenth Amendment.
4 Superseded by the Twentieth Amendment.

Each House shall keep a Journal of its Proceedings, and from time to time publish the same, excepting such Parts as may in their Judgment require Secrecy; and the Yeas and Nays of the Members of either House on any question shall, at the Desire of one fifth of those Present, be entered on the Journal.

Neither House, during the Session of Congress, shall, without the Consent of the other, adjourn for more than three days, nor to any other Place than that in which the two Houses shall be sitting.

Section 6. The Senators and Representatives shall receive a Compensation for their Services, to be ascertained by Law, and paid out of the Treasury of the United States. They shall in all Cases, except Treason, Felony and Breach of the Peace, be privileged from Arrest during their Attendance at the Session of their respective Houses, and in going to and returning from the same; and for any Speech or Debate in either House, they shall not be questioned in any other Place.

No Senator or Representative shall, during the Time for which he was elected, be appointed to any civil Office under the Authority of the United States, which shall have been created, or the Emoluments whereof shall have been encreased during such time; and no Person holding any Office under the United States, shall be a Member of either House during his Continuance in Office.

Section 7. All bills for raising Revenue shall originate in the House of Representatives; but the Senate may propose or concur with Amendments as on other Bills.

Every Bill which shall have passed the House of Representatives and the Senate, shall, before it become a Law, be presented to the President of the United States; If he approve he shall sign it, but if not he shall return it, with his Objections to that House in which it shall have originated, who shall enter the Objections at large on their Journal, and proceed to reconsider it. If after such Reconsideration two thirds of that House shall agree to pass the Bill, it shall be sent, together with the Objections, to the other House, by which it shall likewise be reconsidered, and if approved by two thirds of that House, it shall become a Law. But in all such Cases the Votes of both Houses shall be determined by yeas and Nays, and the Names of the Persons voting for and against the Bill shall be entered on the Journal of each House respectively. If any Bill shall not be returned by the President within ten Days (Sundays excepted) after it shall have been presented to him, the Same shall be a Law, in like Manner as if he had signed it, unless the Congress by their Adjournment prevent its Return, in which Case it shall not be a Law.

Every Order, Resolution, or Vote to which the Concurrence of the Senate and House of Representatives may be necessary (except on a question of Adjournment) shall be presented to the President of the United States; and before the Same shall take Effect, shall be approved by him, or being disapproved by him, shall be repassed by two thirds of the Senate and House of Representatives, according to the Rules and Limitations prescribed in the Case of a Bill.

Section 8. The Congress shall have Power To lay and collect Taxes, Duties, Imposts and Excises, to pay the Debts and provide for the common Defence and general Welfare of the United States; but all Duties, Imposts and Excises shall be uniform throughout the United States;

To borrow Money on the credit of the United States;

To regulate Commerce with foreign Nations, and among the several States, and with the Indian Tribes;

To establish a uniform Rule of Naturalization, and uniform Laws on the subject of Bankruptcies throughout the United States;

To coin Money, regulate the Value thereof, and of foreign Coin, and fix the Standard of Weights and Measures;

To provide for the Punishment of counterfeiting the Securities and current Coin of the United States;

To establish Post Offices and post Roads;

To promote the Progress of Science and useful Arts, by securing for limited Times to Authors and Inventors the exclusive Right to their respective Writings and Discoveries;

To constitute Tribunals inferior to the supreme Court;

To define and punish Piracies and Felonies committed on the high Seas, and Offences against the Law of Nations;

To declare War, grant Letters of Marque and Reprisal, and make Rules concerning Captures on Land and Water;

To raise and support Armies, but no Appropriation of Money to that Use shall be for a longer Term than two Years;

To provide and maintain a Navy;

To make Rules for the Government and Regulation of the land and naval Forces;

To provide for calling forth the Militia to execute the Laws of the Union, suppress Insurrections and repel Invasions;

To provide for organizing, arming, and disciplining, the Militia, and for governing such Part of them as may be employed in the Service of the United States, reserving to the States respectively, the Appointment of the Officers, and the Authority of training the Militia according to the discipline prescribed by Congress;

To exercise exclusive Legislation in all Cases whatsoever, over such District (not exceeding ten Miles square) as may, by Cession of particular States, and the Acceptance of Congress, become the Seat of the Government of the United States, and to exercise like Authority over all Places purchased by the Consent of the Legislature of the State in which the Same shall be, for the Erection of Forts, Magazines, Arsenals, dock-Yards, and other needful Buildings;—And

To make all Laws which shall be necessary and proper for carrying into Execution the foregoing Powers, and all other Powers vested by this Constitution in the Government of the United States, or in any Department or Officer thereof.

Section 9. The Migration or Importation of such Persons as any of the States now existing shall think proper to admit, shall not be prohibited by the Congress prior to the Year one thousand eight hundred and eight, but a Tax or duty may be imposed on such Importation, not exceeding ten dollars for each Person.

The Privilege of the Writ of Habeas Corpus shall not be suspended, unless when in Cases of Rebellion or Invasion the public safety may require it.

No Bill of Attainder or ex post facto Law shall be passed.

No Capitation, or other direct, Tax shall be laid, unless in Proportion to the Census or Enumeration herein before directed to be taken.[5]

No Tax or Duty shall be laid on Articles exported from any State.

No Preference shall be given by any Regulation of Commerce or Revenue to the Ports of one State over those of another; nor shall Vessels bound to, or from, one State, be obliged to enter, clear, or pay Duties in another.

No money shall be drawn from the Treasury, but in Consequence of Appropriations made by Law; and a regular Statement and Account of the Receipts and Expenditures of all public Money shall be published from time to time.

No Title of Nobility shall be granted by the United States: And no Person holding any Office of Profit or Trust under them, shall, without the Consent of the Congress, accept any present, Emolument, Office, or Title, of any kind whatever, from any King, Prince, or foreign State.

Section 10. No State shall enter into any Treaty, Alliance, or Confederation; grant Letters of Marque and Reprisal; coin Money; emit Bills of Credit; make any Thing but gold and silver Coin a Tender in Payment of Debts; pass any Bill of Attainder, ex post facto Law, or Law impairing the Obligation of Contracts, or grant any Title of Nobility.

No State shall, without the Consent of the Congress, lay any Imposts or Duties on Imports or Exports, except what may be absolutely necessary for executing its inspection laws; and the net Produce of all Duties and Imposts, laid by any State on Imports or Exports, shall be for the Use of the Treasury of the United States; and all such Laws shall be subject to the Revision, and Control of the Congress.

No State shall, without the Consent of Congress, lay any Duty of Tonnage, keep Troops, or Ships of War in time of Peace, enter into any Agreement or Compact with another State, or with a foreign Power, or engage in War, unless actually invaded, or in such imminent Danger as will not admit of delay.

ARTICLE II

Section 1. The executive Power shall be vested in a President of the United States of America. He shall hold his Office during the Term of four Years, and, together with the Vice President, chosen for the same Term, be elected, as follows.

Each State shall appoint, in such Manner as the Legislature thereof may direct, a Number of Electors, equal to the whole Number of Senators and Representatives to which the State may be entitled in the Congress: but no Senator or Representative, or Person holding an Office of Trust or Profit under the United States, shall be appointed an Elector.

[The Electors shall meet in their respective States, and vote by Ballot for two Persons, of whom one at least shall not be an Inhabitant of the same State with themselves. And they shall make a List of all the Persons voted for, and the Number of Votes for each; which list they shall sign and certify, and transmit sealed to the Seat of the Government of the United States, directed to the President of the Senate. The President of the Senate shall, in the Presence of the Sen-

[5] Modified by the Sixteenth Amendment.

ate and House of Representatives, open all the Certificates, and the Votes shall then be counted. The person having the greatest Number of Votes shall be the President, if such Number be a Majority of the whole Number of Electors appointed; and if there be more than one who have such Majority, and have an equal Number of Votes, then the House of Representatives shall immediately chuse by Ballot one of them for President; and if no Person have a Majority, then from the five highest on the List the said House shall in like Manner chuse the President. But in chusing the President, the Votes shall be taken by States, the Representation from each State having one Vote; A quorum for this purpose shall consist of a Member or Members from two thirds of the States, and a Majority of all the States shall be necessary to a Choice. In every Case, after the Choice of the President, the Person having the greatest Number of Votes of the Electors shall be the Vice President. But if there should remain two or more who have equal Votes, the Senate chuse from them by Ballot the Vice President.][6]

The Congress may determine the Time of chusing the Electors, and the Day on which they shall give their Votes; which Day shall be the same throughout the United States.

No Person except a natural born Citizen, or a Citizen of the United States, at the time of the Adoption of this Constitution, shall be eligible to the Office of President; neither shall any Person be eligible to that Office who shall not have attained to the Age of thirty five Years, and been fourteen Years a Resident within the United States.

In Case of the Removal of the President from Office, or of his Death, Resignation, or Inability to discharge the Powers and Duties of the said Office, the Same shall devolve on the Vice President, and the Congress may by Law provide for the Case of Removal, Death, Resignation or Inability, both of the President and Vice President, declaring what Officer shall then act as President, and such Officer shall act accordingly, until the Disability be removed, or a President shall be elected.

The President shall, at stated Times receive for his Services, a Compensation, which shall neither be encreased nor diminished during the Period for which he shall have been elected, and he shall not receive within that Period any other Emolument from the United States, or any of them.

Before he enter on the Execution of his Office, he shall take the following Oath or Affirmation:—"I do solemnly swear (or affirm) that I will faithfully execute the Office of President of the United States, and will to the best of my Ability, preserve, protect and defend the Constitution of the United States."

Section 2. The President shall be Commander in Chief of the Army and Navy of the United States, and of the Militia of the several States, when called into the actual Service of the United States; he may require the Opinion, in writing, of the principal Officer in each of the executive Departments, upon any Subject relating to the Duties of their respective Offices, and he shall have Power to grant Reprieves and Pardons for Offenses against the United States, except in Cases of Impeachment.

He shall have Power, by and with the Advice and Consent of the Senate, to make Treaties, provided two thirds of the Senators present concur; and he shall

[6] Superseded by the Twelfth Amendment.

nominate, and by and with the Advice and Consent of the Senate, shall appoint Ambassadors, other public Ministers and Consuls, Judges of the supreme Court, and all other Officers of the United States, whose Appointments are not herein otherwise provided for, and which shall be established by Law: but the Congress may by Law vest the Appointment of such inferior Officers, as they think proper, in the President alone, in the Courts of Law, or in the Heads of Departments.

The President shall have Power to fill up all Vacancies that may happen during the Recess of the Senate, by granting Commissions which shall expire at the End of their next Session.

Section 3. He shall from time to time give to the Congress Information of the State of the Union, and recommend to their Consideration such Measures as he shall judge necessary and expedient; he may, on extraordinary Occasions, convene both Houses, or either of them, and in Case of Disagreement between them, with Respect to the Time of Adjournment, he may adjourn them to such Time as he shall think proper; he shall receive Ambassadors and other public Ministers; he shall take Care that the Laws be faithfully executed, and shall Commission all Officers of the United States.

Section 4. The President, Vice President and all civil Officers of the United States, shall be removed from Office on Impeachment for, and Conviction of, Treason, Bribery, or other high Crimes and Misdemeanors.

ARTICLE III

Section 1. The judicial Power of the United States, shall be vested in one supreme Court, and in such inferior Courts as the Congress may from time to time ordain and establish. The Judges, both of the supreme and inferior Courts, shall hold their Offices during good Behaviour, and shall, at stated Times, receive for their Services, a Compensation, which shall not be diminished during their Continuance in Office.

Section 2. The judicial Power shall extend to all Cases, in Law and Equity, arising under this Constitution, the Laws of the United States, and Treaties made, or which shall be made, under their Authority;—to all Cases affecting Ambassadors, other public Ministers and Consuls;—to all Cases of admiralty and maritime Jurisdiction;—to Controversies to which the United States shall be a Party;—to Controversies between two or more States;—between a State and Citizens of another State;[7]—between Citizens of different States,—between Citizens of the same State claiming Lands under Grants of different States, and between a State, or the Citizens thereof, and foreign States, Citizens or Subjects.

In all cases affecting Ambassadors, other public Ministers and Consuls, and those in which a State shall be Party, the supreme Court shall have original Jurisdiction. In all the other Cases before mentioned, the supreme Court shall have appellate Jurisdiction, both as to Law and Fact, with such Exceptions, and under such Regulations as the Congress shall make.

The Trial of all Crimes, except in Cases of Impeachment, shall be by Jury; and such Trial shall be held in the State where the said Crimes shall have been

[7] Modified by the Eleventh Amendment.

committed; but when not committed within any State, the Trial shall be at such Place or Places as the Congress may by Law have directed.

Section 3. Treason against the United States, shall consist only in levying War against them, or in adhering to their Enemies, giving them Aid and Comfort. No Person shall be convicted of Treason unless on the Testimony of two Witnesses to the same overt Act, or on Confession in open Court.

The Congress shall have Power to declare the Punishment of Treason, but no Attainder of Treason shall work Corruption of Blood, or Forfeiture except during the Life of the Person attainted.

ARTICLE IV

Section 1. Full Faith and Credit shall be given in each State to the public Acts, Records, and judicial Proceedings of every other State. And the Congress may by general Laws prescribe the Manner in which such Acts, Records and Proceedings shall be proved, and the Effect thereof.

Section 2. The Citizens of each State shall be entitled to all Privileges and Immunities of Citizens in the several States.

A Person charged in any State with Treason, Felony, or other Crime, who shall flee from Justice, and be found in another State, shall on Demand of the executive Authority of the State from which he fled, be delivered up, to be removed to the State having Jurisdiction of the Crime.

No Person held to Service or Labour in one State, under the Laws thereof, escaping into another, shall, in Consequence of any Law or Regulation therein, be discharged from such Service or Labour, but shall be delivered up on Claim of the Party to whom such Service or Labour may be due.

Section 3. New States may be admitted by the Congress into this Union; but no new State shall be formed or erected within the Jurisdiction of any other State; nor any State be formed by the Junction of two or more States, or Parts of States, without the Consent of the Legislatures of the States concerned as well as of the Congress.

The Congress shall have Power to dispose of and make all needful Rules and Regulations respecting the Territory or other Property belonging to the United States; and nothing in this Constitution shall be so construed as to Prejudice any Claims of the United States, or of any particular State.

Section 4. The United States shall guarantee to every State in this Union a Republican Form of Government, and shall protect each of them against Invasion; and on Application of the Legislature, or of the Executive (when the Legislature cannot be convened) against domestic Violence.

ARTICLE V

The Congress, whenever two thirds of both Houses shall deem it necessary, shall propose Amendments to this Constitution, or, on the Application of the Legislatures of two thirds of the several States, shall call a Convention for proposing Amendments, which, in either Case, shall be valid to all Intents and Purposes, as

Part of this Constitution, when ratified by the Legislatures of three fourths of the several States, or by Conventions in three fourths thereof, as the one or the other Mode of Ratification may be proposed by the Congress; Provided that no Amendment which may be made prior to the Year One thousand eight hundred and eight shall in any Manner affect the first and fourth Clauses in the Ninth Section of the first Article; and that no State, without its Consent, shall be deprived of its equal Suffrage in the Senate.

ARTICLE VI

All Debts contracted and Engagements entered into, before the Adoption of this Constitution, shall be as valid against the United States under this Constitution, as under the Confederation.

This Constitution, and the Laws of the United States which shall be made in Pursuance thereof; and all Treaties made, or which shall be made, under the Authority of the United States, shall be the supreme Law of the Land; and the Judges in every State shall be bound thereby, any Thing in the Constitution or Laws of any State to the Contrary notwithstanding.

The Senators and Representatives before mentioned, and the Members of the several State Legislatures, and all executive and judicial Officers, both of the United States and of the several States, shall be bound by Oath or Affirmation, to support this Constitution; but no religious Test shall ever be required as a Qualification to any Office or public Trust under the United States.

ARTICLE VII

The Ratification of the Conventions of nine States, shall be sufficient for the Establishment of this Constitution between the States so ratifying the Same.

[Signatures omitted.]

[AMENDMENTS]

ARTICLES in addition to, and Amendment of the Constitution of the United States of America, proposed by Congress, and ratified by the Legislatures of the several States, pursuant to the fifth Article of the original Constitution.

[The first ten articles proposed 25 Sept. 1789; declared in force 15 Dec. 1791]

ARTICLE I

Congress shall make no law respecting an establishment of religion, or prohibiting the free exercise thereof; or abridging the freedom of speech, or of the press; or the right of the people peaceably to assemble, and to petition the Government for a redress of grievances.

ARTICLE II

A well regulated Militia, being necessary to the security of a free State, the right of the people to keep and bear Arms, shall not be infringed.

ARTICLE III

No Soldier shall, in time of peace, be quartered in any house, without the consent of the Owner, nor in time of war, but in a manner to be prescribed by law.

ARTICLE IV

The right of the people to be secure in their persons, houses, papers, and effects, against unreasonable searches and seizures, shall not be violated, and no Warrants shall issue, but upon probable cause, supported by Oath or affirmation, and particularly describing the place to be searched, and the persons or things to be seized.

ARTICLE V

No person shall be held to answer for a capital, or otherwise infamous crime, unless on a presentment or indictment of a Grand Jury, except in cases arising in the land or naval forces, or in the Militia, when in actual service in time of War or public danger; nor shall any person be subject for the same offense to be twice put in jeopardy of life or limb; nor shall be compelled in any criminal case to be a witness against himself, nor be deprived of life, liberty, or property, without due process of law; nor shall private property be taken for public use, without just compensation.

ARTICLE VI

In all criminal prosecutions, the accused shall enjoy the right to a speedy and public trial, by an impartial jury of the State and district wherein the crime shall have been committed, which district shall have been previously ascertained by law, and to be informed of the nature and cause of the accusation; to be confronted with the witnesses against him; to have compulsory process for obtaining witnesses in his favor, and to have the Assistance of Counsel for his defense.

ARTICLE VII

In Suits at common law, where the value in controversy shall exceed twenty dollars, the right of trial by jury shall be preserved, and no fact tried by a jury, shall be otherwise re-examined in any Court of the United States, than according to the rules of the common law.

ARTICLE VIII

Excessive bail shall not be required, nor excessive fines imposed, nor cruel and unusual punishments inflicted.

ARTICLE IX

The enumeration in the Constitution, of certain rights, shall not be construed to deny or disparage others retained by the people.

ARTICLE X

The powers not delegated to the United States by the Constitution, nor prohibited by it to the States, are reserved to the States respectively, or to the people.

ARTICLE XI

[proposed 5 Mar. 1794; declared ratified 8 Jan. 1798]

The Judicial power of the United States shall not be construed to extend to any suit in law or equity, commenced or prosecuted against one of the United States by Citizens of another State, or by Citizens or Subjects of any Foreign State.

ARTICLE XII

[proposed 12 Dec. 1803; declared ratified 25 Sept. 1804]

The Electors shall meet in their respective states, and vote by ballot for President and Vice-President, one of whom, at least, shall not be an inhabitant of the same state with themselves; they shall name in their ballots the person voted for as President, and in distinct ballots the person voted for as Vice-President, and they shall make distinct lists of all persons voted for as President, and of all persons voted for as Vice-President, and of the number of votes for each, which lists they shall sign and certify, and transmit sealed to the seat of the government of the United States, directed to the President of the Senate;—The President of the Senate shall, in the presence of the Senate and House of Representatives, open all certificates and the votes shall then be counted;—The person having the greatest number of votes for President, shall be the President, if such number be a majority of the whole number of Electors appointed; and if no person have such majority, then from the persons having the highest numbers not exceeding three on the list of those voted for as President, the House of Representatives shall choose immediately, by ballot, the President. But in choosing the President, the votes shall be taken by states, the representation from each state having one vote; a quorum for this purpose shall consist of a member or members from two-thirds of the states, and a majority of all the states shall be necessary to a choice. [And if the House of Representatives shall not choose a President whenever the right of choice shall devolve upon them, before the fourth day of March next following, then the Vice-President shall act as President, as in the case of the death or other constitutional disability of the President.—][8] The person having the greatest number of votes as Vice-President, shall be the Vice-President, if such number be a majority of the whole number of Electors appointed, and if no person have a majority, then from the two highest numbers on the list, the Senate shall choose the Vice-President; a quorum for the purpose shall consist of two-thirds of the whole number of Senators, and a majority of the whole number shall be necessary to a choice. But no person constitutionally ineligible to the office of President shall be eligible to that of Vice-President of the United States.

ARTICLE XIII

[proposed 1 Feb. 1865; declared ratified 18 Dec. 1865]

Section 1. Neither slavery nor involuntary servitude, except as a punishment for crime whereof the party shall have been duly convicted, shall exist within the United States, or any place subject to their jurisdiction.

Section 2. Congress shall have power to enforce this article by appropriate legislation.

ARTICLE XIV

[proposed 16 June 1866; declared ratified 28 July 1868]

Section 1. All persons born or naturalized in the United States, and subject to the jurisdiction thereof, are citizens of the United States and of the State wherein they reside. No State shall make or enforce any law which shall abridge the privileges or immunities of citizens of the United States; nor shall any State deprive any person of life, liberty, or property, without due process of law; nor deny to any person within its jurisdiction the equal protection of the laws.

Section 2. Representatives shall be apportioned among the several States according to their respective numbers, counting the whole number of persons in each State, excluding Indians not taxed. But when the right to vote at any election for the choice of electors for President and Vice President of the United States, Representatives in Congress, the Executive and Judicial officers of a State, or the members of the Legislature thereof, is denied to any of the male inhabitants of such State, being twenty-one years of age, and citizens of the United States, or in any way abridged, except for participation in rebellion, or other crime, the basis of representation therein shall be reduced in the proportion which the number of such male citizens shall bear to the whole number of male citizens twenty-one years of age in such State.

Section 3. No person shall be a Senator or Representative in Congress, or elector of President and Vice President, or hold any office, civil or military, under

8 Superseded by the Twentieth Amendment.

the United States, or under any State, who, having previously taken an oath, as a member of Congress, or as an officer of the United States, or as a member of any State legislature, or as an executive or judicial officer of any State, to support the Constitution of the United States, shall have engaged in insurrection or rebellion against the same, or given aid and comfort to the enemies thereof. But Congress may by a vote of two-thirds of each House, remove such disability.

Section 4. The validity of the public debt of the United States authorized by law, including debts incurred for payment of pensions and bounties for services in suppressing insurrection or rebellion, shall not be questioned. But neither the United States nor any state shall assume or pay any debt or obligation incurred in aid of insurrection or rebellion against the United States, or any claim for the loss or emancipation of any slave; but all such debts, obligations, and claims shall be held illegal and void.

Section 5. The Congress shall have power to enforce, by appropriate legislation, the provisions of this article.

ARTICLE XV

[proposed 27 Feb. 1869; declared ratified 30 Mar. 1870]

Section 1. The right of citizens of the United States to vote shall not be denied or abridged by the United States or by any State on account of race, color, or previous condition of servitude.

Section 2. The Congress shall have power to enforce this article by appropriate legislation.

ARTICLE XVI

[proposed 12 July 1909; declared ratified 25 Feb. 1913]

The Congress shall have power to lay and collect taxes on incomes, from whatever source derived, without apportionment among the several States, and without regard to any census or enumeration.

ARTICLE XVII

[proposed 16 May 1912; declared ratified 31 May 1913]

The Senate of the United States shall be composed of two Senators from each State, elected by the people thereof, for six years; and each Senator shall have one vote. The electors in each State shall have the qualifications requisite for electors of the most numerous branch of the State legislatures.

When vacancies happen in the representation of any State in the Senate, the executive authority of such State shall issue writs of election to fill such vacancies: *Provided,* That the legislature of any State may empower the executive thereof to make temporary appointments until the people fill the vacancies by election as the legislature may direct.

This amendment shall not be so construed as to affect the election or term of any Senator chosen before it becomes valid as part of the Constitution.

ARTICLE XVIII

[proposed 18 Dec. 1917; declared ratified 29 Jan. 1919; repealed by the 21st Amendment]

Section 1. After one year from the ratification of this article the manufacture, sale, or transportation of intoxicating liquors within, the importation thereof into, or the exportation thereof from the United States and all territory subject to the jurisdiction thereof for beverage purposes is hereby prohibited.

Section 2. The Congress and the several States shall have concurrent power to enforce this article by appropriate legislation.

Section 3. This article shall be inoperative unless it shall have been ratified as an amendment to the Constitution by the legislatures of the several States, as provided in the Constitution, within seven years from the date of the submission hereof to the States by the Congress.[9]

ARTICLE XIX

[proposed 4 June 1919; declared ratified 26 Aug. 1920]

The right of citizens of the United States to vote shall not be denied or abridged by the United States or by any State on account of sex.

Congress shall have power to enforce this article by appropriate legislation.

ARTICLE XX

[proposed 2 Mar. 1932; declared ratified 6 Feb. 1933]

Section 1. The terms of the President and Vice President shall end at noon on the 20th day of January, and the terms of Senators and Representatives at noon on the 3d day of January, of the years in which such terms would have ended if this article had not been ratified; and the terms of their successors shall then begin.

Section 2. The Congress shall assemble at least once in every year, and such meeting shall begin at noon on the 3d day of January, unless they shall by law appoint a different day.

Section 3. If, at the time fixed for the beginning of the term of the President, the President elect shall have died, the Vice President elect shall become President. If a President shall not have been chosen before the time fixed for the beginning of his term, or if the President elect shall have failed to qualify, then the Vice President elect shall act as President until a President shall have qualified; and the Congress may by law provide for the case wherein neither a Presi-

---

[9] Superseded by the Twenty-first Amendment.

dent elect nor a Vice President elect shall have qualified, declaring who shall then act as President, or the manner in which one who is to act shall be selected, and such person shall act accordingly until a President or Vice President shall have qualified.

Section 4. The Congress may by law provide for the case of the death of any of the persons from whom the House of Representatives may choose a President whenever the right of choice shall have devolved upon them, and for the case of the death of any of the persons from whom the Senate may choose a Vice-President whenever the right of choice shall have devolved upon them.

Section 5. Sections 1 and 2 shall take effect on the 15th day of October following the ratification of this article.

Section 6. This article shall be inoperative unless it shall have been ratified as an amendment to the Constitution by the legislatures of three-fourths of the several States within seven years from the date of its submission.

ARTICLE XXI

[proposed 20 Feb. 1933; declared ratified 5 Dec. 1933]

Section 1. The Eighteenth article of amendment to the Constitution of the United States is hereby repealed.

Section 2. The transportation or importation into any State, Territory, or possession of the United States for delivery or use therein of intoxicating liquors, in violation of the laws thereof, is hereby prohibited.

Section 3. This article shall be inoperative unless it shall have been ratified as an amendment to the Constitution by conventions in the several States, as provided in the Constitution, within seven years from the date of the submission hereof to the States by the Congress.

ARTICLE XXII

[proposed 24 Mar. 1947; declared ratified 26 Feb. 1951]

Section 1. No person shall be elected to the office of the President more than twice, and no person who has held the office of President, or acted as President, for more than two years of a term to which some other person was elected President shall be elected to the office of the President more than once. But this Article shall not apply to any person holding the office of President when this Article was proposed by the Congress, and shall not prevent any person who may be holding the office of President, or acting as President, during the term within which this Article becomes operative from holding the office of President or acting as President during the remainder of such term.

Section 2. This article shall be inoperative unless it shall have been ratified as an amendment to the Constitution by the legislatures of three-fourths of the several States within seven years from the date of its submission to the States by the Congress.

ARTICLE XXIII

[proposed 16 June 1960; ratified 29 Mar. 1961]

Section 1. The district constituting the seat of government of the United States shall appoint in such manner as the Congress may direct:

A number of electors of President and Vice President equal to the whole number of Senators and Representatives in Congress to which the District would be entitled if it were a State, but in no event more than the least populous state; they shall be in addition to those appointed by the States, but they shall be considered, for the purpose of the election of President and Vice President, to be electors appointed by a State; and they shall meet in the District and perform such duties as provided by the twelfth article of amendment.

Section 2. The Congress shall have power to enforce this article by appropriate legislation.

JUSTICES OF THE UNITED STATES SUPREME COURT

Name Chief Justices in SMALL CAPITALS	Service Term	Yrs.	Name Chief Justices in SMALL CAPITALS	Service Term	Yrs.
JOHN JAY, N.Y.	1789–1795	6	Samuel Blatchford, N.Y.	1882–1893	11
John Rutledge, S.C.	1789–1791	2	Lucius Q. C. Lamar, Miss.	1888–1893	5
William Cushing, Mass.	1789–1810	21	MELVILLE W. FULLER, Ill.	1888–1910	22
James Wilson, Pa.	1789–1798	9	David J. Brewer, Kan.	1889–1910	21
John Blair, Va.	1789–1796	7	Henry B. Brown, Mich.	1890–1906	16
Robert H. Harrison, Md.	1789–1790	1	George Shiras, Jr., Pa.	1892–1903	11
James Iredell, N.C.	1790–1799	9	Howell E. Jackson, Tenn.	1893–1895	2
Thomas Johnson, Md.	1791–1793	2	Edward D. White, La.	1894–1910	16
William Paterson, N.J.	1793–1806	13	Rufus W. Peckham, N.Y.	1895–1910	14
JOHN RUTLEDGE, S.C.*	1795–1795	—	Joseph McKenna, Cal.	1898–1925	27
Samuel Chase, Md.	1796–1811	15	Oliver W. Holmes, Mass.	1902–1932	29
OLIVER ELLSWORTH, Conn.	1796–1799	4	William R. Day, Ohio	1903–1922	19
Bushrod Washington, Va.	1798–1829	31	William H. Moody, Mass.	1906–1910	4
Alfred Moore, N.C.	1799–1804	5	Horace H. Lurton, Tenn.	1910–1914	5
JOHN MARSHALL, Va.	1801–1835	34	Charles E. Hughes, N.Y.	1910–1916	6
William Johnson, S.C.	1804–1834	30	Willis Van Devanter, Wyo.	1911–1937	26
Henry B. Livingston, N.Y.	1806–1823	17	Joseph R. Lamar, Ga.	1911–1916	6
Thomas Todd, Ky.	1807–1826	19	EDWARD D. WHITE, La.	1910–1921	11
Joseph Story, Mass.	1811–1845	34	Mahlon Pitney, N.J.	1912–1922	12
Gabriel Duval, Md.	1811–1836	25	Jas. C. McReynolds, Tenn.	1914–1941	27
Smith Thompson, N.Y.	1823–1843	20	Louis D. Brandeis, Mass.	1916–1939	23
Robert Trimble, Ky.	1826–1828	2	John H. Clarke, Ohio	1916–1922	6
John McLean, Ohio	1829–1861	32	WILLIAM H. TAFT, Conn.	1921–1930	9
Henry Baldwin, Pa.	1830–1844	14	George Sutherland, Utah	1922–1938	16
James M. Wayne, Ga.	1835–1867	32	Pierce Butler, Minn.	1922–1939	17
ROGER B. TANEY, Md.	1836–1864	28	Edward T. Sanford, Tenn.	1923–1930	7
Philip P. Barbour, Va.	1836–1841	5	Harlan F. Stone, N.Y.	1925–1941	16
John Catron, Tenn.	1837–1865	28	CHARLES E. HUGHES, N.Y.	1930–1941	11
John McKinley, Ala.	1837–1852	15	Owen J. Roberts, Penn.	1930–1945	15
Peter V. Daniel, Va.	1841–1860	19	Benjamin N. Cardozo, N.Y.	1932–1938	6
Samuel Nelson, N.Y.	1845–1872	27	Hugo Black, Ala.	1937–	—
Levi Woodbury, N.H.	1845–1851	6	Stanley Reed, Ky.	1938–1957	19
Robert C. Grier, Pa.	1846–1870	24	Felix Frankfurter, Mass.	1939–	—
Benj. R. Curtis, Mass.	1851–1857	6	William O. Douglas, Conn.	1939–	—
John A. Campbell, Ala.	1853–1861	8	Frank Murphy, Mich.	1940–1949	9
Nathan Clifford, Me.	1858–1881	23	HARLAN F. STONE, N.Y.	1941–1946	5
Noah H. Swayne, Ohio	1862–1881	20	James F. Byrnes, S.C.	1941–1942	2
Samuel F. Miller, Iowa	1862–1890	28	Robert H. Jackson, N.Y.	1941–1954	13
David Davis, Ill.	1862–1877	15	Wiley B. Rutledge, Iowa	1943–1949	6
Stephen J. Field, Cal.	1863–1897	34	Harold H. Burton, Ohio	1945–1958	13
SALMON P. CHASE, Ohio	1864–1873	9	FRED M. VINSON, Ky.	1946–1953	7
William Strong, Pa.	1870–1880	10	Thomas C. Clark, Tex.	1949–	—
Joseph P. Bradley, N.J.	1870–1892	22	Sherman Minton, Ind.	1949–1956	7
Ward Hunt, N.Y.	1872–1882	10	EARL WARREN, Calif.	1953–	—
MORRISON R. WAITE, Ohio	1874–1888	14	John Marshall Harlan, N.Y.	1955–	—
John M. Harlan, Ky.	1877–1911	34	William J. Brennan, Jr., N.J.	1956–	—
William B. Woods, Ga.	1880–1887	7	Charles E. Whittaker, Mo.	1957–	—
Stanley Matthews, Ohio	1881–1889	8	Potter Stewart, Ohio	1958–	—
Horace Gray, Mass.	1881–1902	21			

* Acting chief justice; the Senate refused to confirm nomination.

President and Vice-President		Secretary of State		Secretary of Treasury		Secretary of War	
George Washington	1789	T. Jefferson	1789	A. Hamilton	1789	H. Knox	1789
John Adams		E. Randolph	1794	O. Wolcott	1795	T. Pickering	1795
		T. Pickering	1795			J. McHenry	1796
John Adams	1797	T. Pickering	1797	O. Wolcott	1797	J. McHenry	1797
Thomas Jefferson		J. Marshall	1800	S. Dexter	1801	J. Marshall	1800
						S. Dexter	1800
						R. Griswold	1801
Thomas Jefferson	1801	J. Madison	1801	S. Dexter	1801	H. Dearborn	1801
Aaron Burr				A. Gallatin	1801		
George Clinton	1805						
James Madison	1809	R. Smith	1809	A. Gallatin	1809	W. Eustis	1809
George Clinton		J. Monroe	1811	G. W. Campbell	1814	J. Armstrong	1813
Elbridge Gerry	1813			A. J. Dallas	1814	J. Monroe	1814
				W. H. Crawford	1816	W. H. Crawford	1815
James Monroe	1817	J. Q. Adams	1817	W. H. Crawford	1817	I. Shelby	1817
D. D. Tompkins						G. Graham	1817
						J. C. Calhoun	1817
John Q. Adams	1825	H. Clay	1825	R. Rush	1825	J. Barbour	1825
John C. Calhoun						P. B. Porter	1828
Andrew Jackson	1829	M. Van Buren	1829	S. D. Ingham	1829	J. H. Eaton	1829
John C. Calhoun		E. Livingston	1831	L. McLane	1831	L. Cass	1831
Martin Van Buren	1833	L. McLane	1833	W. J. Duane	1833	B. F. Butler	1837
		J. Forsyth	1834	R. B. Taney	1833		
				L. Woodbury	1834		
Martin Van Buren	1837	J. Forsyth	1837	L. Woodbury	1837	J. R. Poinsett	1837
R. M. Johnson							
William H. Harrison	1841	D. Webster	1841	T. Ewing	1841	J. Bell	1841
John Tyler							
John Tyler	1841	D. Webster	1841	T. Ewing	1841	J. Bell	1841
		H. S. Legaré	1843	W. Forward	1841	J. McLean	1841
		A. P. Upshur	1843	J. C. Spencer	1843	J. C. Spencer	1841
		J. C. Calhoun	1844	G. M. Bibb	1844	J. M. Porter	1843
						W. Wilkins	1844
James K. Polk	1845	J. Buchanan	1845	R. J. Walker	1845	W. L. Marcy	1845
George M. Dallas							
Zachary Taylor	1849	J. M. Clayton	1849	W. M. Meredith	1849	G. W. Crawford	1849
Millard Fillmore							
Millard Fillmore	1850	D. Webster	1850	T. Corwin	1850	C. M. Conrad	1850
		E. Everett	1852				
Franklin Pierce	1853	W. L. Marcy	1853	J. Guthrie	1853	J. Davis	1853
William R. King							
James Buchanan	1857	L. Cass	1857	H. Cobb	1857	J. B. Floyd	1857
J. C. Breckinridge		J. S. Black	1860	P. F. Thomas	1860	J. Holt	1861
				J. A. Dix	1861		
Abraham Lincoln	1861	W. H. Seward	1861	S. P. Chase	1861	S. Cameron	1861
Hannibal Hamlin				W. P. Fessenden	1864	E. M. Stanton	1862
Andrew Johnson	1865			H. McCulloch	1865		
Andrew Johnson	1865	W. H. Seward	1865	H. McCulloch	1865	E. M. Stanton	1865
						U. S. Grant	1867
						L. Thomas	1868
						J. M. Schofield	1868
Ulysses S. Grant	1869	E. B. Washburne	1869	G. S. Boutwell	1869	J. A. Rawlins	1869
Schuyler Colfax		H. Fish	1869	W. A. Richardson	1873	W. T. Sherman	1869
Henry Wilson	1873			B. H. Bristow	1874	W. W. Belknap	1869
				L. M. Morrill	1876	A. Taft	1876
						J. D. Cameron	1876

THEIR CABINETS

Secretary of Navy		Secretary of Interior		Postmaster General		Attorney General		Other Members
		Established March 3, 1849		S. Osgood	1789	E. Randolph	1789	Secretary of Agriculture
				T. Pickering	1791	W. Bradford	1794	
				J. Habersham	1795	C. Lee	1795	
B. Stoddert	1798			J. Habersham	1797	C. Lee	1797	Established February 11, 1889
						T. Parsons	1801	
								N. J. Colman 1889
B. Stoddert	1801			J. Habersham	1801	L. Lincoln	1801	J. M. Rusk 1889
R. Smith	1801			G. Granger	1801	R. Smith	1805	J. S. Morton 1893
J. Crowninshield	1805					J. Breckinridge	1805	J. Wilson 1897
						C. A. Rodney	1807	J. Wilson 1901
P. Hamilton	1809			G. Granger	1809	C. A. Rodney	1809	J. Wilson 1909
W. Jones	1813			R. J. Meigs, Jr.	1814	W. Pinkney	1811	D. F. Houston 1913
B. W. Crownin-shield	1814					R. Rush	1814	E. T. Meredith 1920
								H. C. Wallace 1921
								H. M. Gore 1924
B. W. Crownin-shield	1817			R. J. Meigs, Jr.	1817	R. Rush	1817	W. M. Jardine 1925
S. Thompson	1818			J. McLean	1823	W. Wirt	1817	A. M. Hyde 1929
S. L. Southard	1823							H. A. Wallace 1933
S. L. Southard	1825			J. McLean	1825	W. Wirt	1825	C. R. Wickard 1940
								C. P. Anderson 1945
								C. F. Brannan 1948
J. Branch	1829			W. T. Barry	1829	J. M. Berrien	1829	E. T. Benson 1953
L. Woodbury	1831			A. Kendall	1835	R. B. Taney	1831	O. L. Freeman 1961
M. Dickerson	1834					B. F. Butler	1833	
								Secretary of Commerce and Labor
M. Dickerson	1837			A. Kendall	1837	B. F. Butler	1837	
J. K. Paulding	1838			J. M. Niles	1840	F. Grundy	1838	
						H. D. Gilpin	1840	Established February 14, 1903
G. E. Badger	1841			F. Granger	1841	J. J. Crittenden	1841	
G. E. Badger	1841			F. Granger	1841	J. J. Crittenden	1841	G. B. Cortelyou 1903
A. P. Upshur	1841			C. A. Wickliffe	1841	H. S. Legaré	1841	V. H. Metcalf 1904
D. Henshaw	1843					J. Nelson	1843	O. S. Straus 1906
T. W. Gilmer	1844							C. Nagel 1909
J. Y. Mason	1844							
G. Bancroft	1845			C. Johnson	1845	J. Y. Mason	1845	(This department was divided in 1913.)
J. Y. Mason	1846					N. Clifford	1846	
						I. Toucey	1848	
W. B. Preston	1849	T. Ewing	1849	J. Collamer	1849	R. Johnson	1849	Secretary of Commerce
W. A. Graham	1850	A. H. H. Stuart	1850	N. K. Hall	1850	J. J. Crittenden	1850	W. C. Redfield 1913
J. P. Kennedy	1852			S. D. Hubbard	1852			J. W. Alexander 1919
J. C. Dobbin	1853	R. McClelland	1853	J. Campbell	1853	C. Cushing	1853	H. C. Hoover 1921
								H. C. Hoover 1925
I. Toucey	1857	J. Thompson	1857	A. V. Brown	1857	J. S. Black	1857	W. F. Whiting 1928
				J. Holt	1859	E. M. Stanton	1860	R. P. Lamont 1929
								R. D. Chapin 1932
G. Welles	1861	C. B. Smith	1861	H. King	1861	E. Bates	1861	D. C. Roper 1933
		J. P. Usher	1863	M. Blair	1861	T. J. Coffey	1863	H. L. Hopkins 1939
				W. Dennison	1864	J. Speed	1864	J. Jones 1940
G. Welles	1865	J. P. Usher	1865	W. Dennison	1865	J. Speed	1865	H. A. Wallace 1945
		J. Harlan	1865	A. W. Randall	1866	H. Stanbery	1866	W. A. Harriman 1946
		O. H. Browning	1866			W. M. Evarts	1868	C. Sawyer 1948
								S. Weeks 1953
								L. Hodges 1961
A. E. Borie	1869	J. D. Cox	1869	J. A. J. Creswell	1869	E. R. Hoar	1869	
G. M. Robeson	1869	C. Delano	1870	J. W. Marshall	1874	A. T. Ackerman	1870	
		Z. Chandler	1875	M. Jewell	1874	G. H. Williams	1871	
				J. N. Tyner	1876	E. Pierrepont	1875	
						A. Taft	1876	

President and Vice-President		Secretary of State		Secretary of Treasury		Secretary of War	
Rutherford B. Hayes	1877	W. M. Evarts	1877	J. Sherman	1877	G. W. McCray	1877
William A. Wheeler						A. Ramsey	1879
James A. Garfield	1881	J. G. Blaine	1881	W. Windom	1881	R. T. Lincoln	1881
Chester A. Arthur							
Chester A. Arthur	1881	F. T. Frelinghuy-		C. J. Folger	1881	R. T. Lincoln	1881
		sen	1881	W. Q. Gresham	1884		
				H. McCulloch	1884		
Grover Cleveland	1885	T. F. Bayard	1885	D. Manning	1885	W. C. Endicott	1885
T. A. Hendricks				C. S. Fairchild	1887		
Benjamin Harrison	1889	J. G. Blaine	1889	W. Windom	1889	R. Proctor	1889
Levi P. Morton		J. W. Foster	1892	C. Foster	1891	S. B. Elkins	1891
Grover Cleveland	1893	W. Q. Gresham	1893	J. G. Carlisle	1893	D. S. Lamont	1893
Adlai E. Stevenson		R. Olney	1895				
William McKinley	1897	J. Sherman	1897	L. J. Gage	1897	R. A. Alger	1897
Garret A. Hobart		W. R. Day	1897			E. Root	1899
Theodore Roosevelt	1901	J. Hay	1898				
Theodore Roosevelt	1901	J. Hay	1901	L. J. Gage	1901	E. Root	1901
Charles Fairbanks	1905	E. Root	1905	L. M. Shaw	1902	W. H. Taft	1904
		R. Bacon	1909	G. B. Cortelyou	1907	L. E. Wright	1908
William H. Taft	1909	P. C. Knox	1909	F. MacVeagh	1909	J. M. Dickinson	1909
James S. Sherman						H. L. Stimson	1911
Woodrow Wilson	1913	W. J. Bryan	1913	W. G. McAdoo	1913	L. M. Garrison	1913
Thomas Marshall		R. Lansing	1915	C. Glass	1918	N. D. Baker	1916
		B. Colby	1920	D. F. Houston	1929		
Warren G. Harding	1921	C. E. Hughes	1921	A. W. Mellon	1921	J. W. Weeks	1921
Calvin Coolidge							
Calvin Coolidge	1923	C. E. Hughes	1923	A. W. Mellon	1923	J. W. Weeks	1923
Charles G. Dawes		F. B. Kellogg	1925			D. F. Davis	1925
Herbert C. Hoover	1929	H. L. Stimson	1929	A. W. Mellon	1929	J. W. Good	1929
Charles Curtis				O. L. Mills	1932	P. J. Hurley	1929
Franklin D. Roosevelt	1933	C. Hull	1933	W. H. Woodlin	1933	G. H. Dern	1933
John Nance Garner				H. Morgenthau,		H. A. Woodring	1936
Henry A. Wallace	1941			Jr.	1934	H. L. Stimson	1940
Harry S Truman	1945						
Harry S Truman	1945	J. F. Byrnes	1945	F. M. Vinson	1945	R. P. Patterson	1945
Alben W. Barkley	1949	G. C. Marshall	1947	J. W. Snyder	1946	K. C. Royall	1947*
		D. G. Acheson	1949				
Dwight D. Eisenhower	1953	J. F. Dulles	1953	G. M. Humphrey	1953		
Richard M. Nixon		C. A. Herter	1959	R. B. Anderson	1957		
John F. Kennedy	1961	D. Rusk	1961	D. Dillon	1961		
Lyndon Johnson							

* On July 26, 1947, the War and Navy Departments were incorporated in the Department of Defense.

THEIR CABINETS (*Continued*)

Secretary of Navy	Secretary of Interior	Postmaster General	Attorney General	Other Members
R. W. Thompson 1877	C. Schurz 1877	D. M. Key 1877	C. Devens 1877	Secretary of Labor
N. Goff, Jr. 1881		H. Maynard 1880		
W. H. Hunt 1881	S. J. Kirkwood 1881	T. L. James 1881	W. MacVeagh 1881	Established March 4, 1913
W. E. Chandler 1881	H. M. Teller 1881	T. O. Howe 1881	B. H. Brewster 1881	
		W. Q. Gresham 1883		W. B. Wilson 1913
		F. Hatton 1884		J. J. Davis 1921
W. C. Whitney 1885	L. Q. C. Lamar 1885	W. F. Vilas 1885	A. H. Garland 1885	J. J. Davis 1923
	W. F. Vilas 1888	D. M. Dickinson 1888		J. J. Davis 1929
B. F. Tracy 1889	J. W. Noble 1889	J. Wanamaker 1889	W. H. H. Miller 1889	W. N. Doak 1930
				F. Perkins 1933
H. A. Herbert 1893	H. Smith 1893	W. S. Bissell 1893	R. Olney 1893	L. B. Schwellenbach 1945
	D. R. Francis 1896	W. L. Wilson 1895	J. Harmon 1895	M. J. Tobin 1948
J. D. Long 1897	C. N. Bliss 1897	J. A. Gary 1897	J. McKenna 1897	M. P. Durkin 1953
	E. A. Hitchcock 1899	C. E. Smith 1898	J. W. Griggs 1897	J. P. Mitchell 1953
			P. C. Knox 1901	A. J. Goldberg 1961
J. D. Long 1901	E. A. Hitchcock 1901	C. E. Smith 1901	P. C. Knox 1901	
W. H. Moody 1902	J. R. Garfield 1907	H. C. Payne 1902	W. H. Moody 1904	Secretary of Defense
P. Morton 1904		R. J. Wynne 1904	C. J. Bonaparte 1907	
C. J. Bonaparte 1905		G. B. Cortelyou 1905		Established July 26, 1947
V. H. Metcalf 1907		G. von L. Meyer 1907		
T. H. Newberry 1908			G. W. Wickersham 1909	J. V. Forrestal 1947
G. von L. Meyer 1909	R. A. Ballinger 1909	F. H. Hitchcock 1909		L. A. Johnson 1949
	W. L. Fisher 1911			G. C. Marshall 1950
J. Daniels 1913	F. K. Lane 1913	A. S. Burleson 1913	J. C. McReynolds 1913	R. A. Lovett 1951
	J. B. Payne 1920		T. W. Gregory 1914	C. E. Wilson 1953
			A. M. Palmer 1919	N. H. McElroy 1957
E. Denby 1921	A. B. Fall 1921	W. H. Hays 1921	H. M. Daugherty 1921	T. S. Gates, Jr. 1959
	H. Work 1923	H. Work 1922		R. S. McNamara 1961
		H. S. New 1923		
E. Denby 1923	H. Work 1923	H. S. New 1923	H. M. Daugherty 1923	Secretary of Health, Education, and Welfare
C. D. Wilbur 1924	R. O. West 1928		H. F. Stone 1924	
			J. G. Sargent 1925	Established April 1, 1953
C. F. Adams 1929	R. L. Wilbur 1929	W. F. Brown 1929	W. D. Mitchell 1929	
C. A. Swanson 1933	H. L. Ickes 1933	J. A. Farley 1933	H. S. Cummings 1933	O. Culp Hobby 1953
C. Edison 1940		F. C. Walker 1940	F. Murphy 1939	M. B. Folsom 1955
F. Knox 1940			R. H. Jackson 1940	A. S. Flemming 1958
			F. Biddle 1941	A. A. Ribicoff 1961
J. V. Forrestal 1945°	H. L. Ickes 1945	F. C. Walker 1945	T. C. Clark 1945	
	J. C. Krug 1946	R. E. Hannegan 1945	J. H. McGrath 1949	
	O. L. Chapman 1949	J. M. Donaldson 1947	J. P. McGranery 1952	
	D. McKay 1953	A. E. Summerfield 1953	H. Brownell, Jr. 1953	
	F. A. Seaton 1956		W. P. Rogers 1957	
	S. L. Udall 1961	J. E. Day 1961	R. F. Kennedy 1961	

INDEX

INDEX

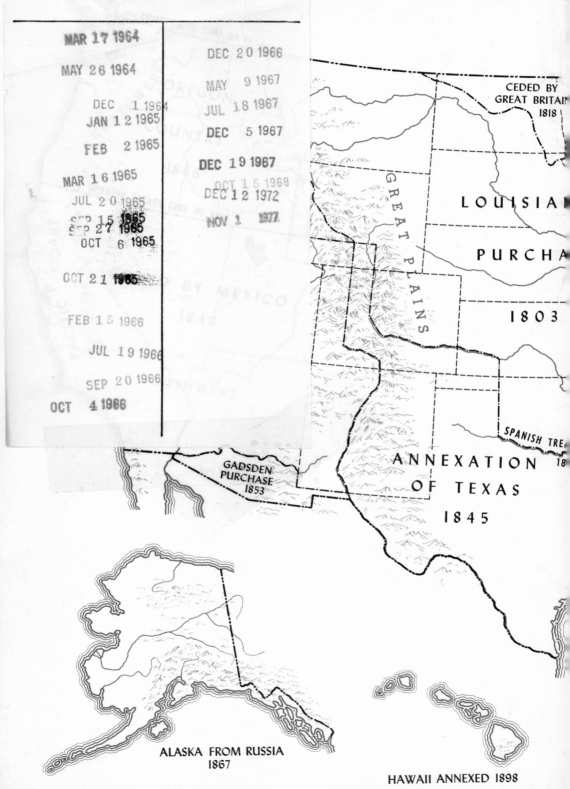

CEDED BY GREAT BRITAIN 1818

LOUISIANA

PURCHASE

1803

GREAT PLAINS

SPANISH TREATY 18

GADSDEN PURCHASE 1853

ANNEXATION OF TEXAS 1845

ALASKA FROM RUSSIA 1867

HAWAII ANNEXED 1898